JIMMY SWAGGART
BIBLE COMMENTARY

Matthew

JIMMY SWAGGART BIBLE COMMENTARY

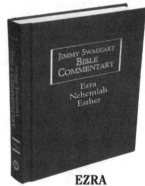

Jimmy Swaggart
Bible
Commentary

Matthew

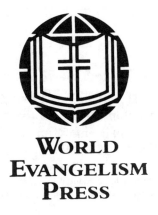

World
Evangelism
Press

ISBN 978-1-934655-04-7

11-073 • COPYRIGHT © 1995 World Evangelism Press®
P.O. Box 262550 • Baton Rouge, Louisiana 70826-2550
Website: www.jsm.org • Email: info@jsm.org • (225) 768-7000
11 12 13 14 15 16 17 18 19 20 21 22 23 24 25 26 / CW / 19 18 17 16 15 14 13 12 11 10 9 8 7 6 5 4

TABLE OF CONTENTS

INTRODUCTION

—■—

Upon beginning this first Volume on the New Testament (Matthew), it is difficult to put into words exactly how I felt. Having spent some three years in writing Commentaries on the Old Testament (and if the truth be known, about fifty years), the bridge from the Old to the New produced a sensation in my heart that is difficult to describe. As all know who are students of the Old Testament, it teems with types, shadows, and symbols of Christ. In other words, I think one could basically say, and without being contradicted, that everything in the Old Testament points to Christ. The Tabernacle and everything in it was a type of Christ. The Sacrifices were a type of Christ. The same could be said for the Temple. As well, Christ was not only the Giver of the Law, but, as well, the embodiment of the Law and the fulfillment of the Law. Consequently, the Prophets proclaimed His Message, whether of Grace or Judgment.

When I began to write Commentary on Matthew, I sensed in my spirit a jubilee that produced an excitement such as I don't think I have ever experienced. It was like the One Whose shadow I had been seeing all along, now appears! The Prophets had said He was coming, and now, John the Baptist says, *"Behold the Lamb of God,"* which, in effect, says *"He is here!"* (Jn. 1:29). It is as if a new day has dawned, and, to be certain, that is exactly what it was, *"A new day!"*

Since the time the Lord moved upon me to begin these Commentaries, it has proven to be such a labor of love that I devote every single hour possible to their completion. However, when I began writing this first Volume of the New Testament, it seems like, if possible, the joy increased. Time and time again the Spirit of the Lord would fall upon me as particular Truths began to be brought out. I would sit at my desk at times and weep, not for sorrow, but for joy. At times the Word would become so alive that I would have to stop writing and sit for a moment as my mind and spirit absorbed that which I believe, the Holy Spirit was giving me. This I believe! If what I have experienced in writing this Commentary is transferred to you, the Bible student, prayerfully, I trust it will be the same blessing to you as it has been to me.

The Word of God is inexhaustible, and, as such, irrespective of what Truths are brought out, consequently given by the Holy Spirit, there remains an unending supply yet untapped. That becomes more understandable as one comes to the realization that the Word of God is alive, and, as such, produces constantly that which Life can produce.

It always amazes me as I dig into a Passage of Scripture, rejoicing greatly as the Holy Spirit opens up new vistas of Truth (not new to the Bible, but new to me), consequently thinking that I have gleaned every possible nugget that can be gleaned. And then I will go over to our Bible College Chapel (WEBC&S), and hear some first-year Bible student preach a Message on the very Scripture that I had been dealing with, and bring out a Truth that I had never heard of or thought of before. As stated, the Bible is inexhaustible!

A dear brother wrote me some time ago and told me of his securing the Volumes of the Commentary which were then completed. He went on to say how he felt they would help him with his Bible study in providing research, etc. *"However, even though the research proved to be helpful,"* he said, *"I have experienced tremendous spiritual growth since beginning my study of these Volumes."* From the framework of his letter, the brother seemed to be one of the most educated men I had ever had the privilege of corresponding with. Inasmuch as he was taken beyond the educational aspect and into the spiritual, i.e., *"Christian Growth,"* this, to be sure, is the intention of our effort. If that which is written does not have a tendency to draw one closer to Christ, then I will not have achieved that which I believe the Lord has called me to do.

Just the other day, another dear brother wrote, listing the number of Bible Colleges and Seminaries he had attended, and then said, *"Brother Swaggart, these Commentaries have helped me to learn more about the Bible than anything I have come across, or any place I have studied, in all of my life."*

These two letters from which we have drawn excerpts, explain totally what we are trying to do with these Volumes.

First of all, we want you to be drawn closer to Christ.

Second, we want you to learn the Bible. To be sure, if you learn the Bible, and learn it with your heart as well as with your head, you <u>will</u> be drawn closer to Christ.

In the midst of the writing of these Volumes, Frances and I are, as well, airing television programs all over the world. And then there is the pastoring of Family Worship Center in Baton Rouge, but with Donnie taking many of those duties. There is the Radio Ministry as well! Consequently, my time is limited. Therefore, I will often come to the office before daylight to begin work, which is, to me, the most productive time of all. And then, Frances and Donnie do so many things in the Ministry that I once did, in order to give me more time to devote to the writing of this material.

As well, I am indebted to scores of scholars who have gone before me (and a scholar I am not!), who have made a contribution, for which I am so thankful. Not being a Greek or Hebrew student, I have had to rely on others, and, of course, my thanks and appreciation to these know no bounds. They have made my task immeasurably easier.

When the word, *"Commentaries,"* is mentioned, most people think of Preachers, and rightly so. However, I have attempted to write these not only for the Preacher, but, as well, for the layman. In Truth, the layman should know the Bible just as much as the Preacher of the Gospel. And considering the available tools, there is no excuse not to! Consequently, even though we pray that these efforts will be a blessing to Preachers, at the same time, we want it to be such to the layman.

Through the years, I have had countless laymen exclaim to me of their inability to understand particular passages of Scripture. Hopefully, these Commentaries will help solve that problem. And if they do, there is no limit to their worth or value, because understanding the Word of God is the single most important thing in which one could ever engage.

If the reader could devote the time of reading one Chapter plus the Commentary each day, I believe one's Bible education, at least for many, will greatly improve! Considering that every Scripture is given along with the Commentary, makes it very simple to study these Volumes. In essence, when you read them, you are reading the Word of God.

In the writing of these Commentaries is the spirit of the Evangelist, for that's what I am! As such, it is colored and flavored by that particular style. Truthfully, it may be offensive to some, but I trust, never boring!

The Church too often follows generals who have never been in battle. They have never heard the cries of the wounded or smelled the smoke, spiritually speaking, of the conflict. They know how to dress pretty and they march well, but the heat of the battle they have never experienced. To be sure, those who have suffered that heat may be scarred, they may even walk with a limp as Jacob of old, but their very survival speaks volumes. As the British poet, John Dryden, said:

"I am wounded,
"But I am not slain.
"I shall lay me down and bleed a while,
"Then I shall rise and fight again."

Once again, allow me to thank Frances and Donnie for their immeasurable help in the operation of this Ministry, in order that I might have time to devote to this task.

THE
BOOK OF MATTHEW

From the time of Malachi to Matthew, a period of nearly 450 years, other than the voice of John the Baptist, the forerunner of Christ, Israel heard the voice of no Prophet. No doubt, with the voice of John the Baptist, a fresh wind began to blow in Israel, and, in Truth, for the entirety of the world, because John's voice would herald the coming of the One Who the Prophets of old had spoken of, the Messiah. Accordingly, the Holy Spirit would use Matthew, a Publican, to first of all herald the greatest event to date in the annals of human history. The honor and distinction of such cannot be adequately portrayed by mere verbiage. One can only proclaim such, using Matthew in this high and honored position, as an act of the Grace of God. Nothing else could explain it!

In this First Gospel, Jesus is presented as the King of Israel (Jer. 23:5-6; 33:15; Zech. 9:9). Hence His Pedigree is given from Abraham and David, and He is portrayed as The Branch, The King.

In the other Three Gospels, He is presented as The Branch, The Servant (Mark); The Branch, The Man (Luke); and The Branch, Jehovah (John).

Consequently, this Gospel sets forth the Messiah's claim as King. Events in His Ministry are therefore recorded and emphasized which do not appear in the other Gospels.

As is obvious, and with very little dispute, Matthew is the author of the Gospel which bears his name. He is called, as well, *"Levi, son of Alphaesus."* He was also said to have been the brother of James (not James who was brother to John), Judas (not Iscariot), and Simon Zelotes.

It is also thought, that he, along with his brothers, was a cousin to Jesus, as his mother

NOTES

was the wife of Cleopas and sister of Mary the mother of Christ (Mat. 27:56; Mk. 15:40; Jn. 19:25).

It is thought that Matthew wrote his Gospel in Judea, and maybe even in Jerusalem, in the year 37 A.D.

It is thought that he ministered in Judea for about fifteen years, then going to Ethiopia and other lands afterwards (Acts 2:43).

Some claim he suffered martyrdom, being thrust through with a spear, with others claiming he died of natural causes.

At any rate, and as stated, he had the distinct privilege of being chosen by Christ as one of the twelve, and by the Holy Spirit to write the very first Gospel, and, therefore, to be the first herald of the Ministry and Person of Christ, which is the introduction to the New Covenant. Consequently, the day he left his tax-collector's business to follow Christ, would be the greatest decision he ever made, and would lead him to sublime heights, such as the human heart could never begin to imagine.

And so it is with all who hear that clarion call, *"Follow Me,"* and who gladly take up their Cross to follow the lowly Galilean.

It, as with Matthew, is a journey that really never ends, but leads to life eternal!

CHAPTER 1

(1) "THE BOOK OF THE GENERATION OF JESUS CHRIST, THE SON OF DAVID, THE SON OF ABRAHAM."

The phrase, *"The Book of the Generation of Jesus Christ,"* is meant to introduce the Pedigree or genealogy of Christ.

"Jesus" is the Greek pronunciation of the Hebrew, *"Joshua, and means Saviour."*

"Christ" means *"Anointed,"* or *"Anointed One."*

Therefore, the Name of Christ actually means *"Saviour Anointed,"* or *"Anointed Saviour."*

As well, His Name had no reference to Deity, but to His humanity as the Son of God.

If one studies the two genealogies given by the Holy Spirit, through Matthew and Luke, one will find them a little different, and by design.

Matthew's Pedigree is that of Joseph, the foster father of Christ, who was the regal heir begotten of Solomon and David. In other words, if the kingly dynasty of Judah had continued, Joseph would have been king of Israel.

In Luke (Lk. 3:23), the Pedigree is not given through Joseph, but instead through Mary the mother of Christ, as she was, as well, a direct descendant from David and Adam through Nathan, Solomon's elder brother.

Even though she was not in the kingly line, as Joseph, still, her genealogy back to David, and to Abraham and Adam, was as flawless as Joseph her husband. Therefore, and, inasmuch as these genealogies were kept in the Temple for all to see, the Religious Leaders of Israel were without excuse respecting the identification of Christ.

They knew from the Prophecies of Daniel, that the Messiah was expected at about this time, and they also knew that He was to be in the direct lineage of David, and, of Abraham, which fit Jesus perfectly (Dan. 9:24-26). To be sure, if there had been the slightest flaw in the genealogy of Christ, respecting these all-important aspects, the Pharisees, as well as others, would have quickly pointed it out.

(Incidentally, in reading these names in the genealogy, one may see that some of them are spelled differently than in the Old Testament. This is because the New Testament was originally written in Greek, with the Old Testament originally written in Hebrew. Consequently, the spelling is somewhat different, but is actually the same name.)

The beginning Bible student may wonder at the necessity of these names, or even their significance! However, the two Chapters in the Bible containing these genealogies (Mat. 1 and Lk. 3), are at least two of the most important

NOTES

Chapters in the entirety of the Word of God. The reason is this:

THE FALL

As all Bible students know, the human family and the world are in a perilous condition because of the Fall of Adam in the Garden of Eden. In a sense, Adam was the federal head of the entirety of the human family, at least in the manner of procreation. (Christ was actually the Federal Head, and because He was the Maker and Creator of man — Gen. 2:7; Jn. 1:1).

The manner in which God created man, and, therefore, mankind, by giving him the ability to bring offspring into the world (procreation), placed a tremendous responsibility on the original Adam. In effect, the entirety of the human family was in his loins, and whatever he did would affect all who would be born in the future, even the entirety of the billions of mankind.

Consequently, had he obeyed God and not fallen, all the children who would have been born to the union of Adam and Eve would have been born *"sons of God,"* instead of *"sons of Adam"* (Lk. 3:38; Gen. 5:3).

Regrettably, he did not obey God and consequently fell, which meant that the entirety of the human family would be born *"fallen."* This is the cause of all the misery, heartache, war, pain, sickness, suffering, and dying which fill the world. Actually, if Adam had not fallen, he would never have died, because, in effect, he was created to live forever. He died as a result of disobeying God, which, in effect, was spiritual death, which ultimately brought physical death, with a pall of death actually over everything (Gen. 2:17).

The type of *"death"* the Lord was speaking of in Gen. 2:17 was *"spiritual death,"* which meant *"separation from God,"* Who is the Source of all life. When spiritual death came, ultimately, physical death came as well!

Inasmuch as Adam was poisoned as a result of the Fall, all who would be born to him, as well as his offspring, which includes the entirety of the human family, and for all time, would be born poisoned as well, i.e., born in sin, or born a *"sinner,"* i.e., original sin.

(If Eve had only sinned, due to the fact that the woman did not contain the seed of procreation, she could have asked forgiveness from the Lord, which would have been granted, with this terrible horror stopping with her. However, inasmuch as the seed of procreation — the bringing of offspring into the world — was in Adam, his Fall destroyed the entirety of the human family. To be sure, he could have obtained forgiveness from the Lord, at least as far as his own action was concerned, even though there is no record that he sought such, but still, the damage to future offspring, which included the entirety of the human family, could not be undone, at least by Adam. Consequently, as a result of his personal action, the entirety of the human family was doomed!)

In effect, with the Fall in the Garden of Eden, Adam and Eve changed Lords, making Satan their Lord, instead of Jehovah. Consequently, Satan, and due to the Fall of Adam, became the *"god of this world,"* and the *"prince of the power of the air"* (II Cor. 4:4; Eph. 2:2). Hence the reason for the blight of humanity, as Satan can only *"steal, kill and destroy"* (Jn. 10:10). Now the question remains as to how man can be redeemed from this terrible condition that he finds himself in?

In respect to this sordid situation, it looks as if Satan has won the day, inasmuch as man, at least within himself certainly cannot extricate himself from this terrible condition.

The story of the Fall of man is the story of the destruction of man, God's choice creation, with all its resultant misery. The essence of all sin, consequently, is displayed in the first sin of Adam and Eve. Man was tempted to doubt God's Word, which he did, and was consequently led to disbelieve, and then disobey. Sin is man's rebellion against the authority of God, and pride is his own supposed self-adequacy (you will be like God — Gen. 3:5).

The consequences of sin, and, therefore, the Fall, were and are twofold:

1. Awareness of guilt and immediate separation from God (they hid themselves).

2. The sentence of the curse, decreeing toil, sorrow and wrath for man himself, and in addition, inevitably, and as stated, involving the whole of the created order, of which man is the crown.

THE EFFECT ON MAN

Man henceforth, and as a result of the Fall, is a perverted creature. In revolting against

the purpose of his being, which is to live and act entirely to the glory of his beneficent Creator and to fulfill His Will, he ceases to be truly man.

His true manhood consists in conformity to the image of God in which he was created. This image of God is manifested in man's original capacity of communion with His Creator; in his enjoyment exclusively of what is good; in his rationality which makes it possible for him alone of all creatures to hear and respond to the Word of God; in his knowledge of the Truth and in the freedom which that knowledge ensures; and in government, as the head of God's creation, in obedience to the mandate to have dominion over every living thing and to subdue the earth (Gen. 1:26).

THE IMAGE OF GOD IS EVIDENT IN MAN

Yet, rebel as he will against the image of God with which he has been stamped, man cannot erase it, because it is part of his very constitution as man. It is evident, for example, in his pursuit of scientific knowledge, in his harnessing of the forces of nature and in his development of culture, art and civilization.

But at the same time, the efforts of fallen man are cursed with frustration. This frustration is itself a proof of the perversity of the human heart. Thus history shows that the very discoveries and advances which have promised most good to mankind have through misuse brought great evils in their train. The man who does not love God does not love his fellowmen. He is driven by selfish motives, which are a result of the Fall. The image of Satan, the greater hater of God and man, is superimposed upon him. The result of the Fall is that man now knows good <u>and</u> evil.

THE RESULTS OF THE FALL

These results are graphically described by Paul in Romans 1:18. All men, however ungodly and unrighteous they may be, know the Truth about God and themselves; but they wickedly suppress this Truth. It is, however, an inescapable Truth, for the fact of the *"eternal power and Godhead"* of the Creator is both manifested within them, by their very constitution as God's creatures made in His image, and also manifested all around them in the whole created order of the universe which bears eloquent testimony to its origin as God's handiwork (Ps. 19:1).

Basically, therefore, man's state is not one of ignorance but of knowledge. His condemnation is that he loves darkness rather than light. His refusal to glorify God as God and his ingratitude lead him into intellectual vanity and futility. Arrogantly professing himself to be wise, he in fact becomes a fool (Rom. 1:21).

Having wilfully cast himself adrift from the Creator in Whom Alone the meaning of his existence is to be found, he must seek that meaning elsewhere, for his creaturely finitude makes it impossible for him to cease from being a spiritual as well as a physical creature.

To make it even worse, his search becomes ever more foolish and degrading, as he continues to go further away from God. It carries him into the gross irrationality of superstition and idolatry, into vileness and unnatural vice, and into all those evils, social and international, which give rise to the hatreds and miseries that disfigure our world. The Fall has, in brief, overthrown the true dignity of man (Rom. 1:23).

Consequently, man is becoming more and more wicked, instead of the opposite, therefore, completely debunking the foolish theory of moral evolution.

THE BIBLICAL DOCTRINE

As we have alluded to, the Scriptural Doctrine of the Fall altogether contradicts the popular modern view of man as a being, who, by a slow evolutionary development, has succeeded in rising from the primeval fear and groping ignorance of a humble origin to proud heights of religious sensitivity and insight.

The Bible does not portray man as risen, but as fallen, and in the most desperate of situations. As well, if one will only look about at the present state of man in the world, and despite education, etc., and the passing of time, such becomes painfully obvious.

It is only against this background that God's saving action in Christ takes on its proper significance. Through the grateful appropriation by Faith in Christ's Atoning Work, what was forfeited by the Fall is restored to man: his true and intended dignity is recovered, the purpose of life recaptured, the image of God restored, and the way into

NOTES

the paradise of intimate communion with God reopened.

OTHER TEACHINGS CONCERNING THE FALL OF MAN

1. The Pelagran Heresy: This theory taught that Adam's sin affected only himself and not the human race as a whole, and that every individual is born free from sin and capable in his own power of living a sinless life, and that there have even been persons who have succeeded in doing so. However, precious few, if any, living examples were pointed out, only those who were dead. Augustine, back in the Fifth Century, strongly opposed this heresy.

2. The Teaching of the Roman Catholic Church: Catholic teaching states that what man lost through the Fall was a supernatural gift of original righteousness that did not belong properly to his being as man but was something added extra by God. As a result of the Fall, they teach that man was merely left in his natural state as originally created, but with this Gift of Righteousness taken away.

This teaching opens the door for the affirmation of the ability and necessity of unregenerate man to contribute by his works toward the achievement of his Salvation. Hence the Roman Catholic, *"Salvation by works."*

3. Liberal Theology: This denies the historicity of the event of the Fall. Every man, it is said, is his own Adam. As a result, modernism teaches that man can solve his problems by proper education and psychological advancement.

However, and in contrast to the above, the Bible teaches the Fall as a definite event in human history — an event, moreover, of such critical consequences for the whole human family that it stands side by side with and explains the other great crucial event of history, namely the coming of Christ to save the world (Rom. 5:12; I Cor. 15:21).

As well, and according to the Bible, mankind, having been liberated from the effects of sin, and, thereby, the Fall, by the crucifixion of Christ at Calvary, which paid for our sins, now awaits a second, and conclusive event in history, namely the Second Advent of Christ at the end of this age, when the effects of the Fall will be finally abolished, with unbelievers eternally judged, and the renewed creation, the new heavens and new earth, wherein Righteousness dwells, being established in accordance with Almighty God's immutable purposes (Acts 3:20; Rom. 8:19; II Pet. 3:13; Rev. Chpts. 21, 22). Thus by God's Grace all that was lost in Adam, and much more than that, is restored in Christ.

THE LAST ADAM

Taking the Bible student back to the Fall, Satan now becomes the ruler of this world's system, and by default on the part of Adam. As stated, it seems as if he has won the day, and has forever spoiled man, God's greatest creation. There is no way that man can save himself, inasmuch, as all will be born spoiled as Adam now is.

As well, Angels cannot redeem man, simply because Angels are another creation altogether. However, the Lord will do something, that it seems Satan had no knowledge of, the sending into the world of a Second Adam, namely, the Lord Jesus Christ, His Only Son (Jn. 3:16).

Paul dwelt on this at length, by mentioning the *"first man Adam"* as being a living soul, while the *"Last Adam"* (the Lord Jesus Christ), was made *"a quickening spirit"* (I Cor. 15:45).

He also said, *"For as in Adam all die, even so in Christ shall all be made alive"* (I Cor. 15:22).

So, God, in effect, would send a Second Adam into the world, the Lord Jesus Christ, Who would become Man, and would not fail as the first one failed (Rom. 5:12).

Paul said, *"For if through the offense of one (Adam) many be dead, much more the Grace of God, and the Gift by Grace, which is by One Man, Jesus Christ, hath abounded unto many"* (Rom. 5:15).

As Jesus, in order to redeem man, had to become a Man Himself, hence the genealogy becomes extremely important, as is obvious!

If one is to notice, the phrase, *"the Son of David, the Son of Abraham,"* does not mention Adam, and because all of the human family goes back to Adam, therefore, his name was not necessary.

"David" is here mentioned first, and because it was to David and his family that the Promise was given, through which the Messiah would come (II Sam. Ch. 7). Consequently, the lineage, at least up to the time of Christ, must not be broken, hence the giving of these names.

NOTES

As well, the Lord made the same Promise to Abraham, *"And I will make of thee a great nation, and I will bless thee, and make thy name great; and thou shalt be a blessing:*

"And I will bless them that bless Thee, and curse him that curseth Thee: and in Thee shall all families of the earth be blessed" (Gen. 12:2-3).

Therefore, Jesus' Pedigree went all the way back to David, and then to Abraham, and ultimately in an unbroken line to Adam (Lk. 3:38).

So, Christ became the Second Man, the Last Adam, and did what the First Adam did not do. He walked perfect before God, and as a man. He did not do so as Deity, but in the same context which you and I are forced to live, even though we all have failed, whereas He never failed. He did this as a man, *"The Man Christ Jesus"* (I Tim. 2:5).

In effect, the Last Adam, the Lord Jesus Christ, did so much more than the First Adam, that God's intention for the First Adam is no comparison to that which was done by Jesus Christ, the Last Adam. The following are just a few of the great differences:

1. The First Adam failed in a perfect environment, while the Last Adam, succeeded in a very hostile environment.

2. The Last Adam walked perfect before God, which the First Adam was supposed to do, but did not!

3. As well, the Last Adam had to offer up Himself as a Sacrifice, which the First Adam was not required to do.

4. The Last Adam had to rise from the dead, which, of course, was not required by God respecting the First Adam.

So, the task required of the Last Adam was far more difficult than the First Adam, but, still, was gloriously carried out and flawlessly so!

As such, all who believe in Him will not perish, but have everlasting life (Jn. 3:16).

Consequently, He purchased back, and by His Own precious Blood at that, what the First Adam lost.

With the First Adam, it was paradise lost; with the Last Adam, it is paradise regained!

Christ, by linking His Name with poor fallen humanity, exemplifies the Grace of God.

It is no honor for Jesus to be called *"the Son of David, the Son of Abraham,"* but it is an honor unsurpassed for *"David,"* and *"Abraham,"* as well as all of us, to have His Name attached to ours. He had everything to offer, while we had nothing, and yet, *"He is not ashamed to call them brethren"* (Heb. 2:11).

I realize that my pitiful attempts to properly elucidate the significance of the genealogy, i.e., *"the generation of Jesus Christ,"* is woefully lacking. But yet, is it possible for any man, and no matter how studiously learned, to successfully treat this subject as it should be treated?

Each and every name in this genealogy, represents poor fallen humanity, and with no way to extricate themselves from the terrible morass of sin. And yet, through this very fallen family, Jesus Christ, God's Only Son, came, and as such, was the consummate Man, and, consequently, the Perfect Sacrifice. Even though it was not possible for the diseased tree of man to bring forth such a One, still, God could do so, and, in fact, did do so, by *"sending His Own Son in the likeness of sinful flesh,"* even though He had no sin in His Flesh, or Spirit (Rom. 8:3; II Cor. 5:21).

(2-5) "ABRAHAM BEGAT ISAAC; AND ISAAC BEGAT JACOB; AND JACOB BEGAT JUDAS AND HIS BRETHREN;

"AND JUDAS BEGAT PHARES AND ZARA OF THAMAR; AND PHARES BEGAT ESROM; AND ESROM BEGAT ARAM;

"AND ARAM BEGAT AMINADAB; AND AMINADAB BEGAT NAASSON; AND NAASSON BEGAT SALMON;

"AND SALMON BEGAT BOOZ OF RACHAB; AND BOOZ BEGAT OBED OF RUTH; AND OBED BEGAT JESSE;"

"Judas" (Judah) is mentioned in vs. 2, and not his other brothers who headed up the other Tribes of Israel, because Christ came through the lineage of *"Judah,"* and as was prophesied by Jacob (Gen. 49:10). Hence, Christ is called *"The Lion of the Tribe of Judah"* (Rev. 5:5).

In verse 3, *"Thamar"* is mentioned, and is the first woman of four in this genealogy to be spoken of. The four are, *"Thamar, Rahab, Ruth, and Bathsheba."* They are placed in this order, a Hebrew, a Gentile; a Gentile, a Hebrew. These women emphasize Christ's condescension in taking human nature, for two of them were Gentiles, and only one was of good character.

Rahab was a harlot before she came to the

Lord (James 2:25). Both Thamar and Bathsheba committed adultery (Gen. 38; II Sam. 11:1-5). Ruth was pure, although a Gentile (Ruth 3:11).

Consequently, Christ descended from both Jews and Gentiles.

The story of *"Ruth"* is one of the most beautiful in the Bible, inasmuch, and as stated, she was a Gentile, but more importantly, she became the great-grandmother of David.

(6) "AND JESSE BEGAT DAVID THE KING; AND DAVID THE KING BEGAT SOLOMON OF HER THAT HAD BEEN THE WIFE OF URIAS;"

In this Scripture, we are told that the kingly line through David was through *"Solomon,"* even though David had other sons. Actually, the genealogy of Christ, and as stated, went back to David through both Joseph and Mary. Joseph, who would have been the king had the dynasty continued, went back through Solomon, while Mary went through Nathan, another son (II Sam. 5:14).

To fulfill Prophecy, both lines were necessary. The Lord had placed a curse upon Jeconiah (also called Coniah or Jehoiachin), who was of the royal line, proclaiming that none of his children would ever sit on the Throne of David (Jer. 22:24-30). But at the same time, the Lord told David that his line through Solomon would forever occupy the throne (II Sam., Chpt. 7).

Mary went back to David through Nathan, a son of David, while Joseph went back to David through Solomon. Therefore, the lineage was perfect (Lk. 1:32-33; Isa. 9:6-7; Rev. 5:5; 22:16). Consequently, to fulfill Prophecy, Mary not only had to be a Virgin, but as well the wife of Joseph (Isa. 7:14; Mat. 1:19-20).

This 6th verse is beautiful in another respect as well, portraying the Grace of God, in that it states, *"begat Solomon of her* (Bathsheba) *that had been the wife of Urias."*

Inasmuch as this was Satan's great effort to destroy David, and, therefore, the Promise of God made to him, that through his family the Messiah would come, this Passage is here placed as a constant reminder to Satan, and all concerned, of the Grace of God.

The phrase, *"And Jesse begat David the king,"* is meant to portray him, instead of Saul, as God's choice, a man after God's Own Heart.

In this, the Lord causes Grace to abound over sin, in that the offense of the people in demanding Saul as a king became a channel of blessing, by the giving of David.

As well, and even though what Bathsheba did, as David, was extremely sinful and wicked in the eyes of God and man, still, there is every evidence that she made this thing right with God, as David, and truly followed the Lord.

It is believed by most scholars that the lady spoken of in Proverbs 31 is, in fact, Bathsheba. As such, the advice she gives in this Chapter, speaks of a Righteousness which only God could give, and which she certainly seems to have been a recipient of.

Therefore, even though not for a moment condoning the terrible sin of David and Bathsheba, and even though they paid a terrible price for this sin, still, in this 6th verse of Matthew's genealogy of Christ, the Grace of God shines brightly.

Only the Blood of Jesus could cleanse and wash away such sin, hence, David's 51st Psalm.

(7) "AND SOLOMON BEGAT ROBOAM; AND ROBOAM BEGAT ABIA; AND ABIA BEGAT ASA;"

Under *"Rehoboam,"* the Kingdom of Israel split into two separate nations, with the Northern Kingdom consisting of Ten Tribes, and called either Israel, Samaria, or Ephraim. The Southern Kingdom, which included the Tribes of Judah, Benjamin, and Levi, was called Judah.

During the reign of Solomon, and especially his beginning years, Israel was the mightiest nation in the world. Actually, it was a type of the coming Kingdom Age, when Israel will once again be the supreme nation in the world. As well, Solomon was a type of Christ, Who ruled in wisdom, honor and greatness, with ambassadors coming from many of the nations of the world seeking his counsel and advice (II Chron. 9:23).

Rehoboam only walked in the way of David for some three years, and then *"forsook the Law of the Lord, and all Israel with him"* (II Chron. 11:17; 12:1).

Evidently, Solomon did not heed the instructions given to him by the Holy Spirit

NOTES

concerning *"the raising up of a child, in the way he should go, and when he is old, he will not depart from it,"* because Rehoboam did not turn out very well! (Prov. 22:6).

"Abijah" (called Abijam) in I Kings, did not begin too well, but seemed to come closer to the Lord in his latter years, inasmuch as his name was changed from *"Abijam,"* which means *"the sea, is tumultuous,"* to *"Abijah,"* meaning *"Jehovah is my Father."* Therefore, Grace, in Chronicles, omits the sadness of Abijah's beginnings, and describes at length his bold testimony for God and the Bible, and his valor and success in battle.

Conversely, *"Asa,"* began well, and ended poorly (II Chron. 16:10-13).

(8) "AND ASA BEGAT JOSAPHAT; AND JOSAPHAT BEGAT JORAM; AND JORAM BEGAT OZIAS;"

"Jehoshaphat" was one of the Godliest kings of Judah.

Between Joram and Ozias (Uzziah), three names are omitted. Ahaziah immediately succeeded Joram (II Ki. 8:24), and was followed by his son Joash (II Ki. 12:1), and he by his son Amaziah (II Ki. 14:1).

As well, the word *"begat"* does not necessarily mean the direct succession of son to father, but just that the individual is in the lineage.

As to why some of the names are omitted, the only answer is that the Holy Spirit had more interest in proving the linkage, rather than each individual.

(9-11) "AND OZIAS BEGAT JOATHAM; AND JOATHAM BEGAT ACHAZ; AND ACHAZ BEGAT EZEKIAS;

"AND EZEKIAS BEGAT MANASSES; AND MANASSES BEGAT AMON; AND AMON BEGAT JOSIAS;"

"AND JOSIAS BEGAT JECHONIAS AND HIS BRETHREN, ABOUT THE TIME THEY WERE CARRIED AWAY TO BABYLON:"

The phrase in vs. 11, *"And Josias begat Jechonias and his brethren,"* portrays this king (Jechonias) as being the last one, at least in the lineage of David to sit on the Throne, before the destruction of Judah and Jerusalem. However, he was followed by his uncle, Zedekiah, who reigned eleven years, who is referred to in the phrase, *"his brethren."* He was on the Throne *"about the time they were carried away to Babylon."*

(12) "AND AFTER THEY WERE BROUGHT TO BABYLON, JECHONIAS BEGAT SALATHIEL; AND SALATHIEL BEGAT ZOROBABEL:"

From Jeremiah 22:30, it has sometimes been thought that Jechoniah died childless. However, that is not what the prediction in Jeremiah meant. It only referred to none of his descendants actually sitting on the Throne of David, which they did not.

"Zerubbabel" was the one who built the Temple after the seventy-year dispersion had ended, and the Children of Israel were allowed back in the land by the Medes and the Persians (Ezra 1:1-4).

(13-14) "AND ZOROBABEL BEGAT ABIUD; AND ABIUD BEGAT ELIAKIM; AND ELIAKIM BEGAT AZOR;

"AND AZOR BEGAT SADOC; AND SADOC BEGAT ACHIM; AND ACHIM BEGAT ELIUD;"

Some have felt that the family of David fell to a low state after the kingly dynasty was stopped, which no doubt it did! However, the perfection of the lineage of Christ had nothing to do with the social status of these individuals, or even their spiritual status.

(15) "AND ELIUD BEGAT ELEAZAR; AND ELEAZAR BEGAT MATTHAN; AND MATTHAN BEGAT JACOB;"

Of this, one can be sure, the most careful records of every branch of the family of David, and all the families of Israel for that matter, were meticulously kept (Gen. 49:10; II Sam. 7).

(16) "AND JACOB BEGAT JOSEPH THE HUSBAND OF MARY, OF WHOM WAS BORN JESUS, WHO IS CALLED CHRIST."

Even though this statement is made matter of factly, still, this one verse of Scripture portrays, at least to date, the announcement of the greatest event in human history, i.e., the birth of Christ.

The phrase, *"And Jacob begat Joseph the husband of Mary,"* portrays Joseph as in the direct lineage of David, and, as stated, if the kingly line had continued, Joseph would have been the king of Israel.

Consequently, Matthew's Pedigree of Christ, is that of Joseph as regal heir begotten of Solomon and David. Mary was the daughter of Eli and cousin to Joseph. Both Joseph and Mary, consequently, were of the

House of David, as Luke narrates (Lk. 3:23).

Even though Mary's name is not mentioned in Luke's account, and because women are never reckoned in genealogies, still, she is there inferred.

Joseph was the legal son of Heli by marriage. In this particular genealogy, he took the place of Mary, with the natural line going back to Adam. The natural line always begins with the man himself and goes backward. However, in the royal line, as in Matthew, Chapter 1, it begins at the source of the dynasty and ends with Christ.

(Some have thought there was a discrepancy in Matthew 1:16, where it says, *"Jacob begat Joseph,"* and Luke 3:23, where it says, *"Joseph, which was the son of Heli."* Actually, Joseph was the son-in-law of Heli, having married Mary the daughter of Heli. It does not say Joseph was begotten by Heli, as it does in the case of Jacob.)

Jesus therefore, united in His Person the two only claims to the Throne of Israel; and, as he still lives there can be no other claimant.

(17) "SO ALL THE GENERATIONS FROM ABRAHAM TO DAVID ARE FOURTEEN GENERATIONS; AND FROM DAVID UNTIL THE CARRYING AWAY INTO BABYLON ARE FOURTEEN GENERATIONS; AND FROM THE CARRYING AWAY INTO BABYLON UNTO CHRIST ARE FOURTEEN GENERATIONS."

From Abraham *"unto Christ,"* was approximately 2,000 years.

(Incidentally, from Adam to Abraham was approximately 2,000 years, and as well, from Christ to the present, called *"the Church age,"* has been approximately 2,000 years. Inasmuch as the call of Abraham signified the people through whom Christ would come, with the conclusion of the next 2,000 years signifying the Birth of Christ, and insomuch as approximately 2,000 more years have passed, should not we very soon expect another great event of Christ, i.e., the Rapture and then the Second Coming!)

The word, *"generation,"* has different meanings, sometimes referring to a particular span of time, such as forty years, or even referring to the entirety of the life span of a particular individual, which could be any number of years. Consequently, the phrase, *"all the generations,"* as given by the Holy Spirit through Matthew, could only refer to His Own designation.

From Abraham to David was about 900 years. From David to *"the carrying away into Babylon,"* was about 500 years, and from that time *"unto Christ,"* about 600 years.

Therefore, for the Holy Spirit to label *"fourteen generations,"* between each of these designations, and considering that the time spans are so different, one can only conclude that the Holy Spirit formed His Own designations regarding the even *"fourteen generations"* between each specification, i.e., *"Abraham to David,"* etc. This we do know, the number *"fourteen"* is not derived from the number of individuals named, especially considering those who were, in fact, in the genealogy, but not specified. Neither is the number *"fourteen"* derived from the span of time, as these times vary by as much as 400 years.

(18) "NOW THE BIRTH OF JESUS CHRIST WAS ON THIS WISE: WHEN AS HIS MOTHER MARY WAS ESPOUSED TO JOSEPH, BEFORE THEY CAME TOGETHER, SHE WAS FOUND WITH CHILD OF THE HOLY GHOST."

The word, *"Now,"* would have probably been better translated *"But,"* in order to mark the contrast between His Birth and that of the preceding births; for they were by natural procreation, but His by spiritual procuration.

The phrase, *"Now the Birth of Jesus Christ was on this wise,"* expresses the Incarnation, for God had to become Man, as here described, in order to redeem fallen man.

The phrase, *"When as His mother Mary was espoused to Joseph,"* was actually an engagement, signified by a legal document, which specified a particular period of time between the espousal and actual marriage relationship (Gen. 29:18; Deut. 20).

Consequently, Mary and Joseph were only engaged, and had not yet come together as man and wife, i.e., no sexual relations.

The phrase, *"Before they came together,"* has to do with Joseph and Mary consummating the marriage, which included sexual relations. Mary was probably about sixteen or seventeen years old at the time, and as prophesied by Isaiah, was a *"Virgin"* (Isa. 7:14).

The phrase, *"She was found with child of*

the Holy Ghost," merely refers to the Truth that the Child was by Divine origin.

The phrase does not refer to any type of physical act, but rather a spiritual act. It has the same connotation as Genesis 1:2, *"And the Spirit of God moved upon the face of the waters."* This, as the conception of Mary, was a spiritual act with a physical result.

The word, *"Virgin,"* as given by Isaiah, is in the Hebrew, *"Ha-alma,"* and means, *"the virgin — the only one that ever was, or ever will be a mother in this way."*

Some would attempt to argue that the word, *"almah"* could mean a young married woman, but is not supported in any Scripture; and in view of the plain record of Mary being a pure Virgin who had not known man and one who conceived by the Holy Spirit, it only shows unbelief and rebellion against God's Word and the Perfect Plan of Redemption through a virgin-born man-God manifest in the flesh — if we accept anything but what is plainly declared in Scripture (Lk. 1:30-38; Jn. 1:1-14; Rom. 8:3; Gal. 4:4; I Tim. 3:16; Heb. 1:5-7; 2:6-18).

If Jesus had been conceived by the normal manner of husband and wife coming together, He would have been born in sin just as all the sons of Adam had been born in sin. As a consequence, He would have needed Redemption as all others, and could in no way have served as the Perfect Sacrifice which, in Truth, He was. Due to the Fall, the seed of man was corrupt, and, therefore, could not bring any *"sons of God"* into the world, as the Lord originally intended, but only *"sons of Adam"* (Gen. 5:3).

However, as Mary was not impregnated by man, but rather by the Holy Ghost, as He decreed her conception, the terrible taint of sin did not pass on to Christ.

(Mary's conception was much the same, at least as far as the act was concerned, as the account in Genesis, *"And God said, Let there be light: and there was light."* The Holy Spirit simply said, and regarding Mary, *"Let there be . . . and there was . . ."* — Gen. 1:3).

All serious Bible students read these words, *"before they came together, she was found with child of the Holy Ghost,"* with wonder, awe, and tremendous reverence. However, this was a stigma that Mary would live with all of her life, in that the enemies of Christ would ever claim that He was conceived out of wedlock, and, consequently, was a *"bastard."*

John records the words that His enemies threw at Him, *"Then said they to Him, We be not born of fornication"* (Jn. 8:41).

Among other things, they were implying that He was born of fornication, and, as such, was illegitimate! In Truth, His Birth was the only legitimate birth ever recorded.

Immediately after the Fall in the Garden of Eden, the Lord said to Satan, *"And I will put enmity between thee and the woman, and between thy seed and her seed; it shall bruise thy head, and thou shalt bruise His Heel"* (Gen. 3:15).

If one is to notice, the Lord referred to *"The Seed of the woman,"* and not the seed of man. In effect, the woman has no *"seed,"* except in this one case, where it refers to the Birth of the Messiah, the Son of God.

(19) "THEN JOSEPH HER HUSBAND, BEING A JUST MAN, AND NOT WILLING TO MAKE HER A PUBLICK EXAMPLE, WAS MINDED TO PUT HER AWAY PRIVILY."

The phrase, *"Then Joseph her husband, being a just man,"* is a statement by the Holy Spirit, referring to the consecration of Joseph, by referring to him as a *"just,"* i.e., *"a Righteous man."* This implies that *"Joseph"* was a true son of David, and desired in every respect to obey the Law.

In these words, *"Then Joseph her husband,"* we find that the engagement to be married in those times, was of far greater weight than the present. Even though the actual wedding had not yet taken place, and they had not come together, still, they were looked at because of the engagement as *"man and wife."*

Even though it is unsaid, one can well imagine the heartache that Joseph went through when Mary informed him of her condition. To be frank, unless the Lord had appeared to him in a dream, as the next verse proclaims, Joseph would not have believed Mary's story.

And before we criticize him for such action, we must realize that Mary was relating something to him that had never happened in human history. To be sure, he had known her all her life, and no doubt had observed a flawless, spotless life, at least in these matters; therefore, he must have been totally without understanding. Knowing her, he could not conceive that she had been unfaithful, but yet, he could not, as well, believe the story of her pregnancy,

as she related how the Angel *"Gabriel"* came to her, and said, *"And, behold, thou shalt conceive in thy womb, and bring forth a son, and shall call His Name JESUS.*

"He shall be great, and shall be called the Son of the Highest: and the Lord God shall give unto Him the Throne of His father David:

"And He shall reign over the House of Jacob for ever; and of His Kingdom there shall be no end."

Then, no doubt, Mary told Joseph that she answered the Angel by saying, *"How shall this be, seeing I know not a man?"*

And then she further related to Joseph, *"And the Angel answered and said unto me, The Holy Ghost shall come upon thee, and the Power of the Highest shall overshadow thee: therefore also that holy thing which shall be born of thee shall be called the Son of God"* (Lk. 1:31-35).

In Truth, such an explanation would have been virtually impossible for any man, no matter how *"righteous"* to comprehend and believe, unless the Lord had intervened, which He did!

The phrase, *"And not willing to make her a publick example,"* proclaims his love for her, and wanting to do all within his power to save her as much embarrassment as possible.

The phrase, *"Was minded to put her away privily,"* means to divorce her privately.

In Truth, the Law of Moses demanded the death penalty for a woman in such cases, along with the man who had committed the deed; however, there is very little record of such action being actually carried out (Deut. 22:20-22).

In Joseph's case, and after hearing Mary's explanation, and being, no doubt, extremely confused, he had decided to avail himself of Deuteronomy 24:1, which meant to divorce her privately, and not put her to death.

(20) "BUT WHILE HE THOUGHT ON THESE THINGS, BEHOLD, THE ANGEL OF THE LORD APPEARED UNTO HIM IN A DREAM, SAYING, JOSEPH, THOU SON OF DAVID, FEAR NOT TO TAKE UNTO THEE MARY THY WIFE: FOR THAT WHICH IS CONCEIVED IN HER IS OF THE HOLY GHOST."

The phrase, *"But while he thought on these things,"* proclaims him carefully digesting her story, but yet finding it so incredible he simply could not believe it.

As stated, he had known her all her life, and could not remotely conceive of her doing such a thing, but yet, according to her own words she was pregnant, and knowing that he had not come together with her, the only plausible explanation was that she had been unfaithful. From the Text, it seems that he strongly desired to believe her, but, logically, simply could not accept her explanation.

The phrase, *"Behold, the Angel of the Lord appeared unto him in a dream,"* first of all proclaims the element of surprise, by using the word *"behold!"* In other words, Joseph had already made up his mind to *"put her away,"* when the *"Angel of the Lord"* appeared to him in a *"dream,"* confirming Mary's story. This must have been, and was without a doubt, the greatest moment in Joseph's life, for this happening to occur.

The phrase, *"Saying, Joseph, thou son of David,"* reminds Joseph of the greatness of his ancestry, which, as well, spoke of the Great Promise given to David in II Samuel 7:12-16.

Even though Joseph was only a carpenter, certainly a noble trade, but, nevertheless, of far lesser station than the King of Israel, still, in God's Eyes, and, actually, the only Eyes that mattered, Joseph was held in very high regard. As stated, had the kingly line continued, Joseph would now be the king of Israel. In a sense, and even though there was no throne presently in Israel, in God's Mind, and which He had originally intended, Joseph was king.

The Message of the Angel was simple, *"fear not to take unto thee Mary thy wife."*

In a moment, and without doubt, Joseph's fears were gone! Irrespective of what others may say or think, the wedding plans will continue, and Mary will become his *"wife,"* in name and in fact.

The Angel then states, *"for that which is conceived in her is of the Holy Ghost,"* thus verifying Mary's explanation, and, as well, laying special stress on the Divine origin of Jesus.

(21) "AND SHE SHALL BRING FORTH A SON, AND THOU SHALT CALL HIS NAME JESUS: FOR HE SHALL SAVE HIS PEOPLE FROM THEIR SINS."

The Angel's announcement to Joseph concerning Jesus, is very similar to what the Lord said to Sarah concerning Isaac, in Genesis 17:19.

The phrase, *"And she shall bring forth a son,"* is virtually that which was given to Isaiah, *"Behold a virgin shall conceive, and bear a son, and shall call His Name Immanuel"* (Isa. 7:14). This *"Son"* was the fulfillment of the Prophecies, which began in the Garden of Eden (Gen. 3:15), and was taken up later with Abraham (Gen. 12:3), and then a little later to Sarah concerning Isaac (Gen. 17:19). Then the Lord confirmed the Promise again to Jacob in the great Prophecy given to him shortly before he died, *"The Sceptre shall not depart from Judah, nor a lawgiver from between his feet, until Shiloh come: and unto Him shall the gathering of the people be"* (Gen. 49:10). (*"Shiloh"* is another Name for the Messiah.)

And then, of course, Isaiah's Prophecies were so pointed and detailed respecting the coming Messiah, that there was no reason for Israel not to know who this *"Son"* was! (Isa. 7:14; 53:1-12).

To date, this was the greatest event in human history, and yet, its announcement and action were given not to the Religious Leaders of Israel, or to its nobility, but to a little teenage girl and her carpenter husband. Jesus would later say, *"O Father, Lord of Heaven and earth, because Thou hast hid these things from the wise and prudent, and hast revealed them unto babes."*

And then He said, *"Even so, Father: for so it seemed good in Thy sight"* (Mat. 11:25-26).

The phrase, *"And thou shalt call His Name JESUS,"* is actually in the Hebrew form, *"Yehoshua,"* or, *"Joshua,"* and means *"Saviour, Who is Salvation."*

Of all the Names given to God in the Old Testament, *"Jehovah-Elohim," "Adonai-Jehovah," "Jehovah-Jireh," "Jehovah-Nissi,"* etc., the greatest Name He was ever given, in both the Old and New Testaments, is *"JESUS."*

The phrase, *"For He shall save His people from their sins,"* actually says, *"For it is He who shall save, He and none other!"*

This Glorious Name, *"JESUS,"* answers to the fact, for He Himself, in His Own Person, by virtue of what and who He is, shall save.

Regrettably, Israel did not want a Messiah Who would save them from their *"sins,"* but, instead, from the Romans, etc.

However, Israel's problem was not Rome, but, instead, herself, which spoke of her sins.

As well, *"sin"* is the cause of all the problems of the human family.

THE CAUSE IS SIN

Washington, along with many other capitals of the world, attempts to solve the problems with more laws, but to no avail. As well, education attempts to solve these problems. Wall Street thinks that a positive market will ensure financial and social stability. However, the problems continue to exacerbate, and despite the new laws, education, and hundreds of billions of dollars being thrown at these social and economic cancers. The reason is simple, only the symptoms are being treated, instead of the cause.

The cause is sin! And that can only be handled by Jesus Christ, and, regrettably, His Name is little allowed to be mentioned in any public institution or building.

The word, *"save,"* in the Greek is *"sodzo,"* and means *"Salvation from sin."*

Man is loathe to admit that he is a sinner, and that he needs a Saviour. The element of pride, which became man's crowning sin as a result of the Fall, makes man think he can save himself. Consequently, he has ever attempted to rebuild the Garden of Eden, but without the Tree of Life, i.e., The Lord Jesus Christ.

Back in the 1960's, Lyndon Johnson, then the President of the United States, launched his *"Great Society"* program, which, he said, would eliminate poverty in America.

During this past thirty odd years (to the mid 90's), and despite trillions being poured into this effort, the problem is worse than ever.

The reason is simple; the problem is not economical or social, but, instead, spiritual. These problems are caused by the wicked hearts of wicked men. Consequently, until the heart is changed, which can only come about by Jesus Christ, the problem will not be solved.

ONLY CHRIST CAN SAVE

If one is to notice, the Angel said, *"He shall save,"* which means that the Church cannot save, nor psychology, nor any other effort of man! Regrettably, Satan has been very successful in substituting other things in place of *"He shall save!"*

For example, when the Catholics speak of accepting Christ, their meaning is entirely

NOTES

different than this proclaimed in the Word of God. They equate the Church with Christ, and, they say, one abiding by its tenets of Faith, whether Scriptural or not, ensures Salvation, and is, therefore, constituted as *"accepting Christ."* Tragically, many Protestant Churches more or less do the same!

Virtually all Catholics and Protestants advocate psychology as the panacea for the ills of man, which is totally contrary to Scripture. Either Jesus is the only One Who can save, as the Bible proclaims, or else the Bible is a lie, and man, by his various philosophies, can save himself.

The record fully shows that man cannot save himself, and that Jesus Alone can save from sin!

WHAT IS SIN?

The Old Testament and the New Testament proclaim sin as *"missing the mark."* In clearer terms, it means to disobey God, which means to disobey His Word. Consequently, the Word of God provides the only true, and, thereby, unchanging standard for *"sin."* It alone is the Revelation of Divine expectations, which provide valid standards for humanity. Regrettably, Congress and the Supreme Court in America have attempted to usurp authority over the Bible. Consequently, those standards change almost constantly, while Bible Standards remain consistent.

In the 51st Psalm, David confessed to God his terrible sin involving Bathsheba and her husband, Uriah. David said, *"Against You, You only, have I sinned"* (Ps. 51:4).

This does not mean his sin did not harm Bathsheba or her husband. Instead, it is an admission that God is the One Who establishes the standard of right and wrong. A relative morality that measures sin by harm done to others must always fall short of the Biblical position. Other people belong to God, and He has established His standards for their protection as well as for our own.

So sin is against God, and because it is against God, the Lord is *"proved right"* and *"justified"* when He acts in Judgment.

Thus, the Old Testament sees sin as involving a person's conscience, pointing to a responsible choice measured against a known Divine standard. But sin is more basic than that; the individual's propensity to react against the Divine norm can be traced back to human nature itself. In other words, human nature is wicked, and is so from birth, and because of the Fall in the Garden of Eden. Against this wickedness, man, at least within himself, is helpless. Consequently, people can only recognize their need and appeal to God for forgiveness, inner cleansing, and spiritual power, which is supplied upon one's Faith in Christ.

Paul, in the New Testament, takes the concept of sin hinted at in Psalm 51:5 and implied in the Old Testament Doctrine of the New Covenant, and develops the portrait of a humanity distorted and twisted by the brutal power of sin. Therefore, sin in the New Testament is explained as in the Old as not only missing God's mark; it is an inner reality, a warp in human nature, and a malignant power that holds each individual in an unbreakable grip.

SIN AS A DISTORTION OF HUMAN NATURE

In Paul's writings, as in the Old Testament, sin represents acts that fall short of the Divine Standard.

Paul brings it out that Pagans sinned without knowledge of the Mosaic Law; but in light of the fact that God has planted in human nature a testimony to moral issues, they are actually sinning against their own standards (Rom. 2:12).

Paul adequately describes this by the entry of sin and death into the race by Adam's act (Rom. 5:12-13). Sin and death now *"dwell"* in the human personality; these are twin principles that distort individual personality and society (Rom. 7:17-8:2).

Ephesians 2 describes the human condition of those dead in trespasses and sins, a condition Believers used to live in and that unbelievers still live in (Eph. 2:2-3).

Thus, acts of sin are portrayed in the New Testament, as in the Old, as an expression of an inner flaw so serious that humanity is a willing slave to hostile spiritual forces and to the cravings of a warped nature.

Consequently, the solution to sin must involve an inner transformation, so that individuals can be freed from the domination of

NOTES

evil, which psychology, or no other self-help program devised by man can ever do.

JESUS' DEATH

Insight into the true nature of sin explains the meaning of Jesus' death. Only when we sense the full extent of our inner bondage can we appreciate the release that Salvation brings, which was brought about by what Christ did at Calvary.

As a result of the hostile spiritual forces within man, and the cravings of his warped nature, the proper understanding of sin, with an understanding of Christ, is central to the Christian understanding of reality.

Jesus located the source of sin in the human heart. Uncleanness is not a matter of externals. The true issue of relationship with God must focus on the human heart as the source from which all evils spring (Mat. 15:16-20).

Despite sin's warp within, and despite some people's choice of a lifestyle of sin, even *"sinners"* do good to those who are good to them.

Consequently, what some call *"total depravity"* may well mean that no human act, flowing as it does from a distorted nature, can meet the Divine Standard. But it does not mean that there is no potential in lost humanity for kindness, friendship, loyalty, or a base type of love. Even as sinners, human beings bear the stamp of the eternal and wear the image of God (Lk. 6:32-34; Rom. 5:6-7).

However, we must not mistake human good as something acceptable to the Lord, for God requires a perfection of motive and action that no person can achieve.

BELIEF IN CHRIST

Without belief in Jesus, people die in their sins. In fact, a person's inner condition is demonstrated by the outward positive or negative response to Jesus. The only freedom from slavery to sin comes from Jesus (St. Jn. 8:21-42).

Paul demonstrates that all human beings lack Righteousness. This is seen by the failure of Gentiles and Jews to live up to the standards they themselves hold. It is proven by Scripture, which charges that all are under sin (Rom. Chpts. 1-3). In fact, the Law of Moses established the Divine Standard against which human actions can be measured. So measured, all people are guilty, and when they compare their own lives to the Standard (the Bible), they become aware of their guilt (Rom. 3:19-20).

God's Love is demonstrated by the fact that Jesus willingly died for sinners. Consequently, the Bible totally portrays the state of lost humanity. Human beings in the bondage of sin are powerless, ungodly, and enemies of God. Sin's warping influence is expressed in human motives, character, and attitude, as well as in sinful acts (Rom. 5:1-11).

THE IMPACT OF JESUS' DEATH AND RESURRECTION ON THE BELIEVER

Through union with Christ, Believers have *"died to sin."* The point made is that the influence of sin on the human personality is *"rendered powerless,"* so sin and death no longer exert mastery. This frees the Believer through Faith expressed in obedience, to live a righteous rather than a sinful life. Paul points out that as creatures, human beings must always surrender their will to some greater power. By surrendering ourselves to God, to obey Him, we can be free of sin's domination (Rom. 6).

In Romans 7, Paul explored the interrelationships between the Believer, sin, and the Law. Drawing from personal experience, Paul shows that sin is an inner reality for the Believer. One who tries to counter its influence by struggling to keep the Law invariably fails.

And then in Romans 8, Paul affirmed deliverance through the Power of the Holy Spirit. Christians rely, not on themselves or their efforts, but completely on the Power of God to *"give life to* (their) *mortal bodies"* (Rom. 8:11). When they rely on the Spirit of God and respond to His promptings, *"the righteous requirements of the Law"* are *"fully met"* by them (Rom. 8:4).

Paul, in Ephesians 2:1-4, described the impact of sin upon the individual. Because human beings by nature are spiritually dead, they are in the grip of the cravings and desires of their warped nature. Only by Christ's gift of new life, accepted by Faith, can we be saved from these ungodly cravings and desires.

SIN IN THE BELIEVER

John explored the inter-play between sin and sins. The sin principle still exists in Believers and issues, at times, in acts of sin. But

confession of sins restores to fellowship with the Lord and opens us to the process of inner cleansing He has begun. Only if we deny the existence of sin within do we lose contact with this reality. Actually, in these Passages, John negates the erroneous teaching of *"sinless perfection."* Even though the Holy Spirit through the Believer says, *"sin not,"* He quickly adds, *"And if any man sin, we have an advocate with the Father, Jesus Christ the Righteous"* (I Jn. 1:8-10; 2:1).

In Truth, the assurance of forgiveness for failures is a motivator of holiness, and not for continued sin. In other words, the act of forgiveness quickly extended to the Believer upon proper confession of sin, in no way breeds license to sin, but, in reality, creates in the life of the Believer a strong desire to overcome any and all sin.

Jesus came to earth to remove sin, first legally (by forgiveness) and then experimentally (by victory over sin in our daily lives). Believers, consequently, must be known for their lack of sin, and not for constant sinning, even though forgiveness is available!

Both the Old and New Testaments view sin in the terms of human response to Divine Standards. People fall short, deviate, and rebel against the norms that God has established.

Such actions result in guilt, but a remedy is implied in the very Hebrew terms themselves. Thus, *"sin"* and *"sin offering"* like *"trespass"* and *"trespass offering"* are from the same roots. God calls on human beings to acknowledge their sin, and in that call God invites the Believer to look to Him for forgiveness.

The New Testament actually carries the explanation of sin a little further, by proclaiming it as not only a deviation from Divinely-established norms, but, as well, something that is deeply rooted in the nature of the fallen race, a reality that holds human beings in slavery to hostile spiritual powers and to baser passions and desires.

Because of the corruption of human nature by sin, no person can achieve, at least within himself, the Standard God must require, and no one apart from Redemption, can please the Lord.

JESUS

Jesus' entry into the world to deal with sin must be understood on multiple levels.

1. Jesus does forgive sins, and His Death on Calvary was a Sacrifice that satisfied the demands of justice that sins be punished.

2. Jesus is also the source of a new life that renews the individual from within. Through Jesus, we are provided with the capacity not to sin.

3. By surrender to God and reliance on the Holy Spirit Whom Jesus has sent, the influence of the sin nature in the Believer can be dampened, and the Christian can live according to God's Will. The Promise of Resurrection's full release from every taint of sin is tasted here, and at each moment the possibility of living without sin's corrupting impact does exist.

In I John, we even have that Promise extended. God will not guarantee us sinlessness. But the reality and the power of His Life within is a major motivation to a life of holiness.

(The exposition on sin was taken from the writings of Reverend Lawrence O. Richards.)

(22) "NOW ALL THIS WAS DONE, THAT IT MIGHT BE FULFILLED WHICH WAS SPOKEN OF THE LORD BY THE PROPHET, SAYING,"

The phrase, *"Now all this was done,"* refers to God becoming Man, in order to redeem man from sin. Actually, the two words, *"all this,"* constitute a gross understatement. What was done to redeem man, which originated with God, is of such magnitude and so far outstrips the ability of man to comprehend it all, that quite possibly it will never be fully comprehended by the natural resources of man, other than being revealed by the Holy Spirit (I Cor. 2:9-10).

The phrase, *"That it might be fulfilled,"* concerns the Lord bringing to pass that which was promised. His Word cannot fail!

The phrase, *"Which was spoken of the Lord by the Prophet, saying,"* refers to these great things having already been predicted by the Prophets of old, and in this case, Isaiah.

Consequently, any and all of the great happenings in the New Testament were already promised in the Old, with Isaiah being the first prophet mentioned.

It must be remembered, that the Angel is continuing to speak to Joseph in the dream, and is patiently explaining what all of this means!

(23) "BEHOLD, A VIRGIN SHALL BE WITH CHILD, AND SHALL BRING FORTH A SON, AND THEY SHALL CALL HIS NAME EMMANUEL, WHICH BEING INTERPRETED IS, GOD WITH US."

The phrase, *"Behold, a Virgin shall be with child,"* proclaims the Angel laying great stress on the word, *"Virgin."*

The phrase, *"And shall bring forth a Son,"* proclaims this *"Son"* as being of such origin that, in the highest sense, He could truly be called *"Immanuel."*

The phrase, *"And they shall call His Name Emmanuel,"* refers to the great titles of Jehovah, Immanuel, Messiah, God, Son of God, Son of David, and Jesus as being grouped together, and is proclaimed so by the phrase, which being interpreted is, *"God with us."*

Consequently, the phrase, *"God with us,"* proclaims the Deity of Christ, even while in human form. In other words, He was Very God, and Very Man.

That does not mean that He was half-God and half-man, but rather fully God and fully man.

However, in the Incarnation, which this verse portrays (God becoming Man), Christ, while never losing His possession of Deity, nevertheless, did lose His expressions of Deity. Irrespective, He was no less God!

This teaches that Jesus perfectly expressed the image of God. The Greek word for image is *"eikon,"* which means *"representation."* In classical Greek thought, the "eikon" had a share in the reality it expressed.

Paul called Jesus *"The image of God"* (II Cor. 4:4) and *"The image of the invisible God"* (Col. 1:15). The word expresses the relationship of a coin to its die, that is, there is no comparison here, but rather an exact expression of the thing from which the coin is molded.

In Hebrews 1:3, Jesus is described as the *"exact representation of His* (God's) *Being,"* and means, *"exact representation."*

God is so perfectly expressed in Jesus that when Philip asked to be shown the Father, Jesus could say, *"Anyone who has seen Me has seen the Father"* (Jn. 14:9).

As well as Jesus being an exact representation of God, which in fact He was God, He, as well, was an exact representation of man, at least in most respects. Several times the New Testament affirms that in the Incarnation, Jesus was made *"like His brothers"* (Heb. 9:17) and *"in the likeness of sinful man"* (Rom. 8:3), or *"in human likeness"* (Phil. 2:7).

Although the New Testament never speaks of Jesus as being in the image of man, as it does in the *"image of God,"* still, we should not conclude that He simply seemed to be human; for the Scripture never says that Jesus was *"like God"* or in the *"likeness of God,"* for He was fully God.

Consequently, He was *"in the likeness of sinful man,"* but only in that He was fully Man, and not *"sinful."*

In Jesus, even though His Person perfectly represented God as He truly is, still, He could not perfectly represent man as he is, for humanity is tainted by sin. Jesus' human nature was untainted by sin. Thus, Jesus is in the image of redeemed humanity, as it will ultimately be renewed when the drama of Redemption is complete.

In respect to all this, one must believe in the *"Virgin Birth"* in order to be saved. To disbelieve it, threatens a rebellion against God and His Word, which undermines the very fabric of one's Salvation. Therefore, those who claim to be saved, and yet disavow the Virgin Birth, are basing their claims on a lie, which cannot have any validity.

God is with us through the Virgin Birth, and in the form of Christ, or else He is not with us at all!

(24) "THEN JOSEPH BEING RAISED FROM SLEEP DID AS THE ANGEL OF THE LORD HAD BIDDEN HIM, AND TOOK UNTO HIM HIS WIFE:"

This Passage proclaims the fact that the dream of the Angel, and what was said, and as given by the Lord, satisfied every question that Joseph had.

The phrase, *"Then Joseph being raised from sleep,"* means that he had a full assurance in his heart upon awakening, of what Mary had said, and that this *"Son"* would, in fact, be the Messiah. There is no way that Joseph could not come to this conclusion after the statements made by the Angel.

The phrase, *"Did as the Angel of the Lord had bidden him,"* refers to obedience to the heavenly vision, and an immediate setting forth to carry out the course of action.

The phrase, *"And took unto him his wife,"* tells us what that course of action was!

Being fully satisfied in his heart, the original plans made in their engagement will now

NOTES

be carried out, and Mary will be *"his wife."*

(25) "AND KNEW HER NOT TILL SHE HAD BROUGHT FORTH HER FIRSTBORN SON: AND HE CALLED HIS NAME JESUS."

The Phrase, *"And knew her not till she had brought forth her firstborn Son,"* proved that after the birth of the Divine Child, Mary physically became Joseph's wife; for *"He took unto him his wife, and knew her not until"* (imperfect tense in the Greek Text), that is, *"was not accustomed to co-habit with her as his wife until."*

Four sons and at least two daughters were the fruit of this marriage, as appears from Chapter 13:55-56. These facts destroy the Roman Catholic Doctrine of the perpetual virginity of Mary of Nazareth.

The phrase, *"And he called His Name JESUS,"* confirms that what Gabriel had told Mary, and, as well, the Name that the Angel had confirmed to Joseph (Lk. 1:26-31).

CHAPTER 2

(1) "NOW WHEN JESUS WAS BORN IN BETHLEHEM OF JUDAEA IN THE DAYS OF HEROD THE KING, BEHOLD, THERE CAME WISE MEN FROM THE EAST TO JERUSALEM."

The phrase, *"Now when Jesus was born in Bethlehem of Judaea,"* proclaims this Bethlehem, for the other was in Zebulon.

As well, Matthew gives no details on the Birth of Christ, as Luke did (Lk. 2). However, Matthew would mention the *"wise men"* which Luke did not!

Incidentally, Jesus being born in *"Bethlehem"* was a fulfillment of Micah 5:2. This little village was about five miles south of Jerusalem.

The phrase, *"In the days of Herod the King,"* proclaims this time as approximately two years after the Birth of Christ.

This was Herod the Great, son of Antipater, an Idumean, and, consequently, a descendant of Esau, and so by nature hated and resolved to murder the son of Jacob.

Antipater, the father of Herod the Great, was made Procurator of Judaea by Julius Caesar in 47 B.C. Herod, only twenty-five years old, was made Governor of Galilee, and then eventually King of Judaea in 37 B.C.

He is the one who rebuilt the Jewish Temple (Jn. 2:20).

When he died, in 4 B.C., his kingdom was divided. Galilee and Perea were given to his son, Herod Antipas. He reigned from 4 B.C. to A.D. 39 (Lk. 3:1-2). This is the man who murdered John the Baptist (Mat. 14:1-11).

Judaea and Samaria were given to Archelaus, another son of Herod the Great (Mat. 2:22). He was succeeded by Herod Agrippa I in A.D. 37. He is called *"Philip"* in Matthew 14:3.

In A.D. 40, he took over all the original territory of Herod the Great. He was succeeded by Herod Agrippa II (Acts 25:13; 26:32).

Even though Herod the Great (the Herod mentioned by Matthew) expended lavish sums on the Temple, it did not endear him to his Jewish subjects. His Edomite descent was never forgotten; if he was a Jew by religion and rebuilt the Temple of the God of Israel in Jerusalem, which he did, that, still, did not deter him from erecting Temples to Pagan deities elsewhere.

This man, keeping with his murderous nature, later executed his own sons, Alexander and Aristobulus. As well, his oldest son, Antipater (named after his grandfather), who had poisoned Herod's mind against his half-brothers, derived no advantage from their death, for three years later he too fell victim to Herod's suspicions and was executed only a few days before Herod's own death. This suspicious murderous nature is well illustrated by the story of the visit of the wise men and the slaughter of the infants of Bethlehem, as Matthew will relate. Few men have been so ungodly!

The phrase, *"Behold, there came wise men from the East to Jerusalem,"* does not give their number, nor their particular country, nor that they were kings. It is just known that they were from the *"East."*

Tacitus and Suetonius, both Romans, testified to the fact that in the east at that time it was believed that a king would be born in Judaea who would rule the whole world.

In fact, Daniel predicted the Coming of our Lord and His being *"cut off"* some 483 years after the Babylonian captivity commandment to restore Jerusalem (Dan. 9:24-26).

Consequently, these *"wise men"* were probably from the area that Daniel had served about 500 years before, and, therefore, would be well aware of his Prophecies concerning this coming King, and would be, no doubt,

guided by their pronouncements.

Incidentally, the meaning of the word *"Bethlehem"* is *"House of Bread."* Consequently, it was fitting that Jesus would be born here, and because He was *"The True Bread."*

(2) "SAYING, WHERE IS HE THAT IS BORN KING OF THE JEWS? FOR WE HAVE SEEN HIS STAR IN THE EAST, AND ARE COME TO WORSHIP HIM."

The question, *"Saying, Where is He that is born King of the Jews?",* proclaims the certitude of the knowledge of these *"wise men,"* in that they did not ask *"Whether there is?"* but *"Where is?"* They show no sign of doubt.

The title *"King of the Jews"* was used first by these Gentiles, and was not used again until used by another Gentile, Pontius Pilate, as well as Roman soldiers (Mat. 27:11, 29, 37).

In actuality, the statement, *"King of the Jews,"* as used by the *"wise men,"* would have probably deeply offended the Jews, as they preferred the term, *"King of Israel"* (Mat. 27:42; Mk. 15:32).

The term, *"Jews,"* was not a term of endearment, at least in the ears of Israel, while the term, *"Israel,"* reminded them of their great privileges according to the Scriptures.

The phrase, *"For we have seen His Star in the East,"* probably would have been better translated, *"We, dwelling in the East saw His Star."*

This Passage with vss. 9 and 10, seem to make it clear that the Star did not precede them in their journey to Jerusalem, as is popularly supposed, but upon seeing it in the *"East,"* they knew it was *"His Star."*

Many questions beg to be asked concerning that statement, of which are few definitive answers.

1. What was this Star they saw in the heavens? Astronomy can suggest nothing which satisfies all these conditions, and, therefore, the appearance must have been strictly miraculous.

About 1600 years before, Balaam had prophesied, *"there shall come a Star out of Jacob...,"* a Prophecy which they may well have been acquainted with (Num. 24:15-19). And yet, this Prophecy alone would have given them precious little information!

2. How did they know it was *"His"* Star? They were emphatic in their statement, and could have only achieved this knowledge

through Revelation from God, which they no doubt had received.

No doubt they had hungrily studied the Prophecies of Daniel, and had been convinced of this coming King.

From these brief statements, there is every evidence that they knew Who He was, and What He was, at least up to a point!

The phrase, *"And are come to worship Him,"* does not necessarily mean the acceptance of Him as God, but as Lord and King.

However, for these *"wise men"* to come without delay, and especially a journey of several hundred miles, requiring several weeks, would not have been undertaken without something powerful happening to them far greater than the ordinary.

Having tabulated Daniel's Prophecies, and knowing this was the approximate time for the Birth of this King, quite possibly they had accepted Daniel's God, and had sought Him earnestly pertaining to these all-important events, and, consequently, experienced a Revelation from Him of some magnitude. Little else could explain their attention, haste, and knowledge!

(3) "WHEN HEROD THE KING HAD HEARD THESE THINGS, HE WAS TROUBLED, AND ALL JERUSALEM WITH HIM."

The phrase, *"Herod the king,"* is in contradistinction to Jesus as *"King of the Jews."*

They are here placed side by side in order to portray the contrast. One was notoriously wicked, while the Other was Gloriously Righteous. One was a murderer, while the Other was a Giver of Life. One helped drag a nation down, while the other picked it up, at least as much as they would allow Him!

As we have stated, had Israel not sinned terribly, bluntly refusing to repent, which necessitated their destruction by the Gentiles, Joseph would now be king, and not this murderous Herod.

Consequently, it becomes obviously clear that to disobey God brings destruction and heartache, while obeying Him brings joy and abundant life (Jn. 10:10).

However, man would disavow this, claiming that God's restrictions hamper his lifestyle, and the way to make a better world is to ignore God, and, instead, for man, himself, to become god, which he has, and with disastrous results!

Consequently, the Bible is presently held up to ridicule all over America, when, in reality, every single freedom and prosperity known in America has its origination in the Word of God. But sadly, blind men lead blind men, and they all fall in the ditch (Mat. 15:14).

The phrase, *"Heard these things,"* refers to the information given him from the *"wise men,"* who had journeyed from the East to Jerusalem.

Little did he realize it, and because the evil heart cannot understand spiritual things; however, he could have been one of the most blessed kings in history to have been reigning when the *"King of kings"* was born! What a privilege he would have had, to have used his position to herald the arrival of the Saviour of mankind. *"These things"* were the single most important things he would ever hear in all of his life, and, yet, he did the very opposite, as most!

As well, how so very important *"these things"* are to the whole of mankind, which constitutes the Word of God. And yet, most have no concern or regard, but, instead, label *"these things"* as fables, and, therefore, little worthy of attention!

The phrase, *"He was troubled,"* has reference, at least in a sense, to the Spirit of God dealing with him concerning what he had heard.

The Word of God never leaves one static. In other words, after hearing the Word, one is either better or worse for the hearing of it. If properly heeded, they are better, and in a way that is beyond one's imagination. If rejected, they do not remain as they were, but, instead, become progressively worse, and because they have rejected Light; therefore, the darkness becomes deeper, as it did with Herod.

The phrase, *"And all Jerusalem with him,"* was true as far as the whole was concerned. However, some few, some two years before, had gathered around Elizabeth and Zacharias, and Mary and Joseph, concerning the two babes. As well, Simeon and Anna, and others were thrilled at the prospect of the Birth of Christ (Lk. 2:38).

The phrase concerning *"All Jerusalem,"* must mean that the news was noised abroad in the city, but which aroused, it seems, little interest in the hearts of the Religious Leaders.

They were so lifted up within themselves that they could not even begin to admit that these Gentile *"wise men"* from the East could tell them anything, and especially concerning the coming Messiah! Therefore, because of hardness of heart and unbelief, they would miss the greatest event to date in human history.

(4) "AND WHEN HE HAD GATHERED ALL THE CHIEF PRIESTS AND SCRIBES OF THE PEOPLE TOGETHER, HE DEMANDED OF THEM WHERE CHRIST SHOULD BE BORN."

This Scripture says the Priests knew the Bible well. However, knowledge of the Scriptures is not the same as heart knowledge. It can be used against Christ.

The phrase, *"And when he had gathered all the Chief Priests and Scribes of the people together,"* means that he did this forthwith and without delay.

He was gathering them together for a very negative result, which would constitute one of the most brutal acts in history. Had he gathered them together in order to worship Christ, as the *"wise men,"* what a difference his life would have been!

The phrase, *"He demanded of them where Christ should be born,"* speaks of the Jewish Sanhedrin, i.e., *"Chief Priests,"* and exactly *"where"* this act spoken of by the *"wise men"* had taken place.

The use of the title *"Christ"* indicates that the Priests informed him that the One he was speaking of was, in fact, the Messiah, i.e., *"The Anointed."* Consequently, he, as well as the *"Chief Priests and Scribes"* was sinning against Light.

As stated, Christ was probably pretty close to two years old at this present time, and these Religious Leaders of Israel had no knowledge of Him. They were so wrapped up in their own religious world, that they had long since departed from the Word of God. Regrettably, it has pretty much always been that way, with the present no exception!

Most of that which God truly does, is unknown completely by the religious world. Not only do they know nothing about it, but they will actively oppose it, as these Priests and Scribes, if given the opportunity. Such characterizes all religion, which is always man-devised, and makes up the far greater part of that which calls itself *"Church!"*

(5) "AND THEY SAID UNTO HIM, IN BETHLEHEM OF JUDAEA; FOR THUS IT IS

WRITTEN BY THE PROPHET,"

The *"Chief Priests and Scribes,"* in answering the question of the King, was speaking of the Prophecy of Micah 5:2. They knew where it was to be, but had absolutely no knowledge that it had happened.

This is startling! The greatest event to date in the annals of human history had recently taken place, and that which the Prophets had spoken of so grandly, and these, the Religious Leaders of Israel, knew absolutely nothing about it. They knew the Word of God, but they did not know its Author. They were versed in its content, but were not versed in its true meaning! Such characterizes much, if not most of modern Christendom.

(6) "AND THOU BETHLEHEM, IN THE LAND OF JUDA, ART NOT THE LEAST AMONG THE PRINCES OF JUDA: FOR OUT OF THEE SHALL COME A GOVERNOR, THAT SHALL RULE MY PEOPLE ISRAEL."

Bethlehem of Judea was where David was born, and now it was where the Son of David had been born.

The women who attended the birth of Obed, who was born to Ruth and Boaz, prophesied, and concerning Boaz, *"that his name may be famous in Israel"* (Ruth 4:14).

Even though the Holy Spirit through them was speaking of Boaz, still, Bethlehem, as a place, would gain that fame also. In fact, and at the present, Bethlehem is one of the most famous cities in the world, and because it was here that Christ was born.

The phrase, *"Art not the least among the Princes of Juda,"* in effect says, *"Art in no wise least among the Princes of Juda."*

The idea is that Bethlehem was very small, but still, and despite its smallness of size, it would gain notoriety and fame, and because of Who was born there, namely Christ.

The phrase, *"For out of Thee shall come a Governor, that shall rule My people Israel,"* refers solely to The Messiah, i.e., Christ.

Even though Christ was denied that *"rule"* at His First Coming, He, at the Second Coming, will definitely rule all of Israel as well as all other nations of the world, and forever (Isa. 9:6-7; Dan. 2:44-45; 7:13-14, 27; Zech. 14; Lk. 1:32-33; Rev. 11:15; 20:1-15; 22:4-5).

(7) "THEN HEROD, WHEN HE HAD PRIVILY CALLED THE WISE MEN, INQUIRED

OF THEM DILIGENTLY WHAT TIME THE STAR APPEARED."

The phrase, *"Then Herod, when he had privily called the wise men,"* indicates his plot of treachery was already beginning.

The phrase, *"Inquired of them diligently what time the Star appeared,"* means that he inquired *"most carefully."*

In this question, he was probably inquiring of the first appearance of the *"Star,"* when it appeared to the *"wise men"* in the *"East"* even before their journey began! He may have reasoned, and no doubt did, that the first appearance of the *"Star"* some time before, signaled the Birth of the Child.

In fact, a time frame of some two years could easily have passed from its first appearance, to the present. When the *"wise men"* first saw the Star, a period of time, no doubt, then passed, as they sought direction, and possibly a Revelation from the Lord.

As well, their preparation for such a long journey, could have easily taken several months. And then adding several months which it took to make the journey of several hundred miles, two years could easily have passed.

(8) "AND HE SENT THEM TO BETHLEHEM, AND SAID, GO AND SEARCH DILIGENTLY FOR THE YOUNG CHILD; AND WHEN YE HAVE FOUND HIM, BRING ME WORD AGAIN, THAT I MAY COME AND WORSHIP HIM ALSO."

The phrase, *"And he sent them to Bethlehem,"* refers to what the *"Chief Priest and Scribes"* had told him concerning the place of the Birth of this miracle Child. Of course, it was the wrong place, because Joseph and Mary had long since departed from Bethlehem. However, the King would have had no knowledge of that!

The phrase, *"Go and search diligently for the young Child,"* refers to him being older than a mere infant, i.e., *"young child."* As stated, he was probably about two years old at this present time.

The phrase, *"And when ye have found Him, bring me word again, that I may come and worship Him also,"* was probably spoken only to the *"wise men,"* because had Jews heard him say this, they would not have believed him.

Little did he realize that if he had truly desired to *"worship Him,"* it would have been,

NOTES

without doubt, the greatest moment of his life. However, he was lying; he, instead, desired to murder Him! In that he was no different than the *"Chief Priests and Scribes,"* who some thirty years later would do that very thing!

So, this evil, wicked King desired to murder Him, and so did the Religious Leaders of Israel!

In this, we find the seed of the opposition against Christ in this present world. It constitutes two directions:

1. Herod: He represents the world which follows in his train and desires nothing to interfere with their place, position, or sins. This is the world system which greatly opposes Christ, as then, so now!

It may pay lip service to Him in some remote circumstances, but as a whole it wants no part of Him, and if given the opportunity will do anything to hinder His Message, and to stop His Work. It may be done under the auspices of many and varied things, but, still, its end result is to hinder the Work of God.

For instance, in 1990, the Supreme Court of the United States rendered a decision respecting Jimmy Swaggart Ministries, that any recordings, Bibles, or Bible Study Courses, etc., we sold through the mail would be deemed taxable, and would be retroactive. This decision was rendered, despite the fact that all secular items ordered in mail-order catalogues are exempt, etc. When the decision was passed down, the defendants in the case, namely the State of California, exclaimed in surprise, *"We are flabbergasted, we never dreamed we would win this case!"*

Of course, they were *"flabbergasted,"* because they should not have won the case. The decision was a direct affront to the Gospel, and was meant to hinder its progress. It was the spirit of Herod pure and simple, although not nearly as vehement, at least in this case. However, if the trend in America continues, Herod's murderous intent will ultimately prevail against Christ.

At this present time (mid 1995), the seed is being sown in America for hostility toward all true Christians. For instance, the *"militia groups,"* as they call themselves, at least in some cases are claiming the Bible and Christianity as their authority in their activities, whatever those activities may be. While it is certainly true that some such activities may possibly be Biblical in some rare circumstances, still, the general thrust of these organizations is totally unscriptural, and, therefore, has absolutely nothing with True Bible Christianity.

At any rate, the news media are picking up on this, and subtly laying the groundwork for Christianity and these groups to be linked together. In this manner, True Bible Christianity can be lampooned, and subtly held up to ridicule.

To give another example, in 1987 (I believe it was), a major newscaster who then worked for PBS went down to Haiti to do what they called an *"expose"* on us.

We had built some thirty-five schools in Haiti, which gave an elementary education, plus one hot meal each day, to an average of 300 students per school. Our organization (Jimmy Swaggart Ministries) funded the building of the schools, as well as their monthly support for the one hot meal a day, etc.

They claimed we were lying about this, and, therefore, took television crews to Haiti for their *"expose."*

They came back and ran their program in several cities in America, claiming that they could only find one school we had built, and it was in a rich area of Haiti, with the insinuation that this one school was for rich kids, etc.

To at least one of the major television stations this program was aired on, we sent irrefutable proof as to the number of schools we had built, plus the number of children attending these schools, and that none of them were *"rich kids,"* but, instead, the poorest of the poor.

The station had their lawyer check out our claims, and then went on the air apologizing to us publicly for allowing this *"expose"* program to be aired. The Manager of the Television Station wrote us a letter, and among other things said, *"I cannot believe that this lady* (the female newscaster) *would air something like this that she knew to be totally untrue!"*

However, she did air such a program, even though she knew it was untrue, because her hatred of the Gospel of Jesus Christ was greater than her love for Truth, that is, if she even knew what Truth was!

I realize that is minor, in comparison to Herod brutally murdering little innocent babies, but, to be sure, and considering that in

NOTES

these last days, *"perilous times shall come,"* America, unless she has Revival, is heading toward the same murderous action.

2. *"The Chief Priests and Scribes":* This speaks of institutionalized religion, which has always been the greatest enemy of the Work of God. It is an enemy to God because it is man-devised, man-instigated, man-operated, and man-inspired! As such, the Lord has no part in it. Such was the Israel of Jesus' day, and such is the Church, at least for the most part, presently!

True Christianity is not a *"religion,"* but, instead, a relationship, i.e., a relationship with Christ.

Religion is a system, as we have stated, which is man-devised, and consists of rules, stipulations, regulations, constitutions and bylaws, etc., designed to reach God, or some desired purpose. Such efforts always sound good to the carnal mind; therefore, it has a large following, and it appeases the conscience very well!

It must be remembered, that it was not the drunks, harlots, thieves, or robbers who murdered Christ, but, instead, the *"Church"* of that day. Even though the world is an enemy of Christ, still, His greatest enemy has always been organized religion.

That doesn't mean that *"organization"* is wicked or evil, neither does it mean that some rules or regulations are evil. It just means that within these things one can find no Salvation. Redemption can only be found in Christ.

However, what I have just said is not so easily defined, inasmuch as God, Christ, and the Bible are most always cleverly intertwined with man's religion. As such, it easily deceives most of the human family.

In Truth, more blood has been spilled over religion than anything else. When Lenin, the father of Communism, made the statement, *"Religion is the opiate of the masses,"* he was actually telling the truth.

What turned him off in Russia, and as it should have, was the Russian Orthodox Church, which is basically the same as the Roman Catholic Church, but without allegiance to Rome. He no doubt observed the foolishness of people kissing the feet of the Priests, rubbing silly icons, and going through religious motion, which have absolutely no relationship whatsoever to the True Gospel of Jesus Christ.

Witnessing this foolishness, he erroneously concluded that this was Christianity, and, consequently, he wanted nothing to do with it. Hence, out of this error of judgment, the evil of Communism was born.

Likewise, in Durban, South Africa, a man slight of stature, hungry for God, and sick of Hinduism, for he was an Indian, walked into a Church in that city. Regrettably, the Church he happened to attend, was cold, formal, lethargic, and without life, because it had degenerated into a mere religious formality. Sadly, he concluded that all Christianity was after this fashion, and, thereby, rejected God and the Bible. That man's name was Mahatma Ghandi. Through a religion of self-denial and human willpower, he wrested control of the great nation of India from Great Britain.

Nevertheless, even though India gained her independence politically, she did not gain it spiritually, and, consequently, continues to be mired in superstitious heathenism, which, in effect, means that the nation is controlled by Demon Spirits.

If Ghandi had truly met Christ, quite possibly India would not only have gained her political freedom, but the door would have been opened for the Gospel to penetrate this land.

No! These *"Chief Priests and Scribes"* were no less murderous than Herod. In Truth, they were more murderous!

Sadly, most of the Churches in America, and in Christianity in general the world over, fall under the category of *"institutionalized religion,"* and, as such, their work is the work of Satan, and not the Work of God.

To be sure, any Religious Denomination, and no matter how true and Biblical its beginnings, unless a Revival Spirit is maintained, will invariably sink into man-devised and man-operated religion.

(9) "WHEN THEY HAD HEARD THE KING, THEY DEPARTED; AND, LO, THE STAR, WHICH THEY SAW IN THE EAST, WENT BEFORE THEM, TILL IT CAME AND STOOD OVER WHERE THE YOUNG CHILD WAS."

The phrase, *"When they had heard the king, they departed,"* means they were proceeding on their journey, more than likely, with every thought of going toward Bethlehem. However,

NOTES

something was to happen that would change their destination.

The phrase, *"And, lo, the Star, which they saw in the East, went before them,"* refers to the miraculous reappearing of this *"Star"* which they had originally seen in their native country. There is every evidence, and as stated, that the Star did not lead them from the East to Jerusalem, but that it appeared to them some time before in their home country, and by some type of Revelation from the Lord, they knew that it signified the Birth of the Messiah. They journeyed to Jerusalem, because they knew that Daniel, in his Prophecies, had alluded to Jerusalem as the *"Holy City"* (Dan. 9:24-26).

As they leave the palace in Jerusalem, no doubt starting toward Bethlehem, the *"Star,"* as stated, reappears.

Inasmuch as it *"went before them,"* it must have been different than any *"Star"* that one could imagine! As well, it must not have been too high in the heavens for them to be able to follow it as they did.

The phrase, *"Till it came and stood over where the young Child was,"* actually refers to the city of Nazareth. For this is where it led them (Lk. 2:39).

As well, if one is to notice, the phrase *"Young Child"* is used, signifying that Jesus is no longer an infant, but actually about two years of age.

If a heart is earnest, honest, and sincere before God, that *"Star,"* which is the Guiding Light of the Holy Spirit, will appear to any and all who truly seek the Lord, and they will be led to Christ. For the Holy Spirit always leads people to Christ.

Herod was not led there because he had no desire for Him. Likewise, the Chief Priests and Scribes were not led there, because they had no desire for Christ as well! But if the heart truly seeks Him, the heart will truly find Him.

It is ironical, that precious few in Israel knew anything about Him, even though they were the very people through whom He came. But, yet, several Gentile *"wise men"* would find Him. Truly, they were *"wise!"* Truly, the others were not!

(10) "WHEN THEY SAW THE STAR, THEY REJOICED WITH EXCEEDING GREAT JOY."

The phrase, *"When they saw the Star,"* actually refers to the *"Star"* stopping over the house where Mary and Joseph lived in Nazareth with the little boy Jesus.

The phrase, *"They rejoiced with exceeding great joy,"* is understandable, and portrays hearts hungry for God, and now knowing that their long quest had finally led them to the One they sought!

It is so sad, when one realizes that hundreds of millions ignore the Gospel even though it is so near them, when these *"wise men"* would go to great expense, journeying many hundreds of miles enduring great hardship, in order that they may find the One they eagerly sought. Their quest was not in vain, and neither will the quest of any sincere soul be in vain, who truly seeks the Lord. The Scripture says, *"And ye shall seek Me, and find Me, when ye shall search for Me with all your heart"* (Jer. 29:13).

It also says, *"Let all those that seek Thee rejoice and be glad in Thee,"* inferring that those who *"seek"* will find, and, consequently, will *"rejoice,"* even as these *"wise men"* (Ps. 40:16).

(11) "AND WHEN THEY WERE COME INTO THE HOUSE, THEY SAW THE YOUNG CHILD WITH MARY HIS MOTHER, AND FELL DOWN, AND WORSHIPPED HIM: AND WHEN THEY HAD OPENED THEIR TREASURES, THEY PRESENTED UNTO HIM GIFTS; GOLD, AND FRANKINCENSE AND MYRRH."

The phrase, *"And when they had come into the house,"* further proves that it was not the stable at Bethlehem where He had been born, but rather a house in Nazareth where He had lived since being presented to the Lord forty-one days after His Birth (Lk. 2:7, 21-39). As stated, He was probably about two years of age at this time.

As well, the *"house"* over which the *"Star"* stopped, no doubt was of humble design. But yet, this seemed not to hinder these *"wise men"* at all! They knew this was the place, and the One they were looking for, because this is where the *"Star"* had led them. Consequently, they were guided by Revelation instead of appearances.

Regrettably, most of the world never finds the Lord, because they look for Him in all the wrong places.

Many people attend a particular Church

because of the richness of its appointments and costly construction. While the Lord may certainly be in some of these places, He is not in many of that nature.

In fact, I think one can say without fear of contradiction, that most every Move of God that has ever taken place, has begun in humble surroundings, and, as such, despised by the world! Referring to the Lord, appearances can be, and usually are deceiving!

Whatever the appearance of the humble dwelling resided in by Joseph and Mary, and the little boy Jesus, this did not deter these *"wise men"* at all! They rejoiced when they arrived, and, no doubt, entered into the house continuing to rejoice.

The phrase, *"They saw the young Child with Mary His Mother,"* infers that the moment they beheld Him, they knew this was the One!

How did they know?

Being strangers, they had no actual knowledge of where they were, and its circumstances. However, the moment they laid eyes on Jesus, something about His countenance told them, *"This is the One!"*

As a result, they *"fell down, and worshipped Him."*

No doubt, the furnishings of the house were spartan, with nothing there that spoke of royalty. But yet, they knew this was the *"King"* they had learned about by Revelation, and, in Truth, they knew He was more than a King, but, instead, *"The King."* Consequently, they *"worshipped Him!"* Every evidence is that they were in no way disappointed, but rather exhilarated to the point that the moment of their destination far exceeded their hopes and expectations. They had found Christ!

If one can properly see this picture in one's mind, one can see what True Christianity really is!

If one seeks religion, one will find what religion brings, which is buildings, ceremony, ritual, etc., and will find no lasting satisfaction or joy. However, when one finds Christ, and regardless of the circumstances or surroundings, one has found the secret of life, and the Source of all fulfillment and joy.

The phrase, *"And when they had opened their treasures,"* presents them giving to God, because He had given so much to them.

What exactly had He given them?

If one truly knows the Lord, one truly knows what they received in that hour.

Were these *"wise men"* truly *"born again"* at that time?

Even though the phrase *"born again"* was not in use at that particular time, still, every indication is that they accepted Jesus as their Lord. This is proven by three things, I believe!

1. They had had a Revelation from the Lord, and, consequently, had eagerly sought the Source of that Revelation. And as we have stated, every evidence in Scripture is that those who seek the Lord always find Him!

2. The finding Him, resulted in great *"rejoicing,"* which always follows the finding of Christ.

3. They worshipped Him: Some have passed this off as merely the culture of these particular individuals. However, every evidence is, and according to their seeking, and rejoicing, that this was more than mere culture, but instead the worshipping of Him as the Lord of Glory.

While it is true that they may not have known near as much about the Bible as their Jewish counterparts, still, what little they did know, which they had possibly learned from the writings of Daniel, they acted on it, whereas, the Religious Leaders in Israel did not act whatsoever on what they knew.

4. They gave gifts to Him, which the next phrase will show, which always follows true conversion.

It is not that one purchases something from the Lord with such gifts, but, instead, *"to prove the sincerity of one's love"* (II Cor. 8:8).

The phrase, *"They presented unto Him Gifts; Gold, and Frankincense and Myrrh,"* infers by the word, *"Gifts,"* that they placed Him in the position of Deity, and with themselves placed in a subordinate position.

Why the three Gifts, *"Gold, and Frankincense and Myrrh?"*

First of all, not only was their journey by Revelation, but, as well, their *"Gifts."*

1. *"Gold"*: Joseph and Mary, being poor, this was no doubt very much needed. As well, within days they would have to flee to Egypt, which this *"Gold"* no doubt financed.

Also, the *"Gold"* represented Deity.

2. *"Frankincense"*: This is a very precious perfume of sorts, and was used in the Holy Incense, which was poured on the coals of fire

which were placed on the Altar of Worship in the Tabernacle and Temple (Ex. 30:34-38).

It was very valuable, inasmuch as it was derived from only one type of tree.

The *"Frankincense,"* along with the other spices, which were poured over the coals from the Brazen Altar, spoke of worship accepted by God, only as it came through Calvary, of which the Brazen Altar was a type. Consequently, the *"Frankincense,"* and whether the *"wise men"* understood it or not, means that God accepted their worship of His Only Son, as He will always accept the worship of such.

3. *"Myrrh"*: This was a spice which came from the stem, of a low, thorny, ragged tree which grew in Arabia and East Africa.

As the Frankincense was used in the *"Holy Incense,"* likewise, the *"Myrrh"* was used in the *"Holy Anointing Oil"* (Ex. 30:22-33).

This was used with a mixture of other spices to anoint the Priests, as well as all the furniture of the Tabernacle, etc. It was a type of the Holy Spirit.

Therefore, their *"Gifts"* spoke of Deity (Gold), Worship (Frankincense), and the Holy Spirit (Myrrh).

(12) "AND BEING WARNED OF GOD IN A DREAM THAT THEY SHOULD NOT RETURN TO HEROD, THEY DEPARTED INTO THEIR OWN COUNTRY ANOTHER WAY."

The phrase, *"And being warned of God in a dream,"* means that they spent the night in Nazareth, and were given further Revelation by the Lord, that they should not have anything else to do with Herod, but, instead, ignore his instructions for them to come back and report what they had found.

So, the Lord would lead them to what they sought, and back again! What a privilege to be led by such a sure Word!

The phrase, *"They departed into their own country another way,"* was, no doubt, the way the Lord instructed them.

However, there is every evidence that the *"rejoicing"* that began upon their finding Christ, continued on their journey back *"into their own country."*

What a testimony to the faithfulness of the Lord, and His eagerness to satisfy the hunger of the searching heart. The great tragedy is that so few search for Him, and, consequently, so few actually find Him!

(13) "AND WHEN THEY WERE DEPARTED, BEHOLD, THE ANGEL OF THE LORD APPEARETH TO JOSEPH IN A DREAM, SAYING, ARISE, AND TAKE THE YOUNG CHILD AND HIS MOTHER, AND FLEE INTO EGYPT, AND BE THOU THERE UNTIL I BRING THEE WORD: FOR HEROD WILL SEEK THE YOUNG CHILD TO DESTROY HIM."

Israel, as God's Son, (Ex. 4:22-23) having failed in obedience and love, it was necessary that a true Israel should appear to vindicate God's Character, and prove that He could be loved and obeyed. Hence the necessity of the departure into Egypt, even over and above Herod's murderous intent.

The phrase, "And when they were departed," insinuates that the action that followed, was almost immediately after the departure of the "wise men," and could very well have taken place the next night.

The phrase, "Behold, the Angel of the Lord appeareth to Joseph in a dream," which is the same manner the Lord had spoken to him nearly three years earlier, when Mary had informed him of her pregnancy.

The phrase, "Saying, Arise, and take the young Child and His mother, and flee into Egypt," once again proves by the phrase, "Young Child," that Jesus was not an infant.

Now, as the Lord had told Jacob to go into Egypt (Gen. 46:1-4), He now tells Jacob's Son to do so as well! The insinuation was that they should go immediately!

The phrase, "And be thou there until I bring thee word," insinuates them being led entirely by the Lord.

What a delightful way to live!

As well, this is the way the Lord desires that all His people live! He desires to lead and guide us, and will, in fact, if we will only seek His leading (Jn. 16:13-15).

The phrase, "For Herod will seek the young Child to destroy Him," infers premeditation and not momentary emotion.

Satan knew that this "Seed of the women" was to crush his head and restore man's dominion (Gen. 3:15; I Jn. 3:8), so he tried many times to kill Christ, even before He could get to the Cross to defeat him (Mat. 26:3-4; Col. 2:14-17; I Pet. 2:24).

(14) "WHEN HE AROSE, HE TOOK THE YOUNG CHILD AND HIS MOTHER BY NIGHT, AND DEPARTED INTO EGYPT:"

The evidence is that Joseph awakened after the dream, immediately "arose," with he and Mary, along with Jesus, leaving for Egypt at once, even that very night. The Message of the Angel, as is obvious, was one of urgency.

(15) "AND WAS THERE UNTIL THE DEATH OF HEROD: THAT IT MIGHT BE FULFILLED WHICH WAS SPOKEN OF THE LORD BY THE PROPHET, SAYING, OUT OF EGYPT HAVE I CALLED MY SON."

The phrase, "And was there until the death of Herod," probably spoke of only a few months, as Herod died shortly thereafter the Advent of the "wise men."

The phrase, "That it might be fulfilled which was spoken of the Lord by the Prophet," is speaking of Hosea, and his Prophecy in 11:1, "When Israel was a child, then I loved him, and called my son out of Egypt."

Even though in effect, Hosea was speaking of Israel being delivered from Egyptian bondage, as recorded in Ex. 14, still, what was spoken of Israel, was clearly true of the Greater Israel, the Lord Jesus Christ.

In effect, the crowning purpose of the Jewish nation was to give the world the Son of God. Ideally, they were, at least in a sense, to be the same, and exactly as the Church and Christ are ideally to be the same!

Consequently, as they rejected Christ, they, as well, have been rejected by the world.

And, as Herod attempted to destroy Christ by murdering all the little boy babies in Bethlehem two years old and under, likewise, the Antichrist, the future Herod, will attempt to destroy Israel in the coming Great Tribulation.

Nevertheless, as Christ was raised from the dead, in a sense, Israel, and for all practical purposes, will be raised from the dead as well, at the Second Coming.

Therefore, when Hosea spoke of Israel coming out of Egypt, likewise, he spoke of the Son of God coming out of Egypt, even as He did!

(16) "THEN HEROD, WHEN HE SAW THAT HE WAS MOCKED OF THE WISE MEN, WAS EXCEEDING WROTH, AND SENT FORTH, AND SLEW ALL THE CHILDREN THAT WERE IN BETHLEHEM, AND IN ALL THE COASTS THEREOF, FROM TWO YEARS OLD AND UNDER, ACCORDING TO

NOTES

THE TIME WHICH HE HAD DILIGENTLY IN-QUIRED OF THE WISE MEN."

The phrase, *"Then Herod, when he saw that he was mocked of the wise men, was exceeding wroth,"* has reference to the fact that the *"wise men"* obeyed God rather than Herod.

While it is certainly true that Believers, and according to the Bible (Rom. 13:1-7), are to obey Civil Rulers, still, this is to be done only when the laws or instructions of such Rulers do not violate the Word of God. The Bible takes precedent over everything, and is to be obeyed at all cost! Consequently, the *"wise men"* were told by the Lord not to report to Herod as previously instructed, but, instead, to go back to their land another way, which they did! They had no intention of *"mocking"* Herod, but only of obeying the Lord.

However, Herod, in his lifted up state, was exceedingly angry, as such despots are, that they did not obey his every whim. Consequently, the Scripture says, *"He was exceeding wroth!"*

The phrase, *"And sent forth, and slew all the children that were in Bethlehem, and in all the coasts thereof, from two years old and under,"* portrays in glaring detail the murderous heart of this despot.

The idea of the passage is that this included Bethlehem, as well as the outlying countryside.

Incidentally, the phrase, *"Two years old and under,"* indicates the age of Christ at that time. The Greek word for a child of about two years old is *"pais,"* and is used in verse 11.

The Greek word for infant is *"brephos,"* which means, *"a newly-born babe,"* and which refers to what the shepherds found nearly two years before at His Birth (Lk. 2:16).

The phrase, *"According to the time which he had diligently inquired of the wise men,"* proclaims the *"wise men"* no doubt telling Herod that they had first seen the Star approximately two years before. These words decide that two years, or nearly so, had elapsed since the apparition of the Star in the East.

(17) "THEN WAS FULFILLED THAT WHICH WAS SPOKEN BY JEREMY THE PROPHET, SAYING,"

This pertains to Jeremiah's Prophecy given about 500 years before, and recorded in his Book (Jer. 31:15).

Consequently, all the happenings to Christ,

even from His very Birth, at least of any magnitude, had already been predicted by the Prophets, which the Religious Leaders of Israel could have easily verified if they had only taken the time to connect these Prophecies with Christ. However, by the time of His Ministry, they had already made up their minds that He was not the Messiah, and, therefore, they, as most, would not allow the Word of God to deter them. In other words, their own wicked ambitions made their decisions instead of the Bible.

(18) "IN RAMA WAS THERE A VOICE HEARD, LAMENTATION, AND WEEPING, AND GREAT MOURNING, RACHEL WEEPING FOR HER CHILDREN, AND WOULD NOT BE COMFORTED, BECAUSE THEY ARE NOT."

Some have claimed that inasmuch as Bethlehem was so small, only about twenty little boy babies were murdered. However, the phrase, *"In Rama was there a voice heard, lamentation, and weeping, and great mourning,"* tells us that the slaughter of the children extended at least ten miles around Bethlehem, including Jerusalem, for *"Rama"* was about five miles north of Jerusalem, which was the opposite direction of Bethlehem, which was about five miles south of Jerusalem. Consequently, there could have been several hundred little boys murdered.

The phrase, *"Rachel weeping for her children,"* refers to Jacob's wife, *"Rachel,"* who was looked upon also, at least in a sense, as the mother of the Tribes of Israel, as Sarah was looked at, as the mother of Israel in general (Gen. 30:1, 22).

While it was true that Rachel only bore Jacob two sons, Joseph and Benjamin, with Leah, Jacob's other wife bearing him six, still, and because of Rachel being Jacob's choice, she was looked upon, at least in the titular sense, as being the mother of the Tribes. (Two servant women, and according to the blessings of both Rachel and Leah, bore two sons each to Jacob, making a total of twelve.)

As well, Rachel was buried at Ramah (Jer. 31:15).

Regrettably, and because of Israel's rejection of her Messiah, the Lord Jesus Christ, Rachel has wept almost from that time until now, and will weep even more so in the coming Great Tribulation.

The word, *"weeping,"* and the fact that they cannot be *"comforted,"* adequately describes these ancient people.

As I write these words in May of 1995, the News Media have just portrayed the surrender of Nazi Germany on May 7, 1945, with that same date in 1995 portraying fifty years. In this portrayal were graphic pictures of the Holocaust, with what allied soldiers found in the death camps at the end of the war. Over six million Jews were ruthlessly slaughtered, including women and children, by demon-possessed Adolph Hitler. Such horror, at least on this magnitude, has never been seen in human history. There is no way that words could adequately describe what really took place! Consequently, Herod's beastly action was only a prelude of what was to come!

First of all, had Israel listened to the pleadings of the Holy Spirit through the Prophet Jeremiah, and repented, they would not have had such an animal on the Throne, as Herod, at this time! However, they did not repent, and suffered terribly, and then, worst of all, they rejected their Messiah, saying, *"We have no king but Caesar"* (Jn. 19:15). To be sure, Caesar has been a hard taskmaster!

Consequently, the phrase, *"Because they are not,"* symbolizes the many millions of Jews who have died in a most horrible manner, and because of their rebellion, of which the Bethlehem slaughter is only a tiny part.

(19) "BUT WHEN HEROD WAS DEAD, BEHOLD, AN ANGEL OF THE LORD APPEARETH IN A DREAM TO JOSEPH IN EGYPT,"

This is the third of four dreams given to Joseph by the Lord.

The phrase, *"But when Herod was dead,"* portrays, and as we have stated, the passing of only a few months from the time of the slaughter.

The phrase, *"Behold, an Angel of the Lord appeareth in a dream to Joseph in Egypt,"* leaves absolutely no doubt as to where Joseph and Mary were, along with Jesus.

In the entirety of the Bible, dreams and visions are portrayed as a vehicle through which the Lord at times speaks (Acts 2:17). In effect, Matthew records five dreams in connection with the birth and infancy of Jesus, in three of which an Angel, as here recorded, appeared

with God's Message. Later, Matthew will record the troubled dream of Pilate's wife (27:19).

However, one must not take any and all dreams as from the Lord. When it is from the Lord, it should be clear according to its description. Nevertheless, the true meaning may need further clarification and revelation (I Cor. 14:29).

(20) "SAYING, ARISE, AND TAKE THE YOUNG CHILD AND HIS MOTHER, AND GO INTO THE LAND OF ISRAEL: FOR THEY ARE DEAD WHICH SOUGHT THE YOUNG CHILD'S LIFE."

The phrase, *"Saying, Arise, and take the young Child and His mother,"* refers to the Lord honoring Joseph as the head of the house, and not giving Mary, the Mother of Jesus, the deified position as given by the Roman Catholics! Even though Mary was greatly loved and respected, as she certainly should have been, still, Joseph is here given the preeminence, as he should have been.

The phrase, *"And go into the Land of Israel,"* does not specify which part, but only back to Israel proper! According to Luke 2:39, every evidence is that they lived in Nazareth before going into Egypt, and, as well, after coming back from Egypt.

The phrase, *"For they are dead which sought the young Child's life,"* speaks of Herod and those who were advising him.

It, as well, speaks of all rebels who one day will suffer the same fate, with all rebellion against Christ ultimately being brought to an end.

(21) "AND HE AROSE, AND TOOK THE YOUNG CHILD AND HIS MOTHER, AND CAME INTO THE LAND OF ISRAEL."

This Passage marks Joseph's immediate obedience. The Angel said, *"Arise,"* and, therefore, *"he arose."* Such should be the obedience of all!

The phrase, *"Young Child,"* refers to Jesus being a little over two years old at this time.

Some time back, while Frances and I were in Cairo, Egypt, we were shown the place where it is said that Joseph and Mary lived during their sojourn in this land. Whether the location is correct or not is anyone's guess.

(22) "BUT WHEN HE HEARD THAT ARCHELAUS DID REIGN IN JUDAEA IN THE ROOM OF HIS FATHER HEROD, HE

WAS AFRAID TO GO THITHER, NOTWITH-
STANDING, BEING WARNED OF GOD IN A
DREAM, HE TURNED ASIDE INTO THE
PARTS OF GALILEE:"

The phrase, *"But when he heard that
Archelaus did reign in Judaea in the room of
his father Herod,"* proclaims, at least in a
sense, the struggle for supremacy that took
place after the death of Herod.

It had been Herod's wish that his oldest son,
Antipater, would succeed him. However, he
too was murdered by his father only four days
from Herod's own death. Consequently, he
appointed the area spoken of to *"Archelaus."*

Nevertheless, the succession was far from certain until the consent of Caesar Augustus, and,
was, in fact, jeopardized for a while by certain
actions of Archelaus. Eventually, however, his
appointment was confirmed by Caesar, but only
in a limited way, promising him that he would
make him king *"if he governed virtuously."*

However, he did not rule virtuously, and was
just as guilty of cruelty and murder as his father, Herod. Consequently, a short time later,
he was deposed for his cruelty, and banished
to Vienne in Gaul.

Nevertheless, he was reigning in Judea,
when Joseph and Mary came back from Egypt.

The phrase, *"Notwithstanding, being
warned of God in a dream,"* records the fourth
and final dream of Joseph.

The phrase, *"He turned aside into the parts
of Galilee,"* refers to the region north of Samaria. It was where most of Christ's Ministry
would be carried out as well.

The disposition of the phrase, seems to indicate that plans had originally been made by
Joseph and Mary to come to another part of
Israel, other than Nazareth where they had
lived after the Birth of Christ, and before going into Egypt. However, that would not be
realized, as Christ could not approach the
Throne of His Father's, at least at this time,
and would have to take the position of a despised Nazarene.

(23) "AND HE CAME AND DWELT IN A
CITY CALLED NAZARETH: THAT IT
MIGHT BE FULFILLED WHICH WAS SPO-
KEN BY THE PROPHETS, HE SHALL BE
CALLED A NAZARENE."

Galilee was despised by Jerusalem, and the
town of Nazareth was especially contemptible

NOTES

(Jn. 1:46). However, it was Joseph's native place;
and there he plied his trade as a carpenter.

The phrase, *"That it might be fulfilled
which was spoken by the Prophets, He shall
be called a Nazarene,"* is not found verbatim
among the Prophecies.

However, the quotation, *"He shall be called
a Nazarene,"* is meant to portray the action
instead of the location.

All the Prophets predicted that the Messiah, in His First Advent, would be despised;
that is, He would be a *"Nazarene."*

Some think that at this particular time, a
Roman garrison was located near Nazareth,
and with all its corrupting influence made
Nazareth a despised place. Hence the question of Nathanael, *"Can there any good thing
come out of Nazareth?"* (Jn. 1:46).

In effect, the Jews in later years, would claim
that Mary was actually impregnated by a
drunken Roman soldier, making Christ's Birth,
and because of their lies, even more despicable!

In fact, Nazareth is a beautiful place, located
on the northern edge of the Plain of Esdraelon.

It was said by Quaresimus, *"Nazareth is a rose,
and, like a rose, has the same rounded form, en-
closed by mountains as the flower by its leaves."*

Some time back, I was in Nazareth, along
with Frances and members of our Television
team. I asked to be taken to the brow of the
hill, where it is reputed that the town fathers
attempted to kill Christ, after He preached in
their synagogue (Lk. 4:18-30). Being taken to
the place, and standing in the exact area that
had been quoted in Scripture, from its high
point, I was able to see a panorama view of
Nazareth, as well as all surrounding areas.

Nazareth is situated in the cove of a horse-
shoe-type hill. Part of that hill has been cut
into, with the mining of bauxite in the area,
but, of course, in Jesus' day, it was intact.

Standing on the extreme northwest part of
the hill, most of Nazareth was to my back. Immediately in front was the Plain of Esdraelon,
or, as it is sometimes called, Megiddo.

At about 11 o'clock, according to direction, if I remember correctly, I could see Mt.
Gilboa where Saul and Jonathan were killed
by the Philistines.

At about 10 o'clock, further in the distance,
I could see Mt. Carmel, situated on the Mediterranean, where Elijah called fire from Heaven.

Immediately to my back, at about 8 o'clock, is the Mountain where some think the Transfiguration took place.

Immediately to my right, at about 2 o'clock, is a range of hills that separates this area from the Sea of Galilee, and Capernum, where Jesus eventually made His Headquarters.

As I stood there that day, I realized that Christ, no doubt, many times, stood in this exact spot, and especially because of its solitude, meditating on the Prophecies, and seeking the Face of His Heavenly Father.

However, and despite its beauty, it was then looked at as a place of ill-fame, and He would consequently be called *"a Nazarene,"* which was then a statement of derision!

Why would the Holy Spirit desire that the Son of God be raised in a place of this nature, if, in fact, it really was a place of ill-repute?

First of all, the Lord's Ways are not our ways. He seldom, if ever, goes by appearances, as most do, even Christians! He has little interest in what people think or say, at least in respect to what He does.

It is the Will of God that all His people, even at the present, view things as He does, and not as the world does. We are not to judge from appearances, but, sadly, most Christians do just that!

To hypothetically state the case, if Christ were born now, instead of 2000 years ago, most modern Christians, sadly and regrettably, would little think of Him as the Messiah, and most of all, because of His surrounding circumstances, as even this place where He was brought up.

How so much have all of us fallen into this trap of judging by appearances, which is almost never according to the Word of God, or according to the way things really are.

We should pray that all of us would allow even this small example of where Christ was brought up to be an example to us.

CHAPTER 3

(1) "IN THOSE DAYS CAME JOHN THE BAPTIST, PREACHING IN THE WILDERNESS OF JUDAEA,"

The phrase, *"In those days,"* represented Israel's greatest day. The Ministry of John the Baptist has now commenced, with the Ministry of Christ to follow just a few months later. All that the Prophets had spoken of, at least in these particulars, was now coming to pass. And yet, *"those days,"* which could have meant Israel's Salvation, instead turned to her destruction, and because of her rebellion!

The phrase, *"Came John the Baptist,"* refers to the son of Zacharias and Elizabeth. As foretold by Malachi (Mal. 3:1; 4:5), John the Baptist appears. He was the last and greatest of the Prophets and would have been to be reckoned Elijah, or as Elijah, had the nation repented. He was the greatest, for he went immediately before the face of Jehovah Messiah.

It seems that the name, *"the Baptist,"* was given to him after the commencement of his Ministry, and because Water Baptism was the visible and external aim and result of his preaching.

The phrase, *"Preaching . . . ,"* proclaims the manner in which the Lord has chosen to deliver His Message. That method is still in force.

The closer to God a Church or religious institution is, which, of course, is exemplified in the individuals in its confines who are called to preach the Gospel, the more forceful will be its preaching. Conversely, the further away from God, the less its preaching until there is little if any at all! Hence, there is very little preaching in the Catholic Church, and because its religion is made up mostly of ceremony.

As well, many Protestant Religious Denominations have long since followed suit!

As well, it must be *"preaching,"* not just for the sake of *"preaching,"* but, instead, *"preaching"* that is anointed and inspired by the Holy Spirit. Hence, Christ would say, *"The Spirit of the Lord is upon Me, because He hath anointed Me to preach the Gospel to the poor"* (Lk. 4:18).

As well, it should be obvious from John's *"preaching,"* that he pulled no punches, minced no words, saying exactly what the Lord told him to say, which ultimately resulted in his life being taken, but only after his Ministry was finished!

The phrase, *"In the wilderness of Judaea,"* refers to the area near Jericho.

The *"wilderness"* was a part of the symbolism of his whole life. The expectation of the Messiah must lead to separation, but separation

NOTES

deeper than that of those who called themselves the *"separated"* (Pharisees).

(2) "AND SAYING, REPENT YE: FOR THE KINGDOM OF HEAVEN IS AT HAND."

The phrase, *"And saying, Repent ye,"* consisted of the body of his Message, and literally made up its content.

As well, his Message was not to the heathen, but to Israel! In effect, he was telling the Church to *"Repent!"*

Actually, the Message of Repentance had to be preached before the First Advent of Christ. Consequently, it stands to reason that it must be preached as well before the Second Advent of Christ.

What is Repentance?

The simple meaning of Repentance is *"to be sorry,"* or *"to regret,"* and to be sorry enough to turn from evil to God, from evil ways to God's Ways. It is a commitment to a faith and way of life that involves turning from a previous way toward the Lord. Such means to make a decision that changes the total direction of one's life.

The Message of John the Baptist to Israel was that they were to ready themselves for the Messiah by making a decision to turn from their evil ways back to Holiness (Mat. 3:2; Mk. 1:15). Actually, Jesus concentrated on the same theme (Mat. 4:17; Mk. 6:12).

It is, in effect, impossible for one to be born again without at least entering into the spirit of repentance. Such is an absolute requirement before realization in Christ can become a reality. The idea of having Faith in Christ for Salvation, and not be willing to repent, or at least entering into the spirit of such, abrogates the entirety of what Faith is all about. Actually, the real problem with most modern conversions is that many attempt to have Faith in Christ without repenting of their sinful life, and, in fact, have no intention of turning from sin. To do such is to frustrate the Grace of God. Paul said, *"What shall we say then? Shall we continue in sin, that Grace may abound?"*

He then went on to say, *"God forbid. How shall we, that are dead to sin, live any longer therein?"* (Rom. 6:1-2).

Several things happen upon the Advent of Repentance. Some of them are as follows:

1. When a person removes himself by his self-will, and by God's help, from Satan's direction, he finds the God-willed consequence of his action toward Righteousness is more Righteousness. As well, when man removes himself by his self-will from God's direction and care, he finds that the God-willed consequence of his evil is more evil (Gen. 6:6; I Sam. 15:11, 35; II Sam. 24:16; Jer. 18:10).

2. Whoever repents, even at the eleventh hour, finds a God of Mercy and Love, and not of Judgment (Jer. 18:8; 26:3, 13, 19; Jn. 3:9).

3. The call for Repentance on the part of man is a call for him to return to his dependence on God.

4. Repentance means to completely change one's mind over the view previously held. It means a complete alteration of the basic motivation and direction of one's life. That is the reason John the Baptist demanded Baptism as an expression of this Repentance.

5. Repentance is for one to be willing to say the same thing of himself that God says about him.

As well, it is obvious from the preaching of the Prophets, John the Baptist, and Christ, as well as the Apostles, that Repentance is demanded for Believers as well as non-believers. However, it is always very difficult to get Believers to repent. But at the same time, when the Holy Spirit is able to bring such into vogue, it always signals Revival.

In effect, the very word, *"Revival,"* contains in its usage and meaning, the very nature of Repentance. Upon Repentance, Revival comes; upon lack of Repentance, there is no Revival!

The phrase, *"For the Kingdom of Heaven is at hand,"* in one sense of the word, was meant to imply the Kingdom that was to succeed the Fourth Empire (the Roman) of Daniel's Prophecy (Dan. 7:9-10).

The actual meaning of the phrase, *"Kingdom of Heaven,"* is *"Kingdom from the Heavens."* It was to be a Kingdom, and, in the future, shall be a Kingdom, headed up by Jesus Christ for the purpose of reestablishing the Kingdom of God over this rebellious part of God's realm. It is only found in Matthew, at least in this fashion, because it is the Gospel of Jehovah's King, of which Matthew symbolized.

As well, it is a Dispensational term and refers to Messiah's Kingdom on earth. It was offered by both John and Jesus (Mat. 3:2; 4:17; 10:7).

Sadly, it was rejected by Israel, and was consequently postponed until the Second Coming.

During the 1,000 year reign of Christ on earth, commonly known as the Millennial Reign, Christ will put down all rebellion and rid the earth of all rebels. Then God will become all in all as before rebellion (Rev. 20:1-10; 21:1-22; I Cor. 15:24-28; Eph. 1:10).

Anything said of the Kingdom of Heaven can also be said of the Kingdom of God, because the former is only the earthly dispensational aspect of the latter. However, there are many things said of the Kingdom of God which cannot be said of the Kingdom of Heaven, which we will give in later notes.

(3) "FOR THIS IS HE THAT WAS SPOKEN OF BY THE PROPHET ESAIAS, SAYING, THE VOICE OF ONE CRYING IN THE WILDERNESS, PREPARE YE THE WAY OF THE LORD, MAKE HIS PATHS STRAIGHT."

The phrase, *"For this is he that was spoken of by the Prophet Esaias,"* refers to Isaiah, with this Prophet being quoted by seven inspired writers some 21 times in the New Testament. This completely refutes the idea of a second Isaiah, as some claim!

The phrase, *"The voice of one crying in the wilderness,"* refers to deep, heartfelt, emotional preaching. It was not the studious type of preaching or teaching, which was given in a calm, collected voice, but, instead, animation which resulted in strong emotional effort, both from the soul of the Baptist, as well as physical exertion.

John had to get the attention of the people, and this was at least one of the ways used by the Holy Spirit.

As well, John felt what he preached. It came from his heart, and was meant to penetrate the hearts of his listeners, which it did!

It was an anxious cry, and because the failure to do what he was commanding, *"Repent ye,"* would result in severe consequences, which it did, the destruction of Israel as a nation by the Roman General, Titus.

The phrase, *"Prepare ye the way of the Lord, make His paths straight,"* is taken from Isaiah 40:3 and Malachi 3:1.

The idea was of repairing roads before a great personage comes along them. The Messiah was about to make His Advent, therefore, Israel must *"make His paths straight."* It spoke of Repentance!

(4) "AND THE SAME JOHN HAD HIS

RAIMENT OF CAMEL'S HAIR, AND A LEATHERN GIRDLE ABOUT HIS LOINS; AND HIS MEAT WAS LOCUSTS AND WILD HONEY."

The phrase, *"And the same John had his raiment of camel's hair,"* spoke of rough garments which were the mark of Prophets (Zech. 13:4).

The phrase, *"And a leathern girdle about his loins,"* probably referred to a sheep or goat skin worn over the garment. It would have been very similar to Elijah's (II Ki. 1:8). Consequently, every part of John's dress was for use, not ornament.

The phrase, *"And his meat was locusts and wild honey,"* refers to a clean food, in which the wings and legs would be torn off, and the remainder sprinkled with salt, and either boiled or eaten roasted, with *"honey."*

If one is to notice, there was nothing ostentatious about John or his lifestyle. Actually, his lifestyle was meant to set him apart as a symbolism of what Israel should be from the other nations of the world.

In effect, they were different, but in all the wrong ways. They were not separate in the ways that really counted, which spoke of God's Righteousness, but, instead, in a sectarian self-righteous way, which meant they held themselves aloof from all others, concluding themselves to be God's chosen, with all others looked at as *"dogs."* Therefore, John's preaching which demanded repentance, would have been a terrible shock and affront to them, and especially to the religious elite.

(5) "THEN WENT OUT TO HIM JERUSALEM, AND ALL JUDAEA, AND ALL THE REGION ROUND ABOUT JORDAN."

"All Judaea," was an idiom for a great multitude. They came for many and varied reasons.

John's voice was the first voice of a Prophet since Malachi, which was a time frame of a little over 400 years. Consequently, the interest of Israel should have been substantial! As well, his Message was strong, to the point, and, no doubt, was heavily anointed by the Holy Spirit.

However, and as the next verse proclaims, many were truly sincere in their desire to walk closer to God, and were consequently moved by the Holy Spirit under his preaching, and, thereby, yielded to the Lord. These days, and as previously stated, were Israel's finest.

It is interesting that the Holy Spirit moved

upon *"Jerusalem"* first of all! Consequently, the very center of Israel's religious life, and, hence, the influence of the entirety of the nation was dealt with first. The Scripture would later be given by Peter, *"For the time has come that judgment must begin at the House of God"* (I Pet. 4:17).

To be sure, Judgment was now beginning!

(6) "AND WERE BAPTIZED OF HIM IN JORDAN, CONFESSING THEIR SINS."

To baptize Gentiles was usual, but to baptize Hebrews was unknown. It would be about the same today as the Pastor of a well-known Church calling to Repentance, and Baptizing extensively members of that Church.

In actuality, that is exactly what needs to be done.

Incidentally, the word, *"baptize,"* used here in the Greek is *"baptidzo,"* which is derived from the Greek word, *"bapto,"* and means *"to dip completely under."* It has no reference to sprinkling.

BAPTISMS APPLICABLE TO MODERN BELIEVERS

While a number of Baptisms are mentioned in Scripture, there are only three which are applicable to modern Believers. They are:

1. BAPTISM INTO CHRIST: At conversion, the believing sinner is baptized into Christ, actually baptized into His Death, His Burial, and His Resurrection (Rom. 6:3-5).

It is derived solely by Faith. It is, as should be obvious, the single most important Baptism afforded the individual. Unfortunately, many read this Passage in Romans 6:3-5 and think that it speaks of Water Baptism. It doesn't. It is the Baptism into Christ, which refers to His Crucifixion and Resurrection.

2. WATER BAPTISM: After the person comes to Christ, they are then to be baptized in water (Mat. 28:19).

3. BAPTISM WITH THE HOLY SPIRIT: This Baptism can take place at any time after conversion, and always will be accompanied by speaking with other tongues (Acts 1:4-8; 2:1-11; 8:12-21; 10:44-48; 19:1-7).

When the individual comes to Christ, it is the Holy Spirit Who baptizes the individual into Christ and into His Body (I Cor. 12:13). After a person is saved, it is the Lord Jesus Christ Who

baptizes one into the Holy Spirit. In other words, Jesus is the Baptizer with the Holy Spirit (Mat. 3:11; Jn. 1:31-33); it is the Preacher of the Gospel who serves as the agent to baptize into water (Mat. 28:19).

(7) "BUT WHEN HE SAW MANY OF THE PHARISEES AND SADDUCEES COME TO HIS BAPTISM, HE SAID UNTO THEM, O GENERATION OF VIPERS, WHO HATH WARNED YOU TO FLEE FROM THE WRATH TO COME?"

People ignorantly speak of the spirit of the New Testament being different from that of the Old respecting sin. However, verses 7-12 overthrow this belief; as do many other Passages in the Bible.

How could God's attitude towards sin change?

The truth is, whether under the Old or New Covenants, God's attitude towards sin does not change. The Baptist called these men children of Satan; he declared the Wrath of God was coming; that the acts of Judgment were even then lying at the root of the tree of religious profession; and that if these moralists did not repent they would be burned up as chaff in the unquenchable fire.

Thus the Doctrines of the Baptist differed fundamentally from those of the Disciples of modern thought.

The phrase, *"But when he saw many of the Pharisees and Sadducees,"* pertains to two sects of self-righteous and zealous Jews who held to the letter of their interpretations of the Law and to their own traditions, regardless of whether they nullified the Word of God or not. They were Christ's bitterest enemies, and would have been considered in modern terminology, the Church of their day (Mat. 15:2; 23:1-33; Mk. 7:8-13; Lk. 11:42; Gal. 1:14; Phil. 3:4-6).

THE PHARISEES

In Jesus' day, the Pharisees were the most respected and influential group in Judaism. Having originated about 135 B.C., they were a committed fellowship of men, determined to follow in exact detail everything required in the Mosaic Law. That, within itself, was not wrong, and every indication is that their early beginnings were very good. However, by now, they had drifted into acute self-righteousness, and, as stated, were bitter enemies of Christ, even though of *"impeccable"* reputations.

The Pharisees would be called the theological conservatives of their day, and would have corresponded to the fundamentalists of our day. (Fundamentalism meaning that one believes the entirety of the Bible, which is certainly required, but can degenerate into self-righteousness, as the Pharisees of old!)

The major mistake of the Pharisees was in their adding to the Word of God. They were constantly interpreting and reinterpreting the Mosaic Law to show how it might apply to every aspect of contemporary life. To the Pharisee, these interpretations and additions were the oral Law, which they placed beside the written Law as having equal authority.

The oral tradition focused on behavior, prescribing in detail each acceptable and each forbidden action. Consequently, the attention of the Pharisees was drawn away from the great themes of the Word of God. Jesus faced the opposition of these committed and orthodox men, and in many confrontations He pointed out their errors.

In effect, they had fallen into hypocrisy, as Jesus accused them (Mat. 23:23).

Jesus also attacked the Pharisees' devotion to the oral Law. He pointed out how their interpretations actually nullified God's clear intent. He applied the words of Isaiah to them: *"These people honour Me with their lips, but their hearts are far from Me. They worship Me in vain; their teachings are but rules taught by men"* (Mat. 15:8-9).

Tragically, in attempting to establish their own Righteousness, the followers of this approach missed Scripture's great revelation of human need and Divine Forgiveness. Mistakingly thinking the Mosaic Law was a way of Salvation, they wandered further and further from Faith and further and further from the Heart of God.

There is no doubt that there were many sincere individuals among the Pharisees. However, they were sincerely on the wrong path! Their Spirituality and Holiness were based on a total misunderstanding of what God requires; truly, they were *"blind guides"* (Mat. 15:14; 23:16-17, 19, 24, 26; Lk. 6:39; Jn. 9:39-40).

Their final state is powerfully portrayed by

Jesus in His last confrontation with this group, as reported in Matthew 23.

Sadly and tragically, the spirit of the Pharisees did not die with this group, but is alive and well at present!

THE SADDUCEES

The Sadducees, as the Pharisees, were a religious party in New Testament times.

Unlike the Pharisees, they rejected the idea of an oral Law and accepted only the Pentateuch as authoritative. However, their orientation was worldly. They did not believe in the Resurrection, personal existence after death, or Divine intervention in history. Thus, they denied the possibility of rewards or punishments after death. In this, they would have been very similar to the Modernists of the present time.

Though naturally hostile to the Pharisees, with whom they differed on nearly every theological issue, they joined with them to resist Jesus and His teaching.

This was in part because they were antagonistic to Jesus' supernaturalism, which resulted in healing and miracles, etc.

But a more basic reason was that they feared Jesus would upset the accommodation they had made with Rome to preserve their hold on priestly and ritual offices, from which they gained many financial advantages.

It is not known exactly as to their origination. As well, they had little following among the populace, but were restricted to the well-to-do. Many, but not all, Priests were Sadducees. Also, nearly all Sadducees appeared to have been Priests, especially of the most powerful priestly families. Under the Herods and Romans, the Sadducees predominated in the Sanhedrin, the ruling body in Israel.

The party died out with the destruction of the Temple in 70 A.D.

The phrase, *"He said unto them,"* refers to not curtailing his Message whatsoever even to the Pharisees and Sadducees, the ruling clique of Israel.

Even though many people, and from all walks of life, were present, still, the Baptist addressed at least some of his Message directly to these cliques, and actually reserved his strongest denunciation for them. No one certainly could have accused John of softening his

Message to appeal to the Religious and Financial Leaders!

The question, *"O generation of vipers, who hath warned you to flee from the wrath to come?"*, actually refers to them as poisonous asps or adders, which were not ordinary snakes, but instead, very deadly and aggressive serpents.

Inasmuch as John used this terminology, every evidence is that the Holy Spirit penetrated their smooth exterior and religious facade, and went deep into their hearts, where lay hidden malice and venom, and hinted that they belonged in the truest sense to the seed of the serpent (Gen. 3:15). Consequently, the Holy Spirit through the Baptist, struck at the very heart of the greatest opposition to the Gospel, religious self-righteousness and self-will! Consequently, the biggest enemy of the Church is the Church.

As well, the biggest enemy to Christianity is Christianity, i.e., perverted, demented, religious philosophies of man, which only claim Biblical Christianity, but, in Truth, do not possess it.

John called them *"vipers,"* and Jesus did the same (Mat. 23:33).

Tragically, the modern counterpart is alive and well! In 1988, one of the Religious Leaders in America, and the Denomination to which I had formerly belonged, said, *"We will get Jimmy Swaggart off of Television, and we will do anything we have to do to do it!"*

Why?

That is a good question!

As the Pharisees and Sadducees did not like what Christ preached, neither did he or his counterparts like what I preached. Their concern was little about souls with people being set free from the ravages of sin, but was rather control, property, and money, and possibly in that order!

No! They did not take this position because of what happened to me, but, instead, used it as an excuse. If it had not been that, they would have found something else, or if unable to find it, would have devised it, exactly as with Christ.

If one does the work of Satan, as the Pharisees and Sadducees of old, and, as well, their modern counterparts, the word *"vipers"* is the only word that is suitable for such!

The phrase, *"Wrath to come,"* is a Scriptural

Doctrine that runs all the way from Genesis through Revelation. God's Wrath against sin is evident from page one in the Bible. Thankfully and wondrously, such *"Wrath"* was expended against Christ on Calvary, instead of the human family. And yet, for all who will not believe in Christ, and accept what He did for this fallen race, *"Wrath"* is sure to come upon them, as surely as it came upon Christ as our Substitute.

Consequently, the modern Gospel which denies this coming *"Wrath,"* and which incorporates almost all of modern Christianity, is purely and simply, *"another Gospel, proclaiming another Jesus, by another Spirit"* (II Cor. 11:4).

This includes all Modernists, as well as many, if not most of those who promote the *"prosperity message and political message."*

The Bible view of God's Anger, which is portrayed in *"Wrath,"* brings us to the concept of Righteous Anger. God's Anger is righteous in all senses. It is provoked only by sin. It is expressed with only good in mind. And, strikingly, the Bible insists that God's Anger is never a controlling element in His choices.

It is impossible for human beings to exhibit truly Righteous Anger, because in us anger tends to dominate and to control. Conversely, God's Anger is always in harmony with His Compassion, Grace, Love, Faithfulness, eagerness to Forgive, and Commitment to do Justice.

Nine times the Old Testament reminds us that God is *"slow to anger"* (Ex. 34:6; Num. 14:18; Neh. 9:17; Ps. 86:15; 103:8; 145:8; Joel 2:13; Jonah 4:2; Nah. 1:3). Conversely, human beings are unable to maintain the balance that God does — a balance that makes it possible for Him to be lovingly angry and to show Compassion and Wrath.

However, it is to never be misunderstood that God's Anger is expressed in Judgment, and evidenced by Wrath. History has shown again and again the impact of God's fury at persistent rebelliousness (Deut. 4:25; 9:1-8; II Ki. 21:1-26). In the last days, God's Wrath will be fully expressed in final Judgment (Isa. 63; Zeph. 2).

(8) "BRING FORTH THEREFORE FRUITS MEET FOR REPENTANCE:"

The words, *"meet for,"* should have been translated *"befitting,"* and spoke of the proof of genuine Repentance to discourage mere profession and outward show (Lk. 3:8-14; 19:8; II Cor. 5:17; 7:9-11).

What kind of *"fruit"* was John speaking of? Two things were here being said:

1. The Water Baptism as a mere ceremony or act, and without the suitable Heart Repentance, was of no consequence. These Pharisees and Sadducees had so long since succumbed to mere ceremony, that John knew that many of them were attempting to carry such over into this ordinance.

Tragically, the far greater number of modern Christians so-called, do the same. They think that *"Water Baptism,"* or *"The Lord's Supper,"* within themselves, and by their ceremony, contain some type of Salvation.

They do not!

These Holy Ordinances must not be engaged in until one has first found Christ as one's Saviour. Only then will their true meaning become obvious.

As well, the true meaning of the Water Baptism offered by John could not be entered into, unless it was prefaced by Repentance, as he constantly said.

2. The *"fruits"* spoken of, would have meant of an inward work, which had already been attended by the Holy Spirit, thereby bringing the people to the realization of their need. As such, it probably would have been obvious, at least in some way on their countenances, or in their demeanors. However, it is not a request for emotionalism, but, instead, a request for the *"fruit"* of sincerity.

(9) "AND THINK NOT TO SAY WITHIN YOURSELVES, WE HAVE ABRAHAM TO OUR FATHER: FOR I SAY UNTO YOU, THAT GOD IS ABLE OF THESE STONES TO RAISE UP CHILDREN UNTO ABRAHAM."

The phrase, *"And think not to say within yourselves,"* concerns the Holy Spirit going to the very heart of the problem of most of these Pharisees and Sadducees. It is a warning against the false feeling of security based on natural privileges. As this feeling was common to most Jews. Quite possibly this reference was not only to the selected group, but to all!

Consequently, with this phrase, and boring to the very seat of their emotions and passions, the Holy Spirit hits the heart of their problem, stripping away their self-righteousness, and placing them on the level of all sinners desperately needing God.

Such preaching will do one of two things:

It will make the hearer intensely angry, or else break him down in humble contrition, which it is actually designed to do.

This, within itself, is the very reason that True Bible Christianity is totally different from the religions of the world. It does not seek to educate nearly so much as it seeks to convict. Consequently, the preaching of the Evangelist, as John, is meant to cut through the hype, facade, and pretense. As such, it is as a *"twoedged sword, piercing even to the dividing asunder of soul and spirit, and of the joints and marrow, and is a discerner of the thoughts and intents of the heart"* (Heb. 4:12).

How many people have been saved, and in their conviction just before Salvation, thought surely someone had told the Preacher all about them? In effect, they were right! However, it was the Holy Spirit Who did the telling, and did so without favor or partiality.

The phrase, *"We have Abraham to our father,"* hit at the very heart of the sectarianism of these Jews.

Israel had come to the place that many, if not most of them thought that being born a Jew meant, *"that the everlasting Kingdom will be assuredly given to those who are of the seed of Abraham according to the flesh,"* and that, although they be sinners and unbelieving and disobedient towards God.

This is what Paul referred to so often when he spoke that Salvation was not by natural descent, but by the spiritual relationship of Faith, which led to the inheriting of the Promises (Gal. 3:9, 29).

They had taken the Promises of God, distorted them, and in this distortion, had completely missed the point which God intended relative to His Revelation to Abraham, in essence, *"The just shall live by Faith"* (Gen. 15:6).

The phrase, *"For I say unto you,"* portrays in its original structure as spoken by John the Baptist, the idea that he desires to say only what the Lord wants him to say, and irrespective of how it sits with his listeners. There is no doubt that it was heavily anointed by the Holy Spirit, and that it had a powerful effect on those who heard it.

The phrase, *"That God is able of these stones to raise up children unto Abraham,"* is actually what happened, in the raising up of the Gentile Church.

As John made this statement, he, no doubt, pointed to stones at his feet, and their obvious deadness, and then exclaimed the Power of God which is able to do whatever needs to be done.

As previously stated, Israel, and especially at this time, was lifted up highly in their own self-righteousness. They were the people of the Promises, the people of the Patriarchs. Therefore, they who called themselves Pharisees, who were the Religious Leaders of Israel, certainly had no need to repent, as the Prophet was demanding!

While it is true that some of the Pharisees and Sadducees who were baptized of John, had truly experienced a change of heart, still, the far greater number considered themselves far above such action. They were the Religious Leaders of Israel, and, as such, the idea that they needed to repent was preposterous to say the least! As a result, and because of their self-righteousness, they would ultimately kill the Lord in the Name of the Lord. That is how deceived they were!

The modern Pentecostals are a case in point. They began with a true hunger for God, and in the most humble of circumstances. Most in those early days who were recipients of the mighty Baptism in the Holy Spirit were uneducated and had very little of this world's goods. As a result, they were called *"holy rollers,"* among other names! As well, they were ostracized by the remainder of the Church world, who labeled them *"emotional fanatics,"* and predicted that the fad would soon die out.

As a result, they had no choice but to seek God day and night. And as a further result, God blessed them abundantly so! With only a handful of people, and from the proverbial wrong side of the tracks, they touched this world with the Gospel of Jesus Christ. They were people who believed that God was real. They believed that He answered prayer and performed miracles! They believed in living a holy separated life! Consequently, this *"fad"* did not die, but rather grew larger than any effort of the Gospel in the entirety of the world.

But sadly, as the third and fourth generations began to come on, many of these had never really had a Pentecost of their own. While it was true they were born into the Church (the Pentecostal Way), many of them, and

despite the fact that they knew how to talk the talk, were not truly born again. As well, the characteristics of Israel of old, sectarianism, self-righteousness, etc., began to rear their ugly heads.

Consequently, at this present hour, most of that which calls itself *"Pentecostal"* is such in name only! Many, if not most, of its modern adherents have little, if any knowledge of the moving and operation of the Holy Spirit. Also, they, as Israel of old, see little need for Repentance!

Of course, the question must be asked, *"Will the Lord raise up, out of dead stones if necessary, a people who are not ashamed to worship Him in Spirit and in Truth?"*

I believe He will!

(10) "AND NOW ALSO THE AXE IS LAID UNTO THE ROOT OF THE TREES: THEREFORE EVERY TREE WHICH BRINGETH NOT FORTH GOOD FRUIT IS HEWN DOWN, AND CAST INTO THE FIRE."

The phrase, *"And now also the axe is laid unto the root of the trees,"* is a sober note indeed! To strike off a branch is partial destruction, but to lay the axe at the root means total destruction. The tree pictures the professor of religion. His destruction will not be his extinction; for after being cut down he will be cast into the fire. Strangely enough, the only good trees in existence are those who confess that they are bad; just as an honest heart is one which accepts the Divine testimony that it is incurably diseased.

This is what makes True Bible Christianity so hard to swallow, and especially for the self-righteous! For one to admit he is bad, and, in fact, must do so, before he can truly bring forth fruit, is well nigh impossible for the professor of religion. The entirety of their religious claims is based upon their heritage, and their present religious status.

To be sure, John's Message was not idle chatter. The Holy Spirit through him was saying exactly what He meant, and He meant exactly what He said.

The phrase, *"Therefore every tree which bringeth not forth good fruit is hewn down, and cast into the fire,"* in effect was saying, that if Israel did not repent, and, consequently, begin to bring forth *"good fruit,"* they were going to be *"hewn down, and cast into the fire."*

Tragically, that is exactly what happened! They did not repent; therefore, the Lord did exactly what He said He would do! From this time, they had about forty years before total destruction.

To be sure, to be *"hewn down,"* i.e., to lose their status as a nation, was bad enough! However, to be *"cast into the fire,"* meant not only the Judgment of God, but, as well, the eternal loss of their souls.

Even though a few were brought to Christ in the Early Church, still, for the most part, almost all of the Jewish people have died lost from that time until now. It is a chilling thought!

(11) "I INDEED BAPTIZE YOU WITH WATER UNTO REPENTANCE: BUT HE THAT COMETH AFTER ME IS MIGHTIER THAN I, WHOSE SHOES I AM NOT WORTHY TO BEAR: HE SHALL BAPTIZE YOU WITH THE HOLY GHOST, AND WITH FIRE:"

The phrase, *"I indeed baptize you with water unto repentance,"* is in no way meant to imply that the act of Water Baptism constitutes Salvation. In fact, the Baptism of John was only a symbol, even as at present, of an inward work that had already been carried out in the heart of the participant.

WATER BAPTISM

While Water Baptism is one of the great Ordinances of the Church, it is not a requirement for Salvation. In fact, Water Baptism is a symbol of the Death, Burial, and Resurrection of Christ (I Pet. 3:21).

The phrase, *"I indeed baptize you with water unto repentance,"* could have and should have been translated, *"I indeed baptize you with water because of repentance."* In other words, when John baptized his converts, they were not baptized in order to be saved, but were baptized because they already had been saved.

Unfortunately, untold millions down through the centuries have placed their faith in Baptismal Regeneration, and have died eternally lost. It is what Jesus did at the Cross and our Faith in Him and His Finished Work which constitutes Salvation — and that alone! (Jn. 3:3, 16; Rom. 5:1-2; 10:9-10, 13; Eph. 2:8-10).

THE CROSS OF CHRIST

Water Baptism is an outward act of an inward

NOTES

work which already has been carried out, and therefore is very important. Still, it carries no Salvation Grace. Likewise, the Lord's Supper is of extreme significance; it also, however, carries no Salvation.

Men love ceremonies, and they have a bad habit of attaching Salvation to ceremonies. There is no Salvation in such, and there never is in works of any nature. Salvation is always by Faith — Faith in Christ and what Christ did at the Cross. We do not *"do"* anything to be saved; rather, we *"believe"* something in order to be saved, which pertains to Faith in Christ and the Cross, and that exclusively.

As well, the type of *"Repentance"* preached by John was far more personal than in the past.

In former years, the Message of the Prophets, although certainly dealing in a personal sense, still, for the most part, spoke to the Spiritual and Civil Leaders of Israel, with the people to follow. However, even though John's Message certainly addressed the Leaders, still, and even more importantly, it was a pointed Message directed to each individual, irrespective of who they were.

And then more pointedly, to lock it in, they were told to be baptized in water, following their Repentance, which, no doubt, thousands did!

The phrase, *"But He that cometh after me is mightier than I,"* now proclaims the real purpose and intent of John's Ministry. He was *"preparing the way of the Lord."*

The word, *"after me,"* is meant to proclaim the soon appearance of Christ.

The word, *"mightier,"* is meant to speak to the power of his own presence and delivery, which, no doubt, awed the people!

In effect, he is saying, *"If you think what you are hearing now is powerful, you have not seen anything yet. The One soon to come is far mightier than I!"*

To extol the *"might"* of the Lord Jesus Christ, no adjectives or superlatives would be adequate! The Scripture says, *"therefore God, thy God, hath anointed Thee with the oil of gladness above thy fellows"* (Ps. 45:7). He was truly *"mightier"* and greatly so, than all who had preceded Him, or those who would follow Him!

He was manifested to *"destroy the works of the devil"* (I Jn. 3:8), and that He did!

The phrase, *"Whose shoes I am not worthy to bear,"* denotes the humility of John.

The people knew what John was saying. He was speaking of the duty of slaves of the lowest rank.

People in those days mostly wore sandals, and the streets not being paved, and consequently dirty, would result in their feet becoming dirty as well!

Consequently, when a guest arrived at someone's house, and especially if it was a house of note, the job of the lowliest servant was to first of all remove the sandals from the feet of the guest, and then with a pail of water, wash their feet. As stated, this was the duty of servants or slaves of the lowest rank.

Therefore, John in comparing himself to Christ, does so as a slave of the lowest rank.

As well, and whether he knew it or not, he is detailing the sole requirement of being Baptized in the Holy Spirit, other than first being saved and believing. That requirement is humility, and the lack of it, the reason that many are not Baptized in the Holy Spirit (Acts 2:4).

BIBLE HUMILITY

The Bible places a high value on humility. God saves (Ps. 18:27), sustains (Ps. 147:6), and gives grace to the humble (Prov. 3:34).

In humility, God's people are called to humble themselves and so to face the pain of self-examination and confession of sins.

Humbled before God, human beings are able to experience the blessings He has for all who will submit completely to Him.

THE HUMBLE LIFESTYLE

What does the New Testament, over the Old, add to our understanding of humility?

Matthew 18:1-4 helps us to see humility expressed in relationship with God. The Disciples asked Jesus who was greatest in the Kingdom of Heaven. The Text tells us that Jesus *"called a little child and had him stand among them."*

Jesus then told them that unless they were to *"change and become like little children,"* they would be unable to enter Heaven's Kingdom. He explained, *"whoever humbles himself like this child is the greatest in the Kingdom of Heaven."*

Just before this, Jesus had presented Himself

NOTES

to Israel as God's Son and their promised Messiah. Israel refused to respond. But what of the child? When he was called, he came immediately, responding to Jesus' Word.

Humility in our relationship with God is seen when we refuse to stand in judgment on His Word, but instead respond immediately, recognizing God as the ultimate Authority in our life. The dependence and responsiveness of the child is to mark our attitude in our personal relationship with the Lord.

PAUL'S TEACHINGS ON HUMILITY

Paul gave an example of Jesus' humility (Phil. 2:5-8), and encouraged compliance with his exhortation: *"In humility consider others better than yourselves. Each of you should look not only to your own interest, but also to the interest of others."*

This attitude is explored further in Romans 12:3-16. The introductory instruction goes like this: *"Do not think of yourself more highly than you ought, but rather think of yourself with sober judgment, in accordance with the measure of Faith God has given you."*

That Faith is to find expression within the Body of Christ, as each member of the Body uses his gifts to serve his fellows. Moved by sincere love, each is told, *"Honor one another above yourselves."* And *"Do not be proud, but be willing to associate with people of low position. Do not be conceited."*

It is in seeing others as persons of great worth because they are loved by God and in seeing ourselves as their servants that we find the fulfilling lifestyle of humility.

Consequently, and as evidenced here by John, humility is a requirement to be Baptized in the Holy Spirit.

(Some of the notes on humility were derived from Dr. Lawrence Richards.)

The phrase, *"He shall Baptize you with the Holy Ghost, and with fire,"* speaks of the Spirit Baptism which every Believer should go on and receive after being saved. It is actually a Second Work of Grace, and is given for power (Acts 1:8).

It is interesting that John would use this type of terminology, especially considering that his listeners would have had little knowledge of the *"Baptism in the Holy Spirit."*

He is here comparing his Baptism in Water

to Christ's Baptism in the Holy Spirit. Of course, there is little comparison! The idea was this:

As John immersed the candidate completely beneath the water, which constitutes the act of Baptism, likewise, the Lord Jesus Christ would do the same to those who were Baptized in the Holy Spirit, i.e., completely immerse them in the Holy Spirit, with the Holy Spirit in them, and them in the Holy Spirit, which is the true meaning of *"Baptism."* That basically was the comparison.

As well, this of which John speaks, is not received at Salvation, even though the Holy Spirit is the primary factor in bringing one to Christ. Upon Salvation, the Believer is definitely regenerated by the Holy Spirit, because that is the only way one can be saved (Rom. 8:14-16). However, there is a vast difference in being *"Born of the Spirit,"* than being *"Baptized in the Spirit"* (Acts 2:4).

In fact, one must truly be saved before one can be *"Baptized in the Spirit"* (Jn 14:17).

Of course, at the time of John, and even in the Ministry of Christ, Believers could not at that time be Baptized in the Holy Spirit, because Christ had not completed His Mission, and, in fact, had not been Glorified (Jn. 7:39).

However, upon completion of Christ's Mission at Calvary and the Resurrection, and then with Him being ascended, the Holy Spirit was sent back exactly as He promised, and then Believers, beginning on the Day of Pentecost, were Baptized in the Holy Spirit, and spoke with other tongues as the Spirit gave utterance (Jn. 16:7; Acts 2:4), fulfilling the Prophecy of the Baptist.

So, John was telling his listeners of that which they could not at the moment receive, but would be able to receive in a short time!

The phrase, *"And with fire,"* has to do with the burning away of *"the flesh"* out of the Godly, and the consuming of the ungodly if they cleave to *"the flesh."*

In that this *"fire"* is *"unquenchable,"* it will, and to be sure, perform its intended purpose!

(12) "WHOSE FAN IS IN HIS HAND, AND HE WILL THROUGHLY PURGE HIS FLOOR, AND GATHER HIS WHEAT INTO THE GARNER; BUT HE WILL BURN UP THE CHAFF WITH UNQUENCHABLE FIRE."

The work of the Holy Spirit is here outlined, which will, without fail, take place in

the hearts and lives of Believers.

The phrase, *"Whose fan is in His Hand,"* refers to the ancient method of winnowing grain.

After the stalks had been pulverized on the threshingfloor, a worker would use a pitchfork, throwing the grain and the husks in the air.

Another worker, that is if there was no wind, would use giant palm fronds, or some other type apparatus, fanning the grain and the husks. Consequently, the husks which were much lighter, would be blown to the side of the threshingfloor, with the grain falling back to the floor.

This would be continued until all the husks were separated from the grain, with the grain being placed into the garner.

The idea is, that the primary task of the Holy Spirit in the life of the Believer, is to bring about this process, using whatever is necessary in order to separate the chaff from the grain. This *"wind"* created by the *"fan,"* may come in various ways, such as adversity, persecution, chastisement, etc., but, to be sure, it will come.

As well, it speaks of a violent process, which is not at all appetizing to the flesh, but will prove to be invigorating to the spirit.

As an example, one would ask as to why the Lord, after having Samuel anoint David to be the future King of Israel, would allow Saul to persecute him as he did, even causing great tribulation, and for a period of about 15 years?

The answer is found in this verse. Even though David was anointed by God to be the King of Israel, still, there were traits in David's life that needed to be removed. Regrettably, those traits, as in all of us, could not be removed easily, but only by adversity and persecution, which are meant to teach us trust and dependence on the Lord, and to humble the flesh.

David was anointed, but he was not ready! It would take this crucible of persecution by Saul to make him ready!

The phrase, *"And He will throughly purge his floor,"* is actually the violent part of the process.

The threshingfloor of old, generally consisted of a large flat portion of rock which could be used for this purpose.

The grain would be piled on top of this rock (floor), with several different methods used to purge the grain from the husks. At times, an ox cart was used, with it being pulled back and forth across the grain, with its heavy wheels breaking the grain loose from the husks. This was done repeatedly, until it was ready to be thrown in the air, as just stated.

The purging process has to do with what Jesus spoke of in taking away the branches from the tree that did not bear fruit, and, consequently, *"purging it, that it may bring forth more fruit"* (Jn. 15:2).

As stated, this is a violent process, which at times makes the Believer think he will not survive it. This has to do with the aged struggle of the *"flesh and the Spirit."* They constantly war against one another, because one or the other must ultimately go. To be sure, this war is not quick, and the battle is not won easily.

Many have attempted to circumvent the *"threshingfloor"* with many and varied schemes, not the least of them being the modern confession principle. However, the flesh cannot be confessed out, neither can hands be laid on someone, as Scripturally valid as that may be in its place, with this work effected in one's heart. Too oftentimes, this method only produces more religious flesh. And even though such is covered up with religious phraseology, petted and pampered, and made to seem holy to a carnal world, still, it is *"flesh,"* and must ultimately be purged.

The phrase, *"And gather His wheat into the garner,"* concerns the end product as developed by the Spirit.

Even after conversion, and especially after conversion, our spiritual lives are still a mixture of *"chaff"* and *"wheat."* The *"chaff"* constitutes the work of the flesh, while the *"wheat"* constitutes the work of the Spirit. They must, and without fail, be separated. The reason is obvious!

Any and all accepted by God, can only be that which is the product of the Holy Spirit. Any product of man, i.e., the flesh, must be rejected out of hand, and not only rejected, but separated, and ultimately burned. As stated, this is the great basic work of the Holy Spirit in the life of the Believer, and it is a work that He will carry out with vigor and faithfulness, with one view in mind, and that is to *"present us faultless before the presence of His Glory with exceeding joy"* (Jude 24).

That is also the reason Jude said, *"And others save with fear, pulling them out of the fire;*

hating even the garment spotted by the flesh" (Jude 23).

He was speaking of this *"fire"* mentioned by John the Baptist!

The phrase, *"But He will burn up the chaff with unquenchable fire,"* pertains to that which will be done to the *"chaff."* This speaks of all our trust in our good works, plus religious acceptance, place and position, and all we prize so highly other than Christ.

Regrettably, this *"chaff"* abides even in the most Godly, and must, consequently, be separated, and at whatever price.

If I remember correctly, the year was 1982. We were getting ready for a crusade in Guatemala City, Guatemala. It would be conducted in the stadium in that city, which would seat approximately 40,000 people.

A couple of days before Frances and I, along with Donnie and Debbie, and the entirety of the team, were to leave, a strong controversy developed over a statement I had made respecting Catholicism over our worldwide Telecast.

The statement concerned *"Salvation by works"* versus *"Salvation by Faith."*

I had merely stated that Catholicism was basically *"Salvation by works,"* which, in reality, was no Salvation at all! I then went on to define *"Salvation by Faith."*

A firestorm erupted! The program was actually taken off two or three stations. In reality, this did not hurt us, as we were on other stations in each particular city. I think that which hurt the most was Pat Robertson taking us off his station in Atlanta, because several Catholics complained!

For some days, or even weeks, we were the subject of countless newspaper columns, along with opposition, it seemed, from every source. I do not remember hearing very much encouragement at that time, as it seemed the entire nation demanded the removal of our Telecast from the airwaves.

However, in all of the confrontation, quite a number of Catholics came to the Lord Jesus Christ, and truly made Him their Saviour. (To be sure, multiple thousands all over the world came to Christ as a result of those programs.)

I want the reader to understand that my statements were not sarcastic or demeaning. But instead, a simple statement, that there was no Salvation in works, but only by Faith in Christ. I attempted with all of my ability to be as diplomatic as possible, but yet, not to compromise the Truth.

I had addressed the Catholics personally, because I believed the Lord had spoken to me strongly about doing so. Consequently, I attempted to the very best of my ability to obey the Lord.

At any rate, when we left for Guatemala City, our hearts were heavy with these pressing problems!

Almost immediately after arriving in that Central American country, I could hardly wait until I could get alone in prayer. Actually, I had quietly sought the Lord almost all the way there, asking Him for direction and guidance as to how to handle this problem.

In looking back, I feel I was far too concerned and should have trusted Him more. Nevertheless, such place and position of trust does not come easily or quickly, which is, in reality, the subject of the statement of John the Baptist.

After arriving and retiring to bed that night, I quickly fell asleep, being very tired. If I remember correctly, I awakened about midnight. I quietly arose, so as not to awaken Frances, and went into the next room (we had a two-room suite).

I then began to importune the Lord concerning the events at hand, as well as our coming crusade in this city. At that time, our Telecast aired in Guatemala, along with most other Central and South American countries. We were expecting tremendous crowds and great results, which the Lord did actually give us.

After seeking the Lord for a period of time, I began to sense a heavy moving of His Spirit. That which transpired, I believe can only be explained as a vision.

In my spirit, this of which John spoke, the threshingfloor, and the chaff, etc., I saw in this vision.

Actually, I did not see the purging of the grain, but only the grain and husks being thrown into the air, with the husks being blown to the side of the threshingfloor.

That which stood out so graphically in the vision, was the chaff at the side of the threshingfloor, and the fire that was consuming it. I remember, as I watched the flames of fire lick up the chaff, asking the Lord as to why this was so important?

I mentioned to Him that the chaff had been

separated from the wheat, and was actually no more a part of the grain, but was off to the side, even off the threshingfloor. Therefore, why was it so important that it be burned?

In my spirit, I could see the flames eagerly consuming the chaff until there was absolutely nothing left.

I knew that the separation of the grain from the husks was all-important. As well, I knew that the husks had to be gotten off the threshingfloor, but inasmuch as it was totally separated, and no longer a part of the grain, why was it so important that it be burned?

As I asked this question of the Lord, His answer after a few moments' time was forthcoming.

This is what He said:

"The flesh and all its works, are so abominable, they not only must be separated from that produced by the Spirit, they must as well be consumed by the fire of the Spirit, that there be no trace left whatsoever."

I will never forget that moment! The Spirit of God was upon me so heavily, that I was nearly bent double sobbing before God. I knew what He was showing me was so very important. I as well knew that it had to do with something of far greater significance, even than the problems we were presently having concerning the Telecast and Catholicism.

Little did I realize the purging that lay ahead for me, and which the Lord was even then showing me. To be sure, it has been violent, so violent in fact that at times I thought I would not survive.

But I have survived! And I believe I am closer to God than ever, which is the intent of the Holy Spirit. I have no idea as to how much more purging is needed, but I do know that much has been purged.

And one other thing I know, that which I have seen the Lord do in my own personal life, drawing me ever closer to Him, I want Him to finish the task, and irrespective of the price. To be sure, no price is too high to pay in order to be drawn closer to God.

Someone has well said, that even though our actions are so very important, still, our reactions are more important! That tells us where we really are.

When our reactions become totally Christlike, then our actions will as well be Christlike, which will then require very little reaction.

(13) "THEN COMETH JESUS FROM GA-LILEE TO JORDAN UNTO JOHN, TO BE BAPTIZED OF HIM."

The word, *"Then,"* signifies the greatest moment in human history to date. The earthly Ministry of Christ will now begin, with it concluding at Calvary, which is the real purpose of His Coming. He must redeem man, and as the Last Adam, His Life and His Death must be perfect. The word, *"Then,"* signifies all that the Prophets had spoken of. To be sure, He was the focal point of all these Prophecies, and now He makes His debut.

The phrase, *"Then cometh Jesus from Galilee to Jordan unto John,"* speaks of them having lived in two different places. Christ had been raised in Nazareth, which was in Galilee, while John had been raised in Judaea, which was close to Jerusalem, and not far from where he is now baptizing in the Jordan River.

As a result, Jesus and John probably saw very little of each other, due to the fact that they lived about 80 miles apart. That is not very far at present, but then, and due to the slow method of transportation, it was quite a distance.

The phrase, *"To be baptized of him,"* meant that John must do the baptizing, which he did! In this, Christ would link His Own Work to that of John's, who was His forerunner.

(14) "BUT JOHN FORBAD HIM, SAYING, I HAVE NEED TO BE BAPTIZED OF THEE, AND COMEST THOU TO ME?"

The phrase, *"But John forbad him,"* signals upon the request of Christ, John's reluctance. To be sure, John's reaction is normal, especially considering the statement he had made, which was certainly true, *"Whose shoes I am not worthy to bear!"* He feels terribly unworthy to perform such a task!

The question, *"I have need to be baptized of Thee, and comest Thou to me?",* proclaims a further assessment by John of his own unworthiness.

In fact, many may ask the question as to why Christ had to be baptized at the hands of John?

1. As a man, Christ must submit Himself to this, in order to *"fulfill all Righteousness."* Water Baptism portrayed His coming Death, Burial, and Resurrection. As a result, it would signal a Baptism far greater even than the Baptism of Repentance presently engaged by John.

NOTES

As the Sacrifices of old only pointed to the coming One Great Sacrifice, namely Christ, likewise, John's Baptism only pointed to the Great Baptism which was coming, the Death, Burial, and Resurrection of Christ, which would purchase man's Redemption, and of which our present Water Baptism symbolizes.

2. As well, this Baptism must be performed by John, because he was the one called of God to *"Prepare ye the way of the Lord, make His paths straight."* As such, and as stated, Jesus linked His Ministry with that of John's, which validated it.

He little had the validation of the Religious Leaders of Israel, but he had it of God, and that's really all that mattered!

(15) "AND JESUS ANSWERING SAID UNTO HIM, SUFFER IT TO BE SO NOW: FOR THUS IT BECOMETH US TO FULFILL ALL RIGHTEOUSNESS. THEN HE SUFFERED HIM."

The phrase, *"And Jesus answering said unto him,"* concerns the Will of God which must be carried out.

The phrase, *"Suffer it to be so now,"* means *"Permit Me to be baptized."*

The phrase, *"For thus it becometh us to fulfill all Righteousness,"* means that John was commanded to baptize, as every Godly Israelite was now commanded to be baptized.

Jesus was a Godly Israelite, and was such in order to save. Hence the obedience of Righteousness rested on them both in relation to this Baptism. But there was this difference, — Righteousness brought Christ there; sin brought His fellow-countrymen there.

The phrase, *"Then he suffered Him,"* proclaims John's obedience.

What must John have thought when Christ walked out into the waters of the Jordan to him? How much he knew before now, concerning the Messiahship of Christ, is not known. But now he will know, and beyond the shadow of a doubt, that this is the Messiah. And yet, a little later while in prison, doubt will overcome him, and he will once again ask for verification (Mat. 11:3). However, John would not be reprimanded by Christ for that later act, but would send John the answer, and then speak the highest of him that had been spoken of any man (Mat. 11:11).

(16) "AND JESUS, WHEN HE WAS BAPTIZED, WENT UP STRAIGHTWAY OUT OF

THE WATER: AND, LO, THE HEAVENS WERE OPENED UNTO HIM, AND HE SAW THE SPIRIT OF GOD DESCENDING LIKE A DOVE, AND LIGHTING UPON HIM."

The phrase, *"And Jesus, when He was baptized,"* marks the ending of His private life, and the beginning of His public one. This, in essence, was the beginning of His Ministry.

The phrase, *"Went up straightway out of the water,"* refers to Baptism by immersion and not by sprinkling!

The phrase, *"And, lo, the heavens were opened unto Him,"* respects the only One, the Lord Jesus Christ, to Whom the heavens would be opened.

Men have tried to open the heavens with Mohammed, Buddha, Confucius, and others, but without success!

About 1800 years earlier, Jacob had seen in a vision *"a ladder set up on the earth, and the top of it reached to Heaven."*

He saw, *"the Angels of God ascending and descending on it."*

He then saw, *"the Lord standing above it, and saying, I am the Lord God of Abraham thy Father, and the God of Isaac"* (Gen. 28:12-13).

In effect, Jacob saw a pre-incarnate appearance of Christ, with Him showing Jacob that He was the Ladder that led to Heaven, and He Alone!

The phrase, *"And he saw the Spirit of God descending like a Dove, and lighting upon him,"* portrays the heavens being opened in order that God would come down to man in a fashion as never before.

This is the only time in the Bible, at least up to this present moment, where God would do this! The reason was obvious, He was perfect, whereas all others woefully came short of the Glory of God.

While it is certainly true, that the *"Spirit of God"* had come upon others in times past, still, not in this fashion. Here, the Spirit of God descends upon the Word made Flesh, by Whom objectively God is revealed to men.

This Passage does not say that the Holy Spirit in this instance, took the form of a *"Dove,"* but, instead, *"like a Dove."* Consequently, we can only assume from John's statement, that he saw the Holy Spirit in a visible appearance *"in bodily form, as a Dove."*

However, at the same time, that in no way means that the Holy Spirit was at all Incarnate,

but that John saw something that reminded him of a *"Dove."*

The structure of the terminology leads us to believe, that John was not merely speaking of the gentleness of a Dove, but, instead, some type of form that was seen by the naked eye. All four Gospels carry the account, and there is no record that others saw it, even though they no doubt felt its effect.

In Truth, the Holy Spirit is a Person, and as such, has a Spirit Body. Even though He proceeded from the Father onto the Son, in no way means that He was not distinct in His Own Personality.

From this moment on, the *"Spirit of God"* would begin to work within Christ relative to His Ministry. Jesus would say, *"The Spirit of the Lord is upon Me, because He hath Anointed Me to . . ."* (Lk. 4:18-19).

(17) "AND LO A VOICE FROM HEAVEN, SAYING, THIS IS MY BELOVED SON, IN WHOM I AM WELL PLEASED."

The phrase, *"And lo a voice from Heaven, saying,"* was the Voice of God, and was heard at least by John, and possibly others!

The phrase, And as spoken by God, *"This is My Beloved Son, in Whom I am well pleased,"* could be translated, *"This is My Son, My Beloved, in Whom is all My delight."*

In Mark and Luke, the formula of the utterance is given: *"Thou art,"* etc. Here, the import: *"This is,"* etc.

But as suggested by John 1:33, it is possible that there were two utterances, one addressed to Jesus as the Spirit was descending, saying, *"Thou art,"* etc., and the other addressed to John after the descent of the Spirit and His repose upon Jesus, saying: *"This is,"* etc.

The three Persons of the Trinity here immediately appear upon the front page of the New Testament; the Father speaking, the Spirit descending, and the Son praying (Lk. 3:21).

"This is My Beloved Son," was the Divine formula of Anointing the Messiah for the Office of Prophet (Mat. 3:17); Priest (Mat. 17:5); and King (Ps. 2:7).

There are several things in Scripture that are said to *"please the Lord."*

1. It pleased the Lord to bless Israel (Num. 24:1).

2. It pleased the Lord to make Israel His people (I Sam. 12:22).

3. Solomon's petition pleased the Lord (I Ki. 3:10).

4. Jehovah is well pleased with the Righteousness that He demands by His Law (Isa. 42:21).

5. It pleased the Lord to bruise Christ (Isa. 53:10).

6. Jehovah was pleased with His Beloved Son (Mat. 3:17).

7. It pleased God by the foolishness of preaching to present His Gospel (I Cor. 1:21).

8. The Lord has set in the Body of Christ, members as it hath pleased Him (I Cor. 12:18).

9. In the Resurrection, God will give the Resurrected a body as it has pleased Him (I Cor. 15:38).

10. It pleased God to call Paul to preach the Gospel (Gal. 1:15).

11. It pleased God that in Christ should all fullness dwell (Col. 1:19).

12. Enoch had this testimony, that he pleased God (Heb. 11:5).

13. God is well pleased with the Sacrifice of Praise (Heb. 13:16).

CHAPTER 4

(1) "THEN WAS JESUS LED UP OF THE SPIRIT INTO THE WILDERNESS TO BE TEMPTED OF THE DEVIL."

The word, *"Then,"* refers to the time immediately after the descent of the Holy Spirit upon Him.

The phrase, *"Then was Jesus led up of the Spirit,"* refers to strong action! In other words, the word, *"led,"* is similar to the word, *"driveth,"* as used by Mark, and refers to the Holy Spirit coming close to forcing Christ to the time of temptation.

It does not refer to any reluctance on the part of Christ, but, instead, to the urgency of the Holy Spirit to bring it about.

The phrase, *"Into the wilderness,"* probably refers to the wilderness area close to Jericho and the Jordan River, where Jesus had been baptized.

The phrase, *"To be tempted of the Devil,"* does not mean that the Holy Spirit tempted Him, but, in fact, does mean that the Holy Spirit can and does lead us into circumstances where temptation is permitted, that we may thereby

be proved and disciplined for future work.

The First Adam was tempted in a garden; the Second in a wilderness. *"Tempted"* means *"Put to the test."* Adam was tested in innocence; Jesus was tempted as knowing both good and evil, though in Himself sinless.

He entered the wilderness of this world's misery and evil to render in it a life of absolute obedience and dependence; and it was therefore necessary that that perfect obedience and dependence should be tested.

It demanded that He should have no other will than that of His Father; and that He would accept that Will, and delight in it, no matter what might be the consequences to Himself.

It was this obedience and dependence that the tempter sought to impair; and so he invited Christ to use His privileges as the Son of God, and as the Messiah, and as the Son of Man, to work a miracle in His Own favor, and to manifest Himself to Israel, and to take up the sovereignty of the earth promised to Him.

But Satan failed!

In the Garden, the First Adam failed, and Satan succeeded! In the wilderness, the Last Adam succeeded, and Satan failed!

WHAT IS TEMPTATION?

Temptation is a difficult situation, a pressure that brings a reaction through which the character or commitment of the Believer is demonstrated, and is instigated by Satan, and, as here, allowed by God, although God never tempts (James 1:13).

JESUS, AS IS HERE RELATED, WAS TEMPTED

The three temptations recorded of Christ parallel pressures under which ancient Israel bridled and turned from God's Way. Yet, Jesus trusted God fully for provision, protection, and purpose. Jesus' submission to God's Will stands in contrast with Israel's refusal to trust and her resultant disobedience.

Thus, Jesus shows Himself to be One Who has a perfect and whole relationship with the Father, One Who thus can lead us to such a relationship.

JESUS' EXPERIENCE

The Book of Hebrews looks back to Jesus' experience and to all the pressures under which

Jesus labored as a human being, and it reassures us. Understanding perfectly the human experience, and *"Because He Himself suffered when He was tempted,"* Jesus is *"able to help those who are being tempted"* (Heb. 2:18).

He Who endured the full weight of suffering in testing situations is fully able to understand and sympathize with us.

GOD CANNOT BE BLAMED

James points out that God cannot be blamed when someone fails to respond in a Godly way under pressure (James 1:13-15). The source of human failure is to be found, not in the situation that God permits, but in *"his own evil desire"* (James 1:14). While all temptation within itself is evil, still, it is not evil that can be transferred to another, unless yielded to. However, if yielded to, the evil that emerges comes from within the human personality.

Temptation is allowed by God in order to test us. However, we have His Promise, *"No temptation has seized you except what is common to man. And God is faithful; He will not let you be tempted beyond what you can bear. But when you are tempted, He will also provide a way out so that you can stand up under it"* (I Cor. 10:13).

The victory demonstrated by Jesus is available to us. Like Jesus, we can commit ourselves to obedience, and we will then find God's Own Way to escape failure.

We must ever remember, that God has not permitted the situation of temptation in order to trap us. He does, however, use difficult situations in our lives. As we remain close to Him, we find His Way of escape, and our Godly response to pressure demonstrates the genuineness of our Faith.

However, we are to never seek temptation in order to prove to ourselves that our Faith is real. Instead, we should follow Jesus' guidance, and when we pray say, *"Lead us not into temptation"* (Mat. 6:13; 26:41; Mk. 14:38; Lk. 11:4; 22:40, 46).

SATAN IS THE AUTHOR OF TEMPTATION, ALTHOUGH GOD ALLOWS IT

Satan tests God's people by manipulating circumstances, within the limits that God allows him (Job 1:12; 2:6; I Cor. 10:13), in an attempt to make them desert God's Will. Actually, the New

NOTES

Testament knows him as *"the tempter,"* as is stated in the verse of our Commentary. Satan is the implacable foe of both God and men (I Pet. 5:8; Rev. 12).

Christians must constantly be watchful (Mk. 14:38; II Cor. 2:11; Gal. 6:1) and active (Eph. 6:10; James 4:7; I Pet. 5:9) against the Devil, for he is always at work trying to make them fall; whether by crushing them under the weight of hardship or pain (Job 1:11-2:7; Heb. 2:18; I Pet. 5:9; Rev. 2:10; 3:10), or by urging them to wrong fulfillment of natural desires (Mat. 4:3; I Cor. 7:5), or by making them complacent, careless and self-assertive (Gal. 6:1; Eph. 4:27), or by misrepresenting God to them and engendering false ideas of His Truth and His Will (Gen. 3:1-5; Mat. 4:5; II Cor. 11:3, 14; Eph. 6:11).

In the art of temptation, Satan can, and often does, quote Scripture for his purpose. However, much of the time he misquotes it (Mat. 4:5).

WHY DOES GOD ALLOW TEMPTATION OF THE BELIEVER?

1. Even though Satan is the tempter, still, he is God's tool as well as His foe (Job 1:11; 2:5). Consequently, it is God Who allows His Child to be led into temptation, and allows Satan to tempt, at least under certain parameters.

2. Even though temptations do not overtake man apart from God's Will, the actual prompting to do wrong is not of God, nor does it express His Command (James 1:12). The desire which impels to sin is not God's, but one's own, and it is fatal to yield to it (James 1:14). Temptation, within itself, is not sin, for Christ was tempted as we are, yet remained sinless (Mat. 4:1; Lk. 22:28; Heb. 4:15). Temptation becomes sin only when and as the suggestion of evil is accepted and yielded to.

3. Temptation is allowed by God in order to test one's Faith (I Pet. 1:6-7).

4. God allows temptation that we may learn reliance on the Word, of which Jesus was an example (Mat. 4:4, 7, 10).

5. The Lord allows temptations in order that the Believer may choose only the Will of God (Lk. 22:42). Actually, all temptation is an effort by Satan to entice the Believer to do that other than the will of God.

And yet, the Believer is importuned to pray that he not be led into temptation (Mat. 6:13; Lk. 22:40).

6. Temptation is allowed by the Lord in order that the Believer may realize how truly weak he actually is, and that he must learn to depend on the Grace of God (II Cor. 12:7-10).

Of this, all of us can be sure! Christ was tempted far above that which any Believer might be tempted. And, as well, He faced Satan with no more spiritual armaments than we have. In other words, He did not, and, in fact, could not draw on His powers of Deity. To have done so, would have completely nullified His very mission as the Last Adam. As well, the manner in which He faced Satan is the pattern laid down for all of us!

(2) "AND WHEN HE HAD FASTED FORTY DAYS AND FORTY NIGHTS, HE WAS AFTERWARD AN HUNGERED."

Three men are recorded in the Bible as having fasted forty days other than Christ. They are: A. Moses (Deut. 9:9, 18, 25; 10:10), B. Joshua (Ex. 24:13-18; 32:15-17), C. Elijah (I Ki. 19:7-8).

The purpose of this fast by Christ, as the others related, was to subdue the flesh. It was through the senses of the flesh that man first yielded to Satan, and fell. Consequently, from that time until now, Satan's greatest area of attack has been in this area.

The original temptation in the Garden of Eden involved the *"pride of life,"* the *"lust of the eyes,"* and the *"lust of the flesh."* This is found in Genesis 3:6, and again in I John 2:15-17).

The denial of food for the body, as done here by Christ, subdues the very area of these temptations. As such, Christ, in the wilderness, was doing the very opposite of what Adam and Eve did in the Garden. They ate of the forbidden fruit, while Christ denied Himself any fruit whatsoever! Consequently, the very area of disobedience, the flesh, was brought into subjection.

It should be quickly added, that what Christ did in the wilderness, respecting the forty-day fast, and the victory over the flesh, was done basically for us, and not for Himself. The victory He won by this forty-day fast, is transferred to us upon Faith in Him, and what He did.

And yet, the Believer should engage periodically in short fasts, which emulates Christ, and helps in the constant struggle of the flesh and the Spirit. However, long fasts should not be engaged unless specifically ordered by the Lord.

Throughout the Old Testament, other than the fasts mentioned by Moses, Joshua, and

NOTES

Elijah, only one fast a day a year was ordered by the Lord, which was the *"Great Day of Atonement"* (Lev. 16:29).

By the time of Christ, the Pharisees had increased the number of fasts from one day a year to two days a week. However, these were commandments of men, and not of the Lord. As such, they were of no consequence.

Paul mentioned *"Fastings often,"* without giving any length of time, etc. (II Cor. 11:27).

The fourteen-day fast Paul spoke of in Acts 27:33, seems to not have been a total fast, but only from meat. He said in verse 34 of that Chapter, *"Wherefore I pray you to take some meat: for this is for your health."*

Exactly as to how many had engaged in this two-week fast is not known, but, as stated, it seems to have been an abstention only from meat, although it could have referred to a total fast.

The phrase, *"He was afterward an hungered,"* refers to the conclusion of the forty-day fast.

Hunger leaves the body after a few days of fast and returns after a period of time, in this case forty days and nights.

During this time, all toxic poisons are expelled from the body, with the breath becoming sweet. It is said that any normal healthy person can fast this long (forty days and nights) without harm. Starvation only begins after hunger returns in such cases.

(3) "AND WHEN THE TEMPTER CAME TO HIM, HE SAID, IF THOU BE THE SON OF GOD, COMMAND THAT THESE STONES BE MADE BREAD."

The phrase, *"And when the Tempter came to Him,"* suggests that Satan appeared to Him personally, which he no doubt did!

The phrase, *"He said, If Thou be the Son of God,"* would have been better translated, *"Since Thou art . . . ."*

It was not meant to cast reflection upon Jesus as the Son of God, but was rather meant for Him to use His privilege as the Son of God in a wrongful way.

The phrase, *"Command that these stones be made bread,"* is a temptation by Satan to get Christ to demonstrate that He believes the heavenly utterance of 3:17, and so provide for His hunger.

It was a subtle snare into which any other

would have fallen, but with one Text from the Written Word (Deut. 8:3) the Tempter was defeated.

Jesus began a Ministry rich in miracles by refusing to work one. He fed others, Himself He would not feed; just as He saved others, but Himself He would not save.

Had Christ done so, He would have acted independently of God, and so failed in a perfect obedience and perfect dependence; and failure would have been sin.

(4) "BUT HE ANSWERED AND SAID, IT IS WRITTEN, MAN SHALL NOT LIVE BY BREAD ALONE, BUT BY EVERY WORD THAT PROCEEDETH OUT OF THE MOUTH OF GOD."

Jesus used Deuteronomy 8:3 in His answer to Satan, which recalled Israel's hunger in the desert. They murmured when hungry; the True Israel trusted, and waited, and He too received Angel's food, as verse 11 will portray.

The phrase, *"But He answered and said, It is written,"* proclaims Jesus using the Word of God as His weapon. Consequently, He set an example for us.

In Truth, and as alluded to, Christ was limited as to the weaponry He could use against Satan. In other words, in the Incarnation (God becoming man), He was limited to only what man can use.

The phrase, *"Man shall not live by bread alone,"* not only stifled Satan, but, as well, struck at the very heart of man's dependency on God. However, almost all of the human family, and for all time, has attempted to live only by physical bread. As such, and because man is a spiritual being as well as a physical being, he is woefully undeveloped, unfulfilled, and unsatisfied! For the finest bread in the world (material sustenance), and irrespective of its quantity, cannot take the place of the spiritual.

The phrase, *"But by every Word that proceedeth out of the Mouth of God,"* pertains to the spiritual which man must have, as well! So, man lives by physical bread, and by spiritual bread.

The physical bread has to do not only with food, but education, money, and what it can buy, as well as creative abilities such as scientific quests.

The spiritual part of man, and because man was created in the image of God, demands

sustenance, as well, from the Creator. Jesus plainly tells us in this Passage, that the spiritual man can only be satisfied and fulfilled by the Bible. It alone is the *"Word of God."* Consequently, the Bible should be a lifelong project for every Believer.

It must be studied daily, as well as diligently, and prayerfully. The idea that some Christians have not even read the Bible completely through at least once, is almost beyond belief. In the natural, it would be the same thing as a pilot flying an airplane, who knew very little about the plane, or about flying. Sooner or later, he will probably kill himself or others, which, in fact, happens constantly!

I think it is obvious that Jesus knew the Word of God, and, in fact, He had to learn it exactly as we do. It was not something that He just automatically knew, just because He was the Son of God. Had that been the case, He would have had an advantage that we do not have.

Actually, we are told in the Psalms exactly how He learned the Word. It says, *"O how I love Thy Law! it is my meditation all the day"* (Ps. 119:97). He meditated on it constantly; therefore, He knew what it said and understood it. If we did the same, our understanding and knowledge of it would be greatly enhanced.

It is a cop-out of the highest order, for any Believer to not read the Bible, claiming they do not understand it!

If anyone will diligently study the Bible, as other things, ultimately it will become clear and understandable. The trouble is, many Christians make little effort, and, consequently, their spiritual lives are weak and anemic.

As the Bible is the Word of God, it is alive, and, consequently, never grows old. Its passages always contain leading, guidance, and direction. As well, it is a constant refreshing!

To give an example, some time back, I was preparing for a service I was to preach in a particular city. The building would be packed, and, in effect, there would be a tremendous moving of the Holy Spirit that night.

At any rate, as Frances and I were getting dressed for the service that evening, the Spirit of the Lord spoke to my heart, saying, *"There is something about the Passage of Scripture that you are going to use tonight, that is different than any other miracle or healing performed by Christ."* The Spirit of the Lord then began to simply outline to me what He was speaking of, which proved to be a tremendous blessing to the people that night, and especially to this Evangelist.

To be sure, I had preached from that particular Text many times in the past, but had not seen that of which the Holy Spirit mentioned, neither had I heard any other Preacher speak of it.

As all know and understand, who truly know the Word of God, it is impossible to exhaust its resources. One may think that a particular Passage of Scripture has been gleaned of all its content, and then the Holy Spirit will open up something else that has never been seen previously, exactly as I have just mentioned! As stated, it is alive, and inasmuch as it is alive, it continues to grow, without ever contradicting itself.

At World Evangelism Bible College and Seminary, we teach the Word of God exclusively! We do not teach psychology, because we believe it is error, and an affront to God's Word.

As well, we only deal with philosophy as it pertains to particular errors contradicting the Word of God. We believe, as Peter said, *"According as His Divine Power hath given unto us all things that pertain unto life and Godliness, through the knowledge of Him that hath called us to glory and virtue.*

"Whereby are given unto us exceeding great and precious promises: that by these ye might be partakers of the Divine nature, having escaped the corruption that is in the world through lust" (II Pet. 1:3-4).

Consequently, it is tragic when many Christians little feed their soul with the Word of God, and are, consequently, as spiritually anemic as those in the world who only attempt to satisfy the entirety of the man by *"bread alone."*

Incidentally, the three temptations of Christ by Satan, perfectly paralleled the temptation of Adam and Eve in the Garden. This temptation concerning the bread, was *"the lust of the flesh."*

(5) "THEN THE DEVIL TAKETH HIM UP INTO THE HOLY CITY, AND SETTETH HIM ON A PINNACLE OF THE TEMPLE,"

The phrase, *"Then the Devil taketh Him up into the Holy City,"* refers to a powerful effort by the evil one. The words, *"taketh Him,"* refer

to a pressure so overwhelming that it speaks of near force.

Consequently, if one had seen Christ at that time, as He left the wilderness after this forty days and nights of fasting, and now under great attack by Satan, while walking toward Jerusalem, the scene would not have been desirous to behold.

Yes! He went physically to the Temple, for to claim that it was only a mental image, does violence to the Text. He actually went to Jerusalem from the wilderness, which was a distance of approximately ten to twenty miles, according to where He was in the wilderness.

If one had seen Him at this time, one would have seen a disheveled figure, thin and emaciated after the long fast, walking, no doubt, with head bowed, and under tremendous pressure, which no doubt showed extensively on His countenance.

Many may take umbrage at such a description, but only because they do not fully understand the totality of the Incarnation. As well, many have the erroneous concept that Jesus, by a mere quotation of Scripture, defeated Satan, with no consequent struggle! That is incorrect!

His temptations were as severe as ours, and even much more so. He felt all the powers of darkness exactly as we feel, with all its attendant misery, pain, and suffering. Satan's attacks are real! They are not mere figments of one's imagination. To be sure, his attack against Christ, was to a degree that none of us have ever experienced.

For instance, the latitude that God allows Satan in any and all temptation, concerns itself with the degree of spiritual maturity, Faith, and the Call of God on a person's life.

For example, the Lord would not allow a new Christian to be tempted by Satan, as much as He would a mature Christian. Consequently, few people have undergone temptation as Abraham, Moses, or David, etc., with none as Christ. Of course, I am speaking of the degree of temptation, for all are tempted in some manner.

The phrase, *"And setteth Him on a pinnacle of the Temple,"* concerns its highest point. Josephus implies that it referred to the top of the Royal Portico which from its highest point to the bottom of the ravine below was nearly 700 feet.

Irrespective of where this *"pinnacle"* was,

the idea was that Jesus make an extravagant show of Himself, which would have been contrary to the Will of God.

(6) "AND SAITH UNTO HIM, IF THOU BE THE SON OF GOD, CAST THYSELF DOWN: FOR IT IS WRITTEN, HE SHALL GIVE HIS ANGELS CHARGE CONCERNING THEE: AND IN THEIR HANDS THEY SHALL BEAR THEE UP, LEST AT ANY TIME THOU DASH THY FOOT AGAINST A STONE."

The order of the Temptations in Matthew is historical; in Luke it is dispensational. There is, therefore, an inner harmony, for Matthew presents Him as the Messiah coming to His Temple, and then as the Son of Man reigning over the earth.

But the Spirit in Luke places His relation to the earth in the foreground, and His connection with Israel in the background. There are many other instances in the Scriptures of a dispensational or moral order designedly differing from the historical.

In this temptation concerning the pinnacle of the Temple, Satan recognizes that the Psalms belong to the Messiah, and that their Promises are His. Jesus did not deny this, but said that it was also written that the servant should not test God to keep His Promises.

Malachi predicted that the Messiah would come suddenly to His Temple (Mal. 3:1). Satan, therefore, proposed that Christ should fulfill this Prophecy by suddenly descending from the pinnacle of the Temple, and, even maybe into the Temple Court — adding that He need not fear, for the Angels were commanded to safeguard Him.

In his quotation of Scripture, Satan added and subtracted words, as a reference to Psalm 91:11-12 shows. When the Holy Spirit quotes the Scripture, He is at liberty to vary them as He often does, for He is their Author, and, consequently, never changes their meaning.

Had the Lord done as Satan suggested, leap from the pinnacle, He would not only have made Himself an agent of Satan's will, but He would have compelled the Angels to become agents as well.

Also, had He commanded the stones to be made bread, and the Angels to safeguard Him, He would have forsaken His position as a servant, for a servant does not command.

The phrase, "And saith unto Him, If Thou

be the Son of God," once again is not meant to cast doubt on Who He was, but instead says, "Since You are the Son of God . . . ."

The phrase, "Cast Thyself down," was no doubt literally spoken, when Jesus was standing on the very "pinnacle of the Temple." As we have stated, the construction of the sentence does not lend credence to the thought that this was done only in the mental sense, but rather literally in the physical.

Was Jesus actually tempted to do so?

He certainly was, or it would not have been a literal temptation!

As we have stated, to be tempted is not sin; only yielding is sin!

To give tremendous weight to the temptation, Satan says, "For it is written, He shall give His Angels charge concerning Thee: and in their hands they shall bear thee up, lest at any time thou dash thy foot against a stone."

However, and as we have stated, Satan subtly misquoted the Word of God, as he is prone to do!

The actual Scripture reads, "For He shall give His Angels charge over Thee, to keep Thee in all Thy ways.

"They shall bear Thee up in their hands, lest Thou dash Thy foot against a stone" (Ps. 91:11-12).

Satan left out the words, "To keep Thee in all Thy ways," in verse 11, and added the words, "At any time," to verse 12. Consequently, as is obvious, Satan adds to the Word of God, and takes away from it.

The words, "To keep Thee in all Thy ways," are critical, inasmuch as it speaks of the Ways of God, and not man. Consequently, Satan, leaving out that phrase, completely distorted the meaning of the Passage.

As well, Satan did not dare continue quoting from Psalms, because the next verse, "Thou shalt tread upon the lion and the adder: the young lion and the dragon shalt Thou trample under feet," predicts his defeat (Ps. 91:13).

(7) "JESUS SAID UNTO HIM, IT IS WRITTEN AGAIN, THOU SHALT NOT TEMPT THE LORD THY GOD."

This is quoted from Deuteronomy 6:16.

What does it mean to tempt God?

Human beings have no right to test, or tempt God, unless specifically invited by God to do so as in Malachi 3:10.

The historic incident referred to in Deuteronomy 6:16 is instructive. God had promised to be with His people and had demonstrated His Presence in the fiery cloud that accompanied them. Yet Israel demanded proof, saying, *"Is the Lord among us, or not?"* (Ex. 17:7). Because God is totally trustworthy, demanding proof of His Power or Presence is an insult, demonstrating a failure to walk by Faith, and, therefore, expressing unbelief.

Therefore, to tempt God is to question His Word, which casts doubt on His ability to do what He has promised. As stated, it is unbelief, which is the foundation of all sin (Jn. 16:9).

So, for Jesus to have cast Himself off the Temple, as Satan suggested, would not have been a proof of His Faith, but, instead, daring or tempting God.

Regrettably, much of the modern *"Prosperity Gospel,"* falls into the same category! Individuals take God's Word, and try to force it into circumstances where it does not apply, or else, attempt to make it mean something that it does not mean. Whether done in ignorance or not, the results are a *"tempting of God,"* which is a grievous sin!

As the first temptation of turning the stones to bread constituted the *"lust of the flesh,"* this second temptation speaks of the *"lust of the eyes."* Satan tempted Christ to do this thing, in order that people might look at Him with their eyes, watching as He performed this great miracle of casting Himself from the pinnacle of the Temple, without suffering harm. In this way, He would make His grand entrance, which, sadly, characterizes so much of modern Ministry. It was the *"lust of the eyes,"* pure and simple!

(8) "AGAIN, THE DEVIL TAKETH HIM UP INTO AN EXCEEDING HIGH MOUNTAIN, AND SHEWETH HIM ALL THE KINGDOMS OF THE WORLD, AND THE GLORY OF THEM;"

The phrase, *"Again, the Devil taketh Him up into an exceeding high mountain,"* does not actually specify what mountain it was. Actually, it doesn't really matter what mountain it was, but the fact is that Jesus literally went to the top of this particular mountain, which was in the general area of Jericho. It could well have been Mt. Nebo, where Moses viewed the Promised Land, but such is only speculation.

NOTES

The phrase, *"And sheweth Him all the kingdoms of the world, and the glory of them,"* did not refer to Jesus being shown these kingdoms physically, but, instead, in a spiritual sense!

(9) "AND SAITH UNTO HIM, ALL THESE THINGS WILL I GIVE THEE, IF THOU WILT FALL DOWN AND WORSHIP ME."

Satan now abandoned all disguise and boldly called upon Jesus to worship Him. Then it was that the Lord dismissed him. This dismissal concluded the temptations, and so declares their historic order.

Satan has captured many kings by the offer of a part of the glory of earthly dominion, and he now tried by the offer of the whole to capture the heart of the Carpenter of Nazareth. But the object of that heart was God and His Will and not earth and its glory.

He did not despise the Throne of the earth, but He would only have it as His Father's gift; and it was as such that He prized it. Every heart that puts God first and seeks to please Him only, is certain to escape Satan's most subtle snares; for to that heart there is given a clearness of vision that discovers these snares.

The phrase, *"And saith unto Him, All these things will I give Thee,"* was not disputed by Christ as being owned by Satan.

While it is certainly true that God owns the world, and all that is in it, still, the world system, and because of the Fall in the Garden of Eden, now belongs to Satan. As such, he is the *"prince"* and *"god"* of this world's system (Jn. 8:44; 12:31; 14:30; II Cor. 4:4; Eph. 2:1-3; I Jn. 5:19).

This is the reason that Christian man is foolish to think that he can *"Christianize"* society. While it is certainly true that he can make it better, still, it will not be wrested from the evil hands of Satan, until the Second Coming of Christ.

Such thoughts (of Christianizing the society) only show the pride and consequent deception of the modern Church. Christians are not called upon to save society, but, instead, to save men out of society (II Cor. 6:14-18).

The phrase, *"If Thou wilt fall down and worship me,"* is, in effect, what Satan was able to make Adam and Eve do! Now he promotes the same tactic with Christ, although in an aggrandized manner.

There are two schools of thought regarding this request by Satan. They are as follows:

1. Satan wants to be God, as the Holy Spirit through Isaiah proclaimed (Isa. 14:12-15). As such, he demands worship! Consequently, almost the entirety of the world, and from the beginning, have worshiped him.

In the past, it was done through idols, with it now being done through various religions of which Satan is the author, such as Islam, Buddhism, Hinduism, Shintoism, Mormonism, and Catholicism.

As well, modern Humanism deifies Satan, by worshiping self which is corrupted by Satan. This latter, humanism, incorporates much of the modern world including America, and especially America. Regrettably, it has made great inroads into the Church as well! Its philosophy is psychology, and its savior is man himself. It is not new. It began with Adam and Eve in the Garden of Eden when they covered themselves with fig leaves, attempting to hide their nakedness (Gen. 3:7).

2. Some propose that Satan's invitation did not really refer to Christ worshiping him as God, for that would have been too blatant, but to simply acknowledge his rights as over-lord of the earth.

Quite possibly both viewpoints are correct, inasmuch as if he could get Christ to take the first step, acknowledging him as over-lord, the worshiping him as God would easily follow!

In Truth, was it possible for Jesus to succumb to temptation, and sin?

Many have claimed that He could not sin, in that He was the Son of God, etc. However, such is not correct!

Were it not possible for Jesus to have sinned in His Incarnation, then Satan's efforts were futile and foolish. While it is certainly true that Jesus could not have sinned as God, still, as God manifest in the flesh it certainly was possible for Him to sin. (Rom. 8:3)

Were it not so, He would not have truly been Incarnate. The Incarnation demanded that He be *"made in the likeness of men"* (Phil. 2:7).

Paul further said, *"God sending His Own Son in the likeness of sinful flesh, and for sin, condemned sin in the flesh,"* meaning that the possibility of sin was present in Christ exactly as it is in all men (Rom. 8:3).

However, there was one great difference! He did not sin, where all others have.

The writer of Hebrews said, *"Seeing then*

that we have a Great High Priest, that is passed into the heavens, Jesus the Son of God, let us hold fast our profession.

"For we have not an High Priest which cannot be touched with the feeling of our infirmities; but was in all points tempted like as we are, yet without sin" (Heb. 4:14-15).

Several things are said in these verses:

1. If He had not suffered the same pressure of temptation as we, and with the possibility of failure, He could not have been *"touched with the feeling of our infirmities."* In that He has undergone the same thing that we undergo, yet without failure, He can empathize with us.

2. As the Last Adam, He must face Satan on the same ground that all other human beings face him, with all the potential for failure. Were it impossible for Him to succumb to these temptations, as some claim, then He was not truly the Last Adam (I Cor. 15:45).

3. Satan would not have wasted his time tempting Christ in all points as we are, if there were no possibility of failure. In fact, this was Satan's greatest opportunity! And to be sure, he took full advantage of it, but without success!

In Truth, Jesus as a Man, overcame Satan in every respect, and as our Substitute, the Representative Man, we are allowed to identify with Him by Faith, and, consequently, are given His victory (II Cor. 5:17, 21).

Thus Satan concludes, at least at this time, his temptation of Christ, with the *"pride of life."* All three are as follows:

1. *"The lust of the flesh,"* i.e., the turning of the stones to bread.

2. *"The lust of the eyes,"* i.e., that all would see Him make His grand entrance, by leaping from the pinnacle of the Temple.

3. *"The pride of life,"* i.e., offering Jesus the kingdoms of the world.

This is Satan's basic manner of temptation for all, but not necessarily in that order.

(10) "THEN SAITH JESUS UNTO HIM, GET THEE HENCE, SATAN: FOR IT IS WRITTEN, THOU SHALT WORSHIP THE LORD THY GOD, AND HIM ONLY SHALT THOU SERVE."

The phrase, *"Then saith Jesus unto him, Get thee hence, Satan,"* proclaims Christ for the first time, addressing Satan directly.

The Bible, as is here proclaimed, presents Satan as a personal being. He was created originally as Lucifer (*"light bearer"*) and carries a number of names in both Testaments. These include the Devil, the Serpent, the accuser of the brethren, and the ruler of the kingdom of the air.

The Hebrew word is *"Satan,"* which means *"adversary."* The Greek *"Satanas"* carries the same meaning. The common name of Satan in the New Testament is *"diabolos,"* and means *"devil,"* which means, *"one who slanders or accuses."*

Both Testaments reveal Satan as God's adversary and the enemy of mankind. He hates man because God originally made man in His image. As well, he is the cause of all the suffering, pain, heartache, brutality, murder and greed in the world, and is, in effect, the fountainhead of evil.

Satan did not make his beginning as one who is evil, but, instead, Righteous. He was created by God along with all the other Angels, with some indication that he was the most beautiful, powerful, and wisest of all (Isa. 14:12-15; Ezek. 28:11-19).

Becoming lifted up in his own beauty, he fell through pride, and led a revolution against God. He then attempted to take God's place and introduce sin into the universe. His initial rebellion included the defection of many Angels and led to the expulsion of that Host from Heaven (Rev. 12:4).

Satan was the power influencing the serpent in Eden, and thus he was an instrument in mankind's Fall, by which he introduced sin's corruption into the human race. As such, and as we have stated, he is the author of all evil in the world, which has bathed it with blood.

Despite what Christ did at Calvary and the Resurrection, Satan still exercises great power in the world. He is called the *"ruler of the kingdom of the air"* in Ephesians 2:2, and is at work in all who are disobedient to God. Despite his powers and the devices he uses to deceive humanity, Satan, as is here obvious, was decisively defeated in every confrontation he had with Jesus (Lk. 11:14-22; 13:10-16).

His greatest thrust is yet to be made, which will take place in the coming Great Tribulation, when he will empower the man of sin, in an effort to abrogate the predictions of the Prophets, and, consequently, to make himself God (II Thess. 2). However, the final destiny of this evil being is fixed.

NOTES

At the Second Coming, he will be cast into the bottomless pit, along with all his fallen angels and demon spirits, and, therefore, not allowed to corrupt the earth during the coming Kingdom Age (Rev. 20:1-3).

At the end of the Kingdom Age, Satan will be allowed out of the pit for one final attempt to overthrow the Lord, which will be short lived, and after which he will be thrown into the Lake of Fire, to be *"tormented day and night for ever and ever"* (Rev. 20:7-10).

After that, there will be a *"new heaven and a new earth . . . And God shall wipe away all tears from their eyes; and there shall be no more death, neither sorrow, nor crying, neither shall there be any more pain: for the former things are passed away"* (Rev. 21:1, 4).

The phrase, *"For it is written,"* once again portrays Christ using the greatest weapon of all, and that which is available to any and all, *"The Word of God."*

The phrase, *"Thou shalt worship the Lord thy God, and Him only shalt thou serve,"* proclaims Christ, in effect, saying to Satan, *"I acknowledge thee not."*

In effect, He was saying, *"God Alone is the Supreme Being, and Alone is to be worshipped."* As well, *"I have come to destroy you and your works, and that I shall do"* (I Jn. 3:8).

However, even though Satan was unable to get Christ to worship him, still, he has succeeded with the far greater majority of mankind.

For instance, all religions, which constitute a work of man, originated by Satan, such as Islam, Hinduism, Shintoism, Mormonism, Buddhism, and corrupt Christianity, is, in effect, man worshiping Satan.

As a case in point, and closer to home, at least respecting Christianity, all Mary worship by the Catholic Church is, in effect, the worship of Satan. As well, millions of Protestants worship their Denomination, even though they would little think of themselves as doing such. However, anything that is made a part of one's Salvation other than Christ, constitutes not only error, but whether realized or not, a form of worship given to Satan, for he is the author of all error.

The Scripture is emphatic, *"And Him only shalt thou serve,"* but yet, is abrogated daily with men serving a Doctrine, a Church, a Denomination, or men, etc.

So, even though Satan was totally unsuccessful with Christ, he has been successful with most others!

(11) "THEN THE DEVIL LEAVETH HIM, AND, BEHOLD, ANGELS CAME AND MINISTERED UNTO HIM."

Luke said that Satan *"Departed from Him for a season,"* meaning that there would be other temptations (Lk. 4:13).

In the phrase, *"Then the devil leaveth Him,"* we have the assurance that no matter how severe the attack, ultimately it will come to an end, and the evil one will leave. God help us, as Christ, that when he does leave, it is not in victory but defeat.

The phrase, *"And, behold, Angels came and ministered unto Him,"* gives us little clue as to exactly how they *"ministered unto Him."*

One can well imagine that after a 40-day fast, and suffering the terrible rigors of combat with Satan, which within itself is far worse than one could ever begin to realize, Jesus was emaciated, physically, mentally, and spiritually.

As well, one can well imagine the Angels keenly observing Christ during the entirety of the 40 days and nights of fasting, and especially during the tryst with Satan. However, during this time they were not allowed to interfere, for Christ must bear the full brunt of this Alone. However, the moment Satan left, they instantly came, ministering to Christ.

Doesn't it follow that similar activities by Angels are carried out with all Believers who are under attack by Satan? The writer of Hebrews said, *"Wherefore seeing we also are compassed about with so great a cloud of witnesses, let us lay aside every weight, and the sin which doth so easily beset us, and let us run with patience the race that is set before us, Looking unto Jesus ..."* (Heb. 12:1-2).

If the Angels beheld and attended Christ, they do likewise with all Believers.

As well, it is noted that these Angels did not speak to Satan, even though they knew him well, having all been created by God at the same time. Actually, there is no record in the Bible of any Righteous Angel addressing Satan or other fallen angels, other than *"Michael the Archangel, contending with the Devil about the body of Moses."* Even then it says, that he *"Durst not bring against him a railing accusation, but said, The Lord rebuke thee"* (Jude 9).

NOTES

Yet to come in the Great Tribulation, *"Michael and his Angels"* will fight against Satan and his Angels, and will cast them out of Heaven (Rev. 12:7-9).

Satan and his Angels still have access to Heaven, and even the Throne of God at present, but this will end with that coming conflict (Job. 1).

(12) "NOW WHEN JESUS HAD HEARD THAT JOHN WAS CAST INTO PRISON, HE DEPARTED INTO GALILEE;"

The long predicted day at last arrived and the King presented himself to Israel (vss. 12-17). However, His reception will not be favorable!

The phrase, *"Now when Jesus had heard...,"* portrays Him as a Man, who had to learn things as all others learn them, unless His Heavenly Father revealed them unto Him, which He often did!

The phrase, *"That John was cast into prison,"* means that such was done to John, only after he had completed his Ministry of preparing the way for Christ. Now that he had accomplished his task, the Lord would allow him to be taken thusly.

The phrase, *"He departed into Galilee,"* refers to the area around the Sea of Galilee where He made His Headquarters, and carried out much of His Ministry.

I will never forget the first time that I had the privilege of seeing this beautiful area, the area that God had selected for the earthly Headquarters of the Ministry of His Son and my Saviour.

Coming from Jerusalem, we topped the last line of hills before the area of the Sea of Galilee. If I remember correctly, I had the driver to stop, and all of us disembarked from the vehicles, observing this panorama which lay before us.

The Sea of Galilee is about 7 miles wide and 14 miles long, and from our vantage point we could see much of it.

I don't think I have ever seen anything so beautiful in all my life! Perhaps my definition of beauty was colored with the thought that this is where Jesus had launched His Ministry of the Redemption of mankind. I stood there for a long while lost in my own thoughts, endeavoring to fill my mind with this scene, and yet, I could not keep back the tears.

He did not settle here by accident, for it was the place selected by His Heavenly Father.

Now, there is only one city on the banks of the Sea of Galilee, Tiberias, but then towns ringed its shore.

Josephus, the Jewish Historian, said that approximately 250,000 lived around the Sea of Galilee during the time of Christ. Then it had a thriving fishing industry, as well as other pursuits, and was prosperous.

Now those cities are gone, and because of a just judgment, with the exception, and as stated, of Tiberius, which lays at its southern extremity.

(13) "AND LEAVING NAZARETH, HE CAME AND DWELT IN CAPERNAUM, WHICH IS UPON THE SEA COAST, IN THE BORDERS OF ZABULON AND NEPHTHALIM:"

The phrase, *"And leaving Nazareth,"* probably refers to His rejection at Nazareth, as detailed in Luke 4:16-30.

The phrase, *"He came and dwelt in Capernaum,"* refers to Him making this small city His Headquarters.

Some have thought that Capernaum was the *"Village of Nahum,"* where this Prophet resided, which it probably was!

Capernaum is located on the northwest shores of the Sea of Galilee. It was near a most copious spring which watered Gennesaret, and was called by some, *"the Town of Seven Springs."*

As late as the early Fifth Century, it was said that Jewish Christians lived in Capernaum, and healed and spoke in the Name of Jesus. They were called *"Nazaraeans."*

I have visited the ruins of Capernaum, and actually did a short Television Special there. It is said that archaeologists have found the site where the Synagogue sat in which Jesus ministered. As well, they claimed to have found the site of Simon Peter's home, where Jesus often resided. Whether they are correct in this latter assumption, is anyone's guess. However, the Scripture is clear, that Capernaum was chosen by God for a very special purpose, but, sadly, little realized the significance of its visitation, and was ultimately judged by Christ.

The phrase, *"Which is upon the sea coast,"* refers to the Sea of Galilee.

The phrase, *"In the borders of Zabulon and Nephthalim,"* refers to these two Tribes bordering the Sea of Galilee, at least after a fashion. In fact, Naphtali did border it on the north

and west. However, the eastern border of Zebulun was several miles away, but with many of its people coming to the Sea of Galilee area to its markets.

(14) "THAT IT MIGHT BE FULFILLED WHICH WAS SPOKEN BY ESAIAS THE PROPHET, SAYING,"

Once again the Prophet Isaiah is referred to, proclaiming the abundance of his Prophecies which dealt with both the First and Second Advents of Christ.

(15) "THE LAND OF ZABULON, AND THE LAND OF NEPHTHALIM, BY THE WAY OF THE SEA, BEYOND JORDAN, GALILEE OF THE GENTILES;"

This area which once contained the Tribes of *"Zebulun and Naphtali"* are especially singled out by the Holy Spirit. And for what reason?

Of course, it is obvious that in this area Jesus carried out much of His Ministry, with His Headquarters actually in the confines of the Tribe of Naphtali.

The meaning of the names of all the ancient Tribes of Israel, in a way, prefigured Christ. That which their names meant, He did!

The firstborn of Leah, Jacob's wife, was *"Reuben"* which meant *"See a Son,"* and refers to the Birth of Christ.

Her second son was *"Simeon,"* with his name meaning *"Hearing,"* and spoke of Christ hearing the Father.

The third son born to her was *"Levi,"* and meant *"Joined,"* and referred to Christ joining the human family to God by His Death and Resurrection.

The fourth son born to Leah was *"Judah,"* and meant *"Praise,"* which typified Jesus as being the ultimate Praise of God.

Leah's fifth son was *"Issachar,"* and meant *"Reward,"* which speaks of the Great Salvation that Jesus has won for us.

Her sixth son was *"Zebulun,"* which meant, *"Dwelling,"* which spoke of Jesus opening up the way for man to dwell with God.

All of this, as well, typifies humanity, with the child being born, and then hearing the Gospel, and when it is old enough, being joined to Christ. He then learns to *"Praise God,"* and receives great *"Reward,"* and will *"Dwell"* with the Lord for ever.

"Naphtali" was born to Bilhah, Rachel's maid, with Rachel also being Jacob's wife. Naphtali

means *"Wrestlings,"* and refers to Jesus defeating Satan, exactly as the temptation in the wilderness proved, as well as the entirety of His Life, Death, Resurrection, and Ascension.

So, He *"wrestled,"* and defeated Satan, that we might *"Dwell"* with Him forever!

As well, *"Dan,"* was born to Bilhah, and before Naphtali, and means *"judging."* Consequently, Jesus judged Satan (Jn. 16:11).

"Gad" was born to Zilpal, Leah's maid, and means *"an army or troop,"* prefiguring Christ leading the armies of Heaven against Satan (Rev. 19).

"Joseph" was born to Rachel, and means *"adding."* Jesus will add to our lives all that has been lost.

"Benjamin," as well, was born to Rachel, and means *"the son of My Right Hand,"* i.e., *"Christ at the Father's Right Hand."*

The phrase, *"By the way of the sea, beyond Jordan,"* refers to the Sea of Galilee.

The phrase, *"Galilee of the Gentiles,"* refers to the great Roman Road which ran near the Sea of Galilee from Damascus. Most all Gentiles traveling in this direction did so on this road.

(16) "THE PEOPLE WHICH SAT IN DARKNESS SAW GREAT LIGHT; AND TO THEM WHICH SAT IN THE REGION AND SHADOW OF DEATH LIGHT IS SPRUNG UP."

His apparition as the Great Light found Zebulun and Naphtali in greater affliction under the Romans than previously under the Assyrians (Isa. 9); and the moral darkness was greater than the national misery.

The depth of this great darkness and the people sitting in it are contrasted with the fame of the Great Light and the people following it.

The phrase, *"The people which sat in darkness saw Great Light,"* refers to Christ, and the people being in spiritual darkness irrespective of their religion of Judaism. In fact, the people, and because of their Spiritual Leaders, had departed so far from the Law of Moses, that the Holy Spirit could only describe it as *"darkness."* And such is all religion! Outside of Christ there is nothing but darkness, and irrespective of its source. Not only is He the *"Light,"* but, and as the Holy Spirit says it, *"Great Light."*

The Greek word is *"phos,"* and means *"underived and absolute light — the opposite of all darkness."*

NOTES

As well, the word, *"sat,"* implies a settled acceptance of this *"darkness,"* which characterizes most of humanity, and for all time.

The phrase, *"And to them which sat in the region and shadow of death light is sprung up,"* refers to the result of that darkness, which is *"death,"* and referred to *"spiritual death,"* which meant separation from God.

The *"Light"* that sprang up around them, and among them, was Christ. As we have repeatedly stated, there is no other *"Light,"* and this is the only *"Light"* which will dispel the *"darkness."*

In the last nearly four years, this Passage of Scripture has burned in my heart. Most of the world lies in darkness, and, as such, they are dying, and with no way to extricate themselves. The great educational universities of the world hold no answers! Neither is the solution found on Wall Street, or even the Church. The only *"Light"* is Jesus.

That is the reason I have struggled, even against insurmountable odds, to attempt to take the Gospel to the world by Television and Crusades, which the Lord has called me to do. It is certainly not that I am anything, because as Paul said, *"I be nothing."* However, the Gospel I preach is everything. It has resulted, even in this Ministry, in hundreds of thousands, if not millions being brought to a saving knowledge of Jesus Christ. It alone can break the chains and shackles of humanity! It alone can set the captive free! It alone can bring hope where there is no hope! It alone can save, because it alone presents Christ!

As the *"Light"* sprang up that day of so long ago in the Galilee area, it, as well, must *"spring up"* all over the world. That is the reason that Christ said, *"Go ye into all the world, and preach the Gospel to every creature"* (Mk. 16:15). Consequently, there is nothing more important in the Mind of God than this task! And yet, and sorrowfully so, most of the Church gives it little attention.

Too many modern Christians, especially in the Pentecostal and Charismatic realm, of which I am a part, are chasing fads, or else, trying to confess their way to wealth. It is ironical, most Christians are trying to get God to make them rich, while He is trying to make them Christlike! The end result is, and because of an improper desire, they don't get rich or Christlike!

(17) "FROM THAT TIME JESUS BEGAN TO PREACH, AND TO SAY, REPENT: FOR THE KINGDOM OF HEAVEN IS AT HAND."

The Messiah's Advent was signaled by three great words, *"Repent"* (vs. 17), *"Follow"* (vs. 19), *and "Blessed"* (5:3). So, *"Repent, Follow, and be Blessed."*

As John, so Jesus, He *"began to preach."* As stated, this is God's method, and has not changed from then until now. Symposiums, Seminars, Counseling, Dramas, etc., may have their place, but it is by *"Preaching"* that the Lord has chosen to present His Gospel.

It is interesting that the very first word used by Christ, as recorded by Matthew, respecting the beginning of His Ministry, is *"Repent."* This surely proclaims the great significance of this all-important Doctrine. And yet, the modern Church little alludes to it.

As well, those to whom Jesus was ministering, were God's chosen people, and, in effect, constituted the Church of its day. Therefore, He was telling the *"Church"* to *"Repent!"*

The phrase, *"For the Kingdom of Heaven is at hand,"* has reference to the fact that entrance into this Kingdom, could not be made unless the people first *"repented."*

THE KINGDOM OF HEAVEN

The *"Kingdom of Heaven,"* which could be translated *"The Kingdom from the Heavens,"* was offered to Israel at the First Advent of Christ. It was rejected!

Regrettably, the rejection of the Kingdom by Israel has submitted the world to nearly 2,000 years more of sadness, trouble, war, and heartache. That finally will be rectified when Jesus comes back and is accepted by Israel, which will take place at the Second Coming (I Cor. 15:24-28; Eph. 1:10).

This *"Kingdom"* was *"at hand,"* because Jesus was there proclaiming it, but, sadly, and as stated, it was rejected.

(18) "AND JESUS, WALKING BY THE SEA OF GALILEE, SAW TWO BRETHREN, SIMON CALLED PETER, AND ANDREW HIS BROTHER, CASTING A NET INTO THE SEA: FOR THEY WERE FISHERS."

The phrase, *"And Jesus, walking by the Sea of Galilee,"* probably refers to Him walking on a road which skirted the bank of the lake, all the way from the mouth of the Jordan northward.

NOTES

Jesus, as should be understood, would be on the western side of the lake.

The phrase, *"Saw two brethren, Simon called Peter, and Andrew his brother,"* along with *"James and John"* of verse 21, constitutes the first calling of His Disciples.

These four had previously met Him in Judea, where no doubt they had gone to be baptized of John, and then had returned to their home in Capernaum.

The phrase, *"Casting a net into the sea: for they were fishers,"* proclaims Christ calling busy men to His service.

The brothers Andrew and Peter were casting their net, and the other brothers James and John were mending their net. He called them to a higher fishing as He called David to a higher feeding (Ps. 78:70-71).

(19) "AND HE SAITH UNTO THEM, FOLLOW ME, AND I WILL MAKE YOU FISHERS OF MEN."

Someone said to me the other day, *"You are a leader!"* I immediately responded to them by saying, *"No! I am not a leader, I am a follower, a follower of Christ."*

The phrase, *"And He saith unto them, Follow Me,"* has a far greater meaning than the simple following from place to place. It meant an immediate detachment from their present occupation, and of a solid attachment to Christ as their Leader.

It is the call that He gives to all, even though to different types of service. It was the greatest journey that these Disciples could ever think of embarking upon, and means the same for all, and irrespective of their place or position in life.

First of all, the following of Him will lead to eternal life, but with a fulfillment and development of such proportions that it beggars description!

Notice, He said, *"Follow Me,"* not other men, Religious Denominations, Doctrines, or personal ambitions or desires. Regrettably, many, if not most, little truly follow Him. But for those who do, it is an unparalleled journey that cannot be matched by anything the world has to offer.

The phrase, *"And I will make you fishers of men,"* constitutes the greatest calling of all!

If one is to notice, for the most important task on earth, the continuing and proclamation of His Gospel, which alone is the Salvation of men, He called for the most part, fishermen. This means that the Religious Leaders, the learned Scholars, the Scribes, as well as the Pharisees, who considered themselves to be the Religious Elite of Israel, were studiously ignored. This, as well, would not endear Him at all to these groups.

In their minds, the very idea that One would be alluded to as the Messiah, and would choose these types of men as His Chief Lieutenants, was unthinkable!

Regrettably, and even after the passing of some 2,000 years, it continues to be unthinkable! And yet, the Scripture says, *"Not many wise men after the flesh, not many mighty, not many noble, are called:"* (I Cor. 1:26).

Paul went on to say, *"But God hath chosen the foolish things of the world to confound the wise; and God hath chosen the weak things of the world to confound the things which are mighty;*

"And base things of the world, and things which are despised, hath God chosen, yea, and things which are not, to bring to nought things that are." (I Cor. 1:27-28).

There is a reason for all that, and Paul said that too, *"That no flesh should glory in His Presence"* (I Cor. 1:29).

(20) "AND THEY STRAIGHTWAY LEFT THEIR NETS, AND FOLLOWED HIM."

The phrase, *"And they straightway,"* means they left immediately.

The phrase, *"Left their nets, and followed Him,"* means that they left their occupation behind forever. They had heard a Higher Calling!

As we have stated, they had already become acquainted with Jesus, as John records in his first Chapter. Without a doubt, they had been tremendously moved by that experience, with it unable to leave their minds, and, consequently, upon His Call, they immediately responded. The Holy Spirit had already performed the work within their hearts.

Little did they realize where this journey would lead. They were unlearned fishermen, never dreaming that God would use them in the capacity He did, and their conclusion, other than Judas, would be to have their names inscribed on the *"twelve foundations"* of the New Jerusalem. They would be called, *"The Twelve Apostles of the Lamb"* (Rev. 21:14).

As far as this earthly life was concerned, tradition says that Peter was crucified, and upon his request, upside down.

NOTES

Tradition also says that both Peter and Andrew were of the Tribe of Reuben, with Andrew evangelizing Scythia, becoming Russia's patron Saint, and that he was stoned and crucified in Greece or Scythia.

(21) "AND GOING ON FROM THENCE, HE SAW OTHER TWO BRETHREN, JAMES THE SON OF ZEBEDEE, AND JOHN HIS BROTHER, IN A SHIP WITH ZEBEDEE THEIR FATHER, MENDING THEIR NETS; AND HE CALLED THEM."

The phrase, *"And going on from thence,"* refers to the same walk beside the lake, which would result in the call of *"James and John,"* as well!

The phrase, *"He saw other two brethren,"* records the second set of brothers He called. In fact, there were several sets of brothers called among the Apostles:

1. Peter and Andrew (Mat. 4:18).

2. James and John (Mat. 4:21).

3. Philip and Bartholomew, sometimes called Nathanael (Jn. 1:43-51).

4. James (known as James the Less), and Judas (not Iscariot). This Judas is called Lebbaeus or Thaddaeus (Mat. 10:3; Mk. 3:18).

It is thought that Matthew (Mk. 2:14; Lk. 6:16; Acts 1:13), along with Simon Zelotes were also brothers of James and Judas. If this is true, then Jesus called four brothers from one family as a part of the twelve Apostles.

The phrase, *"James the son of Zebedee and John his brother,"* concludes the trio who were most intimate with Jesus, *"Peter, James, and John"* (Mat. 17:1-8; 26:36-46; Mk. 5:37).

Luke also states they were partners with Peter and Andrew in the fishing business (Lk. 5:10).

James was the first martyr among the Apostles (Acts 12:1-2). Tradition says that he was of the Tribe of Levi through his father and of Judah through his mother — of both the priestly and royal house, that he preached in India with Peter, and later in Spain, becoming the patron Saint of Spain.

"John his brother," became very close to Christ, and is the only one, tradition says, who died a natural death.

Peter wrote two Books in the New Testament, while John wrote five. It is said that he lived to be about 100 years old, writing the Book of Revelation, which closed out the

Canon of Scripture, when he was near the century mark. He lived the longest of any of the twelve, and was the last to die.

The phrase, *"In a ship with Zebedee their father,"* probably proclaims Zebedee as the owner, or at least partner with his sons, along with Peter and Andrew, of this fishing business.

It is not known why the father of James and John is mentioned, and the father of Peter and Andrew never mentioned, save incidentally, and by our Lord (Mat. 16:17; Jn. 1:42; 21:15-17).

The phrase, *"Mending their nets; and He called them,"* refers to them being busy exactly as Peter and Andrew.

There is evidence, that these sets of brothers, along with Zebedee, were not poverty stricken, but, in fact, were successful businessmen. Mark said as well, that they had servants (Mk. 1:20).

Therefore, the idea that they had nothing to leave in order to follow Christ, is erroneous. Every evidence is, that they were partners in a successful fishing business, and, consequently, most would have thought them foolish for taking the step they did. However, it was the greatest decision they ever made.

(22) "AND THEY IMMEDIATELY LEFT THE SHIP AND THEIR FATHER, AND FOLLOWED HIM."

"Immediately" and *"straightway"* basically mean the same thing!

How well Zebedee was able to run this business after the departure of these four men is anyone's guess. However, I am certain the Lord, as He is prone to do, rewarded him greatly for giving up these sons and partners. To be sure, he was not left in the lurch, for the Lord would provide, and abundantly so!

The phrase, *"Left the ship and their father, and followed Him,"* means that they stopped *"mending their nets,"* at the call of Christ, and immediately began to follow Him.

As stated, they had already met Christ, and had become convinced that He was the Messiah, and being moved upon by the Holy Spirit from the time they first met Him, they were now overjoyed at the opportunity to serve in this capacity.

(23) "AND JESUS WENT ABOUT ALL GALILEE, TEACHING IN THEIR SYNAGOGUES, AND PREACHING THE GOSPEL OF THE KINGDOM, AND HEALING ALL

NOTES

MANNER OF SICKNESS AND ALL MANNER OF DISEASE AMONG THE PEOPLE."

The phrase, *"And Jesus went about all Galilee,"* proclaims the beginning of His Ministry which took place in this area of *"Zebulon, and Nephthalim."*

In this Scripture, the Holy Spirit brings out the method of presenting the Gospel, *"Teaching, Preaching, and Healing."* He has not changed that method until now, despite the fact, that most Christian Denominations, so-called, little *"teach"* or *"preach"* the Gospel anymore! There are even less who believe in *"healing,"* claiming that such is not for today, etc.

The phrase, *"Teaching in their Synagogues,"* proclaims Him beginning in the Synagogues of the area, exactly as He had done in Nazareth, that is if His visit to Nazareth preceded this occasion, which it possibly did not.

Someone has said that *"Preaching"* calls attention to Truth, while *"Teaching"* explains it.

Jesus was recognized in His society as a Teacher, and the New Testament shows He was often addressed as *"Teacher."*

As other teachers in that day in Judea, Jesus' teaching focused on shaping the hearers' perception of God and God's Kingdom, and thus it dealt with the implications of a personal relationship with God.

In John's Gospel, much of Jesus' public instruction focused on Himself and His Own place as Son of God.

Teaching situations with Christ are varied and complex. He taught great crowds in Synagogues, on a mountain or a boat anchored by the seashore. As well, He dialogued.

He illustrated Truth by pointing to the commonplace, and by telling obscure parables. He answered questions and asked questions. Over and over again, events like the healing of a man with a paralyzed hand led to discussion in which the character and purposes of God were more sharply unveiled. In other words, He used any and all occasions to teach His listeners.

As well, Christ maintained an intimate teaching Ministry with His Disciples. He answered their questions about a day's events and questioned them in turn. The Disciples observed Jesus' life while traveling with Him, and Jesus gave them life assignments, as when He sent them out two by two.

This powerful, intimate form of instruction is best understood as discipling, and it is significant that Jesus' instructions to the Disciples after His Resurrection were that they should *"Go and make Disciples of all nations, . . . Teaching them to obey everything"* He had commanded them (Mat. 28:19-20).

Consequently, His Teaching not only provided information, but also created Disciples who desired to live in responsive obedience to God's Will, which should be the goal of every God-called Teacher.

The phrase, *"And preaching the Gospel of the Kingdom,"* in effect was meant to proclaim the Good News of the Kingdom. The entrance into it is by Repentance, as evidenced in verse 17.

The Good News of the *"Gospel of the Kingdom,"* actually knew no bounds.

It meant that first of all, those who *"Sat in spiritual darkness,"* would now see the Light. It meant they did not have to die eternally lost, but upon making Christ their Saviour, could enjoy *"More abundant life,"* with, as Peter said, it being *"Joy unspeakable and full of glory."*

As well, this *"Gospel of the Kingdom,"* not only meant Salvation for the soul, but as well, *"Healing for the body."* The phrase, *"And healing all manner of sickness and all manner of disease among the people,"* proclaims this abundantly!

Even though unbelievers claim that such passed away with the Apostles, the Word of God says the very opposite, even in the Words of Christ, *"Verily, verily, I say unto you, He that believeth on Me, the works that I do shall he do also; and greater works than these shall he do; because I go unto My Father."*

He then said, *"And whatsoever ye shall ask in My Name, that will I do, that the Father may be glorified in the Son"* (Jn. 14:12-13).

As well, this *"Gospel of the Kingdom,"* includes the casting out of *"Devils,"* even as the next verse proclaims.

(24) "AND HIS FAME WENT THROUGHOUT ALL SYRIA: AND THEY BROUGHT UNTO HIM ALL SICK PEOPLE THAT WERE TAKEN WITH DIVERS DISEASES AND TORMENTS, AND THOSE WHICH WERE POSSESSED WITH DEVILS, AND THOSE WHICH WERE LUNATICK, AND THOSE THAT HAD THE PALSY; AND HE HEALED THEM."

The phrase, *"And His fame went throughout all Syria,"* means that it went beyond Israel, into the whole of Syria. It did not mean that Jesus went there personally.

The phrase, *"And they brought unto Him all sick people that were taken with divers diseases and torments,"* respects any and all types of sicknesses and diseases, irrespective of how serious they were.

The phrase, *"And those which were possessed with devils,"* refers to those who were demon possessed.

Modern science, as well as most of the modern Church, discounts all such activity, calling it *"mere folklore."* Nevertheless, and despite the plethora of unbelief, demon spirits are just as real now as then. As well, they cause just as much difficulty and problems.

In fact, many sicknesses (but not all) are caused by demons, along with behavior problems and insanity. (Much insanity, however, is physical and not spiritual.)

Demons do not have bodies, but, in fact, seek those they may inhabit, whether human or animal.

We are not told of their origin in the Bible, therefore, as to exactly where they came from is speculation. This we do know, God did not originally create them in this manner, but they became this way at some point in time. It is said, *"And God saw every thing that He had made, and, behold, it was very good"* (Gen. 1:31).

Some claim these are Fallen Angels; however, Angels are not disembodied, and there is no Scriptural record of any Angel possessing anyone, whether the Angel is fallen or otherwise!

Some think demons are the remnants of a pre-Adamic race, which occupied the earth before Adam and Eve, and before the chaos of Genesis 1:2.

At any rate, it seems as if Israel was infested with them at the time of Christ, which meant that Satan had either brought in reinforcements to oppose Christ, or else, the Ministry of Jesus of necessity, exposed them, which highlighted their activity. More than likely, both causes are correct!

The phrase, *"And those which were lunatick,"* refers to those who were insane, whether by demon possession, or physical disabilities.

The phrase, *"And those that had the palsy,"* refers to those who were paralyzed, among other things.

NOTES

At any rate, and irrespective of their problem, the Scripture said, *"And He healed them."*

If one is to notice, *"He healed them all,"* and irrespective of their spiritual condition. This Grace delights in doing!

In fact, in all the hundreds or even thousands healed and delivered by Christ, not one time does it mention Jesus refusing to heal anyone because of their spiritual condition. No doubt, many who came to Him were not living as they should, with many living in outright sin. Of course, this in no way meant that He condoned sin, but simply that He loved the sinner at least as much, if not more than He hated the sin.

How wonderful is our Lord!

When one reads these verses, one is reading the only hope for humanity. Regrettably, the modern Church has almost ceased to believe Him, at least in this capacity, if any capacity at all. They rather resort to the counselor and psychologist, completely discounting the Power of God.

Nevertheless, and irrespective of all the unbelief, and even though Medical Science can certainly be of help in many areas, still, in many of these cases, if not ultimately all, Christ is the only Answer.

When I was about 10 years old, the Lord gloriously healed me.

Even though my parents had taken me to several doctors, they were unable to find the cause of my problem. I stayed nauseated almost constantly, and had deteriorated to the place where I would go unconscious at times.

When this happened at school, of course, it greatly alarmed the teachers, and after happening several times, they had informed my parents that unless the situation improved, I would have to be taken out of school.

I had been prayed for quite a number of times, but to no avail. However, on this memorable Sunday, the Lord would do wonders.

Service had ended at our Church, and my Mother and Dad were taking the Pastor and his wife to lunch. However, first of all, they went to pray for a particular brother who was ill, and had not been able to be in service that Sunday Morning.

I remember walking into the small frame house with my parents and the Pastor and his wife. We all went to the back room and prayed

NOTES

for the brother in question, and then prepared to leave.

I was standing by the front door prepared to open it to exit the house, with the others behind me, when my Dad said to the Pastor, *"Brother Culbreth, anoint Jimmy with oil, and pray for him."* He then went on to say some things about my illness, and that if the Lord did not heal me, I would have to be taken out of school.

I remember Brother Culbreth walking over to me, with the little bottle of oil in his hand, which he had just used to pray for the man.

He reached up, anointing my head with oil, and began to pray over me, rebuking the sickness in the Name of Jesus. As I have stated, he had done this quite a number of times before, but this time was to be different.

All of a sudden, I felt the Power of God as I've seldom felt it before. It was like something hot poured over my head and going all over my body. As well, all others in the room experienced it too. There was no doubt that God had moved, and I had no doubt that I was healed.

In fact, I have seldom been sick a day in my life since then, and with that sickness, not at all. I was totally and completely healed by the Power of God.

Now, as to why the Lord did not heal me when prayer was offered on my behalf the other times, I have no idea.

I am just so pleased that my Mother and Dad did not lose Faith because I had not been healed the other times, but continued to ask. I was healed, at least in part, because of their persistence.

As well, I have seen many healed by the Power of God through the years, and expect to see even greater things in the future.

Also, Frances experienced a tremendous healing in the mid 1970's, when the doctor said that it was imperative that she have surgery. In fact, the pain was so bad that she was already preparing to enter the hospital.

As well, she had been prayed for several times previously, but to no avail! However, that particular day was different.

I remember laying hands on her and the Power of God coming on her, just as it had on me those many years before. Instantly the pain left, and upon further examination by the doctors, they shook their heads in disbelief, not knowing what had happened, and pronounced that she no longer had any need for surgery.

Let us shout it from the housetops, that what He did so long ago, He still does for those who will dare to believe His Great and Glorious Name!

I am so glad the phrase, *"He healed them,"* included not only those in Israel of so long ago, but myself and my wife, and it has included countless others!

(25) "AND THERE FOLLOWED HIM GREAT MULTITUDES OF PEOPLE FROM GALILEE, AND FROM DECAPOLIS, AND FROM JERUSALEM, AND FROM JUDAEA, AND FROM BEYOND JORDAN."

The association in the Four Gospels of the Name *"Jesus"* with the words *"Multitude," "Great multitudes," "Very great multitudes,"* and *"An innumerable multitude,"* does not surprise the reader who has experimental knowledge of the Saving Grace and Power and Loveliness of Christ.

Regrettably, the following of these *"Great multitudes,"* did not endear Him at all with the Religious Leaders of Israel, who became greatly envious of Him, and thereby set out to destroy Him.

The phrase says, *"And there followed Him great multitudes of people,"* refers not only to those mentioned, but as well to all of us who have heard that Clarion Call, *"Follow Me,"* and have taken up lockstep with Him, for the greatest journey any could ever know.

The song says:

"I heard about His healing, of His
　cleansing power revealing,
"How He made the lame to walk
　again, and caused the blind to see;
"And then I cried 'Dear Jesus,
　come and heal my broken spirit,'
"And somehow Jesus came and bro't to
　me the victory."

Chorus:

"Oh victory in Jesus, My Saviour,
　forever,
"He sought me and bo't me with His
　Redeeming Blood;
"He loved me ere I knew Him, and
　all my love is due Him,
"He plunged me to victory, beneath
　the cleansing flood."

CHAPTER 5

(1) "AND SEEING THE MULTITUDES, HE WENT UP INTO A MOUNTAIN: AND WHEN HE WAS SET, HIS DISCIPLES CAME UNTO HIM:"

The phrase, *"And seeing the multitudes,"* portrays the beginning of the Master's Ministry. Considering the tremendous miracles, healings, and deliverances, there was no reason for Israel not to know Who He was! Daniel had prophesied basically as to the time of His appearance, which, no doubt, the Scribes studied intently; and considering that such miracles, at least in such a wholesale manner, had never been brought about by the Prophets of the past, there was no excuse regarding His identification (Dan. 9:25-26). Consequently, the *"multitudes"* came for two reasons: A. The miracles and healings He performed; and, B. The gracious words that proceeded out of His mouth.

Sadly, at the conclusion of His Ministry, the crowds would thin out dramatically (Jn. 6:66), and for two reasons: A. The things He taught, *"Except ye eat the flesh of the Son of Man, and drink His Blood, ye have no life in you"* (Jn. 6:53); and, B. The tremendous opposition by the Pharisees, with their threatening excommunication for anyone who followed Him (Jn. 9:22).

It is almost unbelievable, and considering His miracles, that the people would allow their Religious Leaders to dictate their choice, but they did! Such is Religion!

The phrase, *"He went up into a mountain,"* does not say which mountain, but is thought to be a small mountain near the Sea of Galilee. More than likely that is correct!

The phrase, *"And when He was set, His Disciples came unto Him,"* refers to Him sitting down when He taught, with the word *"Disciples"* referring to any and all who closely followed Him at that particular time.

(2) "AND HE OPENED HIS MOUTH, AND TAUGHT THEM, SAYING,"

The phrase, *"And He opened His mouth,"* indicates that the words spoken are not the utterance of spur of the moment, but, instead, a carefully thought-out Message of purpose and will.

The phrase, *"And taught them, saying,"* begins the greatest moment of Spiritual and Scriptural instruction that had ever been given in the history of mankind.

It is said that men marvelled at the gracious words which proceeded out of His mouth, and rightly so!

Two sermons, both delivered on mountains, opened and closed the Lord's public Ministry. The first, as here recorded, and probably delivered on a mountain near Capernaum, and the last upon Olivet near Jerusalem (Mat. 24).

The theme of each was the Kingdom from the heavens — its moral characteristics in the first discourse; its fortunes and its future in the second.

(3) "BLESSED ARE THE POOR IN SPIRIT: FOR THEIRS IS THE KINGDOM OF HEAVEN."

The word, *"Blessed,"* begins that which is commonly called *"The Beatitudes."*

The word, *"Blessed,"* as used in the Beatitudes is somewhat different than the word *"Blessed"* as used in the Psalms. However, there are similarities.

The *"Blessed are"* statements in the Psalms describe human attitudes or actions that lead to blessing.

The Beatitudes also look at human attitudes. However, Jesus moves beyond the Old Testament Covenant. He makes the startling statement that God's Kingdom is a present Kingdom, and that His *"Blessed"* ones already know (*"are happy with"*) a unique joy, which comes from living in that Kingdom. For the word *"Blessed,"* as Jesus uses it in the Beatitudes, means *"to be happy,"* which is derived not from external sources, but from internal sources, which speak of the Joy of the Lord.

Consequently, these Beatitudes describe the inner experience of the Believer, who, in comforting others, etc., knows the supernatural comfort provided by God and senses the healing touch of God that rests on those who mourn.

The Old Testament type of Blessing describes the path that leads to God's Blessing. Jesus describes that Blessing itself. In effect, Christ states that God's Blessing comes to us in all our circumstances and makes us fortunate and *"Blessed,"* no matter how others may view our lives.

However, the Beatitudes express a Gospel

NOTES

that is totally contrary to much of that being taught presently in that which is referred to as the *"Prosperity Gospel,"* etc.

Jesus portrays an experience of the Kingdom's inner riches amid external poverty and trial, which presents a Divine paradox. It is so important that the reader must allow us to say it again:

"That which Christ gave as the very foundation of the Christian experience, does not by any means guarantee a life free of trials, tests, or other vicissitudes of life, but does guarantee inner riches, which produce happiness based on joy, and despite the external circumstances."

As should be obvious, this is True Christianity, and is a far cry from much which is promoted presently.

The phrase, *"Blessed are the poor in spirit,"* constitutes the opening recorded phrase of Christ's public teaching Ministry. As this is the first utterance, it is done so with design and purpose. The phrase, *"Poor in spirit,"* means to be conscious of moral and spiritual poverty, and struck at the very heart of Israel's present situation, which was self-righteousness, and the very heart of the problems of all, and for all time. Actually, this first Beatitude is the sum and substance of the entirety of Christ's Teaching. Poverty of spirit stands in contrast to self-sufficiency (Rev. 3:17).

As well, this Beatitude strikes at the very heart of man's problem of self-righteousness and self-sufficiency which came about as a result of the Fall in the Garden of Eden. Therefore, the very first word strikes at the very heart of man's basic problem, a problem so anchored in the human psyche that only the Power of God can affect its direction.

As this phrase *"Poor in spirit"* set the stage for Christ's Ministry, we find His Teaching constant in this regard throughout His Ministry. For instance, the parable of the Pharisee and the Publican, as given in Luke 18:9-14, is an excellent example.

The former extolled his goodness, while the latter extolled his moral poverty.

Jesus said that the latter *"Went down to his house justified rather than the other."* He then went on to say, *"For every one that exalted himself shall be abased; and he that humbleth himself shall be exalted"* (Lk. 18:14).

The phrase, *"For theirs is the Kingdom of*

Heaven," refers to the fact that such were already in the Kingdom.

Even though this *"Kingdom of Heaven,"* was not then realized materially or physically, and because of Israel's rejection of Christ, still, it was realized spiritually, and continues to be so.

Nevertheless, at the Second Coming, it will be realized materially, physically, and spiritually. Consequently, it will also be geographical, i.e., covering the entirety of the world. In other words, the *"Kingdom of Heaven"* will then be brought down to earth.

(4) "BLESSED ARE THEY THAT MOURN: FOR THEY SHALL BE COMFORTED."

This Beatitude dovetails the first, because it means to grieve because of one's personal moral poverty.

Someone asked me the other day as to exactly how they could tell they were close to God?

I thought for a moment, realizing that most of us are prone to answer in respect to all the things we do concerning Bible Study, Church attendance, the giving of money to the Work of God, witnessing to souls, etc.

Of course, these things are important; however, that is the very thing the Pharisee extolled in Luke 18, and even though commendable, and, at least in most cases, certainly approved of by the Lord, still, is no sign of that which speaks of closeness to God.

The answer I believe the Lord gave me, and was startling even to me, was in this vein:

"The more the Holy Spirit is correcting you, the closer you are to God."

Some time back, after seeking the Lord incessantly, drawing nearer to Him, and sensing the result of that nearness, I asked the Lord in prayer that if this was the case (nearness to Him), why did I feel so undone in my spirit?

The answer was immediately forthcoming: The Lord said, *"The further away one is from the Light, the less the flaws show up. The closer one gets, the more the Light exposes the flaws, stains, and inconsistencies."*

The present attitude of too many Christians, which extols their great place and position in Christ, and done with much bravado, is totally contrary to that which Christ taught.

While it is certainly true that all Believers have great place and station in Christ, still, this was given to us only by His Grace, and not at all because of our self-worthiness. As a result,

NOTES

realizing what has been truly and wonderfully given to us, and honestly observing our state of moral imperfection, causes the True Christian to *"mourn,"* and rightly so! This is what Paul was speaking of when he said, *"For we that are in this Tabernacle do groan, being burdened: not for that we would be unclothed, but clothed upon, that mortality might be swallowed up of life"* (II Cor. 5:4).

The phrase, *"For they shall be comforted,"* speaks of that which the Holy Spirit will give to those who properly evaluate their spiritual poverty.

(5) "BLESSED ARE THE MEEK: FOR THEY SHALL INHERIT THE EARTH."

The *"meek"* are the opposite of the self-righteous, and logically follow in order the *"poor in spirit,"* and *"they that mourn."* In other words, the first two guarantee the *"meekness."*

Its general thrust is toward God, as all three of these Beatitudes speak, but such will result in *"meekness"* toward men.

Therefore, *"meekness"* is not possible to those who are not *"poor in spirit"* or do not *"mourn"* over their spiritual poverty.

Someone mentioning a Godly soul, made mention of the fact, *"They were so full of God, because they were so empty of self."*

The Greek word for *"meek"* is *"praus,"* and pictures a humble, gentle attitude that maintains patience despite offenses and is untainted by vengefulness or malice.

A beautiful picture of this attitude as shown in Christ is found in I Peter 2:21-23.

"For even hereunto were ye called: because Christ also suffered for us, leaving us an example, that we should follow His steps:

"Who did no sin, neither was guile found in His mouth:

"Who, when He was reviled, reviled not again; when He suffered, He threatened not; but committed Himself to Him that judgeth righteously:"

The phrase, *"For they shall inherit the earth,"* speaks of the coming Kingdom Age, when the *"Kingdom of Heaven"* will be brought down to earth, when the Saints will rule, with Christ as its Supreme Lord.

(6) "BLESSED ARE THEY WHICH DO HUNGER AND THIRST AFTER RIGHTEOUSNESS: FOR THEY SHALL BE FILLED."

The phrase, *"Blessed are they which do*

hunger and thirst," speaks of intense desire even as a man starving for natural food. He must receive sustenance or else he will die. Consequently, the idea is, that if the seeker does not receive what he so hungrily desires, *"Righteousness"* in this case, he will die.

The very idea of the verse proclaims the *"poverty of Righteousness"* in the human life, which speaks of God's Righteousness. This is one totally empty of all self-righteousness, realizing, as the previous Beatitudes portray, that this is a commodity they do not have, and cannot obtain through any self-worth or merit. It is one totally void of self-righteousness, and hungering for the *"Righteousness of God."*

This individual senses strongly his moral poverty, the absolute destitution of his own merit, and, consequently, his desperate need for the Righteousness of God, which can only be given by Grace.

Jesus said, and concerning this state of mind, and with an unqualified guarantee, *"For they shall be filled."*

However, the *"being filled"* can only come about if we are truly empty of all self-worth, and realize it! He cannot *"fill"* that which is already filled with something else.

(7) "BLESSED ARE THE MERCIFUL: FOR THEY SHALL OBTAIN MERCY."

If one is to notice, there is a progression about these Beatitudes.

First of all, the absolute beginning requirement is to be *"poor in spirit,"* which will result in a *"mourning"* over one's moral and spiritual poverty.

This will result in one being *"meek,"* as should be obvious, which will bring about a *"hunger and thirst after Righteousness."*

As a further result, and properly knowing and realizing his own poverty of self-worthiness, and realizing that the *"Righteousness"* he possess is given solely by the Grace of God, this individual is quick to show *"Mercy"* to others.

However, the word *"Mercy,"* as it is expressed in *"being merciful,"* portrays far more than just a feeling of pity, but, instead, shows itself in action which goes beyond the thought.

The idea is, that as God has shown so much *"Mercy"* to the individual, he, in turn, (the individual) will be quick to *"show Mercy"* to others. Even though the phrase, *"For they shall*

obtain," is in the positive sense, still, it has a tremendous negative sense to it as well.

The idea is, that if one does not show Mercy to others, and this means in action as well as thought, God will not show Mercy. Realizing how dependent we are on the Mercy of God, we should be quick to obey.

The type of *"Mercy"* that God is speaking of is that which He shows to those who are *"poor in spirit."* It is the *"Mercy"* shown to those who *"hunger and thirst after Righteousness,"* with no way to obtain such themselves, and, as well, no fit receptacle for God's Righteousness. Yet, He shows *"Mercy"* and gives the *"Righteousness"* anyway, and simply because we realize our destitute condition, and hungrily desire Him to change it, even though we in no way are worthy of such. He then shows *"Mercy"* and gives us what we need. We are to do the same to others. However, what does that mean?

As the previous verses speak of the poverty of soul, and God's Mercy granted despite such, it, as well, speaks to the Believer who does not condemn, and because he has no right to condemn.

This is what Paul was speaking of when he said, *"Brethren, if a man be overtaken in a fault* (a moral fault), *ye which are spiritual, restore such an one in the spirit of meekness; considering thyself, lest thou also be tempted."*

He then said, *"Bear ye one another's burdens,"* which means to sympathize, show Mercy and Love, and not brow-beat a fallen brother. He said this would *"fulfil the Law of Christ,"* which no doubt spoke of this Beatitude.

He then went on to say, *"For if a man think himself to be something, when he is nothing, he deceiveth himself,"* meaning that if he puts himself above the one with the *"fault,"* he is only *"deceiving himself"* (Gal. 6:1-3).

(8) "BLESSED ARE THE PURE IN HEART: FOR THEY SHALL SEE GOD."

The *"Pure in heart"* speaks of those who have received a new moral nature in regeneration. It is not man's standard of purity, but God's, which is of far greater magnitude than man could ever begin to think.

There is only One Who has been truly *"Pure in heart"* and that is Christ. All of the above, as expressed in the previous Beatitudes, have not *"Purity of heart,"* at least within themselves. However, they realize such, and, therefore, the

"Purity of Christ" is freely given unto them. Consequently, they have a purity which far exceeds any standard of man.

Regrettably, man, even most of the Church, will not accept God's freely given *"Purity of heart,"* which can be brought about in a very short period of time, and, conversely, God will not accept man's standard of purity.

Man's standard consists of religious rules and regulations, which deal altogether with the externals. God's *"Purity"* deals with the heart, which is the seat of one's passions and emotions, which then expresses itself in the externals.

The phrase, *"For they shall see God,"* is a beautiful and wonderful Promise!

"Seeing God" does not speak of seeing Him with the physical eyes, but, instead, seeing Him manifested in one's life. In other words, they will cease to see their own efforts in trying to make themselves pure, but will rather see that which God brings about, which will be glorious and wonderful indeed!

Consequently, the progression continues, as it ascends from *"poverty of spirit"* to *"pureness of heart."*

One can only shout *"Hallelujah!"*

(9) "BLESSED ARE THE PEACEMAKERS: FOR THEY SHALL BE CALLED THE CHILDREN OF GOD."

The idea of this Beatitude is not so much the individual attempting to make peace between warring factions in the material and physical sense, as it is the proclaiming of God's Way, as expressed in these Beatitudes, which, upon acceptance, brings *"peace"* to the individual.

The self-righteous man, whether Believer or otherwise, has no peace within his heart, because he has no peace with God. Self-righteousness just might be the worst sin there is, and because in its pride it is so deceptive.

This sin of self-ability or self-righteousness, resulted from the Fall, and characterizes the war that constantly rages between God and man. Man keeps thinking he can save himself, and despite the fact that the Bible constantly states that man is spiritually and morally bankrupt. And, as such, there is nothing he can do, and despite all his efforts, to extricate himself from this morass. Actually, the more he tries, the deeper he goes into this moral quicksand. That is the reason David said, *"He brought me up also out of an horrible pit, out of the miry*

NOTES

clay, and set my feet upon a rock, and established my goings" (Ps. 40:2).

The more David struggled to get out of that pit by his own strength, the deeper he sank in the *"miry clay,"* as all moralist do! Only God can extricate one from such!

The road to that extrication begins with being *"poor in spirit."* And all who proclaim such to the world and the Church, and upon their accepting it, that is, God's Way, guarantees *"Peace with God"* for themselves, with those who proclaim such, called *"peacemakers."*

The phrase, *"For they shall be called the Children of God,"* expresses the *"peacemaker"* and the one who has received the *"Peace."*

The *"New Birth"* is an absolute requirement to get into this *"Kingdom of Heaven,"* and can only be entered into by these Beatitudes. In other words, to be saved, one has to be *"poor in spirit,"* realizing he cannot save himself, that he is spiritually bankrupt, and desperately needs a Redeemer.

Even though the individual who comes to Christ may not know nor understand these things said, still, his very *"spirit"* must characterize such, upon which the New Birth will be instantly granted by Christ.

Tragically, millions truly get in properly, *"poor in spirit,"* and once in, begin to be lifted up in self-righteousness, which frustrates the Grace of God, and stifles any and all spiritual growth (Gal. 2:21).

(10) "BLESSED ARE THEY WHICH ARE PERSECUTED FOR RIGHTEOUSNESS' SAKE: FOR THEIRS IS THE KINGDOM OF HEAVEN."

The progression continues!

The phrase, *"Blessed are they which are persecuted for Righteousness' sake,"* means that those who operate from the realm of self-righteousness, will persecute those who trust in God's *"Righteousness."*

This is a *"persecution"* that will come without fail! This is the war that began even in the Garden of Eden.

Adam attempted to cover his and Eve's nakedness with *"fig leaves,"* which God would not accept. He slew an animal, which typified Calvary, and covered them with the skin of the slain victim (Gen. 3:7, 21).

A short time later, Cain killed Abel, and because of this same conflict. Cain presented to the Lord as a Sacrifice, *"the fruit of the ground,"* which the Lord would not accept because it portrayed man's self-righteousness.

Abel, in contrast, offered a Lamb unto the Lord, which was a type of the Death of Christ on the Cross, and the Bible said, *"And the Lord had respect unto Abel and to his offering"* (Gen. 4:3-4). It was self-righteousness versus God's Imputed Righteousness. The battle has continued to rage from that day until this.

This was the very seat of the opposition against Christ. Israel could not even begin to think that they were spiritually destitute, and, therefore, spiritually bankrupt. In their minds they were quite holy, and, surely, acceptable to God. The Lord said otherwise, which brought about a self-righteous anger within them, which resulted in their murdering their Messiah.

To be sure, for all those who trust solely in the *"Righteousness of Christ,"* they will be persecuted by the self-righteous.

The phrase, *"For theirs is the Kingdom of Heaven,"* proclaims that one of the ways one can know that one is trusting in the Righteousness of Christ instead of their own, is because one is persecuted. This is one of the signs of being in the *"Kingdom of Heaven."*

(11) "BLESSED ARE YE, WHEN MEN SHALL REVILE YOU, AND PERSECUTE YOU, AND SHALL SAY ALL MANNER OF EVIL AGAINST YOU FALSELY, FOR MY SAKE."

The phrase, *"Blessed are ye, when men shall revile you . . . ,"* speaks of men doing this, which will almost exclusively come from the apostate Church. Consequently, the war referred to in the previous Beatitude, now is extended and enlarged. He said they would do three things:

1. *"Revile you":* This means to make light of your total trust in Christ. In effect, these same individuals who are doing the reviling, claim to trust Christ, at least for the most part. However, they link other things to Christ, in other words, making it *"Christ plus!"* Consequently, one's total trust in Christ will be *"reviled."*

2. *"Persecute you":* Jesus further said, *"They shall put you out of the Synagogues: yea, the time cometh, that whosoever killed you will think that he doeth God service."*

He went on to say, *"And these things will they do unto you, because they have not known the Father, nor Me"* (Jn. 16:2-3).

NOTES

In other words, they think they know the Lord, but in reality they don't, and, consequently, will *"persecute you for Righteousness' sake,"* i.e., Christ's Imputed Righteousness.

3. They will lie about you: The word, *"falsely,"* at least in part, means they will bring up sins which are washed in the Blood of Christ, and, consequently, should be forgiven and forgotten. Consequently, the Lord says that all claims against such a one are *"false,"* and because such sins have been properly handled by the Blood of Jesus, with God's Righteousness freely imputed to the believing sinner.

The phrase, *"For My sake,"* proclaims the nature of the accusations. In other words, they will not accept the Righteousness afforded by Christ, but demand religious rules and regulations of man's devising be honored, trusted, and kept. However, one cannot have God's Righteousness, and man's righteousness at the same time! One or the other must go!

And thus, the Beatitudes conclude by giving the entire foundation of what it means to enter into the *"Kingdom of Heaven."* It is a way totally contrary to the world, and, for the most part, totally contrary to the Church.

(12) "REJOICE, AND BE EXCEEDING GLAD: FOR GREAT IS YOUR REWARD IN HEAVEN: FOR SO PERSECUTED THEY THE PROPHETS WHICH WERE BEFORE YOU."

The word, *"Rejoice,"* proclaims the present inner result of one who is *"blessed"* as a result of entering into the *"Kingdom of Heaven"* and despite the persecution, etc.

The word, *"Rejoice,"* corresponds with David's account, as we have stated, of being brought *"out of the miry clay,"* and as a result, *"He hath put a new song in my mouth, even praise unto our God"* (Ps. 40:3).

The phrase, *"For great is your reward in Heaven,"* speaks of the results of eternal life granted unto the Believer, which can only be obtained in the manner that Christ has given in the Beatitudes.

The phrase, *"For so persecuted they the Prophets which were before you,"* once again draws attention to the fact that this way, *"God's Way,"* will bring *"persecution,"* severely so, by both the world and the Church.

The idea of *"the Prophets"* being named, is meant to not merely speak of a temporal fact, but instead, to indicate spiritual relationship.

(13) "YE ARE THE SALT OF THE EARTH: BUT IF THE SALT HAVE LOST HIS SAVOUR, WHEREWITH SHALL IT BE SALTED? IT IS THENCEFORTH GOOD FOR NOTHING, BUT TO BE CAST OUT, AND TO BE TRODDEN UNDER FOOT OF MEN."

The phrase, *"Ye are the salt of the earth,"* is meant to portray the Believer as *"salt"* (a preservative) in the world.

Therefore, the Lord is saying that only those who fall into the category of the Beatitudes, really constitute a deterrent to evil, and a preservative of Righteousness.

At the same time He is saying, that all of man's self efforts at improvement only adds to the problem, instead of solving it.

The question, *"But if the salt have lost his savour, wherewith shall it be salted?",* refers to the fact that if the salt loses its preservative power, there is nothing to take its place! It is the one and only property to prevent corruption.

The Christian's one mission in life is to guard the Church from corruption by Conduct and Doctrine . That is the reason Jude said, *"That ye should earnestly contend for the Faith which was once delivered unto the Saints."*

Jude further said, *"For there are certain men crept in unawares, who were before of old ordained to this condemnation, ungodly men, turning the Grace of our God into lasciviousness, and denying the only Lord God, and our Lord Jesus Christ"* (Jude 3-4).

If, therefore, one does not shine for Jesus, one is useless; and men treat him with contempt. This is symbolized in the phrase, *"It is thenceforth good for nothing, but to be cast out, and to be trodden under foot of men."*

This corresponds with the statement of Christ, *"Remember therefore from whence thou art fallen, and repent, and do the first works; or else I will come unto thee quickly, and remove thy candlestick out of his place, except thou repent"* (Rev. 2:5).

(14) "YE ARE THE LIGHT OF THE WORLD. A CITY THAT IS SET ON AN HILL CANNOT BE HID."

The phrase, *"Ye are the Light of the world,"* is powerful indeed!

This means that the Believer is not only *"Light,"* but, in fact, the *"only Light."* However, this is Light that is derived solely from Christ, hence, Him saying in verse 11, *"for My sake."*

The Believer, within himself, as Christ graphically brought out in the Beatitudes, has no Light, as he has no Salvation. Consequently, all must be drawn from Christ, for He Alone is that Light, with those making Him Lord of their lives, becoming reflectors of that Light.

This means that the great universities of the world provide no *"Light,"* except that which is derived from the Word of God, whether advertently or inadvertently.

This is the reason (the Light), that the Christlike Child of God is of such value and consequence wherever he may be. However, such worth will not at all be recognized by the world, and seldom by the Church.

The phrase, *"A city that is set on an hill cannot be hid,"* simply means that as such a city is obvious to all, likewise, the Christian should have *"Light"* which is obvious to all!

(15) "NEITHER DO MEN LIGHT A CANDLE, AND PUT IT UNDER A BUSHEL, BUT ON A CANDLESTICK; AND IT GIVETH LIGHT UNTO ALL THAT ARE IN THE HOUSE."

The idea of this verse concerns the purpose of the True Believer in this world.

The phrase, *"Neither do men light a candle, and put it under a bushel,"* really speaks of asceticism, which refers to an individual who shuts himself away as a hermit.

Jesus is saying that if His followers, who are truly endowed with His Righteousness, and, therefore, His Light, hide themselves away, as some have advocated, their very purpose, as least as far as the world is concerned, will be lost. Consequently, it is not God's intention that His people bunch up in little communities, as some have tried, in order to build a paradise, incidentally, which has always failed, but, instead, to live in the very midst of society as *"Salt"* and *"Light,"* and, therefore, to be a restraining influence against evil.

The phrase, *"But on a candlestick; and it giveth Light unto all that are in the house,"* is meant to proclaim, as is obvious, the place where He wants His Children, which is where they can give Light, which is in the midst of the darkness.

So, if you are the only Believer in the midst of a group of unbelievers at your daily employment, etc., do not lament the fact, but, instead, thank the Lord that He has put you in a place of darkness, where your *"Light"* can shine. It is designed thusly by the Lord.

Years ago, when Frances and I first married, and I was just beginning in the Ministry, I secured a job with a plumbing contractor. It was not a large operation with only about eight or ten employees, of which I was one.

The man who owned the company was one of the most profile, profane, and wicked men that I had personally known. It seemed like every word out of his mouth was profanity. The men who worked with him, although professing to know the Lord, were little better than he.

After a very short time, they knew of my devotion to Christ, with him exclaiming with a sardonic laugh, that in just a few days I would be exactly like them — telling dirty jokes, cursing, etc.

By the Grace of God, the very opposite happened! Little by little those men began to ask me questions about the Bible, often which took the place of their profane conversation of the past.

I was even able to get many of them in Church with me, even though, at least to my knowledge, none of them truly accepted the Lord.

However, I was unable whatsoever to get the owner of the company to Church, or anything that looked like Church.

I only worked there about six months, and then left for other endeavors.

Many years passed, with our Ministry growing, until our Telecast covered a sizeable part of the earth.

In the early part of 1987, I believe it was, I received a letter from the daughter of the contractor who I had worked with so long ago — the one, incidentally, who was so profane. She told me how that her Dad was faithfully watching the Telecast, and had made the statement, *"If I ever get it, I want what Jimmy Swaggart had,"* and speaking of those days I worked with him those many years before.

A few months later, I received another letter from her, telling me that her Dad had passed away. But then she added, *"Brother Swaggart, just before he died, he prayed the Sinner's Prayer with you, as he was watching the Telecast, and truly gave his heart and life to Jesus Christ."*

When I read the letter, I could not help but

weep, but for joy. I didn't think that *"Light"* had shown too brightly. But, it had!

In fact, no True *"Light"* of the Gospel is wasted. It always garners its intended results, even though it may take time to do so!

(16) "LET YOUR LIGHT SO SHINE BEFORE MEN, THAT THEY MAY SEE YOUR GOOD WORKS, AND GLORIFY YOUR FATHER WHICH IS IN HEAVEN."

As we have briefly alluded to, these verses (3-16) set out the moral characteristics of the citizens of the *"Kingdom of the Heavens"*; and so it is apparent that the New Birth is an absolute necessity for entrance into that Kingdom.

The idea of this verse, is a continuance of the previous. The Lord lays stress on personal possession of Light, personal action, personal relationship and origin.

In other words, the *"Light"* should produce *"good works,"* which will be *"seen by men,"* but not necessarily done just for that purpose, but rather to carry out the Commandment of the Lord, which will *"glorify God."*

Christianity made inroads into the mighty Roman Empire, and because of this very thing. The morality of Christianity was so much higher than that espoused by Rome, which gradually won many over.

It will do, and in fact, does the same presently!

However, this is not to be confused with the effort of modern Christendom to *"Christianize society."* The two are completely different!

One attempts to serve as a Light, which will glorify God, and show men the way, while the other, by political means, seeks to change society, which in fact, cannot be done, as the temper of these verses brings out. The True Believer is, and as stated, *"Salt"* and *"Light"* which have great reference to making things better, for which they are intended. However, the whole of society will not, and, in fact, cannot be changed until the Second Coming of Christ.

(17) "THINK NOT THAT I AM COME TO DESTROY THE LAW, OR THE PROPHETS: I AM NOT COME TO DESTROY, BUT TO FULFIL."

The phrase, *"Think not that I am come to destroy the Law, or the Prophets,"* was probably said in order counter the idea that some were accusing Him of that.

It was not that His Teaching was removed

from the Law and the Prophets, for actually all that He said could be found one way or the other in the Old Testament. (What is now referred to as the Old Testament was actually the Bible of that day, and consisted of Genesis through Malachi.)

The problem was, that the Pharisees had added so many oral laws to the written Law, that there was little true meaning left anymore to the true intent of the Law and the Prophets. That is why Jesus later asked the question, *"Why do ye also transgress the Commandment of God by your tradition?"* (Mat. 15:3).

They were accusing Him of destroying the Law, and His answer was, *"I am not come to destroy, but to fulfil."*

What did it mean to fulfill the Law?

It meant to satisfy the demands of the Law.

Let's look at the Law of Moses in general, for this is what is being spoken of, and hopefully we will have a better understanding.

THE LAW IN THE OLD TESTAMENT

The Hebrew word for Law is *"Torah."* Its basic meaning is *"teaching"* or *"instruction."* It denotes instruction focused on how one should live, rather than on abstract or academic subjects. In other words, it was very pointed, plain and clear in its demands.

The Law as given to Moses by Jesus Christ in a preincarnate appearance, was a Code, with its Ten Commandments and with instructions covering every aspect of Israel's personal and national life. It was the moral, ceremonial, and civil way of life God ordained for His Old Testament, and, thereby, Covenant people.

In this sense, the Law consisted of all the Statutes, Ordinances, Precepts, Commandments, and Testimonies given by God to guide His people. But the Mosaic Law — those Teachings included in the first five Books of the Old Testament — includes even more.

It included Moses' review of and interpretation of history, his record of God's mighty acts, and his report of Creation.

When the word *"Law"* in the Old Testament is read, it is helpful to remember that it may have many references.

It may refer to God's Revelation in a general way. It may point to a specific set of instructions — e.g., the Law of Passover, or the Ten Commandments, etc. It may indicate the

moral or ceremonial codes, or the writings of Moses.

What is clear; however, is that whatever a particular use of *"Law"* points to, the Old Testament views it as Divine Instruction. It is God's Gift, intended to show Israel how to live a holy and happy life in this world.

To be sure, the Law of Moses was not the only law in the world, as other codes of law had been given previously. However, it was the only Law given by God, and, as such, it so far exceeded the viability of all other law, that there was no comparison. It was the only Law in the world of that day that truly taught man how to live, and gave a complete code directing attention to every facet of life.

THE EXTENT OF THE LAW

To be sure, the Law was a moral code as delivered by Moses; however, it encompassed far more than that.

It functioned as the A. Constitution of the Nation; B. The basis for determining civil and criminal cases; C. A guide to worship; D. A personal guide to good family and social relationships; and, E. A personal guide to relationship with the Lord.

It comprised not only those regulations that defined sin and established guilt, but also the Sacrificial System through which the Believer might find Atonement for sins. In essence, everything in the experience of the people of Israel was guided by the Law.

Despite the all-encompassing nature of Law and despite the fact that Law is seen in the Old Testament as one of God's Great Gifts, Israel fell far short of becoming a just and holy community.

In effect, and even though the Law was a pattern for living, and, given by God, still, it contained no Salvation, nor did it offer any power to give man the ability to keep it.

Even though the keeping of it was the objective, and demanded by God, still, all fell short, which brought upon them its penalty, which is the custom of all law.

In effect, the Law was not meant to save man from sin, but was meant to show man his inability to keep the Law, and that despite all his efforts, he still needed a Redeemer. That Redeemer was Christ!

Consequently, the Law in the Old Testament

was good. But it was not meant to be permanent, for Law has never been effective in making the people of God righteous.

JESUS AND THE LAW

In Jesus' time, the Rabbis (the teachers of the Law), focused their Faith on the Law.

They taught that the first five Books of the Old Testament were the Law, and all the other Writings and Prophets were but Commentary on this core.

The Religious Leaders in Jesus' day were sure not only that these Mosaic Books were the key to life and death, but also that the individual could keep the Law and please God. The young ruler's question, *"What shall I do to inherit eternal life?"* (Lk. 18:18), sums up the understanding of religion held by most of the religious people in his generation.

When Jesus appeared, He did not deny the Law (the Books of Moses). But He did directly challenge the understanding of the Old Testament on which contemporary Jewish Faith was based. To understand the challenge and to sense Jesus' Own view of *"Law"* as the term is used in the Gospels, we need to examine several significant Gospel Passages.

Jesus began by stating His Own allegiance to the Old Testament, as is outlined in the very verse on which we are writing Commentary, which extends to the conclusion of the Chapter. But then He made this dramatic declaration concerning His purpose for coming to earth. He told them that He had not come to abolish the Law or the Prophets, but to fulfill them.

Jesus continued with the warning: The Commandments are to be practiced. But then He said, *"I tell you that unless your righteousness surpasses that of the Pharisees and the teachers of the Law, you will certainly not enter the Kingdom of Heaven"* (Mat. 5:20).

This, of course, exploded like a bombshell, and, if possible, only exacerbated the anger of these groups against Him.

Jesus further taught that the Law and the Prophets could be summed up simply: *"In everything, do to others what you would have them do to you"* (Mat. 7:12).

An expansion on this statement came when Jesus was questioned by one *"expert in the Law."* Asked which is the greatest Commandment, Jesus answered, *"Love the Lord*

your God with all your heart and with all your soul and with all your mind. This is the first and greatest Commandment. And the second is like it: Love your neighbour as yourself. All the Law and the Prophets hang on these two Commandments" (Mat. 22:37-40).

Again, Jesus shifted the issue from strict compliance with the detailed instructions of the Old Testament, of which the Pharisees demanded, to one's heart attitude. Love for God and love for others is the key to Godliness, He says!

When He said that He had come to *"fulfil"* the Law, in effect, He was saying that the day the Mosaic Law would be superseded had arrived.

In a sense, one could say that Jesus was the Law, but when He came to this earth as God manifested in the flesh, He did not come to bring the Law, but, instead, Grace and Truth. As such, the *"Grace"* and *"Truth"* would fulfill the Law.

The Old Testament economy was not rejected. Not at all. Instead, all that the Old Testament foretold had come with Jesus. He was the Prophet Who was destined to bring the Message that superseded that of Moses (Deut. 18:15). Consequently, the way of life He introduced did not abolish the Mosaic Code, but superseded it with a new and better Code called the *"New Covenant,"* in which the Prophets had promised (Jer. 31).

When the Pharisees came to Jesus to raise a point of Law concerning divorce, Jesus answered them by stating God's intentions for marriage, which preceded the Law. From the time of creation God had intended marriage to be a permanent union.

The Pharisees then questioned Him by asking, *"Why then did Moses command that a man give his wife a certificate of divorce and send her away?"* (Mat. 19:7).

Jesus' response is stunning, cutting the ground from underneath those who saw the Mosaic Law as a perfect expression of God's Righteousness. He said, *"Moses permitted you to divorce your wives because your hearts were hard"* (Mat. 19:8).

The point of Jesus' response is this: God, in the Law, established a requirement for His people that was less than ideal. Rather than being the highest possible standard, the Mosaic Law was what one might call a Divine compromise.

What God truly desired was utterly beyond the possibility for people whose hearts were hardened by sin. To make it possible for Israel to even approximate God's real standards, He gave them a Law that made allowances for less than — perfect Righteousness!

No wonder, then, that Jesus taught that our Righteousness must surpass that of the Scribes and Pharisees. God called on the Believer to find a Righteousness that is greater than that expressed in Law: A Righteousness that flows from and finds expression in love for God and love for others.

Consequently, Jesus fulfilled the Old Testament Law, both in the sense of explaining it correctly and in the sense of being Himself the Goal toward which the Old Testament points. As far as the specific Commands contained in the Mosaic Law are concerned, Jesus introduced a Righteousness surpassing them.

This is possible because the moral regulations of the Law are simply practical guidelines on how to love God and neighbor. When love fills the Believer's heart, the reality to which the Law points will come.

JESUS' TEACHING

Jesus' teaching shifted the focus of Righteousness from behavior to character and motivation. God was concerned with a Righteousness that surpassed that of the Rabbi and the Pharisee, who concluded their Righteousness as being in what they called obedience to the Law, but, in effect, was no obedience at all.

That it is not necessary to express such Righteousness by detailed Commandments, is shown in Jesus' response when He was asked the greatest Commandment. *"Love God and love others,"* Jesus replied. And He added, *"All the Law and the Prophets hang on these two Commandments"* (Mat. 22:40).

The Gospels show us that the Old Testament way was to be superseded and transformed by Jesus. Actually, He is the focus of the Old Testament, the One of Whom it testifies. Now that He has come, that era is brought to a close. It is fulfilled, and because it pointed to Him Who would bring a better way, and, therefore, a new era with new patterns of life would replace it.

NOTES

To be sure, that new era was explained and developed in the Epistles. Paul showed that the Law's statements of Righteousness in Commandments and as an aid to being good, could not function in the Believer's life. Faith, not Law, was always the way to Salvation. Reliance on the Spirit, not a struggle to keep the Law, is the way to live a righteous life. It seems clear from Paul's analysis of the weakness of the Law, that the Old Testament Saint, like the Christian today, lived a Godly life by trusting God and having a personal relationship with Him, rather than by looking to Law in order that it might save by trying to keep it.

Of course, the Old Testament Saint was to try to keep the Law, but the idea was that the Law could not save, but only the One it pointed to, namely Christ, and what He would do, which was symbolized in the Sacrifices.

As a result of what Christ did, and that which He gave in the Epistles through the Apostle Paul, and others, Christians today are to understand that the *"do's"* and *"do not's"* of Scripture, can only be fulfilled in our lives by us giving ourselves over to Christ, and the Power of the Holy Spirit.

We then find that in our loving God and others, we suddenly realize the Truth. The requirements of the Law begin to find expression in our lives — not because we are trying to be good, but because the Love of Jesus is working to transform us from within, and the Holy Spirit is prompting us to acts of love that fulfill every demand of the Law, but which the Law, within itself, could never do!

To sum up, Jesus *"fulfilled the Law,"* by meeting its requirements, which meant to walk perfect in its demands, which we could never do.

As a startling example, when the woman was caught in the act of adultery, the Law demanded that she be stoned (Jn. 8:1-11). Jesus satisfied the Law by dying in her place, as He did in the place of all of us. Therefore, He fulfilled it down to its most minute detail, and then, in turn, freely gives His victory to all who will believe Him, and allow His life to become their life. (Most of the statement on *"Law"* were derived from the Commentary of Lawrence O. Richards.)

(18) "FOR VERILY I SAY UNTO YOU, TILL HEAVEN AND EARTH PASS, ONE JOT OR

ONE TITTLE SHALL IN NO WISE PASS FROM THE LAW, TILL ALL BE FULFILLED."

The phrase, *"For verily I say unto you,"* proclaims the ultimate authority!

The Scribes and the Pharisees seldom had a definitive answer, generally going into detail about things that had little to do about the question at hand. Consequently, the people had very little qualitative leadership, if any!

The phrase, *"Till heaven and earth pass,"* does not mean that they will ultimately be destroyed. The Greek word for *"pass,"* is *"parerchomai,"* and means to be changed, or pass from one condition to another. Actually, the heavens and the earth will never pass out of existence, but will be changed and purified by fire, thereby, being renewed (Rom. 8:21-24; Heb. 1:10-12; 12:25-29; II Pet. 3:10-13; Rev. 21:1).

The Bible teaches that the heavens and the earth will remain forever (Ps. 72:17; 89:36-37; 104:5; Eccl. 1:4).

The phrase, *"One jot or one tittle shall in no wise pass from the Law,"* refers to the word *"jot"* as the smallest letter in the Hebrew alphabet, with the word *"tittle"* referring to the smallest ornament placed upon certain Hebrew letters.

The phrase, *"Till all be fulfilled,"* saw this brought to pass in Christ.

Every *"jot"* and *"tittle"* of the whole Law, given at Sinai, was fulfilled, ended, and abolished in Christ, and *"done away"* by Him in His Life, Death, and Resurrection, with a New Testament or Covenant being brought about (Acts 15:5-29; Rom. 10:4; II Cor. 3:6-15; Gal. 3:19-25; 4:21-31; 5:1-5, 18; Eph. 2:15; Col. 2:14-17; Heb. 7:11-28; 8:6-18; 9:1-22; 10:1-18).

(19) "WHOSOEVER THEREFORE SHALL BREAK ONE OF THESE LEAST COMMANDMENTS, AND SHALL TEACH MEN SO, HE SHALL BE CALLED THE LEAST IN THE KINGDOM OF HEAVEN: BUT WHOSOEVER SHALL DO AND TEACH THEM, THE SAME SHALL BE CALLED GREAT IN THE KINGDOM OF HEAVEN."

In this verse, the Lord begins to lay down the foundation for the New Covenant. As well, verses 18 and 19 proclaim the tremendous significance of the Word of God, whether the Old Covenant or the New, a significance, in fact, that is so great that it defies description.

Of course, the world not at all understands

NOTES

the absolute validity of the Word of God, and neither does most of the Church. Even good Christians seldom understand how absolutely important it is, and in every respect. Actually, the Word of God should be a life-long project in the heart and life of every single Believer. Inasmuch as it is the Word of God, and there is no other in the world, and, consequently, the only Revealed Truth in the world, it should be studied diligently by every Believer until its contents are thoroughly mastered, at least as the Lord helps one to do so. In all fairness and honesty, and inasmuch as it is the Word of God, I think I can say without fear of contradiction, that it is impossible for one to exhaust its teaching and knowledge.

The word, *"Whosoever,"* lays the ground of impartiality for all, and, as well, lays the Word of God as the foundation of all teaching and instruction.

The phrase, *"Whosoever therefore shall break one of these least Commandments,"* concerns the abrogation of any part of the Word of God, even that thought to be the least significant!

This Passage does not speak of a lack of light on a given Biblical Subject, but, instead, a direct denial of the Word of God, fostered by unbelief.

In fact, no one has all the light on the Bible, but all must hunger and thirst for more light to be given, and a desire to be corrected by the Holy Spirit, with whatever method He chooses.

The Word of God is such, that if men allow leaven to creep in, unless the leaven is removed, it will ultimately color the whole. Consequently, the Believer should constantly pray that the Holy Spirit, *"Leadeth me in the Paths of Righteousness for His Name's sake"* (Ps. 23:3).

If self-will enters into our study and understanding of the Bible, the Lord will allow a judicial blindness to settle upon such people. However, if we study it with the intention of it correcting us, the Holy Spirit will superintend its direction of Truth within our lives.

As an example, if a Church Body, such as a Religious Denomination, allows error to creep in, and allows that error to become a part of its belief structure, it will ultimately color and corrupt the entirety of all that is believed.

For instance, the unscriptural Doctrine of Unconditional Eternal Security, as it is embraced by many Baptists, pretty well colors the entirety of their theology. Consequently, the *"little leaven"* has now leavened the entire lump (Gal. 5:9).

This does not mean that one cannot be saved and believe in the Doctrine of Unconditional Eternal Security, because Salvation is a matter of trusting Christ, and not the correct understanding of all peripheral Doctrines of Scripture. And yet, any erroneous understanding definitely does weaken our daily walk and advancement in Christ.

Consequently, the phrase, *"And shall teach men so, he shall be called least in the Kingdom of Heaven,"* means to flat-out disbelieve parts of the Bible. *"He shall be called the least,"* means that he will not be in the Kingdom at all!

As an example, many have asked if an individual can disbelieve the Virgin Birth of Christ and still be saved?

No they cannot, simply because to disbelieve that strikes at the very heart of God's Plan of Salvation for the human family, and denies the Faith that saves.

This is basically what Paul was speaking of in Hebrews Chapters 6 and 10. Both Chapters speak of rejecting the Atoning Work of Christ, in which one must believe in order to be saved. If that is denied, there is no way for one to be saved.

The same is true for evolution! One cannot believe such a fabrication and be saved.

While it is certainly true that some new converts may not have light on such subjects, and to be sure the Holy Spirit will be patient, nevertheless, one will definitely line up with the Word of God respecting the soul-saving subjects, if he is to be saved.

So as not to cause misunderstanding, we are speaking of subjects that pertain to the fundamentals of the Faith, and not to peripheral subjects, although extremely important.

As another example, if a Catholic truly makes Christ his Saviour, and not the Church, the Holy Spirit will invariably lead the individual out of this system, because it is His purpose to always *"guide you into all Truth"* (Jn. 16:13).

Even though my statement is blunt, I must say it: *"One, after coming to Christ cannot remain in the Catholic Church embracing its erroneous tenets of Faith and be saved!"* The entire fabric of Catholic Faith is contrary to

the Word of God. And if we are to use the Word of God as the rule of Faith, which we certainly must do, it is impossible to wed the two!

The phrase, *"But whosoever shall do and teach them,"* concerns one making the Word of God as His Rule of Faith for Salvation, and nothing else!

The phrase, *"The same shall be called great in the Kingdom of Heaven,"* means that the Lord sets the Bible as the Standard of all Righteousness, and that He recognizes no other.

(20) "FOR I SAY UNTO YOU, THAT EXCEPT YOUR RIGHTEOUSNESS SHALL EXCEED THE RIGHTEOUSNESS OF THE SCRIBES AND PHARISEES, YE SHALL IN NO CASE ENTER INTO THE KINGDOM OF HEAVEN."

The absolute necessity of the New Birth is here declared as imperative in every case.

The phrase, *"For I say unto you,"* is meant to be in contrast to the Scribes and Pharisees. In other words, there was a direct clash respecting the teaching of the Bible, with Christ claiming His Word as Law and Gospel, and, as well, denouncing the teaching of the Pharisees, that He later called *"leaven"* (Mat. 16:11-12).

Consequently, one can see, even at the very beginning, the animosity that could not help but intensify between Christ and the Religious Leaders of Israel.

The phrase, *"That except your Righteousness shall exceed the Righteousness of the Scribes and Pharisees,"* refers to two types of Righteousness, which can be summed up in several categories:

1. Self-righteousness: This constitutes dependence on one's own ability, and seeks to justify self on real or fancied grounds (Lk. 18:9)! One must come to the realization that God is always justified, while man is always condemned.

2. Relative Righteousness: This *"Righteousness"* compares itself to others, and always finds some that it thinks is of less stature than itself, hence the Pharisee claiming, *"I am not as other men are, extortioners, unjust, adulterers, or even as this Publican"* (Lk. 18:11).

This type of Righteousness, as self-righteousness, is practiced by all of the world, and most of the Church. However, comparing our Righteousness with others, is entirely the wrong measuring rod. The Standard is Christ and not others. When compared with Him, our answer can be only as Isaiah, *"Woe is me!"* (Isa. 6:5), and Job, *"Behold, I am vile"* (Job 40:4), and as John on the Isle of Patmos when he saw Christ in His Glorified Form, *"I fell at His Feet as dead"* (Rev. 1:17).

3. Works Righteousness: This once again goes back to the parable of the Pharisee and Publican, with the Pharisee extolling his good works, *"I fast twice in the week, I give tithes of all that I possess"* (Lk. 18:12). Regrettably, most all the world and the Church depend on this type of Righteousness, which God will not accept!

4. Imputed Righteousness: This is the Righteousness freely imputed by Christ to all who believe. The Publican (criminal) is used as an example, *"And the Publican, standing afar off, would not lift up so much as his eyes unto heaven, but smote upon his breast, saying, God be merciful to me a sinner."*

Jesus said, *"I tell you, this man went down to his house justified rather than the other: for every one that exalted himself shall be abased; and he that humbleth himself shall be exalted"* (Lk. 18:13-14).

This Righteousness freely imputed by Christ, is something the Believer does not deserve, and in fact, can do nothing to earn it. It is given freely, and by Grace.

In other words, the only qualification for this type of Righteousness, is to be unqualified, and know it!

The phrase, *"Ye shall in no case enter into the Kingdom of Heaven,"* proclaims, and loudly so, that the only type of Righteousness God will accept, is the Righteousness freely given by Christ to all who will agree that they have none themselves, and, in fact, cannot obtain any by their own ability, and, are not worthy of any. This is the reason that it is so difficult for most people to be saved.

Most establish their own standards for Salvation, standards which basically balance the good against the bad. It is a standard that God will not accept. Consequently, most of the world has died lost, and most are dying lost at present!

(21) "YE HAVE HEARD THAT IT WAS SAID BY THEM OF OLD TIME, THOU SHALT NOT KILL; AND WHOSOEVER SHALL KILL SHALL BE IN DANGER OF THE JUDGMENT:"

The phrase, *"Ye have heard that it was said*

by them of old time," refers back to the Law of Moses.

The Lord is now going to compare the New Covenant, for which He is laying the foundation, to the Old Covenant. To be sure, it will far exceed the Old in demands and penalties. However, whereas the Old looked to the individual, the New looks to Christ.

The phrase, *"Thou shalt not kill,"* should have been translated, *"Thou shalt do no murder";* for the Magistrate is ordered by God to put capital offenders to death (Gen. 9:6; Rom. 13:1-6).

The phrase, *"And whosoever shall kill shall be in danger of the Judgment,"* is not derived from a direct quotation of Scripture, but it based in substance on Exodus 20:13; Leviticus 24:21; Numbers 35; Deuteronomy 5:17; 19:12.

Under both Covenants, the Bible teaches capital punishment for capital crimes.

Some, while disclaiming the Bible, also claim that capital punishment is no deterrent to crime. While that may or may not be true (a deterrent to crime), such has no relationship to God's Command for capital punishment.

God's value of human life, and the fact that man was originally made in God's image, is the reason that He said, *"Whoso sheddeth man's blood, by man shall his blood be shed: for in the image of God made He man"* (Gen. 9:6). As stated, this is carried over into the New Testament as well (Rom. 13:1-6).

(22) "BUT I SAY UNTO YOU, THAT WHOSOEVER IS ANGRY WITH HIS BROTHER WITHOUT A CAUSE SHALL BE IN DANGER OF THE JUDGMENT: AND WHOSOEVER SHALL SAY TO HIS BROTHER, RACA, SHALL BE IN DANGER OF THE COUNCIL: BUT WHOSOEVER SHALL SAY, THOU FOOL, SHALL BE IN DANGER OF HELL FIRE."

The phrase, *"But I say unto you,"* is emphatic, with the Lord, once again, making Himself the Authority. As such, the Bible and Christ are the same. The former is the Written Word, while the latter is the Living Word. As such, they are indivisible.

The phrase, *"That whosoever is angry with his brother without a cause shall be in danger of the judgment,"* places unjust anger in the same category as murder. Consequently, Jesus addresses not only the act, but the source from which it springs, i.e., the evil heart.

The next two statements are meant to contrast the Jewish Law with the Law of God.

The phrase, *"And whosoever shall say to his brother, Raca, shall be in danger of the council,"* has reference to the Jewish Sanhedrin, composed of 71 Judges, presided over by the High Priest, or a local council of each Synagogue composed of three or more men.

The word, *"Raca,"* was a word used to describe severe contention between parties, with the situation deteriorating to the point of bodily harm. Such, as is obvious, would find themselves in a Court of Law, as is here described.

The phrase, *"But whosoever shall say, Thou fool, shall be in danger of hell fire,"* has reference to the denying of Salvation to anyone, calling them a *"wicked reprobate, destitute of all spirituality."*

While such certainly may be true, with many falling into this category, still, if anyone, even of this description, will turn to the Lord, they can be saved (Jn. 3:16).

The idea of the phrase is, desiring a person to go to hell, and to be, thereby, eternally lost. Jesus is saying, that in the strict interpretation of the Law of Moses, if the situation is carried far enough, one may find himself before the council. However, the Judgment of God is that which is to really be feared, because He can, and, in fact, will, condemn such a murderous heart, baring Repentance, to *"hell fire."*

Once again, Christ is contrasting the Law under the Old Covenant, with that which is required under the New.

It actually goes back to the statement of Jehovah, *"For the Lord seeth not as man seeth; for man looketh on the outward appearance, but the Lord looketh on the heart"* (I Sam. 16:7).

To put it another way, men may beat justice in a human Court of Law, but will never do such in God's Court of Law.

(23) "THEREFORE IF THOU BRING THY GIFT TO THE ALTAR, AND THERE REMEMBEREST THAT THY BROTHER HATH OUGHT AGAINST THEE;"

The phrase, *"Therefore if thou bring thy gift to the Altar,"* is meant to refer to the Brazen Altar as used in the offering of Sacrifices in the Law of Moses.

Because Jesus was speaking to Jews, He would use the terminology of the Old Covenant, i.e., the Altar; however, under the New

Covenant it would have reference to one coming before the Lord, asking forgiveness for wrongdoing. Consequently, the statement is of extreme importance!

The phrase, *"And there rememberest that thy brother hath ought against thee,"* is meant to describe our relationship with our fellowman.

In other words, if we hold unforgiveness in our hearts toward others, our petition to the Lord for forgiveness on His part cannot be brought about until reconciliation is made with the offended party. This, in effect, goes along with Christ's statement, *"For if ye forgive men their trespasses, your Heavenly Father will also forgive you:*

"But if ye forgive not men their trespasses, neither will your Father forgive your trespasses" (Mat. 6:14-15).

(24) "LEAVE THERE THY GIFT BEFORE THE ALTAR, AND GO THY WAY; FIRST BE RECONCILED TO THY BROTHER, AND THEN COME AND OFFER THY GIFT."

The phrase, *"Leave there thy gift before the Altar,"* is meant to put first things first.

In other words, the intimation is that the Lord will not accept our *"gift"* unless we do all within our power to make things right with the offended party.

This makes Christianity so superior to all religions. The idea once again, is that the heart be addressed, and that if the heart is truly addressed, it will be kept free from guilt toward one's fellowman.

The phrase, *"And go thy way,"* refers to making whatever effort is necessary to bring about this reconciliation, if at all possible!

The phrase, *"First be reconciled to thy brother,"* emphasizes the significance that God places on right relationships with others.

Of course, there are some situations that cannot be reconciled, due to one or more parties not desiring such. God does not hold us accountable in such cases, but does hold us accountable to make every effort.

The phrase, *"And then come and offer thy gift,"* has reference to the personal relationship being handled first, or at least, doing all within our power to do so, and *"then"* the Lord will hear our prayers, and forgive us if, in fact, forgiveness is necessary, etc.

Sadly, most Christians little heed these Commands, even though they strike at the very heart of that which we call *"Christianity."* As a result, many prayers and petitions to the Lord go unanswered, and many sins remain unforgiven.

It is a sobering thought!

(25) "AGREE WITH THINE ADVERSARY QUICKLY, WHILES THOU ART IN THE WAY WITH HIM; LEST AT ANY TIME THE ADVERSARY DELIVER THEE TO THE JUDGE, AND THE JUDGE DELIVER THEE TO THE OFFICER, AND THOU BE CAST INTO PRISON."

Many misunderstand verses 25 and 26, thinking they pertain to legal matters, and the need to settle before going to court. However, that is not the intention of Christ, as these two verses relate to verses 23 and 24, and, in a way, to verses 21 and 22, as well!

The idea as tendered by Christ, is that offenses against man are here represented in their true character as offenses against God, Who is therefore depicted as the Adversary in a lawsuit. As well, He is also depicted as the Judge, and that His decision will be rendered in a very disagreeable manner, if His Word is not followed.

The phrase, *"Agree with thine adversary quickly, whiles thou art in the way with him,"* refers to the absolute necessity of making doubly certain that one's fellowman is treated right. This is an absolute requirement by Christ. To offend a brother, is to offend Christ, and is here made glaringly evident.

The phrase, *"Lest at any time the adversary deliver thee to the Judge,"* refers to one's unscriptural actions delivering him to the Judge, i.e., the Lord Jesus Christ.

An example is Moses who fell on his face before the Lord, when Korah, Dathan, and Abram, led a rebellion against him, as is recorded in Numbers 16.

First of all, the unholy trio was dealing with Moses, but then, and quickly, they found themselves dealing with the Lord, Who is the Righteous Judge.

The phrase, *"And the Judge deliver thee to the officer, and thou be cast into prison,"* in effect, refers to a spiritual judgment which is the worst of all! Consequently, millions of Christians are presently *"in prison,"* at least in a spiritual sense, simply because they have harmed their Brother or Sister in the Lord, and have not sought to make it right. To offend God's is to offend God.

NOTES

The *"prison"* can consist of sickness, poverty, or any number of things devised by the Lord.

(26) "VERILY I SAY UNTO THEE, THOU SHALT BY NO MEANS COME OUT THENCE, TILL THOU HAST PAID THE UTTERMOST FARTHING."

I think the idea is glaringly obvious in this verse!

If wrongdoing is carried out against a fellow Believer, upon proper repentance before the Lord, and with proper restitution to the individual, the matter, as proclaimed in verses 23 and 24 can be handled readily and without penalty. However, to fail to do so, which is, sadly, the case much, if not most of the time, invites extremely harsh penalties.

The phrase, *"Verily I say unto thee,"* is meant to impress upon the reader the absolute solemnity of this statement as given by Christ.

The phrase, *"Thou shalt by no means come out thence,"* means that if God's Way (Repentance and seeking of forgiveness from the offended party), is not entered into, the consequences will be dire indeed!

The phrase, *"Till thou hast paid the uttermost farthing,"* concerns itself by payment in installments. In other words, there will not be just one reverse, but one after the other, and with no end in sight.

This goes not only for matters between Believers, but, as well, for entire Religious Denominations. There is no license given in the Word of God, for anyone to mistreat someone else, and irrespective as to whom they may be!

The other day, a very able lawyer spoke to me concerning a major Religious Denomination. He said, *"Brother Swaggart, until the Leadership of this Denomination makes things right, the problems they are now experiencing, will only exacerbate."*

He is right, as the debt draws interest, and, in effect, the payments never end!

How so much easier it is, and as Christ here defines, if in fact one has been wronged, for the offending party to simply say in sincerity, *"I have wronged you, would you please forgive me? I will do whatever I can to make restitution before God and man."* The statement just made, constitutes only a few simple words, but is so difficult for most to carry out.

(27) "YE HAVE HEARD THAT IT WAS

SAID BY THEM OF OLD TIME, THOU SHALT NOT COMMIT ADULTERY.'"

The Believer's conduct toward his fellow-man continues, with Jesus' command respecting divorce and remarriage, but, as well, addresses the true intent of the Law, which was completely different than the interpretation of the Pharisees.

The Commandment, *"Thou shalt not commit adultery,"* is the Seventh Commandment of the Ten (Ex. 20:14).

(28) "BUT I SAY UNTO YOU, THAT WHOSOEVER LOOKETH ON A WOMAN TO LUST AFTER HER HATH COMMITTED ADULTERY WITH HER ALREADY IN HIS HEART."

The Law was based on behavior, which is as all Law, directed toward the act itself. However, the New Covenant is far more stringent than the Old, directing attention to the heart of the individual, instead of the act.

The phrase, *"But I say unto you,"* does not deny the Law of Moses, but rather takes it to its conclusion, which could only be done by Christ. In other words, the Old Covenant pointed the way to the New Covenant, which came with Christ.

As well, the Pharisees were continuously arguing over the divorce question, and now Jesus by His statement, settles the issue completely, at least for His followers. He takes it much further than the act itself, and directs attention to the heart, which gives birth to the act.

In retrospect, the Law, at least in some measure, did actually go beyond the act, even directing attention to the heart by the Tenth Commandment *"Thou shalt not covet."* In other words, the Tenth Commandment said, that not only must the act (whatever infraction) not be committed, but, as well, the individual must not even have a desire to do so. (The word *"desire"* is used in the sense of one wanting to do something, and, in fact, would do it, if the occasion presented itself, and could be done without being found out.)

The phrase, *"That whosoever looketh on a woman to lust after her,"* means to look at one in order to lust, and with a look that stimulates the lust. It is not merely *"looking"* at someone, with a temptation crossing the mind, but, instead, with a desire to carry it out if the consequences could be avoided.

The phrase, *"Hath committed adultery with her already in his heart,"* is a serious charge indeed! It means that God chalks it up as if the sin was committed.

Quite possibly, Christ was directing His attention, not only to the general public, and for all time, but, as well, to a sect called the *"Bleeding Pharisees."*

These individuals wore a heavy bandage around their forehead because they walked about, at least much of the time with their eyes closed, and would, consequently, bump into objects, and especially with their head, hence called *"Bleeding Pharisees."* They were doing so, at least they said, to keep from looking at members of the opposite sex, which made others think of them as extremely holy.

Despite Jesus using the word *"look,"* He is, in effect, saying that the sin is in the heart, and not the eyes. Therefore, His statement must have angered them greatly, as it completely blew away their hypotheses.

(29) "AND IF THY RIGHT EYE OFFEND THEE, PLUCK IT OUT, AND CAST IT FROM THEE: FOR IT IS PROFITABLE FOR THEE THAT ONE OF THY MEMBERS SHOULD PERISH, AND NOT THAT THY WHOLE BODY SHOULD BE CAST INTO HELL."

The Lord does not intend for His statement to be taken literally, as He has already explained that the offense is not in the *"eye"* or *"hand,"* but, instead, the heart! In effect, a blind man can lust.

The idea is, that sin is so bad, with the possibility of such damning the soul, that drastic action must be taken to subdue such passions.

As well, if we think these sins are seldom committed, and by few, we are of all people most mistaken. In fact, the areas addressed by Christ in this Sermon on the Mount, which covers Chapters 5-7, address every major life concern. Therefore, in the aggregate, it is something that all grapple with on a continuing basis.

The phrase, *"For it is profitable for thee...,"* proves the necessity of obeying God in these matters, and, as well, allowing Him to set the Standard, rather than man!

The seriousness of this matter is emphasized in the first phrase, *"And if thy right eye offend thee, pluck it out, and cast it from thee."*

Adultery was once a crime in America, and

because the Law of man was based on the Law of God. However, the Bible is no longer the Standard for moral measurement in America, and, consequently, man's laws change with each administration.

The phrase, *"And not that thy whole body should be cast into hell,"* unequivocally lets man know just how serious these matters are!

Regrettably, most modern Preachers do not even believe there is a *"hell,"* and despite the Words of Christ.

(30) "AND IF THY RIGHT HAND OFFEND THEE, CUT IT OFF, AND CAST IT FROM THEE: FOR IT IS PROFITABLE FOR THEE THAT ONE OF THY MEMBERS SHOULD PERISH, AND NOT THAT THY WHOLE BODY SHOULD BE CAST INTO HELL."

For the Lord to say something once, signifies its importance. For Him to say it twice, as here, signifies its extreme importance!

The Lord's method of teaching was symbolic and figurative. It is better to destroy what tempts to wrongdoing, though it be as precious as an eye or a hand, than to suffer eternal torments.

Few people on earth presently believe verses 29 and 30, while every single person in hell now believes it readily!

(31) "IT HATH BEEN SAID, WHOSOEVER SHALL PUT AWAY HIS WIFE, LET HIM GIVE HER A WRITING OF DIVORCEMENT:"

The phrase, *"It hath been said,"* refers to Deuteronomy 24:1-4.

The phrase, *"Whosoever shall put away his wife,"* refers to divorce proceedings.

The phrase, *"Let him give her a writing of divorcement,"* now placed the emphasis on this legal form. Jesus will change that by dealing with the very heart of the problem.

(32) "BUT I SAY UNTO YOU, THAT WHOSOEVER SHALL PUT AWAY HIS WIFE, SAVING FOR THE CAUSE OF FORNICATION, CAUSETH HER TO COMMIT ADULTERY: AND WHOSOEVER SHALL MARRY HER THAT IS DIVORCED COMMITTETH ADULTERY."

The phrase, *"But I say unto you,"* is, once again, designed to settle the matter once and for all. As such, and even though Incarnate, He places Himself in the position of Deity, which He was!

The phrase, *"That whosoever shall put*

away his wife," places the emphasis on the seriousness of this matter, which was far above any and all legal forms. In effect, and due to the fact that divorce strikes at the very heart of the family, great attention is given to it by Christ, and if it is not followed to the letter, catastrophe, and on a nationwide, or even worldwide scale, is the result.

The phrase, *"Saving for the cause of fornication, causeth her to commit adultery,"* gives the only allowance for divorce, with the exception of the second allowance as referred to by Paul in I Corinthians 7:10-11.

The Word, *"put away,"* means divorce and was so understood by the Jews. If the divorce was granted for fornication, a sin God looked upon as most serious, the putting away was legal, and sanctioned by Christ. It made the contract null and void as before marriage.

Many people misunderstand the true meaning of adultery and fornication. They think fornication applies only to single people, while adultery applies to those who are married. Such is error.

Adultery is unlawful relationship between men and women, single or married. In fact, all fornication is adultery, but all adultery is not fornication.

As an example, David was an adulterer, but he was not a fornicator, as Esau (Heb. 12:16).

Fornication in the Bible means *"adultery of married or single people, committed over and over again with different partners"* (Mat. 19:9; I Cor. 7:2; 10:8; I Thess. 4:3; Rev. 9:21); *"incest"* (I Cor. 5:1; 10:8); *"idolatry,"* which speaks of adultery in honor of idol gods (II Chron. 21:11; Isa. 23:17; Ezek. 16:15, 26, 29; Acts 15:20, 29; 21:25; Rev. 2:14-21; 14:8; 17:2-4; 18:3-9; 19:2); *"sodomy and male prostitution"* (Rom. 1:24-29; I Cor. 6:9-11; II Cor. 12:21; Gal. 5:19; Eph. 5:3; Col. 3:5; Heb. 12:16; Jude: 6-7).

The phrase, *"And whosoever shall marry her that is divorced committeth adultery,"* means one who is divorced with no Scriptural grounds.

(For a more detailed treatment of this important subject of divorce and remarriage, please see Commentary on Malachi 2.)

(33) "AGAIN, YE HAVE HEARD THAT IT HATH BEEN SAID BY THEM OF OLD TIME, THOU SHALT NOT FORSWEAR THYSELF, BUT SHALT PERFORM UNTO THE LORD THINE OATHS:"

As verses 21-26 had to do with the Sixth Commandment, *"Thou shalt not kill"* (murder), and verses 27-32 had to do with the Seventh Commandment, *"Thou shalt not commit adultery,"* verses 33-37 have to do with the Third Commandment, *"Thou shalt not take the Name of the Lord thy God in vain"* (Ex. 20:7).

The phrase, *"Again, ye have heard that it hath been said by them of old time,"* once again alludes to tradition.

Over and over again, Jesus used terms such as, *"Ye have heard,"* or *"It hath been said,"* meaning that the Word of God had been twisted to mean something it did not say. This has ever been the case with professors of religion. In reality, most of the people in Israel did not know the Bible, and even most of those who did, attempted to make it fit their beliefs, instead of allowing it to mold their beliefs. It has little changed presently!

The phrase, *"Thou shalt not forswear thyself, but shalt perform unto the Lord thine oaths,"* concerns that which was commonly done among the people. Consequently, they made the Lord, by their actions, a part of their exaggerations, lies, and fabrications.

(34-36) "BUT I SAY UNTO YOU, SWEAR NOT AT ALL; NEITHER BY HEAVEN; FOR IT IS GOD'S THRONE:

"NOR BY THE EARTH; FOR IT IS HIS FOOTSTOOL: NEITHER BY JERUSALEM; FOR IT IS THE CITY OF THE GREAT KING.

"NEITHER SHALT THOU SWEAR BY THY HEAD, BECAUSE THOU CANST NOT MAKE ONE HAIR WHITE OR BLACK."

The phrase in verse 34, *"But I say unto you, Swear not at all,"* has nothing to do with profanity, at least in this case, but rather the making of vows by Heaven, earth, or any other thing.

The idea of these verses is, that it had become commonplace for individuals to pull God's Name into their declarations. It was done in a flippant, light, irresponsible manner. This is what the Lord is forbidding.

It does not refer to solemn oaths which must be taken in some circumstances, such as Courts of Law, etc.

Actually, the Apostle Paul took oaths in his writings (II Cor. 1:23; 11:31).

Once again, we emphasize that the Lord is addressing Himself to the wholesale use of His Name, and in whatever capacity respecting

NOTES

ordinary conversation, etc. In fact, modern Christians also fall into this same trap.

Many Christians profane the Name of God by exclaiming, *"My God,"* whether upon hearing some type of unusual announcement, or attempting to make their statement stronger. Others use the phrase, *"By God,"* once again taking an oath in flippant conversation, or else in anger. Others use the name, *"Jesus Christ,"* in a flippant exclamation, which is meant to express surprise, etc.

As well, outright profanity has become so common over Television, and in normal usage, that many Christians are not offended by it anymore, or at least raise little objection.

As a consequence, many Christians think little of using the expletives, *"damn,"* or, *"hell,"* in expressing themselves, thinking to lend weight to their statements, not stopping to realize that these two words, plus others of similar comport, are, in effect, words describing acts of God, or places of designation created by God.

At any rate, it is *"swearing"* pure and simple, and is absolutely forbidden by the Lord. His Name is to be regarded, respected, revered, and held above all such thinking, and especially conversation. The failure to do such, shows an improper relationship with Him, with little understanding as to exactly Who He is, the Creator and Redeemer, and who exactly we are, the created, and, therefore, absolutely dependent upon Him.

(37) "BUT LET YOUR COMMUNICATION BE, YEA, YEA; NAY, NAY: FOR WHATSOEVER IS MORE THAN THESE COMETH OF EVIL."

The phrase, *"But let your communication be, Yea, yea; Nay, nay,"* is meant to express the following:

The word of the Believer should be such, that it seldom requires an oath to substantiate what is being said. If one says *"yes,"* it means *"yes."* If one says *"no,"* it means *"no!"*

It is regrettable, that such responsible truthfulness is little adhered to anymore! When the Bible was adhered to more fully, a man's word was his bond. Now, at least in most cases, a man's word, even among Believers, means little!

Christ is here stating, that His followers must stand out by their truthfulness, honesty, and integrity.

The phrase, *"For whatsoever is more than these cometh of evil,"* is meant to say that if *"yes"* does not mean *"yes,"* or *"no"* does not mean *"no,"* evil is then the result. Regrettably, even among many Christians, *"evil"* is the result, more so than Righteousness!

(38) "YE HAVE HEARD THAT IT HATH BEEN SAID, AN EYE FOR AN EYE, AND A TOOTH FOR A TOOTH:"

Someone has said that this phrase more accurately describes the spirit of Mosaic Legislation than any other!

Even though this admonition was carried out literally at times, by the time of the Advent of Christ, such infractions were often handled by the payment of money.

Even though there were jails in those days, still, many, if not most things of this nature were handled in a different manner than incarceration. The guilty party was made to pay either in money, or in work on behalf of the injured party.

By using the phrase again, *"Ye have heard that it hath been said,"* Christ is attempting to pull Israel away from the Letter of the Law, to the Spirit of the Law.

(39) "BUT I SAY UNTO YOU, THAT YE RESIST NOT EVIL: BUT WHOSOEVER SHALL SMITE THEE ON THY RIGHT CHEEK, TURN TO HIM THE OTHER ALSO."

The phrase, *"But I say unto you, That ye resist not evil,"* is not meant to refer to the official duties of Governments, but, instead, is meant to address the individual Believer. In fact, if *"evil"* is not resisted by Government, anarchy is the result. Actually, Government as ordained by God, is said to be, *"The Minister of God, a revenger to execute wrath upon him that doeth evil"* (Rom. 13:4).

The phrase, *"But whosoever shall smite thee on thy right cheek, turn to him the other also,"* is meant to be taken in the figurative. In fact, the offering of the other cheek may be done outwardly, while the opposite is in the heart. If it is done only inwardly, can it always be right.

Actually, when the Lord was smitten on the cheek (Jn. 18:22-23), He did not turn the other cheek but with dignity rebuked the assailant.

The idea of these Passages is, that the heavenly citizen is not to be ready to take offense (vs. 39), nor prompt to go to law (vs. 40), nor

NOTES

disobliging (vs. 41), nor heartless (vs. 42), nor revengeful (vs. 44), but like his Father in Heaven, he is to be kind to both evil and good men; and so, in that sense, be perfect as His Father, for his actions will correspond.

(40) "AND IF ANY MAN WILL SUE THEE AT THE LAW, AND TAKE AWAY THY COAT, LET HIM HAVE THY CLOAK ALSO."

Once again, this Scripture is not meant to be obeyed in the literal sense, for Paul, at least in the literal sense, did the opposite. When the Jews were determined to hold court on him in Jerusalem, he said, *"I stand at Caesar's judgment seat, where I ought to be judged"* (Acts 25:10). In other words, he did not take the position that whatever you want to do to me you may do! In effect, he *"resisted this evil,"* as he should have done.

The idea of these verses is, that we not be so quick to try to defend ourselves, but instead place the situation in the Hands of the Lord.

And yet, there are times, as we have attempted to bring out, that the spirit of these Commands as given by Christ, will be kept totally, while, at times, the actions are forced otherwise.

Paul could have easily stated, and attempting to keep the letter of Christ's Statements, that if the Jews desired to try him in a Court of Law in Jerusalem (before the Sanhedrin), that they were welcome to do so. However, that was not God's Will, inasmuch as they were only seeking to kill Paul. Consequently, while continuing to love them, despite their gross evil, he took advantage of Roman Law, by appealing to Caesar, which, as a Roman citizen, he had the right to do.

And yet, Paul at the same time, and by the action of the Holy Spirit, absolutely forbade Christians to go to court before unbelievers, against other Christians (I Cor. 6:1-8).

As a further example, some time back, the State of California demanded that Jimmy Swaggart Ministries pay sales taxes on Bibles, Bible Study Courses, or religious recordings sold in their State by mail or in crusades. We felt this was unconstitutional, as none of the profits accrued (if any) were for personal or corporate use, but rather for the propagation of the Gospel. Consequently, we sued the State of California, which ultimately went to the Supreme Court of the United States.

In doing so, we did not violate the Command of Christ, and neither did the Apostle Paul in his appeal to Caesar.

On the other side of the coin, we have suffered many injustices, and blatantly so, by fellow Christians, even to the point of suffering great loss, but we have never taken a fellow Christian to court, no matter how blatantly wrong their actions, and have no intentions of doing so. We have rather suffered ourselves to be defrauded (I Cor. 6:7).

(41) "AND WHOSOEVER SHALL COMPEL THEE TO GO A MILE, GO WITH HIM TWAIN."

Once again, let's see what this does not mean.

As is known, Rome ruled in Christ's day. Consequently, the soldiers were at times harsh, demanding that citizens, at times, carry baggage, etc.

At times of such actions, Christ was not meaning that the individual should carry the baggage the distance demanded, and then carefully measure off an added similar distance, and when done, congratulate themselves on the fulfilling of this command. To do so, would completely misdirect the intention of the teaching of Christ.

The idea was, that the Believer was to have a good attitude and spirit, seeking to be helpful and kind at all times, even under the most adverse circumstances. This is what Christ was teaching, and not the measurement of some distance, etc. The entirety of the idea, had to do with the heart of man, and not so much his outward actions, but which most surely would guide his actions accordingly.

(42) "GIVE TO HIM THAT ASKETH THEE, AND FROM HIM THAT WOULD BORROW OF THEE TURN NOT THOU AWAY."

The idea is, that the Child of God should walk in fellowship with the Father, and to imitate Him. He is, for example, to help those of his fellowmen whom God would help, and to help them in the same way. He is not, for example, to give money to a lazy man, to be spent by him in vice, for the Heavenly Father also says: *"If any will not work, neither shall he eat"* (II Thess. 3:10).

Regrettably, many have attempted to turn these admonitions into rules and laws, which completely circumvent the true teachings of Christ. As we have stated, one can easily turn the other cheek outwardly, but only when he

NOTES

turns the other cheek inwardly, can the true spirit of these admonitions be kept, which is intended by Christ.

(43) "YE HAVE HEARD THAT IT HATH BEEN SAID, THOU SHALT LOVE THY NEIGHBOUR, AND HATE THINE ENEMY."

Once again, the Lord resorts to the phrase, *"Ye have heard that it hath been said,"* which once again refers to a twisting of Scripture, to make it mean something that it really does not say.

The phrase, *"Thou shalt love thy neighbour, and hate thine enemy,"* was probably derived from Exodus 17:14-16; Leviticus 19:17-18; and Deuteronomy 7:1-2; 23:3-6. As such, these Scriptures really do not say *"hate thine enemy,"* but had to do with the actions of enemy nations toward Israel, which, if not stopped, would have circumvented the Plan of God. Actually, it was the actions of these enemies of goodness and of Righteousness that were to be *"hated"* with a holy hatred. And inasmuch as these *"enemies"* were determined to destroy the people of God, measures were commanded to be taken against them. It was definitely not supposed to degenerate into a personal hatred.

For instance, the wars fought in my lifetime, consisting of World War II and Korea, with possibly Vietnam at its beginning, were wars carried out in order to stop the encroachment of evil. When Hitler's death camps in Europe were opened, where some 6,000,000 Jews were ruthlessly executed, then it became painfully obvious, just exactly how evil these opponents were. As such, they had to be resisted, which fulfilled Romans 13:1-7.

And yet, as a Believer, particular individuals in these foreign armies, were not to be hated, only their evil and wicked actions.

(44) "BUT I SAY UNTO YOU, LOVE YOUR ENEMIES, BLESS THEM THAT CURSE YOU, DO GOOD TO THEM THAT HATE YOU, AND PRAY FOR THEM WHICH DESPITEFULLY USE YOU, AND PERSECUTE YOU;"

Once again, the phrase, *"But I say unto you,"* proclaims the true intent of the Law, as well as the Command of Christ.

The Teaching of Christ on this subject was so contrary to what was presently being practiced, which was perversion of the Law, that Christ's Words were as revolutionary as anything could possibly be. When the Jews, and especially the Religious Leaders, heard these words, they must have been dumbfounded. The Teaching of Christ was totally opposite of that being presently practiced, and, in effect, this one verse totally sets True Christianity apart from all the religions of the world. Sadly, it is not too much practiced, even by professing Believers, but, still, these admonitions lie at the very heart of what True Christianity is all about. Four things are said in this verse:

1. *"Love your enemies"*: Such a concept was unthinkable even among the Jews, much less among the heathen!

Actually, the *"love"* spoken of here by Christ, is the God kind of Love, which totally transcends that which is called *"love"* by man. The phrase, *"For God so loved the world…"* (Jn. 3:16), is speaking of a world that hated Him.

When Christ is accepted into the heart, the heart is changed, with the Love of God being instilled, which gives the Believer the capacity to love as God loves. Within oneself and abilities, such cannot be done! But with the true born-again experience, and Christ reigning supremely within one's life, such not only can be done, but, in Truth, will be done!

This is the only true answer to racism, bigotry, and prejudice.

As well, it must be remembered that true love as expressed in the heart, will, as well, find itself in corresponding action. In other words, it is not just love that is spoken loudly, as happens in most cases, but, instead, which shows itself in actions.

Love awakened must find expression in a transformed lifestyle. The Divine principle of love infuses the Believer, moving Christians as it moved God to love even enemies.

The New Testament explores in depth the impact of the Divine Love on our relationships in this world. Love creates a new community, as Brothers and Sisters in Christ are bonded together.

Love prompts obedience and provides the motivation that moves Believers to respond to the Lord.

Love transforms the character of the individual and provides a sense of purpose. Love stabilizes relationships, enabling us to overcome the tensions that shatter friendships.

Love compels a practical concern for others that leads us to reach out and meet their needs.

It is love that moves us toward the Righteousness that Law calls for but cannot produce.

The phrase, *"Love your enemies,"* has to do with all types of infractions. It speaks of those who wrong you in any capacity, or even children who disobey their parents, etc. Such, and in whatever capacity, is to be responded to by love, while never condoning the wrongdoing. In other words, if we want to help someone change, let us love them as Jesus loves us and them.

However, true love will, at times, result in chastisement of the loved one, at least in cases of personal relationships, such as parents to children, etc. The chastisement is not carried out when needed, despite love, but, instead, because of love (Heb. 12:6).

2. *"Bless them that curse you"*: This means that no matter how the Believer is treated, we are to respond in a positive way and seek to introduce others to the life in Christ that brings blessing.

Incidentally, the word, *"curse,"* as here used, does not refer to swearing or profanity. It refers to one who wishes you ill, hurt, or harm, and would attempt to bring their wishes into a state of action if possible. Consequently, the True Believer is absolutely forbidden to curse (wish harm upon) anyone.

James says, *"Therewith bless we God, even the Father; and therewith curse we men, which are made after the similitude of God.*

"Out of the same mouth proceedeth blessing and cursing. My brethren, these things ought not so to be" (James 3:9-10).

Although the Believer does have the capacity to *"curse,"* in which will cause harm, and especially because he is a Believer; however, to do so is to take the God-given attributes of Faith and Love, and pervert them, which sends bitter water out of a fountain that is supposed to send only sweet (James 3:11).

The effect, while causing momentary harm on the intended victim, will rather destroy the perpetrator. Consequently, to fail to do what Christ here admonishes, not only robs the victim of blessing, but, as well, destroys the Believer. The True Christian is designed by God to *"bless"* and not *"curse."* To disobey is a perversion of the highest order.

Whenever the Believer *"blesses"* those who *"curse"* them, they are unleashing upon that individual, the only power on earth which can truly change them. Therefore, the best, and, in fact, only way, to stop the adverse actions of such a person, is to truly bless them. Upon the advent of such *"blessing,"* the guilty party will either respond favorably, or else rebel even further, consequently, destroying himself.

The actions and statements of a True Believer are so powerful, at least in the spirit world, that either a positive or a negative effect is had on the individual or victim, even though unseen or unheard. In other words, a blessing extended by a Believer toward an individual, even though unknown by that individual, will be positively felt. They will be blessed, and will sense it, even though they do not know the source. The same can be said for *"curses,"* in a negative way.

For example: Due to happenings since 1988, Frances and I have many times, if not all times, felt the negative response of fellow Believers, even though we would not be aware of the source.

For instance: Oftentimes when feeling a tremendously heavy oppressive spirit on our persons, we learn to watch for negative articles written by fellow Believers, or some such device carried out against us. Of course, many times, and especially if uttered by Christians, and on a worldwide basis, we would have no knowledge of the perpetrators, but would definitely feel in our spirits the effect of the *"cursing."* James said, *"The tongue is a fire . . . setteth on fire the course of nature; and it is set on fire of hell"* (James 3:6).

To survive this, Frances and I have had to constantly, and gladly so, *"bless them who curse us."*

Thankfully, with some few it has changed them, but, sadly, with most, they have continued to rebel, which always results in ultimate destruction.

What does it mean to *"bless those that curse us?"*

To *"bless"* someone, is to speak kindly of the person, irrespective of how they speak of you. It means to speak a positive word about them if at all possible.

And yet, Christ spoke very harshly of the Pharisees, even calling them hypocrites, serpents, and vipers (Mat. 23:29-33).

Was He violating His Own Word?

No! Many modern Believers have confused

these issues, thinking it is wrong for Preachers of the Gospel to say anything negative concerning false Doctrine, or the propagators of such Doctrine.

In Truth, the Pharisees had spurned the Love of God, refusing to be blessed, and had set themselves to destroy the Gospel, therefore, causing many souls to be lost. As such, Christ, as all Godly Preachers, was obligated to point out not only the error of the false Doctrine, which would cause many souls to be lost, but, as well, the perpetrators of that Doctrine, at least the name of their group. To have not done so, would have been a crime of the highest order.

It is the same as the Law of God in Romans 13:5, where it says, and concerning human Government, *"ye must needs be subject."* However, if human law abrogates God's Law, the Believer must not be subject to such law. God's Law is a higher Law, and all law must be subject to that Law. So, Believers in the Early Church, did not violate the Law of God, when they refused to obey Caesar's law, demanding that they call Caesar *"Lord,"* etc.

Neither did Jesus violate His Own Law of *"loving one's enemies, or blessing those who curse us,"* by speaking of the Pharisees as He did! And neither do modern Preachers of the Gospel, when they obey God in pointing out gross error, and the perpetrators of such error, and even in a very negative way, as Christ.

3. *"Do good to them that hate you":* This means, as is obvious, to return unkindness with kindness.

The story is told of a Chinese Christian who was working a plot of land under Communist rule. His plot was immediately above the adjoining plot worked by another man, who was not a Christian, and who fervently avowed Communist Atheism.

The Chinese Christian had gone to much labor and trouble to irrigate his plot of ground, which he had to do in order to secure the crop.

The unbeliever, who had his plot immediately below the plot worked by the Christian, went in during the night, and made a breach in the mound of earth, which released all the water onto his land, thereby watering it with a minimum of trouble, while causing the Christian to have to irrigate his all over again at the expense of much labor.

Without saying anything, the Christian hauled the water by hand to his plot, irrigating it all over again, and beside that, went in that night and performed some needed work on the unbeliever's plot.

The next morning, the unbeliever observed the situation, and noted the work, but not knowing how it was done.

That night, he carried out further damage to the Christian's plot, which necessitates more labor on the part of the Believer. Again, nothing was said or done by the Believer to the unbeliever, but he instead went in, working several hours on the unbelievers plot, performing much needed work.

This went on for quite some time, with kindness being extended each and every time on the part of the Believer for every act of unkindness on the part of the unbeliever.

It took several weeks, while during this time not a word was exchanged between them, but finally, the unbeliever came to the Christian, saying, *"I have disavowed your Jesus, but seeing your actions in the face of my unkindness, I want to know your Christ."* He went on to say, *"Anything that can put such actions of kindness and love in one's heart, should be strongly desired, and to be sure, I want what you have."*

That is the general idea, but, regrettably, not too often carried out.

4. *"Pray for them which despitefully use you, and persecute you":* To pray thusly, is to come very near to the Spirit of Christ. One person said, *"Such persons would have never had a particular place in my prayers, but for the injuries they have done to me."*

How should we pray for such a person?

We should pray that God would move upon them, showing them His Way of Love. This will turn them around, that is, if they will allow it to do so, as nothing else! Actually, this is the only real weapon, prayer, that can be successfully used against any and all.

All of these things done in the true Spirit of Christ, helps the participant at least as much, if not more than the intended offender. The worst thing that can happen to a Believer, is for hate to get in his heart over real or imagined wrongs. Such poisons the system, and causes sickness, as well as terrible discomfort, and, as well, and more importantly, violates

NOTES

the Word of God. So, the idea that only the offender is being helped, is grossly in error.

(45) "THAT YE MAY BE THE CHILDREN OF YOUR FATHER WHICH IS IN HEAVEN: FOR HE MAKETH HIS SUN TO RISE ON THE EVIL AND ON THE GOOD, AND SENDETH RAIN ON THE JUST AND ON THE UNJUST."

The phrase, *"That ye may be the children of your Father which is in Heaven,"* means as the Father does, so shall true sons do!

The phrase, *"For He maketh His sun to rise on the evil and on the good,"* portrays the Lord sending good on both alike!

While it is true that the Lord will ultimately send Judgment if sin is not dealt with, still, even this is done in a corrective sense, instead of the sake of mere punishment.

The phrase, *"And sendeth rain on the just and on the unjust,"* is meant to emphasize that the Lord does good to both groups. Consequently, we are to do likewise, which the entirety of these Passages emphasize.

The next verse explains the higher action of the True Child of God, versus the child of Satan.

(46) "FOR IF YE LOVE THEM WHICH LOVE YOU, WHAT REWARD HAVE YE? DO NOT EVEN THE PUBLICANS THE SAME?"

This verse is meant to proclaim the superiority of True Bible Christianity. The question, *"For if ye love them which love you, what reward have ye?",* is meant to proclaim the type of love the world has, which, in effect, says, *"scratch my back, and I'll scratch yours."*

Asking the question, *"Do not even the Publicans the same?",* Christ is saying that such spurious love can be had by anyone, and, in fact, is shared by anyone. As a result, it is of precious little consequence!

"Publicans" were tax-gatherers. They were despised by the Jews, so any reference to being less than this class was the lowest thing that could be said of anyone religious. In other words, in Israel, a *"Publican"* was the lowest form of human life, at least in the minds of their countrymen.

Rome, at that time, sold certain districts in Israel (as well as other countries) to the highest bidder, respecting the collecting of taxes. The winner of the bid was then allowed to collect taxes in that area, and could keep all that he collected.

So, if he paid $1,000,000 for a certain district, and was able to collect $1,500,000, he had profited himself a half-million dollars.

In the collection of taxes, he was given great latitude and authority, and backed by Rome. Consequently, many, if not most *"Publicans"* grew very rich.

They were considered by Israel to be renegade Jews, who had sold out their country for the sake of money, and were, in turn, greatly despised.

Wondrously enough, the man who wrote this Book, Matthew, had been a *"Publican."*

So, Jesus is saying that if we only love those who love us, we are no better than the *"Publicans"* who were greatly despised by the Jews.

(47) "AND IF YE SALUTE YOUR BRETHREN ONLY, WHAT DO YE MORE THAN OTHERS? DO NOT EVEN THE PUBLICANS SO?"

In verse 46, Jesus touches those of like action, while in this verse He touches those in kind. There was a reason for this!

The various different parties in Israel at that time, such as the Pharisees, Sadducees, and Herodians, virtually hated each other. Also, almost all Jews hated the Samaritans, who they looked at as half-breeds, and not, therefore, Jews.

So, in the phrase, *"And if ye salute your brethren only,"* He was addressing one of the basic problems and sins in Israel. Likewise, any and all who feel that people in their Church only are saved, fall into this category.

Christ is saying that if one's love does not rise any higher than that, they are no better than those considered to be the worst sinners and criminals in Israel, i.e., Publicans.

This must have hit the Pharisees, and others of like ilk extremely hard.

(48) "BE YE THEREFORE PERFECT, EVEN AS YOUR FATHER WHICH IS IN HEAVEN IS PERFECT."

The idea of this Scripture is not that one can attain perfection, *"Even as your Father which is in Heaven,"* but that he will fully and completely attain to that measure of love to which he as a created being was intended to attain.

In other words, it is God's Standard of measurement that is to be used, rather than man's.

The word, *"perfect,"* even though meaning *"sinless perfection,"* as it applies to God, does not refer to such in the life of the Believer,

because such is impossible. However, a perfect God can command no less in His Disciples, and, to be sure, it is a state to which every Believer must aspire, although continually falling short (Rom. 3:23).

The Mosaic Law demanded perfection, although never attained in any individual, even Moses, but only by Christ. As a result, Faith in Christ, as the Representative man, makes one a participant of the perfect walk of Christ.

So, in the Mind of God, the acceptance of Christ, Who is *"perfect,"* gives one Christ's perfection.

CHAPTER 6

(1) "TAKE HEED THAT YE DO NOT YOUR ALMS BEFORE MEN, TO BE SEEN OF THEM: OTHERWISE YE HAVE NO REWARD OF YOUR FATHER WHICH IS IN HEAVEN."

As the Lord dealt with issues in the previous Chapter, in this Chapter He deals with relationship. His teaching concerns itself with the most basic fundamentals of Righteous Living, but yet, that which forms the foundation of our relationship with God.

The phrase, *"Take heed that ye do not your alms before men, to be seen of them,"* strikes at the very heart of our reason for giving.

Why do we give to God?

In beginning this phrase with the words, *"Take heed,"* He is proclaiming the seriousness of the matter, as it is seen by God.

Sadly, many people give to get, while others give, as here stated, to be seen. Paul said we should give to God, *"to prove the sincerity of our love"* (II Cor. 8:8).

The phrase, *"Otherwise ye have no reward of your Father which is in Heaven,"* means that an awful lot of Believers will not be rewarded by the Lord for their giving, and, in Truth, it is not even looked at as giving by the Lord. If it is given in the wrong spirit and attitude, it is counted by the Lord as nothing at all!

If these stipulations are to be followed, as they certainly must be, this means that only a tiny percentage of money given to that which purports to be of God, is actually recognized by Him as such. Let's look at that which God will not honor or recognize as true giving to His Work:

1. Giving to that which is a lie or a sham, and no matter how much the lie is believed, is not honored by God as true giving. The Believer should have more discernment than that.

Some time back, I looked at a structure built at a cost of between $10,000,000 and $20,000,000, which was used not at all, and for all basic purposes was setting empty. And yet, multiple tens of thousands of people had given sums of money, to build this structure because they were told the work carried on within its confines would facilitate the taking of the Gospel to the world.

It was a money-raising ploy pure and simple, and it succeeded very well. Without a doubt, two or three times the amount needed was actually raised, with virtually all of it being wasted. Regrettably, tens of millions of dollars each year, if not more, go into such grandiose projects, which serve no purpose at all, but are merely fund-raising schemes, but believed by the people to be a genuine Work of God. As stated, True Christians would have better discernment, but, sadly, there aren't many True Christians!

Irrespective as to how sincere people may be in the giving of money to such projects, still, it is a scam pure and simple, and cannot be honored by God. It is simply a bad investment regarding that which proposes to the Work of God, but, in reality, is not!

2. Money given to propagate false doctrine certainly cannot be concluded as one truly giving to the Work of God. In effect, all erroneous doctrines are initially instigated by Demon Spirits. Consequently, no matter how sincere the individuals may be in their giving to such error, still, it is not of God, and cannot be blessed by God. In effect, such giving aids and abets the work of Satan. Tragically, this includes the far greater majority of that which is labeled "Christianity."

This does not mean that all True, Godly Preachers have all the light on all Biblical subjects, for such certainly is not the case. However, we are speaking of obvious false doctrine, which is contrary to Scripture, and is error plain and simple, and no matter how sincerely believed.

I hardly think that God would have honored the giving to the false teachers at Corinth who were preaching *"another Jesus,"* and by *"another Spirit,"* which constituted *"another Gospel"*

NOTES

(II Cor. 11:4). And yet, this one verse of Scripture in II Corinthians constitutes most of modern Christianity.

3. As well, God will not bless the *"giving to get"* teaching. This constitutes much, if not all of the *"prosperity message."* It is a heady doctrine because it promises riches. Consequently, most Christians, who are shallow in the Lord, want to be rich. It is ironical that many Christians today are asking the Lord to make them rich, while the Lord is endeavoring to make them Christlike! As a result, they attain neither!

Regrettably, this which the Holy Spirit calls *"another Gospel,"* works about the same as the lottery, etc. The one out of several millions who hits the jackpot in the lottery is held up as the great example of instant riches. Likewise, and sadly, the occasional individual in Christianity who does get rich, and by his own ingenuity, is held up as the great example, which provides an allurement for all others.

To be sure, it certainly is Scripturally possible for God to make someone rich, as He has done in the past, and no doubt does occasionally at present. Nevertheless, and I will hasten to say it, those who involve themselves in the modern *"Prosperity Gospel,"* which breeds covetousness, are not blessed accordingly by the Lord. If, in fact, there are riches, it is by their own ingenuity, and not the Lord's.

Ultimately in this Passage on *"giving,"* the Lord plainly tells us what God will honor, and, consequently, bless!

(2) "THEREFORE WHEN THOU DOEST THINE ALMS, DO NOT SOUND A TRUMPET BEFORE THEE, AS THE HYPOCRITES DO IN THE SYNAGOGUES AND IN THE STREETS, THAT THEY MAY HAVE GLORY OF MEN. VERILY I SAY UNTO YOU, THEY HAVE THEIR REWARD."

The phrase, *"Therefore when thou doest thine alms,"* proclaims the necessity of giving, and in whatever capacity. Now the Lord tells us what not to do:

1. *"Do not sound a trumpet before thee":* The idea was taken from the Pharisees, who, for the most part, made a great show of their giving, so that all would know exactly as to who it came from, and how much was given, especially if it was a sum of notable size.

Consequently, that which was being done was but for one purpose, to be seen of men.

2. *"As the hypocrites do in the Synagogues and in the streets":* Therefore Jesus labels all who do such things as hypocrites. The word, *"hypocrite,"* refers to an actor who plays a part, but is really not the part. In other words, it was only *"play acting."*

3. *"That they may have glory of men":* Regrettably, so much of that which purports to be the Work of God is done for this very purpose.

4. *"They have their reward":* Consequently, don't expect anything from God, because what is done is not true giving, at least in the sense that He will reward.

(3) "BUT WHEN THOU DOEST ALMS, LET NOT THY LEFT HAND KNOW WHAT THY RIGHT HAND DOETH:"

Many people have attempted to take this Scripture literally, completely missing the intent and purpose of what Christ is saying. The idea is, simply, that one not give to receive glory from men.

For instance, many times in Church Services, the Holy Spirit will move upon individuals to give certain amounts of money, and to make it public what they are giving. Such, at times, is used by the Holy Spirit, which encourages others to give, and builds Faith.

While it certainly may be true that some people, even in these Holy Spirit-inspired circumstances, may be giving for self-glory, still, that is a problem with their own heart, and not with the method. In other words, the method is not wrong, only the heart of the individual.

As well, some have attempted to twist this Scripture to make it mean, that anyone who gave publicly was violating this Scripture, and, consequently, the Commands of Christ.

To do so, is to judge in a negative way the motives of every single individual who is giving, which, within itself, violates the Words of Christ to *"judge not"* (Mat. 7:1).

Jesus was not teaching that the giving of these individuals was wrong, or even necessarily the method in which they chose to give, but, instead, the purpose of their heart, which was to receive glory from men. That is what Christ is opposing.

(4) "THAT THINE ALMS MAY BE IN SECRET: AND THY FATHER WHICH SEETH IN SECRET HIMSELF SHALL REWARD THEE OPENLY."

The phrase, *"That thine alms may be in*

secret," simply means that from the heart it is done as unto the Lord.

This would go not only for the giving of money, but any and all work, labor, service, and effort expended for the cause of Christ. It must not be done for show, but, instead, for the Lord's eyes only.

The phrase, *"And thy Father which seeth in secret Himself,"* refers to the Lord Alone Who is to guide and direct one's actions, and because the person and all his goods actually belong to the Lord.

In this manner, the Spirit guides the destiny of all, while in the manner opposed by Christ, such is guided by the flesh, which can never be accepted by God.

The phrase, *"Shall reward thee openly,"* refers to what the Lord will do if we abide by His Word.

In other words, one can be rewarded by man or God, but not by both! If one wants the glory of men, one cannot have the Glory of God! And, conversely, if one has the Glory of God, he will not have the glory of men!

(5) "AND WHEN THOU PRAYEST, THOU SHALT NOT BE AS THE HYPOCRITES ARE: FOR THEY LOVE TO PRAY STANDING IN THE SYNAGOGUES AND IN THE CORNERS OF THE STREETS, THAT THEY MAY BE SEEN OF MEN. VERILY I SAY UNTO YOU, THEY HAVE THEIR REWARD."

As the Lord dealt with giving, which is very important in His sight, He now deals with prayer, which is likewise important.

In these Passages, we learn that those who make God's interest their own, are assured that He will make their interest His.

The phrase, *"And when thou prayest,"* assumes that True Christians, in fact, pray! Tragically, in the modern Church, it would probably be better stated, *"And if thou prayest?"*

Prayer is the most powerful force that a Believer can engage in, that is, if it is truly done in humility, and Scripturally. Shortly, the Lord will give the model prayer, which will embody, as we shall see, the very attitude and spiritual posture that all should strive for.

The phrase, *"Thou shalt not be as the hypocrites are,"* was, by and large, referring to the Pharisees.

The *"standing in the Synagogues,"* and *"in the corners of the street,"* did not mean that it was wrong to pray there, but, instead, that the Pharisees' love of praise made them choose these places specifically, *"that they may be seen of men."*

To be sure, such is a waste of time, and is the very opposite of the truly humble heart.

It is strange, the *"flesh"* while in the world, doesn't want anyone to know that it has any thoughts of God. However, once it gets in the Church, the same *"flesh"* desires that all know, see, and understand just how much their thoughts are on God. Consequently, the *"flesh"* in the Christian is far more deadly than in the unbeliever.

The phrase, *"Verily I say unto you, They have their reward,"* proclaims the foolishness of such action, and that God does not hear such prayers, at least to answer them, and, therefore, they are in vain.

(6) "BUT THOU, WHEN THOU PRAYEST, ENTER INTO THY CLOSET, AND WHEN THOU HAST SHUT THY DOOR, PRAY TO THY FATHER WHICH IS IN SECRET; AND THY FATHER WHICH SEETH IN SECRET SHALL REWARD THEE OPENLY."

The phrase, *"But thou, when thou prayest,"* now refers to the true manner of prayer, and that which God will honor and reward.

The phrase, *"Enter into thy closet, and when thou hast shut thy door,"* refers to secrecy and privacy respecting communion with the Lord, whether petitions asked, or consecration requested.

It does not mean that one is to literally enter into a closet, nor pray alone, but simply that our praying must not be to be heard of men, but rather of God.

The phrase, *"Pray to thy Father which is in secret,"* has reference to a very personal communion between the Lord and His Child.

In our prayer meetings conducted at Family Worship Center, there will be anywhere from 10 to 100 people all praying together, with some praying quietly and some not so quietly.

During these times, there are many things which I desire to say to the Lord, which I would rather others not know about, with others in a similar posture, no doubt!

While it is true that I desire others to pray with me, thereby agreeing with me, concerning many things, still, there are things which are very personal and private between me and the Lord, and, therefore, when I speak to Him about

these things, I do so only in my heart, or else in a manner that cannot be discerned by others. As is obvious, this phrase encourages such praying.

The phrase, *"And thy Father which seeth in secret shall reward thee openly,"* refers to a secret petition (at least, at times), receiving a public answer.

As well, in this Scripture we are plainly told that the Lord will answer prayer.

Respecting the *"answer to prayer,"* some Christians adhere to the practice of praying about a need very loudly so that others will hear it, which, in effect, is not to the Lord at all, as should be obvious.

Some time back, a dear brother whom I did not know, stopped by one of our nightly prayer meetings. He began to loudly petition the Lord that money would be forthcoming for him to repair his bus, or whatever! Of course, it was very obvious as to what he was doing, and, the only label that could be put on him, and all such like, would be *"hypocrite"* (6:2).

I don't remember exactly what happened after prayer meeting, but in some manner I remember telling him that he would be better off somewhere else.

(7) "BUT WHEN YE PRAY, USE NOT VAIN REPETITIONS, AS THE HEATHEN DO: FOR THEY THINK THAT THEY SHALL BE HEARD FOR THEIR MUCH SPEAKING."

The phrase, *"But when ye pray, use not vain repetitions,"* speaks to the practice of the Hindus, Roman Catholics, and others, who believe that by repeating the same prayer hundreds of times, *"they shall be heard for their much speaking."*

Regrettably, the Jews at this time, and especially the Pharisees, were coming perilously close to the heathen by their use of certain phrases over and over again, which constituted *"vain repetition."*

Such is not a prayer from the heart, but is rather a formula, or doing something by *"rote,"* which seems to think that the act itself carries some type of spiritual power. The Moslems pray five times a day; however, it is not prayer heard by God, as is here plainly stated!

The Lord uses the words, *"They think,"* and respecting their being heard, which in effect says, as well, that they are not heard!

(8) "BE NOT YE THEREFORE LIKE UNTO THEM: FOR YOUR FATHER KNOWETH

WHAT THINGS YE HAVE NEED OF, BEFORE YE ASK HIM."

Three things are said in this verse:

1. *"Be not ye therefore like unto them"*: First of all, True Prayer to the Lord is not the easiest task there is. Therefore, when we pray, we surely should desire that we obey the Lord, and guarantee that our prayers be heard. To do otherwise, is a fruitless exercise!

2. *"For your Father knoweth what things ye have need of"*: This phrase is meant to extol the Omniscience of God. He knows all things, and irrespective of what it might be, and does not have to be stirred to action by *"vain repetition."* Actually, many Godly people pray and say very little, at least as far as the mouth is concerned. However, what little is said, comes from the heart, and is greatly honored by God.

3. *"Before ye ask Him"*: The idea is that God is not lacking in knowledge, in that we have to remind Him of what is needed. Actually, and as plainly stated, He already knows.

Consequently, many would ask if, in fact, that is the case, why should we need to pray at all?

First of all, prayer is not just petition. It includes worship, communion, fellowship, and consecration. It involves far more than just asking the Lord for something.

In Truth, many times the Believer will pray for long periods of time, and ask the Lord for very little, if anything! The time will be spent in worshiping the Lord, which He justly deserves, and which strengthens us greatly.

That should not seem so strange. The ties between a parent and his child are strengthened greatly, when the child tenderly and kindly tells the parent how much he is loved. God is a Person, He is not a machine. And as such, He has feelings exactly as we have, although to a different degree. As such, He wants communion between His Children and Himself. While prayer is not the only way such can be done, still, it is a way, and, without a doubt, one of the most important ways.

As well, He desires that we *"ask Him"* respecting our petitions, and irrespective of His previous knowledge. Such builds Faith, Trust, and Responsibility.

(9) "AFTER THIS MANNER, THEREFORE, PRAY YE: OUR FATHER WHICH ART IN HEAVEN, HALLOWED BE THY NAME."

Now we come to that which is commonly

NOTES

referred to as *"The Lord's Prayer."* It contains seven petitions — three respecting God, and four respecting man. Those respecting God come first.

This prayer is also recorded in Luke, although in a shortened version. Consequently, controversy has raged as to the original version.

Inasmuch as Matthew was written first, no doubt, the Holy Spirit superintended the entirety of the version in this Gospel, with a slightly abbreviated form in Luke's Gospel.

The phrase, *"After this manner, therefore pray ye,"* is meant to be in total contrast to the heathen practice. As well, in picking up on the previous verse, it is to be prayed in full confidence, that the Father will hear and answer according to His Will.

To hopefully help us understand this prayer a little better, I am going to address it in sections.

1. "OUR FATHER WHICH ART IN HEAVEN": The first two words, *"Our Father,"* destroy the doctrine of a false humility that teaches that in prayer the suppliant should take up a position as far from God as possible, addressing Him by many august titles, and that only after a very lengthened prayer the term *"Father"* may be used with much timidity. But to be timid when God commands boldness is to be disobedient (Heb. 4:16).

First of all, for Jesus to address Jehovah as *"Father,"* and to instruct His followers to do so, was completely revolutionary to the Jews. In their false humility, they would never have assumed such familiarity.

The main reason was that few really knew Him! Therefore, only His Children can address Him accordingly.

As well, this in no way promotes the unscriptural doctrine of the *"Fatherhood of God, and the brotherhood of man,"* which teaches that God is the Father of all, and that all men are brothers.

While it may sound good to the carnal ear, it is totally untrue. God is the Father only of those who have accepted Him as Lord and Saviour, and, consequently, have become His Children. Otherwise, all men are *"sons of Adam,"* and not *"sons of God"* (Gen. 5:3).

Also, even though God is everywhere, and, therefore, Omnipresent, still, His Spirit Body occupies His Throne in Heaven.

As well, Heaven is a place, and not just the endless stretch of the universe, etc.

Heaven, as described in the Word of God, has cities which have streets, walls, rivers, plants, etc., along with people and Angels, with a Government and society (Rev. Chpts. 4-8, 12, 14-16, 19, 21-22).

Some people object to the statement that God has a Spirit Body. We know He does not have a flesh, blood and bone body, even though the Scripture mentions Him having a head, hands, eyes, etc., therefore, we must conclude that He has some type of Spirit Body (Job 11:5; Dan. 7:9; Rev. 4:2-3).

All the statements in the Bible concerning God, recognizes Him to be a Person, not some invisible nothingness floating around everywhere filling all matter and space.

Even though the Bible teaches the Omnipresence of God, it does not teach the Omnibody of God, in other words, that His Body (Spirit Body), is in many different places at the same time.

When God appeared to Abraham in His Spirit Body, even though His Presence was still in Heaven, as well as everywhere else, still, His Body was in front of Abraham, and, at least at that time, no place else (Gen. 18:1).

Some object to these statements, claiming that such descriptions as given by the Bible regarding the bodily appearances of God, plus body parts such as *"eyes, ears, hands,"* etc., are but anthropomorphic, meaning *"human parts ascribed to God, which He really does not have, but given so that we may understand Him better."*

If that is true, that puts the Holy Spirit, Who superintended the writing of the Bible in the position of encouraging lies. Of course, we know that is untrue!

Therefore, why not simply believe what the Bible says about God, which means to *"rightly divide the Word of Truth,"* which means, among other things, to compare Scripture with Scripture. The Bible never contradicts itself, and neither does it say that things are, when they really aren't!

So, when people pray to God the Father, they are not praying to some disembodied spirit floating around in space, but, instead, to a person, with attributes, feelings, passions, likes and desires. But yet, One Who is Omniscient

NOTES

(All-knowing), Omnipotent (All-powerful), Omnipresent (Everywhere).

As well, He is uncaused, unformed, unmade, and, in fact, has always existed (Isa. 40:12-15; 45:5-7).

2. "HALLOWED BE THY NAME": After addressing the Heavenly Father, immediately the praise and worship begin.

Here we are told how important the *"Name"* of God actually is. He went under many names in the Old Testament in order to express His personality, and, above all, that which He meant to be to His people. The following are some of His Names:

A. *"Elohim":* This is the plural of *"Eloah,"* and means *"Gods."*

This Name indicates the relation of God to man as Creator, and is in contrast with *"Jehovah"* which indicates Him in Covenant relationship with creation. As well, it speaks of Him as an object of worship (Gen. 1:1; 2:3).

This Name is used 2,701 times in the Old Testament.

B. *"Yehovah":* (Jehovah). This Name is used 6,437 times in the Old Testament, and means the Self-existent or Eternal One; Lord. It was the Jewish national Name of God.

Where translated God, it is used with another Name, *"Adonai, Lord. Adonai-Jehovah, Lord God"* (Gen. 15:2, 8; Deut. 3:24; 9:26; Josh. 7:7).

C. *"El":* This means Strength. *"El"* is the Strong and Mighty One; the Almighty; the Most High God (Gen. 14:18-22; 16:13; 17:1).

This is used 220 times in the Old Testament.

D. *"Eloah":* This means Deity; God, the Divine One (Deut. 32:15, 17; II Chron. 32:15; Neh. 9:17).

This Name is used 56 times in the Old Testament.

E. *"Elah":* This simply means *"God"* (Ezra 4:24; 5:1-17; 6:3-18; 7:12-27; Dan. 2:11-47).

F. *"Tsur":* This means *"Rock"* or *"Refuge"* (Isa. 44:8).

G. *"Theos":* This is the main Greek word for *"God"* in the New Testament, and means *"Deity; the Supreme God"* (Mat. 1:23; 3:9, 16; 4:3-10). As well, this word *"Theos"* is used in various combinations.)

H. *"Jehovah-Jireh":* The Lord will provide (Gen. 22:8-14).

I. *"Jehovah-Nissi":* The Lord our Banner (Ex. 17:15).

J. *"Jehovah-Ropheka":* The Lord our Healer (Ex. 15:26).

K. *"Jehovah-Shalom":* The Lord our Peace (Jud. 6:24).

L. *"Jehovah-Tsidkeenu":* The Lord our Righteousness (Jer. 23:6; 33:16).

M. *"Jehovah-Mekaddishkem":* The Lord our Sanctifier (Ex. 31:13; Lev. 20:8; 21:8).

N. *"Jehovah-Saboath":* The Lord of Hosts (I Sam. 1:3).

O. *"Jehovah-Shammah":* The Lord is present (Ezek. 48:35).

P. *"Jehovah-Elyon":* The Lord Most High (Ps. 7:17; 47:2; 97:9).

Q. *"Jehovah-Rohi":* The Lord my Shepherd (Ps. 23:1).

R. *"Jehovah-Hoseenu":* The Lord our Maker (Ps. 95:6).

S. *"Jehovah-Eloheenu":* The Lord our God (Ps. 99:5, 8-9).

T. *"Jehovah-Eloheka":* The Lord thy God (Ex. 20:2, 5, 7).

U. *"Jehovah-Elohay":* The Lord my God (Zech. 14:5).

V. *"Jesus":* His Name given in the Incarnation, and means *"Saviour."*

Of all His Names, this is, without a doubt, His greatest (Mat. 1:21).

All the Names in the Old Testament under which God expressed Himself were designed but for one purpose, and that was to lead up to His Name, as Saviour. For that was His purpose from the very beginning — to redeem mankind. As well, it could only be done under the Name *"Jesus"* (Joshua in the Hebrew).

As such, we worship Him, and, in actuality, worship Him through His Name, which expresses more than anything else Who He is, and what He has done for us.

As Fanny Crosby wrote so long ago:

"To God be the glory great things He hath done,

"So loved He the world that He gave us His Son,

"Who yielded His life an atonement for sin,

"And opened the life gate that all may go in."

"Oh perfect Redemption, the purchase of Blood!

"To every Believer the Promise of God;

"The vilest offender who truly believes,

"That moment from Jesus a pardon receives."

"Great things He hath taught us, great things He hath done,

"And great our rejoicing thro' Jesus the Son;

"But purer and higher and greater will be,

"Our wonder, our transport, when Jesus we see."

CHORUS:

"Praise the Lord, praise the Lord, let the earth hear His Voice!

"Praise the Lord, praise the Lord, let the people rejoice!

"Oh come to the Father thro' Jesus the Son,

"And give Him the glory great things He hath done."

3. (Vs. 10) "THY KINGDOM COME": After offering the Lord praise and worship, which should begin our supplication before Him, and especially considering that the Psalmist also said, *"Enter into His gates with thanksgiving, and into His courts with praise"* (Ps. 100:4), our next concern should be for the entrance of the Kingdom of God on earth. The suffering and heartache which have invaded this world due to Satan and the Fall of man, must be healed!

As far as is known, God's Kingdom now reigns supreme throughout His entire creation, with the exception of Satan, his fallen angels, and planet earth. Jesus came that this might be rectified, and, to be sure, it ultimately will.

The coming of the Kingdom of God to this earth, will dispel all sin, wickedness, and iniquity, which cause all heartache, pain, sickness, suffering, and death. When His Kingdom is firmly established, which it soon shall be, then *"this corruptible shall have put on incorruption, and this mortal shall have put on immortality, then shall be brought to pass the saying that is written, Death is swallowed up in victory"* (I Cor. 15:54).

Since the Fall in the Garden of Eden, man has constantly attempted to reestablish Paradise, without the Tree of Life, i.e., Jesus Christ. He has ever failed, as fail he must!

And now, and even more regrettably, a great segment of the modern Church is promoting the *"political message,"* which, in effect, teaches that the Church will Christianize society in all the nations of the world, and, consequently, usher in the Kingdom. Such sounds good only to the carnal ear. In Truth, this teaching is not found in the Bible, and is, in fact, the opposite of the teaching of Scripture.

To be sure, such is going to be brought about, but not by a gradual process as society is gradually Christianized, but, instead, cataclysmically, with the Second Coming of Christ (Rev. 19).

Through the dream that God gave to Nebuchadnezzar, and with Daniel interpreting it, we know that this world's evil society is going to be smitten by *"The Stone,"* which comes from Heaven, Who is Christ (Dan. 2:34, 45).

4. "THY WILL BE DONE IN EARTH, AS IT IS IN HEAVEN": It should be obvious that the Will of God is not being done on earth presently, as it is in Heaven.

It is not the Will of God for all the sin which causes all heartache, pain and suffering. Neither is it His Will for sickness to ravage the human frame. Neither is death His Will, as we have already stated.

In Truth, almost nothing that is done in the world, or the Church for that matter, is His Will. While it is true that some few attempt to carry out His Will, and with all their strength, still, that number is small.

There are several things about the Will of God which are supposed to become a part of the Christian experience.

THE WILL OF GOD

Every Believer should want, desire, and ardently seek the Will of God in all things; however, if the Word of Lord has already promised us something in His Word, then it's not proper for us to ask for those things and then close our prayer by saying, *"If it be Your Will."* He already has told us in His Word exactly what His Will is. For us to add *"if"* to our prayer in this regard means we actually are questioning the Word of God, which no Believer desires to do.

Christ prayed for the Will of God to be done, in totality and by all individuals, on Earth. One day very soon that prayer will be answered. It will be during the coming Kingdom Age!

One day, and soon, this prayer of Christ, that

we are to constantly pray as well, shall be answered. Of that one can be sure!

5. (Vs. 11) "GIVE US THIS DAY OUR DAILY BREAD": This is a petition for both natural bread, and Spiritual Bread, Who is Christ. Notice it says *"daily"* which applies to both types of bread.

Many Christians, having accepted Christ as their Saviour, leave Him there, foregoing that which He desires to be to us each and every day. An example is the Manna which was given in the Old Testament, and was a type of Christ (Ex. 16).

In the giving of the Manna, it was on a daily basis, with the exception of the Sabbath. Regarding that, twice as much was given on Friday in order to sustain the Sabbath.

The Lord could have given the Manna any way He desired, but He chose to do it in this manner, because it was a type of Christ, Who is needed on a daily basis in our lives.

As well, if much Manna was gathered, with the idea in mind, that one would not have to gather it the next day, it would breed worms and stink. Consequently, the importance of the *"daily"* sustenance was magnified each day (Ex. 16:13-36).

Many Christians are attempting to live on Manna received yesterday, or even many days before. Then they wonder why there are problems in their lives. Jesus, on a daily basis, will lessen such, or, else, give strength to overcome.

In this petition, the natural bread is held up as a necessity, as is obvious, and portrays God as the Divine Benefactor Who provides such for His Believing Children. Consequently, whatever is needed should be asked for, and on a daily basis.

6. (Vs. 12) "AND FORGIVE US OUR DEBTS, AS WE FORGIVE OUR DEBTORS": The word, *"debts,"* does not refer to money that is owed, but, instead, to trespasses or sins.

First of all, this statement by Christ, *"Forgive us our debts,"* i.e., trespasses, denigrates the false teaching of sinless perfection, and despite our great struggles to attain this lofty goal. To be sure, that day will come, when *"corruption will put on incorruption,"* but until then, the struggle between the flesh and the spirit continues.

Actually, the Christian, and despite his best efforts, is continually *"coming short of the Glory of God"* (Rom. 3:23). Consequently, as we daily ask Him for *"bread,"* we are, as well, to ask Him for *"forgiveness."*

However, as is plainly obvious, His forgiving us is tied to our forgiving others their trespasses against us, and whether they ask or not.

To be sure, the only type of forgiveness that Christ will recognize, is the same type of forgiveness that He gives us.

THREE DIFFERENT GREEK WORDS FOR FORGIVENESS

The first Greek word is *"Charizomai,"* and means *"to be gracious"* or *"to give freely."* It is used in the sense of *"forgive"* (II Cor. 2:7, 10; 12:13; Eph. 4:32; Col. 2:13; 3:13).

The word is also used in regard to canceling a debt, as Christ here uses it, a concept analogous to forgiving a sin (Lk. 7:42-43).

Paul not only urged the Church at Corinth to be gracious to a repentant who had sinned seriously (II Cor. 2:7-10); he also insisted that the Believers in every Church show the same compassion to each other that God had shown in forgiving them: *"Bear with each other and forgive whatever grievances you may have against one another. Forgive as the Lord forgave you"* (Eph. 4:32; Col. 2:13; 3:13).

Another Greek word is *"Aphiemi,"* and is used in the sense of forgiveness of sins, of debts, and of crimes. However, the meaning is extended to convey more than mere forgiveness, but means to dismiss, release, leave, or abandon the claim against one.

Divine Forgiveness does not overlook sin or dismiss it lightly, rather, forgiveness is an act of God by which He deals, not only with our guilt, but with sins themselves. In forgiveness, God removes the sins and makes the guilt moot. No wonder the teachers of the Law objected when Jesus said to a paralytic, *"Your sins are forgiven"* (Mk. 2:5). The offended onlookers thought angrily, *"Who can forgive sin but God Alone?"* However, He could do so because He was God. (Mk. 2:7)

You and I may be compassionate to another who falls, but we cannot remit his sins. However, God not only forgives sins, but, as well, remits or cancels them, as if they never happened.

"Aphesis," is another Greek word which speaks of remission of sins (Mat. 26:28; Mk. 1:4; 3:29; Lk. 1:77; 3:3; 24:47; Acts 2:38; 5:31; 10:43;

NOTES

13:38; 26:18; Eph. 1:7; Col. 1:14; Heb. 9:22; 10:18).

It also is rendered *"freedom"* and *"release"* (Lk. 4:18).

The preaching of the Early Church always linked forgiveness with Jesus. He Alone is able to *"give repentance and forgiveness of sins to Israel"* and all others (Acts 5:31).

The Death and Resurrection of Jesus put the Promises of the Old Testament Prophets in perspective, for *"All the Prophets testify about Him that everyone who believes in Him receives forgiveness of sins through His Name"* (Acts 10:43).

Paul specifically links forgiveness with the Death of Christ. He announces it twice in rather similar terms: *"We have redemption through His Blood, the forgiveness of sin, in accordance with the riches of God's Grace"* (Eph. 1:7; Col. 1:14).

GOD'S FORGIVENESS IN THE NEW TESTAMENT

Both Testaments extend the promise of forgiveness to the human race. In the Old Testament, as well as the New, human beings are recognized as sinners in need of pardon. The Old Testament links God's Forgiveness with Sacrifices of Atonement.

The New Testament relates forgiveness to Jesus, specifically to His Sacrificial Death, to which the Sacrifices of the Old Testament pointed.

The basis on which God can forgive sin and remain righteous, has been provided by Jesus' Sacrifice of Himself as an Atonement in that ultimate Sacrifice to which Old Testament offerings, as we have stated, merely pointed. As Hebrews puts it, *"By one Sacrifice He has made perfect forever those who are being made holy"* (Heb. 10:14).

However, Jesus not only forgives sins, but also through His Death at Calvary, provided us with the possibility of a dynamic inner transformation. Jesus has done a perfecting work for us, to make us new and holy; it was not simply a remedial work, wiping out past sins.

Consequently, it is important when thinking of forgiveness, to realize that it is simply the doorway through which we pass into a new life. Jesus' Sacrifice did take away our sins. They are so completely gone that God no longer recalls them against those whom He has saved, for He says, *"Their sins and lawless acts I will remember no more"* (Heb. 10:17).

The Blood of Christ is the basis on which God can righteously provide the promised forgiveness (Rom. 3:25-26).

Christ's Atoning Death is also the basis for our continuing relationship with God (I Jn. 2:1-2). Sadly, all of us stumble and fall at times, as we journey in our new life toward Holiness. But even though we do, we have the promise of forgiveness for every sin. All anyone needs to do is confess sin; then God will forgive and the Holy Spirit will keep on working to cleanse from all unrighteousness (I Jn. 1:7-9).

FORGIVING ONE ANOTHER

The New Testament, as 6:12 emphasizes, places great stress on the importance of forgiving others.

In Matthew 18, Jesus tells three stories to illustrate forgiveness. He portrays human beings as sheep prone to go astray. When this happens, we are to seek the straying. We are to bring the straying home, bearing them in our arms, rejoicing. The image is of a forgiveness that frees us from bitterness or recrimination and provides a joy that is able to heal every hurt (Mat. 18:10-14).

Jesus then spoke of the hurts and sins that mar family relationships, whether Church or personal.

"If your brother sins against you," He began, and then He went on to explain that we are to take the initiative when we are hurt, and we should seek reconciliation. Peter recognized the difficulty of this teaching, and objected. He asked how often such hurts should be forgiven? Jesus answered, *"seventy times seven"*—a phrase indicating unlimited forgiveness (Mat. 18:15, 22).

Following this, Jesus told a parable about a servant with a debt equivalent to staggering sums of money (in modern terms and rates). When the servant could not pay and begged for time, the ruler to whom he owed the sum simply forgave the entire obligation.

But the same servant later demanded the minor amount a fellow servant owed him (equivalent to a few dollars). He actually went so far as to throw the fellow servant into prison for non-payment. Jesus' intention is clear: We who are forgiven an unimaginable debt by God, surely must be so moved by gratitude that we treat our fellowman as we have been treated.

NOTES

This theme — forgive as you are forgiven — is often stressed in the New Testament, and the theme has two applications.

First, God's treatment of us provides an example that we are to follow in our relationships with other persons. We are to be *"kind and compassionate to one another, forgiving one another, just as in Christ in God forgave us"* (Eph. 4:32).

The second application seems to introduce a conditional aspect to the promise of forgiveness. In Matthew 6:14-15 we read, and which we will comment on directly, *"For if you forgive men when they sin against you, your Heavenly Father will also forgive you. But if you do not forgive men their sins, your Father will not forgive your sins."*

In Mark 11:25, the thought is expressed this way: *"And when you stand praying, if you hold anything against anyone, forgive him, so that your Father in Heaven may forgive you your sin."*

Such Passages trouble many. Elsewhere in the Scriptures, forgiveness is spoken as something provided freely through Jesus. It is promised to all who come to Him. How can the Gospel offer and these warnings of Jesus both be true?

The best answer seems to lie in the way forgiveness affects our personality. Just as every coin has two sides, never only one, so forgiveness has two aspects that can never be separated. The two sides of forgiveness are accepting and extending.

The person who accepts forgiveness becomes deeply aware of his own weakness and need. Pride is ruled out as we take our place as supplicants before the Lord. This basic attitude releases us from our tendency to become angry with, or judgmental of, others. We begin to see others as creatures, who are, like us, flawed by weakness.

Rather than react with inflamed pride (He can't do this to me!), we are freed to respond as God does, with loving concern and forgiveness.

It isn't that God will not forgive the unforgiving, it is simply that the unforgiving lack the humble attitude that both permits them to accept forgiveness and frees them to extend forgiveness.

THAT WHICH HAPPENS TO THE BELIEVER UPON FORGIVENESS

One who accepts forgiveness adopts an attitude toward himself that transforms his or her attitude toward others. The person who accepts forgiveness becomes forgiving.

But there are other effects of forgiveness as well. Jesus once confronted a critical Pharisee who observed with contempt the tearful devotion a fallen woman had for Jesus. The Pharisee thought, *"If this man were a Prophet, He would know who is touching Him and what kind of woman she is"* (Lk. 7:39).

Jesus responded to the Pharisee's unexpressed thought. He told a story of two men in debt to a money lender. The one owed $50 and the other $500 (a dollar was equal to a day's wage). If the money lender should cancel the debts, Jesus asked, *"Which man would love him more?"* The Pharisee answered, *"I suppose the one who had the bigger debt canceled"* (Lk. 7:43).

Jesus then nodded toward the weeping woman and confirmed the principle. Her sins were many, but when she was forgiven, she knew the wonder of God's Gift of Love, and she responded with love.

As we meditate on God's Forgiveness and realize how much we have been forgiven, love for the Lord is nurtured in our hearts.
Hebrews develops yet another aspect of forgiveness. The writer compares the Sacrifice of Jesus with the Old Testament Sacrifices that prefigured Him.

Had the earlier Sacrifices had the power to make the worshipers perfect, they *"would have been cleansed once for all, and would no longer have felt guilty for their sins"* (Heb. 10:2).

But Jesus' Sacrifice does make us perfect, at least at the time of forgiveness! Through Jesus our sins are actually taken away! Thus the Believer who realizes that he is truly forgiven is released from a sense of guilt and from bondage to past mistakes. Because God has forgiven our sins (Heb. 10:17), we can forget our past. Forgiven, we can concentrate all our energies on living a Godly life.

(The thoughts on forgiveness were derived from the teaching of Lawrence O. Richards.)

7. (Vs. 13) "AND LEAD US NOT INTO TEMPTATION, BUT DELIVER US FROM EVIL": This Scripture has been misunderstood by many, thinking that God, at times, leads us into temptation. That is not the idea!

The word, *"temptation,"* actually means *"testing."*

NOTES

Peter boldly challenged testing and fell. The instructed child prays that he may not be tested.

The verb, *"To lead,"* is not the same word as 4:1, but, instead, suggests the leading of self-confidence.

The idea is; *"In my self-confidence, which stems from the flesh and not the Spirit, please do not allow me to be led into temptation, for I will surely fail!"*

The phrase, *"But deliver us from evil,"* actually says several things:

A. This is *"evil"* from the evil one himself, Satan, and is designed to destroy. It speaks of a cleverly designed trap put together by all the subtly of Satan, and is powerful indeed!

Nevertheless, the prior phrase, *"And lead us not into temptation,"* lets us know that God draws the parameters, exactly as He did for Job when Satan desired to do certain things to him (Job 1).

Satan no doubt desires many things against Believers, especially those who are doing him great damage; however, the Lord seldom, if ever, allows him unlimited latitude. Satan designs the temptation for our destruction, while the Lord allows it, at least up to a certain point, as a part of our spiritual growth. So, the prayer is that the Lord would allow only small parameters.

B. The word, *"deliver,"* is used, because it signifies a snare or trap set by the evil one, in which the individual, at least on his own, cannot extricate himself. Consequently, he must be *"delivered"* by the Power of God.

Regrettably, the modern Church, at least for the most part, knows little or nothing about *"deliverance."* There is a reason for that, as the next point will bring out.

C. These areas of *"testing"* or *"temptation"* fall into many and varied categories. Even though they may, and, in fact, do affect the domestical, physical, and financial, still, the source is spiritual. As such, it can only be addressed spiritually. Regrettably, the modern Church attempts to address these areas with psychology. Such is not possible!

In these situations, whether realizing it or not, one is dealing with demon spirits, or some other types of satanic minions of darkness. These *"powers,"* and powers they are, do not respond to man's machinations. They respond only to the *"Name of Jesus,"* and the *"Word of God."* However, in the modern Church, Freud has taken the place of Philemon, and Maslow has taken the place of Matthew, with Rogers taking the place of Romans. (These names, other than the Bible, are noted psychologists, whether dead or alive.)

8. "FOR THINE IS THE KINGDOM, AND THE POWER, AND THE GLORY, FOR EVER. AMEN.": The idea is that the Kingdom does not belong to the evil one, but, instead, to the Lord. In fact, Satan is a usurper, attempting to destroy the Kingdom which belongs to God. As a result, he has attempted to take the *"Power,"* and the *"Glory."* However, as the *"Kingdom,"* belongs to God, as well, the *"Power,"* and *"Glory,"* belong to Him.

The word, *"forever,"* means that this will never change, and despite Satan's attempts, and, in effect, predicts Satan's ultimate doom.

And then added to the word, *"forever,"* a double guarantee is given by the added word, *"Amen,"* which means, *"to express a solemn ratification."* In other words, in the Mind of God, the defeat and destruction of Satan, and, therefore, all evil in the world, is a foregone conclusion. As someone has said, *"I have read the last page in the Bible, and we win!"*

So, as one theologian of the past said, *"Inasmuch as this last phrase has guaranteed the whole of the prayer, it could be translated accordingly."*

"Hallowed be the Name of our God. His Kingdom has come; His Will is done. He has forgiven us our sins. He has brought our temptation to an end; He has delivered us from the evil one. His is the Kingdom and the Power and the Glory forever. Amen."

(14) "FOR IF YE FORGIVE MEN THEIR TRESPASSES, YOUR HEAVENLY FATHER WILL ALSO FORGIVE YOU."

The foundation of forgiveness, and as stated, is that of Ephesians 4:32, *"And be ye kind one to another, tenderhearted, forgiving one another, even as God for Christ's sake hath forgiven you."*

Its super-structure is that of verses 14 and 15. If the super-structure is not visible, its invisibility declares the absence of the foundation, for those who have truly experienced the forgiveness of their sins for Christ's sake do forgive those who sin against them, or else they stand in

NOTES

danger of losing their soul.

Inasmuch as the matter of forgiveness is so important, the Lord once again addresses Himself to the part of the Lord's Prayer which spoke of forgiveness. As well, He uses the word, *"trespasses,"* which speaks of even the largest sins, and not just small matters. The idea is this:

As God has forgiven us, we are to forgive others. The doing so shows that we fully understand just how much He has forgiven us, and of serious matters. If one does not understand that, one is not truly saved, or else he has forgotten the pit from which he was digged (Ps. 40:2). If he does understand it, he will be quick to forgive others.

Regrettably, these two verses of Scripture (14 and 15) portray to us that many, if not most, who call themselves Christians, are not truly Believers.

What does it mean to truly forgive someone?

It means to forgive them exactly as God forgave you.

For instance, what type of forgiveness would it be, if the Lord said, *"I forgive you, but every so often I will bring up the wrongdoing you committed, holding it over your head, so that you will never forget it, and you will, therefore, be constantly reminded as to how undependable you really are!"*

In Truth, such a forgiveness would be no forgiveness at all. And yet, that is the type of forgiveness most Christians engage in.

Or, as another example, what type of forgiveness would it be, if the Lord said, *"I forgive you; however, I am going to put you on probation for a particular period of time, and if you come through that probationary period satisfactorily, I will review your situation again, determining if restoration is then possible!"*

In fact, what kind of forgiveness would that be?

Actually, it is no forgiveness at all, and yet, it is the type of forgiveness that most Religious Denominations engage in, and, therefore, their followers do the same.

Such breeds hypocrisy, self-righteousness, portraying a total departure from the Word of God. It is a travesty of Scriptural Grace, which excludes the very foundation of True Bible Christianity, which is Love, Mercy, and Compassion.

Forgiveness by and through Jesus Christ

means forgiveness arising from all that He is and all that He does.

Forgiveness rests totally on the Atoning Work of Christ, that is to say, it is an act of sheer Grace. Therefore, forgiveness is rooted in the Nature of God as gracious, and upon the fact of True Repentance, is always instantly given.

(15) "BUT IF YE FORGIVE NOT MEN THEIR TRESPASSES, NEITHER WILL YOUR FATHER FORGIVE YOUR TRESPASSES."

Perhaps a series of questions with answers hopefully provided, will shed more light on this all-important subject.

Questions: Are Christians to forgive people who have wronged them, when they do not ask for forgiveness, or even consider they have done anything wrong?

Answer: Yes! The forgiveness process is not only for the offender, but, as well, for the offended. The offended is to forgive, in order that ill feelings or a vengeful spirit not arise within his heart. As well, upon doing this, we are fulfilling Christ's Command to *"Love your enemies, bless them that curse you, do good to them that hate you, and pray for them which despitefully use you, and persecute you"* (5:44).

Question: What happens if a Believer refuses to forgive?

Answer: All fellowship and communion with the Lord comes to an abrupt conclusion. Upon refusing to forgive, consequently, the Lord immediately refuses His Forgiveness for us as well! This, as is obvious, means all sins that we commit remain against us, with no prayers being answered. It is a chilling prospect! Sadly, this involves far more Christians than one realizes.

Question: If a Believer continues in this posture of unforgiveness, will he ultimately lose his soul?

Answer: Yes! Matthew 18:15-17 tells us that such a person becomes *"an heathen to us."* If that is the case with the former Believer, it is the case with God as well!

However, this does not mean that we should discontinue loving the person, and praying for him. In fact, we must forgive even though fellowship is discontinued.

Question: How far should forgiveness be extended, in the case of something as serious as child molestation, etc.?

Answer: While forgiveness of such a one

certainly must be carried out, still, correct precautions must be taken until one is absolutely certain that the problem no longer exists.

In other words, if one were guilty of such a crime, and then asked for forgiveness, it must be given. However, one should not associate with that person until they are absolutely certain that the person has truly been delivered. Knowing the consequences of such actions, one surely would not desire their child, or themselves for that matter, to be placed in a situation where further acts of abuse could be carried out.

As well, the offender, that is, if truly repentant, will understand such matters, and would not at all blame the persons involved for such actions.

Question: If someone truly repents, thereby, asking for forgiveness, how should one conduct themselves toward that person?

Answer: Our attitude toward that person should be, and, in fact, must be, exactly as God's attitude toward them and us. We should conduct ourselves toward them as if nothing ever happened in an adverse manner, with the exception of some such like situation as addressed in the previous question. Even then, they should be treated with kindness and love, although with proper precautions taken.

Question: Would not a probationary period of time be proper?

Answer: If that were the case, everybody in the world would be on probation. No! There is nothing in Scripture that even remotely suggests such a thing. As we have previously stated, what if the Lord did us that way, when we go to Him asking for forgiveness? Once again, the type of forgiveness we are to offer to others, and without fail, is the type of forgiveness that God offers to us. No other type will be entertained or accepted by the Lord.

(Once again, there certainly should be a probationary period of time regarding offenses such as child molestation, etc., as we have mentioned!)

Question: What does it mean to forgive as God forgives?

Answer: The only type of forgiveness God will honor, is the type that looks upon the offender, who has properly repented, as if their sin was never committed. That is the way the Lord looks at us, and that is the way He demands that we look at others who truly repent.

While it may not be possible for us to truly forget, as the Lord does, still, if we properly understand how much the Lord has forgiven us, it will then become much easier to put it out of mind what the other individual has done.

When one considers that Christ again broached this subject of forgiveness, even after mentioning it in His *"prayer,"* then we begin to understand just how serious this matter really is. Every Believer should readily take it to heart!

(16) "MOREOVER WHEN YE FAST, BE NOT, AS THE HYPOCRITES, OF A SAD COUNTENANCE: FOR THEY DISFIGURE THEIR FACES, THAT THEY MAY APPEAR UNTO MEN TO FAST. VERILY I SAY UNTO YOU, THEY HAVE THEIR REWARD."

In verses 16-18, the Lord lays down some rudimentary instructions respecting *"fasting."* It, once again, goes to the heart of the matter, instead of the externals.

The phrase, *"Moreover when ye fast,"* sets no specific time. In other words, one should fast as they feel led of the Lord to do so, or as the Lord moves upon them to do so!

The phrase, *"Be not, as the hypocrites, of a sad countenance,"* in effect, addresses the Pharisees who made a big show of their fasting, in order to cause the people to think of them as very holy. Christ is saying that it doesn't matter what people think, but what God thinks!

As fasting was done by the Pharisees for *"show,"* so much in the religious realm falls into this category. It is done for *"show,"* whether it be fasting or giving, etc.

The phrase, *"For they disfigure their faces, that they may appear unto men to fast,"* portrays the actions of hypocrisy. In other words, they were playing a part as an actor, which was a cleverly designed charade. In Truth, the Lord didn't even enter the picture, with them carrying forth their religious activities in order to *"appear unto men!"*

How much presently in the realm of Christendom is done in order to impress men?

I think one would be shocked to realize that this problem is probably, as acute now, as then!

The phrase, *"Verily I say unto you, They have their reward,"* tells us exactly what the Lord thinks of their actions.

It should be quickly stated, that all things done in the realm of the spiritual, must be for

the Heavenly Father only, or else it is of no consequence.

(17) "BUT THOU, WHEN THOU FASTEST, ANOINT THINE HEAD, AND WASH THY FACE;"

The phrase, *"But thou,"* is meant to set apart those who are truly God's Children, in contrast to those who only profess to be, but actually aren't. In effect, the Lord is saying that the Pharisees, and all who follow in their train, are not His Children. Their so-called spirituality was, in effect, man-made religion, which would not, and, in fact, could not be accepted by God.

The phrase, *"When thou fastest,"* once again, places the frequency in the heart of the individual, and not according to some type of rules and regulations.

There was only one day of fasting each year that was commanded in the Law of Moses, and that was on the Great Day of Atonement. However, by the time of Christ, the Pharisees had ruled that two fast days a week should be carried out, and, in fact, if they were not carried out, the individuals were looked at as spiritually inferior. However, these two fast days a week, were strictly man devised and not God.

Men love to play God! And modern-day Christianity is rife with these little gods.

The phrase, *"Anoint thy head, and wash thy face,"* is meant to show the very opposite than that shown by the Pharisees. These two things, the *"anointing of the head,"* and *"washing of the face,"* were actually symbols of joy.

The *"anointing of the head,"* was to be with oil, and was, in effect, a symbol of the Holy Spirit. It meant, at least in this instance, to consecrate a person to God's service. It is taken from Psalms 23:5, *"Thou anointest my head with oil; my cup runneth over."*

(18) "THAT THOU APPEAR NOT UNTO MEN TO FAST, BUT UNTO THY FATHER WHICH IS IN SECRET: AND THY FATHER, WHICH SEETH IN SECRET, SHALL REWARD THEE OPENLY."

With this Passage, the Lord takes the spiritual activity of *"fasting"* completely out of the hands of the Pharisees, where it had been made of none effect, and placed it in its proper position as designed by the Holy Spirit.

They wanted to *"appear unto men to fast,"* while the Lord proclaims the very opposite.

It is to be done only to *"thy Father,"* and is to be done *"in secret."*

This is done in order to assuage spiritual pride, which had so occupied the Pharisees. Tragically, it occupies many today as well!

The phrase, *"And thy Father,"* is meant to imply that God was not the *"Father"* of the Pharisees, and will not be the *"Father"* of any who follow in their train. Therefore, one can follow man or follow God, but cannot follow both!

The phrase, *"Which seeth in secret, shall reward thee openly,"* refers to the *"Father,"* and what He will do for those who truly follow Him, instead of following man.

The Text, although it may appear to address itself only to *"fasting,"* rather extends itself to one of, if not the single most important thing in living for God, the following of man or the Lord!

Sadly, most of Christendom follows men, and if continuing to do so, will see their spirituality gradually, or even speedily degenerating into religion.

While Godly men are certainly to be respected, and, in a sense, followed, the individual must be versed enough in the Bible, that he will always know what is right and wrong, and will follow accordingly. Tragically, as with the Pharisees of old, many, if not most Christians, follow their Religious Denomination irrespective of its Scriptural direction. Such has led millions to hell, and such is leading millions astray at present!

(19) "LAY NOT UP FOR YOURSELVES TREASURES UPON EARTH, WHERE MOTH AND RUST DOTH CORRUPT, AND WHERE THIEVES BREAK THROUGH AND STEAL:"

If the eye be set upon treasures in Heaven, this single purpose will make the character and life simple and straight, and the Christian will shine for Jesus.

If the eye be set upon treasures on earth, the life and character of the Believer will be shrouded in moral darkness. A man's aim determines his character. If that aim be not simple and heavenward, but earthward and double, all the faculties and principles of his nature will become a mass of darkness. It is impossible to give a divided allegiance.

The phrase, *"Lay not up for yourselves treasures upon earth,"* concerns itself with far more than the giving of money to the Work of God. It concerns itself with the entirety of the

lifestyle, aims, and purposes of the Believer. Tragically, as the previous admonishing concerning fasting, this one is little heeded as well!

Upon proper obedience, the Lord will bless His Children respecting financial reward, and the things money can buy, and all other ways. Accordingly, it is not wrong for the Believer to comfortably provide for his family, etc. However, after that is done, and if the Lord has given the individual the ability to make large sums of money, his purpose should be for the spread of the Gospel around the world. As a good steward, he should minutely investigate where his money should go, thereby diligently seeking the Mind of the Lord in these all-important matters.

Even though his earthly business may be whatever, still, his heavenly business should be, and, in fact, must be priority.

Sadly, in the far greater majority of the cases, this is little true, and even with money given, most of the time it is given to worthless projects.

The phrase, *"Where moth and rust doth corrupt, and where thieves break through and steal,"* concerns itself with the *"treasures on earth."*

There is so much good that could be done for the Cause of Christ, with money placed in the proper hands, but most of the time *"moths"* eat it, and *"rust"* corrupts it, with *"thieves"* stealing the rest.

(20) "BUT LAY UP FOR YOURSELVES TREASURES IN HEAVEN, WHERE NEITHER MOTH NOR RUST DOTH CORRUPT, AND WHERE THIEVES DO NOT BREAK THROUGH AND STEAL:"

The phrase, *"But lay up for yourselves treasures in Heaven,"* is the direct opposite of *"laying up treasures on earth."*

What kind of *"treasures"* is the Lord speaking of?

He is speaking of anything that is truly done and carried out for the Work of God. Nothing small goes unnoticed, and nothing large fails to accomplish its purpose, that is, if it is given in the right spirit.

When men ask for an accounting, they are almost all of the time speaking of *"earthly treasures."* However, in this Passage, Jesus is asking for an accounting respecting *"heavenly treasures."*

It is easy to check up on *"earthly treasures"*

by looking at a financial statement. It is not so easy respecting *"heavenly treasures."*

There are many who cannot lay up *"earthly treasures,"* and, in fact, none should! However, all, and irrespective of their state or station in this present life, can lay up great amounts of *"heavenly treasures."*

All, and irrespective of whom they may be, can have an effective prayer life, which is probably the most powerful *"treasure"* of all. As well, all can be a daily witness.

As well, the giving of money falls under the category of *"all,"* simply because God doesn't judge us so much on how much we give, but, instead, how much we have left (Mk. 12:42).

As someone has said:

"It's not what you would do with a million, should riches ere be your lot,

"But what you're doing at present with the dollar and a quarter you got."

And yet, small amounts, though greatly honored by God, cannot usually perform great works for the Lord, due to the smallness of the amount. Therefore, for those whom the Lord has blessed with great business ability, must in turn bless the Work of God by using it accordingly.

(21) "FOR WHERE YOUR TREASURE IS, THERE WILL YOUR HEART BE ALSO."

With this Passage, the Lord is speaking to each person individually.

He speaks of *"your treasure,"* and asks where it is! Wherever it is, earth or Heaven, there the *"heart will be also!"*

This does not necessarily mean that one should sell everything they have and give it to the Work of God, but, instead, they should use the increase for God's Work.

Too many times, Christian businessmen continue to invest heavily, while giving the Lord a minimum, until eventually *"thieves,"* in one way or the other, cause it to be lost.

If the *"heart"* is where it truly ought to be, one will seek the Lord earnestly about any and all transactions, directions, and investments. If that is done, with a heart desired to carry out the Will of God, the Lord will lead and guide, with great benefit, not only for the Believer, but for the Work of God as well!

(22) "THE LIGHT OF THE BODY IS THE EYE: IF THEREFORE THINE EYE BE SINGLE, THY WHOLE BODY SHALL BE FULL OF LIGHT."

NOTES

The phrase, *"The light of the body is the eye,"* is used metaphorically, which is a figure of speech in which a work or phrase is used in place of another to suggest a likeness or analogy between them.

He is, in effect, saying that the light of the soul is the spirit.

The phrase, *"If therefore thine eye be single,"* means that the spirit of man should have but one purpose, and that is to glorify God. (The soul is the part of man that feels, Job 14:22, while the spirit is the part of man which knows, I Cor. 2:11.)

The phrase, *"Thy whole body shall be full of light,"* in effect says if the spirit of man is *"single"* in its devotion to God (meaning not divided), then all of the soul will be full of light.

(23) "BUT IF THINE EYE BE EVIL, THY WHOLE BODY SHALL BE FULL OF DARKNESS. IF THEREFORE THE LIGHT THAT IS IN THEE BE DARKNESS, HOW GREAT IS THAT DARKNESS!"

The phrase, *"But if thine eye be evil, thy whole body shall be full of darkness,"* in effect says, if the *"spirit be evil, the entirety of the soul will be full of darkness."*

The phrase, *"If therefore the light that is in thee be darkness, how great is that darkness,"* is a startling statement!

It means that even right or righteous things that come into such a person's spirit, and because of the darkness of their spirit, such Righteousness is turned to unrighteousness. Because their *"eye"* is evil, i.e., spirit is evil, everything about them is evil, even that which should be right.

In other words, when they hear the Word of God in any form, which is Light, because of their evil spirit, it is twisted and perverted to mean something, in fact, it does not mean!

This is the reason that appealing only to the intellect by the Preacher of the Gospel is a fruitless exercise. If the individual is unsaved, everything that goes to their intellect, which is a product of their spirit, is perverted, consequently, perverting the message. Therefore, the spirit of such a person must be seized by the Power of the Holy Spirit, which is done through the heart which is the seat of one's emotions, which, in effect, goes to the person's spirit through the soul. This is the reason that a spiritual experience most, if not all the time, involves the emotions. Probably one could say that it involves the emotions all of the time, even though, not all the time evident (Jer. 4:14).

So, when some modernist Preachers claim that it is only emotionalism when a person is moved upon by the Holy Spirit, with them reacting by weeping, etc., that Preacher simply does not know what he is talking about. He is portraying a lack of understanding as to how the Holy Spirit moves upon the individual. As stated, He does not deal with the intellect, even though the intellect is, in fact, greatly affected, but with the heart (Heb. 10:16).

In that manner, the darkened spirit of man can be liberated and set free. That is the reason that people can be saved without fully understanding, at least at the outset, what has happened to them. Their spirit, which is the seat of their will and intellect, has been moved upon greatly by the Holy Spirit, through the soul, with the emotions of the person affected, which allows the Holy Spirit to instantly drive away the darkness of the spirit. It is called *"born again,"* and instantly replaces the *"darkness"* with *"Light."*

Ideally, the Believer must continue in this mode, with the spirit (eye) *"single,"* i.e., undivided toward God in its devotion; however, too oftentimes the spirit, i.e., *"eye"* does not remain *"single,"* but, in fact, is allowed to become double in its devotion which occasions the next verse.

(24) "NO MAN CAN SERVE TWO MASTERS: FOR EITHER HE WILL HATE THE ONE, AND LOVE THE OTHER; OR ELSE HE WILL HOLD TO THE ONE, AND DESPISE THE OTHER. YE CANNOT SERVE GOD AND MAMMON."

The phrase, *"No man can serve two masters,"* has to do with the singleness of the spirit of man, which has now become double. In other words, he is attempting to serve God and the world at the same time. Actually, this is a conflict that rages constantly! Men attempt to hold onto God with one hand, while holding onto the world with the other. To be sure, one or the other will have to go.

The phrase, *"For either he will hate the one, and love the other; or else he will hold to the one and despise the other,"* portrays the ultimate conclusion of that man.

Regrettably, many, if not most, let go of God

instead of the world, while continuing to serve the Lord in Name only!

The phrase, *"Ye cannot serve God and mammon,"* is flat out stated as an impossibility.

So, it is total devotion to God, or ultimately it will be total devotion to the world. This is what Jesus was speaking of when He said, *"So then because thou art lukewarm, and neither cold nor hot, I will spew thee out of My Mouth"* (Rev. 3:16).

The word, *"mammon,"* as here used, refers to an egocentric covetousness which claims man's heart and thereby estranges him from God. When a man *"owns"* anything, in reality it owns him.

The word, *"mammon"* is derived from the Babylonian *"Mimma,"* which means *"anything at all."*

Consequently, it is not speaking only of money, but anything which would come in between a person and God.

(25) "THEREFORE I SAY UNTO YOU, TAKE NO THOUGHT FOR YOUR LIFE, WHAT YE SHALL EAT, OR WHAT YE SHALL DRINK; NOR YET FOR YOUR BODY, WHAT YE SHALL PUT ON. IS NOT THE LIFE MORE THAN MEAT, AND THE BODY THAN RAIMENT?"

The phrase, *"Therefore I say unto you,"* is meant to refer back to the previous statements concerning the *"laying up of treasures on earth."*

The phrase, *"Take no thought for your life,"* is strong indeed! It is meant to refer to what we *"eat,"* *"drink,"* and *"wear."* With the words, *"put on,"* and referring to the *"body,"* applying as well to the home we live in, as well as methods of transportation, along with education, etc., the entirety of the physical and material life is addressed.

No! This does not mean that individuals are not to seek gainful employment, or to seek growth for their business, thereby, expecting the Lord to do for them, what they should be doing for themselves. That is not the thought at all!

The idea is that one not spend their time consumed by worry and care respecting these things, which shows a lack of Trust and Faith in God.

As an aside, it is ironic that those who truly adhere to the *"Prosperity Gospel,"* think of little else, while Christ says to *"take no thought."*

Some time back, Frances and I were in a particular city visiting friends. In this city, about all, I suppose, of the Christian Television Channels are received, while in Baton Rouge, we receive very little of this type of programming.

If I remember correctly, I had the occasion to peruse four different Christian programs. Out of the four, three were extolling the *"Prosperity Message,"* consequently, telling people how to get rich, all in the Name of the Lord, etc. The remaining one seemed to be some type of Marriage Seminar, etc.

Of that which I say and heard, there was very little True Gospel actually preached or taught.

The Preachers and Teachers proclaiming the *"Prosperity Message,"* would, no doubt, claim to be preaching the Gospel. While it is certainly true that at least some of what they preach is Gospel; however, the emphasis and priority is all out of balance concerning the true need of man, which is to be saved and become Christlike.

An overemphasis on any subject, which means to place the emphasis contrary to the teaching of the Word of God, constitutes heresy. To explain it in the physical sense, it would refer to an ear on someone's head, which was six or seven times larger than the other ear. While it is an ear, still, it is no longer in proportion, and, consequently, constitutes a deformity.

The question, *"Is not the life more than meat, and the body than raiment?"*, places the priority where it rightly belongs.

Jesus is saying that one's *"life"* is far more than mere things, such as fine foods and beautiful clothes. Those things, in fact, are necessary, but only in their proper proportion.

The Lord is attempting to lead men away from these things, which are in fact necessary, but definitely not the most important. And yet, almost all the world centers up on *"things,"* while neglecting the far more significant purpose of life, which pertains to God and His Work.

It is understandable that the world would place the emphasis on *"things,"* but not so understandable, when that which purports to be the Gospel does the same thing. Then the *"eye"* (spirit) becomes double, while the body (soul) is filled with darkness!

Some time back, while Frances and I were in California, I happened to hear part of a Message over Television by a noted Preacher. He was

explaining the *"Blessing of Abraham,"* and very dogmatically stating that it had nothing to do with spiritual things, but concerned itself altogether with the financial. In other words, and as he said, the *"Blessing of Abraham"* was material riches.

I found myself standing in the middle of the floor, shouting at the Television set, and saying, *"No! That is untrue."*

Whether he knew it or not, he was denying the real purpose for which Christ came, which is the Salvation of man from sin. The *"Blessing of Abraham"* is *"Justification by Faith"* (Gen. 15:6; Gal. 3:14).

(26) "BEHOLD THE FOWLS OF THE AIR: FOR THEY SOW NOT, NEITHER DO THEY REAP, NOR GATHER INTO BARNS; YET YOUR HEAVENLY FATHER FEEDETH THEM. ARE YE NOT MUCH BETTER THAN THEY?"

In effect, and according to this Scripture, the great emphasis of the *"Prosperity Message"* on money, shows a lack of Faith, instead of the opposite, as constantly proclaimed!

The phrase, *"Behold the fowls of the air,"* is meant to draw attention to that which is, at least, a smaller part of God's great creation.

The phrase, *"For they sow not, neither do they reap, nor gather into barns,"* is meant to portray the absolute lack of that on which man spends much, if not most of his time.

Once again, the Lord is not demeaning honest industry, especially considering that the very *"image of God,"* calls for such, at least as far as man retains that image! It is the absolute priority on such to the exclusion of the true mission of man, which is to serve his Creator, that is commanded by the Lord.

The phrase, *"Yet your Heavenly Father feedeth them,"* proclaims an orderly system set up by the Creator in order that even the lowest forms of His creation would be provided for, which they are!

In effect, the Lord is saying, that if the Creator would do such with *"birds of the air,"* how much more would He see to the same needs of His highest creation?

The question, *"Are ye not much better than they?"*, proclaims man's true worth, and sets him apart from the animal kingdom, which completely debunks the foolishness of humanistic evolution.

Such is meant to portray trust that one should

have in God, and more than all, pertains to His Children. Actually, He is not speaking of mankind in general, even though some provision has been made for them, as is obvious, but, more particularly, to those who call Jesus, *"Lord."*

(27) "WHICH OF YOU BY TAKING THOUGHT CAN ADD ONE CUBIT UNTO HIS STATURE?"

Once again, He is teaching trust!

One is to be diligent, industrious, and energetic, respecting all efforts in this realm, and then leave the rest to God. To fret, worry, and live in anxiety, shows a lack of Faith, and constitutes sin (Rom. 14:23).

WORRY AND THE CROSS OF CHRIST

The problems of worry and excess concern have undoubtedly plagued every single Believer at one time or another; however, despite the fact that it has, and does, worry shows a lack of trust in the Lord, and it also shows a lack of love. If we trust the Lord as we ought to and love Him as we should, there will be no worry.

With most Christians, however, it is not so much that they doubt the Lord in these circumstances, but rather that they doubt themselves. In other words, we wonder if we have done something wrong, if we have made a false turn, etc., which would cause us difficulties and problems. When we have those thoughts, we tend to worry.

There is an answer for that!

It is impossible for any Believer to live a life of trust and obedience, a life free of worry and concern, unless such a Believer understands the Cross as it regards Sanctification. I don't care how many formulas Preachers may give you, or how many things they claim will give you the answer. Truthfully, there is only one answer. I speak of the Believer placing his Faith exclusively in Christ and the Cross, and not allowing it to be moved to something else (Rom. 6:1-14).

Only then can the Believer think upon the things he should think upon (Phil. 4:4-8).

I personally know what it is try to live this Christian experience and not understand the Cross as it regards Sanctification. I recall those days, but not with gladness. How many nights did I lay awake, hour upon hour, plagued with care and concern, and all because I did not understand fully what Christ had done for me at the Cross!

Being on this side of the fence now, and I

NOTES

speak of the side of the Cross of Christ as it refers to our Sanctification (actually every single thing we receive from the Lord), there is no worry or fear. The Believer cannot fully trust the Lord and cannot fully love the Lord unless such a Believer understands the Cross of Christ as it refers to Sanctification. The Cross is God's solution to all problems. The Cross is His only solution!

(28) "AND WHY TAKE YE THOUGHT FOR RAIMENT? CONSIDER THE LILIES OF THE FIELD, HOW THEY GROW; THEY TOIL NOT, NEITHER DO THEY SPIN:"

Once again, the Lord uses a metaphor to describe that which He is teaching. He asks this question, *"And why take ye thought for raiment?"*, simply meaning that worry and anxiety will never produce any. The idea is to trust God, which He further explains!

The phrase, *"Consider the lilies of the field, how they grow,"* is meant to point to a system that God has devised to ensure its growth and beauty.

The phrase, *"They toil not, neither do they spin,"* is meant to state that their beauty has nothing to do with their effort, but is given completely by the Creator.

The emphasis is strong, that the Lord will do the same for His Children, and without anxiety, worry, or fear.

We continue to emphasize that this only pertains to God's Children, which are truly born again, and not mankind in general.

(29) "AND YET I SAY UNTO YOU, THAT EVEN SOLOMON IN ALL HIS GLORY WAS NOT ARRAYED LIKE ONE OF THESE."

The phrase, *"And yet I say unto you,"* is meant to draw attention to the fact that He is removing His statements from the hypothesis of the Pharisees.

The phrase, *"That even Solomon in all his glory was not arrayed like one of these,"* uses this King as the epitome of glory, which he was!

In other words, Solomon, and with all the money and wisdom in the world, could not make himself as beautiful as a lowly *"lily."*

It is said that the lilies of Israel had brilliant coloring, and especially the purple and white Huleh lily found near Nazareth.

(30) "WHEREFORE, IF GOD SO CLOTHE THE GRASS OF THE FIELD, WHICH TO DAY IS, AND TOMORROW IS CAST INTO THE OVEN, SHALL HE NOT MUCH MORE

CLOTHE YOU, O YE OF LITTLE FAITH?"

Instead of *"if,"* the word, *"since,"* should be inserted in the phrase, *"Wherefore, since God so clothes the grass of the field,"* is meant to portray God's guarantee.

The phrase, *"Which to day is, and tomorrow is cast into the oven,"* portrays how inconsequential this part of His creation, and yet, how much care He expends on it.

In Israel in those days, the baker's furnace was heated, at times, with grass for fuel.

The question, *"Shall He not much more clothe you, O ye of little Faith?",* is meant to proclaim God's much greater care over His Children.

We are here told the reason for our lack, which is *"little Faith."*

One of the Hebrew words to describe *"Faith"* or *"Faithfulness,"* is *"Munah,"* and means *"firmness, steadiness, and fidelity."* The Old Testament often uses this word as an attribute of God, to express the total dependability of His Character or Promises.

Its first use in describing the Lord is found in Deuteronomy 32:4, *"He is the Rock, His Works are perfect, and all His Ways are just. A Faithful God Who does no wrong. Upright and just is He."*

Many other Passages apply this great Old Testament term to God, or to His Words and Works (I Sam. 26:23; Ps. 33:4; 36:5; 40:10; 88:11; 89:1-2, 5, 8, 24, 33, 49; 92:2; 98:3; 100:5; 110:75, 86, 90, 138; 143:1; Isa. 11:5; 25:1; Lam. 3:23; Hos. 2:20).

The Greek word for *"Faith"* or *"Faithful"* is *"Pistos,"* and means *"trusting, and believing."* It can also be translated *"trustworthy, reliable, faithful."*

It meant that we can trust God to remain faithful to His Commitments. As well, and in view of the fact that God entrusts so much to us, we are to use our opportunities to show loyalty to Him, and, above all, not doubt Him.

Because God is faithful, He can be trusted fully to completely carry out His Commitments to us in Christ (I Cor. 1:9; 10:13; II Cor. 1:18; I Thess. 5:24; II Thess. 3:3; II Tim. 2:13; Heb. 2:17; 10:23; 11:11; I Pet. 4:19; I Jn. 1:9; Rev. 1:5; 3:14; 19:11).

(31) "THEREFORE TAKE NO THOUGHT, SAYING, WHAT SHALL WE EAT? OR, WHAT SHALL WE DRINK? OR, WHEREWITHAL SHALL WE BE CLOTHED?"

The phrase, *"Therefore take no thought,"*

NOTES

means simply to not worry about it in the least!

This verse is similar to verse 25, but yet with a difference.

The *"take no thought for your life"* in verse 25, concerns a state of anxiety, where this statement in verse 31 actually means that even one anxious thought is forbidden.

So He is saying, to have even one single thought regarding *"What we shall eat,"* or *"What we shall drink,"* or *"How we shall be clothed,"* is a waste of time, and is actually forbidden by the Lord.

In view of the fact that He spends so much time in this one area, shows us that the problem is acute, even among God's Children.

Once again, allow us to emphasize the fact that He is not meaning that we take a cavalier attitude toward such things, but that we should do our very best in these areas, and then trust God for the results.

Some who are indolent have erroneously thought that in view of these Passages, they do not have to work, etc. However, this is not, and as stated, the meaning by the Lord at all, for He also says, *"That if any would not work, neither should he eat"* (II Thess 3:10).

(32) "(FOR AFTER ALL THESE THINGS DO THE GENTILES SEEK:) FOR YOUR HEAVENLY FATHER KNOWETH THAT YE HAVE NEED OF ALL THESE THINGS."

The word, *"Gentiles,"* in the phrase, *"For after all these things do the Gentiles seek,"* is meant to portray all who do not know God, and, in effect, are strangers to the commonwealth of Israel. In effect, He is saying that such do not have the help, care, and Promises of the *"Heavenly Father,"* as do God's Children. Consequently, these *"Gentiles,"* i.e., unsaved, have to fend for themselves as best as possible! As a result of not having the help of the Lord, and because they are not His Children, some few of these have their material needs met, while many, if not most in the world go lacking. Hence, the reason for so much poverty, starvation, and dire circumstances.

The phrase, *"For your Heavenly Father knoweth,"* is meant to express the contrast between those who do not know the Lord and those who do!

To be sure, the Lord *"knows"* all things. However, the word, *"ye"* in the last phrase, *"That ye have need of all these things,"* sets the Believer apart as alone the recipient of God's care, oversight, and provision.

What a Promise!

(33) "BUT SEEK YE FIRST THE KINGDOM OF GOD, AND HIS RIGHTEOUSNESS; AND ALL THESE THINGS SHALL BE ADDED UNTO YOU."

The phrase, *"But seek ye first the Kingdom of God, and His Righteousness,"* gives the condition for God's Blessings.

Inasmuch as the unconverted are not seeking such, it is left up to the Believer to do so, and, in turn, receive God's benefits.

As well, we are plainly told to put the Kingdom of God, and His Righteousness, *"first."* This means, as is obvious, that we not spend our time and abilities as the unconverted, seeking the things of this world, but, instead, attend to God's business *"first."*

How many truly do this?

Of course, the Lord is the only One Who truly knows the answer to that question. Nevertheless, I think it is obvious, at least in many, if not most experiences, the Lord's Work comes second, or even further down the line!

Let it be known that all who do such, are not only hurting the Work of God, but they are short-changing themselves as well!

The phrase, *"And all these things shall be added unto you,"* is the guarantee of God's provision.

And what a provision it is!

However, we should understand that *"all these things"* are the things the Lord desires that we have, and not many things that some of us foolishly desire.

(34) "TAKE THEREFORE NO THOUGHT FOR THE MORROW: FOR THE MORROW SHALL TAKE THOUGHT FOR THE THINGS OF ITSELF. SUFFICIENT UNTO THE DAY IS THE EVIL THEREOF."

The phrase, *"Take therefore no thought for the morrow,"* is meant for us to direct our attention to the cares of the present day, and not be in anxiety over the future.

The phrase, *"For the morrow shall take thought for the things of itself,"* is meant to refer back to verse 27.

No matter how much we may be concerned about a situation, and may spend sleepless nights over it, all of the fretting, worry, and anxiety, will not change anything. However, Faith in God

can change it. This is the idea of that phrase.

The phrase, *"Sufficient unto the day is the evil thereof,"* means that we should handle daily difficulties in Faith, and have Faith for the future that the present difficulties will not grow into larger ones.

We have God's assurance that they won't, that is, if we will sufficiently believe Him.

CHAPTER 7

(1) "JUDGE NOT, THAT YE BE NOT JUDGED."

Even though a Chapter insertion is placed between the last verse of Chapter 6 and this verse, still, it is all the *"Sermon on the Mount."* Consequently, the statement concerning *"judging"* harks back to verses 25-34 of the previous Chapter.

The idea is, that God may permit poverty to test His Child, but fellow Believers are not to err, as Job's friends did, and believe the trial to be a judgment for secret sin.

However, the word, *"judging,"* as here used, covers every aspect of dealing with our fellowman.

FIRST OF ALL, GOD ALONE IS JUDGE

The New Testament, like the Old Testament, strongly affirms God as ultimately the only qualified Judge. James emphasizes the Old Testament concept of a judge as a ruler when he writes, *"There is only one Lawgiver and Judge, the One Who is able to save and destroy. But you — who are you to judge your neighbour?"* (James 4:12).

In this dominant legal or judicial sense, only God has the right or knowledge to judge (Jn. 8:15-16). All will have to *"give an account to Him Who is ready to judge the living and the dead"* (II Tim. 4:1, 8; Heb. 10:30; 12:23; 13:4; I Pet. 4:5).

The fact that God Alone is competent to pronounce judgment upon human beings is basic to our grasp of what the Bible says about judging.

Yet, God is not eager to judge. John writes that Jesus was sent into the world, not to condemn, but so that all who believe might be saved (Jn. 3:17). The verdict of condemnation is passed on the lost by their own condition and actions. Jesus, the Light, has come into the world; those who love darkness will reject Him and turn away. The Father *"hast entrusted all judgment to the Son"* (Jn. 5:22).

A person's response to Jesus has become the dividing line between life and death (Jn. 5:19-30). So Jesus announced to the crowds during the week of His Death: *"As for the person who hears My Words but does not keep them, I do not judge him. For I did not come to judge the world, but to save it. There is a judge for the one who rejects Me and does not accept My Word; that very Word which I spoke will condemn him at the last day. For I did not speak of My Own accord, but the Father Who sent Me commanded Me what to say and how to say it"* (Jn. 12:47-49).

ROMANS

Romans picks up the theme and portrays God, moved by kindness, waiting patiently in order that people will respond and repent (Rom. 2:4). But, *"For those who are self-seeking and who reject the Truth and follow evil, there will be wrath and anger"* (Rom. 2:8).

Consequently, those who reject the Divine pardon must in the end stand before God as Judge. In that Judgment, based on evaluation of each person's works (Rev. 20:12), God will *"give to each person according to what he has done"* (Rom. 2:6).

Those who know the Revealed Law of God will be judged by its Standard. But even those who do not know the Will of God as unveiled in the Written Word have *"the requirements of the Law... written on their hearts"* (Rom. 2:15).

God has created human beings with a moral sense, which gives inner testimony to right and wrong. Tragically, human beings are so warped by sin that the inner witness accuses but does not lead to righteous living.

And so the day is coming when God will act as the moral Governor of our universe. He will put aside His patience to carry out the verdict that people pronounce against themselves by their actions and by their refusal to accept God's pardon in Jesus.

WHAT THE CHRISTIAN IS NOT TO JUDGE

In affirming God as Judge, the Scripture also limits those ways in which human beings are to judge others. A number of Passages help us understand the limitations.

NOTES

This Passage in Matthew, plus the corresponding in Luke 6:37-38, give us the warning of Christ.

In the command not to judge, the thought is that we must not assume the right to condemn others. Luke adds, *"Forgive, and ye will be forgiven."* The faults of others are to occasion forgiveness, not condemnation.

AGAIN ROMANS

In Romans 2:1-3, Paul speaks passionately of passing judgment on others. He warns, *"At whatever point you judge the other, you are condemning yourself."* To pass judgment applies the assumption of a moral superiority that we simply do not possess. We are all sinners; no human being is able to judge others without becoming vulnerable to the same judgment.

In Romans 14:1-18, Paul looks at convictions in the Christian community. Then, as today, Believers differed about what was right to eat, or drink, or do. While each person should develop his or her own convictions and live by them, no one has the right to look down on or condemn a brother or a sister for his or her practices, at least in areas not plainly forbidden in Scripture. We must see Jesus as the sole Lord and each other as His servants.

So, each Believer is responsible to the Lord, not to the conscience of other Christians. Paul does appeal for unity. But Christian unity is based on A. The freedom of each individual to be responsible to Christ; B. A nonjudgmental approach to differences of conviction, but not that plainly condemned in the Word of God; and, C. A willingness to consider others when deciding whether or not to use one's freedom to follow one's own convictions.

CORINTHIANS

In I Corinthians 4:3-5, Paul portrays himself as being judged by Believers in Corinth. He wrote, *"I care very little if I am judged by you or by any human court."* The word here is *"anakrino,"* which refers to undertaking an investigative process that is intended to lead to a verdict.

Paul rejected the right of the Corinthians to convene such a court or call his faithfulness as Jesus' servant into question. Paul, though his conscience was clear, was not even competent to judge himself and his possibly hidden motives. What were Paul conclusions?

"It is the Lord Who judges me," he said; *"Therefore judge nothing before the appointed time: wait till the Lord comes."*

Paul taught the Corinthian Believers that they were not to judge sinners outside the Body of Christ. Even though their sins are many, and, they actually live in a constant state of sin due to their unredeemed state, still, it is not the business of Christians to *"judge"* those outside the Body.

Actually, the issue is not the morality of unbelievers which is obvious, but, instead, the lack of their relationship with Christ. Only when they come to Christ, will they, and in fact, can they change (I Cor. 6:9-11).

COLOSSIANS

In Colossians 2:16, Paul said, *"Let no man therefore judge you in meat, or in drink, or in respect of an holy day, or of the new moon, or of Sabbath days."*

This is an extremely important Passage, at least as it relates to judging, simply because to violate this Passage brings on a demanded conformity to particular rules and regulations which have no basis in the Word of God. Consequently, the Holy Spirit through Paul urges all Believers everywhere to resist such teaching.

The idea is, that particular groups or Religious Denominations subscribe to certain manmade rules, and then judge everyone accordingly. Such denies not only Christian freedom, which Christianity espouses, but, above all, the Lordship of Christ.

It has always been man's problem, and especially religious man, to attempt to usurp authority over the Lordship of Christ. All extracurricular activities, unless they are especially condemned in the Word of God, should be left up to the conscience of each Believer. To be sure, even if made to conform to man-made rules, still, the spiritual condition of such a one is certainly not improved, but, instead, diminished. As someone has said, Christ must be Lord of all, or He is not Lord at all!

JAMES

James dealt with judging, as perhaps no other writer, by saying, *"Speak not evil one of another, brethren. He that speaketh evil of his brother, and judgeth his brother, speaketh evil of the Law, and judgeth the Law: but if thou judge the*

NOTES

Law, thou art not a doer of the Law, but a judge.

"There is One Lawgiver, Who is able to save and to destroy: who art thou that judgeth another?" (James 4:11-12)

Actually, James is speaking of *"slander,"* which is another form of judging. He argues, and by the inspiration of the Holy Spirit, that to speak against our brother and sister in the Lord is wrong because it implies becoming a judge of the Law rather than a doer. His argument is, that God gave the Law, not to use against others, but that we might be responsive to it.

In Truth, only God, Who as Governor of the universe gave the Law, has the right to judge human beings by it.

THE LEGAL ASPECT OF JUDGING

When one judges another, the motives of one are called into question, with a condemning verdict passed on the individual. James says that human beings are not competent to call another's motives or practices into question. Even when actions are clearly wrong, forgiveness, not condemnation, is the appropriate response. A judgmental attitude with punitive measures taken is wrong.

In these cases, which in fact occur constantly, we are to always refrain from passing judgment on such a person, remembering that God Alone is competent to judge.

The moment we think we are capable of doing such, we have just taken the place of God, and our sin is far worse than the sin of the one we are judging, whatever his infraction may be!

ARE THERE ANY OCCASIONS IN WHICH IT IS SCRIPTURALLY PROPER TO JUDGE?

Yes! And as is obvious, there are matters in which the Believer has to evaluate certain situations, and, consequently, make a quick or studied judgment.

ROMANS

In Romans 13:1-7, we are given the continuance of government as it is ordained by God, and carried over into the New Covenant.

In effect, God has established human government, and has given governing authorities responsibility for rule, including judicial functions. Thus the administration of Criminal and Civil Law by Judges is a right and a responsibility delegated to organized society.

I CORINTHIANS 2:15

In this Passage, Paul said, *"But he that is spiritual judgeth all things, yet he himself is judged of no man."*

The word, *"judging,"* in this Passage is *"anakrino,"* and means to *"examine or discern."* As such, Believers, possessing the Holy Spirit, are to make value judgments *"about all things."* This concerns itself with Civil issues, Doctrines, or actions, but are always to be kept in the confines of the Word of God. In other words, as things are *"examined,"* people or motives are not to be judged.

The idea is that such a *"spiritual man"* knows *"the very Mind of Christ,"* and is thus able to evaluate from the Divine perspective, sensing God's individual guidance.

In effect, this is the greatest need of the Church. Actually, those who are of such spiritual depth, who can offer guidance and direction, are in short supply, and probably always have been!

COURTS OF LAW AMONG BELIEVERS

In I Corinthians 6:2-5, Paul, and by the guidance of the Holy Spirit, condemns Believers taking their disputes into secular Law Courts. Paul urged Believers to sit in judgment in order to resolve such matters, rather than go to Court before unbelievers.

Therefore, in such cases, wise Believers are to make a judgment, based upon the evidence at hand, and especially after seeking the Mind of the Lord.

Regrettably, such is seldom done at present, with Believers too often ignoring the Word of God about such matters.

JUDGE FOR YOURSELVES

Paul made two statements respecting the judging of particular doctrine, etc. He said, *"I speak as to wise men; judge ye what I say"* (I Cor. 10:15).

He also said, *"Judge in yourselves…"* (I Cor. 11:13).

In both instances, at least in these cases, Paul suggests that the right answer is obvious. However, not every matter Christians are called on to examine has an obvious answer.

In these cases, the Lord expects us to examine the issues of our lives and develop convictions

based on principles found in God's Word.

TO JUDGE OURSELVES

"For if we would judge ourselves, we should not be judged" (I Cor. 11:31).

This manner of judging is obvious, in that the Holy Spirit through the Apostle calls on us to judge ourselves. This is speaking of known wrongdoing within our lives, which should be rightly judged by evaluating our own actions, and recognizing them as sin, and, consequently, putting them away.

If such is done, we will not come under the *"chastening of the Lord."*

WHAT ABOUT CHURCH DISCIPLINE THAT CALLS FOR A JUDGMENT?

I Corinthians 5 outlines the method of Church Discipline, and the basis on which it is carried out.

This particular case, as took place in the Corinthian Church, involved a man who had taken up with *"his father's wife"* (step-mother) (I Cor. 5:1). As well, it seems from II Corinthians 7:12, that the father was alive, for that Passage refers to the one *"that suffered wrong,"* as well as the one who had *"done the wrong,"* that is, if the same case is, in fact, being addressed.

Whenever the news came to Paul concerning this situation, he said, *"For I verily, as absent in body, but present in spirit, have judged already, as though I were present, concerning him that hath so done this deed"* (I Cor. 5:3).

It seems from the description, and no doubt was, that the individual concerned was refusing to cease such immoral activity, or even admit it was wrong. In other words, he was openly practicing immorality, and it seems, with some in the Church, not too very much concerned about it.

Paul judges, and says that several things should be done:

1. In view of this individual refusing to repent and, thereby, cease his immoral activities, the Church should *"deliver such an one unto Satan for the destruction of the flesh, that the spirit may be saved in the day of the Lord Jesus"* (I Cor. 5:5).

This meant that the Believers were to withdraw all spiritual influence from this individual, and even cease praying for him, so as to permit Satan to afflict his body, hopefully, bringing him to repentance.

2. The Church was *"not to associate with anyone who calls himself a brother and consistently practices sin."* He said that fellowship should be withdrawn to such an extent that *"with such a man do not even eat"* (I Cor. 5:11).

3. This was to be done by the local Church at Corinth, because the wrongdoing had taken place there, and the leaders of the local Assembly were more qualified, therefore, to judge.

HOW DOES THIS TEACHING SQUARE WITH THE MANY NEW TESTAMENT PASSAGES THAT TELL CHRISTIANS NOT TO JUDGE ONE ANOTHER?

The answer is found in the affirmation of Scripture that God is the Ruler of the Universe and is the final moral Arbiter. He, the Judge, had already announced His verdict on the practices of which Paul was writing. He had identified these practices as sin, as was given in the Old Testament, and carried over, of course, into the New.

What the local Assembly is called upon to do, is to agree with God in the Divine assessment of the actions of this one who *"calls himself a brother."*

If the individual insists upon continuing in the wrongdoing, the Church is to *"expel the wicked from its fellowship"* (I Cor. 5:13).

Condemning someone by calling into question that person's motives, actions, or personal convictions, is vastly different from accepting God's verdict that certain actions are sins and that those who practice them must be ostracized.

There are certain things carried out in I Corinthians 5, which give us guidelines, as laid down by the Holy Spirit through the Apostle.

They are as follows:

1. What necessitates discipline is an individual's choice to practice what the Bible identifies as sin. The identifying word in this action is *"practice,"* which is obvious in this Chapter.

All of us, in fact, may fail, having to come to the Lord in confession and repentance. For this, there is no call for discipline. Discipline is applied only when a person refuses to acknowledge that his practices are sin and refuses to change his ways.

2. However, the goal of all Church discipline should always be restoration. In the case mentioned by Paul, the *"punishment inflicted on the offender"* (II Cor. 2:6) was sufficient, and it

seems the guilty man repented. Paul then called on the Corinthians to accept him back and to *"reaffirm"* their love for him (II Cor. 2:8).

Yet, in such a case, even if the individual refused to repent, even though fellowship would be withdrawn, Paul said, *"Yet count him not as an enemy, but admonish him as a brother"* (II Thess. 3:15).

In other words, everything that is done, is done with the thought in mind of the person ultimately repenting and being restored to fellowship.

3. The rationale for Church discipline is found in spiritual reality. Sin alienates from God, cutting off the individual from fellowship (I Jn. 1:6). In Church discipline, the Body of Christ acts out this spiritual reality in its relationship with the unrepentant one. A person expelled from the local Church, and for these reasons, senses the fact of lost fellowship, which, hopefully, will cause him to repent, and cease his sinful activities.

4. The occasion for Church discipline, as is found in this Chapter, pertains to moral fault: The practice of sin. However, it should be understood that no Church discipline is called for respecting the committing of sin, but for the practice of sin, as is obvious in these Passages. Upon admonishment, if the brother in question had ceased and, thereby, repented before the Lord, no action would have been called for, or needed!

Respecting other deviations, there is little example in Scripture that Church discipline is called for. Difference in convictions or even doctrinal differences, unless heretical, do not seem to call for Church discipline.

It is only the consistent practice of sin without acknowledgement of the fault that occasions discipline.

5. The responsibility for such discipline rests on the local Christian Body. Matthew 18:15-17 is generally understood to outline a process that Christians should follow.

The offender could be approached by one person, first of all, with, hopefully, the situation rectified, and the individual brought to repentance. However, if the effort is fruitless, two or three members of the local congregation should approach the individual.

If the offender refuses to listen, the whole Church should be informed, with the person being disfellowshipped. This joint responsibility is reflected, where Paul writes of expelling the sinning person when the Church is *"assembled in the Name of our Lord Jesus"* (I Cor. 5:4).

The situation outlined in Matthew 18, can apply, as well, to personal differences.

Also, it should be added, and as stated, that the local Church is to be the arbiter in all cases of discipline. It is not Scriptural for some group, committee, or board, many miles away, to sit in judgment on these matters. Such deprives the local Assembly of its God-given spiritual authority.

Even though Paul sought the Lord earnestly respecting this situation at Corinth, and was given an answer to give to the Church, still, it was the local Church which carried out these actions as laid down by the Holy Spirit. To deviate from these directions, is to usurp authority over the Holy Spirit.

As should be obvious, exercising Church discipline is very different from adopting the judgmental and condemning attitude against which Scripture speaks.

In Scriptural Church discipline, we see the loving action of the Christian community, committed to obedience, intending through the discipline to help the brother or sister turn from sin and find renewed fellowship with the Lord.

6. As well, and as is obvious, the moment repentance is engaged by the offending party, which necessitates a ceasing of the sinful practice (whatever it is), the person is to be instantly restored (II Cor. 2:6-7). The idea that some probationary period should be instituted is not found in Scripture, and, in fact, is foreign to all Scriptural practice, which proclaims the Love and Grace of God. Paul told these Corinthians, *"I beseech you that you would confirm your love toward him"* (II Cor. 2:8).

Then he said, *"For to this end also did I write, that I might know the proof of you, whether ye be obedient in all things"* (II Cor. 2:9).

In I Corinthians, the man was on trial, and now the Church is on trial! They are to restore this brother immediately, *"lest perhaps such a one should be swallowed up with overmuch sorrow"* (II Cor. 2:7).

Consequently, it should be understood, and is obvious in Scripture, that the Holy Spirit not only takes the discipline seriously, but the restoration as well!

Of course, the question is often asked, *"But what if the individual commits the same sin, or other similar sins again?"*

In fact, that may well be the case, and, sadly, sometimes is! However, the Lord does not respond to our petition for Mercy and Forgiveness on the basis of what we might do in the future, but, instead, on the condition of the heart and actions at the present (I Jn. 1:9).

If the Lord treats His Children in this manner, our attitude and actions must be identical.

Some would argue that such actions of probationary periods must be enacted in order to keep the Church pure.

First of all, the Church is not pure, and, in fact, never has been, and, in Truth, never will be, at least until the Trump sounds (I Cor. 15:51-54).

In Truth, man cannot legislate Holiness. His efforts can only bring legalism. It is the business of the Holy Spirit to bring about Holiness, which alone He can do (Rom. 8:1-16).

IN SUMMARY

The New Testament helps us make distinctions about judging, which we have attempted to bring out.

God has established human government and assigned it judicial functions relating to criminal acts in society (Rom. 13). But God has not given Believers any right, apart from Scripture, to examine or condemn other persons.

No one but God is competent to measure motives, or to establish convictions for others. Jesus is Lord and, as God, He is able to discern rightly. Thus we are freed from the responsibility of judging others in these areas.

Instead, we can relate to them in love, with acceptance, and freely extend forgiveness.

Neither are we burdened with the responsibility of punishing others, or exerting discipline, other than that given by the Apostle Paul, as it regards the local Church. Neither are we given the responsibility of forcing others to conform to our notions of what God desires. God will judge — at the appointed time (I Cor. 4:5).

Yet, and as stated, there are certain practices that God has already spoken about. It is our responsibility on moral issues to take our stand with the Lord. Thus, when one who claims to be a Believer habitually practices sin, and, consequently, refuses to repent, the believing community is to expel that person from the local Church.

In Church discipline, the Church judges, not the person, but the actions of that person. When the actions are those that God has identified as sin, then the Church must act in obedience and expel the unrepentant person.

By judging only those things that God calls on us to judge, and by refusing to be trapped into judging others, we will be enabled to live productive and peaceful lives.

(Many of the thoughts on *"judging"* were compiled from the Commentary of Reverend Lawrence O. Richards.)

(2) "FOR WITH WHAT JUDGMENT YE JUDGE, YE SHALL BE JUDGED: AND WITH WHAT MEASURE YE METE, IT SHALL BE MEASURED TO YOU AGAIN."

As we have attempted to bring out, other than that which is outlined by the Lord, the Believer is never to judge others. The penalties are severe!

The phrase, *"For with what judgment ye judge, ye shall be judged,"* proclaims that whatever motive we ascribe to others, such motive will ultimately be ascribed to us.

Likewise, the phrase, *"And with what measure ye mete, it shall be measured to you again,"* is meant to impress upon the Believer the harshness of what he is doing. The judgment is the verdict; the measure is the severity of the verdict.

The idea is, and to turn it around, that we are to judge others exactly as we would judge ourselves, for, in fact, that is exactly what we are doing!

To carefully weigh the consequences, should give us room for pause!

(3) "AND WHY BEHOLDEST THOU THE MOTE THAT IS IN THY BROTHER'S EYE, BUT CONSIDEREST NOT THE BEAM THAT IS IN THINE OWN EYE?"

The idea behind these statements points to the Pharisees, who were constantly looking for small infractions of the Law, whether real or imagined.

The question, *"And why beholdest thou the mote that is in thy brother's eye?"*, is meant to condemn mote hunting. In other words, the Believer, to whom the Lord is speaking, is not to be looking for fault or wrongdoing in the lives of fellow Believers.

Inspecting others was a favorite pastime of the Pharisees, and, regrettably, continues presently.

The Lord now tells us why we should not do such a thing!

The question, *"But considerest not the beam in thine own eye?"*, is meant to proclaim the fact that we have plenty about ourselves that is wrong, which should occupy all of our time in eliminating, instead of looking for infractions in others!

In fact, the *"mote"* and *"beam"* are contrasted! The constant judging of others, portrays the fact that we are much worse off than the one we are judging.

(4) "OR HOW WILT THOU SAY TO THY BROTHER, LET ME PULL OUT THE MOTE OUT OF THINE EYE; AND, BEHOLD, A BEAM IS IN THINE OWN EYE?"

The question, *"Or how wilt thou say to thy brother?"*, is meant to impress upon us the seriousness of setting ourselves up as judge, jury, and executioner. Plainly, the impression is that we are not qualified!

The phrase, *"Let me pull out the mote out of thine eye,"* portrays the individual, as the Pharisees of old, who constantly knew how to set everyone straight, while he was not walking straight himself.

The conclusion of the question, *"And, behold, a beam is in thine own eye?"*, once again draws attention to the fact that the person doing the judging is in far worse spiritual condition, than the one being judged.

(5) "THOU HYPOCRITE, FIRST CAST OUT THE BEAM OUT OF THINE OWN EYE; AND THEN SHALT THOU SEE CLEARLY TO CAST OUT THE MOTE OUT OF THY BROTHER'S EYE."

The phrase, *"Thou hypocrite,"* aptly describes such a person. They are acting the part, without possessing the reality. In other words, what they are claiming that the other person should have, or do, they do not in fact possess themselves.

The phrase, *"First cast out the beam out of thine own eye,"* is meant to proclaim the fact that we constantly have enough faults, and even sins, within ourselves, that should occupy all of our time in elimination.

The phrase, *"And then shalt thou see clearly to cast out the mote out of thy brother's eye,"* has the emphasis on the word *"then."*

When we properly analyze ourselves, then, and only then, can we *"see clearly."*

If, per chance, we then see a *"mote"* in someone else's eye, we will not at all be censoriousness, which means to come from a superior attitude, but, will rather deal in kindness and love. Only then can our actions be effective anyway!

The probable intent of Christ in this scenario is that we not censor our brother or sister in any respect, but, instead, portray to them a loving example of us handling our own faults in a Scriptural way, which will set its own example of Righteousness.

In other words, the victories we win in our own lives, serve as the greatest example of all, which eliminates all finger-pointing.

(6) "GIVE NOT THAT WHICH IS HOLY UNTO THE DOGS, NEITHER CAST YE YOUR PEARLS BEFORE SWINE, LEST THEY TRAMPLE THEM UNDER THEIR FEET, AND TURN AGAIN AND REND YOU."

This Passage tells us that judgment, however, is to be made respecting the actions of the ungodly, and heavenly treasure is not to be exposed to their contempt and hostility. To these, the Gospel, and the ensuing Wrath of God if it be rejected, are to be preached.

The phrase, *"Give not that which is holy unto the dogs, neither cast ye your pearls before swine,"* is speaking of those known to be antagonistic to the Gospel, and, therefore, its proclaimer.

Regrettably and sadly, major Religious Denominations have, at times, ignored this Command of the Lord, and have engaged the News Media to carry out the destruction they desired. In these cases, there is little desire to handle the situation, whatever it may be, in a Scriptural manner, but rather to destroy. As such, the sin becomes abominable!

The phrase, *"Lest they trample them under their feet, and turn again and rend you,"* proclaims the penalty for such action. It may be a while in coming, but, to be sure, it will come! Then, that which is truly *"holy,"* if, in fact, any holiness remains, as well as the *"pearls"* of the Gospel, will be destroyed!

As stated, it may seem as if the statement of verse 6 has no relationship with the preceding verses concerning *"judging,"* but, in fact, it does!

The idea is, that even though there are problems in the Church, as verses 1-5 proclaim,

NOTES

still, the Church is never to reach out into the world (dogs) for help in order to solve its internal disputes.

No! It is not speaking of things akin to Paul's appeal to Caesar, because ungodly men in the reprobate Jewish Church were attempting to take his life (Acts 25:9-10). In all such actions, the Believer, especially if his life is at stake, as Paul's was, should take advantage of the laws of the land, if, in fact, help can be derived from such.

(7) "ASK, AND IT SHALL BE GIVEN YOU; SEEK, AND YE SHALL FIND; KNOCK, AND IT SHALL BE OPENED UNTO YOU."

The thrust of this verse, and the following, is that the Believer in such situations as are common in the Church, does not have to go to the world for help, but, instead, should seek the Lord for wisdom and guidance in whatever is needed.

The idea is, why would the Believer go to the world for help in matters pertaining solely to the Work of God, and especially when the world system has no knowledge of such, when we can easily go to the Lord for whatever wisdom, judgment, or help that is needed!

The phrase, *"Ask, and it shall be given you,"* is also an open invitation for all Believers everywhere to *"ask"* for whatever they need. It implies a Heavenly Father Who has resources which are inexhaustible.

The phrase, *"Seek, and ye shall find,"* is meant to imply that our *"asking"* may not be immediately answered, with the word, *"seek,"* referring to a casting about as to the reason why.

Many times, if not all times, the Lord takes advantage of our petitions to straighten out matters within our lives which need attention. As a result, the answer, at least at times, is not immediately forthcoming. That is when the *"seeking"* is brought into play, which means to seek the reason why the answer is not immediate.

In these occasions, the Lord deals with our heart, portraying to us areas of spiritual pride, or whatever the problem may be. Therefore, if the answer does not come immediately, we should seek the Lord as to the reason why, which is designed within itself to draw us nearer to Him.

Regrettably, many modern Christians are taught that if the answer is not immediately forthcoming, their Faith is deficient. While that at times may be true, the inference is that most of the time it pertains to something else, such as lack of consecration, or wrong direction, etc.

At any rate, the Believer must not cease his asking, but should *"seek"* the reason for the delay. It is promised that he will find that reason.

The phrase, *"Knock, and it shall be opened unto you,"* as well, implies a door that does not immediately open. Jesus dealt with this in Luke 11 to a far greater degree, which we will not now comment on, except to say that if you continue to *"knock,"* it shall be *"opened unto you."*

Regrettably, many Christians quit *"asking"* immediately before the answer is forthcoming, and discontinue *"seeking,"* just before it is to be found, and stop *"knocking,"* thereby, turning away, just before the door opens.

The delay, if, in fact, there is a delay, is for a purpose, and is designed by the Holy Spirit for our good, and not for our harm.

(8) "FOR EVERY ONE THAT ASKETH RECEIVETH; AND HE THAT SEEKETH FINDETH; AND TO HIM THAT KNOCKETH IT SHALL BE OPENED."

If one is to notice, the Lord habitually makes certain statements, while, turning right around and saying the same thing in a different way, but with the same meaning, and with added emphasis!

This is done, no doubt, to emphasize the significance of the statement, and uses a form of teaching, which should be copied by all, which makes the subject easier to remember and understand.

The phrase, *"For every one that asketh receiveth,"* is a wide open, Carte Blanche statement, that refers to *"every one,"* that is, if they, in fact, do what the 7th verse says.

Sometimes the *"asking," "seeking,"* and *"knocking,"* may take quite a period of time, even years.

If the request pertains to the Plan of God, or depends on the will of others, such may, in fact, take an involved period of time. However, many requests would not fall under that category, and will be answered speedily. Nevertheless, the idea of these Passages is that we are not to give up, but to keep believing, and not let hindrances, obstacles, or difficulties deter us from that which we rightly seek.

As well, I am sure the reader would understand that the very tenor of the words precludes frivolous requests!

Regrettably, in the past few years, the deep and abiding intercession once practiced by some Believers, which, in fact, ushered in, among other things, tremendous moves of God, has been replaced, by and large, with frivolity. Too many modern Christians are taught the very opposite of what these Passages demand!

For instance, requests for bigger houses and bigger cars, etc., have replaced, at least for the most part, intercession for Revival and the Salvation of Souls.

As well, most modern Christians are taught the *"confession principle,"* which certainly has some validity, but definitely not in the way it is presently adhered to. They are taught to ask one time, and then begin to confess the answer into existence.

In the first place, such attitude automatically assumes that it knows the Will of God in any and all cases, when, in reality, there may be times what we are asking is not the Will of God, and which the waiting period, as described in these Passages, brings this out, and shifts us to the direction desired by the Holy Spirit.

The idea that Believers always know the Will of God in any and all situations, is preposterous indeed! Also, the very requirement of the Child of God, is to desire what Jesus said, *"Thy will be done in earth, as it is Heaven"* (6:10).

The phrase, *"And he that seeketh findeth,"* is a little different, as also the *"asking,"* than the statements made in verse 7.

Whereas verse 7 concerns itself more so with generalized terms, verse 8 makes the matter personal, and, therefore, the guarantee of an even greater moment, if possible!

The phrase, *"And to him that knocketh it shall be opened,"* once again, takes it from the general realm to the personal position.

It is as if Christ is saying, *"I personally guarantee you...."*

Even as I write these words, I sense the Presence of God.

What beautiful Promises, and, even more so, what a great and wonderful God we serve!

To be sure, and on a personal basis, I have proven these Promises over and over. And yet, there are some petitions of my own personal request that have not yet been answered. However, I know, and beyond the shadow of a doubt, they will be answered!

How do I know that? I know it because of what He has done in the past, and because, *"He has magnified His Word above all His Name"* (Ps. 138:2).

(9-10) "OR WHAT MAN IS THERE OF YOU, WHOM IF HIS SON ASK BREAD, WILL HE GIVE HIM A STONE?

"OR IF HE ASK A FISH, WILL HE GIVE HIM A SERPENT?"

The antidote for care is to betake oneself to the Royal Treasury. Application there will meet with certain response. But the mode of application must follow the pattern as outlined in 6:9-13.

There, God's interests come first. They occur in a descending scale from Himself to His Kingdom and from His Kingdom to the earth.

The four human petitions occur in an ascending scale — from daily bread to final deliverance. The Lord does something in these two verses that is beautiful to behold! He lets the Disciple know that God is not a machine, but, in reality, a *"Father,"* albeit, a *"Heavenly Father."* Even though He is God, and, as such, His thoughts and ways are not ours. Nevertheless, He, as is evidenced by His Only Son, has feelings, emotions, and passions, and will respond accordingly.

Also, these two verses allay all fears that some have respecting relationship with the Lord. In fact, the entirety of verses 7-12 concerns relationship. Every Word breathes with a parental concern and with sonship obligation.

Many Believers have very little prayer life, because they fear that the Lord will ask them to do something which is sorely displeasing to them! Both of these verses assure such an one that *"If his son ask bread, he will not be given a stone, or if he ask a fish, he will not, instead, be given a serpent."*

The Promise is inviolable.

Actually, it has a double meaning, which gives us a double security.

1. It means that the Lord will give us what we ask for, and not substitute something else in its place.

2. If, in fact, what we are asking for is not God's Will, and would turn out to be a *"stone,"* or *"serpent,"* He will guard us from receiving such, and during the time of waiting and consecration, will show us what we truly need.

Tragically, all of us, at one time or the other, may have asked for things which we truly

NOTES

thought we should have, but, which would have turned out <u>not</u> to be the *"bread"* or *"fish"* we had first thought, but our Heavenly Father in His sagacity, instead, steered us in another direction. Such is the reason for the delay sometimes experienced.

(11) "IF YE THEN, BEING EVIL, KNOW HOW TO GIVE GOOD GIFTS UNTO YOUR CHILDREN, HOW MUCH MORE SHALL YOUR FATHER WHICH IS IN HEAVEN GIVE GOOD THINGS TO THEM THAT ASK HIM?"

The phrase, *"If ye then, being evil,"* refers to parents sometimes giving their children things which are not good for them, as well as things which are good.

The phrase, *"Know how to give good gifts unto your children,"* portrays the efforts by fallen human nature to do the best for their children.

The idea is, that if some wicked fathers see to it that their children get what they ask and that they are fed, clothed, and protected, at least as far as is possible, *"how much more"* will the Heavenly Father do for His Children *"that ask Him."*

Luke adds, *"Give the Holy Spirit to them that ask Him,"* which is meant to emphasize the gift which ultimately produces all others (Lk. 11:13).

The phrase, *"Good things,"* should include deliverance from dangers, preservation from evil, bodily healing and health, material prosperity, or any other answer to prayer, which is a *"good thing."*

As such, we should ask to receive it and no longer question the Will of God in the matter. It is already His Will or this teaching of verses 7-11 is false.

However, the Lord allows Himself to interpret what these *"good things"* actually are. And, as well, the wise Christian will not only allow such, but will insist upon it.

(12) "THEREFORE ALL THINGS WHATSOEVER YE WOULD THAT MEN SHOULD DO TO YOU, DO YE EVEN SO TO THEM: FOR THIS IS THE LAW AND THE PROPHETS."

This verse sums up the statutes and precepts of the Kingdom; but this Golden Rule does not authorize capricious benevolent action, but only what is reasonable and morally helpful, and controlled by Divine imitation (5:48).

This principle of action and mode of life is, in fact, the sum of all Bible teaching.

Jesus had a way of summing up extremely complex subjects, into a short statement, which beautifully and wonderfully said what needed to be said!

The phrase, *"For this is the Law and the Prophets,"* proclaims in this one statement, commonly referred to as the *"Golden Rule,"* everything said in the Old Testament. As well, it sums up the New.

Inasmuch as He has been dealing with the harsh judgmental spirit, He is now admonishing His followers to let the opposite feeling rule in their conduct toward others. Let all (the word *"all"* is emphatic) your dealings with men be conducted in the same spirit in which you would desire them to deal with you.

In effect, the Statement by Christ, in the summing up of the Law, *"Thou shalt love thy neighbour as thyself,"* is essentially the same as this statement, but provides the foundation of Love, without which the *"Golden Rule"* cannot be done (Mat. 22:39-40).

(13) "ENTER YE IN AT THE STRAIT GATE: FOR WIDE IS THE GATE, AND BROAD IS THE WAY, THAT LEADETH TO DESTRUCTION, AND MANY THERE BE WHICH GO IN THEREAT:"

The entrance into the Kingdom is declared the narrow gate of conversion, i.e., the acceptance of Christ as Saviour; and the Lord adds that precious few take the opportunity to pass in by it.

This double statement as given in both verses 13 and 14 is offensive to the moralist, for it declares him to be so hopelessly corrupt that he needs a moral re-creation; and it states that few are thus reborn.

The phrase, *"Enter ye in at the strait gate,"* proclaims that the process of conversion must take place in order to be saved. *"The strait gate"* is the door, Who is Jesus (Jn. 10:1).

The word, *"strait,"* also refers to being *"narrow."* Consequently, that means only one way, which excludes all other ways. That *"way,"* i.e., gate, is the Bible. This excludes all Catholicism, Humanism, Islam, Mormonism, Buddhism, Confucianism, Shintoism, etc., as well as the part of Christianity which is corrupt.

Consequently, it is very sad, that in 1994 a group of Religious Leaders in America, signed a concordant, stating that no effort would be made to convert Catholics, because, as they

NOTES

stated it, Catholics are already saved. These Religious Leaders were from every religious background, including Pentecostals and Charismatics. Regrettably, they knew little of the Word of God or they would not have signed such a paper.

A lady asked me one time, as to why we were carrying out missions works in foreign countries, such as, among other things, the airing of our Telecast. She claimed that by doing so, we were affecting their culture and meddling with their religion, which pleased them very well, etc.

It is difficult to understand how someone who called herself a Christian, could come up with such a hypotheses. Evidently, the woman knew absolutely nothing about the Bible.

Most definitely, the Gospel was greatly affecting their culture, which is, in fact, demented, as all culture, but for the better I might add! True Bible Christianity has its own culture, and far exceeds all else!

Whether these individuals are satisfied with their religion or not, which most certainly aren't, is of little consequence! The Truth is, *"their religion,"* is of Satan, and will cause their souls to be eternally lost.

This is the very reason for the Command of Christ, *"Go ye into all the world to preach the Gospel"* (Mk. 16:15).

The phrase, *"For wide is the gate, and broad is the way, that leadeth to destruction,"* proclaims, and as we have stated, the many and varied religions of the world, which are false, and will lead to eternal hell fire.

As well, these evil ways are *"broad,"* which speak, as well, of being very enticing and alluring. As such, most fall easily into its maw.

By contrast, the *"strait gate,"* or door, is narrow, which means that most often one must search to find it.

These Passages completely refute the fallacious idea that approach to God is like the many spokes of a wheel, with all leading to the same hub. No! They do not lead to the same hub, but, instead, to *"destruction."*

To be sure, Preachers who espouse the *"narrow way"* are called *"narrow"* themselves. As such, they are hated, reviled, laughed at, lampooned, and, most, if not all of the time, ostracized!

The phrase, *"And many there be which go*

in thereat," refers to most of the world, and for all time!

Tragically, many, if not most of these people, thought they were *"saved,"* or *"ready,"* or *"prepared,"* or any other terminology that one may apply to the subject. However, these who entered this *"wide gate,"* were not saved. There is nothing in the world worse than a false way of Salvation! But, tragically, and as Christ said, *"Many there be which go in thereat."*

(14) "BECAUSE STRAIT IS THE GATE, AND NARROW IS THE WAY, WHICH LEADETH UNTO LIFE, AND FEW THERE BE THAT FIND IT."

Every contrite heart earnestly desires to be among the *"few."*

The phrase, *"Because strait is the gate,"* means that the requirements are greater than most are willing to accept. At the outset, much determination is required, and afterwards, much self-denial.

Men do not enter this *"strait gate,"* because they cannot carry their sins with them, and they love their sins. However, what they do not realize, is that whatever the Lord takes away, is always that which is harming us, no matter how enjoyable at the present it may seem to be, and then, He always gives us something far greater to take its place.

Religion can only take away; it can add nothing. However, Jesus, even though taking away, then gives eternal life, with all its attendant joys, developments, and fulfillment.

In other words, that which He takes away from us, our sins, and self-will, even though at times seeming attractive, can, in reality, do nothing but hurt. Sadly, many people have to come to a place of great hurt before they will finally say *"yes"* to Christ.

The phrase, *"And narrow is the way,"* means exactly what it says. However, it is *"narrow"* only in the sense of the things of this world, and, definitely not in the sense of the things of God.

The world's system is the enemy of the Believer, and that means everything in it, with the exception of the *"narrow way"* carved out by the Lord. Admittedly, many Preachers, Churches, and entire Religious Denominations have attempted to broaden the way, but they only succeed in destroying it. This *"Way"* is His Way, and, as such, must not be tampered with by man.

This means that the Believer should be very careful as to what he reads, where he goes, friends he associates with, business ventures he enters into, and even the thoughts he thinks. Is this restrictive?

It definitely is restrictive as far as the world is concerned; however, the True Child of God has no interest in the world, so, rather than be restrictive to him, it has the opposite effect.

It enables him, by such restrictions, to draw closer to the Lord, Who expands every legitimate horizon in a manner that the world could never even begin to approach.

The phrase, *"Which leadeth unto life,"* bears out exactly what I have just said.

Actually, Christ, even though speaking of eternal life, is mostly referring to the present in the fullest nature — life as *"the fulfillment of the highest idea of being."*

Without Jesus there is no life! And only in Jesus, can one truly find the meaning of life.

That means that the richest man in the world without Jesus, doesn't know what life means! It also means that the most educated man in the world, doesn't know what life is unless he has Christ. That is the reason Jesus said, *"I am the Way, the Truth, and the Life"* (Jn. 14:6).

Consequently, this *"life"* is not a religion, philosophy, or Church, but, instead, a Person, The Man, Christ Jesus.

The phrase, *"And few there be that find it,"* is sad indeed!

The words, *"find it,"* actually mean that some do search, at least for a little while, and then give up.

Also, the phrase means that this *"strait gate"* and *"narrow way,"* are not easily found.

The reason for that is the deception used by Satan which throws people onto another track, which, in effect, leads to *"destruction."* Satan is a master at this procedure, and, inasmuch as the Fall of man in the Garden of Eden was brought about by deception, man continues to be deceived.

However, if one truly seeks, one will truly find (vs. 8).

(15) "BEWARE OF FALSE PROPHETS, WHICH COME TO YOU IN SHEEP'S CLOTHING, BUT INWARDLY THEY ARE RAVENING WOLVES."

The preachers of falsehood are now at once introduced because they denied the need of

Christ, or else they attempt to add something to Christ, or else they *"use"* Christ to promote some man-made philosophy.

The phrase, *"Beware of false prophets,"* is said in the sternest of measures!

First of all, this means that there definitely will be *"false prophets,"* and, as such, they are at least one of, if not, Satan's greatest weapon.

If one is to notice, Christ did not refer to *"false teachers"* as Peter did (II Pet. 2:1), which refers to persons falsely interpreting fundamental truths, but, instead, *"false prophets."* These falsely claimed to bring messages direct from God. They claimed to bring from God the True Message of Salvation, but their claim was false. Regrettably, millions have followed, and do follow these *"false prophets."*

The phrase, *"Which come to you in sheep's clothing,"* proclaims their deception.

They have on the clothing of *"sheep,"* and, as a result, look like the real thing.

As well, *"sheep's clothing"* denotes their false humility, gentle ways and soothing mannerisms, all designed to deceive.

The phrase, *"But inwardly they are ravening wolves,"* proclaims that the outward is not nearly as reliable as the *"inward."* But sadly, most are fooled by the *"outward,"* i.e., *"sheep's clothing."*

The nature of a wolf is the opposite of the *"sheep."*

The thought of *"ravening"* speaks of violence and greed.

This means that their message is designed but for one purpose, and that is oppose the Truth, and to injure you, and that for their own gain.

These *"false prophets"* could probably be said to fall in two categories:

1. These proclamators of a false Gospel, who actually think they are preaching the Truth, but, in reality, are deceived themselves. As such, they do not know the Lord, and even though carrying the trappings of profession, inwardly they have never been changed. And no matter how cultured or cultivated, and because of not truly knowing Christ, even though professing Him, inwardly they are *"ravening wolves."* These would fall into many areas of corrupt Christianity.

As such, they do not preach the Truth, because they do not know the Truth. They preach a lie, pure and simple, and those who are deceived, which number into the multiple millions, will be eternally lost!

2. The second category of these *"false prophets,"* have at their core a lust for money. Consequently, they take one of three approaches, or a combination of all three:

A. The first category would consist of those who are in the ministry for intellectual, personal, or monetary reasons. They are not called of God. They are *"hirelings"* pure and simple. They preach what their congregations want to hear, instead of what they need to hear, i.e., the Word of God. Sadly, the Churches of the land are filled with this type.

B. The promoters of the *"Prosperity Message,"* who *"use"* Christ to promote this philosophy. Much, if not most, of their message is tailored, designed, and directed in a manner to get people to give money. It is done under the guise of *"Faith,"* or gargantuan returns, in other words, a quick way to get rich. It is a vain philosophy pure and simple.

In fact, their philosophy is subtly presented, with much of the trappings of the True Gospel around it, which makes it extremely easy to believe, and deceptive, because it appeals to the base nature of man, even Christian man, which desires to be rich. All of it is done under a cloak of *"the Blessings of God,"* etc.

Consequently, this *"gospel"* is showcased by the make of car one drives, the cut of their clothes, the type of house they live in, and the amount of money they have. If one is to notice, all of these things are externals, which appeal to the self-life, which, in Truth, must be crucified in Christ, before one can truly know the Will of God.

The adherents of this philosophy, which are many, are asking the Lord to make them rich, while the Lord is attempting to make them Christlike!

They totally forget the Words of Christ, *"A man's life consisteth not in the abundance of things which he possesseth"* (Lk. 12:15).

What makes this all the more appealing, is that it contains a kernel of Truth. And as someone has said, *"Most lies ride into the Church on the back of Truth."*

In fact, God does wondrously bless His people, even financially so. However, to make this one's priority, is to completely twist and subvert the True Gospel of Jesus Christ. This is, as Paul said, *"Perverse disputings of men of corrupt minds, and destitute of the Truth, supposing that gain is Godliness: from such withdraw thyself."*

He went on to say, *"But Godliness with contentment is great gain.*

"For we brought nothing into this world, and it is certain we can carry nothing out.

"And having food and raiment let us be therewith content.

"But they that will be rich fall into temptation and to snare, and into many foolish and hurtful lusts, which drown men in destruction and perdition.

"For the love of money is the root of all evil: which while some coveted after, they have erred from the faith, and pierce themselves through with many sorrows" (I Tim. 6:5-10).

Paul further said, *"But thou, O man of God, flee these things: and follow after Righteousness, Godliness, Faith, Love, Patience, Meekness"* (I Tim. 6:11).

Need I say more!

C. Where the first group shrouded their philosophy in a canopy of selected Scriptures, and, therefore, presented it on a very religions platter, this second group is raw and blunt with their approach. They simply tell you, and without all the philosophical jargon, which attempts to shroud their philosophy with a Biblical Message, that if you will give so much money, and right then, and to them, you will gain for yourself all type of wonderful things.

As a result, they claim to be hearing from God, and at that very moment, which always tells them that you are to give a certain sum of money, and, as stated, to them.

Let all and sundry know and understand that their visions are false.

Others ask for certain amounts of money, and they, in turn, will send you *"blessed water,"* *"blessed pocketbooks,"* *"blessed string"* — yes, blessed string — or any other such foolish thing they can get you to believe. It is a con job pure and simple. They are *"false prophets."*

As such, it is my firm conviction from these Passages, that all who give under these pretenses at the very least, are wasting their money, and at worst are committing sin, and because they are aiding and abetting these *"false prophets."*

John said, *"If there come any unto you, and bring not this Doctrine* (the True Doctrine of Christ), *receive him not into your house, and*

neither bid him Godspeed:

"For he that biddeth him Godspeed is partaker of his evil deeds" (II Jn. 1:11).

(16) "YE SHALL KNOW THEM BY THEIR FRUITS. DO MEN GATHER GRAPES OF THORNS, OR FIGS OF THISTLES?"

The phrase, *"Ye shall know them by their fruits,"* is meant to express that the appearance and claims of these *"false prophets"* are no proof of their true character. Claims and prophecies abound, which have no validity and, in fact, and do not come to pass.

The question, *"Do men gather grapes of thorns, or figs of thistles?",* does not ask the question, *"Do thorns produce grapes?",* etc., because men automatically knew that such does not produce grapes or figs.

So, He is telling His followers to use the same common sense in spiritual matters which they show in matters of everyday life.

What a blessing it would be if all Christians did this!

I am amazed at some Christian Businessmen who will go to meticulous lengths to check the validity of claims made by certain products, etc. And yet, those same Businessmen, at times, will accept the wild extravagant claims of some Preachers, without checking into it. Jesus is saying, that they should use as much sense with the one as with the other!

Years ago, a Businessman, who, in fact, gave large sums of money to the Work of God, came to me, speaking of a particular Preacher who he was planning to sponsor, which involved quite a sum of money.

I was not acquainted with the Preacher, but strongly urged him to check the matter out.

I said to him, *"Sadly and regrettably, many of the claims made by many Preachers simply will not hold water. In other words, it is not true."*

He went on to tell me how he certainly believed what this man said, even though he had no proof of what was being said!

About three months later, he came to me, very distraught I might add!

He said, *"I had occasion to visit the place where my money was supposed to be spent building a certain project, and, in fact, there was no project there, and nothing being planned."*

He then said, *"I threw my money away!"*

Yes he did, which meant that it could have

been used for a legitimate Work of God, but instead was not only wasted, but supported a *"false prophet."*

Some time back, one of our supporters, and a man, I might quickly add, who had given strongly to our Work and Ministry, spoke of going overseas and seeing firsthand the work of our ChildCare Ministry in Africa. I strongly encouraged him to do so, which he did.

When he came back, and after having stayed for nearly two weeks, he said, *"Brother Swaggart, if you could get all your supporters to see this work, and exactly how much good it is doing, you wouldn't have to plead for funds any longer!"*

He has been back several times since.

What type of fruit is Jesus speaking of?

1. The True Gospel of Jesus Christ will always be the foundation of *"good fruit."* Of course, every Preacher claims to be preaching the True Gospel, when, in fact, many aren't!

However, and irrespective of the good intentions, if the Gospel is not being proclaimed as it should be, whatever else is being done will be inconsequential as well!

2. The fruit will be souls saved, Believers baptized in the Holy Spirit, and sick bodies healed, with lives being changed, developing Righteousness (I Tim. 6:11).

Regrettably, wild extravagant claims are made all the time of great numbers being saved, etc. However, some of these claims are spurious, with very precious few of these people being found.

Once again, claims are one thing, while the actual fruit is something else altogether. Before anything is supported, it ought to be checked into, and diligently.

In the last few years, such claims of healings and miracles have been bandied about as if commonplace. In fact, some few are true, and for that we are thankful. However, most, and sadly, are spurious.

Some time back, I had the occasion to visit briefly with a man about this very subject. I did not at all agree with his hypotheses, but, still, I could not deny his findings.

Claiming to be of sincere heart, in which I hope he was, and regarding a particular Evangelist, he *"checked out"* several of the proposed outstanding healings.

He said to me, *"Brother Swaggart, I sincerely*

wanted to find that which was genuine, but there was no way that anyone could conclude, at least honestly, that anything of a physical nature had changed in these particular people."

The Truth is, the Lord still heals the sick, and performs miracles. He answers prayer, and still does great and mighty things. However, false claims in no way glorify God, because nowhere in the Bible does one find God placing a premium on dishonesty.

Regrettably, it seems that the much money in Christian giving, goes more so to wild extravagant claims, than to the actual *"fruit."* This proclaims, that many Christians are not truthfully heeding the admonitions of Christ, if, in fact, they know them at all!

Some time ago, I wrote on this very subject in our publication called *"The Evangelist."* A brother wrote me back, somewhat disturbed with my article, asking me why I did not *"call names?"*

I answered him by saying, that if he was to notice, Jesus did not call names either. He taught in this manner, because He wanted His followers to learn how to detect the *"false prophets,"* rather than naming the individuals.

That a person is a *"false prophet,"* is one thing, while being able to know why they are, is something else altogether.

3. The True Gospel will produce Righteousness in the life of the Believer. Peter said, *"As obedient children, not fashioning yourselves according to the former lusts in your ignorance:*

"But as He which hath called you is holy, so be ye holy in all manner of conversation" (I Pet. 1:14-15).

(17) "EVEN SO EVERY GOOD TREE BRINGETH FORTH GOOD FRUIT; BUT A CORRUPT TREE BRINGETH FORTH EVIL FRUIT."

The phrase, *"Even so every good tree bringeth forth good fruit,"* should be the obvious conclusion of all! Therefore, allow us to say it again, *"Every Christian ought to be a fruit inspector and diligently so!"*

Regrettably, there aren't a whole lot of *"good trees"* around. As a result, there isn't a whole lot of *"good fruit."*

Modern Christendom has been amazingly influenced by the *"hype"* of Hollywood and the ad agencies. In fact, the *"hype"* is so bad, that it is very difficult anymore to know the Truth unless it is minutely inspected. As this is the single most important thing in the world, *"good fruit,"* every Christian should be diligent in their inspection. To heed reports of biased individuals, whether pro or con, is unwise indeed! Regrettably, this is the course that most Christians follow. They simply do not inspect for themselves, at least for the most part. Consequently, the far greater majority, probably one could say without exaggeration, supports a *"corrupt tree bringing forth evil fruit."*

One of, if not the greatest hindrance in the Early Church was these *"false prophets."* They hindered Paul greatly, by denigrating his character, claiming to have a deeper revelation, or outright making false claims. Many of Paul's Epistles were written to refute the error they brought into the Early Church. In fact, the Church at Corinth, even though Paul had planted this work, with almost all of the converts having come to Christ through his Ministry, nevertheless, came very close to turning on Paul, simply because the Corinthians were lax in checking out the *"fruit."* II Corinthians Chapter 7 proclaims their repentance, which greatly gladdened the heart of Paul, as would be obvious!

He was strong in his denunciation of these individuals, calling them *"false apostles, deceitful workers, transforming themselves into the Apostles of Christ."*

He then went on to say, that they were, in effect, *"Satan's ministers"* (II Cor. 11:13-15).

When the Corinthians, who had been saved under his Ministry, demanded his (Paul's) credentials, and because they had been corrupted by these *"false apostles,"* he told them, *"Ye are our Epistle* (fruit) *written in our hearts, known and read of all men"* (II Cor. 3:2). The greatest *"fruit"* of all was their conversion, which they were too blind to see.

He brought forth *"good fruit,"* while these *"false apostles"* brought forth *"evil fruit."*

What is evil fruit?

1. First of all, it is a false gospel.

2. The *"evil fruit"* is greed, selfishness, and self-will generated by this false gospel, which is the opposite of Righteousness.

To be frank, it is very easy to look at the product of most Churches, and determine what kind of Gospel is being preached by the *"fruit"*

NOTES

it produces. Most Churches, and I exaggerate not, are filled with people whose lives have never been changed. They do the same things, act in the same manner, and conduct themselves in the same way as those who profess nothing. No! One is not talking about sinless perfection, for that, in fact, does not exist.

As well, one is not speaking of incidents, which will affect even the most Righteous at one time or the other, demanding Repentance and Forgiveness. We are speaking of the overall lifestyle, which has experienced no change.

If people associate themselves with a Church of any kind, most claim to *"be saved."* While it is certainly true that some are, still, if one looks at all the Churches in the aggregate, most are not saved, and, actually, produce *"evil fruit."*

Truthfully, many Churches are filled with *"moralists."* These individuals attempt to live by a set of rules, which they break as often as not, and think by that they are *"saved."* They think that *"good morals,"* which, in reality, are not so good at all, constitute Salvation. They have never really made Christ their Saviour. Many may have made a mental affirmation, but really did not experience a *"changed heart."* As such, they continue to produce *"evil fruit,"* even though it is of the moral type, which, in fact, is a man-devised morality, which God will not accept.

(18) "A GOOD TREE CANNOT BRING FORTH EVIL FRUIT, NEITHER CAN A CORRUPT TREE BRING FORTH GOOD FRUIT."

The phrase, *"A good tree cannot bring forth evil fruit,"* is strong indeed!

It means that no matter the storms, or vicissitudes of life that affect this *"good tree,"* it will continue to bear *"good fruit."* Regrettably, and even though it is a *"good tree,"* storms, or problems of one kind or the other, and despite the continuing to bear *"good fruit,"* cause many Believers to turn away. The sadness is, that there are so few *"good trees"* that often, such Believers turn to a *"corrupt tree"* which cannot *"bring forth good fruit."*

As well, it should be hastily said, that if it is a *"good tree,"* all the people in the world saying otherwise, will not make it any less good. Approval or disapproval on the part of people change nothing. The Lord is the One Who owns the *"good tree."* While it is true that He may have to *"purge it,"* and, no doubt, will, still, such is done only that it may *"bring forth more fruit"* (Jn. 15:2).

However, the *"purging process"* is not pretty to behold, because it constitutes the dying of certain things, and no one likes to watch something die. It is not pleasant, and most turn away, even the best of Christians. What they think is destruction, is, oftentimes, the very opposite!

To the contrary, it does no good to *"purge"* a *"corrupt tree,"* and because it is corrupt not in just some individual *"branches,"* but, in fact, down to the very roots.

This brings us to our next verse!

(19) "EVERY TREE THAT BRINGETH NOT FORTH GOOD FRUIT IS HEWN DOWN, AND CAST INTO THE FIRE."

As just stated, this *"corrupt tree"* will lose far more than just *"unproductive branches,"* but, in Truth, will be cut down entirely.

This is what John the Baptist was speaking of in his Ministry, which introduced Christ, *"And now also the ax is laid unto the root of the trees: therefore every tree which bringeth not forth good fruit is hewn down, and cast into the fire"* (Mat. 3:10).

In fact, at that time, he was speaking of Israel, which, in A.D. 70, was totally cut down, and because of their rejection of Christ.

It should be understood, that if the Lord would do an entire nation this way, and, especially those who were called *"His chosen,"* would He certainly not do the same to individual *"false prophets?"*

Even as the *"good fruit"* is proof positive, still, the durability of the *"good tree,"* and despite the storms, etc., means that it will continue to bear *"good fruit."*

(20) "WHEREFORE BY THEIR FRUITS YE SHALL KNOW THEM."

The Lord concludes His statement on *"false prophets"* by telling Christians to be *"fruit inspectors."*

Once again, He is talking about *"fruit,"* and not *"hype!"*

If one is to notice, Christ did not say, *"By the good recommendation of others you shall know them,"* or, *"Because major Religious Denominations approve of them,"* or, *"Because they are popular,"* or, *"Everybody likes them,"* etc.

NOTES

In fact, almost none of the above will be true if they are truly bearing *"good fruit."* One is to inspect the *"fruit,"* and not the things just mentioned.

In Truth, not a single Religious Leader, except two members of the Sanhedrin, approved of Christ. Actually, they disapproved of Him so much that they killed Him.

As well, and despite the greatest miracles the world had ever known, His crowds greatly thinned in the last year of His public Ministry, and because His popularity had greatly waned (Jn. 6:66-67).

However, He was known by the *"fruits"* He produced, in changed lives, great miracles of healing, and, above all, the presentation of the Gospel, by His great Sacrifice at Calvary.

Therefore, if the people were going to *"know Him"* by the well wishes of the Religious Leaders, they would have rejected Him out of hand, as, in fact, most did!

(21) "NOT EVERY ONE THAT SAITH UNTO ME, LORD, LORD, SHALL ENTER INTO THE KINGDOM OF HEAVEN; BUT HE THAT DOETH THE WILL OF MY FATHER WHICH IS IN HEAVEN."

The phrase, *"Not every one that saith unto Me, Lord, Lord,"* is wide in its sweeping statement!

First of all, these individuals claimed to recognize Christ as *"Lord."* However, their claim was bogus, or else they had only mentally affirmed their recognition of Christ, without actually experiencing True Conversion.

As well, the repetition of the word *"Lord"* expresses astonishment, as if to say: *"Are we to be disowned?"*

This one Scripture proclaims the fact, that many profess, but do not actually possess. In Truth, and according to the *"few there be that find it,"* in verse 14, most fall into this saddened category.

The phrase, *"Shall enter into the Kingdom of Heaven,"* means to be truly converted, and thereby, at least in a spiritual sense, having already entered into this *"Kingdom."*

The phrase, *"But he that doeth the Will of My Father which is in Heaven,"* refers to those who also say, *"Lord, Lord,"* but, in fact, have been truly saved, and entered into a family relationship with Christ.

So, all the professors and the possessors, say,

"Lord, Lord," but the Truth is here illustrated, that a mere confession, without corresponding results in the heart, is not enough. Regrettably, this adversely affects the far greater majority of those who call themselves *"Christians."*

What is the Will of the Father?

Verse 24 tells us what the *"Will of My Father"* is: *"Therefore whosoever heareth these sayings of mine, and doeth them...."*

In other words, the Word of God is the criteria, and the measuring rod, which will always correspond with Christ, as He is the Living Word, which means that He and the Written Word are indivisible.

This one verse of Scripture, is going to keep many, if not most, out of the Kingdom.

(22) "MANY WILL SAY TO ME IN THAT DAY, LORD, LORD, HAVE WE NOT PROPHESIED IN THY NAME? AND IN THY NAME HAVE CAST OUT DEVILS? AND IN THY NAME DONE MANY WONDERFUL WORKS?"

Many have stumbled over this Scripture, not actually understanding it. Its meaning is clear.

"Miracles" and *"Prophecies"* can truly be of God, or even of Satan. Jesus later said, *"For there shall arise false Christs, and false prophets, and shall shew great signs and wonders; insomuch that if it were possible, they shall deceive the very elect"* (Mat. 24:24).

Therefore, the admonition is clear, that such, even if performed by a True Prophet of the Lord, should not, and, in fact, must not be the yardstick by which such is judged. The Word of God is to be the alone judge of Doctrine.

It is regrettable, that too many Pentecostals, of which I am one, and Charismatics, put entirely too much credit in these things, as helpful and violable as they may be, and are, therefore, led astray by wild claims and exaggerations.

It should be pointed out as well, that even though these things were done, or claimed to be, *"in His Name,"* still, this within itself was no validity.

One might could say that most every Preacher in the world, at least in Christianity, does what they do *"in His Name."* However, miracles performed, and Prophecies given, along with the ready use of His Name, proves nothing. It is abiding by the Word of God, which is the acid test.

As we have already alluded to, *"Are casting out devils, and prophesying Scriptural, and*

especially in the Name of the Lord?" Yes! However, these things, although Scriptural, will not cover the disregarded balance of the Word of God.

In this scenario, and according to verse 21, the *"will of man"* and the *"Will of the Father"* are placed side by side. One cannot have man's will, whether his or others, and God's Will at the same time!

So, the *"Will of God"* is the criteria, which is the Word of God in its entirety.

(23) "AND THEN WILL I PROFESS UNTO THEM, I NEVER KNEW YOU: DEPART FROM ME, YE THAT WORK INIQUITY."

This verse tells us that false teachers are workers of iniquity, however attractive their personal character may be. This judgment is today called narrow, unchristian, violent and bigoted; but it is the Master's Judgment, and therefore perfect.

The moral fruit of these false teachers is corruption in the Church and in the world; and how can such produce changed lives?

The phrase, *"And then will I profess unto them,"* proclaims a coming day of reckoning, which we all should heed very carefully!

This will be at the *"Great White Throne Judgment,"* and will be professed openly in the face of all men (Rev. 20:11-15).

The phrase, *"I never knew you,"* means that even while all this religious activity was taking place, there was, in fact, no personal relationship with Christ. It was all profession, and the use of His Name, without really knowing Who the Person was Who carried the Name.

The Name of Jesus can be used to gain riches, place and position, at least in some circles, and the accolades of men. Therefore, it was used, but without any relationship with Him Personally, and, also by not abiding by all His Word.

Regrettably, this is the case in the far greater majority!

The phrase, *"Depart from Me, ye that work iniquity,"* is chilling indeed!

Depart where?

John said, *"And whosoever was not found written in the Book of Life was cast into the Lake of Fire"* (Rev. 20:15).

It should be readily understood, that what is being spoken of here is not merely the loss of reward, but the loss of one's soul.

As well, the word, *"iniquity,"* is not speaking of sin generally, because every Christian is troubled in some way by fault and failure. This type of *"iniquity"* refers to those who were attempting to serve two masters as described in verses 22-24.

Their *"eye"* (spirit) was evil, and, consequently, the *"Light"* that went into them was darkness, and *"How great is that darkness!"*

As previously stated in Commentary on those verses, this meant that such are so spiritually twisted, and despite the *"miracles"* and the *"use of His Name,"* that whatever *"Light"* of the Gospel that went into them, was immediately turned to *"darkness."*

In other words, they twisted the Scripture to make it mean something they desired, instead of what it actually meant.

It speaks of a false way, a wrong direction, a wrong-headedness, which meant these *"false prophets"* earnestly *"worked"* at this false way.

I have heard Preachers do this, finding a Scripture that they could twist in order to cause people to give money, and, with that only in mind.

I have heard Preachers twist the Scripture, as well, concerning the Baptism in the Holy Spirit, which they had denied, and, therefore, the *"Light"* that went into them was turned to darkness.

Sorrowfully, millions are in the religion business, but they really do not know Jesus as Saviour, and, sadder still, this fact will one day be exclaimed before all!

(24) "THEREFORE WHOSOEVER HEAR-ETH THESE SAYINGS OF MINE, AND DOETH THEM, I WILL LIKEN HIM UNTO A WISE MAN, WHICH BUILT HIS HOUSE UPON A ROCK:"

The phrase, *"Therefore whosoever heareth these sayings of Mine, and doeth them,"* characterizes, and in very simple words, that which it will take to have eternal life. The implication is, that many, if not most, hear *"His sayings,"* but do not *"do them!"* Consequently, Salvation is pronounced in two directives; *"hearing and doing."*

This lays to rest the fallacious doctrine that one can claim to have believed Christ, and therefore have been saved, and then continue to live in sin, as, in fact, multiple millions do!

Many claim that the only difference in the

Believer and the unbeliever, is the Blood of Jesus Christ having been applied to the heart and life of the Believer. They claim that the Believer sins just as the unbeliever, etc.

While it is certainly true that the Blood of Jesus Christ having been applied by Faith to the Believer's heart, is the beginning of the great Salvation process, still, if it has truly been applied, a changed life will be the result, a change so remarkable in fact, that it will be obvious to all!

In other words, the drunk quits drinking, the thief quits stealing, the liar quits lying, the immoral cease their immoral activities, etc. In Truth, Paul said, *"Therefore if any man be in Christ, he is a new creature: old things are passed away; behold, all things are become new"* (II Cor. 5:17).

If this does not happen in the life of an individual, it is a sure sign that the individual has not truly believed with his heart, but, in fact, has only proclaimed a mental affirmation, which is not acceptable to the Lord, and of which these Passages speak.

However, truly being Born Again, and becoming a new creature in Christ Jesus, does not mean sinless perfection. While struggles with certain things may continue, still, the change that is produced will be obvious to all, and with Grace given to further subdue every unholy trait.

The phrase, *"I will liken him unto a wise man, which built his house upon a rock,"* now proclaims that which will actually stand the acid test.

The area in which Jesus was speaking, contained *"rock"* very near the surface, and sometimes even on the surface. Therefore, there was no excuse for not providing the suitable foundation for the *"House of Salvation."*

The only reason that one would not find a suitable place, and especially with such places obvious, is because of self-will. Too many individuals want Salvation but they desire their own will at the same time! Such is not to be.

When Jesus died on Calvary, He died to save us not only from sin, but also from the very receptacle of that sin, *"self-will."*

Once again, the criteria is obedience to the Word of God. If one knows and obeys the Word, this, and this alone, is constituted as the *"Rock."* A house built on anything else, no matter how acceptable to the world, and no matter how much approved by men, will not stand. This means that all the religions of the world, along with all false doctrine perpetrated by *"false prophets,"* will ultimately come crashing down. It may be in this life, or it may be in the Judgment to come, but whichever, it will be *"found wanting."*

(25) "AND THE RAIN DESCENDED, AND THE FLOODS CAME, AND THE WINDS BLEW, AND BEAT UPON THAT HOUSE; AND IT FELL NOT: FOR IT WAS FOUNDED UPON A ROCK."

The phrase, *"And the rain descended, and the floods came, and the winds blew, and beat upon that house,"* completely destroys the erroneous hypotheses of our friends who say that if a Christian has enough Faith, he can confess these things away.

The implication is not that these things might come, but that they definitely will come, and there is no way that one with a proper confession so-called can forego these tests.

The word, *"beat,"* in this Text means *"struck with violence."* It has reference to Satan bringing the full brunt of his attack against this *"house."* However, the Holy Spirit simply says, and with a note of finality, *"and it fell not."*

The idea is, that the only thing that will stand this type of test is the Word of God, and, one might quickly add, the Word of God rightly divided, and not twisted as 6:22-24 proclaims.

The reason the *"house"* stood, is not because of its grand and glorious appointments, but simply because its foundation was sure.

Regrettably, many in these modern times, while viewing the *"storm,"* claim, as we have alluded to, that if the individual had Faith, such would not come, or else, there must be sin or wrongdoing, which brought the storm.

No! The *"storm"* has not come because of a lack of Faith, but because of one's Faith. Faith will always be tested, and great Faith will always be tested greatly!

In Truth, there just possibly may be wrongdoing involved, but because the *"house"* is built upon the *"Rock,"* the only thing that will be destroyed about it will be the unproductive *"branches"* (Jn. 15:2).

No one can claim flawless Faith, or sinless perfection, therefore the storms are allowed by

the Lord to perform a noble work of consecration in the life of the Believer, although Satan's idea is to destroy, but without success!

I believe one can say, and without contradiction, that the Bible teaches, and conclusively so, that in the spiritual sense, these *"floods and winds"* are necessary for our spiritual growth.

Joseph of old, so long ago, said it so beautifully, *"But as for you, ye thought evil against me; but God meant it unto good . . ."* (Gen. 50:20).

(26) "AND EVERY ONE THAT HEARETH THESE SAYINGS OF MINE, AND DOETH THEM NOT, SHALL BE LIKENED UNTO A FOOLISH MAN, WHICH BUILT HIS HOUSE UPON THE SAND:"

The phrase, *"And every one that heareth these sayings of Mine, and doeth them not,"* once again proclaims the fallacy of claiming Salvation, when one is not attempting to obey the Word of God, but, instead, relying on a false doctrine such as *"Once saved always saved,"* or *"Sin a little bit every day religion,"* or *"Associating with a certain Church, such as Catholicism, etc., thinking it brings Salvation."*

If one is to notice, Christ said to *"hear these sayings of Mine,"* not the sayings of other men, Churches, Religious Organizations, etc. If whatever is taught or preached does not line up 100% with the Word of God, it must be rejected out of hand!

I spoke once to the Religious Leader of a major Pentecostal Denomination, as he made a certain statement. I kindly said to him, *"Brother, what you are saying is not Scriptural!"*

I was speaking to him by phone, and I remember him stammering and stuttering for a few moments, and finally saying, *"But that is our tradition!"*

It was sad! He could not deny my statement, and could not buttress his with the Word of God, but he still clung to his unscriptural position.

From that day, that particular Religious Denomination has experienced no growth, but, instead, the opposite; and I say that with no joy.

The phrase, *"Shall be likened unto a foolish man, which built his house upon the sand,"* proclaims every other way of Salvation in the world as false, and irrespective of how it looks on the surface, it will not stand the test when the storms come. The Lord calls that man *"foolish!"*

Regrettably, the *"sand builders"* constitute almost all the world, and for all time!

The *"Rock builders,"* even though, and as Jesus proclaimed, it is clearly defined in the Bible, still, *"few there be that find it"* (vs. 14).

(27) "AND THE RAIN DESCENDED, AND THE FLOODS CAME, AND THE WINDS BLEW, AND BEAT UPON THAT HOUSE; AND IT FELL: AND GREAT WAS THE FALL OF IT."

Just as storms came against the house built upon the *"Rock,"* likewise, storms came against this house.

However, the word, *"beat,"* in this verse is different than the word, *"beat,"* in verse 25.

There it meant, and as stated, violent action, where here it means *"lightly struck."*

In other words, the storm against the house built upon the *"Rock"* was fierce indeed, but *"it fell not,"* whereas, the storm described against the *"house built upon the sand,"* was of small power. However, this *"house"* had no endurance at all, *"and it fell,"* even at the beginning of the storm.

The phrase, *"And great was the fall of it,"* meant that all the elaborate religious preparation, and no matter how applauded by the world, will not stand before God, nor at the *"Great White Throne Judgment"* (Rev. 20:11-15).

(28) "AND IT CAME TO PASS, WHEN JESUS HAD ENDED THESE SAYINGS, THE PEOPLE WERE ASTONISHED AT HIS DOCTRINE:"

The phrase, *"And it came to pass, when Jesus had ended these sayings,"* proclaims the conclusion of the most powerful Message ever uttered on this earth, *"The Sermon on the Mount."*

This Message proclaimed the true intent of the Law of Moses, and, above all, laid the foundation for the New Covenant, which Christ would introduce, but would be given in fullness to the Apostle Paul (Col. 1:25-29).

"These Sayings of Mine," as Christ put it, so far eclipses the wisdom of this world, that it beggars description!

For instance, some time ago, I had the privilege of reading the testimony of a dear lady who was saved by the Blood of Jesus in the country of Pakistan. She had been born and raised a Moslem, with her family quite prominent in Pakistan, and going back hundreds of years as a part of the cultured Elite.

She had the misfortune of suffering a divorce,

NOTES

and found herself lonely, heartbroken, and desperately needing help.

During this time of great trouble, being a Moslem, she turned to the Koran for solace, even though she had really never read it.

The words held no meaning, produced no comfort, and despite her diligence to peruse the texts, no solace was forthcoming.

Still desperate, her mind wandered to thoughts of the Bible, which she had not read either, and, in fact, had been taught against it all her life.

Through her Uncle, she was able to secure a copy of the Word of God. Having never seen one before, she hardly knew where to begin, but started in the Book of Matthew. When she came to the Beatitudes, they were a great solace to her, and were the most beautiful statements she had ever read in all of her life. It seemed like the Words were alive!

Day after day, she hungrily devoured the Texts, receiving comfort, solace, and strength.

Nevertheless, Satan, at this time, began to make his entrance. Which was truly the Word of God, the Koran or the Bible?

Even though still unconverted, she began to pray asking the Lord to show her the Truth. To be sure, an honest, sincere heart will always receive an answer from the Lord.

The Lord gently spoke to her heart, saying, in answer to her request, *"You have asked which book is truly the Word of God, the Bible or the Koran?"*

He then said, *"The Book which calls Me 'Father,' is My Word!"*

A short time later, she was gloriously saved, and then Baptized in the Holy Spirit. Her testimony, and especially concerning the manner in which the Lord led her on a daily basis, was one of the most interesting and inspiring that I've ever had the privilege to read. It was a perfect example of a false house being forsaken, with one being *"built on the Rock,"* i.e., *"these Sayings of Mine."*

The phrase, *"The people were astonished at His Doctrine,"* proclaims them hearing words they had never heard before!

Especially considering that these were the very people (the Jews) to whom the Bible had been given, and to whom the Prophets had been sent, and exclusive of anyone else in the world, why were they astonished at His Teaching?

They were astonished, because, first of all, He taught, as the next verse proclaims, with such authority and power, which was produced by the Anointing of the Holy Spirit (Lk. 4:18).

As well, they had not heard the Word of God truly and honestly proclaimed, at least for the most part, in all of their lives. They were like most people presently in most Churches, who hear a watered-down version, or no version at all!

Even in many Pentecostal and Charismatic Churches, which claim to believe and preach the entirety of the Word of God, still, many, if not most, proclaim a mixture of psychology and Bible, which constitutes *"houses built on sand."* In Truth, and sadly, modern humanistic psychology has become the cure-all for the ills of man. Regrettably, many, even the Fundamentalists, which include the Pentecostals, Charismatics, Baptists, and Holiness, are claiming that the Bible does not hold all the answers for the behavioral problems of modern man. Therefore, they claim, a wedding of the Bible and psychology is the only answer!

Such drivel proclaims a total lack of knowledge of the Word of God, or of man, for that matter!

Such constitutes rank, raw unbelief. As such, it is sin, and decidedly so!

Once again, we come back to the *"Rock"* or the sand. I think it is obvious that one cannot build a *"house"* on part rock and part sand. The idea is foolish to say the least!

Any building contractor knows that if half of the foundation is insecure, such will destroy the good half as well!

That is why Jesus said, *"Beware of the leaven of the Pharisees"* (Mk. 8:15), and Paul said, *"A little leaven leaventh the whole lump"* (I Cor. 5:6).

What Jesus taught was the pure, unadulterated, uncompromised, undiluted, and unassailable Word of God. Its clarity, perfection, purity, clearness, and power evoked an *"astonishment"* among the people, as it will any people.

That is the reason Paul said, *"I charge thee therefore before God, and the Lord Jesus Christ, Who shall judge the quick and the dead at His appearing and His Kingdom;*

"Preach the Word; be instant in season, out of season; reprove, rebuke, exhort with all

NOTES

longsuffering and doctrine" (II Tim. 4:1-2).

He then added, *"For the time will come when they will not endure sound doctrine; but after their own lusts shall they heap to themselves teachers, having itching ears;*

"And they shall turn away their ears from the Truth, and shall be turned unto fables" (II Tim. 4:3-4).

(29) "FOR HE TAUGHT THEM AS ONE HAVING AUTHORITY, AND NOT AS THE SCRIBES."

The phrase, *"For He taught them as One having authority,"* refers to Divine Authority, which He had by the Power of the Holy Spirit.

As well, every single God-called Preacher, filled with the Holy Ghost, can, and, in fact, must minister, at least with a measure of that *"authority."*

Going back to verses 21 and 22, Jesus said, *"Many will say to Me in that day...."* In those verses, He declared Himself to be God the Great Judge Eternal. Hence He spoke with authority; and the people felt it. None of the great Prophets could use such words.

The phrase, *"And not as the Scribes,"* spoke of them always referring to tradition, or to what some other teacher had said.

These individuals, along with the Pharisees and Sadducees, were constantly arguing over Scripture, attempting to devise tricky questions, which they thought portrayed their great cleverness, but, instead, only portrayed their ignorance.

They seldom told anyone how to keep the Law, but, instead, how not to break it. Consequently, they devised over 600 added laws, which were tradition, and, therefore, man-devised. There was seldom, if ever, a *"Thus saith the Lord!"*

Therefore, Jesus' Message was a gush of sunshine on their darkened spiritual world.

This *"Sermon on the Mount,"* and that of Luke 6, were possibly one and the same. The Lord descended the mountain a certain distance and meeting the multitude He re-ascended a little to *"a plain"* or level place suitable for the purpose, and there taught.

Emphasis is laid in Matthew on the necessity of a new moral birth, hence the points about sin in the heart; in Luke, outward actions are reviewed. The distinction between *"standing"* and *"state"* is apparent.

CHAPTER 8

(1) "WHEN HE WAS COME DOWN FROM THE MOUNTAIN, GREAT MULTITUDES FOLLOWED HIM."

The phrase, *"When He was come down from the mountain,"* portrays the conclusion of the *"Sermon on the Mount,"* which exhibited the statutes of the Kingdom which He proposed to set up on the earth, and which, in Truth, have already come to millions of hearts and lives, and will ultimately fill the earth. He now descends into the midst of the people demonstrating His Power as God over disease (2-16), over nature (24-26), and over Demons (28-32), and His ability, by vanquishing evil, to fill the earth with happiness and destroy the works and kingdom of the Devil; but men preferred Satanic domination, and disease, and Demons, and swine (vs. 34).

The phrase, *"Great multitudes followed Him,"* is a result of the *"authority"* with which He taught.

(2) "AND, BEHOLD, THERE CAME A LEPER AND WORSHIPPED HIM, SAYING, LORD, IF THOU WILT, THOU CANST MAKE ME CLEAN."

The time-frame of the coming of the leper, does not necessarily mean that this happened immediately after Jesus came down from the mountain, as Matthew does not seem to be concerned with chronological connection of the incidents here narrated, for this is evidently to him a matter of but secondary importance, and was sanctioned by the Holy Spirit. He only desires to bring out different aspects of the Lord's life.

So, exactly when the leper came is not that important, but what happened to him!

The phrase, *"And, behold, there came a leper,"* is meant by the Holy Spirit to portray several things:

1. In the Old Testament, leprosy was a portrayal or symbol of sin, and how it affected the sinner. It was the most loathsome disease that could affect a human being, with the extremities of their bodies, such as fingers, toes, nose, and even lips, etc., literally falling off the body as the disease took its deadly toll! In fact, there could be no more fitting example, as leprosy

affected the physical, sin affected the spiritual.

2. The manner of the leper is a fitting example as to the manner of the sinner. The account is given in Leviticus:

A. *"His clothes shall be rent":* The garment worn by the leper was to be torn in the back from the bottom to the top, leaving only the hem at the top of the garment intact, in order to hold it together. Such was meant to symbolize his undone condition. Such, as well, portrayed man's pitiful efforts to save himself, which are looked at by God as a torn, wasted garment. It symbolized the *"fig leaves"* of Adam and Eve which the Lord would not accept, along with Cain's unsuitable Sacrifice, as well as all of man's futile attempts to form his own religion in order to reach God (Gen. 3:7, 21; 4:4, 5; Prov. 14:12).

B. *"And his head bare":* The men among the Jews in those days wore a type of cap on their heads, which signified that their covering was the Lord, and that peace had been established with Him. The leper, not being allowed to cover his head, symbolized that he had no protection from the anger of God, and that he was open to the Judgment of God, of which his leprosy was a type. There is the *"enmity"* between God and man, and because of man's sin. The Scripture says that *"God is angry with the wicked every day"* (Ps. 7:11).

Actually, man does not feel this enmity near as much as God, because man is the cause of the estrangement, and has offended God.

However, the Death of Christ on the Cross, settled this *"enmity,"* at least for all who will believe. Paul said, *"And that He might reconcile both unto God in one body by the Cross, having slain the enmity thereby:*

"And came and preached peace to you which were afar off, and to them that were nigh.

"For through Him we both have access by one Spirit unto the Father" (Eph. 2:16-18).

So, the anger of God against wicked man, was assuaged at Calvary by the Death of Christ on the Cross, and was ratified by His Resurrection. Now, and as the Scripture says, there can be *"peace"* between God and man.

(Incidentally, under the New Covenant, and because of what Christ did at Calvary and the Resurrection, the Believer wears no religious covering on his head, because Christ is now his covering, I Cor. 11:4).

C. *"And He shall put a covering upon his upper lip, and shall cry, Unclean, unclean":* Not only were his garments to portray his uncleanliness, along with his uncovered head, as well, the leper was to constantly cry, *"Unclean, unclean."*

Consequently, every action by the unsaved, whether spoken or committed, is crying, *"Unclean, unclean!"*

For example, when someone is asked if they are saved, and they reply, *"I am a Baptist,"* or *"Methodist,"* or *"Pentecostal,"* or *"Catholic,"* they are, whether they realize it or not, crying, *"Unclean, unclean."*

No! It does not mean that one is necessarily wrong to belong to one of these particular Churches, but their speech identifies, as the leper of old, that they do not know what Salvation really is, thinking it is contained in the Church. Therefore, their answer betrays them! Only the Blood of Jesus can cleanse, which means that no Church, or all the religious ritual in the world, can wash away one single sin. Those who depend on such are crying, *"Unclean, unclean!"*

D. *"He shall dwell alone":* Despite the crowds, the activity, and the excitement, there is a terrible loneliness to sin. This is because man, originally created in the *"Image of God,"* has now violated that image, and is estranged from his Creator. Consequently, there is a loneliness that nothing in the world can acquiesce. That is the reason for much of the alcoholism, drug addiction, and other means of escapism. Only Christ can assuage that loneliness (Lev. 13:45-46).

Moses, in Leviticus, also gave the remedy for the terrible disease of leprosy, which was a type of the Death and Resurrection of Christ. It is as follows:

1. *"And the Priest shall go forth out of the camp; and the Priest shall look":* The *"Priest"* was a type of Christ, and, consequently, went looking for the leper, as Christ came from Heaven looking for lost souls.

Redeemed man is accustomed to saying, *"I found the Lord,"* when, in reality, *"The Lord found the man."*

2. *"Two birds alive and clean":* One of these would represent Christ in His Death, with the other representing Him in His Resurrection.

3. *"Cedar wood":* The Cedar Wood represented the Cross of Christ, which He would die upon.

4. *"And scarlet":* This represented His shed Blood.

NOTES

5. *"And hyssop":* This represented His Incarnation, and, thereby, paying the price for man.

6. *"One of the birds be killed in an earthen vessel over running water":* This signified the Death of Christ, with the *"earthen vessel"* representing His human Body, and the *"running water"* representing the Holy Spirit, Who superintended His Death.

7. *"And shall dip them and the living bird in the blood of the bird that was killed over the running water":* The bird that was left alive, and with all the *"wood, scarlet, and hyssop,"* held beside it, would be dipped in the blood of the bird that was killed over the running water. This spoke of the Blood applied to the lost soul, which Faith alone in that Blood could cleanse the sinner.

8. *"And he shall sprinkle upon him that is to be cleansed from the leprosy seven times":* The Blood must be applied, and the *"seven times"* spoke of a perfect Salvation, as *"seven"* is God's number of perfection.

9. *"And shall let the living bird loose into the opened field":* This spoke of Christ's Resurrection, which ratified what He did at Calvary. As well, it spoke of the sinner going free! (Lev. 14:3-7).

A. Such could come to Christ, and were, in fact, invited to come.

B. Only Christ could heal such a one, as only Christ can save such a one from sin.

C. All of humanity is a moral leper, of which this is meant to imply, with all needing Salvation.

D. The answer is Jesus and not the Church, or anything else!

In all of the miracles of Christ, I think one will find that the miracle or healing, was meant to portray far more than the actual event itself. As with the *"leper,"* a lesson was taught, not only to Israel, but to the world in general. Therefore, it is up to the Bible Student, to glean that which the Master intended!

The phrase, *"And worshipped Him,"* proclaims the leper doing that which he actually was not supposed to do, approach Christ, or anyone else, for that matter! He was supposed to remain at approximately 100 feet distance from anyone. So how could he have the nerve to approach Christ as he did!

As stated, Matthew did not give these

incidents in chronological order, but, instead, in spiritual order. Consequently, Jesus had probably performed a number of miracles before this incident, of which the leper had heard, or maybe even seen.

The word, *"worshipped,"* portrays not only his desperation, but, as well, the thought in his heart that this One may truly be the Messiah, which He was!

At any rate, the manner in which he came portrays the correct approach for all. He came properly *"worshipping,"* which will never be denied, and especially considering his proper attitude.

The phrase, *"Saying, Lord,"* further proclaims him addressing Jesus as the Messiah.

The phrase, *"If Thou wilt, Thou canst make me clean,"* contains a wealth of information!

First of all, the exclamation, *"If Thou wilt,"* denotes that quite possibly no leper had yet been cleansed by Christ, although other miracles had by now been performed. The man's utterance, therefore, marks a distinct advance in Faith.

Knowing that Christ was able, he appeals beyond His power to His heart.

What a lesson for all!

This portrays to us that Faith will find a way, and irrespective of the obstacles and hindrances, and which will always abound! In fact, he could have been stoned for approaching so close to Christ. However, he was dying anyway, and his heart must have reasoned, *"I would rather go toward Him and risk everything, rather than not go at all and remain in this horrible condition."*

The phrase, *"Thou canst make me clean,"* has a far greater meaning than being merely *"healed,"* as great as that would have been! It meant healing and its consequences — restoration to social and spiritual privileges.

In other words, he would no more be a *"leper,"* and would be allowed once again into society.

The word, *"clean,"* is beautiful, in that it expresses the terrible malignancy of leprosy, as it typifies sin. That is the reason the Lord not only forgives sin, but He *"cleanses from all sin"* (I Jn. 1:9).

In every aspect, and in every way it can be observed, sin is filthy. This speaks of a moral and spiritual filth that carries with it such a stain, that it can be cleansed only, and as stated,

NOTES

by the Precious Blood of Christ. All the education, money, religion, Churches, and good works, in the world can never cleanse the horrible stain of sin. Only the Blood of Christ, and Faith in that Atoning Work, can effect this miracle of Redemption. As Jesus Alone could make the leper clean, Jesus Alone can make the sinner clean!

(3) "AND JESUS PUT FORTH HIS HAND, AND TOUCHED HIM, SAYING, I WILL; BE THOU CLEAN. AND IMMEDIATELY HIS LEPROSY WAS CLEANSED."

The phrase, *"And Jesus put forth His Hand, and touched him,"* was meant, at least in the spiritual, to describe the actions of Christ in respect to the sinner.

God, by decree, could say, *"Let there be light,"* and there was light! However, He could not decree or speak Salvation into existence, but, instead, *"He hath made Him to be sin for us, Who knew no sin; that we might be made the Righteousness of God in Him"* (II Cor. 5:21).

Christ, by becoming the *"Last Adam"* touched man's sin, in order to deliver man from its death, but because of His purity, was undefiled.

As well, according to the Law of Moses (Lev. 13:46; 11:40), touching a leper meant that one would be unclean until the evening. Therefore, why was Christ not defiled, as others?

He was not defiled, as He was perfectly pure, and, as well, because He healed and cleansed the leper, and there was nothing left to defile. Also, if the Pharisees had dared to accuse Him, there would be no proof of their accusation, because the leper now stands *"cleansed, well, and whole"*

It was in this manner that Jesus bore our sins at Calvary, and, in effect, *"Being made to be sin for us,"* even though He never sinned. He took the judgment and the penalty for sin, which should have come to us, but the terrible effects of sin, as this leprosy, could not attach itself to Him, because of His absolute purity. What man touches, he defiles, and because he is defiled. What Christ touches, He purifies, because He is pure!

The phrase, *"Saying, I will; be thou clean,"* was Christ's immediate response, as it always will be to any and all who come truly seeking Him.

The phrase, *"And immediately his leprosy was cleansed,"* expresses the simplicity and actuality of Salvation!

No one is saved by degrees, but always *"immediately!"*

One moment a precious soul is lost and undone without God, and the next moment, upon Faith in Christ, that soul is immediately cleansed!

As well, as it happened to this leper, possibly in a city, or the suburbs, or at the foot of the mountain, Salvation can take place as well!

Some erroneously equate going to Church with being Saved. It isn't! Salvation comes only through Christ, and Christ Alone!

The *"cleansing"* of this leper, no doubt, meant the healing of the parts of his body which had suffered loss. Consequently, the possibility definitely exists, that fingers, or other extremities, which may have fallen off due to the rotting of this terrible disease, were, in fact, instantly replaced!

Luke said he was *"full of leprosy,"* and if the same man, which he no doubt was, this miracle included that of which we have spoken (Lk. 5:12-13).

(4) "AND JESUS SAITH UNTO HIM, SEE THOU TELL NO MAN; BUT GO THY WAY, SHEW THYSELF TO THE PRIEST, AND OFFER THE GIFT THAT MOSES COMMANDED, FOR A TESTIMONY UNTO THEM."

Only God could cleanse the leper, hence Jesus was God; but yet, as a Servant, He veiled His Glory, and, as a Hebrew, in subjection to the Law, commanded the man to fulfill its requirements.

Thus the Law, through the activities of the Priest, confirmed the miracle wrought by the Law-giver.

But Immanuel's mission in His First Advent was to deal with sin and suffer its judgment at Calvary. He suppressed anything that would hinder that purpose of Grace, and so forbade the man to publish the fact of his healing.

The phrase, *"And Jesus said unto him, See you tell no man,"* was done, it seems, for several reason. But the greatest reason of all was the purpose for which He came.

THE CROSS OF CHRIST

It should be abundantly obvious that everything Jesus did was of utmost significance. But the primary reason that God became Man was to go to the Cross, because there alone could the demands of a Thrice-Holy God be met.

So, nothing must stand in the way of that: not healings, not miracles, not anything else!

The only answer for sin is the Cross of Calvary. There is no other, because there need be no other. The Cross of Christ is to be the foundation of all Biblical doctrine.

Peter said this:

"Forasmuch as you know that you were not Redeemed with corruptible things, as silver and gold (presents the fact that the most precious commodities [silver and gold] could not Redeem fallen man), *from your vain conversation* (vain lifestyle) *received by tradition from your fathers* (speaks of original sin that is passed on at conception from father to child);

"But with the Precious Blood of Christ (presents the payment, which proclaims the poured out Life of Christ on behalf of sinners), *as of a Lamb without blemish and without spot* (speaks of the lambs offered as substitutes in the Old Jewish economy; the Death of Christ was not an execution or assassination, but rather a Sacrifice; the Offering of Himself presented a Perfect Sacrifice, for He was perfect in every respect [Ex. 12:5]):

"Who verily was foreordained before the foundation of the world (refers to the fact that God, in His Omniscience, knew He would create man, man would Fall, and man would be Redeemed by Christ going to the Cross; this was all done before the Universe was created; this means the Cross of Christ is the Foundation Doctrine of all Doctrine, referring to the fact that all Doctrine must be built upon that Foundation or else it is specious), *but was manifest in these last times for you"* (refers to the invisible God Who, in the Person of the Son, was made visible to human eyesight by assuming a human body and human limitations) (I Pet. 1:18-19).

Let us say it again:

Every doctrine that is not built squarely upon the Foundation of the Cross of Christ is the cause of error.

The phrase, *"But go thy way, shew thyself to the Priest,"* relates to Leviticus 13:49, and 14:2. Actually, without this official verdict, the man could not be restored to the privileges of society.

The phrase, *"And offer the gift that Moses commanded,"* concerned, and as we have said, *"two living clean birds, and cedar wood, and scarlet and hyssop"* (Lev. 14:4). Other Sacrifices were to be offered as well!

The phrase, *"For a testimony unto them,"* had reference to what Christ had done, and which only the Messiah could do. Therefore, there was no excuse whatsoever for them not knowing exactly Who Jesus was.

(5) "AND WHEN JESUS WAS ENTERED INTO CAPERNAUM, THERE CAME UNTO HIM A CENTURION, BESEECHING HIM,"

Christ came not only to cleanse Israel, but to liberate the Gentile, and accordingly, the servant of the Roman Officer was set free from his malady.

The phrase, *"And when Jesus was entered into Capernaum,"* probably referred to the time when He initially made His Headquarters in this city.

The phrase, *"There came unto Him a Centurion, beseeching Him,"* referred to a captain of 100 men, a 60th part of a Roman Legion.

As well, Matthew's account is abbreviated with, more than likely, the *"Centurion,"* not actually coming himself, but sending emissaries. According to Luke's account, which is much more detailed, this seems to be what happened!

As well, it is not wrong for such action to be portrayed in such a manner as Matthew did!

The one who speaks for, and, on behalf of another, is the same as the first person speaking.

(6) "AND SAYING, LORD, MY SERVANT LIETH AT HOME SICK OF THE PALSY, GRIEVOUSLY TORMENTED."

The leprous Jew had called Jesus, *"Lord,"* and now, the Gentile *"Centurion"* calls Him *"Lord,"* proclaiming Him Lord of all!

The phrase, *"And saying, Lord, my servant lieth at home sick of the palsy,"* spoke of great concern for the servant on the part of the Centurion, and, as well, denoted this sickness, which was a *"paralysis with contraction of the joints, accompanied with intense suffering."*

The phrase, *"Grievously tormented,"* places the sickness in the realm of acute pain, which was not only getting worse, but was threatening the man's life.

If one is to notice, all the healings and miracles of Christ were carried out, regardless of the spirituality of the recipients. There is precious little record of any accusation of any nature, except a brief *"Go, and sin no more,"* concerning the woman taken in adultery (Jn. 8:11). No doubt, Jesus healed many who were not living as they should live, and, in fact, had sin in their lives. Considering the tremendous number involved, and the manner in which the healings

NOTES

were carried out, which, oftentimes, were instantaneous, and carried out by a touch, with little, if any, preliminary conversation (vs. 16), one must come to this conclusion.

Such was done in this manner to present the Grace of God, which came by Jesus Christ. Grace never condemns the sinner, while it also never condones the sin.

An example is this Centurion's servant, who was, no doubt, a Gentile, and, *"a stranger to the Promises."* Nevertheless, he was not excluded, because Grace cannot exclude anyone, and, in fact, will never exclude anyone who comes to Christ.

(7) "AND JESUS SAITH UNTO HIM, I WILL COME AND HEAL HIM."

The emphasis is not on the coming, but, instead, on the One Who is coming, namely Christ. The *"I"* is emphatic, meaning, *"I can, and I will!"*

It is said in the same spirit, as the answer given to the leper, *"I will; be thou clean."*

He says the same today to any and all who will dare to believe Him. He has not changed, and, in Truth, can never change!

He Alone can heal the brokenhearted. He Alone can heal broken marriages, twisted lives, dreams and hurting hopes! He Alone!

(8) "THE CENTURION ANSWERED AND SAID, LORD, I AM NOT WORTHY THAT THOU SHOULDEST COME UNDER MY ROOF: BUT SPEAK THE WORD ONLY, AND MY SERVANT SHALL BE HEALED."

The phrase, *"The Centurion answered and said,"* does not necessarily mean that the Centurion answered personally to Christ, for Luke proclaims him sending friends to Christ with this message.

Matthew does not explain how this was done, as Luke, but just that it was done.

The phrase, *"Lord, I am not worthy that Thou shouldest come under my roof,"* was probably his referral to being a Gentile. Knowing the bias of the Jews, quite possibly he thought that Christ may have felt the same way. However, if those were his thoughts, they could not have been more wrong!

The phrase, *"But speak the word only, and my servant shall be healed,"* proclaims remarkable Faith.

Being a military man, he knew what authority and orders were. If he gave an order, he expected it to be carried out, and because the authority of the Emperor was behind him. He felt that Christ had the same authority in the spiritual sense.

Whether he understood it or not, his hypotheses respecting the military was very close to the spiritual.

There is actually a war in the spirit world, which has been carried on since the Fall of Satan, and as far as this world is concerned, since the Fall of Adam and Eve in the Garden of Eden. Satan's Fallen Angels have ranks, as is proclaimed in Scripture (Eph. 6:12). As well, the Angels of the Lord serve Righteousness in the same manner, with Michael being the only Archangel spoken of in Scripture, placing him in the highest rank of all (Jude 9).

Likewise, Paul told Timothy, *"War a good warfare"* (I Tim. 1:18). As well, he said, *"The weapons of our warfare are not carnal . . ."* (II Cor. 10:4).

Quite possibly the Centurion knew nothing of this, but, still, he came closer to Great Faith than any in Israel.

(9) "FOR I AM A MAN UNDER AUTHORITY, HAVING SOLDIERS UNDER ME: AND I SAY TO THIS MAN, GO, AND HE GOETH; AND TO ANOTHER, COME, AND HE COMETH; AND TO MY SERVANT, DO THIS, AND HE DOETH IT."

The phrase, *"For I am a man under authority,"* referred to his being under the authority of the Emperor, and making certain that he always carried out his orders.

The phrase, *"Having soldiers under me: and say to this man, Go, and he goeth; and to another, Come, and he cometh; and to my servant, Do this, and he doeth it,"* proclaims the order of command.

Actually, the entirety of this verse, very systematically, portrays true *"authority."* As stated, the Centurion received his orders and was quick to obey, and when he gave orders, he expected full and immediate obedience as well!

Authority simply means *"the one in command,"* or, more specifically, *"delegated power."*

The Centurion had Rome behind him, while Jesus had the *"Father,"* i.e., Almighty God, behind Him.

Whatever the Centurion had heard of Christ, he felt at least that His authority was as great as Caesar's, and even greater, because Caesar could not heal his servant, while Jesus could!

(10) "WHEN JESUS HEARD IT, HE

MARVELLED, AND SAID TO THEM THAT FOLLOWED, VERILY I SAY UNTO YOU, I HAVE NOT FOUND SO GREAT FAITH, NO, NOT IN ISRAEL."

The phrase, *"When Jesus heard it, He marvelled,"* records one of the only two times He marvelled; the Faith of this Gentile, and the unbelief of the Jews (Mk. 6:6).

The phrase, *"And said to them that followed, Verily I say unto you,"* is a statement meant to be heard by all, even His Disciples.

The phrase, *"I have not found so great Faith, no, not in Israel,"* actually refers to the individuals He had by now met!

He is saying, and surprisingly so, that a Gentile surpassed them all. As well, the Centurion is put above the Apostles, but only in the realm of his Faith.

Actually, Israel would lose her way, because she had no *"Faith!"* The Gentiles would accept Him, of whom this one is an example, because they had Faith.

"Faith in what?", one may ask.

The man had Faith in Jesus Alone, while the Jews had Faith in their system, but no Faith in Christ!

(11) "AND I SAY UNTO YOU, THAT MANY SHALL COME FROM THE EAST AND WEST, AND SHALL SIT DOWN WITH ABRAHAM, AND ISAAC, AND JACOB, IN THE KINGDOM OF HEAVEN."

In this Scripture, Christ foretells the coming of the Gentile Church, even though His listeners would in no way have understood that.

The phrase, *"And I say unto you,"* proclaims the coming announcement in dogmatic style, which would be chilling indeed, at least for the Jews.

The phrase, *"That many shall come from the east and west,"* refers to the furtherest limits of the earth. As such, and as stated, it proclaims the Church.

The phrase, *"And shall sit down with Abraham, and Isaac, and Jacob, in the Kingdom of Heaven,"* proclaims this great number of Gentiles being saved, which, no doubt, was a shock to the Jews who heard this pronouncement.

Gentiles were looked at by the Jews as dogs, and the idea that *"many"* would be saved, was preposterous to say the least!

Consequently, it was very difficult, even for the Early Church to open the door wide to the

Gentiles. Peter was given the privilege of being the first one to do this (Acts 10). Even then, it came slow with the Apostle Paul leading the spearhead, proclaiming Jesus saying to him, *"I will send thee far hence unto the Gentiles"* (Acts 22:21).

(12) "BUT THE CHILDREN OF THE KINGDOM SHALL BE CAST OUT INTO OUTER DARKNESS: THERE SHALL BE WEEPING AND GNASHING OF TEETH."

The phrase, *"But the children of the Kingdom shall be cast out into outer darkness,"* refers to Israel being lost, as they were!

They were lost because they rejected Christ, as all are lost who reject Christ!

There are some who erroneously think that God has provided another way of Salvation for the Jews. He has not! All must come the same way, for all can be saved in Christ, and none can be saved without Christ.

The *"Outer darkness"* speaks of hell itself, and even with emphasis, *"There shall be weeping and gnashing of teeth."*

No one on earth was more religious than the Jews, and, yet, they died lost, proclaiming the Truth, that religion cannot save!

They came so close, but yet were so far away. They had greater opportunity than any, and, therefore, their hell will be the greatest of all!

(13) "AND JESUS SAID UNTO THE CENTURION, GO THY WAY; AND AS THOU HAST BELIEVED, SO BE IT DONE UNTO THEE. AND HIS SERVANT WAS HEALED IN THE SELFSAME HOUR."

The phrase, *"And Jesus said unto the Centurion,"* was rather meant that the Message was to be given to the Centurion, which it was!

The phrase, *"Go thy way; and as thou hast believed, so be it done unto thee,"* was exactly as the Centurion felt it would be. He had Faith that Jesus' Word was enough, and Jesus responded in kind, *"as thou hast believed, so be it done unto thee."*

The phrase, *"And his servant was healed in the selfsame hour,"* did not mean that he was healed an hour from then, but in the same hour in which Jesus spoke, which was immediately.

One can only say, *"What Faith! What Power!"*

To be sure, there was rejoicing in the Centurion's house that night, and there will be rejoicing in any house that Jesus visits!

As well, this entire episode is meant to portray the *"Word of God"* coming into a life, or a

house. Even now, some 2,000 years later, if men, as the Centurion, will only believe, this *"Word"* will have the same effect, and respecting any problem!

(14) "AND WHEN JESUS WAS COME INTO PETER'S HOUSE, HE SAW HIS WIFE'S MOTHER LAID, AND SICK OF A FEVER."

It seems clear that Jesus, by now, had left his boyhood home of Nazareth, and would now make Capernaum His Headquarters. This is after He had preached in the Synagogue in Nazareth, which seemed, extensively so, to have aroused the ire of the good city fathers, in which they then attempted to take His life by taking Him to the top of the hill and casting Him off. However, Luke said, *"But He passing through the midst of them went His way"* (Lk. 4:28-30).

I have visited the ruins of Capernaum, and have seen the site where it is claimed that Peter's house stood. How this could be determined is anyone's guess.

At any rate, the site is very near the site of where the Synagogue stood, and is very near the shore of the Sea of Galilee.

The phrase, *"He saw his wife's mother laid, and sick of a fever,"* proclaims Peter as a family man, so he could hardly have started celibacy in the Roman Church (I Cor. 9:5).

The Text seems to imply that Jesus had not been told about the lady's physical condition. Matthew said she had *"a fever,"* while Luke, who was a physician, said she had a *"great fever."* At any rate, she was very ill, and it seems unable to even stand.

(15) "AND HE TOUCHED HER HAND, AND THE FEVER LEFT HER: AND SHE AROSE, AND MINISTERED UNTO THEM."

The phrase, *"And He touched her hand, and the fever left her,"* refers to an instantaneous healing. One moment she was sick, and seriously so, and the next moment she was well!

Almost everything that Christ did respecting healings and miracles, was in this fashion. The deliverance was instantaneous.

Likewise, when Christ truly comes into a heart, the deliverance from sin is instantaneous there as well!

With man it is the very opposite! The treatments are of lengthy duration, with the help being minimal, if any at all! The Holy Spirit through the Prophet Jeremiah, said, *"They have healed also the hurt of the daughter of My people slightly, saying, Peace, peace; when there is no peace"* (Jer. 6:14).

And yet, men continue to seek men, rather than the Lord, and, sadder still, the Church follows suit!

The phrase, *"And she arose, and ministered unto them,"* signifies, as stated, an immediate healing, with her, it seems, going about to prepare the evening meal.

There was, no doubt, great joy in that house that night, as great joy will always characterize any place where Jesus is. The entrance of Christ into any home, changes the disposition of that home, and always for the good.

The sadness of some 50 percent of the marriages presently concluding in divorce, with all its attendant misery and suffering, could be instantly dispelled by one visit of Christ, and a yielding unto Him. He never leaves the house as He found it, but always makes it better!

And it doesn't matter what the problem is, be it domestical, financial, physical, or spiritual, Christ is the Answer, and, in fact, the only Answer.

I can remember the day that Jesus came into our house. I was five years old when my parents were saved. Of course, I loved both of them very much.

But yet, before they came to Christ, and despite their love for each other, it seemed like the quarrelling and the fussing were almost continuous. I remember as a little child, grieving, when I would witness these quarrels, and the harsh things my parents said to each other.

But, oh happy day! When my Mother and Dad came to Jesus there was an instantaneous change in our home, and even though I was only five years old, I noticed it immediately.

The fussing, quarrelling and fighting instantly stopped. Peace and harmony reigned! Even though as I write this, it has been some 55 years ago, I can still remember that moment as if it were yesterday. Joy filled my heart, because my Mother and Dad did not quarrel anymore; instead, they talked sweet and kind to each other. There was a different spirit in the house altogether.

When Jesus comes in, the spirit changes! The song says:

"What the world needs is Jesus, just one glimpse of Him.
"What the world needs is Jesus, just one glimpse of Him.
"He will bring joy and gladness, take

NOTES

away sin and sadness,
"What the world needs is Jesus, just one glimpse of Him!"

I suspect that Peter's Mother-in-law was so very thrilled and glad to be able to prepare an evening meal for Christ, along with the others, and especially after what He had done for her. This question must be asked:

"After what Christ has done for us in the Salvation of our souls, would not it be prudent for us to 'minister' unto Him, by helping to take the Good News of His Glorious Word to the entirety of the world?"

(16) "WHEN THE EVEN WAS COME, THEY BROUGHT UNTO HIM MANY THAT WERE POSSESSED WITH DEVILS: AND HE CAST OUT THE SPIRITS WITH HIS WORD, AND HEALED ALL THAT WERE SICK:"

The phrase, *"When the even was come,"* referred to the Sabbath ending at sundown. (It began at sundown on Friday night, and ended at sundown Saturday night.)

The people now felt free to walk about, performing duties, with no fear of breaking the Sabbath, which had just ended.

The phrase, *"They brought unto Him many that were possessed with devils,"* speaks of a horror that has plagued humanity even from the Fall. Demon spirits seek to possess human beings. If they are not able to possess, they seek to oppress, with the latter being experienced by all at one time or the other, whether understood or not! (Acts 10:38).

Actually, the unsaved are dramatically influenced by demon spirits, hence, the terrible things which are constantly done.

Demon possession is what Satan seeks the most, and demons probably possess far more people than is realized. Such is a torture almost beyond belief.

An individual so occupied, loses control of his will and faculties, doing things beyond his power to resist.

Demon spirits are disembodied intelligent spirits, who do the bidding of their master, Satan. They are sent to steal, kill, and destroy (Jn. 10:10).

There is no relief from these spirits in the medical or the psychological field. In other words, medicine and psychology are helpless against these spirits of darkness, and because it is a spiritual matter, albeit affecting the physical and the mental.

Preachers of the Gospel are supposed to be filled with the Holy Ghost, enabling them to use the Name of Jesus to cast out Devils (Mat. 10:1; Mk. 16:17).

Regrettably, most Preachers, lacking the Holy Spirit, refer such cases to the psychologists, even though there is no help from that source, instead of casting them out. These spirits of darkness operate in the realm of the spirit world, and do not, and in fact will not, respond to anything other than the Name of Jesus.

Some years ago, I, with one of my associates, was in Addis Ababa, Ethiopia, where we were proposing to carry out a particular Missions work. Ethiopia, at that time, was under Communist rule, and tightly regulated by that Totalitarian Government.

Despite the danger involved, a meeting was being conducted that night where nearly 50 Preachers would be present. I was privileged to be there and speak to them for a few moments.

In talking with these men, some who would shortly give their lives for the Cause of Christ, I asked a number of them how they had found the Lord. Their testimonies were remarkable, to say the least; however, one stood out in particular.

One young man, now preaching the Gospel, told me that he had been converted from Islam. His story, as stated, was immensely interesting!

He had developed a friendship with a young Christian, with both of them attending the university in Addis Ababa. He went on to tell how they had friendly conversations with each other respecting the merits of Christianity vs. Islam. Of course, each strongly upheld his own beliefs.

The converted former Moslem told me how on one particular day, his friend came to him, stating that he was going to pray for a man who was demon-possessed, and asking if he (the Moslem friend), would like to come along? He instantly accepted, desiring to see what might take place.

They were both ushered into a room, where several people were, along with the man who was demon-possessed, which was obvious for all to see. His condition was so terrible, he had to be held down by others.

The young Christian laid hands on him, and began to pray for him, but without any obvious success.

After a few minutes, the young Christian

turned to his Moslem friend, stating that he was going to get other Christians to come help him pray, and for the Moslem to wait, and he would return shortly.

The converted Moslem stood there that night telling me how he observed this demon-possessed man, after his Christian friend had left! The thought came into his mind, *"Why not lay hands on him in the name of Mohammed, and command this Demon to come out?"*

This he attempted, but with no success whatsoever!

Then another thought came to him, *"Why not try the Name of Jesus?"*

He reasoned within himself that this was futile, because all knew that Mohammed was the greater Prophet, and, besides, his Christian friend had already used the Name of Jesus, but without success.

However, the thought kept pushing at him, try the *"Name of Jesus!"*

Very slowly, he walked back to the demon-possessed man, laid his hand on his head and quietly said, *"In the Name of Jesus, come out of him!"*

That night, as I stood in that room with him and all the other Preachers, he looked at me and said, *"Brother Swaggart, even though I was a Moslem and did not believe that Jesus was the Son of God, still, when I uttered that Name, the Power of God came all over me, and all over him."*

And then he said, *"Before my very eyes, I watched that man instantly delivered and restored to his right mind, and I knew that something greater than I had ever known before had just taken place."*

I stood there that night, asking him, *"What did you do?"*

"I stood there," he said, *"trembling all over, feeling the Presence of God for the first time in my life, and knowing in my heart, and in a moment, that Jesus Christ was Lord, and, Mohammed was not His Prophet!*

"I bowed my head," he said, *"and at that moment I accepted Jesus as my Saviour."*

I asked him what his friend thought when he finally returned, and, if, in fact, he did return?

"Oh yes," he said, *"in a few minutes time, he came back, with others; however, the scene that greeted him was not what he had left.*

"My Christian friend left a demon-possessed man, and a Moslem. He came back to a man no

longer demon-possessed, and his friend no longer a Moslem, but now a brand-new Child of God."

Instantly noting the change, he asked, *"What happened?"*

He said, *"I then told him what had happened to me, and how I had used the Name of Jesus, and both of us, the demon-possessed man and myself, had been instantly delivered."*

He then turned to me that night, with tears filling his eyes, and said, *"Brother Swaggart, a short time later Jesus filled me with the Holy Ghost and called me to preach His Gospel, which I have been doing ever since."*

Let all know and understand that there is Power in that Mighty Name of Jesus. He Alone can set the captive free! As well, as He did it then, He will do it now for all who will believe Him.

The phrase, *"And He cast out the spirits with His Word,"* simply means, that with a short word, He commanded them to come out, and they instantly obeyed. They had to obey, because they were in the Presence of One Who was stronger than they.

Some time back, I saw over television a documentary of a Catholic Priest attempting to cast out a Demon by using a long formula of exorcism, which was to no avail. Sadly, the man did not know Christ, and there was no favorable result.

When Jesus spoke, the Demons obeyed! To be sure, they will obey now, when His Name is used by Holy Ghost-filled men and women.

As well, one does not have to be a Preacher to exercise this Mighty Name, only, a Believer. The Scripture says, *"These signs shall follow them that believe,"* and irrespective as to whom they may be (Mk. 16:17). The only criteria is *"believing."*

The phrase, *"And healed all that were sick,"* places those who were physically ill in a different category than those who were *"possessed with devils."*

While Demons certainly can cause sickness, still, Jesus placed these in two categories, one group being delivered, while the other was healed.

To be sure, that's what the world needs, deliverance and healing.

If one is to notice, the stress is on the word *"all,"* meaning that none were excluded, and none were so bound as to be beyond His Power, and no kind of disease too great for Him to subdue.

Hallelujah!

(17) "THAT IT MIGHT BE FULFILLED WHICH WAS SPOKEN BY ESAIAS THE PROPHET, SAYING, HIMSELF TOOK OUR INFIRMITIES, AND BARE OUR SICKNESSES."

It has been argued many times as to whether healing is in the Atonement, i.e., that which Christ did at Calvary in delivering mankind. This Scripture should settle it once and for all, even as the Holy Spirit gave it through Matthew. Healing definitely is in the Atonement.

The phrase, *"That it might be fulfilled which was spoken by Esaias* (Isaiah) *the Prophet,"* refers to Isaiah 53.

The phrase, *"Saying, Himself took our infirmities, and bare our sicknesses,"* expresses what He did at Calvary and the Resurrection.

THE FINISHED WORK OF THE CROSS

What Jesus did at the Cross is of far greater magnitude than anyone ever even begins to realize.

It has been argued for centuries as to what the Atonement included. Some claim that the Atonement addressed only sin and not sickness. Others claim the Atonement did address sickness, disease, and other bondages.

Which is correct?

Truly, when Jesus went to the Cross, He answered every single problem, no matter what it is, which faces humanity as a result of Adam's Fall.

Paul said, and I quote from THE EXPOSITOR'S STUDY BIBLE:

"But not as the offense, so also is the free gift (would probably have been better translated, *"as the offense, much more the Free Gift";* the *"Free Gift"* refers to Christ and what He did at the Cross, which addressed all that was lost at the Fall). *For if through the offense of one* (Adam) *many be dead, much more the Grace of God* (proclaims the inexhaustible power of this attribute), *and the Gift by Grace* (presents Jesus as that *"Gift"*), *which is by One Man, Jesus Christ* (what He did at the Cross), *has abounded unto many* (this *"One Man,"* the Lord Jesus Christ, nullified the offense of the *"One Man,"* Adam).

"And not as it was by one who sinned, so is the gift (so much greater is the Gift): *for the judgment was by one to condemnation* (by Adam), *but the Free Gift is of many offenses unto Justification* (cleanses from all sin).

"For if by one man's offense death reigned by one (Adam's Fall); *much more they which*

receive abundance of Grace (not just *"Grace,"* but *"Abundance of Grace";* all made possible by the Cross) *and of the Gift of Righteousness* (Righteousness is a Gift from God which comes solely through Jesus Christ, and is received by Faith) *shall reign in life by One, Jesus Christ.* (This proclaims the Believer *"reigning,"* even as death had reigned, but from a position of much greater power than that of death.)

"Therefore as by the offense of one judgment came upon all men to condemnation (Judged by God to be lost); *even so by the Righteousness of One* (Christ) *the Free Gift came upon all men unto Justification of Life* (received by simply believing in Christ and what He did at the Cross, which is the only answer for sin).

"For as by one man's disobedience many were made sinners (the *"many"* referred to all), *so by the obedience of One* (obedient unto death, even the death of the Cross [Phil. 2:8]) *shall many be made Righteous"* (*"many"* refers to all who will believe) (Rom. 5:15-19).

So Jesus not only addressed everything that was lost at the Fall, but He also addressed the revolution engineered by Satan sometime in eternity past (Eph. 1:10).

WHAT CHRIST TOOK UPON HIMSELF AT THE CROSS

As well, there is indication in the Text, with the words, *"Himself took,"* that all His miracles were performed at His Own expense, and that expense the greatest. It has reference that each miracle of healing meant for Him a fresh realization of what bearing the sin of the world included.

In other words, Christ suffered a foretaste of what He would suffer on the Cross, with each miracle He performed.

This may well have been the cause of His sigh at one miracle (Mk. 7:34), and His deep emotion at another (Jn. 11:33).

As well, Luke 8:46 records the miracle of the woman who touched Him, and *"power went out of Him."* He then asked, *"Who touched Me?"*

This miracle of healing, though performed in momentary unconsciousness of what was taking place, still necessitated personal contact with sin, which was the cause of all sickness to begin with, which to Christ's whole nature meant moral effort.

Origen said concerning Christ, and probably correctly, *"For those that are sick I was sick, and*

NOTES

for those that hunger I suffered hunger, and for those that thirst I suffered thirst."

Some object to healing being in the Atonement, *"For if that were so,"* they say, *"no Christian would ever be sick!"*

Such thinking is erroneous, which, I think, the following proves:

For those who believe in the Atonement, they will agree that all sins were paid for by Christ at Calvary. And yet, even though that is the case, still, Christians sin at times! However, this in no way means that the Atonement was less than sufficient, but simply that the sin nature is still present in the Believer, although *"born again."* It is called *"corruption,"* or *"this corruptible"* (I Cor. 15:53), and refers to Believers continuing at times to sin, and despite the Atonement.

As victory over sin was guaranteed in the Atonement, likewise, healing was as well. Nevertheless, the word *"mortal"* continues to be used of the Believer, which speaks of death and dying, and with sicknesses which cause it.

The idea is as follows:

The Believer is presently *"Sanctified"* and *"Justified in the Name of the Lord Jesus and by the Spirit of our God"* (I Cor. 6:11).

However, the Believer is not yet Glorified, which will take place when *"This corruptible puts on incorruption, and this mortal puts on immortality"* (I Cor. 15:53).

Then with *"incorruption,"* i.e., the elimination of the sin nature, and the putting on of the Glorified State, the Believer will never sin again. Likewise, with the *"putting on of immortality,"* i.e., a Glorified Body which will never get sick and die, then, as is obvious, all sickness will end.

Therefore, as the Atonement does not guarantee freedom from all future sin, even though delivered from sin, likewise, it does not guarantee freedom from all future sickness, even though delivered from sickness at Calvary.

The answer is, and as we have stated, that even though the Believer is now fully saved from sin, and all that sin brings, which is sickness, etc., still, the completed State of the Salvation experience has not yet been realized, and will not be realized until the First Resurrection of Life, when the Believer will then be Glorified. Then, and only then, will the Believer be complete, then fully realizing all that Jesus did at Calvary.

Paul said it this way, *"Who also hath given unto us the earnest of the Spirit,"* meaning a down-payment, on that which is to come, which refers to the Resurrection, when the Saints will put on immortality (II Cor. 5:5).

He also said, *"For the earnest expectation of the creature waiteth for the manifestation of the sons of God"* (Rom. 8:19).

That *"manifestation"* has not yet come, but, come it shall! (I Thess. 4:16-18).

Actually, it is impossible to separate sickness from sin, as both come from the same source, Satan. No! It does not mean that every Christian who gets sick has sinned, but that sickness has its roots in sin, which is a result of the Fall of man. Consequently, the deliverance that Jesus wrought at Calvary was a complete deliverance, which included all the effects of the Fall, which spoke of everything sin has caused, including death.

As is obvious, Christians, though delivered, and appropriating the benefits of the Atonement at Calvary, still die. However, death will be abolished, as well, at the First Resurrection, along with all sin, sickness and disease (I Cor. 15:54).

Hallelujah!

(18) "NOW WHEN JESUS SAW GREAT MULTITUDES ABOUT HIM, HE GAVE COMMANDMENT TO DEPART UNTO THE OTHER SIDE."

The phrase, *"Now when Jesus saw great multitudes about Him,"* indicates that something here was not quite right. Perhaps, the people on seeing His miracles, desired to make Him King, or else their eyes were off Him, onto that which He was doing. At any rate, He left them, no doubt, in a state of great rejoicing, because of the tremendous number of miracles and healings which had taken place. Those who came sick, went away well! Those who came demon-possessed, went away free of that horrible bondage.

"Oh happy day, Oh happy day,

"When Jesus washed, my sins away."

Ironically, and beautifully enough, Jesus will leave the *"multitudes,"* travelling across the lake, in order to set a captive free, who was so possessed that quite possibly 2,000 demon spirits inhabited him.

The phrase, *"He gave commandment to depart unto the other side,"* speaks of Him knowing exactly where He was going, even though the Disciples, at least at this time, seemingly did not!

The *"other side"* was not at all like this side, but, instead, inhabited by tombs filled with men's

bones, and demon-possessed maniacs.

Thank God, that Jesus *"departed"* and came to this *"other side,"* of man's fallen condition.

Even though He was a King, He did not come to be crowned King, but, instead, to lift man from his pitiful, pathetic, fallen state, of which these maniacs symbolized!

As well, and as we shall see, it will not be easy for Him to get to the *"other side."* Satan does not give up his prey easily! And yet, Jesus came, and despite the storms of hindrance.

(19) "AND A CERTAIN SCRIBE CAME, AND SAID UNTO HIM, MASTER, I WILL FOLLOW THEE WHITHERSOEVER THOU GOEST."

The nature of the *"flesh"* and the claim of the Lord appear in verses 19-22. The *"flesh"* is either too forward (vs. 19) or too backward (vs. 21).

The Lord understood its impotency in relation to spiritual facts and rebuked it with Divine wisdom, showing that He Himself claimed to be everything or to be nothing.

Thus two moral facts appear — the one: Christ must be everything or nothing; the other: That man's boasting of the majesty and value of his religious will is folly.

The phrase, *"And a certain Scribe came, and said unto Him,"* pertained to this group who were experts, so-called, in the study of the Law of Moses. They were the professional students of the Law and its defenders. They attempted to apply the Mosaic Law to daily life. They claimed that the oral Law was even more important than the written Law. By their efforts, the Law of Moses was, by and large, reduced to heartless formalism.

They were also referred to as *"lawyers,"* and *"teachers of the Law."*

Many of them clashed with Christ, for He taught with authority, and He condemned external formalism which they fostered.

And yet, it seems that some of them may have been Believers!

The phrase, *"Master, I will follow thee whithersoever thou goest,"* proclaims the impression that Christ had made on this particular *"Scribe."*

From the answer that Christ gave, it seems that He looked by the Power of the Holy Spirit into the heart of this man, and saw that he did not quite mean what he had said.

The Scribe had seen the miracles, witnessed the healings, heard the accolades of the crowds, and, consequently, did not really count the cost.

Jesus' answer reveals the opposite side of the momentary fame and popularity.

(20) "AND JESUS SAITH UNTO HIM, THE FOXES HAVE HOLES, AND THE BIRDS OF THE AIR HAVE NESTS; BUT THE SON OF MAN HATH NOT WHERE TO LAY HIS HEAD."

The phrase, *"And Jesus saith unto him,"* reflects the idea that the man had not counted the cost of following Christ.

The phrase, *"The foxes have holes, and the birds of the air have nests,"* refers to His creation, which He provided for. And yet, this same creation, and because of the Fall in the Garden of Eden, which greatly affected the reptile and animal world, presently *"groaneth and travaileth in pain together until now,"* awaiting deliverance (Rom. 8:22). They have been affected by the curse, as well as man!

The phrase, *"But the Son of Man hath not where to lay His Head,"* records this as the first of the 88 occurrences of this Name, and is Christ's title as having dominion in the earth — the earth which had room for foxes and birds, but not for Him.

The title, *"Son of Man,"* is God's answer to Satan to guarantee his defeat and restore man's original dominion.

In Jesus' answer to the *"Scribe,"* He is, in fact, proclaiming that His Kingdom is not of this world's system. The Scribe may have had in his mind, even as the Disciples of Christ, that Christ would use His great Power to overthrow Rome, and, once again, make Israel the dominating power in the world. If that was the case, he, the Scribe, would have for himself an important position in this coming Kingdom.

However, Christ, if, in fact, these were His thoughts, deflated this erroneous idea!

I wonder how the Scribe equated the great miracles of Christ, with Him having no place to *"lay His Head?"*

(21) "AND ANOTHER OF HIS DISCIPLES SAID UNTO HIM, LORD, SUFFER ME FIRST TO GO AND BURY MY FATHER."

The phrase, *"And another of His Disciples said unto Him,"* probably does not refer to one of the original twelve, but to a follower.

As we go along, many will be found who began, but did not finish this journey. Actually, most would ultimately leave, and despite the miracles and the healings (Jn. 6:66).

The phrase, *"Lord, suffer me first to go and bury my father,"* does not mean that the father had now died, but, instead, to take care of him until he died, ever how long that was!

Even though the Text is sparse, still, there is indication that the Lord had extended an invitation to this man to follow Him. Were that the case, which it no doubt was, it was the greatest invitation he would ever receive. And yet, all presently receive the same invitation, but with almost all making the same type of excuse as this Disciple.

(22) "BUT JESUS SAID UNTO HIM, FOLLOW ME; AND LET THE DEAD BURY THEIR DEAD."

The phrase, *"But Jesus said unto him,"* implies an answer of censure.

The words, *"Follow me,"* are emphatic, meaning that nothing, absolutely nothing, must stand in the way!

This is what Christ demands, and why many refuse to follow.

Everything must be to the exclusion of Christ, and, the Holy Spirit means, *"everything."* (It was the Holy Spirit Who instructed Christ in this answer.)

The phrase, *"And let the dead bury their dead,"* actually means, *"Let the spiritually dead bury their physically dead."*

In the statement, and when properly understood, Christ was not showing disrespect for the dead. Neither was He denying, even in the slightest way, the desired devotion and commitment to the man's parent.

The idea is, that all who do not follow Him are *"spiritually dead,"* and there are plenty of them who can attend to all the duties brought about because of the vicissitudes of life. Those who are *"spiritually alive"* are those who follow Him, and are consequently so involved in very important duties, in fact, the most important of all, that everything else must be attended to by others.

(23) "AND WHEN HE WAS ENTERED INTO A SHIP, HIS DISCIPLES FOLLOWED HIM."

Several things are implied in this Text:

First of all, there is some indication that the ship He entered into was not one that belonged to any one of His Disciples.

Second, the phrase, *"His Disciples followed Him,"* implies that they little understood, if at all, where He was going, or why He was going. But nevertheless, they *"followed Him,"* which they were instructed to do, and which was their training ground (Mat. 4:19). This was His manner of instruction. They were to observe all that He did, and hear all that He said.

Tragically, in modern times, many in the Church have drifted away from this manner of training which was instituted by the Holy Spirit, and have substituted their own, which little works!

The modern method is for students to enroll in a Bible College, or institute of sorts, and be taught various subjects by a professor, etc. Actually, that method is not wrong, as far as it goes. What is lacking oftentimes, is the principal figure, such as Christ or the Apostle Paul, who can inspire leading, guidance, and direction. In other words, the Disciple (learner) was to catch the Spirit of Christ, and then later the Apostle Paul, and others. If the principal figure is absent, very little is going to be accomplished for the Cause of Christ. With all the professors, instructors, and accouterments of whatever type of training given in the realm of the Work of God, there must be a principal individual, who has been signally called by God, with a proven Ministry, whose spirit can be transferred to the students. If that is lacking, nothing else done, irrespective of its quality, can make up for this all-important shortfall. To do otherwise, is to forsake the manner of instruction designed by the Holy Spirit.

As we have previously stated, every single thing done by Christ had a far greater degree of magnitude and significance than the act performed, as great as it may have been. Each healing and miracle and action, was a portrayal, in some manner, of His Mission, which was the Salvation of mankind.

Consequently, this great miracle of the calming of the storm, as well as the deliverance of the maniacs of Gergesa, was meant, among other things, to portray the terrible destitution of mankind, and the Mission of Christ to deliver man from the terrible bondage of darkness. Some may blanch at such stark symbolism as these maniacs; however, the description is appropriate, and especially considering the condition of the world. The answer, and, in fact, the only answer, is Christ!

(24) "AND, BEHOLD, THERE AROSE A GREAT TEMPEST IN THE SEA, INSOMUCH

THAT THE SHIP WAS COVERED WITH THE WAVES: BUT HE WAS ASLEEP."

To follow Christ involves suffering with Him, and ensures the hatred of Satan; for the storm designed to hurt Him would have destroyed them. This principle operates presently as well!

The phrase, *"And, behold, there arose a great tempest in the sea,"* emphasizes the idea that inasmuch as Christ was with them, they hardly expected a storm.

The terminology implies that the storm was violent.

It was designed by Satan, but allowed by the Heavenly Father.

Would it have been possible for Satan to have killed Christ and the Disciples?

No! Actually, Christ, and because He was born without sin, and lived without sin, could not have been killed. When He was crucified, He made the statement, *"I lay down My Life, that I might take it again.*

"No man taketh it from Me, but I lay it down of Myself. I have power to lay it down, and I have power to take it again. This Commandment have I received of My Father" (Jn. 10:17-18).

Could Satan have killed the Disciples?

Not as long as Jesus was in the boat with them, and they were walking in Faith and believing. That being the case, neither they, nor any Child of God, can be taken until the Lord desires that such be taken. All who follow the Lord are the property of the Lord, and, as such, do not answer to Satan.

Nevertheless, the evil one would attempt to cause as much consternation and damage as he could, hence the storm!

The phrase, *"Insomuch that the ship was covered with the waves,"* refers to the intensity of the storm, and Satan trying to sink the ship while Christ was asleep.

The phrase, *"But He was asleep,"* portrays several things:

1. Christ, as man, became tired like all other men, and was probably very tired at this time especially after healing the sick and performing miracles. Many Christians not understanding the Incarnation, cannot feature Christ having the same limitations as all other men. However, even though He was God, still, He never once used His attributes of Deity, but, instead, functioned as a man, filled with the Holy Spirit. As a man, He grew tired, needed rest, and had to find

out about things exactly as all other men, unless the Holy Spirit revealed things to Him, which He often did.

2. Inasmuch as everything He did was designed by the Holy Spirit, His being asleep, at least at this particular time, was designed by the Spirit of God. It would be used to teach the Disciples, A. Their need of Him; B. His Power; and, C. The manner in which He used it.

Most every Child of God has gone through similar circumstances, when the storm was raging and it seemed like the boat was sinking, and it seemed, as well, as if God were asleep! However, though He delay, does not necessarily mean, and in similar cases will never mean, that He denies.

(25) "AND HIS DISCIPLES CAME TO HIM, AND AWOKE HIM, SAYING, LORD, SAVE US: WE PERISH."

The phrase, *"And His Disciples came to Him, and awoke Him,"* specifies their dire need of His services. The Sea of Galilee was known to them, greater than any area of the world. They had plied these waters all of their lives, and had, no doubt, faced many storms. However, the intensity of this storm was such that they must have His help. Likewise, there is no way that one can properly get through this life without His help!

As well, one will find that a true Call of God will arouse the enmity and hatred of Satan as nothing else.

The phrase, *"Saying, Lord, save us: we perish,"* means that they had exhausted all of their resources in keeping the ship afloat, and despite their vast knowledge in these things now had no hope of escape except through Him.

Psychology calls Christianity a *"crutch,"* and, therefore, implying that man is able to get by without such dependents. However, they completely misunderstand man's relationship with God, inasmuch as the roots of psychology does not even believe there is a God.

While religion may in fact be a crutch, True Bible Christianity is not a religion, but, instead, a relationship, and, most of all, with a Person, the Man, Christ Jesus. Inasmuch as a child cannot get by without its parent, at least as it should, likewise, man cannot get by without God.

The entire thrust of the Fall of man in the Garden, is that he, in effect, in changing Lords from God to Satan, has attempted to survive without Jehovah. That he cannot do, at least, properly so!

NOTES

In effect, the biggest problem with man is to get him to admit that he needs the Lord. The idea of self-sustenance is strong in the rebellious heart. That is the reason the song, or such like, *"I did it my way,"* sounds macho to most.

The Truth is, if man does it *"his way,"* which, in effect, is the Devil's way, he will certainly be lost. Actually, the entirety of the conflict is over God's Way vs. man's way!

So, to admit the need of help, is not only not wrong, it is very much right. However, most of mankind, and even the Church, seek help other than from the right source. They seek it in other men, which is the thrust of psychology, which is no help at all. The idea of the entirety of this scenario is as follows:

1. The journey: There is a journey of life that all must take, and, at times, and especially for most, it is not pleasant.

2. The storm: Probably one can say that storms will come in every life, many of them with the same intensity as here recorded.

Sadly, much of the modern teaching in Christian circles is that if one properly confesses the Word of God, all such storms can be eliminated. I think it should be obvious that according to this Text, such is foolishness. This storm came even though Christ was in the boat. However, some of the purveyors of this false doctrine of modern confession, would probably even suggest that if Christ had the Faith they had, He could have eliminated the storm; but, of course, false doctrine knows no limitations in its boundaries of impropriety.

No! The storms are going to come, of that, one can be sure.

3. Christ: As long as Christ is in the boat, whatever the storm, it is going to make it to the other side. Actually that is at least a part of the lesson being taught in this scenario.

4. Proper petition: Even though Christ was in the boat, His help had to be properly solicited. No, the Disciples saying, *"we perish,"* was not a bad confession, it was the Truth. The Lord, as the next verse will show, did not admonish them for this statement, but, instead, for their lack of Faith.

In Truth, they would learn the lesson here taught, as they would face many similar storms in later years, and would weather them because of their Faith in God.

The idea was, that their Faith was misplaced,

as the next verse will show.

(26) "AND HE SAITH UNTO THEM, WHY ARE YE FEARFUL, O YE OF LITTLE FAITH? THEN HE AROSE, AND REBUKED THE WINDS AND THE SEA; AND THERE WAS A GREAT CALM."

The phrase, *"And He saith unto them,"* is meant to portray the reason for their dilemma. If one will properly discern what Christ is saying, the answer will be forthcoming.

The question, *"Why are ye fearful, O ye of little Faith?"*, is a question that should be applied to all.

Why were they fearful?

In this case, their Faith was in His bodily presence. As such, it was misplaced, which this scenario is meant to portray, at least in part!

As long as He was bodily present, they were, in effect, not using any Faith at all. This episode would portray the wrong of such action.

He was, in effect, telling them, that whether He was bodily present or not, He was still present, and they were to have Faith in Him accordingly. The lesson would not be lost on them, for they would exhibit great Faith after His Ascension.

"Little Faith," always produces fear, and *"Fear hath torment,"* as John would later say (I Jn. 4:18). He would further say, *"There is no fear in love; but perfect love casteth out fear,"* probably drawing from this very episode.

"Little Faith," which produces *"fear,"* is the plight of the human family. And, the *"Faith,"* as well, must not be misplaced, as here, as too often it is, but rather in Him. Strong Faith is brought about only by properly knowing and understanding the Word of God, for, *"Faith cometh by hearing, and hearing by the Word of God,"* which means to properly hear and understand the Bible (Rom. 10:17).

So, Christians who little know their Bible, have *"little Faith."*

The phrase, *"Then He arose, and rebuked the winds and the sea; and there was a great calm,"* portrays His Power as unexcelled. The actual words stated by Christ are recorded by St. Mark.

The rebuke of *"O ye of little Faith,"* occurs four times — combating care (6:30); fear (8:26); doubt (14:31); and reasoning (16:8).

(27) "BUT THE MEN MARVELLED, SAYING, WHAT MANNER OF MAN IS THIS, THAT EVEN THE WINDS AND THE SEA OBEY HIM!"

The phrase, *"But the men marvelled,"* proclaims their reaction as one of astonishment. They had never seen such power exhibited which would calm a storm, especially of this ferocity, and in a moment's time.

The exclamation, *"Saying, What manner of man is this, that even the winds and the sea obey Him!"*, proclaims this display of power, as greater than any heretofore seen.

The two words, *"obey Him,"* sums up the entirety of the matter. In effect, it was Satan who obeyed Him, because the storm was caused by Satan, but with the permission of God.

Not only did they *"marvel"* over the calming of the storm, but, as well, the rapidity of the calming, which took place in a moments time.

Such portrays what the Lord can do in a human heart, and irrespective of the severity of the situation.

In the first place, man (psychology) can do nothing, and, what tiny bit it might do, is carried out over a period of many months, or even years. What Jesus does is instant!

In a short time we shall see two maniacs who were instantly delivered by the Power of God.

Therefore, the question, *"What manner of Man is this?"*, can never be fully answered, because such vocabulary is not possible. While He is a Man, still, He is God, and, as such, He has the Power to do anything that is needed to save humanity. He actually did it 2,000 years ago at Calvary, and it was ratified at the Resurrection.

As a consequence, Satan will obey Him only, and to be sure, Him he will obey!

(28) "AND WHEN HE WAS COME TO THE OTHER SIDE INTO THE COUNTRY OF THE GERGESENES, THERE MET HIM TWO POSSESSED WITH DEVILS, COMING OUT OF THE TOMBS, EXCEEDING FIERCE, SO THAT NO MAN MIGHT PASS BY THAT WAY."

The phrase, *"And when He was come to the other side into the country of the Gergesenes,"* establishes the purpose of His journey. There was a mission to perform. As well, it would typify the entirety of His Mission from Heaven to earth.

Man was in a desperate terrible plight, as evidenced by these two maniacs, and the only solution was the Coming of Christ. There was no way they could be delivered otherwise!

As we have previously stated, the intellectuals and the moralists may disagree with the extremity of this statement, claiming that man is not near as bad as the two maniacs here represented. However, man has always underestimated his true spiritual condition, even though he knows something is wrong, but thinking it is only a slight maladjustment, which can be properly handled with education, money, psychological counseling, etc.

However, it is not a slight maladjustment, but, instead, a total spiritual wreckage which adversely affects every part of being and life. For to be without God (and man is without God) is to be without proper life. Consequently, Christ came to rectify this horrid situation, which only He could do!

The phrase, *"There met Him two possessed with devils,"* proclaims the reason for His coming to this deserted area on the other side of the Sea of Galilee.

Matthew mentions *"two,"* while Mark and Luke only speak of one; just as they only speak of one blind man at Jericho and one colt at the entry to Jerusalem. This shows design, not discrepancy. It could be explained in one of two ways.

1. Even though there were two maniacs, as here portrayed, still, it could well have been only one who figured as the principle in the scenario, and was consequently mentioned by Mark and Luke, as they also spoke of only one blind man at Jericho, etc. Even though Matthew recorded two blind men being in Jericho, and healed by Christ, still, Bartimaeus stood out, and was therefore highlighted by the Holy Spirit.

(Some have claimed these were entirely different incidents altogether, but that seems unlikely.)

2. The Prophecies immediately preceding Matthew predicted the Advent of Christ as King of Israel and Prince of Judah. The Holy Spirit in this first Gospel, therefore, records the historic facts that there were two demoniacs, and two blind men, and two animals, for these represented Israel and Judah. No such duality was needed in the other Gospels.

If the Holy Spirit was intending that the two in each case serve as a type of Israel and Judah, and as Matthew presented Christ as King, this, perhaps, was the reason for the *"two,"* while the others, who presented Christ differently, mentioned only *"one."*

These two individuals were demon possessed, as the Scripture relates, which spoke of insanity.

I think the possibility at least exists that

"demon possession," along with its other debilitation, always speaks of insanity in one form or the other.

There were other cases of Jesus casting out, or expelling demon spirits from individuals, which had caused particular physical deformities, but I think it could not be said that these individuals were *"demon possessed"* (Lk. 13:16; Mat. 15:22).

Peter spoke of Jesus *"healing all that were oppressed of the Devil"* (Acts 10:38). These individuals would need the spirits rebuked, or even *"cast out,"* which were causing the physical difficulties, but it would not mean they were *"demon possessed."*

I believe that the Scripture, as stated, will bear out that *"demon possession,"* expresses insanity, at least in one way or the other. It may not be total insanity, as here represented by the maniacs, but, at least, will express itself in that direction in one form or the other.

The phrase, *"Coming out of the tombs,"* proclaims these demon-possessed maniacs as living in these particular places. Their presence there signified their kindred spirit with death, hence, their occupying these places.

Death is the effect of all sin, and characterizes all that Satan touches. Therefore, those who would be totally possessed by demon spirits, as these, would seek such association.

As well, as death signified spiritual uncleanliness, these tombs would have been the epitome of such, and, therefore, desired greatly by these demon spirits.

As we have stated in previous Commentary, the Bible does not inform us as to exactly where demon spirits originated. Some have claimed they are Fallen Angels, however, this is unscriptural, as the Bible never refers to Angels, fallen or otherwise, inhabiting anyone. Actually, Angels have spirit bodies, whereas demon spirits are disembodied, and, consequently, seek a body to inhabit.

Some Bible Scholars feel that these may be the spirits of a pre-Adamic creation on earth. In other words, that there was a creation on earth, and even possibly ruled by Lucifer before his fall, and these fell with him in his revolution against God. This we do know:

The earth was not originally created *"without form, and void,"* as expressed in Genesis 1:2, but, became that way after some type of chaotic upheaval, which quite well could have been the Fall of Lucifer, which introduced sin into God's creation.

At any rate, we do know that God did not create these demon spirits in this fashion, as He did not create man in the manner in which man now is. They became that way after some type of disruption, as man became as he is after the Fall (Gen. 1:31; 3:17-19).

The phrase, *"Exceeding fierce,"* expresses not only these demon-possessed maniacs, but, as well, the spirit of the entirety of the unconverted world. *"Fierceness"* describes man's attitude toward his fellowman, and toward God.

Men are perplexed at man's inhumanity to man, thinking that proper education will assuage these problems. However, such is not the case. The problem is not ignorance, but, instead, the rule of Satan in the hearts of men, which *"steals, kills, and destroys"* (Jn. 10:10).

The phrase, *"So that no man might pass by that way,"* spoke of this particular locality, and the danger represented by these two maniacs. However, it also speaks of the entirety of the world.

In most cities of the world, men cannot quietly or safely pass through because of the *"fierceness,"* as here described. The same can be said for most all the earth, and will not be ameliorated until the Coming of Christ, when all that which causes fear will be done away with (Rev. 20:1-3).

(29) "AND, BEHOLD, THEY CRIED OUT, SAYING, WHAT HAVE WE TO DO WITH THEE, JESUS, THOU SON OF GOD? ART THOU COME HITHER TO TORMENT US BEFORE THE TIME?"

The phrase, *"And, behold, they cried out, saying,"* refers to the demon spirits speaking to Christ, but using the voices of the two men.

The question, *"What have we to do with Thee, Jesus, Thou Son of God?",* proclaims these demons as having more intelligence than the Disciples of modern religious thought.

They declared the Godhead of Jesus; that He has appointed a time for Judgment; that the Judgment involves torment; and that He will command it.

Many Preachers today deny that Jesus could, or would torment any creature. So dreadful is hell that the demons preferred to indwell swine than to be banished thither. The entry of the

NOTES

demons into them shows that the misery of these two men was not a question of disease or of passion, but of wicked spirits.

The question, *"Art Thou come hither to torment us before the time?",* proclaims a coming time of Judgment, which is outlined in Revelation 20:1-3. At that time, when Satan is shut up, every Fallen Angel, along with demon spirits, will be incarcerated as well! This will happen at the Second Coming of the Lord.

Satan will only be loose one other short time after that, which will be a thousand years after his incarceration, and at the conclusion of the Kingdom Age. However, his efforts then will be short-lived, when he will then be *"cast into the lake of fire and brimstone"* (Rev. 20:7-10).

(30) "AND THERE WAS A GOOD WAY OFF FROM THEM AN HERD OF MANY SWINE FEEDING."

The presence of this *"herd of swine,"* at least in this fashion, was prohibited by the Law of Moses, and because hogs were labeled as unclean by the Holy Spirit (Lev. 12:26). However, this area, especially at this particular time, was probably occupied mostly by Gentiles, or else Jews who had taken on Gentile ways, thereby, departing from the Law of Moses.

(31) "SO THE DEVILS BESOUGHT HIM, SAYING, IF THOU CAST US OUT, SUFFER US TO GO AWAY INTO THE HERD OF SWINE."

Even though Matthew does not mention it, Mark stated that Jesus had commanded the unclean spirit to come out of the man. Therefore, the phrase, *"If Thou cast us out,"* should have been translated, *"Since Thou art casting us out...."*

The phrase, *"Suffer us to go away into the herd of swine,"* refers to about 2,000 according to Mark 5:1-16.

Why did they ask permission to go into the swine?

As we have previously stated, demon spirits are disembodied, and must inhabit some type of physical body in order to properly exert their will, which is always evil. It is obvious that their first choice is a human being, while they will go into an animal as here portrayed, if they have no other choice. However, the entrance into the swine occasioned the death of the animals.

(32) "AND HE SAID UNTO THEM, GO. AND WHEN THEY WERE COME OUT, THEY WENT INTO THE HERD OF SWINE:

AND, BEHOLD, THE WHOLE HERD OF SWINE RAN VIOLENTLY DOWN A STEEP PLACE INTO THE SEA, AND PERISHED IN THE WATERS."

The phrase, *"And He said unto them, Go,"* proclaims His approval.

The phrase, *"And when they were come out, they went into the herd of swine,"* refers to them obeying Him explicitly, exactly as the wind and the sea.

The phrase, *"And, behold, the whole herd of swine ran violently down a steep place into the sea, and perished in the waters,"* proclaims the reaction of the hogs to the demons. As the men had been insane, the hogs, likewise, went insane, but as a lower form of life, they ran over the cliff and perished in the waters below. Several questions beg to be asked concerning this episode:

1. Why did the demons desire to go into the swine, inasmuch as their purpose would be foiled by the swine killing themselves?

Obviously, the demon spirits did not know that the hogs would be so affected. Therefore, they helped themselves not at all by their choice.

2. Why would Christ give permission for such, knowing that it would mean the loss of many thousands of dollars to the owners of the swine?

The Scripture is silent as to exactly why Christ did this, therefore, we can only surmise.

It could definitely have been revealed to the Lord by the Holy Spirit the need for such chastisement of the owners, but if not that, at least He did this on instructions from the Heavenly Father. He did nothing, especially of this nature, without the Father expressly telling Him to do it (Jn. 5:19).

God as the ultimate Owner of all things, has the right to use those things as He desires and sees fit. For instance, He destroys many things through inclement weather, or that referred to as accidents, etc., and for His Own implicit purposes. This we do know, concerning whatever is done, as said by Abraham, *"Shall not the Judge of the earth do right?"* (Gen. 18:25).

(33) "AND THEY THAT KEPT THEM FLED, AND WENT THEIR WAYS INTO THE CITY, AND TOLD EVERYTHING, AND WHAT WAS BEFALLEN TO THE POSSESSED OF THE DEVILS."

The phrase, *"And they that kept them fled,"* implies that they did so speedily, and with some,

if not great, fear respecting what they had seen.

The phrase, *"And went their ways into the city, and told everything,"* concerned itself with quite a story.

The phrase, *"And what was befallen to the possessed of the devils,"* did not mean that they by any means ignored the death of all the swine, as the next verse portrays, but, most of all, at the sudden and instant change of those who had formerly been *"possessed of the devils."*

(34) "AND, BEHOLD, THE WHOLE CITY CAME OUT TO MEET JESUS: AND WHEN THEY SAW HIM, THEY BESOUGHT HIM THAT HE WOULD DEPART OUT OF THEIR COASTS."

This verse proclaims that men can beseech Christ to leave them, and — fearful fact — He hears their prayer.

The phrase, *"And, behold, the whole city came out to meet Jesus,"* actually uses a part for a whole. The leaders, along with the business people of the city, plus others, are referred to.

Even though they came to meet Jesus, still, it was not intended to be a positive meeting.

The phrase, *"And when they saw Him,"* refers to the fact that they probably did not find Him immediately, but after a short time of seeking, did come upon Him.

The phrase, *"They besought Him that He would depart out of their coasts,"* is sad indeed! It seems, they, as most, were only concerned about the money they had lost respecting the death of the swine, and, therefore, completely missed what He could have done for them had they only sought His help.

There were many sick among them who would not be healed, because Jesus would not be asked. Many others were no doubt demon possessed, just as the maniacs had been, but would not receive deliverance.

As well, all, except for the newly-delivered former maniacs, were in sin, but would receive no Salvation.

Due to the power He possessed, and the manner in which He had used it, they were fearful of taking Him to task, which they no doubt would have done otherwise, but, instead, *"besought Him to depart."*

Men never ask the Lord to depart for good reasons, but only for bad. They wanted nothing to interfere with their activities, and, therefore, lost the opportunity of eternity.

Perhaps the loss was meant by the Lord to bring them to Him, as He intends for many losses to do such! However, it only embittered the owners of the hogs, and they chose to demand His departure. The loss was great, but not of the hogs, but rather their souls.

Some time back, I had occasion to read a book written in the 1800's. It spoke of this very area. An account was being given of someone who visited this area back in the 1700's, that is, if I remember correctly.

They told of how the area had long been inhabited by wild hogs, which had used their snouts to uproot the earth, until the entirety of the area was completely destroyed, with the earth rooted up into hundreds, if not thousands of mounds, with the hogs foraging for roots or food of any nature.

The people had a choice to make. It was Christ or hogs, and, regrettably, they chose the hogs. Consequently, and as the illustration proclaims, hogs they got!

The choice is presently no different! Men have to make the choice between Christ and immorality, or alcohol, or drugs, or greed, etc. Irrespective of how it looks, other than Christ is always a sorry choice. In other words, it would seem that it would be no choice at all, that men would immediately run to Christ. However, most do exactly what the good city fathers of this area did. They choose hogs!

CHAPTER 9

(1) "AND HE ENTERED INTO A SHIP, AND PASSED OVER, AND CAME INTO HIS OWN CITY."

The phrase, *"And He entered into a ship, and passed over,"* refers to Him coming back to Capernaum, as is evidenced by the phrase, *"And came into His Own city."*

However, His mission was completed, in that the maniacs were delivered, and, as well, the figure of His mission to the world was exampled.

Out of all the population of the area of the maniacs, only two were delivered, with all the rest desiring not at all that which He had to give, but, instead, their own sins and bondage. Likewise, the great price paid by Christ at Calvary and the Resurrection, even though affordable

to the entirety of the world, and for all time, nevertheless, is accepted by only a few. Most love their sin, and, therefore, have no time for Him, and even demand His departure.

This Chapter discloses the character of Messiah's Ministry; the prior one, the dignity of His Person. In them, He reveals Himself as Jehovah visiting Israel and the world, in Grace and Power; healing all manner of disease (vs. 35); forgiving iniquity (vs. 2); electing sinners to Salvation (vss. 9-13); proposing gladness to a sad world (14-17), and so manifesting Himself as the God of Psalm 103, Who first forgiveth iniquity and then healeth disease.

In Chapter 8, He appears as the God of Psalm 93, ruling the mighty waves of the sea.

But the Power which healed in Chapter 9 is the same Power which will torment in 8:29.

(2) "AND, BEHOLD, THEY BROUGHT TO HIM A MAN SICK OF THE PALSY, LYING ON A BED: AND JESUS SEEING THEIR FAITH SAID UNTO THE SICK OF THE PALSY; SON, BE OF GOOD CHEER; THY SINS BE FORGIVEN THEE."

The phrase, *"And, behold, they brought to Him a man sick of the palsy, lying on a bed,"* will occasion not only the healing of the sick, but the forgiving of sin as well!

The *"palsy"* here described, seems to have been some type of paralysis.

The phrase, *"And Jesus seeing their Faith said unto the sick of the palsy,"* refers not only to the Faith of the sick man, but, as well, to those who brought him. He was lying on a cot of sorts, and was being carried by at least two men, and possibly four.

The phrase, *"Seeing their Faith,"* refers to the action of Faith. True Faith will always have corresponding action. If there is not such action, there is no Faith.

The saying, *"Acting upon one's Faith,"* is here exampled. These men acted on their Faith, and Jesus saw their actions, which resulted in not only the healing of the man, but forgiveness of his sins.

The idea is, that God will always respond to the proper type of Faith.

The phrase, *"Son, be of good cheer; thy sins be forgiven thee,"* denoted the Salvation of this man.

This is the only time in Scripture, at least in this fashion, when it seems the man who had come originally for healing, was first addressed by the forgiveness of sins. However, quite possibly some conversation took place between the man and Christ that is not here recorded. This is evidenced by the phrase, *"Son, be of good cheer,"* indicating that the possibility at least existed that the man may have related to Christ a life of a certain type of sin, which, he felt, may have brought about the *"palsy."*

If that indeed happened, or, at any rate, Christ said to him, *"Thy sins be forgiven thee,"* such was of far greater magnitude than the healing that was to come.

However, Salvation and Healing, of which this episode is no doubt meant to portray, usually go hand in hand. It does not necessarily mean that all sickness is caused by particular sins in the lives of individuals, but many times the two are connected. Consequently, when the sins are forgiven, oftentimes the healing follows.

(Originally, all sickness stems from sin, i.e., original sin.)

(3) "AND, BEHOLD, CERTAIN OF THE SCRIBES SAID WITHIN THEMSELVES, THIS MAN BLASPHEMETH."

The phrase, *"And, behold, certain of the Scribes said within themselves,"* pertained to a goodly number of Pharisees and Teachers of the Law, who, having heard of the Miracles of Christ, came from cities all around Capernaum, and even as far away as Jerusalem (Lk. 5:17). However, they had not come with an open heart, but only to find fault. Consequently, nothing said or done, irrespective of its might or power, would convince them. Their problem was unbelief!

They had already envisioned within their hearts and minds what the Messiah would be like, and the persona of Christ did not fit their description. They were looking for a kingly Messiah who would throw off the yoke of Rome, and, as well, make them (the Pharisees and Scribes) His chief lieutenants.

Jesus little mentioned Rome, and up to this time, at least for all practical purposes, completely ignored the Pharisees and Scribes, although He would denounce them roundly as the months wore on and their criticism of Him increased.

The phrase, *"This man blasphemeth,"* was in response to Jesus forgiving the sins of the one sick of the palsy.

NOTES

Actually, no Passage in the Old Testament plainly affirmed that the Messiah would forgive sins, although it was implied by Isaiah (Isa. 42:1-7).

In their minds eye, Jesus was merely a peasant, and, consequently, the idea that He was the Messiah was preposterous, therefore, they were there solely to find fault.

The truth was, they did not know the Word of God, and what little of it they did know, they had twisted until the *"Light that was in them was darkness"* (6:23).

So, as they stand there watching Jesus speak to the man sick of the palsy, their evil hearts are imagining only evil!

(4) "AND JESUS KNOWING THEIR THOUGHTS SAID, WHEREFORE THINK YE EVIL IN YOUR HEARTS?"

The phrase, *"And Jesus knowing their thoughts said,"* proclaims the Holy Spirit revealing such to Christ.

Jesus did not *"know their thoughts"* because He was the Son of God, because as a man, He knew little more than any other man, but knew such only as the Holy Spirit revealed these things unto Him. As well, such power was not constant, but only given as the Holy Spirit desired.

The question, *"Wherefore think ye evil in your hearts?"*, appeals to the very core of their being.

Their unbelief, however, was of such magnitude that even this revelation had little or no effect on them.

The Lord works from the premise of Faith, and if men will not believe, even miracles little attract them.

As well, it should be added, that the *"evil"* in the hearts of these Scribes, as it was registered against Him, is judged accordingly respecting those who serve Him (Mat. 25:40).

(5) "FOR WHETHER IS EASIER, TO SAY, THY SINS BE FORGIVEN THEE; OR TO SAY, ARISE, AND WALK?"

The question, *"For whether is easier, to say,"* directs attention to the sins of man and one of the corresponding results, which is sickness.

Jesus is here proclaiming that man's resultant physical misery is a direct result of the Fall in the Garden of Eden. Consequently, to address one without addressing the other is impossible! They, sin and sickness, both stem from the same source, Satan.

So, the skeptic who denounces God because of the terrible sicknesses upon mankind, and especially the innocent, such as babies and little children, simply has no understanding of the original cause. All of man's misery, even the innocent, stems from the Fall, which he is loathe to admit!

The skeptic would continue to argue, that if such really did happen, it was something that took place thousands of years ago, of which they share no blame. However, that argument is groundless.

Every human being, and for all time, suffers because of things over which they have no control, and at least, at times, in a personal sense, are not culpable.

At any rate, Christ came from Heaven to liberate man from this terrible fallen condition. And that liberation includes not only sin, but all that sin causes, such as sickness, poverty, etc.

The question, *"Thy sins be forgiven thee; or to say, Arise, and walk?"*, puts it all, both sin and sickness, into the same category. No! It does not mean that all who are sick have sinned, but that sickness had its birth in original sin.

The word, *"easier,"* in the first phrase, implies that it is not easy at all, and, in fact, it is so difficult that it is impossible for man to effect either one, forgiveness of his sins or healing within himself.

In other words, Christ is saying to these skeptics, *"Not only can you not forgive sins, but you cannot heal the result of sin, which is sickness."* Consequently, by His statement, and especially His actions, He proclaims Himself *"God manifest in the flesh, the Messiah."*

(6) "BUT THAT YE MAY KNOW THAT THE SON OF MAN HATH POWER ON EARTH TO FORGIVE SINS, (THEN SAITH HE TO THE SICK OF THE PALSY,) ARISE, TAKE UP THY BED, AND GO UNTO THINE HOUSE."

The phrase, *"But that ye may know that the Son of Man hath power on earth to forgive sins,"* refers to these Scribes now being without excuse. The *"power"* that He manifested, was *"power"* possessed only by God. For these skeptics had said, as Luke recorded it, *"Who can forgive sins, but God Alone?"* (Lk. 5:21).

As well, the two words, *"on earth,"* mean that He is the only One on earth Who has the power to do this, which negates the claims of the Catholic Priesthood.

The *"forgiving of sins"* by Christ, is the single greatest experience that can happen to an individual. To be sure, it will be done readily, upon the request of the unbeliever or Believer.

Actually, the very state or nature of sin is forgiven in the life of the unbeliever upon his confession of Christ (Jn. 3:16; Rom. 10:9-10). At that time, all sin is washed and cleansed in the penitent one, and he, in effect, becomes *"a new creature in Christ Jesus"* (II Cor. 5:17).

As well, any Believer, after coming to Christ, and upon the committing of sin, has instant recourse for forgiveness by simply confessing the sin to the Lord, which will immediately bring about forgiveness (I Jn. 1:9). However, the Believer, inasmuch as he is a *"new creature,"* does not fall into sin easily, and, in Truth, should not do so at all. Nevertheless, due to the frailties of the flesh, every Believer, occasionally, and even often, fails God and must seek forgiveness, which is granted automatically upon obedience to the Word of God. However, falling into sin is totally different than one who habitually practices sin. If such is the case, one is not truly converted (I Jn. 3:9).

The phrase, *"Then saith He to the sick of the palsy,"* now proclaims Jesus turning His attention away from the skeptics to the man in question. He had Faith, and, consequently, would receive forgiveness of sins and healing for his paralyzed body. The others had no Faith, and would receive nothing!

The phrase, *"Arise, take up thy bed, and go unto thine house,"* was the second greatest Word this man had ever heard in all his life, with the greatest Word being that his sins were forgiven, as spoken by Christ just a few moments earlier.

The scenario is meant to convey to the skeptical Scribes, the condition of Israel which is presently *"sick,"* and because of *"sin."* However, the self-righteousness of the spiritual leadership of Israel, as evidenced in these Scribes, could in no way admit such.

The man admitted he was a sinner, and, therefore, received forgiveness, and, as well, received healing. Israel would not admit such, and, therefore, received no forgiveness or healing.

Tragically, almost all the world falls into the category of the skeptical Scribes, while only a precious few fall into the category of the forgiven, healed man!

(7) "AND HE AROSE, AND DEPARTED TO HIS HOUSE."

The song says:

"Oh the joys that's sent from Heaven, Oh the bliss the blood-washed know,

"Oh the peace of sins forgiven, where the healing waters flow."

CHORUS:

"Where the healing waters flow, where the joys celestial glow.

"Where there is peace, and rest and love, where the healing waters flow."

The phrase, *"And he arose,"* portrays the physical action of a spiritual result. Jesus raises men up, while Satan knocks them down!

The phrase, *"And departed to his house,"* proclaims a rejoicing that would gladden *"his house"* forever!

How many millions have experienced the same touch from Heaven, but how few in comparison to the whole!

His *"house"* had formerly been one of suffering, privation and sinfulness. Now it is a *"house"* of Salvation, and because of Jesus. He Alone can change the heart, thereby, changing the *"house."*

All who believe Him will experience the same, while all who reside in unbelief, as the Scribes, receive nothing.

(8) "BUT WHEN THE MULTITUDES SAW IT, THEY MARVELLED, AND GLORIFIED GOD, WHICH HAD GIVEN SUCH POWER UNTO MEN."

The people *"marvelled, and glorified God"*; however, the Scribes, who were the spiritual leaders, did no such thing.

And yet, there is no indication in these words that these *"multitudes"* understood that these actions of Christ proclaimed Him as Messiah. The Scribes, no doubt, understood it well, but rejected it and withheld it from the people. Due to such corrupt spiritual leadership, millions would die lost. As it was then, so it is now!

The phrase, *"Which had given such power unto men,"* proclaims these *"multitudes"* as seeing Jesus only as man, and not as God manifest in the flesh.

However, even though the people only saw Jesus as a miracle-working man, and their Religious Leaders denouncing Him as a Satanic agent (vs. 34), Jesus, unchilled by the blindness

of the one and the hostility of the other, persisted in His mission of Love (vss. 35-38).

But men did not want God in their midst, even though He was there in Grace — a Grace that while on the way to raise to life the dead maiden of vs. 18, who was a figure of Israel, healed whoever touched Him (vs. 20).

What a wonderful Lord we serve!

(9) "AND AS JESUS PASSED FORTH FROM THENCE, HE SAW A MAN, NAMED MATTHEW, SITTING AT THE RECEIPT OF CUSTOM: AND HE SAITH UNTO HIM, FOLLOW ME. AND HE AROSE, AND FOLLOWED HIM."

Matthew will now proclaim the moment of his call to follow Christ. It will be the greatest day in this man's life, and with occasion and honor that begs description.

The phrase, *"And as Jesus passed forth from thence, He saw a man, named Matthew,"* records the instance of this call.

This *"man, named Matthew,"* was a Roman tax-collector, who had bought for an annual sum of money the privilege of enforcing tax assessments. They were called publicans, and were, therefore, hated and despised by the people — whom they often defrauded. They were looked at as having sold out to the heathen power of Rome, and were called renegade Jews, and often were very wealthy, and, one might say, at the expense of their fellow Jews. The Pharisees, as well as much of Israel, did not even believe that a publican such as Matthew could be saved. And yet, Jesus would choose him as a Disciple.

(Matthew is also called *"Levi."*)

The phrase, *"Sitting at the receipt of custom,"* is interesting indeed!

Due to the shame attached to one such as this, as well as the animosity, many publicans, such as Matthew, did not collect the taxes themselves, but hired others to *"sit at the receipt of custom."* However, it seems that Matthew, by sitting in the toll booth himself, had little regard for what the people thought. In other words, his actions portrayed a bold and brazen attitude toward the thinking of that particular time.

Actually, there was no wrongdoing attached, at least by the Lord, to this particular position. Jesus said as much, when He later said, and concerning the paying of taxes to

Rome, *"Render therefore unto Caesar the things which are Caesar's"* (Mat. 22:21).

Of course, if the tax-collector showed partiality in dealing with the public, or else overcharged, this definitely would have been wrong in the eyes of God. Whether Matthew was guilty of such, is anyone's guess!

The phrase, *"And He saith unto him, Follow Me,"* proclaims two things:

1. Christ, as well, had little concern for the taboos and social mores of the religious leadership of Israel. He did not come to abide by their restrictions, but, instead, to introduce the New Covenant, which was the total opposite of their thinking.

2. He would call Matthew to be one of His Disciples, simply because the Heavenly Father, through the agency of the Holy Spirit, would tell Him to do so. Of course, choosing this man would fly in the face of the Religious Leaders of Israel, and would cause them to hate Christ even more.

Actually, the question should be asked, as to why Christ did choose this man?

As stated, He did this only by the guidance of the Holy Spirit (Jn. 5:19).

The answer is found in the statement, *"For the Lord seeth not as man seeth; for man looketh on the outward appearance, but the Lord looketh on the heart"* (I Sam. 16:7).

The words, *"Follow Me,"* constituted an entirely different scenario to Matthew than the religion of his day. As well, it constitutes the very embodiment of Christianity.

As we have stated, Christianity is not a religion, but, instead, a relationship with a Person, the Man, Christ Jesus.

Jesus did not say to Matthew that he was to follow a creed, dogma, theory, or religion, but, instead, Himself, namely Christ. This put an entirely different light on the matter.

The Law of Moses had been so perverted by the Jews, that its original intent was completely lost. Now it was a system of rules, which were grievous to be borne and which provided no life whatsoever, and because they were man-devised. As such, Matthew was sick of them, which evidenced itself in his bold defiance.

This was different! Jesus was telling him not to follow this man-devised system which afforded no life whatsoever, but, instead, His Person. As well, when Jesus said the words, *"Follow Me,"*

they, no doubt, were accompanied by the convicting Power of the Holy Spirit. How they registered on Matthew's heart is anyone's guess. But, to be sure, one can conclude that it was no matter-of-fact transaction. For this publican to have done what he did, *"And he arose, and followed Him,"* would have evidenced a powerful emotion in Matthew's heart. The evidence is clear that he did what he did immediately!

Quite possibly, he would have lost much money by following Jesus so instantaneously. And yet, he gained eternal life, which totally eclipses any immediate loss respecting finances. It was the greatest trade he ever made!

To be sure, Matthew's conversion, and a conversion it was, is the true manner of Salvation. One must make a clean break, and instantly! One cannot serve God by degree, but only with the whole heart, which is evidenced in this former tax-collector.

As Peter and John had been fishers of fish, Matthew was a fisher of money. Now, all will become *"fishers of men."*

(10) "AND IT CAME TO PASS, AS JESUS SAT AT MEAT IN THE HOUSE, BEHOLD, MANY PUBLICANS AND SINNERS CAME AND SAT DOWN WITH HIM AND HIS DISCIPLES."

The phrase, *"And it came to pass, as Jesus sat at meat in the house,"* referred to Matthew's house (Lk. 5:29), which Matthew modestly did not mention.

The structure of the sentence emphasizes the fact that this gathering did not necessarily happen the same day that Matthew left his *"receipt of custom,"* but, possibly, some days later, after Matthew had made it known to all the other tax-collectors, and even others, as to his new-found calling. This proclaims the fact that Matthew was not only <u>not</u> ashamed of what he had done following Jesus, but, instead, was thrilled at the new-found prospect. This, as well, portrays true conversion.

The phrase, *"Many publicans and sinners came,"* portrays, once again, Jesus totally breaking from the manner and ways of the Pharisees. It seems all were welcome to Matthew's house, which included *"sinners."*

The Pharisees were so self-righteous that they would have never done such, and, no doubt, grandly criticized Christ and His Disciples being associated with such.

In reality, and tragically, the Pharisees, and due to their self-righteousness, were in much worse spiritual condition than these *"sinners,"* whom they despised. As well, these were the very people for whom Jesus came.

The phrase, *"And sat down with Him and His Disciples,"* speaks of fellowship, but on Christ's terms, and not their's. But yet, them *"sitting down"* with Him implied welcome.

The word, *"Him,"* is emphatic, implying that He Personally made them welcome, but does not mean that He condoned their sin.

(11) "AND WHEN THE PHARISEES SAW IT, THEY SAID UNTO HIS DISCIPLES, WHY EATETH YOUR MASTER WITH PUBLICANS AND SINNERS?"

The phrase, *"And when the Pharisees saw it,"* implies that the gathering was noised abroad even before it happened, and the Pharisees took great exception.

Once again, they were only interested in finding fault, and had little desire to know the real purpose and mission of the Messiah.

The phrase, *"They said unto His Disciples,"* finds them attacking Christ through those who followed Him, rather than attacking Him directly.

The question, *"Why eateth your Master with publicans and sinners?"*, constituted in their thinking a great wrong.

As we have stated, the publicans were tax-collectors, and the *"sinners"* were those who made no profession of religion whatsoever, and were openly living in sin.

Notice they said to the Disciples, *"your Master,"* signifying that they would never accept Him as such! As well, they were attempting to drive a breach between the Disciples and Christ by inferring that they were foolish for following Him. In effect, they are saying that such a Teacher should know better than to do what He was doing by eating with these *"publicans and sinners."*

(12) "BUT WHEN JESUS HEARD THAT, HE SAID UNTO THEM, THEY THAT BE WHOLE NEED NOT A PHYSICIAN, BUT THEY THAT ARE SICK."

The phrase, *"But when Jesus heard that, He said unto them,"* infers that the Disciples relayed to Him the statement of the Pharisees.

The phrase, *"They that be whole need not a physician, but they that are sick,"* proclaims the very reason why Jesus came. His statement is of far greater import than meets the eye.

In effect, He is telling the Pharisees that He did not come for them, and because such would have been pointless anyway. In their self-righteousness, they would never admit their need for Him, and, therefore, any overture toward them was pointless.

By making the statement, *"They that be whole,"* He was not inferring that the Pharisees were *"whole,"* i.e., Righteous, but, instead, that the unrighteous, i.e., *"sick,"* were the ones He came for. Actually, the Pharisees were in worse condition than the *"publicans and sinners,"* and because of their self-righteousness, but, of course, did not think so, but, instead, thought the very opposite.

So, the statement of Christ disarmed them, and, at the same time, pointed to their terrible self-righteousness by their ignoring these *"publicans and sinners,"* and even despising them.

In this statement made by Christ, He fully exposed what the Pharisees actually were, and, at the same time, what they ought to have been. And yet, there was nothing they could say contrary to His statement.

(13) "BUT GO YE AND LEARN WHAT THAT MEANETH, I WILL HAVE MERCY AND NOT SACRIFICE: FOR I AM NOT COME TO CALL THE RIGHTEOUS, BUT SINNERS TO REPENTANCE."

The phrase, *"But go ye and learn what that meaneth,"* and referring to His statement concerning the *"physician"* and the *"sick,"* is chilling indeed! It means that there is no Saviour for the self-righteous, and because they will never admit that they need a Saviour, thinking their own *"good works"* will save them.

The phrase, *"I will have Mercy and not Sacrifice,"* means that these Pharisees thought that the offering of Sacrifices, plus all the religious rituals in which they engaged, made them Righteous. Consequently, they gauged everyone's Salvation by how faithful they engaged in all of these rituals.

Christ is telling them that if their religion made them exalted and self-righteous, which it did, and that they considered themselves to be defiled by associating with sinners, then their Sacrifices were in vain.

He was stating that they needed to show

"Mercy," instead of finding fault with everyone else, because they did not measure up to their standards.

"Mercy" is a beautiful and life-giving attribute, which originates with God. Inasmuch as He shows Mercy to us, He demands that we show Mercy to others. To be sure, if one does not show Mercy to others, it's a pretty good sign that Mercy has not been shown to him. In other words, they, as the Pharisees, have never truly been saved.

If one is truly *"born again,"* they will truly realize the Mercy that God has shown to them, and will be quick to show it to others.

The phrase, *"For I am not come to call the Righteous, but sinners to repentance,"* once again, did not mean that these Pharisees were Righteous. The statement is rather tendered to explain the true mission of Christ.

He did come to *"call the sinners to repentance,"* but, the manner that He chose to do that was not by telling them how truly bad they were, but, instead, to show them Mercy.

The Scripture does not say, *"For God saw how bad the world was, and sent His Only Begotten Son...,"* but, instead, *"For God so loved the world..."* (Jn. 3:16).

Of course, it is obvious that the world was bad! But telling it how bad it is will not make it any better. Therefore, the duty of the God-called Preacher is to call men to *"repentance,"* but to do it with Love, Compassion, and *"Mercy."*

If one is to notice, Christ had three approaches to humanity. They are as follows:

1. To the *"publicans and sinners,"* which included most of the common people, etc., and irrespective of the depth of their sin, He had nothing but Love and Compassion. In other words, even though He hated the sin, He loved the sinner and showed it. There was not a word of condemnation for this class of people, which made up the far greater majority.

2. To the Pharisees and the self-righteous of such like, He had nothing but scathing denunciation (Mat. 23).

3. To the worldlings such as the Herodians, who were not of the Religious Elite, but were mostly of the wealthy class and who ignored God, He ignored them. If there was any statement toward them, it was generally in sarcasm.

Whenever it was mentioned to Him that Herod would kill Him, His response to Herod and his followers was, *"Go ye, and tell that fox..."* (Lk. 13:31-32).

(14) "THEN CAME TO HIM THE DISCIPLES OF JOHN, SAYING, WHY DO WE AND THE PHARISEES FAST OFT, BUT THY DISCIPLES FAST NOT?"

The phrase, *"Then came to Him the Disciples of John,"* records the first visit of John's Disciples, whose ministry was now beginning to wane, and because his work of introducing Christ, which he had gloriously done, was now complete. (Actually, John, by this time, may have already been put in prison.)

The question, *"Why do we and the Pharisees fast oft, but Thy Disciples fast not?",* is revealing indeed!

The linkage of the Disciples of John and the Pharisees is not meant to portray similarity. Actually, John the Baptist strongly denounced this group (3:7). These Disciples are simply referring to the fact that they fasted often, as well as the Pharisees, while it seems the Disciples of Christ, at least at that time, fasted not at all.

If, in fact, John had already been imprisoned, his Disciples, as here, it seems, had drifted, at least somewhat, into ritualism. Jesus' explanation will properly answer their question. The life and liberty of the Gospel destroy the wineskins of ritualism, as the next verse will proclaim.

(The Pharisees, at least at this time, fasted twice a week, even though such was not commanded in the Scripture. Quite possibly, John's Disciples were doing the same, and thought it strange that Jesus' Disciples did not follow suit.)

(15) "AND JESUS SAID UNTO THEM, CAN THE CHILDREN OF THE BRIDECHAMBER MOURN, AS LONG AS THE BRIDEGROOM IS WITH THEM? BUT THE DAYS WILL COME, WHEN THE BRIDEGROOM SHALL BE TAKEN FROM THEM, AND THEN SHALL THEY FAST."

The phrase, *"And Jesus said unto them,"* entails the introduction of the New Covenant, which would take the place of the Old, and, of necessity, would be much better!

The question, *"Can the children of the bridechamber mourn, as long as the bridegroom is with them?",* is speaking of Himself being personally present with them, with such being likened to a marriage feast, which certainly would not be the time to fast.

In effect, Christ is telling the Disciples of John, that they, as well, should be rejoicing instead of mourning.

While it may have been true that John had now been imprisoned, and, if so, would occasion sorrow among his Disciples, still, John fulfilled his mission in introducing Christ, and, therefore, they should rejoice!

In effect, Christ is telling them that they have not properly understood the mission of John, and the glorious manner in which he fulfilled it. If they had understood it properly, even though sorry, and extremely so, concerning John's present plight, still, in the total aspect of all things, John's present position should not be mourned, but instead celebrated, and because the One he pointed to (the Bridegroom) is now here.

Actually, it should have been a time of unparalleled rejoicing throughout the entirety of Israel! The One the Prophets had spoken of was now here. In effect, the very reason for Israel's existence (the womb of the Messiah), had brought forth That for which she was raised up. Such should have been the occasion of much joy and celebration. Jesus here says as much by describing His Presence as a marriage feast, which always occasioned tremendous joy.

However, Israel did not rejoice because she did not know Who He was. The Religious Leaders not only did not rejoice, but were extremely agitated at His Presence, and, because of their unbelief, totally missed the single most important moment in all history.

The phrase, *"But the days will come, when the bridegroom shall be taken from them,"* in effect, spoke of the Death, Resurrection, and Ascension of Christ, i.e., *"taken from them."*

The *"days to come,"* of which Jesus spoke, was about two and one-half to three years away.

The phrase, *"And then shall they fast,"* is filled with meaning!

"Fasting" implies sorrow or mourning over personal weakness, or the present spiritual plight of one's person, or even a Church, or the entirety of a nation.

When a Christian fasts at present, even though he may be fasting for his own personal reasons, which certainly are spiritually and scripturally legitimate, still, whether he understands

NOTES

it or not, a part of the sorrow incorporated in his fast respects the rejection of Christ by Israel, which hindered the coming of the Kingdom of Heaven in its totality, which rejection brought misery, and, as well, mourns for Christ to come back.

Therefore, fasting pictures something which is wrong and which desperately needs to be remedied, which only the Second Coming of Christ can bring about. Even though fasting, and as stated, may be for personal reasons, still, its full meaning points to all that is wrong in this world, and that Christ Alone can set things right.

(16) "NO MAN PUTTETH A PIECE OF NEW CLOTH ONTO AN OLD GARMENT, FOR THAT WHICH IS PUT IN TO FILL IT UP TAKETH FROM THE GARMENT, AND THE RENT IS MADE WORSE."

The phrase, *"No man putteth a piece of new cloth onto an old garment,"* will now begin to answer their question as to exactly Who John the Baptist introduced, Who was Christ, the Giver of the New Covenant.

Jesus here likens the Law of Moses to *"an old garment,"* implying that it has served its purpose, and, is worn out, and must be replaced. The *"old garment"* spoke of all the ritual of the past, which clung to Israel like a cloth, and even John's Disciples.

The *"new cloth"* is the *"New Covenant,"* which Christ would introduce, but would be given in totality to the Apostle Paul (Gal. 1:11-12).

In effect, Christ is saying that He did not come to patch up the *"old garment,"* with pieces of the *"new,"* but, instead, will replace it altogether.

Regrettably, even in the Early Church, many continued to attempt to apply the *"New"* to the *"Old."* This was the occasion of Paul's greatest difficulty. They kept trying to cling to the Old, even after the New had been introduced.

Sadly, the Modern Church, even after some 2,000 years, continues to revert back to the *"old garment."*

For instance, the attempting to keep the old Jewish Sabbath, is an attempt to cling to the *"old garment."* As well, any time the Church reverts back to legalism, which possibly we all have done at one time or the other, it is an attempt to revive the *"old garment."*

The Lord tells us what happens whenever the Church reverts to legalism!

The phrase, *"For that which is put in to fill it up taketh from the garment, and the rent is made worse,"* means that the Child of God does not help himself by resorting to legalism, but, instead, makes the matter *"worse."* Please allow us, and because of its significance, to say it again:

"Any time the Believer attempts to revert back to Law, thinking it will help his present plight, whatever it is, the situation will not only not be improved, but will actually worsen."

(17) "NEITHER DO MEN PUT NEW WINE INTO OLD BOTTLES: ELSE THE BOTTLES BREAK, AND THE WINE RUNNETH OUT, AND THE BOTTLES PERISH: BUT THEY PUT NEW WINE INTO NEW BOTTLES, AND BOTH ARE PRESERVED."

The subject is so important that Jesus will say the same thing all over again, using an entirely different illustration, which was His custom.

The phrase, *"Neither do men put new wine into old bottles,"* was referring to something that all of His listeners would have been very well acquainted with.

The *"bottles"* here spoken of were actually containers made out of the skin of lambs, etc.

The *"old bottles"* or *"skins,"* referred to skins which were cracked because of age and could not stand much pressure.

If *"new wine"* was put into *"old bottles,"* i.e., *"old skins,"* the wine upon expanding, which it did, and which would exert pressure, would burst the skins, with the resultant loss of the wine.

Jesus described it by using the phrase, *"Else the bottles break, and the wine runneth out, and the bottles perish."* In other words, both the *"wine"* and the *"skins"* would be lost.

This is what happens when the Church reverts to Law! Not only does the *"Law"* (old bottles) not work for them, but, as well, the *"new wine,"* as given by the New Covenant, is lost. Consequently, the Believer receives no help whatsoever.

To be sure, the lesson, as intended by Christ, is so strong that if one insists on attempting to put *"new wine into old bottles,"* they will *"perish,"* i.e., *"fall from Grace"* (Gal. 5:4). This is exactly what Paul was speaking of when he said, *"Stand fast therefore in the liberty* (new wine) *wherewith Christ hath made us free, and be not*

NOTES

entangled again with the yoke of bondage (old bottles)*"* (Gal. 5:1).

The phrase, *"But they put new wine into new bottles, and both are preserved,"* simply means that the Gospel, *"new wine,"* cannot be tacked on to the Law, i.e., *"old bottles,"* but must be placed in *"new bottles,"* i.e., *"New Covenant."*

Did the Disciples of John understand what Christ was talking about?

Quite possibly they did, at least as far as was possible at that time. It would not have been possible for them to have understood it totally, because the New Covenant had not even then been given. However, at least they were made to understand that something new was coming, which was so much better than what had been, and which was occasioned by His Presence, and introduced by John.

The difference between the Old Covenant and the New Covenant is striking. The Old Covenant knew a Law that was carved in cold stone.

The New Covenant takes the Righteousness that was expressed in Law and supernaturally infuses that Righteousness into the very character of the Believer. Thus Hebrews quotes the Old Testament foreview as something that is now, through Christ, our own: *"I will put My Laws in their hearts and I will write them on their minds . . . . Their sins and lawless acts I will remember no more"* (Heb. 10:16-17).

There is none of the Laws called *"Do this and live"* in the New Covenant. Instead, we meet again the great *"I will"* of God, Who promises that He Himself will transform us from within (Gal. 2:20).

Paul carefully explains that all of God's Promises are appropriated by Faith. Today, to us, who, like Abraham, are *"fully persuaded that God* (has) *power to do what He promises"* (Rom. 4:21), comes the promised Salvation, and with it comes forgiveness and inner transformation. Such are the benefits of Covenant relationship with the Lord.

Even though we have only touched on the benefits of the New Covenant, still, to fully proclaim all that it entails would probably be impossible. Truly, Christ *"is the Mediator of a Better Covenant which was established upon better promises"* (Heb. 8:6).

If one is forced to attempt to portray the New Covenant in one Passage, possibly the following says it best of all:

"For He hath made Him to be sin for us, Who knew no sin; that we might be made the Righteousness of God in Him" (II Cor. 5:21).

Hallelujah!

(18) "WHILE HE SPAKE THESE THINGS UNTO THEM, BEHOLD, THERE CAME A CERTAIN RULER, AND WORSHIPPED HIM, SAYING, MY DAUGHTER IS EVEN NOW DEAD: BUT COME AND LAY THY HAND UPON HER, AND SHE SHALL LIVE."

The phrase, *"While He spake these things unto them,"* pertains to the subject matter just given; however, Mark and Luke seem to place it at another time (Mk. 2:21; Lk. 5:36).

As should be obvious, the chronological order of events is not always adhered to in the Gospels. This is not a discrepancy, but, actually, by design. The Holy Spirit, in superintending the writing of these Books, had each Message and illustration placed exactly where He desired it, but still in its rightful place, if all the facts were known (II Pet. 1:21).

As is obvious in the Gospels, they are not identical, with some accounts given in one which will not be given in the others, etc. However, if one carefully analyzes these Books and uses the same common sense that is used in the giving of any accounts in books other than the Bible, it quickly becomes obvious that there are no discrepancy, distortion, or contradiction.

Sometimes the same illustration will be shown in a little different manner, simply because the Holy Spirit is placing the emphasis a little different in each account.

So, if the happenings of the raising of the daughter of Jarius took place immediately after Jesus' short dissertation on the *"old garments"* and *"old bottles,"* we are not sure! Neither does the Text specifically say that it does, but merely speaks of *"these things,"* which could have referred to other teachings as well! And yet, more probably, the chronology here is correct, and meant to be, whereas in Mark and Luke, the same account of the teaching on the Law is placed elsewhere in the Text.

The phrase, *"Behold, there came a certain ruler, and worshipped him, saying,"* speaks of Jarius who was a ruler of the Synagogue. Incidentally, both Mark and Luke carry this account, with each giving a little added information, which verifies what I have been attempting to say concerning the recording of these events.

INSPIRATION

The Bible is inspired by the Holy Spirit. As such, it is without error. The word, *"Inspiration,"* in the Greek, is *"theopneustos,"* which means *"God-breathed."*

Every Bible writer was inspired by the Holy Spirit in all things that were written.

Inspiration guarantees more, much more, than the mere thought being inspired. It guarantees that each and every word has proceeded from the Mouth of God.

The Holy Spirit searched through the vocabularies of each and every writer and actually selected the word He desired to use for each and every subject matter He dealt with. This means the Holy Spirit selected every Word. That's why Jesus said:

"Man shall not live by bread alone, but by every Word that proceeds out of the Mouth of God" (Mat. 4:4).

Concerning Inspiration, Peter said, and I quote from THE EXPOSITOR'S STUDY BIBLE:

"Knowing this first (harks back, as stated, to the Old Testament, which, in effect, was the Bible of Peter's day), *that no Prophecy of the Scripture is of any private interpretation.* (This refers to the fact that the Word of God did not originate in the human mind.)

"For the Prophecy (the word *"Prophecy"* is used in a general sense, covering the entirety of the Word of God, which means it's not limited merely to predictions regarding the future) *came not in old time by the will of man* (did not originate with man): *but holy men of God spoke as they were moved by the Holy Spirit.* (This proclaims the manner in which the Word of God was written and thereby given unto us) (II Pet. 1:20-21).

All of this means that there are no errors or contradictions in the original Text. There is no book in the world that can even remotely compare with the Bible as it regards the veracity of its content. It has been investigated in every manner possible. No one ever has been able honestly to refute its claims.

Incidentally, as a Believer, if you do not own a *"word-for-word"* translation of the Bible, such as the King James Version, then you really do not have a Bible, but something else entirely.

(I strongly recommend THE EXPOSITOR'S STUDY BIBLE as one of the most helpful Study

Bibles ever produced.)

The phrase, *"My daughter is even now dead,"* is said by Matthew, while Mark says, *"My little daughter lieth at the point of death"* (Mk. 5:23).

Once again, there is no discrepancy. Matthew does not give the entirety of the account as Mark and Luke did, but greatly abbreviates it. If the entirety of all three of the accounts are placed together, then it becomes obvious as to what Matthew did, and, as stated, by design.

As well, Mark mentioned that the little girl was 12 years old, whereas Matthew said nothing of her age (Mk. 5:42).

The Faith of Jarius is amazing, especially considering that the child is dead.

Still, it possibly would not have matched the Faith of the Centurion, simply because that man was a Gentile, and would not have had access to the Word of God, as Jarius (8:5-10).

The phrase, *"But come and lay Thy hand upon her, and she shall live,"* proclaims great Faith in the Son of God.

(The Centurion had merely requested of Christ that He *"speak the Word,"* whereas, Jarius had asked for a personal visit. However, the former was sick while the latter was dead, which definitely would have necessitated greater Faith.)

Jarius was to get exactly what he asked for!

(19) "AND JESUS AROSE, AND FOLLOWED HIM, AND SO DID HIS DISCIPLES."

The phrase, *"And Jesus arose, and followed him,"* means that He did so promptly.

If one is to notice, the entirety of the Life of Christ, at least during His earthly Ministry of approximately three and one-half years, was spent in service to others. What an example for us to follow!

The cause of most problems in the human life is self-will; in other words, selfishness. When our life is lived for others, exactly as this example portrays, one would be surprised as to how quickly a lot of our own personal problems would disappear.

The phrase, *"And so did His Disciples,"* presents them doing exactly as He had demanded, *"Follow Me!"*

What the Disciples were to see, and, more particularly, three of them, was the greatest display of power they had seen thus far, even eclipsing the calming of the storm, for Jesus would raise the dead.

Following Him, that is if one truly follows, is the most exciting, thrilling, fulfilling, rewarding, and instructive life that one could ever begin to live.

(20) "AND, BEHOLD, A WOMAN, WHICH WAS DISEASED WITH AN ISSUE OF BLOOD TWELVE YEARS, CAME BEHIND HIM, AND TOUCHED THE HEM OF HIS GARMENT:"

The phrase, *"And, behold, a woman,"* is addressed thusly, in order that this particular woman would stand out, and because of her Faith.

The phrase, *"Which was diseased with an issue of blood twelve years,"* speaks of her being physically and ceremonially unclean (Lev. 15:25).

Exactly what her disease was, the Bible does not say. Perhaps it was a female disorder. At any rate, Mark said that she had *"suffered many things of many physicians,"* but was not helped, but instead grew worse.

The phrase, *"Came behind Him,"* refers to an action on her part that no doubt had come to her a short time before.

Exactly what she had heard of Jesus is anyone's guess. No doubt, His working of miracles was being discussed by everyone. Whatever she had heard and however she heard it, caused her to believe that if she could just get to Him this terrible problem that had plagued her for so long would be healed. As well, the implication is that her physical situation was deteriorating rapidly, and, quite possibly, if His help was not forthcoming, she would lose her life.

However, upon arriving at the scene where she felt He would be, her Faith was to encounter many obstacles. First of all, even though Matthew does not mention it, Mark said that the people *"thronged Him."* Consequently, it was not going to be easy to get to Him. Even if she could, there would be little time to explain to Him her problem, and due to the press of the crowd. However, a thought, no doubt born of the Spirit, entered her mind. The phrase, *"And touched the hem of His garment,"* as the next verse portrays, was not done by accident, but was a settled thought in her mind, even though of short duration.

This lady's Faith is remarkable, and yet a portrayal of all of humanity who attempts to come to Christ. Regrettably, many, upon reaching the obstacles, as Faith always encounters, allow the obstacles to overcome them, and retire without getting what they came for. However, True Faith, at least that which is born of the Spirit, will not take *"No"* for an answer. Neither will it allow obstacles to stop it, even though they may hinder. Irrespective, it will press through, and the result will always be the same, as it was for this precious lady.

The *"Hem of His garment,"* referred to the (either blue or white) tassels or fringes worn by every Israelite at the four corners of their upper garments (Num. 15:37-41).

Tradition maintains that the threads of the tassels were white to symbolize Righteousness, along with a conspicuous blue thread among them to symbolize that the Commandments were of heavenly origin.

Such was commanded by the Lord, that every time it was noticed, they would be reminded of the Law and their responsibility to obey it, and their calling to be a holy people unto Jehovah.

This is what the woman saw, and, evidently, knowing the Law, she reasoned that the Promises of God were wrapped up in that tassel, and, even more importantly, the One Who wore it was different than anyone she had ever seen. This, we have to believe.

Jesus was Anointed by the Holy Spirit more than any other man who had ever lived, and inasmuch as He was perfect, Faith could, no doubt, see within Him the attributes of Godliness as they had never been seen in any other man (Ps. 45:7; Heb. 1:9).

(21) "FOR SHE SAID WITHIN HERSELF, IF I MAY BUT TOUCH HIS GARMENT, I SHALL BE WHOLE."

The phrase, *"For she said within herself,"* concerns her response to the seeming impossibility of securing a private audience. As stated, Faith will find a way.

How many millions come part way, and with Christ within grasp, but then turn away?

Possibly, one can say that the hindrances will always be there. Satan will see to that! And as well, it seems that the Lord allows such in order that the true asker will receive, the true seeker will find, and the one who truly knocks will have the door opened unto him. The merely curious and the doubtful mind receive nothing!

The phrase, *"If I may but touch His garment, I shall be whole,"* proclaims her Faith. To be sure, it was not any garment, but *"His garment!"*

NOTES

Actually, such garments with the blue and white tassels were worn by most all. Therefore, it was not the garment, but the One Who wore it. That One was the Creator of the worlds, the Saviour of mankind, and the Giver of eternal life. This was God manifest in the flesh. This is why Christianity, at least True Bible Christianity, is so important, and so far ahead of the religions of this world. Christianity is Christ. Consequently, when Christianity becomes mere philosophy, Christ is no longer the focal point, and, therefore, it degenerates into mere religion. Then, in fact, it is no different than all the others.

However, if we remember Who is wearing the garment and keep our eyes on Him, the miraculous results experienced by this dear lady of so long ago will be ours as well!

Among the great lessons taught in this episode, no doubt, this is at least one.

No matter how beautiful the garments of others were, or how prominent this *"tassel"* was displayed, there was no miracle in them. However, when worn by Christ, and with eyes upon Him, that which she sought for became hers.

(22) "BUT JESUS TURNED HIM ABOUT, AND WHEN HE SAW HER, HE SAID, DAUGHTER, BE OF GOOD COMFORT; THY FAITH HATH MADE THEE WHOLE. AND THE WOMAN WAS MADE WHOLE FROM THAT HOUR."

The phrase, *"But Jesus turned Him about,"* refers to His response to her touching His garment, and, as Mark said, *"At the moment of the touch, virtue* (power) *went out of Him,"* and healed this dear soul.

The phrase, *"And when He saw her,"* refers to Him not finding her immediately. Actually, He did not know she was in the crowd, nor her need, nor her action. To be sure, the Holy Spirit designed it this way in order that we may learn this valuable lesson of Faith, of which I will speak more directly momentarily.

The phrase, *"He said, Daughter, be of good comfort,"* refers to a total change of relationship.

At first, it was just *"a woman,"* now, it is *"Daughter!"*

Yesterday, she was one of the world's nobodies, now, she is one of Heaven's somebodies.

The phrase, *"Thy Faith hath made thee whole,"* portrays an extremely valuable lesson. It teaches us something about God that we should readily understand.

First of all, the Lord does not respond to *"need"* nearly as much as He responds to *"Faith."* Actually, there were scores that day thronging Him and pressing Him, who, no doubt, had many needs. But yet, there is no record of any of them being healed. The reason, and as we have stated, is that He responds to Faith, and not necessarily to need. Of course, He is mindful of our needs, but it is Faith in God to which He responds.

The phrase, *"And the woman was made whole from that hour,"* refers to the exact moment of her touch. In other words, she was healed immediately.

There is a beautiful sermon outlined in this illustration that is apropos respecting the whole of humanity. It is as follows:

1. Chained: This dear woman was chained by disease and sickness which had taken their deadly toll. As well, physicians could not help her, which means there was no help for her in this world other than Christ.

Likewise, the world is chained by sin, and there is no help in this world for that terrible malady. To be sure, neither money nor education nor even the Church is a remedy for sin. Actually, there is no earthly remedy, but there is a remedy and that remedy is Christ. He Alone can break the terrible chains of sin, as the chains of this woman's sickness were broken so long ago.

2. Changed: As Jesus changed her, He can change all who come to Him.

The world tries to change humanity, and calls it *"rehabilitation."* However, such is only a charade, for man cannot change man. Sickness cannot heal sickness, and disease cannot heal disease. So much for man's *"rehabilitation!"* The change can only come about as Christ reveals Himself to the soul. Then the *"change"* will be instantaneous, miraculous, and glorious. Such is described in the glorious *"born-again"* experience.

3. Claimed: As the person *"chained"* by sin, sickness, disease, and hopelessness comes to Christ, then they are *"changed"* by the mighty Power of God. However, it doesn't stop there, as glorious and wonderful as that is! Then He claims us, which means that we enter into the family of God, and, as such, are made a part of that family.

As He claimed her by calling her *"Daughter,"* He claims all who come to Him.

This scenario has a personal application to

me, that I would like to share:

In April of 1995, Frances and I went into Old Mexico for a series of meetings, which also included several meetings on the U. S. side of the border.

In this tour, the last service was conducted in Harlengin, Texas, a beautiful city in the Rio Grande Valley.

The service was to be conducted in the Civic Center in Harlengin, and that which began as a very special lesson to me took place as Frances and I were getting ready for the service that night, even minutes before we were picked up to be taken to the Auditorium.

What I'm about to tell is not earth-shaking, but yet, anything that God gives us is very special, and will be not only of great help to us, but, as well, of great help to others.

As I was getting dressed that evening, all of a sudden, I sensed the Presence of God respecting what I was going to preach that night. The Lord spoke this to my heart:

"I am going to show you," He said, *"something about this Passage of Scripture that you do not know."* And then He said, *"This is the only incident in the New Testament where someone was healed without Jesus even knowing they were there."*

That was all that was said, but yet, I sensed the Presence of God greatly, and sensed that something special would take place in the service that night, which it did.

When we arrived at the Auditorium just a few minutes later, it was packed to absolute capacity. There must have been 20 to 25 Preachers on the platform, with the service already having started.

From the moment the service was turned to me, the Spirit of God seemed to permeate the place. Every song was powerfully Anointed by the Holy Spirit, but that Anointing seemed to intensify as I began to preach.

And then, in the middle of the Message, as I began to elaborate regarding the woman who touched the hem of Jesus' garment, the Lord unfolded to me an expansion on that which He had already revealed.

As I continued preaching, I sensed an even heavier Anointing of the Holy Spirit. And then the Lord began to reveal to me a Truth that I had not seen previously regarding the illustration of the woman with the issue of blood.

As stated, Jesus did not even know she was there. Consequently, He did not know of her need. And, as stated, this was by design.

However, her Faith pulled power out of Christ, even though He did not know who she was, or that she was there, or what she had touched Him for. To be sure, many were touching Him, but, seemingly, without results. However, her touch brought tremendous results to her, and was felt immediately by Christ.

The Truth, as simple as it may be, is that Faith will move God, and irrespective of the circumstances. He did not even know she was there, and yet, Faith pulled power out of Him into her need, and it was instantly met. If it did it for her, it will do it for all who dare to believe Him.

The Truth of this is, that it doesn't really matter how difficult the situation is, or how problematic the circumstances. Faith will move God.

Some may take exception to that statement, *"Faith will move God"*; however, according to the Text, there is no other way it can be explained. Faith pulled the answer for her need out of Him, even though He did not even know of her presence. As we have previously stated, allow us to state it again; *"The Lord does not necessarily respond to need, but, instead, to Faith."* Of course, that is Faith in Him, and not in other things, etc.

I might also quickly add, that one of the most erroneous teachings in modern Christendom is that Faith is to be used only to get what we need. That is wrong, and blatantly so!

Of course, Faith gets us what we need, but its primary purpose is of far greater magnitude. Faith is intended by God to help us to be what we ought to be, instead of merely receiving things we want, etc.

This is borne out in Jesus calling the woman *"Daughter,"* which spoke of relationship. Yes! She got what she needed, but, more importantly, she became something she desperately needed to be, which her Faith claimed, which spoke of relationship to Christ, which is the most important of all. Yes! She was healed, but, more importantly, she became His Daughter.

This is evidenced even more so by the principle foundation of one's Faith, as it is found in Abraham:

The Scripture says, *"And he believed in the Lord; and He counted it to him for Righteousness"* (Gen. 15:6).

NOTES

This means that Abraham had Faith in God, and God helped him to literally *"be"* Righteousness.

So, to cheapen Faith by placing it in the realm of receiving only, is a corruption of that which is the basic foundation of relationship with Christ. Our Faith is to instead help us to be what He wants us to be, which definitely will include receiving the things we need, but which will not stop there.

(23) "AND WHEN JESUS CAME INTO THE RULER'S HOUSE, AND SAW THE MINSTRELS AND THE PEOPLE MAKING A NOISE,"

Whenever Jairus first came to Christ, his daughter, the evidence proclaims, even though extremely ill, was not yet dead. However, during the incident of the healing of the woman, news had come to him that his daughter had died. He would then say, *"My daughter is even now dead: but come and lay Thy Hand upon her, and she shall live."* Jesus will do accordingly.

These *"minstrels"* were those who were paid mourners who attended houses of the dead and made great lamentation, etc.

As is obvious, these were called in immediately after the demise of the loved one. When Jesus arrived, they were already *"making a noise,"* i.e., making lamentation over the death of the child.

(24) "HE SAID UNTO THEM, GIVE PLACE: FOR THE MAID IS NOT DEAD, BUT SLEEPETH. AND THEY LAUGHED HIM TO SCORN."

The phrase, *"He said unto them, Give place,"* in effect, says, *"Get out of the room!"* The idea is, and due to their *"noise making,"* that His admonition was not too gentle.

The phrase, *"For the maid is not dead, but sleepeth,"* infers two things:

1. These paid mourners did not want to leave, even at His Command that they do so. Quite possibly, they were concerned that they would not be paid for their services if they left. At any rate, the exchange was somewhat sharp between them and Christ.

2. His statement about her not being dead was not meant as they took it. He was looking forward to the result of Him raising her from the dead, and they were thinking of her at the present. In Truth, she was dead, but, as well, in Truth, she would not remain dead.

The phrase, *"And they laughed Him to*

scorn," refers to them having no Faith at all in what He was about to do, that is, if they even knew the reason for His Presence.

Their *"laughter"* was such of total ridicule. All knew the girl was dead, and, therefore, they met His demands with *"scorn."*

(25) "BUT WHEN THE PEOPLE WERE PUT FORTH, HE WENT IN, AND TOOK HER BY THE HAND, AND THE MAID AROSE."

The phrase, *"But when the people were put forth, He went in,"* refers to them not leaving easily. The idea is that they left only short of force being used.

The words, *"He went in,"* means that He would not go in until they had left, or, even more directly, had been removed.

To be sure, their presence would not have affected His Power at all, but, inasmuch as they had no Faith whatsoever, He would not allow them to be a part of this grand and glorious miracle.

By their *"scorn,"* they lost so much, as all lose so much when using *"scorn"* regarding Christ. Regrettably, almost the entirety of the world meets Christ with *"scorn"* instead of Faith. As a result, as these were put out, they, likewise, will be put out (7:23).

The phrase, *"And took her by the hand,"* refers to life touching death. Matthew, in giving only an abbreviated account, does not mention Christ's exact words as Mark, but simply refers to the action.

However, that which took place between the words, *"And took her by the hand,"* connected to the following phrase, *"And the maid arose,"* is startling indeed!

One moment she was dead, and now she is alive, arising, and walking about. I wonder what the thoughts of those *"mourners"* were upon this Advent?

The next verse tells us what happened!

(26) "AND THE FAME HEREOF WENT ABROAD INTO ALL THAT LAND."

The news spread like wildfire all over the area of the little girl being raised from the dead, and no wonder!

Inasmuch as Jairus was a *"ruler"* in the local Synagogue, and especially considering that the mourners had already been brought in, the astonishment of this miracle of the raising of the girl from the dead knew no bounds.

Likewise, Jairus' Faith is to be commended, in that he did not give up, even when told the child was dead. He believed that Christ could raise her from the dead, and his Faith was rewarded with exactly that which he requested.

Is it possible to comprehend the happiness that filled that home after this great miracle? For weeks, or perhaps months, the child had steadily grown worse, with all the attendant hurt of the parents, especially realizing that they were about to lose her. But now, in a moments time, that darkness has turned to light, and that death has turned to life.

One can well imagine that as long as Jairus lived, he would bring people into his house, showing them exactly where Jesus stood when He took his dead daughter by the hand and life flooded her body. The moment of such a happening would never be lost.

As well, at least speaking from a spiritual sense, Jesus has entered into millions of houses, and has turned night to day. He Alone is the Answer to the ills of this world.

(27) "AND WHEN JESUS DEPARTED THENCE, TWO BLIND MEN FOLLOWED HIM, CRYING, AND SAYING, THOU SON OF DAVID, HAVE MERCY ON US."

I think it is apparent that one can say with little fear of contradiction that the account of the healing of the two blind men given here is totally different than that of the two healed in Jericho (20:29-34), even though the terminology is very similar in both. Actually according to John, only a small number of the miracles performed by Christ were placed in the Sacred Text (Jn. 21:25). So unless it is obvious that the accounts of the incidents given are similar, it would be wise to consider each, as here, separate incidents altogether.

The phrase, *"And when Jesus departed thence,"* implies that the healing of the *"two blind men"* happened not too very long after the raising of the girl from the dead.

The phrase, *"Two blind men followed Him,"* refers, no doubt, to His *"fame"* that had gone out in all that land.

The word, *"Crying,"* implies great passion!

The phrase, *"And saying, Thou Son of David, have mercy on us,"* refers to this title being used only by a heathen woman (15:22) and four blind men (20:30-31).

The phrase, *"Son of David,"* was a Messianic title, and implied the fulfillment of the prophetic promises in Christ.

As to this title being used by a Gentile woman plus four blind men, is not without spiritual significance.

1. The Gentiles would receive Him, as symbolized by the *"Woman of Canaan"* (Mat. 15:21-22), while Israel would reject Him.

2. The four blind men exclaiming Him as the *"Son of David,"* proclaims Israel being blind to His true identity. The Religious Leaders of Israel rejected Him, with their blindness only deepening, which spoke of a fourfold or complete spiritual blindness.

The phrase, *"Have mercy on us,"* was that which Israel should have said, as spoken by these *"two blind men,"* but which they did not say. Mercy unasked, is Mercy ungiven. Conversely, Mercy asked, as these blind men, is Mercy given.

It is a simple statement, *"Have mercy on us,"* but, yet, a request the Lord always answers. Men do not need justice, they need Mercy!

The writer of Hebrews tells us, *"Let us therefore come boldly unto the Throne of Grace, that we may obtain Mercy, and find Grace to help in time of need"* (Heb. 4:16).

(28) "AND WHEN HE WAS COME INTO THE HOUSE, THE BLIND MEN CAME TO HIM: AND JESUS SAITH UNTO THEM, BELIEVE YE THAT I AM ABLE TO DO THIS? THEY SAID UNTO HIM, YEA, LORD."

The phrase, *"And when He was come into the house,"* could very well refer to the house of Matthew, or even Peter's home. At any rate, what an honor and privilege to have Him in *"the house."*

The phrase, *"The blind men came to Him,"* in a spiritual sense, refers to all who are without God, for all in this condition are *"spiritually blind."* As such, it is not possible for the spiritual eyes of an individual to be opened, except by the Power of the Holy Spirit. Such cannot be opened by intellect or education, and Preachers who attempt to do so are wasting their time. It is only when the Word of God is preached and Anointed by the Holy Spirit, that *"recovery of sight to the blind"* can be effected (Lk. 4:18).

They came *"to Him,"* because no other could effect this miracle, as no other can open eyes which are blind spiritually.

The phrase, *"And Jesus saith unto them,"* refers to a simple question they will be asked!

The question, *"Believe ye that I am able to do this?",* pretty much sums up about all He ever said to those who approached Him.

Not one time did He ever refuse to heal anyone, nor did He question them about their spiritual condition!

Considering the great number of people healed by Him, one would have to come to the conclusion that many of these people were not living as they should, and, yet, Jesus never one time reprimanded them or refused to heal them under any circumstances. He only asked if they had Faith, and, seemingly, if they did not have it, He would impart such to them (Mk. 9:24).

As Faith was required for healing, likewise, it is required for Salvation. Consequently, basically, the same statement is given regarding the *"born-again"* experience (Jn. 3:16).

The Lord does not ask that one understand all about Salvation, or how it is afforded, as He did not require of these *"blind men"* to understand how He performed the miracle. He only asked that they believe that He could to such. He asks no more for Salvation.

The phrase, *"They said unto Him, Yea, Lord,"* was all He required.

Some folk misunderstand Faith, and, consequently, believe that one must understand all about it before one can have it. Such is not the case.

Jesus does not ask us to understand all about it, and, in Truth, it is impossible for one to understand all its ramifications. The Lord simply asks that one believe and answer as the two blind men, *"Yea, Lord."*

Nothing could be more simple than that, and, yet, most of the world is loathe to say these two simple words. Therefore, they go unhealed and unsaved!

(29) "THEN TOUCHED HE THEIR EYES, SAYING, ACCORDING TO YOUR FAITH BE IT UNTO YOU."

The phrase, *"Then touched He their eyes,"* was probably done according to their level of Faith. Perhaps it was weak, and, accordingly, required the *"touch."*

As well, the *"touching"* of the blinded eyes speaks of the Incarnation of Christ, and His association with the hurting as well as wicked and sinful.

There was no way the *"blinded eyes"* of a darkened world could be opened without Him Personally touching the darkness.

To cure the darkness of a chaotic world, all He had to do was say, *"Let there be light: and there was light"* (Gen. 1:3). However, to cure the darkness of man, and because it was a willful darkness, it could not be dispelled with a word, but required the *"touch."*

That *"touch"* would mean the contamination of Himself with the sin of the world, as *"He Who knew no sin, was made to be sin, that we might become the Righteousness of God in Him"* (II Cor. 5:21).

The phrase, *"According to your Faith be it unto you,"* could be said to be, *"The Law of Faith."*

(30) "AND THEIR EYES WERE OPENED; AND JESUS STRAITLY CHARGED THEM, SAYING, SEE THAT NO MAN KNOW IT."

The phrase, *"And their eyes were opened,"* records in simple statement an outstanding miracle. It was instant!

Likewise, in the spiritual sense, upon Faith in Christ, the spiritual eyes are opened instantly. Anyone who is truly born again, will relate the glory of this happening.

One moment the knowledge of God is non-existent, while the next moment, and with the entrance into Christ, knowledge is imparted. The individual cannot really tell how it is done, but the fact is, it is done, and instantly! Paul said, *"According as God hath dealt to every man the measure of Faith"* (Rom. 12:3).

The phrase, *"And Jesus straitly charged them,"* refers to a strong charge, even at the risk of displeasure, that they tell no man as to how they had come by this glorious miracle.

The phrase, *"Saying, See that no man know it,"* may have been done as much for them, as for Himself.

Some have argued that He desired to keep the account of these miracles as quiet as possible, so as not to arouse the enmity of His enemies. However, as the next verse proclaims, such is well nigh impossible to keep quiet, and especially considering that He was healing so many, and even raising the dead.

While He no doubt desired that attention not be directed at Him, especially this early in His Ministry, still, the greater thrust of His Command may well have been for the benefit of those who were healed. The *"display"* of such, could cause spiritual harm, in that it might degenerate into spiritual pride.

While it is certainly true, that one who has had blinded eyes instantly opened could hardly

be expected to be less than ecstatically happy. Still, special care should be taken on such an occasion, should one be privileged to come by such, that whatever is said and done, personal merit be ruled out in every circumstance.

Presently speaking, in the last thirty or forty years, the *"display"* of healings and alleged miracles have become gaudy beyond compare. The Lord must be sorely displeased with such actions.

The present demand for *"display"* is so great, that oftentimes that which is displayed so grandly is often found out to have little substance in fact. It is tragic but true!

In too many cases, the Evangelist is aggrandized, with the person grandly showcased as they give their *"testimony."* Such is done, it is said, to build Faith in others, etc. However, one has to wonder, that if it is rather done to build up the individual, be it the Preacher or the person.

And then, far too often an already deplorable situation is vulgarized by the slight hint, or sometimes not so slight a hint, that if large gifts of money are forthcoming, great miracles will come to the giver.

All of it is saddled with great quantities of Scripture, but one must wonder as to what the Lord actually thinks?

If these Scriptures are to be taken at face value, as they certainly should be, then I think it is obvious as to what He thinks! He is sorely displeased and, quite possibly, that is at least one of the reasons precious few true healings or miracles are seen at present.

(31) "BUT THEY, WHEN THEY WERE DEPARTED, SPREAD ABROAD HIS FAME IN ALL THAT COUNTRY."

At least they spread abroad *"His fame"* instead of their own!

Considering that the opening of blinded eyes was a miracle of astounding proportions, and considering the tremendous joy they experienced from being liberated from a darkened world, both spiritually and physically, it would have been almost impossible for them to have contained themselves.

(32) "AND AS THEY WENT OUT, BEHOLD, THEY BROUGHT TO HIM A DUMB MAN POSSESSED WITH A DEVIL."

The phrase, *"As they went out,"* probably refers to leaving out of the home of Matthew, or maybe Simon Peter. The *"two blind men"* who were miraculously healed had obviously followed Him into the house where the miracle was performed. And now, He, along with the former blind men, as well as the Disciples, are leaving the house when the following happened.

The phrase, *"Behold, they brought to Him a dumb man possessed with a devil,"* suggesting that his not being able to speak was caused by demon possession.

Some would claim that this was only their superstitious ideas, while his problem was physical. However, the Holy Spirit says that he was *"possessed with a devil,"* and that *"the devil was cast out."* Consequently, we see that some forms of dumbness are caused by demon possession.

This would not always be the case, but was the case here, and, no doubt, is the cause many other times.

(33) "AND WHEN THE DEVIL WAS CAST OUT, THE DUMB SPAKE: AND THE MULTITUDES MARVELLED, SAYING, IT WAS NEVER SO SEEN IN ISRAEL."

The phrase, *"And when the Devil was cast out, the dumb spake,"* does not tell us how Jesus did it, but only that it was done.

If one is to notice, Matthew, and because he portrays Jesus as King, gives very little information respecting his illustrations. It is done in this manner, because a King does not have to explain or clarify, whereas a servant would do the opposite by going into great detail, exactly as given in Mark. Jesus, in the Gospel of Mark, is portrayed as a Servant.

The phrase, *"And the multitudes marvelled,"* must have occasioned this individual being known over the area which was probably Capernaum. Knowing he could not speak, and quite possibly had not spoken in some length of time, maybe even years, and seeing him instantly able to speak, and, doing so, they *"marvelled."*

The phrase, *"Saying, It was never so seen in Israel,"* is coming close to suggest that Jesus is the Messiah. Where Jesus is, great and glorious things happen!

If one is to notice in this scenario, one is faced with demon spirits and Christ. Likewise, the majority of the nations of the world are under the sway of demon spirits. It is this way because they will have none of Christ.

As a result, poverty, ignorance, superstition, witchcraft, disease, crime and sickness are rampant. Where Jesus is, devils have to go. Where

NOTES

He is not, devils abound!

Regrettably, the Churches in America once proclaimed Jesus, at least for the most part. However, He has been quietly set aside in most Churches, with man being placed in the center, and, consequently, man's humanistic ideas of psychology have taken the place of Christ. As a result, the spirituality of the nation has seriously dropped, with demon spirits holding greater and greater sway. The next verse tells us why!

(34) "BUT THE PHARISEES SAID, HE CASTETH OUT DEVILS THROUGH THE PRINCE OF THE DEVILS."

The phrase, *"But the Pharisees said,"* concerns the Religious Leaders of Israel. What they *"said"* will constitute blasphemy of the Holy Spirit, for which there is no forgiveness.

The phrase, *"He casteth out devils through the prince of the devils,"* asserted not only that Jesus effected this cure by the instrumentality of Satan, but, as well, by means of union with him.

In attributing the Works of God to Satan, even though the Holy Spirit was not mentioned, still, they blasphemed Him as Jesus will later assert (Mat. 12:22-32). Several things are said in this verse:

1. The *"Church"* of that day would greatly oppose Christ. Tragically, the greatest enemy of Christ at present is not the many vices of the hour, but, instead, the *"Church."* It is tragic but true!

2. In effect, the Church is Satan's greatest area of operation. It is obvious as to what vice is, but not so obvious at all respecting the deception of religion. Consequently, much of the world is led astray.

3. Satan's greatest work is done in this area, even though it is little spoken of. Most of the time, the poor alcoholic, or drug addict, is held up as the greatest example of Satan's handiwork. To be sure, it is his handiwork. However, his greatest handiwork is not that at all. It is rather the popular Preacher who stands behind the pulpit on Sunday mornings, espousing *"another Gospel, and, another Jesus, by another Spirit"* (II Cor. 11:4).

It would be bad enough were these in the minority; however, they are in the majority, the far greater majority.

Sadly, most of the Baptists, Methodists and

Holiness have denied the Holy Spirit, and, therefore, all the things He does, leaving them, for the most part, man-originated institutions, which means they are of no spiritual help.

Regrettably, as well, many of the Pentecostals and Charismatics have abandoned the Word of God to such an extent, that they little know anymore what is of God and what is not. Too often, they run here and there, saying, *"Here is Christ, or there is Christ."* But Jesus said, *"Believe it not."*

He also said, *"For there shall arise false Christs and false Prophets, and shall shew great signs and wonders; insomuch that, if it were possible, they shall deceive the very elect"* (Mat. 24:23-24).

Yes, and sadly so, the greatest hindrance to the Work of God is not the gross sin and iniquity of this world, but, instead, that which calls itself *"the Church."* True, there is a Remnant who loves God, and seeks to follow His Word, but it is only a small Remnant.

(35) "AND JESUS WENT ABOUT ALL THE CITIES AND VILLAGES, TEACHING IN THEIR SYNAGOGUES, AND PREACHING THE GOSPEL OF THE KINGDOM, AND HEALING EVERY SICKNESS AND EVERY DISEASE AMONG THE PEOPLE."

In this one verse we find what the true order of the Gospel should be. It is as follows:

1. *"And Jesus went about all the cities and villages"*: Someone has said that two-thirds of the Name of God is *"Go."* The method of Christ in going to all the cities and villages in Israel is the example we are to follow. The Apostle Paul, under the guidance of the Holy Spirit, extended that to the entirety of the world, obeying the Great Commission of Jesus Christ (Mk. 16:15).

The very Heart of God, which means priority, is the taking of the Message of Redemption to the world. If that is not paramount in any Church, or heart and life, then the pattern laid down by Christ has been abandoned, and, to be sure, whatever has replaced it is of man, and will receive no blessing from the Lord, and, consequently, will reap no spiritual results.

One can tell the spiritual temperature of any Christian effort, or even of a single individual, by their burden, or the lack of it, regarding the taking of the Gospel to the world. If there is a small burden, there is a small amount of God.

Sadder still, most of the money given by

Christendom for that which purports to be World Missions, is used to support bloated religious bureaucracies, or else to support false doctrine. Precious little actually gets to that which is the True Gospel of Jesus Christ. Most of it goes to support the *"Pharisees"* of the previous verse, with precious little going to support Christ.

2. *"Teaching in their Synagogues"*: The word, *"teaching,"* refers to imparting Scriptural knowledge and instilling doctrine. It simply means to explain the Word of God.

Christ was the greatest Teacher of men. His listeners marvelled at what He said, and because of two things: A. His knowledge of the Word of God; and, B. The Anointing of the Holy Spirit upon Him.

3. *"Preaching the Gospel of the Kingdom"*: Someone has said that preaching proclaims Truth, while teaching explains it.

Teaching is referred to about 168 times in the Bible, and is about equal in both Testaments. But preaching is referred to only 5 times in the Old Testament, and 138 times in the New.

The reason for such little preaching in the Old Testament is because the Gospel of the New Covenant had not yet been given, but only pointed to.

Now, and with the Advent of the New Covenant, preaching is predominant in the New Testament.

As well, it was the *"Gospel of the Kingdom"* that was preached, and which should be preached today. It simply refers to all that Christ brought and bought at Calvary and the Resurrection.

4. *"And healing every sickness and every disease among the people"*: This was the Ministry of Christ, and, as well, He commanded every Gospel Minister thereafter to do this work (Mat. 10:1-8; 28:20; Mk. 3:15; 6:7-13; 16:15-20; Lk. 9:2; 10:9; James 5:14-16).

This is part and parcel of the Gospel, and if eliminated, means that a part of the *"Gospel of the Kingdom"* is no longer being preached. Sadly, most present preaching falls into this category of unbelief.

As well, anything that claims to be a move of God, with any one of these four things absent, cannot be said to truly be such, and irrespective of whatever other phenomenon is present.

(36) "BUT WHEN HE SAW THE MULTITUDES, HE WAS MOVED WITH COMPASSION

ON THEM, BECAUSE THEY FAINTED, AND WERE SCATTERED ABROAD, AS SHEEP HAVING NO SHEPHERD."

The phrase, *"But when he saw the multitudes, He was moved with compassion on them,"* refers to the True Heart of God, and should be, and, in fact, will be, the attitude of all Believers who truly know Christ.

The word, *"moved,"* refers to pity and sympathy, which had its foundation in the very heart of Christ, i.e., His bowels, His innermost being.

The word, *"compassion,"* has its roots in heathen sacrifices, which spoke of the intestines being taken from the victim, and held up before the sun in the hands of the offerer. It spoke of the very *"guts"* or inner being of the victim. It was called *"the compassion."*

Consequently, when the word is used, it speaks of far more than just a feeling of sympathy, but, instead, sympathy and pity that is born in the very being of the individual, which affects the entire person.

The phrase, *"Because they fainted,"* tells the reason for this *"compassion."*

The people are pictured as sheep harassed and prostrated by fatigue. The reason is found in the next phrase.

The phrase, *"And were scattered abroad, as sheep having no shepherd,"* proclaims Israel as having precious few spiritual shepherds, if any!

Oh, yes, the *"Pharisees"* of verse 34 were loud and boisterous concerning their religious claims, but they had no heart for God. Consequently, they were not *"True Shepherds."* As a result, the *"sheep"* did not know what to do, where to go, what to believe, etc. Is it any less true today!

In my travels around the world, at least as Christianity is concerned, I see the Catholic Church ruling the people by fear and superstition. Too often the Protestants are little better, having no leadership at all.

What does it mean to be a True Shepherd?

Every under Shepherd, and that is what men are, is to heed the Lord Jesus, *"that Great Shepherd of the sheep"* (Heb. 13:20).

Peter referred to Him as the *"Shepherd and Bishop of our souls"* (I Pet. 2:25).

If this is done, the people will be truly led. But if, instead, under Shepherds listen to the voice of themselves or other men, they will be the same as the Pharisees. They are known as *"thieves and robbers"* (Jn. 10:8).

It might quickly be said that in Jesus' day, if one followed organization, they could not follow Christ, and, conversely, if they followed Christ, they could not follow organized religion.

I think the present is not far from that which prevailed in the time of Christ. When Denominational Heads demand that they be listened to, and explicitly obeyed or else, one can be certain that what they are saying is not of God. All of this boils down, then and now, to who is the True Head of the Church! It is either man or Christ, but it cannot be both.

Paul said, *"Let no man beguile you . . ."* into, *"not holding the Head,"* i.e., Christ (Col. 2:18-19).

(37) "THEN SAITH HE UNTO HIS DISCIPLES, THE HARVEST TRULY IS PLENTEOUS, BUT THE LABOURERS ARE FEW;

The phrase, *"Then saith He unto His Disciples,"* refers to a Truth that is now to be given, which has not changed from then to the present.

The phrase, *"The harvest truly is plenteous,"* refers to two things: A. The great number of souls who were in desperate need of God; and, B. The harvest was ready to be gathered, but it could not be gathered for lack of *"labourers."*

As then, so now!

The phrase, *"But the labourers are few,"* refers to True Preachers of the Gospel.

There were thousands of Pharisees who constantly trumpeted their knowledge of God, but, in reality, did not know Him. However, the few who did know Him were few indeed!

Out of all the hundreds of thousands of Preachers presently in Christendom, true laborers, as well, are few and far between. Most are hirelings, false prophets, or false apostles. It was true in the day of Christ, as well as in the time of the Apostle Paul, and it is true now.

When Paul was in prison in Rome, he desired to send a Preacher to the Church at Philippi. However, he said, *"For I have no man like minded, who will naturally care for your state. For all seek their own, not the things which are Jesus Christ's"* (Phil. 2:20-21).

What did he mean, *"For all seek their own"*?

He meant that they did not seek the Will of God, but sought only their own comfort and enrichment.

To be sure, there are multitudes of *"labourers,"* but most are laboring for themselves and not Christ.

(38) "PRAY YE THEREFORE THE LORD OF THE HARVEST, THAT HE WILL SEND FORTH LABOURERS INTO HIS HARVEST."

The two words, *"Pray ye,"* begins this admonition, but is little followed by the Modern Church.

Instead of *"prayer,"* too oftentimes men who call themselves *"shepherds,"* i.e., *"labourers,"* are sent by committees, or else go to a place of their own choosing. They do this because they do not have the Mind of the Lord, and because they have not truly sought His Face. Consequently, the result is man-appointed works, which will accomplish nothing for the Cause of Christ.

There was a time, at least in Pentecostal circles, when men sought God, and He laid a burden on their hearts and lives for a certain part of the world, to which they responded. At the present, this is little adhered to, with religious hierarchy demanding the Headship, and, therefore, designating where Preachers can and cannot go. While these might be *"labourers,"* they are not *"God's labourers."*

His *"labourers"* hear His Voice, and follow Him (Jn. 10:4).

When the little Church in my hometown of Ferriday, Louisiana, was planted, it was done so by two women (a mother and her daughter), who, upon seeking the Lord earnestly, was told by the Holy Spirit, *"Go to Ferriday, Louisiana."*

They knew no one in this small back-water town in Louisiana, and, in the natural, had no desire to go to this place. However, the Lord spoke to them and they obeyed, which resulted in many souls being saved and many lives being changed. My family was a part of that number.

As a result, and speaking only of my own Ministry, and to be sure there were others, many have been brought to Christ, and all because of the obedience of two women. They were led by the Lord, and, consequently, a Work for God was established, with astounding results. Had they listened to man, as most do, they would have never come to this little back-water town, but thank the Lord they did not listen to man!

Those were some of the early days of the great Pentecostal move, and men, in those times, heard from Heaven. Too often at the present, they have heard only from man, which accrues no spiritual results.

NOTES

When the Lord said, *"Pray ye,"* He meant exactly what He said! Men were to seek God until the Lord answered, and gave them guidance and direction respecting their particular ministries. But, tragically, too many modern Christians little believe in prayer.

The entirety of the phrase, *"Pray ye therefore the Lord of the harvest,"* proclaims Jesus Christ as being the Head and President of this all-important task — the most important task there is.

Inasmuch as the *"harvest"* is His, and that He is an active Head, and not a passive Head, we are, as stated, to seek His leading and guidance in all things respecting this all-important task.

The entirety of the thrust of this Passage is Leadership, and, more importantly, His Leadership. That is to never be abrogated in any sense, but adhered to faithfully.

The phrase, *"That He will send forth labourers into His harvest,"* is the single most important statement that could be made regarding this worldwide work.

He does the calling of the *"labourers,"* and, as such, designates their field of service.

Please allow me to emphasize again, that more and more this is being taken over by religious hierarchy, and, as such, the Lord will have nothing to do with it. Only those who He calls and sends is approved, and, therefore, blessed by Him. All other is man-directed, and unapproved, at least by the Lord.

It might be quickly added as well, that those He calls and sends will be opposed greatly by those sent by men. As the Pharisees opposed Christ, modern counterparts will continue to do the same.

And yet, despite all the hindrances from the powers of darkness, the *"labourers"* sent into this harvest, and by Him, the *"Lord of the harvest,"* we might quickly add, are greatly rewarded and blessed by reaping many souls.

CHAPTER 10

(1) "AND WHEN HE HAD CALLED UNTO HIM HIS TWELVE DISCIPLES, HE GAVE THEM POWER AGAINST UNCLEAN SPIRITS, TO CAST THEM OUT, AND TO HEAL

ALL MANNER OF SICKNESS AND ALL MANNER OF DISEASE."

The phrase, *"And when He had called unto Him His twelve Disciples,"* refers to Him doing this, only after He had done exactly what He told us to do, *"pray."* Luke said He *"continued all night in prayer to God,"* concerning those who He would choose (Lk. 6:12-16). Thus, prayer and action interact; but prayer precedes action.

As a result of His interceding in prayer, He *"called unto Him His twelve Disciples."*

The call to Discipleship and the call to Apostleship should not be confounded. Verse 1 speaks of *"Disciples,"* while verse 2 speaks of *"Apostles."* The Election to the one precedes that to the other. A Disciple is a pupil; an Apostle is a messenger; but an Apostle can never leave the Spirit's School, but must remain a Learner to the end, therefore ever continuing to be a Disciple.

This *"call"* is not by personal choice. It originates in Heaven, and comes from the Throne of God. Consequently, the Lord calls today exactly as He did then.

Those in the Ministry who have really not been called of God are the bane of the Church. They have no distinct call, and are there for personal benefit and self-aggrandizement. They almost always oppose the truly called.

As well, and respecting the calling of the original Disciples, the number *"twelve"* is of great significance. It was not a random choice, but ordained by God.

The number *"twelve"* speaks of government, i.e., God's Government. Consequently, there were Twelve Tribes of Israel. The High Priest wore twelve stones on his Breastplate.

Accordingly, the New Jerusalem, which as well typifies God's Government, is *"twelve thousand furlongs"* in measurement, which speaks of 1,500 miles square. It has *"twelve foundations,"* and in them *"the names of the twelve Apostles of the Lamb."*

There are *"twelve gates"* in the wall of this city, where stands *"twelve Angels,"* and with the *"names of the Twelve Tribes of the Children of Israel"* written on the *"twelve gates."*

The foundations are garnished with *"twelve precious stones."* As well, the *"twelve gates"* are made of *"twelve pearls."*

Within the city, a *"pure river of Water of Life"* proceeds out of the *"Throne of God and of the Lamb."* By this river is the *"Tree of Life,"* which bears *"twelve manner of fruits"* (Rev. Chpts. 21-22).

God's Government, of which the number *"twelve"* represents, is a perfect Government, in contrast to man's government, which is imperfect.

The establishment of God's Government in the world is the purpose of the Holy Spirit, and it will ultimately be done, with that *"Government upon His* (Christ's) *shoulder"* (Isa. 9:6-7).

As well, it is Satan's effort to usurp authority over God's Government in the Church, by the insertion of his government, which is brought about through religious hierarchy. (This does not speak of civil government, but, instead, religious government.)

The phrase, *"He gave them power against unclean spirits, to cast them out,"* concerns two things.

1. This power was given to them, and by God, Who is the only Source. Man cannot bestow such power on any other man, neither can man earn such power. It is a free gift from God to those He has called.

2. He is still giving this power today, as it was not limited to the original twelve. Jesus said, *"And these signs shall follow them that believe; In My Name shall they cast out devils"* (Mk. 16:17). As stated, it is not limited to the original twelve, but is given to all who *"believe,"* irrespective of them being Apostles or not!

This is God's method of opposing the Powers of Darkness, and He has not changed that method. Regrettably, religious man has been very successful in substituting other methods, which, as should be obvious, will not work.

As an example, much of the Church world at present is busily engaged with time, energy and money, attempting to promote the *"political message,"* proposing to put the *"right"* politicians into public office, which, in their thinking, will change the nation. Regrettably, such will have little effect.

First of all, most of these individuals who are touted so highly, are merely *"political,"* and not spiritual, i.e., not born again.

As well, this world's system can only be assuaged slightly, but cannot be changed, irrespective of all such efforts. So, Satan has been successful in changing God's method of opposing evil to another man-made method entirely.

While it is certainly true that Christians should involve themselves in the political process, still, they must do so with the understanding that their efforts will make only a slight difference.

Conversely, Preachers of the Gospel, who are full of the Holy Ghost and carrying out the Commands of Christ to *"Cast out devils,"* can, and, in Truth, make an eternal difference.

This is done, not only by the laying on of hands, but even more so by the preaching of the Gospel of Jesus Christ under the Anointing of the Holy Spirit. As the Gospel fills men's hearts, demon spirits are overthrown and cast out.

The phrase, *"And to heal all manner of sickness and all manner of disease,"* harks back to Christ *"healing every sickness and every disease among the people"* (9:35).

Therefore, it is obvious that what He did, He expects those He calls to do, as well!

It is sad, that the far greater majority of the Modern Church does not even believe in *"casting out devils,"* nor that modern Preachers are to pray for, and expect sickness to be healed. Consequently, they constitute no more than a man-made organization, which, for all practical purposes, is of no more spiritual use than a local chapter of the Kiwanis Club. It is done God's Way or no way at all!

(2-4) "NOW THE NAMES OF THE TWELVE APOSTLES ARE THESE; THE FIRST, SIMON, WHO IS CALLED PETER, AND ANDREW HIS BROTHER; JAMES THE SON OF ZEBEDEE, AND JOHN HIS BROTHER;

"PHILIP, AND BARTHOLOMEW; THOMAS, AND MATTHEW THE PUBLICAN; JAMES THE SON OF ALPHAEUS, AND LEBBAEUS, WHOSE SURNAME WAS THADDAEUS;

"SIMON THE CANAANITE, AND JUDAS ISCARIOT, WHO ALSO BETRAYED HIM."

If one is to notice, the Apostles are grouped in *"twos."*

Actually, the twelve were sent forth in couples (Mk. 6:7); hence the word *"two"* may be supplied after the word *"first."* This word does not here mean *"chief,"* as many think.

The first two, therefore, were Peter and his brother Andrew; the second two, James and

his brother John; the third two, Philip and his friend Bartholomew (Nathaniel) (Jn. 1:45; 21:2); the fourth pair, Thomas and Matthew; the fifth, James and his brother Thaddaeus, i.e., Judas; and the last pair, Simon the Zealot and Judas Iscariot.

Eleven of these men were Galileans; one, Judas Iscariot was a Judaean. Iscariot most probably means *"of Kerioth"* (Josh. 15:25), a town in Judaea.

James and Judas were sons of Alphaeus, i.e., Cleopas. He was married to a *"sister"* (relative) of the Virgin Mary. These brothers were, therefore, first cousins to the Lord.

James, the brother of John, was the first to suffer martyrdom (Acts 12:2); and John himself was the last to die, and some have said the only one of the original twelve to die a natural death.

As well, it should be noted that none of these men were a part of the aristocracy of Israel, nor the religious Elite. Most were fishermen, with Matthew being a hated tax-collector. They had very little formal education, and yet, three of them would be used to write Books in the New Testament, Matthew, John and Peter.

Their names will, as well, be inscribed on the twelve foundations of the New Jerusalem (Rev. 21:14). (This does not include Judas Iscariot, who was replaced by Matthias — Acts 1:26.)

The name, *"Simon the Canaanite,"* probably should have been translated, *"Simon the Zealot,"* as in Luke 6:15.

(5) "THESE TWELVE JESUS SENT FORTH, AND COMMANDED THEM, SAYING, GO NOT INTO THE WAY OF THE GENTILES, AND INTO ANY CITY OF THE SAMARITANS ENTER YE NOT."

The phrase, *"These twelve Jesus sent forth,"* refers to a select number which will never be added to. In other words, even though the Lord continues to call *"Apostles and Prophets,"* etc., still, all future Apostles are somewhat different than the original twelve, and because of their personal and direct association with Christ. In other words, no more of the same authority as the original twelve will be called and sent forth, even though multiple tens of thousands have been called since that time, and sent forth, some even as *"Apostles"* (Eph. 4:11).

The phrase, *"And commanded them,"* concerns their present Commission, which would apply to the length of the Ministry of Christ (a little over three years), but would be changed after His Death, Resurrection, and Ascension.

The phrase, *"Saying, Go not into the way of the Gentiles,"* was given for a specific purpose.

It was not time for the Message of Redemption to be taken to the Gentiles at the present, and for several reasons.

First of all, the New Covenant, based entirely upon Faith in Christ, had not yet been given, but was even then being made possible by Christ. For a Gentile to be saved at this time, and previous, they, in effect, had to become a proselyte Jew. This would change with the giving of the New Covenant, even with Peter being the first one to take the Gospel to the Gentiles (Acts 10).

The phrase, *"And into any city of the Samaritans enter ye not,"* referred to the area of Samaria north of Judaea, and south of Galilee. In other words, this district was sandwiched between Judaea and Galilee.

These *"Samaritans"* were not looked at as Jews by Israel, but rather a half-breed, part Jew and part Gentile.

In this Commission, Jesus was speaking only of His Disciples at this present time, for He Himself would minister to the Samaritans (Jn. 4). As well, after the Day of Pentecost the Apostles would go to Samaria and see a tremendous Work of God brought about (Acts 8).

(6) "BUT GO RATHER TO THE LOST SHEEP OF THE HOUSE OF ISRAEL."

The reason for this Commission respecting *"Israel,"* was because of its unique and peculiar position. These were the people of God, or, rather, were supposed to be people of God, and, as such, were due the first presentation under Christ, and despite their faithlessness as described by *"lost sheep."*

This did not mean that the Gospel was not to be presented to the rest of the world, which it was. Actually, Jesus came for the entirety of the world, as described in St. John 3:16. But the first presentation was to go to Israel, and because they were God's Own special property, and despite their teachers having proved faithless, which made them now as shepherdless as the Gentiles.

The phrase, *"Lost sheep,"* is interesting, inasmuch as it refutes the unscriptural contention of unconditional eternal security. This false doctrine claims, *"once a sheep, always a sheep."*

However, as here graphically given, *"sheep"* can be *"lost,"* exactly as Israel here was. In fact, they did not heed the Master's Message, and, therefore, went into eternal spiritual oblivion.

(7) "AND AS YE GO, PREACH, SAYING, THE KINGDOM OF HEAVEN IS AT HAND."

Actually, this is basically the same Message preached by John the Baptist (3:2), and Christ, Himself (4:17).

The Apostles were to *"preach,"* which refers to a proclamation of Truth.

The phrase, *"Saying, The Kingdom of Heaven is at hand,"* was actually a dispensational term. It refers to the Messiah's Kingdom on earth. Sadly, it was rejected, and, therefore, postponed until Christ comes again, at which time the Kingdom will be set up (Lk. 19:11-27; Acts 1:6-7; 3:19-26).

Now, it is in the realm of profession, or spiritually realized in all Believers, but not in the material sense. In the coming Kingdom Age, it will be realized in every aspect, physical, material, and spiritual.

Israel did not necessarily reject the *"Kingdom,"* but, instead, rejected Christ Who Alone could bring it. Many want Salvation without Christ, but such is not to be.

(8) "HEAL THE SICK, CLEANSE THE LEPERS, RAISE THE DEAD, CAST OUT DEVILS: FREELY YE HAVE RECEIVED, FREELY GIVE."

The following, as derived from these Passages, constitutes the manner in which the Lord operates His Work:

1. As He called the twelve, He calls all who truly work in His service (vs. 1).

2. As He gave the Apostles power, He, as well, gives power to all who are truly called by Him, and truly believe Him (vs. 1).

3. As the names of the twelve were given, likewise, the calling of each and all is a personal calling by the Lord, with a specific call going to a specific person (vss. 2-4).

4. As He sent the twelve, likewise, He sends all who are called by Him, and to their designated field of operation (vs. 5-6).

5. As the Disciples were told to *"preach,"* likewise, this particular call is the same for all, and especially the very Message that is to be preached (vs. 7).

6. Along with preaching, they were to deliver men from the bondage of darkness by the

presentation of the Gospel. Modern Preachers are to do no less, at least if they are called by God.

The action in the work of these Preachers was fourfold:

A. *"Heal the sick"*: In His Name, sickness was to be dispelled.

B. *"Cleanse the lepers"*: This spoke of contagious diseases that were to be healed as well!

C. *"Raise the dead"*: Even though these would be few, as is obvious in the Word of God, still, such powerful miracles would, at times, characterize the True Gospel Ministry.

D. *"Cast out devils"*: This was a major part of the Ministry of Christ, and should be a major part of all Gospel Ministers.

E. *"Freely ye have received, freely give"*: This refers not only to the designations just given, but, as well, to any and all other types of spiritual needs which must be met, and can only be met by the Power of God.

Also, as they had freely received this power, they were to freely give this power.

The connotation of the Text is such that by the words, *"Freely give,"* we are made to understand that not even the hint of charge, or monetary return is to be expected for such services. The moment that monetary return is attached in any way, the insinuation is that the power will be lifted.

I wonder what that presently says about the modern Gospel which has become so commercialized?

While it certainly takes money, and, at times, much of it, to take the Gospel to the world, still, never under any circumstances must the idea be presented that if people give so much money, *"healing"* or any such like will be forthcoming. At all times this power must be *"freely given,"* and because it has been *"freely received."*

These Passages from verse 1 through verse 8 are very special to me on a personal basis.

If I remember correctly, this of which I will speak took place in late 1992. That morning, early, I had arisen and had, as was my custom, gone out to pray. I generally would walk back and forth in front of our house on the circular drive for a period of time, seeking the Lord. That morning was to be no different.

After a protracted season of prayer, I came back into our small family room, picking up

my Bible, and began to read. I began with the first part of this tenth Chapter of Matthew, because I had finished reading the previous Chapter the day before.

As I started to read, these great Truths began to sharply stand out in the Scripture. The Holy Spirit, to a great degree, directed my attention to the Lord giving this power to His Disciples. It lingered down through the 8th verse, but, more particularly, summed up by saying, *"He gave them power against unclean spirits, to cast them out, and to heal all manner of sickness and all manner of disease."*

As these Passages began to unfold before me, I greatly began to sense the Presence of God, even weeping as the Holy Spirit made them so real. To be sure, in all my years of studying the Word of God, I had probably read these very Passages 50 times or more. But now, the Spirit of God would highlight them in a graphic manner, and for a particular purpose and reason.

I am not totally certain as to what that purpose and reason is, but I do know that whenever the Spirit of God does something of this nature, it is by design.

From that experience in 1992, and the tremendous moving of the Holy Spirit upon my heart, I believe this is what the Spirit of God was telling me.

"There is going to be a tremendous Move of God that is going to come upon this world, which will result in many of these great miracles taking place, exactly as it happened in the Ministry of Christ, and by the Apostles."

I believe the Lord told me, that He was going to give particular individuals, whomever they may be, the same type of power which He gave His Apostles of so long ago. As well, they would bring about the same results.

In the last few months, and especially the last few weeks, in our daily prayer meetings, I have sensed a moving and operation of the Holy Spirit as I have seldom experienced. Even this morning (6-13-95), it seemed like the moving of the Holy Spirit was heavier than ever. Basically, He was imploring through me, and helping me, to pray that I would be filled with the Spirit in a greater degree than I had ever known in all my life. Actually, this same type of petition, accompanied by a great moving of the Holy Spirit, has been in this same fashion for weeks.

In this morning prayer meeting, as at other times, the moving and operation of the Holy Spirit was so pronounced, that it was as if my very insides would be turned outward. To attempt to describe it is difficult, but it is as if He washes of every impurity and uncleanliness.

He is telling me that all chaff must be burned, which can only be done by the fire of the Spirit, until no impurity remains. In this cleansing, so much is exposed which heretofore was thought of the Spirit, but, in reality, was of the flesh. All of this must go, with nothing left but the Spirit, which will, of necessity, result in an infilling as not previously known.

I have lived for the Lord long enough to know that when the Spirit of God does such, it is for a purpose and reason. I believe it has to do with these very Passages of Matthew 10:1-8.

(9-10) "PROVIDE NEITHER GOLD, NOR SILVER, NOR BRASS IN YOUR PURSES,

"NOR SCRIP FOR YOUR JOURNEY, NEITHER TWO COATS, NEITHER SHOES, NOR YET STAVES: FOR THE WORKMAN IS WORTHY OF HIS MEAT."

The word, *"two,"* is to be understood before pairs of shoes and staves. In effect, they were to go just as they were — without additional coats, shoes or staves.

Immanuel was to be depended on entirely for everything.

The words, *"Provide neither,"* refers to Believers being called of the Lord, and then waiting to respond to that call until they have a certain amount of money saved, etc. *"This is not to be,"* says Christ.

The moment the call is given, the response is to be accordingly. The idea is that God will provide what is needed.

The phrase, *"For the workman is worthy of his meat,"* unequivocally states that provision is to be made for Ministers of the Gospel by those to whom they minister. Consequently, Jesus sanctions and ordains the support of Ministers.

In respect to this phrase, I have noticed through years of preaching all over the world, that Churches which abundantly prepared for their Pastors, and were generous and kind with Evangelists, were singly honored and blessed by God.

As well, I noticed those who were the opposite were not blessed by the Lord. If the Lord

says they are *"worthy,"* then those to whom they minister must, as well, know they are *"worthy,"* and, as such, should be cared for.

As well, the word, *"workman,"* as it is applied to a Minister of the Gospel, means exactly what it says, in that he truly labors for the Lord. As someone has said, *"Preachers ought to consider how criminal it is to receive the fruit of labor, without labor."*

(11) "AND INTO WHATSOEVER CITY OR TOWN YE SHALL ENTER, ENQUIRE WHO IN IT IS WORTHY; AND THERE ABIDE TILL YE GO THENCE."

The phrase, *"And into whatsoever city or town ye shall enter,"* refers to the propagation of the Gospel everywhere.

The phrase, *"Enquire who in it is worthy,"* basically speaks of like or similar Faith. It also speaks of those who have a burden for souls and desire to see the Work of God expanded in their particular area.

The phrase, *"And there abide till ye go thence,"* is conditional, as the next two verses proclaim.

This scenario is speaking of a *"workman,"* which means the opposite of laziness! Consequently, all freeloaders and spongers are excluded. Too many of these have given Ministry a bad name for obvious reasons. Consequently, we are speaking of a *"worthy workman"* and a *"worthy house."* The combination can bring great blessing to both, and is guaranteed, as the following verses tell us.

(12) "AND WHEN YE COME INTO AN HOUSE, SALUTE IT."

This refers to bestowing *"Peace"* on the house, which implies that the presence of this *"worthy workman"* is a blessing instead of an imposition.

Once again, a *"workman"* is *"worthy"* not only because he is called of God, but because he conducts himself accordingly. He is thoughtful, never demanding, appreciative of the slightest kindness, carries his own weight, is never an imposition to others, and instead of a burden, is a blessing. As stated, there have been far too many of the other kind, i.e., *"unworthy workmen."*

(13) "AND IF THE HOUSE BE WORTHY, LET YOUR PEACE COME UPON IT: BUT IF IT BE NOT WORTHY, LET YOUR PEACE RETURN TO YOU."

The phrase, *"And if the house be worthy,"* implies that at times the situation may not be as it appears.

The phrase, *"Let your peace come upon it,"* shows the blessing that can come to such a house, and in every capacity.

The phrase, *"But if it be not worthy, let your peace return to you,"* speaks of the blessing brought to a halt.

The implication is, and rightly so, that to bless or not to bless is left up to the *"worthy workman."* It also implies that he is not to bless a house that is *"not worthy."*

What would constitute not being worthy?

It would simply refer to the occupants of a particular house not earnestly attempting to live for God. In other words, hypocrisy would be obvious!

The idea of verses 11-13, as is obvious, has to do with the accommodations of a Minister of the Gospel; however, it also includes, and even more so, an area of Ministry. In other words, the word, *"house,"* could refer to the entirety of a *"city,"* as the next verse portrays.

All of these verses are not only speaking of the presentation of the Gospel, but also include the conduct of a single *"house,"* or *"workman,"* i.e., Preacher.

(14) "AND WHOSOEVER SHALL NOT RECEIVE YOU, NOR HEAR YOUR WORDS, WHEN YE DEPART OUT OF THAT HOUSE OR CITY, SHAKE OFF THE DUST OF YOUR FEET."

The phrase, *"And whosoever shall not receive you, nor hear your words,"* represents in the eyes of God a serious consequence.

The single most important *"words"* in the world is the Word of God. Consequently, the bringing of the True Message is a tremendous blessing for any community, and actually is the only True Blessing there really is! Upon acceptance of these *"words,"* Heaven's gates are opened. Upon rejection, they are closed.

The phrase, *"When ye depart out of that house or city, shake off the dust of your feet,"* concerns itself with a witness against that *"house or city."* It means they have had the opportunity to hear, but refused it.

This is what Jesus was talking about when He said, *"And I will give unto thee the keys of the Kingdom of Heaven: and whatsoever thou shalt bind on earth shall be bound in Heaven:*

NOTES

and whatsoever thou shalt loose on earth shall be loosed in Heaven" (16:19).

Any *"house or city"* privileged to hear the Message of Redemption brought by a Preacher of the Gospel, in effect, that Preacher uses the *"key"* to unlock the door of Salvation.

As well, this is what Jesus was speaking of when He said, *"Whose soever sins ye remit, they are remitted unto them; and whose soever sins ye retain, they are retained"* (Jn. 20:23).

If accepted, the Preacher, in effect, serves as the agent through which sins are remitted.

If rejected, he still serves as the agent through which sins are retained.

It is so important, this presentation of the Gospel, and its acceptance or rejection, that stern symbolism is used respecting rejection. The very *"dust"* of the area now comes under a curse. That's how important the acceptance or rejection of the Gospel actually is!

(15) "VERILY I SAY UNTO YOU, IT SHALL BE MORE TOLERABLE FOR THE LAND OF SODOM AND GOMORRAH IN THE DAY OF JUDGMENT, THAN FOR THAT CITY."

Several extremely important things are said in this Scripture. They are as follows:

1. *"Verily I say unto you"*: The phrase is meant to denote an extremely important announcement, as will be obvious. It is said in respect to final authority, meaning that God *"hath committed all judgment unto the Son"* (Jn. 5:22).

2. *"It shall be more tolerable"*: The word, *"tolerable,"* emphasizes the fact that in the judgment of the wicked that is coming, there will be degrees of punishment.

3. *"For the land of Sodom and Gomorrah"*: These twin cities are used as an example of the Judgment of God upon sin and sinners. Its account is found in Genesis 19.

Strangely enough, Jesus would liken Capernaum, where He had made His headquarters, as well as other nearby cities, as more evil and wicked than Sodom. This was because they had the opportunity to hear the Gospel as perhaps no other cities in the world, whereas Sodom had little opportunity!

4. *"In the day of Judgment, than for that city"*: This means the wicked are still in existence, and that there will be a Judgment. It is outlined in Revelation 20:11-15, and is called *"The Great White Throne Judgment."*

(16) "BEHOLD, I SEND YOU FORTH AS

SHEEP IN THE MIDST OF WOLVES: BE YE THEREFORE WISE AS SERPENTS, AND HARMLESS AS DOVES."

The phrase, *"Behold, I send you forth,"* has the *"I"* as emphatic, emphasizing that He is the One doing the sending, and if the Messenger is rejected, Christ is rejected as well!

The phrase, *"As sheep in the midst of wolves,"* denotes the powerful opposition that is coming, and, most of all, that it will be religious opposition.

The phrase, *"Be ye therefore wise as serpents,"* portrays the wisdom of the serpent in avoiding danger.

The phrase, *"And harmless as doves,"* refers to the simplicity and gentleness of the dove to escape danger.

A combination of the two saves Christian people from courting persecution on the one hand, and from human planning to avoid it on the other.

(17) "BUT BEWARE OF MEN: FOR THEY WILL DELIVER YOU UP TO THE COUNCILS, AND THEY WILL SCOURGE YOU IN THEIR SYNAGOGUES;"

The phrase, *"But beware of men,"* is a warning to distrust men, for they are wolves by nature (vs. 16); they are cruel (vs. 17); they are unnatural (vs. 21); and they hate goodness, or at least God's goodness (vs. 22). This moral description of man is denied by modern popular Preachers, and arouses their anger.

The phrase, *"For they will deliver you up to the councils,"* concerns itself with the opposition to the Message.

Most Christians do not understand that the greatest enemy to the True Work of God is the Church. Of course, it speaks of the apostate Church.

The phrase, *"And they will scourge you in their Synagogues,"* means they could excommunicate (Jn. 9:22), scourge (Deut. 25:3; II Cor. 11:24), or stone to death (Deut. 22:24; Jn. 8:5; Acts 7:58; 14:19).

Very shortly, the Lord's Apostles, as well as the Apostle Paul, would face these very things. Tragically, it did not die with the demise of Judaism, but continues unto the present hour.

Some time back, Frances and I were in Toledo, Spain, and had the opportunity to observe the torture rooms where hundreds, if not thousands, were tortured to death in the Spanish

Inquisition. Rome held sway over the State, and over religion, and demanded that all come under its authority.

Those who refused this blasphemous religion, faced torture and death exactly as Jesus portrayed. Throughout a period of years, hundreds of thousands, if not millions, died for their testimony of Christ, rather than come under the yoke of Roman Catholicism.

As well, we saw the torture rooms in the largest Catholic Church in Lima, Peru. The instruments of extreme pain were there for all to see.

The Catholic Church now boasts that such activities are no longer carried out; however, in their heart they have not really changed, only subdued by secular government, which they no longer control, at least in a total sense.

However, institutionalized religion, even in the Protestant circles, at times, carries the same intent, although hindered by the law of the land from carrying out that intent. The evil of this system has always been, will continue, and even increase in these last days, becoming paramount under the Antichrist, and only stopped by the Second Coming of the Lord.

(18) "AND YE SHALL BE BROUGHT BEFORE GOVERNORS AND KINGS FOR MY SAKE, FOR A TESTIMONY AGAINST THEM AND THE GENTILES."

Persecution by the Church, as outlined in verse 17, has been, and is, always followed by that of the State.

The phrase, *"And ye shall be brought before Governors and Kings for My sake,"* refers to the successors of Nebuchadnezzar, in which Israel, as the Church of its day, was put in subjection under them as a just judgment for its corruption. This principle rules still in Christendom.

The words, *"My sake,"* refer to an animosity which exists in the entirety of the world against Jesus Christ.

The animosity is not so much directed against *"God,"* because He is looked at by the world as an abstract idea, with the humanists even claiming themselves, and mankind in general, as being God. Consequently, the hatred and animosity is reserved for Jesus, because He claims to be, and actually is, the only access to God.

In opposition to His claim, the Moslems claim instead that Mohammed is the way to God, with Hinduism the worship of many gods, while Buddhism declares the *"god in us."*

As well, Catholicism places Mary above Christ, with her actually acting as the Mediator.

Among the Protestants, too oftentimes the Headship of Christ is abrogated in favor of men.

The phrase, *"For a testimony against them and the Gentiles,"* refers to the opportunity to proclaim the Gospel to these *"Governors and Kings,"* exactly as Paul preached before Felix, Festus, Agrippa, and possibly even Nero, who otherwise would not have heard the Gospel.

(19-20) "BUT WHEN THEY DELIVER YOU UP, TAKE NO THOUGHT HOW OR WHAT YE SHALL SPEAK: FOR IT SHALL BE GIVEN YOU IN THAT SAME HOUR WHAT YE SHALL SPEAK.

"FOR IT IS NOT YE THAT SPEAK, BUT THE SPIRIT OF YOUR FATHER WHICH SPEAKETH IN YOU."

The phrase, *"But when they deliver you up,"* does not say, *"if,"* but *"when,"* denoting the persecution which will definitely come.

The phrase, *"Take no thought how or what ye shall speak,"* actually refers to one's own defense. In effect, the defense is to be left in the hands of God.

The phrase, *"For it shall be given you in that same hour what ye shall speak,"* denotes the unction of the Holy Spirit Who superintends all the actions of the Spirit-filled Believer.

The phrase, *"For it is not ye that speak,"* denotes the Anointing of the Holy Spirit on what is spoken, but, as well, the actual terminology given, with it being spoken in power.

The phrase, *"But the Spirit of your Father which speaketh in you,"* denotes the Holy Spirit within the Believer, Who is greater and more powerful than all the Religious Leaders or *"Governors and Kings."*

Consequently, these Passages spoken by Christ, predict the descent of the Holy Spirit at Pentecost.

(21) "AND THE BROTHER SHALL DELIVER UP THE BROTHER TO DEATH, AND THE FATHER THE CHILD: AND THE CHILDREN SHALL RISE UP AGAINST THEIR PARENTS, AND CAUSE THEM TO BE PUT TO DEATH."

Judas Iscariot, at that moment listening to Jesus, and himself an Apostle, was to be the first to fulfill the Prophecy of this verse.

The phrase, *"And the brother shall deliver up the brother to death,"* etc., is meant to

NOTES

unequivocally state that all, when brought before Religious Leaders or *"Governors and Kings,"* will not be delivered, but, some, instead, will die. It has nothing, at least for the most part, to do with their Faith, but rather the Will of God.

As well, this Scripture portrays even in a deeper sense, the animosity against the Messenger, and because of Christ. It is an animosity that will divide families, even to *"death."*

The entirety of the language in all of these verses, proclaims the Truth of deeper families ties with the One above, than even one's own personal family. The spirit of this Text brings out the total devotion, with the exclusion of all else and all others, to Christ. He must come before *"brother," "father,"* or *"children."*

(22) "AND YE SHALL BE HATED OF ALL MEN FOR MY NAME'S SAKE: BUT HE THAT ENDURETH TO THE END SHALL BE SAVED."

The phrase, *"And ye shall be hated of all men for My Name's sake,"* simply means that a true testimony to Christ's Name ensures man's hatred.

If the *"hatred"* and enmity of the world is not forthcoming, then something is wrong with the *"testimony"* (vs. 18).

It means that popular Preachers are not preaching the Gospel. If they were, the world would hate them. The statement by Christ is flat out, and means that there are no exceptions to the rule! Devotion to Him ensures the hatred of the world.

The phrase, *"But He that endureth to the end shall be saved,"* refers to bravely facing suffering.

Some have claimed that Jesus was referring to the coming destruction of Jerusalem, which would take place in 70 A.D., which He may well have been! However, the principle holds true, and irrespective of the time and place.

The phrase, *"Endureth to the end,"* means that these problems of intensive persecution will remain until the Second Coming.

As well, the words, *"Shall be saved,"* refer to maintaining the testimony to the end, whatever that end may be! To compromise the testimony in order to gain the plaudits of the world, as many have done, ensures the loss of the soul.

Some have claimed that this only refers to preservation from death at the time of the persecution. However, the tenor of the Text says otherwise, with the preceding verse speaking of *"death."* No! It refers to the loss of soul, if, in fact, one does not *"endure."*

(23) "BUT WHEN THEY PERSECUTE YOU IN THIS CITY, FLEE YE INTO ANOTHER: FOR VERILY I SAY UNTO YOU, YE SHALL NOT HAVE GONE OVER THE CITIES OF IS-RAEL, TILL THE SON OF MAN BE COME."

The phrase, *"But when they persecute you in this city, flee ye into another,"* refers back to the *"shaking off the dust of the feet."* This is not a cowardly flight, but a wise act to further the Gospel. There is no point in staying where the Gospel is not desired, and due to its great importance the Messenger should take it to another city where he may be more gladly received.

The phrase, *"For verily I say unto you,"* is meant to denote the significance of the next phrase, even beyond what appears on the surface.

The phrase, *"Ye shall not have gone over the cities of Israel, till the Son of Man be come,"* tells us several things:

1. The very heart of the Gospel is Evangelism, here noted by the going from one city to another. If that is lacking in the heart, or the Church, it is a sure sign of spiritual declension.

2. The entire complexion of the Passages denotes the certitude of persecution.

3. Israel was to be evangelized first, and then the rest of the world according to Acts 1:8.

4. The task of evangelizing all the *"cities of Israel"* would not be completed, due to persecution and the rejection of the Gospel. This was evident in the Early Church, when Jesus told Paul, *"Depart: for I will send thee far hence unto the Gentiles"* (Acts 22:21).

5. This Scripture boldly pronounces the Second Coming, and which will most surely happen!

(24) "THE DISCIPLE IS NOT ABOVE HIS MASTER, NOR THE SERVANT ABOVE HIS LORD."

The idea of the phrase, *"The Disciple is not above his Master,"* is that as Christ was persecuted, reviled, and opposed, so shall His followers.

As was the Master's custom, He makes the same statement in another way by saying, *"Nor the servant above his Lord."*

Many foolish practitioners of what is commonly referred to as the *"Faith Ministry,"*

which, in reality, is no Faith at all, claim that if the Apostle Paul and others would have had stronger Faith, they would not have had to undergo such extensive persecution, etc. I think it is obvious from these Passages just exactly how facetious such statements are! And yet this error has many followers, who opt for its *"prosperity message,"* and, thereby, lay claim to a gospel, which, in effect, is *"another gospel,"* which promises freedom from all suffering, etc.

(25) "IT IS ENOUGH FOR THE DISCIPLE THAT HE BE AS HIS MASTER, AND THE SERVANT AS HIS LORD. IF THEY HAVE CALLED THE MASTER OF THE HOUSE BEELZEBUB, HOW MUCH MORE SHALL THEY CALL THEM OF HIS HOUSEHOLD?"

The phrase, *"It is enough for the Disciple that he be as his master, and the servant as his lord,"* is not meant, even in the slightest fashion, to proclaim equality between the *"Disciple and Master."* It simply means the following:

1. If the Disciple is truly like his Master, and is seeking to emulate Him in all respects, he will suffer persecution.

2. The idea is, that one can somewhat gauge one's spirituality and nearness to Christ, by his being persecuted exactly as Christ was!

The phrase, *"If they have called the master of the house Beelzebub,"* has reference to the lord of the dunghill, a most contemptuous and vile idol. It was identified as Prince of Demons, and was what the Religious Leaders of Israel called Christ. In other words, they said that He was the Devil.

The question, *"How much more shall they call them of His household?"*, refers to the followers of the Lord receiving the same type of treatment.

It is natural that the religious opposers of the True Gospel would claim their way as right, and, if so, they would be forced to claim all else as of Satan. It is impossible for it to be otherwise!

If one is truly of the Lord, and truly doing the Work of God, with its evidential fruit, to oppose that is to oppose God. However, the opposition is never content to merely oppose it, it must try to destroy it by persecution, and by labeling it as *"Satan."* Now we are speaking of blaspheming the Holy Spirit!

In travelling all over the world in Crusades,

our opposition, as here, is far more from the religious sector than it is from the secular.

Almost everywhere we go the Catholic Church fights us intently, and not because anything is overtly said or done respecting Catholicism, but that our Message is totally contrary to Catholicism as every True Message of the Gospel shall be, and, consequently, many Catholics have been saved. Therefore, one does not have to take up spiritual arms against such to ensure persecution, for it will automatically come!

And now, sadder still, tremendous opposition comes from certain segments of the Pentecostal and Charismatic Churches joining in with the Catholics, attempting to hinder the Crusades in any way possible!

Such opposition is carried out for many and varied reasons. The greatest reason of all is *"control and money."* Many Preachers want to totally control their people, even as the Religious Leaders in Israel did during the time of Christ. Consequently, they did not want them listening to Christ, and threatened them with excommunication if they did so (Jn. 9:34). This same spirit prevails even now.

As well, and as stated, *"money"* plays an important part, inasmuch as the *"control"* exercised includes the finances. In other words, the Lord is no longer telling the people where to give, with direction now coming from man.

To be sure, this spirit that prevailed in the time of Christ, prevails at present!

It is impossible for God to oppose Himself. If He is with the Disciple (follower), then He certainly will not sanction him being called *"Beelzebub."* So, even though both claim to be of God, it should be obvious that one isn't!

We have gone into cities in both America and abroad, and, at times, had tremendous movings of the Holy Spirit, with a goodly number of people being saved, etc. At the same time, we were experiencing tremendous opposition from some of the Churches just mentioned. By their opposition, they were saying, whether the words were used or not, that we were of the Devil. However, Satan does not bring people to Christ.

The Truth is, if they are fighting God as the evidence proclaims, it should be obvious as to what spirit they are of.

It is understandable at the opposition from Catholicism, and even from the Denominational

Churches, which for all practical purposes, deny the Holy Spirit. However, opposition from one's own is not so readily understandable. Nevertheless, it was from Jesus' Own that He received His greatest persecution. They called Him *"Beelzebub,"* and, will do the same *"of His household."*

(26) "FEAR THEM NOT THEREFORE: FOR THERE IS NOTHING COVERED, THAT SHALL NOT BE REVEALED; AND HID, THAT SHALL NOT BE KNOWN."

The phrase, *"Fear them not therefore,"* refers to compromising the Message. Irrespective of what the opposition says and attempts to do, the Message is not to be weakened, glossed, compromised, or weakened!

The one word, *"fear,"* is probably the greatest cause of all watered-down Gospel, and is, consequently, Satan's greatest weapon. Too many Preachers *"fear"* what other men may say or think.

They fear that if the Truth is preached, some of their tithe payers will quit. Others fear they will lose their place and position; therefore, they trim their Message.

If *"fear"* is allowed in the heart of the Preacher, or anyone who witnesses for Christ, more fear will be added, while, at the same time, if boldness is used, more boldness will be added.

The phrase, *"For there is nothing covered that shall not be revealed; and hid, that shall not be known,"* reveals several things:

1. All will stand before God one day to give account for their Ministries, and then the true motive of all hearts will be *"revealed."*

2. Inasmuch as false doctrine is going to be revealed at the Judgment, why not uncover it now, and thereby turn people to Christ!

3. Ancient religions were based upon mysteries withheld from the public. The Gospel has no such mysteries. All its Truths are to be publicly proclaimed.

(27) "WHAT I TELL YOU IN DARKNESS, THAT SPEAK YE IN LIGHT: AND WHAT YE HEAR IN THE EAR, THAT PREACH YE UPON THE HOUSETOPS."

The phrase, *"What I tell you in darkness,"* is meant to refer to the seasons of prayer as the person is alone with God, and, thereby, hearing from Heaven.

The phrase, *"That speak ye in light,"* concerns a Message to be delivered that has been received in privacy. As well, it is not to be trimmed, glossed, or compromised. Exactly what *"I tell you,"* that alone is to be spoken.

The phrase, *"And what ye hear in the ear,"* is meant to relate that which God gives.

These Passages completely refute the contention by entire Religious Denominations that God no longer speaks to His people. In fact, He speaks constantly, as here described. If He doesn't, it is a sign that the person does not know Him. If He does, and He certainly shall upon proper obedience, the Message in its exact detail is to be delivered, and irrespective as to how it may affect others.

Years ago, I felt led of the Lord to make certain statements respecting certain Doctrine, that I will not now reveal, but which was swaying, at least at that time, many people.

The words, I believe, the Lord gave me were strong and to the point, and left absolutely no room of not knowing what I was speaking about. The Message was not met with great approval, but turned out some time later to be exactly as I had said.

At any rate, after the service, and upon retiring to bed, I slept very little that night. I was troubled in spirit if I had done the right thing. I knew the Message had angered some, and I realized that no one desired to hear what I had to say, and yet, I felt the Lord had told me to say it.

I had no qualms about obeying God, but I had qualms about the source of my Message. Could I be sure it was from the Lord, or was I speaking out of my own mind? This is what troubled me.

The next day being Sunday, and with our service to convene in the Auditorium that afternoon at 2:30, Frances and I, along with friends, left our hotel rooms at about 11 a.m. for lunch.

We were in the back room of a tiny little restaurant, and were sitting there waiting for the meal which we had ordered. All of a sudden a young lady walked up to my table. I did not know her, but she knew us.

She introduced herself, and then, stammering somewhat, proceeded to say the following to me:

"Brother Swaggart," she said, *"in prayer this morning, I strongly felt led of the Lord to give you this Message. And yet,"* she continued to

say, *"I wondered how I could do it, simply because I had no idea that I would even see you, and I certainly did not know you would be in this restaurant."*

She then said, and with great consternation, *"I feel so insignificant and foolish attempting to say these things to you. But the Lord told me to tell you, 'What you have preached is of Me. Do not be fearful about it.'"*

She then said, *"Brother Swaggart, I don't even know what that means, and if I have offended you, please forgive me."*

I slowly arose from the table, and there before Frances and the others, I took her hand in mine and assured her that I was in no way offended, but, instead, blessed. I then thanked her greatly for her obedience.

When she finally left, I turned around to all of my friends at the table, and could hardly talk for weeping, while I related to them how I had been troubled all night and fearful over what I had preached in the service the evening before.

I then related to them how gloriously wonderful the Lord is, that He would send this young lady as He did and give me a Word of reassurance.

It was so very real to me, and I was so very thankful for what the Lord had done and, as well, how He had done it.

I excused myself from the table and walked over to a window, standing there alone, as no one else but our party was in the room. I could not help but weep and praise the Lord for His kindness and graciousness.

The phrase, *"That preach ye upon the housetops,"* referred to the style or design of that time, when the tops of houses were flat and individuals would, at times, use that heightened structure for public proclamation.

However, knowing that the Holy Spirit knows all things, past, present, and future, I cannot help but believe that this phrase concerning the *"housetops"* has somewhat to do with modern television, which, as is obvious, did not come about until nearly 2,000 years after this utterance.

News reporters through the years have asked me if I thought Jesus would have used Television had it been available at that time? They were asking such, not with a desire to know, but with sarcasm, insinuating that preaching over Television was somewhat crass and vulgar.

My answer always was *"Yes!"* Had Television been available, Jesus would have used this medium. The reason I know is because He preached everywhere that was available, whether Synagogues, houses, boats, or on the side of mountains.

Television, for all its attendant irresponsible use (both secular and religious), is the greatest medium the world has ever known to reach masses of people in a short period of time, and yet on a one-to-one basis.

In 1968, the Lord laid a burden on my heart, and greatly so, to go on radio, which we did in January of 1969. Our program was called *"The Campmeeting Hour,"* and despite its name, was 15 minutes in duration, Monday-Friday. In about 1974, the Holy Spirit began to deal with me greatly about going on Television, which we did in 1975.

Our beginning efforts were elementary and clumsy to say the least! But, ultimately, the Lord gave us help, guidance and direction, and began to use the program to touch the hearts and lives of literally millions of people.

During the 1980's, the program covered almost all of South and Central America, along with all of North America, excluding the majority of Mexico.

As well, it aired in great parts of Africa, Australia, the Philippines, along with parts of Europe and Asia.

At the present, we are airing over great parts of America, along with Canada, the Philippines, Russia, and parts of Africa. I firmly believe that the Lord will ultimately help us to cover the entirety of the earth, or at least where He will open the door.

At any rate, we have received several million letters from people, with many of these telling us of glorious and miraculous conversions within their lives as a result of the Gospel we preach over Television.

As is known, for everyone who takes the time to write, there are several, if not many who simply do not bother to write, but, nevertheless, have been greatly touched by the Lord.

This I do know, almost everywhere we go, and irrespective of its locality, I meet people who have been saved as a result of the Telecast, whether years ago or recently. We give the Lord all the praise and glory, and as should be obvious, He, and He alone, deserves it.

I am not on Television because I merely saw a need and am responding to it. But I am there because God has directly called me to this all-important task of World Evangelism. And as Paul said, *"I was not disobedient to the heavenly vision"* (Acts 26:19).

(28) "AND FEAR NOT THEM WHICH KILL THE BODY, BUT ARE NOT ABLE TO KILL THE SOUL: BUT RATHER FEAR HIM WHICH IS ABLE TO DESTROY BOTH SOUL AND BODY IN HELL."

The phrase, *"And fear not them which kill the body, but are not able to kill the soul,"* has to do with the fear of man.

The implication is, that the very worst man can do is to *"kill the body"* which is temporal anyway, but irrespective of what he does, he cannot *"kill the soul."*

At least one of, if not the greatest hindrance to the proclamation of the Gospel is the fear of man. Even though secular government is alluded to (vs. 18), still, the greater attention is directed toward religious activity. In other words, the greatest opposition will come from organized religion, and their cruelty will be worse than all. There is no limitation to the cruelty which can be carried out when men attempt to justify their actions in the realm of religion. That is the reason the religious hierarchy of Israel could kill the Lord in the Name of the Lord!

(Our statement is not meant to imply that all organized religion is wrong, but that most opposition to the True Gospel comes from that source.)

The phrase, *"But rather fear Him which is able to destroy both soul and body in hell,"* refers to God.

The entire essence of this Passage is that men are to look to God seeking to please Him, rather than looking to other men. Whatever man does can only affect the body, while that which God does affects both *"soul and body."*

The Roman Catholic Church claims that if one does not adhere to their tenets of faith, they (Roman Catholic Hierarchy) have the power to banish a soul to *"hell."* To be frank, some Protestant Denominations claim the same thing, at least in a round-about way. However, in this Passage, Christ tells us that only God has that prerogative. Consequently, such threats are not to be given serious consideration.

NOTES

As well, Christ, in this Passage, proclaims the certitude of a place called *"hell."* The Greek word is *"gehenna,"* and means eternal hell where the bodies and souls of all wicked will be marred and tormented forever.

For years I have preached a Message entitled, *"Can A Loving God, Send An Eternal Soul To An Eternal Hell, Where It Will Burn There Forever And Forever?"*

The answer of course is in the affirmative!

In Truth, the Lord has done everything conceivably possible to keep man from this place, even to giving His Only Begotten Son to die on a cruel Cross at Calvary in order that men may be saved. Therefore, the reason that men die eternally lost and go to a Devil's hell is not the fault of God, but their own.

The fault appears in two ways:

1. Men hear the Gospel, as millions do, but reject it. Therefore, they have only themselves to blame.

2. Many do not have the opportunity to hear the Gospel, for which the Church is to blame. Nevertheless, they will still die eternally lost because ignorance is not Salvation, and their blood will be required at the hands of those who were commissioned to warn them (Ezek. 3:18).

The failure to warn, as well, is in two categories: A. Men fail to preach the True Gospel, causing men to believe a lie and be eternally lost; and, B. The Church does not tell them at all, thereby, giving them no opportunity to reject or accept.

(29) "ARE NOT TWO SPARROWS SOLD FOR A FARTHING? AND ONE OF THEM SHALL NOT FALL ON THE GROUND WITHOUT YOUR FATHER."

The idea of this verse is that every event is taken notice of by God.

The Jewish Rabbis had a saying, *"A bird perishes not without God, much less a man."*

"Sparrows" here were chosen by Christ as an example, because they were some of the least of God's creation, and, as well, there was an abundance of them.

Consequently, one would normally think that one sparrow more or less would not be noticed by God.

However, Christ proclaims the infinite knowledge and care exhibited by the Heavenly Father in noting the loss of even one of these little birds.

The phrase, *"Without your Father,"* means without His Knowledge or Will.

Sinful men receive no comfort concerning such august knowledge on the part of God, because it is obvious that He knows and sees every act of disobedience.

However, the Child of God relishes in this information, knowing that his Heavenly Father is observing and superintending all that happens to him.

(30) "BUT THE VERY HAIRS OF YOUR HEAD ARE ALL NUMBERED."

Several things are said in this wonderful Passage:

1. God is Omniscient, therefore, He knows everything. However, the unlimited expanse of such knowledge is beyond the comprehension of mere mortals.

For instance, Psalm 147:4 says, *"He telleth the number of the stars; He calleth them all by their names."*

Astronomers claim there are over 40,000,000,000,000,000,000,000 (40 sextillion) stars which are suns to other planets. God knows the exact number of them, for He made them (Isa. 45:18).

There are over 500,000 words in the Webster's Unabridged Dictionary. If God has every star named, then there are enough such names to fill about 80,000,000,000,000,000 (80 quadrillion) books that size. It would be hard to estimate how many more it would take to record all the other words God uses concerning the whole of His vast universes.

2. Considering such vast creation, which is derived from a knowledge far past the comprehension of mere mortals, that God would take such infinite care of even the smallest details, is, once again, beyond our comprehension.

3. Considering such knowledge, man should have a consummate desire that such a One would rule and reign in his life, especially considering that the Lord freely and abundantly offers His Ability, Grace and Knowledge to all who will accept Him (Jn. 10:10).

4. That one can have fellowship, communion, companionship, and friendship with such a One, is, once again, beyond our comprehension. Why the Lord would even desire fellowship with mere mortals, is again a mystery to all. But yet, He does! What a privilege on our part, and yet, how so few take advantage of it,

and especially considering the tremendous rewards and blessings of such union.

(31) "FEAR YE NOT THEREFORE, YE ARE OF MORE VALUE THAN MANY SPARROWS."

The statement, *"Fear ye not therefore,"* goes in several directions.

First of all, it means that the threats, and even actions of the evil men involved, as portrayed in verse 28, should hold no fear for the Child of God, for the Lord is ruling and guiding all destiny, and these individuals can do nothing but what the Lord allows. As well, and to be sure, He will allow only that which He desires, and which in the long run is best for His Children.

As well, the statement expresses an infinite care, solicitude and protection that is beyond the pale of one's understanding. Consequently, the minuteness of this care forbids one to fear.

This not only pertains to the fear of man, but, as well, to one's livelihood, whether in the realm of the physical, material, or spiritual. To love Him is to trust Him, which absolves all fear (I Jn. 4:18).

The phrase, *"Ye are of more valuable than many sparrows,"* is meant to express the idea, that if the Heavenly Father will express such infinite care regarding a little *"sparrow,"* how much more will He take regarding His Child.

Also, this statement completely debunks the contention by the evolutionists that man is merely a higher form of life. Man was created in the *"Image of God,"* while the animal kingdom was created for man, and that he might *"have dominion over the fish of the sea, and over the fowl of the air, and over ever living thing that moveth upon the earth"* (Gen. 1:27-28).

Actually, the *"value"* of man is so high in the Eyes of God that in order to redeem man, He would give His Only Begotten Son to die on Calvary to effect that Redemption.

Regrettably, the evolutionists put such a low value on the worth of man, that millions of little babies yet unborn are murdered in their mothers' wombs. It is obvious that the less of the worship of God there is in any respective country, the less value is placed on life.

(32) "WHOSOEVER THEREFORE SHALL CONFESS ME BEFORE MEN, HIM WILL I CONFESS ALSO BEFORE MY FATHER WHICH IS IN HEAVEN."

NOTES

The phrase, *"Whosoever therefore shall confess Me before men,"* is meant to tie man to God.

This statement is meant to proclaim the fact that something has happened which has estranged man from God, and despite the fact that God is the Creator of man. Consequently, this estrangement has placed fear in the heart of men and causes them to be disassociated from their Creator. This estrangement came from the Fall in the Garden of Eden.

As well, the words, *"Confess Me,"* proclaim Jesus as the only way to the Father. He Alone is the bridge over these troubled waters. He Alone is the link to the Father. Consequently, for the union to be reestablished, there is an absolute requirement of the confession of Christ.

What does it mean to confess Christ to the world?

It means to confess Him with the voice, but not only with the voice, but that our actions coincide with our voices. In the days of the Early Church, thousands died in the Roman Arenas simply because they would not say *"Caesar is Lord."* And yet, some, if not many, mouthed *"Caesar is Lord,"* while claiming that in their heart they were saying *"Jesus is Lord."* However, by thinking to save their life in this manner, they, in effect, lost it.

Conversely, those who were thought to have lost their life by refusing to acclaim Caesar, in effect, gained it.

It is not possible, at least in the Eyes of God, to say one thing with the mouth, while believing something else with the heart, except in a negative sense.

In other words, millions claim to know Christ with their mouths, but in their hearts allegiance goes in another direction. The idea is that if one truly believes in the heart, he, as well, will confess with the mouth.

To confess Him, as well, proclaims an unshakable Faith in what He did at Calvary and the Resurrection. Also, it means to confess the Bible because it testifies of Him. As stated, this is done not only in the heart, but, as well, *"before men."*

The phrase, *"Him will I confess also before My Father which is in Heaven,"* places the pronoun, *"Him,"* in an emphatic position. In other words, to this particular person who *"confesses Me before men . . . ."*

Upon one's confession of Christ, a corresponding confession is made by Christ, *"before My Father which is in Heaven."* This speaks as well of the Throne of God, and proclaims Salvation for the one who rightly *"confesses Me."*

What a wonder it is for Christ to boldly confess the name of the Believer before the Father and all the Host of Heaven. Jesus further said, *"I say unto you, that likewise joy shall be in Heaven over one sinner that repenteth"* (Lk. 15:7).

(33) "BUT WHOSOEVER SHALL DENY ME BEFORE MEN, HIM WILL I ALSO DENY BEFORE MY FATHER WHICH IS IN HEAVEN."

The entirety of the statement in verses 32 and 33, and continuing through verse 39, involves separation from the dearest upon earth, with the claims of Christ being paramount. As well, on one's relation to those things depends everything hereafter.

The phrase, *"But whosoever shall deny Me before men,"* once again places the emphasis on Christ. He, and He Alone, is the focal point. As we have stated, much of the world believes in God in one way or the other, whether personal or impersonal; however, the great contention is the way to God, which the Bible claims, and especially in the Words of Christ, is Christ, and Christ Alone. One cannot reach God apart from Christ, and especially considering that it was Christ Who paid the price for man's Redemption.

The phrase, *"Him will I also deny before My Father which is in Heaven,"* proclaims the horror of all horrors.

Many people do not consider Peter's denial of Christ as very serious. However, this verse tells us differently. In Truth, it is one of, if not the most serious sin that one could ever commit. And yet, Christ, in His Grace and Kindness, willingly and quickly forgave Peter, and, furthermore, made him one of the greatest men of God who ever lived. Only the Grace of God could do such a thing, for as He did it for Simon of old, He has done it as well for all of us.

(34) THINK NOT THAT I AM COME TO SEND PEACE ON EARTH: I CAME NOT TO SEND PEACE, BUT A SWORD."

In recent days, some foolish men in America have claimed this Scripture as the foundation of their actions, in forming their militias and fomenting threatened anarchy. However, they completely misunderstand

what Christ has said, for His statement is not meant for arms to be taken against the government, or even against one's fellowman. Actually, it means the very opposite!

The phrase, *"Think not that I am come to send peace on earth,"* means that His entrance into the world manifests the hidden evil of the heart, as light manifests impurity in a dungeon. The meaning is that His very Presence will arouse enmity, anger and rebellion in the hearts of evildoers, and that without His followers doing anything.

The phrase, *"I came not to send peace, but a sword,"* is explained in the following verses, and means not that His followers would take up swords against their fellowman, but, instead, that evildoers would take up swords against His followers. Righteousness in the heart arouses enmity in the hearts of the unrighteous, and that without any action on the part of the Righteous.

(35) "FOR I AM COME TO SET A MAN AT VARIANCE AGAINST HIS FATHER, AND THE DAUGHTER AGAINST HER MOTHER, AND THE DAUGHTER IN LAW AGAINST HER MOTHER IN LAW."

As stated, such *"variance"* is not enjoined because of action on the part of the Righteous, but because of the evil in the hearts of those who are unrighteous. In other words, the Presence of Christ automatically tenders this type of unholy response, and, at times, even violent response.

This verse teaches us that a man's family must be subordinate to Christ. In fact, the tenderest human affection must fall into the same category. If not, it will expel Him.

The phrase, *"For I am come...,"* is meant to proclaim what His coming into the heart and life of the individual means, and that His followers would have absolutely no doubt of what the immediate result would be.

Actually, the entirety of the terminology in this Passage proclaims not only enmity, which by its very nature implies separation, but, as well, complete severance. Relation to God is the great line of cleavage, and it must be a cleavage so distinct that there is absolutely no doubt as to the disposition.

Such does not mean that one will not love *"his father"* or *"mother in law,"* etc., but that now Christ is all in all.

It also means that Christ is not only first, but second, third, fourth, etc.

(36) "AND A MAN'S FOES SHALL BE THEY OF HIS OWN HOUSEHOLD."

This "household" not only speaks of the immediate family, but, as well, of one's Church family. Millions have died eternally lost because they allowed their family to come in between them and God, and, the greatest number lost has come about because individuals allowed their "Church household" to take pre-eminence over Christ. This is probably the greatest culprit of all, and because of its heavy religious connotations. If the Church comes before Christ, then the Church has become an idol, as surely as the heathen idols of old. Tragically, this is not an isolated case, but is rather, and sadly so, the rule!

I wrote a short article some time ago for our publication, "THE EVANGELIST," on the subject of "Accountability," and feel that it would be worthwhile to reprint. It is as follows:

The question was, "To whom are you accountable?"

The answer is as follows:

Having heard that question asked scores of times in the last few years, virtually every time it has been asked it has been from an unscriptural perspective.

I am assuming that the one posing this question desires a Scriptural answer, since any other answer is of no value whatsoever.

Some time back, a friend of mine was going to a place to conduct a series of meetings. She was called by a particular Preacher and asked the very question of my subject, "To whom are you accountable?"

I don't know her answer to him, but had she asked him the same question, more than likely he would have given the name of one or more Preachers.

WHAT IS ACCOUNTABILITY?

Webster's Dictionary says that the words, "accountable," or "accountability" simply mean "to furnish a justifying analysis or its explanation."

However, the word, "accountability," is really not the correct word for this subject, even though it is used constantly. The real word is "accountant," which means "one who gives an account or is accountable." This definition has nothing to do with the system of recording and summarizing business and financial transactions.

To boil away all the froth from the top, and despite all the noble and lofty statements, it simply means that some man or group of men, desire to serve as a "hierarchy" above a person in order to tell him what he should and should not do. In the field of religion, probably more blood has been spilled over this than anything else, and, as well, more people, as stated, have died lost because of it.

While accountability to a hierarchy in the civil, political, and business world is acceptable and necessary, such practices have no place or part in the Work of God. Religious men, attempting to bring the ways of the world into the Ways of God have been the bane of the Church from the time of Adam and Eve.

This concept of accountability, as used by the Modern Church, is the way of the world and not of God. To bring the system of the world into the Church is sure death because it always necessitates a departure from the Word of God. God's Ways are not man's ways and never will be!

Therefore, if the reader desires man's ways, then to read further will be a waste of time. However, if the reader desires God's Ways, perhaps the balance of this statement will be of some benefit.

A MEDIATOR BETWEEN GOD AND MEN?

Modern religious accountability (and religious it is) in the truest sense of the word, demands that there be a mediator between the individual and God, with a man or men serving in that position. However, the Scripture says, "For there is One God, and One Mediator between God and men, the Man Christ Jesus" (I Tim. 2:5).

Actually, the entire Catholic Church is built on this premise, claiming the Priest as a "mediator" between God and men. In fact, such a circumstance was correct under the old economy of God with the Law of Moses. In that time, Priests after the Aaronic Priesthood actually did serve as mediators between God and men. However, upon the First Advent of Christ and His finished work at Calvary and the Resurrection, He Alone serves as our Great High Priest (Heb. 3:1; 4:14; 5:6; 8:1-6). Consequently, those who would desire to serve as modern "mediators," or "Priests," are somewhat late. They will need to go back about 3,000 years, become a Jew, belong to the Tribe of Levi, and be after the lineage of Aaron.

NOT ONLY CATHOLICS

Regrettably, Catholics are not the only ones who claim a mediatorship between God and men: the Protestant world is not far behind, although not nearly as practiced at it.

One Evangelist of my acquaintance was heralded far and wide as being the example of *"accountability,"* because he had submitted himself to a group of Preachers, and, consequently, was accountable to them.

In my presence, a man stood to his feet and related with glowing reports this outstanding (as he thought) position. When he had finished, I quietly asked him how this *"accountability"* could really be considered as such, especially considering that this Evangelist would see these particular Preachers only once or twice a year?

Especially among the Charismatics, this foolishness is rife as men love to lord it over other men, and, surprisingly enough, some men love being lorded over.

RELIGIOUS DENOMINATIONS

Religious Denominations practice this same type of *"accountability."* It is thought that if one is associated with a Religious Denomination, this spells *"accountability,"* while, at the same time, pointing to a lack of *"accountability"* in all those who do not belong to such Denominations.

However, a little common sense should inform one that the accountability that God demands could hardly be carried out under the scrutinizing eye of Denominational Heads who may see a Preacher only once a year, if that!

No! Associating oneself with a Religious Denomination affords no type of accountability of the type that the Lord will accept. The same must be said for all man-made groups.

Men love to say that they are accountable to certain groups, which in their eyes or in the eyes of others give them status and credibility. Conversely, men love to say that certain others are accountable to them, which makes them feel important.

Those who will not join or associate with this type of thinking are labeled *"lone rangers,"* and, therefore, as the thinking goes, they

NOTES

must have something to hide. If not, they would certainly desire to be *"accountable"* to some individual or group, wouldn't they!

The Truth is, it is very easy to be accountable to men, that is, if one does not desire to obey God. It is easy because men can easily lie to other men, which they constantly do. However, one cannot lie to God. It's not what men think that matters anyway; it is what God knows.

The Apostle Paul said, *"But they measuring themselves by themselves, and comparing themselves among themselves, are not wise"* (II Cor. 10:12).

What is Scriptural accountability?

Throughout the entire Word of God, man is importuned, even commanded, to look to God and not to other men. This entire scenario began in the Garden of Eden with Adam listening to his wife instead of the Lord. Then it followed with Cain listening to himself or others, rather than the Word of the Lord, offering up his own man-made sacrifice instead of what God commanded (Gen. 4:3-8).

Israel's problem was listening to other nations instead of Jehovah. The Early Church was faced with this at its very beginning. The Apostles were commanded *"not to speak at all nor teach in the Name of Jesus. But Peter and John answered and said unto them, Whether it be right in the sight of God to hearken unto you more than unto God, judge ye"* (Acts 4:18-19).

While all Believers should appreciate fellow Believers and, when appropriate, actively seek their counsel and advice, the only thing owed one another is love.

In Romans 13:1-7, Paul, by the inspiration of the Holy Spirit, laid down the criteria for obedience with respect to human governments and civil rulers. He said that, *"every soul"* must be *"subject"* to these higher powers.

However, that applies only to civil government; it has nothing to do with the Work of God.

When he came to the Work of God, he said that no Christian owed any other Christian anything except to *"love one another."* He went on to say, *"He that loveth another hath fulfilled the Law."* He was speaking of the Law of Moses (Rom. 13:8-10).

In other words, no Christian owes Religious Leaders or any other Christians obedience and subjection the way he does civil authorities.

The Scriptures, as we have quoted, are plain regarding that.

Some men enjoy being accountable to others, at least as the world describes accountability, because they do not want to shoulder responsibility themselves.

AN EXAMPLE

One Religious Leader said to another Preacher of my acquaintance, *"You obey what I say because you are accountable to me; if it is wrong, then I will be responsible and not you."*

This is fallacy and totally unscriptural. There is no such circumstance in the Bible of one person doing something wrong and someone else being responsible for it. Almost the entire Catholic Church is made up of this falsehood, while many Protestants fall into the same category. However, everyone is ultimately going to answer to God for their own actions; at that time, they will not be able to point a finger at anyone else, but they will have to take responsibility themselves. The Scripture says, *"The soul that sinneth, it shall die"* (Ezek. 18:4). Likewise, they must take responsibility now!

The Scripture also says, *"Looking unto Jesus the Author and Finisher of our Faith..."* (Heb. 12:2).

This doesn't say to look to a Religious Denomination or to an earthly Priest or even a Preacher, but *"unto Jesus."*

SCRIPTURAL AUTHORITY

While it is certainly true that the Lord has set in the Church *"Apostles, Prophets, Evangelists, Pastors, and Teachers"* (Eph. 4:11), these leaders have no authority over people, even their followers, only over evil spirits (Mk. 16:17-18). Actually, no Christian, of any capacity, has any authority over another; submission as taught in the Bible is on a horizontal plane, not on a vertical plane. The Scripture says, *"Submitting yourselves one to another..."* (Eph. 5:21).

When the Apostle Paul wrote to the various Churches (most of which he had planted), he never one time ordered anyone to do anything, but always politely made his request: *"I beseech you, brethren"* (Rom. 12:1; 15:30; 16:17; I Cor. 1:10; 4:16).

If anyone were to have the right to claim spiritual authority or require that people be

accountable to him, Paul certainly would have been one who did. However, Paul followed the Lord, and such authority was not given to him or to any other man. The Lord reserves that exclusively unto Himself as the *"Head of ... the Church"* (Col. 1:18).

Actually, the highest and only spiritual authority on earth is the local Church, made up of *"called out Believers."*

When Jesus addressed Himself to the Work of God on earth and to its individual members, He addressed Himself to local Churches, and more specifically to the Pastors of those Churches, such as *"the Angel of the Church at Ephesus,"* and so forth (Rev. 2:1).

He did not address Himself to the headquarters Church in Jerusalem or to a denominational headquarters because, in Truth, such did not exist. While there was certainly a Church in Jerusalem, and even though it was a very strong Church, it did not serve as an imperial religious headquarters.

Correspondingly, the Bible teaches that the local Church carries the highest spiritual authority there is. As a result, accountability should be confined to the leadership and people of the local assembly. Nothing from the outside should take authority over that particular assembly or its people (II Cor. 2:10; Rev. Chpts. 2-3).

Accordingly, younger Ministers in the local Church should submit themselves to the leadership of that Church (Heb. 13:17). Peter said, *"Likewise, ye younger, submit yourselves unto the elder..."* (I Pet. 5:5).

However, both Hebrews 13:17 and I Peter 5:5 are speaking of the local Church, not some outside, unscriptural denominational religious office.

There is every evidence in Scripture that accountability should be to a local Church: both to its apostolic leadership and to its people (Acts 13:1-5).

When there was a problem in the Church in Corinth, and it seems to have been with one of its leaders, Paul dealt directly with the Church relative to what should be done, because he had been asked to do so (I Cor. 5:1; II Cor. 2:3-11).

There is no incident in the New Testament Church in which problems were handled other than through the local Church, other than the one meeting recorded in Acts 15 which had to do with Doctrine, and which involved all the Apostles.

It should be understood that when we speak of the Church, it is not an all-inclusive term covering all Churches of a particular Religious Denomination, for example, but, instead, refers to a local, indigenous assembly which might well have branches, but which answers to that one particular Church and not to a Denomination or group of Churches.

As we have previously stated, when Christ addressed the seven Churches of Asia, He addressed each Church individually and did not link them together in the slightest, except that they were all a part of His Body.

Even though particular Churches may have a common bond of Doctrine and a like sense of purpose, spiritual authority and accountability begin and end with each assembly, and even more specifically with the Pastor of that Church. He answers directly to the Word of God and to Christ through the agency of the Person of the Holy Spirit.

HOW ACCOUNTABLE SHOULD A PERSON BE TO HIS LOCAL CHURCH?

Of course, the answer to that question is simple inasmuch as all accountability begins and ends with the Word of God. While the Scripture commands that younger or Associate Ministers in the local Church submit to its leadership, such submission can only be given as long as the Word of God is fully adhered to. This would hold true for the lay membership as well as for the Ministerial Leadership.

To give an example, since the 1960's, quite a number of people have been Baptized in the Holy Spirit with the evidence of speaking with other tongues in Churches which do not believe this Biblical Doctrine.

As a consequence, if the leadership of those particular Churches demands that all such actions cease and desist, then submission comes to an end simply because its leadership is unscriptural.

However, such individuals should not cause problems in that particular Church, neither should they attempt to usurp authority over its leadership. To be Scripturally accountable, they should quietly leave and associate themselves with a different Church that adheres to sound Biblical Doctrine.

NOTES

Man-made accountability has no validity with God, and most of what is labeled accountability in modern circles will find no counterpart whatsoever in the New Testament Church.

True accountability is demanded by God and is far more stringent than that demanded by man, because the accountability required by the Lord covers every aspect of one's life and service, not just a part.

(37) "HE THAT LOVETH FATHER OR MOTHER MORE THAN ME IS NOT WORTHY OF ME: AND HE THAT LOVETH SON OR DAUGHTER MORE THAN ME IS NOT WORTHY OF ME."

While it is true that Bible Christianity gives Eternal Life, plus all of its associate values to the Believer, while the religions of the world give nothing, still, that which is demanded by the Lord is far more than that demanded by the major religions of the world.

To be sure, this verse of Scripture is the dividing line of Christianity. Many claim Christ, but few measure up to these standards.

Anything could have been inserted in the place of one's dearest family relationships; however, Jesus used that which is the dearest, or at least should be!

Sooner or later, one's love will be tested, and it is on that test, "our love," that we stand or fall.

The phrase, "He that loveth father or mother more than Me is not worthy of Me," is meant to emphasize that which Christ did for us. He gave His all, His very life, and in turn He demands all.

Nevertheless, if one strictly follows the Lord in this test of Discipleship, one will find that his love for his dearest, such as family relationships, is not lessened, but rather increased. Then the love is pure, and untainted by selfishness or self-will.

Therefore, Christ, in making these demands, is not taking anything from His Disciple, but, instead, adding to him.

To not follow this admonition, one loses both; the favor of God, and the true love for our loved ones, which only God can give.

(38) "AND HE THAT TAKETH NOT HIS CROSS, AND FOLLOWETH AFTER ME, IS NOT WORTHY OF ME."

Crosses were placed at the doors of Roman Courts of Justice, and convicted prisoners on passing out to execution had to take up their cross and carry it to the place of death.

Christ's followers are here pictured following Him to death, each one bearing his or her cross. This destroys the popular notion that the word, *"cross"* in this verse means a trial, such as ill health or poverty, etc.

Actually, to suffer anything that the unsaved can suffer, does not constitute bearing the cross. Consequently, this would rule out almost all that which is referred to as *"cross-bearing."*

What does bearing the cross mean?

1. First of all, there is a *"cross."* Therefore, this negates the claims of the *"Faith Teachers"* regarding the confessing away all troubles and difficulties. Such is not to be, and would not be for the good of the Child of God even if it could be. The Scripture says that Jesus learned obedience by the things He suffered (Heb. 5:8). No! That certainly does not mean that one should look for suffering; however, to the True Child of God such will come!

Even though at times it is difficult, still, the Lord brings such about in order that our spiritual growth may be enhanced.

2. As we have stated, the cross is not the normal vicissitudes of life, as disagreeable and debilitating as they may be.

3. The words, *"Followeth after Me,"* constitute bearing the cross. It is following Jesus.

Inasmuch as His earthly journey ended at Calvary, with His Death, likewise, our earthly journey must end with the death of self-will. Whatever that takes, and at times it takes much, must be done.

Hebrews 11 bears this out. While tremendous victories of Faith are proclaimed, one must notice that the trial of Faith is balanced. It says:

"Who through Faith subdued kingdoms, wrought Righteousness, obtained Promises, stopped the mouths of lions,

"Quenched the violence of fire, escaped the edge of the sword, out of weakness were made strong, waxed valiant in fight, turned to flight the armies of the aliens.

"Women received their dead raised to life again; and others were tortured, not accepting deliverance; that they might obtain a better resurrection:

"And others had trial of cruel mockings and scourgings, yea, moreover of bonds and imprisonment:

NOTES

"They were stoned, they were sawn asunder, were tempted, were slain with the sword: they wandered about in sheepskins and goatskins; being destitute, afflicted, tormented;"

And then the Holy Spirit adds, *("Of Whom the world was not worthy:) they wandered in deserts, and in mountains, and in dens and caves of the earth."*

And then the Holy Spirit concluded this tremendous statement by saying, *"And these all, having obtained a good report through Faith . . ."* (Heb. 11:33-39).

These did bear the cross, and irrespective of whether it was a tremendous feat of Faith or that which seemed to be the very opposite! They followed Jesus to the death, and whatever kind of death it was. That is bearing the cross.

4. Bearing the cross ensures that one's love and devotion is not divided. As stated, the tests will come as to the sincerity of one's love. If the love is not pure, the cross, and sadly, will be laid aside. Only pure love will continue to bear it.

(39) "HE THAT FINDETH HIS LIFE SHALL LOSE IT: AND HE THAT LOSETH HIS LIFE FOR MY SAKE SHALL FIND IT."

As Christ continues His discourse, and knowing the thoughts of men respecting such stern demands, He answers the question before it is asked.

No! To obey Him, thereby *"following Him,"* and *"bearing the cross,"* does not cause one's life to be lost, instead, it causes one to find it.

One only need look at the idle rich, a place and position one might quickly add, which most of the world seeks. These individuals, having all the money one could desire, are thought to really enjoy life, etc. However, the opposite is the truth.

If one will bother to make a detailed search of the lives of those in question, one will find, at least if the person doesn't know Christ, that misery and heartache are the result, simply because in attempting to *"find their life"* without God, they *"lose it."*

Conversely, he that makes Christ everything in his life, placing all else behind him, finds that he loses his old life with all its attendant problems and difficulties, and in its place finds new life. However, one must notice that to find this new life, one must do so *"for Jesus' sake."*

In fact, millions, down through the years, have tried to lose their life in efforts which did not include Christ. In that quest, they found no life.

As an example, some years ago I saw a documentary over Television concerning a Catholic Monk. He was spending his life in seclusion, engaging in certain rituals which were supposed to make him holy, etc.

He, through the Television cameras, showed us his room which was spartan indeed! His bed was a simple cot, with only a blanket thrown over hard boards. There was no pillow.

He arose each morning at 4 a.m. and engaged in reciting prayers, as well as certain other rituals. Actually, the entirety of his day was made up of similar circumstances.

He only ate two meals a day, allowing himself a diet that was Spartan, plain and simple.

Once every six months he went into town for an hour or so. Other than that, he did not deviate from his rigorous, Spartan schedule.

After all these things were explained, the man doing the documentary asked him, *"Do you feel close to God?"*

I will never forget the answer of this Catholic Monk. He turned and looked at the man who had posed the question, and said: *"I have done this now for nearly three years, and I have never felt God one time, and, in fact, I don't even know if there is a God."*

His answer was not surprising, and yet sad! He was truly losing his life, but despite all the religious ritual, it was not for the sake of Christ, but, instead, a misguided quest. What is done must be for *"Jesus' sake,"* and not for the sake of religion, charity, or even others, as noble as that might be. It must be for Christ's sake alone, which if properly done, will definitely include others, but not others alone.

The offer here given is the greatest offer to mankind that could ever be made. It is the secret and source of happiness and joy. It alone proclaims the fulfillment which only Christ can give. Other than this which is laid down by Christ, there is no *"life,"* and irrespective of money, education, place, position, or status. All else is emptiness, unfulfillment, darkness and waste!

However, this *"life"* spoken of by Christ, which is found only in Him, is somewhat like the Tabernacle of old. There was nothing outwardly

about it that was beautiful. Nothing attractive, nothing enticing! In fact, there was no allurement whatsoever.

Upon looking at it, the merely curious would have little desire or inclination to inquire further. However, for those who did inquire further, that which awaited them was glorious indeed!

Even though the outside held nothing attractive, upon walking inside one would have found walls made of gold. As well, they would have found articles of furniture, and designed by none other than the Holy Spirit. They would find a beauty beyond description. However, none of that is obvious from the outside.

Likewise, this *"life"* spoken of by Christ, which is only given to those who truly *"bear their cross after Him,"* is not easily understood at all by outward observance. From the outward there is nothing enticing. However, upon losing one's life for His sake, and then, wonder of wonders, *"finding it,"* only then is it understood.

Regrettably, precious few are there who find it.

(40) "HE THAT RECEIVETH YOU RECEIVETH ME, AND HE THAT RECEIVETH ME RECEIVETH HIM THAT SENT ME."

Even though the persecution, at least for the True Servant of the Lord, will be great, even as the Lord warns, still, great promises of blessings are tendered toward those who show even the slightest favor to God's Anointed.

Someone has said, *"A man's messenger is as himself."*

The phrase, *"He that receiveth you receiveth Me,"* places the servant of the Lord in close proximity to his Master. He actually is an Ambassador, speaking for the Lord and on His behalf. The relationship could not be closer, at least in the Mind of the Lord.

Consequently, the servant of the Lord must conduct himself accordingly at all times. He is representing Christ, and his every action is to be the action of Christ. He is to speak with the same authority, yet with the same love. In other words, he is to conduct himself as the Lord conducted Himself, at least as far as is possible!

In this one phrase is the responsibility of the Ambassador, the close tie of the Lord to the Ambassador, and the blessing promised to those who *"receive you."*

The phrase, *"And he that receiveth Me receiveth Him that sent Me,"* refers to the Heavenly Father Who sent Christ to redeem humanity. Consequently, the kind action on the part of the one who *"receives you,"* sets in motion a series of events that involve both God the Son and God the Father. There is no more sure road to blessing than this promised in verses 40-42.

Knowing that most will be unkind, and even hateful to the servant of the Lord, for the few who truly show kindness tremendous things are promised. To be sure, those promises are kept!

Even though it is not spoken in these Passages, still, the inference is that those who conduct themselves in the opposite manner than here spoken, will, to be sure, be the recipient of stern measures from both the Father and the Son. Because to persecute His, is to persecute Him. To be sure, He will take far sterner measures on behalf of that done to His, even than that done to Him.

(41) "HE THAT RECEIVETH A PROPHET IN THE NAME OF A PROPHET SHALL RECEIVE A PROPHET'S REWARD; AND HE THAT RECEIVETH A RIGHTEOUS MAN IN THE NAME OF A RIGHTEOUS MAN SHALL RECEIVE A RIGHTEOUS MAN'S REWARD."

So as there will be no misunderstanding, the Lord vividly portrays the entirety of the disposition of His followers, be they *"Prophet"* or a *"Believer"* who does not have one of the fivefold callings (Eph. 4:11).

The difference in the reward for the kindness shown to the *"Prophet"* or the *"Believer"* (Righteous man), is not stated! But, to be sure, a reward is promised to all who show any type of kindness toward any of God's Children.

The phrase, *"He that receiveth a Prophet in the name of a Prophet shall received a Prophet's reward,"* refers to only those who are truly the Lord's. Receiving a false prophet as a true one or a wicked one posing as a Righteous man, will not be rewarded.

Actually, if a person receives such or bids him Godspeed, John says he is a partaker of his evil deeds (II Jn. 9-11). Consequently, one must be certain that these are truly from the Lord.

These Passages are far more important than meets the eye. Regrettably, most modern Christians little think for themselves, allowing Religious Leaders, so-called, to make

NOTES

the identification. In most cases this is extremely untrustworthy.

In Jesus' day, if one had listened to the Religious Leaders, as many did, Jesus was labeled by these apostates as a false prophet, or even a servant of Satan (vs. 25). Therefore, I think one can say without any fear of Scriptural contradiction or exaggeration, that in all ages the True Prophets of God have seldom been accepted by the majority, and especially the Church. It is sad but true!

In Paul's day it had not changed. He wrote of himself while imprisoned in Rome, *"Some indeed preach Christ even of envy and strife; and some also of good will:*

"The one preached Christ of contention, not sincerely, supposing to add affliction to my bonds" (Phil. 1:15-16).

He would also write to the Church at Corinth, a Church we might quickly add which he had planted himself, which meant that most, if not all the converts in that Church were his. And yet, he would ask of the people in that Church, *"Do we begin again to commend ourselves? or need we, as some others, epistles of commendation to you, or letters of commendation from you?"* (II Cor. 3:1).

The reason for the letter was that Paul's own converts in Corinth were in danger of turning against him, and because of false prophets. Consequently, Satan is very adept at deceiving people. Therefore, the Child of God must live close to the Lord, knowing God's Word, and have a discerning spirit that they may know for themselves what is false and what is true.

The situation is so critical, and because of the things I have said, that the Lord, knowing that the True Prophet would have few who would kindly receive Him, a *"Prophet's reward"* is promised to those who exhibit such kindness. To be sure, the return is great on such an investment.

As an example, when David was fleeing from Absalom, three men showed him kindness, *"Shobi," "Machir,"* and *"Barzillai,"* and did so even though they did not know if David would be alive the next day, or what the results of their kindness would be, at least as far as David's enemies were concerned. However, the Holy Spirit preserved a record of their kindness for all generations, and recorded it in II Samuel 17:27-29.

Whatever David's reward will be, Christ said that these three men will receive the same reward at the Judgment Seat of Christ. This is how highly the Lord thinks of such action.

Consequently, a *"Righteous man's reward"* actually speaks of one sent by the Lord on a Righteous mission of whatever capacity. Those who help Him even in the slightest degree to fulfill this mission, will receive the same type of reward that the Righteous man receives upon the completion of the mission.

(42) "AND WHOSOEVER SHALL GIVE TO DRINK UNTO ONE OF THESE LITTLE ONES A CUP OF COLD WATER ONLY IN THE NAME OF A DISCIPLE, VERILY I SAY UNTO YOU, HE SHALL IN NO WISE LOSE HIS REWARD."

The *"little ones"* spoken of here, and the *"Disciple,"* are one and the same.

The phrase, *"And whosoever shall give to drink unto one of these little ones a cup of cold water,"* is meant to point to the smallest help, at least if that is all that can be given, that it does not go unnoticed by the Lord, and will be remembered in His Book, and amply rewarded (Rev. 20:12).

Once again, we stress the fact that the Lord is speaking of those who are sent on particular missions in His Name. Knowing that Satan will do all to hinder, and, sadly, much of that hindrance will come from those who should be helping instead of hurting, even the smallest detail of kindness exhibited toward the Lord's servant who helps him on his way is extremely important in the Eyes of the Lord. Knowing there will be few who do such and how important it is, great reward is promised.

The phrase, *"In the name of a Disciple,"* actually means *"Because he is a Disciple"* and is on a mission from the Lord.

The phrase, *"Verily I say unto you, he shall in no wise lose his reward,"* is meant to imply the certitude of such action. The Lord will Personally see to it that such kindness is rewarded, not only in this life, but the one to come!

CHAPTER 11

(1) "AND IT CAME TO PASS, WHEN JESUS HAD MADE AN END OF COMMANDING HIS

NOTES

TWELVE DISCIPLES, HE DEPARTED THENCE TO TEACH AND TO PREACH IN THEIR CITIES."

This Chapter predicts a turning point in the Ministry of Christ. The people refused to repent or to believe (vss. 16-17); their leaders declared Jesus to be Satan (10:25); and, greatest blow of all, His beloved forerunner doubted His Messiahship (vs. 3).

But this seeming failure of His mission did not confound the Lord, for He was bearing the easy yoke and the light burden (vs. 30) of the Father's Will (vs. 26), and in that Will He exulted (vs. 25).

Surrounded by ruin, for that's what it was, He triumphantly declared that all things were delivered unto Him, and that He dwelt in a realm of mutual knowledge in the Godhead that was the perfection of bliss, and that nothing could effect. He rested in Isaiah 49.

The phrase, *"And it came to pass, when Jesus had made an end of commanding His twelve Disciples,"* refers to the teaching of the previous Chapter. To be sure, the information given and the instruction offered, would not be appealing at all to the carnal heart. For the most part, it promises persecution, opposition, and even death. However, it also promises that if one faithfully takes up this journey, in the *"losing of his life, he shall find it."* To be truthful, it is the only True Life there is!

Many contend that this teaching was only for the *"twelve Disciples,"* and does not pertain to the modern Church. However, that is error!

The number *"twelve"* is the number of the Church, as we plainly see in the Book of Revelation, and as stated. It was the number of the Jewish Church, for He chose twelve Patriarchs, and the number of the Christian Church, for it is the Church of the twelve Apostles. Therefore, what is given to them, in effect, is given to the entirety of the Church.

Twelve implies Covenant. Thus, the very number of the Apostles reminds us that we are brought by the Grace of Christ into very close relations with God, into a New Covenant with God. Consequently, all things commanded the first Disciples are still in force (Mat. 28:20). Teaching that excludes such from the modern Church, is the teaching of unbelief.

If one is to notice, He *"commanded,"* which means they were not suggestions.

If one properly studies and understands the Work of God, one understands that the statements and orders are basically all military in principle. Consequently, it is to be looked at accordingly.

The phrase, *"He departed thence to teach and to preach in their cities,"* does not say exactly where, but probably covers all of Galilee. Once again, Christ portrays the mission of the Church, in that its priority must be the taking of the Gospel to the entirety of the world. Of course, for this to be done and carried out properly, Disciples have to be called, taught, instructed and guided, as here shown.

So, in this one verse we have the proper methods of our Lord, and that which Christianity is all about. He called unto Him Disciples, inviting them to *"follow Me,"* and then proceeded to take the Gospel to the world.

(2) "NOW WHEN JOHN HAD HEARD IN THE PRISON THE WORKS OF CHRIST, HE SENT TWO OF HIS DISCIPLES,"

This must have been an extremely hard time for John the Baptist. Thousands are flocking to the side of Christ, with tremendous miracles being performed, and yet John languishes in prison.

It was not that he did not know His Ministry and Message, for that he did. He was the forerunner, the way preparer, for the Messiah. He had performed his task admirably so, preparing the hearts of the people for the Advent of the greatest One Who would ever be, the Lord of Glory, the Lord Jesus Christ, the Son of God.

However, John, as strong as he was and as heavily anointed as he had been, was still human. As such, the doubts began to fill his mind. He stares at the walls of a lonely prison cell, and he cannot help but wonder as to why the Lord did not perform a miracle in order that he may be released from prison.

Too oftentimes it is easy to criticize the Bible Giants who stumbled in one way or the other, never stopping to realize the tremendous pressure that was brought against them. Even though John's lapse of Faith was wrong, still, as we shall see, there was no reprimand from Christ, and neither should there be from us. We should ask ourselves, that if we had been in his shoes, would we have done any better, or even as well?

I think the answer to that is obvious!

NOTES

The phrase, *"He sent two of his Disciples,"* represents men who are in a quandary, disappointed, hurt, and not quite understanding all that has befallen them.

A short time before, thousands of people were thronging to hear John, now, and abruptly, it is all over. He is in prison, while these same thousands are going now to hear Christ. They are almost like orphans.

Once again, it is easy for us to say as to what they should have done, and probably ultimately did do, but not so easy when experiencing the same yourself.

(3) "AND SAID UNTO HIM, ART THOU HE THAT SHOULD COME, OR DO WE LOOK FOR ANOTHER?"

When John heard of the great miracles of Christ, no doubt, he was elated, and yet, the questions crowd his mind. He probably thought of nothing else, as day by day he languished in this prison. And yet, the gloom of this prison cell is occasion for the evil one to fill John's mind with thoughts that are not of Faith.

He was the one who introduced Christ. He was the one who baptized Him. He possibly had even heard the Voice of God, *"This is My Beloved Son, in Whom I am well pleased . . ."* (3:17). And yet, doubts fill his mind.

Unless one has been there, one little knows the struggle that John faced. The answer lies in the frailty of human flesh, the propensity to doubt, plus the ability of Satan to present his lie dressed up in all that seems plausible.

It has been said that God's Saints fail sometimes in that very Grace which is their most striking characteristic; Elijah, for instance, in courage; Moses, in meekness; Peter, in steadfastness.

After many years of living for the Lord, I am persuaded that it is seldom in the weak areas of a person's life that they fail. It is almost always in the strong areas. They are on guard respecting the weak places, consequently, providing Satan with excellent opportunity respecting the areas in which they think they are most strong. As stated, I think if one will carefully study the lives of the Bible Giants, they will find this to be true.

It only shows how weak we really are, even in that which we feel is the strongest. It has been said that if enough pressure is applied, the strongest will fail. I think the Bible is replete with that Truth, inasmuch as the only One Who never failed is Jesus. All others stand wanting. That is at least one of the reasons He said in the Beatitudes, *"Blessed are they that mourn."* He was speaking of those who mourned over their own shortcomings, flaws, inconsistencies and failures, as all should!

In the question the Disciples of John are told to ask Jesus, we find that the Baptist had less than perfect understanding respecting what Christ would really do. He, however, cannot be faulted, because it seems that no one else understood either. All believed that Jesus was going to set up His Kingdom at that time, throwing off the yoke of Rome, and delivering Israel. The two Disciples who walked on the road to Emmaus said, and concerning Christ, and before they knew or believed He had been raised from the dead, *"But we trusted that it had been He which should have redeemed Israel"* (Lk. 24:21).

Doubt is the nemesis of Faith, and plagues every Christian at one time or the other. The Greek word is *"diakrino,"* and suggests uncertainty about something sent forward as an object of Faith, and in this case, Christ. Rather than the quiet confidence that rests completely in God's Word and thus responds with an obedience capable of giving focus and direction to life, doubt suggests a defective Faith — a Faith that believes and yet cannot bring itself to trust.

This type of doubt is not expressed in some intellectual quest for logical certainty. It invades experience, hindering prayer (Mat. 21:21; James 1:6), and trapping us in actions about which our consciences are unsure (Rom. 14:22-23).

The type of doubt that plagued John was the reality of Christ — in other words, was Christ really the Messiah? A bevy of circumstances brings about the doubt. If He was the Messiah, why did He not deliver him from this prison?

If He was the Messiah, why did He not set up His Kingdom and give him a place in it?

All of this is generated by a lack of knowledge of the Word of God. However, before we criticize him for such, let it be understood that it is much easier at present to look back at reality which has already happened, than to look forward to that which is only in shadow, and dim at that!

As well, there was almost nothing in the Old Testament, of which John would have been familiar, regarding the coming Church. This was something he could not see, nor could the others see it. The Church would be brought into being as a result of Israel's rejection of Christ, and, therefore, the Kingdom. And shortly, Jesus would announce this. But, at present, these are things yet unsaid.

So he asks, *"Art Thou He that should come, or do we look for another?"*

(4) "JESUS ANSWERED AND SAID UNTO THEM, GO AND SHEW JOHN AGAIN THOSE THINGS WHICH YE DO HEAR AND SEE:"

The phrase, *"Jesus answered and said unto them,"* will reveal the beautiful attitude of Christ, as an example to all of us. As we study the answer that He gave to John through His Disciples, we will hopefully learn much.

As well, Christ will always *"answer,"* and irrespective of the doubt or unbelief, providing the question is sincere.

The phrase, *"Go and shew John again those things which ye do hear and see,"* proclaims the answer!

Even though Christ pointedly said to the woman at Jacob's well, and concerning His Messiahship, *"I that speak unto thee am He"* (Jn. 4:25-26), still, He would answer John in a different manner. The woman had little true knowledge of the Word of God, while John did! Consequently, Jesus directed him to Isaiah 35:5-6 and Isaiah 61:1-2.

These were the particular miracles, and this the particular preaching which should accredit His Person. His claim was not that He worked miracles, but that He worked certain predicted miracles and preached in a certain predicted manner.

Thus He appealed to the Scriptures, and having quoted their testimony to Himself, He then gave His testimony to John, declaring him to be blessed, as well as all others who found nothing to stumble at in His (Christ's) Person, teachings, or actions.

(5) "THE BLIND RECEIVE THEIR SIGHT, AND THE LAME WALK, THE LEPERS ARE CLEANSED, AND THE DEAF HEAR, THE DEAD ARE RAISED UP, AND THE POOR HAVE THE GOSPEL PREACHED TO THEM."

Jesus called John's attention away from the political scene (restoring at that time the

Kingdom to Israel), to the true purpose of His mission, the restoration of the individual.

To be sure, the Lord is attempting to do the same presently! Regrettably, great segments of the modern Church are just as steeped presently in the *"political message"* as they were during the time of Christ. At this time, all the Disciples could see was the restoration of Israel, which pertained to Christ using His great Power to overthrow Rome, and politically make Israel a great nation once again. It has little changed at present.

As men misunderstood the true purpose and mission of Christ at that time, they still misunderstand His true purpose and mission.

While it is true that eventually an earthly kingdom will ultimately come about, still, this, as then, is not the time or the place.

It is not political liberty so much that is needed, but, instead, spiritual liberty, and that can only be afforded by Christ. As well, it is by far the most important. If that is done, then the other will come!

Even though these great statements of victory, as given to John, pertain to the physical, still, they even more so pertain to the spiritual.

1. *"The blind receive their sight"*: Physically, this was done, and, as well, many had their spiritual eyes opened.

2. *"The lame walk"*: This happened physically as well, but, more so, man is spiritually lame, and that because of the Fall, and within himself cannot walk upright. Jesus lifts men up that they may walk properly.

3. *"The lepers are cleansed"*: He literally cleansed lepers from this loathsome disease, but, even more importantly, their cleansing was meant to serve as a symbol of the spiritual cleansing from sin, of which leprosy was a type, and which only Jesus could give.

4. *"And the deaf hear"*: Men were literally healed from physical deafness; however, their far greater problem was spiritual deafness, hence, Jesus would say, *"Who hath ears to hear, let him hear"* (Mat. 13:9). Because of the power of the Gospel and Revelation given by the Holy Spirit, many did *"hear."*

5. *"The dead are raised up"*: Even though the dead were raised physically according to the Word of Christ, still, due to the Fall, man is spiritually dead, which means to be separated from God. Consequently, the raising of the dead

in the physical sense was meant to serve as an example of the great *"born-again"* experience, which brings the dead spiritually to life.

6. *"The poor have the Gospel preached to them"*: This phrase is used last in this scenario, where it was used first in Luke 4:18. Such was designed accordingly by the Holy Spirit.

As the Luke account was given first, it was meant to imply that all that would follow would be based upon the *"Gospel preached to the poor"* (poor in spirit).

Now, and as it is quoted later, it is given last, and meant to imply that as a result of the Power of the Holy Spirit and the preaching of the Gospel, these great and glorious things took place.

This which is given is the True Mission of Christ, and should be the True Mission of the Church. However, and sadly, much of the modern Church, as we have stated, opts for the *"political message,"* simply because it requires no Power of God, only the carnality of man. Whereas to do the Works of Christ, which the Church is intended to do, requires a close walk with God and a tremendous infilling of the Holy Spirit. Tragically, the far greater majority of the modern Church does not have this, and, in fact, does not even believe in it.

Consequently, precious few *"blind receive their sight,"* whether physical or spiritual, and precious few *"lame walk,"* whether physical or spiritual, etc.

(6) "AND BLESSED IS HE, WHOSOEVER SHALL NOT BE OFFENDED IN ME."

The phrase, *"And blessed is he,"* now proclaims the Lord adding another Beatitude to those given in Chapter 5.

The phrase, *"Whosoever shall not be offended in Me,"* refers to several things:

1. To not be offended at Him because of His Mission, i.e., not using His Power to overthrow Rome.

2. Many were offended at the lowly exterior of the Great King. But God manifest in flesh, had not come to display the pomp of Royalty, but to forgive the sins and to heal the diseases of humanity. This mission was far more Divine and Glorious than a seizure of the Throne of David, though that might have liberated John.

3. A carnal heart could not understand Immanuel descending to the depths of human

sin and misery, loading Himself with mens burdens and sorrows, and offering up Himself as a Sacrifice in expiation of their sins. However, such action revealed the Heart of God as no Imperial splendor could possibly have done.

(7) "AND AS THEY DEPARTED, JESUS BEGAN TO SAY UNTO THE MULTITUDES CONCERNING JOHN, WHAT WENT YE OUT INTO THE WILDERNESS TO SEE? A REED SHAKEN WITH THE WIND?"

The phrase, *"And as they departed,"* refers to the two Disciples of John who now returned from Christ back to John. I believe, and without a doubt, their answer satisfied John to the very core of his being.

The phrase, *"Jesus began to say unto the multitudes concerning John,"* is meant to portray to this crowd, who had no doubt overheard the exchange regarding John's question, exactly as to what type of man John really was.

Perhaps some had thought ill in their hearts regarding John, and because of the question of the Disciples. Maybe they had even begun to have doubts about his prophetic office, and because of his question, thinking that it made him look weak, and he was not the strong man they thought he was after all!

At any rate, Jesus plainly answered them, and if such questions and criticism arose in their hearts, such were quickly stilled.

The question, *"What went ye out into the wilderness to see?"*, was pertaining to the type of man John was.

Consequently, the thoughts no doubt were in the minds of the people, that if John had truly been what they thought he was when they saw him in the *"wilderness,"* surely he would not now be in prison, and if he was genuine, Jesus would surely use His great Power to set him free.

In effect, Jesus is saying that what John was as he preached in the wilderness and the thousands thronged to Him, and the entirety of the nation of Israel exclaimed this first prophetic voice in over 400 years, this John, yes, this John, was exactly what they thought he was, and was still the same at the present!

The question, *"A reed shaken with the wind?"*, speaks of the type of reeds which grew in great quantities on the Jordan River, and with which the people were very familiar. Whichever way the wind blew, the reed blew.

NOTES

However, Jesus is saying, John is not like a *"reed shaken with the wind."* In fact, he is the very opposite!

Whichever way the wind blew, John stood resolute, and was unbending and unyielding in his proclamation of the introduction of Christ.

(8) "BUT WHAT WENT YE OUT FOR TO SEE? A MAN CLOTHED IN SOFT RAIMENT? BEHOLD, THEY THAT WEAR SOFT CLOTHING ARE IN KINGS' HOUSES."

The question, *"But what went ye out for to see?"*, is the same question asked in the previous verse, and by design. These people had heard of John's preaching and had gone out to see him. And what did they see?

The question, *"A man clothed in soft raiment?"*, was meant to point to those who were the opposite of True Prophets.

False prophets lived for luxury, and preached for money.

True Prophets, and in the custom of the Prophets of old, wore rough garments, which in effect made a statement. That statement was, that they could not be bought or sold by any man, and they were not preaching for money or predicting for gold. They heard only the Voice of God, and that Message only would they deliver.

In effect, Jesus is saying, *"That is the type of Prophet you saw. Men could not buy Him, and, in effect, if Herod's gold could have done so, John would not now be in prison."*

The phrase, *"Behold, they that wear soft clothing are in kings' houses,"* is actually referring to John being in prison.

If he had sold out, he would now be wearing beautiful clothing, and serving as the Court Preacher for Herod. Instead, he is in a dungeon, so that should tell you something!

(9) "BUT WHAT WENT YE OUT FOR TO SEE? A PROPHET? YEA, I SAY UNTO YOU, AND MORE THAN A PROPHET."

The question, *"But what went ye out for to see?"*, is the third time this question is posed. Jesus wants to make certain by repeating this phrase, that they know exactly who John is, and not be swayed by him being in prison or sending his Disciples respecting the Messiahship.

The question, *"A Prophet?"*, is said emphatically!

He is saying, *"You went out to see a Prophet, and a Prophet you saw!"* Consequently, His answer to them lays to rest any question they may have had regarding the validity of his prophetic office. But now He will tell them something which will place John in a position higher than any Prophet who had ever lived.

The phrase, *"Yea, I say unto you, and more than a Prophet,"* is meant to proclaim what the other Prophets only predicted, John actually saw and handled (Jn. 1:31-34; I Jn. 1:1).

This would have been somewhat difficult for the listeners to have understood, considering that Prophets like Isaiah and Jeremiah, along with Ezekiel and others had written great Books, which were actually a part of their Bible.

As well, David, the sweet singer of Israel, had prophesied of the coming of this One, and had written many Psalms about Him. Therefore, in their minds at least, how could John be greater than these, especially considering that he never wrote a single Book, or performed a single miracle? And yet, Jesus says about John, *"He is more than a Prophet,"* i.e., more than all Prophets!

The next verse tells us what Jesus was speaking of:

(10) "FOR THIS IS HE, OF WHOM IT IS WRITTEN, BEHOLD, I SEND MY MESSENGER BEFORE THY FACE, WHICH SHALL PREPARE THY WAY BEFORE THEE."

This verse affirms the Godhead of Jesus of Nazareth.

The phrase, *"For this is he, of whom it is written,"* proclaims John, although portrayed in the New Testament, as, in fact, the last of the Old Testament Prophets. All the others said, *"He is coming,"* speaking of Jesus, while John said, *"He has come!"*

The *"written"* phrase concerning John is found in Malachi 3:1. It says, *"Behold, I send My Messenger before Thy Face,"* and is meant to speak of the forerunner of Christ, John the Baptist. He was called by the Lord, *"My Messenger."* There could be no higher distinction.

As well, where the other Prophets only could point to one who was coming, John would behold *"His Face."*

The phrase, *"Which shall prepare Thy way before Thee,"* proclaimed John preaching the Message of Repentance, which had to be preached before the First Advent of Christ. As well, He introduced Christ.

As wonderful and glorious as all the great

things done by the other Prophets and Patriarchs, still, direct association with Christ is by far the most wonderful of all. Proximity to Him signals a greatness that nothing else, and no matter how lofty, could ever hope to attain. That is the reason the Disciples were what they were, and the reason such is spoken of John.

Consequently, the Prophets, such as Isaiah, who spoke more of His Coming, were quoted more in the New Testament, and Isaiah was quoted more than all. All of this because of the greatness and glory of Christ.

Consequently, those who had the privilege and honor of being near the lowly Galilean are considered to be the greatest of all.

To be sure, nothing they had done would merit such, but strictly their nearness to Christ.

Regrettably and sadly, Israel had the opportunity to experience that greatness as well, for the very thing they wanted, national freedom, they could have had, but only by accepting Christ. He was their Greatness, and they did not know it! He was their Glory, and they did not know it! Just having Him in their midst, was the single greatest thing that could ever happen to any people and for all time, and they did not know it!

Likewise, to have His Glorious Gospel proclaimed is the greatest sound any listener will hear, but most do not know it!

(11) "VERILY I SAY UNTO YOU, AMONG THEM THAT ARE BORN OF WOMEN THERE HATH NOT RISEN A GREATER THAN JOHN THE BAPTIST: NOTWITHSTANDING HE THAT IS LEAST IN THE KINGDOM OF HEAVEN IS GREATER THAN HE."

The phrase, *"Verily I say unto you,"* is meant to proclaim in no uncertain terms exactly who John was. Christ's Word is definitive and omniscient.

The phrase, *"Among them that are born of women there hath not risen a greater than John the Baptist,"* places John in the forefront of the Prophets.

As we have previously asked, why would Jesus say this when John had not written a single Book in the Bible, nor performed a single miracle, nor, at least as far as we know, seen one sick person healed?

When one considers the glowing statements written by the Prophet Isaiah, as well as others, what did Jesus mean by this statement?

Isaiah only pointed toward Christ, and said He was coming, while John the Baptist said, *"Behold the Lamb of God!"* All the other Prophets only pointed toward Him in the distant future, while John announced Him.

The others told what He would be like, but John actually placed his hands upon Him, baptizing Him in the River Jordan.

The idea is that nearness to Christ automatically proclaims greatness, at least if Christ is accepted.

Isaiah and the other Prophets were great because they spoke of Him, but John was greater because he was with Him, and actually touched Him.

Proximity to Christ is what ensured that greatness, and of the original twelve as well!

The phrase, *"Notwithstanding he that is least in the Kingdom of Heaven is greater than he,"* is meant to proclaim the New Covenant.

The idea is, *"The weakest Christian is greater in privileges than the greatest of the Old Testament Saints."*

John the Baptist told of the Great Redemption Plan that was coming, but the actual joys of Redemption he could not know because Jesus had not yet been glorified (Jn. 7:39).

However, allow us to say that the words, *"Greater than he,"* referring to Believers in the New Covenant, only refer to its privileges, which are all God given, and not to anything personally done or accomplished by the individual.

(12) "AND FROM THE DAYS OF JOHN THE BAPTIST UNTIL NOW THE KINGDOM OF HEAVEN SUFFERETH VIOLENCE, AND THE VIOLENT TAKE IT BY FORCE."

The idea of this Scripture concerns the *"violent"* nature of the transition from the Old Covenant to the New. It did not come about easily!

The phrase, *"And from the days of John the Baptist,"* proclaims John introducing the *"Kingdom of Heaven."*

The phrase, *"Until now,"* speaks of Christ Himself, Whose sole purpose and mission was to bring in the New Covenant, which would usher in the *"Kingdom of Heaven."*

The phrase, *"The Kingdom of Heaven suffereth violence,"* speaks of the extremely violent nature of the price Jesus paid to usher in the *"Kingdom of Heaven."*

He was opposed greatly by the Religious Leaders of Israel, who would have killed Him

NOTES

prior to the Crucifixion if He had not been protected by the Holy Spirit.

As well, His violent Death on Calvary was, in fact, *"violent"* beyond comprehension. It took this to bruise the head of Satan (Gen. 3:15).

As well, His Resurrection was violent in nature, in that it had to overthrow death in order to be brought about.

Paul uses violent terminology in exclaiming His Death and Resurrection, by saying, *"Blotting out the handwriting of ordinances that was against us, which was contrary to us, and took it out of the way, nailing it to His Cross;*

"And having spoiled principalities and powers, He made a shew of them openly, triumphing over them in it" (Col. 2:14-15).

If one is to notice, the terminology used by Paul speaks of violent conflict, which was necessary in order that the penalty for sin could be paid, and the price for Redemption could be afforded.

The phrase, *"And the violent take it by force,"* speaks of Christ taking the dominion away from Satan, who had taken it from Adam.

As well, and in a lesser sense, everyone who comes to Christ experiences, at least somewhat, a violent overthrow of the old nature, with the coming in of the new. Satan does not give up his prey easily, and the consequences are violent in nature.

In a narrow sense, it also has reference to Religious Leaders who will not enter in themselves, and attempt to hinder all who would enter.

And the last struggle that is mentioned, which actually never ends in the life of the Christian, is the *"violent"* struggle between the flesh and the spirit. It is called *"warfare"* by the Apostle Paul (II Cor. 10:1-4; I Tim. 1:18).

(13) "FOR ALL THE PROPHETS AND THE LAW PROPHESIED UNTIL JOHN."

This Statement by Christ is meant to proclaim the conclusion of the Old Law of Moses.

In a greater sense, it proclaims that the *"Prophets"* and the *"Law,"* all pointed toward the coming of the New Covenant, i.e., the Kingdom of Heaven.

The phrase, *"Until John,"* is meant to proclaim John as the last Prophet under the Old Covenant. To be sure, Prophets would continue to be called by God, with this office viable even now (Eph. 4:11), still, the Prophets after John would enjoy a *"Kingdom"* already come, instead of *"prophesying"* about one that was to come (Mat. 3:2).

If one is to notice, both John and Jesus talked about the *"Kingdom that was at hand,"* i.e., in the process of being introduced (3:2; 4:17). It would not really be in full bloom until after Calvary and the Resurrection, and even the Day of Pentecost. The full ingredients of it would be given to the Apostle Paul, as is outlined in his Epistles.

(14) "AND IF YE WILL RECEIVE IT, THIS IS ELIAS, WHICH WAS FOR TO COME."

This Passage is freighted with meaning.

The phrase, *"And if ye will receive it,"* has to do with the *"Kingdom of Heaven,"* which Israel, in fact, would not receive.

Had the nation received John, he would have represented Elijah to them, and would have been reckoned by God as Elijah. The pronoun *"it"* should have been translated *"him,"* and referring to John the Baptist.

If Israel had received Christ as their Messiah, the Kingdom of Heaven would have come about at that time, not only in the spiritual sense, which it did come, with tens of millions having it in their hearts, but materially and physically as well!

Of course, the question must be asked that if this had happened, how would Jesus have died on Calvary to redeem man and purchase his Redemption?

Of course, God being God, could have brought it about in any number of ways. However, the question is moot because such did not happen, and, as well, all of the Prophecies proclaimed Israel's rejection of Him, which is exactly what happened.

As well, it should be quickly added, that Israel was definitely not forced into this position by God in order to fulfill Prophecy, but that Prophecy was simply the foreknowledge of God as to what they actually would do, and of their own volition.

The phrase, *"This is Elias* (Elijah), *which was for to come,"* refers to Malachi 4:5-6.

As stated, if Israel had accepted Christ, the Lord would have allowed John to serve as Elijah, even though he was not actually that Prophet, but only represented Elijah in spirit and power (Lk. 1:17).

In fact, Elijah, who was translated that he did not see death (II Ki. 2:11), will come back with Enoch in the middle of the coming Great Tribulation, and will witness and prophesy to Israel for *"a thousand two hundred and three-score days, clothed in sackcloth"* (Rev. 11:3).

During this time, which is even yet to come, the Lord will protect them from their enemies, as they, in thundering tones, pronounce judgment upon Israel and the world.

At the end of that time (about 3 1/2 years), the Lord will allow them to be killed, but will raise them from the dead (Rev. 11:7-12).

(15) "HE THAT HATH EARS TO HEAR, LET HIM HEAR."

This phrase means that he that has had the privilege to hear these words as they came from Christ, will be held responsible to hear, and hear correctly. This solemn injunction occurs some 15 times in the New Testament.

The inference as well is that Israel had the privilege of hearing these words, while the rest of the world, at least at that time, did not. Also, the idea is that they will be held accountable for them.

(16) "BUT WHEREUNTO SHALL I LIKEN THIS GENERATION? IT IS LIKE UNTO CHILDREN SITTING IN THE MARKETS, AND CALLING UNTO THEIR FELLOWS,"

The question, *"But whereunto shall I liken this generation?",* is meant to call attention to the fact that Israel would not *"hear,"* and despite the miracles and works performed by Christ, or the manner in which the Message was presented.

The words, *"This generation,"* are spoken in a very negative sense. In respect to *"This generation,"* Jesus used such words as *"evil and adulterous"* (Mat. 12:39, 45; 16:4; Mk. 8:38; Lk. 11:29); *"faithless and perverse"* (Mat. 17:17; Mk. 9:19; Lk. 9:41); and *"untoward"* (Acts 2:40).

In rejecting Christ, *"This generation"* would not only doom themselves, but all who would follow thereafter, for Israel would be destroyed by Rome a little over 35 years later, and would wander as outcasts around the world for nearly 2,000 years.

The phrase, *"It is like unto children sitting in the markets, and calling unto their fellows,"* is speaking of children playing in public at weddings and funerals, and are disappointed and displeased if the onlookers do not dance or lament.

(17) "AND SAYING, WE HAVE PIPED UNTO YOU, AND YE HAVE NOT DANCED;

WE HAVE MOURNED UNTO YOU, AND YE HAVE NOT LAMENTED."

The idea is that Israel refused to mourn with the Baptist when he demanded Repentance, or to rejoice with Christ when He came healing the sick, performing miracles, and casting out devils. They responded favorably to neither!

(18) "FOR JOHN CAME NEITHER EATING NOR DRINKING, AND THEY SAY, HE HATH A DEVIL."

The idea is that John, who lived in the wilderness, had no social life whatsoever, and, therefore, nothing that Israel could point to in a negative way respecting his lifestyle. And yet Israel said of him, *"He hath a devil."*

(19) "THE SON OF MAN CAME EATING AND DRINKING, AND THEY SAY, BEHOLD A MAN GLUTTONOUS, AND A WINEBIBBER, A FRIEND OF PUBLICANS AND SINNERS. BUT WISDOM IS JUSTIFIED OF HER CHILDREN."

The phrase, *"The Son of Man came eating and drinking,"* refers to the lifestyle of Jesus, which was totally opposite to that of John.

As stated, John's lifestyle was one of absolutely no social life, and for a purpose and reason. His lifestyle was meant to portray the spiritual condition of Israel. In other words, Israel should have separated herself from her activities in mourning and travail respecting their spiritual condition. But she did not!

Jesus came, presenting the Gospel of the Kingdom, which should have brought great joy, and, likewise, His lifestyle of mixing and mingling with the people exemplified His Mission.

If the people had properly lamented their own sinfulness and separated themselves in mourning and repentance, as the lifestyle of John proclaimed, there would have been great rejoicing throughout the entirety of Israel, upon the Advent of Christ. But, regrettably, they did neither!

The phrase, *"And they say,"* and pertaining to the balance of the Scripture, is what Christ's enemies said of Him, and not what was actually true.

The phrase, *"Behold a man gluttonous, and a winebibber, a friend of publicans and sinners,"* was only partially true. Jesus was not *"gluttonous,"* or a *"winebibber,"* but He definitely was a *"friend of publicans and sinners,"* and, thank God He was!

NOTES

Israel said of John, *"He hath a devil,"* and that was not true, and, as well, they said things of Christ which were not true.

Being a *"friend of publicans and sinners,"* did not, and by the greatest stretch of the imagination, mean that Jesus condoned their sin, but that He loved them despite their sin.

The phrase, *"But wisdom is justified of her children,"* means that wisdom justified both courses, that of John and Christ. In other words, the Holy Spirit was appealing to them in two totally different ways, with both ways being right. However, Israel rejected both.

(20) "THEN BEGAN HE TO UPBRAID THE CITIES WHEREIN MOST OF HIS MIGHTY WORKS WERE DONE, BECAUSE THEY REPENTED NOT:"

The idea is that the Holy Spirit devised every means possible to touch Israel, all to no avail! Likewise, the same manner in which He dealt with Israel, He also deals with individuals. He speaks to them one way and then the other, being a wise fisherman of men, but, tragically, most, as Israel of old, refuse and reject. That is the reason for that which Christ will now say.

The phrase, *"Then began He to upbraid the cities,"* refers to those near Capernaum where He had made His Headquarters, and where His *"mighty works"* of miracles and healings, and even the dead being raised, were performed. It harks back to the Prophecy of Isaiah; *"The land of Zabulon, and the land of Nephthalim, by the way of the sea, beyond Jordan, Galilee of the Gentiles;*

"The people which sat in darkness saw great light; and to them which sat in the region and shadow of death light is sprung up" (Mat. 4:15-16).

Sadly, they rejected the Light!

The phrase, *"Wherein most of His mighty works were done,"* has to do, as stated, with His miracles.

Each miracle and each healing was a witness to the people of the claims of Christ, and the majesty of His Person. There was no excuse for them not knowing He was the Messiah. Consequently, that which was done, the miracles, was not only, and as we have stated, for the individuals who needed the miracles, but, as well, was meant to serve as a sign for all of Israel as to Who Christ actually was.

The phrase, *"Because they repented not,"* has a reference far greater than that which appears on the surface.

Repentance is far more than confessing before the Lord something that is wrong, but, instead, confessing before the Lord what we actually are. Israel would not confess the wrong they were doing, because they would not confess the wrong they were.

Repentance does not so much speak of an action, as much as it does a state — the state of one's being.

The Publican exemplified this of which Jesus was speaking, when he said, *"God be merciful to me a sinner."* It was not so hard for him to do this, because he was a sinner and knew it.

However, on the other hand, the Pharisee did not even remotely think of himself as such, when, in reality, he was a sinner just as much, if not more so than the Publican.

This was wrapped up not so much in the actions of the Pharisee, nearly as much as his state, which was one of self-righteousness (Lk. 18:9-14).

When the word, *"repentance,"* is used respecting the modern Church, most little understand it.

Actually, most Charismatics do not even believe in repentance, claiming it to be an Old Testament Doctrine which has no validity in the New Covenant. They claim that repentance has no place in the New Covenant, because repentance admits that something is wrong, and nothing can be wrong, they say, in the new creation man.

And if, by chance, something is wrong, it has nothing to do with repentance, they would say, it simply being a matter of a wrong or bad confession.

As Jesus said, *"They do not know the Scriptures,"* and as I might say, *"Nor the depravity of man, even the new creation man, if he ceases for a moment to depend wholly on God."*

Paul said concerning repentance, and as is obvious, under the New Covenant, *"But now commandeth all men every where to repent"* (Acts 17:30).

He also said, *"Testifying both to the Jews, and also to the Greeks, repentance toward God, and Faith toward our Lord Jesus Christ"* (Acts 20:21).

To be sure, *"repentance,"* is definitely an

NOTES

Old Testament Doctrine, but, as well, it is a New Testament Doctrine!

When repentance is spoken of, many modern Believers automatically think of some particular sin or sins, with most concluding that they are not guilty of such, and, therefore, in no need of repentance.

However, as stated, repentance definitely does deal with acts of sin, but even more so it deals with one's spiritual state.

By that, we speak of complacency, lethargy, self-righteousness, lukewarmness, a lack of burden for the lost, etc., of which most of the modern Church is plagued. But yet, most of the modern Church, as Israel of old, sees no need for repentance.

(21) "WOE UNTO THEE, CHORAZIN! WOE UNTO THEE, BETHSAIDA! FOR IF THE MIGHTY WORKS, WHICH WERE DONE IN YOU, HAD BEEN DONE IN TYRE AND SIDON, THEY WOULD HAVE REPENTED LONG AGO IN SACKCLOTH AND ASHES."

Why would Christ say *"Woe"* to the cities of *"Chorazin and Bethsaida"*? And why would He compare them to *"Tyre and Sidon"*?

The answer is obvious! Christ had personally ministered in these cities, even with *"mighty works"* being performed in them, while He had not ministered in *"Tyre and Sidon."* As a result, there was far greater opportunity for these cities in Galilee to repent, than *"Tyre and Sidon"* which had not had such visitation. In fact, and as Jesus said, if *"Tyre and Sidon"* had seen such miracles, and had such visitation, *"they would have repented long ago in sackcloth and ashes."*

Such tells us that the entrance of the Gospel never leaves one static, or, more plainly said, in the same condition as at the beginning. The person is either better or worse; better, if the Gospel is accepted, but worse, if it is rejected. It is like the sun which softens wax, but, at the same time, hardens clay. The result is not in the sun, but in the material.

This is the reason that America is in such acute danger at present. This nation, and without a doubt, has experienced the Gospel more than any nation in the world. Tragically, it has rejected the Gospel, which is now resulting in a spiritual hardness, exactly as the cities of Galilee.

(22) "BUT I SAY UNTO YOU, IT SHALL BE MORE TOLERABLE FOR TYRE AND

SIDON AT THE DAY OF JUDGMENT, THAN FOR YOU."

Two things are here said:

1. The words, *"More tolerable,"* tell us that there will be degrees of punishment, and because some sins are worse than others. The sin of rejecting Christ when having the opportunity to accept Him, is the worst of all!

2. There is a coming *"Day of Judgment,"* and despite the denial by the modernists and unbelievers. At that *"Day of Judgment,"* the people of these cities here mentioned by Christ, along with all others who have had opportunity, and greatly so, to hear the Gospel, but rejected it, will be judged far more harshly than the people of the cities of the world who have had little opportunity to accept Christ.

The phrase, *"Than for you,"* is emphatic respecting the pronoun *"you."* In the Mind of God, the *"Judgment"* has already been pronounced.

(23) "AND THOU, CAPERNAUM, WHICH ART EXALTED UNTO HEAVEN, SHALT BE BROUGHT DOWN TO HELL: FOR IF THE MIGHTY WORKS, WHICH HAVE BEEN DONE IN THEE, HAD BEEN DONE IN SODOM, IT WOULD HAVE REMAINED UNTIL THIS DAY."

The phrase, *"And thou, Capernaum,"* is once again emphatic, reserving this city for the worst Judgment of all.

Capernaum had the unique dignity of being the Lord's Ministry Headquarters. Consequently, it was chosen thusly by the Holy Spirit, and, accordingly, was the most favored spot on earth.

Nazareth was the family home; but there was no room for Him there, for not only did they not want Him, but His Own family did not believe in Him (Jn. 7:5), and reckoned Him to not be of sound mind (Mk. 3:21). But He, as wisdom, was vindicated by His Children.

Capernaum rejected Him exactly as Chorazin and Bethsaida.

The phrase, *"Which art exalted unto Heaven,"* refers to its great prosperity by the Sea of Galilee, and, therefore, a city to which many people looked.

The idea is that it was *"exalted"* because of its prosperity, and not because of Who resided in its midst, namely Christ.

Is it any different than most cities today, which have had a visitation of the Lord?

Capernaum did not know Who or What was in its midst, even as plainly visible as He was, and, likewise, the Righteous who live in certain cities today are not known by the city proper.

The phrase, *"Shall be brought down to hell,"* has two meanings:

1. The Romans, a few years later, destroyed all these cities by the Lake, with the exception of Tiberius. Consequently, and according to the prediction of Christ, none presently remain, with the exception of Tiberius.

2. Most of its inhabitants went to *"hell,"* are there today, and will be in the Lake of Fire forever. As well, their *"hell"* will be more horrible than most, and because the Son of God was in their very midst and they did not know it, or if they did, they purposely rejected Him, which actually was the case!

"Sodom" is here used, referring to Capernaum, where *"Tyre and Sidon"* had been used respecting the other cities. The reason being, that Jesus made His Headquarters in Capernaum, and, therefore, they had the greatest opportunity of all for Salvation.

By comparison, *"Sodom"* only had the testimony of Lot, Abraham's nephew. At any rate, Jesus said that if greater testimony had been given in Sodom, it would not have been destroyed, because enough people would have repented to have stopped the Judgment. As it was, there were not even ten Righteous in the city, and considering its terrible sin of sodomy as well as other great sins, Judgment took it away.

This shows how important the Gospel is to any area. That is the reason we labor day and night to fulfill the mission God has called us to do, to take the Gospel to the world by Television and Crusades. Actually, the Lord has given me a specific call to do this very thing.

(24) "BUT I SAY UNTO YOU, THAT IT SHALL BE MORE TOLERABLE FOR THE LAND OF SODOM IN THE DAY OF JUDGMENT, THAN FOR THEE."

To be classified below Sodom is the worst thing that could be said of any city or people. Considering that Sodom was so bad that the Lord had to take it out by extreme Judgment, one is made to understand the severity with which God looked at Capernaum.

If we properly understand that, then we more properly understand God's dealings with the human family, and the Church.

To be sure, no one in Capernaum would have even dreamed of making such a comparison that Capernaum was more evil than Sodom, which was guilty of the most heinous of sins. There were two reasons that God looked at Capernaum, as the other cities mentioned, in the capacity that He did!

1. Mighty works of Righteousness were carried out in them, and by no less than Christ, which afforded them a wide open door of opportunity, but rejected.

2. Self-righteousness: Not only was this the sin of these cities of Galilee, but, as well, it is the sin of the modern Church.

In the eye of these Jews, they were, at least in their minds, God's chosen people, the people of the Prophets, and had given the world the Word of God. (Never mind that they killed many of the Prophets, and rejected the Word!)

At the present, the Pharisees had heavily enmeshed Israel in a blanket of religion. They were minute in every aspect of the Law of Moses, or at least their twisting of it, and, in their thinking, were close to God, and were, therefore, Righteous and Holy. However, the Lord concluded them as being the very opposite, even so bad that they were worse than Sodom.

What an indictment!

And yet, in speaking of the cities in America and Canada, would His indictment be any less at the present?

Capernaum, as well as the other cities in question, never really saw themselves as God saw them. And that is the blight of the Church!

A short time ago, at our own Church, Family Worship Center in Baton Rouge, Louisiana, in a Sunday morning service, a young lady, who was, by and large, a stranger to the Church, came during the Altar Call. One look at her, and one could pretty much tell that she had seen some difficult times. I speak of sin and wrongdoing in the eyes of God! Nevertheless, she wept before God, crying out to Him with bitter tears, to which He responded immediately.

Sitting in the Church that morning were hundreds of Believers, who were not at all guilty of some of the sins this girl was possibly guilty of, but yet, in the Eyes of God, I wonder if His thoughts toward some of them were not the same as His thoughts toward Capernaum! I form no judgment, or even opinion, but I do ask the question.

NOTES

The sins of complacency, lethargy, and self-righteousness, of which many of us are afflicted, must be terrible in the Eyes of God, possibly even worse than sins of immorality!

(25) "AT THAT TIME JESUS ANSWERED AND SAID, I THANK THEE, O FATHER, LORD OF HEAVEN AND EARTH, BECAUSE THOU HAST HID THESE THINGS FROM THE WISE AND PRUDENT, AND HAST REVEALED THEM UNTO BABES."

The phrase, *"At that time Jesus answered and said,"* is probably a reference to one or several people nearby, who agreed with what He had said about Capernaum and the other cities.

In answer to their statement of agreement, if, in fact, that is what happened, He will, in turn, praise the Lord.

The phrase, *"I thank Thee, O Father, Lord of Heaven and earth,"* speaks of relationship and the owning of the *"Lord"* as the Creator of all things, whether in Heaven or earth.

The phrase, *"Because Thou hast hid these things from the wise and prudent,"* concerns a judicial judgment on the Religious Leaders of Israel who had the opportunity to hear and understand, but refused to do so.

Their refusal caused the Lord to deepen the darkness. If one wills Righteousness, more Righteousness is willed unto him. Conversely, if one wills unrighteousness, further unrighteousness is willed as well!

The phrase, *"And hast revealed them unto babes,"* reveals that Salvation is not a matter of education but of Revelation. All the elaborate machinery of man's religious ceremonial and all his self-determination at Righteousness avails nothing!

The Lord *"revealed"* these Great Truths unto the simple folk, simply because they *"believed."*

(26) "EVEN SO, FATHER: FOR SO IT SEEMED GOOD IN THY SIGHT."

It was *"good"* and because it was fair and equitable to all. Had the presentation of these great Truths been dependent on education, the far greater majority of the world would have been excluded. Therefore, the presentation of these great Truths, and by the God of Truth, was carried out solely according to the state of one's heart regarding such Truths.

That is the reason the Holy Spirit said, *"For the Lord seeth not as man seeth; for man looketh on the outward appearance, but the Lord looketh on the heart"* (I Sam. 16:7).

(27) "ALL THINGS ARE DELIVERED UNTO ME OF MY FATHER: AND NO MAN KNOWETH THE SON, BUT THE FATHER; NEITHER KNOWETH ANY MAN THE FATHER, SAVE THE SON, AND HE TO WHOMSOEVER THE SON WILL REVEAL HIM."

The tenor of this verse, as important as it is, is that only those to whom the Son wills to reveal the Father possesses a saving knowledge of God, and He wills to reveal Himself to the sinful and guilty.

In fact, all are sinful and guilty, but all will not admit it, as Israel, and, consequently, there is no revelation for them.

The phrase, *"All things are delivered unto Me of My Father,"* coincides with 28:18, where Jesus said, *"All power is given unto Me in Heaven and in earth."*

This is done because Jesus is the Member of the Godhead, Who came from Heaven, paying the price, and, thereby, effecting the Redemption of mankind.

Paul spoke of this when he said, *"Wherefore God also hath highly exalted Him, and given Him a Name which is above every name"* (Phil. 2:9-11).

The *"All things"* not only mean that Salvation is delivered unto Christ to give unto men, but, as well, the Judgment of men is delivered unto Christ. Now, He is the Saviour; then, He will be the Judge (Jn. 5:22).

The phrase, *"And no man knoweth the Son, but the Father,"* speaks of His being an eternal member of the Godhead. In other words, Jesus is God!

The phrase means that no man knew Him fully in all the mystery and glory of His Divine Personality, save only God the Father. The word, *"knoweth,"* means to *"fully comprehend,"* in which no man has fully comprehended the Son, but, as stated, the Father.

The phrase, *"Neither knoweth any man the Father, save the Son,"* says the same thing in reverse.

The only One, Who fully *"comprehends"* the Father, is His Son, the Lord Jesus Christ.

These statements are made for many reasons, but primarily, at least at that time, because of Israel claiming their great knowledge of God, and the Pharisees boasting that their

tradition came from God, although through many hands. Christ rather claimed to have received His Revelation from God Himself. The transmission was always immediate, with no links between the Giver and the Receiver.

Actually, the Revelation of God as Father was introduced by Jesus. He often spoke of God as *"My Father in Heaven."*

In addition, in His public and private supplication to God, Jesus addressed God as Father, as is recorded in 11:26.

This claim that He had a Father-Son relationship with God was shocking to the Religious Leaders of Israel. When Jesus spoke of God as His Father, the Jews (John's term for the Religious Leaders) *"tried all the harder to kill Him."*

Jesus not only violated their traditions, *"but He was even calling God His Own Father, making Himself equal with God"* (Jn. 5:18).

RELATIONSHIP

Many of the things Jesus taught explored the relationship between the Father and the Son. When Jesus claimed, *"I and the Father are One"* (Jn. 10:30), He aroused hostility. Rather than accept His claim, the Jews made attempts to stone Him because, they told Him, *"You, a mere man, claim to be God"* (Jn. 10:33). Yet the claims of Jesus were authenticated over and over again. The Oneness existing between Jesus and the Father was expressed in Christ's Words and in His miraculous Works (Jn. 14:10-11).

THAT WHICH JESUS DID

God the Father was at work in all Jesus did so that Christ perfectly expressed the Will and Character of the Father (Jn. 5:17-23). The Father and Jesus were One in Authority and Power. Jesus had the Divine right to judge and the Divine power to give life (Jn. 5:21-22). Pre-existent as God with the Father (Jn. 1:1-5; 8:56-58), the Son is One with the Father as an object of our love and worship (Jn. 14:21-23).

HIS STATEMENTS

The statements made by Jesus and recorded in the Gospels affirm the Son's identity with the Father. Jesus could say, *"Any one who has seen Me has seen the Father"* (Jn. 14:9), for *"I am in the Father and the Father is in Me"* (Jn. 14:10).

Jesus fully and perfectly expresses the very character of God the Father. And yet, Jesus remains as the Second Person of the Trinity, distinct from the Father. Jesus said the Father is greater than He (Jn. 14:28), portrayed Himself as sent by the Father (Jn. 5:36-37; 6:57; 8:16, 18, 42; 12:49), and lived His Life on earth according to the Father's Will (Mat. 26:39-42; Jn. 5:36; 12:49).

While the existence of one God as a Trinity of Father, Son, and Holy Spirit, involves concepts beyond man's total comprehension, what is most important is that in the coming of the Son we have a stunning revelation of the fact that God is Father. This could only come through Jesus. As Christ said, *"No one knows the Son except the Father, and no one knows the Father except the Son and those to who the Son chooses to reveal Him."*

In presenting Himself as the Son, Jesus presented an aspect of God completely unknown before the Incarnation. He spoke of God as His Father — the One they claimed as their God — saying to the Jewish Leaders, *"Though you do not know Him, I know Him"* (Jn. 8:54-55).

Only in Jesus do we learn that God is Father. Only in seeing God as Father do we begin to realize the intimacy of the relationship that can exist between the Believer and the Lord.

(The notes on God the Father as related by Christ, were derived from the writings of Lawrence O. Richards.)

The phrase, *"And He to whomsoever the Son will reveal Him,"* is, as stated, the sinful and guilty. The Scripture is clear, that all who feel they have a claim on God, are excluded. In other words, one comes not by pedigree, works, status, position, or merit, but, instead, by exclaiming what one truly is, *"sinful and guilty."* Then the Son will *"reveal"* the Father to that person.

That is the reason the entirety of the Plan of Salvation is based upon Grace, which extends Mercy, and not on works. However, such is very difficult for man to accept! Man loves to point to the good things he has done, and the bad things he has not done, thinking that such earns merit with God. Such are mistaken, and because of such thinking, no revelation from God comes to them, as no revelation came to the Jews.

They thought themselves to be Righteous and Holy, and, thereby, called the Gentiles

"dogs." Jesus responded to that by saying, *"But the children of the Kingdom shall be cast out into outer darkness"* (Mat. 8:12).

Consequently, self-righteousness is lethal indeed!

As well, the present attitude of many who are quick to claim their *"Kingdom rights,"* and in a manner which hints at self-worth, are the exact opposite of the Beatitude, *"Blessed are the poor in spirit . . ."* (Mat. 5:3).

(28) "COME UNTO ME, ALL YE THAT LABOUR AND ARE HEAVY LADEN, AND I WILL GIVE YOU REST."

Verses 28-30 proclaim the first recorded general invitation to all men. It is very similar to the last recorded one (Rev. 22:17).

The phrase, *"Come unto Me,"* is meant by Jesus to reveal Himself as the Giver of Salvation.

The phrase, *"All ye that labour and are heavy laden,"* refers to the subject matter of the last phrase of the previous verse.

Men, then, as now, were *"laboring"* to enter the Kingdom of God, attempting to earn Salvation by their works. As a result, they were *"heavy laden"* in their spiritual toil of finding Righteousness through legalism (Rom. 10:2-3). They were burdened under the Pharisaic rules and regulations, which were not Scriptural, and as Jesus later said, *"They bind heavy burdens and grievous to be borne, and lay them on men's shoulders"* (Mat. 23:4).

The phrase, *"And I will give you rest,"* means rest from all of these man-made laws, with the word, *"rest,"* actually meaning *"vacation."*

In other words, He was saying that He would give them a vacation from all this legalism, as well as guilt and sin.

Religion is a sorry thing! And that is what the Jews had done to the Law of Moses. They had added so much to it, that it was referred to by Paul as the *"Jews' religion"* (Gal. 1:13-14).

Consequently, the biggest word in religion, of which much of Christianity, as well as its Jewish counterpart, has degenerated into, is the word *"do!"* In other words, *"do"* this, or don't *"do"* that!

By contrast, the greatest word in True Bible Christianity is *"done,"* meaning that there is nothing else to *"do"* except believe, because all has been *"done"* by Christ.

(29) "TAKE MY YOKE UPON YOU, AND LEARN OF ME; FOR I AM MEEK AND LOWLY

IN HEART: AND YE SHALL FIND REST UNTO YOUR SOULS."

The phrase, *"Take My yoke upon you,"* actually refers to the exchange of yokes, from that of the Law and legalism to that of Christ. However, there is a vast difference in *"His yoke,"* as He will momentarily say.

This *"yoke"* consists of accepting the Divine Will and so imitating Christ, and working in harmony with that Will, which will bring about the promised rest.

The phrase, *"And learn of Me,"* is the key to all that Christ is, and does. It is tragic, but even most Christians learn of everything else other than *"Him."* He, Alone, was what He claimed to teach. Inasmuch as He is God, there is no limit to what can be learned. Also, it must be learned by the heart before it really can be learned by the head.

The phrase, *"For I am meek and lowly in heart,"* expresses the only personal thing Jesus ever said of Himself. Consequently, this, of all things, is what we are to learn.

The *"meek and lowly"* spirit is the very opposite of the spirit of the world, which is pomp and strut. To be sure, how can one learn *"meekness and lowliness of heart"*?

The answer is found in the first three Beatitudes.

First of all, Jesus said, and as we expressed in the Commentary on Matthew 5, *"Blessed are the poor in spirit,"* which refers to the acknowledgement of one's moral and spiritual poverty. This is not easy to do, and especially considering that it is by and large the opposite of that which is mostly taught at present.

The second Beatitude is, *"Blessed are they that mourn,"* which speaks of mourning over one's faults, flaws, inconsistencies, and the *"poverty of spirit"* of the first Beatitude.

The third Beatitude says, *"Blessed are the meek,"* which means that which will automatically come, if one has a proper poverty of spirit, and mourns over that poverty of spirit. *"Meekness"* will be the natural result!

Now, it must be quickly stated that Christ was not plagued, as we, by a *"spiritual and moral poverty."* However, His *"meekness and lowliness of heart"* was even more pronounced because of that.

On our behalf, He *"Made Himself of no*

reputation, and took upon Him the form of a servant, and was made in the likeness of men.

"And being found in fashion as a man, He humbled Himself, and became obedient unto death, even the death of the Cross" (Phil. 2:7-8).

That is the example we are to follow.

However, it is very difficult for man to do such, and, more particularly, religious man, simply because when Adam and Eve lost God-consciousness due to the Fall, in its place they received self-consciousness. As a result, self has been boosted and boasted from the very beginning. Unchristlike self is the seed-bed of all sin. Therefore, it is hard for man to humble *"self,"* admitting that he desperately needs a Redeemer, and that Redeemer Alone is Christ.

As well, religious man, as Israel of old, has an even harder struggle because he thinks that surely all his religious good works earn him some merit with God. To be told that all must be thrown out, even admitting that he is spiritually bankrupt, is difficult indeed! Consequently, it is easier for the *"thieves and harlots"* to do so, than the religious man (Mat. 21:31-32).

The phrase, *"And ye shall find rest unto your souls,"* refers to the cessation of labor in attempting to earn our Salvation, and trusting totally in Christ. When this is done, the *"rest"* or *"vacation"* takes place in our repose in Christ.

To this *"rest,"* Christ calls all His servants — that is, to the yoke of full submission to the Father's Will — willing to be meek and lowly in heart — willing not to be self-willed and proud, but to occupy the lowest place and to accept seeming failure as a true donation of all things.

Nothing can overthrow the servant who takes that place; it is the place of perfect rest to the heart.

As an example, in the perfection of His Faith in the Father's Love, and of His (Christ's) submission to the Father's Will, standing amid the ruins of His Mission, as it seemed, yet He still proclaimed, *"All things are delivered unto Me"* (vs. 27).

It is the privilege of the servant, when confronted with apparent failure, as well, to imitate the Faith and Triumph of his Master. For in the total fulfillment of all things, there is no real failure for the Child of God. The way is a way of *"rest,"* and whatever direction it may lead, because Christ is being followed.

(30) "FOR MY YOKE IS EASY, AND MY BURDEN IS LIGHT."

The *"yoke"* and *"burden"* of Judaism were extremely heavy, as all religion is heavy; however, by contrast, and even though He does have a *"yoke,"* it is *"easy,"* with its *"burden"* pronounced as *"light."*

Even though He asks something of us, actually, the entirety of our life, still, once submitted to His *"yoke,"* we will find it is not difficult, as many think, but rather *"easy."*

Also, one immediately finds that even though He does demand things of us, still, *"His Commandments are not grievous"* (I Jn. 5:3).

If what He asks seems to be hard, it is because we have made it hard. In other words, we have added more *"yoke"* and *"burden"* of our own, or else others! Regrettably, this has probably happened to all of us at one time or the other.

The reason being is that we have not properly *"learned of Him."* To do so, more than all, means to learn the Word of God, which will give God's Divine Will, which will enable the Believer to truly take a *"vacation."*

Hallelujah!

In doing God's Will, one will find that living for God, is truly a *"vacation."*

CHAPTER 12

(1) "AT THAT TIME JESUS WENT ON THE SABBATH DAY THROUGH THE CORN; AND HIS DISCIPLES WERE AN HUNGERED, AND BEGAN TO PLUCK THE EARS OF CORN AND TO EAT."

This Chapter will portray the animosity of the Religious Leaders of Israel intensifying toward Christ. Tremendous miracles will be performed, but yet ignored by the Pharisees, with them entering into the darkness of blaspheming the Holy Spirit.

Rejected by the nation as Messiah the King, He now presented Himself to them as Elohim the Creator of the Sabbath (vss. 1-14), and as Jehovah the Redeemer (vss. 22-37), and Saviour (vss. 38-50) of men.

The phrase, *"At that time Jesus went on the Sabbath Day through the corn,"* referred to a distance of approximately two-thirds of a

NOTES

mile, which constituted the length one could travel under the Mosaic Law on the Sabbath Day (2,000 cubits).

As well, the word, *"corn,"* should have been translated either *"wheat"* or *"barley,"* for Indian corn, as we know it, was not then grown in Israel.

The phrase, *"And His Disciples were an hungered, and began to pluck the ears of corn and to eat,"* was permitted according to Deuteronomy 23:25. This was probably the time of the wheat harvest.

(2) "BUT WHEN THE PHARISEES SAW IT, THEY SAID UNTO HIM, BEHOLD, THY DISCIPLES DO THAT WHICH IS NOT LAWFUL TO DO UPON THE SABBATH DAY."

The phrase, *"But when the Pharisees saw it, they said unto Him,"* proclaims these Religious Leaders by now, watching every move made by Christ and His Disciples. They dogged His steps, attempting to find something of which they could accuse Him. Neither the miracles He performed, nor the powerful and gracious words that came from His mouth, moved them at all!

Why did they hate Him so?

They were Disciples of Satan, and, as such, they were opposed to all He did, for He, the epitome of Righteousness, was by nature opposed to the epitome of evil, and it Him! Paul calls such *"Satan's ministers,"* and so they are (II Cor. 11:15).

Satan's greatest area of opposition to the True Body of Christ, and, therefore, to the Work of God, is the apostate Church.

And what is the chief sign of the apostate Church?

Its chief sign is its opposition to the True Child of God, and, therefore, the True Work of God.

Regrettably, many, if not most, Christians are so shallow in the Word of God, that they little know which is which, the True Church or the apostate Church?

The phrase, *"Behold, thy Disciples do that which is not lawful to do upon the Sabbath Day,"* was not Scripturally correct. The phrase, *"Not lawful,"* applied to their man-made laws, and not to the Law of Moses. By now, the Pharisees had added a little over 600 laws to the original Law of Moses, consequently, making it non-effective by their tradition (Mk. 7:7-8).

The entirety of their man-made salvation, which, in reality, was no salvation at all, was in keeping these rituals they had devised themselves. In Truth, they did not know God. Adding to the Word of God or taking away from it, is always the action of apostates.

(3) "BUT HE SAID UNTO THEM, HAVE YE NOT READ WHAT DAVID DID, WHEN HE WAS AN HUNGERED, AND THEY THAT WERE WITH HIM;"

This action of His Disciples was the first that revealed the nature of His Person and of His Authority to open and close dispensations.

The phrase, *"But He said unto them,"* proclaims His custom of referring these critics to the Word of God.

The question, *"Have ye not read what David did . . . ?",* refers them to I Samuel 21:1-7.

His defense was that if David the King when rejected ate the shewbread, the Son of David when in a similar case might enjoy a similar privilege.

The phrase, *"When he was an hungered, and they that were with him,"* places David's situation and His as similar.

David was fleeing from Saul as this demon-possessed reprobate was attempting to kill him. Likewise, Jesus was being hounded by the demon-influenced Pharisees. The same spirit that was in Saul was in them.

The question, *"Have ye not read?",* was asked by the Lord on six occasions, in attempts to pull them away from their traditions to the Word of God (Mat. 12:3; 12:5; 19:4; 21:16; 21:42; 22:31-32).

(4) "HOW HE ENTERED INTO THE HOUSE OF GOD, AND DID EAT THE SHEWBREAD, WHICH WAS NOT LAWFUL FOR HIM TO EAT, NEITHER FOR THEM WHICH WERE WITH HIM, BUT ONLY FOR THE PRIESTS?"

The lesson that Jesus taught is obvious, at least to those who are truly sincere concerning the Word of God.

In fact, David did break the Mosaic Law in two ways: A. By *"entering into the House of God"* (the area he, not being a Priest, was not supposed to enter.); and, B. By *"eating the Shewbread"* which was to be eaten only by the Priests.

By mentioning this, was Jesus sanctioning the breaking of the Mosaic Law?

No! It was only a ceremonial law which David broke, and not a moral law.

The lesson being taught is that inasmuch as David and his men were physically destitute because of a lack of food, the eating of this bread was permissible, and because they were of more worth than the bread. Actually, the *"Shewbread,"* under the old Mosaic Law, was a Type of Christ, Who came into the world to save man. Therefore, the eating of it by David and his men was a portrayal of this Salvation.

Tragically, the Pharisees could not see this great Truth, because they had no regard for what the Law intended, but only for its letter.

(5) "OR HAVE YE NOT READ IN THE LAW, HOW THAT ON THE SABBATH DAYS THE PRIESTS IN THE TEMPLE PROFANE THE SABBATH, AND ARE BLAMELESS?"

The idea of this verse is that the Priests did as much work, if not more, on the Sabbath Day in their preparing the Sacrifices, plus other duties, as any other day! And yet they were not accused of breaking the Law.

Why?

The duty of the Priest was to serve as a mediator between God and men. Consequently, their carrying out these duties on the Sabbath Day was more important than obeying the strict letter of the Law. Actually, they were commanded in the Law of Moses to do these things on the Sabbath, and because of its greater significance.

Jesus will once again point to His Messiahship by likening Himself to the Priests, which He actually was. He is our Great High Priest (Heb. 4:14).

In this role as Great High Priest, which the Pharisees denied, Jesus would do many things on the Sabbath, but He did these things to save men exactly as the Priests of old!

(6) "BUT I SAY UNTO YOU, THAT IN THIS PLACE IS ONE GREATER THAN THE TEMPLE."

The phrase, *"But I say unto you,"* is once again meant to portray the Truth of the Word of God.

The phrase, *"That in this place is One greater than the Temple,"* is speaking of Himself.

Actually, the Temple plus all its accouterments was a Type of Christ. The Antitype is, out of necessity, greater than the Type. As the Antitype, He fulfilled all that the Type pointed to, and was of necessity *"greater."*

In fact, He was a greater *"Temple"*; a greater *"Prophet"* (vs. 41); and a greater *"King"* (vs. 42); i.e., God Himself.

Lest one misunderstand, this statement has no reference to the idea of breaking the Law of Moses, because of Who He was, but, instead, to point to the very purpose of the Temple, which was a Type of Christ, and which was constructed that man may have communion with God, and, as a consequence, be forgiven of his sins, etc.

The Jews had lost all sight of what the Temple or the Sacrifices were for. The entire purpose of its being was to point men to One Who was coming, Who could truly save. Instead, the Jews, having lost sight of this Truth, in effect, began to worship the Temple. Thus it became an idol, and they idolaters!

That spirit then is identical to the spirit now of men losing sight of what their Religious Denominations are supposed to be all about — the pointing of men to Christ. Instead, the *"Church"* itself is worshiped, with it, as of old, becoming an idol and they idolaters!

(7) "BUT IF YE HAD KNOWN WHAT THIS MEANETH, I WILL HAVE MERCY, AND NOT SACRIFICE, YE WOULD NOT HAVE CONDEMNED THE GUILTLESS."

The phrase, *"But if ye had known what this meaneth, I will have Mercy, and not Sacrifice,"* is stated again, as it was in 9:13.

The Jews had placed their Salvation in the Sacrifice itself, instead of Who it pointed to, namely Christ.

The entire act of Sacrifice was an act of Mercy on the part of God, in that it pointed to Christ and what He would do at Calvary, and, therefore, made a way for man to have his sins forgiven, and for peace to be established between him and God.

The Jews lost sight of this, thinking that the ritual of Sacrifice itself afforded Salvation. It is the same with the modern Church.

The Church within itself contains no Salvation, as the Sacrifices within themselves contained no Salvation. When the Church degenerates to legalism, as the Sacrifices of old, it no longer serves its purpose of pointing people to Christ.

The phrase, *"Ye would not have condemned*

the guiltless," refers to them condemning Christ, Who was *"guiltless."*

They condemned Him because they did not know Who He was and because of their unbelief, and, as well, they had lost all understanding as to what the Law of Moses was all about.

As well, much of the modern Church in the making of its rules and regulations, apart from the Bible, as well, *"condemns the guiltless."* While it is true that no man in the strict sense of the word is *"guiltless,"* still, if the Word of God is fully obeyed, with sins properly confessed and, thereby, washed and cleansed, God looks at that individual as *"guiltless."* The Church is to do likewise, but seldom does! As such, it condemns itself.

Paul said as much when he demanded that the Church at Corinth forgive one of its erring members who had truly repented. In I Corinthians 5 the man was on trial, while now the Church is on trial, and as Paul said, *"That I might know the proof of you, whether you be obedient in all things"* (II Cor. 2:6-11).

(8) "FOR THE SON OF MAN IS LORD EVEN OF THE SABBATH DAY."

The entire complexion of this verse presents Jesus as the Messiah, and, therefore, as the Son of God, i.e., *"Son of Man."*

The phrase, *"For the Son of Man is Lord,"* in effect, means that all the things the Pharisees were discussing, such as the Sabbath, etc., were, in reality, the creation of Christ, and for the very purpose of pointing men to Himself.

The Sabbath was a token of the Covenant between Jehovah and the nation (Ezek. 20:12-20). Hence the Son of Man had power over it. If His dominion over the Sabbath was denied, then was the Covenant destroyed, because He was the Giver of the Sabbath and the Maker of the Covenant.

These Passages, as is obvious, are extremely significant inasmuch as they are intended to draw the eyes of men away from religious ritual, no matter how Scriptural it may be, to its intended purpose and, thereby, to Christ. Jesus is the focal point of all. When He ceases to be, there is no Salvation.

An example is *"Water Baptism"* and *"The Lord's Supper."* Both are Scriptural and, thereby, sacred ordinances; however, there is no Salvation in the water or the cup. There is Salvation only in that, or, more preferable,

Who they represent, namely Christ! And yet, millions of people think by being baptized in water or taking the Lord's Supper, that such ensures their Salvation!

In doing so, they have done the same as the Pharisees of old.

(9) "AND WHEN HE WAS DEPARTED THENCE, HE WENT INTO THEIR SYNAGOGUE:"

The words, *"And when He was departed thence,"* refers to the following as taking place several days, or perhaps several weeks later than the exchange in the corn fields (wheat or barley fields).

The phrase, *"He went into their Synagogue,"* concerned itself with approximately the first two and half years of His Ministry. In His last year, He was little allowed in their Synagogues, and because of the hatred of the Pharisees.

It is ironic! In the very place they are supposed to worship Him, He will not be allowed.

Is not that the same with most modern Churches?

(10) "AND, BEHOLD, THERE WAS A MAN WHICH HAD HIS HAND WITHERED. AND THEY ASKED HIM, SAYING, IS IT LAWFUL TO HEAL ON THE SABBATH DAYS? THAT THEY MIGHT ACCUSE HIM."

The *"Withered hand,"* is a portrayal of the spiritual condition of Israel and, as well, of all mankind. Its *"healing"* refers to Salvation, and which could be given only by Christ. The man's hand was made whole, but Israel would not allow Christ to make them whole, as most of mankind.

The phrase, *"And, behold, there was a man which had his hand withered,"* proclaims him being in the Synagogue and meeting Christ. Sadly, and despite religious activities being carried on in this Synagogue constantly, this was the only time it truly contained the Presence of the Lord, and because it contained the Person of the Lord. The only time God was in the place, He was confronted.

Likewise, most Churches have never seen a visitation from the Lord, and I speak of His Presence and Spirit. And even by chance, if the Lord does attempt to come, as evidenced by a manifestation of His Spirit, He is quickly told to leave because He is not desired.

Is it fully realized that a person baptized in the Holy Spirit is not welcome in most

Churches? If the Spirit is not welcome, then Christ is not welcome, and irrespective of how much He is talked about.

The word, *"withered,"* refers to the hand being shrunken, and with very little use, if any at all! As stated, it typifies man's spiritual condition.

The question, *"And they asked Him, saying, Is it lawful to heal on the Sabbath Days?"*, refers to the Pharisees completely devoid of the understanding and purpose of Christ or the Sabbath. The further statement of Christ will portray that the Pharisees had precious little regard for man or his needs, but only for their religion.

They concluded that *"healing"* was work, and, therefore, unlawful, when the very purpose of the Sabbath was to point to the *"rest"* which one would have in Christ, which could come about only by spiritual healing, of which this healing was a type.

Many Christians confuse Saturday and Sunday, calling Sunday the Sabbath, which it is not.

The old Jewish Sabbath of Saturday was to be a day of *"rest,"* pointing to the One Who would come, Who would truly provide *"rest"* for the soul.

Conversely, Sunday is a day of worship, commemorating the Death, Burial, and Resurrection of Christ. We worship Him Who fulfilled that day of *"rest,"* which means that it is no longer to be kept, and because He has come and fulfilled it. To keep the Jewish Sabbath, is, in effect, saying that Christ has not yet come.

As well, and for that reason, Sunday is not to be referred to as the Christian Sabbath. To do so, proclaims a misunderstanding of what the Sabbath was all about and Who it pointed to (Mat. 28:1; Mk. 16:2; Lk. 24:1; Jn. 20:19; I Cor. 16:2; Heb. 10:9; Rev. 1:10).

The phrase, *"That they might accuse Him,"* portrays a closed mind as a result of a hardened heart. As well, to accuse His is to accuse Him!

Satan is the *"accuser of the brethren,"* and Satan's children, and no matter how religious they are, as the Pharisees, accuse as well! (Rev. 12:10).

(11) "AND HE SAID UNTO THEM, WHAT MAN SHALL THERE BE AMONG YOU, THAT SHALL HAVE ONE SHEEP, AND IF IT FALL INTO A PIT ON THE SABBATH DAY,

WILL HE NOT LAY HOLD ON IT, AND LIFT IT OUT?"

The phrase, *"And He said unto them,"* is meant to draw them to common sense, which characterizes the Word of God. In Truth, the Word of God is the greatest *"common sense"* Book in the world. If properly understood, there is nothing in it that is weird, nonsensical, or strange. To be sure, man-made religion is weird and strange, and because it has deviated from the Word of God.

Jesus draws their attention to something that all were familiar with. He spoke of an animal, and in this case a *"sheep, falling into a pit on the Sabbath Day."* He then asked the question, *"Will he not lay hold on it, and lift it out?"*

Of course, the answer to the question was obvious! Most definitely this would be done even on the Sabbath Day, and even by these Pharisees. Inasmuch as the question called for a positive answer, He then asked another question.

(12) "HOW MUCH THEN IS A MAN BETTER THAN A SHEEP? WHEREFORE IT IS LAWFUL TO DO WELL ON THE SABBATH DAYS."

The question, *"How much then is a man better than a sheep?"*, surely would have shamed them! However, the hardened heart has no shame, and because the One Who makes the heart tender is no longer there, if, in fact, He ever has been! These Pharisees would pull a *"sheep"* out of a pit, even if it was on a Sabbath Day, but would do nothing to help a fellowman.

They had completely lost sight of what God was all about. Likewise, that is the fault of the Church at present!

The sole business and responsibility of the Church is to point men to Christ, just exactly as the Tabernacle and Temple of old were to point men to Christ. However, they lost sight of that as most do today.

When this happens, priorities are confused. Things then become more important than people.

The phrase, *"Wherefore it is lawful to do well on the Sabbath Days,"* answers their question of verse 10, and in few words proclaims exactly what the Sabbath is all about.

There is no evidence that they attempted to answer His question or His statement. In Truth, how could they answer? A *"man"* was certainly

NOTES

of more value than a *"sheep,"* and how could anyone fault doing *"well on the Sabbath?"*

His answer was kind and gracious and yet to the point, and answered their accusations completely. But yet, they were not moved at all to repent.

In their thinking, how could anyone even dare to suggest that someone as Righteous as they needed to repent? (Mat. 4:17).

(13) "THEN SAITH HE TO THE MAN, STRETCH FORTH THINE HAND, AND HE STRETCHED IT FORTH; AND IT WAS RESTORED WHOLE, LIKE AS THE OTHER."

So much is said in this verse which pertains to any and all!

1. *"Then saith He to the man"*: One of the reasons the Pharisees hated Christ so much is because they could not control Him. He asked their advice, permission or counsel on nothing. How could He, the Lord of Glory, ask permission of His creation? Also, they had absolutely nothing they could contribute to Him. Consequently, His independent nature angered them greatly!

However, His action was Scriptural and right, and for the sole reason that God is dependent on nothing or no one. He is sufficient within Himself.

Religious men love to control what is spoken and to whom it is spoken, and no less today than then!

Such has existed in the Catholic Church since its inception, but is now pandemic in the Protestant Church as well! Even in religious organizations which once boasted that they were not a Denomination, but, instead, a *"Movement,"* have forsaken those principles, now boasting of their denominational status.

As the world heads toward the Antichrist, religious control is going to become more and more severe, with the time coming shortly, if it has not already arrived, that it is going to be well nigh impossible to belong to organized religion and properly serve God at the same time.

2. *"Stretch forth thine hand"*: This, of course, spoke of the withered hand. It was symbolic of the spiritual state of Israel, and of mankind in general. But yet, and despite the obvious helplessness of this *"withered hand,"* and that which it symbolized, man does not at all think of himself as helpless or withered. In fact, he has a very high opinion of himself, thinking he is able to

solve his problems and ultimately to make a verdant garden out of this world. However, his attempts always fail because he tries to do so without the *"Tree of Life,"* i.e., Jesus.

As Christ told the man to *"Stretch forth his hand,"* He, likewise, is telling all of mankind to do the same, and by the presentation of the Gospel.

The *"Withered hand,"* with its obvious inability to function properly, portrays man's inability to save himself spiritually. And yet he keeps trying, and religious man most of all!

3. *"And it was restored whole":* About the best that man can do is to put a Band-Aid over the tremendous problems that plague him, while Christ makes one *"whole."*

What happened to the man's hand is not exactly stated, but definitely inferred. Inasmuch as it became like the healthy hand, then a miracle of outstanding proportions was performed. Before the very eyes of the onlookers, this *"withered hand"* fleshed out, with life, feeling and ability instantly returning. Such is Salvation as afforded by Christ, which, in Truth, can be afforded by no other.

The word, *"whole,"* means every part and ability being completely restored. This is the only answer for hurting humanity. Half measures are no good, because it actually leaves the person still in need of help.

Regrettably, modern psychology, which has its roots in humanism and, therefore, atheism, is man's answer to the ills of the world. Regrettably, the modern Church has fallen for this lie as well!

Let it be known, and dogmatically so, that there is no answer for the ills of man other than Christ. Man must have a miraculous intervention, and only Jesus can do that.

I asked a professor at one of the nation's largest universities, who, incidentally, was a Moslem, if Islam could effect a miraculous change in the life of an alcoholic, drug addict, etc.?

He looked away and lied, answering softly in the affirmative. However, Islam is a religion of man, as all other religions, and can effect no change in one's life except for the worse. Only Jesus can truly change a person, and, to be sure, He can do it instantly.

4. *"Like as the other":* Of course, this was speaking of the healthy, normal other hand of the man. However, in symbolism, it could

NOTES

refer to man before the Fall. Then he was *"whole"* because he was a Child of God. The Fall robbed him of that, causing him to be *"spiritually withered."*

Nevertheless, with the Advent of Christ and the price paid at Calvary, the *"born-again"* experience is possible, once again making a man *"whole"* and, consequently, a *"Child of God."*

Whereas now only a few, as this man, have been made *"whole,"* upon the Second Advent of Christ, the entirety of mankind will be made *"whole."* The Kingdom will then have truly come!

(14) "THEN THE PHARISEES WENT OUT, AND HELD A COUNCIL AGAINST HIM, HOW THEY MIGHT DESTROY HIM."

The Grace and Power that provided food on the Sabbath Day, furnished also healing; but His Love only excited their hatred, as is here made evident. But yet, and as the next verse will show, their hatred could not restrain the founts of Grace that perpetually did well up in His Heart, which resulted in Him healing everyone.

The phrase, *"Then the Pharisees went out,"* infers that they may have even left before the healing of the man with the withered hand. The structure of the phrase is that they could no longer stay in the same building with one who would do such an awful thing as the healing of a man on the Sabbath.

I wonder if the entirety of the Church world of Christianity was placed in the same position, as to how much difference there would be?

When one considers that the far greater majority of the denominational Church no longer believes that Jesus heals today, to be sure, their attitude would little change even in His Presence. Consequently, they would leave as the Pharisees.

Regrettably, too many of my own Pentecostal and Charismatic friends would, instead, make merchandise of the miracle performed, and even though they would not leave, Christ, I am afraid, would put them out accordingly as He cleansed the Temple (Mat. 7:22; 21:12-13).

The phrase, *"And held a council against Him,"* proclaims Mark stating that the Herodians joined the Pharisees in this council (Mk. 3:6). One must remember, these were the Religious Leaders of Israel.

Of all the Church services presently conducted this Sunday morning, how many of them, and irrespective of what they claim, are actually *"against"* the Lord instead of for Him? Millions worship Him with their mouths, while their hearts are far from Him (Mat. 15:8-9).

The phrase, *"How they might destroy Him,"* is sad indeed!

They did not realize that in destroying Him they were destroying themselves.

Of course, they could not really destroy Him, except that which He allowed, for no man could take His Life from Him. When He died, as He would shortly, He would lay down His life freely (Jn. 10:18).

It should also be remembered that if one seeks to destroy those who belong to Him, as well, they are destroying Him. He said, *"Inasmuch as ye have done it unto one of the least of these My brethren, ye have done it unto Me"* (Mat. 25:40).

(15) "BUT WHEN JESUS KNEW IT, HE WITHDREW HIMSELF FROM THENCE: AND GREAT MULTITUDES FOLLOWED HIM, AND HE HEALED THEM ALL;"

The phrase, *"But when Jesus knew it,"* refers to the plotting of the Pharisees and Herodians against Him. The structure of the sentence seems to infer that the information was given to Him by His Disciples, or others.

The phrase, *"He withdrew Himself from thence,"* refers to Him leaving that particular city and going to another.

The phrase, *"And great multitudes followed Him,"* was partly the reason the Pharisees hated Him. They were envious of His popularity, and, as well, the crowds who followed Him threatened their position of leadership.

It might be quickly added that their leadership was man-appointed and not God-given. Such always opposes the Work of the Spirit.

The phrase, *"And He healed them all,"* is emphatic respecting the word *"all."* As is obvious, this means that not a single person left without healing. This no doubt would have included blinded eyes being opened, lepers being cleansed, and paralysis being healed, etc.

(16) "AND CHARGED THEM THAT THEY SHOULD NOT MAKE HIM KNOWN:"

He hid Himself and would not even allow the fame of His miracles to hinder His purpose of offering up Himself as a Sacrifice for sin. That day would come when He would reign (*"show judgment over the Gentiles"*).

Meanwhile, He would not demand His rights, as the 19th verse will declare.

How so much this spirit is needed by the modern Church, in that modern advertisement too often does the very opposite! However, the more the flesh is exalted, the less the Spirit will work. Perhaps that is the reason the Holy Spirit moves very little at present!

(17) "THAT IT MIGHT BE FULFILLED WHICH WAS SPOKEN BY ESAIAS THE PROPHET, SAYING,"

As always, His actions fulfill the Scriptures. To be sure, He did such not just that the Scriptures be fulfilled, but that the Scriptures, through the foreknowledge of God, proclaimed what He would be like.

In other words, He was not acting out a part, but was portraying instead what He really was, *"Meek and lowly in heart."*

Isaiah is quoted in the Gospels more than any other Prophet.

(18) "BEHOLD MY SERVANT, WHOM I HAVE CHOSEN; MY BELOVED, IN WHOM MY SOUL IS WELL PLEASED: I WILL PUT MY SPIRIT UPON HIM, AND HE SHALL SHEW JUDGMENT TO THE GENTILES."

The phrase, *"Behold My Servant,"* as given by the Holy Spirit some 800 years before to the Prophet Isaiah, proclaims Christ as a *"Servant,"* but, more importantly, the Father's Servant. As a Servant, and due to the humble station of such, the Religious Leaders of Israel gave Him no respect or regard, but treated Him insultingly! However, the Servant they were treating in this manner was unlike any other servant they had ever known, inasmuch as This Servant belonged to God, and even more so was God! Consequently, their actions would ultimately reap a bitter harvest.

As well, Christ exemplified the *"Servant spirit,"* as no other man, setting an example before us of the truly *"meek and lowly in heart."*

Actually, this is the hallmark of True Christianity, and yet evidenced so little by most all of us.

And yet, Christ was moved not at all by the insults of the Pharisees and their rejection, because His motive in its entirety was to please the Father, which He did in totality.

Likewise, the proper servant spirit in our own hearts will cause us to act accordingly, not taking offense, but rather looking to the

Father. Regrettably, the servant spirit is not easily attained, and, as a matter of experience, does not come quickly or without price.

The phrase, *"Whom I have chosen,"* refers to every facet of Christ's Demeanor, Personality, Actions, Message, and Ministry, being designed wholly by the Holy Spirit. God chose not only Him, but the Way in which He faithfully walked.

As well, He was meant to serve as an example in this capacity, that we may allow the Father to choose for us. But sadly, and as well, how so little we do this, too many times charting our own course and, as always, reaping the bitter results.

The phrase, *"My Beloved in Whom My soul is well pleased,"* proclaims Jesus faithfully carrying out that which was planned by the Father, which caused Him to be greatly loved, and because it greatly pleased the Father.

To please God and not man, must be the goal of every Believer. To be sure, to do His Will is to please Him!

The phrase, *"I will put My Spirit upon Him,"* regards the results of having pleased the Father. He was Anointed by the Holy Spirit *"above all his fellows,"* and *"without measure"* (Ps. 45:7; Jn. 3:34).

As I dictate these notes in mid 1995, for the last few months, and especially the last few weeks, there has been a strong moving and operation of the Holy Spirit within my heart, which at times seem to be deeper than any move of God I have ever known. Never in all of my life have I been Anointed to pray and seek God, at least in this manner.

The ingredient of my petition, and I believe inspired by the Holy Spirit, is that I would have a greater infilling of the Spirit of God, and that He would have greater latitude within my life in order that the Anointing be pronounced.

However, in these petitions and the moving of the Holy Spirit, there have been, as well, and as I have previously stated, a cleansing action by the Spirit that all things displeasing to the Lord would be eliminated. To be sure, and again as I have stated, there are many things in our lives which are not pleasing to Him, which are not at all recognized at first, and can only be revealed by the Spirit. That is the reason that seeking His Face in brokenness of spirit is so very important! The fallow ground must be broken! The will must be emersed in Christ!

NOTES

Consequently, the degree of the Holy Spirit we are given and the manner in which He uses us, is predicated, and according to this verse, <u>as to how we please the Father</u>.

God help us that we may do that which is pleasing in His sight.

The phrase, *"And He shall shew judgment to the Gentiles,"* actually speaks of the coming Church, which is made up virtually of Gentiles.

It was always the intention of the Lord that the Gospel go to the entirety of the world, and not to the Jews only (Jn. 3:16). However, the Jews became so sectarian in their thinking that they excluded all but themselves, calling the Gentiles *"dogs."*

In their thinking, a Gentile could be saved, but only by becoming a proselyte Jew, and entering into all the Mosaic Law with all its rituals and ceremonies. As well, this thinking was embedded even in the Disciples.

It took the vision given to Simon Peter declaring God's purpose to cleanse the Gentiles, and by Faith in Christ only, and not by rituals and ceremonies (Acts 10), to open this door. Even then, great segments of the Early Church attempted to bring parts, if not all, of the Old Covenant into the New, completely ignoring the Words of Christ in Matthew 9:16-17, concerning *"putting a piece of new cloth onto an old garment"* or *"putting new wine into old bottles."*

Nevertheless, through the Ministry and persistence of the Apostle Paul, the New Covenant as given to him was kept free from this which would have destroyed it. Consequently, every Gentile who reads these words is reading the fulfillment of that prophesied by Isaiah some 2800 years ago, and fulfilled by Christ.

Therefore, His Mission, although seemingly a failure due to His rejection by the Jews, we now know did not fail and, in fact, could not fail!

(19) "HE SHALL NOT STRIVE, NOR CRY; NEITHER SHALL ANY MAN HEAR HIS VOICE IN THE STREETS."

This Passage is beautiful in its meaning, powerful in its application, and should be, and in fact must be, the goal to which we all aspire.

The phrase, *"He shall not strive, nor cry,"* refers to Him not defending Himself against the accusations of the Pharisees, even though He did correct their error and strongly denounced them (Mat. 23).

The idea is that inasmuch as tremendous

crowds followed Him, at least in the first two years of His Ministry, He could have strongly whipped up insurrection against the Pharisees and the Religious Leaders of Israel, especially considering His great miracles, but this He never did.

The phrase, *"Neither shall any man hear His voice in the streets,"* does not refer to Him preaching and teaching, etc., but rather extolling His abilities and accomplishments. In other words, He never promoted Himself, but, instead, allowed the works to speak for themselves.

How so different than the madding craze of modern self-promotion, using the glitz of Hollywood and the techniques of the world! How so unlike Him, Who Alone had the right to boast, but never did so because He would do only the Father's Will.

(20) "A BRUISED REED SHALL HE NOT BREAK, AND SMOKING FLAX SHALL HE NOT QUENCH, TILL HE SEND FORTH JUDGMENT UNTO VICTORY."

This verse has a double meaning:

1. Christ would endure the discordance of the *"bruised reed"* and the offensiveness of the *"smoking flax,"* i.e., the unbelief and rebellion of Israel, but only up to the day that He would bring forth judgment unto victory. In that day will the bruised reed be broken and the smoking flax quenched, which it was!

It is impossible to produce melody with a bruised reed, and the smell of a smoking wick is unendurable. Such was Israel; and such is man. Grace endures these for a time; but judgment, as the Scripture here plainly says, is certain to fall eventually upon them.

2. The *"bruised reed"* and the *"smoking flax"* does speak of and symbolizes the feeble Believer. This proclaims Christ's treatment of such as marked by long-suffering and gentleness. Consequently, the actions of the Church should be identical!

This was carried through by the Apostle Paul in his statement concerning a man who would not repent, but insisted on being disobedient to the Word of God. He said, *"And if any man obey not our Word by this Epistle, note that man, and have no company with him, that he may be ashamed."*

But then he said, *"Yet count him not as an enemy, but admonish him as a brother"* (II Thess. 3:14-15).

A *"reed"* was a type of plant which grew in abundance in the marshes of Israel. It was hollow, and after being cut could easily be notched and made into a whistle or flute. Also, it was delicate and would *"bruise"* or break easily.

Inasmuch as they grew in abundance, it was easier to throw away the makeshift musical instrument after it was bruised, and make a new one, rather than attempting to repair it.

Jesus proclaims, by using the *"bruised reed"* as an example, that He would not throw away the weak Believer, but would repair him.

As well, the *"smoking flax"* consisted of a wick which floated in an open lamp. If the oil is used up or the wick is not trimmed, it will smoke giving no light, but rather soot up the lamp.

Christ declares that He will replenish the oil and trim the wick in order that it may again burn brightly rather than *"quench it."*

The phrase, *"Till He send forth judgment unto victory,"* has two meanings as well:

1. If the Believer, as Israel, continues to live in unbelief, which, within itself, is an oxymoron, judgment, and as stated, will ultimately come.

This happened with Israel in A.D. 70, when Titus completely destroyed Jerusalem, with over 1,000,000 Jews being massacred, and hundreds of thousands of others being sold as slaves all over the world.

As well, the individual Believer, if continuing to resist the pleadings of the Holy Spirit, to him, at some point in time Judgment will come. Grace will cause the Blood of Jesus to wash away all sin, that is, if properly repented of (I Jn. 1:9); however, if the Believer will not allow the Lord to repair the *"bruise"* or *"cleanse"* the wick, sin ultimately has to be judged.

To be sure, the Holy Spirit is constantly striving to effect Righteousness in the life of the Believer, in which all failure and sin can be overcome, and will do so as here described if allowed to have His way (Jn. 16:7-11).

However, Satan is very successful in maneuvering Believers into Churches which little believe in the convicting power of the Holy Spirit, which greatly hinders the Work of the Holy Spirit in this all-important process. Consequently, the *"bruised reed"* is then broken and the *"smoking flax"* is then quenched!

2. Even though Israel was destroyed in A.D. 70, still, at the Second Coming of the Lord,

Israel will then accept Christ, consequently *"Sending forth judgment unto victory."*

As well, in the life of every Believer, if one is to notice, even though the struggle may be great and at times looking as if the *"Bruised reed"* will break or the *"Smoking flax"* will be quenched, still, many, if not most, ultimately find their way to *"victory."*

Respecting the individual Believer, of which this verse also speaks, the idea is that if the Holy Spirit is given any latitude at all, and irrespective as to how severe the problem may be, He will, and without fail, repair the *"bruised reed"* and the *"smoking flax," "Sending forth judgment unto victory,"* i.e., with the emphasis on *"Victory!"*

(21) "AND IN HIS NAME SHALL THE GENTILES TRUST."

The idea of the entirety of the statement as given by Isaiah, and as it pertained to Christ, concerned the Mission of Christ in presenting the Gospel to the Jews, which they rejected, and the way being made for the Church, which would consist almost exclusively of Gentiles. The Jews, even though His people, would put no trust in His Name, while the Gentiles would, which pertains to the Church.

Also, the idea expressed in this verse, and especially in the phrase, *"In His Name,"* reflects that Christianity is emphatically trust in a Person rather than a religion or system. His Mission, although tenuous at the outset, was ultimately, and will ultimately be totally victorious, which was brought about first with the Gentiles, but will eventually be brought about with the Jews as well!

(22) "THEN WAS BROUGHT UNTO HIM ONE POSSESSED WITH A DEVIL, BLIND, AND DUMB: AND HE HEALED HIM, INSOMUCH THAT THE BLIND AND DUMB BOTH SPAKE AND SAW."

The phrase, *"Then was brought unto Him one possessed with a Devil, blind, and dumb,"* points toward one who was in terrible straits, as would be obvious!

The idea is that one or more individuals brought this man to Christ, and because they had Faith that Christ could deliver him. Either one or more demon spirits, in whatever else they had done to this man, also caused him to be *"blind,"* and deaf, which brought on the *"dumbness,"* i.e., unable to speak. Consequently, Satan had pretty

NOTES

much, if not altogether, shut up each entrance by which he might come to Faith. Therefore, the possibility definitely exists that the Faith of the ones who brought him effected his healing, inasmuch, and due to his restrictions, that he in all likelihood did not have Faith.

The lesson here portrayed consequently is twofold:

1. This man in his terrible condition represented the spiritual condition of Israel and all of mankind. Man is spiritually blind, deaf and dumb, and, consequently, cannot, at least within himself, have Faith in God. Therefore, the initiation must be made by the Spirit in revealing Himself to man, with *"a measure of Faith"* freely given in order that man may believe, as here represented (Rom. 12:3).

2. As this man could not have Faith for himself, others had to have it for him. This action teaches us that unbelievers cannot be brought to Christ unless someone intercedes for them, which speaks of the *"Ministry of Reconciliation"* (II Cor. 5:18-19).

Regrettably, at this particular time, precious little intercession is going on for the lost, and because the Church has been, at least for the most part, deterred by the *"Prosperity Message,"* etc. In other words, most modern Christians, instead of interceding for the lost, are instead spending their energies in attempting to use their Faith, such as it is, in trying to get rich. It is sad but true!

The way of Faith is so effected, that if Believers do not intercede for unbelievers, they, as this poor man represented in this Text, cannot come to Christ. If one is to notice, at this present time, precious few people are coming to the Lord around the world, and due to the reasons given.

To be sure, all blindness and deafness producing this muteness are not caused by demon spirits; however, this particular case was!

The phrase, *"And He healed him,"* does not exactly tell us what happened. However, it would go without saying that Jesus cast out this *"Devil,"* which automatically caused his eyes to open and his ears to be unstopped.

The *"healing"* registered on the damage done by these spirits which was effected immediately.

The phrase, *"Insomuch that the blind and dumb both spake and saw,"* constitutes another miracle within itself. While it is obvious for eyes to *"see"* after they have been opened, it is not ordinary for the mute to instantly speak after having their ears opened, at least to any degree. However, the word *"spake"* indicates that there was a flow of conversation, which, as stated, was a miracle within itself.

As well, when the unbeliever comes to Christ and is *"born again,"* the spiritual blindness is lifted along with the spiritual dumbness, and then they can spiritually speak and spiritually see.

(23) "AND ALL THE PEOPLE WERE AMAZED, AND SAID, IS NOT THIS THE SON OF DAVID?"

The people, and as stated, were pictured in the unhappy man of verse 22; and though they cried out, *"Can this be the Son of David?"*, yet they failed to recognize Immanuel.

The basic reason was their Spiritual Leaders, as the following verses proclaim.

People can seldom rise higher than their Spiritual Leaders. Some few will push past such apostasy, but only a few! Most allow others to think for them, and, consequently, speak for them.

(24) "BUT WHEN THE PHARISEES HEARD IT, THEY SAID, THIS FELLOW DOTH NOT CAST OUT DEVILS, BUT BY BEELZEBUB THE PRINCE OF THE DEVILS."

The Pharisees here declared their belief in an organized kingdom of demons, having Satan as its chief. The Lord affirmed that truth, but rebuked and destroyed their cruel attack upon Himself.

The phrase, *"But when the Pharisees heard it,"* speaks of the deliverance of the man who was *"blind and dumb."* It caused no joy in them, only the opposite, insomuch that they would accuse Christ of being in league with Satan. As such, and as the following verses proclaim, they would blaspheme the Holy Spirit, thereby sealing their doom.

In Truth, they were in league with Satan, and were what they were accusing Him of. Tragically, this apostasy did not die with the Pharisees, but is alive and well presently. This means that many, if not most, who presently call themselves Religious Leaders, are, as well, in league with Satan. The evil one operates this procedure in two different ways:

1. It is done as the Pharisees, by opposing all that is truly of God. Consequently, in the

NOTES

mind of these skeptics the Lord no longer heals, performs miracles, answers prayer, baptizes in the Holy Spirit, etc.

When these things do happen, their response to it is, *"It is of the Devil."*

As here, to attribute to the Devil that which is truly of God is serious indeed!

2. Satan reverses himself at times, actually bringing about healings, etc., or even miracles, by that which purports to be of God but actually isn't!

Jesus said, *"For there shall arise false Christs, and false Prophets, and shall shew great signs and wonders, insomuch that, if it were possible, they shall deceive the very elect"* (Mat. 24:24).

Therefore, *"signs and wonders"* do not necessarily mean that such is of the Lord. It may be, or it may not be!

The criteria is the Word of God, which Jesus fulfilled in every respect.

In other words, everything must line up with the Bible for it to truly be of God.

The phrase, *"This fellow,"* is said with derisive contempt.

If it is to be noticed, not one time did the Pharisees refer to Christ as *"Jesus."* The Name, *"Jesus,"* means *"Saviour,"* consequently, they would address Him by other names, such as *"Master,"* which meant *"Teacher,"* which was also said with contempt, as here!

The phrase, *"Doth not cast out devils, but by Beelzebub the prince of devils,"* is a charge so serious that, as stated, by this accusation the Pharisees blasphemed the Holy Spirit.

The spirit world of darkness, and controlled by Satan, with a host of Fallen Angels and demon spirits, is in contrast to the Spirit World of Light, with God at its Head, along with the Holy Spirit and Christ, with a host of Angels. Between these two, a war rages, with man caught in the middle.

Due to the Fall, most of mankind serves Satan, and, therefore, is a participant in the world of darkness, whether they realize it or not.

Conversely, a few serve the Lord and are part of the World of Light. Consequently, the spirit world plays a powerful part in all activity of humanity, even though most do not realize it.

For instance, every unbeliever is influenced more or less, and constantly, by demon spirits, even though they little realize it. Some are even *"demon possessed,"* as spoken of in verse 22.

Christians are greatly opposed by demon spirits, and constantly, and must take authority over them by using the Name of Jesus and the Word of God (Mk. 16:17; Mat. 4:1-11).

Ultimately, the cause of all evil in the world is Satan and his world of darkness. He uses unredeemed man to carry out his insidious desires, to *"steal, kill and destroy"* (Jn. 10:10).

In contrast to this, Christ died on Calvary to redeem man from the powers of darkness, and then gave redeemed man the Holy Spirit, Who actually takes up abode in the heart and life of the Believer (I Cor. 3:16).

At the Second Coming of Christ, Satan will be defeated, and along with all his minions of darkness will be locked away in the *"bottomless pit"* for a thousand years (Rev. 20:1-3).

For this thousand years the world will know a time without evil, with Jesus Christ, Personally, ruling from Jerusalem. It is called the *"Kingdom Age."*

At the end of the one thousand years, Satan will be loosed for a short period of time, and will attempt to overthrow this *"Kingdom Age,"* but will be given short shift, and will be *"Cast into the lake of fire and brimstone, where the beast and the false prophet are, and shall be tormented day and night forever and ever"* (Rev. 20:10).

Thus will end Satan's domain, with his kingdom of darkness destroyed, and at that time a *"New Heaven and a new earth,"* will be prepared by God. The *"New Jerusalem"* will then come down from God out of Heaven, and established on planet earth, and *"There shall be no more curse: but the Throne of God and of the Lamb shall be in it; and His servant shall serve Him:*

"And they shall see His Face; and His Name shall be in their foreheads.

"And there shall be no night there; and they need no candle, neither light of the sun; for the Lord God giveth them Light: and they shall reign for ever and ever" (Rev. 21:1-2; 22:3-5).

(25) "AND JESUS KNEW THEIR THOUGHTS, AND SAID UNTO THEM, EVERY KINGDOM DIVIDED AGAINST ITSELF IS BROUGHT TO DESOLATION; AND EVERY CITY OR HOUSE DIVIDED AGAINST ITSELF SHALL NOT STAND:"

The phrase, *"And Jesus knew their thoughts,"* proclaims Jesus not hearing what was said, but, instead, was revealed to Him by the Holy Spirit.

As such, the very Power of the One Who Jesus used to effect this great miracle on the one *"possessed with a devil,"* is listening as always and hears these Pharisees attribute this miracle to Satan.

The phrase, *"And said unto them, every kingdom divided against itself is brought to desolation,"* proclaims Christ's answer to their absurd accusation.

As was His method, He made this same statement in another way by saying, *"And every city or house divided against itself shall not stand."*

In this Passage, Jesus attributes a *"kingdom"* to Satan, which means that he is more than a mere individual, but that he is bound up with his kingdom and his kingdom with him. It is, as stated, a kingdom of darkness.

The idea of the statement is that Satan does not oppose himself! He does not possess one with an evil spirit and then cast out that spirit.

Even a natural kingdom could not stand under such an onslaught. Actually, the Roman Empire, which ruled at the time of Christ and was the strongest the world ever knew up to that time, was ultimately ripped apart by internal division, until they were so weakened that outside enemies could bring them down, which they did!

Consequently, division is one of Satan's greatest weapons against the True Work of God. Someone has said that God gives man a *"vision"* and then gives *"provision"* respecting the carrying out of the *"vision,"* while Satan attempts to bring into the *"vision"* the destructive force of *"division."*

The very word, *"division,"* speaks of a disruption which causes the vision to die; hence, *"di-vision."*

(26) "AND IF SATAN CAST OUT SATAN, HE IS DIVIDED AGAINST HIMSELF; HOW SHALL THEN HIS KINGDOM STAND?"

Satan can, and often does, take off sicknesses which he has placed on a person by demon spirits in order to help false religions.

False religions damn many souls, and, to be sure, Satan can as easily take off what he has placed on, in order to deceive those who are drawn to these false religions.

However, when he does such, he is not casting himself out nor divided against himself. In fact, his web of deception by such actions is woven even tighter by causing people to believe a lie, and, thereby, be damned (II Thess. 2:9-12).

For instance, many point to the alleged miracles and healings at Lourdes and elsewhere of similar nature, claiming that such proves the veracity of Catholicism.

Even if some healings are genuine, it proves nothing! Catholicism is error, and, therefore, not Biblical, and the Holy Spirit will not, and, in Truth, cannot function in that arena. He is Truth, and, as such, can never condone error, and irrespective of the so-called Faith of an individual (I Jn. 5:6). As well, He always leads one to Truth, and never to error (Jn. 16:13).

The claims at Lourdes, and all such other type places in Catholicism, are based on allegiance to Mary and not Christ. Such is error and cannot be honored or blessed by the Holy Spirit. He *"glorifies Christ,"* and not Mary or anyone else (Jn. 16:14).

(27) "AND IF I BY BEELZEBUB CAST OUT DEVILS, BY WHOM DO YOUR CHILDREN CAST THEM OUT? THEREFORE THEY SHALL BE YOUR JUDGES."

Jesus now turns attention to the claims of the Pharisees themselves in casting out devils. He does so by asking the question, *"By Whom do your children cast them out?"*, while neither denying or affirming that they, in fact, actually did cast out devils. He was using the statement only as argument to prove His point.

Had they answered the question, they most certainly would have claimed that they did so by the Power of God, and, consequently, in view of His previous argument about Satan casting out Satan, which they knew to be true, they were then forced to admit that what He did was by the Power of God also!

In Truth, they did not cast out any devils, nor did their children, i.e., disciples for Satan, as stated, cast out Satan.

However, the possibility did exist that in their exorcisms, so-called, as we have stated, Satan may well have lifted his bondage momentarily from someone in order to deceive the people in believing that the Pharisees were of God, etc.

(28) "BUT IF I CAST OUT DEVILS BY THE SPIRIT OF GOD, THEN THE KINGDOM OF GOD IS COME UNTO YOU."

NOTES

The phrase, *"But if I cast out devils by the Spirit of God,"* places the emphasis on the *"Spirit of God."*

As well, His statement here infers that while He, and by the Spirit of God, was really casting out devils, they actually were not! The *"Spirit of God,"* and as we have stated, will not endorse error in any capacity; and, to be sure, these people did not know God, and, consequently, were actually of Satan.

The phrase, *"Then the Kingdom of God is come unto you,"* places the Pharisees in an untenable position. If the *"Spirit of God"* was actually helping Him and He had already made it clear that such could not be done without the Spirit of God, then they must admit that He is the Messiah.

Their accusation backfired on them!

(29) "OR ELSE HOW CAN ONE ENTER INTO A STRONG MAN'S HOUSE, AND SPOIL HIS GOODS, EXCEPT HE FIRST BIND THE STRONG MAN? AND THEN HE WILL SPOIL HIS HOUSE."

The idea of this verse is that even though Satan is *"strong,"* still, Jesus is much stronger, able to *"Bind the strong man,"* *"Spoil his goods,"* and even *"Spoil his house."*

The question, *"Or else how can one enter into a strong man's house...?"*, speaks of Jesus coming to invade Satan's domain. In fact, He had already entered this *"strong man's house,"* and, to be sure, there was nothing Satan could do about it.

The *"house"* spoke of Satan's dominion over mankind, which Jesus would destroy. John said, *"For this purpose the Son of God was manifested, that He might destroy the works of the Devil"* (I Jn. 3:8).

The continuance of the question, *"And spoil his goods...?"*, refers to Jesus destroying the stranglehold over individuals by casting out devils or healing the sick, with such sickness being caused by the powers of darkness.

However, the greatest *"spoiling"* would be the bondage of sin that was broken at Calvary. There Christ completely *"destroyed the works of Satan."*

The conclusion of the question, *"Except he first bind the strong man?"*, then proclaims He would do it, and now He has done it.

The phrase, *"And then He will spoil his house,"* is more than merely a conclusion. It is an emphatic statement that He will do this, yes, utterly plunder the whole house.

As a result of what Christ has already done, no person now need be bound by the powers of darkness. Satan is a defeated foe, and his house is *"spoiled!"* Now every captive can go free, because what Jesus did at His First Advent was for the entirety of mankind.

As a footnote, if Satan could have stopped Him, he would have done so; but he was powerless to do anything!

(30) "HE THAT IS NOT WITH ME IS AGAINST ME; AND HE THAT GATHERETH NOT WITH ME SCATTERETH ABROAD."

The argument of this verse is that the Presence of Immanuel tested everything and everybody.

The phrase, *"He that is not with Me is against Me,"* presents the Truth that there is no such thing as neutrality with Christ. Due to its significance, allow us to say that again:

"It is impossible to take a neutral position regarding Christ."

The very nature of His Person and Being and, above all, that He is God, demands either acceptance or rejection.

Furthermore, the word, *"against,"* denotes opposition, and not only opposition, but *"intense opposition!"*

However, this statement does not address itself to those who have never heard the Gospel, or even to those who have not been especially dealt with by the Holy Spirit, but, instead, to those the Holy Spirit has dealt with, as these Pharisees and others who heard Christ and then purposely rejected Him.

The idea is that such rejection opens the door wider for the entrance of Satan, with opposition to Christ intensifying.

The phrase, *"And he that gathered not with Me scattereth abroad,"* refers to the Truth that one cannot be *"with Christ"* and *"against"* His True Servants. Such a position cannot be.

In other words, one cannot love Christ and at the same time be opposed to His Disciples. If one truly loves Jesus, one will truly love Peter, James, and John, etc.

As well, if a person is truly *"for Christ,"* he will truly attempt to bring souls to Him. He will serve as a True Shepherd.

Otherwise, he will be as a wolf, serving for personal gain, and will, of necessity, *"scatter the flock."*

(31) "WHEREFORE I SAY UNTO YOU, ALL MANNER OF SIN AND BLASPHEMY SHALL BE FORGIVEN UNTO MEN: BUT THE BLASPHEMY AGAINST THE HOLY GHOST SHALL NOT BE FORGIVEN UNTO MEN."

The words, *"Wherefore I say unto you,"* are meant to address the most fearsome statement that Christ would make. It concerns the awful sin of blaspheming the Holy Spirit, for which there is no forgiveness, and which therefore consigns one to an eternal doom.

Directly, He is speaking to the Pharisees and the statement they have made regarding His casting out demons, and them saying that He did this *"By Beelzebub the prince of the devils!"* They were attributing the Powerful Work of God, which had been brought about by the Holy Spirit through Christ as a work of Satan. Nothing could be more serious!

The phrase, *"All manner of sin and blasphemy shall be forgiven unto men,"* speaks of all types of sins, even as severe as murder, adultery, hate, pride, or any other despicable act that men are so accustomed to engage in. However, this does not mean an automatic forgiveness, but, instead, forgiveness predicated on such being earnestly solicited from the Lord, whether through John 3:16 or I John 1:9.

The phrase, *"But the blasphemy against the Holy Ghost shall not be forgiven unto men,"* is, without a doubt, the most chilling warning given in the entirety of the Bible.

Of course, the question is immediately asked, *"What constitutes the sin of blaspheming the Holy Spirit for which there is no forgiveness?"*

First, one must know and understand exactly Who the Holy Spirit is!

The Holy Spirit is God; however, it is not this role as Deity which calls into question this sin, for the next verse tells us that words or even blasphemy spoken against Christ or even God the Father, will be forgiven.

What is being spoken of here is the role played by the Holy Spirit as it regards the Redemption of man. While it is true that the Holy Spirit involves Himself in all aspects of creation and maintaining that creation, still, it is His specific role in drawing men to Christ, plus His Work and Operation in the Body, and the role He plays in delivering men from the powers of darkness that is here referred to.

SPECIFICALLY, WHAT IS THIS SIN?

It is any insulting remark or curse — or specifically attributing to Satan works actually performed by the Holy Spirit. This is unforgivable when it is done maliciously and knowingly. It is unpardonable because it is willful rejection of Light (Jn. 3:19).

As such, it is a deliberate insult to the last and only instrument of God held out to man for the purpose of bringing about the remission of sin.

(This is not meant to place one in fear, because many, if not most, have made some statement respecting the Holy Spirit they knew was wrong, or even insulting. Many have grieved over such, thinking they have blasphemed the Holy Spirit, with Satan taking full advantage, attempting to make them believe that they have sinned away their day of Grace and cannot be saved. Such is not true, as we will elaborate on more fully as we proceed.)

When men reject and spurn God's only agent for Redemption — and His only avenue for forgiveness — there is no other person to plead their cases before God! The Holy Spirit is the specific Person of the Godhead, Who presents the case of the individual before God. Those who willfully and blatantly reject this representation are therefore left with no further recourse. They have gratuitously rejected their last resort, for it is the Holy Spirit Who draws the person to Christ (Jn. 6:44).

While it is the Father, as John proclaims, Who really draws the person to Christ, still, He does so by the Agency of the Holy Spirit (Jn. 16:8-11).

The reason this sin is so uniquely appalling is because of Whom it is directed against. God the Father made this world and administers it whether or not men like or approve of the things He does. Likewise, Jesus Christ came down from Heaven and went to the Cross at Calvary regardless of men's desires, preferences, or anything they may have tried to do to prevent Him. The Holy Spirit, however, is totally different.

He responds to the wishes — to the reception or rejection — of men. He never imposes His Will on anyone. God the Father and Jesus the Son will, under good and sufficient provocation,

NOTES

impose Their Wills. God's Holy Spirit does not, at least in this capacity.

The Holy Spirit, at least in His dealings with man, always operates *"as gently as a dove."* Man can invite or reject the ministrations of the Holy Spirit, and the reaction of the Holy Spirit will conform to the *"signal"* sent out by the individual.

There is nothing in life more repugnant than to see an individual mistreating a gentle being. When that gentle being also happens to be a member of the very Godhead, what could be less forgivable?

If one is to notice, the Scribes or the Pharisees actually never referred by Name to the Holy Spirit. The title wasn't used. They merely attributed the Works of God (via the Lord Jesus Christ) to Satan. They, therefore, at the same time, blasphemed the Holy Spirit Who brought about these works. The Holy Spirit was the instrument by which Jesus cast out devils, but the Pharisees gave credit for this action to Satan.

The Holy Ghost is God, and He is the only Member of the Godhead Who:

1. Is on this earth to administer the affairs of God the Father and God the Son.

2. Pleads the case of the individual before God the Father and God the Son. (In other words, He is the Intercessor. No one else on or from this earth can do this.)

3. Is sensitive to rejection. When you willfully reject Him, there is no other avenue or approach to God.

The Pharisees deliberately confused God with Satan. They called good evil, and evil good. They willfully rejected (and therefore sinned against) Light.

These considered themselves to be masters of the Law of Moses. They knew (or were supposed to know) the entirety of God's communication with man. For them to so act meant they were evil at heart. They desired and wallowed in iniquity and wickedness.

So, blasphemy against the Holy Spirit is willful rejection of Light by identifying Satan with God, and knowing the difference.

WHO CAN COMMIT THIS UNFORGIVABLE SIN?

I think it would be proper to ask the following:

1. Can a Christian commit this sin?
2. Can an unsaved person commit this sin?
3. Can a backslider commit this sin?

THE CHRISTIAN

No, a Christian cannot commit this sin, as a Christian is a Believer and, therefore, Christlike. Such a one loves the Lord, and would not do anything as reprehensible and malicious as this, and for any number of reasons.

Admittedly, some Christians — in times of discouragement — have said things about God they would later like to retract. Some Christians have even held a grudge against God for something they thought He did, or could have prevented and did not.

But God will forgive all this when an individual seeks forgiveness. Consequently, there is nothing in the Word of God that suggests that a Christian would commit the sin of blasphemy against the Holy Ghost.

To begin with, the Christian (the True Christian) is doing everything within his power to be Christlike and to do precisely what God wants him to do. Admittedly, there is such a thing as the lukewarm Christian or the weak Christian. But, at the same time, there is no record within the Word of God that any Child of God living for the Lord would or could commit this particular sin.

THE UNSAVED

First of all, allow me to say that there are many things people say in ignorance about the Holy Spirit, but which is not the unpardonable sin, and because it is done in ignorance.

Actually, one may blaspheme and insult the Holy Spirit in ignorance and still be saved. Of course, we are speaking of the unsaved, who do things in their unsaved state.

Paul said in I Timothy 1:13, and referring to himself, *"Who was before a blasphemer, a persecutor, and injurious: but I obtained Mercy, because I did it ignorantly in unbelief."*

Paul, therefore, specifically states that he was a blasphemer but that he didn't know any better.

Unsaved people do many unsavory things and make innumerable silly, foolish, wicked statements — not realizing the true import of their actions or words. And, more than likely, if God held the unsaved accountable for everything

NOTES

they said or did, there would be very few unsaved left alive — and thus very few potential candidates for Salvation would survive long enough to become Christians.

Consequently, Christians do not need to worry about something they said or did while living in an unsaved condition, fearing the possibility that they may have blasphemed the Holy Spirit. The Devil delights in using this type of guilt trip as a weapon of condemnation. But what did Paul say in Romans 8:1?

"There is therefore now no condemnation to them which are in Christ Jesus, who walk not after the flesh, but after the Spirit."

This is one of Satan's favorite ploys. He will bring up things the Christian did before he was saved. Satan does this, hoping the Christian is not familiar enough with the Word of God to know that he is now a new creature in the Lord Jesus Christ (II Cor. 5:17). So, upon Faith in Christ, it is as if the Christian never committed those old sins because he is now a totally new person — from the ground up and the heart out. Old sins have no reference to the Christian. They were committed by the entirely different person that Christian was before he became a new creature in Christ Jesus.

Actually, there is precious little (if any) record in the Word of God suggesting blasphemy of the Holy Spirit by those who have never known the Lord and who thus never had an opportunity to understand His Mercy and His Grace. It would seem from Paul's statement that whatever was done would have been done in ignorance. To be sure, these persons are lost. But, at any moment they choose, they may come to the Lord Jesus Christ (irrespective of what they may have done in the past). At this point their sins are forgiven and they become cleansed and washed in the Blood, and become new creatures in Christ Jesus.

So that one will not misunderstand, if a person is unsaved — even though he does the things he does in ignorance — he is not forgiven these sins unless he accepts the Lord Jesus Christ as his Saviour. Otherwise, he will be eternally lost (Acts 17:30), just as if he did commit the unpardonable sin.

However, any time the unsaved comes to Christ, and irrespective of what type of sins they have committed in their unsaved state, they will be accepted by the Lord. That Promise is held out to all! Jesus said, *"All that the Father giveth Me shall come to Me; and him that cometh to Me I will in no wise cast out"* (Jn. 6:37).

He also said, *"And the Spirit and the bride say, Come. And let him that heareth say, Come. And let him that is athirst come. And whosoever will, let him take the Water of Life freely"* (Rev. 22:17).

To make certain there was no misunderstanding respecting the great invitation to be saved, the entirety of the Canon of Scripture is closed out by the great invitation just given. Jesus died for all, and all may come (Jn. 3:16).

THE BACKSLIDER

Some would claim that this is an Old Testament term and really does not apply to the New Covenant. While it is certainly true that the word, *"backslider,"* or, *"backsliding,"* does not appear in the New Testament, still, the inference is there.

The word, *"backsliding,"* simply refers to one who has fallen back or lost ground in his devotion to Christ. Therefore, if the word does not appear in the New Testament, the spirit of the word does.

For instance, the Holy Spirit through Paul gave the great dissertation on Believers being *"unequally yoked together with unbelievers,"* and with the demand that such was not to be (II Cor. 6:14-18). If such were disobeyed, as it often has been, the person could only be labeled as *"backslidden,"* at least to whatever degree they had disobeyed.

Jesus spoke of the individual who was neither *"cold nor hot,"* but *"lukewarm,"* which meant that such a one had cooled off, spiritually speaking, and which could be labeled as none other than *"backslidden"* (Rev. 3:15-16).

As well, some individuals, and sadly so, will completely turn their back on God going into deep sin, as many have. The prodigal son, as Jesus related, is a case in point (Lk. 15:3-24).

In this state, it is possible for one to blaspheme the Holy Spirit, but it is not likely.

Actually, one of Satan's greatest ploys regarding the backslider is attempting to convince him that he has blasphemed the Holy Spirit, and, consequently, cannot be saved even if he tried. Any time this happens it is always untrue, because Satan would not bother to suggest this lie if such were the case.

The Truth is, if a person wants to be saved, there is no record in the Word of God that the Lord has ever turned one away. In fact, and as we have stated, the entirety of the Bible is an invitation to the sinner to come to Jesus. If the desire is there, acceptance will always be given, and that includes the backslider, no matter what he has done.

SO WHO EXACTLY CAN BLASPHEME THE HOLY SPIRIT?

Paul said, *"For it is impossible for those who were once enlightened, and have tasted of the heavenly gift, and were made partakers of the Holy Ghost,*

"And have tasted the good Word of God, and the powers of the world to come,

"If they shall fall away, to renew them again unto repentance; seeing they crucify to themselves the Son of God afresh, and put Him to an open shame" (Heb. 6:4-6).

This Passage speaks of individuals who have truly once known God or else claim to have known Him, as the Pharisees, but have apostatized.

This means to completely reject His Atoning Work, in that they do not even believe it anymore. Consequently, it is impossible for such a person to be saved, because he has turned from the only thing that can save him, and counted it *"an unholy thing,"* as this next Passage will proclaim.

Paul also said (that is, if Paul wrote Hebrews), *"For if we sin wilfully after that we have received the knowledge of the Truth, there remaineth no more sacrifice for sins,*

"But a certain fearful looking for of judgment and fiery indignation, which shall devour the adversaries" (Heb. 10:26-27).

Then Paul, speaking under Holy Spirit unction, says in the 29th verse, *"Of how much sorer punishment, suppose ye, shall he be thought worthy, who hath trodden under foot the Son of God, and hath counted the Blood of the Covenant, wherewith he was sanctified, an unholy thing, and hath done despite unto the Spirit of Grace?"*

Paul is not saying that if a Christian sins after being saved he cannot be forgiven. That is not the idea at all. He is speaking of those who were once Believers, but who turned their back on God and went their own way, actually into apostasy. Almost always, these individuals continue to profess themselves as the Pharisees, as being Believers, but in the wrong thing. These individuals repudiate the work of Grace — openly blaspheming the Sacrifice of the Lord Jesus Christ and rejecting His universal and unique Sacrifice for sin. In doing so, they blasphemed the Holy Spirit, exactly as the Pharisees.

If any backslider retains his Faith in Christ and the Lord's Atonement, he can be renewed to repentance if he comes back to the Lord and asks for forgiveness. It is when he totally rejects Christ and His Gospel that He becomes hopeless.

As an example, a particular Methodist Bishop is said to have trusted Christ as his Saviour as a young man. Then, after becoming a Bishop in the Church, he turned his back upon God and openly repudiated the Sacrifice of the Lord Jesus, saying that the Blood of Jesus was no more than the blood of a dead dog. This man, if he made these statements and continued in that belief, which he seems to have done, blasphemed the Holy Ghost because he knew what he was doing. He had full knowledge of his statements and he made them wilfully, thus rejecting Light.

At this point there was no more Sacrifice for his sins. In other words, the only way a person can be saved is by trusting in the Atoning Work of the Lord Jesus Christ; that is, in the Blood He shed at Calvary as recompense for our sins. If one does not trust in this or believe it, or ceases to believe it, as this Bishop, he cannot be saved.

So, it would seem from the Word of God that basically the only individuals who could blaspheme the Holy Spirit and thus commit the unpardonable sin, are those who have once known God (or at least made a conscious profession of knowing Him) who then wilfully turned their backs on that knowledge. Thus they sin against Light. Consequently, they, as the Pharisees, blaspheme the Holy Spirit, thus committing the unpardonable sin.

It should be quickly added that they who do these things, and once again as the Pharisees, have no desire to follow Christ, but only to follow their own way.

A WARNING

In the last several decades the world has seen a great outpouring of the Holy Spirit. This outpouring has taken place in direct fulfillment of Joel's Prophecy (Joel 2:28), which was repeated for confirmation by Peter (Acts 2:17). He said, *"And it shall come to pass in the last days, saith God, I will pour out of My Spirit upon all flesh...."*

However, all Church Leaders have not been in sympathy with this outpouring. In fact, many have rejected this outpouring of the Holy Spirit. Some, in denying the legitimacy of the Holy Spirit Baptism, have made slanderous remarks, consigning the modern manifestation of the Pentecostal experience to *"the Devil."* Some have even said, *"People who speak in other tongues are of the Devil."* What are they doing? To be sure, they are attributing the Work of the Holy Ghost to Satan!

When this is done, do these people blaspheme the Holy Spirit?

Of course, the Lord Alone is the Judge of this. However, a word of caution should be given.

There may be many reading this who do not agree with our teaching respecting the Baptism in the Holy Spirit with the evidence of speaking with other tongues (Acts 2:4). Of course, anyone can believe whatever he or she chooses to believe, but it would be far wiser to restrict comment concerning the Person of the Holy Spirit — and Holy Spirit manifestations.

I remind all concerned that when the Pharisees blasphemed the Holy Spirit, they never mentioned the Holy Spirit. They were talking about the miracles of Jesus which were performed through the Agency of the Holy Spirit. Yet, in the unimpeachable Judgment of Jesus Christ, they blasphemed the Holy Ghost.

So, individuals who are supposed to know the Word of God and understand (or at least claim to understand) it, should be extremely cautious about their statements. As the wise man Gamaliel said so long ago, *"lest haply ye be found even to fight against God"* (Acts 5:39).

It would seem from the Word of God that only those who have knowledge of God and His Ways can blaspheme the Holy Spirit. It would also seem that the unsaved who do things in ignorance are not held accountable for this sin, if they subsequently turn to the Blood of Jesus for Salvation!

HOW CAN ONE KNOW IF HE HAS BLASPHEMED THE HOLY SPIRIT?

I see no evidence in the Word of God that one will know or care if this has happened.

There is no record in the Word that an individual who wants Mercy and cries out for it would not receive it. It would seem that every soul who desires to come to the Lord Jesus Christ, whoever they may be, will always be welcomed with open arms.

It does say, however, that individuals who apostatize (separate themselves) and consciously turn their backs on God and sin against Light (just as the Scribes and the Pharisees did by accusing Jesus by casting out devils through Satan), even though they may continue to profess, which most do, have sinned so wilfully that there is no further desire to return to God's Ways. They seem to then become incapable of developing such a desire in the future. This would seem to be the situation for those who have blasphemed the Holy Spirit. They have no more desire for God. There is no more attraction to His Ways. At this point, any tendency toward Righteousness is replaced in their hearts by hatred for God and everything He stands for. There is no Scriptural evidence that such even tried to return to the Lord. Consequently, they can no longer be saved.

I have heard stories of individuals who rejected the Call of God many times but then would eventually desire Salvation, but, it is said, could not be saved.

There may be such cases, but it is not because God won't accept them, but rather because they won't accept His Plan for their lives. They won't accept the restrictions they envision as changing their lifestyles. Were they to will to do so, at that moment they can be instantly and gloriously saved. Such cases are not God's fault; they are the fault of the attitude of the sinner.

In cases of blaspheming the Holy Spirit, however, it is not only the individual who does not want to be saved — God also rejects them. They don't want Him, and He doesn't want them. It is a twofold situation. They close the door through their own willful apostasy, and then God seals the door. Their sin is unpardonable. It cannot be forgiven, and because there is no desire for it to be forgiven.

It is the door that is shut and no man can open.

Even though we have previously said it in this short dissertation, still, because of its significance, allow us to say it again.

NOTES

Christians need never worry that something they said while in the unsaved state against the Holy Spirit, amounts to blasphemy. Satan, to be sure, will bring this accusation, but he is merely an accuser of the brethren. He is a liar and the father of all lies. God is well aware of this, so don't you believe it. It is all washed away, cleansed by the Blood of Jesus Christ.

Also, no unsaved person need listen to Satan and allow the evil one to tell them they did something unforgivable or unpardonable so they are now ineligible for Salvation. Satan wants sinners to believe there is no use hoping for Salvation. He wants them to believe they've blasphemed the Holy Spirit so they won't move forward to Salvation. However, this is just one more lie of Satan. If they believe it, true enough, the end purposes of Satan will be realized, and they will end up eternally damned as if they had blasphemed the Holy Spirit.

In actuality though, they did not commit the unpardonable sin, and they could have come to the Lord at any time they wished. If they had believed with all their hearts that God saves from sin, their Salvation would become an instant reality.

In summation: One who has truly been a Believer or else professed to be so, but then turns his back on God's Way of Salvation and blasphemes by denying the very precious Blood of Jesus (the only agent that can cleanse from sin) — that person has apostatized. He has turned his back upon God and God's Way, willfully, and sinned against Light. He has done this with his eyes wide open as to the consequences of his actions. He has become calloused and hardened. Having rejected God, there is no further chance (or avenue) to petition God for Salvation.

Although this person may try to save himself in other ways, he has finally and irreversibly rejected the Blood of the Lord Jesus Christ for all time. He has blasphemed the Holy Ghost and there is no way he can be saved. He has, as the Pharisees, committed the unpardonable sin.

One may well ask that if such has been done, and the individual then sees the error of his ways and cries out to God for Mercy and Pardon, can that person be saved?

Yes he can! God has never turned His back on one who truly comes to Him, and irrespective of past actions. In Truth, quite possibly this has been done many times.

If one has truly blasphemed the Holy Spirit, there will be no desire in that person's heart for Salvation. The very One Who truly draws him to Christ, the Holy Spirit, is no longer wanted or desired, or even believed in, therefore, Salvation is impossible.

IN CONCLUSION

Years ago, in Atlanta, after the Altar Call at the conclusion of the service, I noticed a man (among the many who had come) kneeling at the right side of the Altar. I felt led of the Holy Spirit to go down to where he was kneeling. I knelt beside him, putting my arm around his shoulder, and began to pray for him.

I sensed the struggle he was having even before he told me this: *"Brother Swaggart, I'm a murderer. I've just been released from prison. I've paid my debt to society, but I killed a man.*

"I see that man in my dreams. I see the smoking gun. I see the blood flowing from his body. I did this horrible thing, and it was so evil and wicked that I can't believe God can forgive me."

Weeping, I told him the words of Isaiah. *"... though your sins abe as scarlet, they shall be as white as snow; though they be red like crimson, they shall be as wool"* (Isa. 1:18).

In a moment's time, the Light of the Gospel and the Mercy of Jesus Christ broke through into his heart and life. Suddenly, he trusted Jesus for forgiveness. He asked the Lord to cleanse his heart and his hands from the stain of blood that he had shed those years before. In a moment's time, *"... the Blood of Jesus Christ, God's Son, cleansed him from all sin"* (I Jn. 1:7). He was totally forgiven, cleansed and restored. His name was immediately entered into the Lamb's Book of Life, and he was just as saved as anyone who had committed lesser sins.

God will forgive any sin, no matter how despicable. Any person who comes to Him, He will in no wise cast out. But if men wilfully sin against Light and turn their backs upon God and put Christ to an open shame by denying His Precious Blood — if they wilfully with eyes wide open ascribe the Works of the

NOTES

Holy Spirit to the Devil — if they wilfully and knowing apostatize themselves — then there is no way for them to be saved, for they have denied the very Agency which brings them to Christ, and that which saves them, the Blood of Christ. They have blasphemed the Holy Spirit; they have committed the unpardonable sin. Man is not the judge of this, God is.

Paul said in Hebrews 10:31, *"It is a fearful thing to fall into the hands of the Living God."* Some Christians, constantly fed on the pabulum of a God Who is Love only and not justice or vengeance, are disturbed by this Scripture. But the fact is, God does have limits beyond which He cannot go if He is to be the God of Truth, Honesty, and Justice. Those who reject God's Love and Mercy must realize that fairness demands a consequence for such actions.

Those who brazenly defy God and those who constantly tempt God by tiptoeing about the edges of His Mercy and Forbearance, should read Proverbs 1:24-33. This is God's very Word directed at those who have been described in this Message.

"Because I have called, and ye refused; I have stretched out My Hand, and no man regarded;

"But ye have set at nought all My counsel, and would none of My reproof:

"I also will laugh at your calamity; I will mock when your fear cometh;

"When your fear cometh as desolation, and your destruction cometh as a whirlwind; when distress and anguish cometh upon you.

"Then shall they call upon Me, but I will not answer; they shall seek Me early, but they shall not find Me:

"For that they hated knowledge, and did not choose the fear of the Lord:

"They would (have) *none of My counsel: they despised all of My reproof.*

"Therefore shall they eat of the fruit of their own way, and be filled with their own devices.

"For the turning away of the simple shall slay them, and the prosperity of fools shall destroy them.

"But whoso hearkeneth unto Me shall dwell safely, and shall be quiet from fear of evil."

(32) "AND WHOSOEVER SPEAKETH A WORD AGAINST THE SON OF MAN, IT SHALL BE FORGIVEN HIM: BUT WHOSOEVER SPEAKETH AGAINST THE HOLY GHOST, IT SHALL NOT BE FORGIVEN HIM,

NEITHER IN THIS WORLD, NEITHER IN THE WORLD TO COME."

The phrase, *"And whosoever speaketh a word against the Son of Man,"* involves many, because many, even as Paul, have blasphemed Him, but forgiveness is promised if it is asked (I Jn. 1:9).

The phrase, *"But whosoever speaketh against the Holy Ghost, it shall not be forgiven him,"* proclaims the finality of such an act.

The phrase, *"Neither in this world, neither in the world to come,"* concerns two dispensations.

"This world," referred to the dispensation of Law that was then closing.

"The world to come," referred to the dispensation of Grace that was even then beginning.

In other words, God's attitude concerning this sin would not change from one dispensation to the other. As it was under Law, it is under Grace.

(33) "EITHER MAKE THE TREE GOOD, AND HIS FRUIT GOOD; OR ELSE MAKE THE TREE CORRUPT, AND HIS FRUIT CORRUPT: FOR THE TREE IS KNOWN BY HIS FRUIT."

This statement of Christ goes back to verse 30, *"He that is not with Me is against Me."* The idea is that the *"tree"* cannot be both *"good"* and *"corrupt"* at the same time. He was speaking of the Pharisees and all such like!

The phrase, *"For the tree is known by his fruit,"* placed them and all such like on one side and Him on the other, as all who followed Him.

His *"tree"* was good, because the *"fruit"* was good.

Their *"tree"* was corrupt, because the *"fruit"* was corrupt!

Under Him and His teaching, lives were changed, people were drawn to God, sick bodies were healed, demons were cast out, and bondages were broken. In other words, the evidence was the *"good fruit."*

The tree of the Pharisees, and despite their claims, produced no good fruit. No lives were changed; no sick bodies were healed; no demons were cast out; no bondages were broken.

Conversely, by their teaching, people were pulled away from God toward ritualism, and away from the Word of God to their own rules and regulations.

This Statement of Christ is actually a continuance of His dissertation on *"false*

prophets,*"* and their *"fruits,"* as expressed in Matthew 7:15-20.

His definition is clear and plain, and yet, many if not most Christians little check the fruit or else believe great claims of such, while little or no evidence can be produced.

Tragically, at the time of Christ, many if not most were labelling the *"corrupt fruit"* as good, and the *"good fruit"* as corrupt!

As then, so now!

If the fruit is good, the tree is good, and despite whatever difficulties there may be.

(34) "O GENERATION OF VIPERS, HOW CAN YE, BEING EVIL, SPEAK GOOD THINGS? FOR OUT OF THE ABUNDANCE OF THE HEART THE MOUTH SPEAKETH."

The phrase, *"O generation of vipers,"* is a strong statement indeed! He was speaking of the Pharisees, and likened them to *"vipers,"* i.e., snakes, because that old serpent, the Devil, was their father.

As well, virtually the entirety of this *"generation"* had been influenced by these *"vipers."* Consequently, they would be lost.

The question, *"How can ye, being evil, speak good things?",* meant that because of the evil of the Pharisees, it was impossible for them to know Who He was or the source of His Works. Consequently, there was nothing good they could say about Him, because there was nothing good in them.

The phrase, *"For out of the abundance of the heart the mouth speaketh,"* is meant to point to total depravity. Such proclaims the Truth, and especially the *"good tree"* and the *"corrupt tree"* of the previous verse, that man is either one or the other. He is either a follower of Christ and produces *"good fruit,"* or he is *"evil."*

This puts all the religions of the world in the *"evil"* category, plus all who have not accepted Christ. Allow us to emphasize again, there is no middle ground. While there are degrees of evil, still, it comes from the *"corrupt tree."*

The question then must be asked, if it is possible for *"good things"* to be done out of an *"evil heart?"*

Yes, evil man is capable of producing some good things, and because the influence of his being originally created in the Image of God is still prevalent. However, these *"good things"* are the exception and in no way produces Salvation, and does not mean that one is saved.

However, most of the world base their judgment on the good things, so-called, equating it with Salvation, etc.

(35) "A GOOD MAN OUT OF THE GOOD TREASURE OF THE HEART BRINGETH FORTH GOOD THINGS: AND AN EVIL MAN OUT OF THE EVIL TREASURE BRINGETH FORTH EVIL THINGS."

As was the method of Christ, He once again says the same thing as said in verse 33, but in a different way.

The *"good man"* of this verse is the same as the *"good tree"* of verse 33, as the *"evil man"* is the same as the *"corrupt tree."*

As the *"good tree"* will bring forth *"good fruit,"* likewise, the *"good man"* will bring forth *"good treasure"* out of his heart. If one is truly born again, these *"good things"* will be evident, and because of the state of the transformed heart, and is the sign of true conversion.

Irrespective of the claims, and irrespective of great religious activity, if one has not truly been born again, the heart as a result is not changed, because religious activity cannot change it. Consequently, and despite all the religious accouterments, the man is still *"evil"* and will continue to bring forth *"evil things."*

Churches are full of individuals who claim Salvation. They claim to have accepted Christ as their Saviour, and claim to believe what He did at Calvary, etc. However, their lives have not changed!

The same lifestyle they had *"before joining the Church,"* they continue to have. In effect, the only change that has come about is that they are now somewhat religious and attend Church fairly often. Other than that, there is no change, and especially in their lifestyle.

The Truth is, these individuals, who in fact are the majority of Church-goers, have not truly been *"born again,"* consequently, their hearts remain *"evil."*

Years ago, an acquaintance of mine, a famous sports figure, gave his heart and life to the Lord, and, as well, was Baptized in the Holy Spirit. His life drastically and gloriously changed, and, of course, for the better!

I saw him some time later, asking him about his situation, and casually asked how his Church had accepted the beautiful thing that had happened within his life?

He laughed, exclaiming that he was no

longer a part of that Church. The Pastor had called him in, politely suggesting that he might be happier somewhere else.

He laughed again, and said, *"Brother Swaggart, when I was drinking, cursing, being unfaithful to my wife, and doing about anything else I was big enough to do, I was a member in good standing in my Church.*

"But now that I have been Baptized in the Holy Spirit and speak with other tongues, consequently ceasing my past activities, and, as well, having fallen in love with Jesus, I am no longer welcome at my Church."

In Truth, the Church he formerly attended, which, incidentally, was one of the major Churches in the city, was, in Truth, no Church at all, at least as far as God was concerned. It was a *"social club,"* which describes most of the Churches in America and the world.

(36) "BUT I SAY UNTO YOU, THAT EVERY IDLE WORD THAT MEN SHALL SPEAK, THEY SHALL GIVE ACCOUNT THEREOF IN THE DAY OF JUDGMENT."

The phrase, *"But I say unto you,"* is meant to portray an even more severe announcement.

The phrase, *"That every idle word that men shall speak,"* concerns their claims of Salvation, and accompanied by many words, claiming that the *"corrupt tree"* is *"good,"* when, in reality, it is not.

The phrase, *"They shall give account thereof in the day of Judgment,"* says two things:

1. It is God, and not man, Who lays the standard as to whether the tree is *"good"* or *"corrupt."* Actually, His Word is the standard!

That is the reason Jesus had previously said to *"Fear God,"* and not man (10:28-33).

2. Despite the denial of much of the world, Jesus says, there will be a *"Day of Judgment,"* and of that, one can be sure! It is called the *"Great White Throne Judgment,"* and all of these things that men say and do are *"written in the Books, according to their works,"* to which they will answer (Rev. 20:11-15).

(37) "FOR BY THY WORDS THOU SHALT BE JUSTIFIED, AND BY THY WORDS THOU SHALT BE CONDEMNED."

The idea is that words proceed out of the heart.

If the person is truly a follower of Christ, his words will portray such, because he has confessed Christ with his mouth as Lord, and, even more so, the Lord of his own life (Rom. 10:9-10).

As well, and despite contrary claims, the evil heart will show itself in the very words of the converted person. As the first was *"justified"* by his words, the latter will be *"condemned"* by his words.

It is somewhat like knowing the password. You either do, or you don't, and your words will portray such.

The words of the Pharisees portrayed them as followers of Satan, and despite their claims, while the Words of Christ portrayed Him as being of God. Consequently, there was really no excuse for the people being deceived.

Neither is there any excuse for people being deceived today!

(38) "THEN CERTAIN OF THE SCRIBES AND OF THE PHARISEES ANSWERED, SAYING, MASTER, WE WOULD SEE A SIGN FROM THEE."

The phrase, *"Then certain of the Scribes,"* were distinct from those of verse 24; but just as unbelieving and guilty, as appears from the Lord's Language to them.

The phrase, *"And of the Pharisees,"* refers to the fact that the Scribes were a part of the Pharisees, and because they shared the same Doctrine.

It is strange, both these groups claimed to believe the Bible from cover to cover, and took it literally.

The Sadducees were another party who did not take the Bible literally, along with the Herodians, who did not take it at all. These, as well, were enemies of Christ, but not nearly so as the Scribes and Pharisees.

How could anyone claim to believe the Bible and be as strict about it as they claimed they were, and still oppose Christ, Who was, in reality, the Living Word of God?

The Truth is, they really did not believe the Bible, having twisted and turned it to make it say what they desired, and then made their Salvation out of their twisted version of it.

Millions today do the same thing!

The Bible, which then consisted of Genesis through Malachi, was just as real, true, and life-giving as Jesus Himself. Actually, the Written Word and the Living Word were indivisible. So, these hypocrites really did not believe the Bible as they claimed!

The phrase, *"Answered, saying, Master, we*

would see a sign from Thee," proclaims further their evil hearts.

After hearing the Words of Christ respecting blaspheming the Holy Spirit and the *"good tree"* and the *"bad tree,"* and even knowing of His great miracles and healings, they demanded a different type of *"sign."*

They were probably demanding a sign from Heaven, something that would be very obvious and would be instant and at His Command!

The True signs of His Messiahship, as given in the Word of God, which are found in Isaiah 61:1 as well as other places, of these they had no interest. They demanded something the Scriptures did not promise, and, in reality, if done, would have been a sign that He was not the Messiah!

Consequently, when the modern Church seeks signs which have little Scriptural validity, what does that say?

These *"Scribes,"* who were supposed to be sticklers for the Word of God, had, in reality, drifted so far from the Bible that their words, and exactly as Christ had stated, betrayed them. They were asking for something which was not Biblical, and if they had been truly converted and had known the Word as they claimed, they would not have asked such!

If it is to be noticed, they called Him *"Master,"* which meant *"Teacher,"* but it was said with sarcasm. In their heart they had no regard for Him as the Messiah and no respect for Him as a True Teacher of the Word of God, which He really was.

(39) "BUT HE ANSWERED AND SAID UNTO THEM, AN EVIL AND ADULTEROUS GENERATION SEEKEST AFTER A SIGN; AND THERE SHALL NO SIGN BE GIVEN TO IT, BUT THE SIGN OF THE PROPHET JONAS:"

The phrase, *"But He answered and said unto them,"* consists of a startling rebuke!

The phrase, *"An evil and adulterous generation seekest after a sign,"* spoke of that present *"generation,"* and was called *"evil and adulterous."*

They were *"seeking after a sign,"* means that they were not at all satisfied with the true signs, which were Biblical and were taking place constantly.

If it is to be noticed, the true *"signs"* He performed set people free, while the *"sign"* they asked for would have delivered no one, but, in effect, would have been only a stunt, if performed.

Even though the sin of *"adultery"* may have been common at this time, still, the manner in which Jesus used this word, spoke instead of Israel's spiritual unfaithfulness to God, and, therefore, the worship of something else which, in effect, was their own religion, a twisted version of the Law of Moses.

The phrase, *"And there shall no sign be given to it, but the sign of the Prophet Jonas,"* was not exactly what they expected, and neither would they have understood it.

Inasmuch as they could easily understand the true signs of healings and miracles that Christ performed, but would not accept them, He would give them a *"sign"* they could not understand, and because of their unbelief. Had they accepted the first, they would have understood the latter. He was speaking of His Resurrection.

(40) "FOR AS JONAS WAS THREE DAYS AND THREE NIGHTS IN THE WHALE'S BELLY; SO SHALL THE SON OF MAN BE THREE DAYS AND THREE NIGHTS IN THE HEART OF THE EARTH."

This Statement of Christ tells us several things:

1. Jesus was referring to Jonah 1:17, which spoke of the great fish swallowing Jonah, and his *"three days and three nights"* in this fish.

2. The word, *"whale,"* is here used, while the term, *"great fish,"* is used in Jonah 1:17. There is no discrepancy, for a *"whale"* is a *"great fish."*

THE MIRACLE-WORKING POWER OF GOD

Many claim that the account of the *"whale"* swallowing Jonah is nothing more than a fable. To state such, however, is to doubt God, to question His Word, and to question His Power.

There truly are some whales which are up to one hundred feet long and weigh as much as 300,000 pounds.

The *"Literary Digest"* in 1896 printed the story of a Mediterranean whale that was so large that it demolished a harpoon boat and also attacked two men. One man was killed and the other man was swallowed by the whale.

About a day and a half after the episode, the whale was killed and the man was rescued. His name was James Bartley, and he lived with no aftereffects except his skin was tanned by the gastric juices of the whale.

The facts are these: If the Bible says it, irrespective of the scoffers and the doubters, one

NOTES

can be absolutely certain that whatever the Bible says about a situation, that's exactly what has happened.

Once again, we state: To doubt the Word of God is to doubt God. Such portrays tremendous ignorance, to say the least.

3. Christ, as portraying His Death, and being in the grave *"three days and three nights,"* means that He could not have been crucified on Good Friday, as most suppose. Actually, there is no statement in the Scripture that says He was crucified and buried on Friday. This would put Him in the grave only one day and one night, proving His Own Words untrue.

Actually, He stayed in the grave three full days and three full nights, exactly as He stated. He was put in the grave Wednesday just before sunset and was resurrected at the end of Saturday at sunset.

Some people are confused by the Sabbath of John 19:31. However, the Sabbath spoken of in that verse is not the regular weekly Saturday Sabbath, but the special Sabbath of the Feast, which fell on a Thursday.

4. The *"heart of the earth,"* refers to the lower parts of the earth, and actually speaks of Paradise, which occupants Jesus liberated during the time His Body was in the grave, as well as His preaching to the *"spirits in prison"* (Eph. 4:9; I Pet. 3:19). Exactly what this referred to, His preaching to the spirits in prison, is not stated. We know that it was a part of hell, but not much more than that.

As well, the word, *"preaching,"* at least in this instance, does not mean the proclamation of Good News as it normally does, but, instead, an announcement. As well, we have no knowledge as to what that announcement was!

5. Some have concluded that Jonah, in the belly of the whale, actually died, and was resurrected after three days and three nights. They contend this was necessary in order to properly serve as a True Type of Christ. However, His *"three days and three nights in the whale's belly,"* while in the deep of the sea, could have served the same purpose without him actually dying.

It is my opinion that he did not die, and especially considering that Jesus said, *"he was three days and three nights in the whale's belly,"* with no mention that he actually died.

As well, Jonah's account of himself does not anywhere relate the plain statement that he died.

6. The greatest *"sign"* of all would be the Resurrection of Christ after being dead three days and three nights. His Resurrection validated His Messiahship, His miracles, and what He did at Calvary.

If, in fact, He would not be able to come out of the grave as Jonah came out of the whale, then everything else was a moot point.

About a year and a half later, Israel, which included these Scribes and Pharisees, would be given this sign, but would not believe it either!

To be sure, there is no *"sign"* that could be given, and irrespective of its power, that would be as great as the *"sign"* of His Resurrection.

(41) "THE MEN OF NINEVEH SHALL RISE IN JUDGMENT WITH THIS GENERATION, AND SHALL CONDEMN IT: BECAUSE THEY REPENTED AT THE PREACHING OF JONAS; AND, BEHOLD, A GREATER THAN JONAS IS HERE."

The two statements of Christ in verses 41 and 42 are powerful indeed!

Once again, Jesus used as an example the Gentiles (Ninevites), which would have infuriated the Scribes and Pharisees. The very idea that these Gentile dogs, and irrespective of their repentance, were better than they was preposterous, at least according to their thinking!

The phrase, *"The men of Nineveh,"* proclaims the idea that the men of this heathen city, and as evil as they were, took the lead in coming to God, which occasioned the following of their wives and children.

In effect, Nineveh was very evil, and was being threatened by the Judgment of God unless they repented. Miracle of miracles, they did repent.

The people of this city were the cruelest of the cruel, and yet in their generation more Righteous than Israel at this time in her generation, and because they repented.

The phrase, *"Shall rise in judgment,"* i.e., stands in mute judgment of Israel, and because they repented, and Israel would not.

The phrase, *"With this generation,"* is said with contempt by Christ.

They were evil beyond evil; wicked beyond wicked, and despite all their claims to the contrary.

"This generation" of Israel, was visited by no less than the Son of God, whereas Nineveh was privileged to hear only the Prophet Jonah.

NOTES

As well, Christ performed the greatest miracles the world had ever known, while Jonah performed none.

The words, *"And shall condemn it,"* is because of the very things mentioned.

The phrase, *"Because they repented at the preaching of Jonas,"* signifies that this was the only witness they had, while Israel had every other type of witness that could be given by Heaven.

They had the miracles, healings, Christ Himself, along with preaching that was such as the world had never heard before.

Consequently, this leads to the next phrase, *"And, behold, a greater than Jonas is here."* And yet Israel still would not repent!

(42) "THE QUEEN OF THE SOUTH SHALL RISE UP IN THE JUDGMENT WITH THIS GENERATION, AND SHALL CONDEMN IT: FOR SHE CAME FROM THE UTTERMOST PARTS OF THE EARTH TO HEAR THE WISDOM OF SOLOMON; AND, BEHOLD, A GREATER THAN SOLOMON IS HERE."

Once again, the Lord uses a Gentile as an example.

The heathen, represented by the men of Nineveh and the Queen of Sheba, believed the Word of the Lord proclaimed by a Prophet and by a King, but Israel refused to believe that Word at the Mouth of Him Who was Greater than Jonah, and greater than Solomon; as He was also Greater than the Temple.

As well, we might quickly add, if the story of Jonah is only a parable, as many say, and not historically true, then is the story of the Queen of Sheba also untrue; but the Lord here puts them on the same historic basis; and He insisted repeatedly that He only spake Truth because He only said what God told Him to say.

As well, if the illustration of Nineveh was condemning, the illustration of the Queen of Sheba is even more so.

The Message of Repentance was brought to the Ninevites by Jonah to their own city, and possibly even to their own homes. However, the Queen of Sheba marks a higher stage of inquiry and Faith, inasmuch as she traveled *"From the uttermost parts of the earth to hear the wisdom of Solomon."*

The idea is that at great expense, time and trouble, she would make this long arduous trip, and would be amply rewarded.

By contrast, Jesus came to Israel with them having to expend no money, time or energy to hear Him, but despite the convenience still would not receive Him.

As well, this woman went to all of this trouble and distance to hear Solomon, while Israel had no interest in Christ, even though He was far greater than Solomon in both wisdom and power.

What an indictment!

Also, Solomon had only *"wisdom"* to offer, while Christ could offer eternal life, but with few takers!

There are still few takers!

(43) "WHEN THE UNCLEAN SPIRIT IS GONE OUT OF A MAN, HE WALKETH THROUGH DRY PLACES, SEEKING REST, AND FINDETH NONE."

The phrase, *"When the unclean spirit is gone out of a man,"* refers to these spirits of darkness which went out of Israel when she was destroyed by Nebuchadnezzar. At that time, the nation ceased to be, and was only restored some 70 years later, albeit in a very diminished form.

To be sure, the spirit of darkness *"went out,"* but not because it was cast out by the Power of God, as the man was delivered of verse 22.

The phrase, *"He walketh through dry places, seeking rest, and findeth none,"* proclaims the manner of *"Unclean spirits"* and, in particular, the manner of the *"Unclean spirit"* which now inhabited Israel.

As well, the language implies that impure spirits have once had bodies, and hence their eagerness to re-embody themselves in men or even in swine.

(44) "THEN HE SAITH, I WILL RETURN INTO MY HOUSE FROM WHENCE I CAME OUT; AND WHEN HE IS COME, HE FINDETH IT EMPTY, SWEPT, AND GARNISHED."

The phrase, *"Then he saith,"* refers to the intelligence possessed by these spirits as they function in the domain of darkness and under the authority of their master, Satan.

The phrase, *"I will return into my house from whence I came out,"* refers to the possibility at least existing that such could be done.

In fact, there was a short time of Revival upon Israel's return from captivity, under the leading of Ezra and Nehemiah, along with the prophesying of Haggai and Zechariah.

NOTES

However, it was short-lived. There is even some evidence that Zechariah, who wrote the Book that bears his name, was stoned to death by these good people of Israel (Mat. 23:35).

About a hundred years later, Malachi served as the last Prophet of Israel until the Advent of John the Baptist, a time of nearly 400 years. Due to the silence of the prophetic voice at this time, the spirituality of Israel was weak to say the least, and steadily grew weaker. With the absence of the Spirit of God, Israel became a fertile field for *"Evil spirits."* By the time of the Advent of John the Baptist, these *"Unclean spirits"* controlled the nation through its Religious Leadership. Therefore, Satan's greatest trump card of all was played in his infestation of the people and the land, with *"Unclean spirits,"* i.e., religious spirits. There could be no worse bondage!

At the present, religious spirits, i.e., unclean spirits, control India, Saudi Arabia, Syria, Egypt, Jordan, along with all Moslem countries, as well as Japan with its ancestor worship, along with most if not all the Far East, i.e., Buddhism and Confucianism.

Actually, most of the world is controlled by either Islam, Buddhism, Hinduism, Confucianism, Catholicism or Spiritism. This is all in the realm of unclean spirits, i.e., religious spirits.

The reason that America, Canada, and England, plus a few others, have known such greatness is because a modicum of True Bible Christianity, i.e., that which is Truly Christ, was introduced to these nations. Even though it was only partially embraced, still, it brought about a greatness and glory such as the world has never known before, making these nations the envy of the world. Regrettably, this greatness and glory is being lost, and speedily, and because the vision of Christ is being lost.

The phrase, *"And when he is come, he findeth it empty, swept, and garnished,"* respecting an emptiness of the Glory of God.

To be sure, the vacuum will be filled, whether in a nation or an individual. If it is not filled with God, it will be instantly filled with demon spirits. This means that almost the entirety of the world is filled and occupied by *"Unclean spirits;"* hence the murder, rape, robbery, stealing, hatred, racism, pride, poverty, starvation, and war, along with man's inhumanity to man.

The statement, *"Empty, swept, and garnished,"* is meant to portray Israel after the captivity, when, for a period of time, the nation was possessed by neither God nor Satan.

Inasmuch as these were God's people, the possession did not come about until the Lord and His Ways had been abandoned. Therefore, with no one to protect them, Satan filled the vacuum. He found it *"empty"* of God, but *"garnished"* with religious ritual, which he only increased until it destroyed the land.

(45) "THEN GOETH HE, AND TAKETH WITH HIMSELF SEVEN OTHER SPIRITS MORE WICKED THAN HIMSELF, AND THEY ENTER IN AND DWELL THERE: AND THE LAST STATE OF THAT MAN IS WORSE THAN THE FIRST. EVEN SO SHALL IT BE ALSO UNTO THIS WICKED GENERATION."

The phrase, *"Then goeth he,"* concerns the *"Unclean spirit."* The time period spoken of here by Christ is after Israel has rejected and, consequently, crucified Christ. As a result, the way is open for a greater and deeper alignment with the Powers of Darkness. Due to their actions of denying the Son of God, they opened the door for self-destruction as possibly no other nation of the world. They were given tremendous opportunity by the Coming of Christ, their Messiah, and with all His attendant visitation concerning miracles, healings, and the most powerful Word of God which proceeded out of His Mouth they had ever known. But yet, they rejected it with a cool dedicated precision and brought upon themselves a judicial judgment from which there was no escape.

They said they did not want Christ, actually saying, *"We have no king but Caesar,"* and then demanding the crucifixion of Christ. So now they will have an invasion of demon spirits such as they, or any other, have never known.

The phrase, *"And taketh with himself seven other spirits more wicked than himself,"* concerns the infestation of Israel after the rejection of Christ and after He had ascended back to Glory. *"Seven"* being God's number, and inferring totality among other things, emphasizes the fact that the nation was totally and completely taken over by demon spirits. As stated, it was the most diabolical kind of all, i.e., religious spirits. Consequently, they were not only seven times more wicked than they

were at the Advent of Christ, but due to these spirits being *"more wicked,"* they were, in effect, *"total wickedness."*

Israel, had known terrible wickedness previously, which occasioned their destruction by the Babylonians. That wickedness was idolatry. However, idolatry is somewhat clumsy and stupid, but a false Gospel which characterized Israel after its rejection of Christ is neither clumsy nor stupid, and is more wicked than idolatry (I Cor. 2:4; Gal. 1:8).

In effect, and even though Israel was destroyed in 70 A.D., still, this phrase and those following will also pertain to the coming Great Tribulation, when Israel will accept the Antichrist, thinking he is the Messiah.

As a result, Judah will reach the lowest depth of moral and religious degradation immediately prior to the Second Advent; for energized by the unclean spirit of verse 43, and assisted by the seven other spirits, she will reach the *"last state."*

The phrase, *"And they enter in and dwell there,"* concerned Israel, as stated, immediately after her rejection of Christ. The Lord having been rejected, Satan now has an open door.

Regrettably and sadly, even though Israel was scattered all over the world after her terrible defeat by the Romans, these spirits have continued to dwell in these people, and because of their rejection of Christ, with their hatred of Him only increasing, if possible!

The phrase, *"And the last state of that man is worse than the first,"* concerns Israel after her rejection of Christ, which made her *"worse"* and, in effect, *"seven times worse."* As stated, this terrible condition will continue, and even exacerbate during the coming Great Tribulation.

The phrase, *"Even so shall it be also unto this wicked generation,"* places the time frame of Christ's discourse in the generation that rejected Him. Consequently, it was called *"This wicked generation."*

Therefore, what would happen to Israel is here foretold by Christ, which has come to pass to the letter.

(46) "WHILE HE YET TALKED TO THE PEOPLE, BEHOLD, HIS MOTHER AND HIS BRETHREN STOOD WITHOUT, DESIRING TO SPEAK WITH HIM."

The phrase, *"While He yet talked to the people,"* concerns the terrible Word He has just delivered concerning Israel's present and future state.

The phrase, *"Behold, His mother and His brethren stood without,"* refers to the probability that He was in a particular house with His Disciples and many others to whom He was speaking. As well, there must have been a sizable crowd outside, with which *"His mother and His brethren"* had joined, due to their being no more room in the house.

The phrase, *"Desiring to speak with Him,"* proclaims, and due to the following statements, that their desire to speak with Him was not in a positive sense.

Actually, they came to capture and confine Him — thus in spirit uniting with the Pharisees who planned to destroy Him. Such is man, and such is the flesh!

The Scripture says plainly that they did not at this time believe in Him (Jn. 7:5).

Mary was willing to be the honored mother of the King of Israel, but unwilling to be the despised Disciple of the hated Nazarene (Mk. 3:21-31). Thankfully this would change!

The reasons for their opposition are not so readily obvious. More than likely it was the *"flesh"* which opposed the *"Spirit."*

His life had been one of perfection; however, this perfection did not gladden their hearts, as it only showed up their imperfection. Consequently, they, as most, opposed Him.

Such proclaims the Truth that environment, even though it may have some influence, cannot affect one's Salvation. Salvation is a matter of the heart and must be obtained on a personal basis, and irrespective of environment, education, ability, or state!

In connection with their present objections, they see the whole of the religious establishment of Israel turning against Him, and strongly so! To them, His rhetoric, as obvious concerning His Message respecting the demon possession of Israel, seemed to only enflame an already incendiary situation. They fear the worst, so, consequently, they will attempt to restrain Him. But, of course, they will meet with no success, and because His allegiance was to the Father and not them, even though His dearest relatives.

As well, the Scripture is emphatic in including *"His mother"* in this situation. Such debunks the fallacious Mary Doctrine of the Catholic Church, of which we will say more momentarily.

NOTES

(47) "THEN ONE SAID UNTO HIM, BEHOLD, THY MOTHER AND THY BRETHREN STAND WITHOUT, DESIRING TO SPEAK WITH THEE."

The phrase, *"Then one said to Him, Behold,"* proclaims a Message having been given to this man by the mother and brethren of Christ, in order that He may speak with them.

Not desiring to read more into the statement than is actually there, still, the sentence structure lends credence to the thought that they somewhat demanded an audience, and because of family relationship. There is a hint of impatience in the request and, as well, a lack of respect for His present discourse, as it seems they were not hesitant to interrupt it.

The phrase, *"Thy mother and Thy brethren standing without,"* infers that they were tired of waiting, and especially due to the fact that they were family relations and felt they deserved better treatment. Truly, and yet sadly, they were not only, at least at this time, *"standing without"* physically, but spiritually as well! As stated, and thankfully, this would change!

The phrase, *"Desiring to speak with Thee,"* emphasizes that they had things to say to Him, whatever they were, but that they little desired to hear what He had to say to them, inasmuch as it seems that His great discourses, such as the *"Sermon on the Mount,"* etc., were all but ignored by them.

Such is difficult to understand, and must have been a delight to the Pharisees, who, no doubt, exclaimed that even His Own family did not believe in Him!

(48) "BUT HE ANSWERED AND SAID UNTO HIM THAT TOLD HIM, WHO IS MY MOTHER? AND WHO ARE MY BRETHREN?"

His answer is startling!

The phrase, *"But He answered and said unto him that told Him,"* lends credence to the idea that all that has been proposed in my Commentary is correct. Quite possibly, and due to His answer, the situation was even worse than we now know.

The question, *"Who is My mother?",* was said for a purpose. It will totally refute the claims later made by the Catholic Church.

To be sure, the question is not asked with unkindness, but only intending to set the record straight.

The question, *"And who are My brethren?"*, as well, is in the same vein.

Jesus knew the purpose of His relatives, which, at least at that time, was not according to the Will of God. Whatever they wanted or desired, and which His answer proves, was not what the Father wanted and desired! How subject He was to the Will of God, and how little His followers are!

He had previously stated that *"He that loveth father or mother more than Me is not worthy of Me"* (10:37). And now, that which He demanded of His followers, He demonstrates by His allegiance to the Heavenly Father.

As alluded to, the question, *"Who is My mother?"*, completely refutes the fallacious Doctrine of the Catholic Church that Mary is the mother of God.

The Catholic Church, and inasmuch as it is guided by demon spirits, has actually made Mary instead of Christ a mediatrix between God and man.

They pray, *"Hail Mary, full of Grace, the Lord is with thee. Blessed are thou among women, and blessed is the fruit of thy womb, Jesus. Holy Mary, Mother of God, pray for us sinners, now and at the hour of our death. Amen."*

A former Catholic Priest wrote:

"I could personally testify to the fact that the Jesus Christ I knew, loved, and served as a Roman Catholic is not the same Jesus Christ I know, love, and serve today. The Jesus I once knew was a wafer of bread and a cup of wine — and He had a mother called Mary who stood between Him and me. I couldn't get through to Him except through her, and He couldn't get through to me except through her.

"In other words, my religion back then was tantamount to — let's say — Buddhism or the Muslim religion.

"There was no difference, objectively speaking, between me as a Catholic Priest and a Moslem Priest, for example."

Some Catholics pose the question, *"Can't find Jesus?"*; they then say, *"Look for His mother."*

Mary dominates every aspect of Catholic religious life. Unfortunately, this is the opposite of Biblical Christianity.

Regrettably, this terrible error of Mary worship in the Catholic Church has only exacerbated in the last few years, inasmuch as Pope John Paul II claims his position as Pope as a

NOTES

gift from Mary. He claims to have had a vision of her in earlier years, in which she predicted his enthronement to the highest position in Catholicism. Consequently, and due to the heavy promotion by this Pope, the Catholic Church has sunk only deeper into this darkness, making this Pope the opposite of what many Protestants claim, a man of terrible wickedness.

In the following statements, I want to look at Mary as the Catholic sees her, Mary as the mediator between Jesus Christ and man, and Mary as the Bible describes her, of which we have already alluded to.

MARY — AS THE CATHOLIC SEES HER

In this prayer of consecration to Mary, the Catholic says, *"Oh, Mary, my Queen and my Mother, I give myself entirely to thee. And to show my devotion to thee, I consecrate to thee this day my eyes, my ears, my mouth, my heart, my whole being without reserve. Wherefore, oh, good Mother, as I am thine own, keep me and guard me as thy property and possession."*

Catholics feel that Mary occupies a unique and tremendously influential position as a result of her role as Christ's human mother. They are taught that they can safely entrust all their problems to her. She provides, they say, the spiritual key to Salvation of the soul and to receiving miraculous answers to prayers concerning earthly problems.

Catholics are taught (although they will deny this) that Mary is to be given worship equal to God — and higher even than worship afforded Christ. She is to be addressed as *"My Mother."* Even casual observation of Catholics reveals that both conversations and services bring forth more references to the *"Blessed Virgin"* than to the three Persons of the Holy Trinity, God the Father, God the Son, and God the Holy Ghost. Obviously, the Catholic religion strongly is oriented toward veneration of Mary. She is called the following:

- The Mother of Divine Grace
- Help of Christians
- Ark of the Covenant
- Queen of Angels
- Morning Star
- Health of the sick
- The Gate of Heaven

The Catholic *"cult of Mary"* is based fundamentally on her sacred motherhood. The 4th

Century title bestowed upon her by the Catholic Church — Theotokos (Greek for *"Bearer of God"*) — was equivalent to *"Mother of God."*

Rome reasoned this way:

"Mary is the mother of Jesus. Jesus is God. Ergo, Mary is the mother of God."

Furthermore, Catholics state and believe that to deny honor to Mary actually is to deny the Deity of Christ. Of course, if a person accepts this, he opens a flood gate of ensuing theological absurdities that must be accepted as logical developments of the original fallacy.

IS MARY THE MOTHER OF GOD?

No, Mary is not the mother of God. Mary was the mother of the human being, Jesus. Mary served a biological function that was necessary to bring about a unique situation. The preexistent Son of God was to take on human form. As He walked the earth (in human form), He was very God and very Man. His *"God"* component had always been. While Mary was essential to harbor His developing human form (for nine months), she had nothing whatsoever to do with His Godhead! Mary was, therefore, the Mother of Jesus, the Man. She was not, by any stretch of the imagination, the mother of God.

God has no mother. If one understands the Incarnation, one understands that God, while never ceasing to be God, became completely Man.

"Wherefore when He cometh into the world, He saith, Sacrifice and offering Thou wouldest not, but a body hast Thou prepared Me" (Heb. 10:5).

It was this Body that God prepared for His Son — Jesus Christ — Who would become Man. Of necessity, He would be born into the world as are all other human beings, but with one tremendous difference, His Virgin Birth:

"Therefore the Lord Himself shall give you a sign; Behold, a Virgin shall conceive, and bear a Son, and shall call His Name Immanuel" (Isa. 7:14).

This Virgin was the teenaged maiden called Mary. She was to bring the Son of God into the world. But it was not God Who would be born; it was *"The Man Christ Jesus"* (I Tim. 2:5).

THE ANNUNCIATION OF JESUS

The Bible tells us that the Angel Gabriel was sent from God to a Virgin named Mary.

"And the Angel came in unto her, and said,

Hail, thou that art highly favoured, the Lord is with thee: Blessed art thou among women" (Lk. 1:28).

Using this Passage, the Catholic Church has altered the words to read: *"Hail, Mary, full of Grace."* The Church then interprets its own words by advancing the argument that since Mary is full of Grace, she must have been the finest and holiest of all created beings. Further, Catholic Doctrine concludes that through the Grace bestowed on her, she received from God the degree of purity and holiness necessary to be worthy of serving in the role of *"Mother of God."*

Now, let us pause to examine for a moment the *"Hail, Mary"* prayer, which is quoted in its entirety at the beginning of this dissertation. Because this prayer is based (albeit loosely) on Scripture (Lk. 1:28), it seems that Catholics have attempted to place God's stamp of approval on their position in regard to Mary.

The *"Hail, Mary"* begins:

"Hail, Mary, full of Grace, the Lord is with thee. Blessed art thou among women and blessed is the fruit of thy womb, Jesus."

WORD USAGE CAN CHANGE, AND, IN FACT, HAS CHANGED

Now, let us digress for a moment to discuss semantics — the study of language. Language changes constantly. Word meanings change constantly. For example, a few years ago a person who was *"gay"* was *"happy."* Today a *"gay"* person is a *"homosexual,"* and the old definition has fallen completely out of usage.

By the same token, the word, *"blessed,"* has, through usage, taken on two meanings. *"Blessed"* — pronounced as one syllable — describes someone who has received a blessing. In modern thinking, when someone is blessed, he has come suddenly into money, he has been cured of an illness, or what-have-you. On the other hand, when pronounced as two syllables *"bless-ed,"* the word implies a person of superior spirituality, someone who is more saintly in moral character; for example, *"That blessed man returned my lost wallet and wouldn't even accept a reward."*

At the time the Bible was written (and when it was translated by the King James translators), the word *"blessed"* had only one meaning — referring to one who had received a blessing, such as Mary.

Similarly, the word, *"grace,"* has come to have a meaning that is not the Biblical definition. *"Grace"* — within Scripture — means a gift from God that is undeserved. *"Grace"* is a free gift from God with no preconditions or strings attached. But today *"grace"* has come to be used to imply an inherent human quality of goodness that is closely allied to bless-ed-ness.

So the wording of the *"Hail, Mary"* prayer, taken in the context of today's language usage, appears to give Scriptural support to Catholic contentions that Mary was eternally without sin. Turning to the actual words of Scripture, however, we receive a different picture. The Angel Gabriel's actual words were:

"Hail, thou that art highly favoured, the Lord is with thee. Blessed are thou among women" (Lk. 1:28).

Mary was unquestionably highly favored by God, in that He chose her to receive this honor. And it was certainly a blessing to be singled out to hold such a distinctive position in the history of the world. But the rest of the words within this prayer simply were composed by the Catholic Church and have no basis in Scripture whatsoever.

Delving further into this matter, we read where Mary's cousin Elisabeth said:

"And whence is this to me, that the mother of my Lord should come to me?" (Lk. 1:43).

Here, Elisabeth called Jesus *"Lord."* She was talking about the unborn Holy Child then occupying Mary's womb. He definitely is Lord. He is called *"The Lord Jesus Christ"* many times within the Word of God.

But, once again, it must be emphasized that it was not God Who was born of Mary, it was the human Child — the Lord Jesus Christ.

The unbiblical worship of Mary by the Catholic Church has its perverted foundation in the insupportable misnomer, *"Mother of God."* The correct Scriptural description of Mary is the simple Biblical expression, *"Mary the Mother of Jesus"* (Acts 1:14).

THE IMMACULATE CONCEPTION

This erroneous (and confusing) term does not refer to the conception of Jesus Christ (as most non-Catholics and many Catholics believe). It refers to the conception of Mary in her mother's womb.

The Catholic Catechism says:

NOTES

"The Blessed Virgin Mary alone, from the first instant of her conception, through the foreseen merits of Jesus Christ, by a unique privilege granted her by God, was kept free from the stain of original sin . . . . From the first moment of her conception (she) *possessed justice and holiness, even the fullness of Grace, with the infused virtues and the gifts of the Holy Ghost."*

This Doctrine, a total fiction with no Scriptural support, was *"infallibly"* defined by Pope Pius IX as part of the *"revealed deposit of Catholic Faith"* in 1854. There was great opposition to this pronouncement at the time within the Catholic Church.

The Doctrine of the Immaculate Conception implies that for Mary to be born without original sin, her mother also had to be a sinless virgin. The only other alternative is that God granted her a unique immunity to the all-pervasive original sin that is an inescapable element of the human condition.

To be frank, Roman Catholic Theologians lamely defend their assertion of the Immaculate Conception by saying that *"God could have done it"* or *"It was fitting that He should do so — and therefore He did it."*

But, of course, if God had decided on such a course, it would have meant that He was replacing the Plan of Salvation described in the Bible with a totally new concept.

If this had happened, we would have a quadrinity instead of the Trinity. God's Word then would have stated that the Godhead consists of God the Father, God the Son, God the Holy Spirit, and Mary, the Mother of God. The Bible does not so state, so we can then conclude that this aberrant Doctrine is not of God.

THE ORIGIN OF "MARY,
THE MOTHER OF GOD"

The veneration of Mary, the Mother of God, and the use of the term, *"Mother of God,"* originated about A.D. 381. It was officially decreed by the Council of Ephesus in A.D. 431.

Prayers started to be directed to Mary as well as to the other Saints about A.D. 600.

The *"Immaculate Conception of Mary"* was proclaimed by Pius IX, as previously stated, in A.D. 1854.

In 1931, Pope Pius XI reaffirmed the Doctrine that Mary is the *"Mother of God."*

In 1950, Pope Pius XII pronounced the Doctrine of the *"Assumption of Mary."* This states that Mary, at the completion of her earthly life, was bodily taken up into Heaven without knowing death. Oddly enough, this mystical belief had been a peripheral precept within the Catholic Church since the Middle Ages, but was only given official certification in 1950. There was a great deal of resistance to the issuance of this Doctrine by Pius XII, but he insisted that it was his infallible right to declare such a *"fact."*

THE BABYLONIAN CULT

Fundamentally, the worship of Mary originated with the worship of *"The Queen of Heaven"* — a pagan deity. It seems that the Roman Church — in altering its Doctrines to conform to those formerly observed by conscripted pagans — saw that it would be politically desirable to supply the populace with a satisfying parallel figure within their newly-imposed Christian religion. Thus was Mary elevated to Divine status.

The image of mother and child had been a primary object of Babylonian worship for centuries before the birth of Christ. From Babylon, this spread to the ends of the earth. The original mother figure in this tableau was Semiramis — the personification of unbridled lust and sexual gratification. And once we start to study the worship practices of heathen nations, we find amazing similarities embraced over wide areas and through long periods of time.

For instance: In Egypt, the mother and child are known as Isis and Horus; in India, Isi and Iswara; in Asia, Cybele and Edoius; in Pagan Rome, Fortuna and Jupiter-puer; in Greece, Ceres with Plutus in arms. In isolated Tibet and in China and Japan, early Roman Catholic Missionaries were stunned to find counterparts of the Madonna (the Italian name for the Virgin Mary) and her child being worshiped as devoutly as in Rome itself. Shing Moo (the *"Mother of China"*) is represented with child in arms and with a halo around her head — exactly as if she had been painted by a Roman painter.

These nations all trace their common worship from Babylon — before its dispersion in the days of Nimrod. Thus, worship of Mary is

Babylonian in origin. There is absolutely no suggestion of such worship in Scripture.

MARY AS THE MEDIATOR BETWEEN JESUS AND MAN

Mary is looked upon by the Catholic Church as an intercessor, a mediator, and a redemptress. Some Catholics say this is not a *"defined article of the Faith."* Others say it is. In any case, in practice, it is part and parcel of what is known as the *"Ordinary Teaching Authority"* of the Church.

These titles signify that Mary is a universal intercessor — that is, she seeks God's favors for all mankind. They clearly imply that Mary is so intimately associated with our Redemption that she may be considered a co-Saviour with Christ, although subordinate to Him. Church Doctrine further alleges that Mary *"mediates Grace universally."*

What does this mean in plain language? Incredibly, the Catholic position is that no Grace flows from God to any person without passing through the good offices of Mary!

Some Church Leaders state that Doctrines concerning Mary were modified and tempered by the Second Vatican Council of 1962-1965. However, this is what Catholic Priest Anthony Wildhelm stated in his book, *"Christ Among Us: A Modern Presentation of the Catholic Faith:"*

• On page 90: *"God the Son became a Man through Mary, His human mother, whom we call the Mother of God. We can say that God has relatives, that God has a mother."*

• On page 91: *"The Hail, Mary is one of the most ancient prayers of the Church..."* *"Hail, Mary, full of Grace.*

'By these privileges, which God gave to Mary, we can see that He always prepares people for their roles in His Plan."

• On page 367: *"We particularly honor Mary, the Mother of Christ, because of her great role in God's Plan of Salvation. She was closer to Christ than anyone else."*

• On page 368: *"Mary is God's masterpiece. To honor her is to honor God, Who made her what she is.*

"Because of Mary's great role, she was conceived without sin, remained sinless throughout life, and was perpetually a virgin.

"We believe in Mary's Assumption, that she was taken into Heaven, body and soul, at the end of her earthly life."

• On page 369: *"We give special place to Mary's intercession and sometimes consider her to be our 'spiritual mother.'"*

• On page 370: *"Mary is the model Christian, the preeminent member of the Church."*

• On page 371: *"Mary is particularly the model of our worship."*

"The devotion of the rosary has been a tremendous influence in helping hundreds of millions to pray."

The Roman cult of Mary erects a barrier between the individual and the Trinity. It confuses the Catholic Believer's perception of the work and functions of the individual members of Godhead. It robs Christ of His unique Creatorship.

Rome's theologians insist that Mary's role and function is to lead souls to Christ. However, Jesus said:

"That which is born of the Spirit is Spirit . . . So is everyone that is born of the Spirit" (Jn. 3:6-8).

He further stated:

"No man can come to Me, except the Father which hath sent Me draw him" (Jn. 6:43-44).

So, according to the Bible, Mary has no role to play in the Salvation of a soul.

I go back once again to our quote from a former Catholic Priest:

"The Jesus I once knew was a wafer of bread and a cup of wine, and He had a mother called Mary who stood between Him and me . . . ."

Does his statement sound like he was *"led to Christ by Mary?"*

DO CATHOLICS WORSHIP MARY?

Catholics maintain that they do not worship Mary, that she only aids them in their worship of God.

However, when the Catholic attributes the Immaculate Conception to Mary, they are conferring Divinity upon her by this claim. The term *"worship,"* as defined by *"Webster's New Collegiate Dictionary,"* is *"Reverence paid to a Divine being and extravagant respect or admiration for, or devotion to, an object of esteem."* In ascribing the Immaculate Conception to Mary, the Catholic Church has, in effect, declared her Divine, and thus renders her worship that should be reserved only for Deity. By their constant reference to her, worship is afforded.

Yes, Catholics do worship Mary. To be tragically concise, most Catholics do not understand

the worship of God the Father or of His Son, Jesus Christ. The real focus and conception of their worship is directed to Mary. And, of course, their perception of worshiping God is the worship of God through Mary. Everything must go through Mary to God — and everything must come from God through Mary, they say.

MARY AS THE BIBLE DESCRIBES HER

To be brutally frank, there is little mention of Mary within the Word of God.

MATTHEW

In Matthew, Chapter 2, we read of Mary's witnessing the adoration of the wise men. This Chapter also recounts the events leading to the trip to Egypt. Then it gives account of an experience from the childhood of Jesus and describes Mary's concern.

As well, Mary is mentioned, and as we are commenting on, as desiring to see Jesus, but with the response of Christ not favorable.

MARK

Mary is mentioned only briefly in this Gospel: Once as simply the mother of the Carpenter Jesus (Mk. 6:3) and again as a family member (Mk. 3:32).

LUKE

Luke, Chapter 1, describes the visit of the Angel Gabriel to Mary. The same Chapter tells of Mary's visit to Elisabeth. We can conclude from the statements made by Mary that she had a wide-ranging knowledge of the Old Testament — which is commentary on her spiritual perceptions.

Luke, Chapter 2, describes Mary as giving birth to the Lord Jesus Christ in the stable. She also pondered here the words of the shepherds.

JOHN

In John, Chapter 2, Mary asks Jesus to perform His first public miracle at Cana. (Obviously, because of the confidence with which she approached the situation, she knew His capabilities.) Oddly enough, in Mark 3, Matthew 12, and Luke 8, it seems she either opposed His Ministry or at least harbored some confusion about His Mission.

John, Chapter 19, talks about how Mary stood at the foot of the Cross and observed with great sorrow the death of her Son — her Saviour and our Saviour — the Lord Jesus Christ.

ACTS

According to Acts 1:14, Mary was numbered among the 120 who tarried in the Upper Room waiting for the enduement of Power on the Day of Pentecost. She, like other Believers, needed that infilling of the Holy Spirit as power for service.

This is all the Bible reveals about Mary. (And, incidentally, in the Gospels, Jesus never did call her *"Mother."* He addressed her as *"Woman."* But going back to the ancient Hebrew, this was not an expression of disrespect.)

So, let us look now without superimposed opinions or doctrines, at the bare bones of what the Bible does say about Mary.

HIGHLY FAVOURED

When the Angel Gabriel appeared to her, as described in Luke 1, he used the word *"Hail."* This simply means *"Hello,"* a salutation used to get a person's attention. He also used the phrase, *"highly favoured,"* which means *"blessed"* or *"endued with Grace."* As discussed earlier, these terms do not imply anymore than that the person has received an unmerited favor.

Mary was highly favored. No doubt hundreds of thousands (or even millions) of pious, young Israelite maidens had aspired to be the one so highly favored. They had known from ancient Prophecies, that the *"Seed,"* the *"Redeemer,"* would be born to a Hebrew maiden. And from Isaiah's Prophecy they further knew that she had to be a virgin.

"Therefore the Lord Himself shall give you a sign; Behold, a Virgin shall conceive, and bear a Son, and shall call His Name Immanuel" (Isa. 7:14).

Very importantly, the lineage had to come through David. Matthew gives the genealogy in the royal line through Solomon. In Luke, the royal line was given through Nathan, another son of David, and then through Heli, the father of Mary. Both lines were necessary in fulfilling Prophecy.

God had placed a curse upon Jechoniah of the royal line and sworn that no seed of his should ever sit on the Throne of David and reign in Jerusalem (Jer. 22:24-30).

God had also sworn to David that his line (through Solomon) would forever sit on his

Throne (II Sam. 7). The only way this could be fulfilled was for Jesus, the Son of David (through Nathan and Mary), to become legal heir to the Throne of David through his stepfather, Joseph, of the Kingly Line (Lk. 1:32-33).

Jesus, as the foster Son of Joseph and the firstborn of His family, became the legal Heir to David's Throne through Joseph. However, it must be remembered, the Royal Line in Matthew was given through Solomon which culminates in Joseph. The Royal Line in Luke was given through Nathan, culminating in the father of Mary, Heli.

So, Mary, in the Royal Lineage through Nathan, David's son, became the mother of the Lord Jesus Christ.

Yes, Mary was highly favored.

And certainly it could be said that the Lord was with her and she would be blessed among many.

HANDMAIDEN OF THE LORD

Mary called herself . . . *"The Handmaid of the Lord"* (Lk. 1:38).

This shows the beautiful humility characterized by Mary and is a statement that might well be studied by Catholic Theologians.

However, there is a tremendous difference between *"The Handmaid of the Lord"* and *"Mother of God."*

By her own words, Mary refuted the Catholic Doctrine of the Immaculate Conception:

"And my spirit hath rejoiced in God my Saviour" (Lk. 1:47).

This statement by Mary totally discounts the theory of an Immaculate Conception and the Catholic contention that Mary was ever without sin. If God was her Saviour, then she must have needed Salvation, which presupposes some history of normal human sin. No Scripture even hints that Mary was sinless.

This false cult of Mary worship is another effort by Satan who knows that one cannot completely accept Christ as long as one retains heretical concepts of Mary. Incidentally, Luke's statement in 1:28 quotes Gabriel's words as being *"Blessed art thou among women."* It does not say, *"Blessed art thou above women."*

ACCORDING TO THE BIBLE, IS MARY AN INTERCESSOR AND A MEDIATRIX?

"Wherefore He is able also to save them to the uttermost that come unto God by Him,

seeing He ever liveth to make intercession for them" (Heb. 7:25).

Jesus Christ is our only Intercessor. There is no hint or suggestion in the Word of God that Mary should or would occupy such a role. Whenever Mary is inserted into the role of intercessor (as she is by the Catholic Church, to intercede with her Son, Jesus Christ, on behalf of individuals on earth), this, in effect, robs Christ of the rightful position He earned through His tremendous Sacrifice on Calvary. He paid the full price on that Cross with the shedding of His Precious Blood.

Christ Alone is worthy to make intercession for us. Christ Alone paid the price. Mary did not suffer and die on the Cross. She did not shed her blood. And neither does Christ need an assistant to motivate Him to intercede for the Saints. He is perfectly capable of performing this duty Himself, as He ever sits at the Right Hand of God making intercession for us.

"It is Christ that died, yea rather, that is risen again, Who is even at the Right Hand of God, Who also maketh intercession for us" (Rom. 8:34).

There is no hint in the Bible that Christ will have a *"staff"* to assist Him or that Mary has any role to perform in such a position. In fact, there is no need for additional mediators or motivators.

We blaspheme when we imply that Jesus Christ could not satisfactorily accomplish His eternal work of intercession without persuasion from His earthly mother.

We blaspheme when we add to the Word of God:

"For there is one God, and one Mediator between God and men, The Man Christ Jesus; Who gave Himself a ransom for all" (I Tim. 2:5-6).

This states boldly that there is one God. We then are told further in equally clear terms that there is one Mediator between God and man.

Please note that fact well.

There are not two mediators, nor three or four, just One! And then if there is any confusion, the identity of that One Mediator is revealed:

"For there is One God, and One Mediator between God and men, The Man Christ Jesus" (I Tim. 2:5).

NOTES

Why is He the Mediator? Again, Scripture spells it out clearly:

"Who gave Himself a ransom for all" (I Tim. 2:6).

Obviously, we blaspheme when we intrude Mary (or anyone else for that matter) into a mediatory role that is distinctively that of the Lord Jesus Christ Alone. And, once again, there is no hint or suggestion in Scripture that any such role ever has been considered for her by God.

The Roman Catholic position is that God the Father and His Son, Jesus Christ, are, through normal human efforts, unreachable. By extension, they then propose that since Christ's mother is available, positions delivered by her will not be ignored. Who would turn away his own mother if she came seeking a minor favor?

Thus, in Catholic tradition, when a person goes through the mother, he gets through more quickly and more surely. No doubt Jesus will look with more favor on her requests than on any delivered directly. Hence, the Catholic bumper stickers: *"Can't find Jesus? Look for His mother."*

Such statements totally misinterpret the Person of God and the Incarnation, Redemption, and Plan of God for the human race. The Apostle Paul said it well:

"Now the Spirit speaketh expressly, that in the latter times some shall depart from the Faith, giving heed to seducing spirits, and doctrines of devils; Speaking lies in hypocrisy; having their conscience seared with a hot iron; Forbidding to marry, and commanding to abstain from meats, which God hath created to be received with thanksgiving of them which believe and know the Truth" (I Tim. 4:1-3).

In all the Early Church, no statement is reported of an Apostle referring to Mary as the *"Mother of God."* There is no hint of prayers being offered to her, nor admonitions given to the Saints to honor her beyond what the Bible suggests as normal deference.

Surely, if this great fabrication were valid, we would have at least a word from the Early Church concerning Mary.

The silence is deafening!

Only when the Church began to apostatize, were these errors gradually brought in, with the *"leaven"* ultimately corrupting the whole.

(49) "AND HE STRETCHED FORTH HIS HAND TOWARD HIS DISCIPLES, AND SAID, BEHOLD MY MOTHER AND MY BRETHREN!"

The phrase, *"And He stretched forth His Hand toward His Disciples,"* refers to the original Twelve, but is not limited to them, as it refers to any and all who follow Him, as the next Scripture proclaims.

The phrase, *"And said, Behold My mother and My brethren,"* proclaims, and as stated, Jesus publicly breaking the bond that existed between Him and His family relatives after the flesh. He pointed to His Disciples and owned them as His nearest relatives in a family transcending any earthly one. This Word, like a sword, must have pierced Mary's heart.

"Stretching forth His Hand," is a graphic statement indicating even greater force behind His remarks.

(50) "FOR WHOSOEVER SHALL DO THE WILL OF MY FATHER WHICH IS IN HEAVEN, THE SAME IS MY BROTHER, AND SISTER, AND MOTHER."

The two words, *"For whosoever,"* and as stated, increase the dimensions of His family to include all who follow Him.

Natural relationship has influence in earthly governments (I Ki. 2:20), but no influence in Messiah's government. This fact, and as stated, destroys the Doctrine of the intercession of Mary.

The phrase, *"Shall do the Will of My Father which is in Heaven,"* proclaims the qualifications for being a part of the Family of God.

With this statement, Jesus completely severs any favored claims that His personal family may have had, and, consequently, claims His unique relationship with the Father, which underscored His Incarnation. In other words, His total allegiance was to the Father, and not to anyone or anything else.

He, no less, demands the same from all who would follow Him. As He severed all personal family relationships, as least as far as claims were concerned, He demands that we do the same. The *"Will of God"* must take preeminence over the will of personal family, or even Church family. It is the *"Will of My Father,"* and not the will of some Church or human organization.

Regrettably, this excludes almost all who call themselves *"Christian!"* The allegiance of many, if not most, and despite what they say, is to the Church, and not *"The Heavenly Father!"*

This was the problem then, and is the problem now!

The people had to make a decision as to whether they would follow the Pharisees or Christ. They, regrettably, chose the former and were called by Christ, *"This wicked generation"* (vs. 45).

The phrase, *"The same is My brother, and sister, and mother,"* proclaims the great Family of God. And wonder of wonders, *"He is not ashamed to call them brethren"* (Heb. 2:11).

CHAPTER 13

(1) "THE SAME DAY WENT JESUS OUT OF THE HOUSE, AND SAT BY THE SEA SIDE."

The phrase, *"The same day went Jesus out of the house,"* probably referred to Peter's house in Capernaum in which He had been teaching, as the last Chapter records.

The phrase, *"And sat by the sea side,"* refers to the Sea of Galilee. It is referred to by several names, *"Sea of Chinnereth"* (Num. 34:11) or *"Chemmeroth"* (Josh. 12:3), and in the New Testament as the *"Lake of Gennesaret"* (Lk. 5:1) and the *"Sea of Tiberias"* (Jn. 21:1).

The lake is about seven miles wide and twelve miles long. The River Jordan flows through it from north to south. Its waters are fresh, and therefore sweet — unlike those of the Dead Sea.

In Jesus' day, it was famous for its fish throughout the Roman Empire and produced a flourishing export trade. Consequently, at that time, it was a very prosperous region, with towns which ringed its shore. This is where much of Christ's Ministry was carried out. Today, only Tiberias remains as a town, with the others having been swept away as predicted by Christ, and because of their refusal to repent (Mat. 11:20-24).

There is no record in the Bible that Jesus ever visited Tiberias. It was a thoroughly Gentile city, having been founded by Herod Antipas about 20 A.D., and named after the Roman

Emperor Tiberius.

Herod made it his capital, with many of its buildings situated on a former graveyard, and so rendered the city unclean in Jewish eyes.

Probably the reason Jesus did not minister in this city, if, in fact, He did not, was because, as stated, it was thoroughly Gentile. Even though He came for the entirety of the world, which certainly included all Gentiles (Jn. 3:16), still, His Ministry at His First Advent was to the Jews, and for many and varied reasons.

Inasmuch as He did not condemn this city, it remains unto today.

As the site of the Headquarters of Christ at His First Advent, the Sea of Galilee area, was selected by the Holy Spirit. It is, in my opinion, one of the most beautiful places on earth.

On our last trip to Israel, we had a Water Baptismal Service in the Jordan River, as it flows out of the southern extremity of the Sea of Galilee. I had the privilege of baptizing all three of my Grandchildren, Jennifer, Gabriel, and Matthew, and other people who were with us. Even though Water Baptism at the Jordan River is of no greater spiritual significance than Water Baptism elsewhere, it was still a privilege and a delight to experience this moment, especially regarding my Grandchildren.

(2) "AND GREAT MULTITUDES WERE GATHERED TOGETHER UNTO HIM, SO THAT HE WENT INTO A SHIP, AND SAT; AND THE WHOLE MULTITUDE STOOD ON THE SHORE."

The phrase, *"And great multitudes were gathered together unto Him,"* concerned His Teaching. This could have numbered hundreds, but more likely thousands of people. If the people had had proper spiritual guidance among the Jewish Leaders, quite possibly the entirety of the situation would have been different, because the common people loved Him. But, regrettably, that leadership was lacking, and the last year of Jesus' public Ministry His crowds thinned out considerably because of threatened excommunication from the Synagogue of all those who followed Him. What a travesty and tragedy!

As the thousands gathered around Him that day, and bent close in order to hear, little did they realize they were listening to the One Who created the worlds, and, in reality, was the very

Maker of mankind, and all things!

The phrase, *"So that He went into a ship, and sat,"* respects the great multitude who pressed Him, and necessitated Him using the *"ship"* as a platform. No doubt, it pushed a few feet out into the water, with Him sitting on its bow teaching the Gospel.

The phrase, *"And the whole multitude stood on the shore,"* proclaims them listening to Him and hearing the greatest Message they had ever heard in all of their lives. It would be the Message of Eternal Life, and, yet, it would be couched in Parables, which was a unique way of teaching, and used by design.

Quite possibly, many of them waded out into the water up to their knees or even deeper to be nearer to Him, and with the bank, constituted the *"shore."*

(3) "AND HE SPAKE MANY THINGS UNTO THEM IN PARABLES, SAYING, BEHOLD, A SOWER WENT FORTH TO SOW;"

The phrase, *"And He spake many things unto them in Parables,"* constituted a unique way of teaching. As stated, it was used by design, and, no doubt, instructed by the Holy Spirit.

Why did He use this method?

PARABLES

Jesus used Parables quite often. Basically, He used them in such a way as to create curiosity rather than to explain a particular subject.

This is the idea:

Parables were used in order that those who truly were hungry to learn more about God's Ways would press in and seek more because the Parable invited such.

Conversely, Parables would cause the merely curious to turn away; therefore, the Holy Spirit designed the Parables in a way that they would satisfy the hunger of the searching heart and close the door on the skeptic at the same time.

True Faith always is honored, while the merely curious are left more confused than ever. The Holy Spirit was the Designer of this manner of speech and He moved upon Christ thus to speak.

The Parables uttered by Christ were at times very difficult to understand. But when they were understood, they always opened tremendous Truths that greatly rewarded the earnest and honest seeker.

In whatever form the Word of God is given, it is something like precious metals hidden in the ground. One must earnestly dig for these metals before they can be found. It is the same way with the Gospel.

The phrase, *"Behold, a sower went forth to sow,"* concerns an illustration all would have been familiar with.

The ground was first prepared for the reception of the seed, with the *"sower"* (a man) walking about the prepared ground, flinging the seeds in every direction.

This same method was used by my Dad when I was a child, as he would plant mustard seed. In flinging the seed here and there, and if the ground was properly prepared, it would germinate where it fell, with the mustard plants coming up shortly, etc.

For the Message that Christ wanted to portray, which was the presentation of the Gospel to the world, its reception in different hearts, and the results that would follow, this Parable would beautifully illustrate.

(4) "AND WHEN HE SOWED, SOME SEEDS FELL BY THE WAY SIDE, AND THE FOWLS CAME AND DEVOURED THEM UP:"

Inasmuch as this Parable is explained in verses 18-23, we will not attempt to give the explanation now, but will only comment on the illustration itself.

The *"way side"* here portrayed, probably pertained to a road which ran the length of the field in question. As such, it was not adequately prepared for seed, even though some fell on it.

As the road was hard, the seeds were fully exposed, which were an invitation to the *"fowls"* flying above, which swooped down and quickly *"devoured them."*

(5) "SOME FELL UPON STONY PLACES, WHERE THEY HAD NOT MUCH EARTH: AND FORTHWITH THEY SPRUNG UP, BECAUSE THEY HAD NO DEEPNESS OF EARTH:"

The *"stony places"* here mentioned were common in that part of the world.

In the fields and in certain areas, the rock was very near the surface, with only a thin layer of soil over it.

Even though the seed would germinate in this soil, still, it was very shallow and, therefore, the root structure was not sufficient.

(6) "AND WHEN THE SUN WAS UP, THEY WERE SCORCHED; AND BECAUSE THEY HAD NO ROOT, THEY WITHERED AWAY."

The *"sun"* coming up, referred to the heat of the day, in which the plants, if not healthy, would be greatly distressed.

Even though these particular plants did have roots, they were very shallow because of the thin depth of the earth. The roots quickly hit the rocks and were stunted, which if normal would have reached down deep into the soil. As a result of the shallow root system, there was no sustenance for the plant, therefore it withered under the scorching rays of the sun.

These were illustrations that all the people understood very well, and because they were very familiar with all the things Christ was saying.

In this first of seven Parables, He begins with such simplicity that even the children knew exactly what He was talking about. And yet, even though they fully understood the illustration, if its spiritual application was not given to them, as stated, the Truth would be lost.

Also, it seems, at least on some occasions, that a short period of time lapsed between the giving of the Parable and its explanation. And in some, the explanation was not given at all, unless pressed.

By using this method, and as stated, the skeptics vanished away, while those who were truly desirous of knowing more would press in for the explanation.

It seems that four of the Parables were given on the sea shore, while the latter three were given in the house (vs. 36).

(7) "AND SOME FELL AMONG THORNS; AND THE THORNS SPRUNG UP, AND CHOKED THEM:"

The idea of the verse seems to be that the *"thorns"* were not there when the seeds were sown, or at least had not sprung up. However, as the seeds germinated and grew into plants, likewise, over certain parts of the field the thorn bushes grew likewise and *"choked"* the plants. They should have been cleared out, but evidently were not.

(8) "BUT OTHER FELL INTO GOOD GROUND, AND BROUGHT FORTH FRUIT, SOME AN HUNDREDFOLD, SOME SIXTYFOLD, SOME THIRTYFOLD."

This ground was *"good,"* and produced

different quantities, because it had been cleared of *"thorns"* and other obstructions, etc.

(9) "WHO HATH EARS TO HEAR, LET HIM HEAR."

The idea of this verse is that whoever hears is responsible to hear and to obey, and will be accordingly judged.

Consequently, those who have the privilege to hear the Gospel are to devote the entirety of their lives to learning more and telling others.

Regrettably, precious few fall into that category. Most who have the privilege to *"hear,"* little understand what they have heard, and little make it the crowning love and labor of their lives.

Too much and too often, serving Christ is relegated to a couple of hours on Sunday morning, if that!

(10) "AND THE DISCIPLES CAME, AND SAID UNTO HIM, WHY SPEAKEST THOU UNTO THEM IN PARABLES?"

The phrase, *"And the Disciples came, and said unto Him,"* seems to pertain to a later time when they were alone. There is no evidence that He was still on the boat when their question concerning the Parables was posed to Him.

Even though the illustration was very clear to them, even as it had been to the people, still, they did not know nor understand what it represented.

The question, *"Why speakest Thou unto them in Parables?",* portrays a consternation on their part! They did not understand His Message, even though they understood the illustration, and neither did the people, and they are at a loss as to why He was now teaching in this manner?

In the Sermon on the Mount, and at other times, He had been very clear, concise, forthright, and to the point, even brutally frank. The new method confuses them, and now He will answer.

(11) "HE ANSWERED AND SAID UNTO THEM, BECAUSE IT IS GIVEN UNTO YOU TO KNOW THE MYSTERIES OF THE KINGDOM OF HEAVEN, BUT TO THEM IT IS NOT GIVEN."

The phrase, *"He answered and said unto them,"* concerns the Lord's method of dealing with two different classes of people, those who really wanted to know God's Ways and those who were merely curious.

NOTES

The phrase, *"Because it is given unto you to know . . . ,"* draws out the first group, of which the Disciples were a part, and speaks of those who truly desire to learn God's Ways.

Unfortunately, this group is small in comparison to the other, as the next phrase will bear out.

The phrase, *"The mysteries of the Kingdom of Heaven,"* at least in this case, of the first Parable, is that only about one-fourth of the expended effort succeeds, while three-fourths fail. Subsequent history demonstrates the accuracy of this Prophecy.

The phrase, *"But to them it is not given,"* concerns the second group who is far larger, who have little interest, and as the next verse proclaims, what little interest they have is lost.

We do not mean to claim by the previous or following statements that Christ meant for the world to be divided into four sections, or that only about a fourth would heed the Word, because that is not the thrust of the Text. The thrust, as conveyed by the Holy Spirit through Christ, is to give the reasons why many, if not most, who hear the Gospel bring forth no fruit, or less fruit.

However, having said that, it is amazing as to the accuracy of the percentage of one-fourth, even though that was not, or so it seems, the full intention of the Holy Spirit.

There are about 5.5 billion people in the world presently. Of this number, approximately one-fourth makes some type of claim toward Christ, whether philosophical or genuine. (Only the Lord knows the number of those who are truly born again.)

The rest of the world is divided up accordingly: Catholicism, about 1 billion. (Although many would disagree, I do not consider Catholicism to be Christian, although claimed.) Islam, as well, has about a billion adherents. The last segment is divided up between Hinduism, Buddhism, Shintoism, Confucianism, Spiritism, and Atheism. The latter group would encompass a little over 2 billion people.

This percentage will hold true even in the local Church. If a Godly Pastor tries to analyze his local congregation, and irrespective of its size, he will find that about one-fourth are truly dedicated, sincerely consecrated people, in other words who can be depended on. The other three-fourths fall into any number of categories.

(12) "FOR WHOSOEVER HATH, TO HIM SHALL BE GIVEN, AND HE SHALL HAVE MORE ABUNDANCE: BUT WHOSOEVER HATH NOT, FROM HIM SHALL BE TAKEN AWAY EVEN THAT HE HATH."

This is the Passage from which I have drawn the thought that if one wills Righteousness, the Lord wills more Righteousness to them. Conversely, if one wills unrighteousness, more unrighteousness comes. The same is true for the knowledge of the Ways of God.

A gift unused, whether moral, physical, or material, sooner or later is lost; but on the contrary if used develops.

The phrase, *"For whosoever hath, to him shall be given,"* is the exact opposite of carnal thinking, but yet continues to hold true even in the secular world. It comes under the adage of the *"rich getting richer, with the poor getting poorer."*

In this case, it is speaking of the knowledge of the Ways of God and the desire to know more.

The idea is not so much the amount possessed, but, instead, the desire for more or no desire at all!

So, the promise is given that if one wants to know the Ways of God, the Holy Spirit will see to it that *"He shall have more abundance."*

The phrase, *"But whosoever hath not, from him shall be taken away even that he hath,"* means that whatever Word of God has been given, in such no interest is expressed, therefore, the Holy Spirit withdraws, and, consequently, that which the person has is lost.

The spiritual get more spiritual, while the carnal get more carnal. It is sad but true. It all has to do with the desire of the heart.

The idea is that the prepared ground will ensure growth, while the unprepared ground loses even the seed it receives.

(13) "THEREFORE SPEAK I TO THEM IN PARABLES: BECAUSE THEY SEEING SEE NOT; AND HEARING THEY HEAR NOT, NEITHER DO THEY UNDERSTAND."

The phrase, *"Therefore speak I to them in Parables,"* is meant to refer to the group which *"hath not,"* and because they desire not. Actually, it says that there is no point in the Holy Spirit wasting time on this group, *"because"* they do not wish to see or hear or understand; and hence by a just judgment they lose their triple moral ability.

It is not because they can't see, but it is because they have no desire to see. It is not because they can't hear, but because they have no desire to hear. Neither do they have a desire to understand.

An illustration is those found in every Church who never seem to be touched or moved by anything the Lord does. Others are praising God; but they seldom, if ever, offer any praise.

Others are moved to tears, while they are dry-eyed.

Others express great joy on their countenance, while no emotion is registered on these individuals. They never seem to grow in the Lord and they express little interest. Sadly and regrettably, they fall into this category here mentioned by Christ.

Such was Israel at the time of Christ, and such is much of the modern Church!

(14) "AND IN THEM IS FULFILLED THE PROPHECY OF ESAIAS, WHICH SAITH, BY HEARING YE SHALL HEAR, AND SHALL NOT UNDERSTAND; AND SEEING YE SHALL SEE, AND SHALL NOT PERCEIVE:"

This is found in Isaiah 6:9-10, and was prophesied approximately 800 years previous.

This Passage is actually quoted some seven times in the New Testament, therefore proclaiming this as the great sin of all time, at least among those who refer to themselves as *"Believers"* (Mat. 13:14-15; Mk. 4:12; Lk. 8:10; Jn. 12:39-40; Acts 28:26-27; Rom. 11:8).

The phrase, *"And in them is fulfilled the Prophecy of Esaias,"* in the Greek literally means, *"Being fulfilled,"* which includes the present because the process is still continuing.

The phrase, *"Which saith, By hearing ye shall hear,"* more specifically referred to Israel hearing Christ, but really not hearing Him, and because they had no desire to *"hear."*

The phrase, *"And shall not understand,"* has no bearing on their incapacity to understand, but, instead, that they made no effort to understand.

The phrase, *"And seeing ye shall see, and shall not perceive,"* means that they saw Christ, and thus an image was formed in the retina of the eye, yet no impression was conveyed to the mind and spirit.

As stated, such condition continues unto the present.

The next verse tells us why!

(15) "FOR THIS PEOPLE'S HEART IS WAXED GROSS, AND THEIR EARS ARE DULL OF HEARING, AND THEIR EYES THEY HAVE CLOSED; LEST AT ANY TIME THEY SHOULD SEE WITH THEIR EYES, AND HEAR WITH THEIR EARS, AND SHOULD UNDERSTAND WITH THEIR HEART, AND SHOULD BE CONVERTED, AND I SHOULD HEAL THEM."

The phrase, *"For this people's heart is waxed gross,"* gives the reason for their spiritual dullness and, therefore, rejection of Christ.

Even though the words, *"This people,"* spoke of the *"wicked generation"* of Christ's day, still, its structure refers to the type of individuals spoken of, and irrespective of the time in which they lived.

This phrase tells us that the spiritual dullness began in the *"heart."* It was not an intellectual problem, neither was it a social problem. It was a spiritual problem, and began in their soul, gradually increasing until the *"heart"* was insensitive to the moving and operation of the Holy Spirit. What we are speaking of here is the single most dangerous thing that can happen to any person who hears the Gospel, and makes a profession of receiving it. It is something that every Believer, and no matter how close to the Lord, must guard against continuously.

As well, it speaks to a Gospel-hardened people who profess much, as Israel of old, but, in reality, have become hardened to the Holy Spirit until they are *"past feeling."* The Spirit of God moves and it does not touch them. By and large, they think they are beyond and above that which the Holy Spirit is presently doing.

In their minds, others may certainly need such, but they have outgrown that which is presently happening.

The Truth is not at all as they think it is, but, in reality, is the opposite.

The phrase, *"And their ears are dull of hearing,"* means they have heard and heard, and little acted on what they heard, and now the Holy Spirit pulls back until they lose even that which they have had.

This pertains to those who have lost their first love, with them now not using what they have heard, and, therefore, the Holy Spirit takes away what they do have.

The phrase, *"And their eyes they have closed,"* means that with deliberation they have closed their eyes.

If one is to notice, the Holy Spirit begins the Scripture with the *"heart,"* where all spiritual declension begins, and then proceeds to the *"ears,"* and then the *"eyes."*

The phrase, *"Lest at any time they should see with their eyes, and hear with their ears, and should understand with their heart,"* is now inverted.

In other words, the Holy Spirit in this phrase places the *"eyes"* first, and the *"heart"* last.

Why?

Conversion begins with the heart, as spiritual declension begins with the heart. However, once the heart has *"waxed gross,"* it is that which the Holy Spirit can no longer reach. As a result, it is now placed last, and because it is last.

The *"eyes"* now come first, and it becomes obvious that they cannot see in the spiritual sense.

The *"ears"* are next, and it is obvious that the person cannot spiritually *"hear."*

As the *"heart"* is spiritually dead, there is no spiritual comprehension.

The phrase, *"And should be converted, and I should heal them,"* means they purposely would not turn to Him; had they done so He would most certainly have healed them morally and spiritually.

Many who cling to the erroneous doctrine of Hyper-Calvinism (misunderstood Predestination), have attempted to twist these Passages, making them mean something else entirely.

In the darkness of this erroneous doctrine, they have concluded God as the Author of the spiritual condition of these, indicating they were predestined to be lost. However, even to the elementary Greek student, in which the original Text was written, it is obvious, and plainly so, that the initiation is with the individual, and despite the efforts of the Holy Spirit to move them otherwise.

This fallacious doctrine of misunderstood Predestination is another effort by Satan and believed by many people to negate the True Purpose of God, which is to save humanity, and the responsibility of the individual to earnestly seek the Lord.

While it is certainly true that all before conversion, are totally depraved and cannot, at least within themselves, initiate a spiritual response, or even desire. However, the Scripture is clear that the Holy Spirit does initiate the response, and not to a select few, but to all (Jn. 3:16; Acts 17:30; II Pet. 3:9; Rev. 22:17).

The last invitation in the Bible is, *"Whosoever will,"* and it means exactly what it says.

The terrible spiritual condition is not, therefore, the fault of the Holy Spirit or some grossly evil idea of limited selection for Salvation, as taught by some, but rather on the part of the people who, despite the movings of the Holy Spirit, refuse to *"see," "hear,"* or *"understand."* In other words, their rejection is by cool, calculating, studied rejection.

In Truth, so that all will have the same opportunity respecting acceptance or rejection of the Lord, the playing field starts out level. The Psalmist said, *"He fashioneth their hearts alike"* (Ps. 33:15), meaning that each person at birth is given by God a heart identical regarding spiritual perception. What happens thereafter, at least as it regards the acceptance and rejection of Christ, and upon their opportunity to hear the Gospel, is according to their own free will. All indication in Scripture is that such (the free will) is never tampered with by God. He deals, speaks, moves, impresses and calls, but never forces one in either direction.

(16) "BUT BLESSED ARE YOUR EYES, FOR THEY SEE: AND YOUR EARS, FOR THEY HEAR."

This Passage has two meanings:

1. It means that their *"eyes"* had the opportunity to *"see,"* and their *"ears"* had the opportunity to *"hear"* the Gospel as it was presented by Christ. In this, they were *"blessed,"* and exceedingly so!

Not all in the world had or have that glorious and wonderful opportunity!

2. It also means that they not only had the opportunity to *"see"* and *"hear,"* even as the skeptics did, but they hungrily desired to *"see"* and *"hear"* and, as such, they received that which such attention and desire brought, eternal life in Christ.

Even though the others were not healed morally, these were, and wondrously so!

"Oh happy day, Oh happy day,
"When Jesus washed my sins away."

As a result, their *"eyes"* and *"ears"* were *"blessed!"*

(17) "FOR VERILY I SAY UNTO YOU, THAT MANY PROPHETS AND RIGHTEOUS MEN HAVE DESIRED TO SEE THOSE THINGS WHICH YE SEE, AND HAVE NOT SEEN THEM; AND TO HEAR THOSE THINGS WHICH YE HEAR, AND HAVE NOT HEARD THEM."

The phrase, *"For verily I say unto you,"* even though repetitive, always signals a very important statement. Considering that it comes from the Son of God, the far-reaching effects of what is said could not be exhausted were one to devote to it a lifetime of study. God is speaking, and yet few heeded!

The phrase, *"That many Prophets and Righteous men desired to see those things which ye see,"* concerned itself with the First Advent of Christ, the incomparable, infallible One, Who performed miracles of such astounding proportions that John the Beloved said, *"And there are also many other things which Jesus did, the which, if they should be written every one, I suppose that even the world itself could not contain the books that should be written"* (Jn. 21:25).

The phrase, *"And have not seen them,"* refers to two things:

1. The Spirit of God told these *"Prophets"* and *"Righteous men"* that such was coming and, as a result, they longed to see that, and, more particularly, the One Who they had been told about.

This statement by Christ refers to an intense longing on the part of these individuals.

2. Even though they did not see it, they held on by Faith, believing God that ultimately it would come. And even though they would not be privileged to personally partake of it, still, they had been privileged to have been told about it, and in that they would rejoice.

Even though what was coming was distant, still, they did not lose their Faith, and for this they were commended by Christ, which is the highest commendation of all.

The phrase, *"And to hear those things which ye hear, and have not heard them,"* concerns the Words of Life as given by Christ. An excellent example is the *"Sermon on the Mount,"* and, as well, these Parables!

They did not hear these things, but at least they heard about the gracious things He would say.

An example is this statement by Isaiah concerning the coming Messiah, *"And He hath made My Mouth like a sharp sword; in the shadow of His Hand hath He hid Me, and made Me a polished shaft; in His quiver hath He hid Me"* (Isa. 49:2).

The idea of this statement by Christ is to contrast the many who desired to see and to hear and to understand with those who had no interest.

(18) "HEAR YE THEREFORE THE PARABLE OF THE SOWER."

This verse emphasizes the necessity and significance of hearing the Word of God. As well, the *"Parable of the sower"* will now be explained.

The words, *"Hear ye,"* are spoken to His Disciples, plus anyone else who was there, signifying the privilege they had of hearing it, and is meant to be contrasted with those just mentioned who had no such privilege.

As well, this is meant to refer to all who have the privilege of hearing the Word of God presently, as contrasted by those who do not have that privilege.

Even though I have related it elsewhere in these Volumes, still, I think the following is worth repeating:

In the 1980's, Frances and I, along with Donnie and others, had the privilege of going into Communist China. Actually, we did a Television Special there, which was shown a little later to our American and Canadian audiences.

As we went in, we took several hundred Bibles printed in Chinese that we were to give to a particular contact in Beijing. Thankfully, upon checking our bags, the Customs officials in China either overlooked them or for whatever reason said nothing. (There were 30 or 40 in each suitcase, which probably numbered several hundred, if not a couple thousand.)

After getting situated in our hotel, we learned that the man to whom we were to deliver the Bibles had been placed under house arrest. He was not allowed to go in or come out. As well, no foreigner would be allowed into his home. For a while we did not know what to do.

After going to prayer, someone in our party was given direction by the Lord. It concerned a young Chinese couple who had made the trip with us from America to see the land of their forefathers. They said later that they had not

even really known why they came, simply because they really did not have the money to spare for such a trip. But, nevertheless, something kept urging them to come. Of course, that reason would now become obvious, as they would be used to take in the Bibles.

Inasmuch as they were Chinese, quite possibly they would not be noticed and would be allowed entrance. At any rate, they agreed to make the effort, realizing the danger involved.

If I remember correctly, one or two taxis were rented, with a couple of people going with them, with the taxis stopping a hundred yards or so away from the man's dwelling.

This they did, and with all the Bibles!

I don't know how many trips the young man and his wife had to make between the taxis and the man's dwelling, but, at any rate, all the Bibles were delivered, and without incident.

After coming back to the hotel, the young Chinese couple related this to us.

They said all the Bibles were stacked on the table, as stated, totalling several hundred, or maybe up to as many as two thousand. When they finally finished, they said the dear Chinese brother stood there for a moment looking at them and then dropped to his knees on the floor, weeping and crying, and thanking God for the *"bread,"* as he put it.

The young couple related to us the tremendous feeling of that moment, knowing that most Chinese Christians had no Bibles, and longed for one, whereas Americans, plus many others in the world, have all the Bibles they want and too oftentimes little read or study them.

There is no way that one could overemphasize the necessity of all Christians taking advantage of the Word of God and its many Promises. The mastering of its contents should be a lifelong project. And God help any Christian who reads and studies his Bible less than he would the newspaper or particular periodicals, etc.

(19) "WHEN ANY ONE HEARETH THE WORD OF THE KINGDOM, AND UNDERSTANDETH IT NOT, THEN COMETH THE WICKED ONE, AND CATCHETH AWAY THAT WHICH WAS SOWN IN HIS HEART. THIS IS HE WHICH RECEIVED SEED BY THE WAY SIDE."

Jesus will now break down the *"Parable of the sower,"* explaining what He was speaking of.

The phrase, *"When any one heareth the Word of the Kingdom,"* refers to the Word of God, i.e., the Bible.

It is expressed here as *"The Word of the Kingdom,"* because it speaks of God's Way vs. Satan's way.

The entirety of the world system, upon the Fall of Adam and Eve, was changed over from a *"Kingdom of Light"* to a *"Kingdom of Darkness."* Consequently, the story of the Bible is the bringing back of the *"Kingdom of Light."* The *"Word of the Kingdom"* is the greatest thing one could ever *"hear."*

The phrase, *"And understandeth it not,"* does not refer to one who is incapable of understanding, but, instead, to one who has no desire to understand. Regrettably, this makes up a great percentage of the human family.

The phrase, *"Then cometh the wicked one,"* refers to Jesus comparing Satan to a vulture, because in the telling of the Parable, He said, *"And the fowls came and devoured them up."*

The phrase, *"And catcheth away that which was sown in his heart,"* refers to Satan being allowed to do such a thing by the individual involved.

In other words, the individual who has had the privilege of hearing the Word is not a pawn in this scenario, but, instead, has the option of desiring to understand it or giving it no heed. The initiative does not lie with the Lord or with Satan, but with the person. Their free will is never tampered with by God, neither is Satan allowed to go beyond a certain point in his persuasion.

To be sure, both the Lord and Satan move upon, persuade, deal with, and speak to the person involved; however, whether to accept or reject is strictly the initiative of the individual.

The phrase, *"This is he which received seed by the way side,"* refers to the area not prepared for planting, as described in verse 4. It concerned the road which ran the distance of the field, and inasmuch as it was a road, its surface was packed hard and would not have been a fit receptacle for seed. There would be no way for them to germinate and take root. Consequently, the fowls would swoop down and eat the seed, here likened to the Devil snatching the Word from the hard hearts of those who had no desire to receive it.

(20) "BUT HE THAT RECEIVED THE

SEED INTO STONY PLACES, THE SAME IS HE THAT HEARETH THE WORD, AND ANON WITH JOY RECEIVETH IT;"

The phrase, *"But he that received the seed into stony places,"* concerns the second group, and pertained to the area of earth which was very shallow, with rock just beneath the surface.

The phrase, *"The same is he that heareth the Word,"* refers to this one hearing the Word exactly as the previous one. However, there is a difference in the two.

Whereas the first one did not receive it, this one, *"Anon with joy receiveth it."* (The word *"anon"* means immediately.)

Not only do they receive it, but they do so with *"joy,"* registering delight in the privilege of having heard the Word of God. Every True Preacher of the Gospel is well familiar with this group. They make such a good start, but then fall by the way side.

Why?

(21) "YET HATH HE NOT ROOT IN HIMSELF, BUT DURETH FOR A WHILE: FOR WHEN TRIBULATION OR PERSECUTION ARISETH BECAUSE OF THE WORD, BY AND BY HE IS OFFENDED."

The phrase, *"Yet hath he not root in himself,"* refers to the *"stony places."* In other words, and as Jesus said in the Parable, the Seed (the Word of God), upon striking the earth (the heart), immediately germinates because there is some soil. However, when the roots attempt to go down deep into the ground, they meet resistance, which is the *"stony place."* Consequently, the roots are very shallow and cannot support the plant.

The phrase, *"But dureth for a while,"* refers to the plant living a short time because of having at least some root structure. It refers to the individual hearing the Word of God, believing it, and accepting Christ. It is all done with joy, with the beginning looking very promising. However, something then happens which is described next.

The phrase, *"For when tribulation or persecution ariseth because of the Word,"* refers to the *"stony places."*

Inasmuch as this individual is now a Believer, and because he has believed the *"Word of God,"* without fail, *"tribulation or even persecution,"* will now come. It is not a question of *"if,"* but, instead, *"when."*

The phrase, *"By and by he is offended,"* means that he allows the *"tribulation or persecution"* to stop him in his progress, with him falling by the way side. It is described by Jesus in the Parable as the sun coming up, and then beginning to shine in its strength, and during the heat of the day the root of the plant withers away, causing the plant to die (vs. 6).

(22) "HE ALSO THAT RECEIVED SEED AMONG THE THORNS IS HE THAT HEARETH THE WORD; AND THE CARE OF THIS WORLD, AND THE DECEITFULNESS OF RICHES, CHOKE THE WORD, AND HE BECOMETH UNFRUITFUL."

The phrase, *"He also that received seed among the thorns,"* concerns the third group who makes even greater progress than the previous two.

The seed is properly planted, and the soil is fertile and good with plenty depth; however, as the seed comes up and begins to mature, *"thorns"* come up as well, and because they are not pulled out, they choke the plant to death.

The phrase, *"Is he that heareth the Word,"* again, as the others, concerns the Word of God.

If one is to notice, the Word of God is always the criteria. It is impossible for one to know the Gospel without it coming from the Word of God. That is the reason the Bible and its study is so very important. It is also the reason that it is so important for the Preacher of the Gospel to make certain that he preaches the Word instead of other things. These *"other things"* may be important, interesting, titillating, or even exciting and helpful in some areas; however, the Bible only is the *"Seed,"* which can take root and grow in a person's heart, thereby developing the Ways of God.

The phrase, *"And the care of this world,"* concerns itself with the ways of this world and is likened by Jesus as *"thorns."*

This, plus the following are the two greatest hindrances to the progress of the Child of God.

The Christian must understand that while we are in this world, still, we are not of this world. Its system may have passing interest, but that interest is always to be short-lived. Therefore, he that is too comfortable in this world system, will soon be very uncomfortable in God's system, and will be *"choked"* exactly as Christ here affirms.

NOTES

The phrase, *"And the deceitfulness of riches,"* is the second and equal greatest danger.

Jesus called riches *"deceitful,"* simply because the acquiring of such makes a person believe several erroneous things. Some who obtain riches believe they are more intelligent than others and, therefore, above others. Some think that riches give them a special place and position. And inasmuch as *"riches"* are the standard of this world, the special place and position is definitely true in that category, but definitely not with God.

Sadder still, great segments of the Christian Church have opted for the *"Prosperity Message,"* which is in direct contrast to this statement by Christ.

It is not wrong to be rich, but it is wrong to place emphasis on riches, or to make it priority, or if God does bless one with such, not to use it for His Work and Glory. Regrettably, only a precious few do use acquired wealth for the Gory of God, while far more allow these *"riches"* to *"choke the Word"* in their lives, and they become unfruitful.

Many would ask as to what is the *"Prosperity Message?"*

In a very brief synopsis, it is the emphasis placed by some on using the Word of God to acquire riches. In other words, the basic foundation of this teaching is that God wants everybody to be rich. Consequently, this becomes the goal, the priority, and actually the entirety of the embodiment of the message of these individuals, with their *"Faith"* so-called being used toward this end.

Getting souls saved is given precedent not at all in this teaching, with *"Christian growth"* tied to the price of one's suit of clothes, or the make of one's car.

In other words, if the person acquires wealth, this means they have a lot of Faith, and if they are poor, they have no Faith.

It is a heady teaching and attracts many adherents, because it appeals to the greed in people's hearts which, sadly, seems to reside at least somewhat, if not greatly so, in most if not all!

No! It does not work. And the reason is simple, it is not the Word of God. About the only ones who get rich are the Preachers who espouse this false doctrine.

The phrase, *"Choke the Word,"* means

exactly what it says! The intended growth is never realized, and because as *"thorns"* will choke to death any plant unless they are removed, likewise, the *"care of this world, and the deceitfulness of riches,"* will do the same in the life of the Christian.

The phrase, *"And he becometh unfruitful,"* actually means he loses his soul. Jesus said as much when He said, *"Every branch in Me that beareth not fruit He taketh away"* (Jn. 15:2).

He then said that, *"Such are cast into the fire, and are burned"* (Jn. 15:6).

So, it is not just a matter of not living up to their full spiritual potential, but, instead, losing their soul.

This *"Parable of the sower,"* completely refutes, as is glaringly obvious, the unscriptural doctrine of *"Unconditional eternal security."*

As is obvious in this Parable, the illustration is given of the first group who hears the Word, but does not accept it. The numbers are legend.

The second group hears it, receives it, and begins to live for God, thereby, truly saved, but after a while falls by the wayside, and because of *"tribulation or persecution."*

The third group, as we have just commented on, as well, hears the Word and receives the Word, but the *"care of this world and the deceitfulness of riches,"* ultimately, and after a good period of time, *"Choke the Word,"* and they lose their way. The numbers of these lost, as well as the previous group, are legend as well!

(23) "BUT HE THAT RECEIVED SEED INTO THE GOOD GROUND IS HE THAT HEARETH THE WORD, AND UNDERSTANDETH IT; WHICH ALSO BEARETH FRUIT, AND BRINGETH FORTH, SOME AN HUNDREDFOLD, SOME SIXTY, SOME THIRTY."

The phrase, *"But he that received Seed,"* once again refers to hearing the Word of God, with the Word being likened to *"Seed."*

The implication is that this *"Seed"* will take root and grow, bearing forth *"Good fruit."*

While all other things, such as intellectual pursuits, scientific quests, etc., may be *"seed"* as well, still, those things, and as attractive as they may be, can bring forth no *"good fruit."* Only the Word of God can do that (Mat. 7:17).

Consequently, and throughout the entirety

of the world and for all time, every truly good thing that has been done is because of the entrance of the *"Seed"* which is *"The Word of God!"*

The phrase, *"Into the good ground,"* refers to the soil of verse 8, which had been properly cultivated and prepared. It refers to the hungry heart of the individual, and could refer back to the Sermon on the Mount, *"Blessed are they which do hunger and thirst after Righteousness: for they shall be filled"* (Mat. 5:6).

The phrase, *"Is he that heareth the Word, and understandeth it,"* means that not only did he hear it, even as the others, but he wanted to understand it, and, consequently, the desire for understanding is automatically rewarded by the Lord by giving more understanding.

Those of verse 19 who do not understand the Word, and because they have no desire to understand it, as Jesus said, *"From him shall be taken away even that he hath"* (vs. 12).

So, as we have stated, the response, whether favorable or unfavorable, is strictly with the individual. Their free will is never tampered with by God, and He will not allow Satan, at least at this stage, to interfere beyond the parameters laid out.

So, this person wants the Word, desires the Word, actively seeks the Word, and as a result is given the Word, and more Word.

The phrase, *"Which also beareth fruit,"* is that which is desired, and which Jesus elaborates on in John Chapter 15.

What type of *"fruit"* is being spoken of?

It speaks of Christian Growth with all its parameters, but if it would be possible for it to be summed up in two words, those two words would probably be *"Holiness and Righteousness."* And of course, this is that which Christ gives, and not that which is devised by man.

The phrase, *"And bringeth forth,"* speaks of a process which is explained in the last phrase.

The phrase, *"Some an hundredfold, some sixty, some thirty,"* with the *"hundredfold"* being given first, means that this is what the Holy Spirit strives for in the heart and life of the individual. Nothing else is acceptable, hence the *"Father"* purging the branch, *"that it may bring forth more fruit"* (Jn. 15:2).

The idea is not, as many have believed, that some can only bring forth *"sixtyfold,"* and others *"thirtyfold,"* and because of their talents and abilities, etc. Actually, this has nothing to do with one's talents or abilities, but altogether with God, and the individual yielding to Him by providing his heart as a fertile field for growth.

The idea is that one does not automatically begin to bring forth an *"hundredfold,"* but begins with the *"thirtyfold,"* and then onto the *"sixtyfold,"* with the *"hundredfold"* as the goal. The Holy Spirit can be satisfied with no less than an *"hundredfold,"* and we must not be satisfied with less either!

As well, this has nothing to do with the size of one's Church, the amount of money given, or the largeness of one's Ministry, or the great show made by some in the Church, and in whatever capacity.

It strictly refers to Christian Growth, which entails the Will of God, which develops Holiness and Righteousness, and pertains to any and all Christians, irrespective of who they are or where they may abe.

The one who is at *"thirtyfold"* is expected by the Holy Spirit to go on to *"sixtyfold,"* and then, ultimately, to an *"hundredfold."*

It is tragic when one drops from *"sixtyfold"* down to *"thirtyfold,"* and then ultimately *"becometh unfruitful"* as the previous group is spoken of, because of allowing *"the thorns"* of the *"world"* and *"riches"* to *"choke the Word."* Tragically, this happens often! However, it is so unnecessary.

What a joy to bring forth fruit an *"hundredfold,"* which is within the reach of every single Christian.

Incidentally, the *"good ground"* is ground that is prepared, that is, plowed up by the Spirit of conviction because of sin. The Truth is, the heart is incurably diseased (Jer. 17:9); but it becomes good, that is, honest, when it accepts this testimony (Lk. 8:15).

(24) "ANOTHER PARABLE PUT HE FORTH UNTO THEM, SAYING, THE KINGDOM OF HEAVEN IS LIKENED UNTO A MAN WHICH SOWED GOOD SEED IN HIS FIELD:"

This is the second Parable given by Jesus.

The Parable of the Tares (24-30 and 37-43) conflicts with modern religious thought. It asserts the existence of the Devil (vs. 39); declares him to be a moral father, and, as such, to have children (vs. 38); that these children are human beings (vs. 41); that after death they will be cast into the furnace of conscious suffering (vs. 42);

that evolution is a myth, for no system of cultivation can develop wheat out of tares; and that people may be so morally perfect as to be indistinguishable from True Christians and yet be the seed of the serpent.

Such is Christ's Own Teaching, and it moves the contrite heart to trembling and weeping.

Once again, Jesus uses the example of a man sowing *"Good seed in his field."* This speaks, as we by now know, of the Word of God.

As verse 37 proclaims, the *"Man"* who sows the good seed is the Lord Jesus Christ. Even though the Holy Spirit is the One Who does the actual sowing, still, the Church and its presentation of the Gospel, belongs to Christ (Mat. 16:18).

The *"Sowing of the Seed"* (Word of God) is the single most important work on the face of the earth, and because of its eternal consequences. And yet, most modern Believers show little concern for this all-important task.

Every Believer, and irrespective as to whom they may be, should take it upon themselves to do four things:

1. To draw as close to God as is humanly possible, being extensively familiar with His Word, and truly consecrated to Jesus Christ. Tragically, too many Believers are consecrated merely to the Church, and not actually to Christ.

2. He should pray daily for the furtherance of the Gospel, even asking the Lord to give him a burden not only for those who are his close loved ones or friends, but even certain parts of the world which he will never visit. By this means the Holy Spirit through prayer will bring about a mighty Move of God in certain areas. That is the reason Jesus said, *"Pray ye therefore the Lord of the harvest, that He will send forth labourers into His harvest"* (Mat. 9:38).

Tragically, the number of Believers who are True Intercessors before the Lord are few and far between. However, it is this manner in which the Holy Spirit brings a Move of God to certain parts of the world.

3. Along with the prayer life, every Christian ought to witness for Christ to whoever the Lord puts him in contact with. As well as his verbal testimony, his life should be a living testimony to Jesus Christ.

4. Every Believer, other than their tithes, ought to as well set aside another portion for

World Evangelism. How large that portion should be, should be according to the leading of the Holy Spirit. With some it may be small, even as low as five percent of their income, while with others it may be far higher, and because of the Blessings of the Lord.

This should be earmarked for the taking of the Gospel to other parts of the world than their own locality.

Also, it is incumbent upon the Believer to make certain that his money is going to truly reach the lost. Regrettably, this is at times not easy to do.

Many modern Believers take the position that they will just give to their local Church and allow them to disperse it according to the Denominational program. This is extremely unwise!

Inasmuch as I have many years of experience in Foreign Missions programs and the taking of the Gospel to the world (for that's what the Lord has called me to do), I think I can say without any fear of exaggeration or contradiction, that up to ninety-nine percent of that given in this capacity is wasted. Tragically, most of the modern Missionaries now sent to the foreign field are little more than amateur psychologists. That is sad but true!

As well, too many Christians give to that which claims great Missions works, but in reality have very little to show for it. The Believer should consider the following before making an all-important decision regarding as to where his money goes concerning Foreign Missions:

1. Is the Preacher he is supporting truly called of God for this all-important task? As I have stated, many Believers in their giving to Religious Denominations in this capacity, do not even really know who they are supporting. They should know!

2. Does the Preacher have a proven track record of winning souls to Christ by his (or her) Ministry?

3. Does all the money go for the winning of souls, by preaching of the Gospel, whether by Radio or Television, or in person, or the building of Churches or Bible Schools, etc.? Tragically, far too much money earmarked for the presentation of the Gospel around the world goes to grandiose schemes which may look good on the surface, but, in reality, serve

NOTES

no purpose, at least as far as the Work of God is concerned.

4. Is the Gospel preached by the individual, and in whatever capacity, the True Gospel of the Bible? God cannot bless error, and neither can the Holy Spirit anoint it, no matter how cleverly presented. Sadly, the far greater presentation, at least at the present time, is error!

I realize I have been extremely pointed and direct in this presentation, but I do so because I have vast experience in this area, and because I know that most Christians are wasting their money, at least in this respect. I will give an example.

Some time ago, I received a letter and a contribution from a dear lady respecting an appeal we had made for the presentation of the Gospel by Television in the former Soviet Union. Of course, we were very grateful for her contribution.

In the short note that she sent, she mentioned that she was supporting another particular *"Ministry,"* and, as well, they were covering Russia with the Gospel. The way she worded her statement, it seemed she had given quite a bit to that particular Ministry. While I am not familiar with all Ministries, I was familiar, and very much so, with this particular one.

Even though they had given the public the impression that they were reaching the entirety of Russia with the Gospel by Television, and, consequently, had raised many millions of dollars for this task, in Truth, they were only on Television in one city. Even that particular program was of no consequence, because it was not translated into Russian, and because it mostly featured rock n' roll music. That was their presentation, and yet Believers had given millions of dollars thinking they were truly evangelizing this extremely needy part of the world. (I would to God they had been truly evangelizing Russia.) The Truth is, the money was totally wasted, and not only wasted, but they, in effect, were supporting a work of Satan, as this very Parable will bring out. It is Satan's business to hinder the *"Good seed,"* and he does it wondrously well!

(25) "BUT WHILE MEN SLEPT, HIS ENEMY CAME AND SOWED TARES AMONG THE WHEAT, AND WENT HIS WAY."

The phrase, *"But while men slept,"* has the obvious meaning, which we will direct our attention to momentarily, still, its greater meaning has to do with that which I have been attempting to portray, Christians actually supporting the spreading of *"tares"* instead of *"wheat."*

Tragically and sadly, too many Christians, spiritually speaking, are *"asleep,"* thereby failing to heed the words of the Apostle Paul, *"Therefore let us not sleep, as do others; but let us watch and be sober"* (I Thess. 5:6).

The phrase, *"His enemy came and sowed tares among the wheat,"* represents something that was quite common in Jesus' day.

It was quite common in the East for enemies to sow tares and other poisonous seeds in the fields of those they wished to hurt. So, those who were listening to Jesus understood full well of that which He spoke.

"Tares" are a particular species of the grass family, the seeds of which are poisonous.

The phrase, *"And went his way,"* refers to the mission of sowing the *"tares"* as being completed and successful!

(In verses 36-42, we will give a more detailed Commentary on this Parable, as in those verses, Jesus gives the explanation.)

(26) BUT WHEN THE BLADE WAS SPRUNG UP, AND BROUGHT FORTH FRUIT, THEN APPEARED THE TARES ALSO."

The phrase, *"But when the blade was sprung up,"* refers to the *"good seed"* taking root, growing, and having a healthy start.

The phrase, *"And brought forth fruit,"* refers to its intended purpose!

The phrase, *"Then appeared the tares also,"* represents this poisonous grain which looks like wheat while growing, but when fully grown and ripe has ears which are long, the grains being black and poisonous. As is obvious, this would create great difficulty, especially in the attempt to harvest the true grain, i.e., *"the wheat."*

(27) "SO THE SERVANTS OF THE HOUSEHOLDER CAME AND SAID UNTO HIM, SIR, DIDST NOT THOU SOW GOOD SEED IN THY FIELD? FROM WHENCE THEN HATH IT TARES?"

The phrase, *"So the servants of the householder came and said unto him,"* refers to those who had helped sow the *"good seed,"* but, more particularly, refers to True Ministers of the Gospel of Jesus Christ.

NOTES

The question, *"Sir, didst not thou sow good seed in thy field?",* has reference to the seed sowed, and if it really was *"good seed,"* why would the tares be there as well?

The question, *"From whence then hath it tares?",* proclaims a lack of understanding as to how the *"tares"* had come to be there!

They knew the ground was properly cultivated, which should have destroyed all such seed, and, as well, they knew they had sowed *"good seed!"* Therefore, how was it, at least in their thinking, that this came to be?

(28) "HE SAID UNTO THEM, AN ENEMY HATH DONE THIS. THE SERVANTS SAID UNTO HIM, WILT THOU THEN THAT WE GO AND GATHER THEM UP?"

The phrase, *"He said unto them,"* will proclaim a far greater consternation than that which they have shown. To be sure, the Lord is far more grieved at this turn of events than even those who labor for Him. This circumvents, and successfully so, all that He did at Calvary! To be sure, it does not destroy the effort, but it does seriously hinder it.

The phrase, *"An enemy hath done this,"* refers to Satan and his helpers. Regrettably, his helpers constitute mostly that which calls itself *"The Church,"* and incorporates the Religious Ministry. Actually, the next verse will give us more information respecting this.

The question, *"The servants said unto him, Wilt thou then that we go and gather them up?",* refers to a task that is nearly, if not totally impossible respecting the growing stage.

(29) "BUT HE SAID, NAY; LEST WHILE YE GATHER UP THE TARES, YE ROOT UP ALSO THE WHEAT WITH THEM."

The phrase, *"But he said, Nay,"* is said for a very good reason. The following tells us why!

The phrase, *"Lest while ye gather up the tares, ye root up also the wheat with them,"* refers to the destruction that would be incumbent upon the *"wheat"* if such were done.

The idea is that even though the *"tares"* are obvious, at least to those who truly know what wheat looks like, still, their root systems are entangled with the root systems of the wheat. Therefore, if they take the obvious tares and pull them out, the wheat will be uprooted as well, and, consequently, destroyed.

The idea is that True Gospel Ministers, even though able to properly identify the *"tares,"* i.e., false doctrine, still, they are not to use force to stop it.

This is commanded for a number of reasons:

1. First of all, zealous Believers may think they have all the light on particular Gospel subjects, but in reality do not! In other words, unless what is being preached is obviously *"false doctrine,"* one should be very careful.

As an example, many good Baptist friends, thinking they have all the light on the Holy Spirit, will attempt to hinder, or even stop any presentation of the Holy Spirit which does not agree with their own Doctrine.

2. The attitude should be, and I think is Scriptural, that even though the *"tares,"* i.e., false doctrine, should be pointed out, and graphically so, still, that is as far as it should go.

America founded on the principle of *"Freedom of Religion,"* was done, I think, by the Will of the Lord. In other words, every man has the right to preach whatever he feels he should preach, at least within certain parameters. (Something that would instigate riots, or the hurting of others, should not be allowed.)

If I demand the right to preach what I feel is Scripturally correct, I should, at the same time, give that right to others!

Of course, I am referring to *"rights."* However, that does not mean that one has the *"right"* to preach any doctrine they so desire in my Church. Actually, it is my responsibility as a *"watchman"* to not only point out false doctrine, but, as well, to make certain that what is preached in my Church is *"Sound Doctrine."*

But, at the same time, those who I consider to not be preaching the Truth, have the right to build their own Churches and proclaim what they believe is right by any means at their disposal.

It would come as a shock to many Christians, but there are scores of Preachers who, if they had their way, would not allow any type of Church except their own, nor any type of Gospel except that which they preach. If they had the power to do so, they would stop all others, even by force if necessary. History is replete with such action.

This is what Jesus is talking about, at least in part. To have such an attitude is not only wrong, but in direct opposition to the Command of Christ as here stated. The reason is obvious!

While the *"tares,"* at least at times, would

NOTES

be uprooted, still, *"wheat"* would be uprooted as well!

3. Whenever Churches or Preachers fight, almost always *"wheat,"* i.e., young Christians, are destroyed.

While false doctrine, and as we have already stated, should be graphically pointed out, and in no uncertain terms, still, that is as far as it should go! It is unwise, except in very limited circumstances, to even call the names of those we feel are not preaching the Truth. If one is to notice, Paul always pointed out the error, but he seldom called names.

The idea is that people would learn to recognize the error, and irrespective as to who preaches it.

(30) "LET BOTH GROW TOGETHER UNTIL THE HARVEST: AND IN THE TIME OF HARVEST I WILL SAY TO THE REAPERS, GATHER YE TOGETHER FIRST THE TARES, AND BIND THEM IN BUNDLES TO BURN THEM: BUT GATHER THE WHEAT INTO MY BARN."

The phrase, *"Let both grow together until the harvest,"* refers to the end of the age or, more specifically, the First Resurrection of Life. To be sure, that time is coming!

The phrase, *"And in the time of the harvest I will say to the reapers,"* refers to the Lord performing this all-important task, because only He has the wisdom and ability to do so.

The *"reapers"* are the Angels, as He will later say.

The phrase, *"Gather ye together first the tares,"* in a sense points them out for destruction, exactly as was done in Jerusalem immediately before its destruction, which is proclaimed in Ezekiel Chapter 9.

The phrase, *"And bind them in bundles to burn them,"* refers to all those who did not have the True Gospel and, consequently, were not saved but will die eternally lost.

The phrase, *"But gather the wheat into My barn,"* refers to those who truly followed the Lord, and were washed in the Blood of the Lamb.

(31) "ANOTHER PARABLE PUT HE FORTH UNTO THEM, SAYING, THE KINGDOM OF HEAVEN IS LIKE TO A GRAIN OF MUSTARD SEED, WHICH A MAN TOOK, AND SOWED IN HIS FIELD:"

The Parable of the Mustard Seed and of the Leaven are popularly understood to predict the prosperity of the Church. However, that is not so!

The Text declares their relation to the Kingdom and not to the Church. Paul revealed this in Ephesians 3:3-6.

The Parables foretell the outward failure, and the inward corruption of God's moral kingdom upon earth — introduced by the Son of Man, and the Apostles, in consequence of the rejection of the actual kingdom of Israel. This moral kingdom would become outwardly big as, in fact, it has, like an abnormal mustard tree, but the Devil, symbolized by the fowls of the air, would make his home in it, at the same time that idolatry, symbolized by the woman, would corrupt it internally.

Thus in conduct and in doctrine, the failure of what is called Christianity is here revealed beforehand. We will explain that further momentarily!

The phrase, *"Another Parable put He forth unto them,"* refers to the third Parable.

The *"mustard seed,"* was chosen to represent the *"Kingdom of Heaven,"* and because of its small size. And yet, it would grow very rapidly and become a large tree in a short period of time. Likewise, did the Gospel! However, with the insertion of the *"tares,"* i.e., demon powers, it became corrupt.

The fault is not in the *"mustard seed,"* but in the *"tares"* which are sowed among the good seed, which causes all the problems.

(32) "WHICH INDEED IS THE LEAST OF ALL SEEDS: BUT WHEN IT IS GROWN, IT IS THE GREATEST AMONG HERBS, AND BECOMETH A TREE, SO THAT THE BIRDS OF THE AIR COME AND LODGE IN THE BRANCHES THEREOF."

The phrase, *"Which indeed is the least of all seeds,"* concerns the small beginnings of the Gospel of Jesus Christ.

When Jesus ascended back to Heaven, only 120 went according to His Command to wait for the *"Promise of the Father,"* i.e., the Holy Spirit. Therefore, one could well say that this 120 constituted the beginnings of the *"Church."* As obvious, it was small, and with tremendous opposition arrayed against it.

Still, because of the Power of the Holy Spirit, in just a few days *"there were added to them about three thousand souls"* (Acts 2:41).

From that moment it began to grow, and, as the *"mustard seed,"* extremely fast.

The phrase, *"But when it is grown, it is the greatest among herbs, and becometh a tree,"* concerns the growth of Christianity until presently. Despite the tremendous opposition down through the ages, it is the largest *"Faith"* in the world, claiming nearly two billion people as adherents, if one is to include Catholicism. Consequently, it is exactly as Christ said, *"The greatest among herbs."*

The phrase, *"So that the birds of the air come and lodge in the branches thereof,"* speaks not only of its size, but, as well, of every kind of bird, which speaks of every type of doctrine. In other words the false is mixed with the good, which makes a large number and refers to the large size. However, even though it is large, even the largest, still, only a small part of it is truly of God, and, thereby, true followers of Christ.

As all of these Parables are linked together in one way or the other, quite possibly the *"Parable of the sower"* proclaims just how much of this *"tree"* is truly of the Lord.

It was only about a fourth in the *"Parable of the sower"* who truly heard the Gospel, lived the Gospel, and brought forth *"fruit."*

(Even though we have used a fourth as an example, still, it is not our intention to place a number of certainty on those who truly follow the Lord. While it is certainly known that God knows the exact number, still, no man does. Therefore, our using this number is only meant to serve as direction, and not definition.)

(33) "ANOTHER PARABLE SPAKE HE UNTO THEM; THE KINGDOM OF HEAVEN IS LIKE UNTO LEAVEN, WHICH A WOMAN TOOK, AND HID IN THREE MEASURES OF MEAL, TILL THE WHOLE WAS LEAVENED."

The phrase, *"Another Parable spake He unto them,"* represents the fourth, and has reference to the others. Even though the shortest, it is one of the most powerful!

The phrase, *"The Kingdom of Heaven is like unto leaven,"* is figurative of sin (I Cor. 5:6-8; Gal. 5:9); false doctrines (Mat. 16:6-12; Mk. 8:15-21); and hypocrisy (Lk. 12:1). As is obvious, it is not used in a good sense.

The phrase, *"Which a woman took,"* is, likewise, used figuratively in an evil sense, and represents wickedness, fallacy, uncleanness, and unfaithfulness (Lam. 1:17); harlotry (Ezek. 16:15, 22, 26, 28-59; 23:1-49; 36:17; Hos. 1:2; 2:2-17; 3:1; Rev. 17); wickedness (Zech. 5:5-11; Rev. 17:5); and false religion (Rev. 17).

Even though the designation, *"woman,"* is used sometimes in a good sense, it is only when Israel is symbolized (Gen. 37:9-10; Ezek. 16; Rev. 12).

It also pertains to the Two Covenants as outlined in Galatians 4:21-31; however, this, as well, pertains to Israel.

On all other occasions, as in verse 33, the *"woman"* represents evil. An example is found in Zechariah 5:7. In the 8th verse of that same Chapter, the Angel said that this woman *"represented wickedness."* That has reference to the rebuilding of Babylon, which is even yet to come, and which will be the epitome of wickedness in these last days.

The phrase, *"And hid in three measures of meal,"* represents the Word of God.

This *"woman,"* representing wickedness, false teaching, false prophets, religious programs, etc., and representing the *"tares,"* will infiltrate the Work of God on earth, until the whole is corrupted.

The phrase, *"Till the whole was leavened,"* represents the entirety of the *"Kingdom of Heaven,"* which includes the Church being totally corrupted in these last days.

As we have stated, this refers to the failure of Christianity in general to subjugate the world. To be sure, it will accomplish its intended purpose of drawing many, even millions into the Kingdom. However, due to it being totally corrupted, Christianity will not take over the entirety of the world, thereby, ushering in the Millennium, as many presently teach.

This false doctrine is the *"Kingdom Age"* philosophy, which is now taught by many and goes under many names, and with many variations. However, it basically teaches that the Millennium will be ushered in by Christianity growing more and more powerful until it ultimately subdues the religions of the world either by conversion or unification. Consequently, many of its leaders are openly advocating that the doctrines of Catholicism are Scriptural and proper. As a result, no effort is to be made to convert Catholics, because they are *"brothers in the Lord, the same as we,"* they say!

They also advocate that this process will

come into being by political means rather than spiritual means, even though they conclude it all to be spiritual. Consequently, the major thrust of many if not most segments of the modern Church is furiously engaged in the political process.

Tragically, the far greater majority of what is presently being done, and called *"evangelism,"* is unscriptural, and, in Truth, only fulfills the prediction of this very *"Parable."*

Daniel prophesied that for sure the *"Kingdom of Heaven"* would prevail in this world, but denies emphatically that such will be brought about by political means, etc. In fact, he predicts the opposite!

He saw a *"Stone"* which was *"cut out without hands,"* which spoke of it being all of the Lord, and none of man, which completely negates this present false gospel.

As well, Daniel said, that this Stone, Who is Christ, *"Smote the image upon his feet that were of iron and clay, and brake them to pieces"* (Dan. 2:34).

This speaks of the Coming of the Lord, and, more specifically, the Battle of Armageddon, when He will come back with great power, destroying the Antichrist and his armies, and, as well, completely disrupting and even destroying the system of nations which have existed for so long.

Daniel said, and concerning these nations, *"And the wind carried them away, that no place was found for them."*

He went on to say, *"And the Stone that smote the image became a great mountain, and filled the whole earth"* (Dan. 2:35).

These Passages, along with others, definitely speak of the earth being taken over by Christ and what one might call *"Christianity;"* however, it will not be by the process of Christianity gradually taking over the whole world, but, instead, the opposite, which speaks of Christ coming in great Power and Glory.

To be sure, much of what is presently called Christianity will have become so corrupt that it will join forces with the Antichrist, and will have to be destroyed in totality by Christ at His Second Coming.

Therefore, the unity message is going to become stronger and stronger, with the True Gospel of Jesus Christ becoming less and less. To be sure, the Lord will always have a Holy

Remnant, which will make up the True Church, but in comparison to the whole, it will be small.

The word, *"whole,"* means, and speaks of organized religion.

It is fearsome to realize how close the modern Church is to the fulfillment of this Parable. If one is to look at modern Christendom, there is not much left which speaks of Holiness and Righteousness, which is the hallmark of the Work of the Holy Spirit. By and large it is corruption!

For the most part, the far greater majority of the Denominational Church World have completely turned their backs on the Holy Spirit, even denying His Power and Veracity.

Tragically, this is happening as well even in the Pentecostal and Charismatic segments! At the present, the *"political gospel,"* to which we have been alluding, and the *"prosperity gospel,"* comprises the larger part by far of the Pentecostal and Charismatic segments.

Repentance is presently scoffed at in most of the modern Church. As a result, the great Biblical Principles of Righteousness and Holiness are little considered, or even understood. Mighty Religious Denominations, which once espoused the Gospel of Jesus Christ, are now bloated and fat, and mistake this sickly condition for spiritual prosperity.

As a result, Believers run hither and yon, seeking the latest fad, basically standing for nothing, and, thereby, falling for anything.

Even though my words are not exactly positive, and, consequently, do not subscribe to the feel-good gospel, still, they are, and according to this 33rd verse, the Truth. Paul said as much (I Tim. 4:1-8; II Tim. 3:5; 4:3-4); as well as Simon Peter (II Pet. 3:3-4).

(34) "ALL THESE THINGS SPAKE JESUS UNTO THE MULTITUDE IN PARABLES; AND WITHOUT A PARABLE SPAKE HE NOT UNTO THEM:"

The phrase, *"All these things spake Jesus unto the multitude in Parables,"* relates only to this segment of His Teaching.

The phrase, *"And without a Parable spake He not unto them,"* refers to these illustrations given concerning the presentation of the Gospel, how it affects, and is effected, and more specifically to the end times, which sees Christendom as being wholly corrupted.

NOTES

As we have stated, leaven is invariably presented in Scripture as a symbol of evil, and frequently a woman as an agent of idolatry. The meal was pure, which symbolizes the Word of God. However, the leaven introduced an element into it which produced corruption. At the present time, and getting worse daily, modern Christendom, at least as it influences the world, is wholly corrupted. To be sure, this does not include the Holy Remnant, wherever and whoever they may be, which makes up the True Body of Christ. But it does include all else!

If one is to notice, Jesus gave very little personal instruction regarding Salvation, etc., in these Parables, but, instead, gave that, as stated, which pertained to the disposition of the Kingdom of Heaven.

(35) "THAT IT MIGHT BE FULFILLED WHICH WAS SPOKEN BY THE PROPHET, SAYING, I WILL OPEN MY MOUTH IN PARABLES; I WILL UTTER THINGS WHICH HAVE BEEN KEPT SECRET FROM THE FOUNDATION OF THE WORLD."

The phrase, *"That it might be fulfilled which was spoken by the Prophet,"* refers to Psalm 78:2, which was written by or for Asaph. Most Bible Scholars would not call this a Messianic Psalm; however, it is!

This shaft of light from verse 35 actually illuminates the entire Book of the Psalms, which, I think, if properly investigated, will be found that the entirety of the Psalms pertains to Christ in His Intercessory or Mediatorial role.

The phrase, *"Saying, I will open My Mouth in Parables,"* refers to the *"dark sayings"* of Psalm 78:2.

The phrase, *"I will utter things which have been kept secret from the foundation of the world,"* refers to Truths which have never before been revealed, but are now given, albeit in shadow.

These things which have been *"kept secret,"* refers to the Gentiles being brought in, the establishment of the Church, although not so boldly stated here, and how all the nations of the world would become permeated, or at least influenced by its principles.

To be sure, the Jews could not have even remotely thought or considered that which Christ is speaking of, even though pointed to by the Law of Moses.

The word, *"foundation,"* in *"Foundation of the world,"* means in the Greek, *"katabole,"* which means to cast down or throw down. It should have been translated, *"From the casting down of the world."*

It refers to the overthrow of the pre-Adamite world by the flood of Genesis 1:2, and does not refer to the Fall of Adam and Eve.

As well, *"katabole,"* is not the ordinary word for founding or foundation. This would require the use of the word, *"themelios,"* and refers to the word, *"foundation,"* as found in Luke 6:48-49 and 14:29.

Katabole, therefore, means the disruption, overthrow, or ruin of the social system before Adam. In Genesis 1:1, we have the *"themelioo,"* of the world, which means the founding of the earth, and in Genesis 1:2, we have the *"katabole"* which means the overthrow of the social system on the earth by the flood, which does not refer to Noah's flood, but a flood which preceded Adam and Eve.

So, the statement as made by Christ, actually refers to the rebellion of Lucifer as he attempted to overthrow the Kingdom of God, which continues even unto this very hour (Isa. 14:12-15; Ezek. 28:11-19). This statement given by Christ also announces the defeat of Satan, which took place at the Cross.

To sum up, the great Truths that Jesus is here presenting, concerns the entire disposition of the Gospel from His time and forward. It would greatly influence the earth, but would become totally corrupt, even as we are now seeing. In other words, the true nature of the Gospel would be rejected by all but a few. However, that which was rejected was not rejected totally, but for the most part would be turned, twisted, and corrupted. It includes all of Catholicism and Protestantism, except, and as stated, a tiny Remnant.

(36) "THEN JESUS SENT THE MULTITUDE AWAY, AND WENT INTO THE HOUSE: AND HIS DISCIPLES CAME UNTO HIM, SAYING, DECLARE UNTO US THE PARABLE OF THE TARES OF THE FIELD."

The phrase, *"Then Jesus sent the multitude away,"* means that these Truths which were presented in the first four Parables, for the *"Parable of the leaven"* was the fourth, was given not only to His Disciples, but, as well, to the *"multitudes."*

It is doubtful that many of them understood what He was talking about, and He as good as said so in verses 14 and 15.

To be sure, even His Own Disciples little understood His statements until they were more properly explained.

The phrase, *"And went into the house,"* respects a private session. It was quite possibly the home of Simon Peter!

The phrase, *"And His Disciples came unto Him, saying,"* refers to their lacking in understanding respecting the Parables they had just heard, and more particularly the *"Parable of the tares and the wheat."* Therefore, as they asked Him to explain the *"Parable of the sower,"* they will, likewise, ask for an explanation of this Parable.

(37) "HE ANSWERED AND SAID UNTO THEM, HE THAT SOWETH THE GOOD SEED IS THE SON OF MAN;"

The answer, if one is to notice, is very clear, pointed, and concise.

He says that the One doing the sowing is *"The Son of Man,"* i.e., *"Himself."* He, and He Alone, is the Lord of the harvest (Mat. 9:38).

As well, it is *"His Church"* (Mat. 16:18).

(38) "THE FIELD IS THE WORLD; THE GOOD SEED ARE THE CHILDREN OF THE KINGDOM; BUT THE TARES ARE THE CHILDREN OF THE WICKED ONE;"

The phrase, *"The field is the world,"* enlarges it considerably so over Judaism, which encompassed only the Land of Israel, and, furthermore, proclaimed the coming of the Church, which would be made up mostly of Gentiles.

In effect, this is what He said in the Great Commission, *"Go ye into all the world, and preach the Gospel to every person"* (Mk. 16:15).

The phrase, *"The good seed are the Children of the Kingdom,"* refers to True Believers of the Word of God. It refers to everyone, and everywhere, both Jew and Gentile, who is truly *"born again"* (Jn. 3:3).

As well, it would have no central base as Judaism had Jerusalem. In fact, after the Day of Pentecost, the Holy Spirit gradually shifted away from Jerusalem to Antioch, where it seems as if the greater part of World Missions, at least at that time, was carried forth (Acts 13:1). After that, it shifted to many capitals of the world, with the Holy Spirit moving anywhere there was a hunger for God, and irrespective of the place. Actually, the place had little to do with what the Holy Spirit was doing, only the thirsty hearts of men.

The phrase, *"But the tares are the children of the wicked one,"* in many ways resemble the *"Children of the Kingdom."*

Jesus would tell the Pharisees, *"Ye are of your father the devil, and the lust of your father ye will do"* (Jn. 8:44).

However, at the same time, they professed to be *"Children of the Kingdom,"* and with most of the people believing they were. Nevertheless, Christ portrayed them for what they really were.

If all professing Christians, along with all Religious Leaders, were to stand before Christ, how many would He point out as *"Children of the Kingdom"* and *"children of the wicked one?"*

The answer would probably be shocking! And to be sure, and exactly as He shall state, such identification and separation ultimately will be brought about.

(39) "THE ENEMY THAT SOWED THEM IS THE DEVIL; THE HARVEST IS THE END OF THE WORLD; AND THE REAPERS ARE THE ANGELS."

The phrase, *"The enemy that sowed them is the Devil,"* proclaims in the Words of Christ, Satan as the arch-enemy of all that is holy, good, and true, and, more specifically, the arch- enemy of God.

The *"Devil,"* i.e., Satan, heads the Kingdom of Darkness, in his effort to overthrow the Kingdom of God. In this Kingdom of Darkness, billions have died eternally lost, and the world has been bathed in blood, with suffering, sorrow, poverty and heartache having riddled the sons of men, and continues to this hour.

Most of the world does not believe there is such a one as Satan, and because they do not believe the Bible. Consequently, they do not believe that the only power which can overcome Satan is the Power of God. Therefore, they continue to attempt to assuage the sorrow and suffering of the world by human wisdom which has little effect. Regrettably, the Church follows suit by *"denying the Power of God"* (II Tim. 3:5).

Satan is responsible for all the evil, sorrow and sadness that fill the world, as it comes from the evil hearts of his children. As stated,

many of these *"children,"* if not most, are in the religious sector.

The phrase, *"The harvest is the end of the world,"* should have been rather translated, *"The end of the age."* It is the age that will end at the Second Coming of Christ (Zech. 14:1-5; Mat. 24:29-31; 25:31-46; Rev. 19:11-21). Then the *"Kingdom of Heaven,"* which now resides in a spiritual sense in the hearts of many, will then reside as well in the physical and material sense. It will be the ending of one age, the age here spoken of, and the beginning of another, i.e., the Millennium.

The *"Harvest"* represents the First Resurrection of Life, which Paul spoke about in I Thessalonians 4:16-17, where all the Righteous will be taken out of the world, and which many of those remaining will be *"burned."* As well, it concerns the judgment of the nations (Dan. 7:9; Mat. 25:31-46).

The phrase, *"And the reapers are the Angels,"* refers to the *"Holy Angels"* coming back with Christ at the Second Coming, thereby helping Him to establish His Throne, i.e., *"The Throne of His Glory."* As here stated, the Angels will play a great part in all that is done in the setting up of the *"Kingdom of Heaven"* on earth.

(40) "AS THEREFORE THE TARES ARE GATHERED AND BURNED IN THE FIRE; SO SHALL IT BE IN THE END OF THIS WORLD."

The phrase, *"As therefore the tares are gathered and burned in the fire,"* proclaims a coming Judgment. That Judgment is the *"Great White Throne Judgment,"* and is recorded in Revelation 20:11-15.

If it is to be noticed, the Lord draws special attention to this coming Judgment, outlining it to a far greater degree than when the Parable of the tares and wheat was given. He wants the certitude of such action to be clearly understood.

This offends the modernists and even most religionists, and because the lie of psychology has made such penetration into the modern Church, that the idea of a coming reckoning, or that one is responsible for his actions, is foreign to much of the modern Church.

As well, most modern religionists do not believe there is a literal Hell. However, the words, *"burned in the fire,"* are not merely a figure of speech, but an actuality.

Years ago, I preached a city-wide crusade

in a particular state, with the chairman of the meeting being a member of the largest Pentecostal Denomination in the world.

On Saturday night of the meeting, which drew several thousand in attendance, I preached on the subject of *"Hell."* If I remember correctly, my subject was *"Can a loving God condemn a person to Hell, burning him there forever and forever, and justify Himself in doing so?"*

After the service, which had, incidentally, seen a goodly number respond to the Altar Call, this Pastor made a statement to me that let me know he little believed in this place called *"Hell."* Sadder still, he was a member, as stated, of this large Pentecostal Denomination which claims to believe all the Bible.

I also knew that this man was an advocate of the *"self-esteem gospel,"* and, as such, he would little adhere to any message that he considered to be *"negative."*

Some may claim that these negative Truths do not have to be believed in order for one to preach the Gospel. I disagree!

If one does not preach all the Gospel, then one does not preach the Gospel! Paul said, *"For I have not shunned to declare to you all the Counsel of God"* (Acts 20:27).

The problem with most Preachers, and a great problem it is, is that they do not declare the *"Whole Counsel of God!"*

That Hell is a literal place and not an attitude or symbolism, was proclaimed by Christ in His relating the story of the rich man who went to Hell and Lazarus who went to Paradise (Lk. 16:19-31). He had much to say elsewhere concerning this place as well! (Mat. 5:22, 29-30; 10:28; 18:9; 23:15, 33; Mk. 9:43, 45, 47; Lk. 12:5; James 3:6).

Hell is depicted as a place of unquenchable fire — with the general idea that fire expresses Divine Judgment. Jesus said that the fire of Hell is unquenchable (Mk. 9:43), eternal (Mat. 18:8), with its punishment being eternal, but the opposite of eternal life (Mat. 25:46).

There is no suggestion that those who enter Hell ever emerge from it, with but one exception, when all in Hell will stand before God at the Great White Throne Judgment (Rev. 20:11-15). However, it (the emergence from Hell) will not be pleasant, because the conclusion of this Judgment is an eternal consignment to the Lake of Fire (Rev. 20:11-15; 21:8).

Hell is a picture of the awfulness of sin, as Calvary is a picture of the great Love of God for the sinner. To be sure, it is not God's Will that any go to Hell, and irrespective as to whom they may be. As stated, He has done everything possible to keep man from this place, even to the sending of His Own Son to die on Calvary.

So, one cannot fault the Love of God, and neither can they honestly condemn Him. As a result of what God has done to save man from Hell, man can blame no one but himself if he dies eternally lost, with but one exception!

That exception is that no one told him of the Gospel Plan of Salvation through Jesus Christ. In that case, he will have the Church to blame, but, still, such will not save him from this dreadful place.

God told Ezekiel to warn the unrighteous, and whether they believed the warning or not, they would know that a Prophet had been among them.

However, if Ezekiel did not warn them, their blood would be required at his (Ezekiel's) hands (Ezek. 3:17-21).

Regrettably, much of the Church has bloody hands!

As well, many, when hearing what is called the Gospel, in Truth, is no Gospel at all, but rather a *"false message"* delivered by a *"false prophet."* Consequently, hundreds of millions have died and gone to Hell because they believed a lie.

A Preacher acquaintance of mine was given a dream by the Lord. In the dream he saw Hell! He described the burning sea of flame and the millions who resided there, in *"weeping, wailing, and gnashing of teeth."*

In the dream, he saw individuals reach down into the Lake of Fire, taking other persons by the hair of the head, pulling them up and looking into their faces. He asked the Angel who was with him as to what they were doing?

The Angel answered, saying, *"They are looking for the Preacher who preached a lie to them, which caused them to be lost!"*

Sadly, the Doctrine of Hell, as an eternal Lake of Fire where all unbelievers go, is seldom preached behind modern pulpits. In fact, most Preachers do not even believe there is a place called *"Hell,"* declaring that a loving God could not send a person to such a place!

While it is certainly true that God is a God of Love, and, as well, of Mercy, Compassion, Grace, and Longsuffering, still, in order to be that, which He has readily made evident, He, as well, must be a God of Justice and Judgment. If not, the whole thing falls down!

If Preachers preach the whole Gospel, they will have to preach on this subject, as negative as it may be, warning men, and because they love them so much, about this terrible place. Jesus did, and we must as well!

The phrase, *"So shall it be in the end of this world,"* should have been translated, *"in the end of this age,"* and speaks of the conclusion of this Dispensation.

Actually, the world will never end, but, instead, will be changed, i.e., refurbished, remade (Rev. 21:1).

(41) "THE SON OF MAN SHALL SEND FORTH HIS ANGELS, AND THEY SHALL GATHER OUT OF HIS KINGDOM ALL THINGS THAT OFFEND, AND THEM WHICH DO INIQUITY:"

The phrase, *"The Son of Man shall send forth His Angels,"* proclaims Christ as the Authority in these matters, and directing that which is to be done.

Today, Christ is our Saviour, whereas then He will be the Judge.

To say it another way, if men do not say *"yes"* to Him as Saviour, they will answer to Him as Judge. It is one or the other and cannot be escaped!

The phrase, *"And they shall gather out of His Kingdom,"* refers to the *"Angels"* separating all who do not serve Christ, and consigning them to the Lake of Fire.

This will take place at the conclusion of the Kingdom Age. During the Kingdom Age, which will last for a thousand years, Jesus will rule Personally from Jerusalem with his Angels, and which Satan and demon spirits will be consigned to the bottomless pit (Rev. 20:1-3). The world during this one-thousand-year reign of Christ will know prosperity, both spiritually and economically, as it has never known before.

However, at the end of the thousand years, Satan will be *"loosed out of his prison."*

At that time, he will *"go out to deceive the nations,"* and will *"gather"* all the people on the earth who do not want to serve Christ, and will, once again, attempt to destroy *"the beloved*

city," Jerusalem, where Christ resides, fulfilling verse 41. However, the Scripture says, *"And fire came down from God out of Heaven, and devoured them"* (Rev. 20:4-10). No doubt, Angels will be used, as here described by Christ, during this momentous time at the conclusion of the Kingdom Age.

The words, *"His Kingdom,"* refers to this coming Kingdom Age.

The phrase, *"All things that offend, and them which do iniquity,"* includes all on the earth at that time, who will, and as stated, be forced to serve Christ, but in their hearts will not want Him. These, at that time (when Satan is loosed), will join Satan, which will prove to be his very last effort, and will write *"finish"* for all sin and *"iniquity."* Then the New Heavens and New Earth will come into being (Rev. 21:1).

Sin, which comes from Satan and is disobedience to God, has been the cause of all the pain and suffering in this world. At that time (the new heavens and the new earth), the terrible horror of sin and iniquity will be brought to an eternal conclusion. And then all things will be as God intended for them to be at the beginning. Christ will then be all in all (Rev. 22:1-5).

(42) "AND SHALL CAST THEM INTO A FURNACE OF FIRE: THERE SHALL BE WAILING AND GNASHING OF TEETH."

The phrase, *"And shall cast them into a furnace of fire,"* is the Second Resurrection of Damnation. It is called *"The Second Death,"* and is the end result of the Great White Throne Judgment (Rev. 20:11-15).

The phrase, *"There shall be wailing and gnashing of teeth,"* speaks of the eternal suffering and pain in Hell, and as Jesus described in Luke 16.

One noted Communications Baron in America said some time ago, *"I want to go to Hell, because that's where all the fun is going to be,"* or words to that effect!

Regrettably, there will be no *"fun"* in Hell, but only that which Christ speaks of, *"Wailing and gnashing of teeth,"* which speaks of terrible pain, suffering, and regret.

(43) "THEN SHALL THE RIGHTEOUS SHINE FORTH AS THE SUN IN THE KINGDOM OF THEIR FATHER. WHO HATH EARS TO HEAR, LET HIM HEAR."

The phrase, *"Then shall the Righteous shine forth as the sun,"* is basically the same thing as said by Daniel, *"And they that be wise shall shine as the brightness of the firmament"* (Dan. 12:3).

This Passage by Christ refers to that which was said by John on the Isle of Patmos, *"And the city had no need of the sun, neither of the moon, to shine in it: for the Glory of God did lighten it, and the Lamb is the Light thereof"* (Rev. 21:23).

The *"Righteous"* will be a reflection of the Glory of the *"Lamb,"* i.e., Christ. This has to do with the Glory of God which will outshine the sun.

The phrase, *"In the Kingdom of their Father,"* has reference to the statement made by Paul, *"Then, at the end, when He shall deliver up the Kingdom to God, even the Father"* (I Cor. 15:24).

The phrase, *"Who hath ears to hear, let him hear,"* proclaims the certitude of such action, and that upon hearing these predictions, it would be very wise to believe and obey.

(44) "AGAIN, THE KINGDOM OF HEAVEN IS LIKE UNTO TREASURE HID IN A FIELD; THE WHICH WHEN A MAN HATH FOUND, HE HIDETH, AND FOR JOY THEREOF GOETH AND SELLETH ALL THAT HE HATH, AND BUYETH THAT FIELD."

This is the fifth Parable, and is given to His Disciples as they repose *"in the House"* (vs. 36). This, as well as the next two Parables, was probably spoken to the Disciples in private.

The first Parable was begun by simply the telling of it, with the next three beginning with the word, *"Another."* These were spoken to the multitudes.

The last three begin with the word, *"Again,"* and are spoken, as stated, in the house privately to His Disciples.

The phrase, *"The Kingdom of Heaven is like unto Treasure hid in a field,"* refers to the Gospel (Treasure) hid in the world (field).

Some have claimed that this *"Treasure"* is Israel, etc. However, the Parables of *"The Kingdom of Heaven,"* pertain to the Gospel going to the entirety of the world, whether Jew or Gentile, and man's acceptance or rejection of it. Therefore, it cannot be limited to Israel.

Paul said, *"We have this treasure in earthen vessels"* (II Cor. 4:7).

The word, *"hid,"* refers to the knowledge of the *"Kingdom of Heaven"* during Old Testament times. Paul also said, *"Even the mystery*

which hath been hid from ages and from generations, but now is made manifest to His Saints" (Col. 1:26).

That *"Treasure,"* even though proclaimed in the Gospel, is actually Christ (Col. 1:27).

Paul also said, *"In Whom* (Christ) *are hid all the treasures of wisdom and knowledge,"* referring to the Truth of this Parable, which one has to dig in order to find the Treasure, somewhat as a miner who digs for gold, etc. (Col. 2:3).

Paul, when giving these statements in the Book of Colossians, was, no doubt, drawing from this very Parable by Christ.

The phrase, *"The which when a man hath found,"* refers to a man finding this great Treasure, i.e., Christ. Christ is that which the heart truly craves, and yet men attempt to assuage this spiritual thirst by other things, which is impossible to do. He is truly a *"Treasure,"* but One Who is not easily found.

It is not the idea that one does not know He exists, but before accepting Him, it is impossible to know Who He really is, or What He really is!

It is somewhat like the Tabernacle in the wilderness, which design was given by God to Moses. Outwardly, there was nothing about it that was attractive; however, upon entering it, the beauty of it defied description. It was all of gold! And such is Christ.

The words, *"He hideth,"* is not meant to say that those who find Christ, hide Him, but, instead, is meant only to illustrate the Parable that he has found the Treasure in a certain field, and he does not want anyone to know about it until he has purchased the field, which he does not at present own.

In fact, Jewish Law in those days stipulated that any type of treasure found in any field was the property of the owner of the field.

What Jesus was telling would have been common to the ears of the people, and because of the many centuries of wars and conflicts which had been fought in that part of the world, and, at times, due to these conflicts, *"treasures"* of whatever variety would sometimes be found buried in a field or hidden in a cave.

As well, Jesus is not addressing Himself to the morality of what the man did by finding the treasure and not telling the owner, but, instead, buying the field. He was only illustrating His Parable by referring to something which quite possibly happened not infrequently in a country like Israel.

The phrase, *"And for joy thereof goeth and selleth all that he hath, and buyeth that field,"* refers to the *"Treasure,"* i.e., Christ, of the *"Kingdom of Heaven"* being so valuable, that everything must be done which can possibly be done in order to obtain Him.

Actually, that is the moral of this Parable. The *"selling all that he hath,"* means that everything else pales by comparison to this *"Treasure."*

There is a parallel in this to Jesus telling His prospective Disciples to *"Follow Me!"* They were to do so to the exclusion of all else. They had found the *"Treasure,"* and nothing else matters.

The words, *"Buyeth that field,"* does not mean that one can earn or merit or purchase Salvation, but, instead, that such is used as a metaphor describing that whatever price has to be paid, must be paid! One must put family behind them, as well as all else.

(45) "AGAIN, THE KINGDOM OF HEAVEN IS LIKE UNTO A MERCHANT MAN, SEEKING GOODLY PEARLS:"

Jesus now deals with the individual who is already obviously wealthy, and, as such, is accustomed to all the good things that wealth can buy. However, he seeks *"goodly pearls,"* meaning that he is still searching for something better than what he has.

In the phrase, *"Seeking goodly pearls,"* is found the thirst and the hunger which fills the hearts of men, and can only be satisfied by Christ. As well, such portrays that all else little satisfies.

As well, the plural in *"pearls,"* means that he has the very best the world can offer, and from several sources, i.e., money, intellectualism, place and position, as well as acclaim.

Also, he does not really know that a *"Pearl"* of such infinite value actually exists, which would make all others undesirable. But yet he keeps searching because that which he has, though valuable, does not satisfy his desires.

(46) WHO, WHEN HE HAD FOUND ONE PEARL OF GREAT PRICE, WENT AND SOLD ALL THAT HE HAD, AND BOUGHT IT."

This is the story of Salvation. Men try to satisfy the longing of their heart with *"things,"* and despite Jesus saying, *"A man's life consisteth not in the abundance of things he*

possesseth" (Lk. 12:15). What the soul cries for in every man is Jesus. He Alone can satisfy; He Alone can fill the void in every heart and life.

The phrase, *"When he had found one Pearl of great price,"* signifies Christ. He had been seeking *"goodly pearls,"* i.e., many goodly pearls, but now he will find *"One"* of such *"great price,"* i.e., inestimable value, that it alone will be of far greater value than all else he has had, and by far!

The phrase, *"Went and sold all that he had, and bought it,"* has the same connotation as the previous Parable, where the man sold all he had to buy the field. This one buys the "One Pearl of great price."

This *"merchant,"* who was, no doubt, a jeweler as well, minutely inspected this *"One Pearl"* when it was found, seeking flaws, but found none! In other words, it was flawless, without discoloration, perfectly round, in other words, perfect. Such alone describes Christ! Such alone is Christ!

As well, this *"merchant"* was smart enough to know the value of this *"One Pearl"* when he found it. Regrettably, many upon seeing it do not know what they have seen, and do not realize its value.

(47) "AGAIN, THE KINGDOM OF HEAVEN IS LIKE UNTO A NET, THAT WAS CAST INTO THE SEA, AND GATHERED OF EVERY KIND:"

This Parable is very similar to the Parable of the tares and wheat, but with a single difference.

In the former Parable, faithfulness was heralded, while in this Parable, warning is given that some of those now within the sphere of the *"Kingdom of Heaven"* in fact will ultimately be cast out.

The phrase, *"Again, the Kingdom of Heaven is like unto a net,"* is intended to reference the understanding of a net which catches fish. His Disciples, formerly being fishermen, would have understood perfectly what He was talking about.

The phrase, *"That was cast into the sea,"* refers to a place where fish can be caught and are accustomed to being caught. The illustration is meant to speak of fishing for men, with some responding favorably.

The phrase, *"And gathered of every kind,"* referred to all types of people who respond favorably to the Gospel, at least at the outset.

The *"net,"* being what it was, and with the invitation, *"Come unto Me, all..."* (Mat. 11:28-30), many will respond who truly profess, but do not truly possess. Regrettably, the Church is filled with this kind.

(48) "WHICH, WHEN IT WAS FULL, THEY DREW TO SHORE, AND SAT DOWN, AND GATHERED THE GOOD INTO VESSELS, BUT CAST THE BAD AWAY."

The word, *"Which,"* is meant to denote that a large catch *"gathered of every kind,"* is not exactly the purpose, but, rather, a quality catch.

The phrase, *"When it was full, they drew to shore,"* denotes a specific time when all of this will be brought to pass.

Paul's statement, and referring to the Birth of Christ, *"But when the fulness of time was come, God sent forth His Son,"* refers to a specific set time that this was to take place, which could not be delayed or rushed by man's actions (Gal. 4:4). Likewise, the *"Times of the Gentiles,"* has a certain limitation, when certain things will happen, *"until the times of the Gentiles be fulfilled,"* signifying that there is a specific date when this will happen (Lk. 21:24).

Likewise, when the *"net is full,"* i.e., a specified time, the last Altar Call will be given, and the last invitation by the Holy Spirit will be extended. The Lord Alone knows that particular time. It cannot be, as stated, delayed or hastened by man's actions.

Many have claimed that Jesus can be brought back earlier if the Church will do thus and so! However, there is no Passage in the Word of God that lends credence to such thinking.

Actually, the Lord has a specific date, which is unmovable, in which the great things promised will be fulfilled. In other words, the Rapture and the Second Coming, as well as other things, have a fixed time and cannot be hastened or delayed by man's actions, etc.

The phrase, *"And sat down,"* refers to the Throne of Judgment. However, the Judgment will be divided into two types of Judgment, with the first being the Judgment Seat of Christ, which will deal only with the Righteous, and the second Judgment being only for the unrighteous, which will be about a thousand years removed from the first.

At the Judgment Seat of Christ, no souls will be lost, but rewards, and because of wrong motivation, definitely will be.

At the Great White Throne Judgment, no one will be saved, but all will be lost (II Cor. 5:10; Rev. 20:11-15).

The very fact of the First and Second Resurrections will make the distinction between the *"good and bad."*

The phrase, *"And gathered the good into vessels,"* speaks of those who are truly saved. In other words, the *"vessel"* as here contains the *"good,"* i.e., *"good fish."*

The phrase, *"But cast the bad away,"* refers to the fisherman culling the bad from the good, because they were not fit for the marketplace. The bad were thrown away, as the tares.

This Parable proclaims the absolute necessity of the *"born again"* experience, and not mere profession, as characterizes the far greater majority of the Church. The warning is that the Lord knows those who are His, and there will come a time that he will say, *"Rise up, My love, My fair one, and come away"* (Song of Sol. 2:10). To be sure, at that time, His sheep will respond *"for they know His Voice"* (Jn. 10:4).

The others will not respond because they do not know His Voice.

(49) "SO SHALL IT BE AT THE END OF THE WORLD: THE ANGELS SHALL COME FORTH, AND SEVER THE WICKED FROM AMONG THE JUST."

The phrase, *"So shall it be at the end of the world,"* should have been translated, and as we have stated, *"At the end of the age."*

The phrase, *"The Angels shall come forth,"* refers to these celestial beings playing a great part in all that is done.

At the Second Coming, enumerable Angels will accompany Him, who will help Israel, among other things (Mat. 24:31; 25:31). According to Christ, the Angels will be very much involved in the event at hand.

The phrase, *"And sever the wicked from among the just,"* has the same connotations as verse 41, when the Angels will *"Gather out of His Kingdom all things that offend, and them which do iniquity."*

As stated, this particular *"severing"* will take place at the end of the Millennial Reign, when Satan will be loosed from his pit, and will make his final appearance, getting multiple millions on earth to join him. However, and as stated, his efforts will be short-lived, with him and his followers being defeated and placed in the Lake of Fire where he will never be released (Rev. 20:10).

(50) "AND SHALL CAST THEM INTO THE FURNACE OF FIRE: THERE SHALL BE WAILING AND GNASHING OF TEETH."

This verse is word for word the same as verse 42, and by design. Inasmuch as what is being said is fearful indeed and that it has eternal consequences, the Holy Spirit has Matthew to repeat it in order that men may have another warning.

As stated, there are seven Parables of which the *"Parable of the drag net"* is the last. Seven is God's number of completion, and, therefore, the messages contained in the Parables cover the entirety of the order of the *"Kingdom of Heaven,"* and as it refers to men. Its order, nature, scope, qualifications, and length are here proclaimed in these Parables. Consequently, they are of extreme importance, even though difficult at times to understand. As stated, they were designed in this manner accordingly in order that the merely curious would not know, while the truly interested would press through until the information became clear.

The correspondences between the Parables support the belief that all of them relate to the earth during the period between the First and Second Advents, with the final results of the Kingdom of Heaven taking place, at least as far as the wicked are concerned, at the conclusion of the Kingdom Age.

The eternal destiny of the tares and of the wicked as one of conscious misery is here revealed by God Himself.

(51) "JESUS SAITH UNTO THEM, HAVE YE UNDERSTOOD ALL THESE THINGS? THEY SAY UNTO HIM, YEA, LORD."

The question as asked of Christ of His Disciples, and of us as well, *"Have ye understood all these things?",* is meant to signify their importance. Even though they were spoken in a manner which purposely placed them in shadow, still, they were meant to be understood. And, if they had been easy to understand, Jesus would not have asked the question!

And yet, most modern Christians have little understanding as to the meaning of these Parables, or any knowledge of future events as predicted in the Word of God.

If one does not understand what the Bible says about the future, one may well

lack understanding in what it says about the present.

As a whole, these Parables teach several things:

1. The meaning of the *"Kingdom of Heaven,"* or as it is in the Greek, *"The Kingdom from the Heavens."*

It is headed up by Jesus Christ for the purpose of reestablishing the Kingdom of God over this rebellious part of God's realm. It is only found in Matthew because it is the Gospel of Jehovah's King. As well, it is a Dispensational term and refers to the Messiah's Kingdom on earth.

It could have made its entrance at Christ's First Advent, but was rejected.

Even though from that time it can be received in the heart, still, its total fulfillment has been postponed until the Second Coming. It is now in the realm of profession, but then, the coming Kingdom Age, it will be in the realm of possession.

These Parables apply, as stated, to this age. At the end Christ will come and set up a literal earthly Kingdom forever.

During the first one thousand years of His eternal reign, He will put down all rebellion and rid the earth of all rebels. Then God will become all in all as before rebellion (I Cor. 15:24-28; Eph. 1:10; Rev. 20:1-10; 21:1-22:5).

2. These Parables proclaim the scope of this coming Kingdom, which will include the entirety of the world. The Gospel is to be preached to all the world, that all may have amply opportunity.

3. They teach us, as well, that most will not accept the Gospel, but will, and for their own reasons, reject it.

4. They exclaim the tremendous worth of the Kingdom of Heaven, and that no price is too high to enter into it.

5. They teach us that many will enter in, but all will not be allowed to remain, and because of their unfaithfulness.

6. They exclaim the efforts of Satan to hinder, and graphically so.

7. The Parables exclaim the Coming Judgment and eternal punishment, even hellfire.

The phrase, *"They say unto Him, Yea, Lord,"* proclaims the understanding of the Disciples regarding this all-important subject.

They understood it, while the learned

Religious Leaders of Israel did not understand it, and because they had no desire to do so.

They (the Religious Leaders) had no desire for the Sermon on the Mount, consequently, the Lord would see to it that this all-important information was withheld from them.

Also, the Apostles had the Teacher of all teachers as their Instructor. What an honor to have sat where they sat.

(52) "THEN SAID HE UNTO THEM, THEREFORE EVERY SCRIBE WHICH IS INSTRUCTED UNTO THE KINGDOM OF HEAVEN IS LIKE UNTO A MAN THAT IS AN HOUSEHOLDER, WHICH BRINGETH FORTH OUT OF HIS TREASURE THINGS NEW AND OLD."

The phrase, *"Then said He unto them,"* proclaims a pick-up on the answer they have just given to Him.

The phrase, *"Therefore every Scribe which is instructed unto the Kingdom of Heaven,"* is a term every Christian should heed and regard highly.

The word, *"Scribe,"* as Christ uses it is interesting! It is interesting, because He applies it to His Disciples, as well as all Believers from then forward. The purpose of a Scribe was threefold:

1. They preserved the Law. They were professional students of the Law and its defenders.

Consequently, every Believer is to have the spirit of the Scribe in being a constant student of the Word and its defender.

2. They gathered around them many pupils to instruct them in the Law.

Consequently, every modern Believer should be versed enough in the Word of God to be ready, as Peter said, *"Always to give an answer to every man that asketh you a reason of the hope that is in you with meekness and fear"* (I Pet. 3:15). Peter may well have been thinking back to this Statement of Christ.

3. The Scribes were referred to as *"Teachers of the Law,"* and, as well, every Believer, and as here signified by Christ, should be versed enough in the Word that they would be Teachers as well!

Paul said, and chiding some of the Believers of his day, *"For when for the time you ought to be teachers, ye have need that one teach you again which be the first principles of the oracles of God; and are become such as have need of milk, and not of strong meat"* (Heb. 5:12).

What a rebuke!

Even though *"Scribes"* were a select group in Jesus' day, still, the Lord is, in effect, saying that all Believers should be *"Scribes."*

He was referring to their dedication to the Bible, instead of their attitude and spirit, which for most of this class was *"self-righteousness."*

The phrase, *"Is like unto a man that is an householder,"* in the thoughts of some, classifies this as another Parable, and, therefore, the eighth and final one in this series. However, the identifying marks which characterized all the other Parables are missing in this statement.

To take this phrase and stretching it to include all the other identifying marks is not sound Scriptural practice regarding interpretation.

The man in this statement is like unto a *"householder,"* who has many things in his house both old and new.

The phrase, *"Which bringeth forth out of his treasure things new and old,"* refers to his willingness to put these valuable items on display. They are valuable because they are called *"his treasure."*

As well, the words, *"new and old,"* probably have a triple meaning:

1. The instructed Christian Teacher can enrich others out of his store of Divine Truth. That Truth as to time is *"old,"* i.e., eternal; as to experience, power and character perpetually *"new."*

2. It could refer, at least in a limited sense, to both *"old"* and *"new"* Testaments. The *"old"* would certainly be old Truths, while the *"new"* would, as well, be new Truths. And yet, even the *"new"* would be *"old"* after a short period of time.

3. The *"old"* Truths are given *"new"* light, and inasmuch as it is the Word of God, it is impossible for one to exhaust the meaning of the old Truths, even as old as they may be.

As well, and which is probably the correct interpretation, the Holy Spirit is constantly giving *"new"* Truths, which always agree, and one hundred percent, with the Word of God, and never takes away from the *"old"* Truths, but merely sheds more light on them. Hence, *"old"* is mentioned after *"new,"* for it implies greater knowledge and skill.

NOTES

(53) "AND IT CAME TO PASS, THAT WHEN JESUS HAD FINISHED THESE PARABLES, HE DEPARTED THENCE."

The phrase, *"And it came to pass, that when Jesus had finished these Parables,"* refers to the ones just given, and not to those He would give at a later time (Chpts. 18, 20-22, 24-25).

The phrase, *"He departed thence,"* refers to His going to Nazareth. It will not be a pleasant reception.

(54) "AND WHEN HE WAS COME INTO HIS OWN COUNTRY, HE TAUGHT THEM IN THEIR SYNAGOGUE, INSOMUCH THAT THEY WERE ASTONISHED, AND SAID, WHENCE HATH THIS MAN THIS WISDOM, AND THESE MIGHTY WORKS?"

The phrase, *"And when He was come into His Own country,"* refers, as stated, to Nazareth.

Some think that the Lord visited Nazareth twice; but a comparison of all the records points to only one visit.

On reaching the town, He had no public and believing reception as elsewhere, nor did the multitudes press around Him for healing.

The phrase, *"He taught them in their Synagogue,"* could mean that He taught them for several days.

They did not at all understand Who He was, or what He was about.

As well, the great Truths He taught them, which are recorded in part in Luke 4, were rejected. They were rejected because the implications of these Truths from Isaiah pointed to Him as the Messiah. He said in Luke's account, *"This day is this Scripture fulfilled in your ears"* (Lk. 4:21).

The phrase, *"Insomuch that they were astonished,"* means they were astonished over what He said in that which He taught them. They were flabbergasted! In effect, they were rendered speechless.

What was proposed in Him astonished them because it referred to Him as the One the Prophets pointed to and proclaimed. Were that the case, the Messiah had been living among them for some thirty years, although not revealed.

The question, *"And said, Whence hath this Man this wisdom, and these mighty works?",* is meant to cast aspersions on Jesus referring to Him as *"this."* The word, *"Man,"* was inserted by

NOTES

the translators, and, therefore, they did not even do Him the honor of calling Him a *"Man,"* but, merely, *"this."*

It was a practiced insult meant to show not only their displeasure, but absolute ridicule of His Person and what some may have thought concerning His Person, i.e., Messiah.

They wanted to know where He had obtained all of *"this wisdom,"* because they had known Him, as stated, for some thirty years, and, consequently, they knew He was not of the educated aristocracy of Israel.

Actually, they were not denying the *"wisdom"* He exhibited, but really wanted to know where He had obtained it. This implied that He was not really wise, but that His statements, although very wise, were borrowed from someone else, memorized, and then presented. In other words, they did not accredit Him with such *"wisdom,"* even though it came out of His Mouth.

Concerning the *"mighty works,"* quite possibly they were speaking of that which they had heard, and not necessarily that which they had seen, because the Scripture says He did not do many mighty works there *"because of their unbelief."*

Their hearts were closed to all He had to say, or as to Who He was. There was nothing He could have said or done that would have changed their minds. To them He was no more than a joke, and they will exclaim such in the next verse.

(55) "IS NOT THIS THE CARPENTER'S SON? IS NOT HIS MOTHER CALLED MARY? AND HIS BRETHREN, JAMES, AND JOSES, AND SIMON, AND JUDAS?"

The question, *"Is not this the carpenter's son?",* portrays their denial of His claim regarding the Messiahship.

Actually, it seemed that He was far more open with them respecting this all-important subject than He was with anyone else in Israel. He had read to them the Scriptures from Isaiah, which clearly pointed to the Messiah, and which they knew. And then, as we have stated, He plainly said to them, *"This day is this Scripture fulfilled in your ears!"* Consequently, there was no way to misunderstand His explanation of these Passages.

That a carpenter, the Son of a carpenter, whom they had all known for some thirty years, and Whose mother and brothers and sisters they knew, should claim to be Jehovah Messiah, the Promised King of Israel, and should say such things about the Prophets Elijah and Elisha was an offense to them. But they could not deny His Wisdom nor His Miracles; and their statements about His Person, and His parents and His brothers and sisters provide irrefutable evidence of His actual humanity.

With their statement in the form of a question, *"Is not this the carpenter's Son?"*, they were denying His Virgin Birth. But, of course, very little if anything had been said about this all-important aspect of His life. It is obvious, and from their actions presented here, that no one would have believed it anyway (the Virgin Birth).

One has to wonder what their attitude toward Him was as they saw Him grow up in their midst. Considering that He was perfect in His conduct, speech, attitude and demeanor, such a life should have told them something. Luke said, and concerning the times of His young manhood, *"And Jesus increased in wisdom and stature, and in favour with God and man"* (Lk. 2:52).

As well, inasmuch as He was a carpenter's son, or so they thought, He, no doubt in helping his foster father, had helped build many of the houses and furniture in the little town of Nazareth. Consequently, they would have had more contact with Him than they would have with most.

However, there is not much True Faith in the hearts of men. Most, even Christians, make judgments according to appearances.

In their eyes, Jesus was a peasant and nothing else!

Even though the Scripture contained in the Old Testament, which they then had, said very little if anything about this period of His life, still, enough was said, and especially in Isaiah 53, that they should have had some clue, at least at this stage. However, they had no such knowledge because there were very few among them, if any, who truly studied the Scriptures, thereby asking the Lord to reveal His Word to them. As then, so now!

The question, *"Is not His Mother called Mary?"*, portrays her being well known, as would be obvious.

The Greek for *"Mary"* is *"Miriam."* Actually,

there were six Marys mentioned in the New Testament.

They are: The mother of Jesus, as is obvious; Mary Magdalene (Lk. 8:2; 24:10); Sister of Lazarus (Mat. 26:7; Lk. 10:39-42; Jn. 11; 12:3); Mother of James (Mat. 27:56; Mk. 15:40; Jn. 19:25); Mother of Mark (Acts 12:12); a helper of Paul (Rom. 16:6).

Even though privileged to be the Mother of the Lord Jesus Christ, still, Mary would suffer as few women have ever suffered. Truly as Simeon prophesied before Mary and Joseph, as they brought Baby Jesus for His dedication according to Exodus 13:12, and specifically to Mary, *"Yea, a sword shall pierce through thine own soul also"* (Lk. 2:35). This was to be fulfilled graphically so! It must have been very difficult for her, the rejection of Jesus by her neighbors, and, more particularly, the manner in which they rejected Him. They actually wanted to kill Him (Lk. 4:28-29).

The question, *"And His brethren, James, and Joses, and Simon, and Judas?"*, denies the claims of the Catholic Church that these were merely next of kin instead of His actual brothers.

This Passage plainly tells us that Mary had other children, and that these four brothers (half brothers) were the sons of Mary and Joseph.

MARY'S FIRSTBORN

The Lord is called *"Mary's Firstborn"* (Mat. 1:25; Lk. 2:7). From that statement alone it is known that she had other children.

Concerning this very thing, David said that Mary would have other children and the Messiah would have brothers. He wrote, *"I am become a stranger unto My Brethren, and an alien unto My Mother's children"* (Ps. 69:8-9).

Clearly and plainly, James is referred to as *"the Lord's Brother"* (Gal. 1:19).

Further, the Scripture tells us that *"His Mother and His Brethren"* followed Him to Capernaum (Mat. 12:46-50).

The Catholic Church claims that Mary had no other children and that His Brethren actually were cousins by another Mary and Cleophas. They claim that Joseph was too old to have children by Mary or that he had children by a former marriage.

The twisting of Scriptures in order to buttress a lie does not make it any less a lie. None of what our Catholic friends claim is mentioned in Scripture or even history. If Joseph did have children before Jesus was born, then Jesus could not be the legal heir to David's Throne, which, by Law, went to the firstborn.

Exactly as the Scripture said, Jesus was *"Mary's Firstborn."*

"James" and *"Jude"* (Judas), the half-brothers of Jesus here noted, wrote the two Books in the New Testament which bear their names. However, there is evidence that they did not believe on Jesus until after the Resurrection (Jn. 7:5).

It seems that James became the Pastor of the Church in Jerusalem, and during the times of the Early Church was looked at by all of the Apostles as an Elder (Acts 15:13; Gal. 1:19).

Of the other two, *"Joses and Simon,"* very little, if anything, is known!

(56) "AND HIS SISTERS, ARE THEY NOT ALL WITH US? WHENCE THEN HATH THIS MAN ALL THESE THINGS?"

The phrase, *"And His sisters,"* is all that is known of these, which numbered at least three, and possibly more.

The question, *"Are they not all with us?"*, refers to both the brothers and the sisters, and portrays them all living in Nazareth, at least at this time.

The idea of these statements by the people, and more particularly the Religious Leaders of Nazareth, was obvious. If He was the Messiah, it seems as if His brothers and sisters, along with His Mother surely would have known so! (It seems by now that Joseph had died.) Inasmuch as not a single word had ever been uttered by any of them concerning this high and lofty claim, that, at least in the minds of these people, was proof enough that His claims were false.

Also, the questions asked concerning His family are, as well, asked in a sarcastic manner in order to note that this was not a family of education, or means, and most certainly not of the aristocracy!

The question, *"Whence then hath this Man all these things?"*, once again portrays the word *"Man"* added by the translators. Therefore, they once again use the word, *"this,"* and speaking of Christ, with the spokesman as he asks the question possibly extending his arm toward Christ in a sweeping motion, which was meant

to add emphasis to his contempt.

Not only were his claims preposterous, at least in their eyes, they would not even show Him enough respect to address Him by the Name, *"Jesus."* Their contempt was such, and as we have stated, that they wanted to kill Him.

Quite likely in the months that followed, and as the darkness deepened with Israel's rejection of Him, the Pharisees, no doubt, used this occasion, claiming that even His Own townspeople did not believe in Him, nor even His family. The contention would have been that surely if He were genuine, these would have been the first to have believed.

There is no way that one can fully understand the pain that Jesus must have endured at this time, and, more specifically, because He knew what that rejection meant!

(57) "AND THEY WERE OFFENDED IN HIM. BUT JESUS SAID UNTO THEM, A PROPHET IS NOT WITHOUT HONOUR, SAVE IN HIS OWN COUNTRY, AND IN HIS OWN HOUSE."

The phrase, *"And they were offended in Him,"* is an understatement to say the least! Luke said they were *"filled with wrath,"* and would have killed Him had they been able to (Lk. 4:28-30).

The word, *"offended,"* in the Greek is *"skandalidzo,"* which means, *"to be scandalized."*

In other words, they were concerned that the reputation of their town would be sullied by these preposterous claims, with all of Israel laughing at them.

Their Faith was in appearances, which is no Faith at all!

The phrase, *"But Jesus said unto them,"* pertains to the following phrase, and, as well, what He said about Elijah and Elisha concerning Gentiles only who received from God in their day, and as recorded by Luke. His answer is revealing!

The phrase, *"A Prophet is not without honour, save in His Own country,"* speaks of His city of Nazareth.

However, the phrase, *"And in His Own house,"* is more revealing. It pertains to His Own brothers and sisters here mentioned.

There is no evidence that Mary opposed Him in any sense, but there is every evidence that His brethren opposed Him greatly, and as recorded, as stated in John 7:5. Just exactly how far their opposition went at this time, is not stated! Surely, they would not have been a part of the group who, at this time, tried to kill Him! But yet, they did not believe He was the Messiah, and had no regard for His Ministry, and despite His *"wisdom"* and *"mighty works."* But yet, and as referred to, two of them would become stalwarts for Christ after the Resurrection, with the others, no doubt, following suit.

This was a sad day for Christ, but a sadder day still for Nazareth. For they would reject the only One Who had the Power to Save.

(58) "AND HE DID NOT MANY MIGHTY WORKS THERE BECAUSE OF THEIR UNBELIEF."

The idea of this verse is not that He could not perform these works, but that they would not bring the sick to Him, save a few.

Christ exhibited no failure in any case respecting those who came to Him for healing and help. Nor did unbelief of anyone present hinder His healing everyone who came to Him. On the contrary, 23 times it is stated, He healed *"them all"* and *"every one"* (Mat. 4:23-24; 8:14-18; 9:35; 11:5; 12:15; etc.).

The phrase, *"And He did not many mighty works there,"* refers to Nazareth alone! He did *"Many mighty works"* elsewhere. How sad!

No doubt, there were blind, maimed, halt and withered in this city which desperately needed healing, but would not come to Him, and remained in their terrible condition. Such is so sad when healing and deliverance was so close.

Likewise, almost all of the world conducts itself exactly as Nazareth of old. They will go to anyone and everyone except Christ. Consequently, their sin, sickness, and sorrow remains. Why?

The phrase, *"Because of their unbelief,"* was the reason then and is the reason now!

They did not believe He was the Son of God, and neither do men believe it today.

They did not believe He was the fulfillment of the Prophecies, and neither do men believe it today!

They did not believe what the Bible said about Him, and because they did not believe the Bible!

"Unbelief" is the foundation sin of all sin. Jesus said that the Holy Spirit would *"Convict*

the world of sin, because they believe not on Me" (Jn. 16:8-9).

CHAPTER 14

(1) "AT THAT TIME HEROD THE TETRARCH HEARD OF THE FAME OF JESUS,"

The phrase, *"At that time Herod the tetrarch,"* refers to the son of the Herod who slew the infants of Bethlehem, and was, consequently, a descendant of Esau.

His wife was a daughter of Aretas the King of Arabia; but he dishonored her by his connection with Herodias, who was his sister-in-law and niece. Herodias' daughter was Salome. King Aretas, to avenge his daughter who had fled from Herod, attacked Herod, and would have destroyed him but for the intervention of the Romans.

Herod was courteously called *"king"* (vs. 9) but officially *"tetrarch."* This is a compound Greek word meaning ruler of a fourth. In other words, of the entire area of Israel, he only ruled a fourth part, which was Galilee and Perea.

Urged by the ambitious Herodias, Herod went to Rome with her and begged the Emperor to make him a king officially. But the Emperor, hearing of his maladministration, banished him to Lyons in France, from whence he went to Spain, and it is supposed died there. He was called *"Herod Antipas."*

The phrase, *"Heard of the fame of Jesus,"* spoke of the miracles Christ performed, even to the raising of the dead.

This *"fame"* would bring fear to the heart of Herod, while it brought envy to the hearts of the Pharisees and other Religious Leaders. However, this *"fame,"* which spoke of Healings, Deliverances and great Salvations, brought great joy to the hearts of the recipients.

So it is today!

(2) "AND SAID UNTO HIS SERVANTS, THIS IS JOHN THE BAPTIST; HE IS RISEN FROM THE DEAD; AND THEREFORE MIGHTY WORKS DO SHEW FORTH THEMSELVES IN HIM."

The phrase, *"And said unto his servants, This is John the Baptist,"* proposes a terribly guilty conscience that plagued Herod because of his murdering the Prophet.

As one observes the actions of this man, he observes the misery of one who has had the opportunity to accept the Lord, but for whatever reason failed to do so. The failure is then compounded by a terrible crime, as Herod's murder of the Baptist, which now leaves him an object of extreme misery.

It is said that while he was in Rome in A.D. 39, and at a banquet celebrating his birthday, someone made an appearance at the celebration dressed as a Prophet and impersonating John the Baptist. It is said that it terrified Herod.

Therefore, it must have been common knowledge of his extreme consternation respecting the murdered Prophet. Such is the wages of sin.

The phrase, *"He is risen from the dead,"* refers to Herod thinking that Jesus was actually John the Baptist who had come back to life. Luke mentions that others may have fostered this idea as well! (Lk. 9:7-9).

The phrase, *"And therefore mighty works do shew forth themselves in him,"* portrays great fear.

He is concerned that it really might be John the Baptist, and that these *"mighty works"* may extend to him in the form of vengeance. The ridiculous that plagues a guilty heart knows no bounds in its absurdities. As Solomon said, *"The wicked flee when no man pursueth"* (Prov. 28:1).

Herod is a perfect example of the command, *"Touch not Mine Anointed, and do my Prophets no harm"* (Ps. 105:15).

(3) "FOR HEROD HAD LAID HOLD ON JOHN, AND BOUND HIM, AND PUT HIM IN PRISON FOR HERODIAS' SAKE, HIS BROTHER PHILIP'S WIFE."

The phrase, *"For Herod had laid hold on John, and bound him, and put him in prison,"* refers to the gloomy castle of Machaerus on the shores of the Dead Sea. The Baptist was a prisoner here for more than a year prior to his death.

The phrase, *"For Herodias' sake, his brother Philip's wife,"* refers to the reason John had been arrested by Herod and placed in prison.

"This infamous woman was both niece and wife to Philip and Herod, being the daughter of Aristobulus, son of Herod the Great. She

first married Philip, her uncle, by whom she had Salome. Later she left him to live publicly with her brother-in-law, Herod, who had been before married to the daughter of Aretas, King of Arabia Petra.

"Aretas made war on Herod, because he had deserted the King's daughter in favor of Herodias.

"He destroyed Herod's army, which Josephus says was judgment on him for murdering John the Baptist."

(4) "FOR JOHN SAID UNTO HIM, IT IS NOT LAWFUL FOR THEE TO HAVE HER."

It was not lawful because Herodias was his niece and wife of his brother Philip.

The phrase, *"For John said unto him,"* proclaims the Message as given by John to be pointed, direct, and left absolutely no doubt as to whom he was speaking.

The phrase, *"It is not lawful for thee to have her,"* was stated unequivocally, which, as well, left no doubt as to the wrongness of the act. This Preacher did not pull punches, trim his Message, or compromise the Word of God. There are not many of this stripe today, and, in fact, there have never been many. The reasons are obvious! Such Prophets, who are truly God's Prophets, don't last long! To curry favor, too many trim their Message. And to curry favor, they lose their Message.

(5) "AND WHEN HE WOULD HAVE PUT HIM TO DEATH, HE FEARED THE MULTITUDE, BECAUSE THEY COUNTED HIM AS A PROPHET."

The phrase, *"And when he would have put him to death,"* refers, no doubt, to the first part of John's incarceration. The last months of John's life, and according to Mark, Herod came to highly esteem John (Mk. 6:20).

Herod's conscience was guilty (vs. 2), it was cowardly (vs. 5), and it was degraded (vs. 7).

The phrase, *"He feared the multitude,"* means that he feared if he put John to death, and, as stated, which was at the beginning of his incarceration, that the people might revolt because John, at that time, was popular. If such happened, it could cause him problems with Rome, so he withheld his evil hand.

The phrase, *"Because they counted him as a Prophet,"* gives the reason for John's popularity.

Evidently, throughout Israel there had been an uproar respecting the arrest of John. Little knowing or understanding the Ways of the Lord, he probably had not realized at the outset what the arrest of the Prophet would mean.

Israel had not had the voice of a Prophet for some 400 years, with John's voice being the first since Malachi. Consequently, the people held John in high regard, as they certainly should have!

(6) "BUT WHEN HEROD'S BIRTHDAY WAS KEPT, THE DAUGHTER OF HERODIAS DANCED BEFORE THEM, AND PLEASED HEROD."

The phrase, *"But when Herod's birthday was kept,"* either referred to his natural birth or the day he began to reign. Both were counted as birthdays by such rulers. As well, requests were granted on this day which would not have been granted otherwise!

The Phrase, *"The daughter of Herodias danced before them, and pleased Herod,"* refers to Salome. She was probably about 17 or 18 years old at this time.

There is every evidence that her *"dance"* was lewd, and that it aroused the passions of Herod and those who were with him.

This is a scene not totally unlike millions of such happenings all around the world. Alcohol no doubt flowed abundantly at this *"party."* As well, passions ran high! John the Baptist was not at the party, he was in prison!

However, the modern Gospel places him at the party, while all the time claiming to be a Believer.

At the present, too many call themselves *"Believers"* while making the music for such debauchery.

At the 1994 National Religious Broadcasters' Convention, a Country/Western Star was providing the *"entertainment,"* and when he finished, he told the assembled crowd of radio and television Preachers, etc., *"Now I have to get back to the bars, nightclubs, and smoke-filled dance halls."* His statement was met with applause.

They killed Believers at such parties in John's day, while now the *"Believers"* are the ones throwing the party.

God help us!

(7) "WHEREUPON HE PROMISED WITH AN OATH TO GIVE HER WHATSOEVER SHE WOULD ASK."

The phrase, *"Whereupon he promised*

with an oath," was not an uncommon thing at such parties, but what she asked was definitely uncommon!

The phrase, *"To give her whatsoever she would ask,"* made Herod feel big in the eyes of his guests.

(8) "AND SHE, BEING BEFORE INSTRUCTED OF HER MOTHER, SAID, GIVE ME HERE JOHN BAPTIST'S HEAD IN A CHARGER."

The phrase, *"And she, being before instructed of her mother,"* tells us that the girl went to her mother as to what she should ask.

This woman, Herodias, was one of the most wicked women who ever lived. Her wickedness exceeded even that of Herod's.

The phrase, *"Said, give me here John Baptist's head in a charger,"* proclaims the sickening request.

She was determined to rid herself of the stinging rebuke of John once and for all! She wants him beheaded, and at once!

(9) "AND THE KING WAS SORRY: NEVERTHELESS FOR THE OATH'S SAKE, AND THEM WHICH SAT WITH HIM AT MEAT, HE COMMANDED IT TO BE GIVEN HER."

The phrase, *"And the king was sorry,"* refers now to his fondness for the Prophet. He had probably spent many hours with John, and John had told him many wonderful things respecting the Word of God, so that Herod knew that he was a *"just man,"* and, as well, *"an holy man"* (Mk. 6:20).

In this, one can see the Mercy and the Grace of God. The Lord gave this Monarch an opportunity to make things right, and despite his wicked lifestyle. He came close, but not close enough.

The phrase, *"Nevertheless for the oath's sake,"* proclaims him being impelled to commit this dastardly crime.

The conscience is defiled and needs to be purged (Heb. 9:14), not only from sinful passions, but also from dead religious works. So, Herod's conscience had been stifled, and now it had become hardened.

Yet, many moral teachers proudly say that the conscience is an inward spiritual light, which, if obeyed and followed, will guide to Heaven!

The phrase, *"And them which sat with him at meat,"* referred to his guests, with none of them speaking a word in John's defense.

Who were these guests!

The Scripture does not say, but, no doubt, they were some of the Jewish Leaders of Galilee.

To speak up, especially at this time, could incur the wrath of Herodias, which, later on, if not immediately, could cause them severe financial problems, etc. Therefore, these Jewish Leaders (if, in fact, that's who they were), said nothing, while the greatest Prophet the world had ever known was about to be killed. No wonder they turned on Jesus as well!

The nation was now so evil that Jesus would refer to it as *"this wicked generation"* (12:45).

The phrase, *"He commanded it to be given her,"* insinuates that he looked for a way out of this dilemma, but found none.

He was now on the spot, with the girl standing before him, and with his oath already given, and his guests looking on. So, this son of Satan would acquiesce to her request.

(10) "AND HE SENT, AND BEHEADED JOHN IN THE PRISON."

The phrase, *"And he sent,"* proclaims the carrying out of this dastardly deed!

There is a possibility that John, over the last few months, had been brought to this very room by Herod, where John faithfully pointed him toward the Lord. Herod, no doubt, was brought under great conviction by John's words which bore heavily upon his mind, and constantly. But now, instead of sending a messenger, he would send an executioner. It would be a deed that would haunt him for the rest of his life, causing a fear to penetrate his mind and reside there, which would make life miserable to say the least!

The phrase, *"And beheaded John in the prison,"* proclaims the killing of the greatest Prophet who ever lived.

However, his Message and his Ministry were complete. He had done, and admirably so, what God had called him to do.

He was the one who introduced the Son of God, and, as such, he was privileged as no Prophet had ever been privileged.

That his life ended in this fashion, is a testimony to his faithfulness even unto the very end. He died upholding the Gospel, and it would be said of him, that he never compromised even at the expense of his own life.

Exactly where Herod was conducting this celebration is not exactly known. Wherever

it was, it had to be very near the prison, because the entirety of this bloody event took place, it seems, in a very short time.

(11) "AND HIS HEAD WAS BROUGHT IN A CHARGER, AND GIVEN TO THE DAMSEL: AND SHE BROUGHT IT TO HER MOTHER."

The phrase, *"And his head was brought in a charger,"* proclaims the horror of this scene.

What must have been the attitude of these drunken guests, or even the attitude of Herod when the head of the Prophet was brought in?

The phrase, *"And given to the damsel,"* refers to Salome.

The phrase, *"And she brought it to her mother,"* refers to one of the most wicked women who ever lived.

Jerome says that she was so wicked that after gloating over the head of John, she drew out his tongue and pierced it with a needle.

In this manner, she was proclaiming to one and all that His Voice was now stopped and his tongue would say no more words against her.

This is but one of the many ways and efforts used by Satan to stop the Voice of the Man of God. This wicked woman would stop John's voice, while the Pharisees would stop the Voice of Christ.

Every voice that God has raised up has been opposed greatly, not only by the world, but, as well, and sadly so, by the Church.

(12) "AND HIS DISCIPLES CAME, AND TOOK UP THE BODY, AND BURIED IT, AND WENT AND TOLD JESUS."

The phrase, *"And his disciples came, and took up the body, and buried it,"* refers to the disciples of John.

I wonder what their thoughts were as they took up this headless body, and now knowing the reason and the manner in which he died?

John was probably killed the night before, with his disciples coming the next day for the remains.

The phrase, *"And went and told Jesus,"* refers to their love for the Lord. The reaction of Christ is given in the following verse:

(13) "WHEN JESUS HEARD OF IT, HE DEPARTED THENCE BY SHIP INTO A DESERT PLACE APART: AND WHEN THE PEOPLE HAD HEARD THEREOF, THEY FOLLOWED HIM ON FOOT OUT OF THE CITIES."

The phrase, *"When Jesus heard of it,"* means that the Holy Spirit did not impart this knowledge to Jesus, but, as the previous verse proclaims, by the disciples of John.

The phrase, *"He departed thence by ship into a desert place apart,"* affirms the real humanity of our Lord Jesus Christ. Deep emotion demanded solitude. No doubt, He sought a place where He could give vent to the sorrow that burdened His Heart because of the cruel murder of His beloved forerunner; but in the perfection of His Nature, He deferred the indulgence of His grief in order to teach, heal and feed the multitude, as the next verse will show.

The *"desert place"* here spoken of was probably near the northeast corner of the Sea of Galilee. He came from Capernaum. Of this one can be sure, even though Jesus was God manifest in the flesh, still, He was *"very Man,"* and with all the emotions attached to man. But yet, grief, sorrow and pain would be far more deeply felt by Him than by anyone else, and because of His perfection. Consequently, one can only guess at the deep sorrow and emotion felt by Christ at this time.

He knew John had instantly gone to Paradise, where he now resided with Abraham, Isaac and Jacob, along with all the Prophets of the past. But He also felt this loss keenly, because death is an enemy and the result of the Fall in the Garden of Eden. This monster called death was at least a great part of the reason for His coming.

In a little while the fear of death would be completely abolished by Christ, at least for Believers, and in the future death will be completely eliminated (I Cor. 15:54-57).

The phrase, *"And when the people had heard thereof,"* refers to many who were seeking Him, no doubt bringing their sick and afflicted, but had heard He had departed.

The phrase, *"They followed Him on foot out of the cities,"* referred to them walking around the western rim of the lake, which, from Capernaum, would have probably been about two or three miles. (He and His Disciples had taken a boat, cutting across the corner of the lake, with their destination, as Luke said, *"a city called Bethsaida"* (Lk. 9:10). The *"desert place,"* meaning a country area with few if any inhabitants, was near Bethsaida.

The inference by the word, *"cities,"* is that the crowd following Him swelled due to it

being joined by others from various towns along the way.

Their *"following Him"* was not to be in vain, for they would experience healings and miracles of unprecedented proportions.

All who *"follow Him,"* are treated accordingly, but, regrettably, most, presently, will not follow Him. Even the great crowds evidenced here will soon thin out, and because of persecution.

While it is true that to all who follow Christ, great and glorious things happen, still, it will not be done without price. Satan bitterly opposes all who set out to follow the Lord, and much, if not most, of the opposition comes from that which calls itself *"The Church."*

(14) "AND JESUS WENT FORTH, AND SAW A GREAT MULTITUDE, AND WAS MOVED WITH COMPASSION TOWARD THEM, AND HE HEALED THEIR SICK."

The phrase, *"And Jesus went forth,"* refers to Him going to them.

The phrase, *"And saw a great multitude,"* probably refers to some 10,000 to 15,000 people. The Scripture says there were 5,000 men besides women and children (vs. 21).

The phrase, *"And was moved with compassion toward them,"* refers to Him seeing the destitute condition of many who were sick and desperately needing help. No doubt, there was every type of disease that one could imagine represented. Some were no doubt heart-rending in their appearance.

Whatever the situation, it moved Him greatly as He observed it, with the word *"compassion"* being used.

This refers to pity and concern that comes from the very depths of one's being.

As we have stated in past Commentary, when Jesus healed people, it seems that in some way He felt in His Body, if not the pain of the person, at least the energy of the Spirit it took to bring about these healings.

Even though the healings were done oftentimes by a mere word, or, at the most, a touch, still, there was something that took place in the very heart of His Being. Hence, when the woman who had the issue of blood touched Him, even though many others were touching Him as well, He would say, *"Virtue is gone out of Me"* (Lk. 8:46).

The phrase, *"And He healed their sick,"* tells us what He did, what they received, and, as well, that sickness is of the Devil.

No, it does not mean that all who are sick are of Satan. But it does mean that sickness, as well as poverty, want, sin and sorrow, have their origination in the evil one.

Were it God's Will for people to be sick, Jesus by no means would have healed them!

As well, if it were God's Will for people to be sick some of the time, then Jesus would not have healed all the people all the time, because had He done so, He would have been violating the Father's Will in healing some that the Lord wanted to be sick.

No! Jesus never turned one away, saying, *"God has a purpose for you being sick,"* etc. He healed them all, proving that it is always God's Will for all the sick to always be healed.

This is proven beyond the shadow of a doubt by the action of Christ.

So, many would ask, if it is always God's Will for the sick to be healed, why are many Christians sick, with healing at times not forthcoming?

In the last few years, many in the Church, seeing this which looks like an inconsistency, have ventured all types of reasons, such as *"lack of Faith,"* etc. And yet, Jesus never refused one for lack of Faith. Actually, He would give such a one Faith if necessary (Mk. 9:24).

Others claim that unconfessed sin stops the healing Power of God! And yet, Jesus healed them all, never turning anyone down no matter how sinful they were.

Considering the thousands He healed, it stands to reason that at least some of these people were not living right, but Jesus healed them anyway!

Others, trying to skirt the issue, claim that it is not always God's Will to heal, when, and as we have stated, the very action of Christ shows otherwise!

It is easy to blame the individual who is sick by claiming he does not have enough Faith, etc. However, these accusations are without foundation, that is, if we use the multitudes healed by Christ as an example. As stated, Jesus never turned one away.

The answer to this dilemma lies in Christ. Even though all Believers are given the authority to freely use the Name of Jesus as well as the Power of the Holy Spirit, still, there is a great difference in Christ and all others, and no matter how holy or consecrated they may be!

Christ was perfect, while we aren't!

Christ <u>always</u> did the Will of the Father, while no Preacher, or anyone else for that matter, can claim such distinction.

Christ was filled with the Holy Spirit without measure, while no other can claim such (Jn. 3:34).

Paul and Peter were used extensively in the healing of the sick and the performing of miracles, still, neither they, nor any others could boast of the measure of Christ.

To argue over whether it is God's Will to always heal the sick is a moot point. The answer is automatically given by the actions of Christ. However, the Will of God is one thing, with it always being carried out something else entirely.

In Truth, and if one looks at the entirety of the world, the Will of God is seldom carried out, at least up to this time. If so, Jesus would not have prayed, *"Thy Will be done in earth, as it is in Heaven"* (Mat. 6:10). He prayed this prayer because the Will of God is seldom carried out, at least presently! One day, thank God, it will be!

Therefore, the answer to this dilemma, and as stated, is that some few men may be holy, consecrated, and dedicated to God, but, still, they are not Christ. We are forever coming short of the Glory of God, while Jesus never came short at all (Rom. 3:23).

Every once in a while, some poor individual comes along and tries to make people think he can do anything Jesus did, and papering his claims with chosen Scriptures, he attracts a following. However, in a short period of time, and despite the good intentions, all are shown that they are not Jesus, nor anything close!

Despite the frailties and flaws of poor humans, even the Godliest, the Lord at times does heal, and even performs glorious miracles, and even now. However, that is done solely on the merit of His Grace, and never on our greatness.

Back in the early 1980's, I had a dream that I believe was from the Lord.

I dreamed that I had taken a friend to see my old home place in Ferriday, Louisiana, actually, the house in which I had been raised. That is somewhat strange, because the house had been torn down about ten or fifteen years before I had the dream.

At any rate, I remember walking into the house with my friend, which was now empty. We both stood in the middle of the living room, with me pointing out to him where my piano had sat, etc. All of a sudden the entire complexion of the room changed.

I looked to my left, actually where the old upright piano sat on which I learned to play as a child, and in its place was a casket. It had not been there when we walked into the room, but now suddenly appeared.

To say the least, I was very startled! The lid was up, and I stood there only a few feet from it, wondering why it was there, and if anyone was in it?

All of a sudden, and to my amazement, a figure began to rise out of the casket. It was a woman, and she seemed to have power over gravity, as she seemed to float, and, in just a few moments, came to stand immediately before me.

The person I saw in the casket and who was now standing before me was Kathryn Kuhlman.

When I had the dream, Kathryn Kuhlman was still alive and actually continuing her Ministry. However, I really did not know her, except by reputation, having never had the privilege to meet her, nor had I ever heard her preach, or been in one of her meetings. I knew that God had used her greatly in praying for the sick, but that was about the extent of my knowledge. Why she was the one I saw in this dream, I have no idea, especially considering that I personally knew so little about her.

In the dream, I was overwhelmed by what had taken place, as I suppose would be normal with anyone. My reaction, however, was not predictable.

I looked at her for a few moments, with no greeting taking place or words exchanged.

Instead, I began to sob as I fell on my knees, weeping almost uncontrollably. Then I asked her, *"Does Jesus really heal the sick today as He did so long ago?"*

I do not know why I asked the question, simply because I have always believed and preached that He does heal the sick now exactly as He did in His earthly Ministry, although not nearly with the frequency that He did then!

However, that was the question I asked, and I will never forget Miss Kuhlman's answer.

She said, *"Look unto Him, look unto Him!"*

And then with a sweep of her left hand, and

without really looking, she motioned toward the wall to her left, on which hung a picture of what some artist thought Jesus may have looked like.

I looked up to where she pointed and saw the picture, which actually had not been there when we came into the room.

As stated, it was a picture of Christ. But the amazing thing about the picture was His Eyes. Flames of fire were shooting out of them, and I suppose I would have to say the flames were shooting toward me.

The dream ended.

When I awakened the next morning, it was heavy on my mind, and especially the flames of fire coming from the Eyes of Christ. And then I remembered that John the Beloved said, when he was given the vision of Christ on the Isle of Patmos, *"And His Eyes were as a flame of fire"* (Rev. 1:14).

Kathryn Kuhlman died a short time later. As well, the Lord gave me a dream concerning that also!

I dreamed we were in a particular city conducting a Revival Crusade. In the dream, I was in a hotel room, and actually lying on the bed, when I heard a knock at the door.

I arose from the left side of the bed, walking around the bed to go to the door. I opened the door and a man was standing there, and he said, *"Kathryn Kuhlman died last night!"*

The dream ended.

Several months after the dream, we were in Birmingham, Alabama in a Crusade. We had checked into a hotel in that city on a Thursday afternoon.

The following Saturday afternoon I was in the room alone, as Frances had stepped out for a few minutes. I was lying on the left-hand side of the bed, studying, if I remember correctly, for the service that night. The bed was situated in the room exactly as I had seen it in the dream.

I heard a knock at the door, and swung my feet to the left side of the bed, arising, and walked around the end of the bed exactly as I had seen in the dream as well!

When I opened the door, Donnie was standing there. (I had seen a man in the dream, but did not know who it was.)

Donnie said to me, *"Daddy, Kathryn Kuhlman has just died!"*

It was exactly as I had seen it in the dream.

Why the Lord gave me these dreams about her, and especially considering how little I knew her, I have no idea. And yet, everything the Lord does is for a purpose, even though it may not be discernable at the time.

I do believe that a mighty Move of God is coming, and, as well, I believe this Move is going to incorporate, at least to some degree, the same type of healings and miracles which were prevalent in the Ministry of Christ.

Some evil times are coming in these last days, but, as well, it will, I believe, signal a great Move of God. Peter said, and quoting the Prophet Joel, *"And it shall come to pass in the last days, saith God, I will pour out of My Spirit upon all flesh"* (Acts 2:17).

Again, the *"last days,"* as spoken of here, concerns itself, and according to the following verses of Acts 2, with the *"end time"* or the last of the *"last days."*

(15) "AND WHEN IT WAS EVENING, HIS DISCIPLES CAME TO HIM, SAYING, THIS IS A DESERT PLACE, AND THE TIME IS NOW PAST; SEND THE MULTITUDE AWAY, THAT THEY MAY GO INTO THE VILLAGES, AND BUY THEMSELVES VICTUALS."

The phrase, *"And when it was evening, His Disciples came to Him,"* refers to approximately 3 p.m.

The Jews actually had two evenings, the time of the evening sacrifice, which was 3 p.m., and the later evening, which was 6 p.m.

For the people to be sent away and for them to have time to get to various places where they could obtain food, etc., it would have to be the first evening of which Matthew speaks. At any rate, it was after several hours of Jesus healing the sick and performing miracles.

The phrase, *"Saying, This is a desert place, and the time is now past,"* refers to the time the people should leave, that is, if they were to find food, and because they had been without nourishment all day, except for the few who may have brought food with them.

The phrase, *"Send the multitude away,"* refers to about the best that man can do. Even the Church, for the most part, sends them away unhelped and unfed, while Jesus says, *"They need not depart."*

The phrase, *"That they may go into the villages, and buy themselves victuals,"* refers to

NOTES

about the best that man can do. In other words, *"You're on your own!"*

However, Jesus, as the Light of the world and the Bread of Life, is about to perform a miracle of unprecedented proportions. This miracle will portray What and Who Christ really is.

He not only is our Saviour, but, as well, He is our Healer and our Provider. He is everything, all in all!

(16) "BUT JESUS SAID UNTO THEM, THEY NEED NOT DEPART; GIVE YE THEM TO EAT."

The phrase, *"But Jesus said unto them,"* is about to signal a great miracle. He will now take them into a new dimension. As the lesson was for them, so it is for us.

The phrase, *"They need not depart,"* emphasizes the Truth that everything one needs is in Jesus, whether it be spirit, soul, or body. He is teaching the Disciples, as well as all His followers then and now, that He is to be looked to for everything. It speaks of that which is spiritual, physical, material, and domestical.

Whereas the spiritual is the same and, therefore, identical for all, Healing and Provision may come in many and varied ways, as this illustration amply proclaims.

In other words, we are to trust the Lord to keep us in health, and irrespective as to how He chooses to do so. He may heal outright or He may use doctors in various ways to correct situations, but neither doctors, nor any mortal for that matter, can heal.

As well, He may bring about the provision in many and varied ways. Concerning the paying of Tithes and His Blessings on such, He told Malachi, *"Prove Me now herewith, saith the Lord of Hosts, if I will not open you the windows of Heaven, and pour you out a Blessing, that there shall not be room enough to receive it"* (Mal. 3:10).

In this Passage, He pictures Himself doing these things by *"rebuking the devourer"* and by giving good crops, or whatever is called for respecting Blessing (Mal. 3:11).

In Luke, He said, *"Give, and it shall be given unto you; good measure, pressed down, and shaken together, and running over, shall men give into your bosom"* (Lk. 6:38).

In the first Promise, He pictures Himself bringing about the Blessing, whereas in Luke, He uses other men to bring about the Blessing.

However, the lesson being taught is that it is all the Blessing of the Lord, irrespective of the way or the method He chooses to bring it about.

So, we are to look to Him for everything! However, it is sad when almost all of the modern Church no longer looks to the Lord for deliverance or victory regarding spiritual problems which the world labels as *"behavior problems."* Instead, humanistic psychology is looked to instead of Christ.

To be sure, if there is help from that source, and regarding the problems at hand, then the entire Bible is a fabrication, and Jesus Christ needlessly came to this earth with the idea of correcting something that man within himself can correct.

Of course, the Bible is not a fabrication and the Mission of Christ was not a misconceived idea.

While it is true that man, and by his own initiative, can solve some physical problems as well as material needs; however, he is woefully helpless, at least in the realm of his own capabilities, regarding the spiritual. Only Jesus can handle those problems, and as we are attempting to bring out, He is the only One Who can, as well, really handle the physical and the material! Consequently, He says, *"They need not depart."*

The phrase, *"Give ye them to eat,"* proclaims the duty of the Gospel Minister in trusting Christ, and, thereby, spiritually feeding the multitudes. This will be a tremendous miracle in which the Disciples will participate; however, they can only do so with Christ's guidance, leading and miracle-working Power.

Even though, and as the narrative will suggest, they could do very little within themselves, still, they were commanded to do that, while the Lord would take care of the balance by multiplying what they had done. This is God's Way, and it is a method which He has not changed from then until now.

(17) "AND THEY SAY UNTO HIM, WE HAVE HERE BUT FIVE LOAVES, AND TWO FISHES."

There were probably between 10,000 and 20,000 people which needed to be fed, and to perform this task, the Disciples could come up with only a handful of bread and fish. Nevertheless, this would prove to be sufficient.

In the service of the Lord, those who are called of God must do what little they can with the expectation that God is going to bless it and multiply it exceedingly so. To be sure, at least for those who trust Him and believe Him, this happens constantly. He takes what little we have, multiplies it, and what started out as almost nothing now becomes a miracle of gargantuan proportions. This is the story of the Church, the Work of God in general, and the efforts of even the least of us.

It is our feeble effort coupled with Faith in Him, and with Him supplying the miracle-working Power, that brings about the miraculous results.

That is the reason True Bible Christianity so far exceeds all else! Everything else in the world, including all religion, along with man's efforts in any and every capacity, are limited to whatever man can do. However, this of which we speak and which Jesus portrayed is limited only by what God can do, which is actually unlimited — unless we limit Him by our own lack of Faith, which we are often prone to do.

It was said of Israel, *"How oft did they provoke Him in the wilderness, and grieve Him in the desert!*

"Yea, they turned back and tempted God, and limited the Holy One of Israel" (Ps. 78:40-41).

They limited Him by their lack of Faith, as we, too often, do the same!

He does not expect us to produce the miracle, at least within our own ability, but He does expect us to produce what we can, as little and insignificant as it may be, with Faith in Him that He is able to do what needs to be done.

Someone has said that the greatest thing a Believer can do is believe.

(18) "HE SAID, BRING THEM HITHER TO ME."

This is the secret! We are to bring what little we have to Him, expecting Him to do great and mighty things with it. This is the moral of this story, the thrust of this illustration.

I can see the Disciples taking the *"five loaves and two fishes,"* which might have been contained in a small basket, and handing it to Him. It was a simple task, the handing of this small amount of foodstuff to Him, but some of us find it so difficult to do.

Instead, Churches fight unceasingly over what shape the loaves of bread ought to be, or whether they are to lay on top of the fish or

NOTES

the fish on top of them. If we can't fight over that, we fight over the size of the basket in which it is placed, or so it seems!

There are all types of schools teaching prospective Preachers how to bake the bread and buy the fish. There are even myriads of schools teaching students how to make the baskets. Consequently, there are all types of bakeries for the bread, and factories for the baskets, but almost no schools telling people how to take it to Jesus.

We are all so concerned, and especially in each other's eyes, as to how our little gift looks, when that is of little consequence to Him anyway. He is not going to allow it to remain in its present status. He is going to change it, multiply it, and use it in unprecedented ways.

(19) "AND HE COMMANDED THE MULTITUDE TO SIT DOWN ON THE GRASS, AND TOOK THE FIVE LOAVES, AND THE TWO FISHES, AND LOOKING UP TO HEAVEN, HE BLESSED, AND BRAKE, AND GAVE THE LOAVES TO HIS DISCIPLES, AND THE DISCIPLES TO THE MULTITUDE."

The phrase, *"And He commanded the multitude to sit down on the grass,"* presents order and a method by which the distribution was made.

God's Work is an orderly Work. It has a plan, a motive, a direction to it, which is devised, and to be sure, by the Holy Spirit.

When the Children of Israel came out of Egypt and started their trek through the wilderness, they did not march as a mob, but, instead, as a well-ordered group with each Tribe given a respective place and position according to the other Tribes, and especially in relationship to the Sanctuary. Everything was in *"order,"* which spoke of God's Government. The Church is to be conducted accordingly.

The order is, *"And ye shall be witnesses unto Me both in Jerusalem, and in all Judaea, and in Samaria, and unto the uttermost part of the earth"* (Acts 1:8).

According to Mark, they were ordered to sit down in companies of 50 and 100. As would be obvious, and especially considering a crowd this size, some would be very close to Jesus and the Disciples, while, of necessity, others would have been seated quite a distance away at the very back of the multitude.

Nevertheless, and to be sure, those at the

NOTES

back received just as much food as those at the very front. That is the way the Lord intended for it to be.

However, I am afraid that some parts of the world, at least as far as the Gospel is concerned, receives a far larger portion than other parts. This is not God's Will!

Admittedly, there are some areas which are closed to the Gospel. Nevertheless, even regarding these areas, the Saints should seek the Lord incessantly that these doors would be opened.

However, where doors are open around the world, it is imperative that all receive a like share of the *"bread."* Nevertheless, and sadly so, this is little being done!

If one is to take the Book of Acts as the criteria and the Early Church portrayed in that Book as an example, it is obvious that the very thrust of the Church, and, in reality, the only thrust, was the taking of the Gospel to areas which did not have it. The Apostle Paul headed up this thrust, with the Holy Spirit portraying through him that which the Lord wanted and desired. It is an example we must follow today, that is, if we are to follow the Lord.

As an example, and as a small part of the great Work of God, the Lord has called me to take the Gospel to the world by Television and Crusades. That is my mission and my calling, and, as a result, we have seen literally hundreds of thousands all over the world, brought to a saving knowledge of the Lord Jesus Christ. That is the reason, even in the face of impossible circumstances, that we continue to make every effort to carry out this task, and will do so until the Trump sounds or the Lord calls us home.

However, this is not just my calling, but it is actually the calling of every single Child of God. We have the Bread! It must be given to a starving world.

The phrase, *"And took the five loaves, and the two fishes,"* presents the lad who gave the bread and the fish (Jn. 6:9), along with the Disciples who took it and gave it to Jesus. Consequently, the method of God's manner is here presented.

The boy represents all Believers who do what they can do to take the Gospel to the world.

The Disciples represent the called Ministers of the Gospel, who will follow the Lord's directions respecting the distribution of the bread.

Of course, Jesus is here presented as the One

Who provides the miracle and gives instructions as to how the bread is to be distributed.

The phrase, *"And looking up to Heaven,"* signifies where the help truly comes from respecting the miracle and the blessing. God is the Source! The others, the lad and the Disciples, were allowed to play a part, but not because such was needed by the Lord, but that they might learn Faith and Trust.

The phrase, *"He blessed,"* simply meant that He acknowledged God as the Provider and properly gave thanks, as we must do constantly.

As well, it should be remembered that these *"five loaves and two fishes,"* were not special. To be frank, any loaves or fishes would do. Therefore, we should not become lifted up over our small contribution.

The phrase, *"And brake,"* meant that each loaf of Bread was broken by Christ, symbolizing that the Gospel we receive and which saves our souls is meant to be shared with others. That is what Paul meant when he said, *"I am debtor both to the Greeks, and to the Barbarians; both to the wise, and to the unwise.*

"So, as much as in me is, I am ready to preach the Gospel to you that are at Rome also" (Rom. 1:14-15).

In Truth, if this is not carried out, the power and effectiveness of the Gospel soon dies in the heart of the recipient.

The phrase, *"And gave the loaves to His Disciples,"* represents the beginning of the distribution.

Even though all played a part, the ones who grew the grain for the bread and the ones who caught the fish, and then the one who baked the bread and prepared the fish, along with the boy who freely donated it, the main part of the distribution was expected to be carried out by the Disciples. It has not changed unto this hour.

As well, it is incumbent upon the Disciples to hand it out properly, evenly, and according to the instructions of Christ. Even though all the others played a part, which, in effect, made it possible, still, it is the responsibility of each and every Preacher to play their part in the distribution.

As well, those who supplied the ingredients, labored in the putting of the ingredients together, and supplied the *"loaves and fishes,"* must make certain that it properly gets to those in need.

NOTES

Sadly and regrettably, too many squander all the bread and fish on themselves, leaving almost nothing for the multitudes who have none, and, worse still, too many Preachers do not distribute it properly, if at all!

The phrase, *"And the Disciples to the multitude,"* concerns the final link in this chain which refers to the Gospel being taken to where it is needed.

When Jesus blessed the bread and began to break it, this is quite possibly when the miracle began. He just kept breaking and breaking, and the containers of whatever sort they had just kept filling up and being distributed. That is the way with the Gospel.

It is given to one, and he shares it with another, and he shares it with another, etc. As a result, one Message of the Word of God properly received, multiples many times over as it is properly given to others. In fact, it never ends!

There is another lesson to be learned in this scenario as well. It is as follows:

1. *"And took":* This refers, as well, to the Lord taking the individual from a life of sin, and bringing them into His Great Saving Grace. He *"took"* all of us out of sin, and from the world of darkness, and translated us into the Kingdom of His Dear Son.

2. *"He blessed":* Almost immediately after conversion, if one is to notice and remember, the Blessings of God come upon the new convert readily. It is a great and blessed time, when it seems, at least in many cases, everything the new convert asks for is given by the Lord, and speedily so. However, this lasts for a period of time and then begins to subside.

The new convert, young in the Lord, is encouraged greatly by the Lord respecting blessing and great gifts given. However, if the convert remains in this posture, there will be very little growth.

It is as a child who asks his parent for any and all things, with these things being supplied according to ability and need. But after a while, the parent, and because of maturity, expects the child to grow beyond the *"gimme stage."* The Lord expects no less from us, with the next stage portraying His method.

3. *"And brake":* This is one of the most difficult times of a Believer's life, and, yet, the most rewarding. It is the stage of maturity which the Lord takes us to, which requires a

"breaking" in our lives. It is not pleasant, as the subduing of the flesh is never pleasant. Self must be subdued and placed in Christ. This is the time when Christlikeness is expected of us.

The methods used by the Lord to bring about this *"breaking"* are many and varied. And quite possibly, it is a process which really never ends.

An example is found in the *"alabaster box of ointment of spikenard very precious,"* which was used to anoint Jesus in the house of Simon the leper. However, even though the ointment was very precious, it was of no consequence until the box was broken, when it could then be *"poured on His* (Jesus') *Head"* (Mk. 14:3).

It is the same with the Believer! The precious fragrance of Salvation which is possessed is of no use to others until it is given to them. To be sure, the Believer, as the container of ointment, has to be broken before Christ can be properly presented. Otherwise, it is *"self"* being presented which is of no use whatsoever. The *"Precious Ointment"* is Christ, and He Alone is the sweet fragrance to a hurting and dying world.

This is the great task that the Holy Spirit is constantly working at within our lives. Too often, we try to give a hurting world our talent, ability, education, knowledge, ad infinitum. It is of no consequence. It is only when Christ is presented, and without a mixture of self, that the hurting soul can receive and be blessed.

4. *"And gave"*: After the breaking comes the giving. As we have stated, whatever is given prior to this is of little or no consequence. What is given after the breaking, is the True Bread, which is Christ.

There is an awful lot of *"giving"* at the present time, but very little of which does any good, and because it has not yet been *"broken."*

Scores of Christians who have beautiful voices and can sing well, nevertheless bless precious few, if any! The reason being that the flesh is evident and obvious, which no matter how properly dressed and pleasantly presented, is still flesh, and, consequently, of no value.

And yet, every once in a while, even using this one example, a voice greatly blesses others, pointing them to Jesus, with them leaving encouraged, strengthened, and refreshed. It is because the *"singer"* has been *"broken!"*

NOTES

The same goes for Preachers, witnesses, or efforts of any kind, be it layman or Minister.

Regrettably, the last few decades have seen a large portion of the Church catering to the *"Prosperity Message,"* which basically denies what we are saying, and because it is still in the baby stage of *"gimme!"* It is clouded under a panoply of *"giving,"* when, in reality, the entire thrust of the message is a *"giving to get."* Such is not in harmony with the Word of God, and, consequently, a false message, although extremely attractive.

Much, if not most, of the Church relishes in giving to a hurting world, but too often it is the giving of self instead of Christ. It is because the giver has not properly been *"broken,"* and is still back in the *"blessing"* stage. Consequently, he is very proficient in telling others how to be *"blessed."*

This method of blessing, however, is not God's method, but, instead, man's. God's method is the giving of Christ to a hurting world, which, within itself, will definitely bring blessing, but then, not the selfish kind, but will develop the spirit instead of gratifying the flesh.

As a closing note, too much bread is going to the Disciples (Preachers), with them never giving it to Jesus, and, consequently, it accomplishes very little, if anything.

If it goes to Jesus, as it must do, when it is given back to the Disciples, then as they give it to the multitudes, it is anointed, multiplied, and performs great miracles. This is God's Way, and there is no other.

The Disciples had to keep constantly going to Jesus for fresh supplies for the need of the multitude. They had no resources of their own. They were dependent upon Him.

(20) "AND THEY DID ALL EAT, AND WERE FILLED: AND THEY TOOK UP OF THE FRAGMENTS THAT REMAINED TWELVE BASKETS FULL."

The phrase, *"And they did all eat,"* refers to all being able to eat if they so desired. What a privilege it was to be able to eat bread which had been blessed by Christ, and even miraculously multiplied. Such is the one who partakes of the Gospel.

As well, and as stated, it is God's Will that *"all"* in the entirety of the world be given the opportunity to *"eat"* if they so desire. Whether they *"eat"* or not is up to them! However, it is imperative that they be given the opportunity. Regrettably, and considering how little True Gospel is preached, many, if not most, never have that opportunity.

The phrase, *"And were filled,"* tells us what the Gospel will do for the human heart. It alone satisfies! It alone meets every need! And, of course, the Gospel and Christ are indivisible.

The phrase, *"And they took up of the fragments that remained,"* portrays nothing wasted, with these *"fragments"* no doubt being given to others.

The idea is that the Gospel is so precious that it must never be wasted by being given to the same person over and over again, without them also giving it out to others. Consequently, the *"fragments"* were gathered up.

The phrase, *"Twelve baskets full,"* signifies this number not by chance, but by design.

"Twelve" in the Bible signifies God's Government. It signified the Twelve Tribes of Israel, and it signified the Church, as there were Twelve Apostles who formed the nucleus of the Early Church.

The idea is that if God's method for the propagation of the Gospel is followed, all will be fed, and not just a few.

As well, the number *"seven"* as pertaining to the *"five loaves and two fishes,"* speaks of perfection, as it is God's number, and here speaks of the perfection of the Gospel as it applied to this scenario (Josh. 6:4-15; I Ki. 18:43; II Ki. 5:10; Rev. 1:4-20; 2:1; 3:1; 4:5).

(21) "AND THEY THAT HAD EATEN WERE ABOUT FIVE THOUSAND MEN, BESIDE WOMEN AND CHILDREN."

It is claimed by some that there were possibly very few *"women and children"* in the crowds, simply because of the distance that at least some of them had to walk. However, this was no ordinary meeting.

As well as to hear Christ speak, even more so, many were coming for healing, which would have included just as many women as men and possibly great numbers of children. So, what would have normally happened under normal circumstances would not have applied to this crowd. Consequently, there could have been as many as 15,000 people present.

Also, that it was about 5,000 men, was not by accident.

The number *"five"* in the Bible is thought

by many to be the number representing Grace. Definitely, it was Grace that fed this multitude, because there was nothing within themselves that could have earned this which Christ did (Ex. 26:3-9, 26-27, 37; 27:1; Isa. 9:6; Eph. 4:11).

The Gospel, as well, is the same for *"women and children"* as it is for *"men."* All must *"eat"* and if so, all will be *"filled."*

(22) "AND STRAIGHTWAY JESUS CONSTRAINED HIS DISCIPLES TO GET INTO A SHIP, AND TO GO BEFORE HIM UNTO THE OTHER SIDE, WHILE HE SENT THE MULTITUDES AWAY."

The phrase, *"And straightway Jesus constrained His Disciples to get into a ship,"* pertains to it being late in the day.

At that time, He told His Disciples to get in the *"ship"* and go on back to Capernaum without Him, as He would follow later. They did not at all desire to do so, that is, to leave Him, and possibly for several reasons.

Due to the healings and the great miracle performed by the feeding of the thousands with the five loaves and two fishes, John related as to how the people wanted to make him King (Jn. 6:15). The Disciples were not adverse to this either, not really understanding, at least at this time, the purpose of His Mission.

The word, *"constrained,"* means that Jesus had to be very firm in His demands that they do what He asked.

The word also suggests that the anguish which filled the Lord's Heart concerning the death of John the Baptist demanded relief and could no longer be restrained; so He constrained them to leave, as He desired privacy.

As well, this episode should teach us, as I am sure it taught the Disciples, that we are to obey even when we are not certain as to the reason, and, in fact, do not understand.

The Lord gave them no explanation, as, in reality, He owed them none. Neither is He obligated to explain all things to us either!

The phrase, *"And to go before Him unto the other side,"* pertained to them going back to Capernaum. The distance wasn't far, possibly two or three miles, with them cutting across the northwest corner of the Sea of Galilee. If the wind was right, it should take less than an hour. However, even though the wind may have been right to begin with, the situation was soon to change, and for the worse.

The phrase, *"While He sent the multitudes away,"* means they went away quite different than when they came.

When they came, many sick were among them, with many no doubt oppressed or even possessed by demon spirits. When they left after spending the day with Christ, there was not a sick one among them, and not a single one who was oppressed or possessed by spirits of darkness. As well, they had been fed physically.

There is no way that one could fully express the joy and the happiness that must have filled the hearts of these thousands, as it does with all who come in contact with Jesus. Without a doubt, some who had left their homes with blinded eyes came back able to see perfectly.

Others had left their homes so sick they could hardly walk and needing the help of others to make the journey. However, they were to come back totally different than when they left, completely healed and made every whit whole.

The Scripture is replete with the knowledge that Jesus did not leave one sick person among them. They were all healed, delivered, and set free!

There would be many *"Hallelujahs"* on the way home that night. As well, there must have been much joy.

And then when they arrived home, the joy was even greater, as one might well could imagine, as children gathered around a brother or a sister, or even a father or mother, who had left very ill, but came back totally well.

"Come, every soul by sin oppressed,
   There's mercy with the Lord,
"And He will surely give you rest by
   trusting in His Word."

(23) "AND WHEN HE HAD SENT THE MULTITUDES AWAY, HE WENT UP INTO A MOUNTAIN APART TO PRAY: AND WHEN THE EVENING WAS COME, HE WAS THERE ALONE."

The phrase, *"And when He had sent the multitudes away,"* alludes to the thought that the multitudes, as the Disciples, did not leave easily or quickly.

No doubt, and especially the ones He had healed and delivered, desired to thank Him and express the gratitude of their hearts. What must one say who has just been healed of blindness, and all of a sudden he can now see? For

NOTES

such a miracle, there is no way that one could even begin to adequately express the thanksgiving that would fill the heart. As well, neither can anyone properly thank the Lord for what He has done for them. Such a task, even though we spend eternity, could never be adequately accomplished. It took some time, but finally they left happy and joyous!

Do you, the reader, remember the day or night that Jesus saved your soul? Do you remember how you felt? Did it seem to you, as it did with me, that a thousand pounds had rolled off your shoulders?

Please forgive me for repeating myself, but going home that night, and even though for many of them it would have taken several hours, still, the roads must have been filled with singing, happy people, for they had been with Jesus!

The phrase, *"He went into a mountain apart to pray,"* expresses that which Christ did often (Mat. 26:36; Mk. 6:46; 14:32; Lk. 6:12; 9:28; Jn. 17:9-20).

Prayer, and without a doubt, is the most powerful force in which a Believer can be engaged. And yet, so few Christians take advantage of this glorious privilege.

A Prophecy was given a little while after the turn of the Century, during the great Azuza Street outpouring, which said, *"The day will shortly come when My people will praise Me, to Whom they no longer pray."*

Tragically, that day has already come! I thank the Lord that my Grandmother who has long since gone to be with Jesus, taught me the value of prayer when I was but a child. From the time I was 8 years old until about 11 or 12, I was in prayer meetings constantly. During the Summer months when I was not in school, I would be in a prayer meeting most every day with my Grandmother and a few others who gathered, in which Heaven never failed to come down.

Being a child, the Spirit of the Lord would deal with me so greatly that at times I would begin to pray and literally go into a trance, and then awaken some time later. I would think a few minutes had passed, when, in reality, it had been several hours.

The year was 1944, and I was nine years old. America was at war. During that Summer, we gathered at least once a day and sometimes twice at my Grandmother's, at our Church, or at my Aunt's. Those were times of Heaven on earth.

Almost every time before we went to prayer, each of us would draw a Promise Card, which usually contained one Scripture, as some are familiar with.

Each of us would read the Promise, and, always, when it came to me, I would read mine with great excitement and thrill. This was the Word of God and the Lord seemed to give me an excellent understanding of it, even though only a child.

Immediately after the Promises, we would all go to prayer, and almost immediately I would be in the Spirit.

As a child, that is the reason I wanted to be in these prayer meetings. The Power would fall, and the Glory would fill the place. It was during these times that the Lord called me to preach His Gospel, and actually told me what type of Ministry I would have. From that moment, the Summer of 1944, I knew this Ministry would be worldwide in scope, and I knew that many souls would be won to Jesus.

To be sure, since that day there have been many hard times. The evil one has fought unceasingly, but the Holy Spirit has fought even more.

My Grandmother taught me that nothing was impossible with God. She was my Bible Teacher, Bible School, Bible College, and Seminary. She taught me to believe God! She taught me that He would answer prayer.

I remember one particular evening in 1953. Frances and I had just married. After getting off from work, I would go over to my Grandmother's for prayer, as she lived near. Some if not most of the time Frances was with me.

In one of those evenings sessions, and after the two of us had prayed for a considerable length of time, we were discussing the Work of God and the call of God on my life. (If I remember correctly, Frances was not present on that particular evening.)

I can still see my Grandmother sitting in the chair and gesturing with her hands. A slight smile was on her lips and her eyes seemed to flash fire as the Glory of God filled her countenance. She said the following, and even though she would probably not have called it Prophecy, I know it was!

In the midst of her conversation, she said, *"Jimmy, God will use you, and you will see some of the largest crowds ever known in Christendom. Many people will come to Christ."*

And then she said something else, of which I do not feel at liberty to reveal, but which has not yet come to pass, but which I definitely believe shall!

She then closed the Prophecy by saying, *"I will not see it because the Lord will take me on, but you will see it."*

She was right! In 1961, if I remember correctly, the Lord took her home to Glory. As stated, I have seen some of this Prophecy come to pass, and I believe I will see all of it.

The prayer life she taught me, which is exampled by Christ, has been my mainstay. It has seen me through some very troubled waters, giving me strength, which most have not understood. Since the Fall of 1991, we have been engaged in prayer meetings every single morning and every single night, with the exception of service nights. Countless times I have met with our group which numbers anywhere from 10 to 100, with me coming in, at times, very discouraged, and leaving some time later literally floating on clouds. The Spirit of God had come down in such a mighty way, filling my heart, and time and time again, which has given me the strength to carry on.

Somebody said, *"If Jesus had to pray, what about us!"*

Prayer is not fully understood by most, with it somewhat being a mystery of our Faith. Yet, prayer is a simple act and a comfort to Believers, who, from the beginning, have turned to the Lord with confidence and Faith.

Prayer is not really a theological exercise, nor is it out of reach of the most immature Believer. Actually, the Bible emphasizes the simplicity of prayer. Believers are encouraged to pray about everything, confident that God hears prayer, cares, and is able to act.

RELATIONSHIP

Prayer is really tied to our relationship with Christ. It is that which the Believer sustains with the Father, the Son, and the Holy Spirit.

Actually, the prayer known as the *"Lord's Prayer,"* sums up our beautiful relationship which we have with God. We approach Him as we would a Father. We acknowledge and praise Him as the Hallowed One in Heaven. We express our joyful submission to His Will. We acknowledge our dependence on the Lord for material and spiritual sustenance, and we ask for forgiveness. We acknowledge His right to direct our lives.

A CONTINUING INTIMATE WALK WITH JESUS

Prayer without the personal relationship, an intimate walk with Christ, will soon weaken and die. Jesus, using the image of the Vine and Branches (Jn. 15) told the Apostles, *"If you remain in Me and My Words remain in you, ask whatever you wish, and it will be given you."* That intimate relationship with Jesus is enhanced as His Words reshape our personalities to fit with His Values and Character, which brings us into so rich a harmony with the Lord that what we wish is what God desires us to ask. That is the union the Holy Spirit desires to bring about in our lives.

THE HOLY SPIRIT AND PRAYER

The Holy Spirit plays a unique role in the intimate exchange known as prayer. Actually, without His involvement, one cannot successfully pray. *"The Spirit Himself intercedes for us with groans that words cannot express"* (Rom. 8:26), and *"The Spirit intercedes for the Saints in accordance with God's Will"* (Rom. 8:27).

While the Spirit may assist us in prayer without our conscious awareness, our understanding clearly must be involved (I Cor. 14:13-15). Jesus told the Apostles that the Spirit would take from what belonged to Jesus and make it known to us (Jn. 16:15).

THE INTERCESSORY NATURE OF PRAYER

One of the most striking features of prayer as it is offered in the New Testament, and especially in the Epistles, is its intercessory nature. We read again and again of prayer being offered by Believers for one another. In this, we learn that prayer is an expression of relationship within the Body of Christ as well as an expression of relationship with God. Out of the intimacy of shared lives grows a deep concern for others and their needs, and this provides the primary content for much of the prayers offered in the Epistles.

In the last few months, I have been encouraged

by the Lord to minister to the people on the value of intercessory prayer. I have also been led to pray by the Holy Spirit that the Lord would give even more people in our Church, Family Worship Center, a burden of intercessory prayer.

I believe that True Revival cannot really come unless it is born by this method. I also believe that every Move of God that has taken place was born somewhere in prayer.

It is unlikely that the Holy Spirit will really deal with hearts and lives until first someone has cried out to God for these individuals. To be sure, the one doing the praying may only experience a burden for a particular area, which may be anywhere in the world, and which may not even be known by the Intercessor. But yet, the Holy Spirit knows, and He would take this of Christ, as we have already stated, and make it known to us (Jn. 16:15).

For every soul that is saved, every sick body healed, every deliverance effected, every Revival that breaks out anywhere in the world, to be sure, began somewhere in intercessory prayer, by somebody, whether acquainted with the individuals or not.

This is the wonder in Glory of praying according to the burden of the Holy Spirit. He knows all things, and He knows what is the Mind of Christ, and He can reveal to us the need without us even really being too acquainted with more than the burden itself.

One dear Preacher friend, who is now with Jesus, and who left such a positive mark upon my life, gave this illustration concerning intercessory prayer.

He told of entering Bible School when he was a very young man. This was many years ago, actually in the early 1920's. The school was small, but yet filled with students who were on fire for God.

He told of one particular incident where the Lord gave almost the entire student body a burden for the country of Brazil. If I remember correctly, he said that not a single student had ever been to Brazil, and actually knew no one there. However, the Holy Spirit dealt heavily with these students until almost any hour of the day or night one or several were in the prayer room crying out to God for this country in South America. This went on for weeks, with the burden so strong that it could only be satisfied by crying out to God on behalf of this country.

My friend went on to tell how that in later years, of which even this Evangelist had the privilege of playing a tiny part by the airing of our Telecast in that country, God began to move greatly, until today, and considering the entirety of the world, the Church in Brazil is among the strongest.

He went on to say that he believed that as God gave them that burden of intercessory prayer, and, no doubt, the same burden to others in other parts of the world, that this was at least a part of the beginning of this great Move of God which has resulted in hundreds of thousands, if not millions being brought to Christ.

I believe what he said, and I also believe that there are no shortcuts to Revival, and if there is a Move of God in this capacity, it must be born through intercessory prayer.

CONDITIONS FOR ANSWERED PRAYER

The New Testament as well as the Old offers us much encouragement respecting God answering prayer (Mat. 7:7-11; 18:19; Jn. 14:13-14; 15:16; 16:23). Therefore, the Child of God must pray believing.

And yet, there are conditions to be met before prayer can be answered. However, in thinking and praying about this, I personally believe that rather than subjecting the reader to many *"dos"* and *"don'ts,"* that suffice to say, relationship, as we have already stated, is the key to answered prayer. If there is little relationship with Christ, there will be little answer to prayer.

As well, if our relationship is what it ought to be, we will only want, seek, and be led by His guidance. Nearness to Him proclaims leading and guidance which only He can give.

Relationship ensures all of this, and relationship cannot be obtained and assured without close communion with Him. Communion is established by the study of His Word, the desire to do His Will, and the seeking of His Face.

Therefore, a proper relationship with Him will ensure a strong prayer life, which will bring about that which God intends.

The phrase, *"And when the evening was come, He was there alone,"* proclaims an awesome picture.

The Lord of Glory enwrapped by the shadows of the night, alone on the mountainside, bewailing the death of the Baptist.

NOTES

He was *"alone,"* but yet with God. Once again, please allow us to say, *"If Jesus had to pray, what about us!"*

(24) "BUT THE SHIP WAS NOW IN THE MIDST OF THE SEA, TOSSED WITH WAVES: FOR THE WIND WAS CONTRARY."

This entire episode is freighted with meaning which was meant to teach the Disciples a tremendous lesson, and is meant for all others as well!

The phrase, *"But the ship was now in the midst of the sea,"* concerns not only the Sea of Galilee, but, as well, the Sea of Life.

The word, *"Now,"* emphasizes a particular time, which, in fact, was between 3 and 6 o'clock in the morning. They had been on the lake for nine or more hours. Consequently, a journey that should have taken an hour or two has now taken almost all night. There is a reason, which the balance of this Scripture will portray.

The phrase, *"Tossed with waves,"* does not imply a storm, but, instead, turbulence.

In the last few years, great segments of the modern Church have attempted to do away with this *"tossing"* by the modern confession principle. Even though a proper confession of the Word of God is necessary, and even mandatory for a victorious Christian life, still, there is nothing in the Bible that lends credence to the idea that all problems can be confessed away, leaving nothing but a trouble-free existence. The Word of God does not teach that, instead, it teaches the very opposite! As an example, Peter said, *"Beloved, think it not strange concerning the fiery trial which is to try you, as though some strange thing happened unto you"* (I Pet. 4:12).

As well, these things are allowed by the Lord that Faith may be tried and Trust may be developed. Consequently, that which is debilitating to the flesh is invigorating to the Spirit.

The phrase, *"For the wind was contrary,"* proclaims not only the present circumstances for the Disciples, but, as well, the difficulties facing mankind as a result of the Fall. Even more particularly, it speaks of an adverse wind which in a far greater manner faces the Child of God.

The entirety of the world system is opposed to the things of God. Consequently, it is opposed or *"contrary"* to the Believer. If it is not, that is a sure sign that the person is not walking as close to God as the Scripture demands.

Even though the Text does not specifically say, every evidence is that Jesus knew He was sending His Disciples into the face of this difficulty. Consequently, He not only allows us to be faced with similar circumstances, but, as well, purposely deals with us accordingly.

The training ground of this Christian Life must include obstacle courses if our training is to be complete.

What type of military would America have, or any other nation for that matter, if its soldiers were not properly trained and if such training did not include severe obstacle courses? I think the answer is obvious.

(25) "AND IN THE FOURTH WATCH OF THE NIGHT JESUS WENT UNTO THEM, WALKING ON THE SEA."

The phrase, *"And in the fourth watch of the night,"* and as stated, refers to 3:00 to 6:00 in the morning.

The Jews divided up their time segments into three parts of four hours each, while the Romans divided theirs into four parts of three hours each. As is obvious, Matthew used the Roman method.

Why did Jesus wait so long to go to them, and, especially considering that they had been laboriously fighting this turbulence and contrary wind for nine or more hours?

All Believers, at one time or the other, ask the same question! We desire that the Lord come to our rescue immediately, but oftentimes He doesn't.

Why?

The delay in these types of circumstances is just as much a part of the lesson as the contrary wind and the turbulence.

Two lessons are taught here:

1. To wait on the Lord: This pertains to consecration, with the Lord dealing with us about certain areas of our lives. We wait *"on Him"* as He performs the needed spiritual surgery, even though it may take some time. It is the problem of subduing self, which is the age-old conflict between the flesh and the Spirit. There is absolutely no other way this task can be carried out. Prayer is an absolute requirement in this consecration. And I might quickly add once again, that *"self"* cannot be *"confessed away,"* as some believe. Regrettably, the modern Church little waits on the Lord, and because it has by and large been

taught that to do so infers that something is wrong. And, according to this false doctrine, nothing can be wrong with the New Creation man. And if something is wrong, they say, that means that we are not confessing properly, and upon getting our confession properly lined up with the Word of God, the situation will be immediately rectified. Such is false!

Even though the Believer is definitely a New Creation, still, the human factor is still present because we have not yet been Glorified. We have been Washed, Sanctified, and Justified, but the last step in this Salvation process, which is to be Glorified, will not be brought about until the Resurrection. Then, *"corruption will put on incorruption, and mortality will put on immortality"* (I Cor. 15:51-54).

Inasmuch as that has not yet happened, there is still *"corruption"* in the Believer, which speaks of the sin nature, as well as *"mortality,"* which speaks of death and dying.

Unfortunately, too many have attempted to bypass the Resurrection and presently claim the Glorified state.

2. To wait for the Lord: In a sense, these Disciples were waiting *"for"* the Lord, even though they had no idea He was coming. Consequently, the episode was meant to teach them, and us, that He will always come, even though it may seem to us that it is overly delayed. Actually, there is no delay.

In fact, He is never delayed, which means that He is never early, nor is He ever late. He desired that some nine or more hours pass, and with great difficulty one might add, that the Disciples would learn that without Him in this ship of life the situation is extremely difficult, if not impossible! As well, and as stated, such incidents are meant to test our Faith and teach Trust. Great Faith must be tested greatly!

No doubt in the years to come, the Disciples would recall this incident which would have taught them great lessons.

The phrase, *"Jesus went unto them,"* proclaims His constant, watchful care, even though the Disciples were not aware of such. He who notes the sparrows fall and numbers the very hairs of our heads, to be sure, knows every action and dilemma of every single one of His Children.

While there would come a day that most of them would die a martyr's death, still, He would not allow it to happen until their Ministry and Mission were complete. Accordingly, He deals with us.

The phrase, *"Walking on the sea,"* presents not only a notable miracle, for such had never happened in human history, but, as well, a miraculous insertion into their own personal dilemma.

The preceding Scripture had said that the ship was *"tossed with waves,"* which meant a very turbulent sea. Therefore, where Jesus walked, the water immediately became calm, or else the walking would have been impossible.

Irrespective of the climatic conditions at the moment, the entire episode suggests the Miracle-working Power of God. The idea is that once the lesson is taught, the Lord will come to us, and irrespective of the circumstances, even if He has to perform a tremendous miracle to do so, as is here portrayed.

(26) "AND WHEN THE DISCIPLES SAW HIM WALKING ON THE SEA, THEY WERE TROUBLED, SAYING, IT IS A SPIRIT; AND THEY CRIED OUT FOR FEAR."

The phrase, *"And when the Disciples saw Him walking on the sea, they were troubled,"* proclaims their state of mind. Why were they troubled?

I suspect that under the circumstances anyone would have been *"troubled."* They had labored almost all night long against the *"contrary wind,"* and now in an exhausted state, they see Jesus walking on the water. Their reaction was normal under the circumstances.

The phrase, *"Saying, it is a spirit,"* means that they did not actually think this was Jesus. The time of the night, the turbulent conditions, with Him doing something that no one had ever done before, placed them in a situation beyond their Faith to believe.

The phrase, *"And they cried out for fear,"* probably means they were placed in a position in which they thought they were about to die.

Too oftentimes, one is prone to speak disparagingly of the Disciples or others in such circumstances. However, Christ did not reprimand or chide them. To be frank, none of us would have done any better, or possibly even as well!

(27) "BUT STRAIGHTWAY JESUS SPAKE UNTO THEM, SAYING, BE OF GOOD CHEER; IT IS I; BE NOT AFRAID."

NOTES

The phrase, *"But straightway Jesus spake unto them,"* means that He was very close to the boat, especially considering that His Voice could be heard above the wind, etc.

To be sure, to earnest, sincere, seeking souls, and whatever the occasion, the Words of Christ were always kind, gracious, and life giving. However, if He spoke to the Pharisees, it was biting, stern and denunciatorial!

The phrase, *"Saying, Be of good cheer; it is I; be not afraid,"* is meant to calm their fears, and to let them know that they were not looking at a *"spirit,"* but, instead, the Person of Christ.

To be sure, and because of His Presence, the complexion of everything instantly changes.

He can handle the *"contrary wind,"* or any other problem that one may have. Even though He tarried for quite some time, He is now here, and things that afore seemed insurmountable are now of no consequence. Such is Jesus, and such is the absolute necessity of having Him with us.

Notice His statement, *"Be of good cheer,"* which has a far greater meaning than appears on the surface.

He is telling the Disciples, and all others as well, that irrespective of the circumstances or how bad they seem, or even how impossible they may be, with Him, the Lord of Glory, one need never be discouraged, distraught, full of anxiety or fear, but, instead, happy, joyful, encouraged, in other words, *"of good cheer."*

The statement contains the idea of one facing difficulties, which no one else knows how they can be solved, but yet the individual with the problems has a twinkle in his eye, knowing he has a Source which the world knows nothings about. That Source is Christ!

So, the problems, difficulties, and vicissitudes of life will come and are allowed by God, and for our own benefit, but yet, Christ will *"never leave us nor forsake us,"* i.e., always be there to handle the situation (Heb. 13:5).

(28) "AND PETER ANSWERED HIM AND SAID, LORD, IF IT BE THOU, BID ME COME UNTO THEE ON THE WATER."

The phrase, *"And Peter answered Him and said,"* is given only by Matthew. It will provide a valuable lesson, not only for the Apostle, but for all of us as well!

Peter's personality was to venture forth while others were more retiring. Sometimes this caused him problems, while at other times, as here, it brought him tremendous Blessing.

The phrase, *"Lord, if it be Thou,"* is not meant to express doubt. Actually, it probably would have been better translated, *"Lord, since it be Thou . . . ."* In other words, since Christ is here, anything is possible!

The phrase, *"Bid me come unto Thee on the water,"* is said by the Greek scholars to have a double meaning.

1. The real reason for Peter's request was not that he would walk on the water as well, but that he loved Christ so much that he wanted to come to Him.

2. However, even though the *"walking on the water"* was not the reason for the initial request, still, Peter's words suggest that he believed that whatever the Lord did, he would enable His followers to do as He Himself did.

(29) "AND HE SAID, COME. AND WHEN PETER WAS COME DOWN OUT OF THE SHIP, HE WALKED ON THE WATER, TO GO TO JESUS."

The phrase, *"And He said, Come,"* proclaims Peter's Faith and the Master's response to it. Jesus always responds to Faith in a positive way.

As well, it is interesting to note that one minute saw Peter as the other Disciples, almost paralyzed by *"fear,"* and now, almost instantly, there is Faith.

How can this be?

The answer lies in the fact that the Presence of Christ ensures Faith, while the lack of His Presence ensures the very opposite of Faith, which is fear.

The moral is this:

Then, Jesus could only be at one place at a time. Consequently, during His earthly Ministry, and because of functioning as a man, He was limited, at least regarding His Personal Presence.

Now, He suffers no limitation, and is with us always. Therefore, as there was no excuse for the Faith of the Disciples to wane after the Ascension of Christ and the Advent of the Holy Spirit, and, in Truth, there is no record that it did, likewise, there is no excuse for any other Believer as well!

Faith comes by hearing and believing the Word of God. However, it is impossible to understand the Word, at least to any degree, without having a personal knowledge of Jesus

Christ as well! So, in effect, having, knowing, and understanding the Word of God is the same as having Christ with one at all times. Consequently, there is no need to fear, and every reason to have Faith.

The phrase, *"And when Peter was come down out of the ship,"* refers to him stepping over the side to go to Jesus. I wonder what the attitude and thoughts of the other Disciples were? To be sure, most won't get out of the ship because of its apparent safety. However, the safety is not in the boat, but in Christ.

The phrase, *"He walked on the water, to go to Jesus,"* presents a notable miracle.

The implication is that as He *"walked on the water,"* he was all the time keeping his eyes directly on Christ. Therefore, Christ gave him the Power to do so. To those who have Faith in Christ, they will find glorious, startling, and miraculous things happening within their lives.

This is what makes Christianity so far ahead of every philosophy, religion, or any other construction of mankind.

Christianity is tied to a Person, and not a ritual or ceremony. That Person is Christ.

As well, He is not a person who lived and died many years ago, with but a memory being respected and built upon, as most religions. He is alive, having risen from the dead, which gives True Bible Christianity a force and power light years above and beyond all else!

To be sure, Peter's walking on the water as such was of little benefit. However, it would show him and all others that the Lord is able to do miraculous things through those who would dare to believe Him. In later years, no doubt, Peter, remembering this incident, would be strengthened and encouraged despite the circumstances.

The key is relationship to Christ, which relationship is brought about only by the Holy Spirit (Jn. 16:14).

(30) "BUT WHEN HE SAW THE WIND BOISTEROUS, HE WAS AFRAID; AND BEGINNING TO SINK, HE CRIED, SAYING, LORD, SAVE ME."

The phrase, *"But when he saw the wind boisterous, he was afraid,"* means that he took his eyes off Jesus.

Evidently, where Jesus was remained calm and where Peter had been walking was calm as well. Nevertheless, all around them, and with the whipping of the wind, the waves must have been rolling and large. Now the fear returns, and because Peter's eyes are on the circumstances instead of Christ.

Herein lies the problem and difficulty of all of us. This which Peter did, the getting his eyes on circumstances, is one of the greatest battles that the Saint of God will ever fight.

The *"boisterous wind"* (difficult circumstances) is almost always present. As the wind, these circumstances are loud, clamorous and demanding attention. As the waves looked like they were going to engulf Peter, likewise, it looks at times like the waves of adversity will engulf us. To be sure, that *"boisterous wind"* can blow in the realm of spiritual problems, finances, physical problems, or domestical problems. Therefore, it takes a stern resolve, especially in these times which come to all Believers, to keep one's eyes directly on Christ.

The phrase, *"And beginning to sink,"* refers to his Faith waning, with fear, once again, taking control.

Even though we sometimes make light of Peter respecting this situation, still, one must remember that he is the only one who got out of the boat and started for Jesus. Consequently, I would rather get out of the boat going toward Christ and make a mess of things than stay in the boat and do nothing! Faith ventured is always Faith rewarded, and irrespective of our faltering.

On this short trip, Peter *"began to sink,"* as all Believers have done at one time or the other when they got out of the boat attempting to walk on the water toward Christ. Even though Jesus had told Peter, *"Come,"* still, this within itself did not ensure lack of failure. Peter must maintain his Faith along the way. His Faith would waver, as Faith has wavered in the life of every single Believer. However, it, at least in Peter's case, was regained. If all would do what Peter did, Faith would be regained for them also.

The phrase, *"He cried, saying, Lord, save me,"* portrays the answer to every dilemma.

This lesson tells us that however foolish man may be, if he cries, *"Lord, save me,"* he is sure of an immediate Salvation.

(31) "AND IMMEDIATELY JESUS STRETCHED FORTH HIS HAND, AND CAUGHT HIM, AND SAID UNTO HIM, O THOU OF LITTLE FAITH, WHEREFORE DIDST THOU DOUBT?"

The phrase, *"And immediately Jesus stretched forth His Hand, and caught him,"* prevented him from sinking further.

The word, *"immediately,"* proclaims the action of Christ to any sinking soul, and irrespective of how wicked or difficult the problem may be. He is *"A very present help in trouble"* (Ps. 46:1).

The phrase, *"And said unto him, O thou of little Faith,"* proclaims the *"boisterous wind"* causing him to get his eyes off Jesus, which caused his Faith to weaken. Jesus did not say that he lost all his Faith, but that it had been reduced to *"little Faith."*

This portrays the fact that our Faith can go up or down, and according to our reaction to circumstances. Do we keep our eyes on Christ and His Promises, or do we start looking at the circumstances?

The question, *"Wherefore didst thou doubt?",* proclaims that which is the ultimate cause of Faith that weakens. We allow the circumstances, which seem to be extremely adverse, to produce the *"doubt,"* which weakens our Faith.

The Greek word for *"doubt"* is *"distadzo,"* and means to *"waver mentally."* It is only used here and in Matthew 28:17.

It is not *"dipsukos,"* which means double-minded as in James 1:8; 4:8; or *"diakrino,"* which means to hesitate, and be at variance with oneself (Mat. 21:21; Mk. 11:23; Acts 10:20; 11:12; Rom. 4:20; 14:23; James 1:6).

The Expositors say in regard to prayer being answered, *"One must not hesitate to the lawfulness of the request; must not stagger over the greatness of the promise; must not say yes and no in his determination; and must not waver mentally as to the outcome."*

Even though I agree with them in respect to their statement, still, I feel that the meaning of the entirety of this episode is of far greater consequence than a Faith formula, but, instead, that one is taught to keep his eyes on Christ, and regardless of the circumstances.

As well, at the same time, he must believe that Christ is going to work out the situation one way or the other, and irrespective of its seeming impossibility.

However, many have tried to use God's

Word against Himself. Such cannot be done! In other words, many have taken a Passage of Scripture such as Matthew 14:31 or Mark 11:24, and claim anything desired, which would span all the way from the ridiculous to that blatantly opposed to the Will of God. As stated, the Lord will not allow His Word to be used against His Will.

The idea is, and with all these great Promises as given in the Word of God, that we are to pray in the Spirit, which will always be according to the Will of God (Rom. 8:26-27).

As an example, Paul, in Romans 4, points to Abraham and describes the Patriarch as being fully aware of his own advanced age and of Sarah's having gone far beyond menopause. The fact is clear: No child can possibly be conceived by these two.

Yet, God appears to them and promises that Abraham will father a multitude. Paul says of him, *"Without weakening in his Faith, he faced the fact that his body was as good as dead — since he was about a hundred years old — and that Sarah's womb was also dead. Yet, Abraham did not waver through unbelief regarding the Promise of God . . . being fully persuaded that God had Power to do what He had promised"* (Rom. 4:19-21).

Some have taken Mark 11:24 and other such great Promises, and have attempted to make them apply to any and every type of request, and using Abraham as an example. However, there is a vast difference:

The Lord promised Abraham that he would father a child, even though 100 years old, while He has not promised that to all others, and irrespective of Mark 11:24, etc.

As another example, Jesus told Peter to come to Him out of the boat, but He has not literally said the same to others. Consequently, anyone else who attempts to get out of a boat and walk on the water, will find themselves immediately sinking, and irrespective that God is no respecter of persons, unless He has spoken specifically to the individual, as to Peter.

It is regrettable that this much space must be used to explain such things; however, in the last two or three decades far too many Believers have misapplied or misunderstood the Word of God, and have actually attempted to use the Word of God against God's Will, which always has hurtful consequences.

NOTES

The Lord does not serve us; we serve Him! He did not tell these Disciples, or anyone else for that matter, that He would follow them, but that they were to follow Him.

In these last few years, the Lord of Glory has too often been treated as a glorified bellhop. While the proclamation of Faith is admirable and desirable, still, it must not be allowed to degenerate into presumption.

There is every indication that when Jesus *"stretched forth His Hand"* and caught Peter, that Peter once again walked the water. Too many Believers major on Peter's *"sinking,"* and rather forget that he began his excursion by walking on water, and concluded it by walking on water. True, there was an unhappy mishap in the midst of this, but it didn't stay unhappy for long!

Sadly, too many in the modern Church are too quick to label Peter, or such like him, in a negative mode. Just because someone begins to *"sink"* does not mean, and despite the gossip, that they will remain in that posture. The Lord of Glory is there with an outstretched hand, and He can help them to *"walk on the water again!"*

(32) "AND WHEN THEY WERE COME INTO THE SHIP, THE WIND CEASED."

The phrase, *"And when they were come into the ship,"* referred to Jesus and Peter. Christ can save one, as Peter, from the depths of defeat, causing one to once again perform the miraculous. Never rule out anything if Jesus is involved.

The following statement which I will quote is not found in the Bible, but was actually given by one of the former Presidents of the United States, Theodore Roosevelt. However, it is based on a Scriptural principle which, I believe, this episode concerning Simon Peter bears out.

"The credit belongs to the man who is actually in the arena, who strives valiantly; who knows the great enthusiasms, the great devotions, and spends himself in a worthy cause; who at the best, know the triumph of high achievement; and who, at the worst, if he fails, at least fails while daring greatly, so that his place shall never be with those cold and timid souls who know neither victory nor defeat."

As well, Britain's John Dryden wrote:

*"I am wounded, but I am not slain.
"I shall lay me down and bleed a while.
"Then I shall rise and fight again."*

The phrase, *"The wind ceased,"* proclaims the Power of Christ over the elements.

Such is the moral life without and with Jesus. Without Him, it takes nine or more hours to go two or three miles, and then the abyss; with Him, the same distance is done in a few seconds. John said, *"Then they willingly received Him into the ship: and immediately the ship was at the land whither they went"* (Jn. 6:21).

(33) "THEN THEY THAT WERE IN THE SHIP CAME AND WORSHIPPED HIM, SAYING, OF A TRUTH THOU ART THE SON OF GOD."

The phrase, *"Then they that were in the ship came and worshipped Him,"* means they worshiped him as God. As well, Jesus accepted their worship, and because of Who He was, and that He was due such worship. Actually, He accepted worship a number of times (Mat. 8:2; 9:18; 14:33; 15:25; 18:26; 28:9, 17; Mk. 5:6; Lk. 24:52; Jn. 9:38).

The phrase, *"Saying, Of a truth Thou art the Son of God,"* means they recognized Him as the Messiah. In their eyes, and now, and especially after seeing all the things He has done, there is no other conclusion that can be arrived at.

Also, the Religious Leaders of Israel could easily have known had they so desired. However, unbelief, which characterized the Pharisees, can see nothing which pertains to God, not even His Only Son.

On this acclamation of Faith that Jesus is the Son of God, hinges the eternal destiny of the entirety of mankind. To be saved, one must affirm this declaration.

However, just believing He is the *"Son of God"* will not guarantee Salvation, as Judas was also in this boat, who worshiped Him and made the same declaration. And yet he died lost. Why?

Possibly, he started out well; however, somewhere along the way he desired the *"reward of iniquity,"* which referred to his way instead of God's Way, and lost his soul, as multiple millions do! (Acts 1:18).

(34) "AND WHEN THEY WERE GONE OVER, THEY CAME INTO THE LAND OF GENNESARET."

The phrase, *"And when they were gone over,"* refers to them being immediately at the shore, as John stated!

The phrase, *"They came into the land of Gennesaret,"* refers to an area about three miles long, which began at the northwest corner of

the Sea of Galilee, and stretched from Chorazin at the northwest corner down to Magdala.

This was an area immediately inland from Capernaum, which is said to have contained many fruit orchards.

(35) "AND WHEN THE MEN OF THAT PLACE HAD KNOWLEDGE OF HIM, THEY SENT OUT INTO ALL THE COUNTRY ROUND ABOUT, AND BROUGHT UNTO HIM ALL THAT WERE DISEASED;"

Josephus said that this area was heavily populated, and, therefore, the crowd that gathered was possibly very large.

The phrase, *"And when the men of that place had knowledge of Him,"* proclaimed what they knew Him to be, i.e., the Healer. Their knowledge of His Saving Grace was not nearly as extensive as their knowledge of His Healing Power. This was because they did not yet fully understand His Mission.

The Prophet Hosea said, *"My people are destroyed for lack of knowledge"* (Hos. 4:6).

Hosea was speaking of the knowledge of the Word of God.

Those who had *"knowledge of Him,"* received glorious and wonderful things, while those who refused such knowledge, even though plainly shown to them, received nothing! It is the same presently.

Those who have *"knowledge of Him,"* see astounding things brought to pass. This is the secret of the blessings and prosperity of America, and every other nation in the world which enjoys a modicum of prosperity and freedom.

Those who have no *"knowledge of Him,"* have no freedom, and little prosperity.

As then, so now, the entirety of the prosperity of the world, both spiritual and economical, are tied to a *"knowledge of Him."*

The phrase, *"They sent out into all that country round about,"* refers to an area of several miles.

The idea is that the moment these individuals, whoever they were, knew of Jesus' Presence, they began sending for every sick person they knew, and then telling individuals to inform everyone who was ill that Jesus is here!

What a glorious Message that must have been when the news was given to one who was blind, leprous, or paralyzed, that Jesus was close and healing was certain. There is no way that words could even begin to describe the joy that must have filled countless hearts and lives.

Likewise, there is coming a day when the news will go out all over the world that Jesus Christ reigns in Jerusalem and, as such, and exactly as it happened those long years ago, the entirety of the human family will be healed of all their diseases, and, as well, all who are sick with sin can be likewise healed (Isa. 2:4; 4:5-6; 9:7; 35:5-6).

The phrase, *"And brought unto Him all that were diseased,"* speaks of instant healing. Not one time did Jesus ever turn a person away. All who came to Him were healed, and irrespective of the severity of their *"disease."*

The offer is still open to the sin-weary soul, even now!

(36) "AND BESOUGHT HIM THAT THEY MIGHT ONLY TOUCH THE HEM OF HIS GARMENT: AND AS MANY AS TOUCHED WERE MADE PERFECTLY WHOLE."

The phrase, *"And besought Him that they might only touch the hem of His garment,"* may well have stemmed from the knowledge of the woman with the issue of blood, who touched the hem of Jesus' garment, and was made whole (Mat. 9:20-21).

No doubt, she told all as to what Jesus had done for her, and with the news spreading far and wide others desired to do the same thing, and rightly so!

The phrase, *"And as many as touched were made perfectly whole,"* does not mean that only these were healed, but that in the midst of Him laying His Hands on many, no doubt, and them receiving healing, as well, all who merely touched the *"hem of His garment"* were healed!

What a glorious time that must have been. Everyone He touches and everyone who touches Him is made *"whole."*

One can only guess at the extreme joy that must have filled the hearts and lives of this score of people. Many came sick, but not a single one left sick. They all left completely and totally healed by the Power of God.

All over this area of Gennesaret, homes were filled with happy and joyous people who had been healed by Christ. Some had arisen that morning with the sentence of death upon them, and because of some dread malady, but will go to bed this night with no sickness whatsoever in their physical bodies. People

who were blind can now see! Others who were deaf can now hear!

Families which were destitute, and because the husband and father was too sick to work, now have a brand-new lease on life. Their entire world has changed, and because of Jesus.

As an Evangelist, I must proclaim to one and all that as He did then, so can He do now, whether spiritual, physical, financial, or domestical.

The word, *"whole,"* in the Greek is *"diasodzo,"* and means to be *"saved throughout or completely healed."* It is used eight times in the New Testament and refers only to bodily healing.

It means that they were not only whole, but perfectly whole.

They didn't leave His Presence gradually getting better, but totally, completely, and absolutely whole, and in every sense of the word.

Someone has said that if the hem of His garment is so rich with blessing, how rich must be His Hand and Heart!

CHAPTER 15

(1) "THEN CAME TO JESUS SCRIBES AND PHARISEES, WHICH WERE OF JERUSALEM, SAYING,"

The phrase, *"Then came to Jesus Scribes and Pharisees,"* illustrates the significance of the statement by the use of the word *"Then."* This important word illustrates the Truth of verse 19.

The hearts of these individuals were filled with evil reasonings, and unaffected by the beauty, love, grace, and tenderness of Jesus, these religious teachers rudely intruded themselves and their ceremonial trivialities and traditions into this scene of amazing miracles and of Divine Power. Sadly, such is the natural heart!

If one is to notice, almost all of the opposition to Christ came from Religious Leaders. The man in the street little opposed Christ, if at all, and irrespective of the bondage of sin he labored under. Neither was Rome antagonistic toward Christ. Almost, if not exclusively, this opposition came from that which called itself the *"Church"* of that day. It is no less today.

Using our own Ministry as an example, almost every place we go to conduct crusades or where the Telecast is aired, the opposition from just about all segments of the *"Church"* is fierce.

Why?

It is for the same reason as the Scribes and Pharisees. Those individuals did not know God, and neither do their modern counterparts. If one truly knows the Lord, one will not oppose that which is of the Lord.

That which is man-devised and, consequently, man-controlled, as the Scribes and Pharisees, always opposes that which is of the Spirit.

During Paul's time the opposition was identical. It came from the religious sector. Concerning Rome, it was said, *"For I will be no judge of such matters"* (Acts 18:15). Therefore, Satan's greatest weapon against the Work of God is the apostate Church. It has always been that way, and it is at present!

The phrase, *"Which were of Jerusalem, saying,"* proclaims this city as the seat of religious activity. Consequently, more religious spirits congregated there than anywhere else.

One will find this true regarding the domicile of almost all Religious Denominations. It is generally the most difficult place to have revival. Likewise, Jesus did not visit Jerusalem unless it was imperative. The reason was that the opposition there was the greatest. Once again, it was because it was man-controlled, and not of the Holy Spirit.

It had not always been that way. In the reign of David and the early years of Solomon, plus certain other kings of Judah, Jerusalem was what God intended for it to be, at least after a fashion. However, by now, there was no spiritual leadership in Jerusalem, just religious leadership, which ultimately caused the city and the nation to be destroyed.

(2) "WHY DO THY DISCIPLES TRANSGRESS THE TRADITION OF THE ELDERS? FOR THEY WASH NOT THEIR HANDS WHEN THEY EAT BREAD."

The question, *"Why do Thy Disciples transgress the tradition of the elders?",* expressed the actual spiritual condition of these Scribes and Pharisees, and portrayed the fact that their confidence was in their man-made rules and regulations rather than the Word of God.

The *"Tradition of the elders,"* had to do with the writings of the Scribes, which the Jews held as more important than those of the Law and the Prophets. If the two clashed, the

Word of God was invariably set aside, with the *"traditions"* given pre-eminence.

I once asked a group of Catholic Priests as to exactly what they did whenever their *"traditions"* obviously contradicted the Word of God? Their answer was somewhat interesting.

They attempted to imply that there was no contradiction, and if it seemed to be, the *"tradition"* was a later revelation from God and must be adhered to. Consequently, the Catholic Church is not guided and ruled by the Word of God, but, instead, by *"the tradition of men."*

Sadly, this problem persists in many Protestant circles as well! The word of man takes precedent over the *"Word of God."*

The phrase, *"For they wash not their hands when they eat bread,"* had nothing to do with sanitary conditions, but rather a ridiculous *"Tradition of the elders."* This particular *"tradition"* stated that an evil spirit by the name of *"Shibta,"* could sit on the hands of people, and when the hands were dipped into water, the evil spirit was removed. Otherwise, he might be ingested while the person was eating, which would cause even greater problems.

One has to wonder at the absurdity of such notions, but, yet, whenever man veers away from the Word of God, ridiculous assertions are put forth.

As well, even more importantly, and as we have stated, these Scribes and Pharisees did not really *"see"* all the people Jesus was healing, nor did they *"hear"* the Messages He preached, which brought eternal life to all those who believed. They only saw their little silly rules being broken.

Regrettably, it has changed not at all today.

(3) "BUT HE ANSWERED AND SAID UNTO THEM, WHY DO YE ALSO TRANSGRESS THE COMMANDMENT OF GOD BY YOUR TRADITION?"

The phrase, *"But He answered and said unto them,"* proclaims Him drawing them back to the Word of God, which must be the criteria in any and all situations.

The question, *"Why do ye also transgress the Commandment of God by your tradition?",* places the real truth of the matter exactly where it ought to be. It is as follows:

1. The word, *"also,"* proclaims Jesus admitting that His Disciples did ignore this *"tradition,"* and because it was of no consequence.

In effect, if the Disciples had observed these *"traditions,"* which were unbiblical, they would have been committing sin. That is a strong statement, but every indication as here given by Matthew has the inference that this is what Christ was saying.

One must ask the question as to how many religious practices are presently observed which have no Scriptural basis or foundation? To observe these practices and whatever they may be is wrong.

Some time ago, as an example, I spoke to a Religious Leader concerning a certain thing he was demanding that I do. I mentioned to him that what he was asking (or rather demanding) was not Scriptural. He stammered for a few moments, and finally said, *"But it's our tradition."*

He was right, it was their tradition, but it was not the Word of God. And for me to acquiesce to his demands would have constituted wrongdoing on my part, because he was demanding that I do something unscriptural.

2. In the eyes of God, the Disciples had committed no transgression, even though in the eyes of these Religious Leaders they did. In the eyes of God, which are the only eyes that matter, there had been a transgression committed, but it was by these Scribes and Pharisees. They had substituted their own rules and regulations for the Word of God, which men are so prone to presently do, as well!

Actually, everything must be guided by the Word of God. It alone holds the true answer to every question of life. It must not be added to or taken from, because it is the *"Commandment of God."*

(4) "FOR GOD COMMANDED, SAYING, HONOUR THY FATHER AND MOTHER: AND, HE THAT CURSETH FATHER OR MOTHER, LET HIM DIE THE DEATH."

The phrase, *"For God commanded, saying,"* proclaims an example that Jesus is about to use regarding the manner in which these religious leaders were abrogating the Word of God.

The words, *"God commanded,"* places the statement beyond a suggestion, but actually a rule of conduct which must be faithfully followed. Even though Jesus would only give one example, still, the entirety of the Bible falls under the same category. It is *"God's Commandments,"* and, as such, must be followed faithfully.

The phrase, *"Honour thy father and mother,"* is drawn from Exodus 20:12, and is the 5th Commandment.

The phrase, *"He that curseth father or mother, let him die the death,"* is taken from Exodus 21:17. It has little to do with profanity, but rather speaks of a son or daughter, who, for whatever reason, would refuse to support their aged parents, who, in some cases, had no means of support. They *"cursed"* them by such actions, in effect, telling them to get by the best way they could, or die if they could not manage.

This was such a sin in the eyes of God that such offspring were to be put to death if they committed such wickedness.

(5) "BUT YE SAY, WHOSOEVER SHALL SAY TO HIS FATHER OR HIS MOTHER, IT IS A GIFT, BY WHATSOEVER THOU MIGHTEST BE PROFITED BY ME;"

The phrase, *"But ye say,"* proclaims them being in direct contradiction to what *"God commanded."*

When the Truth is known, the cause of all problems is the difference in what *"God commands,"* i.e., the Bible, and what *"ye say,"* i.e., man says!

The phrase, *"Whosoever shall say to his father or his mother, It is a gift,"* has reference to a scheme concocted by ungodly Priests, which made the Word of God of none effect.

The idea was that if children did not want to support aged parents, they would make a deal with a corrupt Priest, claiming they were dedicating their entire estate to God, in which the Priest would get a rake-off, and because he legitimized the *"gift,"* which, in effect, was no gift to God at all.

The phrase, *"By whatsoever thou mightest be profited by me,"* means that the children would profit from the transaction by not having to care for their aged parents, claiming that all the money had been given to the Work of God. In effect, they could then use the money for whatever they desired.

It was a neat little scheme which abrogated the responsibility that the children were to show to aged parents, and, as well, was a lie. The money was not going to the Work of God, and even if it truly was meant to do so, the plain and clear Command of God to care for aged parents left no loopholes. This was to be carried out without fail. The next verse gives us a little more insight.

(6) "AND HONOUR NOT HIS FATHER OR HIS MOTHER, HE SHALL BE FREE. THUS HAVE YE MADE THE COMMANDMENT OF GOD OF NONE EFFECT BY YOUR TRADITION."

The phrase, *"And honour not his father or his mother,"* proclaims the real reason why there were to be no exceptions.

In most cases, the aged parents would not need any financial help, and because they had made their own provision. However, in isolated cases, the aged parents would find themselves destitute, consequently, the Command of God that they be cared for by the children.

In some cases, the adult children were negligent in their responsibility, and, therefore, showed little love for their aged parents, hence the shirking of responsibility.

In other cases, the aged parents may be financially destitute because of sinful practices on their part, which no doubt happened at times. Adult children, at times, would not want to shoulder this responsibility, especially in view that the destitute condition was the fault of the individual involved, and not circumstances or the children.

However, the Word of God made it clear that these situations were not to be considered, if, in fact, they were true, but the parents were to be *"honored"* simply because they were the parents, and not because of other reasons.

The phrase, *"He shall be free,"* was not in the original Text, but was added by the translators. It meant that by making such a deal with a corrupt Priest they would be *"free"* from responsibility. However, the Lord is telling them that God's Laws supersede man's laws. They may be *"free"* in the eyes of man, but they are not free in the eyes of God.

The phrase, *"Thus have ye made the Commandment of God of none effect by your tradition,"* concerns hypocrisy on the part of those involved in such schemes, as the next verse portrays.

To try to find ways to get around the Word of God seems to be the pastime of many who claim to be followers of the Lord. For instance, millions of Christians deny the veracity of the Baptism in the Holy Spirit with the evidence of speaking with other tongues, by adding to or

NOTES

taking away from what the Word of God says about this very important subject. The attitude is such that, at least in most cases, it is not a matter of misinterpreting the Word, but, instead, a matter of plainly refusing to believe what God has said, and then attempting to concoct a scheme as the Scribes and Pharisees of old.

God's Word was meant to be taken literally and obeyed literally, except in cases where it is obvious that symbolism is being used. An example is Matthew 5:13.

(7) "YE HYPOCRITES, WELL DID ESAIAS PROPHESY OF YOU, SAYING,"

The phrase, *"Ye hypocrites,"* is said with force, and no doubt angered the Scribes and Pharisees greatly, and especially considering it was said to their faces.

The word, *"hypocrite,"* portrays someone acting out the part of a character in a play.

In Greek drama, the actors held over their faces oversized masks painted to represent the character they were portraying. In life, the hypocrite is a person who masks his real self while he plays a part for his audience.

Following are some characteristics of a hypocrite:

1. A hypocrite does not act spontaneously from the heart, but with calculation to impress observers (Mat. 6:1-3).

2. A hypocrite thinks only of the external trappings of religion, ignoring the central, heart issues of love for God and others (Mat. 15:1-21).

3. A hypocrite uses spiritual talk to hide base motives — (Richards) (Mat. 22:18-22).

The phrase, *"Well did Esaias prophesy of you, saying,"* refers to the Word of God as the foundation for all Christ said and did.

If one is to notice, the Lord often explained the Mind of the Spirit rather than quoting the exact words.

(8) "THIS PEOPLE DRAWETH NIGH UNTO ME WITH THEIR MOUTH, AND HONOURETH ME WITH THEIR LIPS; BUT THEIR HEART IS FAR FROM ME."

The phrase, *"This people draweth nigh unto Me with their mouth,"* portrays, as well, a great percentage of the modern Church.

The phrase, *"And honoureth Me with their lips,"* means that they knew all the phraseology, and, in effect, could talk the talk, but did not walk the walk.

The phrase, *"But their heart is far from Me,"* portrays the true nature of the individual, and despite their profession.

This defines the hypocrite. Normally, *"Out of the heart the mouth speaketh,"* but these had so subverted themselves that they had trained themselves to speak what they were not (Mat. 12:34).

This verse proclaims the absolute fallacy of the observance of outward ceremony and ritual, while the *"heart"* has not been changed by the Power of God. Such characterizes the greater majority of the modern Church.

(9) "BUT IN VAIN THEY DO WORSHIP ME, TEACHING FOR DOCTRINES THE COMMANDMENTS OF MEN."

The phrase, *"But in vain they do worship Me,"* pertains to almost all worship in Christendom, and because of the actions of the previous verse.

For instance, multitudes in corrupt Christendom, when attending religious ceremonies, sprinkle themselves with what is called holy water, a ceremony commanded by men, and their consciences would torment them if they failed to obey this tradition. They then walk out of the Church, thinking nothing of using profanity, which abrogates the 3rd Commandment (Ex. 20:7). A host of other Commandments are casually broken as well! This verse declares their worship to be *"vain."*

The phrase, *"Teaching for doctrines the commandments of men,"* is the great sin of the modern Church, as Israel of old!

What are the *"commandments of men?"*

It is anything that adds to or takes away from the Word of God, or does not *"rightly divide the Word of Truth"* (II Tim. 2:15).

As an example:

1. The doctrine of hyper-Calvinism is a commandment of man, which, in its simplistic form, means that God has predestined some to be eternally lost and some to be eternally saved. The Scripture says the very opposite (Jn. 3:16; Rev. 22:17).

2. The doctrine of ultimate reconciliation, which teaches that ultimately all will come to God, even including Satan and his angels. The Scripture says otherwise (Rev. 20:10; 21:8).

3. The doctrine of unconditional eternal security, that teaches that once one is saved, they cannot lose their Salvation irrespective

NOTES

of what they do. The Scripture says the opposite (Heb. 6:4-6; 10:26-31).

4. The doctrine of a sinning Salvation, in other words, the Believer constantly sins, and, in effect, has no choice but to constantly sin. The Scripture says otherwise (I Jn. 3:4-10).

5. The doctrine of no hell or eternal punishment. The Scripture says otherwise (Rev. 20:10-15).

6. The political gospel, which claims that Christianity will ultimately affect the cultures of the world in a positive way, and by political means, thereby, ushering in the Millennium and the Second Coming of Christ. The Scripture says the very opposite, in that Bible Evangelism can be effected only by the preaching of the Gospel which changes the heart upon Faith, and not by political means (I Cor. 1:21, 26-29).

As well, the world, as this false doctrine proclaims, is not going to gradually become better and better, but actually worse and worse, and will be changed only by the cataclysmic Coming of the Lord, which will smash man's efforts (Dan. 2:34-35; II Tim. 3:1-5).

7. The prosperity message is a doctrine of men, which basically teaches the preeminence of financial gain, which can be obtained by knowing how to use the Word of God, etc. In effect, it denies the real problem of man which is sin, and the only solution which is the Saviour. It would deny that label, but the priority of its message says otherwise!

8. The self-esteem message, which is another commandment of men, basically teaches that man's real problem is a low self-esteem. This error is a product of psychology, and actually denies man's true problem which is sin and self (I Tim. 1:15).

9. Another commandment of men is the denial of Blood Atonement. Such denies the only solution for sin which is Jesus Christ and Him crucified, instead, proclaiming a *"works"* Salvation (I Pet. 1:18-20).

10. *"Works"* Salvation makes up almost all of Catholicism, as well as much of Protestantism. By its propagation of *"works,"* it denies Faith, while the Scripture plainly tells us that Salvation is *"not of works lest any man should boast, but is the Gift of God"* (Eph. 2:8-9).

Above are but a few of the *"commandments of men,"* which are causing millions to be lost or else seriously hindered in their spiritual growth.

(10) "AND HE CALLED THE MULTITUDE, AND SAID UNTO THEM, HEAR, AND UNDERSTAND:"

The phrase, *"And He called the multitude, and said unto them,"* presents Him making a clean break from the Scribes and Pharisees. His teaching was diametrically opposed to them. The antagonism of necessity will now grow deeper.

The Ministry and Methods of Christ completely oppose the unity message as well! Preachers are not looked upon too favorably who oppose and point out that which is false doctrine. They are accused of destroying the unity of the Body. The question might be asked, *"What unity?"*

There could be no unity between Christ and these religious professors, as there can be no unity today with such, at least if a person truly desires to follow the Lord.

Jesus opposed these false doctrines vehemently because they were taking people to hell. For the same reason, every True God-called Preacher must oppose that which brings spiritual ruin to the soul. To do less is to abrogate one's spiritual responsibility and calling.

However, one must be warned, that, as with Christ, the taking of an open stand will arouse bitter opposition and even persecution. They ultimately killed Christ, and will attempt to kill all those who truly follow Him.

The phrase, *"Hear, and understand,"* means that it was difficult for His listeners to understand what He was saying, and due to the practiced deception of the Pharisees who had filled the land with their false doctrine. What Christ will teach them will be totally opposed to what the Pharisees were teaching them. As stated, His Words were not met with approval by the Pharisees.

This is the reason that a mere intellectual presentation can never penetrate the darkness of the human heart. Only that which is the Word of God, and which is mightily Anointed by the Holy Spirit, can perform this task. That is the reason most people remain deceived, with only a few actually knowing and following the Truth. Regrettably, there aren't many Preachers who truly preach the Word of God with an Anointing of the Holy Spirit (Lk. 4:18).

The reason Jesus told the people to *"Hear,*

NOTES

and understand," is because their minds were filled with error. As such, the Holy Spirit had to break down this error with Truth, which would then cause them to *"hear"* correctly, and correspondingly, to *"understand."*

If one is to notice, Jesus used these words, *"Hear, and understand,"* or a derivative, quite often. The statement was as much a command to the spirit world as it was instruction to the listeners.

To be sure, when He uttered these Words, the minds and ears of the people, at least of those who would believe, instantly opened for a favorable reception of the Gospel.

When He said these Words, if one would have had the opportunity to peer into the spirit world, one would have seen demon spirits falling away, which had been hindering the people.

(11) "NOT THAT WHICH GOETH INTO THE MOUTH DEFILETH A MAN; BUT THAT WHICH COMETH OUT OF THE MOUTH, THIS DEFILETH A MAN."

The phrase, *"Not that which goeth into the mouth defileth a man,"* proclaims Christ drawing the minds of the people away from mere externals to the true condition of the heart, as is proclaimed in verse 8. He is speaking of various types of food such as pork, etc., which prohibitions still grip a great part of the world — Buddhists, Hindus, Moslems, etc.

Some would argue that alcohol and drugs, and even gluttonous appetites, would be the exception to this rule. However, that is not correct.

Even though these items are great problems, still, it is what produces the desire for these things, and which stems from the heart, that is the real problem.

This is why programs such as Alcoholics Anonymous or Gamblers Anonymous, etc., which stem from earthly wisdom, can really never set the captive free. While it is true that these self-help programs (mostly called 12-step programs) can have at times some small success in helping a person to stop drinking or gambling, etc., still, these programs can only address the externals and not the true condition of the heart, which is the cause of the problem in the first place. Consequently, the individual, for the balance of his or her life, even though possibly discontinuing the act itself, must constantly say, *"I am a recovering alcoholic,"* etc.

Even though one commends that and is thankful for even that small help, nevertheless, such individuals are not really free until Jesus Christ sets them free. He does so by a change of heart, which destroys the reason and the cause for the unholy desire. Consequently, the problem, and as boldly proclaimed by Christ, is not external, but rather internal, i.e., the heart.

The phrase, *"But that which cometh out of the mouth, this defileth a man,"* speaks of that which has its origin in the evil heart.

Psychology attempts to address itself to the externals because that is all it can do. It can not, and for all its earthly wisdom, deal with that which really makes man do what he does — an evil heart of unbelief. Consequently, this statement made by Christ, is, without a doubt, one of the most profound statements ever made, and hits at the very heart of man's true condition. This is the reason that men must be *"born again"* (Jn. 3:3-8).

For some 6,000 years of recorded history, and with every effort that can possibly be made, man has attempted to prove this statement by Christ wrong. However, the overwhelming evidence proclaims the constant abject failure of all these efforts.

For instance, mighty universities, such as Harvard, Yale, Oxford, etc., attempt to ameliorate this problem, which is actually the cause of all man's difficulties, by educating the mind. While God places no premium on ignorance, still, an educated, unrenewed mind is not changed at all, it is just a little smarter. Consequently, whereas it was only able to kill men one at a time, now it can kill them by the hundreds of thousands in one fell swoop.

Paul said, *"And be not conformed to this world: but be ye transformed by the renewing of your mind, that ye may prove what is that good, and acceptable, and perfect, Will of God"* (Rom. 12:2).

This is the *"renewed mind,"* which can only come about by the born-again experience.

What was Jesus speaking of when He spoke of defilement that came out of the mouth?

He was speaking of that which comes out of an evil, unregenerate heart, and is listed in verse 19. Please allow us to say it again:

All the earthly wisdom in the world, such as psychology and all its derivatives, cannot have any effect whatsoever on this acute problem.

NOTES

If it could, then Jesus wasted His time in coming down to this earth and dying a horrible death on Calvary.

For the unregenerate world to take this position is understandable; however, for the Church to take this position, which it is readily doing, is tragic!

The Church begins this downward slide by continuing to believe that one must accept Christ as his Saviour in order to be saved, but then all continuing problems are handled by psychology. However, a little leaven will ultimately leaven the entirety of the lump. Consequently, and at the present time, a great part of the modern Church no longer even believes in the office work of the Holy Spirit in convicting man of his sins and of the absolute necessity of the New Birth. Many pay lip service to it, as these Jews of old, while, in reality, trusting other things.

(12) "THEN CAME HIS DISCIPLES, AND SAID UNTO HIM, KNOWEST THOU THAT THE PHARISEES WERE OFFENDED, AFTER THEY HEARD THIS SAYING?"

The phrase, *"Then came His Disciples, and said unto Him,"* concerns a time of private contemplation regarding the things recently said by Christ.

We now find them, no doubt the original twelve and possibly others, who are now in effect remonstrating Him. This was, as should be obvious, error on their part. Whereas in a carnal environment, the people may, in some limited circumstances, teach the teacher, still, it is not possible for the Disciple, i.e., student, to teach Christ. Such is preposterous, and yet all of us have been guilty at times of falling into the same trap of the Disciples.

Everything that God does is right, and not simply because He does it, but because it is right. That is the reason, Jesus, at the very outset, told His Disciples to follow Him. Under no circumstances would He follow them, and for the obvious reasons.

The question, *"Knowest Thou that the Pharisees were offended, after they heard this saying?"*, was the reason for their complaint. They knew that the statement by Christ, concerning defilement, had hit at the very heart of Pharisaical doctrine, and had, therefore, greatly antagonized them.

The word, *"offended,"* is a strong word,

meaning *"to scandalize."* In other words, the Disciples were saying that Jesus had so shredded their doctrine that they were scandalized in the public eye and would now seek revenge.

They were exactly right! However, as one divine of old said, *"If offense arises from the statement of the Truth, it is more expedient that offense be permitted to arise than that the Truth should be abandoned."*

Actually, the position that Christ took, which He had to take, and because the souls of men were at stake, is the same position that every True Preacher of the Gospel must take. Truth automatically exposes the lie. The Light automatically dispels the darkness. To be sure, those who project the lie and espouse the darkness will be offended. Nevertheless, the Truth must be upheld.

As an example, I am holding in my hand, even as I dictate these words, an article from one of the major religious magazines. The title is, *"Cutting-edge Rock Bands Attract Teens."*

The article espouses, and places its seal of approval on a particular band that calls itself *"Christian"* and had performed at a dance hall in a certain city.

In conjunction with the same article, the magazine espoused a Church in California where, it said, they have a bar that serves non-alcoholic drinks, a stage for hosting bands, and a large dancing area.

The article went on to say that the Pastor, who incidentally is Charismatic, *"runs the hottest nightclub in town."*

I do not know the motivation of this Pastor nor of these rock-n-roll bands. But I do know that what they are doing is wrong, terribly wrong!

Why?

Borrowing the methods of the world, by no stretch of the imagination, will perform a work for God. The efforts being carried out in this scenario, and whatever the motivation, are works of the flesh, and not of the Spirit. As such, they can effect no change in the lives of the young people who attend these gatherings. They may be entertained, and they may even come by some pseudo-religious experience. However, they will receive nothing from the Lord.

Paul said, *"For to be carnally minded is death; but to be spiritually minded is life and peace.*

"Because the carnal mind is enmity against

NOTES

God, for it is not subject to the Law of God, neither indeed can be.

"So then they that are in the flesh cannot please God" (Rom. 8:6-8).

To use any method of the world, and no matter how enticing, will never draw men to Christ. It may draw them to a Church, and, as stated, to a pseudo-religious experience, but it will never effect a work of the Holy Spirit within their hearts and lives, which must be carried out if there is to be a true change in the life of the individual.

Regrettably, the modern Pentecostal and Charismatic Church, at least for the most part, has drifted so far away from the Bible, and, therefore, the genuine moving and operating of the Holy Spirit, that it is now *"Church"* in name only. For spiritual leadership so-called to have no more spiritual perception than this, proclaims an acute lack of Bible knowledge, as well as an acute lack of the ways of the Holy Spirit.

The modern Church has by and large succumbed to the idea that if it draws a crowd and brings in a large sum of money, this constitutes the blessings, and, therefore, the approval of the Lord. Nothing could be further from the truth.

Is that which I have just mentioned the exception? Regrettably, it is not! In one way or the other, it is more so the norm in the modern Church.

In fact, the most evil place in town is more often the Church than not! This statement may seem harsh, but it is true.

It is evil, because, as these Pharisees of old, its false way is hidden beneath a covering and cloak of religion. Consequently, it is even more deadly than the bar on the corner, or the drug pusher peddling his wares to unsuspecting children. It is obvious as to the wrong of these actions; however, the other is not so obvious, and therefore more deadly.

Now, am I applauded for taking such a stand?

The answer to that should be obvious. I am not only <u>not</u> applauded, but instead I am reviled, demeaned, and dismissed out of hand as someone who is not properly informed.

The false prophets were offended then, and the false prophets are offended now! Nevertheless, the Truth must go forth.

(13) "BUT HE ANSWERED AND SAID, EVERY PLANT, WHICH MY HEAVENLY

FATHER HATH NOT PLANTED, SHALL BE ROOTED UP."

The phrase, *"But He answered and said,"* means, as is obvious, that He did not remain silent, but further proclaimed His position.

One of the great problems in the modern Church is that false doctrine and false ways are presented, and precious few bother to answer.

The short phrase, *"Every plant,"* presents Christ using as a symbolism that which His Disciples, as well as all others, would properly understand.

The phrase, *"Which My Heavenly Father hath not planted, shall be rooted up,"* means that the doctrine of the Pharisees was not of Divine origin, but of earthly origin. As such, it could not be accepted by God, and must not be accepted by His Children.

As well, the words, *"Rooted up,"* refer back to the Parable of the Tares and Wheat (13:24-30).

It is the business of the God-called Preacher to point out these *"tares,"* but it must be left to the Heavenly Father to *"root them up."*

If one is to notice, Jesus led no crusade to overthrow the Pharisees, Scribes, and Sadducees, who, as is obvious, were bitter enemies, and great opposers of the True Work of God.

With the massive crowds He was at this time drawing, along with the tremendous miracles that He was performing, He could have easily done such a thing. Of course, He did not do it because it was not the Father's will to do so, and because that is not God's way. To be sure, and as stated, they will one day be rooted up, but that is in the Father's Own good time, and will be carried out by Him exclusively.

As well, and if it is to be noticed, Christ did not so much oppose these individuals on a personal basis, but more so their doctrine.

There is a fine line drawn here, because the individual and his false doctrine are so closely intertwined that it is very difficult to distinguish between the two. However, the True Preacher of the Gospel must follow the example of Christ in making the false doctrine the chief target instead of the individual. Even then, it is to be more so exposed by preaching the Truth rather than majoring on the error. The next verse exemplifies what I am saying.

(14) "LET THEM ALONE: THEY BE BLIND LEADERS OF THE BLIND. AND IF

THE BLIND LEAD THE BLIND, BOTH SHALL FALL INTO THE DITCH."

The phrase, *"Let them alone,"* and referring to the Pharisees, is a strong statement, meaning that if they are offended, so be it! The idea is that if the Truth offends, under no consideration must it be discontinued on that account. To be sure, Truth often offends; but the servant of Truth must not permit himself to be influenced by the enemies of Truth. Rough Truth is better than polished falsehood, and though sometimes rough, is never rude.

In fact, some few of the Pharisees turned to Christ, such as Nicodemus (Jn. 3:1; 19:39). However, if Jesus had not proclaimed the Truth, none would have been brought to the knowledge of Salvation.

In 1982, the Lord dealt with my heart strongly concerning the tremendous number of Catholics who then viewed our Telecast. He gave me a Message that was to be directed to them. In essence, it was very brief, *"The just shall live by Faith"*; however, the very ramification of the subject, which is probably the single most important principle in Bible Christianity, completely undermines Catholic dogma and doctrine.

After much prayer and soul consternation, in order that I ascertain it was the Lord telling me to do this and not a figment of my own mind, I set about with great trepidation to carry out that which the Lord instructed me to do.

Yes! We had many Catholics brought to Christ, inasmuch as our Telecast was aired in most of Central and South America, along with the U.S.A., as well as other countries of the world which were predominantly Catholic. Nevertheless, the opposition was fierce to say the least!

Many of my own Pentecostal, and especially Charismatic brethren were incensed at the stand I took, and irrespective that tremendous numbers of Catholics were being brought to Christ. As I have stated elsewhere in these Commentaries, I remonstrated to one Brother, who was greatly upset over my position, as to how many Catholics he had won to Christ? If I remember correctly, he said *"None."*

I then related to him how that we had seen multiple thousands brought to Christ. His answer was somewhat interesting.

He claimed that if I had taken no stand

whatsoever, I would have won many more to the Lord. Of course, his position was totally unscriptural, as these very Passages portray.

I then answered him, relating to him how that previous to the stand I had taken, very few, if any, Catholics were saved.

It was only after I began to pointedly preach, directing my attention to their error and answering it with Truth, did I begin to see many Catholics brought to Jesus.

As well, we have seen many alcoholics brought to Christ, not because we agreed with their sin, but, instead, because we opposed it. The same could be said for homosexuals, etc.

However, even though the sin was greatly opposed, the sinner was always met with love. That, as well, was the method of Christ.

Admittedly, whenever a person's pet sin (and religion is a pet sin), is addressed, oftentimes it will make the individual very angry. They take it as a personal attack. However, that is not the case.

And yet, when it comes to professors of religion, as the Pharisees, this is somewhat different than that of which I have just mentioned. At times, Jesus attacked these individuals personally, and with good reason (Mat. 23).

It is one thing for a person to be a sinner, and quite another for one to be a professor of religion, and especially calling himself a Religious Leader. Then, as the Pharisees, it is almost impossible to distinguish between the false doctrine and the false prophet. They are basically indivisible.

So, the Word, *"Let them alone,"* does not mean to not address their error, but means that them being offended is not to be a deterrent to preaching the Truth. The reason is found in the next phrase.

The phrase, *"They be blind leaders of the blind,"* proclaims every false religion in the world, such as Islam, Buddhism, Shintoism, Hinduism, etc., as well as apostate Christianity.

What did Christ mean by calling them *"blind,"* whether leaders or followers?

This designation applied to all who were not following the Word of God. The Bible is the criteria, and the Bible alone! If it is ignored or falsely interpreted, or, as with the Pharisees, subtly twisted, it ceases to be the Word of God.

So, anything that does not agree with the Word of God in totality constitutes spiritual

NOTES

blindness. This does not mean that everyone must have total Light on the entirety of the Word of God. In fact, no one has all the Light on the Bible; however, one must walk in all the Light he has, and earnestly ask the Lord to enlarge that Light and be willing to walk therein when it is given to him.

The trouble is that many people, and especially Preachers, refuse to walk in the Light when it is shown to them.

When this happens, spiritual blindness begins to set in, and ultimately will lead to total blindness if not corrected.

This is what Jesus meant when He said, *"For whosoever hath, to him shall be given, and he shall have more abundance: but whosoever hath not, from him shall be taken away even that he hath"* (Mat. 13:12).

The phrase, *"And if the blind lead the blind, both shall fall in the ditch,"* is an obvious conclusion, which the Disciples should have understood, but regrettably did not!

In fact, the entire nation of Israel in A.D. 70 *"fell in the ditch,"* and actually ceased to be a nation. This was done because the people would not follow Christ, but rather these *"blind leaders,"* i.e., Pharisees, Scribes, and Sadducees.

In modern times, entire Religious Denominations have rejected the True Light of the Gospel, with its leaders actually leading the people to hell. It is a strong statement, but true!

Of course, many ask as to how these *"blind leaders"* are to be recognized and identified?

Jesus addressed that, and pointedly, by saying, *"Ye shall know them by their fruits"* (Mat. 7:16).

Even though we have addressed this previously, because of its tremendous significance and that Jesus addressed it several times, please allow us to repeat ourselves.

What is the fruit that Jesus was speaking of?

To sum up a very complex subject in a very brief statement, probably one could say that the *"fruit"* of *"Righteousness and Holiness"* developed in the life of the Believer is the greatest fruit of all.

Regrettably, entire Churches, at least in some cases, have not a single person with any degree of *"Righteousness."* To be sure, this is something that man cannot devise, but must be a Work of the Holy Spirit.

Such *"Righteousness and Holiness"* will bring about an obviously changed life, and will, as well, be a testimony to others.

Only the True Gospel of Jesus Christ can bring about this Work, because the Holy Spirit can only function in regard to Truth (Jn. 16:13).

These *"blind leaders"* were preaching lies, which means they had subtly twisted the Word of God in order to make it mean something it did not, consequently, the Holy Spirit would not, and, in fact, could not, function in such a circumstance. He can only act on Truth, which is the Word of God. He does not act upon, move upon, or bless error or sin.

So, if the Holy Spirit is to be active in any heart and life, which constitutes the Church, the Word of God must be given preeminence.

(15) THEN ANSWERED PETER AND SAID UNTO HIM, DECLARE UNTO US THIS PARABLE."

The phrase, *"Then answered Peter and said unto Him,"* proclaims the Disciples as led by Peter, asking for further explanation, and because they did not quite understand the total ramifications of what Jesus had said respecting that which defiled a man and these *"blind leaders"* who were preaching error.

The phrase, *"Declare unto us this parable,"* means to explain it further. This request demonstrates the ignorance of the natural heart, even of a Disciple. The reason for this *"blindness"* on their part was because they had been influenced greatly by these *"blind leaders,"* as well as the entirety of Israel.

To be sure, false doctrine dies hard, and it is difficult for one to be emancipated from old modes of thought, even error — and especially error!

This is the reason that Jesus said to the multitude as recorded in the 10th verse, *"Hear, and understand."*

When it comes to spiritual error, it is far different than other types of error of the intellect, etc.

As an example, if an individual misunderstands something about any subject that one might name, such as mathematics, geology, etc., the error can be corrected by merely showing what is correct.

This is employed as well by the Holy Spirit in the presentation of God's Word. However, spiritual error embraced is different than

NOTES

other types of error, in that all spiritual error is accompanied by the powers of darkness, even evil spirits (Mat. 13:39).

As such, the mere presentation of Truth alone is not enough. It must be accompanied by the Power of the Holy Spirit. Whenever the Truth is preached under the Anointing of the Holy Spirit, it is driven home like a sledge hammer striking blows, which shatters the spirits of darkness holding the person in the bondage of error.

That is the reason why many Preachers see very little results for the Lord, even though some of them do preach the Truth. There is little or no Anointing of the Holy Spirit, therefore, no power to overcome the powers of darkness resident in the lives of individuals, in order that the Gospel may have free course. That is part of the reason Paul admonished the Thessalonians to *"Pray for us, that the Word of the Lord may have free course, and be glorified, even as it is with you"* (II Thess. 3:1).

Even though this petition by Paul had as its primary objective the removal of hindrances, still, it also had reference to that of which we speak. He wanted to preach with a powerful Anointing of the Holy Spirit, in order that the Truth would find lodging in the hearts of people.

(16) "AND JESUS SAID, ARE YE ALSO YET WITHOUT UNDERSTANDING?"

To be frank, the Disciples, and despite the many miracles, healings, and strong preaching, little understood the True Mission and Ministry of the Master until the Advent of the Holy Spirit on the Day of Pentecost.

To be sure, they were saved, but still had little understanding of the Ways of God. Jesus said, and concerning the Holy Spirit, *"For He shall receive of Mine, and shall shew it unto you"* (Jn. 16:14).

This one question, *"Are ye also yet without understanding?"*, and coupled with St. John 16, proclaims the absolute necessity of the Holy Spirit in the life of the Believer. Regrettably, almost all the Church world, while professing to believe in the Work and Ministry of the Holy Spirit, in Truth, deny Him, or at least ignore Him. One would be shocked if one knew the actual Truth as to how little latitude He is given in the modern Church. Consequently, the lack of *"understanding"* concerning the Ways of God is acute to say the least, and abominable at its worst! Only with the Advent of the Holy Spirit did the Disciples begin to understand the Mission of Christ and what He wanted in the world.

(17) "DO NOT YE YET UNDERSTAND, THAT WHATSOEVER ENTERETH IN AT THE MOUTH GOETH INTO THE BELLY, AND IS CAST OUT INTO THE DRAUGHT?"

Jesus answers the request of the Disciples, at least at the beginning, with two questions. First of all, He asked them about their lack of understanding, and now He poses another question, *"Do not ye yet understand . . . ?"*, and will proceed to explain it in such simple terms that even the most simple would be able to grasp it.

The part of the question, *"That whatsoever entereth in at the mouth goeth into the belly,"* relates simply to the statement that the eating of food has absolutely nothing to do with the spiritual side of man. It does not affect the heart, the spirit, or the soul. The food enters the stomach, and then into the digestive tract, with its nutriments going to the physical part of the body, and the wastes going into the elimination part of the body, i.e., *"and is cast out into the draught?"*, which concludes this question.

No one could misunderstand His implication, and the meaning is surely not lost upon His Disciples. None of this affects the spiritual part of man, and, consequently, does not add to or take away in the spiritual sense.

The same would hold true for all types of religious customs thought to bring health or relief, etc. For instance, millions bathe in the filthy waters of the Ganges River in India, thinking it affords some type of spiritual healing or even eternal life. As the food Jesus spoke of, it does not!

Likewise, hundreds of millions of Catholics put a piece of bread on their tongue, thinking it turns into the actual Body of Christ, when it does not.

As well, millions of Protestants are baptized in water, thinking this affords some type of Salvation, when, in reality, even though in the spiritual sense it definitely symbolizes something very important (the Death, Burial, and Resurrection of Christ, and thusly the individual), still, the water contains no more spiritual life than the food these people were eating or not eating.

NOTES

At its very core, Jesus was addressing the ridiculous assumption posed by the Pharisees, that a demon spirit could possibly rest on the hands of an individual and could be washed off by water, etc. Such was silly, to say the least, with the statement of Christ proclaiming its absurdity.

The mind of religious man is so warped and twisted, that if people could be caused to believe such foolishness, as well, they could be made to believe that only a certain type of water (holy water) could remove such a spirit.

As this, religion is always absurd, is not practical, and never provides what it claims. Only Christ can do that.

Paul addressed himself to this when he said, *"Wherefore if ye be dead with Christ from the rudiments of the world, why, as though living in the world, are ye subject to ordinances,*

("Touch not; taste not; handle not; Which all are to perish with the using;) after the commandments and doctrines of men?" (Col. 2:20-22).

This problem was rampant in Jesus' day, in Paul's day, and is rampant at present!

Paul also said, *"For the Kingdom of God is not meat and drink; but Righteousness, and peace, and joy in the Holy Ghost"* (Rom. 14:17).

(18) "BUT THOSE THINGS WHICH PROCEED OUT OF THE MOUTH COME FORTH FROM THE HEART; AND THEY DEFILE THE MAN."

The phrase, *"But those things,"* limits that of which Christ is speaking. In other words, not everything that comes out of the mouth of a man is defiling, but only that which proceeds from an evil heart. As well, the implication is strong that it is religious reasonings which help promote the terrible sins of verse 19.

Every single person in the world is religious, with the exception of those who have truly made Christ their Saviour. To be sure, most do not understand that they are religious, but they are.

Whether they are following some false religion or no religion at all, or even consider themselves to be atheistic or agnostic, still, any and all these ways are the ways of Satan, and, thereby, religious. In whatever direction it takes, it is a philosophy devised by man, which actually originates with Satan, that claims it knows the way better than its Creator. Hence it is a religion, whether thought of as such or not!

Years ago, Frances and I were in California with a series of revival meetings. One Sunday immediately after Church, the Pastor asked if I would go with him to pray for one of his parishioners who was in the hospital.

In the hospital room there were two beds, each occupied by an elderly man. The one for whom we had come to pray was on the bed against the wall.

I suppose we must have stayed there pretty close to half an hour talking with this elderly gentleman. Even though he was very close to death, still, he was one of the most joyful persons I had ever met. Of course, he had a tremendous touch of the Lord Jesus Christ in his life.

He began to tell me about some of the great Preachers he had known and heard, and we discussed that for quite some time. As I have stated, it was a joy to be with him. I went there to cheer him up, but I think it worked the other way around.

As we were leaving, I looked at the other man, walked over to him, and asked if he would like us to pray for him. I will never forget his answer.

His eyes blazed with anger, and he very abruptly answered, *"No!"*

I then remonstrated, *"But, Sir, don't you know that you don't have long left here. You desperately need a Saviour, and that Saviour is the Lord Jesus Christ."*

To the best of his ability, he raised up in the bed, glared at me, and I will never forget his answer. *"I don't want your Saviour, I am my own savior,"* he said!

With that, he fell back to the pillow gasping for breath, and one could hear the death rattle that was even then sounding in his throat.

I backed away, looking over at the dear Brother we had just prayed for and he was slowly shaking his head.

I thought, as I looked back at the other man, *"If you are your own savior, what a mess you have made."*

That is the trouble with the human family, they attempt to be their own savior, and one can easily observe the results of that farce.

The phrase, *"Which proceed out of the mouth come forth from the heart,"* speaks for the soul and spirit, which constitute the inner

man and actually make him what he is, a conscious, intelligent, responsible (or irresponsible) being.

(The word, *"heart,"* as spoken of in the Bible, does not speak of the physical organ, but of the soul and spirit.)

The Hebrew word for *"heart"* is *"leb,"* which means the conscious self — the inner person with every function that makes a person human.

As an example, when addressing Pharaoh in Exodus, several statements are made concerning the heart.

The Scripture says, *"I(the Lord) will harden his heart"* (Ex. 4:21).

It also said, *"Pharaoh's heart became hard"* (Ex. 7:13).

It also said, *"Yet his heart was unyielding"* (Ex. 9:7).

These are but a few of the statements made concerning Pharaoh's heart.

In context, Pharaoh's will is clearly in view. In this scenario, the question is whether Pharaoh operated as a free and responsible person in refusing Moses' requests or was caused to act against his will.

The Old Testament views God as a casual force in all that happens, but it also views human beings as fully responsible for their attitudes and actions.

In a sense, God caused the response of Pharaoh, even if in no other way than by confronting him with a choice. Whenever God speaks, we are driven to make a choice to open our hearts to God's Word or to harden them.

However, this implied no course of action forced upon Pharaoh by the Lord. Only the opportunity was presented to him, but the free moral choice was his. It is clear from the Scriptures that Pharaoh *"hardened his own heart,"* and by his own actions, and that any influence exerted by God did not force Pharaoh to act against the inclination of his own character and the free choice of his own will.

JEREMIAH

The Holy Spirit through the Prophet Jeremiah said, *"The heart is deceitful above all things and beyond cure. Who can understand it?"* (Jer. 17:9).

In analyzing this statement, one must come to the conclusion that every aspect of man's personality — the mind, emotion, will, etc. — has been affected by the Fall and is so warped that we cannot trust ourselves.

THE NEW TESTAMENT

In the New Testament, the Greek word for *"heart"* is *"kardia,"* and is used in the same sense as in the Old Testament. The heart of man is his very person: his core, his conscious awareness of all that he sees and knows. It is that which comes from his soul and spirit.

Consequently, a heart response to God begins with belief that Jesus is Lord and that God has raised Him from the dead. This new beginning redirects our total life and experience (Rom. 10:8-13).

It is the failure to respond to God from the heart, which causes the full development and expression of the inner, sinful bent to human nature, which is the cause of all the sin and evil in the world (Rom. 1:21-32).

Before conversion, the inner personality of human beings is warped towards sin, and is the source of sin and of sinful actions. Consequently, we are not to look for causes of sin in externals, as Jesus here responds. We are to look within (Mat. 12:34; 15:18-19; Mk. 7:19; Lk. 6:45).

Whenever the individual responds favorably to the Lord, God's Spirit comes into our renewed personality, bringing God's Own strength and vitality, His Own pure motives and desires (Rom. 5:5; II Cor. 1:22; Gal. 4:6).

As a result, it is easy to see the deep need for Christ that exists in lost humanity (Richards).

The phrase, *"And they defile the man,"* proclaims to us the true source of defilement which is the evil, wicked heart, hence the statement by Jeremiah (Jer. 17:9).

(19) "FOR OUT OF THE HEART PROCEED EVIL THOUGHTS, MURDERS, ADULTERIES, FORNICATIONS, THEFTS, FALSE WITNESS, BLASPHEMIES:"

The phrase, *"For out of the heart proceed,"* proclaims the depravity of the unconverted human heart, which expresses itself in the actions listed here by Christ. It is not a pretty picture! As previously stated, such proclaims the reason for man's inhumanity to man.

1. *"Evil thoughts":* The phrase, *"Evil thoughts,"* provides the foundation for all the other atrocities listed, and state their beginning as coming from an unrenewed mind.

As stated, these are religious reasonings,

even though they are never thought of as such, and are here declared to be evil. They are *"religious,"* because they utilize a way which is not of God and, therefore, can only come from Satan. Therefore, these with such hearts are Satan's children, as almost all the world constitutes *"Satan's children."* He can only steal, kill, and destroy (Jn. 10:10), and his children can only do the same.

These *"Evil thoughts"* issue out of the deep abyss of corruption from which proceed the black catalogue detailed in this verse. Before coming out of the heart, these sins had, of necessity, their home in the heart.

This statement by Christ destroys the belief that the natural heart is good, and makes foolish modern efforts to improve human nature. The assumption that only what goes into the heart defiles it, is here denied; and the necessity of the creation of a new heart declared. It is evident that what comes out of the heart must exist in the heart.

2. *"Murders":* This word is different than the word *"kill."* The type of *"murder"* here mentioned is that which extends from an evil heart, and is first conceived in the heart before the act is carried out. This is what is defined by the law of the land, and rightly so, as *"cold-blooded murder."*

For such crimes, the Bible teaches that capital punishment should be administered to the guilty party. Such Law, as given by God, is registered in both the Old and New Testaments (Gen. 9:6; Rom. 13:1-7). The reason capital punishment is demanded by God for certain crimes is not as a deterrent to crime. It is because man was originally made in the *"Image of God,"* and, as such, human life is sacred.

Among other things, this is what makes the terrible crime of *"abortion"* so horrible. In fact, abortion is murder, pure and simple. That means every doctor who aborts a baby is guilty of murder, and every mother who consents to such is guilty of the same crime. Actually, in the eyes of God, guilty parties of such crimes should have their own lives forfeited. The reasons are obvious.

3. *"Adulteries":* The sin of adultery is the sex act performed between a man and woman before one is married, or unfaithfulness after one is married.

Hollywood has so desecrated this Law of

God until it has little meaning anymore to the average citizen. However, Hollywood, obliterating this line of chastity and purity, makes it no less a sin against God and man. Consequently, the results are obvious all around us, in broken homes, broken marriages, disease and perversion.

As *"murder"* is the 6th Commandment of the Ten Commandments of Exodus 20, *"adultery"* is the 7th Commandment. As such, they are carried over into the New Covenant.

Jesus had previously taught that *"adultery"* did not originate with the act itself, but actually in the heart, as He here proclaims again (Mat. 5:27-28). In other words, this sin begins with an *"Evil thought."*

4. *"Fornications"*: All adulterers are not fornicators, but all fornicators are adulterers.

Some have erroneously thought of adultery as that which was committed by those who are married, with fornication referring to those not married. That is incorrect.

Fornication means adultery committed by married or single people, and refers to going from one partner to the next (I Cor. 7:2; 10:8; I Thess. 4:3; Rev. 9:21).

It also means incest (I Cor. 5:1; 10:8); idolatry, which referred to prostitution of both the male and female respecting idol gods (II Chron. 21:11; Isa. 23:17; Ezek. 16:15, 26, 29; Acts 15:20, 29; 21:25; Rev. 2:14-21; 14:8); natural harlotry (Jn. 8:41; I Cor. 6:13-18); spiritual harlotry (Ezek. 16:15, 26, 29; Rev. 17:2-4; 18:3-9; 19:2); sodomy and male prostitution (Rom. 1:24-29; I Cor. 6:9-11; II Cor. 12:21; Gal. 5:19; Eph. 5:3; Col. 3:5; Heb. 12:16; Jude 6-7).

It is obvious from these Scriptures that they do not apply to single people only, but, as well, to both single and married.

5. *"Thefts"*: This pertains to stealing, and speaks to the 8th Commandment (Ex. 20:15).

It means the secret and open removal of the property of another, any injury done to it, and carelessness about that which belongs to another.

This pertains not only to property, but as well to a person's name, character, and reputation.

6. *"False witness"*: This speaks to the 9th Commandment, and, as is obvious, is brought over into the New Covenant as well! This pertains to untrue testimony, lying.

The reason laws and iron-clad contracts,

so-called, are required, is because man simply will not tell the truth.

Unconverted, man's father, the Devil, is a liar, and the father of it. Consequently, his children continue to do the same (Jn. 8:44).

As well, and as Christ proclaims, lies originate in the heart before they are spoken with the mouth.

7. *"Blasphemies"*: As this dialogue opens with *"Evil thoughts,"* and provides the foundation for all the other sins, likewise, it closes with *"blasphemies,"* which speak of vocal opposition to God, and come in the form of profanity or unbelief.

The actual word *"blasphemy,"* means *"to slander,"* or *"to speak lightly of the sacred."* It is abusive (profane) and damaging speech.

It indicates a hostility toward God and is expressed directly or indirectly in contemptuous or slanderous ways. Consequently, as it stems from the ungodly heart, blasphemy is of far greater consequence than the actual curse or profanity that comes out of the mouth.

All *"blasphemy"* is forgivable if the individual will take the sin to Christ, with the exception of blaspheming the Holy Spirit, which is not forgivable in this world or the one to come (Mat. 12:31).

Actually, all of these sins with the exception of the one mentioned are forgivable by the Lord, if one will only go to Him (Mat. 12:31; Rom. 10:9-10; I Jn. 1:9).

(20) "THESE ARE THE THINGS WHICH DEFILE A MAN: BUT TO EAT WITH UNWASHEN HANDS DEFILETH NOT A MAN."

In no uncertain terms, Christ draws the attention of the Disciples back to the ridiculous assertions of the Pharisees by declaring emphatically, *"These are the things which defile a man,"* which spoke of man's real problem instead of this foolishness.

Likewise, modern man, even modern religious man, holds to foolish thoughts little different than that projected by the Pharisees of old. The fallacy of self-esteem is but one.

The idea that man's problems are caused by a low self-esteem is ludicrous to say the least! It is but another attempt of worldly wisdom to assuage the terrible problems of man, whatever they may be. It is sadder still when the Church buys into this foolishness.

A proper union and relationship with

Christ will solve any and all problems. That is the reason Jesus said, *"Come unto Me, all ye that labour and are heavy laden, and I will give you rest"* (Mat. 11:28).

Christ is the answer for all things, and irrespective of what they may be, and needs no help from worldly wisdom.

The phrase, *"But to eat with unwashen hands defileth not a man,"* as well, lays to rest many of the rules and regulations held in many modern Churches.

For instance, jewelry is not offensive to the Holy Spirit, simply because it cannot, within itself, defile anything.

As well, ladies' make-up is of no consequence respecting spiritual things. While it is true that certain types of make-up could be in bad taste, still, it has nothing to do with one's spirituality.

Clothing, as long as it is modest, falls into the same category.

Likewise, any and all food is acceptable. It has no spiritual connotations in any form.

While it was true that the Jews under the Mosaic Law, which was the Law of God, were not to eat certain types of animal food, with it being called unclean. Contrary to what many think, this did not have a dietary or health purpose, but was rather a constant reminder to Israel that they were linked with Jehovah, and everything they did was to express their position as His special people.

For instance, no unclean animal was allowed to be used in Sacrifice, and because the Sacrifices represented Christ. As well, both the Priest and the offerer of the Sacrifices, in some instances, were to eat a part of the Sacrifice offered. This affirmed the individual being yoked to the Lord.

As well, Israel was to be the dispenser of the Word of God as given by the Holy Spirit (the Bible), and was, as well, to be the womb of the Messiah. As such, they were to carry forth themselves somewhat differently than those under the New Covenant.

Inasmuch as Christ has been born, and has paid the price for man's sins, the restrictions placed upon Israel concerning certain dietary laws no longer apply to those under the New Covenant (Acts 10:15; Col. 2:20-23).

As well, Jesus is plainly telling Israel in these Passages that those type of things had

nothing to do with one's spirituality anyway. Consequently, the dietary laws under the Old Covenant were given for an entirely different reason, as explained.

(21) "THEN JESUS WENT THENCE, AND DEPARTED INTO THE COASTS OF TYRE AND SIDON."

The phrase, *"Then Jesus went thence,"* portrays Him leaving (probably Capernaum), and going to the borders of *"Tyre and Sidon."*

These two cities were located on the Mediterranean Sea, north of Israel. Both are very prominent in Old Testament history.

The Scripture does not say that Jesus went into these cities, but merely to the border between Israel and Lebanon where they were located.

These two areas of *"Tyre and Sidon"* were steeped in heathenistic idol worship. Their gods were Baal and Ashtaroth, which, they, in one form or the other, continued to worship even during the time of Christ.

Coming back to the present, during the last war Israel engaged in when they attempted to expunge the Palestinians from Lebanon, Frances and I, along with Donnie and others, had the opportunity, as invited guests of Israel, to go into Lebanon during the heaviest fighting to tape a Television Special. It was quite an experience.

The present border between Israel and Lebanon, which possibly is very near the location where it was in Jesus' day, is actually a very beautiful place.

Here the cliffs rise up from the Mediterranean. As well, the altitude rises somewhat as the topography changes to a mountainous district.

As we crossed the border that day, Israeli soldiers were everywhere, with long lines of trucks backed up coming from Lebanon bringing back all types of burned-out and destroyed Russian equipment which had been taken from the Palestinians and the Syrians.

As we stopped at the border for the regular regulation ritual, I had the occasion to stand there for a length of time, looking out over the Mediterranean as well as back into Israel. We learned a short time later, that almost immediately below our feet at the bottom of the mountain, where gigantic caves were located which opened up to the sea, huge quantities of weapons and ammunition were located by the Israelis, which had been stored there by the Palestinians.

The closest Jewish town to the border is Nahariyya. It is a resort area of between 10,000 and 20,000 population. We spent the night there just before going into Lebanon.

I do not know if this little city even existed during the time of Christ; however, I do know that somewhere close to here, and possibly this very place, Christ came. Consequently, one of the greatest miracles recorded in the Bible would take place.

To be sure, and within itself, it was no greater than many of the other miracles of Christ. However, the manner in which it took place provides a tremendous lesson for all Bible students.

(22) "AND, BEHOLD, A WOMAN OF CANAAN CAME OUT OF THE SAME COASTS, AND CRIED UNTO HIM, SAYING, HAVE MERCY ON ME, O LORD, THOU SON OF DAVID; MY DAUGHTER IS GRIEVOUSLY VEXED WITH A DEVIL."

The two words, *"And, behold,"* mark the sudden intrusion of this woman into the Mission of Christ. When Matthew wrote these words, no doubt the Holy Spirit moved upon him to say them as he did in order to highlight this unexpected turn of events.

The phrase, *"A woman of Canaan came out of the same coasts,"* concludes her to be a Gentile. Mark called her a *"Greek,"* and a *"Syrophenician."*

At any rate, the phrase, *"A woman of Canaan,"* says it all! She was an *"Alien from the Commonwealth of Israel, and a stranger from the Covenants of Promise, having no hope, and without God in the world"* (Eph. 2:12). As such, she was typical of all Gentiles, and epitomize you who hold this book in your hands.

Her life was one of idol worship, and a cruel worship it was, even employing human sacrifice.

(Whether such sacrifices continued unto the time of Christ is not known, but in centuries past they had been rampant.)

How this woman heard of Jesus is not known. No doubt His fame had spread to this part of the world, and the stories abounded of the tremendous miracles He was performing. And now He was close to her home. It would be the greatest day in her life. If He had not come to this area, she would never have had the

NOTES

privilege of knowing Him, or experiencing the tremendous deliverance afforded her daughter.

This illustration speaks to me the dire necessity of taking the Gospel of Jesus Christ to the world. Paul would later say, *"How then shall they call on Him in Whom they have not believed? and how shall they believe in Him of Whom they have not heard? and how shall they hear without a Preacher"* (Rom. 10:14).

That is the reason we labor day and night at Jimmy Swaggart Ministries to take this Gospel to the world. World Evangelism is my calling. I live it, breathe it, and seek to carry it out with every fiber of my being.

As well, it should be, and, in Truth, must be, the singular goal and mission of every Child of God. None are excluded! All are commanded to take the Gospel to the world (Mk. 16:15). And yet, I am concerned that most Christians have little burden for this all-important task.

How do I know that?

When one considers that the average giving of Christians in America (and I suppose this would go for Canada as well) for World Evangelism is only one penny a day on the average, one must come to the conclusion just stated. Of course, there are a few who have a great burden and do their very best for this all-important task, but the sad truth is that most do not give anything.

The average cost, or expenses, for the operation of a Church in America is pretty close to $15 per person per week in 1995 dollars. In other words, if a Church averages 100 people in attendance in America, its expenses are approximately $1500 per week, averaging, as stated, about $15 per person. (Some Churches, of course, spend far more than that.)

The cost for us to take the Gospel to various countries of the world, oftentimes to people who have had little opportunity to hear, is a little less than one cent, per person, per week. That means it costs about 1500 times more each week to minister to Church members in America than it does to take the Gospel to other countries of the world.

(I am speaking of our own Telecast, and not attempting to factor in the cost of other types of missions projects.)

And yet, we have to plead constantly for funds to even pay this small amount.

When one considers that almost from the

moment the Telecast begins to air people begin to be saved, it would seem as though all Believers would be ready to help. But, sadly, that is not so!

The Apostle Paul had this same difficulty, the raising of support for his Missions works.

In writing to the Church at Philippi, he said, *"But I rejoiced in the Lord greatly, that now at the last your care of me hath flourished again"* (Phil. 4:10).

For a time the Philippians had ceased to help the Apostle, and according to his terminology, this had caused great difficulties. But now they had once again begun to give him financial support, for this is what this Passage speaks of.

Every person in the world has the right to hear the Gospel. And now, more than all, due to the advent of Television, the opportunity presents itself to reach untold hundreds of millions with the Gospel of Jesus Christ. To be sure, each one of us will be held responsible for our part in this task.

Some time ago, I received a telephone call from a Pastor friend who related to me a beautiful testimony. He had just returned from Moscow, where he and other Preachers from America had conducted a week-long teaching seminar, for which they had brought in Russian Pastors from all over the former Soviet Union. He explained to me that they did this once a year, even paying the expenses of these Pastors to Moscow.

Considering that most of these Pastors in the former Soviet Union had very little Bible training, this, of course, was an extremely valuable time for them.

During the course of one of the teaching sessions, he happened to ask the room full of Pastors, numbering somewhat over 100, as to exactly how they had found Christ? Actually, he had each one stand and give a brief testimony to this all-important experience.

He said to me, *"Brother Swaggart, how pleasantly surprised I was when over half of these Pastors, some of them pastoring Churches over 1,000 in attendance, told how they had found Christ as a result of your Telecast."* He said, *"I just had to call you and give you that bit of news."*

Believing that God was going to open the door in this vast land then known as the Soviet Union and that the Lord had told me to

NOTES

do so, we began to translate our Television Program from English to Russian, if I remember correctly, in late 1988.

Then, if memory serves me right, we began to air first of all in Riga, Latvia in 1989. I have been told that the K.G.B. sent an agent from Moscow to Riga to inquire of the Television Station as to why they were airing our program. To my knowledge, it was the very first Gospel program ever aired in the former Soviet Union.

The station management informed this agent that they were airing it because it was what the people wanted. At any rate, even though the agent was very upset, the program was allowed to continue. In 1990, as the result of a miracle, we were able to begin airing the Telecast over TV-One in Moscow, which had formerly been the major Communist Government network, which reached the entirety of all fifteen Republics, some 280,000,000 people. As stated, the program was translated into Russian, as it still is.

For about a year, we had a Post Office Box in Moscow in order that the people could write us if they so desired. In that year, 1991, we received over 1,000,000 letters, even though we told the people we had no means in which to answer their letters. That is how hungry they were for the Gospel.

Considering the vastness of this area, Television is the only way that one could quickly reach these masses. To be sure, that is what the Lord has called me to do. In all honesty, it would take hundreds of thousands of Holy Ghost-filled Missionaries to reach this land, and even many years at that, when we were able to do it in a very short period of time, and with astounding results.

No, I am in no way demeaning the tremendously important role of the Missionary, or any other effort for the propagation of the Gospel. To be sure, all are needed and seriously so. Nevertheless, I do make the statement that what God is helping us to do respecting World Evangelism is tremendously important. It is important enough, I might quickly add, that every True Believer ought to do all he can to help, especially considering the forthcoming results.

All over the world there are multiple hundreds of millions of people just like this *"Woman of Canaan,"* who must have the opportunity to hear the Gospel and to know the Lord Jesus Christ. There is nothing more important than that!

The phrase, *"And cried unto Him,"* constitutes a Message within itself.

This woman was desperate! She had come to receive something from Christ, and she would not leave without getting that which she asked.

Inasmuch as the word, *"cried,"* meant to *"clamor,"* or, in other words, to speak with great emotion, the Holy Spirit through Matthew gives us an idea as to her desperation and the cry of her heart. I dare say that if anyone will come to Christ in this manner, an answer will be forthcoming.

Too many people approach the Lord in a lackadaisical way, and most of the time they receive nothing. To be sure, one is not advocating that the loudness of one's approach assures His answer, but this we do know:

True Bible Faith will not be denied. There is always an urgency about Faith which produces an emotion in the soul of the individual who comes to God. One can see this in the lives of the Bible Greats such as Abraham, who felt the urgency so great to see the Promise of God carried out in his life respecting this coming child that he would even attempt to help the Lord, which, of course, was wrong, but nevertheless portrayed his feelings.

The Apostle Paul is another example! There is an urgency about his Ministry, his life, and his efforts. Faith produces such an urgency, and, as well, it produces an emotion as exampled by this *"Woman of Canaan."*

I am here today saved by the Blood of Jesus, because my Mother cried to God on my behalf. As a teenage boy, and despite the Call of God on my life, I did not want to live for the Lord. However, night after night, and even in the wee small hours of the morning, I would hear my Mother in the adjoining bedroom, as she would cry to God on my behalf. No, she was not praying loudly, but there was an urgency to her petition, even registering in a moan as she importuned the Heavenly Father on my behalf. I can recall that even now, and with a sob from her soul, as she claimed my soul and the Call of God on my life.

She saw the fingers of Satan reaching for me, and realizing the dire danger, and with

great burden of soul, she importuned the Lord on my behalf.

I seriously doubt I would be here today had it not been for that petition and her *"crying to God."* This is a Faith that will not be denied! A Faith that will not take *"no"* for an answer! It is the same type of Faith that this *"Woman of Canaan"* had, even though she did not really know God. However, she did know her need, and she did know Who Jesus was, which is more than could be said for the Religious Leaders of Israel.

The phrase, *"Saying, Have Mercy on me, O Lord, Thou Son of David,"* presents a petition to the Lord which was actually wrong in principle, but not in Faith.

Christ, as a Minister of the circumcision for the Truth of God to fulfill the Promises made to the Fathers, refused to answer the Gentile petition addressed to Him as *"Son of David,"* but when the woman took the place of a *"dog,"* thus admitting she had no claim, and threw herself on His Mercy and Grace as Lord, He at once responded; for the Scripture said that He was so to act that the Gentiles also might glorify God for His Mercy (Rom. 15:8-12).

Why would she have used this phrase, *"Son of David,"* when speaking to Christ?

Living as close as she did to Israel, she was probably well acquainted with the hopes and aspirations of the Jews respecting their Coming Messiah.

Hearing the conversations of His great miracles and the discussion as to whether He was the Messiah, she no doubt concluded in her heart, and irrespective of what others may have said, that Jesus was indeed the Messiah, the *"Son of David,"* and, in effect, the *"Son of God."*

She as a Gentile had no Scriptural right to address Christ as the *"Son of David,"* still, she probably did not know that. Her story is an example to all of us.

If the Lord demanded that our approach to Him be totally proper in every respect, most of us would fall by the wayside. But, thankfully, He does not demand that. He only demands Faith, and Faith this woman had!

Even as I write these words, I strongly sense the Presence of God. Even with tears, I feel the emotion of the moment as she approached Christ. I see myself in her, as you should as well!

She was out of dispensation, even unscriptural, and actually had no right for what she was asking; however, her petition would not be denied, and neither will the petition of anyone else be denied if they come in the manner in which she came — of Humility and Faith. The Holy Spirit had this glorious example portrayed to us by both Matthew and Mark that its great lesson would not be lost upon us. If she received, you can receive as well!

The phrase, *"My daughter is grievously vexed with a devil,"* gives the state of her child, which was serious indeed!

The Lord did not contradict her respecting the diagnosis, so, undoubtedly, demon powers were the cause of this affliction. This is a subject in which not many are knowledgeable, and I speak of even children being influenced or even possessed by demon spirits. Actually, this is not the exception, especially in the world in which she lived, or even in the world in which we live today.

Tragically, most children in America, or any country in the world for that matter, are raised in homes who little know God. They are submitted to profanity, immorality, and a very atmosphere that is charged by the powers of darkness. Consequently, they, even as children, provide a fertile territory for the activity of demon spirits.

If one could look into the spirit world, one would see demon spirits operating graphically so in the lives of many, if not most, teenagers, and even pre-teens.

In a documentary which I saw over Television in the recent past, the commentator was remarking about the callousness of some teenagers who had committed murder. *"They seem to show no remorse whatsoever concerning the terrible thing they have done,"* she said.

"Killing a fellow human being was no more to them than a flick of the wrist," she added.

The ages of the two *"killers"* she interviewed were, if I remember correctly, 12 and 14.

She was nonplussed over their attitude, as well as multiple tens of thousands of other teenagers and pre-teens exhibiting traits that are completely unexplainable to the sociologist or psychologist, etc.

The answer now is the same as it was then, *"Vexed with a devil."*

There is only one answer to this terrible malady, and it, as well, is the same now as then, *"Jesus."* All the sociologists or psychologists in

NOTES

the world cannot help such a one. This is the reason that the Gospel preached in all of its power is so very important. It is the answer, and because it is the Gospel of Christ.

Just three weeks ago, as I dictate these notes (June of 1995), we received a letter that explains what I am attempting to say.

It was addressed to Frances.

"Dear Mrs. Swaggart:

"You probably wonder why I am writing this letter to you instead of your husband, but I feel this is a story that only a mother can understand. I know that you have a son, and I thought you might want to hear what God has done in my life.

"I have always been privileged to stay home and take care of our only son. We live in a very exclusive neighborhood, and have many of the luxuries not afforded to most.

"Up until the past few years, I thought that nothing could touch the peace and prosperity of our world. Then one morning 16 months ago, I awoke to find that our son, who was then 16, had left home in the middle of the night.

"For about year, we had fought an uphill battle with him. He had gotten into the wrong crowd — a gang-type group, whose leader seemed to have much more influence on him than my husband and me. We have found marijuana in his room, pornographic literature, rock music — all the earmarks of teenage trouble.

"We immediately sought professional help for him, which we know now was definitely a mistake. We spent thousands of dollars, only to be told that we had failed in our efforts to raise our son, and that his rebellion was simply a natural response to our erroneous child rearing.

"When he left, I have to admit to you that in one sense I was relieved. I knew that we could not do anymore for him, as the harder we tried, the more rebellious he became.

"When our son was reported missing, we came to realize that he was on the long list of statistics. The Police Department made an earnest effort to locate him; but under the circumstances, we knew that he did not want to be found.

"For a period of about six months, we did not hear from him at all. Then, we only heard through other teenagers who had once been his friends that he was living with this gang, and more or less living on the streets or in 'hop'

houses, where sources of drugs were readily available. I don't think I have to tell you that I died a thousand deaths during this time.

"Tuesday morning, three weeks ago, I answered the phone, and realized that on the other end was my son. He said, 'Mom, I really need to talk to you. Something has happened to me. I am ready to come home.' Words cannot express to you just what went through my mind at that time. Tears ran like a river, and I was so happy — yet, I wondered, is this real? Would he come home, only to repeat the scenario of the past? I don't think that his Dad or I could stand that.

"Late that afternoon, a prodigal son arrived on the doorsteps. He was dirty and bedraggled — his hair long and unkempt — his arms scarred with needle tracks from 'shooting up.' But, in spite of all this, there was a look in his eyes that was bright and happy, like I had not seen in two years.

"After hugging and crying for what seemed like hours, he said, 'Mom, the strangest thing happened to me yesterday. I had gotten totally stoned the night before, had come in about daylight, and crashed on the couch. I had been watching some sort of weird stuff on TV, and went off to sleep. When I woke up, it was about 3:30 in the afternoon. On the Channel where I had been watching, there was this Preacher. Mom, it was the same one that I used to see Grandma watching when I was a kid. (My Mother, until her death six years ago, always watched your program.) I thought about Grandma, and how disappointed she would have been in me if she could see me now, and I started to cry. The Preacher was talking about how no matter how bad you are, God still loves you and wants you to come home to Him. Then he prayed a prayer, and I said it with him. I said, God, I don't want to be like this. I don't want to shoot dope. I can't stop. Please help me.'

"He continued, 'This Preacher's son was there with him praying. I wanted to be able to see my Dad, and to have him be proud of me like this Preacher is of his son. He talked about how his son was a Preacher too. I thought about how I had disappointed Dad and you. I said, God, forgive me for doing this to Mom and Dad. Please let them want me to come home. Then I went to sleep again, and didn't wake up until this morning. When I woke up, I knew that I had to come home, so I called you. Mom, this is

the first time I haven't shot up in the morning for over a year, and I feel great'

"I was in a total state of shock! I wasn't even sure that I believed in miracles, but I had one standing here in front of my eyes. I have to admit that I was skeptical, and, first of all, I had to know just who this Preacher was that my son had seen. (He had not seen the program begin or end, and did not know the name.) I looked at the television listing at 3:30 P.M. on Monday on all the networks, and nothings was there except soaps. On most of the major Cable Stations we had children's programming and miscellaneous programs — nothing religious. I said, 'Do you know what station you were watching?' He said, 'Mom, all I know is that it is a station where they show atheist programs and stuff, and it was on a Monday afternoon.'

"The only thing I could think of that fit this description was People TV — the local Public Channel. Sure enough, when I looked on their listings, it said, 'Jimmy Swaggart.'

"At 3:30 that next Monday, we turned on the program, and there was Jimmy Swaggart, singing and preaching. My son's eyes filled with tears, and he said, 'That's him, Mom, that's him.' We both wept and cried during the entire program.

"My son is finally home. He is clean shaven, has a hair cut, and his clothes are clean. However, these are small, unimportant things. He has a new life. He has had no drugs or alcohol since he walked in my door again. We are looking for a good Bible-based Church to attend.

"Once again, let me thank you for being on People TV Channel 12. Thank God that Brother Swaggart has been able to withstand the attacks launched against him, and is still preaching the Gospel.

"I have no idea just how your program happened to be aired on our little local Channel, but please know that his Father and I are so thankful to Brother Swaggart for helping us get our son back. Only the Lord will be able to relate to you just how your Ministry has blessed this family!"

This letter is just one of the many hundreds of thousands, or even millions, we have received over the years, telling of what Jesus Christ has done within a heart and a life. The only answer to these terrible problems is Christ.

Regrettably and sorrowfully, the modern Church has become one great referral unit. It refers the Alcoholic to Alcoholics Anonymous, and the compulsive gambler to Gamblers Anonymous, etc. As well, it refers those who are influenced, or even possessed by demon spirits, to the psychologists. To be sure and certain, there is little help from these sources. Only Jesus can set the captive free! Only Jesus can break the chains that bind humanity! Only Jesus can save the lost soul!

Why are the Churches, at least for the most part, doing this?

They are doing it because most of them no longer preach the Gospel, or even believe the Gospel. Most have denied, and are denying, the mighty Power of the Holy Spirit. Consequently, there is no power in their services, their worship, or their preaching. As a result, no captives are set free. By and large, it is *"Dead Preachers, preaching dead sermons, to dead congregations."*

However, I will say as Joshua of old, *"As for me and my house we will serve the Lord"* (Josh. 24:15).

(23) "BUT HE ANSWERED HER NOT A WORD. AND HIS DISCIPLES CAME AND BESOUGHT HIM, SAYING, SEND HER AWAY; FOR SHE CRIETH AFTER US."

In the entirety of this scenario, and as intended by the Holy Spirit, we are given a perfect description as to how to approach the Lord, and how to receive from the Lord. It will be an invaluable lesson.

The phrase, *"But He answered her not a word,"* was by design. Everything that Jesus did, even down to the Words He spoke, was guided by the Holy Spirit. Therefore, this scene, as it unfolds before us, is a carefully-crafted plan engineered by the Holy Spirit in order to meet this woman's need, i.e., the healing and deliverance of her daughter.

So, His failure to answer was not meant at all to put her off, or to deny her request, but, instead, in order that she might receive what she has asked.

The Ways of God are not our ways! However, those ways are meant for our good.

The lesson here taught, and to be learned, is that if the Lord does not answer immediately, we are not to stop our petition. The phrase, *"And cried unto Him,"* as given in the

previous verse, meant that she kept crying. In other words, she would not stop.

It is regrettable that a great part of the Church world is taught that we are only to ask the Lord one time, and that any further petitions are a sign of lack of Faith. The Scripture abundantly proclaims that such is not true. If, at first, we do not receive, we are importuned to continue asking (Lk. 11:8).

As well, the delay, if there is delay, is not meant to be antagonizing to the seeker. The Lord does all things for a purpose. Along with giving us what we request, He, as well, always teaches us lessons by the manner in which He gives them.

Regrettably, most Christians presently ask once or twice, if that, and then quickly tire, claiming that God does not answer prayer, or else give some other excuse.

The lesson taught in this experience is that if we do not at first receive, continue to ask, and, as this *"Woman of Canaan,"* to be sure, continue asking in Faith. Delay does not mean denial! It only means that we are to continue asking and believing.

The phrase, *"And His Disciples came and besought Him,"* proclaims them doing this after her repeated petition. However, if one is to notice, there is another potent Truth in this phrase.

This *"Woman of Canaan,"* did not come to the Disciples, but Jesus. It is sad when Catholicism erroneously encourages its people to pray to dead Saints, or even some of these Disciples, or, more particularly, Mary, the Mother of Christ.

In the four Gospels, which give the account of the Ministry of the Master, one finds precious little evidence that individuals in need came to the Disciples, but, instead, directly to Christ. It would surely seem that the Holy Spirit is telling us something in these many accounts of seekers coming to Christ.

The Truth is that all petitions must be made directly to the Father in the Name of Jesus (Jn. 16:23). All other prayers and petitions are useless, with no help forthcoming whatsoever from these other sources, and because to do otherwise is unscriptural.

The phrase, *"Saying, Send her away; for she crieth after us,"* probably would have been better translated in another manner, inasmuch as the true meaning is here obscured. It should have been translated, *"Grant her request; for she crieth after us."*

It seems they were perturbed due to her petition, and a loud petition at that. In other words, she would not stop her *"crying,"* and neither should we!

Every evidence is that the Disciples grew impatient with her. To be frank, and sadly so, most of the hindrance of our present petitions, and especially if the answer is not forthcoming immediately, comes directly from the Saints of God, even as the closest companions of Christ, His Disciples.

As I have mentioned elsewhere in these Volumes, since October of 1991, this Ministry has been engaged in two prayer meetings a day, with the exception of Saturday morning and service nights. We are doing this because I feel that the Lord told me to do it, and, to be sure, it has been the greatest thing that has ever happened to me personally, or this Ministry. And yet, the encouragement from those outside of our own immediate Church has been almost nonexistent. Actually, and if the Truth were fully known, it would be the very opposite.

Why?

The modern Church has been so led astray from the Word of God that, for the most part, it simply no longer believes.

James said, *"Is any among you afflicted? let him pray"* (James 5:13). Instead, the Church has turned to humanistic psychology as the answer for the ills of humanity. Consequently, and despite its statements to the contrary, the modern Church little believes in prayer. The evidence is obvious.

As well, the modern Faith Message (so-called) discourages intercession before the Lord, claiming that to do so admits something is wrong, and nothing can ever be wrong, they say, with the *"new creation man."* If something is wrong, they continue to say, it is because one's confession is erroneous, and if the right confession is once again enjoined, all the problems will disappear.

While a proper confession is certainly important, still, such error, and error it is, is taught nowhere in the Word of God.

First of all, James did not say that if one is afflicted, he should correct his confession, but, instead, that he should *"pray."* The word, *"afflicted,"* means to *"suffer trouble."*

NOTES

While the consecrated Believer will not all the time *"suffer trouble,"* still, there is much trouble in this world otherwise.

This *"Woman of Canaan,"* suffered great trouble in the affliction of her daughter, and was earnestly seeking help from Jesus. However, much more would be done for Christ, if the Church would cry to the Lord at this present time on behalf of individuals such as this *"Woman of Canaan."*

To be sure, the greatest thrust of these prayer meetings we have now been conducting for several years is in that direction. America desperately needs a Move of God, and that could go for any country in the world. I believe the Holy Spirit has shown me that if we will seek the Face of the Lord in deep intercession for lost humanity, bondages of sin and shame will be broken in the lives of those who are bound by sin and Satan. Actually, we have always seen great movings of the Holy Spirit in this capacity, but I believe what the Lord is about to give us is going to be even more pronounced than we have ever seen in the past. Actually, we are already beginning to see it. Bondages of darkness are being broken, bondages so severe as to have no hope other than Christ. To be sure, there is no hope other than Christ!

(24) "BUT HE ANSWERED AND SAID, I AM NOT SENT BUT UNTO THE LOST SHEEP OF THE HOUSE OF ISRAEL."

The phrase, *"But He answered and said,"* presents what seems like another rebuke to the woman. Her Faith would be sorely tested, which, no doubt, the Holy Spirit intended to do.

The phrase, *"I am not sent but unto the lost sheep of the house of Israel,"* proclaims His Mission, at least in His First Advent, as exclusively to the Jews, although it would ultimately fall out to the entirety of the world (Jn. 3:16).

As a *"Man,"* Christ was *"sent";* and was, therefore, a Servant. Hence the silence of verse 23.

As God, He had liberty of action, and, in Grace, He could respond to the need, which He ultimately would, which Faith presented to that Grace; otherwise He would have denied His Own character and nature as God.

Due to the Prophecies and the Plan of God, Jesus must first come to Israel. They were His people, or, at least, should have been! All the great Promises had been made to them.

Therefore, the Gospel should be offered to them first, before it was offered to the Gentiles.

The Plan of God was, and even from the very beginning, that Israel would accept their Messiah and then take His Glorious Message to the entirety of the world. This was God's intention from the very beginning as He told Abraham, *"In thee shall all families of the earth be blessed"* (Gen. 12:3). However, the Jews refused to give that *"Blessing"* to the Gentiles, or even accept it themselves.

The words, *"Lost sheep,"* and respecting Israel, are interesting indeed!

Very few, if any, Jews would even think of admitting they were *"lost."* They had by now come to the place that they believed simply being a Jew constituted their Salvation. In other words, their Salvation was their nationality, and their nationality was their Salvation.

It is the same presently with most modern Believers. Their association with a certain Church is their Salvation, and their Salvation is their association with a certain Church.

However, there is no Salvation in nationality, as there is no Salvation in association with particular Churches.

The words, *"Lost sheep,"* are interesting in another capacity as well!

The modern teaching of unconditional eternal security claims that, *"Once a sheep, always a sheep."* However, Christ here says the very opposite. He calls Israel, or at least the greater part of it, *"Lost sheep."*

It meant that they were supposed to be His people, and, in Truth, some of them had once been His people. But now, these *"sheep"* had refused to recognize Christ as the Messiah, or to accept Him as Saviour. Therefore, in their refusal to do this, they did not discontinue being *"sheep,"* but were, in fact, *"Lost sheep."*

As well, a modern Believer, although at one time in Faith, can cease to believe, and then becomes what one might call, *"a lost Believer."* These individuals were once in Faith, and it certainly was God's Will that they remain in Faith, but by their own volition they removed themselves, and if remaining in that state, as Israel of old, they were *"lost."*

As well, the word, *"lost,"* in the Greek is *"apollumi,"* and means *"to destroy fully,"* to *"perish."* Consequently, it does not mean a loss merely of fellowship, as some teach!

(25) "THEN CAME SHE AND WORSHIPPED HIM, SAYING, LORD, HELP ME."

The phrase, *"Then came she and worshipped Him,"* seems to indicate, according to Mark, that Jesus had left the street where this *"Woman of Canaan"* first approached Him, and now goes into a house, with her following. Once again, and even greatly so, her persistence is proclaimed. She has met two rebuffs already from Christ, or at least what probably seemed to her as such, but she was not deterred. Instead, she falls at His feet and worships Him. If one is to notice, she has graduated from petition to *"worship."* To be sure, this entire episode is remarkable. The lessons contained therein should stand as a beacon of hope for all who believe God and are determined to receive certain things from Him.

The phrase, *"Saying, Lord, help me,"* is actually a completely different petition than her first, when she addressed Christ as *"Thou Son of David."* However, even though this plea, *"Lord, help me,"* was better than her first one, still, she did not get the Blessing until she added: *"I am a dog."* This was the same ground the Publican took when he said, *"Be merciful to me a sinner"* (Lk. 18:13).

There are two things which stand out about this woman so dramatically, and which should be an example to us. They are as follows:

1. Faith: She would not stop her petition. She had a need and she knew that Jesus was the only One Who could meet that need, and she was determined to get what she had come for. We are constantly admonished in the Word of God to do the same (Mat. 21:21-22; Mk. 11:24; Lk. 11:8; Jn. 15:7).

2. Humility: This trait stands out so dramatically in the action of this lady. Despite the seeming rebuffs, she would fall at His feet and worship Him.

How many Believers presently hold a grudge against God because He did not do something they thought He should have done?

The Truth is, none of us are worthy of anything from God, and until we understand that, the granted petitions are going to be few and far between.

Preachers are very fond of talking about one's *"rights"* in Christ. Despite teaching to the contrary, and even despite our having received the great born-again experience and becoming a Child of God, still, we have no *"rights,"* only *"privileges."* Jesus said, *"For whosoever exalteth himself shall be abased; and he that humbleth himself shall be exalted"* (Lk. 14:11).

I wonder what the Lord must think of us demanding our *"rights?"*

Far too often, healing, prosperity, or a host of other things, are demanded as the *"rights"* of the Believer. No! The only One Who has *"rights"* is Christ. He Alone is *"Worthy, to receive glory, and honour, and power"* (Rev. 4:11). All of these things, even being a *"Joint heir with Christ,"* is but a *"privilege,"* but what a *"privilege"* it is!

(26) "BUT HE ANSWERED AND SAID, IT IS NOT MEET TO TAKE THE CHILDREN'S BREAD, AND TO CAST IT TO DOGS."

The phrase, *"But He answered and said,"* will now constitute the third rebuff to this woman (a rebuff, at least as it looked outwardly, but, in actuality, was the manner in which she could receive what she came for).

The phrase, *"It is not meet to take the children's bread, and to cast it to dogs,"* is strong indeed!

In effect, He was calling her a *"dog,"* in which she readily understood! As well, this word, *"dog,"* meant the lowest form of the canine variety, a *"cur dog."*

So, in effect, He was speaking of her and her people as being idol worshipers, and, in fact, some of the worst kind. In fact, and as stated, they were worshipers of Baal and Ashtaroth, which signaled the worst form of depravity and pollution.

The *"Children's bread,"* referred to Israel, who were recipients of the Promises and the Prophets, and, in effect, were the only ones in the world who had any knowledge of Jehovah. Consequently, they are called *"children."*

The word, *"Bread,"* speaks of the Word of God and all that it entailed.

In Truth, Jesus' Own people, the Jews, were in worse spiritual condition even than these heathen. They were worse simply because they had been given the Light, albeit rejected, while the Gentiles had been given precious little Light at all! That is the reason Jesus placed a curse upon Israel, and using the very area that this woman came from as an example, by saying, *"For if the mighty works, which were done in you* (Israel), *had been done in Tyre and Sidon, they would have repented long ago in sackcloth and ashes"* (Mat. 11:21).

So, if these (Tyre and Sidon) were *"dogs,"* what category must Israel fall into?

(27) "AND SHE SAID, TRUTH, LORD: YET THE DOGS EAT OF THE CRUMBS WHICH FALL FROM THEIR MASTERS' TABLE."

She has suffered three rebuffs but is not deterred by any:

1. *"He answered her not a word":* This concerns her first petition when she spoke of her daughter.

2. My Mission is only to Israel: This, in fact, excluded her, but she responded by *"worshiping Him."*

3. He called her a dog, which was the worst cut of all: By this time, most would have left, but not her. In fact, the answer that she gave Him is one of the greatest answers of Faith in recorded history.

The phrase, *"And she said, Truth, Lord,"* proclaims her acknowledging her position as undeserving and without legal Covenant rights to the children's bread.

In other words, she is saying that she knows she has no claim on the Lord. She realizes that she is but a heathen, Gentile, *"dog."* All of this is true and she admits to it.

What made this woman persist in her petition?

Of course, the ready answer would be that her daughter was in a terrible condition and desperately needed help. While all of that is true, still, there must have been something about Christ, and despite His response to her, that caused her to press on until the victory came.

To be sure, there was something about Christ! Even though His statements to her were negative, even extremely so, still, His entire manner and personality was one of pure love. This must have encouraged her to press forward.

This should be a lesson to us that even though the situation may be critical, with even our wrong or sin most terrible, which demands judgment, still, to any and all who come to Him, they will find Him always to be loving, kind, considerate, compassionate, longsuffering and quick to forgive.

The phrase, *"Yet the dogs eat of the crumbs which fall from their masters' table,"* in effect, turns the Words of Christ back to Himself. She uses His Own Words as a means in which to receive healing and deliverance for her daughter, which in no way would abrogate His Mission to Israel, but, at the same time, would grant her request.

She, in effect, is saying, *"The Jews are the children, while we are the dogs, but, as dogs, we claim our portion, even if only crumbs."*

One can sense the Presence of the Lord even in the saying of these words. This lady is an example to us all, as the Holy Spirit intended her to be.

Most Believers (and I do not believe I exaggerate) try to find ways as to why God will <u>not</u> do certain things. To be sure, that list is endless. However, this dear lady did the very opposite. She turned every negative into a positive; every darkness into a light; every no into a yes! And what she was doing was totally Scriptural. Paul would later say, *"For all the Promises of God in Him are Yea, and in Him Amen, unto the Glory of God by us"* (II Cor. 1:20).

(28) "THEN JESUS ANSWERED AND SAID UNTO HER, O WOMAN, GREAT IS THY FAITH: BE IT UNTO THEE EVEN AS THOU WILT. AND HER DAUGHTER WAS MADE WHOLE FROM THAT VERY HOUR."

The phrase, *"Then Jesus answered and said unto her,"* is emphasized by the word, *"Then!"*

All the time the Holy Spirit has been drawing her to this place, and now she will receive what she has come for.

Did Jesus change His mind?

No! He wanted her to have her petition all along, but had to bring her to the place to where she could receive it.

It was true that these other situations were hurdles that had to be overcome; however, Faith can overcome any and every hurdle, as Jesus now proclaims.

The moral of the story, and the lesson the Holy Spirit is teaching, is the lesson of Faith. As well, it is the type of Faith that will not be denied.

The phrase, *"O woman, great is thy Faith,"* proclaims His answer to her persistence. As well, what she had was *"great Faith."* Only two people are spoken of as having *"great Faith."* The first was the Gentile Centurion who came for the healing of his servant (Mat. 8:5-10), and now this Gentile woman. What a rebuke to Israel!

The phrase, *"Be it unto thee even as thou wilt,"* proclaims, as is obvious, her getting exactly what she wanted. What a lesson for all others!

While it is true that the Lord will definitely give to the believing Saint that which they want or desire, still, what we want or desire must be in line with what the Holy Spirit wants as well! The following may seem negative; however, I feel in light of the times, what will be said is necessary.

Since the 1970's, this idea of getting what we want has been taken to excess. Scores of Believers, and thinking they automatically know the Will of God in all things, have begun to ask for all type of things, even foolish things, which shows a terrible spiritual immaturity.

If Believers sincerely and truly want the Will of God in their lives and are constantly seeking that Will, they will, as well, pray in the Will of God. If the Holy Spirit is helping us pray, which He certainly will, at least if we are striving constantly for God's Will, we will never pray for anything that is not desired for us by the Heavenly Father (Rom. 8:26-27).

Many have taken various Scriptures in the Word of God, such as Matthew 21:21-22; Mark 11:24; John 14:14; 15:7, etc., and have attempted to apply these Passages to any and all things, claiming that they portray the Will of God in these matters, and if we do not receive whatever we want, whatever that is, it shows a lack of Faith on our part. Such is presumption!

While it is true that the Word of God means exactly what it says, still, these Promises are meant to carry out His Will and not our will. Even in Scriptures such as Mark 11:24, our will is supposed to be His Will, and we are to desire nothing that He does not desire. If we sincerely want the Will of God, that is exactly what we will want — His Will!

The most dangerous thing a Christian can do is to attempt to use the Word of God against God, as millions have attempted to do!

It is perfectly permissible, and even encouraged, for us to take God's Word and apply it to our situation exactly as this *"Woman of Canaan"* did, still, it must be in the Will of God exactly as the deliverance of this woman's daughter was.

Of course, the Will of God is the Word of God; however, He will not allow His Word to be used against Himself.

As an example, all of these Faith Scriptures we have just noted, could definitely apply to the acquiring of great wealth. In fact, the major thrust of a large segment of the Charismatic community has been exactly this, to acquire riches. However, what does the Bible say?

Paul said, *"But Godliness with contentment is great gain.*

"For we brought nothing into this world, and it is certain we can carry nothing out.

"And having food and raiment let us be therewith content.

"But they that will be rich fall into temptation and a snare, and into many foolish and hurtful lusts, which drown men in destruction and perdition.

"For the love of money is the root of all evil: which while some coveted after, they have erred from the faith, and pierced themselves through with many sorrows."

Then Paul said, *"But thou, O man of God, flee these things; and follow after Righteousness, Godliness, Faith, Love, Patience, Meekness"* (I Tim. 6:6-11).

In Truth, Jesus was the epitome of the Will of God. His actions portrayed God's Will, as well as His Messages. Everything He did was totally in the Will of God. In this, several things become obvious.

First of all, He healed everyone who came to Him, irrespective of their spiritual condition, etc. Therefore, from this example, we must assume that it is always God's Will to heal the sick. However, all of us know that oftentimes, even good Christians fail to receive healing, even though they earnestly petition the Lord. Even Paul said, *"But Trophimus have I left at Miletum sick"* (II Tim. 4:20).

I think all would have to assume that Paul had great Faith, even with many great miracles performed in his Ministry, but, still, at times individuals were not healed, as here recorded.

Of course, the question must be asked that if it is always the Will of God to heal the sick, even as Christ portrayed, why aren't they always healed?

I suppose that question has been asked by every Faith-filled Believer since the time of Christ.

I personally believe that the only answer is, and as I have already commented on, that no Believer can come up to the status of Christ in their Faith or life. While it is true that all sincere Believers truly strive to be like Christ, still, at the same time, all of us fall woefully short (Rom. 3:23).

At the same time, while the Lord desires to bless His people, and, in Truth, constantly blesses them, even financially, nevertheless, I think the Scripture is clear that it is not always His Will that all Christians be rich.

The phrase, *"And her daughter was made whole from that very hour,"* proclaims this woman receiving exactly what she asked for. Mark portrayed Christ, saying, *"For this saying go thy way; the devil is gone out of thy daughter"* (Mk. 7:29). Consequently, this woman's diagnosis of her daughter's condition was exactly right!

Along with all the other many valuable lessons taught us in this portrayal, as well, the tremendous lesson of intercession on behalf of another, as this Mother, should not be lost upon us. To be sure, most, if not all, who come to the Lord do so simply because someone, as this woman, interceded before the Lord for them. Regrettably, most of the energy of the Church in the last few years has been spent on trying to get *"rich"* instead of this all-important task. Satan has successfully appealed to the covetousness in the hearts and lives of many, and successfully drawn them away from that which is all-important, the Salvation of souls.

(29) "AND JESUS DEPARTED FROM THENCE, AND CAME NIGH UNTO THE SEA OF GALILEE; AND WENT UP INTO A MOUNTAIN, AND SAT DOWN THERE."

The phrase, *"And Jesus departed from thence,"* refers to Him leaving the border of Israel, and coming to the East side of the Sea of Galilee. We learn from Mark that Jesus came to the cities of Decapolis, which were located on the eastern side.

The phrase, *"And came nigh unto the Sea of Galilee,"* refers to a hill near this body of water. It was probably near Bethsaida.

The phrase, *"And went up into a mountain, and sat down there,"* indicates that Jesus had come to this place evidently to rest. However, such was not to be!

(30) "AND GREAT MULTITUDES CAME UNTO HIM, HAVING WITH THEM THOSE THAT WERE LAME, BLIND, DUMB, MAIMED, AND MANY OTHERS, AND CAST THEM DOWN AT JESUS' FEET; AND HE HEALED THEM:"

The phrase, *"And great multitudes came unto Him,"* could well have represented several thousand people. This was to be the greatest day of their lives. As well, it is the high point, and by far, for any and all who come to Jesus. There is no life like a life lived for Him. There is no joy like that with which He fills the soul.

The phrase, *"Having with them those that were lame, blind, dumb, maimed, and many others,"* proclaims about every type of physical malady known to man. As well, what is said physically can also be said spiritually for any and all!

It is interesting that the word, *"maimed,"* is used, in that it means one who is crippled, but also one who has been deprived of a limb, such as the loss of an arm or a leg, etc.

There is no passage in the four Gospels that specifically states that Jesus replaced missing limbs, with the exception of the servant's ear which was cut off by Simon Peter in the Garden of Gethsemane (Lk. 22:50-51; Jn. 18:10). In this incident, Jesus, no doubt, had the severed ear replaced on the servant's head where He healed it. However, He could easily have replaced missing limbs even though they had long since been gone, for such was certainly within the realm of His Power.

The phrase, *"And cast them down at Jesus' feet,"* denotes scores, possibly many hundreds, attempting to get to Christ, and even throwing themselves at His feet. For many of them, their situation was desperate, therefore they used desperate measures!

The phrase, *"And He healed them,"* implies that He *"healed them all."*

There is no record in the Word of God of anyone who came to Christ being turned away. Neither does He turn anyone away today, and in fact never has.

(31) "INSOMUCH THAT THE MULTITUDE WONDERED, WHEN THEY SAW THE DUMB TO SPEAK, THE MAIMED TO BE WHOLE, THE LAME TO WALK, AND THE BLIND TO SEE: AND, THEY GLORIFIED THE GOD OF ISRAEL."

The phrase, *"Insomuch that the multitude wondered,"* means they were stricken with astonishment when they saw the tremendous miracles. The attitude was one of tremendous joy, coupled with astonishment, at what was happening before their very eyes.

The phrase, *"When they saw,"* means that they looked intently on what was happening.

Before their very eyes, they watched the blind led to Him, and then in a moment's time the man or woman formerly blind no doubt was shouting, *"I can see, I can see!"*

As well, the cripples were led to Him, and then in a moment's time the crippled leg was made every whit whole, and before the eyes of all who stood nearby. No doubt, there was every type of miracle performed that could be imagined.

Inasmuch as the Holy Spirit through Matthew uses the word, *"lame,"* signifying cripples, along with the word, *"maimed,"* which, as we have stated, could signify a missing limb or finger, etc., could mean that missing limbs were instantly replaced, which no doubt happened, and which happened before the very eyes of the onlookers.

The phrase, *"And, they glorified the God of Israel,"* proclaims the wave of glory and blessing that must have swept that crowd. The Power of God must have been so real at this time that every single individual witnessed and experienced it. Truly, Heaven had come down to earth!

The implication is that they were not only glorifying God for the tremendous miracles performed, but, as well, for the tremendous moving of the Holy Spirit which took place in their midst through the Ministry of Christ.

There had never been another day like this in human history, except for the other times when Jesus did accordingly.

. . . And yet, the Religious Leaders of Israel did not at all glorify God at these wonderful happenings, but, instead, accused Christ of working in league with Satan (12:24). There is no darkness like religious darkness!

This which mankind experienced that glorious day of so long ago, it will once again experience at the Second Coming of Christ. Then the multitudes will come to Him exactly as they did at His First Advent, and, once again, this scene will repeat itself, except on a worldwide basis. Then, thankfully, Israel will not reject Christ, but will accept Him. The world will then know a time of blessing and prosperity it has never known before in all of its history.

As the multitude that day *"Glorified the God of Israel,"* then the entirety of the world will *"Glorify the God of Israel."*

(32) "THEN JESUS CALLED HIS DISCIPLES UNTO HIM, AND SAID, I HAVE

COMPASSION ON THE MULTITUDE, BE-CAUSE THEY CONTINUE WITH ME NOW THREE DAYS, AND HAVE NOTHING TO EAT: AND I WILL NOT SEND THEM AWAY FASTING, LEST THEY FAINT IN THE WAY."

The phrase, *"Then Jesus called His Disciples unto Him,"* seemingly proclaims a private session between them and Him. The intent of the phrase by the Holy Spirit is that it shall be an example to all those who have been called into Ministry. Of course, whatever the Disciples were doing, which no doubt concerned itself with the vast multitude, they dropped immediately and came to Christ.

The lesson should not be lost on those who have been specifically called. In Truth, He calls constantly for private consultation with those on whom He has laid His Hand. The problem is many do not hear, and then oftentimes those who do hear refuse to come.

To be sure, there is no way that God's servants can truly know His Heart unless there are constant times of prayer, communion and fellowship. That which He was about to do, which was to perform another great miracle of feeding some 10,000 to 12,000 people, He will now tell them.

It is His Will that those whom He has called be brought into His close confidence. As such, the Preacher of the Gospel should know what the Lord is about to do, because this He said, *"Surely the Lord God will do nothing, but He revealeth His secret unto His servants the Prophets"* (Amos 3:7).

Using my own Ministry as an example, in 1944, when I was only nine years old, the Lord spoke through me by Prophecy of the invention of the Atomic Bomb. At that time, it was being worked on by a handful of scientists, but the world would know nothing of it until the Summer of 1945. However, the Lord knew, and revealed it to me even though I was only a child. The Prophecy merely stated that a Bomb was being invented that would destroy an entire city.

In about 1980, the Lord told me to place the Telecast in other countries of the world, with it being translated into their languages. He told me at that time that a vast number of people would be saved. That is exactly what has happened, and is happening.

In 1985 (I believe it was), He spoke to me that the Gospel would go to every town, village, and

city, in what was then known as the Soviet Union. This was given to me while I was preaching in the city of Minsk, Russia. Of course, as everyone knows, in the last days of 1989, Communism fell, and about that time our Telecast was placed on TV One in Moscow, covering the entirety of the former Soviet Union. Therefore, the Prophecy was fulfilled in totality.

As well, in early 1992, the Lord, I believe, spoke to my heart that He was going to send a Move of the Holy Spirit that would touch this entire world. To be sure, I believe it will come to pass, and exactly as He has said.

However, these things cannot be given to the Preacher of the Gospel, or anyone for that matter, unless there is a close walk with God and a close communion with Him.

To be sure, the entirety of the Ministry, and in every capacity, belongs to Christ. This is proclaimed in Luke 4:18-19. Consequently, every God-called Preacher must enter into the Ministry of Christ.

The Preacher (and all Believers for that matter) must hear, and thereby know what Jesus wants, and then carry it out by the Power of the Spirit.

The phrase, *"And said, I have compassion on the multitude,"* proclaims in this example the Heart of Christ for people. As well, this should be, and, in fact, must be, the feeling and composure of those who carry out the Work of Christ. Actually, this *"compassion"* is the first requirement. As Paul said, *"Though I speak with the tongues of men and of angels, and have not love, I am become as sounding brass, or a tinkling cymbal"* (I Cor. 13:1). To be sure, if we truly love, we will truly serve.

The phrase, *"Because they continue with Me now three days, and have nothing to eat,"* proclaims several things.

First of all, they who follow Jesus shall never lack. As well, and spiritually speaking, He demands that the people have something to *"eat,"* i.e., fed. Singularly, the nourishment is, and ever has been, the Word of God.

One can well understand that the people would not want to leave, especially considering the miracles which were taking place, as well as the great Moving of the Holy Spirit among them. Many of them having been there for *"three days,"* had literally made the ground their bed during the night, and had existed on what little food they had brought with them, which was probably precious little, if any! At any rate, they were so enamored with what was taking place that they could not, and, in fact, would not pull themselves away from these tremendous happenings, and no wonder!

As an aside, and spiritually speaking, these had been *"three days"* without food, with most people in most Churches having received precious little, if any, food, i.e., the Bible.

The phrase, *"And I will not send them away fasting, lest they faint in the way,"* proclaims the fact that most of these people had had very little, if anything, to eat in the last three days.

Once again, and speaking from a spiritual viewpoint, the majority of the Church world is *"fainting in the way,"* simply because they have not had the spiritual nourishment of the Word of God.

(33) "AND HIS DISCIPLES SAY UNTO HIM, WHENCE SHOULD WE HAVE SO MUCH BREAD IN THE WILDERNESS, AS TO FILL SO GREAT A MULTITUDE?"

The phrase, *"And His Disciples say unto Him,"* as proved by the following, proclaims doubt and unbelief.

Too often when we question the Lord as the Disciples here do, it is in unbelief instead of Faith.

The question, *"Whence should we have so much bread in the wilderness, as to fill so great a multitude?"*, proclaims a serious state of unbelief, which is remarkable, especially considering that just a short time before Jesus had fed more people than were here now with five loaves and two fishes.

Why were they this prone to doubt?

1. First of all, this was before the Advent of the Holy Spirit, Who would come into the hearts and lives of Believers, which changed things dramatically (Jn. 7:39).

The modern Church little knows or understands the Help and Power of the Holy Spirit, and for the simple reason that most do not even believe in Him, or if they claim to do so, only pay Him lip service. If one is to notice, after the Day of Pentecost, the Disciples took on a completely new complexion, spiritually speaking. Timid men became bold as lions, with doubt turning to Faith. This can be accredited to nothing else other than the Holy Spirit (Acts 2:4).

2. Even with those of us who hungrily desire

the infilling of the Holy Spirit, plus His ever-present leading and guidance, still, we are so prone, as the Disciples, to forget past deliverance in the face of present difficulty.

Even after seeing the great miracle of the Red Sea, which, up to that time, was at least one of the greatest miracles ever performed, nevertheless, Israel feared that they would perish of thirst in the wilderness. Even Moses could not understand how the Lord would be able to supply enough flesh to eat in the wilderness for this several million people (Ex. 16:8; Num. 11:21).

So, immediately on the heels of all of these miracles being performed by Christ, with even this very miracle of multiplying the loaves and the fishes having already been performed, the Disciples questioned Christ as to how such could be done!

Looking at the situation in the spiritual sense, which, no doubt, the Holy Spirit desires that we do, we must understand that this world is a wilderness also. Likewise, the only way it can be fed, speaking in the spiritual sense, is by the miracle-working Power of God. That which I am about to say will be contradicted by some, but I believe I have the Scriptural proof to back up the statement.

As will be obvious in the following Scriptures, there will be a few loaves and some fish. However, without the Power of God, those loaves and fish cannot even remotely think of feeding a fraction of this vast assemblage, much less the entirety of the multitude. This is the same as the Word of God without the Power of the Holy Spirit upon it.

I maintain that even though the Truth is preached, unless it is accompanied by the Power of the Holy Spirit, the great miracle of regeneration will not take place in the lives of men and women. There are too many Preachers, who, while preaching the Truth, have no power on what they preach. There must be an Anointing of the Holy Spirit to accompany that which is preached. This much is spoken in Luke 4:18, where Jesus said, *"The Spirit of the Lord is upon Me, because He hath anointed Me to preach the Gospel to the poor . . . ."*

This Passage in Luke tells us that it was not enough to just *"preach the Gospel,"* but it must be preached under the Anointing of the Holy Spirit.

However, *"The Anointing of the Holy Spirit which generates conviction in the hearts and lives of people, is as scarce as the proverbial hen's teeth."*

This is obvious in the serious lack of True Born-again experiences.

So, if the Anointing of the Holy Spirit is upon the *"bread,"* it will multiply to perform its intended task in this *"wilderness"* called the world.

(34) "AND JESUS SAITH UNTO THEM, HOW MANY LOAVES HAVE YE? AND THEY SAID, SEVEN, AND A FEW LITTLE FISHES."

The phrase, *"And Jesus saith unto them,"* constitutes the words that we desire to hear. That is the question of the hour, *"What is Jesus saying?"*

It little matters what others say, or even the entirety of Religious Denominations, only what Jesus says. To be sure, He speaks through His Word, and, as well, in Revelation Knowledge. However, that which is given to the true man of God will always, and without exception, coincide with the Written Word of God, and will never contradict it, add to it, or take away from it.

The question, *"How many loaves have ye?"*, proclaims, once again, Jesus using what is at hand.

Individuals are too often wanting other things, when, if we will allow the Blessings of God to come on that which we already have, that, coupled with those Blessings, will perform tremendous miracles.

As He asked this question of His Disciples so long ago, He is, no doubt, asking the same question of all of us!

If we have loaves, He can multiply them. If we have sickness, He can heal it! If we have sin, He can forgive it! If we have needs, and of any nature, He can meet those needs!

The multitudes had brought their sicknesses unto Him, now they will bring the few loaves and fish unto Him.

One can sense the Presence of God even as we contemplate Jesus in action. There is nothing He cannot do. But, tragically, too many Preachers are looking to a Seminary Graduate Degree to equip them to meet the needs of the people, when, in Truth, it will meet no needs whatsoever. The crying need is for Jesus to become a part and, actually, the whole of our Ministry, and even our very lives.

NOTES

The phrase, *"And they said, Seven, and a few little fishes,"* is not without great meaning.

Beautifully enough, it was five loaves and two fishes in the last miracle of multiplication, which constituted seven, and now the word, *"seven,"* is used again concerning the loaves.

It is obvious in the Word of God that *"seven"* is God's number, denoting fulfillment, completion, totality, and perfection. So, the work He will here perform will be a perfect work of: A. Preaching the Gospel to the poor; B. Healing the sick; and, C. Giving the multitudes physical food. What He did then, He will do now, for all who will believe (Josh. 6:4, 8, 13, 15; Rev. 1:4, 11-13, 16, 20; 2:1; 3:1; 4:5).

(35) "AND HE COMMANDED THE MULTITUDE TO SIT DOWN ON THE GROUND."

The phrase, *"And He commanded,"* is a strong statement referring to the necessity of that being done which He demanded.

The phrase, *"The multitude to sit down on the ground,"* constituted them being prepared to receive that which was about to happen.

Is it possible that some of these had been recipients of the previous miracle of the multiplication of the loaves and the fishes?

I think it was for certain that at least some were present who had also been present at that first miracle. If, in fact that did happen, no doubt they were whispering to the others, *"He's going to do it again!"*

We should always thank the Lord for the tremendous miracles He has performed at a previous time; however, the *"multitude"* present at this particular time on the stage of history must have their miracle as well!

What happened on the Day of Pentecost was wonderful indeed! As well, there have been many wonderful movings of the Holy Spirit from then until now. Nevertheless, as wonderful as those are, they will not suffice for our present needs, even as the prior multiplication of the loaves and the fishes would not suffice for this hungry crowd presently. Jesus must perform this miracle again. And so He did.

I believe this miracle performed twice is meant to convey this very Message unto us. If He did it before, He will do it again, if men will only believe! He is no different now than He was at the previous outpourings of the Holy Spirit.

Why, then, do we not receive as we should receive?

I think if we will become as desperate as this crowd, we too will receive. They remained there for some three days with very little sustenance, or none at all. They would not leave, and because their needs were great. To be sure, those needs were met.

Even after the needs were met, I have every confidence that the people still did not want to leave, but instead hung on to every word spoken by Christ. Had they left, the miracle would not have been performed.

I think we leave too quickly!

(36) "AND HE TOOK THE SEVEN LOAVES AND THE FISHES, AND GAVE THANKS, AND BRAKE THEM, AND GAVE TO HIS DISCIPLES, AND THE DISCIPLES TO THE MULTITUDE."

The phrase, *"And He took the seven loaves and the fishes,"* now commences the miracle. These loaves and fishes in the hands of others were no more than what they were. However, in His Hands the entire complexion changes, which is an understatement of gargantuan proportions.

Therefore, it doesn't really matter exactly what it is. If it is in His Hands . . . .

Men are continually trying to present some great thing to God. But, we must understand that there is nothing we can present to Him that He would think is great. That should be obvious. Whatever it is, and no matter how menial it may seem (as these seven loaves and few fish), when placed in His care it becomes a miracle. That is the secret!

The phrase, *"And gave thanks, and brake them, and gave to His Disciples,"* once again presents the order.

The giving of *"thanks"* is emphasized in both accounts, and constitutes an extremely important part of this scenario.

Do we properly thank the Lord for all that He has done for us?

To be sure, the thanksgiving sets the stage for the miracle.

As He began to *"brake"* the loaves, the action begins, even though only doubling what had previously been there.

If He broke the loaves in half, which He probably did, this would have meant fourteen pieces, plus an undetermined number of fish. If that is what happened, He could have given a piece to each of His twelve Disciples, with

two pieces left over. What He did with the two pieces, we are not told, that is, if the scenario unfolded in this manner.

The phrase, *"And the Disciples to the multitude,"* may have very well proclaimed the manner in which the miracle was carried out.

In this episode, and after *"thanks"* was offered, the *"breaking and giving"* seemed to be the pivot on which this miracle turned.

Quite possibly, and continuing with this method, each Disciple gave a piece of bread and a piece of fish to one of the individuals sitting down, and told them to break the pieces in half, give them to the person sitting beside them, and tell that person to break it as well, continuing in this mode.

Even though it is not possible to explain a miracle, still, this may have been the way it happened, with each piece miraculously growing as it was broken, which is unexplainable.

Once again, and as we have already stated in the previous Chapter, this scenario, as well, portrays the manner in which the Lord uses His Children.

1. *"He took":* This pertains to the person coming to Christ.

2. *"Gave thanks":* Or as the last scenario portrayed, *"He blessed."* Great blessing generally follows the new convert.

3. *"And brake* (break)*":* Not long after the Salvation experience, the Holy Spirit brings us to a place of *"breaking."* Most of the time, it is not a pleasant experience, with the individual at times wondering if there will be anything left.

The *"breaking"* is necessary, simply because of the tremendous amount of self-will resident even in the most consecrated Believer.

4. *"And gave":* Even though the blessings come after He takes us, still, we cannot be the blessing to others we should be until we are properly broken, with self-will eliminated. To give ourselves to others is of no benefit or consequence whatsoever. To give Christ to others is the secret of manifold blessing. However, this can only be done after we have been properly broken.

Regrettably, great segments of the modern Church world are attempting to remain in the *"blessing"* stage, which portrays spiritual immaturity and selfishness. We must be *"broken"* in order that we can be *"given."*

(37) "AND THEY DID ALL EAT, AND WERE FILLED: AND THEY TOOK UP OF THE BROKEN MEAT THAT WAS LEFT SEVEN BASKETS FULL."

The phrase, *"And they did all eat, and were filled,"* means they were all satisfied.

Only Christ can fill the hungry heart.

The tragedy is that in most Churches there is no spiritual food to *"eat,"* therefore, none are *"filled,"* i.e., satisfied.

The phrase, *"And they took up of the broken meat that was left seven baskets full,"* proclaims several truths.

1. It is only the broken bread, i.e., lives, which can be multiplied.

2. They had *"seven"* loaves of bread, besides the fish, and now they take up *"seven baskets,"* portraying the fact that the multiplication must have been enormous, especially considering that approximately 10,000 or more people had been fed.

3. The *"baskets"* here noted were very large, some of them even big enough to hold a man.

4. As the number, *"seven,"* represents perfection, consequently, it was a perfect Gospel that was given to these people, and it continues to be a perfect Gospel today.

In its perfection, the Gospel contains so much that it can never be exhausted irrespective of the number of people who partake. What is left over will even be far and away greater than what we already have. It is impossible to exhaust the Promises of God.

As an aside, *"twelve"* baskets of fragments were taken up regarding the previous miracle of multiplication. Twelve denotes government, and God's Government at that, which means perfect government.

The seven baskets of fragments taken up in this miracle, combined with the twelve baskets taken up in the previous miracle, denotes the perfect Gospel which will always come forth from God's perfect Government.

So, in the two, we have government (12) and perfection (7).

(38) "AND THEY THAT DID EAT WERE FOUR THOUSAND MEN, BESIDE WOMEN AND CHILDREN."

The number in the previous such miracle was *"five thousand"* beside women and children, with this *"four thousand"* constituting one thousand less.

The Holy Spirit, in being so careful to denote the number of *"men"* in each account, is, among other things, letting us know that it is the *"men"* who are supposed to take the spiritual leadership in the home. Regrettably, that is not always the case!

As well, some feel that the number *"five"* in the Bible denotes Grace, while the number *"four"* denotes wholeness, such as the fourfold Gospel, i.e., Salvation, Holy Spirit, Healing, and the Coming of the Lord.

(39) "AND HE SENT AWAY THE MULTITUDE, AND TOOK SHIP, AND CAME INTO THE COASTS OF MAGDALA."

The phrase, *"And He sent away the multitude,"* tells us of such, but only after they had been satisfied spiritually and physically. Only Christ can do such a thing.

Tragically, and far too often, the greater majority of the people are sent away from modern Ministries, but without having received any spiritual sustenance whatsoever.

The phrase, *"And took ship, and came into the coasts of Magdala,"* is actually across the Sea of Galilee to the western side. Magdala was a small town located about ten miles south of Capernaum. This is probably where Mary Magdalene lived, and with her deliverance from seven demons probably having taken place sometime before (Mk. 16:9).

CHAPTER 16

(1) "THE PHARISEES ALSO WITH THE SADDUCEES CAME, AND TEMPTING DESIRED HIM THAT HE WOULD SHEW THEM A SIGN FROM HEAVEN."

The phrase, *"The Pharisees also with the Sadducees came,"* proclaims the joining of these two groups who were normally antagonistic to each other.

The Pharisees would have been called the fundamentalists of their time. They professed to believe all the Bible which then consisted of Genesis through Malachi. They alone set the spiritual tone for Israel, and, sadly, it was a self-righteous, hypocritical tone, which caused Jesus to call it *"a wicked and adulterous generation."* For all of their claims of believing the Bible and of being so holy, they were, in fact, bitter enemies of Christ.

The *"Sadducees"* were another religious party in Israel who believed very little of the Word of God, and would have been called the modernists of their day. They held most of the high religious offices in Israel, which, in effect, were the civil offices as well! They, too, were enemies of Christ, but not nearly as rabid as the Pharisees.

As stated, the coming together of the two was unusual, and because they hated each other. However, they hated Christ more, and, therefore, their mutual hatred of Him overrode their animosity toward each other.

The Pharisees hated Christ because His Righteousness showed up their self-righteousness, and, as well, they were concerned that He would usurp their authority over the people.

The Sadducees were concerned that somehow His Ministry might, in some way, cause Rome to come down on their heads, which would jeopardize their religious/civil offices.

All of them were so far away from God, and despite their claims on God, that they could not see Who Christ actually was. They judged Him by their own wicked, adulterous hearts. Regrettably, organized religion, at least for the most part, functions in the same manner presently!

The phrase, *"And tempting desired Him that He would shew them a sign from Heaven,"* presents an absurd request, and especially considering that they had already made this same demand (12:38). Jesus had just fed 4,000 men beside the women and children with but seven loaves and a few fish; however, they would not accept this.

This demand was really a sarcastic slur against His Messiahship. The type of *"sign"* they demanded was not promised in the Word of God.

In Truth, Jesus fulfilled every sign as given by the Prophets.

1. He was born of the Virgin Mary as prophesied by Isaiah (Isa. 7:14).

2. He was born in Bethlehem as prophesied by Micah (Mic. 5:2).

3. He fulfilled Isaiah's Prophecies of the performing of healings and miracles (Isa. 61:1-2).

However, these signs were not good enough for them, even considering they contained the greatest Miracles the world had ever known in

NOTES

all of its history. In Truth, nothing He did could have satisfied them, and irrespective of how potent or how powerful it would have been.

In effect, the unbelief then parallels the present.

The present *"signs"* are graphic indeed, but largely unnoticed and therefore unheeded by the world and the Church. They are as follows:

1. During the time of Christ religion abounded, possibly more so than ever, with the people talking constantly about God, but with precious few actually knowing Him. It is almost identical at the present.

Church attendance presently is at an all-time high. Man is more religious than possibly he has ever been before. Gigantic crowds are gathering in respect to particular religious fads. However, the ingredient that Jesus demanded is missing now as then.

Solid Bible Preaching under the Anointing of the Holy Spirit, with some small exception, is not a part of the present religious phenomenon. Neither was it in Jesus' day. Consequently, when John the Baptist and Christ came *"preaching,"* it was an oddity to the people.

Presently, and despite the large religious overtones, there is almost no call to Repentance. Actually, a great part of the Pentecostal and Charismatic Church world no longer even believes in Repentance, if, in fact, they ever did. It is called an Old Testament Doctrine that has no relativity to the New Testament. So, the *"signs"* are similar.

2. The *"sign"* of the vast increase in knowledge, and as Daniel prophesied concerning the last days, is being fulfilled to the letter (Dan. 12:4).

Up until the turn of the century, with some few exceptions (the steam engine, telegraph, etc.), man pretty much lived, existed, traveled, etc., as he did two or three thousand years ago. And then about the turn of the century, *"knowledge"* exploded, changing the world dramatically.

When one considers that it was only about 80 years from the Civil War to World War II, then one realizes how fast everything has changed. The Civil War was fought very little differently than wars of a thousand years earlier. And yet, in just 80 years an advancement of knowledge took place that literally beggars description.

3. The outpouring of the Holy Spirit, itself,

NOTES

in these last days is one of the greatest *"signs"* of all! It, too, is in fulfillment of Joel's Prophecies, and as repeated by Simon Peter on the Day of Pentecost, *"And it shall come to pass in the last days, saith God, I will pour out of My Spirit upon all flesh"* (Acts 2:17).

Admittedly, these *"last days"* pertain to the entirety of this last 2,000 years; however, the following Scriptures in the Second Chapter of Acts let us know that the present outpouring is in fulfillment of Joel's *"latter rain"* (Joel 2:23). This, the outpouring of the Holy Spirit, is the greatest *"sign"* of all!

4. Paul prophesied that a *"falling away"* would come in the last days, which we are already seeing (II Thess. 2:3). The Word, *"falling away,"* means *"a defection from Truth,"* which characterizes this hour!

The modern Church has become so psychologized that it little thinks anymore in Biblical terms, but rather in psychological terms. People are no longer delivered, they are rehabilitated. There are no more sinners, only victims.

People no longer need to pray through, but, instead, they need therapy. Preaching is no more, while counseling is in. Salvation is just another religious experience to be woven into the psychological fabric.

It is no longer Sanctification, but, instead, self-esteem. As well, the Baptism in the Holy Spirit with the evidence of speaking with other tongues, is little referred to anymore, but is simply called glossolalia. As well, it is no longer repentance, but rather referral.

. . . A falling away? Yes! And greater than most realize.

Some scholars believe this Chapter closes the first half of Matthew's Gospel. Its subject is: The King presented. The second half has as its subject: The King rejected.

Three forms of unbelief recorded in this Chapter characteristically close this first section of the Book.

The first form of unbelief demanded a sign from Heaven (vss. 1-4), i.e., the hostility of the natural heart.

The second form revealed blindness and inattention to Divine testimony by Miracles to the Person and Nature of Christ (vss. 5-12), i.e., the stupidity of the natural heart.

The third form manifested itself in popular indifference, indolence, or mere curiosity respecting the Messiah Himself (vss. 13 and 14), i.e., the frivolity of the natural heart.

Thus, here, as everywhere, the entry of the Lord Jesus reveals and tests the natural heart and its thoughts and professions. Where there is no sense of sin and need, the heart is uninterested; but when that need is felt, there can be no rest apart from Christ. Curiosity excites a carnal interest, but Faith has wants and only finds them satisfied in the Person and Work of Him Who is the Lamb of God and Son of God. (Williams)

(2) "HE ANSWERED AND SAID UNTO THEM, WHEN IT IS EVENING, YE SAY, IT WILL BE FAIR WEATHER: FOR THE SKY IS RED."

The phrase, *"He answered and said unto them,"* will constitute an extremely strong statement. According to 12:24-32, the Pharisees and Scribes, and possibly the Sadducees, had already blasphemed the Holy Spirit. Consequently, there was no more hope for them, as becomes more and more obvious, even as more and more information is revealed. Consequently, Jesus responds accordingly!

The phrase, *"When it is evening, ye say, It will be fair weather: for the sky is red,"* draws attention to the heavens exactly as they have demanded.

The idea of His Statement is that they had spent much time and effort learning to read the signs of the heavens respecting the weather, but almost no time at all, and despite their claims to the contrary, of learning and understanding the *"signs"* of the Word of God. They knew a lot about a lot of things, but not about that which really mattered, the Word of God.

Is it any different presently?

Many Bible Colleges presently do not even offer a degree in Bible. That is the same as a Law School not offering a degree in Law.

Such a school would be laughed out of existence, but, yet, the Word of God is so frowned upon that anything that demeans it is applauded. Therefore, a Bible College can offer degrees in everything except the Bible, and precious few think anything of it.

Theology, which is the study of God and His Word, was once the queen of the sciences in almost all universities in the land. Today, it holds no credence at all, with psychology having taken its place.

Concerning the secular schools, that is bad enough; however, when one considers that the same is true for most of the Seminaries and Bible Colleges as well, then it becomes a tragedy.

(3) "AND IN THE MORNING, IT WILL BE FOUL WEATHER TO DAY: FOR THE SKY IS RED AND LOWERING. O YE HYPOCRITES, YE CAN DISCERN THE FACE OF THE SKY; BUT CAN YE NOT DISCERN THE SIGNS OF THE TIMES?"

The phrase, *"And in the morning, it will be foul weather to day: for the sky is red and lowering,"* was meant to call their attention to far more than the weather. His statement concerned more than weather prognostications.

When He used the term, *"It will be foul weather to day,"* He was, as well, speaking of what was coming upon Israel. In the Greek, it actually means, *"Today a storm!"*

Spiritually, with Israel's rejection of Christ as their Saviour and Messiah, the storm clouds were already gathering. They would explode in all their fury in 70 A.D., when Titus' tenth legion laid siege to Jerusalem, with over 1,000,000 Jews slaughtered in that carnage, and hundreds of thousands of others sold as slaves all over the world.

The phrase, *"O ye hypocrites,"* refers to the Pharisees and Sadducees acting as if they were really seeking the Messiah, but really desiring Him not at all.

The question, *"Ye can discern the face of the sky; but can ye not discern the signs of the times?",* actually means that they were determined not to recognize Him, and irrespective of how many signs were brought forth.

The phrase, *"The signs of the times,"* actually said, *"The great sign of the great time."* It was the time foretold by Daniel 9:25, and Christ Himself was the Sign.

Christ's statement is twofold.

1. Natural intelligence can observe and study natural phenomena. Only Spirit revelation intelligence can recognize spiritual facts recorded in the Bible. Hence the necessity of a spiritual birth in order to *"see"* the Kingdom of God.

For instance, the world is fastly heading toward the advent of the man of sin, i.e., the Antichrist, which will culminate in Armageddon. The political pundits of this hour have absolutely no knowledge of these soon-to-come events, simply because their sense knowledge cannot understand the Word of God which requires Spirit knowledge (I Cor. 2:14). Beside that, they would not believe it even if they did understand it!

2. If, in fact, these Pharisees and Sadducees had blasphemed the Holy Spirit, which every evidence says they had, it would have been impossible for them to *"see"* or *"believe,"* simply because they had no desire to do so (13:15).

It is remarkable, they were surrounded by *"signs of the times,"* in that Christ was performing miracles such as the world had never seen before, and, as well, speaking as no man ever spoke, but, still, they did not *"see"* because they refused to *"see,"* which meant they had made a conscious choice to reject God and His Son, and irrespective of how much they claimed otherwise. Consequently, a judicial blindness had settled upon them, a blindness which would only deepen as it went toward the dark night of eternity.

The axiom is, and was, the blind get blinder, and those who see, see more!

(4) "A WICKED AND ADULTEROUS GENERATION SEEKETH AFTER A SIGN; AND THERE SHALL NO SIGN BE GIVEN UNTO IT, BUT THE SIGN OF THE PROPHET JONAS. AND HE LEFT THEM, AND DEPARTED."

The phrase, *"A wicked and adulterous generation seeketh after a sign,"* had already been spoken by Christ a short time earlier (12:39).

It is not vain repetition, but rather the proclamation of Truth which does not change.

Was that generation the most wicked of all?

I think one would have to say it was. The generation which saw Jerusalem destroyed some 600 years earlier, and despite the prophesying of Jeremiah, nevertheless, was restored some 70 years later. This generation of which Christ speaks, would be destroyed by Titus, and would not be restored.

Other than John the Baptist, who immediately preceded Christ, Israel had not heard the voice of a Prophet since Malachi, which was a period of some 400 years. Without the prophetic voice, the nation had drifted ever deeper into sin and unbelief. However, the type of sin and unbelief it drifted into, was the most lethal of all! It was the sin of self-righteousness and unbelief of the Word of God, which was proved by their twisting and turning it to their own warped notions.

NOTES

In fact, very few would have labeled Israel's present spiritual posture as *"sin,"* but *"sin"* it was, and labeled by Christ as *"wicked and adulterous."* And yet, they would have thought of themselves as the very opposite.

I wonder what Christ is saying of this Church generation that closes out the 20th Century?

The phrase, *"And there shall no sign be given unto it, but the sign of the Prophet Jonas,"* concerns the Death, Burial, and Resurrection of Christ, of which Jonah was a type, in his being swallowed by the whale and then delivered from this certain death.

As Jesus spoke these words, the Pharisees and Sadducees would not have known in the least as to what He was speaking. They did not even believe His Miracles were from God, much less that He would die and be raised from the dead!

Of course, that *"sign,"* His being raised from the dead, would be the greatest sign that humanity would ever know in all of its history. But, still, they would not believe that either!

The phrase, *"And He left them, and departed,"* proclaims Him saying no more to them. They had refused the Message, therefore no more would be given.

Him departing meant exactly what it said, in that there is no record that He ever taught publicly or worked miracles again at this place.

(5) "AND WHEN HIS DISCIPLES WERE COME TO THE OTHER SIDE, THEY HAD FORGOTTEN TO TAKE BREAD."

As Matthew writes, he places Jesus now on the northeastern shore of the Sea of Galilee. Having been on the western shore, actually close to Magdala, the Master gives instructions to go to the *"other side."* The short trip should have taken an hour or two, or maybe a little longer.

The area to which they had gone was not nearly as thickly populated as the western shore, hence the difficulty in obtaining food, which occasioned the phrase given by Matthew, *"They had forgotten to take bread."*

Exactly what Christ did in this area is not specifically stated, except some of His deepest and most comprehensive teaching was offered at this time. Actually, to begin these tremendous lessons, the Lord will use the bread episode as a springboard for that which He will teach.

(6) "THEN JESUS SAID UNTO THEM, TAKE HEED AND BEWARE OF THE

LEAVEN OF THE PHARISEES AND OF THE SADDUCEES."

The phrase, *"Then Jesus said unto them,"* commences this teaching, and, contrary to popular thought, is in the negative sense.

The phrase, *"Take heed and beware of the leaven of the Pharisees and of the Sadducees,"* is meant to point out the corrupt teaching of these groups. Jesus is now pointing out the *"tares"* as He had given in the Parable of the *"Tares and Wheat"* (Mat. 13:24-30). Jesus will succinctly point it out, but that is as far as He would go. To be sure, this method of operation is to be the example for all to follow.

The word, *"leaven,"* was meant to refer to their corrupt teaching. It penetrated all ranks and classes of society in Israel. Inasmuch as it was corrupt, it pulled astray almost the entirety of the nation. False doctrine has no less effect today!

Most of the time, and as here, false doctrine has a kernel of Truth in it, which makes it plausible to the hearer, and, thereby acceptable. As well, it generally appeals to some base instinct in man, which is generally made to appear very religious. However, anything that is not exactly according to the Word of God, is labeled by Christ as *"leaven."*

Paul would later say, *"A little leaven leaveneth the whole lump"* (Gal. 5:9). He also said, *"Purge out therefore the old leaven, that ye may be a new lump, as ye are unleavened"* (I Cor. 5:7).

He is meaning that the Corinthians (and all) should get the false doctrine out which had attached itself to the True Word of God.

To point out the *"leaven"* then was not popular, and is not popular now. To be sure, it will bring the wrath of the modern Pharisees and Sadducees upon one's head, exactly as it did at the time of Christ. Regrettably, most Preachers are not willing to undergo such opposition, and, therefore, steer another course.

The main reason that many fall prey to this *"leaven,"* is because of a lack of knowledge of the Word of God. For instance, most Catholics have no knowledge whatsoever of the Bible. Even the Priests, at least for the most part, are Scriptural illiterates. Consequently, they believe whatever they are told.

Sadly, most Protestants are little better!

The other night in our own Church, Family Worship Center in Baton Rouge, Louisiana, I asked if there was anyone in the congregation who had not read the Bible completely through at least one time? To my shock and surprise, several people raised their hands, and despite our constant admonishment for them to study the Word of God.

For a Christian, and especially having lived for God for quite some time, to have not read the Bible completely through at least once, is, to be sure, unthinkable! In Truth, the Bible should be read through at least once a year, if not more. As well, good, sound, Bible-study aids should be obtained to help us understand the Word of God even more. When one considers that the Bible is the only Revealed Truth in the world today, and, in fact, ever has been, its contents, above all, should be mastered. But, yet, and sadly, it is an unread Book in many Christian circles. The best defense against error is the Truth! However, Truth unknown is Truth of no value.

And then, again, many Christians do not live close enough to the Lord that the Holy Spirit can make the Word of God real to their hearts and lives. So, too oftentimes what they read, they little understand. Consequently, they are perfect targets for the *"leaven of false doctrine."*

(7) "AND THEY REASONED AMONG THEMSELVES, SAYING, IT IS BECAUSE WE HAVE TAKEN NO BREAD."

The phrase, *"And they reasoned among themselves,"* shows an appalling lack of Scriptural and Spiritual knowledge. It is appalling that they did not understand what He was talking about, even though it seemed so very clear.

Why were they so lacking in understanding?

First of all, allow us to say that these same men after the Day of Pentecost, which occasioned the Coming of the Holy Spirit, were totally changed by the Power of God, and became Scriptural and Spiritual giants. So much so, in fact, that some of them, as Matthew, would write these great accounts of the Ministry of Christ, or Epistles as did John and Peter.

As well, that they would write such unflattering things about themselves, is further proof of the veracity and reliability of the Gospel.

Once again we learn from these Passages, although in an indirect manner, of the tremendous power, authority, and strength or help provided by the Holy Spirit. Consequently, it is sad and exceedingly so, at how little regard the modern Church gives to the Holy Spirit.

NOTES

To be certain, even though they were seriously lacking in Scripture and Spiritual knowledge, and, at that time, seemed hardly to progress at all, still, these Disciples being with Christ was of a value of such magnitude that it defies description. We learn from this that it is the Holy Spirit Who imparts the understanding of the Word and the Ways of God to the Believer (Jn. 16:7-15).

In this account as given by John, Jesus would say, *"It is expedient for you that I go away: for if I go not away, the Comforter* (Holy Spirit) *will not come unto you; but if I depart, I will send Him unto you"* (Jn. 16:7).

He was here extolling the tremendous value of the Holy Spirit as He helps the Believer understand the Word of God, among other things.

It was not that Jesus could not explain it, which He graphically did, and as is outlined in these Passages, but that the hearers, and in this case, the Disciples, did not have the capacity to understand it. The Holy Spirit coming to dwell within the hearts and lives of Believers is what made the great difference, even in the Disciples. This task, Jesus did not do, and, in Truth, was not meant to do, as this was the office work of the Holy Spirit. And yet, in essence, He would abide in the heart and life of the Believer through the agency of the Holy Spirit.

Actually, the Disciples could not properly understand what Christ was saying, and irrespective as to how much He explained it, until the Advent of the Holy Spirit. Consequently, His teaching and explanation to them, was given in order that the Seed of the Word of God might be planted, and that it would be preserved, which it was! Then, upon the Advent of the Holy Spirit, this teaching became crystal clear to them.

This shows us that the mind of man is so perverted by the Fall that it is impossible, even for converted man, to understand the Word of God without the agency of the Holy Spirit.

To answer the question: They could not understand the things being said by Christ because they did not, at this time, have the help of the Holy Spirit as they would later (Acts 2:4). Jesus would later say, *("But this spake He of the Spirit, which they that believe on Him should receive: for the Holy Ghost was not yet given; because that Jesus was not yet glorified")* (Jn. 7:39).

The phrase, *"Saying, It is because we have taken no bread,"* portrays the minds of the Disciples in another direction entirely. They were thinking of physical bread which was to be eaten, and not of the recent exchange between Christ and the Pharisees and Sadducees. They totally misunderstood what He was saying.

(8) "WHICH WHEN JESUS PERCEIVED, HE SAID UNTO THEM, O YE OF LITTLE FAITH, WHY REASON YE AMONG YOURSELVES, BECAUSE YE HAVE BROUGHT NO BREAD?"

The phrase, *"Which when Jesus perceived,"* proclaims the fact that He probably did not overhear them, but that the Holy Spirit told Him what they were *"reasoning."*

Every indication is that they were ashamed that they did not understand what He was saying, and were, consequently, whispering among themselves.

The phrase, *"He said unto them, O ye of little Faith,"* is meant to teach them a lesson. It should be a lesson to us as well!

This Passage proclaims the Truth, that every Miracle He performed was meant to not only meet the need of the moment, whatever that need was, but, as well, to teach Faith in God. To be sure, His deeds constituted the Word in action, because *"Faith cometh by hearing, and hearing by the Word of God"* (Rom. 10:17).

As well, all the things He does for us are meant to increase our Faith, which, again, is His Word in action in our lives.

The point I am attempting to make is that Faith cannot be tendered apart from the Word of God. However, the things He does for us is His Word in action in our lives.

Despite the tremendous Miracles performed by Christ, still, the only thing that could be said at this time of the Disciples and concerning Faith, was that they had little of this precious commodity.

What would He say of us, and, in fact, does say of us?

By contrast, He would say of the Gentile woman, *"Great is thy Faith"* (15:28).

This is remarkable, in view of the fact that this woman had no access to the Word of God, while Israel had total access. The difference is, she took advantage of the little *"crumb"* she had and, thus, saw tremendous things brought

about, while Israel little acted upon the great abundance of the Word that they had. It is not altogether as to how much we know, but how much we are rather acting on.

The question, *"Why reason ye among yourselves, because ye have brought no bread?"*, is meant to draw attention to their foolish reasoning. Consequently, He will teach His Disciples some things about false doctrine, as well as some things about Faith.

(9-10) DO YE NOT YET UNDERSTAND, NEITHER REMEMBER THE FIVE LOAVES OF THE FIVE THOUSAND, AND HOW MANY BASKETS YE TOOK UP?

"NEITHER THE SEVEN LOAVES OF THE FOUR THOUSAND, AND HOW MANY BASKETS YE TOOK UP?"

These two verses portray to us the fact that Christ's numerous Miracles were not wrought at random. Each was carefully designed by the Holy Spirit, which is evident in that the smallest detail such as numbers, baskets, loaves, etc., were carefully noted. If He noted it, we should do likewise.

The insensibility of the Disciples to the Lord's actions and to His teaching, is a humiliating proof of the darkness of man's heart to moral realities. They saw what He did, but they did not really know what He did. Of course, and as stated, that would change upon the Advent of the Holy Spirit.

The question, *"Do ye not yet understand...?"*, portrays, as stated, their insensitivity to the things of the Spirit.

The Mission of Christ was one, and, consequently, His mind and heart was on that constantly. That Mission was the Redemption of Man. Consequently, anything that hindered, such as the false doctrine of the Pharisees and Sadducees, loomed large in His sight. Actually, it was said of Him in the Psalms, *"Through Thy precepts I get understanding: therefore I hate every false way"* (Ps. 119:104). Consequently, He hated the false way of the Pharisees and Sadducees. To be sure, we, as guardians of the Truth, must do no less presently.

The part of the question, *"Neither remember...?"*, and concerning the number fed, with the number of baskets left over, proclaims the necessity of every Believer remembering all that Christ has done for us.

Why?

There are things in life which are certainly important, such as our family, etc. However, the single most important things in our lives are the things done for us by the Lord, with the most important being the time we were saved by the Blood of Jesus and Baptized in the Holy Spirit. Of course, there are many other things He does constantly, such as answers to prayer, healings, etc.

We should remember these things, recalling them from time to time, realizing that anything the Lord does is of extreme significance. As well, what He does is so profound that we seldom learn everything with each exercise. Sometimes years pass before we learn all that He is attempting to show us in things He does for us. Consequently, we should *"remember!"*

Sadly, too many Christians remember everything but those things. They know the batting averages of particular ball players, but very little of what the Lord has done. Such is appalling!

The inference by Christ is that if the Disciples had properly evaluated the Miracles performed, they would not be wondering as to where they were going to get bread to eat. What an insult to Christ! And yet, I wonder if our actions are any better.

(11) "HOW IS IT THAT YE DO NOT UNDERSTAND THAT I SPAKE IT NOT TO YOU CONCERNING BREAD, THAT YE SHOULD BEWARE OF THE LEAVEN OF THE PHARISEES AND OF THE SADDUCEES?"

The question, *"How is it that ye do not understand that I spake it not to you concerning bread . . . ?"*, is meant to censure their want of spiritual discernment. Consequently, the fault of them not understanding, as here implied by Christ, was a moral fault.

To be sure, most would not understand the word, *"moral,"* being used in this circumstance.

However, the word, *"moral,"* has to do with relating to principles of right and wrong behavior. It speaks of one's conscience or ethical judgment. It acts on the mind, character, and will.

Consequently, the Disciples were at moral fault because their behavior toward what Christ was doing was somewhat cavalier. In other words, they were not taking it as seriously as they should have, which constituted a moral breach.

Tragically, this moral fault could be applied to most who call themselves Believers. We

simply do not take the Word of God or the Work of God as seriously as we should!

To be sure, and as stated, they would probably not understand until the Advent of the Holy Spirit. Still, the fact remains that they were not giving the attention and thought that such miracles, and, more particularly, the Person of Christ rightly deserved.

The question continues, *"That ye should be beware of the leaven of the Pharisees and of the Sadducees?"*, which caused them now to understand what He was speaking of.

It seems to suddenly dawn on them that He was not talking about *"bread"* as we think of bread, but rather something else entirely!

(12) "THEN UNDERSTOOD THEY HOW THAT HE BADE THEM NOT BEWARE OF THE LEAVEN OF BREAD, BUT OF THE DOCTRINE OF THE PHARISEES AND OF THE SADDUCEES."

The phrase, *"Then understood they how that He bade them not beware of the leaven of bread,"* as is obvious, proclaims them finally understanding. He was using symbolism, as He often did, which actually made the situation easier to understand, that is, if they had been thinking in the spiritual sense.

Regrettably, many if not most Believers are not spiritually minded, but, instead, the opposite, carnally minded.

Every Believer should have a spiritual mindset to where they see not just a few things in the spiritual sense, but, instead, all things.

In one sense of the word, this is what Paul was speaking of when he said, *"And be not conformed to this world: but be ye transformed by the renewing of your mind, that ye may prove what is that good, and acceptable, and perfect, Will of God"* (Rom. 12:2).

If one thinks constantly in the spiritual sense, in other words looking at a situation as the Spirit of God looks at it, then one will know the Will of God in any and all circumstances.

Paul also said, *"For to be carnally minded is death; but to be spiritually minded is life and peace."*

He then went on to say, *"Because the carnal mind is enmity against God: for it is not subject to the Law of God, neither indeed can be"* (Rom. 8:6-7).

The Disciples here, and, regrettably, for almost all the Ministry of Christ, were carnally minded. As stated, that would change upon the Advent of the Holy Spirit.

Conversely, and sadly so, it has not changed for many, if not most Believers. The reason being that most Believers do not hungrily desire the Lord as the Apostles of old.

The phrase, *"But of the doctrine of the Pharisees and of the Sadducees,"* pertains to error that included practice, precept, manner of life, as well as teaching. This spirit of error permeated everything they did. This is the leaven that corrupts the whole.

Error, and irrespective of what kind, ultimately always affects the whole of the individual, and, if not purged, what he does.

These two parties, the Pharisees and Sadducees, albeit extremely religious, and, as such, able to deceive the people, nevertheless, were going in the opposite direction of God. In fact, they were emissaries of Satan, and despite their heavy religiosity. In Truth, Satan is involved in religion more so than anything else. This is where he deceives many people.

At this stage, should I not as well warn the reader of the doctrine of Catholicism, of the Jehovah's Witnesses, of Christian Science; of Modernism, of the psychologizing of the Church, of the prosperity message, of the political message, and of the unity message?

These, plus many we have not named, are error pure and simple, and if followed to the conclusion, will cause a person to lose their soul, or else be seriously weakened in a spiritual sense.

(13) "WHEN JESUS CAME INTO THE COASTS OF CAESAREA PHILIPPI, HE ASKED HIS DISCIPLES, SAYING, WHOM DO MEN SAY THAT I THE SON OF MAN AM?"

The phrase, *"When Jesus came into the coasts of Caesarea Philippi,"* refers to the northeastern shore of the Sea of Galilee. The ship probably landed close to Bethsaida, with Jesus and His Disciples walking north toward the city of Caesarea Philippi. The area was known as Paneas.

The word, *"coasts,"* probably means that He did not go into the city itself, but somewhere close to the outskirts.

It was an area that was not very heavily populated, and probably chosen in order that He not be disturbed. He would here teach His Disciples some very important things, of which the Chapter proclaims.

NOTES

The question, *"He asked His Disciples, saying, Whom do men say that I the Son of Man am?"*, constitutes one of the most important questions ever asked! Upon the answer to this all-important question hinges the Salvation of man.

If one is to notice, Jesus referred to Himself as *"The Son of Man,"* and for a purpose. This was the term used to portray the Truth of the Incarnation — *"very God and very Man,"* or *"perfect God and perfect Man."*

In other words, He was not half God and half man, but, instead, totally God and totally man.

THE DOCTRINE OF THE INCARNATION

This Doctrine is one of the most important Doctrines in Scripture.

Paul spoke of God sending His Son *"in the likeness of sinful flesh,"* in order that He might *"condemn sin in the flesh"* (Rom. 8:3).

In this respect (flesh), the Incarnation stands in contrast with *"Spirit,"* of which God is. In other words, *"God is a Spirit,"* and not flesh (Jn. 4:24). Therefore, for God to become flesh, as Jesus did, means that He came, lived and died in the state and under the conditions of created physical life. In other words, that He Who died was Man. However, the New Testament also affirms that He Who died, eternally was, and continues to be, God. The formula which enshrines the Incarnation, therefore, is that in some sense God, without ceasing to be God, was made Man.

This is what John was speaking of in His Gospel when he spoke of *"The Word"* (God's agent in creation, Who in the beginning, before the creation, not only was with God, but Himself was God, Jn. 1:1-3) becoming flesh (Jn. 1:14).

This had to be, God becoming Man, in order that He might do what the first Adam failed to do.

In the first Adam, all died, and because of Adam's transgression. In Christ, Who was the last Adam, *"all are made alive,"* at least those who believe (I Cor. 15:22, 45).

Whenever Adam fell in the Garden of Eden, due to the manner in which man was created, he acted for all of humanity.

In other words, when God created the Angels, the evidence is that they were all created at one time, and fully mature. In other words, there has never been a baby Angel, or such a thing as an Angel being born as man.

However, when God created man, He employed a different type of creation by creating only a pair, Adam and Eve, which from them would come the entirety of the human family. It is called procreation, or rather the ability to have offspring.

Consequently, in Adam's loins (his genes), figuratively speaking, was every single human being who would ever live. In other words, what he did affected all.

When Adam was created, due to his being created by God, he was, in essence, *"a son of God"* (Lk. 3:38). Consequently, had he not fallen, through procreation (the bringing of offspring into the world), those born to him would have been, as well, *"sons of God."* Had his offspring not sinned, it would have remained accordingly.

However, when he sinned, and, thereby fell, he and Eve no longer brought *"sons of God"* into the world, but, rather, *"sons of Adam"* (Gen. 5:3). Consequently, every human being born thereafter was born a *"son of Adam"* instead of a *"son of God."* This means that all are born lost!

Due to the fact that it was Adam who caused the Fall and the loss of the human family, only another Adam could redeem the human family. This is the cause and reason for the Incarnation, God becoming Man. Consequently, God became the Second or Last Adam. As such, He lived perfectly, which the first Adam did not do. Then, as the Last Adam, He died on Calvary as the Perfect Man, and, the Perfect Sacrifice, thereby paying the price for man's Redemption.

In the Garden of Eden, the penalty for disobedience was death (Gen. 2:17). As well, the price of Redemption was death (Rom. 5:8-11). However, God could only accept the death of a Perfect Sacrifice, therefore, no other human being would suffice. So God would become flesh, called the Incarnation, serving as the Last Adam, and die on Calvary as the Perfect Sacrifice. This God the Father could accept, and, in Truth, did accept!

So, and as stated, in the first Adam all died, likewise, in the Last Adam all are made alive who believe (Jn. 3:16).

So, as Adam acted as the representative for the entirety of the human family, which resulted in their loss, likewise, Jesus acts as the representative for the entirety of the human

NOTES

family, *"that all who believe in Him should not perish but have everlasting life"* (Jn. 3:16).

That is what is meant by the *"born-again"* experience (Jn. 3:3). Now, sons of Adam can become *"sons of God,"* and by the New Birth. Therefore, what Adam lost, Christ regained. Now, man, formerly a son of Adam, can now be reborn as a *"son of God."*

A DIFFERENCE

However, there is a vast difference in men who are born again by their Faith in Christ, and who become a son of God, than Christ Who is *"The Son of God."* The basic definition is that Jesus is God's Son. This identification is rooted in Jesus' Own thought and teaching. His sense of being *"The Son"* in a unique sense that set Him apart from the rest of men, went back at least to His statement of being about the Father's business, when He was only twelve years old (Lk. 2:49). As well, it was confirmed to Him by His Father's Voice from Heaven at His Baptism: *"Thou art My Beloved Son"* (Mat. 3:17; Mk. 1:11; Lk. 3:22). In other words, His Divine Sonship was no less than Personal Deity.

As a Son, He had no independent initiative, but lived to glorify His Father (Jn. 17:1, 4). He did this by doing His Father's Will (Jn. 4:34; 5:30; 8:28). He came into the world because the Father *"sent"* Him, and gave Him a task to fulfill (Jn. 4:34; 17:4; 19:30). He came in His Father's Name, as His Father's Representative (Jn. 5:43), and, because all that He said and did was according to the Father's Command (Jn. 7:16; 8:26; 12:49; 14:10). In effect, His life on earth revealed His Father perfectly (Jn. 14:7).

When He spoke of the Father being greater than Himself (Jn. 10:29; 14:28), He is referring not to any essential or circumstantial inferiority, but to the fact that He was subordinate to the Father's Will.

However, this does not mean that He is to be subordinated to the Father in men's esteem and worship. Just the reverse; for the Father seeks the Son's Glory no less than the Son seeks the Father's Glory.

The Father has committed to the Son His two great works of giving life and executing judgment, *"That all may honour the Son, even as they honour the Father"* (Jn. 5:23). This amounts to saying that the Father directs all men to do as Thomas did (Jn. 20:28), and acknowledge the Son in the same terms in which they ought to acknowledge the Father Himself — namely, as *"My Lord and my God."*

THE NATURE OF THE INCARNATION

When the Word (Jesus) *"became flesh,"* His Deity was not abandoned, reduced, or contracted, nor did He cease to exercise the Divine functions which had been His before. It is He, we are told, Who sustains the creation in ordered existence, and Who gives and upholds all life (Jn. 1:4; Col. 1:17; Heb. 1:3). And to be sure, these functions were not halted during His time on earth.

However, when He came into the world, He *"emptied Himself"* of outward glory (Jn. 17:5; Phil. 2:7), and in that sense He *"became poor"* (II Cor. 8:9). But this does not at all imply a curtailing of His Divine Powers. Actually, the New Testament stresses instead that the Son's Deity was not reduced through the Incarnation. Paul said, *"In the Man Christ Jesus, dwelleth all the fullness of the Godhead bodily"* (Col. 2:9).

As someone has said, He never lost the possession of His Deity, but rather its expression. The Incarnation of the Son of God, then, was not a diminishing of Deity, but an acquiring of manhood. It was not that God the Son came to indwell a human being as the Spirit was later to do (I Cor. 3:16), but was, instead, the Son in Person coming to live a fully human life.

He did not simply clothe Himself in a human body, taking the place of its soul, as some have claimed, but actually took to Himself a human soul as well as a human body. His Manhood was complete; He became *"The Man Christ Jesus"* (Gal. 4:4; I Tim. 2:5; Heb. 2:14, 17).

As well, His Manhood is permanent. Though now exalted, He *"continues to be God and Man in two distinct natures, but yet, one Person, and forever"* (Heb. 7:24).

HIS INCARNATE LIFESTYLE

Jesus' life was one of dependence and obedience to the Father, because the Incarnation did not change the relationship between the Son and the Father. They continued in unbroken fellowship, the Son saying and doing what the Father gave Him to say and do, and not going beyond the Father's known Will at any single moment (Mat. 4:2).

NOTES

For instance, He confessed ignorance of the time of His return (Mk. 13:32), and can be explained as the Father simply not wanting Him to know at that time this particular piece of information. As the Son, He did not wish or seek to know more than the Father wished Him to know.

He lived a state of sinlessness and His life was impeccable. That His whole life was sinless is several times asserted (Mat. 3:14-17; Jn. 8:46; II Cor. 5:21; Heb. 4:15; I Pet. 2:22; I Jn. 2:1).

That He was exempt from the original sin of Adam due to His Virgin Birth, is evident from the fact that He was not bound to die for sins of His Own (Heb. 7:26), and hence could die as a representative for all of mankind, and as the Perfect Sacrifice, the Righteous taking the place of the unrighteous (Rom. 5:16; II Cor. 5:21; Gal. 3:13; I Pet. 3:18).

WAS IT POSSIBLE FOR JESUS AS THE INCARNATE SON OF GOD TO SIN?

As God, no! As Man, yes!

Even though never ceasing to be God, still, the expression of Deity, at least as far as His earthly walk was concerned, was laid aside, while He, nevertheless, continued to possess it. In this state, and as Man, it would have been possible for Him to have sinned. Otherwise, He could not have been our Perfect Substitute, nor could He have been the Last Adam. He had to function as the first Adam functioned, at least according to attributes, or else He could not have been the proper Substitute.

Had it been impossible for Him in His Incarnation to sin, Satan wasted His time in the temptations (Mat. 4:1-11).

The writer of Hebrews said, and concerning Jesus, *"But was in all points tempted like as we are, yet without sin"* (Heb. 4:15).

Were it not possible for Him to have sinned, then He, as the Scripture says, could not have been *"touched with the feeling of our infirmities"* (Heb. 4:15).

The Truth is that He does feel what we feel as a human being, because He experienced what we experience, except sin.

The reason for Satan's great efforts to cause Christ to fail was because this was the only opportunity Satan would have. As God, Satan could not induce Christ to sin. However, upon becoming Man in the Incarnation,

Satan now has an opportunity, and the greatest of all, to destroy the Plan of God for the human family. Consequently, he would tempt Christ, and greatly so, knowing that it was possible for Christ to fail, inasmuch as He was Man. However, Christ did not fail. Facing Satan on his own ground, He defeated the evil one completely. He never failed even in one point, therefore, Satan had no claim upon Him whatsoever. As such, He was, and remained, the consummate Man, *"The Man Christ Jesus."*

In this, He became our Substitute. That which we could not do, He did on our behalf. Consequently, Faith in His Name and Work guarantees us not only Redemption, because of what He did at Calvary, but, as well, the victorious, overcoming life.

THE CROSS OF CHRIST

As we know and the Bible affirms, Jesus Christ was, and is, Very God and Very Man. He wasn't half God and half Man, but rather totally God and totally Man!

The Lord Jesus Christ was totally different than anyone else ever has been or ever shall be. To classify Him with other men presents a bad classification, because He stands alone. There never has been anyone like Him. There never will be anyone like Him. He truly was God manifest in the flesh.

But yet He was so fully human that most doubted His Deity, despite the fact of the innumerable miracles that He performed, miracles that were so astounding as to defy all description. He did everything from opening blinded eyes to raising the dead. As the late, great, Baptist Preacher, E. V. Hill, stated, *"There is no problem greater than 'dead and buried.'"* And Jesus took care of that 2,000 years ago.

When he made that statement as he preached on a Wednesday evening at Family Worship Center in Baton Rouge, Louisiana, the congregation was powerfully moved. We have not forgotten it from that day until this.

To misunderstand the *"Person"* of Christ and the *"Function"* of Christ (the latter refers to the Cross) is to misunderstand the Lord in totality.

An improper knowledge of Who Jesus is constitutes an improper Salvation which should be obvious!

NOTES

(14) "AND THEY SAID, SOME SAY THAT THOU ART JOHN THE BAPTIST: SOME, ELIAS; AND OTHERS, JEREMIAS, OR ONE OF THE PROPHETS."

The answer given by the Disciples as to what others were saying respecting Who Christ was is very revealing!

If it is to be noticed, it is obvious that precious few, if any, considered Christ to be the Messiah, and that despite the Miracles and the fulfillment of Scripture.

Thinking that He was *"John the Baptist,"* Elijah, or even Jeremiah, was the talk of the hour.

If not led by the Holy Spirit and, therefore, guided by the Word, religious men come up with ridiculous conclusions. That Jesus was the Promised Messiah was so obvious, and yet they were so spiritually blind they could not *"see."*

Why?

Israel, at this time, had been so influenced by the error of the Pharisees and Scribes that their spiritual perception was skewed and perverted. Sadly, and because of false doctrine, it has changed little at present regarding the modern Church.

Coupled with this error, the Pharisees and Scribes were slandering Christ constantly, even accusing Him of performing His Miracles in league with Satan. Due to their rabid opposition, the people were fearful of voicing their thoughts concerning the Messiahship of Christ, even if they believed He truly fulfilled the Prophecies.

It is difficult for the modern Believer to fully understand the rabid opposition Christ faced in these Religious Leaders. They were truly emissaries of Satan, and inasmuch as Satan works best in religious circles, the opposition was fierce. With some few exceptions, the entirety of the religious leadership of Israel fell into this polluted category. Truly, *"He came unto His Own, and His Own received Him not"* (Jn. 1:11).

Two things are noted in the answer of the Disciples, which we have already commented on. However, to bring it more so into focus, and because it is so prevalent today as well, allow us to state it again:

1. The people did not know the Word of God, consequently, they believed all types of foolish things. This is the reason for such error in the modern Church as well, and especially

regarding futuristic events respecting Prophecy.

The Birth and Coming of Christ was a futuristic event until it happened. Inasmuch as the people did not fully understand what the Word of God said about this all-important happening, and due to what they did know being corrupted by the Pharisees, they did not recognize Him when He came.

As well, for those who are presently denying the coming Rapture of the Church, which number is overly large, the confusion concerning the entirety of the Plan of God becomes more and more evident.

The part of the Church which is not looking for the Coming of Christ, is, as well, not looking to carry out His Will. That is a strong statement, but I believe it to be true.

2. Because of not knowing the Word of God, the people arrived at, as is here obvious, foolish speculation, and exactly as is being done presently.

Great segments of the modern Church claim that it is going to Christianize the culture of the world and thereby welcome Christ back. Such thinking is foolishness at its least and blasphemous at its worst. It is the same as thinking Jesus was John the Baptist or Elijah, etc., reincarnated, or having come back.

(15) "HE SAITH UNTO THEM, BUT WHOM SAY YE THAT I AM?"

Even though Christ was Very God, still, He was also Very Man. As such, it must have hurt, and hurt deeply, to know that His Own people did not think of Him as the Messiah. Of course, He knew the reasons why. As such, He must have grieved at their lack of diligence concerning the Word of God, as He must grieve accordingly at the present.

The question, *"But Whom say ye that I am?"*, being addressed personally to His Disciples, in one sense of the word was even more important than what Israel thought of Him.

As that question was addressed personally to the Disciples, it is addressed personally to all.

To be sure, everything hangs on the answer. If men do not know Who Jesus is, men cannot be saved.

Even in Christianized America and Canada, I am afraid that the answer to that question, for the most part, would receive less than a favorable response.

Many in the modern Church deny His Divinity, while claiming He may have been a *"good Man,"* or a *"Prophet,"* etc. Actually, the answer would not be too different than what Israel gave so long ago.

And then again, many would claim Him to be but deluded, and His followers deceived!

(16) "AND SIMON PETER ANSWERED AND SAID, THOU ART THE CHRIST, THE SON OF THE LIVING GOD."

The phrase, *"And Simon Peter answered and said,"* proclaims Peter speaking for all, but yet more so for himself, because the Lord will answer him in a personal sense, as is revealed in the next verse. Peter's answer was actually in two parts. They are as follows:

1. *"Thou art the Christ"*: The Name *"Christ"* meant *"Anointed,"* and at least in this sense referred only to the Messiah.

Beautifully and strangely enough, the first time the term *"Anointed"* was used in referring to the Coming Messiah, was by Hannah when she said, *"And exalt the horn of His Anointed"* (I Sam. 2:10). The Hebrew word for *"Anointed"* is *"Mashiyach,"* i.e., Messiah.

From this point on, others take up the theme of God's Anointed One — the Messiah (vs. 35; Ps. 2:2; 45:7; Isa. 61:1; Dan. 9:25-26; Jn. 1:41; 4:25).

Isaiah 10:27, "And the yoke shall be destroyed because of the Anointing," should have been translated, *"Because of the Anointed One."*

Isaiah is actually referring to Christ destroying the Antichrist in the coming Battle of Armageddon. However, Christ Alone can break the yoke of sin, bondage, and poverty, and will do so for anyone who will believe Him.

2. *"The Son of the Living God"*: This means that the *"Son"* is of the same substance and essence as the Father, and actually One with the Father.

WHAT DOES IT MEAN THAT JESUS IS THE SON OF GOD?

It means that the Lord Jesus Christ in Essence is the same as the Father. In other words, even though He was fully human, He was, at the same time, fully God. God, in fact, declared Jesus to be *"My Beloved Son"* (Mat. 3:17; 17:5).

Of Himself, He said, *"I am the Son of God"* (Jn. 10:36).

John called Him, *"The Only Begotten Son"*

and *"The Son of the Father"* (Jn. 1:18; 3:16-18; I Jn. 4:9; II Jn. 3).

Jesus referring to Himself as *"The Son of God"* is what infuriated the Pharisees. They said, *"He makes Himself equal with God"* (Jn. 5:18).

The charge thus leveled against Christ by the Jews was not at all disclaimed by Jesus because He did in fact make Himself equal with God, and rightly so!

The Lord continued to say, *"The Son can do nothing of Himself* (proclaims the humanity of Christ, with Him freely giving up the expression of His Deity while never losing its possession), *but what He sees the Father do* (proclaims His total subservience to the Father, which as a Man He was to do and did so): *for what things soever He does, these also do the Son likewise* (setting an example of humility and dependence, which the human family seriously lacked).

"For the Father loves the Son (the obedience of the Son is based on the love the Father has for the Son), *and shows Him all things that Himself does* (plainly says that everything Jesus did is that which the Father told Him to do) (Jn. 5:19-20).

The word, *"living"* means that the Father has Life within Himself, and could be translated, *"The Ever Living."*

Actually, this statement of Faith, as made by Peter, must be believed in one form or the other for a person to be saved, even though they may not fully understand it.

The Son of God is of the substance of the Father, begotten from everlasting, God of God, Perfect God, and Perfect Man, Son of God, and Son of Man.

Whether Peter understood all of what He said at this particular time, is not known. To be sure, the subject is so vast, so weighty, and so deep, that it would be impossible for a mere mortal to fully plumb its depths or scale its heights.

It is the Great Confession of Faith!

(17) "AND JESUS ANSWERED AND SAID UNTO HIM, BLESSED ART THOU, SIMON BAR-JONA: FOR FLESH AND BLOOD HATH NOT REVEALED IT UNTO THEE, BUT MY FATHER WHICH IS IN HEAVEN."

The phrase, *"And Jesus answered and said unto him,"* is to proclaim an answer of Blessing.

Too often, and even shortly, Christ will have to rebuke Peter. Here, He commends and

NOTES

blesses him greatly.

The phrase, *"Blessed art thou, Simon Bar-jona,"* is used for several reasons:

1. Even though Jesus had been referred to by the Disciples as such on a previous occasion, still, this was the first time that Jesus had been so pointedly addressed as the Son of God, at least in this fashion.

2. The word, *"blessed,"* refers to a solemn benediction, in a sense, meaning to be blessed forever, rather than a mere celebration of the moment.

3. Jesus addressed him as *"Son of Jonah"* as Peter has addressed him as *"Son of God."* He is in effect saying that Peter is son of Jonah, just as he (Christ) is truly the *"Son of God."*

The phrase, *"For flesh and blood hath not revealed it unto thee,"* simply means that the Ways of God, as well as the Word of God, cannot really be understood in natural human wisdom. Actually, human wisdom produced the ridiculous assertions outlined in verse 4, with thoughts that Jesus was really John the Baptist come back to life, etc. This is the tragedy which is now being carried out in many if not most Bible Colleges and Seminaries.

Some time back, I was shown an advertisement respecting the course offerings of several Seminaries, etc. In all the subjects listed, Bible subjects were the least. Actually, most of the courses offered were either psychology or psychology oriented, i.e., human wisdom.

As I have stated elsewhere in these Volumes, there was a time that theology was the queen of the sciences in all universities in America, both secular and religious. However, theology, which is the study of God, has taken a back seat, if any seat at all, with psychology now serving as the queen of the sciences.

Years ago, a Methodist layman said to me, *"Brother Swaggart, the Methodist Church did not lose its way because of the people attending its Churches, but, instead, because of its Seminaries which turned out Preachers who no longer believed the Bible."* Regrettably, that which happened in Methodism is now happening in Pentecostal circles as well!

The ways of the world, *"flesh and blood,"* have now been brought into the Church. When this happens, the Holy Spirit is no longer wanted or desired. Regrettably, this characterizes the far greater majority of the modern Church!

The word, *"revealed,"* simply means *"to uncover."* Consequently, the question should be asked as to why the Holy Spirit has designed the Ways and Word of God to where it cannot be understood by *"flesh and blood,"* i.e., human wisdom?

It is not that the Holy Spirit has designed such accordingly but that the Fall of man in the Garden of Eden so corrupted his spiritual faculties that it is impossible, at least within himself, to comprehend the Ways of God. That is the reason Paul said, *"They are all gone out of the way, they are together become unprofitable: there is none that doeth good, no, not one"* (Rom. 3:12). Therefore, without a Revelation of the Spirit upon the unregenerate heart of man, it is impossible for him to comprehend or understand that which is of God.

The phrase, *"But My Father which is in Heaven,"* signifies that Peter did not receive his knowledge respecting his great acclamation of Faith from human wisdom, i.e., the Pharisees and Sadducees, etc., but rather as a direct revelation from the Father Himself.

It goes back to Jesus' statement, *"For whosoever hath, to him shall be given, and he shall have more abundance: but whosoever hath not, from him shall be taken away even that he hath"* (Mat. 13:12).

Peter wanted to know more about Christ, therefore, greater revelation was given unto him. Conversely, the Religious Leaders of Israel had no desire to know more, consequently, what little they did know was *"taken away,"* which left them in total darkness.

This answers the question of the Moslem who claims that if Christianity is so viable, why is it that America is so wicked?

Of course, as wicked as America might be, still, the countries of the world ruled by Islam are far more wicked!

The Truth is that the freedoms afforded by America, which have made it the land of choice for most of the population of the world, have been brought about solely because of what little of the Word of God it has adhered to, even though precious little.

The wickedness that is obvious and prevalent, and growing worse we might add, is not because Bible Christianity is not viable, but because America, by and large, has rejected the Ways and Word of God. Consequently, upon its

NOTES

rejection, what little true knowledge of the Word of God it has is being *"taken away."*

Light rejected is darkness deepened!

All the other religions and philosophies of the world are totally different! The rejection of these religions, such as Islam, Buddhism, etc., not only does not hinder, but, instead, leaves one at least static, i.e., unchanged.

This is the reason entire Religious Denominations in Christianity lose their way. They begin to reject the Word of God, which causes them to lose what little knowledge of God they do have. If *"leaven"* is not removed, as Jesus spoke of the *"leaven of the Pharisees,"* it will ultimately corrupt the whole.

This 17th verse proclaims to us that the Believer will receive his knowledge of the Lord either from *"flesh and blood"* or from God. If he receives it from God, or God-called Preachers, whatever is received will always coincide with the Word of God exactly as Peter's confession. The Word of God was replete with the Prophecies concerning the Coming Messiah, and that He would be life and give life. Jesus fulfilled this in totality.

Just a little later, Peter will receive a *"revelation"* from Satan (vss. 22-23), i.e., *"flesh and blood,"* his own human wisdom. Consequently, as he was commended by Christ in verses 17 and 18, he is rebuked by Christ in the later incident.

This proclaims to us that the struggle is constant in the heart of the Believer, referring to *"revelation knowledge."* It can come from God or the flesh, i.e., Satan.

If the Believer stays close to God, thereby staying in the Word, and, consequently, led by the Spirit, the *"revelation"* will always be from the Lord. However, if spiritual coldness sets in due to a lack of consecration, *"revelation"* will begin to come from sense knowledge, i.e., Satan.

If this happens, which it sadly does in the lives of many Believers, they then become prey for *"false apostles,"* preaching *"another gospel,"* which presents *"another Jesus,"* and by *"another spirit"* (II Cor. 11:4, 13).

(18) "AND I SAY ALSO UNTO THEE, THAT THOU ART PETER, AND UPON THIS ROCK I WILL BUILD MY CHURCH; AND THE GATES OF HELL SHALL NOT PREVAIL AGAINST IT."

The phrase, *"And I say also unto thee,"* proclaims two revelations.

1. The revelation by the Father to Peter that Jesus is *"The Son of the Living God."*

2. The word, *"also,"* proves Christ to be a separate Person from the Father. As verse 17 proclaims the Father giving a revelation, verse 18 proclaims Jesus as giving one. It is the revelation of the building of His Church.

The phrase, *"That thou art Peter,"* refers to his name change.

In John 1:41 and 42, Simon confessed Jesus as the *"Son of David"*; here as *"Son of the Living God."*

In John 1, he was promised a new name; here that new name is bestowed.

The name, *"Peter,"* or, *"Cephas,"* means *"A fragment of a rock."* (The Greek for Peter is *"Petros,"* and in Aramaic, is *"Cephas,"* which language Jesus spoke.)

The phrase, *"And upon this Rock,"* refers to Jesus Himself, and not Peter, as some claim.

Peter is, as stated, *"Petros,"* that is, a stone that may be thrown here or there; in this phrase the word, *"Rock,"* is, *"Petra,"* which means a mighty immovable mass of rock — the Godhead of Christ. In other words, the *"Rock"* is Christ. Paul said, *"And did all drink the same spiritual drink: for they drank of that spiritual Rock that followed them, and that Rock was Christ"* (I Cor. 10:4).

The phrase, *"I will build My Church,"* refers to the Church belonging to Christ, and, as well, being headed up by Christ, and not Peter, or any other man for that matter!

Paul said, and speaking of Christ, *"And He is the Head of the Body, the Church: Who* (Christ) *is the Beginning, the Firstborn from the dead; that in all things He* (Christ) *might have the pre-eminence"* (Col. 1:18).

I might also quickly add, as this Passage brings out, Christ is not a passive Head, as some claim, but, instead, an active Head, serving as the Leader of His Church.

Once again, this abrogates the claims of the Catholic Church that Peter was the first Pope, and that apostolic succession resides in the Bishops of the Catholic Church, of which we will have more to say later.

The True Church of Jesus Christ has Christ as its Head, and is, therefore, a spiritual organism.

The Catholic Church is purely a human organization, and, as a result, has no spirituality at all.

WHAT IS A CHURCH?

The Church is basically a New Testament theme, although it was referred to in the Old Testament, with Israel in a shadowy way serving in that capacity (Acts 7:38).

The word, *"Church,"* in the Greek is *"Ekklesia,"* and means, *"called out."* The word is used 115 times and is always translated *"Church,"* except in Acts 19:32-41, where it is translated *"assembly."*

However, the word, *"Church,"* is used in many and varied ways by modern Believers, such as *"The Church on Tenth Street,"* or a Religious Denomination, etc. None of these uses are particularly Biblical.

When the new community of Christians in the Early Church referred to themselves, it was always as an *"Ekklesia,"* i.e., Church, a called-out group. By doing so, it broke with its Jewish roots by rejecting the term synagogue.

To be sure, the choice of *"Ekklesia,"* was appropriate, as it linked two Greek words to mean *"a called-out assembly."* The Gospel proclamation called lost people out of the world to gather together in a unique fellowship. Joined-together Believers formed a new community: a community committed to Jesus and to the radical lifestyle expressed in God's Word. It is the allegiance of the new community to Jesus that makes its members different from those *"outside"* (I Cor. 5:12; 6:4).

"Ekklesia," or Church, in the New Testament encompassed any number of Believers. These Believers consisted of both small and large groups, and met in homes (Rom. 16:5), or wherever they could meet.

Even though the word, *"Church,"* may refer to a single group of Believers, it also refers to the Universal Body of all Believers in all places, and at all times.

JESUS AND THE CHURCH

The Church belongs to God (I Cor. 1:2; 10:32; 11:16, 22; 15:9; II Cor. 1:1; Gal. 1:13; I Thess. 2:14; II Thess. 1:4; I Tim. 3:5, 15).

Yet, the Church stands in a unique relationship to Christ. The Church is Christ's Body, a vital living extension of Jesus Himself. As such,

Christ is *"Appointed Head over everything for the Church, Which is His Body"* (Eph. 1:22-23). Consequently, the Church must recognize Jesus as Lord and corporately submit to Him Who is *"Head of the Church"* (Eph. 5:23-24).

THE CHURCH IS A BODY AND FUNCTIONS ACCORDINGLY

Members of the Body of Christ, like parts of a human body, have different functions (Rom. 12:4-5; I Cor. 12:4-5; Eph. 4:11). God the Holy Spirit gives spiritual gifts — Divine ennoblements for Ministry — so that each person in the Body can function in a ministering way toward other Body members (Rom. 12:6-8; I Cor. 12:7-11; Eph. 4:11). As a result, each member's contribution is essential (Rom. 12:5; I Cor. 12:14-26): only as each Believer's Ministry is performed will the Body grow and *"build itself up in love"* (Eph. 4:14-16).

The image of the Body in the New Testament is far more than just meeting on Sunday mornings for worship and other activities. Unless we also come together to function as the Body of the New Testament, we are not truly being Christ's Church.

The members are to serve one another, and, as well, strive to take the Gospel of Jesus Christ not only to their local community, but to the entirety of the world.

THE CHURCH IS ACTUALLY A FAMILY

This identity as family is derived from God's nature as Father (Eph. 3:14). Paul says further in his letter to the Ephesians that his prayer is that Believers might function as family: that *"rooted and established in love,"* the family members might *"have power, to gather with all the Saints, to grasp how wide and long and high and deep is the Love of Christ"* (Eph. 3:17-18).

As well, family terms are used in the New Testament as identifiers of Believers. Again and again, Believers are identified as Brothers and Sisters and, at times, even as Mothers and Fathers (I Tim. 5:1-2).

In becoming children of one Father, each Believer has been drawn into God's Universal family of Faith, and thus into family relationship with one another.

In essence, we are family. Although there may be differences among members of a family in practice and in convictions, and even in

Doctrine, our basic identity comes from the fact that each person who trusts in Jesus becomes a Child of God (Gal. 3:26). As Children of the same Father, each Believer is to love other Believers as Brothers and Sisters (I Thess. 4:9; I Pet. 1:22; I Jn. 3:11-15; 4:7-21).

ADMISSION INTO THE CHURCH

Admission into the Church is strictly spiritual, but with a physical, domestical and economical result.

Admittance into the *"Church"* is by Faith in Christ, which means to accept what Christ did at Calvary and the Resurrection. Paul stated, *"That if thou shalt confess with thy mouth the Lord Jesus, and shalt believe in thine heart that God hath raised Him from the dead, thou shalt be saved.*

"For with the heart man believeth unto Righteousness; and with the mouth confession is made unto Salvation."

Paul then said, *"For whosoever shall call upon the Name of the Lord shall be saved"* (Rom. 10:9-10, 13).

As well, the invitation is given to all, irrespective of race or nationality. Paul also said, *"For there is no difference between the Jew and the Greek: for the same Lord over all is rich unto all that call upon Him"* (Rom. 10:12).

As is obvious, other than witnessing or preaching the Gospel to individuals, man has nothing to do with admitting the individual into the Church, except to recognize what God has already done, and, likewise, man cannot remove one from the Church.

As well, belonging to a certain congregation, organization, Religious Denomination, or any other type of group, has absolutely nothing to do with being a member of the Body of Christ, i.e., the Church. Unfortunately, many Church groups have led others to believe that association with their group guarantees association with Christ, and disassociation with that group, whatever it may be, causes one to lose association with Christ.

Nothing could be further from the Truth. Association with an earthly group has absolutely nothing to do with one's Salvation and, likewise, disassociation in no way removes one from association and fellowship with Christ.

So, admittance into the Church, the Body of Christ, is the making of Christ as one's Saviour, which results in a heartfelt, born-again experience (Jn. 3:3).

Upon being born again, one should certainly seek to be associated with a group of local Believers, if at all possible, who are attempting to follow the Word of God, with it as their criteria.

The phrase, *"And the gates of hell shall not prevail against it,"* actually means *"The power of death"* shall not prevail against it.

The reference here is to Resurrection and not to infallibility in Doctrine, as asserted by some.

Christ, being the Living God, and His people living stones, they could not be held captive in the mansions of the dead.

On the third day, He, as the True Samson, rose and carried away the gates of hell. They could not prevail against that Rock, i.e., *"It."* He prevailed against them; and when He arose all His people arose in and with Him (I Thess. 4:14).

As well as referring to *"the power of death,"* the *"gates of hell"* also refers to the iron grip of sinful bondage which binds all of unsaved humanity. This includes sin, sickness, poverty and all other domains of darkness. With the Death and Resurrection of Christ, all of these *"gates"* fell. As a result, any authority presently held by Satan is a pseudo-authority, or, more particularly, that allowed him by Believers.

This is what Jesus was speaking of when He said, *"And these signs shall follow them that believe; In My Name shall they cast out devils; they shall speak with new tongues;*

"They shall take up serpents; and if they drink any deadly thing, it shall not hurt them; they shall lay hands on the sick, and they shall recover" (Mk. 16:17-18).

To be sure, most, if not all, of these Promises have to do with demon spirits and their expulsion.

For instance, the words, *"Take up,"* in verse 18, and concerning serpents, have absolutely nothing to do with snakes. The Greek word for *"Take up,"* is *"airo,"* and means to *"take up, in order to remove, to put away."* It refers to the putting away of demon spirits, which takes place when the Gospel is preached in Power and Anointing, and by the authority of the Name of Jesus, as used by Believers.

The Church is meant to tear down the strongholds of Satan, and to do so by the Power of the Holy Spirit, which is brought into focus by the use of the *"Name of Jesus."*

Regrettably, much of the modern Church is no longer a *"Living Organism,"* empowered from On High, but, instead, an intellectual or academic organization. Unfortunately, Satan does not respond to the intellectual or academic posture. He only responds to the Power of God, as evidenced in the Name of Jesus, used by Spirit-filled Believers.

Tragically, most of the modern Church is a far cry from that intended by the Holy Spirit, according to what Jesus built. Actually, the Book of Acts is meant to serve as an ideal of what the *"Church"* ought to be.

Regrettably, many have foolishly claimed that the modern Church has outgrown the Book of Acts.

If that is the case, then it means that mere man is more intelligent than the Holy Spirit, which is ludicrous to say the least!

No! The Book of Acts is meant to serve as the criteria, and should not be deviated from. To do so, institutes man's ways instead of God's Ways, and proves catastrophic.

(19) "AND I WILL GIVE UNTO THEE THE KEYS OF THE KINGDOM OF HEAVEN: AND WHATSOEVER THOU SHALT BIND ON EARTH SHALL BE BOUND IN HEAVEN: AND WHATSOEVER THOU SHALT LOOSE ON EARTH SHALL BE LOOSED IN HEAVEN."

The phrase, *"And I will give unto thee,"* does not refer to Peter only, but definitely includes Peter. Actually, the same Power is promised all Believers (Mat. 17:20; 18:18; 21:22; Mk. 9:23; 11:22-24; 16:15-20; Lk. 10:19; Jn. 14:12-15; 15:7, 17; Acts 1:4-8; 2:38-39; 5:32; I Cor. 12).

The phrase, *"The keys of the Kingdom of Heaven,"* refers to symbols of authority. Here they mean authority and power to do the Works of Christ (Mat. 16:15-20; 18:18; Jn. 14:12-15).

The word, *"keys,"* a symbolism used by Christ, refers back to *"The key of the House of David"* (Isa. 22:22).

This was a literal key held by the treasurer of the nation of Israel. Even then it was symbolic, it referred to authority.

Jesus referred to these *"keys"* twice to John the Beloved on the Isle of Patmos, when He said, *"And have the keys of hell and of death"* (Rev. 1:18), and, *"He that hath the key of David, He that openeth, and no man shutteth; and shutteth, and no man openeth"* (Rev. 3:7).

In the first instance, He spoke of having

these *"Keys of hell and of death"* Himself, but the latter reference refers to the *"keys"* shared by Him with the Church.

Several things are here said:

1. First of all, these are the *"Keys of the Kingdom of Heaven,"* and not the *"key"* to some earthly organization, such as the Catholic Church, or any Protestant Organization.

The *"Kingdom of Heaven"* is the rule of Christ in the heart and life of the Believer.

2. As well, the word, *"thee,"* and as we have stated, refers to the entirety of the Body of Christ, and not to just Peter, or some successor.

3. As well, it does not refer to any religious hierarchy.

4. It actually refers to each and every Believer, irrespective of whom they may be, with Power and Authority given unto each one in order that they may carry out the Work of God on earth, and, in effect, carry on the work started by Jesus.

5. The *"keys"* refer to preaching or proclaiming the Gospel, whether one on one, or to a large gathering, which, if accepted, sets the captive free. Whenever the Believer does this, whether layman or Preacher, he is, in effect, taking the *"key"* and unlocking the spiritual prison which binds humanity. What a privilege it is to have such Power and Authority, as well as the privilege of doing this!

However, these *"keys"* are used not nearly as much as they ought to be, considering that a great percentage of the world knows little or nothing about Jesus Christ and His Power to save. The *"keys"* have been given unto us, and it is our duty and responsibility to use them.

6. Regrettably, most of the *"keys"* used, will not unlock the door, simply because it is the wrong *"key,"* i.e., false doctrine.

Jesus said, *"And this Gospel* (the Gospel He preached and practiced) *of the Kingdom shall be preached in all the world for a witness unto all nations; and then shall the end come"* (Mat. 24:14).

He was speaking here of the *"keys."* However, much, if not most, of the time, it is not *"This Gospel"* being preached, but, instead, *"another gospel"* (II Cor. 11:4), which, in effect, is no Gospel, i.e., *"key"* at all!

The phrase, *"And whatsoever thou shalt bind on earth shall be bound in Heaven,"* refers to Satan and his minions of darkness being

bound, and, therefore, unable to carry out their work of destruction, and because of the Gospel being preached. Christ has given this function of *"binding"* and *"loosing"* to the Church.

We are allowed to use the Name of Jesus, which, in effect, ties Satan's hands, at least regarding all he would like to do.

This *"authority"* guarantees that with the use of the Name of Jesus by Believers, Christ up in Heaven will ratify the action taken, that is, if it is according to His Word.

The phrase, *"And whatsoever thou shalt loose on earth shall be loosed in Heaven,"* is the same as the previous phrase, except in a different direction. Here, the Believer not only binds Satan, but, instead, *"looses"* the Power of God according to the usage of the Name of Jesus.

As the *"binding"* ties Satan's hands and stops his power to *"steal, kill and destroy,"* likewise, the *"loosing"* releases all that Jesus did at Calvary and the Resurrection. This is done by preaching and believing the Gospel, which is carried out by the authority of the Name of Jesus, with each member of the Body of Christ given the authority to *"bind and loose."*

"Binding" has to do with the spirit world of darkness, while *"loosing"* has to do with the spirit world of light. One binds Satan and his efforts, while the other looses or brings to bear, all that Christ did. This power resides, and as stated, in the Believer, who makes up the Body of Christ.

Some have claimed that these terms speak of admitting or barring from the Church. However, even though some men would enjoy that being true, actually, it is totally untrue. Admittance into the Body of Christ is held in the Hands of none other than Christ, and will never be relinquished (Jn. 3:16; 3:3; Rom. 5:8; 10:9-13).

Respecting the Catholic claim of Peter as the first Pope, and the Roman Bishops being his successors, with the *"Keys of the Kingdom of Heaven"* confined to the Catholic Church, or any other earthly organization for that matter, should be addressed at this time.

WAS PETER THE FIRST POPE?

The Pope of Rome stands as the nominal head of all Roman Catholic worship. He represents (according to Catholic Doctrine) the central authority of Christ's Church on earth, and is claimed to be successor in this position to the Apostle Peter. According to Catholic tenets, Christ appointed Peter the first Pope, according to their interpretation of Matthew 16:17-19. Peter then went to Rome (they say) where he served in this capacity for some twenty-five (or more) years.

Beginning with Simon Peter, the Catholic Church traces (or attempts to do so) an unbroken succession right down to this day. And upon this claim, the entire framework of Catholicism is built. It is therefore incumbent upon anyone honestly seeking Truth to ask some questions before blindly accepting such critically-important assertions.

1. Does the Holy Word of God reveal that Christ ordained one man to be above all others in His Church?

2. Can we find any Scriptural authority for an organization in which one man (a Pope) serves as the supreme head?

3. Did early Christians recognize Peter as the Pope, or leader, of the Church?

THE POPE AND THE CATHOLIC CHURCH

Here is what the Catholic Church says about the Pope:

"The Roman Pontiff, when he speaks ex cathedra — that is, when in the exercise of his office as pastor and teacher of all Christians he defines . . . a doctrine of Faith or morals to be held by the whole Church — is, by reason of Divine assistance promised to him in blessed Peter, possessed of that infallibility . . . and consequently such definitions of the Roman Pontiff are irreformable."

In other words, the Catholic Church believes the Pope to be infallible when teaching on matters of Faith and morals, and when speaking authoritatively (ex cathedra — from the chair of Peter) as the vicar of Christ on earth.

Any person of average intelligence who is even superficially conversant with the New Testament can protest that no such ordered hierarchical system is even suggested within Scripture. Only the loosest and most tenuous of authority structures (other than submission to Christ, the Head) can be detected within the pages of the Bible. Knowledgeable Christians search in vain for any evidence of Peter's acting as an authority figure within the New Testament Church — the true beginnings of Christ's Church are recorded in the Book of Acts.

The other Apostles in no way deferred to Peter. When the Apostles and Elders met in Jerusalem (Acts 15:6) to debate how to heal the first major doctrinal schism within the young Church, it was James, the Lord's Brother, who was obviously in charge (Acts 15:13). Peter spoke during this meeting, as did others, but it was James who handed down the decision.

Where is Peter here demonstrating his capacity for infallible decisions and pronouncements as an example for all subsequent Popes? The decision finally reached at this time came not through Peter, nor was this decision transmitted throughout the Church by Peter. The *"Apostles and Elders, with the whole Church,"* sent Paul, Barnabas, Jude, and Silas to announce the determination of this question by the council (Acts 15:22).

It is easy enough to see from this single incident that the Early Church functioned in a manner radically different from that claimed within Catholic theology.

WAS PETER EVER IN ROME?

Peter may have passed through or visited Rome at some time, but there is not a hint of Scriptural evidence to confirm this. (Furthermore, outside of much-quoted Catholic *"traditions,"* neither is there any historical evidence of Peter's presence in Rome.)

As Paul closed out the Book of Romans (his letter to the Church at Rome), he mentioned many people. In fact, Romans 16 consists of little more than a lengthy list of those he greeted there. Now according to the papal catalog of Bishops of Rome, Peter was in Rome at this time. Amazingly, however, Paul did not send greetings to Peter!

Since Peter was not mentioned here by Paul, it can be concluded with some certainty that he was not there at that time! This, of course, undermines the very foundation of the claimed apostolic succession of the Roman Bishops. If Peter had been in Rome as Bishop (as the Roman Catholic Church claims), he would have been the first one to whom Paul would have referred! It is therefore a waste of time to consider such a groundless theory. To be frank, it is unlikely that Peter ever even saw the city of Rome in his lifetime!

We do know a number of things about Simon Peter, however. He was one of the

Twelve. He was a native fisherman of Bethsaida when the Lord called him. He was a married man (Mat. 8:14; I Cor. 9:5). He had no headship over the entire Church. He ministered primarily to Jews (Gal. 2:7). And it seems he was not even the head of the Jewish sector of the Church, much less that of the Gentiles (Acts 15; II Cor. 11:28; Gal. 2:6-21).

Peter was only one Elder among many (I Pet. 5). As previously mentioned, there is not the slightest indication that he ever set foot in Rome. Instead of travelling west (toward Rome), we find Peter in the east writing an Epistle from Babylon (I Pet. 5:13). Furthermore, we know nothing of his death — other than the Prophecy given in John 21:18-19.

Some claim that Peter's reference to Babylon in I Peter actually refers to Rome. This is a ridiculous assertion, however. The city of Babylon still existed when Peter wrote this. It was home to many Jews and was well-known as a major city on the Euphrates River. The great historian, Josephus, wrote of Babylon during this same period. Why then would Peter send salutations from Babylon if he was actually in Rome? This would be as irrational as a person today claiming he was in San Francisco when he was really in New York City. Sad to say, Catholic assertions about this do not hold water when exposed to the facts of the case.

DID JESUS GIVE PETER THE KEYS TO THE CHURCH, MAKING HIM THE FIRST IN A LONG SUCCESSION OF POPES, AS CLAIMED BY THE CATHOLIC CHURCH?

First, and foremost, we know that Christ is the Head of the Church (Eph. 1:22). Peter was never the head of the Church, nor is any other man, as we have already stated — only Christ.

Secondly, Peter himself said that Christ was the True Cornerstone (I Pet. 2:4-8). He also said that Christ is . . .

"... The Stone which was set at nought of you builders, which is become the Head of the corner. Neither is there Salvation in any other: for there is none other Name under Heaven given among men, whereby we must be saved" (Acts 4:11-12).

The Church was built on Christ. He is the only True Foundation and there is no other foundation. The Word of God says:

NOTES

"For other foundation can no man lay than that is laid, which is Jesus Christ" (I Cor. 3:11).

I think it is obvious, from even cursory investigation of Scripture, that the Disciples did not take our Lord's Words "... Upon this Rock I will build My Church," to mean that He was appointing Peter to be their Pope. A short time later, they asked Jesus (Mat. 18:1) "Who among them would be the greatest?" If Jesus had previously stated that Peter was to be their Pope, the Disciples would have automatically assumed that he was the greatest among them. Of course, this was not what Jesus was saying when He made this statement.

Furthermore, it seems obvious that the outstanding role in the Early Church was taken by Paul, not Peter. Paul wrote some 100 Chapters consisting of 2,325 verses within the New Testament. (Actually, it was Paul who defined and delivered the New Covenant, and because it was given to him by Christ.) On the other hand, Peter wrote only eight Chapters, consisting of 166 verses. Thus, it seems that Paul's Ministry was far more important than Peter's, that is, if one is to use this as a yardstick, which one shouldn't. The Apostle Paul stated:

"For I suppose I was not a whit behind the very chiefest Apostles" (II Cor. 11:5; 12:11).

Now, if Peter had been declared the supreme Pontiff, the Pope, then, certainly Paul would have been somewhat behind him. Obviously, this was not the case, as Paul's statement confirms.

Then, in Galatians 2:11, we read that Paul tendered a rebuke to Peter: "Because he was to be blamed."

It would certainly seem that Peter was not demonstrating infallibility in this situation, and that he was not considered by Paul to be "the infallible Pope." It is for sure that today, when papal infallibility had been formalized within the Catholic structure, we find no Bishops publicly rebuking the Pope for his errors.

It was the Apostle Paul who was "... the Apostle of the Gentiles" (Rom. 11:13).

On the other hand, Peter's Ministry was "... unto the circumcision," i.e., the Jews (Gal. 2:9).

This, within itself, is clear evidence that Peter was not the Bishop of Rome (as the Catholics teach), for Rome was a Gentile city.

The Catholic Church claims that Peter went to Rome about A.D. 41 and was martyred there about A.D. 66. However, as we have said, there is not a shred of evidence that Peter was ever in Rome. Certainly, he could have been, but Scripture does not even remotely hint at such.

Actually, I believe that all evidence is to the contrary. The New Testament specifically tells us that Peter visited Antioch, Samaria, Joppa, Caesarea, and other places, but absolutely no mention is ever made of his going to Rome. This would certainly be a strange omission when we realize that Rome was the capital of the Empire and was considered to be the most important city in the world.

Then if we accept A.D. 66 as the date of Peter's martyrdom, this would mean that he was Bishop of Rome from A.D. 41 to A.D. 66. But in about A.D. 44, we know Peter was attending the Council in Jerusalem, and about A.D. 53, we know that Paul joined him in Antioch (Gal. 2:11). Then, about A.D. 58 (as previously mentioned), Paul wrote his letter to the Christians at Rome — and failed completely to mention Peter as among those he was saluting in Rome.

To put this incident in proper perspective, imagine a Missionary writing to his home Church and greeting 27 of its prominent members — while completely ignoring the Pastor!

The entire hierarchy of the Catholic Church is built on the premise of Peter being the first Bishop of Rome. But once we begin to investigate these claims, we find no evidence to support them. In fact, at the same time, we are finding a great deal of evidence to refute them.

KEYS TO THE KINGDOM

In Rome today, at the high altar in St. Peter's Basilica, hundreds of feet above the altar and carved in marble, are the words (in Latin), *"Thou art Peter, and upon this rock I will build My Church."*

Did Jesus actually appoint Peter the first Pope?

I believe our Commentary on Matthew 16:18-19 adequately proves that He did not.

For hundreds of years, at the beginning of the Christian Church, no one ever used these words to claim any kind of papal supremacy or infallibility. Even unto this day, only Catholics do.

It stands to reason, if this had been the case, Peter, being the first Pope of the Church, surely, someone would have mentioned it

during those times. To be sure, the silence speaks volumes.

They did not mention it because it was not so, and the very idea of such would have been a laughing matter among the early Christians.

LET US LOOK AT THE EARLY CHURCH

Nowhere in the Book of Acts (which is the most complete history of the Early Church) is there any suggestion of such a person or position. Only gradually did the concept of an organized Church — governed, directed, and regulated by a hierarchy of Popes, Bishops, and Priests — evolve. And even then it did so despite widespread opposition.

It was Cyprian of Carthage (who died about A.D. 258) who introduced the concepts that were to bring about revolutionary changes in worship patterns within the Church.

Cyprian demanded obedience from the whole Church to the Bishop of Rome, who (he said) derived his authority directly from God. He made awesome claims for the episcopacy.

In the years following, this concept was gradually intruded into existing practice, and Church government eventually became almost completely autocratic.

During the years A.D. 390-461, Leo I, Bishop of Rome, used all his considerable powers to establish recognition for the Bishop of Rome as *"the Universal Bishop."* It was he who first made the claim that Peter had been the first Pope (some 400 years after this supposedly took place).

The eastern branch of the Church emphatically denied these claims. Even the Council of Chalcedon (where Leo exercised great power) refused his request to certify his claims. His assertions of papal supremacy did, however, produce a profound effect in later years.

Please note well that it was Leo I, the first Bishop of Rome, who laid claim to universal authority over the Church, and note also that this did not come about until some 400 years after the time of the Apostles in the Early Church. The Church had long since begun to apostatize.

Leo's claim was enforced through the power of the Roman Emperor, but even then it received only marginal acceptance within the Catholic Church. Further, the doctrine of papal infallibility was not officially promulgated until 1870!

IS THE CATHOLIC CLAIM TO UNIQUE GUIDANCE BY THE HOLY SPIRIT, THROUGH THE OFFICE OF THE POPE, VALID?

The answer to this becomes obvious the moment we consider the Roman Catholic Church's long history of errant and unscriptural doctrines.

If the Catholic Church is uniquely protected from error by the intervention of the Holy Spirit (through the Pope's office), a person can only conclude (and no irreverence is intended) that the Holy Spirit was asleep (or at least had His eyes closed) when the following occurred during the long and checkered career of the Catholic Church.

1. Leo I, Bishop of Rome (A.D. 390-461), advocated the death penalty for heresy — in other words, opposition to the Catholic Church.

2. Leo II, (A.D. 682-684), pronounced one of his predecessors, Pope Honorius I (A.D. 625-640), a heretic.

3. Stephen II (A.D. 752-757), encouraged the military conquest of Italy by Pepin and accepted the conquered lands as papal property.

4. Sergius III (A.D. 904-911), had a mistress, and their illegitimate offspring subsequently became Pope.

5. John X (A.D. 914-928), had multiple mistresses and was killed in the physical act of adultery by an irate husband.

6. Boniface VII (A.D. 984-985), murdered his predecessor, John XIV (A.D. 983-984).

7. Boniface VIII (A.D. 1294-1303), bought his papacy.

8. Benedict IX (A.D. 1032-1045), was made Pope at the age of twelve. He committed public murders and robberies, and was finally driven out of Rome by the people.

9. From A.D. 1045 to A.D. 1046, there were three rival Popes. During the reign of Alexander III (A.D. 1159-1181), there were four rival Popes. (Will the real Pope please stand?)

10. The incredibly cruel inquisition was initiated by Pope Innocent III (A.D. 1198-1216), and was to last for some 500 years. This was a Church court which purpose was ostensibly to root out and punish heretics. The lands and properties of condemned heretics became the

property of the Church. It thus served two practical purposes: Dissenters who disagreed with Catholic doctrines and practice were silenced, while the Pope's coffers were swelled.

The inquisition was responsible for the torture and death of countless Saints who refused to accept the practices of Rome. Any criticism of Pope or Bishop was immediate cause for the most gruesome tortures and executions. It was the most effective weapon ever devised to still criticism.

Not surprisingly, it suppressed for many years the rising tide of Protestantism within the *"holy"* Roman Empire. In fact, it is estimated to have been responsible for the deaths of some 900,000 confessing Christians during this period alone.

In totality, it is estimated that the Roman Catholic Church murdered some 20,000,000 people during the existence of the Inquisition. And a person cannot help asking the sobering question: Is this an example of Holy Spirit guidance that supposedly keeps the Roman Church on its unwavering course of infallibility?

IN CONCLUSION

Traditional Roman Catholicism states that there is only one True Church founded by Jesus Christ that is visible to the world. It is the temporal extension of Christ's Presence on earth, they say! It is vivified (lent life) and guided by the Holy Spirit.

It is endowed with infallibility and will last until the end of time. It cannot err in matters of Faith and morals. It is superior to, and the only reliable interpreter of, the Holy Bible.

It is visible (they say) in an authoritative, hierarchical structure that includes the very vicar of Christ — the Pope — on down through Bishops and Priests to the average layman. It is moreover a living organism, *"The mystical body of Christ."* Union with this organization is, in some manner, they say, necessary for Salvation.

In contrast, Evangelical Christianity sees the Church primarily as the universal and invisible community of born-again Christians. The Church's mission is to witness to Jesus Christ crucified and to His Plan for Salvation — and to foster life in the Holy Spirit through proclamation of the authoritative, written Word of God.

Protestants see the Church in a secondary degree, with its visible congregations as a vehicle instituted by Christ to preach the Word, to celebrate the ordinances of Water Baptism and the Lord's Supper, and to gather saved Christians in fellowship for mutual edification. Its life span in sacred history is limited to that period from Pentecost to the Rapture.

Evangelical Christianity constantly renews itself by submitting to the guidelines of the inerrant Scriptures and by making itself available to the Power of the Holy Spirit, and not some papal authority. No latter-day revelations are accepted if they are not in total agreement with the letter and spirit of God's written Word. It supports no intricate, external, contrived, hierarchical structure, at least not in its true Scriptural state, but conforms to the pattern of the simple pastoral framework revealed within the New Testament.

It relies without reservation on God's sustaining help and claims no infallible gift in regard to interpreting the Word of God. It says the Church is a saved people — not an organization based on the weaknesses of men.

It does not claim to save. It makes God's Plan of Salvation known to man at all times and in all places. It is a slave, and willingly so, to the sovereign Power of Jesus Christ, but enslaves no man's conscience. It believes all born-again people are a part of the Body of Christ — His Universal Church.

(20) "THEN CHARGED HE HIS DISCIPLES THAT THEY SHOULD TELL NO MAN THAT HE WAS JESUS THE CHRIST."

The phrase, *"Then charged He His Disciples,"* is a strong statement, with the word, *"charged,"* referring to a command. It is, in effect, a military term, which has a stern reprimand attached to it if disobeyed.

The phrase, *"That they should tell no man that He was Jesus the Christ,"* is emphatic, i.e., marked by emphasis.

Why?

1. If the people would not believe, even though confronted by a constant performing of Miracles, which was a fulfillment of Scripture, they would not believe if the fact of His Messiahship was proclaimed publicly.

2. As well, the Disciples, at least at this time, were not spiritually mature enough to make such a momentous announcement. In fact, they still did not understand Christ's Mission as the near future would proclaim.

3. By this time, it was painfully obvious that Israel had rejected her Messiah, and, therefore, any further proclamation was pointless!

The title, *"Jesus the Christ,"* is actually a proclamation of Messiahship. The Name, *"Jesus,"* was common among the Jews, meaning *"Joshua"* in Hebrew. However, with the proclamation of *"Christ"* attached to it, which meant *"The Anointed,"* automatically the assertion of Jesus being the Messiah was claimed.

In effect, He was telling His Disciples not to attach the Messianic title of *"Christ"* to Jesus, when speaking to others.

His heart must have broken in commanding the Disciples thusly, because, in effect, it spelled the doom of Israel. But, of course, the Disciples would not have understood that, at least at this particular time!

(21) "FROM THAT TIME FORTH BEGAN JESUS TO SHEW UNTO HIS DISCIPLES, HOW THAT HE MUST GO UNTO JERUSALEM, AND SUFFER MANY THINGS OF THE ELDERS AND CHIEF PRIESTS AND SCRIBES, AND BE KILLED, AND BE RAISED AGAIN THE THIRD DAY."

The phrase, *"From that time forth began Jesus to shew unto His Disciples,"* refers to a marked change in His Ministry. Now, the opposition by the Religious Leadership of Israel turns to outright rejection. Some four times this rejection is announced from here on (16:21; 17:22; 20:17-19, 28). In each announcement a new feature is added, as we shall see!

The phrase, *"How that He must go unto Jerusalem, and suffer many things of the Elders and Chief Priest and Scribes,"* constitutes one of the saddest statements ever made!

It is even sadder that *"Jerusalem"* will be the place, and the Religious Leaders the instigators of His sufferings.

Jerusalem was the city that was chosen by the Lord, *"That My Name might be there"* (II Chron. 6:6), in other words, His city. But now it has been so polluted by Satan, and by a false man-made religion, that it doesn't even know its own King when He comes. Of course, that is Satan's greatest trump, when he can pollute that which belongs to the Lord.

The three classes named here who would persecute Him are intentionally named.

1. *"The Elders":* These were the most aged and venerated members of the Sanhedrin.

They were, in effect, the ruling body of Israel, both politically and spiritually. (In Israel there was no separation of Church and State, both being one and the same.)

2. *"Chief Priests"*: These were the heads of the twenty-four courses respecting the carrying out of the Priestly duties on a day-to-day basis.

All the Priests did not work twelve months of the year in the carrying out of their office, but actually only two weeks out of the year, after which they went back to their families.

This was what was being spoken of when it said, and concerning the coming birth of John the Baptist, *"A certain Priest named Zacharias, of the course of Abia"* (Lk. 1:5).

In other words, Zacharias, the father of John the Baptist, was performing his two weeks of duties at the Temple, when the Angel of the Lord appeared unto him, announcing the coming birth of John.

These twenty-four courses were instituted by the Holy Spirit through David, concerning the Temple which would shortly be built (I Chron. 24).

3. *"Scribes"*: These individuals were supposed to be experts in the study of the Law of Moses. They were the originators of the Synagogue service, and some of them sat as members of the Sanhedrin.

They were oftentimes referred to as *"lawyers"* or *"teachers of the Law."* They belonged mainly to the party of the Pharisees, but as a body were distinct from them. They clashed with Christ, for He taught with authority, and He condemned external formalism which they fostered. Although the majority opposed Christ, some believed (Mat. 8:19).

Consequently, the entire religious world (with the exception of a few leading individuals) is portrayed here as being opposed to Christ.

Regrettably, that has not changed, as it continues accordingly to this present hour.

The phrase, *"And be killed,"* does not say in which manner, but will just a little later (20:19).

It is so startling, as we shall see, that the Disciples could not believe their ears. How could One with such Power be killed? As well, they did not realize the depth of the hatred held by the Religious Leaders against Christ.

The phrase, *"And be raised again the third day,"* proclaims the first time that such a thing

is mentioned, at least in Matthew, respecting this tremendous event.

The announcement, as given by Christ, was said, no doubt, with great sorrow, but, yet, matter of factly! As such, this event, which had never happened before in human history simply was not understood.

It is very easy for us to look down on the Disciples at their lack of understanding, but I doubt if anyone else at that time would have done any better, or even as well!

The evidence will show that the Disciples were far more concerned about Him being killed, than about the Resurrection. They understood what He meant concerning being *"killed,"* but there was no way they could have understood the Resurrection, at least at this stage.

(22) "THEN PETER TOOK HIM, AND BEGAN TO REBUKE HIM, SAYING, BE IT FAR FROM THEE, LORD: THIS SHALL NOT BE UNTO THEE."

The phrase, *"Then Peter took Him,"* means that he was greatly concerned respecting this statement by Christ, and probably laid his hand on His shoulder, within ear-shot of all the other Disciples. (It could mean that he drew Him aside, but probably the other is correct.)

The phrase, *"And began to rebuke Him,"* is fairly strong, with Peter chiding Jesus for speaking of suffering and death.

It was a foolish move on Peter's part, but how often have all of us done the same, at least by our attitude!

The phrase, *"Saying, Be it far from Thee, Lord: this shall not be unto Thee,"* proclaims a mind set of Peter, and, as well, where he was spiritually at this time.

When the Heavenly Father revealed to him that Jesus was indeed *"The Son of God,"* He was perfectly willing to proclaim this, and would have gladly done so publicly had not Christ charged him otherwise. However, his present rebuke of Christ was not a revelation from the Father, but rather a revelation of his own heart.

He had visions of Jesus using His great Power to overthrow Rome, with Israel, once again, becoming the premier nation in the world, and with him occupying a powerful position in this coming government. Consequently, the statement by Christ concerning being *"killed,"* was so foreign to his thinking that he would not hear of such.

To proclaim Jesus as Messiah, fit right in with his plans, but not Christ being killed!

As well, and no doubt, he could in no way understand that one with such power could be killed. In Peter's thinking, these Religious Leaders named by Christ, did not have the power to do this thing. So, in effect, he concludes himself wiser than his Lord.

Any time a Believer attempts to circumvent the Will of God, he is taking the same tact as taken by Peter. They are concluding themselves to be wiser than God. Regrettably, Peter is not alone in this misadventure, as most, if not all of us, have fallen into this trap at one time or the other.

(23) "BUT HE TURNED, AND SAID UNTO PETER, GET THEE BEHIND ME, SATAN: THOU ART AN OFFENCE UNTO ME: FOR THOU SAVOUREST NOT THE THINGS THAT BE OF GOD, BUT THOSE THAT BE OF MEN."

The phrase, *"But He turned, and said unto Peter,"* is a statement respecting a strong action.

The manner in which He *"turned,"* was obvious to all the Disciples, and especially Peter, that something was wrong, and seriously so, concerning Peter's statement.

The indication is that even though all the Disciples heard this exchange, still, Jesus' statement was pointedly directed at Peter. It would be the sternest of rebukes!

The phrase, *"Get thee behind Me, Satan,"* undoubtedly came as a shock to Peter. Jesus used nearly the same words in rebuking Peter that He had used to the Devil in his temptation (4:10).

A short time earlier, Peter had been used greatly by the Lord, while now he is being used by Satan, as he has played the adversary's part by opposing the Divine Plan.

This is a lesson that all of us must learn, that being used gloriously by the Lord at a given time does not ensure that it will continue. Living for God, and walking close to Him, is a constant occupation. There are two times the Believer must constantly be on guard: A. Before being used by God; and, B. After being used by God. As is obvious, this means that the Believer must be on guard at all times.

If the Believer follows *"after the Spirit,"* then the things of the Spirit will be forthcoming. But if *"after the flesh,"* the things of the flesh will be forthcoming, which will ultimately bring spiritual death (Rom. 8:1, 6).

Consequently, and irrespective as to who the person is, as Peter, who was one of the inner three, still, everything must be checked against the Word of God. Even if Peter says it and it is wrong, it must be corrected.

Some years later, Paul would basically do the same with Peter, when he *"withstood him to the face, because he was to be blamed"* (Gal. 2:11). (Peter had reverted to mixing Law with Grace.)

And yet, at the same time, let no one think that Peter was anything other than one of the greatest men of God who ever lived. Concerning the Early Church, the Scripture says, *"Insomuch that they brought forth the sick into the streets, and laid them on beds and couches, that at the least the shadow of Peter passing by might overshadow some of them."*

Then the Scripture said, *"And they were healed every one"* (Acts 5:15-16).

Even as I dictate these words, I sense the Presence of the Lord. Despite Peter's lapse, the Holy Spirit would have us to understand that there are few men in history who would stand the equal of the fisherman.

As an aside, in this Scripture we have the law of double reference.

In such cases, a human being is addressed, but an invisible person is also referred to. Part of what is said applies to each and this is determined by what is applicable to either. Other examples of this Law are Genesis 3:15; Isaiah 14:4-27; Ezekiel 28:11-19.

The phrase, *"Thou art an offence unto Me,"* proclaims anything that is contrary to the Word of God, as being an *"offence"* to the Lord. This, we should well heed!

In Truth, and sadly so, most of that which goes under the guise of Christendom is *"an offence"* to the Lord.

The phrase, *"For thou savourest not the things that be of God, but those that be of men,"* spoke of the grand thinking of the Disciples respecting Jesus overthrowing Rome, etc. That was *"of men,"* and not *"of God,"* as much, if not most, of that which is done presently, and claiming to be of the Lord.

The Child of God is to seek the things *"that be of God,"* and not that which *"be of men."* This is done by following the Word of the Lord, and not the word of men.

NOTES

NOTES

As well, and even more importantly, the Disciples, and according to the statements by Christ which followed, could not think of Christ suffering. They loved Him, and could not think of such a thing.

As well, the strain of modern Christianity, which attempts to eliminate all suffering in the Christian walk, is a thing *"of men,"* and not *"of God."*

A great part of that which calls itself *"the Faith Ministry,"* which, in reality, is no Faith at all, has attempted to eliminate the *"Cross"* from the Christian experience, or else to pervert its meaning. To do such is to deny Christ.

(24) "THEN SAID JESUS UNTO HIS DISCIPLES, IF ANY MAN WILL COME AFTER ME, LET HIM DENY HIMSELF, AND TAKE UP HIS CROSS, AND FOLLOW ME."

The phrase, *"Then said Jesus unto His Disciples,"* is added to by Mark, in that Jesus also called a sizable group of people to Him as well! The Message about to be announced is so important that the people must hear it as well, and because it pertained to them also!

The phrase, *"If any man will come after Me,"* pertains to all followers of Christ, in which the conditions are now laid down for acceptance into this most select group. To be sure, it will not be conditions that the carnal heart desires. And yet, the demands made are absolutely necessary if one is to be a True follower of Christ. As well, what applied to one, applies to all!

The phrase, *"Let him deny himself, and take up his cross, and follow Me,"* spells out that which is demanded.

The poor human heart likes position and glory, and is quite willing to exalt the Messiah even to Heaven, as Peter, but it shrinks from self-mortification, shame, hatred, persecution and death. The term, *"the cross,"* means all this.

If anyone wishes to go after Jesus, he must consent to share His reproach and die with Him. At the door of the Roman Court of Justice, crosses were piled, and the condemned on leaving took up a cross and carried it to the place of execution. The Believer must follow Christ in that path.

It is the only path; there is no other; and if anyone would be His Disciple, he must enter it, for it is the path the Master took.

Three things are here demanded, and they are as follows:

1. *"Deny himself":* The first is self-denial. Consequently, Jesus died on Calvary, not only to deliver man from sin, but, as well, from self. This malady, self, will prove to be the most difficult obstacle in the life of any Christian. Sin can be easily washed and cleansed, with the sinner forgiven, delivered, and restored in quick order, that is, if the Word is fully obeyed (I Jn. 1:9). However, self properly placed in Christ is not so easily or quickly done!

Too much of what the Believer gives to the world in the Name of Christ is self, which will draw no one to the Lord, and reap no spiritual benefits. And yet, much if not most of the Church gives such, thinking all the time it is Christ.

More tragic still, many in the modern Church have sought to glorify self by the promotion of self-esteem. To be sure, man's problem is not a low self-esteem, even though that problem may exist. Man's problem is *"self"* period, whether low self-esteem or high self-esteem. Self must properly be placed in Christ in order that God's Will be carried out in all things.

The major problem with *"self"* is that it desires things which are not the Will of God, hence, the demanded self-denial by Christ. We are to deny self-will in favor of His Will.

2. *"Take up his cross":* Luke adds *"daily."*

Exactly what is the cross spoken of by Christ?

First of all, anything that can be undergone by anyone unsaved does not constitute the *"cross."* Consequently, that lets out all sickness, poverty, rejection, etc., for all of these things are encountered by those who do not follow Christ. Unfortunately, many Christians have thought of such things as *"crosses."*

The *"taking up of the cross,"* simply means to do the Will of God, whatever that Will is, in any and every life.

To be sure, if one truly follows the Will of God, thereby taking up their cross, such will always be met by hostility from the world and opposition from the apostate Church. Therefore, at times, the *"cross"* gets heavy.

Therefore, as the first is self-denial, the second is self-abnegation.

3. *"And follow Me":* The following of Christ will necessitate the taking up of the cross,

because that is the path Christ trod. So, to follow Christ means not only to follow to victory, glory, and eternal life, but, as well, through the many sorrows and heartaches that accompany such a journey. As Jesus bid His Disciples upon calling them to *"follow Me,"* likewise, He bids the same to all others.

However, and irrespective of the difficulty of the journey, and, to be sure, some parts of it will be very difficult, we have the assurance and comfort of knowing that in following Him, He has been there before us, and, consequently, has made a way.

This was done in His earthly walk, and proclaims victory to all who will assiduously follow Him.

As the first is self-denial, with the second being self-abnegation, the last is self-diligence.

(25) "FOR WHOSOEVER WILL SAVE HIS LIFE SHALL LOSE IT: AND WHOSOEVER WILL LOSE HIS LIFE FOR MY SAKE SHALL FIND IT."

The phrase, *"For whosoever will save his life shall lose it,"* means that it is lost in relation to this world, but is found in relationship to the next. Those who refuse, safeguard their life in this world, but suffer eternal loss in the next. As one divine said, *"If you keep your seed, you lose it; if you sow it, you will find it again."*

The idea pertains to self-will! The individual who sets out on this life journey to carry out his own will, of necessity, must deny the Will of God. To do that, will bring no lasting satisfaction in this world, and no eternal life in the world to come. It is so sad and tragic that most of the world follows the footsteps of self-will, instead of following Christ. As such, the world is inundated with misery, heartache, pain and suffering.

How terrible it is when someone of note dies, and about all that can be said of him or her is some inane thing which matters little, if at all.

Recently an announcement was made concerning the death of a movie star. The gist of his life's accomplishment was told in just a few words, with the high point having been his performance in a particular Broadway play which was noted for its abundance of profanity. Even though the public lauded him, his life was wasted and was no benefit to himself or anyone else. What a waste! And yet, that characterizes almost all of the world. It was a life lived

for self; therefore, it was lost, i.e., squandered, misused, wasted, misspent, of no consequence.

The phrase, *"And whosoever will lose his life for My sake shall find it,"* speaks of losing one's own life in service to Christ, which, in Truth, is no loss at all. In other words, to lose that which is of no benefit is no loss, and that is exactly what a life is without Christ.

However, to lay aside our own will, wishes and desires, which, without Christ, are meaningless anyway, and for His sake, give everything to Him, is the greatest trade anyone could ever make. It would seem that the entirety of the world would want to engage in this trade, but, sadly, most do not!

Why?

Satan blinds the world in that it does not know, cannot see, does not think correctly, and, in reality, thinks that up is down, while down is up, while out is in and in is out. It calls evil good and good evil!

In reality, for one to *"lose their life,"* and, as stated, a life without Christ, is no loss whatsoever. But yet, to think that with this *"loss"* the Lord gives us eternal life, then we realize that we have really lost nothing, and gained everything.

The only life that is fulfilling, rewarding, and of benefit, is the life lived for Christ. All other life, and irrespective as to how much money or so-called pleasure the individual may have, is, in reality, no life at all. And yet, one cannot know that until one accepts Christ and enters into His Life.

This is somewhat like the Tabernacle of old! From the outside there was no beauty. However, upon entering its portals, one is dazzled by the greatest display of beauty and wealth that one could ever behold.

Likewise, the unsaved who observes the Christian experience by only looking at the externals, sees very little that is appealing. But upon accepting Christ, everything changes, because for the first time, true life, which can only be given by God, becomes the property of the follower of Christ.

I have prayed with paupers and I have prayed with Presidents, and I have never seen any individual and irrespective of their station in life, who knew true happiness outside of Christ. Such does not exist!

I am always amazed when I hear it said of

some individual, and concerning the plaudits of the world, *"They made it!"*

Of course, they are speaking of fame and glory with its accompanying riches, etc. Still, I always wonder, *"Made what?"*

All of these who have *"made it,"* at least in the vernacular of the world, know no true fulfillment or reward outside of Christ. Most, if not all, live in misery, and all, at least if they do not accept Christ, in some way die in shame and heartache.

Just the other day, a Believer, a dear friend of mine, was speaking disparagingly of a particular situation in his life. He was somewhat distraught and disturbed. I heard him out for a few minutes, and then said to him:

"That which you are speaking of, even if it was perfect, which it never can be, still, can never satisfy the hunger and the thirst of your heart. Only Christ can do that."

His face brightened, and I could tell the truth of the statement sank into his heart.

It is regrettable that all of us at one time or the other, even though Believers, have looked in other directions for that which our heart craves. It can only be found in Christ.

This means that irrespective of what type of house one has to live in, the environment, or the state of one's health, etc., the true meaning and purpose of life can only be realized if Christ is looked to in totality. This is the very opposite of the thinking of the world, as they place all hopes, dreams and aspirations on *"things."* And yet, millions, and even billions, drink of that fountain, and thirst again. While if one drinks of the Water of Life given by Christ, they will never thirst again (Jn. 4:13-14).

(26) "FOR WHAT IS A MAN PROFITED, IF HE SHALL GAIN THE WHOLE WORLD, AND LOSE HIS OWN SOUL? OR WHAT SHALL A MAN GIVE IN EXCHANGE FOR HIS SOUL?"

The question, *"For what is a man profited . . . ?"*, proclaims Christ bringing this all-important transaction down to the level that all can understand, hence the use of the word, *"profit."*

In doing so, He is asking that all consider the stakes. And to be sure, the stakes are very high!

The continuance of the question, *"If he shall gain the whole world, and lose his own soul?"*, puts everything in proper perspective.

First of all, no one has ever gained the *"whole*

world," and no one ever will. To be truthful, most sell their soul for next to nothing.

Here we are, once again, referring to *"gain"* and *"loss,"* as the question that can be understood by all.

Jesus is speaking of the temporal versus the eternal.

Whatever it is that an individual obtains in this world, and no matter of how much of it, is only enjoyed for a short while. However, the soul of man is eternal. If he loses that, he has lost everything.

The truth of the matter is that most people do not believe that man was originally created in the Image of God, and, consequently, will live forever. Most do not even believe that man is created spirit, soul and body (I Thess. 5:23). As such, and due to the lie of evolution, most believe that man is a physical being only, and at death goes into nothingness, or into something that is not now known. They believe this because they do not believe the Bible.

That is the reason that abortion can be practiced without any pangs of conscience. If, in fact, man is only a higher form of animal life, with no soul or spirit, and merely a physical body, then his life is worth very little. In fact, that is what most of the world believes, hence the aborting of a baby is of no consequence.

As well, in the countries of the world which are not influenced by the Bible, life is so cheap that it is sacrificed by the powers that be at will!

This is the reason that some of Hitler's Generals could speak flippantly of working a hundred or more Russians to death, digging an anti-tank ditch, and think nothing of it. In their minds, these (the Russians) were sub-human, while they (the Germans) were the master race. And I might quickly add, this from a nation (Germany) which had once known God! That is the reason Jesus said, *"The last state of that man is worse than the first"* (Lk. 11:26).

Much of the world, not believing the Bible, believes in some form of reincarnation, which, of course, is a lie of Satan, using the vehicle of Hinduism and other Eastern Religions as a springboard for this fabrication.

The truth is, man is an eternal soul, and made that way by God. He will live forever, whether in Heaven or hell. If he accepts Christ as his Saviour, he will have eternal life, and will live forever in the state of that life, and with Christ.

If he does not trust Christ as his Saviour, he will lose his soul exactly as Jesus has spoken, and will continue to exist forever in the *"Lake of Fire"* (Rev. 21:8).

It is this which the scoffers jest about! They do so in unbelief, and, consequently, *"lose their soul."*

The question, *"Or what shall a man give in exchange for his soul?",* takes it a step further.

In other words, Jesus is saying that there is absolutely nothing, and irrespective as to what it is, as important as the saving of one's soul. Everything else pales into insignificance in comparison to the worth of the soul of man, and because it was originally made in the Image of God and is, therefore, eternal.

WHAT IS THE SOUL?

As stated, God created man, spirit, soul and body.

The spirit of man is the part of man which *"knows,"* which includes the intellect, will and intelligence (Rom. 8:26; 12:2; I Cor. 2:11).

The soul is the part of man which feels, which concerns the passions and emotions (Job 14:22).

According to the Greek scholars, the word translated *"life"* in verse 25 should have been translated *"life"* in verse 26, even though *"soul"* is correct.

Actually, the word, *"soul,"* is used in two senses: It is used first of all of the life which now is — the bodily life, and the life which is to come, the spiritual, the everlasting life. Actually, they are two stages of the same life — that which is mortal, and that which is immortal, i.e., *"the Glorified Body in Heaven."*

The body is the only part of man that dies, with the soul and the spirit going to be with Jesus if born again, and, sadly, into hell if not born again (Phil. 1:23; Lk. 16:22-23).

The body goes back to dust, and, therefore, sleeps until the Resurrection, whether of eternal life or eternal death.

If the person is a Believer at the First Resurrection of Life, God will give the soul and the spirit a new body (I Cor. 15:35-38).

If an unbeliever, the body will be raised to join the soul and the spirit at the Second Resurrection of Damnation, which is a thousand

NOTES

years after the First Resurrection of Life. It will then be cast into the Lake of Fire, to burn there forever and forever (Rev. 20:11-15).

So, in view of the eternal consequences, one can well understand why Christ would use this type of startling terminology.

(27) "FOR THE SON OF MAN SHALL COME IN THE GLORY OF HIS FATHER WITH HIS ANGELS; AND THEN HE SHALL REWARD EVERY MAN ACCORDING TO HIS WORKS."

In this one Scripture, Christ alludes to the Rapture, mentions the Second Coming, and speaks of the Judgment, without really defining all of these tremendous events.

The phrase, *"For the Son of Man shall come in the Glory of His Father with His Angels,"* speaks of something totally different than what was said to Peter about how He (Christ) must *"suffer many things . . ."*

In essence, He is saying that the suffering must precede the Glory, and definitely will come; however, the sufferings only declare the *"Glory,"* which will most surely come, and in a splendor such as the world has never known before.

This speaks of the Second Coming, which will be, and without a doubt, the most striking, startling event the world has ever known in all of its history. There is no way the mind of man can imagine, or the tongue can adequately portray the Glory of this event, or even the mind to even fully comprehend it. It is outlined in Revelation 19:11-21.

The phrase, *"And then He shall reward every man according to his works,"* pertains first of all to the Rapture. Between the Rapture and Second Coming, every Believer will be rewarded *"according to his works"* (I Cor. 3:12-15).

The same holds true for unbelievers who will be at the Great White Throne Judgment, where they will be judged as well, at least respecting punishment, *"according to their works"* (Rev. 20:11-15).

Consequently, it speaks of the Judgment, whether of the Righteous at the *"Judgment Seat of Christ,"* or the unrighteous at the *"Great White Throne Judgment."*

The *"works"* are important to the Believer, only pertaining to reward. The Believer will not be judged according to his soul's Salvation, because the Believer's sins were judged at Calvary.

As well, the Great White Throne Judgment, which will be a gathering of unbelievers only, will be conducted not for the judgment of the soul. That has already been determined by the refusal to accept Christ.

This judgment pertains to the degree of punishment, *"according to their works"* (Rev. 20:12).

Regrettably, many of the *"works"* of the Believer are going to be *"burned,"* and *"he shall suffer loss"* respecting reward, even though no Believer will lose their soul (I Cor. 3:15).

Only the *"works"* that are done because of *"Love of God,"* and *"Love of man,"* will stand the acid test, because these two incorporate the entirety of the Commandments of the Lord (Mat. 22:37-40).

All other *"works"* carried out through false doctrines, envying, strife, divisions, bigotry or personal ambition, will not stand the test, and will be *"burned."*

One can add to that, love of praise, pride of Denomination, pride of talents, and love of authority.

(28) "VERILY I SAY UNTO YOU, THERE BE SOME STANDING HERE, WHICH SHALL NOT TASTE OF DEATH, TILL THEY SEE THE SON OF MAN COMING IN HIS KINGDOM."

The phrase, *"Verily I say unto you,"* pertains to the coming transfiguration.

The phrase, *"There be some standing here,"* was referring to His Disciples, with the word, *"some,"* pertaining to Peter, James and John, and not the entirety of the Twelve.

The phrase, *"Which shall not taste of death,"* means they would behold the transfiguration before they died. Actually, it would take place in a very short time.

The phrase, *"Till they see the Son of Man coming in His Kingdom,"* referred to Christ being transfigured, i.e., to change the form from the earthly to the heavenly.

In other words, they would get a glimpse of that which was going to be. They would see the Glory of Christ, while, at the same time, seeing Moses and Elijah. Of course, there is no way that words could describe the astonishment of such a moment. They would look at two men, one who had been dead for about 1500 years, while the other, Elijah, was translated that he should not see death, and, in fact, had lived in Paradise in his natural body for about 900 years. Consequently, Peter, along with James and

John, would now see the Glory of the One he had acclaimed as *"The Son of the Living God."*

CHAPTER 17

(1) "AND AFTER SIX DAYS JESUS TAKETH PETER, JAMES, AND JOHN HIS BROTHER, AND BRINGETH THEM UP INTO AN HIGH MOUNTAIN APART."

The phrase, *"And after six days,"* is in the Hebrew language exclusive, which means all the days and time are not included.

Luke said, *"about eight days,"* but in Hebrew the phrase is inclusive, meaning that two more days of time elements were counted which Matthew and Mark did not include. Consequently, both statements agree.

The phrase, *"Jesus taketh Peter, James, and John his brother,"* proclaims these three in contrast to the other nine. Actually, two other times record Christ taking these three into a deeper experience. All three times portray a revelation.

1. The three Disciples, Peter, James and John, were given a *"Revelation of the Glory of God,"* in the Transfiguration experience.

2. Peter, James and John, were called into the house of Jairus, while the other nine were not, as Jesus raised Jairus' daughter from the dead (Lk. 8:51). They then experienced a *"Revelation of Power."*

3. All the Disciples minus Judas, went into the Garden of Gethsemane with Jesus immediately before His Crucifixion. However, after Jesus told them to remain at a certain place, He took Peter, James and John, with Him a little further into the Garden. Here they experienced a *"Revelation of Suffering"* (Mk. 14:32).

Why did Jesus choose these three to experience a greater witness of Himself than the others?

I believe the Scripture teaches that it was not an arbitrary decision. The Bible teaches *"whosoever will,"* and that God is *"no respecter of persons"* (Rev. 22:17; Acts 10:34).

Therefore, one can only conclude that Jesus saw in the hearts of these three a deeper hunger for a closer walk with Him than the others. That is the only explanation!

Consequently, Peter would be the most powerful of the Twelve chosen by the Holy Spirit to preach the inaugural message of the Church on the Day of Pentecost, and, as well, to be the first one to take the Gospel to the Gentiles (Acts Chpts. 2 and 10). He also wrote two Epistles, I and II Peter.

John wrote the Gospel of John, which is the most in-depth of the Gospels concerning the Teachings of Christ. As well, he wrote I, II and III John.

Even more importantly, and if such can be graded accordingly, the Holy Spirit chose John to write the Book of Revelation, which closed out the Canon of Scripture which began with Moses about 1600 years earlier. He was near a hundred years of age when he wrote this great Prophetic Book, and was the last of the Twelve to die.

Not much is known concerning James, John's brother, who was murdered by Herod in 44 A.D. about eleven years after the Crucifixion of Christ. There is no Biblical evidence of accomplishments regarding him, as with Peter and John. However, one can be certain that the approximate eleven years of ministry he did have was marked by a great touch of God. There had to have been a hunger in his heart for the things of the Lord that was somewhat more pronounced than the nine.

The phrase, *"And bringeth them up into an high mountain apart,"* does not tell us which mountain.

Some have claimed that it was Mt. Tabor, which is close to Nazareth. From what little account that is given, that, to me, seems to be correct.

On one of our trips to Israel, around 1985, we taped a Television Special at Nazareth, the boyhood home of Jesus.

I asked to be taken to the place where the city fathers had determined to kill Christ by throwing Him off this high hill.

As we drove up to this place and unloaded the equipment, while our Television people were preparing for the *"shoot,"* I had the occasion to survey the surrounding countryside.

Standing on that high point, with my back to Nazareth, the Valley of Megiddo was spread out before me. From where I stood, Mt. Gilboa was at about 11 o'clock. This is where Saul and Jonathan were killed fighting the Philistines.

At about 10 o'clock was Mt. Carmel, situated on the Mediterranean, where Elijah called fire

NOTES

down from Heaven. Actually, from this high point I could see a faint glimpse of the Mediterranean Sea.

Immediately behind me at about 8 o'clock was the Mountain where it is thought that Jesus was transfigured, and at its base, as we will soon study, where Jesus delivered a boy from demon spirits.

In all of the times I have travelled to Israel, and considering all the places we have visited, to me, this particular spot stands out as one of the most meaningful.

As I stood there that day, I realized that Jesus as a young boy many times, no doubt, came to this very place, where He found privacy and would seek the Face of His Heavenly Father. No doubt, He spent countless hours at this very spot, meditating on the Scriptures. We know, from Luke's account, that from the time He was twelve years old He knew what His mission was, for He said, *"Wist ye not that I must be about My Father's business?"* (Lk. 2:49).

(2) "AND WAS TRANSFIGURED BEFORE THEM: AND HIS FACE DID SHINE AS THE SUN, AND HIS RAIMENT WAS WHITE AS THE LIGHT."

The phrase, *"And was transfigured before them,"* means that the Glory did not shine upon Jesus, but, instead, shone out from Him through His raiment.

Someone has said that the *"Transfiguration"* was not the real miracle, but the constant veiling of His Glory. In other words, the *"Transfiguration"* was the normal, which He actually was, while the hiding of this Glory, was the marvel.

The Transfiguration marks an important stage in the Revelation of Jesus as the Christ and the Son of God. It is an experience similar to His Baptism.

In the Transfiguration, His Glory is revealed not through His deeds, but in a more personal way. The Glory denotes the Royal Presence, for the Kingdom of God is in the midst of His people.

The phrase, *"And His Face did shine as the sun,"* is similar to His appearance in Revelation 1:16, where it says, *"His countenance was as the sun shineth in His strength."*

Paul would later write, *"For God, Who commanded the light to shine out of darkness, hath shined in our hearts, to give the light of the knowledge of the Glory of God in the Face of Jesus Christ"* (II Cor. 4:6).

The phrase, *"And His raiment was white as the light,"* means that His garment, which was not necessarily white to begin with, seems to be white because of the great *"light"* shining through it.

The Greek word used to express the *"light"* is *"stilbo,"* which means *"Living Light."* So, the word, *"transfigured,"* here means that His outward form of expression was changed, namely, from that of a servant to that of Deity. As stated, the *"light"* was not shining upon Him, but, instead, from Him, and was so bright that it was difficult if not impossible at this time to look directly at Him.

This is the way He will appear in His Coming Glory, when He rules and reigns from Jerusalem in the Coming Kingdom Age.

As alluded to, this is what Christ really was, with His form of a Servant, which He took upon Himself only as an expression of His humanity. He was a Servant, while all the time, God.

(3) "AND, BEHOLD, THERE APPEARED UNTO THEM MOSES AND ELIAS (ELIJAH) TALKING WITH HIM."

The words, *"And, behold,"* speak of something happening suddenly, with one moment it not being there, and the next moment it suddenly appearing.

The phrase, *"There appeared unto them Moses and Elias* (Elijah),*"* means that these two personages appeared suddenly!

Why Moses and Elijah, and not other Prophets?

It is thought by some that Moses represented all who were under the Law, while Elijah, having been translated about 900 years before, represents the Raptured Saints. The appearance of both of them means that all those who were under the Law and those under Grace will be treated accordingly in the First Resurrection of Life.

What purpose did their appearance serve?

The phrase, *"Talking with Him,"* gives us an indication, as Luke said they *"spake of His decease,"* referring to His soon-to-come Crucifixion. Everything depended on this, including man's Salvation, of which the Law pointed to but could not bring about, as well as the Advent of the Holy Spirit, and all that would follow in its train, along with the coming Resurrection of Life.

In speaking of His coming death, they were

proclaiming this Doctrine as the great theme of Heaven (Rev. 1:5; 5:6, 9; 7:14).

(4) "THEN ANSWERED PETER, AND SAID UNTO JESUS, LORD, IT IS GOOD FOR US TO BE HERE: IF THOU WILT, LET US MAKE HERE THREE TABERNACLES; ONE FOR THEE, AND ONE FOR MOSES, AND ONE FOR ELIAS."

The phrase, *"Then answered Peter, and said unto Jesus,"* proclaims the Disciple at this awesome time, commenting on something he had no knowledge of, and making a request that was not appropriate, and, as well, displeasing to the Heavenly Father.

The phrase, *"Lord, it is good for us to be here,"* had reference to Himself, James and John.

According to Luke, when Jesus and the three arrived at the top of the mountain, Jesus began to pray, and as He prayed He experienced the Transfiguration, with the two Prophets then appearing unto Him. How long Jesus prayed before the Transfiguration, the Scripture does not say. At any rate, the tremendous Power of God that seemed to overshadow the mountain, and which brought about the Transfiguration of Christ, also caused the three Disciples to fall into a deep sleep.

While Moses and Elijah were still there, and talking with Christ, Peter and the other two awoke, and were greeted by a sight that no human being had ever beheld.

How they knew these two were Moses and Elijah, the Scripture does not say. Perhaps in overhearing the conversation between Jesus and the two Prophets, it was brought out as to who they were. However, there is a possibility that for a few moments they were given the knowledge that will come to all Believers at the Resurrection, when, as Paul said, *"Now I know in part; but then shall I know even as also I am known"* (I Cor. 13:12). But, regardless of how they knew, they knew who these two men were!

The phrase, *"If Thou wilt, let us make here three tabernacles,"* spoke of three booths, such as the people erected when celebrating the Feast of Tabernacles.

Why did Peter suggest this?

As wrong as he was, there is a possibility that he actually had the Feast of Tabernacles in mind. He may have truly thought such, due to the Glorious Transfiguration of Christ, which was a display of Glory such as the Disciples had never seen. And now, with the appearance of Moses and Elijah, Peter may have thought that the Kingdom of Heaven which Jesus had been preaching about was about to be unveiled in all of its splendor and glory. In fact, in a sense the Feast of Tabernacles, if that is what Peter was thinking, represented that coming day. Peter, possibly thinking this glorious time had now arrived, blurts out that which, at least at that time, made sense.

Even though all have a tendency to berate the Apostle, still, for all the light he presently had, he was probably far more Scriptural than one tends to think.

He had no doubt read the great Prophet Zechariah, when he spoke of the coming Kingdom Age, and the keeping of the *"Feast of Tabernacles,"* and surmised that the time had now come (Zech. 14:18-21).

Even now, after all the Epistles have been given, and we are given much more light on the great Plan of God, still, as Paul said, *"For now we see through a glass, darkly"* (I Cor. 13:12).

Just quite possibly, some of our present thoughts concerning coming or even present events respecting the Work of God are just as inane as those of the Disciple!

The phrase, *"One for Thee, and one for Moses, and one for Elias (Elijah),"* inasmuch as these were the only three he saw, to begin this Feast of Tabernacles, he would build three booths on the top of the mountain, where it had had its beginning.

Considering the mind-set of the Disciples, in that Jesus, they thought, was going to set up His Kingdom now, this no doubt seemed to the Disciple to be the beginning of this great moment. Never mind that Jesus had only a few days earlier rebuked him for denying the coming Crucifixion. The idea that Christ would suffer and be crucified, and despite His plainly saying this would happen, still, they not only did not understand such, but, in fact, did not believe it! Up to hours before the Crucifixion, even at the Last Supper, *"There was also a strife among them, which of them should be accounted the greatest"* (Lk. 22:24).

So, Peter's request, which seems so outlandish now, probably seemed very plausible to him then!

(5) "WHILE HE YET SPAKE, BEHOLD, A BRIGHT CLOUD OVERSHADOWED THEM:

NOTES

AND BEHOLD A VOICE OUT OF THE CLOUD, WHICH SAID, THIS IS MY BELOVED SON, IN WHOM I AM WELL PLEASED; HEAR YE HIM."

The phrase, *"While he yet spake,"* concerns these statements by Peter which the Heavenly Father would not ignore.

The phrase, *"Behold, a bright cloud overshadowed them,"* once again, and because of the word, *"behold,"* refers to the *"bright cloud"* appearing suddenly.

This was a demonstration of the Shechinah, a token of the Presence of the Most High, which had appeared over the Tabernacle in the wilderness.

The words, *"Overshadowed them,"* means that Peter, James and John, were included as being in this *"overshadowing."*

Soon, on the Day of Pentecost, that cloud, so to speak, would come to abide in these three, plus all the others who were there that memorable Day, along with the multiple millions of others who have, as well, experienced the mighty Baptism in the Holy Spirit with the evidence of speaking with other tongues (Acts 2:4).

The *"cloud"* overshadowing them as well, was a fore view of the Work of the Holy Spirit after the Day of Pentecost in glorifying Christ (Jn. 16:14). So, the Glory was not for Peter, James and John, or even for Moses and Elijah, but was totally because of Christ, as the balance of the Scripture will bear out.

The phrase, *"And behold a voice out of the cloud, which said,"* was actually the Voice of God the Father.

Consequently, we have here a portrayal of the Trinity as it is revealed, with the Father speaking with audible voice, with Jesus, His Son, standing in a radiant light, and the Holy Spirit present with the overshadowing cloud.

The phrase, *"Which said, This is My Beloved Son, in Whom I am well pleased,"* presents the same voice, saying the same words that had been heard when Jesus was baptized in the Jordan (Mat. 3:17).

The phrase, *"Here ye Him,"* presents the proclamation of a tremendous Truth.

God will not have even the greatest Saints associated with His Beloved Son in worship or teaching. Regrettably and sadly, Peter's erroneous proposal has been adopted by the Catholic Church, and men are accordingly commanded to listen to that Church as an authoritative teacher, instead of Christ, and to associate mere mortals with Christ.

However, upon Peter placing Moses and Elijah in the same category of Christ, the Divine Voice said: *"Hear Him,"* and, we might add, Him Alone.

Going back to Simon Peter, no sooner did he receive his new name (16:18), than he demonstrated his personal weakness. In 16:22 and 23, he intruded himself as a stumbling block in connection with the Cross, and in this 4th verse a belittler of the Glory.

The carnal nature can mirror Satan, that is, an adversary. It understands neither the Cross nor the Glory; and it refuses to die to the world (16:24).

A Christian who is not dead to the world is an *"offence,"* i.e., a stumbling stone to all who try to walk the path of shame and death with Christ.

As this verse proclaims, Simon was rebuked on the summit of the mountain and Satan was rebuked at its base (vs. 18).

MOSES AND ELIJAH

As an aside, and back to Moses and Elijah, Moses actually had been dead for about 1,600 years and had been in Paradise for that length of time (Deut., Chpt. 4; Jude 9).

In order to make this appearance, he was brought out of Paradise, and he stood with Jesus and Elijah on the Mount of Transfiguration. He then went back to Paradise to await the Coming of Christ after the Crucifixion, when Christ would then deliver all of these Saints held in that place and take them with Him to Heaven (Eph. 4:8).

As we have stated, when the Believer dies, even though the body goes back to dust, the Spirit and soul of the individual go to be with Christ. Paul calls the Spirit and soul, *"the inner man"* (Eph. 3:16), and, as Moses, looks exactly as it did with the body (the outer man).

As well, and back to the Scripture at hand, when God the Father spoke of Jesus and how *"pleased"* He was with Him, in effect, He was, at the same time, saying that He was not pleased with Peter, James and John, as well as Moses and Elijah. In Truth, He is not pleased with any other human being, and because of the obvious reasons, except they have trusted Christ as their Lord and Saviour. As such, all of those on the mountain top were included in the *"well*

pleased" statement, and because all had trusted Christ. This would include, as well, every Believer in Christ who has ever lived.

God the Father cannot be pleased with anyone who is *"out of Christ,"* but of those *"in Christ,"* He is proclaimed as being *"well pleased."*

Also, if Peter, in fact, was thinking of the Feast of Tabernacles when he made his statement, it will yet be realized.

In the coming Kingdom Age, Jesus, in all of His Glory, as here shown, will reign supreme from Jerusalem, and over the entirety of the earth. As well, at that time, and as stated, the entirety of the world will come to keep the *"Feast of Tabernacles."* Consequently, Peter was not so much wrong, as being so much early. It will ultimately come to pass!

(6) "AND WHEN THE DISCIPLES HEARD IT, THEY FELL ON THEIR FACE, AND WERE SORE AFRAID."

The phrase, *"And when the Disciples heard it,"* refers to the *"Voice out of the cloud."* The majesty and power of this was so great that *"They fell on their face, and were sore afraid."*

The action of the phrase is such that is seems they did not *"fall on their face,"* simply because they could not physically stand, but, instead, because they were so awestruck at what they were seeing that fear enveloped them, as they looked at the radiance of this Glory. The words, *"Sore afraid,"* means that they were fearful they would die.

As we have said many times, comparing our righteousness with others is easily done; however, when placed beside the Righteousness of Christ, one easily sees, just as the Disciples did, one's terrible deficiencies.

Men mock Christ, and because they have never seen Him in His Glory. When they do, their reaction will be identical to the Disciples, *"They will fall on their faces, and be sore afraid."*

In this scene on the mount, one is observing absolute pure Righteousness and Holiness on the part of Christ. All others, even Moses and Elijah, and the Disciples, have none except that which comes from Christ, and upon Faith is freely given.

(7) "AND JESUS CAME AND TOUCHED THEM, AND SAID, ARISE, AND BE NOT AFRAID."

The phrase, *"And Jesus came and touched them,"* proclaims a *"touch"* of love and compassion. There was no reprimand whatsoever for

Peter's statement, only the words, *"Arise, and be not afraid."* These are words He ever speaks to all who will come to Him in Faith believing.

To the trembling heart, He says, *"Be not afraid!"* To the troubled mind, He says, *"Be not afraid!"* To the accusations of Satan, He says, *"Be not afraid!"*

As the song says:

"I have found His Grace, is all complete.
"He supplieth every need.
"While I sit and learn, at Jesus' feet,
"I am free, yes free indeed!"
CHORUS:
"It is joy unspeakable, and full of Glory,
"Full of Glory, full of Glory,
"It is joy unspeakable, and full of Glory,
"And the half has never yet been told."

(8) "AND WHEN THEY HAD LIFTED UP THEIR EYES, THEY SAW NO MAN, SAVE JESUS ONLY."

The phrase, *"And when they had lifted up their eyes,"* proclaims them earnestly surveying their present locality where this stupendous miracle had occurred.

The phrase, *"They saw no man, save Jesus only,"* conveys a tremendous Truth.

That Truth is that everything hinges on Jesus, and, in Truth, Jesus is enough. The Father has committed all judgment unto the Son, and as a result of what Jesus did at Calvary and the Resurrection, *"God also hath highly exalted Him, and given Him a Name which is above every name"* (Phil. 2:9).

In reality, the *"Transfiguration"* presented to all Believers a fore glimpse of that which is to come. It will be so glorious, as here depicted, that it will defy description! As well, the miracle-working Power of God is portrayed in this event, in that all Preachers of the Gospel should have the *"cloud"* to overshadow them.

(9) "AND AS THEY CAME DOWN FROM THE MOUNTAIN, JESUS CHARGED THEM, SAYING, TELL THE VISION TO NO MAN, UNTIL THE SON OF MAN BE RISEN AGAIN FROM THE DEAD."

The phrase, *"And as they came down from the mountain,"* pertains to Jesus, Peter, James and John, but after an event that was mind-boggling, to say the least!

As they had witnessed the Power and Glory of God on the mountain, they will now witness the power of Satan at the foot of the mountain.

NOTES

However, the Power of God incorporated in Jesus will prove to be well equal to the task.

The phrase, *"Jesus charged them, saying, Tell the vision to no man,"* is, in essence, a military command. Under no consideration were they to relate this to anyone, at least at this present time, not even to their fellow Disciples.

The Holy Spirit through Matthew proclaims this event as a *"vision."* This does not mean that it did not actually and literally happen, but that it could only been seen in the realm of the Spirit. To be frank, it is doubtful that anyone would have believed them anyway, and, more so, to be a witness of such Glory would have made it very difficult to comprehend the coming Crucifixion, as it did even with Peter, James and John. Surely, anyone, the common thinking would be, who could call people from the grave could ward off any common threat!

The phrase, *"Until the Son of Man be risen again from the dead,"* had reference to the fact that the Resurrection of Christ would tie all of this together.

THE RESURRECTION

The Greek word for the phrase, *"from the dead,"* is *"ek,"* which means *"out from"* or *"from among."* It speaks of Christ being raised from the dead and also all the Saints being raised at the time of the coming Resurrection, of which Christ is the *"Firstfruits."* At that time, all the righteous dead will be raised from among the wicked dead, which is the *"First Resurrection of Life,"* which could take place at any time (I Thess. 4:13-18).

The wicked dead will be raised a thousand years after the First Resurrection of Life (Rev. 20:4-6).

Following are some of the times that the phrase *"Out Resurrection,"* as here, is used, and means, *"Out from among the dead,"* and pertains, as stated, to the First Resurrection of Life (Mk. 6:14; 9:9-10; 12:25; Lk. 9:7; 16:31; 20:35; 24:46; Jn. 2:22; 12:1, 9, 17; 20:9; 21:14; Acts 3:15; 4:2, 10; 10:41; 13:30, 34; 17:3, 31; Rom. 4:24; 6:4, 9, 13; 7:4; 8:11; 10:7, 9; 11:15; I Cor. 15:12, 20; Gal. 1:1; Eph. 5:14; Phil. 3:11; Col. 1:18; 2:12; I Thess. 1:10; II Tim. 2:8; Heb. 13:20; I Pet. 1:3, 21).

(10) "AND HIS DISCIPLES ASKED HIM, SAYING, WHY THEN SAY THE SCRIBES THAT ELIAS (ELIJAH) MUST FIRST COME?"

The phrase, *"And His Disciples asked Him,*

saying," respects Elijah, and was a question that troubled them greatly, as it left them without understanding.

The question, *"Why then say the Scribes that Elias* (Elijah) *must first come?",* concerns the Prophecy of Malachi and the recent appearance of Elijah in the vision. They were confused!

Malachi, who was the last Prophet before John the Baptist, had mentioned, even as he closed out his Book, *"Behold, I will send you Elijah the Prophet before the coming of the great and dreadful day of the Lord"* (Mal. 4:5).

They knew that Malachi, of whom the Scribes were quoting, had said that Elijah must come before the Advent of Christ, and not after His Coming, as they had just witnessed. Christ had been ministering now for nearly three years, and it seemed to them that Elijah's appearance as they had witnessed it, could not be a fulfillment of Malachi's Prophecy.

They were right! However, they were confused on two issues:

1. First of all, they confused the two comings of Christ, only thinking of one coming. They were thinking at this time that He was going to set up His Kingdom. Actually, they continued to think such even after the Resurrection and just before His Ascension, when they asked, *"Lord, wilt Thou at this time restore again the Kingdom to Israel?"* (Acts 1:6). They simply did not discern or rightly divide the Word of Truth as they should have regarding these two great events.

2. They did not understand that John the Baptist came in the spirit and power of Elijah, consequently, fulfilling Malachi's Prophecy, in that he preceded Christ.

Had Israel received John the Baptist, he would have been Elijah to Jerusalem at that time. But, of course, this they did not do! So, Israel's rejection of John the Baptist and Christ necessitated another coming, which has not taken place as of yet, but most surely shall (Rev. 19).

(11) "AND JESUS ANSWERED AND SAID UNTO THEM, ELIAS TRULY SHALL FIRST COME, AND RESTORE ALL THINGS."

At first glance, it seems as though verses 11 and 12 contradict each other. However, when it is understood as to what Jesus was actually saying, the matter concerning Elijah is cleared up.

The phrase, *"And Jesus answered and said*

unto them," proclaims the Master always answering an honest inquiry, as here!

The phrase, *"Elias truly shall first come, and restore all things,"* refers to Elijah who will be sent back to earth along with Enoch, who was also translated that he should not see death. This will take place somewhere along the middle of the coming Great Tribulation, which is even yet future. They will come to Jerusalem, which shall be at that time under the domain of the Antichrist, and will prophesy for approximately three and a half years (Rev. 11:1-13).

During this period of time, they will have great power given to them by God, and will, no doubt, pave the way for the Second Coming by preaching the Truth to Israel.

To be sure, Israel, after having been deceived by the Antichrist for the first three and a half years of the coming Great Tribulation, and having been betrayed by him, will be open to the True Preaching of the Word, which these two will bring forth. At that time, and as Malachi said, *"He* (speaking of Elijah who will be accompanied by Enoch) *shall turn the heart of the fathers to the children, and the heart of the children to their fathers."*

This will be, *"Before the coming of the great and dreadful day of the Lord,"* i.e., the Battle of Armageddon and the Second Coming (Mal. 4:5-6).

However, the Disciples knew that Elijah did not do these things before the Ministry of Christ, as the Prophet Malachi predicted. As well, and if they had any inkling that John the Baptist could have fulfilled this Prophecy, which they probably did not, they knew that Israel did not heed him.

(12) "BUT I SAY UNTO YOU, THAT ELIAS IS COME ALREADY, AND THEY KNEW HIM NOT, BUT HAVE DONE UNTO HIM WHATSOEVER THEY LISTED. LIKEWISE SHALL ALSO THE SON OF MAN SUFFER OF THEM."

The phrase, *"But I say unto you, that Elias* (Elijah) *is come already,"* must have startled Peter, James and John, because they knew He was speaking of John the Baptist.

The phrase, *"And they knew Him not,"* means that Israel did not recognize the true mission of John the Baptist, as the forerunner of Christ, and simply because they did not believe that Jesus was the Messiah. As well, some of the people believed that John was possessed by a devil (Mat. 11:18).

The people were so far away from God and were so wrapped up in their own self-righteousness that they knew neither John nor Jesus, at least as to their true mission. The nation had been so twisted by the erroneous teaching of the Scribes and the Pharisees, that, as Jesus had said, *"They made the Word of God of none effect, by their tradition"* (Mat. 15:6).

The phrase, *"But have done unto him whatsoever they listed,"* refers to John being murdered by Herod. However, the people were just as guilty because they consented to this travesty, and lifted no hand to stop it. Consequently, their actions show that they really did not care!

The phrase, *"Likewise shall also the Son of Man suffer of them,"* is another reference to the coming Crucifixion of Christ.

However, even though they did understand concerning John, as the next verse proves, still, they did not understand about Jesus' coming death.

(13) "THEN THE DISCIPLES UNDERSTOOD THAT HE SPAKE UNTO THEM OF JOHN THE BAPTIST."

This teaching of Christ regarding John the Baptist and Elijah was not new. He had said, *"This is he, of whom it is written, Behold, I send My messenger before Thy Face,"* and *"This is Elijah, which was for to come"* (Mat. 11:10, 14).

As well, the Angel Gabriel, in announcing the birth of John the Baptist, had spoken that he would go before Christ in the spirit and power of Elijah (Lk. 1:17). Consequently, they should have been very familiar with what Jesus was talking about, even before the explanation.

(14) "AND WHEN THEY WERE COME TO THE MULTITUDE, THERE CAME TO HIM A CERTAIN MAN, KNEELING DOWN TO HIM, AND SAYING,"

If Christ manifested His Deity in Glory on the summit of the mountain, Satan manifested his power and cruelty at its foot.

The phrase, *"And when they were come to the multitude,"* concerns the crowd at the foot of the mountain. Luke said this happened the *"next day"* after the Transfiguration.

There are some who think the Transfiguration took place at night, as it very well may have. However, it could just as easily have taken place

during the day, with Christ, along with Peter, James and John spending the night somewhere, and coming the next day to this particular place. The lesson to be taught here, as always, will open up knowledge as to problems and their cause.

The phrase, *"There came to Him a certain man,"* represents an individual with a great need, namely his son who was possessed by a demon spirit.

The phrase, *"Kneeling down to Him, and saying,"* proclaims the man knowing Who Jesus was, and his joy at seeing Him, especially after the failure of the Disciples to help him.

The word, *"kneeling,"* does not refer merely to respect, but, instead, a recognition, at least in some respects, as to Who Jesus was, the Messiah.

As well, it is the posture, at least speaking in a spiritual sense, in which all must come to Christ. This thread of humility and brokenness runs throughout the entirety of the Gospels, and the entirety of the Bible for that matter!

I am afraid that in our eagerness to portray ourselves as champions and overcomers, etc., we, at times, elevate ourselves at the expense of Christ. If one is to notice, many of the modern songs especially in Charismatic circles, extol this very premise, our power, etc., while elevating Christ only in a limited way.

Even though these efforts are oftentimes shrouded in Scripture, still, the final result is a subtle praising of ourselves instead of the Lord. We must be very careful to avoid this!

The Believer never reaches such a place of maturity that he could or should dispense with *"kneeling before Christ."* Actually, the closer to Him we really get, with out lives totally immersed in Him, the more we will ignore ourselves, and because of truly being able to properly evaluate what we really are, and all the more praise Him. A true Christlike spirit will ever seek to hide self in Christ, with self less and less being seen, if at all, and Christ more and more being seen.

This is the place to which the Holy Spirit desires to bring us, while, if we take over the task ourselves, the opposite will be the result.

(15) "LORD, HAVE MERCY ON MY SON: FOR HE IS LUNATICK, AND SORE VEXED: FOR OFTTIMES HE FALLETH INTO THE FIRE, AND OFT INTO THE WATER."

The phrase, *"Lord, have mercy on my son,"* proclaims the need, and the urgency of the father for this need to be met.

Once again, we have the Ministry of Intercession before us, i.e., to intercede on one's behalf. Of course, it is obvious as to the father's concern, as this was his son. However, the True Believer in Christ must, as well, have this Ministry of Intercession on behalf of others. To be frank, unless the Church has that burden, the unsaved, and regardless of their need, will not be brought to Christ. It is called the *"Ministry of Reconciliation,"* and is said to be given to the Body by the Lord (II Cor. 5:18). Actually, the *"Ministry of Intercession"* is the ingredient of *"Reconciliation."* In other words, there will be no Reconciliation without the Intercession.

Regrettably, so much of the Church has been pulled away from this all-important aspect, and now spends too much of their time interceding for themselves, that their economic situation will improve. In doing so, the basic fundamental of the Gospel is ignored, in that Jesus said, *"Seek ye first the Kingdom of God, and His Righteousness; and all these things shall be added unto you"* (Mat. 6:33).

So, if we would seek to intercede before the Lord on behalf of the needs of others, the other things will automatically come.

The phrase, *"For he is lunatick, and sore vexed,"* proclaims the problem. The Greek word for *"lunatick"* is *"seleiazomai,"* which means *"moonstruck."* It was a form of epilepsy, but caused by demon spirits. Actually, Mark has the man referring to the problem being caused by a *"dumb spirit"* (Mk. 9:17). Luke just mentioned *"a spirit"* (Lk. 9:39).

There is no discrepancy in the three accounts, as each gave a portion of what the man actually said.

The phrase, *"For ofttimes he falleth into the fire, and oft into the water,"* proclaims only a part of the problem, with attacks also *"tearing him,"* causing him to *"foam at the mouth,"* and *"gnash with the teeth"* (Mk. 9:18).

Along with this, he had, as stated, a *"dumb spirit,"* which either meant he could not talk nor hear at all, or during certain times could not talk or hear. The latter was probably the case.

Whatever the medical diagnosis would have been, had modern doctors been brought into the case, still, Jesus agreed with the man's

NOTES

diagnosis concerning evil spirits, and *"rebuked the Devil."* From this episode we learn several things:

1. Even children can be taken over and controlled by demon spirits. This does not necessarily mean the child is demon possessed, but, instead, is oppressed, which means to *"exercise dominion over,"* and to do so with such a power and force as to make the individual helpless to defend himself.

As this child was plagued by this evil spirit, likewise, many Believers and unbelievers are plagued as well. As stated, it does not mean that they are possessed, which refers to an evil spirit taking over the spirit of an individual, which can cause bizarre things such as super human strength or murderous intent, and, I think, always rendering the person more or less insane. However, possession can result in insanity which manifests itself in clever ways, such as Adolph Hitler, etc. In these instances, the individual is driven by these spirits to carry out the work of Satan to *"steal, kill, and destroy"* (Jn. 10:10). The Scripture delineates between possession and oppression. The Scripture says, *"How God anointed Jesus of Nazareth with the Holy Ghost and with Power: Who went about doing good, and healing all that were oppressed of the Devil; for God was with Him"* (Acts 10:38).

As referred to, the Greek word for *"oppression"* is *"katadunasteuo,"* and means *"to overpower or exercise hard control, or to use power against one."*

As stated, these spirits can cause certain diseases and afflictions, as well as hurtful and bizarre actions.

Only the Power of God can overcome these spirits. They do not respond to medicine or psychological counseling, etc. They only respond to the Name of Jesus.

If one could pull back the curtain, seeing deeply into the spirit world, one would find the cause of most, if not all bizarre actions, and even some sicknesses, as caused by demon spirits. Unfortunately, the modern Church, which even includes the Pentecostal and Charismatic varieties, who should know better, is, for the most part, responding to this terrible darkness with psychology, instead of the Power of the Holy Spirit in the Name of Jesus.

If one is to notice, despite all the psychological counseling, along with mood-altering drugs, the problem is not diminishing, but rather exacerbating. There needs to be more teaching on the subject in modern Churches, along with the exercising of the Power of God by using Scriptural authority against these spirits.

For years the argument raged as to whether or not a Christian could be demon possessed. It was not without foundation because of certain bizarre actions, etc. However, there is no record in the Word of God of a Believer being demon possessed. But there is definitely a record of Believers being oppressed by these spirits (Acts 10:38).

2. In these cases, the spirits have to be rebuked, with the Believer taught how to exercise the Word of God on his behalf and, consequently, to live in victory over these powers of darkness. That is one of the reasons Paul said, *"For God hath not given us the spirit of fear; but of power, and of love, and of a sound mind"* (II Tim. 1:7).

In a modern situation, this man's son would have been treated by doctors, but with little help forthcoming because the problem was not physical, but spiritual, which manifested itself in physical and mental disturbances.

However, at the same time, this does not mean that all or even most physical problems are caused by demon spirits. In fact they aren't, but, at times, as this episode portrays, such is definitely the case.

As well, a form of insanity is expressed here, which denoted suicidal tendencies, etc.

When one considers the condition of most home life in America, and every other country in the world for that matter, one begins to understand the reason for the abundance of demonic activity.

Most children live in an atmosphere of perversion, filth, profanity, anger, racism and hatred — all a perfect environment for the operation of demon spirits. When one understands this, then one does not wonder why the situation is so bad, but why, instead, it isn't much worse!

As stated, the only answer to this is the Power of God and the knowledge of the Word of God. Regrettably, most Churches do not even believe in the Power of God, and, accordingly, the True Word of God is being less and less taught and preached. As a result, and as the Prophet said, *"My people are destroyed for lack*

of knowledge" (Hos. 4:6). (The *"knowledge"* here spoken of refers to God and His Ways, i.e., the Word of God.)

(16) "AND I BROUGHT HIM TO THY DISCIPLES, AND THEY COULD NOT CURE HIM."

The phrase, *"And I brought him to Thy Disciples,"* refers to the man bringing the child to Jesus, but when Jesus was found not to be there, he appealed to the nine who were present, Peter, James and John being with Christ.

The phrase, *"And they could not cure him,"* proclaims a total failure in the situation to which Jesus will address Himself momentarily.

We do know that in the past Jesus had sent out His Disciples *"Giving them power against unclean spirits, to cast them out, and to heal all manner of sickness and all manner of disease"* (Mat. 10:1). So why did they fail in this case?

(17) THEN JESUS ANSWERED AND SAID, O FAITHLESS AND PERVERSE GENERATION, HOW LONG SHALL I BE WITH YOU? HOW LONG SHALL I SUFFER YOU? BRING HIM HITHER TO ME."

The phrase, *"Then Jesus answered and said,"* will begin to portray the reason for the failure of the Disciples. To be sure, as it applied to them, it applies to us as well!

The phrase, *"O faithless and perverse generation,"* gives the first two reasons for their failure, with three more to follow.

To be sure, this statement as made by Christ was meant to include basically the entirety of Israel, even His Apostles, and especially the nine.

1. *"Faithless":* For whatever reason, the nine had arrived at a place of total lack of Faith. It would seem that the constant miracles performed by Christ would have generated great Faith in them. However, and despite such, they now find themselves *"faithless."*

Among other reasons, the Word of God, which alone generates Faith, was not lodging in their hearts as it should have been. This was caused, as is obvious in past experiences, such as Peter rebuking Christ (16:23), by them not following the Word of God, but, instead, misinterpreting the Word, or being ignorant of its content altogether. As stated, only the Word of God and that Word being properly understood, can generate Faith in the heart of the Believer (Rom. 10:17).

2. *"Perverseness":* This refers to wrong action, and because the Word of God was twisted,

i.e., perverted. The Scribes and Pharisees, who were supposed to be the guardians of the Word for the people, instead, had so twisted it by adding to or taking from, that the people little knew or properly understood the Word, thus producing a perverted generation. To be sure, the Disciples had suffered this perversion along with all others.

The question, *"How long shall I be with you?"*, is raised to express the idea that the three and a half years of His public Ministry, which His Disciples were a part of, seemed to be insufficient.

The question, *"How long shall I suffer you?"*, refers to Him having to bear their Spiritual and Scriptural ignorance. I wonder as to how many of us presently He is asking the same two questions? To be frank, I fear, at least some, if not most of the time, we are no better, or even worse!

As Jesus had to keep telling His Disciples the same thing over and over again, He seems to have to do the same with us presently, and I say that by experience. We seem to learn so slowly.

The phrase, *"Bring him hither to Me,"* is meant to point to Him directly, and not His Disciples.

Thankfully, the Day of Pentecost, with the ushering in of the Holy Spirit, would greatly heal this malady in the lives of the Disciples. Then they would truly exemplify the Name and Person of Christ, with God using them mightily respecting the healing of the sick and miracles (Acts 5:12-16), along with preaching the Word.

(18) "AND JESUS REBUKED THE DEVIL; AND HE DEPARTED OUT OF HIM: AND THE CHILD WAS CURED FROM THAT VERY HOUR."

The phrase, *"And Jesus rebuked the Devil,"* refers to Jesus addressing the demon spirit Personally.

These evil spirits have personalities and intelligence. As well, they do not respond to anything other than the Power of God as manifested in the Person of Christ. (All the power held by Believers, in effect, is power borrowed from Christ, and made possible by the Advent of the Holy Spirit, Acts 1:8.)

The phrase, *"And he departed out of him,"* is here said matter of factly, but Mark records that when this spirit came out, it *"cried, and rent him sore"* (Mk. 9:26).

Matthew only gives the spiritual aspects of this scenario, while Mark and Luke give the physical aspects as well!

NOTES

The Word of Christ is such that devils must obey. They have no alternative or choice!

The phrase, *"And the child was cured from that very hour,"* referred to not only an immediate release, but, as well, that this spirit would never return, with the child remaining healed and delivered.

Over 500 years before, the Prophet Jeremiah had said, *"Heal me, O Lord, and I shall be healed; save me, and I shall be saved: for Thou art my praise"* (Jer. 17:14).

One can well imagine the happiness and joy of this father, along with the child. (The designation *"child"* could refer to a boy in his early teens, which he probably was.)

(19) "THEN CAME THE DISCIPLES TO JESUS APART, AND SAID, WHY COULD NOT WE CAST HIM OUT?"

The phrase, *"Then came the Disciples to Jesus apart,"* refers to them coming to Jesus privately, after He had gone into a house, according to Mark.

The question, *"And said, Why could not we cast him out?"*, proclaims their consternation at their failure. As well, they had no doubt heard Jesus make the statement concerning faithlessness and perverseness, which they knew applied to them as well!

In fact, they had had great results in the past respecting healings, miracles and the casting out of demons, consequently, they were perplexed as to the reason for their present failure.

To be sure, this same question, *"Why could not we . . . ?"*, is being asked by many presently, as it should be.

Regrettably, it is not asked at all by most, and because they are too busy proclaiming what God will not do, instead of what He will do! Far better to ask the reason why, than to deny it altogether, as most of the modern Church is doing!

(20) "AND JESUS SAID UNTO THEM, BECAUSE OF YOUR UNBELIEF: FOR VERILY I SAY UNTO YOU, IF YE HAVE FAITH AS A GRAIN OF MUSTARD SEED, YE SHALL SAY UNTO THIS MOUNTAIN, REMOVE HENCE TO YONDER PLACE; AND IT SHALL REMOVE; AND NOTHING SHALL BE IMPOSSIBLE UNTO YOU."

The phrase, *"And Jesus said unto them,"* portrays some of the most powerful statements uttered by Christ.

The phrase, *"Because of your unbelief,"* adds

the third reason for their not being able to cast out this spirit. Unbelief is the cause of faithlessness, but, within itself, has its roots in far deeper spiritual terrain. Unbelief is a mind-set which speaks of deliberation of action. In other words, it is unbelief spawned by spiritual ignorance (I Tim. 1:13). It has its domicile in an evil heart (Heb. 3:12).

David said, *"He made known His Ways unto Moses, His Acts unto the Children of Israel"* (Ps. 103:7).

From this we know that God's Acts do not necessarily generate Faith, even though they definitely should, and at times do! Actually, His Acts are His Word in action.

However, having said that, it is *"His Ways"* which, in effect, is His Word, which really generates Faith.

Consequently, that generation of Israelites, and despite the great Acts of God, lost their way through unbelief (Heb. 3:19; 4:6).

As well, the Disciples registered faithlessness, perverseness and unbelief in the midst of the greatest Move of God the world had ever known. This shows us that environment and companionship, as important as they may be, are not the actual ingredients of nearness to the Lord; that comes from relationship.

That is the reason some Believers can lose their way while in the midst of a great Church, with the Gospel being preached constantly, souls being saved, and the Power of God being constantly manifested. Environment and companionship will never take the place of relationship.

The phrase, *"For verily I say unto you,"* is meant to pronounce an extremely strong statement.

The phrase, *"If ye have Faith as a grain of mustard seed,"* presents Christ once again using as symbolism something that all were acquainted with. Consequently, in this one statement is tremendous teaching on the subject of Faith.

The *"mustard seed"* was the tiniest of seeds, but if placed in the proper soil, quickly grew to a quite large tree.

Such is Faith! Even though at the beginning it may be small and seemingly insignificant, still, if placed in the proper soil of the Word of God, it will quickly grow.

So, small Faith or little Faith is not necessarily the problem, as this is mostly the case

with all. The secret is using what Faith we have, and with proper use more will be added (Mat. 13:12).

We learn from this that the Lord does not demand great Faith, at least at the beginning, but that we simply use what Faith we have. This means to believe God and stand on His Promises, and not be denied.

"Faith is," as Paul would later explain it, *"the substance of things hoped for, the evidence of things not seen"* (Heb. 11:1).

So, the key is to believe even though the evidence is *"not yet seen."*

The phrase, *"Ye shall say unto this mountain,"* is meant to be taken literally. It is not mere hyperbole (an extravagant exaggeration — hype), but was meant exactly as said. *"This mountain"* was probably a reference to Mt. Tabor, where the Transfiguration had taken place. So, He chooses something that is totally impossible in the natural — the removal of a mountain.

As well, and if one is to notice, He said, *"Ye shall say,"* speaking of words of power, which of necessity are positive. Of course, all of this is said in the context of the Will of God. Jesus didn't move mountains, or anything else, unless the Father wanted it done. This must be our criteria as well, which demands a constant prayer life and consecration.

Too many, and too often, have attempted to go into the mountain-moving business as a figment of their own imagination, and not according to the Will of God.

And yet, according to the Will of God, the mountain-moving business is the business the Lord is in, and, accordingly, should be the business we are in.

The very tenor of these statements is meant to proclaim the impossible being made possible. It is meant to proclaim that which within itself could not be done under any circumstances, and yet by Faith in God can be carried out.

As such, and understanding the tremendous power contained by a Faith-filled (Word-filled) Child of God, we should be very careful what we say. We should speak positive about all things, and especially that which we are believing God for.

In other words, when we pray for a lost loved one to be saved, or any such request, all future statements should be in respect to the request. Despite what the person may be doing at the time, the words out of our mouth should be, *"I believe he* (or she) *will be saved!"*

We should do the same in respect to finances, victory, or anything else that needs removing.

The phrase, *"Remove hence to yonder place; and it shall remove,"* is a startling statement indeed!

To be sure, Jesus, as the Creator and Maker of all things, has moved mountains many times. The entirety of the earth owes its topography to mountains being moved hither and yon (Jn. 1:3).

Once again, I emphasize the Truth that, despite the attempts by some to spiritualize these statements, the emphasis of the Greek means that we are to take His statements literally. The phrase, *"And nothing shall be impossible unto you,"* bears that out!

This includes everything promised by God's Word (Ps. 34:10; 84:11; Mat. 7:11; Mk. 11:22-24; Jn. 14:12-15; 15:7, 16).

This is what makes Bible Christianity the most powerful force on earth. It is because Jesus serves as its Head, and imparts His Power to those who will believe (Acts 1:8). If the Church believes in the miracle-working Power of God, consequently having Faith in His Name, it pales into insignificance every philosophy and religion in the world.

The Church is supposed to be a miracle Church; the Believer is supposed to be a miracle Believer, with Faith in God and His Word producing the most staggering miracles the world has ever known — and all of this from Faith no larger than a *"mustard seed."*

One can only shout *"Hallelujah!"*

(21) "HOWBEIT THIS KIND GOETH NOT OUT BUT BY PRAYER AND FASTING."

The phrase, *"Howbeit this kind,"* and referring back to the demon spirit that oppressed the boy, implies there are different kinds of demons with different degrees of power, which requires a different or greater power to cast them out.

The phrase, *"Goeth not out but by prayer and fasting,"* proclaims the last two reasons the Disciples were unsuccessful.

To their credit, *"fasting"* was not really a priority at the time due to Christ being with them. In fact, Jesus had addressed this earlier when questioned by the Disciples of John the Baptist (Mat 9:14-15). However, after His Ascension,

NOTES

the Disciples would then fast.

Prayer, however, was another matter altogether. The record indicates that Jesus prayed much, while it seems the Disciples, at least before His Resurrection and Ascension, prayed very little. As well, this would change after the Day of Pentecost.

So the five causes for failure according to Christ are as follows:

1. Faithlessness (vs. 17).
2. Perverseness (vs. 17).
3. Unbelief (vs. 20).
4. Lack of prayer (vs. 21).
5. Lack of fasting (vs. 21).

As this Scripture proclaims, Faith needs prayer and fasting, along with the Word of God for its development and full growth.

Prayer is the place we ascertain the Will of God as it is coupled with the Word of God. It is where the Holy Spirit deals with our consecration and helps bring about our spiritual growth.

Many Believers have the idea that prayer is only for making requests to the Lord. While such is included, still, that is only a small part of prayer.

Prayer should begin with Praise, in order to thank the Lord for all He has done, and is doing.

Prayer should be consecration, which portrays a hunger for the Will of God, and for God's Will to be revealed unto us.

Prayer enhances our spiritual growth, as the Holy Spirit points out flaws and inconsistencies in our spiritual walk.

Prayer is communion with God, which is very important to Him and should be very important to us. It is something every Christian should engage in constantly. Actually, we are importuned to *"pray without ceasing"* (I Thess. 5:17), which means to constantly be in a state of prayer, actually breathing a prayer to the Lord on a constant basis.

Regrettably, not many modern Christians engage in prayer. The reasons are varied, but mostly center in unbelief. In other words, they simply do not believe that God will do anything, hence little or no prayer.

Ignorance of communion with the Lord plays a great part in lack of prayer, as well! As stated, many who think of prayer as only a petition, fail to understand the tremendous blessings which come to the Child of God engaging in prayer and having communion with the Heavenly Father. Such produces a euphoria, a comfort, a sense of well-being, and, actually, a peace which passeth all understanding. There is nothing in the world that can remotely take the place of communion with God. As well, and as stated, such can only come about by prayer.

This is the reason that prayer should be habitual, constant, dedicated, earnest and sincere. It is the most powerful force, at least for those who truly believe God, that has ever been known.

FASTING

We aren't told in the Word of God how often Believers should fast.

One could say that fasting humbles the soul before God (Ps. 35:13); in effect, it also chastens the soul (Ps. 69:10), and does have a tendency to curb passions or appetites which aren't right.

However, fasting will not bring about victory over sin. While it will help in the process, the victory is always won through Christ and the Cross and our Faith in that Finished Work. We make a large mistake when we try to find victory over sin in any other capacity other than Christ and the Cross. Fasting, as stated, is important, and definitely will aid in the process. But the final victory always rests with Christ and the Cross and our Faith in that great Work.

(22) "AND WHILE THEY ABODE IN GALILEE, JESUS SAID UNTO THEM, THE SON OF MAN SHALL BE BETRAYED INTO THE HANDS OF MEN:"

The phrase, *"And while they abode in Galilee,"* lends more credence to the thought that it was Mt. Tabor, which was in Galilee, where the Transfiguration took place.

The phrase, *"Jesus said unto them,"* proclaims a total departure from what they had been dealing with respecting the casting out of certain demons, etc.

The phrase, *"The Son of Man shall be betrayed into the hands of men,"* draws the Disciples back to the mission at hand. That mission was the Redemption of humanity, which would require the offering of the Perfect Sacrifice, which was His Body.

The *"betrayal"* would take place through the

NOTES

machinations of Judas.

The *"Hands of men,"* actually referred to the Religious Leaders of Israel. At this time, the Heavenly Father would purposely allow His Son to be taken from His Hands, and placed into evil hands, i.e., *"Hands of men."*

(23) "AND THEY SHALL KILL HIM, AND THE THIRD DAY HE SHALL BE RAISED AGAIN. AND THEY WERE EXCEEDING SORRY."

The phrase, *"And they shall kill Him,"* was a statement they probably now believed, but did not yet understand.

Jesus had just told them how that *"Faith as a grain of mustard seed"* could move mountains. And now He speaks of His coming death, and at the hand of cruel men, and they cannot understand how such could be done to Him, especially considering His Great Power. As well, when He said these words, Judas was listening with the other Disciples, but yet would proceed with his plans just a little later.

The phrase, *"And the third day He shall be raised again,"* proclaims His Resurrection, which was beyond their understanding to an even greater degree than His death. This is proven by the fact that after His death on Calvary, none of them believed that He would come forth from the dead. It was beyond their comprehension!

The phrase, *"And they were exceeding sorry,"* has what one might call a double meaning.

1. They were *"exceeding sorry,"* regarding these terrible things Jesus said would happen to Him, even though they little understood it.

2. There is indication that such statements as He was making, caused great sorrow because it dashed their hopes of Him overthrowing Rome, and setting up Israel as the premier nation in the world, with Him as its Leader and they as His chief lieutenants.

(24) "AND WHEN THEY WERE COME TO CAPERNAUM, THEY THAT RECEIVED TRIBUTE MONEY CAME TO PETER, AND SAID, DOTH NOT YOUR MASTER PAY TRIBUTE?"

The phrase, *"And when they were come to Capernaum,"* finds Jesus with His Disciples back at their headquarters.

The phrase, *"They that received tribute money came to Peter, and said,"* pertained to the Temple tax which every Jew was supposed

NOTES

to pay yearly, and was about a half shekel per person. This was derived from Exodus 30:13, and was a levy to handle expenses regarding the upkeep of the Temple in Jerusalem. It was supposed to be voluntary, but the possibility exists that a heavy hand was being applied that all would participate.

This was not a political tax, and, consequently, Rome had nothing to do with it. To be sure, had Rome been involved, they would have exacted the tax by force, and in quick order!

For what reason they applied to Peter, instead of directly to Christ, we are not told. Perhaps it was because Peter was a citizen of Capernaum, and possibly Jesus was staying with him, with the other Disciples staying with other friends.

The question, *"Doth not your Master pay tribute?"*, was asked, no doubt, for purpose. In other words, there were motives behind the question.

It seems that Priests or Levites were not required to pay the tax. Consequently, at least in their minds, if Jesus paid the tax, by doing so, such was a sign that He laid no claim to a higher origin or Divine Mission. In other words, in their thinking, His paying the tax was Him saying, *"I am not the Messiah!"* However, that was only their thinking, and not the truth.

As well, there was a strong element in Israel at that time who deliberately refused to pay the tax because of the Roman presence in Jerusalem. No doubt, Jesus was being accused constantly of fomenting sedition, and, once again, in the thinking of the authorities, His refusing to pay the tax would give them more ammunition in linking Him with these groups, even though it was not true.

So, whether He paid the tax or refused to pay the tax, they had cleverly laid a trap, it seems, to show Him up either way.

(25) "HE SAITH, YES. AND WHEN HE WAS COME INTO THE HOUSE, JESUS PREVENTED HIM, SAYING, WHAT THINKEST THOU, SIMON? OF WHOM DO THE KINGS OF THE EARTH TAKE CUSTOM OR TRIBUTE? OF THEIR OWN CHILDREN, OR OF STRANGERS?"

The phrase, *"He saith, Yes,"* constitutes the words of Peter. Immediately he answers in the affirmative, and without seeking the advice and counsel of Jesus.

Why did he do this?

What was in his heart, only he and the Lord knows. However, he quite possibly was thinking of the recent statements made by Christ concerning how He (Jesus) was to soon be killed. Trying to do everything possible to stall such horrendous activity and fearful that this very tax situation could precipitate a confrontation, he hurriedly answers, *"Yes!"*

The phrase, *"And when he was come into the house, Jesus prevented him,"* portrays the Lord already knowing the exchange that had taken place, due to the Holy Spirit having revealed it to Him. The word, *"prevented,"* means that Jesus anticipated what Simon would relate.

The question, *"Saying, What thinkest thou, Simon?"*, probably took Peter by surprise, inasmuch as Jesus begins to address Himself to the subject possibly even before Peter brings it up.

He did not necessarily tell Peter that he was wrong in giving the answer as he did, but, He desires that Peter understand His (Jesus') rightful place and position. Peter must not for a moment, and especially out of fear to the authorities, forget his great declaration of Faith that Jesus is *"The Son of the Living God."*

If one is to notice, Jesus, more and more in the closing months of His earthly Ministry, sought to impress upon His Disciples as to Who He really was, and His Mission. But still, the actual fact of the Crucifixion would be so horrible that the Disciples did not have full understanding until after the Resurrection.

The question, *"Of whom do the kings of the earth take custom or tribute? of their own children, or of strangers?"*, places the question in the proper framework. The way the question is posed automatically assumes the answer, even as Peter gave it, as recorded in the next verse.

(26) "PETER SAITH UNTO HIM, OF STRANGERS. JESUS SAITH UNTO HIM, THEN ARE THE CHILDREN FREE."

The phrase, *"Peter saith unto Him, of strangers,"* portrays the correct answer.

The phrase, *"Jesus saith unto him, then are the children free,"* is a declarative statement.

The tax was levied for the Temple expenses, of which Jesus was Lord. As such, He was not obliged to pay, nor His Disciples, who were like the Priests, who were also exempted, and because they served as Ministers of the Temple.

As well, inasmuch as this tax was an *"Offering of Atonement,"* which referred to a Ransom of souls, He, as the Son of God, needed no Atonement or Ransom. His life was perfect, and, in fact, He had come to give His Life a Ransom for others. Consequently, and as stated, He owed no Ransom, therefore, He did not owe any Temple or Atonement tax.

He took Peter beyond whatever subtle trap the collectors of this tax were subtly laying for Him.

He would pay it, as the next verse proclaims, but He wanted Peter to know that doing such was in no way a statement on His part that He was not the Messiah. In essence, He emphatically states otherwise!

As well, by paying it, even though He did not owe it, no one could accuse Him of any type of sedition or insurrection.

(27) "NOTWITHSTANDING, LEST WE SHOULD OFFEND THEM, GO THOU TO THE SEA, AND CAST AN HOOK, AND TAKE UP THE FISH THAT FIRST COMETH UP; AND WHEN THOU HAST OPENED HIS MOUTH, THOU SHALT FIND A PIECE OF MONEY: THAT TAKE, AND GIVE UNTO THEM FOR ME AND THEE."

The phrase, *"Notwithstanding, lest we should offend them,"* proclaims Him paying the tax, even though not owed, in order that His enemies not have any occasion against Him.

As well, if He refused to pay it, the people may have seen such as an attempt to dishonor the Temple.

Also, and in a more thoughtful vein, Peter had said that Jesus would pay it, therefore, He would honor and cover His Disciple. To have done otherwise, would have placed Peter in a precarious position, which Christ never does to anyone.

The phrase, *"Go thou to the sea, and cast an hook, and take up the fish that first cometh up,"* presents one of the strangest miracles performed by Christ. He would pay the tax, but not from money out of the treasury of the group, but as *"found money."* In this manner, He was paying it, but, at the same time, not paying it. The authorities would be satisfied, and, as well, His place and position would not be compromised.

The phrase, *"And when thou hast opened his mouth, thou shalt find a piece of money,"* proclaims the strangest method of fund-raising that could ever be devised.

The *"piece of money"* was a *"stater,"* which constituted a shekel. As the tribute was half a

shekel, this paid for both He and Peter. In fact, several miracles are noted here:

1. It had to be revealed to Christ by the Holy Spirit that there was a fish in the lake with money in its mouth.

2. That particular fish had to respond to the bait on Peter's fishing line, and be the first one to do so!

3. Of all the hundreds of thousands, or even possibly millions of fish in the lake, this particular fish had to be at the right place at the right time, which only the Power of God could have brought about.

The phrase, *"And give unto them for Me and thee,"* proclaims the tax being paid.

I wonder what Peter thought when he felt the tug on the line, and pulling up the fish found the money in its mouth, exactly as Jesus stated?

This shows another example of a miraculous material supply afforded by Christ, proclaiming that nothing is impossible to the Believer who will stand on the Word of God and dare to believe.

This illustration of the coin in the mouth of the fish is very dear to me personally. It was October of 1991, and Jimmy Swaggart Ministries was facing total collapse. To be sure, the fault was mine, and mine alone; however, those situations are never as simple as some make them out to be.

At any rate, I made the decision to place myself and this Ministry into the Hands of the Lord, that He may do with it what He so desired. If I remember correctly, it was October 17, a Thursday night, when the Lord moved so powerfully at our evening prayer meeting giving purpose and sense of direction. I'm certain that had He not done so, we simply could not have survived. Frances was at the point of collapse, and I was little, if any, better at all! There is no way that words can describe the guilt, the heartache, especially knowing that it is your fault. As well, the guilt and grief only increases when it is realized that many other people are hurt as well, and by your actions.

But that night, and in one of the most powerful ways I have ever experienced, the Spirit of God fell among our little group, completely changing the complexion of all that was happening.

However, even though some things instantly changed, still, there were problems galore, not the least of which was our acute financial state.

The Ministry owed millions of dollars; how could we now pay this?

The next Monday morning, just before walking out of the door to leave for the office, the telephone rang. It was my secretary. She was weeping, even sobbing, as I spoke to her, and she proclaimed the seriousness of our situation, of which I was fully aware.

I did my best to console her, and left immediately for the office. During the ten minutes it normally took to make the short trip, I was earnestly seeking the Lord as to what to do. I knew that He had to lead us step by step, or else it would be impossible for us to survive at all.

Very clearly the Lord spoke to my heart, and said, *"Call all the department heads together and have a prayer meeting."*

Upon arriving at the office I had my secretary do this, exactly what the Lord had told me to do. Some fifteen or twenty people gathered in our conference room. Of course, all were distraught, not knowing what to do or how to do it.

I sat down that morning at the head of the long conference table and told them that our only hope was the Lord. If we were to survive He would have to be the One to do it, and in order for Him to do so, we would have to submit to Him in every aspect of this Ministry. To be sure, we had always attempted to do this, but we were to do so now to a much finer degree than ever before.

A few minutes later we all went to prayer. That Monday morning, the Spirit of God moved in a powerful way in that room. Among others, I watched the Spirit of God come upon Donnie like a cloud of Glory, with him being changed almost instantly. He walked into the room totally defeated, and left out totally victorious. Only the Lord could do such a thing, and He did it so beautifully and magnificently that day.

I believe the Moving of the Spirit was a sign of confirmation to our efforts. Actually, I know it was!

I sat on the floor after I had gone to prayer, and began to importune the Lord as to exactly what we ought to do. During the course of my pleading about many things, I recounted to Him our perilous financial condition and I told him I simply did not know how we could survive.

An Evangelist such as myself is supported by the people because of their trust in him. They trust his consecration, the Call of God on

his life, and what he does with the money they give to support the work. Regrettably and sadly, that trust had been broken into a thousand pieces. As well, there was absolutely nothing I could personally do to encourage the few supporters we had left, or give them any assurance at all. Whatever was to be done, had to be done totally and completely by the miracle-working Power of God.

And, of course, almost all of the Church world was, at that time, loudly proclaiming our demise and that we would never rise again.

Furthermore, they were proclaiming that God in no way would help us, and we were therefore hopelessly wrecked. Needless to say, the future in the natural looked like no positive future at all! And yet, I had definitely felt that the Holy Spirit had told me to continue on, and under no circumstances were we to entertain the thought of quitting.

As I began to importune the Lord about the finances, I sensed a strong Moving of the Holy Spirit. It pertained to this episode of Peter, who, according to directions from Christ, found the money in the mouth of the fish. It was, as stated, the most unusual way to raise funds that could ever be imagined!

The Lord said to me, *"As I secured the funds, even in this strange way, for Peter to pay the tax, likewise, I will meet your needs."*

It was just that clear, and just that simple! At that moment, an assurance by the Holy Spirit flooded my heart, and somehow I knew, even though it may be in strange ways, that God would see us through.

However, I will have to confess that, at the same time, there was fear in my heart. I knew the miracle it took for that fish, at that particular time, to be caught by Peter. And then, the money in its mouth constituted one of the strangest ways of funds being obtained that the mind of man could ever begin to imagine! Actually, the mind could not even imagine such a miracle. Such is beyond imagination, and can only be brought about by God.

As I write these words, it is August 8, 1995, nearly four years after that Monday morning prayer meeting. During this time, and against all odds, the Lord has seen us through. Just a few minutes ago, Frances walked into my office, asking how much she could increase the Television budget per week?

I thought for a moment, and then said, *"$10,000 a week, over and above our present budget."*

Where will the money come from?

Out of the mouth of the fish, if necessary, and placed there by Christ!

During this nearly four years, we have seen miracle after miracle. Financially, we literally exist hour by hour. Our budget is over a quarter of a million dollars a week at present, and I have every confidence that in our expansion of World Evangelism, as the Lord has called us and directed us, the budget will increase many times over. He is giving me Faith to believe for whatever is needed.

If I remember correctly, it was in late Spring of 1993. We were about a half million dollars behind. The situation was becoming critical, and we did not really even know if we could meet the coming payroll.

Since that first morning prayer meeting in October of 1991, we have conducted two prayer meetings a day, minus service nights, and with the exception of Saturday morning. I have done this because I felt this is what the Lord has wanted us to do. It has been the greatest thing, as I have repeatedly stated, that has ever happened to us. We have literally had to pray in every single thing that has been done, and, to be sure, we have little by little learned more and more about His leading and guidance.

During these prayer meetings, I, as well as our people, have constantly taken these needs to the Lord. At times, it seems the Lord would allow us to come right up to the wire. It tests our Faith, as Faith must be tested.

In all of this, the Lord has never been late, while, at the same time, not being early. As someone has said, *"He's an on-time God."*

At the particular time in question, with us literally running out of time and room to maneuver, and a half million dollars in the red, the Lord, and as He had done so many times, performed another miracle.

Two lawyers called. The Ministry had been left a substantial sum of money in two particular estates, according to the two lawyers.

The amount? About a half million dollars, exactly what we owed!

If I attempted to relate all the incidents of this nature, I am afraid that this book would have to add another hundred pages to its size.

NOTES

As well, the manner in which the money has been forthcoming, at times, has been so bizarre that it equals exactly what the Lord told me that morning in 1991. It is little different than Peter finding the money, as Christ stated, in the mouth of the fish.

So, many of these Passages in the Word of God are so real to me, and especially this one we have just alluded to, and for the obvious reasons. Along with Peter, or to whomever it happened, I have literally lived these experiences. To be sure, there is no greater way to live.

As well, I must not fail to express my deepest love and appreciation to our many friends and supporters who continued to support this Ministry, even though they, as I, did not understand some things, but because the Lord instructed them to do so. I personally believe that their action has been one of the most important in recent history. I know that the Lord will honor them greatly! They have prayed for us and loved us. Some are able only to give small amounts, as least as far as money is concerned, while others have been able to give larger amounts. All are deeply appreciated, and all are part of this great miracle. There is nothing in the world greater than being a part of what God is doing!

I am expecting the Greatest Move of God that I have ever experienced, and, as well, that this world has ever experienced! These precious souls of Faith will be a part of this thing that God is already beginning to do.

What a privilege for all of us!

CHAPTER 18

(1) "AT THE SAME TIME CAME THE DISCIPLES UNTO JESUS, SAYING, WHO IS THE GREATEST IN THE KINGDOM OF HEAVEN?"

First of all, what would have precipitated such a question?

The chronology of this Chapter suggests that after Jesus came down from the Mt. of Transfiguration, He then delivered the boy at the base of the mountain, which was probably close to Nazareth.

After this deliverance, He then sets out for Capernaum, crossing the range of hills between Nazareth and that city.

On the way, it seems that He once again spoke of His Death and Resurrection. However, the Disciples little understood it, but, instead, discussed places of position and power in the coming Kingdom.

Upon arriving in Capernaum, it seems that Jesus went to the home of Simon Peter, where the issue of the tribute money was settled by Him performing the miracle of the coin in the mouth of the fish.

At some point, after this episode, all the Disciples gathered at Peter's home, where Jesus confronted them about their *"dispute among themselves, as to who should be the greatest"* (Mk. 9:34).

He had either overheard them on the road to Capernaum, or else the Holy Spirit had revealed to Him this seed of carnality in their hearts.

The phrase, *"At the same time came the Disciples unto Jesus,"* concerns this gathering where His question was posed to them.

The question, *"Saying, Who is the greatest in the Kingdom of Heaven?",* concerns them wanting Him to settle this matter.

This entire episode is a sad proof of the indifference and selfishness of the natural heart! Again, on the very eve of the Lord's agony and Crucifixion, this same petty question excited them (Lk. 22:24).

Perhaps it was motivated by the Word spoken to Peter in 16:19, and by the selection of him, James and John to witness the Transfiguration.

Without a doubt, the nine had queried the three as to where they had been with Jesus during the time of the Transfiguration. Surely they obeyed the Command of the Lord in not relating what they had seen (17:9), nevertheless, the attitude of the three could very well have been one of superiority, as this question suggests!

The question portrays to the reader that despite the statements of Christ concerning His coming Death and Resurrection, still, their minds were on other things altogether.

They could see Jesus using His Power to overthrow Rome, and to once again make Israel great. And, of course, when this time came, they, being His trusted lieutenants, would have tremendous places of position and power.

One would like to think that their question was more lofty than this imperial kingdom they saw in their minds; however, Acts 1:6 tells us differently.

In the first place, they did not really understand what the *"Kingdom of Heaven"* actually was! Their present thinking made it a material kingdom more than anything else.

While it is true that when the *"Kingdom of Heaven"* on earth finally materializes in totality, it will definitely have a material side, still, before that can happen, the spiritual side of this Kingdom which is by far the most important, must be realized. This they little understood.

Actually, the *"Kingdom of Heaven"* is tied so inextricably to Israel that it cannot be fully realized on earth until Israel accepts Christ as Redeemer and Messiah. Consequently, this which the Disciples wanted and desired could not come to pass at that time, at least in a material sense, because of Israel's rejection of Christ. While it definitely came in a spiritual sense into the hearts of believing men and women, the fulfillment of the material part of it awaits Israel's acceptance of Christ, which will take place at the Second Coming.

Regarding the question, *"Who is the greatest in the Kingdom of Heaven?",* Jesus did not rebuke their desire for it to come or to have place and position in it, but He did rebuke the carnal motivation of their hearts, which, sadly, makes up so much of modern Christendom.

Regrettably, the very tenor of their question placed them in the category of worldly ambition which is gained by self-reliance, the assertion of self-importance, as well as emulation and disregard for the interests of others.

Even though this spirit was ultimately eradicated from the hearts of the Disciples, still, it has definitely not been eradicated in the lives and hearts of many modern Believers!

(2) "AND JESUS CALLED A LITTLE CHILD UNTO HIM, AND SET HIM IN THE MIDST OF THEM,"

The phrase, *"And Jesus called a little child unto Him,"* suggests to some that this could have been one of Peter's children, while tradition suggests that this was the famous martyr Ignatius.

The phrase, *"And set him in the midst of them,"* is added to by Mark as he spoke of Jesus taking the child in His arms.

Once again, Jesus will use symbolism to explain an extremely important principle.

The words, *"Midst of them,"* suggest that the teaching here applies to all of them, with none excluded. Consequently, Peter, James and

John, even though forming an inner circle, especially must heed this admonition. Of all the lessons taught by Christ, and if it is possible to make one more important than the other, this lesson about to be taught is surely the single most important of all!

(3) "AND HE SAID, VERILY I SAY UNTO YOU, EXCEPT YE BE CONVERTED, AND BECOME AS LITTLE CHILDREN, YE SHALL NOT ENTER INTO THE KINGDOM OF HEAVEN."

The phrase, *"And He said, Verily I say unto you,"* marks Jesus' custom of using terminology respecting an extremely important message about to be given concerning proper Christian growth, etc.

The phrase, *"Except ye be converted,"* proclaims the first condition for entrance into the Kingdom of Heaven, and to have a part in its administration. This is basically the same thing He told Nicodemus when he said, *"Except a man be born again, he cannot see the Kingdom of God"* (Jn. 3:3).

The word, *"converted,"* simply means to *"do an about face."*

In its broadest sense, it speaks of forsaking the ways of the world which are instigated by Satan and entering into the Ways of God which are totally different. Therefore, it speaks of not only being born again, but, as well, allowing the Holy Spirit to form one into the likeness of Christ. It was referred to by Paul as, *"Being conformed to the Image of His Son"* (Rom. 8:29).

He also said, *"And as we have borne the image of the earthy, we shall also bear the image of the heavenly"* (I Cor. 15:49).

The phrase, *"And become as little children,"* is the second requirement, which actually speaks of the conformation, which must take place.

Why did He choose a child to explain this most important principle?

A child, at least within itself, is helpless, absolutely dependent on others, and, as is obvious, has a total absence of personal ambition. Such is the very opposite of the spirit of the world instituted by Satan. To be sure, being *"converted"* is the easy part, while *"becoming as a little child"* is not done easily or quickly.

And yet, to be saved one must admit his helplessness in saving himself and throw himself totally on the Mercy and Grace of God, with total dependence in Christ, which is exactly as

a little child. The reason many people do not give their hearts to the Lord is because they do not want to humble themselves accordingly. The spirit of *"I did it my way,"* is the spirit of the world, and the spirit which has caused so many to be lost.

Man is loathe to admit that he cannot solve his own problems, nor save himself. He keeps trying and he keeps failing, and because of this insidious spirit of pride.

However, after one is truly *"converted,"* i.e., born again, too often the spirit of the *"little child"* is laid aside, once again picking up the spirit of pride, ambition and self-importance. Thankfully, the Holy Spirit does not leave one at that time, but, instead, goes to work to change the *"image of the earthy"* into the *"image of the heavenly"* (I Cor. 15:49).

It took only a short time to get Moses out of Egypt, but it took forty years to get Egypt out of Moses.

The spirit of the Kingdom of Heaven, being totally opposite of the spirit of the world, is the spirit of lowliness. In this condition there is fellowship with God; and then it is easy to be meek and humble and to say *"no"* to self; for He Who tastes the sweetness of that fellowship does not seek greatness upon earth.

This is the reason that religious hierarchy is so foreign to True Biblical experience. Hierarchy is political, with all its selfishness, ambition, self-importance, and political jockeying and in-fighting, which is the spirit of the world so obvious in secular politics. The opposite is demanded by Christ!

The phrase, *"Ye shall not enter into the Kingdom of Heaven,"* is emphatic!

The entirety of this statement by Christ is very similar to the first Beatitude, *"Blessed are the poor in spirit; for theirs is the Kingdom of Heaven"* (5:3).

As stated there, *"poor in spirit"* refers to the individual understanding that he is spiritually and morally bankrupt, i.e., poor in these great attributes of God — spirituality and morality. One must understand that about himself before he can be saved, i.e., *"enter the Kingdom of Heaven."*

This principle is unique to Bible Christianity, and is the trait which makes one Christlike. Even though every Believer of necessity has a measure of child-like simplicity, nevertheless, the flesh, as well, constantly screams to regain supremacy. Too often it does!

Consequently, the battle rages in the heart and life of the Believer constantly concerning this principle, which is actually the struggle between the flesh and the Spirit.

A little child characterizes a lack of personal ambition, is dependent totally on others, and if wrong is committed or slights manifested, is quick to forgive and forget. This is the way the Believer is to be.

A lack of personal ambition does not mean a lack of promotion, etc., but, instead, that the Lord does the promotion and not man as the result of schemes, etc. Hence the Psalmist said, *"For promotion cometh neither from the east, nor from the west, nor from the south.*

"But God is the Judge: He putteth down one, and setteth up another" (Ps. 75:6-7).

To be sure, the *"putting down"* or *"setting up"* is predicated solely on one *"becoming as little children,"* or the failure to do such.

(4) "WHOSOEVER THEREFORE SHALL HUMBLE HIMSELF AS THIS LITTLE CHILD, THE SAME IS GREATEST IN THE KINGDOM OF HEAVEN."

The words, *"Whosoever therefore,"* as is obvious, apply to all! In other words, there are no exceptions to this rule. As stated, Peter, James and John, by virtue of being pulled into an inner circle of leadership, would, of necessity, have to be the more humble, i.e., *"as a little child."*

The phrase, *"Shall humble himself as this little child,"* refers to the requirement for greatness in the Kingdom of Heaven.

To be sure, it certainly does not constitute greatness in the kingdom of this world, as that is gained by self-promotion, ruthlessness, ambition and manipulation of others. Regrettably and sadly, the latter too often characterizes the Church as well!

What does it mean to humble oneself?

A child does not consciously humble itself, but is humble by nature. While the Believer is not humble by nature, still, he can become that way by deliberate choice, as is here proclaimed.

What is that choice?

The choice is really to allow the Lord to be the total Leader and Leadership in one's life. Christ is to be the Example, as He is actually the only One Who perfectly humbled Himself as a little child and assuredly will be the greatest in

NOTES

the Kingdom of Heaven. Consequently, and as stated, we are to emulate Him.

As a Believer, when we are reviled, we make the choice, as Christ, to not revile in return (I Pet. 2:23).

Paul said, *"Being reviled, we bless"* (I Cor. 4:12).

It means that slights, being ignored, or passed over, does not arouse enmity in our hearts. We choose to place such situations in the Hands of Christ, allowing Him to handle it, without being offended.

As stated, we choose to allow Christ to promote us, instead of using manipulation to promote ourselves.

We choose to understand that how we look to others is of little consequence, but, instead, how we look to Christ.

The phrase, *"The same is greatest in the Kingdom of Heaven,"* answers the question as asked by the Disciples. Consequently, the definition of *"greatest"* as given by Christ, is the total opposite of that of the world.

Greatness in the world is money, place, position, adulation by the adoring crowds, promotion by one's peers, bigness and supremacy, which is too often accompanied by ruthlessness. Too often that definition is carried over into the Church. However, it is the spirit of the world, and it cannot enter the *"Kingdom of Heaven."*

Greatness, as defined by Christ, is the very opposite of all that characterizes the world. That is what the Believer must strive for.

(5) "AND WHOSO SHALL RECEIVE ONE SUCH LITTLE CHILD IN MY NAME RECEIVETH ME."

The phrase, *"And whoso shall receive one,"* has a strong meaning.

The phrase speaks first of all of the *"one"* who is Christlike in nature and spirit, and, consequently, does not promote himself, etc.

As well, the one who *"receives"* such a one is to never take advantage, but, instead, is to treat the one as he would treat Christ.

The phrase, *"Such little child,"* concerns the demeanor, attitude and spirit of the Christlike Believer. As is obvious, it is not referring to a *"little child"* per se, but, instead, a Believer who has the spirit of such a one, as is the subject of the entirety of this lesson.

The phrase, *"In My Name receiveth Me,"* means that whatever is done to the least Believer is done to Christ.

(6) "BUT WHOSO SHALL OFFEND ONE OF THESE LITTLE ONES WHICH BELIEVE IN ME, IT WERE BETTER FOR HIM THAT A MILLSTONE WERE HANGED ABOUT HIS NECK, AND THAT HE WERE DROWNED IN THE DEPTH OF THE SEA."

The phrase, *"But whoso shall offend one of these little ones which believe in Me,"* concerns the opposite of the previous verse.

The word, *"offend,"* can have reference to any type of offense, but more so speaks of a spiritual stumbling block placed in the way which causes the offended one to spiritually stumble.

The words, *"Little ones,"* do not refer to children, new converts or weak Christians, as some believe, but, instead, a strong Believer in the Lord who will not defend himself, but has placed all defense in the Hands of the Lord. Actually, such humbling of oneself and committing all such action to the Lord, is the foundation of spiritual strength.

However, due to such a person not defending himself, many, as would be obvious, take advantage of such a one. That is what Paul was speaking of when he said, *"Dearly beloved, avenge not yourselves, but rather give place unto wrath: for it is written, Vengeance is Mine; I will repay, saith the Lord"* (Rom. 12:19).

Many in the Early Church were a perfect example of this, being persecuted severely by Rome. It is estimated that tens, if not hundreds of thousands went to their deaths at this time. Regrettably, some few renounced their allegiance to Christ, which resulted in them momentarily saving their lives, but actually losing them (16:25-26). Over a period of time, and because of this, the Roman Empire was ultimately destroyed.

To be sure, all who fall into this category of persecution and offense against *"these little ones,"* will face the same inglorious end! As those who favorably receive such, receive Christ, likewise, those who offend such, offend Christ!

The phrase, *"It were better for him that a millstone were hanged about his neck, and that he were drowned in the depth of the sea,"* is meant to refer to a type of punishment engaged by the Syrians, Greeks and Egyptians.

Such punishment seems to have been reserved for the worst criminals; and, as well, the size of such a stone would prevent the body rising to the surface and being buried by

NOTES

friends. Consequently, it was considered a horrible death!

The idea is that such a one will come to a horrible end in this life and the one to come!

As this refers to all Believers and for all time, and especially those who have taken upon themselves the humility of Christ. It, as well, referred to Christ.

He did not defend Himself, nor did He use His Power against those who opposed Him and ultimately crucified Him. However, because of Israel's action against Him, they were totally destroyed in 70 A.D. by the Romans armies, until they no longer existed as a nation. Also, generation after generation of Jews have staggered in a stygian night of darkness, which has not ended even yet!

(7) "WOE UNTO THE WORLD BECAUSE OF OFFENCES! FOR IT MUST NEEDS BE THAT OFFENCES COME; BUT WOE TO THAT MAN BY WHOM THE OFFENCE COMETH!"

The phrase, *"Woe unto the world because of offences!"*, refers to the state of the world respecting its opposition to the things of God. To be sure, these *"offences"* have been going on since the Fall in the Garden of Eden. In many cases, they have been atrocious to say the least, even as we spoke of the terrible persecution of the Early Church by Rome. The inquisition of the Dark Ages as instituted by the Catholic Church, is another case in point!

Probably, America has offended less in these matters than most nations, and, consequently, has experienced Blessings by God as few nations in the world. And yet, as the darkness of the last days begins to deepen, the fear of God, even in this country, is beginning to diminish, and greatly!

Consequently, during the time of the coming Great Tribulation, the Judgment of God is going to be poured out on this earth as it has never known before (Rev. 6:17). At the Second Coming, another great judgment of the nations will commence, which will bring this very Scripture into focus.

The phrase, *"For it must needs be that offences come,"* speaks of the entire order of events, which God in His all-wise purposes has allowed for many and varied reasons. Such is done that the Righteous may be proved and purified, and the chaff may be separated from the wheat.

The phrase, *"But woe to that man by whom the offence cometh,"* is meant to emphasize the understanding that even though *"offences"* may be necessary, and for the reasons stated, still, all, including entire nations as well as individuals, will be ultimately called to account for even a single *"offence"* unless repentance is enjoined. This is emphasized by the words, *"that man,"* meaning that nothing is overlooked by the Heavenly Father, especially considering hindrance and hurt toward His *"little ones!"*

(8) "WHEREFORE IF THY HAND OR THY FOOT OFFEND THEE, CUT THEM OFF, AND CAST THEM FROM THEE: IT IS BETTER FOR THEE TO ENTER INTO LIFE HALT OR MAIMED, RATHER THAN HAVING TWO HANDS OR TWO FEET TO BE CAST INTO EVERLASTING FIRE."

The phrase, *"Wherefore if thy hand or thy foot offend thee, cut them off, and cast them from thee,"* refers back to the offences of the previous verse. It would be better for the worldling to do about anything, rather than offend *"one of these little ones,"* i.e., all followers of Christ.

Is Christ speaking in a literal sense?

No! He is using comparables in order to arouse attention and to point to the highest stakes of all, the loss of the soul, which will result if God is opposed, by opposing His Children.

Actually, sin does not begin with the hand or the foot, but, instead, the result of a deceitful heart. Therefore, these body members are used mainly as symbolism.

The phrase, *"It is better for thee to enter into life halt or maimed, rather than having two hands or two feet to be cast into everlasting fire,"* points to the paying of any price, if necessary, to <u>not</u> oppose *"these little ones."* To not oppose them, within itself, will not save the soul, but to oppose them will definitely cast one into *"everlasting fire,"* i.e., eternal hell.

The *"woe"* mentioned in verse 7, has to do with the *"everlasting fire"* spoken of here. The Greek word is *"gehenna"* which means *"eternal hell."*

The entirety of verses 8 and 9 speak to the *"woe"* of verse 7. It speaks of judgment that is coming upon this world and upon each individual who has rejected Christ, and, consequently, has persecuted and opposed the *"little ones,"* i.e., those who follow Christ.

(9) "AND IF THINE EYE OFFEND THEE,

PLUCK IT OUT, AND CAST IT FROM THEE: IT IS BETTER FOR THEE TO ENTER INTO LIFE WITH ONE EYE, RATHER THAN HAVING TWO EYES TO BE CAST INTO HELL FIRE."

The phrase, *"And if thine eye offend thee, pluck it out, and cast it from thee,"* is saying the same thing as the previous verse, and is meant to add weight to an already extremely weighty statement.

Once again, the plucking out of the eye will not really solve one's problem of sin, as such originates with the heart. Therefore, Christ, as stated, is using a comparable to draw attention to the significance of His statement.

The phrase, *"It is better for thee to enter into life with one eye, rather than having two eyes to be cast into hell fire,"* as well, says the same as the previous verse. The repetition is by design, and meant to describe the emphasis.

"Hell fire" is used, and is the same as *"everlasting fire"* of the previous verse. Men may deny the place called hell, and modern Preachers may disavow its existence; however, the terminology used by Christ leaves absolutely no doubt as to the existence of the place and its eternal consequence.

So, if the moral of these two verses could be summed up, we are being told by Christ that irrespective of what the world thinks, these *"little ones"* as they are looked at by the world, i.e., of no consequence and therefore easy prey, are, in fact, the single most important of anything in the world. As a result, sore treatment will result in *"everlasting fire."*

So, if the *"hand"* would seek to hurt them, the *"foot"* seek to walk on them, or the *"eye"* look upon them for evil, it would be far better for one to lose these offending members than to *"offend one of these little ones."*

While it is true that the world thinks little of the followers of Christ, still, God thinks much of them, and He is the One Who should be feared!

(10) "TAKE HEED THAT YE DESPISE NOT ONE OF THESE LITTLE ONES; FOR I SAY UNTO YOU, THAT IN HEAVEN THEIR ANGELS DO ALWAYS BEHOLD THE FACE OF MY FATHER WHICH IS IN HEAVEN."

The phrase, *"Take heed that ye despise not one of these little ones,"* ties in with verse 7, which instigates verses 8 and 9.

Many Commentators have attempted to pull

verses 8 and 9 out of context, claiming they refer to the individual Believer, etc. However, to do so corrupts the train of thought which speaks of these *"little ones"* and continues through the entirety of the Chapter.

As a result of the explosive statements of verses 8 and 9, the words, *"Take heed"* are here enjoined, and speak of the *"little ones,"* i.e., followers of Christ.

The very spirit of the world is to *"despise"* these, which Christ solemnly warns against.

The phrase, *"For I say unto you,"* is meant to point to a declarative statement, and another reason to *"take heed!"*

The phrase, *"That in heaven their Angels do always behold the Face of My Father which is in Heaven,"* is startling indeed!

The statement is clear. Every single Believer is assigned an Angel who reports to the Heavenly Father of any and all doings, whether good or bad, as done by others to the Believer assigned to him. To be sure, this pertains not only to unbelievers attempting to hurt a Believer, but, as well, other Believers who take matters into their own hands attempting to hurt a fellow Believer, as following verses proclaim!

So, the moment anyone looks into the face of a Believer, so to speak, attempting harm, to be sure, the Angel of that Believer is, as well, looking into the face of God Almighty.

That is at least one of the reasons the Believer is to leave retaliation in the Hands of the Lord, because, as stated, *"He will repay"* (Rom. 12:19).

(11) "FOR THE SON OF MAN IS COME TO SAVE THAT WHICH WAS LOST."

The idea of this verse is that the very purpose of God coming to this world as man is to *"save the lost."* As such, and once the lost accepts Him as Saviour, they then become a Child of God, and, consequently, the property of the Lord. Inasmuch as their Salvation was paid for at great price, intended harm, as these Passages suggest, is not looked at lightly.

As well, the entire complexion of these Passages speaks of a terrible contest between the Lord and Satan, between Light and darkness!

All was *"lost"* in the Garden of Eden with the Fall of Adam and Eve. Satan must have danced in hellish glee at what looked like the victory of all victories in the realm of darkness. However, the Lord did not allow His most prized creation, man, to remain in this pitiful condition.

He came down here to seek and to save, and to find that which was *"lost,"* which He did!

Considering the terrible price, one must realize how precious is the soul of those who were once lost, but now found.

(12) "HOW THINK YE? IF A MAN HAVE AN HUNDRED SHEEP, AND ONE OF THEM BE GONE ASTRAY, DOTH HE NOT LEAVE THE NINETY AND NINE, AND GOETH INTO THE MOUNTAINS, AND SEEKETH THAT WHICH IS GONE ASTRAY?"

The question, *"How think ye?"*, now addresses itself to the rationale of the situation.

First of all, the previous verse lets us know, and as stated, just how precious these sheep are, and how they are to be protected. Once again the Lord will use symbolism, even that which all are familiar with, in order to make His case.

The phrase, *"If a man have an hundred sheep, and one of them be gone astray,"* proves that sheep, i.e., Believers, can go astray, and, in fact, according to the following verses, be lost. Once again, this refutes the unscriptural Doctrine of Unconditional Eternal Security, i.e., once saved, always saved.

The question, *"Doth he not leave the ninety and nine, and goeth into the mountains, and seeketh that which is gone astray?"*, proclaims the extensive efforts of the Lord to find the lost one. This illustration of the lost sheep has close ties with the 23rd Psalm. Even though we have given the following elsewhere in these Volumes, due to the nature of this illustration, I think it would be proper to relate it again.

Concerning the 23rd Psalm, it is written, as is obvious, from the perspective of the sheep, instead of the shepherd. In the 3rd verse it says, *"He leadeth me in the paths of righteousness for His Name's sake."*

However, and as this illustration by Christ concerning the lost sheep states, at times a sheep will leave the *"path of righteousness."* The sheep, which is symbolic of the Believer, and, we might quickly add, not being very smart, quickly finds itself in an untenable position, such as a deep ravine or tangled in a thorn bush, etc. Unable to secure its freedom, it will begin to bleat, and according to its cry the Shepherd will then come, as Christ here portrays.

Tenderly and gently, the Shepherd will extricate the sheep from its perilous situation, gently placing it back on the *"path of righteousness."*

At times, and sheep being what they are, this same animal will once again leave the *"path of righteousness,"* and, as before, will find itself very shortly in grievous circumstances. Once again, the cry is heard by the Shepherd, with him quickly retrieving the lost one and replacing it once again on the *"path of righteousness."*

In fact, this may happen several times, with the Shepherd repeating the scenario exactly as before. However, if the wandering sheep continues to be persistent in its straying from the *"path of righteousness,"* there will come a time that the Shepherd will take stringent measures.

At that particular time, he will not come as before, allowing the sheep to *"bleat"* until it has no voice left. The sheep is by now perplexed, because all the previous times, and irrespective of its foolishness, when it began to cry, the Shepherd came. But now he doesn't come!

However, ultimately he will come, that is, after the sheep has no strength left to cry.

Of course the sheep does not know it, but all the time the Shepherd is near, even watching closely that predators do not take advantage of the hapless condition of the sheep.

When the Shepherd finally appears, he once again extricates the sheep from its perilous situation, but now does something different.

He pulls the foreleg of the sheep as far out as it will stretch. He then takes his crook, which is a long staff curved on one end, with which he has retrieved the sheep several times in the past. He will then bring the staff down rather sharply on the outstretched foreleg, breaking the bone. Of course, the pain is sharp, and for a short time the sheep hurts rather severely.

He then lays the sheep on the ground, taking two short sticks and makes a splint, binding up the broken leg. He then picks up the sheep with the broken limb, carrying it gently on his shoulder, even next to his heart, and will do so every time he moves from place to place. He does this until the leg heals.

After it heals, he puts the sheep back on the *"path of righteousness,"* and does so for *"His Name's sake,"* with the excellent probability it will not stray again.

This is what is meant, at least in part, by the phrase, *"He restoreth my soul"* (Ps. 23:3).

The entirety of this scenario, as with many Passages of Scripture, can have several meanings. They are as follows:

1. There is a possibility with some small Scriptural indication that God has created other inhabited worlds other than planet earth. If, in fact, that is true, and according to verse 11, He has come down here to retrieve this one which has *"gone astray."* It might also be added that He has done so at a fearful price in order to *"seek and save."*

2. This illustration could very well apply to Israel which had definitely *"gone astray."* Regrettably, he would not at that time be able to *"find it,"* even as verse 13 portrays. However, ultimately he shall.

3. The illustration definitely applies to the straying Believer, as is obvious, and greatly portrays the tremendous lengths gone to in order to retrieve the straying one.

We serve a great and wonderful Lord!

(13) AND IF SO BE THAT HE FIND IT, VERILY I SAY UNTO YOU, HE REJOICETH MORE OF THAT SHEEP, THAN OF THE NINETY AND NINE WHICH WENT NOT ASTRAY."

The phrase, *"And if so be that he find it,"* portrays, as stated, that at times it may not be found. The idea is this:

It is not possible for the Saint to have Salvation and sin at the same time. No one can safely continue sinning, living in careless unconcern, with the expectation that the Lord will somehow, even against their will, retrieve them from this situation. Man has to cooperate with Grace in order to be found and brought home. God forces no one to be saved against his will.

The phrase, *"Verily I say unto you, he rejoiceth more of that sheep, than of the ninety and nine which went not astray,"* is basically the same as the story of the prodigal son, as proclaimed in Luke 15.

The *"rejoicing"* more so of this straying sheep, even than the ninety and nine which are saved, is meant to express a tremendous victory. It is not meant to place any approval whatsoever on the straying, but, instead, on being found. Such proclaims a great victory over Satan and the retrieval of the formerly straying one from a horrible destruction. As well, there is another great Truth illustrated in this story which must be brought out.

The retrieval of the straying one, and in whatever circumstance, represents a soul being salvaged. The ninety and nine represents those who are already saved.

To be sure, the ninety and nine may do great and glorious things among themselves which certainly is commendable and worthy of note. However, no *"rejoicing"* is spoken of regarding these events, and irrespective of what they may be.

However, with the retrieval of the *"straying one,"* great rejoicing takes place, which tells us that God's priority is the Salvation of souls. In fact, this is glaringly obvious!

To be sure, healings are important as they are registered in the Body of Christ. Prophecies and other manifestations of the gifts are important as well! However, no rejoicing in Heaven (for that is what this implies), is registered respecting these happenings, only with the Salvation of souls.

The business of the Church should be to place its priority where God places His, i.e., the Salvation of souls. Sadly, and especially in Pentecostal and Charismatic circles, with whom I am associated, such is little the case! Too often, religious phenomenon is heralded far and wide, while precious souls coming to Christ, for whom Christ died we may quickly add, are little noticed!

Any time the priority of the Church is misaligned, this is a sure sign that it is little Spirit led, but, instead, man led.

(14) "EVEN SO IT IS NOT THE WILL OF YOUR FATHER WHICH IS IN HEAVEN, THAT ONE OF THESE LITTLE ONES SHOULD PERISH."

The phrase, *"Even so it is not the will of your Father which is in Heaven,"* concerns itself with souls being lost. To be sure, this statement reinforces that which we have written concerning the Heavenly Father's priority.

This phrase teaches that the Heavenly Father Who resides in Heaven, orders, plans and directs the operation of Redemption and Salvation on earth.

The phrase, *"That one of these little ones should perish,"* speaks of the preciousness of each soul, with none being placed in a category of worthlessness. Every single soul is precious in His sight. Sadly, that is not always the case in the modern Church.

Too many times the poor and uneducated are given little thought with the rich and educated catered to. To be sure, if a modern Church is to be a New Testament Church, it will have in its congregation rich and poor, great and small,

along with all colors, or, at least, will welcome all, whether they come or not. Otherwise it is not a New Testament Church, and, in fact, at least in the eyes of God, is no Church at all!

Consequently, it is sad when the poor are not welcome in some Churches, or even people of color, such as in the Southern Baptist. The same would go for the Methodist, Presbyterian, Assemblies of God, Church of God, that is, if such is the case in these respective Religious Denominations! When Jesus said, *"Come unto Me all . . . ,"* He was not meaning all of a certain class, but *"all"* respecting the entirety of the human family (Mat. 11:28).

As well, and as we will see in the next few verses, these Passages are speaking not only of the world which opposes the Believer, but, as well, other Believers who seek to hurt a fellow Believer. To be sure, this should never be, nevertheless it happens, and often, and is therefore addressed by Christ.

(15) "MOREOVER IF THY BROTHER SHALL TRESPASS AGAINST THEE, GO AND TELL HIM HIS FAULT BETWEEN THEE AND HIM ALONE: IF HE SHALL HEAR THEE, THOU HAST GAINED THY BROTHER."

The phrase, *"Moreover if thy brother shall trespass against thee,"* is something that should never happen, but, regrettably, oftentimes does! As is obvious, this is speaking of a fellow Believer who has wronged another Believer.

The procedure which follows and as given by Christ, is the criteria to be used respecting such situations.

The phrase, *"Go and tell him his fault between thee and him alone,"* respects one on one.

The one who has been offended should not wait for the offender to take the first step, but should take the initiative and *"go"* to the man (or woman) and seek to solve the problem.

The *"fault"* as the offended one sees it, is to be related to the *"brother,"* and done so in a gentle, kind and gracious manner. The structure of the Text, and especially the Christlike manner, demands such rather than railing accusations. Such will never solve a problem, but only exacerbate it.

The phrase, *"If he shall hear thee, thou hast gained thy brother,"* proclaims the first step taken, which, at times, is the only step necessary, with the grievance settled between the two.

As well, the structure of the Text demands

that if one feels he has been wronged, he not tell everyone else in the Church about it, but, instead, go to the individual who is responsible.

(16) "BUT IF HE WILL NOT HEAR THEE, THEN TAKE WITH THEE ONE OR TWO MORE, THAT IN THE MOUTH OF TWO OR THREE WITNESSES EVERY WORD MAY BE ESTABLISHED."

The phrase, *"But if he will not hear thee,"* means that step one has failed, with the individual refusing to admit the transgression.

The phrase, *"Then take with thee one or two more,"* could probably refer to the Pastor of the Church, plus one or two others, or else two disinterested parties in whom confidence is placed.

For the one offended to take two or three of his close friends, would hardly constitute the requirement. It would seem they should be disinterested parties so as to be able to judge impartially.

The phrase, *"That in the mouth of two or three witnesses every word may be established,"* proclaims the facts of the case, whatever they may be, laid out before impartial individuals in order that they may make a judgment.

(17) "AND IF HE SHALL NEGLECT TO HEAR THEM, TELL IT UNTO THE CHURCH: BUT IF HE NEGLECT TO HEAR THE CHURCH, LET HIM BE UNTO THEE AS AN HEATHEN MAN AND A PUBLICAN."

The phrase, *"And if he shall neglect to hear them,"* means that the two or three disinterested parties, after hearing the evidence, render their judgment in favor of the offended party.

However, it could mean that these *"two or three witnesses,"* after hearing the evidence, may, in fact, render their judgment in favor of the other party. If that is the case, the offended one, or at least thought to be offended, should let the matter rest, accepting the verdict of the *"two or three witnesses."*

However, if the verdict has been in favor of the one offended and the offender would not accept the verdict of the *"two or three witnesses,"* the offended one should *"tell it unto the Church."*

This would probably refer to all of the Elders in the Church, which would refer to the Ministerial Leadership in whatever capacity, and not to the entirety of the Church Body.

The phrase, *"But if he neglect to hear the Church,"* means that the Elders have decided

in favor of the offended one. Once again, if they decide otherwise the offended one should let the matter drop, placing it in the Hands of Christ.

The phrase, *"Let him be unto thee as an heathen man and a publican,"* refers to having exhausted all efforts, and as Christ here stipulates.

If that be the case, conduct toward such a one should be as to an unbeliever, but yet with kindness. A Believer would seek to win such a one to Christ, and, accordingly, kindness and a forgiving spirit should be shown in these cases as well!

Actually, Jesus will further address Himself to such a situation, as Peter asks Him about forgiveness, and a brother transgressing against Him. Peter, no doubt, had this in mind when he questioned Christ.

The idea of the *"heathen"* and *"publican"* is that fellowship should be stopped, which would probably be unavoidable in any case.

The offended one is to continue to pray for the individual and to bless him, that is, if it lays within his power. He is definitely not to slander him, speak ill of him, or seek to hurt him in any way, and irrespective of his wrong.

Of course, the question must be asked as to how the Lord looks at a Believer who will not admit a wrong, even when the evidence is obvious?

Of course, the Lord is the Judge; however, refusal to admit a wrong, especially when it is obvious, which means refusal to repent, places one in an extremely precarious position. Generally, when this happens, grudges are carried with forgiveness denied, which brings serious consequences to say the least! Jesus said, *"If ye forgive not men their trespasses, neither will your Father forgive your trespasses"* (Mat. 6:15). That is the reason every step must be taken that is possible and exactly as Jesus has outlined, in order that these matters be settled. The consequences are so serious that one could lose his soul.

If one is to notice, Jesus left no door for legal action before unbelievers in these situations. In fact, the Apostle Paul, and being led by the Holy Spirit, said, *"Dare any of you, having a matter against another, go to Law before the unjust, and not before the Saints?"* (I Cor. 6:1).

Grievances, and of whatever kind, should be kept in the Church between Believers. And yet, it is sad when one realizes that Christians presently are constantly going to court against other Christians. To be sure, there may be times, and as Paul suggested, that a proper judgment may not be given by the Church, which no doubt happens, and often. However, if such should happen, one should place the matter in the Hands of the Lord and not seek redress in a court of unbelievers. Such shows that more trust is placed in the faltering hands of weak men rather than in the Lord.

(18) "VERILY I SAY UNTO YOU, WHATSO-EVER YE SHALL BIND ON EARTH SHALL BE BOUND IN HEAVEN: AND WHATSO-EVER YE SHALL LOOSE ON EARTH SHALL BE LOOSED IN HEAVEN."

The phrase, *"Verily I say unto you,"* proclaims Jesus addressing Himself to the very things I have just discussed.

The phrase, *"Whatsoever ye shall bind on earth shall be bound in Heaven,"* refers itself to the previous verses.

The idea is that if proper redress is not administered by the Church, the situation should be placed in the Hands of Christ, Who is the highest court of all, hence, the words, *"Verily I say unto you!"*

The offended individual should take the matter to the Lord in prayer, *"binding"* the intended damage of the situation. The Lord has promised for the party who trusts Him and maintains the posture of a *"little one,"* i.e., one of meekness and humility, that He will bind whatever such a one binds.

The phrase, *"And whatsoever ye shall loose on earth shall be loosed in Heaven,"* carries the same connotation as the previous statement, except in a reverse order.

In Truth, one should *"bind"* the Powers of Darkness, which, undoubtedly, are working in these situations, and *"loose"* the *"Ministering spirits, sent forth to minister for them who shall be heirs of Salvation"* (Heb. 1:14). This refers to Angels who work for Believers.

The entire ingredient of verse 18 proclaims to us that spirits of darkness can, in fact, be working in such cases as outlined in verses 15-17. Regrettably, demon spirits can be very much involved with Christians, as they fail to follow the Lord, causing stubbornness, an unforgiving spirit, producing anger, etc.

As such, the Believer who has been offended and has sought redress but without success,

should turn his attention to binding the spirits of darkness operating within the wayward Believer, instead of opposing the Believer personally. As well, and as stated, he should *"loose"* all the attributes of God in these situations, which the Heavenly Father has promised to ratify in Heaven.

This lets us know the cause of many problems in the lives of recalcitrant Believers, and oftentimes it is difficult if not impossible to deal with them on a personal basis. As such, no court of law can solve the problem, with it only being solved in the spiritual realm. We are told how in verses 18 and 19.

However, the Believer should understand that doing such (binding and loosing) will not automatically guarantee satisfactory results in all cases. Some people simply do not want to do right, with little that can be done in such cases. Even God won't force a person to do right. That being the case, the matter is to be left in the Hands of the Lord, with the Believer knowing that he has done all that is humanly or heavenly possible.

(19) "AGAIN I SAY UNTO YOU, THAT IF TWO OF YOU SHALL AGREE ON EARTH AS TOUCHING ANYTHING THAT THEY SHALL ASK, IT SHALL BE DONE FOR THEM OF MY FATHER WHICH IS IN HEAVEN."

The phrase, *"Again I say unto you,"* proclaims an added prerogative given to the Believer. Inasmuch as it comes from Christ, such is the ultimate authority and should be heeded diligently by all Believers. But sadly, many do not heed, attempting to take matters into their own hands, which always leads to further difficulty.

The phrase, *"That if two of you shall agree on earth as touching anything that they shall ask,"* refers to Believers who are asking in the Will of God. It refers to the grievances of verses 15-17, or anything for that matter. However, the *"any thing"* here noted, as stated, refers to the Will of God. God will never allow His Will to be used against Himself, in other words, to bring things into being which are not His Will.

However, it is obvious that Believers who commit everything to the Lord only want and desire the Will of God, and, consequently, only ask according to that Will.

Why two?

In the order of spiritual events, the Lord has ordained that one Believer added in agreement to another does not merely double the power, but, instead, increases it fivefold.

The Lord said to Israel of old, *"And five of you shall chase an hundred, and an hundred of you shall put ten thousand to flight: and your enemies shall fall before you by the sword"* (Lev. 26:8).

This means that one Believer has the power of one, which is considerable to say the least, while *"two"* has that power quadrupled or more!

As well, it seems that the multiplication of this power is increased dramatically not only by Trust in the Lord, but, as well, by *"agreement"* between Believers.

Also, the two words, *"on earth,"* mean that what is agreed to on earth will be ratified in Heaven.

The idea is that Believers on earth do not rule Heaven, but that the Father in Heaven rules earth. Some modern Believers who have gotten a little carried away in their demands should understand that!

The phrase, *"It shall be done for them of My Father which is in Heaven,"* respects the conditions being met and, consequently, the answer forthcoming.

Once again, it is speaking of Believers taking grievances before the Lord concerning other Believers, but, as well, it is speaking of all things, in other words, anything, and in any category, that is in the Will of God.

Some have taken verses 18 and 19 and attempted to apply them to religious hierarchy or denominational heads. Such is claimed by the Catholic Church, and, regrettably, in many Protestant circles as well!

The erroneous idea is that the *"binding and loosing,"* as well as the *"agreeing,"* apply to Church officials, and that whatever they *"agree"* on will be ratified in Heaven.

Such is nonsense!

It is regrettable that many in Protestant circles have succumbed to the error of the Catholic Church regarding its papal authority, so-called, respecting the Pope, Bishops and Priests.

Actually, there is no such thing as Church hierarchy in the New Testament. One will look in vain in the Early Church for such error. It simply did not exist, and because it was not the Will of God.

These verses have nothing to do with Church officials, religious hierarchy, or denominational

heads as such! These Promises pertain to all Believers, and irrespective as to who they are or where they are. The sentence structure proclaims such in using the pronoun *"ye"* in verse 18 and *"you"* in verse 19.

Satan relishes a false religious structure, which takes power out of the hands of the ordinary Believer placing it in the hands of religious heads. Men, unfortunately, love to lord it over other men and, worse still, some men love being lorded over! Tragically, millions have gone to hell because of such error.

Many have been taught to believe these religious heads rather than the Bible, whether they have gone under the name of Pope, Bishop, Priest, Superintendent, Overseer, etc.

While the Scripture certainly teaches that Believers should respect their Pastors and, in effect, follow them as they follow the Lord, still, the Believer should know the Bible well enough that if these do not follow the Lord, it will be easily ascertained. To do anything less is unscriptural and is to flirt with the destiny of one's soul.

Every Believer has access to the Father the same as any other Believer. In other words, the Pope has no more access to God than the most humble Believer. To be truthful, the Pope has no access to God whatsoever, and because he holds an untenable, unscriptural position which God will not, and, in fact, cannot recognize, unless he comes the way of all men (Lk. 18:13).

And I might quickly add that there is no such thing as a Pentecostal Pope, Baptist Pope, or Charismatic Pope, etc.

What do we mean by those statements?

We are speaking of false spiritual authority. If one is to cut through all the fluff, it refers to some religious head who has been elected by popular ballot, who presumes to interpret the Word of God on behalf of other individuals. In other words, the idea is that they will tell other individuals what to do, even that which is unscriptural, and irrespective as to how obviously unscriptural it is, the individual is to obey. The inference is that if the demand is, in fact, unscriptural, only the religious official will be responsible to God, and not the person upon whom the demand is made.

Actually, this is the entirety of the premise of the Catholic Church, with Bishops and Priests demanding obedience, and irrespective of what is instructed. Unfortunately, this spirit, which is deadly and has caused millions of souls to be lost, has invaded Pentecostal and Charismatic circles as well!

The entirety of the tenor of the Word of God is that no one can take responsibility for someone else and neither can anyone shift responsibility from themselves. Each must answer to God, with the Scripture boldly proclaiming, *"The soul that sinneth, it shall die"* (Ezek. 18:4).

(20) "FOR WHERE TWO OR THREE ARE GATHERED TOGETHER IN MY NAME, THERE AM I IN THE MIDST OF THEM."

The phrase, *"For where two or three are gathered together,"* actually refers to the *"little ones"* of verse 10 and that which constitutes a Church, at least in the Eyes of God. In fact, the far greater number of Churches in the world are small.

However, the idea is not that they be kept this small, but that God recognizes it as a Church, although only constituting two or three people. In fact, many large, thriving congregations started with two or three people.

As well, the idea presents itself that Believers should *"not forsake the assembling of themselves together"* (Heb. 10:25).

Also, and as stated, the structure of the verse is meant to proclaim the absence of any type of religious hierarchy. In religious systems, which have pretty much been dominant, at least in one way or the other since the Church began to apostatize in the second century, Religious Denominations take the position that it is not a Church until they place their seal of approval on it. To be certain, all of that is man-made and man-directed, and is not recognized by God.

The phrase, *"In My Name,"* constitutes the qualifications for recognition by the Lord as a Church.

If the *"two or three"* have gathered for an unscriptural reason, and irrespective as to how much they may claim it is *"in His Name,"* still, the Lord will not recognize it as a Church. Sadly, many Churches are begun on a premise of self-will, pride, or personal ambition. Consequently, the Spirit of God does not abide in such circumstances. While, in fact, it may be a Church recognized by a Religious Denomination, or others, still, in the Eyes of God it is not a Church.

This is the reason that many Church splits are not recognized by the Lord. In fact, it is possible that one side or even both sides of the split

NOTES

are scripturally wrong! In view of the fact that many, if not most, Churches are presently begun in this manner, this is the reason that the Spirit of God is not present in these Churches, and, in fact, possibly never will be. I will give Family Worship Center in Baton Rouge as an example.

This Church was begun as a result of the Lord laying the burden on my heart and moving on me directly to begin this congregation. To be sure, it began small, but quickly began to grow. Actually, many, if not most, of the people in the Church are my converts, and not malcontents from other Churches.

In respect to this, it should be obvious that the Lord would not call me to begin this Church with His Blessings obviously upon it and then, at the same time, call someone else to instigate a split or to take advantage of any malcontents to begin another Church out of Family Worship Center. The Lord does not work against Himself. He does not call one to build and then someone else to destroy that which is built.

Of course, that would go for any other Church begun in a similar manner. In such Churches, the Holy Spirit will not, and, in fact, cannot abide. Such Churches are not begun *"in His Name,"* and irrespective of how much they claim to be, but, instead, because of self-will or personal ambition. The phrase, *"There am I in the midst of them,"* is the ingredient and, in fact, the only ingredient that constitutes a True Church. His Presence is the sole deciding factor.

In fact, some Churches may have elaborate buildings and a large congregation, but if the Presence of the Lord is not in their midst, and irrespective as to what they may call themselves or the approval given by others, in the Eyes of God it is not a Church.

I think I exaggerate not when I say, and sadly so, that most Churches fall into this debilitating category.

Even at the risk of redundancy, and because it is so important, the following bears repeating.

His Presence is the criteria and, in fact, the only criteria for that which constitutes a Church, and not buildings, money, recognition by others, size or religious ceremony.

(21) "THEN CAME PETER TO HIM, AND SAID, LORD, HOW OFT SHALL MY BROTHER SIN AGAINST ME, AND I FORGIVE HIM? TILL SEVEN TIMES?"

The phrase, *"Then came Peter to Him, and*

said, Lord," will bring about one of, if not the most important answers respecting relationship with fellow Believers.

The question, *"How oft shall my brother sin against me, and I forgive him? till seven times?",* was probably asked by Peter in respect to the statement made by Christ in Luke 17:4. It is one of the most important questions asked by any Disciple.

(22) "JESUS SAITH UNTO HIM, I SAY NOT UNTO THEE, UNTIL SEVEN TIMES: BUT, UNTIL SEVENTY TIMES SEVEN."

The phrase, *"Jesus saith unto him,"* and as stated, contains the answer that could solve most problems concerning relationships, and in any capacity.

The phrase, *"I say not unto thee, Until seven times,"* proclaims Christ taking this all-important aspect of forgiveness out from under the Law. In other words, Christ demolished this attempt to define by Law the measure of Grace.

The phrase, *"But Until seventy times seven,"* refers to no limit being placed on forgiveness, but it being practiced wherever the occasion would arise.

Jesus very well in His statement, *"Seventy times seven,"* could have been referring to the vengeance demanded by Lamech in the same amount not long after the Fall of Adam and Eve (Gen. 4:24). Forgiveness in the New Covenant must be extended at least as far as old-world vengeance. To be sure, it has an unending extension!

As well, the 490 times referred to by Christ, and if answering Peter in reference to Luke 17:4, was actually referring to 490 times of forgiveness being extended even in one day if necessary!

Of course, the language is meant to imply, and as stated, an open-ended forgiveness. As well, it refers to individuals who have not asked for forgiveness and will neither acknowledge that wrongdoing has been committed.

Forgiveness in such a case by the Believer, even though one-sided, has a positive effect on both.

1. If forgiveness is quickly enjoined, and irrespective of the attitude or action of the offender, hatred and animosity is automatically suspended in the heart of the offended one.

2. The Believer who is quick to forgive, and irrespective of the actions of others, proclaims

by doing so his deep and abiding appreciation for what Jesus has done for him. He has been forgiven of much and, consequently, he forgives quickly!

3. To fail to forgive someone, and irrespective of their attitude, in effect, places the offender in a prison of sorts, actually making it more difficult for them to come to a place of repentance. Forgiveness acts as a release for the offender, whether they respond favorably or not!

4. It is highly unlikely, if not impossible, for one to be sinned against by another some 490 times in one day. Nevertheless, the Believer who is truly attempting to follow the Lord with all his heart, will forgive as many times as is needed. To do so, places the offender in the Hands of the Lord with no thought of vengeance on the part of the one offended.

In Truth, this aspect of the Christian walk is so important that Jesus had stated earlier that if *"We forgive not men their trespasses, neither will our Father forgive our trespasses"* (Mat. 6:15).

Consequently, this statement by Christ must be linked as well to verses 15-17, respecting an individual who would not admit to his wrong, etc. Even though fellowship cannot be continued with the person who refuses to admit such and seek forgiveness, still, our love for that person must not diminish, with every kindness and consideration continued where possible, and with every hope that such a one will ultimately repent. The patience that God shows with us should, as well, be shown to others!

For the Believer to harbor animosity in his heart because of the actions of another, shows a lack of trust in the Lord as well as a desire to exact vengeance, which is totally contrary to the Word of God (Rom. 12:19-21).

(23) "THEREFORE IS THE KINGDOM OF HEAVEN LIKENED UNTO A CERTAIN KING, WHICH WOULD TAKE ACCOUNT OF HIS SERVANTS."

The phrase, *"Therefore is the Kingdom of Heaven likened unto a certain king,"* is meant to illustrate in this parable the principle of forgiveness that has been spoken of in verses 21 and 22. The example given will be crystal clear, leaving absolutely no room for misunderstanding as to what the Lord requires of His Children.

The phrase, *"Which would take account of his servants,"* is exactly what happens on a continuing basis respecting every Believer. The Lord *"takes account"* and constantly!

(24) "AND WHEN HE HAD BEGUN TO RECKON, ONE WAS BROUGHT UNTO HIM, WHICH OWED HIM TEN THOUSAND TALENTS."

The phrase, *"And when he had begun to reckon, one was brought unto him,"* respects attention given to each individual. This will gladden the heart of those who truly desire to follow the Lord, but will bring fear to those who do not enjoy that consecration.

The phrase, *"Which owed him ten thousand talents,"* represents a tremendous sum of money. If in gold, it represented approximately $4,000,000,000 in 1995 dollars. If silver, it would represent approximately $80,000,000. The numbers, as obvious, are staggering!

Actually, it is meant to represent the sin debt owed by the individual and, as obvious, with absolutely no way of paying such an amount.

The average American earns about a $1,500,000 in the course of his lifetime. Consequently, owing a debt of $4,000,000,000, or even $80,000,000 respecting silver, as is obvious, is an amount that is totally impossible to pay.

(25) "BUT FORASMUCH AS HE HAD NOT TO PAY, HIS LORD COMMANDED HIM TO BE SOLD, AND HIS WIFE, AND CHILDREN, AND ALL THAT HE HAD, AND PAYMENT TO BE MADE."

The phrase, *"But forasmuch as he had not to pay,"* represents the sinner who cannot hope to pay such a staggering amount.

The phrase, *"His Lord commanded him to be sold, and his wife, and children, and all that he had, and payment to be made,"* represented that which was actually carried out in those times. The sin debt, of which Jesus is actually illustrating, must be paid.

However, even if the selling of his wife and children as slaves were carried out, such would not make even a small dent in the enormous amount owed.

To be sure, the Lord is not placing His seal of approval upon such action, but is portraying the severity of the situation and the absolute impossibility of such a sum being paid.

As well, and in a spiritual sense, the entirety of the family is affected adversely if they do not know the Lord. In essence, they do go into slavery, to which the results of sin always take one.

NOTES

(26) THE SERVANT THEREFORE FELL DOWN, AND WORSHIPPED HIM, SAYING, LORD, HAVE PATIENCE WITH ME, AND I WILL PAY THEE ALL."

The phrase, *"The servant therefore fell down, and worshipped him,"* refers to the Salvation experience or, in other words, when a person comes to the Lord.

The phrase, *"Saying, Lord, have patience with me, and I will pay thee all,"* too often characterizes most Believers. Even though we profess to believe that Jesus paid it all, still, some of us continue to attempt to earn our place and position in Christ.

It is interesting that this man claimed he would *"pay thee all,"* when, in reality, the amount was so staggering that such an appeal is ludicrous to say the least! And yet, too many of us keep trying to do the same thing, *"pay all,"* when Jesus has already paid it all.

(27) "THEN THE LORD OF THAT SERVANT WAS MOVED WITH COMPASSION, AND LOOSED HIM, AND FORGAVE HIM THE DEBT."

The phrase, *"Then the Lord of that servant was moved with compassion,"* respects the reason of our Salvation. *"God so loved the world..."* (Jn. 3:16).

The Lord does not save us because we merit such or have earned such, as is here obvious, but simply because of His *"compassion."*

The phrase, *"And loosed him,"* respects that which happens to a person upon Salvation. They are literally released from a spiritual prison where Satan has held them bound, and set free by the Power of God. Isaiah said, *"To bring out the prisoners from the prison, and them that sit in darkness out of the prison house"* (Isa. 42:7).

As well, whenever a Believer refuses to forgive another Believer, in effect, and in a spiritual sense, he is keeping that individual in prison. Here, Christ proclaims by His illustration that they are to be *"loosed"* and irrespective of what they have done.

In a broad sense, this pertains to Christ's statement, *"And whatsoever ye shall loose on earth shall be loosed in Heaven"* (vs. 18).

In other words, the Lord will recognize our action as being Christlike, and in accordance with what He has done for us.

It does not mean that the offender who

refuses to admit his guilt or seek forgiveness, is, in fact, forgiven by the Lord. That cannot be until the individual owns up to his sin and requests forgiveness.

As is obvious, there is a vast difference in us as Believers, and the Lord as the all-knowing One. We are to forgive, even though the individual does not request forgiveness, while the Lord does not forgive, and for the obvious reasons, unless the individual repents.

The phrase, *"And forgave him the debt,"* concerns the forgiveness of this staggering amount.

This is what happens when the sinner comes to Christ. All is forgiven, and irrespective of the amount owing.

(28) "BUT THE SAME SERVANT WENT OUT, AND FOUND ONE OF HIS FELLOW SERVANTS, WHICH OWED HIM AN HUNDRED PENCE: AND HE LAID HANDS ON HIM, AND TOOK HIM BY THE THROAT, SAYING, PAY ME THAT THOU OWEST."

The phrase, *"But the same servant went out,"* denotes a negative action, and one which the Lord instantly recognizes.

The phrase, *"And found one of his fellow servants, which owed him an hundred pence,"* represents this man who has recently been forgiven such a staggering amount, actively seeking out one who owed him a paltry sum.

Too often this represents too many Christians. Every slight or trifle is exaggerated, which portrays self-will, and is the very opposite of a Christlike attitude and spirit.

The *"hundred pence"* represents about $300 in 1995 money. Consequently, the $4,000,000,000 recently forgiven this man, is to be compared with the $300 owed him.

The enormous difference between these two amounts is meant to represent the difference between the offenses of our neighbors against us and those of which we are guilty towards God.

The phrase, *"And he laid hands on him, and took him by the throat,"* is treatment totally unlike that which he received at the hands of the Lord.

Such proclaims that the Lord or His Word is not even remotely considered in this matter, but only the ugly self-will of the man recently forgiven.

This illustration, among other things, is intended to teach us that everything we do is to be done in the light of what God has done for

us, and according to His Word. Regrettably, many, if not most, Believers do not take that tact. The idea is, at least in too many Christian circles, that if he has done it to me, I can do it to him.

Whenever the sinner comes to Jesus, he enters into an entirely different culture. It is the Christlike culture, which is founded on the Word of God, and should rule the attitude, conduct and disposition of all that we do.

The phrase, *"Saying, Pay me that thou owest,"* is a demand which the debtor cannot meet, as the one making the demand could not meet his debt.

(29) "AND HIS FELLOWSERVANT FELL DOWN AT HIS FEET, AND BESOUGHT HIM, SAYING, HAVE PATIENCE WITH ME, AND I WILL PAY THEE ALL."

The phrase, *"And his fellowservant fell down at his feet, and besought him, saying,"* is interesting, as it represents both as *"servants."* In other words, and according to the Lord Who had forgiven the monstrous debt, both were on the same level, and irrespective of their station in life.

Actually, one could easily recognize that the man who owed *"ten thousand talents"* was a man of tremendous importance, at least as far as the world is concerned, and because of the staggering amount he owed. The other man who owed only the approximate $300 was no more than a day laborer, if that, because he could not even pay this paltry sum, and would have been recognized by the world as of no consequence. And yet, the Lord labels them both as *"servants,"* and which they actually were in God's sight.

Some men love to think of themselves as great, while God gives no consideration to that which man calls greatness, placing all on the same level of want.

The phrase, *"Have patience with me, and I will pay thee all,"* is very similar to the terminology employed by the man who owed the *"ten thousand talents."*

Man, and irrespective to who he is, keeps thinking he can somehow pay this monstrous sin debt. The rich man thought he could, and the poor man thinks he can! As stated, such continues to characterize many Believers, and maybe all of us in one way or the other.

(30) "AND HE WOULD NOT: BUT WENT

AND CAST HIM INTO PRISON, TILL HE SHOULD PAY THE DEBT."

The phrase, *"And he would not,"* characterizes the very opposite of what the Lord had shown to him. In other words, he would not even consider it, nor even agree to an extension of time. He was unmerciful in his attitude and unmerciful in his action.

Just a short time before, he had basically appealed in the same manner to the one he owed such a staggering amount, and had received mercy and compassion. However, he shows none to the poor man, even in regard to such a paltry sum owed to him.

The phrase, *"But went and cast him into prison, till he should pay the debt,"* refers to exacting total punishment, and demanding every cent be paid, which, of course, is impossible!

The action, as here presented by the Lord, is meant to portray to us the abomination of the terrible sin of unforgiveness. We who have been forgiven so much should delight in forgiving others. And yet, so few do!

Or else, many claim they forgive, but put such attached conditions to their forgiveness that, in effect, it is no forgiveness at all! In Truth, unless our forgiveness is the same as the Lord's, then it is not recognized by God as forgiveness. Sadly, too many Believers concoct their own type of forgiveness, which the Lord will not recognize.

There is no record here that the Lord demanded penance of any nature or payment of any kind when He forgave the man who owed so much. Actually, to do so is not forgiveness, but, instead, payment toward a debt.

Unfortunately, too many modern Believers, taking a cue from Religious Denominations, demand probation, penance, or some type of payment. Such is denied, but the denial in no way abrogates the truth of what is actually being done.

To tell someone who has truly repented, that you forgive them but that they have to sit in the back of the Church for two years, etc., is, in fact, a mockery of the very word *"forgiveness."*

What if the Lord forgave someone, but said, *"From time to time I will bring up the sin that you committed, making certain that your memory is refreshed concerning this act, so that you will forever realize just how bad it actually was!"*

Of course, such is no forgiveness at all, and is the very opposite of that which the Lord does.

In Truth, that is more akin to that which Satan does than the Lord.

(31) "SO WHEN HIS FELLOWSERVANTS SAW WHAT WAS DONE, THEY WERE VERY SORRY, AND CAME AND TOLD UNTO THEIR LORD ALL THAT WAS DONE."

The phrase, *"So when his fellowservants saw what was done, they were very sorry,"* portrays a tremendously important lesson.

First of all, these individuals, whomever they were, were placed in the same category respecting dependency on the Lord as the man who had owed all the money, or the one who had owed a small amount.

Their being *"sorry"* instead of angry is a very interesting observation and pertains to all, especially considering that what was done was enough to make anyone angry!

Anger against sin is an attribute of God, while sorrow pertains to men. The reason is simple, that is if we all properly evaluate ourselves.

In the heart of every person, even the most dedicated to the Lord, is the germ of evil, which, if unchecked, could lead into similar circumstances. There but for the Grace of God go I, and, one may quickly add, through no attributes of our own!

The phrase, *"And came and told unto their Lord all that was done,"* was an act of justice and mercy, and not one of malice. The reaction of the Lord justified their action.

As well, ultimately, sin will find you out (Num. 32:23).

(32) "THEN HIS LORD, AFTER THAT HE HAD CALLED HIM, SAID UNTO HIM, O THOU WICKED SERVANT, I FORGAVE THEE ALL THAT DEBT, BECAUSE THOU DESIREDST ME:"

The phrase, *"Then his Lord, after that he had called him, said unto him,"* concerns the second time he will now stand before the Lord. Then he was extended Mercy and Grace, where now he will not be extended such, and because he refused to extend such.

The phrase, *"O thou wicked servant,"* is the category he is now placed in, and despite the fact of his no longer owing the *"ten thousand talents,"* i.e., grievous debt of sin. The *"why"* is obvious!

The phrase, *"I forgave thee all that debt, because thou desiredst Me,"* proclaims the reason the Lord now calls him *"wicked!"*

One can easily see how heinous this sin of unforgiveness is in the Eyes of God, and especially considering the enormous debt the man had been forgiven, and mercifully so! As well, for anyone to argue that their original debt was not that much, is completely without merit. All fall into the same category, and, consequently, all are judged guilty (Rom. 3:10-18).

The only requirement for the enormous *"debt"* being forgiven, was that the individual in question *"desire"* that the Lord do so. Nothing else was demanded, as stated, no penance, probation, or repayment schedule. With the simple request, and tendered sincerely, the enormous *"debt"* was wiped away, as if it never existed.

(33) "SHOULDEST NOT THOU ALSO HAVE HAD COMPASSION ON THY FELLOW-SERVANT, EVEN AS I HAD PITY ON THEE?"

The question, *"Shouldest not thou also have had compassion on thy fellowservant . . . ?"*, is a question that every Believer should earnestly consider! It is at least one of the singular most important principles of one's experience with Christ. To refuse forgiveness, and on any grounds, is to close the door to the Mercy and Grace of God. Consequently, one should think very carefully concerning his action in these matters.

The conclusion of the question, *"Even as I had pity on thee?"*, is intended to bring to bear the idea that if an individual who has been forgiven so much does not even have the Grace of God to extend forgiveness in matters which are infinitesimally smaller, there is no hope for that person. As stated, for anyone of us to refuse to forgive, and exactly as the Lord demands, is to stop all forgiveness from the Lord toward us (6:14-15).

In such a situation, many hide behind denominational rulings which clearly violate the Word of God.

Once again, it must be understood that God's dealings with us are not predicated on what Religious Denominations or others do or not do, but on our personal obedience to the Word of God, or the lack of it! Attempting to justify lack of forgiveness on any grounds is not acceptable to the Lord under any circumstances.

As well, the type of forgiveness enjoined must be the same type of forgiveness the Lord has given to us. That is a very important statement and should be thought about very carefully.

NOTES

(34) "AND HIS LORD WAS WROTH, AND DELIVERED HIM TO THE TORMENTORS, TILL HE SHOULD PAY ALL THAT WAS DUE UNTO HIM,"

The phrase, *"And his Lord was wroth,"* expresses anger by the Lord, and at what?

No anger was registered by the Lord when this man originally came before Him, even though he owed *"ten thousand talents."* But now, anger is registered.

Why?

This is considered to be a far worse sin than the original, simply because it is a sin against Light. Before conversion, the individual walked in darkness. Now he walks in Light, and should act accordingly, especially in view of forgiveness.

To be sure, this sin is so heinous in the Eyes of God that it is the only sin in the Bible which closes up Heaven against the offender. To be sure, all of us, even the best, are in constant need of forgiveness, especially considering that all of us continually *"come short of the Glory of God"* (Rom. 3:23). Therefore, to shut up Heaven, stopping the Mercy and Grace of God on our behalf, is the most serious thing that could happen to any individual. And the only sin that will do that is the sin of unforgiveness.

The phrase, *"And delivered him to the tormentors,"* reflects the person being ultimately lost. Such refutes the unscriptural doctrine of unconditional eternal security, as should be blatantly obvious in this illustration.

In other words, if the individual continues in the capacity of unforgiveness, he will lose his soul.

At the same time, anyone who is committing this sin, if he will ask forgiveness from the Lord for that sin and immediately extend forgiveness to the person in question, the Lord will immediately forgive and, once again, re-open the gates of Mercy and Grace.

The phrase, *"Till he should pay all that was due unto him,"* has been argued from the time it was uttered by Christ.

Does it mean his original debt of *"ten thousand talents,"* which was freely forgiven by Christ? Or does it refer to this new sin?

Actually, the question is moot, because sin against God which is unforgiven, as this sin is, and because the man would not forgive the lesser offense, is a debt that no individual could ever hope to pay, and irrespective as to amount or size. In other words, even the smallest sin, whatever that may be, is beyond the ability of anyone to wash or cleanse, at least within their own ability. So, the sentence handed down is a debt the individual cannot hope to pay, and, as such, it will remain there forever.

As well, some have attempted to construe the idea from this Passage that a certain length of time in hell (torment) will ultimately pay the debt. However, there is nothing in the Word of God that even remotely hints at such a thing. Actually, the very opposite is stated, with the use of terms such as *"everlasting fire,"* etc. (Mat. 18:8).

(35) "SO LIKEWISE SHALL MY HEAVENLY FATHER DO ALSO UNTO YOU, IF YE FROM YOUR HEARTS FORGIVE NOT EVERY ONE HIS BROTHER THEIR TRESPASSES."

The words, *"So likewise,"* are given in case the plainly illustrated Truth is lost upon the individual. This concluding verse will leave absolutely no doubt as to what is being said.

The phrase, *"Shall My Heavenly Father do also unto you,"* states exactly what is said, meaning that the individual, if engaging in unforgiveness, will lose their soul, and irrespective of what type of walk they have had with the Lord previously. Actually, that which the Lord has done for us, and our nearness to Him, is the very basis on which we must engage in forgiveness of others, even as the Lord has forgiven us.

The phrase, *"If ye from your hearts forgive not every one his brother their trespasses,"* is a solemn statement indeed!

The idea is that our Heavenly Father requires us to forgive without limit in order that His Mercy and Grace may be extended to us without measure as well!

As here proclaimed, true forgiveness can only come from the *"heart."* As it comes from the heart, it will express itself in similar conduct which is sincere and not merely pretended. Revenge or vengeance must be totally put away. There must be no malice in the heart, no storing up of evil passions for future outlet. This alone enables one to continue in a state of Grace and in reconciliation with God. As well, this alone makes prayer acceptable, which is the reason many Christians do not pray. They harbor unforgiveness, which makes prayer impossible!

Also, if the offender truly repents, the offended must forgive, and immediately, and restore full fellowship (Gal. 6:1). The idea of claiming that forgiveness is extended but no fellowship is possible, even though the individual has truly repented, is not a type of forgiveness that God will recognize.

Also, no one is to be excluded from forgiveness, nor is any *"trespass"* to be off-limits. We must always remember that whatever someone has done, if they truly seek forgiveness, our forgiveness extended to them can never even begin to compare with the forgiveness that God has extended unto us.

In the giving of this illustration concerning the parable of the unmerciful servant, it is related so clearly that no one need have any difficulty whatsoever in understanding perfectly what Jesus is talking about. Inasmuch as the stakes are so very high, even the Salvation of our souls, we must be quick to forgive, and exactly as Jesus has stated. To do otherwise, even in the slightest degree, is the most foolish move that any Believer could ever engage in.

CHAPTER 19

(1) "AND IT CAME TO PASS, THAT WHEN JESUS HAD FINISHED THESE SAYINGS, HE DEPARTED FROM GALILEE, AND CAME INTO THE COASTS OF JUDAEA BEYOND JORDAN;"

The phrase, *"And it came to pass,"* at least at this time, is a momentous statement. The Crucifixion is only a short time ahead. His heart must have been heavy, especially considering His rejection. He has already said that offenses must come, *"But woe to that man by whom the offence cometh!"* Tragically and sadly, *"that man"* will include virtually the entirety of the leadership of Israel, with the *"woe"* extending to the destruction of Israel as a nation.

The phrase, *"That when Jesus had finished these sayings,"* concerns the great 18th Chapter, with all the many warnings given concerning opposition to, and persecution of, those who followed Him. Along with that which was meant to speak to all Believers and for all time, it is as if He is warning Israel of the terrible judgment that will befall them if they continue in their hatred of and their murderous intent toward Him.

The phrase, *"He departed from Galilee, and came into the coasts of Judaea beyond Jordan,"* speaks of Him departing from the area where He had performed so many miracles and had given the greatest part of His teaching. It was His farewell to the scene of His earthly headquarters which had been chosen by the Heavenly Father. He now sets out for Jerusalem in order to give His life a ransom for many. He will not return unto Galilee until after His Resurrection.

Actually, there was no part of the Holy Land in which He did not at some time minister; however, it was the Galilee area in which most of His Ministry was carried out.

The word, *"coasts,"* should have been translated *"borders."*

"Beyond Jordan" speaks of the east side of the Jordan River, which was the area of Perea. It was at this time governed by Herod Antipas, and was greatly prosperous. It was a little over 80 miles from Capernaum to Jerusalem, and would take Jesus through Jericho where He will heal blind Bartimaeus.

His reason for taking the route east of the Jordan River rather than on the other side, could have been for this very reason, the healing of the blind man, as well as the Salvation of Zacchaeus. However, the opposition to His Ministry by the Pharisees on the eastern side, although fierce, was not nearly as bad as the other route.

Many Bible Students do not realize it, but Jesus was banned from most of the Synagogues of Galilee and Judea. As well, those in that area, which actually made up the far greater bulk of Israel who openly followed Him, were threatened with excommunication from the Synagogue, which spoke of a ban and shunning so complete that at times the victim could not even purchase food to eat. It was that serious!

It is difficult to realize that the Saviour of humanity, God's Only Son, the Messiah of Israel, would have the doors of all the religious centers closed to Him. Such seems unthinkable! But yet, is it any different now?

If one truly preaches the Gospel even at this modern time, truly following Jesus, and attempting to obey the Word of God fully, the attitude of the religious community, and basically all parts of it, will take the same attitude now as then! Satan is working no less in religion today than he was then, and the attitude

NOTES

of religion toward Christ is no different now than it was then.

This is what is going to make it so easy for the apostate Church world to accept the Antichrist. One Evangelist from Canada made this statement concerning the Pentecostals, with whom both of us are associated.

He said, *"The last generation of Pentecostals lost the Anointing of the Holy Spirit, and, consequently, this generation of Pentecostals doesn't even know what it is, at least for the most part."*

At the present time, Pentecostals and Charismatics who claim to believe all the Word of God, are, for the most part, rejecting that Word in favor of fads, foibles and phenomenon. If one rejects the Truth, one by design will always accept a lie.

Great crowds are gathering in order to *"laugh"* and roll on the floor, or to watch an Evangelist blow on people and have them fall over. There is very little repentance, if any, at least at this time, and very little preaching of the Word, and, in Truth, precious few people being saved and Baptized in the Holy Spirit. Despite great claims to the contrary, there are precious few healings as well!

Hundreds of millions of dollars are coming from the pockets of Christians, being poured into schemes which are not of God, and, as a result, do nothing for God.

Why?

As stated, if one rejects the Truth, one accepts a lie!

(2) "AND GREAT MULTITUDES FOLLOWED HIM; AND HE HEALED THEM THERE."

The phrase, *"And great multitudes followed Him,"* speaks of that which probably could not have happened had He taken the western side of Jordan. Consequently, even unto the end, He was seeking to reach souls and to free them from their sin and sickness.

The phrase, *"And He healed them there,"* speaks of that which He would have done for the entirety of Israel, both physically and spiritually, had they only allowed Him to do so.

Mark makes mention as well that he taught them, which generally characterized His method of alternating between preaching, teaching and healing.

(3) "THE PHARISEES ALSO CAME UNTO

HIM, TEMPTING HIM, AND SAYING UNTO HIM, IS IT LAWFUL FOR A MAN TO PUT AWAY HIS WIFE FOR EVERY CAUSE?"

The phrase, *"The Pharisees also came unto Him,"* and using the word, *"also,"* places these reprobates as coming to Him for an entirely different reason. These individuals had probably been sent from Jerusalem, dogging His every step, and, as well, seeking, as here, to snare Him with thorny questions. They had absolutely no regard for the Word of God, which they incidentally claimed to meticulously keep, nor for the true purpose of the Gospel, which was to set men free. They were only concerned about their authority and petty rules.

Tragically and sadly, if one looks at the modern Church, one sees little difference! Of people being truly saved by the Blood of Jesus, with lives radically and gloriously changed, there is very little interest at the present. Identically as before, the interest is in authority and money.

The words, *"Tempting Him,"* are interesting in that it was the opposite of the multitudes. They trusted Him, while the Pharisees tempted Him.

Their clever snare, as will be obvious, was to pose a question to Christ that ensnared Him irrespective of His answer. However, their snares never worked because they were dealing with the Lord of Glory, but did not have enough sense to realize it.

The phrase, *"And saying unto Him,"* is a pronouncement of their clever question on divorce, which they had measured carefully and crafted accordingly!

The question, *"Is it lawful for a man to put away his wife for every cause?",* was actually a question which raged in Jerusalem at that time.

Actually, the Lord had already dealt with this subject twice, once in the Sermon on the Mount (5:32), and again with the Pharisees on the observance of the Law (Lk. 16:18).

If one is to notice, the real issue here is divorce for *"every cause,"* and not divorce for fornication which was lawful (Deut. 24:1-4).

This controversy over divorce and remarriage was raging at the time, with the scholars divided between the views of Hillel and Shammai.

Hillel taught that a man could divorce his wife for any cause whatsoever. If he ceased to love her or had seen someone he liked better, or even because she did not prepare his meals as he desired, he could seek and obtain a divorce.

Shammai, on the other hand, permitted divorce only in the case of fornication, adhering to Deuteronomy 24:1-4.

The Pharisees, in their tempting of Him, probably felt if they could get Him to agree with the popular lax view of Hillel, they could then demean Him for lax morality and the weakening of the family unit.

On the other hand, if He came down on the side of Shammai, which allowed divorce for sexual uncleanness only, He might possibly arouse the enmity of Herod as John the Baptist, because Jesus was now in the territory of this wicked Monarch.

So, when they found that Jesus would go to Jerusalem by the eastern route of Jordan, they no doubt felt this would be an excellent time to spring their trap.

(4) "AND HE ANSWERED AND SAID UNTO THEM, HAVE YE NOT READ, THAT HE WHICH MADE THEM AT THE BEGINNING MADE THEM MALE AND FEMALE,"

The phrase, *"And He answered and said unto them,"* proclaims Him completely ignoring these two alleged Biblical scholars, Hillel and Shammai, and going directly to the Word of God.

Regrettably, even at this present time, Religious Denominations, at least for the most part, appeal to their Constitution and Bylaws, instead of the Word of God. Some of them argue that their Constitution and Bylaws are the Word of God. However, many times that is woefully untrue!

Having such documents to satisfy governmental demands is understandable. But in cases of behavior, lifestyle, or disputes, the Word of God, and the Word of God alone, must be the criteria.

The beginning of a question, *"Have ye not read . . . ?",* is asked by the Lord in a somewhat sarcastic tone, exactly as it should have been. These hypocrites claimed to abide by the Word of God, which actually was their chief contention, but, in reality, did not abide by it at all!

The continuing of the question, *"That He which made them at the beginning made them male and female,"* is a tremendously informative statement.

First, with the pronoun, *"He,"* Jesus takes them back to God, Who is the Creator of all things, but definitely not responsible for the direction some of His creation took. For instance,

God, in His creation of Angels and man, gave both the liberty of choice. To secure the desired conclusion, this manner of creation was necessary.

Consequently, a third of the Angels including Lucifer, chose to oppose their Creator, while man, regrettably and sadly, chose the same route of rebellion. As stated, God was not responsible for that choice.

As well, Jesus takes the Pharisees back to the original intention of God by using the words, *"At the beginning."* In other words, He is saying that we must look at God's original intention, and not the direction that man's wicked heart has taken him.

The phrase, *"Male and Female,"* is meant to relate that God made the first members of the human family a male and a female, and from one.

In the creation of animals, the male and female were created separately. However, in the making of the human family, God created only one person, Adam, and from Adam's side made Eve. Two individuals of opposite sexes were thus formed for each other; one was the compliment of the other, and the union was perfect and was to last as long as life.

Consequently, in this original institution, as is clear, there was no room for polygamy, or for divorce.

The manner in which God created man and woman is the manner in which He united them as man and wife, and intended for them to live.

As well, from this we learn that the sin of homosexuality is one of the most wicked of sins, and a direct affront against God's original creation of man and woman. As someone has said, God created Adam and Eve, not Adam and Steve.

To disrupt God's order of the creation of man and woman by claiming that homosexuals were created that way, i.e., born in that manner, is a direct denial of the Word of God, and is one of the greatest signs of the destruction of any civilization, and in this case, western civilization.

Homosexuality is sin, and grievous sin at that! It is the only sin, at least that which we have a record of, which caused God to completely annihilate two cities (Gen. 19:5, 24).

As well, this Passage plus many others destroy the absurd theory of evolution, which is another affront to the Creator in that it lowers His greatest creation, and, consequently, His Image, to the level of the lowest animal or

NOTES

reptile. Consequently, man's sin is great and must of necessity be judged!

(5) "AND SAID, FOR THIS CAUSE SHALL A MAN LEAVE FATHER AND MOTHER, AND SHALL CLEAVE TO HIS WIFE: AND THEY TWAIN SHALL BE ONE FLESH?"

The continuance of the question, *"And said, for this cause,"* proclaims God as not only the Creator of man, but, as well, the Founder of marriage, which makes it a sacred institution.

The phrase, *"Shall a man leave father and mother, and shall cleave to his wife,"* was spoken by Adam in Genesis 2:23-24, but was, in effect, a prophetic utterance, with the words rightly attributed by Christ to the Creator. Adam was only the mouthpiece.

In Truth, and in the natural sense, Adam would have known nothing of *"father and mother,"* inasmuch as he and Eve did not have such.

The conclusion of the question, *"And they twain shall be one flesh?",* proclaims the union of husband and wife as being nearer than all other human relations, even mother and father, as important as that my be!

In marriage, the *"one flesh"* continues, even as the human family began in *"one flesh."*

In marriage there is a spiritual and physical union, so that two persons become virtually one being. Originally, man contained woman in himself before she was separated from him.

As someone has said, man, as a race, was created male and female, the latter being contained in the former. In marriage this unity is acknowledge and continued.

This is the reason that fornication or adultery is such a sin, with Paul quoting Genesis 2:24 in Ephesians 5:31 and I Corinthians 6:16.

(6) "WHEREFORE THEY ARE NO MORE TWAIN, BUT ONE FLESH. WHAT THEREFORE GOD HATH JOINED TOGETHER, LET NOT MAN PUT ASUNDER."

The phrase, *"Wherefore they are no more twain, but one flesh,"* proclaims God as looking at a man and his wife not as two, but, instead, as *"one flesh."*

This tells us that for every young man the Lord has a young lady, and for every young lady a young man. Consequently, the Will of God must be sought earnestly respecting this Divine union, for Divine it is!

The phrase, *"What therefore God hath joined together, let not man put asunder,"* tells us that the institution of marriage is God's appointment.

As well, the manner in which Christ made this statement proclaims to us that He was speaking not just of Adam and Eve, but of all wedlock and for all time.

As well, the phrase, *"God hath joined together,"* concerns the institution of marriage, and irrespective of whether it was the Will of God or not!

Many claim that some married people were not joined together by God, so they are free to divorce and marry the one God intended them to have, etc.

However, this is a corruption of the Text in that the institution of marriage is here spoken of, and not the respective mate for each person. While it is true, and as stated, that God has a woman for each man, and, definitely a will in this matter, still, whether it is His will or not, all marriages are recognized not only by the State but by God as legally joined together as man and wife. As such, they will be held responsible for their vows (Rom. 13:1-10).

The phrase, *"Let not man put asunder,"* specifically gives God's Will concerning divorce. In plain terms, we are told that it is not to be.

When divorce is instituted (saving for the cause of fornication, etc.), man opposes God and acts against nature. He and his wife are one; spiritually, they can no more separate from one another than they can from themselves.

Despite the lax morality of the present time, that is the reason that divorce is the second most traumatic experience one can undergo, with the death of a close loved one being the first.

Why?

The trauma of divorce is present, and despite modern man's lax morality, because of the manner in which God originally created man and woman. Consequently, no matter how the laws of modern man may change or how lax morality may become, the trauma will remain!

(7) "THEY SAY UNTO HIM, WHY DID MOSES THEN COMMAND TO GIVE A WRITING OF DIVORCEMENT, AND TO PUT HER AWAY?"

The phrase, *"They say unto Him,"* proclaims the Pharisees attempting to use the Word of God against God.

Jesus has taken them back to the original

intent of God, completely ignoring the arguments of the modern scholars, and, as stated, making the Bible the foundation for all rule of conduct.

The question, *"Why did Moses then command to give a writing of divorcement, and to put her away?",* is posed by the Pharisees from Deuteronomy 24:1-2.

Now they will attempt to pit Moses against Christ, thinking He will have no answer to their question.

Actually, by using the word, *"command,"* relative to Moses, they were in error. The words Moses gave in Deuteronomy 24:1-2 were from the Lord, with Moses only as the mouthpiece. Even though it was called the *"Law of Moses,"* actually, it only meant that God used him in the giving of the Law. It was really the Law of God.

As well, the *"writing of divorcement,"* spoke of a detailed document outlining what the wife had done, with it being ruled on by the judges, which would necessitate delay and publicity. It was not undertaken rashly or lightly.

(8) "HE SAITH UNTO THEM, MOSES BECAUSE OF THE HARDNESS OF YOUR HEART SUFFERED YOU TO PUT AWAY YOUR WIVES: BUT FROM THE BEGINNING IT WAS NOT SO."

The phrase, *"He saith unto them,"* refers to the answer given by Christ to the Pharisees, which will rightly divide the Word of Truth.

The liberal divorce laws which prevailed at the time of Christ, proclaimed a corruption of the Word of God. In other words, the statement given by Moses in Deuteronomy 24:1-2 had been so enlarged upon that its original meaning had long been lost. Many of the people and Religious Leaders of Israel were attempting to twist the Word of God in order to make it justify their wicked actions.

The phrase, *"Moses because of the hardness of your heart suffered you to put away your wives,"* first of all records Moses *"suffering"* it, and not *"commanding"* it!

The word, *"uncleanness,"* in Deuteronomy 24:1, was the center of controversy.

Shammai held that it referred only to moral and criminal sins of fornication, which is actually correct, while Hillel contended that it referred to anything disliked by the husband, even something trivial.

The *"hardness of the heart"* is what dictated

divorce in any situation. If, in the time of Moses, the Law absolutely forbade divorce in any circumstance, there was a danger that some evil men would seriously mistreat their wives or even murder them.

In those days, and in whatever culture, the wife actually became the property of the husband and he became her lord and master (Ex. 21:7-11). In fact, wives were given far more freedom in Israel under the Law of Moses than in surrounding nations which had no knowledge of the Lord. Consequently, if it is to be noticed, the laws respecting divorce were given concerning the man, with the wife included only in an indirect manner.

If the Lord had not allowed divorce under any circumstance, an intolerable situation would have been forced upon many wives.

The phrase, *"But from the beginning it was not so,"* is saying that God never intended divorce, and for the obvious reasons, but only because of the hardness of heart was it allowed.

(9) "AND I SAY UNTO YOU, WHOSOEVER SHALL PUT AWAY HIS WIFE, EXCEPT IT BE FOR FORNICATION, AND SHALL MARRY ANOTHER, COMMITTETH ADULTERY: AND WHOSO MARRIETH HER WHICH IS PUT AWAY DOTH COMMIT ADULTERY."

The phrase, *"And I say unto you,"* is meant by Christ to put the crowning statement on this extremely volatile question. In essence, the same One Who at the beginning said, *"Therefore shall a man leave his father and his mother, and shall cleave unto his wife: and they shall be one flesh"* (Gen. 2:24), now says the following:

The phrase, *"Whosoever shall put away his wife, except it be for fornication,"* gives us the only Scriptural grounds for divorce, and, at the same time, completely denounced those who wished to put away their wives for *"every cause."*

(For the definition of fornication, please see notes on Matthew 5:32.)

The phrase, *"And shall marry another, committeth adultery,"* states how God looks at the situation in an unlawful marriage. In other words, the only Scriptural grounds for divorce is *"fornication,"* and if for any other reason divorce is entered into, and the man remarries, he *"commits adultery,"* as should be obvious! He has sinned against the order of God, of the two being *"one flesh,"* with that union being unlawfully dissolved.

The reason that *"fornication"* is a cause for divorce, and by either party, is because by the committing of that sin, the same sin of the disrupting of the union of *"one flesh"* has been committed.

The phrase, *"And whoso marrieth her which is put away doth commit adultery,"* means to marry a woman who has been divorced because she has committed the sin of *"fornication."* The man who does such commits *"adultery."*

If one is to notice, the Word is *"commit adultery,"* and not *"living in adultery."* Actually, the phrase, *"living in adultery,"* is not found in the Bible. The idea insinuates that every time a husband and wife enters into relations in such cases, they commit adultery, and are, therefore, *"living in adultery."*

That is unscriptural and, consequently, incorrect. While it is true that the initial act concerning remarriage without proper Scriptural grounds, causes one to *"commit adultery,"* however, that sin is consummated within itself, and does not carry over to repeated relations.

As well, many have argued that divorce allowed for *"fornication"* does not free the man or woman to remarry. However, every indication is that such is incorrect, with remarriage allowed under such circumstances.

Attempting to take the phrase, *"And whoso marrieth her which is put away doth commit adultery,"* and make it mean that such a one can never remarry, even if their partner has engaged in *"fornication,"* does not mean that at all.

It simply means that if and when one remarries, they are not to marry one who has been divorced due to committing the sin of *"fornication."* The man or woman would be free to marry anyone else, but not one guilty of such sin.

There is one more cause allowed for divorce and remarriage, as given by Paul in I Corinthians 7:12-15. It is willful desertion by either the husband or the wife because of Christ and the Gospel.

In other words, if after marriage the husband or wife comes to Christ, and because of this allegiance the mate deserts the marriage bonds, which at times happens, the Christian is no longer bound to that marriage and is free to remarry in the Will of God.

Actually, but without saying so, Christ, by using the phrase, *"Except it be for fornication,"* somewhat came down on the side of Shammai.

(10) "HIS DISCIPLES SAY UNTO HIM, IF THE CASE OF THE MAN BE SO WITH HIS WIFE, IT IS NOT GOOD TO MARRY."

The phrase, *"His Disciples say unto Him,"* once again portrays an erroneous idea held by the Disciples, and because they improperly understood the Word of God. Such erroneous beliefs permeated Israel at that time, and because the Word of God had been made of none effect by man's traditions.

The phrase, *"If the case of the man be so with his wife, it is not good to marry,"* portrays, as stated, a complete misunderstanding.

While it is true that marriage without God is not, and, in fact, cannot be what it should be, and results in much heartache. However, with the Lord's approval and blessing, as it is supposed to be, marriage is truly the greatest of all blessings and the fulfillment of God's intentions.

Israel was arguing over the grounds for divorce, when they should have been seeking God and searching His Word in order to heal whatever problems there may have been in various marriages. They were not seeking God as to how to solve the problem, but, instead, engaging in that which exacerbated the problem.

The Word of God said the very opposite of that which the Disciples now exclaimed! Solomon said, *"Whoso findeth a wife findeth a good thing"* (Prov. 18:22). As well, Solomon said, *"And a prudent wife is from the Lord"* (Prov. 19:14).

(11) "BUT HE SAID UNTO THEM, ALL MEN CANNOT RECEIVE THIS SAYING, SAVE THEY TO WHOM IT IS GIVEN."

The phrase, *"But He said unto them,"* refers to Jesus answering their statement in a totally opposite manner.

They were still dealing with divorce with all its ignoble circumstances, and now coming to the conclusion that if divorce is not made easy, marriage should not even be entered into!

When people are drawn back to the Word of God, as the Disciples here were, oftentimes they come up with ridiculous conclusions, in effect, claiming that the Word of God is too severe.

It must ever be understood that the Bible is not only not severe, but, as well, shows man the only way the difficulties can be addressed, with victory guaranteed. In later years Peter would write, *"According as His Divine Power hath given unto us all things that pertain unto life*

and godliness, through the knowledge of Him that hath called us to glory and virtue:

"Whereby are given unto us exceeding great and precious promises: that by these ye might be partakers of the Divine nature, having escaped the corruption that is in the world through lust" (II Pet. 1:3-4).

Peter, when writing these words, and inspired by the Holy Spirit, may well have thought back to some of these ridiculous statements made to Christ by himself and the other Disciples.

The phrase, *"All men cannot receive this saying, save they to whom it is given,"* is meant to answer the statement of the Disciples concerning it *"not being good to marry."* He, in effect, is saying that all should marry, save the few who are called of God to do otherwise. The next verse tells us what that is.

(12) "FOR THERE ARE SOME EUNUCHS, WHICH WERE SO BORN FROM THEIR MOTHER'S WOMB: AND THERE ARE SOME EUNUCHS, WHICH WERE MADE EUNUCHS OF MEN: AND THERE BE EUNUCHS, WHICH HAVE MADE THEMSELVES EUNUCHS FOR THE KINGDOM OF HEAVEN'S SAKE. HE THAT IS ABLE TO RECEIVE IT, LET HIM RECEIVE IT."

Three classes are here spoken of who should not marry. Conversely, all others should enter into marriage, but according to the Will of God regarding their mate.

Strangely enough, the meaning of the word, *"Eunuch,"* is *"court officer."* In this context, it would refer to one who had given up the pleasures of married life in order to serve the State. The same could be said for some who would purposely give up family life in order to serve the Lord, and because they had been called to do so in this manner, such as the Apostle Paul.

As well, it has the meaning of the word, *"castrate,"* which means the removal of a man's testicles, or concerning a woman, the removal of the ovaries to where she could no longer conceive.

This word *"castrate"* may apply to *"officers of the court,"* but not to those who perform in the service of the Lord.

For instance, Daniel and the Hebrew Children were called *"Eunuchs,"* but they were not castrated, for they were *"without blemish"* (Dan. 1:4).

1. *"For there are some Eunuchs, which were so born from their mother's womb":* This small number speaks of those who have no sex drive

whatsoever, neither any inclination to marry. The intimation is that it would be best that they not marry.

2. *"And there are some Eunuchs, which were made Eunuchs of men"*: This refers to men who were purposely castrated, whether willingly or not, in order that they may serve in king's courts and in various positions. Consequently, they were, in effect, married to the State.

3. *"And there be Eunuchs, which have made themselves Eunuchs for the Kingdom of Heaven's sake"*: This is the third group which involved no castration, but accepted celibacy because they felt called of the Lord to do so.

Hence the Apostle Paul argued that his condition as a celibate was not sinful as his opponents at Corinth contended, but, on the contrary, was a call of God in the highest form of evangelistic effort, with Paul and others given the grace to do so by the Power of the Holy Spirit.

The phrase, *"He that is able to receive it, let him receive it,"* only refers to the last group, and speaks of those called of the Lord for such a task, which would, as is obvious, be few.

In reality, almost all the Bible greats were married. Therefore, from this, we know that the Lord only calls a few for this task. Consequently, the Catholic Church has no Scriptural grounds for the celibacy demanded of its Priests and Nuns. In fact, this imposed condition has caused untold grief for the Catholic Church respecting immorality and hypocrisy, with no intention at all to imply that such resides only in the Catholic Church.

(13) "THEN WERE THERE BROUGHT UNTO HIM LITTLE CHILDREN, THAT HE SHOULD PUT HIS HANDS ON THEM, AND PRAY: AND THE DISCIPLES REBUKED THEM."

The phrase, *"Then were there brought unto Him little children,"* proclaims a number of mothers, accompanied by their children, some of them being infants hearing Jesus' teaching on marriage and enlightened by it, desiring Jesus to bless their children.

The phrase, *"That He should put His Hands on them, and pray,"* proclaims that as Christ had blessed marriage, now He should bless its fruit.

If one is to notice, Jesus elevated women to their true position as intended by God. He did not by His treatment of them place them in a position inferior to man, but on man's equal.

In fact, the Holy Spirit allowed a woman, Mary Magdalene, to be the first to herald the Resurrection (Mk. 16:9-11).

Due to the Fall in the Garden of Eden, and the woman being the first to yield to the temptations of Satan, from thereafter man tended to blame her, with many, if not most, of her rights abrogated.

In fact, a curse had been placed upon woman by the Lord as a result of her action in the Fall, by saying to her, *"And thy desire shall be to thy husband, and he shall rule over thee"* (Gen. 3:16).

However, it seems, that is if one studies history closely, that man took this statement further than God intended, as man is inclined to do! If man does not deny or ignore the Word of God, he has a tendency to pervert it. Consequently, the actions of Christ pulled the Word of God back to its original intention.

The phrase, *"And the Disciples rebuked them,"* proclaims the Disciples attempting to prevent the mothers (or fathers, if any were involved) from carrying out their desires.

Why?

First of all, the laying on of hands, and since the very beginning, was symbolical of blessing (Gen. 48:14). Actually, it remains so unto the present (Acts 6:6).

Perhaps the Disciples thought that such action was beneath Christ, or else His time was not to be wasted in this manner.

No doubt they had seen Jesus touch many babies and little children with healing instantly effected. However, these were not ill, and possibly they thought His time should be spent helping those who were truly in need.

However, Jesus was much displeased, as Mark described it, at their action, and, instead, called them unto Him.

(14) "BUT JESUS SAID, SUFFER LITTLE CHILDREN, AND FORBID THEM NOT, TO COME UNTO ME: FOR OF SUCH IS THE KINGDOM OF HEAVEN."

The phrase, *"But Jesus said,"* proclaims the very opposite of what His Disciples were saying.

This is the reason that the Word of God must be our criteria, and not the word of man. Even the best of men, as the Disciples, can make a mistake, whereas the Word of God contains no mistakes.

Unfortunately, the Word of God, i.e., Jesus, is presently being set aside in favor of the word of man, i.e., psychology. Adhered to in this fashion, it will almost, if not, always be the opposite of what the Lord is saying.

The phrase, *"Suffer little children, and forbid them not, to come unto Me,"* means they are to be permitted, and not hindered. While it was true that many, if not most, of the children were too young to understand the blessing that Christ would give them, still, they were not too incompetent to receive it.

Actually, children can receive far more from the Lord than most realize. First of all, they have no prejudice or bias to overcome. Their hearts are open, and their minds, even at the tenderest of ages, are far more able to receive from the Lord than many realize.

My parents were saved when I was six years old. Naturally, I attended Church with them constantly, and, as well, they witnessed to me, especially my Mother.

I don't remember exactly how old I was when the Lord began dealing with me, but it must have been within weeks of the time I gave my heart to Him, which was not long after my eighth birthday.

Strangely enough, the Lord saved me on a Saturday afternoon. I was going to the movies, and was standing in line with the other kids waiting for the ticket window to open at 3 p.m.

Without warning, the Spirit of God spoke to me, saying, *"Do not go into this place. Give me your heart, for you are a chosen vessel to be used in My service!"*

Even though I was only a child, still, the voice which spoke to my heart (not audible) was so clear that it was unmistakable. I did nothing for the moment, not quite understanding all that was happening, but knowing that it was the Lord.

About that time the ticket window opened and the line began to inch forward as the kids were purchasing their tickets. I must have been about the ninth or tenth in line, and as we inched forward the Spirit of God spoke the second time saying virtually the same thing.

By this time I had reached the ticket window, laying my quarter on the counter to pay for admission.

The reel of tickets was on an old-fashioned spindle hanging from the ceiling, with the ticket lady pulling them down, tearing off each ticket accordingly. The spindle jammed and it took a few moments for her to repair it.

During that time, I said an eternal *"Yes"* to the Lord Jesus Christ. Actually, I said nothing audibly, only in my heart, but it was enough. At that moment, I instantly knew that the Lord had saved me.

About that time I grabbed my quarter, and the lady, whose name was Mrs. Green, looked at me and said in exasperation, *"Jimmy, do you want a ticket or not?"*

"No ma'am," I quickly said, grabbing my quarter and quickly leaving. That which followed is, as well, forever etched in my mind.

Putting the quarter in my pocket, I walked down the street past the Piggly-Wiggly Supermarket, Ellis' Five and Dime, Doris' Dress Shop, and went into Vogt's Drug Store on the corner.

I laid my quarter on the counter and spoke to Vogt Jr., who was behind the counter, asking him to give me a triple-decker ice cream cone. All he had was chocolate, strawberry, and vanilla, which he piled as high as was possible, giving me 10 cents change from my quarter. (Of course, 15 cents then was about the equivalent of $2 now.)

Taking the ice cream cone in hand, I walked outside, and stood on the curb of the sidewalk with my back to the Drug Store. I've never felt so happy in all of my life. I really do not how to describe it!

It seemed like a hundred pounds had rolled off my shoulders as I stood there literally pulsating with joy.

If I felt that good at only eight years of age, I have often wondered how must it feel for someone who has lived a life of hard sin to come to Jesus Christ? There is absolutely nothing like the experience of the New Birth.

Strangely enough, I did not really feel that way when I gave my heart to the Lord in front of the Theater, or even walking down the street immediately afterward. However, when the Spirit of the Lord did move upon me, it was truly *"joy unspeakable, and full of glory."*

Almost immediately I went home, and arriving much earlier than the expected two hours or later, my Mother asked why I was home so soon.

Somewhat matter of factly I said to her, *"I got saved!"*

Actually, it took her a few moments to understand what I was saying, even after I had explained it. I remember the tears rolling down her face as she turned away, after having hugged me.

A few months later I was gloriously Baptized in the Holy Spirit with the evidence of speaking with other tongues.

So, even though I would not have been thought of as a *"little child,"* still, at eight years old I was a child. But yet, the Lord gave me some of the most remarkable experiences that anyone could ever have. Consequently, I will ever be thankful that He said, *"Suffer little children, and forbid them not, to come unto Me!"*

The phrase, *"For of such is the Kingdom of Heaven,"* means that those who enter Christ's Kingdom must be pure, obedient and humble, even as a *"little child."*

That is the reason He said, *"Of such,"* pointing not so much to their age, but to their disposition and character.

In essence, the Kingdom of Heaven belongs to them, or those of such spirit, and they belong to it.

(15) "AND HE LAID HIS HANDS ON THEM, AND DEPARTED THENCE."

This must have been a beautiful scene. Mark says that Jesus *"took them up in His Arms, put His Hands upon them, and blessed them."*

It doesn't say He prayed, even as the parents had requested, and perhaps because there was no need, inasmuch as the laying on of His Hands was all that was necessary.

As well, the sense of the structure of the words concludes that the children eagerly desired to come to Him. With childlike purity and innocence, they recognized in Him the love and compassion which caused them to have no fear at all.

It is remarkable, that little children knew this, but the Religious Leaders of Israel did not know it!

The phrase, *"And departed thence,"* has the flavor of both joy and sadness.

The joy in the mother and the children must have known no bounds. They could not have understood everything, but they did understand something special was taking place when He took these children in His Arms and laid His Hands on them. In effect, the Creator of the heavens and the earth had touched their children. They would never be the same again.

And yet, there was a sadness because He was departing for Jerusalem, where He would be

beaten, spit upon, and crucified. It is very difficult to put the two together. How could people, and especially those who called themselves Religious Leaders, be so heartless, so cruel, and so utterly lacking in anything that pertained to goodness?

The answer is obvious!

"They were of their father the Devil, and the lusts of their father they would do" (Jn. 8:44).

(16) "AND, BEHOLD, ONE CAME AND SAID UNTO HIM, GOOD MASTER, WHAT GOOD THING SHALL I DO, THAT I MAY HAVE ETERNAL LIFE?"

The phrase, *"And, behold, one came and said unto Him,"* is meant to portray a sudden happening. It concerns the rich young ruler, and probably took place immediately after Jesus dealt with the children, or no later than the next day.

The words, *"Good Master,"* refer to this man addressing Christ as a *"Teacher,"* with the word, *"Good,"* added to it seemingly out of respect.

The kernel of his question notes that he did not think of Jesus as the Messiah, i.e., the Son of God, Who could give him *"eternal life,"* but rather a *"Teacher"* Who could tell him how to obtain *"eternal life."*

The question, *"What good thing shall I do, that I may have eternal life?",* is that which is asked in one form or the other by the majority of mankind, and for all time.

Putting together the facts as stated by the three Evangelists, this man was young, noble, wealthy, strong (for he could run and kneel), courteous, educated, and religious. Most would esteem him to be perfectly happy.

But he was conscious that he did not have *"life"* and he desired to get it, and asked what should he do.

ETERNAL LIFE

One cannot do anything to merit Eternal Life. Such is gained totally by accepting Christ and what He has done for us at the Cross.

Almost all the world, even Christian America so-called, operate on this principle. They want to *"do"* something, when, in Truth, it has already been *"done,"* and by Jesus Christ.

In fact the very definition of religion is the doing of certain things (or not doing certain things) which will effect some desired result.

Religion is based on *"works,"* while Christianity is based on *"Faith."* Religion is doing something, while Christianity is trust placed in something which has already been done.

In effect, religion can be summed up in one word, *"do,"* and exactly as this rich young ruler said, while Christianity can be summed up in one word, *"done!"*

The moral effect of Salvation by works and Salvation by Faith is seen in the action of the Philippian jailer in contrast with this nobleman (Acts 16:33-34).

The rich young ruler seeking Salvation by personal moral merit, as we shall see, refused to share his money with others; the jailer obtaining Salvation upon the opposite principle of Faith, at once actively expended on others everything he could.

(17) AND HE SAID UNTO HIM, WHY CALLEST THOU ME GOOD? THERE IS NONE GOOD BUT ONE, THAT IS, GOD: BUT IF THOU WILT ENTER INTO LIFE, KEEP THE COMMANDMENTS."

The question, *"And He said unto him, why callest thou Me good?",* is meant to call his attention to the salutation.

Why exactly did this rich young ruler call Jesus *"good"*?

He did so because he thought that Salvation resided in merit, and all who had anything to do with it, even telling others how to obtain it, must, of necessity, be *"good."*

Of course, his definition of *"good,"* was skewed, as it is with all such people.

Almost all the world bases its definition of *"good"* on what it does or does not do. While those things certainly have some merit, still, good deeds, or the acting in a prescribed manner which is accepted socially, etc., does not make one *"good."*

This man was referring to Jesus as being *"good"* because He healed people and performed miracles. So in the man's mind Jesus was *"good."*

While it was true that He definitely was *"good,"* still, His goodness was a result of Who He was, and not the cause.

The phrase, *"There is none good but One, that is, God,"* is meant to place the word, *"good,"* in its proper perspective.

The statement made by Christ is meant to address itself to the question asked by the rich

young ruler. Jesus was not saying that He was not good, but was attaching this word to God where it rightly belonged. In effect, He was saying that He was God, which the rich young ruler had not admitted.

However, this statement made by Christ tells us that the only thing in this world that is *"good"* is God and that which He does.

It is true that some people are *"good"*; however, it is goodness that is freely given to them by their simple Faith and Trust in Christ, and not through or because of anything they have done. It is the same as Righteousness. Some are Righteous, but only because of what Christ has done in their lives, and not through any of their good works, etc.

As self-righteousness is a terrible problem, likewise, self-good falls into the same category. The world and the Church is filled with both.

That is the reason repentance is not a subject desired by most congregations. True Bible Repentance demands that one repent not only of the bad, but, as well, of the good. Consequently, most will not repent. Men are quick to renounce their bad traits, but not so quick to renounce their good traits. However, it could probably be said that *"good traits"* have caused more people to be lost than otherwise. Men depend on their *"good,"* not realizing that it is a commodity which will not spend in the economy of God.

And yet, Jesus said, *"Let your light so shine before men, that they may see your good works, and glorify your Father which is in Heaven"* (Mat. 5:16).

To be sure, these are *"good works"* which are carried out by *"good people"*; however, these individuals are *"good"* because of their simple Faith in Christ which produces the *"good works."*

Conversely, the world, and even much of the Church, is attempting to produce a good life, just as this rich young ruler, by producing good works. In every aspect they have it backwards.

The phrase, *"But if thou wilt enter into life, keep the Commandments,"* is meant to answer the man on the same grounds which he has asked — the grounds of good works!

He will show him that he has not, and, in fact, cannot attain to eternal life by *"keeping the Commandments,"* i.e, good works.

The Truth was that no one could keep all of them, all of the time! Christ is the only One

Who did it, and as the representative Man, gave His perfect score to all who would have simple Faith in Him.

(18) "HE SAITH UNTO HIM, WHICH? JESUS SAID, THOU SHALT DO NO MURDER, THOU SHALT NOT COMMIT ADULTERY, THOU SHALT NOT STEAL, THOU SHALT NOT BEAR FALSE WITNESS,"

The question, *"He saith uno him, Which?"*, is interesting indeed!

What did he mean by *"Which?"*

Jesus did not say *"Commandment"* in the singular, but, instead, *"Commandments"* in the plural. He was meaning all of them, which, of course, this man had not kept, nor anyone else.

The phrase, *"Jesus said, Thous shalt do no murder,"* referred to the Sixth Commandment, with it rightly translated as *"murder,"* which should have been done in Exodus 20:13.

The phrase, *"Thou shalt not commit adultery,"* was the Seventh Commandment.

The phrase, *"Thou shalt not steal,"* was the Eighth Commandment.

The phrase, *"Thou shalt not bear false witness,"* was the Ninth Commandment (Ex. 20:1-17).

(19) "HONOUR THY FATHER AND THY MOTHER: AND, THOU SHALT LOVE THY NEIGHBOUR AS THYSELF."

The phrase, *"Honour thy Father and thy Mother,"* was the Fifth Commandment.

The phrase, *"And, thou shalt love thy neighbour as thyself,"* was taken from Leviticus 19:18. It was not a part of the original Ten Commandments, at least in letter, but actually summed up all the Commandments, which dealt with one's fellowman, of which there were six, with four dealing with man's relationship to God.

(Jesus summed up all the Commandments into two, with the first being, *"Thou shalt love the Lord thy God with all thy heart, and with all thy soul, and with all thy mind.*

"This is the First and greatest Commandment.

"And the Second is like unto it, Thou shalt love thy neighbour as thyself.

"On these Two Commandments hang all the Law and the Prophets" — Mat. 22:37-40.)

(20) "THE YOUNG MAN SAITH UNTO HIM, ALL THESE THINGS HAVE I KEPT FROM MY YOUTH UP: WHAT LACK I YET?"

The phrase, *"The young man saith unto Him,"* constitutes a statement which is totally wrong.

NOTES

He was too quick to answer. He would have done much better to have thought it over carefully. However, he was so lifted up in himself that he claims that which no human being had ever done.

The phrase, *"All these things have I kept from my youth up,"* was error to say the least, but did not draw condemnation from Christ.

He saw a hunger in the young man for God that warranted an appeal, but, regrettably, the hunger for the things of this world was greater!

Why would this young man have answered as he did?

Perhaps in his self-deception, he actually thought this to be the case. Men, unless probed, as Christ did this man, generally think very highly of themselves. They conveniently forget the negatives, while enlarging upon and building up the positives, such as they are. This would have been very natural for this man.

He has already spoken of the *"good thing"* he wants to do, and because, at least in his own mind, he has already done many *"good things."* So, he concludes particular deeds, which he considers to be positive, as "keeping the Commandments."

He is not alone in his boasts!

The question, *"What lack I yet?"*, proclaims, however, that despite these boasts something is wrong, bad wrong! He was conscious that he did not have *"life,"* and, consequently, he desired to get it, hence, his exchange with Christ.

Almost all the world falls into the same category. They balance the good deeds against the bad deeds, and in their minds the good deeds always win out. Of this, they feel somewhat good about themselves, even as this rich young ruler. But yet, deep down inside something is missing, something of vital importance! There is an emptiness, a lack of fulfillment. They drink of that water and they thirst again!

In this *"lack,"* which almost all experience, they keep trying to find it without really even knowing what they are actually looking for. They are confident that a new car will slake the thirst; however, it does not!

If they can make a certain amount of money, surely, the satisfaction will come. In many cases it does come, but only for a short time. Gradually, and no matter what man tries to do to slake that thirst, it always returns.

There is only One Who can satisfy this thirst where the individual will never thirst again.

That Man is Jesus! He Alone can satisfy the ache, cry, burden, and thirst of the human heart.

(21) "JESUS SAID UNTO HIM, IF THOU WILT BE PERFECT, GO AND SELL THAT THOU HAST, AND GIVE TO THE POOR, AND THOU SHALT HAVE TREASURE IN HEAVEN: AND COME AND FOLLOW ME."

The phrase, *"Jesus said unto him,"* will be the greatest Word this man will ever hear, as to all who hear, believe, and do it.

The phrase, *"If thou wilt be perfect,"* is interesting indeed!

It is said with a tiny bit of sarcasm, as the bold claims of this young man have, in effect, said, and foolishly so, *"I am perfect: what lack I yet?"*

Christ will now show him that his perfection is only in his own mind, as with his goodness.

The phrase, *"Go and sell that thou hast, and give to the poor,"* actually touches on all the Commandments that Jesus has mentioned.

If one is to notice, Jesus did not mention the Tenth Commandment, *"Thou shalt not covet,"* and because it is here given, albeit in a roundabout way.

In effect, Jesus would not make this demand of all, because this would not be the failing of all as it was the rich young ruler. Christ always deals with us where we are. This man had boasted of all the good things he was doing and desired to do, but yet now fails on the very ground he has desired to play the game.

Jesus is showing him, as well as all, that our ways of obtaining eternal life will not accomplish its task, and, as well, man is unable to even do that which he himself has devised.

The phrase, *"And thou shalt have treasure in Heaven,"* is meant to pit that treasure up beside earthly treasure. The choice is there for all, but most choose the earthly variety.

The phrase, *"And come and follow Me,"* is, in effect, saying, *"If you love your neighbor as yourself, then share your wealth with him; and if you love Jehovah your God with all your heart, then follow Me, for One only is good, that is God, and I am He."*

With this final statement, Jesus put His Finger on the Two Great Commandments of the Law.

While the former demand of selling all that one has and giving to the poor may not apply to all, simply because many have nothing to sell, the latter demand, *"Come and follow Me,"* definitely applies to all!

In effect, He gives the same invitation to this man that He gave to His Disciples, and, in effect, gives to all.

To be saved, i.e., receive eternal life, one must accept Christ as Saviour, and if this is truly done, one will truly *"follow Him."*

To follow Him, one must give up his own life, but in doing so he will find life, i.e., eternal life. It is the greatest journey on which man could ever begin to engage.

(22) "BUT WHEN THE YOUNG MAN HEARD THAT SAYING, HE WENT AWAY SORROWFUL: FOR HE HAD GREAT POSSESSIONS."

The phrase, *"But when the young man heard that saying,"* records that which he did not want to hear, nor expect to hear; thus the attitude of almost all the human family.

Many claim they want to do the right thing, but when shown in the Word of God what they must do, they back away.

Some would argue that Jesus asks too much! No! What Jesus asks was more than just the parting with money. In effect, He was dealing with the man's god. The money was only a symptom, with self-will being the real culprit.

Jesus demanded of him a total change of lifestyle. While it was true he would forsake all, still, at the same time he would find all. And, as well, what he would find would be so much greater than what he would lose. Jesus never takes anything from anyone but that He gives in return that which is far better.

The phrase, *"He went away sorrowful,"* proclaims his decision. The Gospel makes men mad, sad, or glad. Naaman went away in a rage; the rich ruler went away sorrowful; but Zaccheus received Christ joyfully.

The phrase, *"For he had great possessions,"* proclaims that which he did have and did not want to give up, but, as well, that which he did not have, eternal life. The difference is this:

All of these *"possessions"* in a short time would be left anyway! Conversely, eternal life could be kept forever!

(23) "THEN SAID JESUS UNTO HIS DISCIPLES, VERILY I SAY UNTO YOU, THAT A RICH MAN SHALL HARDLY ENTER INTO THE KINGDOM OF HEAVEN."

The phrase, *"Then said Jesus unto His Disciples,"* portrays them evidently looking on at this exchange, and as the results will show, somewhat flabbergasted by it!

The phrase, *"Verily I say unto you,"* proclaims that which alone mattered, the Word of God.

The phrase, *"That a rich man shall hardly enter into the Kingdom of Heaven,"* was a startling statement to say the least, and ran counter to virtually all public thought.

In the first place, and considering the young man's confession of the keeping of the Commandments, had he lived at present, he would have been welcome in most any Church and would have been heralded far and wide as a great example for Christ.

In Truth, most people in modern Churches base their Salvation on something they *"do,"* exactly as this rich young ruler. However, God knows the heart, exactly as the heart of this young man was known.

As well, he was rich! In the thinking of the Israel of that day, riches were associated with the Blessings of God, while poverty was associated with His curse. So, one who was rich was automatically labeled as *"right with God."*

In the Words of Christ, why is it more difficult for a rich man to be saved than otherwise?

As this man, they depend on their riches, and almost all place themselves in a different position than others. Consequently, learning they must come to God only in the same manner as the poorest of the poor causes many to turn away, as this young man.

In their eyes they are special and should be treated accordingly. In God's Eyes they are just a poor sinner as spiritually bankrupt as anyone else. With God, the money makes no difference at all, while with the individual it makes all the difference in the world.

Jesus did not say they could not be saved, but only with difficulty, and because of the things mentioned.

(24) "AND AGAIN I SAY UNTO YOU, IT IS EASIER FOR A CAMEL TO GO THROUGH THE EYE OF A NEEDLE, THAN FOR A RICH MAN TO ENTER INTO THE KINGDOM OF GOD."

The phrase, *"And again I say unto you,"* is addressed to the Disciples, but, as well, to all!

The phrase, *"It is easier for a camel to go through the eye of a needle,"* was a favorite saying of that particular time. Actually, it was a proverbial expression for an impossibility.

The idea concerned a small gate that was cut in the confines of a large gate in the wall of

a city. If a camel was unloaded of all its baggage and knelt down on its knees, it could squirm through, but otherwise was impossible!

The illustration would have had its effect on the Disciples as they envisioned in their minds the camel being stripped of baggage, equating with riches, and then getting on its knees which could be equated with humility.

The phrase, *"Than for a rich man to enter into the Kingdom of God,"* equates the *"rich man"* having to do the same as the camel, which is very difficult for most to do, especially considering their pride.

Men equate security with riches, and, consequently, learn to trust in them. As such, they see little need to trust God, and are somewhat independent, at least in their minds, of needing anything. Their riches can purchase all!

However, as this young man portrayed, despite his riches he *"lacked something"* which his riches could not satisfy.

As well, riches have no impact on disease or death, neither will they truly elicit love from one's fellowman. While it is certainly true that rich men have many friends, and for the obvious reasons; however, most of the time the *"friends"* are there for the money and not the person.

So, Jesus tells us that not many rich men *"enter the Kingdom of God."*

This is ironical, considering that much of the Charismatic community makes the acquiring of riches a priority.

No! Jesus is not saying that it is a sin to be rich, but that many allow riches to keep them out of the Kingdom of God, which is obvious!

(25) "WHEN HIS DISCIPLES HEARD IT, THEY WERE EXCEEDINGLY AMAZED, SAYING, WHO THEN CAN BE SAVED?"

The phrase, *"When His Disciples heard it, they were exceedingly amazed,"* proclaims an astonishment among the Disciples, with the inference being that they were even offended. They were not only *"amazed,"* but *"exceedingly amazed!"*

Why?

As stated, the statement of Christ cut through one of the prime Doctrines of Israel in that material riches were equated with Godliness. Consequently, their theology is turned upside down. In Truth, Jesus was continually upsetting their theology, and because the Pharisees had so twisted the Word of God that its pure simplicity was little known anymore.

The question, *"Who then can be saved?"*, portrays their present thinking, and rightly so.

Then, as now, most who were not rich were struggling to be so and therefore fell under the same category. This meant that the majority of mankind was excluded from Salvation, at least if they took the position of the rich young ruler.

Quite possibly their own position came to their minds, as Jesus' statement probed deep into their own hearts.

The following verses proclaim this.

They were envisioning a kingdom which was greatly material, with Jesus at its Head and them by His side. This kingdom would be the greatest in the world with power and riches beyond comprehension. Now, and because of the statement of Christ, the entirety of the fabric of their theology must be re-thought.

To be sure, the theology of the entirety of the world should be re-thought!

Their question, *"Who then can be saved?"*, now points to only a few who will truly obey God and thereby find eternal life. As then, so now!

(26) "BUT JESUS BEHELD THEM, AND SAID UNTO THEM, WITH MEN THIS IS IMPOSSIBLE; BUT WITH GOD ALL THINGS ARE POSSIBLE."

The phrase, *"But Jesus beheld them,"* concerns itself with a calming effect His countenance produced.

They are totally perplexed as they briefly discuss this question among themselves, with the consternation no doubt showing on their faces. However, as they look at Jesus, the Text implies that they noticed a look of serenity and peace which calmed them. It is like a parent calming the fears of a small child.

Even as I dictate these words, I sense the Presence of God. I recall the countless times that I too have been perplexed, astonished, and without an answer. But every time the Presence of the Holy Spirit, as Christ, would bring a soothing effect, and I would be calmed, as here, by His Great and Glorious Promises.

The phrase, *"And said unto them,"* will proclaim a Great Truth which will answer their question, *"Who then can be saved?"*

The phrase, *"With men this is impossible,"* speaks not only of the rich, but the poor as well, actually including all!

Entrance into the Kingdom of God by man,

as man, however cultivated and moral, is here declared by the Infallible Judge to be impossible.

It is impossible to make an Ethiopian white, or to change a leopard's spots, because that which they exhibit externally is in their nature; but God can do it, for with Him all things are possible.

So then, what cannot be obtained by merit may be received by gift; for the Gift of God is eternal life.

It is impossible for a camel to go through the eye of a needle, and it is equally impossible for the most deeply religious man to enter Heaven on the principle of merit.

The phrase, *"But with God all things are possible,"* refers to God as being the only One Who can give Salvation. Such does not lay within the domain of man, and, in fact, never has! It is all of God Who makes the impossible possible! Zaccheus is a case in point, with him being rich but yet accepting Christ (Lk. 19:8-9).

(27) "THEN ANSWERED PETER AND SAID UNTO HIM, BEHOLD, WE HAVE FORSAKEN ALL, AND FOLLOWED THEE; WHAT SHALL WE HAVE THEREFORE?"

The phrase, *"Then answered Peter and said unto Him,"* proclaims the Apostle as the spokesman, which he generally was.

The phrase, *"Behold, we have forsaken all, and followed Thee,"* proclaims it is just as hard for the poor man to leave his little house as it is for the rich noble to forsake his great palace.

In Truth, they had *"forsaken all"* and followed Christ. While it was not much which they forsook, still, it was all they had.

This exchange, which produced this teaching of Christ, proclaims what it means to follow Christ. Jesus had dealt with this before when He spoke of taking up the cross and following Him. However, the rich young ruler coming to Him occasioned a practical application, whereas the taking up of the cross was spiritual.

In Truth, the following of Christ is the most revolutionary concept the world has ever known. It pales all philosophies and religions. The *"forsaking all"* means exactly that, *"forsaking all!"*

This speaks of riches, family, place and position, with all being renounced in favor of Christ.

Paul said, *"But what things were gain to me, those I counted loss for Christ."*

He then went on to say, and speaking of these

things we have mentioned, *"And do count them but dung, that I may win Christ"* (Phil. 3:7-8).

Regrettably, most of the modern Church world has not really *"forsaken all."* Most are quite willing to forsake that which is harmful and bad, and, therefore, destructive, but are quite unwilling to forsake that which is good, i.e., riches, family, approval of the world, place and position.

Hence, too many, and too often, desire to maintain their old lifestyle, while, at the same time, professing Christ. In other words, the nightclub performer claims he can continue to perform, with the gambler claiming he can continue to gamble, etc.

The Church, in times past, has attempted to address this issue by instituting rules and regulations. Such is Law, and, consequently, will not work!

If a person does not forsake the world in his heart, he has not forsaken it, even though a Church rule forbids him accordingly.

The idea, and as Paul said, is *"winning Christ."* If that hunger and desire is prevalent, the Holy Spirit will lead one to make any sacrifice which he will gladly do, and because the winning of Christ is the only thing that really matters.

If men have an imperfect view of Him, they will have an imperfect walk. To clearly see Him is to clearly see all that the soul craves and the heart reaches for. No wonder Paul said, *"Yea doubtless, and I count all things but loss for the excellency of the knowledge of Christ Jesus my Lord."*

He then went on to say, *"For Whom I have suffered the loss of all things"* (Phil. 3:8).

While he did *"suffer the loss of all things,"* which spoke of his family, wealth, as well as place and position in the economy of Israel, he *"won Christ,"* which was so far greater than what he had forsaken, i.e., lost.

The question, *"What shall we have therefore?"*, was asked seemingly in a carnal manner, while the answer given by Jesus will be glorious to say the least!

(28) "AND JESUS SAID UNTO THEM, VERILY I SAY UNTO YOU, THAT YE WHICH HAVE FOLLOWED ME, IN THE REGENERATION WHEN THE SON OF MAN SHALL SIT IN THE THRONE OF HIS GLORY, YE ALSO SHALL SIT UPON TWELVE THRONES, JUDGING THE TWELVE TRIBES OF ISRAEL."

NOTES

The phrase, *"And Jesus said unto them, Verily I say unto you,"* does not contain a reprimand for their question, but rather gives them an answer which is so startling that it must have been a wonder to the Disciples.

The phrase, *"That ye which have followed Me, in the regeneration,"* speaks particularly to the Disciples of which Judas would not partake, and because of the betrayal.

The *"Regeneration"* spoke of the *"born-again"* experience, which will result in the coming Kingdom Age, which will result in the restitution of all things.

The phrase, *"When the Son of Man shall sit in the Throne of His Glory,"* refers to the coming Kingdom Age when Jesus will reign Personally from Jerusalem and, in effect, govern the entirety of the world.

In fact, Peter, James, and John, had seen the Glory of the Lord in the Transfiguration, but not His Throne. The *"Throne"* was absent because Christ was not then ruling except in the hearts of a few.

In that coming Glad Day He will rule in the hearts of all, and, as well, give the world a material kingdom of prosperity and peace such as it has never known before.

The phrase, *"Ye also shall sit upon twelve Thrones,"* proclaims to them a promise which far exceeded their wildest expectations.

They were thinking of temporal advancement and promotion, but what they are here promised far exceeds that! However, it will not come immediately or even in the near future, but, instead, *"when,"* i.e., the coming Kingdom Age.

This statement may well have precipitated the question after Jesus' Crucifixion and Resurrection, *"Lord, wilt Thou at this time restore again the Kingdom to Israel?"* (Acts 1:6).

After the coming of the Holy Spirit at Pentecost their imperfect view was corrected, with them then understanding what Christ was saying.

The phrase, *"Judging the Twelve Tribes of Israel,"* proclaims exactly what they had desired, but on a much greater scale. As stated, this will take place during the coming Kingdom Age.

During the time of Christ and thereafter, the Disciples were given no recognition at all by Israel, but, instead, persecution. In the coming Kingdom Age all of this will change, and all because they exchanged a little fishing boat for a Kingdom.

(Not only will the Apostles have Thrones over Israel, but all Saints will reign with Christ across the entirety of the world as well! — Rev. 20:4-6)

(29) "AND EVERY ONE THAT HATH FORSAKEN HOUSES, OR BRETHREN, OR SISTERS, OR FATHER, OR MOTHER, OR WIFE, OR CHILDREN, OR LANDS, FOR MY NAME'S SAKE, SHALL RECEIVE AN HUNDREDFOLD, AND SHALL INHERIT EVERLASTING LIFE."

The phrase, *"And every one,"* speaks of all followers of Christ, whereas the previous verse concerning the *"judging the Twelve Tribes of Israel"* spoke only of the Twelve.

The phrase, *"That hath forsaken,"* goes back to the statement Peter made of *"forsaking all,"* and the admonition by Christ to the rich young ruler, *"Come and follow Me."*

The phrase, *"Houses, or brethren, or sisters, or father, or mother, or wife, or children, or lands,"* leaves absolutely no doubt as to what is being said. Everything is included. Christ begins and ends with material things, while placing the most precious in the middle, family relations. This pretty well eliminates many if not most of those who call themselves Believers.

The idea in many, if not most, cases does not literally mean to abandon such, but to give these things their proper place in the heart, which is secondary to Christ. In Truth, these things are to have no place at all, being placed in Christ. It is the same with self.

It is impossible to do away with self, inasmuch as that would mean the cessation of life, therefore, the idea is that self be placed in Christ, which then brings out its true worth. These other things fall into the same category.

The phrase, *"For My Name's sake,"* determines that the motive of true surrender is affection for Christ Himself. The reward is an encouragement in service or in suffering after the great decision has been made to follow Him for His Own sake.

The phrase, *"Shall receive an hundredfold,"* is added to by Mark, *"now in this time"* (Mk. 10:30).

What did Jesus mean by that?

He meant exactly what He said!

However, one must take account as He takes account. If one judges only in dollar bills, one will greatly shortchange himself.

If the reader will allow me to use my own life as an example, even though I consider it to be unworthy, perhaps a comparison can be made.

My cousin, Jerry Lee Lewis, and myself, began to play the piano at a very early age. Actually, at the age of 8, I asked the Lord specifically for the talent to play this instrument, even making Him certain promises, and He gave me exactly what I asked.

As we grew older we became somewhat proficient with this instrument, with Jerry Lee going into entertainment, and me into the Ministry. This particular time, the mid 1950's, saw the new craze of rock 'n roll take hold. It was a new genre of music which swept the world like wildfire and fastly degenerated to a point of destruction for millions.

At any rate, this was the time of Jerry Lee, Elvis, and a host of others. They were selling millions of records and making millions of dollars.

In 1958, Frances and I launched out full time into Evangelistic Work. To be sure, our launch was without fanfare and created no excitement anywhere. To be truthful, we were struggling to even provide the necessities of life.

I was preaching a short meeting at our home Church in Ferriday, Louisiana. The meeting was to conclude that Sunday with a dinner on the ground, etc. To be sure, the crowds in the services were small, but with great joy we anticipated this coming day of fellowship. The following scene is etched in my mind, and because I believe it played a tremendous part in all that the Lord has done for this particular Preacher.

The Sunday morning service had ended, and we had all gathered outside, possibly 30 or 40 of us, enjoying the meal that was spread out before us. In the midst of this repast, my Uncle Elmo, Jerry Lee's dad, drove up. If I remember correctly, he was driving a brand-new Cadillac.

Upon getting out of the car, all the people greeted him warmly, and after a few minutes of conversation he walked over to me. I was very glad to see him, and I began to ask him how Jerry Lee was doing, and how things were going, etc.

He said to me, *"Jimmy, I have just returned from Memphis, and a meeting with Sam Phillips."* Sam was the owner of Sun Records, the man who had started Elvis, Jerry Lee, Charlie Rich, Carl Perkins, as well as a host of others. Of course that means little or nothing now, but then it captivated the interest of the world.

My Uncle went on to say, *"I told Sam how you could play the piano and sing as well! He told me to have you in Memphis Monday morning."*

I looked up at him and said, *"Uncle Elmo, I only play and sing Gospel music and I don't think he would be interested in that."*

My Uncle somewhat startled me when he said, *"Oh yes, I told him that, and he said that Sun Records wanted to start a Gospel line and you would be the first artist."*

Of course, at least at the moment, that seemed like an answer to prayer. My Uncle said, *"I'll take you tomorrow."*

I opened my mouth to say that I would be ready to go, when the Holy Spirit quietly spoke to me, *"I don't want you to do this!"*

For a few moments I stood there startled, with questions going through my mind as to why the Holy Spirit did not want me to take this offer? It was Gospel Music, and I wondered what could be wrong with that?

My Uncle looked at me awaiting an answer, noticing the perplexed look on my face.

After a few moments I said, *"Uncle Elmo, I thank you so much for what you've offered, and please express to Mr. Phillips my gratitude; however, I cannot go."*

I remember him looking at me somewhat startled, saying, *"I don't understand, it's Gospel Music and what could be wrong with that?"*

To be frank, I did not understand either, and I mumbled something to him of which I do not remember.

He stood there looking at me for a few moments and finally said, *"Jimmy, I'll give Sam your answer and your gratitude."*

He was kind and gracious. Turning around, he bid *"good bye"* to all of us, got in the new Cadillac and left.

As I watched that car disappear down the road, I overheard one of the ladies nearby say, *"Did you hear what he just did?"*, and speaking of me, *"he turned down that offer!"*

I stood there for a few moments thinking of our needs, with my car in poor shape and, if I remember correctly, having only two suits of clothes, with Frances not having much more. Our offering the night before had been $1.38. Yes, that's what I said, $1.38!

I don't remember what it finally was that Sunday but I know it was precious little.

I excused myself from our small group and walked into the nearby Church.

Going into a small room and closing the door behind me, I began to pray. I asked the Lord, *"Why can I not do this which my Uncle suggested, especially considering that it is Gospel Music, and that we need the money so very badly?"*

I will never forget the answer the Lord gave me. He said, *"Trust Me!"*

That's all it was, *"Trust Me!"*

I dried my tears, saying, *"Yes, Lord, I will trust you!"*, and then walked out of the room.

After we left, I told Frances what the Lord had told me, and, of course, resolved to do exactly what He had told me.

I don't know all the reasons why the Lord did not want me to do this, but looking back I can well imagine why!

To be brief, the Lord did exactly what He told me He would do, plus so much more! The Blessings have been so manifold that I am at a loss for words attempting to describe them. As I dictate these words in mid August of 1995, the Lord has helped us to sell nearly 15,000,000 recordings during the intervening years. We have been able to see untold hundreds of thousands, if not millions, who have been blessed and helped through our Ministry of Music, even though it has been only an auxiliary to the Preaching of the Gospel.

By comparison, my cousin, who I love very much, despite the beginning glamour, has not been treated too well by the evil one. As the entirety of the world knows, Elvis died of a drug overdose at the age of 42 (if I remember his age correctly).

The Lord has not only given me a *"hundredfold,"* but I personally think a *"thousandfold"* or even a *"millionfold."*

On top of that, the joy of living for Him has been the greatest joy of all.

However, it must be remembered that divided allegiance cannot attain the *"hundredfold,"* only Christ being supreme in one's heart.

The phrase, *"And shall inherit everlasting life,"* is an added blessing to the *"hundredfold,"* and actually eclipses it by such margins that it defies description.

What kind of value could be placed on *"everlasting life?"*

The answer is obvious, none! It is beyond value or price and can only be obtained in Christ.

Consequently, the *"forsaking all and following Him,"* is the greatest decision anyone could ever make, and yet so few seem to make that decision!

(30) "BUT MANY THAT ARE FIRST SHALL BE LAST; AND THE LAST SHALL BE FIRST."

The phrase, *"But many that are first be last,"* actually refers to Israel.

They were the *"first"* to be given the Promises of God, and, actually, the first to receive the Gospel through the Ministry of Christ. However, they did not accept it, and, consequently, will be the *"last"* to take advantage of the great Gospel offer as here made. As a result of their refusal, they have wandered as outcasts throughout the world for nearly twenty centuries. However, the fulfillment of the Prophecies concerning their Restoration are even now beginning to be fulfilled, and will be totally fulfilled at the Second Coming. Then they will be restored, although *"last."*

The phrase, *"And the last shall be first,"* refers to the Gentiles who were the last to receive the Gospel. Basically, it refers to the Church.

Even though last to receive the Word, the Gentiles, which make up the Church, received the Gospel, and, consequently, were *"first"* to accept these admonitions of Christ.

As a result, the Church has enjoyed these manifold blessings promised by the Lord and rejected by Israel. As a result, they which were *"last"* are now *"first."*

CHAPTER 20

(1) "FOR THE KINGDOM OF HEAVEN IS LIKE UNTO A MAN THAT IS AN HOUSEHOLDER, WHICH WENT OUT EARLY IN THE MORNING TO HIRE LABOURERS INTO HIS VINEYARD."

The phrase, *"For the Kingdom of Heaven is like unto a man that is an Householder,"* once again portrays Christ using as an illustration something familiar to all in order to portray a great Truth. It is called the Parable of the Labourers in the Vineyard.

In effect, Jesus is answering Peter's question, *"What shall we have therefore?"* The primary lesson we will learn is that the reward of the Kingdom is not of debt, but of Grace.

The phrase, *"Which went out early in the morning,"* refers back to the last verse of the previous Chapter concerning the *"first being last, and the last being first."*

The word, *"early,"* has to do with Israel being the first to receive the Word of the Lord.

The *"Householder"* refers to the Lord of Glory.

The phrase, *"To hire labourers into his vineyard,"* refers first of all to the call of Abraham, Isaac, and Jacob, who formed the basis for the nation of Israel and the presentation of the Word of the Lord.

Even though Jesus uses a common illustration easily understood, still, it has great spiritual meaning far beyond the mere proclamation that the Gift of God is predicated on Grace, and not merit, as important as that lesson is.

Some have claimed that the statement concerning the *"first shall be last,"* merely referred to those who exalted themselves, but rather would be abased, etc. (Mat. 23:12). However, the sentence structure of the statement (19:30) lends no credence to that thought, nor in the 16th verse of this Chapter.

(2) "AND WHEN HE HAD AGREED WITH THE LABOURERS FOR A PENNY A DAY, HE SENT THEM INTO HIS VINEYARD."

The phrase, *"And when he had agreed with the labourers for a penny a day,"* would translate roughly into $40 a day in 1995 value. In keeping with the illustration, the story will proclaim several Truths.

Inasmuch as this agreement was made *"early in the morning,"* the amount of money agreed upon was for an entire day, beginning at 6 a.m. through 6 p.m.

Of course, in the great Promises of God given to the Patriarchs of old, money had nothing to do with it. However, this agreement does illustrate the Promises made by the Lord, which were glorious, abundant, and far reaching (Gen. 12:1-3; Deut. 28:1-14).

The phrase, *"He sent them into his vineyard,"* represents the Householder, after making an agreement with the labourers, sending them into the *"vineyard"* to gather the harvest.

As well, it symbolizes the task which lay ahead for Israel after the Promises of God had been given unto the Patriarchs, etc. Actually, and as stated many times, Israel's task was threefold:

1. In the *"vineyard"* of the world they were to give humanity the Word of God, which they

did. Every writer of the Books of the Bible was Jewish. (Some claim that Luke was Gentile, but every evidence is that he was Jewish as well!)

2. They were to serve as the womb of the Messiah, which they did, but, sadly and regrettably, rejected Him.

3. They were to evangelize the world, in which they failed, but will yet carry out this noble task in the coming Kingdom Age.

Their Blessing was to be Salvation which they were to receive by Faith and actually through trust in Christ, the coming Redeemer. However, the conditions were that it could not be earned by their nationality, call, or favored position. By the time of Christ, however, they actually believed, at least for the most part, that their nationality, call, and favored position, actually referred to Salvation. Consequently, only a few were actually saved.

As well, they were to be the greatest nation in the world, with the treasures of God opened unto them, that is if they obeyed the Lord (Deut. 28:12-13).

(3) "AND HE WENT OUT ABOUT THE THIRD HOUR, AND SAW OTHERS STANDING IDLE IN THE MARKETPLACE."

The phrase, "And he went out about the third hour," refers to 9 a.m.

The Jewish day was primarily divided into four quarters, 6 a.m. to 9 a.m., 9 a.m. to 12 noon, 12 noon to 3 p.m., 3 p.m. to 6 p.m., totalling a 12-hour day.

The phrase, "And saw others standing idle in the marketplace," quite possibly in the mind of Christ referred to no time period at all respecting Israel or the Church, but is given to portray the Truth at the end of the parable.

(4) "AND SAID UNTO THEM; GO YE ALSO INTO THE VINEYARD, AND WHATSOEVER IS RIGHT I WILL GIVE YOU. AND THEY WENT THEIR WAY."

The phrase, "And said unto them; Go ye also into the vineyard," gives these, as the others, the opportunity to serve and to bring in the harvest.

The phrase, "And whatsoever is right I will give you," involves itself with a tremendous Truth.

At the outset, it seems there was haggling with an agreement finally made, but now these labourers consent to work for "whatsoever is right." In other words, the amount of the payment would be left up to the "Householder."

The phrase, "And they went their way,"

NOTES

means that they did so willingly, having placed their trust in the "Householder."

The lesson here taught pertains to our service for the Lord. If we leave the reward up to Him, performing our task from a motivation of love, one can always be certain that He will always do that which is "right." As well, and as here illustrated, He will always give far more than what we deserve, or even expect!

That is at least one of the reasons that our giving to God must be on this basis. Money given with a promised or expected set return, which seems to be presently prevalent, portrays a lack of love for God and a lack of trust in God. To trust Him, means to trust Him in all things, and especially the reward. If we truly love, we will truly trust!

(5) "AGAIN HE WENT OUT ABOUT THE SIXTH AND NINTH HOUR, AND DID LIKEWISE."

Once again more labourers are needed, and even though the day has reached its mid-point, and even toward the last quarter, still, other labourers are hired.

The numbers here would refer to a half day, or quarter day's work.

If the times given have any reference at all to specific periods in Israel, or even the Church, there is no clue. Actually, and as stated, these time periods are not the purpose of the illustration, but rather given to reinforce the Truth which will ultimately be brought out.

(6) "AND ABOUT THE ELEVENTH HOUR HE WENT OUT, AND FOUND OTHERS STANDING IDLE, AND SAITH UNTO THEM, WHY STAND YE HERE ALL THE DAY IDLE?"

The phrase, "And about the eleventh hour he went out," refers to 5 p.m. in the late afternoon, with only an hour left of useful work.

The question, "And saith unto them, Why stand ye here all the day idle?", is asked somewhat with reproach.

There was work to be done, namely the gathering of the harvest, and these had been standing idle all day.

(7) "THEY SAY UNTO HIM, BECAUSE NO MAN HATH HIRED US. HE SAITH UNTO THEM, GO YE ALSO INTO THE VINEYARD; AND WHATSOEVER IS RIGHT, THAT SHALL YE RECEIVE."

The phrase, "They say unto him, Because no man hath hired us," means that they had had no opportunity to work in the vineyard due to not being hired.

Where they were during the early morning hour, or even at the other appointed times, is not stated. For whatever reason, they were not present when the *"Householder"* came looking for help.

However, them standing and waiting to be hired at this late hour portrays an acute need or desperation.

If one desires to attach a time element to the Church pertaining to this, it could well refer to these present times, or even the coming Great Tribulation.

As well, it could even pertain to Israel in the last half of the Great Tribulation. At that time, and in essence, they will be standing and waiting, with all signs pointing toward the end of the day with no one coming for them. However, Christ will come, even at the *"eleventh hour,"* i.e., just before the end — total destruction.

The phrase, *"Go ye also into the vineyard,"* no doubt is a startling announcement to these, and because of the lateness of the hour. But yet, they are hired!

The phrase, *"And whatsoever is right, that shall ye receive,"* once again portrays no agreement on pay, but, instead, trust placed in the *"Householder"* that he would be fair.

(8) "SO WHEN EVEN WAS COME, THE LORD OF THE VINEYARD SAITH UNTO HIS STEWARD, CALL THE LABOURERS, AND GIVE THEM THEIR HIRE, BEGINNING FROM THE LAST UNTO THE FIRST."

The phrase, *"So when even was come,"* refers to 6 p.m.

The phrase, *"The Lord of the vineyard saith unto his Steward,"* refers to the time for settlement.

In the spiritual sense, the *"Steward"* could well represent the *"Holy Spirit."* Even though the *"Householder,"* i.e., God the Father, gives the instructions, it is the *"Steward,"* i.e., the *"Holy Spirit,"* Who carries out the instructions.

The phrase, *"Call the labourers, and give them their hire,"* refers to all the labourers who have been hired, and for the entirety of the day.

Spiritually, this could well refer to the *"Judgment Seat of Christ,"* where rewards will be given out, and, as well, to Israel, who in essence will not be at that Judgment, but will come in when the Lord *"restores again the Kingdom*

unto Israel" which He will do immediately after the Second Coming.

The phrase, *"And give them their hire,"* refers to payment now being made, but with only the first group who has worked from the beginning of the day knowing exactly what they are to receive.

The phrase, *"From the last unto the first,"* refers to all gathered at the same time, but most of them not knowing what their pay is to be.

Ironically enough, the ones last hired are to be paid first, with the ones hired first being paid last.

This has to do with those who haggled for a certain amount and those who mentioned no pay, but left it up to the *"Householder"* to *"do right by them."* They would not be disappointed!

The spirit of the scenario has to do with Israel and the Church. Israel, functioning under the Law, gradually came to believe that their position was honored, special, and, therefore, merited certain favors from the Lord.

Conversely, the Church came in under Grace, which Israel refused, and as a result of Grace, the Church, at least as a rule, sees itself not as favored, but as privileged. Hence, the treatment by the *"Householder,"* i.e., the Lord, is much different. Debt is for an exact amount, while Grace is open ended and therefore freely given as desired by the *"Householder."*

That is the reason the Church is so foolish when she attempts to mix Law with Grace. It is never an advancement, but always a regression.

(9) "AND WHEN THEY CAME THAT WERE HIRED ABOUT THE ELEVENTH HOUR, THEY RECEIVED EVERY MAN A PENNY."

The phrase, *"And when they came that were hired about the eleventh hour,"* proclaims that it is somewhat a surprise to them at being called first, and especially considering that they were hired last.

The phrase, *"They received every man a penny,"* means they were paid just as much as those who had labored all the day, and no doubt received such with great surprise, and pleasantly so!

They had trusted in the *"Householder"* to do *"what was right,"* and they now find that their trust pays off in a bountiful way.

The illustration is meant to be a lesson to all. If we serve God because we love Him and therefore do whatever He asks us to do, regardless of what it is, without complaint or demand, but with gratitude, for the opportunity, as these last-hour labourers did, the reward, will be great, to be sure. This is the major lesson as taught by Christ and one which we certainly should learn.

(10) "BUT WHEN THE FIRST CAME, THEY SUPPOSED THAT THEY SHOULD HAVE RECEIVED MORE; AND THEY LIKEWISE RECEIVED EVERY MAN A PENNY."

The phrase, *"But when the first came,"* actually means they were the last to come. Hence, the first shall be last, and the last shall be first.

The phrase, *"They supposed that they should have received more,"* meant that they were anticipating more.

They had observed all those who came the *"third hour,"* and, likewise, the *"sixth and ninth hour,"* and even the *"eleventh hour,"* watching them receive the same amount, and now they think, surely, due to their having labored all day that their pay will be more than the others.

The phrase, *"And they likewise received every man a penny,"* proclaims them receiving the same as all the others.

(11) "AND WHEN THEY HAD RECEIVED IT, THEY MURMURED AGAINST THE GOODMAN OF THE HOUSE."

The phrase, *"And when they had received it,"* indicated that they did not receive it with joy.

The phrase, *"They murmured against the goodman of the house,"* proclaims them being unhappy, but with no good cause.

For those who function under Law, their nature is to *"murmur,"* while those who function under Grace have nothing to murmur or complain about.

(12) "SAYING, THESE LAST HAVE WROUGHT BUT ONE HOUR, AND THOU HAST MADE THEM EQUAL UNTO US, WHICH HAVE BORNE THE BURDEN AND HEAT OF THE DAY."

The phrase, *"Saying, These last have wrought but one hour, and thou hast made them equal unto us,"* proclaims jealousy on the part of Israel.

In essence, Paul mentioned this when he said, *"I say then, have they stumbled that they should fall? God forbid: but rather through their fall Salvation is come unto the Gentiles, for to provoke them to jealousy"* (Rom. 11:11).

The phrase, *"Which have borne the burden and heat of the day,"* once again refers to service

rendered, and for a certain amount of payment to be expected. However, they had expected more than they had agreed upon, but only after seeing those who had demanded nothing, in effect, receiving as much as they who had labored all the day.

(13) "BUT HE ANSWERED ONE OF THEM, AND SAID, FRIEND, I DO THEE NO WRONG: DIDST NOT THOU AGREE WITH ME FOR A PENNY?"

The phrase, *"But he answered one of them, and said, Friend, I do thee no wrong,"* proclaims that there was no grounds for their murmuring and complaining.

The question, *"Didst not thou agree with me for a penny?"*, brings to the fore that which their haggling had produced — an agreement.

In effect, the Lord is saying that if they had left the payment amount up to Him, it would have been different. However, they demanded so much and that is what they received, while the others demanded nothing and received much.

Such is the Lord, and such is the lesson portrayed!

(14) "TAKE THAT THINE IS, AND GO THY WAY: I WILL GIVE UNTO THIS LAST, EVEN AS UNTO THEE."

The phrase, *"Take that thine is, and go thy way,"* refers to the agreed-upon amount.

In effect, Jesus is telling Peter that if he desires a stipulated answer respecting his question, *"What shall we have therefore?"*, (Mat. 19:27), then such can be given. However, if it is left open ended, in other words according to the Grace of God, this will be pleasing to the Lord and, as well, will guarantee reward far beyond that imagined.

The phrase, *"I will give unto this last, even as unto thee,"* in a sense refers to Christ blessing the Church even as He has blessed Israel, even though the Church was *"last."*

(15) "IS IT NOT LAWFUL FOR ME TO DO WHAT I WILL WITH MINE OWN? IS THINE EYE EVIL, BECAUSE I AM GOOD?"

The question, *"Is it not lawful for me to do what I will with Mine Own?"*, respects the entirety of the Plan of God.

The moment that man, even believing man, attempts to thrust himself into God's Way, with an attempt to change that Way, he always brings harm to himself. The Scripture plainly says, *"For My thoughts are not your thoughts, neither are your ways My Ways, saith the Lord.*

"For as the heavens are higher than the earth, so are My Ways higher than your ways, and My Thoughts than your thoughts" (Isa. 55:8-9).

The question, *"Is thine eye evil, because I am good?"*, proclaims an intrusion even deeper into the Ways of God, but with malice, even more so than the previous question!

The word, *"evil,"* here refers to *"stingy or envious."*

The word, *"good,"* refers to *"generous,"* thereby portraying the nature of man who is envious and the nature of God which is generous.

The Truth is that God is no respecter of persons, and, consequently, does not favor one over the other. His Judgment is predicated on His Own Nature, which treats all according to their heart response to His Ways.

Man attempts to plan and then seeks God's Blessings on such plans, even though envious.

Far better to allow God to plan, accepting His Plan, which will always guarantee Blessings. In Truth, God cannot bless man, only Christ in man. He is *"good,"* while no man, and as Christ said, can be labeled thusly (19:17).

(16) "SO THE LAST SHALL BE FIRST, AND THE FIRST LAST: FOR MANY BE CALLED, BUT FEW CHOSEN."

The phrase, *"So the last shall be first, and the first last,"* is used again, and by design.

As stated, it refers to the Church who came in *"last,"* but will be the *"first"* to receive the Gospel, and because Israel rejected it, and the *"first"* to be honored, blessed, and glorified. The Church will be raptured away at least seven years before the Second Coming, and will actually come back with Christ at this momentous time (Zech. 14:5; Jude 14). Israel, who was *"first"* to receive the Word of the Lord, will then accept Christ, in effect *"last"* to do so. They will then as well be blessed!

The phrase, *"For many be called, but few chosen,"* is meant to give strength to the first phrase.

The word, *"many,"* actually means all were called, but only a few chose to accept. This was true of Israel, and it is true as well regarding the entirety of the world, and respecting the Church.

Many have taken the word, *"chosen,"* attempting to teach election or predestination in an unscriptural manner.

NOTES

There are no reasonable or Scriptural arguments that can be presented to prove that God saves or keeps men contrary to their free choice.

Nothing is hard to understand about election, foreknowledge, or predestination, when we realize that it is God's Plan itself, and not personal conformity to that Plan that has been foreknown and predestinated. God decrees that all who do conform will be saved, and all who do not will be lost, and this is the sum and substance of these doctrines.

God's decrees were never made to determine the choices of free moral agents as to whether some will be saved or others will be lost.

God does not determine our willing and doing, but He does decree the basis of the action for free moral agents that will save or damn them accordingly. This does not mean that the initiative or man's Salvation is with man. It is with God, Who chose to make a way of Salvation for all men, especially of them who believe and who conform to His Plan of their own free choice.

Election (or those chosen) deals with all people as sinners, and therefore must deal with them on the same basis or the Plan is faulty and the Planner is a respecter of persons and unjust in His dealings (Rom. 3:23). The reason God saves only a few is because only a few choose the Way of God and therefore God is free from the final responsibility of the Salvation or damnation of anyone.

If God offers pardon to all, and He most certainly does, then all can accept it alike or the offer of pardon is a fraud. If all can accept it, and all certainly can, then He is fair to all that Salvation and damnation rests with the individual and not with God (Rev. 22:17).

To argue that God offers a pardon to all alike and then to contradict this by saying that He offers it to only a few special ones whom He has chosen to save, does not make sound logic and is not Scriptural.

God does not force one to become willing and another to become unwilling to be saved. He deals with all men, seeking to persuade them to be saved, and because some become willing and others do not is no sign that God is responsible for the choice made.

While it is true that God chose Abraham, David, and others, still, it is a matter of record that there were qualities of character in these individuals that caused God to choose them.

After He began to deal with them, the record is clear that they chose Him. They became willing to obey God, and, to be sure, their will was not forced, but was, at least in this regard, their own personal action.

To sum up the doctrine of election or the ones *"chosen,"* we may say that the elect of God, are the *"whosoever will class"* who come and take of the Water of Life freely, and the non-elect are the *"whosoever will not class"* who choose to reject the Gospel.

The Gospel is presented to all, and all have the right to accept or reject. None are forced one way or the other by the Lord (Rev. 22:17). The Plan of God is that which is *"chosen,"* and all may enter into it who choose, with them then becoming the *"chosen."*

Basically, predestination falls into the same category. It is God's Law or Plan that is predestinated and not the individual conformity to it. All Scripture is clear that men are absolutely free to choose for themselves whether they conform to the predestined plan or not (Jn. 3:16-20; Rev. 22:17).

Those who do conform will enjoy forever the predestined blessings, and those who do not will suffer eternally the predestined judgments of the plan.

It would be foolish to call the entirety of the world as the word *"many"* means, with all not having the opportunity to accept.

(17) "AND JESUS GOING UP TO JERUSALEM TOOK THE TWELVE DISCIPLES APART IN THE WAY, AND SAID UNTO THEM,"

The phrase, *"And Jesus going up to Jerusalem,"* is more than just a statement concerning a particular journey. He is *"going up"* to be crucified, and, as such, His Heart must have been very heavy along the way.

The phrase, *"Took the twelve Disciples apart in the way, and said unto them,"* refers to that which was not to be shared by the multitudes.

The number *"twelve"* includes Judas, and is said in this manner by the Holy Spirit to point to the sadness of the coming betrayal. Judas would *"choose"* the wrong way, as he and all have the power to do, and, as a result, was not one of the *"chosen."* The Lord truly called him, just as he did all the others, but ultimately Judas rejected the call.

(18) "BEHOLD, WE GO UP TO JERUSALEM; AND THE SON OF MAN SHALL BE

BETRAYED UNTO THE CHIEF PRIESTS AND UNTO THE SCRIBES, AND THEY SHALL CONDEMN HIM TO DEATH,"

The phrase, *"Behold, we go up to Jerusalem,"* is meant to call attention to what would happen in this place.

The phrase, *"And the Son of Man shall be betrayed unto the Chief Priests and unto the Scribes,"* refers to what Judas will do, but, of which, at the moment, Judas had probably no thought, the Devil not having yet put it into his heart. And yet, the word, *"betrayed,"* is used specifically by the Holy Spirit through Christ that Judas may be warned.

Ironically enough, the *"Chief Priests and Scribes"* were the religious rulers of Israel. They are the very ones who should have received Christ, but, instead, rejected Him.

The phrase, *"And they shall condemn Him to death,"* referred to this act which would be carried out by the Sanhedrin. Actually, they could condemn but they could not execute, Israel being a vassal state to Rome.

This is the third time that Jesus announced His sufferings (16:21-22), but, still, without much understanding on the part of the Disciples.

Unless the Holy Spirit enlightens the heart, the clearest spiritual teaching has neither meaning nor power. This fact humbles man's pride.

Jesus would not *"condemn"* them even though they were guilty, while they would *"condemn"* Him although innocent. Such is man!

(19) "AND SHALL DELIVER HIM TO THE GENTILES TO MOCK, AND TO SCOURGE, AND TO CRUCIFY HIM: AND THE THIRD DAY HE SHALL RISE AGAIN."

The phrase, *"And shall deliver Him to the Gentiles,"* refers to being delivered to Pilate and the Romans. As stated, the Jews could *"condemn Him to death,"* but they could not carry out the execution. Therefore, the Romans had to be brought in, which they were, and by subterfuge and deceit, claiming that Christ was advocating insurrection against Caesar!

As a result of Him being delivered *"to the Gentiles,"* this made both Jews and Gentiles guilty of His sufferings and death (Acts 2:23-36; 3:14-15; 4:27).

The phrase, *"To mock, and to scourge, and to crucify Him,"* proclaims the first time Jesus distinctly announced that His Death would be by crucifixion. These were words the Disciples could not grasp. Luke said, *"And they understood none of these things: and this saying was hid from them, neither knew they the things which were spoken"* (Lk. 18:34).

They firmly believed that the Messiah would conquer Rome, setting up Israel as the premier nation. They could not grasp His real mission, to die at this time. Even after the Resurrection, this Restoration of Israel was utmost in their minds (Acts 1:6-7).

However, Jesus now says the opposite, in that both Jews and Gentiles will share in His Death.

The phrase, *"And the third day He shall rise again,"* proclaims this great event, but being completely lost on the Disciples exactly as the prediction of His Death.

(20) "THEN CAME TO HIM THE MOTHER OF ZEBEDEE'S CHILDREN WITH HER SONS, WORSHIPPING HIM, AND DESIRING A CERTAIN THING OF HIM."

The phrase, *"Then came to Him the mother of Zebedee's children with her sons,"* refers to Salome, the mother of James and John. The Scripture is clear that James and John were with her respecting the request she is about to make. From the way Mark described it, it seems that the two sons enlisted their mother's help.

Inasmuch as Salome was present at this time, it seems there were others with Jesus and the Disciples as they made their way to Jerusalem.

The phrase, *"Worshipping Him, and desiring a certain thing of Him,"* proclaims her being the spokesperson.

While it was true that they *"worshipped Him,"* still, there is indication they were making their plans and then desiring Him to bless those plans. This, as we shall see, was wrong!

First of all, the *"worship"* was tendered, at least in part, in order to gain a particular desire. While it is certainly not wrong to make proper petitions to the Lord, our worship, however, should be to Him and for Him Alone. But, yet, I am afraid too many Christians worship the Lord from a wrong spiritual posture, even as Salome, James, and John.

While it is true that all of us may want or desire things from Him, which He encourages us to do, still, the *"worship"* should be apart from that.

(21) "AND HE SAID UNTO HER, WHAT WILT THOU? SHE SAITH UNTO HIM, GRANT THAT THESE MY TWO SONS MAY SIT, THE

ONE ON THE RIGHT HAND, AND THE OTHER ON THE LEFT, IN THY KINGDOM."

The question, *"And He said unto her, What wilt thou?"*, in a sense respects the manner in which the Lord responds to our requests. Also, the following will portray that if our requests are not proper, the Lord will not grant them. Selfish motives, as here, always meet with the same response.

The phrase, *"She saith unto Him, grant that these my two sons may sit, the one on the right hand and the other on the left, in Thy Kingdom,"* pertains to a well thought out request. This is something they had talked over at length and now make their petition to Him.

Having heard what Jesus had said earlier respecting the Twelve Disciples sitting on Twelve Thrones judging the Twelve Tribes of Israel, the maneuvering had already begun.

And now with the announcement concerning His Death and Resurrection, even though they did not understand it, still, they must seize the opportunity, with His Resurrection, at least in their thinking, possibly referring to the setting up of *"Thy Kingdom"* (19:28).

We, here, see the first signs of politics in the Church. It is all man-devised and has no place in the Kingdom of God. But yet, men desiring place and position soon abrogate the Ways and Will of God, formulating their own plans as here, which, and sadly so, make up the far greater majority of the modern Church.

(22) "BUT JESUS ANSWERED AND SAID, YE KNOW NOT WHAT YE ASK. ARE YE ABLE TO DRINK OF THE CUP THAT I SHALL DRINK OF, AND TO BE BAPTIZED WITH THE BAPTISM THAT I AM BAPTIZED WITH? THEY SAY UNTO HIM, WE ARE ABLE."

The phrase, *"But Jesus answered and said,"* will not be the answer they desire.

The phrase, *"Ye know not what ye ask,"* characterized not only James and John, but, as well, so many of our petitions presently! If men ask by the Spirit of God, they will always ask in the Will of God. However, selfishness permeates too many of our petitions, as James and John.

The question, *"Are ye able to drink of the cup that I shall drink of, and to be baptized with the Baptism that I am baptized with?"*, proclaims that indeed which they would do, but at this time understood not at all. Two things are here spoken of:

1. *"The cup"*: Even though a *"Cup of Salvation and Blessing"* are spoken of in the Bible (Ps. 16:5; 23:5; 116:13), still, this *"Cup"* spoken of by Christ is the *"Cup"* of sufferings of the Messiah, which the Disciples were to enter into (Mk. 10:38; Jn. 18:11).

All want the *"Cup of Blessings,"* but none want the *"Cup of sufferings."* In fact, many in the modern Church have attempted to eliminate this particular *"Cup"* by declaring, erroneously we might add, that such sufferings can be confessed away, that is, if the Believer has enough Faith. They claim that while it was true that Jesus suffered greatly, still, His suffering meant that we would not have to suffer. However, His statements prove otherwise!

The *"Cup of suffering,"* that must be undergone by all Believers is allowed by the Lord for many and varied reasons. First of all, the world hates Christ, and if they hated Him, they hate us (Jn. 15:18). As well, there is even a greater hatred of the True Believer by the apostate Church. This was evidenced by the Pharisees and Scribes greatly opposing Christ. As well, the greatest opposition has always come from this source, hence, Cain killing Abel, Joseph's brothers hating him, and Saul's opposition to David. Also, Paul's greatest opposition came from those who claimed to be Believers, which instigated the writing of several of his Epistles. That opposition continues no less today.

The Lord also allows suffering in order to teach obedience in the realm of Trust and dependency (Heb. 5:8).

No! Not only can the modern Church not eliminate this *"Cup,"* but, as well, it should not be eliminated.

2. *"The Baptism"*: Whereas the *"Cup"* contains that which must be done, the *"Baptism"* proclaims the actual doing of it. Hence, this is a *"Baptism of Suffering."*

They did, indeed, drink of His Cup and suffer His Baptism, for James was beheaded (Acts 12:2), and John was exiled to Patmos (Rev. 1:9).

If the Believer is to be as he ought to be in Christ, he must enter into the Sufferings of Christ. Paul said, *"If so be that we suffer with Him, that we may be also glorified together."*

He then said, *"For I reckon that the sufferings of this present time are not worthy to be compared with the Glory which shall be revealed in us"* (Rom. 8:17-18).

NOTES

In effect, he says that if we are Children of God, and, consequently, heirs, which means that we are *"heirs of God, and joint-heirs with Christ,"* we will, of necessity, suffer with Him (Rom. 8:17).

As well, the suffering in which every True Believer must engage is a part of the Sanctification process which brings self into Christ.

Jesus died on Calvary to save man from sin and self. It is not so difficult for the sin to be washed and cleansed by the Blood of Christ, only requiring Faith in His Name. However, the proper disposition of self is not so easily or quickly carried out. Actually, it is a lifelong project of which the suffering plays a part (Mat. 16:24).

The phrase, *"They say unto Him, We are able,"* is an answer proclaiming they really did not know what they were saying.

They were thinking of Thrones, Glory, Honor, Place and Position. Hence they would answer, *"We are able!"* He was saying something else entirely.

(23) "AND HE SAITH UNTO THEM, YE SHALL DRINK INDEED OF MY CUP, AND BE BAPTIZED WITH THE BAPTISM THAT I AM BAPTIZED WITH: BUT TO SIT ON MY RIGHT HAND, AND ON MY LEFT, IS NOT MINE TO GIVE, BUT IT SHALL BE GIVEN TO THEM FOR WHOM IT IS PREPARED OF MY FATHER."

The phrase, *"And He saith unto them, ye shall drink indeed of My Cup, and be baptized with the Baptism that I am baptized with,"* proclaims Jesus predicting of them that which was to come, even though they little understood its meaning at that time!

As stated, James was murdered by Herod (Acts 12:2). John, his brother, was the last to die of the original Twelve, and probably died on the Isle of Patmos. Tradition says he was the only one who died a natural death, although hounded and persecuted throughout his life. It seems the Lord allowed him to live to approximately ninety years of age, and then shortly before his death gave him the Book of Revelation.

It should also be said that it seems the closer one is to Christ, as the Early Church and Church history bears out, the greater the suffering. Consequently, all the Disciples with the exception of John, many believe, died a martyr's death. The same could be said for Paul.

The phrase, *"But to sit on My Right Hand, and My left, is not Mine to give,"* means that this prerogative is not His, but, instead, that of the Heavenly Father.

Of course, the request made by Salome regarding her two sons pertains to status. Jesus does not deny that such will be, a Throne on either side of His Throne, but actually infers that such will be. As well, every indication is that these two Thrones could well be occupied by two of the original Twelve, minus Judas, but including Matthias who took the place of Judas (Acts 1:26). Who those two will be, we are not told.

The phrase, *"But it shall be given to them for whom it is prepared of My Father,"* lends credence to the thought that these positions, as well as every other place and position in the *"Kingdom of Heaven"* is granted on the Grace of Love and Faithfulness, and not to ambition or the concession of a request. Paul addressed himself to this in I Corinthians 3:11-15.

(24) "AND WHEN THE TEN HEARD IT, THEY WERE MOVED WITH INDIGNATION AGAINST THE TWO BRETHREN."

The phrase, *"And when the ten heard it,"* portrays dissention and division in the ranks, and because of self-will and personal ambition, both which are unchristlike.

Political maneuvering in the Church always leads to such conclusion, because it portrays man's ambition instead of God's Will. And yet, this short verse characterizes so very much of the modern Church!

The phrase, *"They were moved with indignation against the two brethren,"* means that they likewise coveted these positions sought by James and John for themselves. Were that not so, they would not have been *"moved with indignation!"*

One who is totally moved by the Holy Spirit has no personal ambition, allowing the Lord to make the plans, with the Spirit-led Believer seeking to carry them out. Consequently, those who seek such places and positions, do so from self-will and not God's Will.

In the great Plan of God, God gives men a *"Vision."* That particular vision is for a particular task designed and allotted by the Holy Spirit, with the Believer seeking to carry it out.

In giving the *"Vision,"* the Lord also gives *"Provision,"* whether in the spiritual, material, or any other manner.

However, when this is done, Satan comes in

as here with *"division."* The very word, *"division,"* is to cause the Vision to die, hence, *"die-vision."* To be sure, personal ambition is one of Satan's surest ploys.

(25) "BUT JESUS CALLED THEM UNTO HIM, AND SAID, YE KNOW THAT THE PRINCES OF THE GENTILES EXERCISE DOMINION OVER THEM, AND THEY THAT ARE GREAT EXERCISE AUTHORITY UPON THEM."

The phrase, *"But Jesus called them unto Him, and said,"* concerns a lesson regarding worldly greatness, as well as Christian greatness and preeminence. To say that this lesson is important would be a gross understatement. As we shall see, the desire for greatness among Believers is not condemned by Christ, but rather must be channelled in the right direction. However, many Believers employ the ways of the world respecting greatness, and bring it over into the Church. Regrettably, the standards for greatness in much of the modern Church are probably little different than the standards of the world because they are the standards of the world.

I think that the teaching of Christ will show that true spiritual greatness among Believers is little recognized by other Believers, and because too many are still looking for the standards of the world. However, for those who aspire to true spiritual greatness, lack of recognition is of no consequence whatsoever. The Christlike spirit demands self-abnegation.

The phrase, *"Ye know that the princes of the Gentiles exercise dominion over them,"* gives the definition of worldly greatness. The less Bible there is in any respective country, the more repressive dominion that is exercised. As someone has said, *"Much Bible, much freedom; little Bible, little freedom; no Bible, no freedom!"*

The phrase, *"And they that are great exercise authority upon them,"* refers to the using of authority, and not only having it!

This standard of the world, which is always backed up by force, and actually is necessary respecting government; however, is not the Way of the Lord among His people (Rom. 13:1-8).

And yet, most, if not all, Religious Denominations fall into this category. The reason pertains to *"leaven."* If a little leaven is introduced it ultimately corrupts the whole (I Cor. 5:6).

In the first place, there is nothing in the

Book of Acts or the Epistles which speaks of a Religious Denomination. It simply does not exist! Actually, each Church was its own indigenous Body, with sole spiritual authority, as is evidenced by the seven letters to the seven Churches of Asia, as given by Christ (Rev. Chpts. 2 and 3). Jesus did not write to a Denominational Headquarters because none existed, not even Jerusalem. He wrote, as said, to each individual Church because each individual Church was looked at by Christ as its own indigenous Body, incorporating sole spiritual authority, which was supposed to be derived from the Word of God. While there was fellowship among Churches, along with a strong effort to proclaim the same Doctrine, as evidenced by the letters of the Apostle Paul (I Cor. 1:10), there was no such Church or place designated as any type of Religious Headquarters, at least one that had authority over other Churches.

While it is true that the first Council was held at Jerusalem; however, this was done only because many, if not most, of the Apostles were there, along with James the Lord's brother (Acts 15). Without an agreement among these individuals whom the Lord had chosen, there could be no stated purpose. So the meeting was held there, but there is very little evidence of any other such meetings in Jerusalem, even though this would have been the logical place for a Headquarters if the Holy Spirit had desired. Actually, it is obvious that the Church at Antioch played a greater role in Evangelism, even than Jerusalem (Acts 13:1-5).

And yet there is nothing wrong with a Religious Denomination being formed, providing it is understood that within itself it carries no spiritual connotation or spiritual authority. As well, it must be understood that offices within such a structure must not be labeled as spiritual, but rather administrative. While it is true that spiritual men certainly should occupy these offices, whatever they should be, still, there is no designation in the Word of God for such denominational offices, and, consequently, they carry no spiritual authority.

If Religious Denominations are looked at as an effort to proclaim a common bond of Doctrine as well as the propagation of the Gospel, no spiritual harm is done. However, when men begin to think of their particular Religious Denomination as something ordained of God

and association with it some type of spiritual exercise, then it becomes Denominationalism, and consequently, a sin.

Probably one could say that the moment a religious body begins to interpret itself as a Religious Denomination, the *"leaven"* has already begun, with *"Denominationalism"* as the next step, which the *"leaven"* ultimately leads to.

All of that has been said in order to point to the manner in which such evolves, which is always by the method here spoken of by Christ as worldly *"dominion."* In other words, Church Government now becomes the same type of government of the world, and because it is of the world.

Once Denominationalism is reached, or as it is being reached, *"Religious Hierarchy"* is the next step. (A Religious Hierarchy is a ruling body of clergy organized into orders or ranks each subordinate to the one above it.)

As well, one will look in vain in the New Testament for a Religious Hierarchy, for none existed!

As a hierarchy strengthens, two things begin to develop:

1. It claims sole authority of the Word of God, with God speaking to the hierarchy, with it filtering down to the underlings. As such, the hierarchy speaks for the people and the Preachers. It frowns greatly on those who claim to hear from God without the benefit of the hierarchy.

2. If the hierarchy exercises ultimate control, it will claim infallibility when teaching on matters of Faith and morals. In other words, whatever is said is to be obeyed, and irrespective of its lack of Scripturality.

The idea is that the hierarchy is right in all things, and to obey is a natural conclusion. If something is unscriptural, the hierarchy will be responsible, and not the individual Preacher, etc., they say!

However, Religious Hierarchy generally takes on a tone of infallibility, with its word gradually taking precedent over the Word of God.

The Catholic Church is an excellent example of *"Religious Hierarchy."* Sadly and regrettably, many Protestant Denominations are coming perilously close to the Catholic model.

Worldly men, and especially worldly religious men, love to *"exercise dominion and authority"* over other men. It is the way of the world and the government of the world. As stated, while this type of government is a necessity in the world, it has no place in the Church.

(26) "BUT IT SHALL NOT BE SO AMONG YOU: BUT WHOSOEVER WILL BE GREAT AMONG YOU, LET HIM BE YOUR MINISTER;"

The phrase, *"But it shall not be so among you,"* is emphatic as uttered by Christ, and is meant to point to the personal ambition of James and John, as well as all the other Disciples, as well as every other single follower of the Lord.

In this emphatic statement, Christ plainly denounces the government of the world brought into the Church. And yet, and as stated, much, if not most, of the Church world totally ignores this Command.

Regrettably, the Church is not only plagued with Catholic Popes, but Pentecostal and Charismatic Popes as well! As stated, men love *"authority,"* but not many enjoy being a *"servant."*

The phrase, *"But whosoever will be great among you,"* is meant to address itself to the personal ambition of the Disciples, as well as all!

Jesus does not deny, nor does He condemn, those who would be all they can be in Christ, or to do all they can for Christ. However, His definition of *"greatness"* is the total opposite of the world. Regrettably, it is a definition that many of us have yet to learn!

The phrase, *"Let him be your minister,"* was exampled in His answer to James and John.

The unity of Jesus and the Father, and His wondrous self-renunciation as Son of God, shine forth in His answer.

Positions in the Kingdom of the Son were planned by the Father; and the Son, as the Servant, in the Unity of the Godhead, would only give such positions to those to whom the Father had determined to grant them. He, as the Son, and as the Servant, could indeed lead His followers to suffering and death, but the first places in His Kingdom He would only bestow on those whom the Father had chosen for such positions.

His gentle rebuke of the Disciples explains the spirit of service, the perfection of which was seen in Himself.

WHAT IS A MINISTER?

The Greek word is *"diakonos,"* which means one who executes the command of another, i.e., a servant. Strangely and beautifully enough,

NOTES

the word, as it is broken down, actually means *"one who runs errands,"* or *"one who is attendant,"* or even *"one who is a waiter at a table or other menial duties."*

The true Minister of the Gospel is, as should be obvious, a servant. Christ is the Perfect Example. Again, this should be obvious.

Christ came to this world not to be served, but rather to serve. The greatest example of that *"service"* was the Cross. It was all for the human race and even those who did not love Him. It is to be our greatest example, as well.

Believers cannot be the *"servant"* they ought to be, i.e., *"Minister,"* unless they have a correct knowledge of Christ and the Cross. In other words, they must not confuse Who Christ is and What Christ has done.

Let us say it again:

Every Believer is to be a *"Minister."* Such can be done properly only as the Believer properly understands the Cross. That's the reason Jesus said, *"If any man will come after Me, let him deny himself, and take up his cross daily, and follow Me"* (Lk. 9:23).

(27) "AND WHOSOEVER WILL BE CHIEF AMONG YOU, LET HIM BE YOUR SERVANT:"

The phrase, *"And whosoever will be chief among you,"* directs its attention to that which was desired by James and John, as well as so many of us, but with a definition entirely different than they had supposed!

The phrase, *"Let him be your servant,"* gives the true Christian road to *"greatness."*

The Greek word is *"doulos,"* and means *"one giving himself wholly to another's will,"* at least that which is Scriptural.

No Preacher of the Gospel has a right to be a lord over God's people (I Pet. 5:1-8). The Scripture teaches us that the proper Minister of the Gospel is to be the *"least of all"* and *"a servant of all"* (Mk. 9:35).

This is a demand by our Lord that most in the modern Church seem to have forgotten.

(28) "EVEN AS THE SON OF MAN CAME NOT TO BE MINISTERED UNTO, BUT TO MINISTER, AND TO GIVE HIS LIFE A RANSOM FOR MANY."

The phrase, *"Even as the Son of Man came not to be ministered unto,"* expresses Himself as the perfect example.

He ministered, healed, saved, delivered, and fed the multitudes, while asking nothing in return, at least in a personal way. His Life was to spend and be spent.

The phrase, *"But to minister,"* proclaims these glorious things He constantly did. His life was for others, which epitomizes the True Christlike life. The more Christlike, the less selfish; the less Christlike, the more selfish!

The phrase, *"And to give His life a Ransom for many,"* is meant to proclaim the highest example of all and the obedience of His Own Word in *"losing one's life, to find it!"*

The word, *"Ransom,"* in the Greek is *"lutron,"* and means to pay the price, whatever that price may be. In this instance it was His Life given at Calvary. He literally *"gave His Life,"* in order that others may have life, which is the crowning example to His True Ministers.

As well, the word, *"many,"* refers to the entirety of the world, whatever that number may be and whenever they may have lived.

This *"Ransom"* is the *"Atonement"* of the old Mosaic system, which by the offering of Lambs or Bullocks, could only point to the One Who should come, namely Jesus Christ.

Actually, Jesus said very little about the atoning nature of His Sufferings and Death. Perhaps it is impossible for one to fully understand and comprehend that which Christ did at Calvary and the Resurrection.

As well, there is something in the ingredient of Faith which demands that we accept even though we do not understand fully and completely. Therefore, the Plan of God is predicated on Faith, which anyone can have, rather than a certain level of intellectualism, which many could not have.

To be Christlike is to enter into the Divine, while being worldly, i.e., un-Christlike, is to digress into the Fall of man.

True Christian *"greatness,"* i.e., the servant, is the strength of the Church. Could it be possible that this is the reason we are so weak?

(29) "AND AS THEY DEPARTED FROM JERICHO, A GREAT MULTITUDE FOLLOWED HIM."

The phrase, *"And as they departed from Jericho,"* has a sadness to it, because it is the last time He will pass through this city. He is only days away from the Crucifixion, and, consequently, His Heart must have been heavy.

It is beautiful in its application, that His route lay on the same path His Namesake had taken,

Joshua. Joshua had set forth to conquer the promised land. Such would serve as a material type of our Salvation and spiritual inheritance.

However, Jesus will now go forth to win that spiritual inheritance by His Death at Calvary. As Joshua conquered, He would conquer!

As Joshua defeated all the combined heathen kings, likewise, Jesus defeated Satan and every minion of darkness.

As I dictate these words, I sense greatly the Presence of the Lord. All He did for us on that dark day at Calvary, we will possibly never fully understand. But this we do know, every victory has been won, and every devil has been defeated, and because He lives, we shall live also.

The old song says:
"When the host of Israel, led by God,
"Around the walls of Jericho softly trod;
"Trusting in the Lord, they felt the
    conqu'ror's tread,
"By Faith they saw the victory ahead."
The last verse says:
"When like those who've gone before to
    that land,
"By death's river cold and dark I
    shall stand;
"Trusting in the Lord, I will not fear
    or dread,
"By Faith I see the victory ahead."
Chorus:
"Victory ahead! Victory ahead!
"Thro' the Blood of Jesus, victory ahead;
"Trusting in the Lord, I hear the
    conqu'ror's tread,
"By Faith I see the victory ahead."

From the Jordan River, which lay close to Jericho, to the city itself was called the *"Divine District."* It was said to be the most luxuriant spot in Israel. It has the climate of Lower Egypt, and displayed the vegetation of the tropics.

Its fig trees were preeminently famous; it was unique in its growth of palms of various kinds which exist unto this day. Its crops of dates were a proverb; as well, the balsam plant, which grew principally here, furnished a costly perfume, and was used also as a medicine for healing wounds.

In the time of Christ, this area was spotted by towers and castles. A great stone aqueduct of eleven arches built by the Romans, brought a copious supply of water to the city. As well, the great fountain healed by Elisha poured forth from its copious underground springs, and, as well, continues to do unto the present.

This was *"Jericho,"* and yet none of this would appeal to Christ as He passed through it for the last time.

On one of our trips to Israel, a beautiful and yet strange thing happened at this city. Our group was on the ruins of Old Jericho, the part that Joshua had marched around so long, long ago. Actually, we had held a service at this area, with about 20 or 30 people present.

I had addressed the people for a few moments, pointing out the tremendous things that had taken place in this general area.

As stated, Joshua crossed the Jordan close to Jericho when he came into the Promised Land. As well, it was here, or rather nearby, that Elijah was translated by a Chariot of Fire.

Most believe it was nearby Jericho where John baptized Jesus in the River Jordan. As well, it was near Jericho where Jesus went into the wilderness to be tempted of the Devil. And then of course, as we shall study, the healing of two blind men by Christ, one being Bartimaeus, as well as the Salvation of Zacchaeus (Lk. 19:1-6).

As I related these things to our group, I sensed the Presence of the Lord, but was little aware of what would transpire shortly.

At the conclusion of the short service, people were praising the Lord with uplifted hands, and one could sense the gentle moving of the Holy Spirit.

I walked away from the crowd even to the other side of the ruins, seeking privacy, as I sensed the Holy Spirit beginning to move upon me even in a greater way.

The Spirit of the Lord began to increase in its intensity, until it seemed to fill every part of my being. It was like my heart would break as I began to sob, greatly sensing the Presence of God.

Looking back, I know that the Lord did this for a purpose and reason, but as of yet I am not certain as to what that purpose and reason are, at least in its totality.

In my heart of hearts, I believe that the Lord was speaking to me concerning the great victory won at this place by Joshua. This was the citadel and stronghold of Satan, sitting at the very entrance to the Promised Land.

As it fell to Joshua, and as he followed the Lord, I believe the Lord was telling me, likewise,

every stronghold of Satan would be defeated in my own life, with the Promised Land taken as it was by Joshua.

In Truth, and by the Grace of God, I believe I can say that Jericho is behind me, with tremendous victories just ahead!

The phrase, *"A great multitude followed Him,"* would concern itself as witnessing one of the greatest miracles ever. Jesus would heal two blind men.

This was the Passover season, with thousands going to Jerusalem to keep this all-important Feast. I wonder how many in the crowd who looked at Jesus really understood that He was the Passover.

This great Feast commemorating the deliverance from Egypt would be fulfilled by His Death at Calvary. For some 1600 years it had been kept, and now it was to be fulfilled.

But yet, the multitude then did not know, as the multitude now does not know!

(30) "AND, BEHOLD, TWO BLIND MEN SITTING BY THE WAY SIDE, WHEN THEY HEARD THAT JESUS PASSED BY, CRIED OUT, SAYING, HAVE MERCY ON US, O LORD, THOU SON OF DAVID."

The phrase, *"And, behold, two blind men sitting by the way side,"* portrays two, while Mark and Luke portray only one. Mark gave the name as *"Bartimeus."*

Matthew and Mark portray an exit from the city, while Luke records Jesus and His Disciples coming into Jericho. There is no discrepancy or contradiction.

First of all, there were *"two"* exactly as Matthew stated. Both were healed! However, one of them stood out, namely Bartimeus, hence chronicled by Mark and Luke.

This is quite common with any person as they proclaim something that happened, highlighting one particular individual who may have dramatically stood out, while saying nothing of one or more who may have been there as well! It is not a denial of their presence, nor any intention to do so, as Mark or Luke, but, instead, bringing out that which the Holy Spirit desired, and for particular reasons.

Here, in keeping with the purpose of Matthew's Gospel, both the blind men are mentioned.

It is quite possible that the Holy Spirit spoke of two, because He desired that they represent the Hebrew nation in its two divisions of Israel and Judah; and their receiving sight illustrates and predicts the Light that will shine upon the nation in the future day, when the Son of David shall go up to Jerusalem not to be crucified, but, instead, to be crowned King of kings and Lord of lord!

Respecting the entrance or exit of the city, some have claimed that it was two different cases, with one occurring on the entrance into the city, with the other occurring as the city was exited. This certainly is possible, inasmuch as Jericho was a city of approximately 100,000 population, and, no doubt, with a number of blind men. However, such is highly unlikely, especially considering that the terminology of the request is almost identical.

I personally believe that the account of this Miracle as related by Matthew, Mark, and Luke, is one and the same.

When Luke gave the account, he spoke of Jesus coming into Jericho, while Matthew and Mark spoke of Him performing this Miracle as He left the city.

It could well be that they came into the city and stopped to refresh themselves, or for whatever reason. At some point during this day the experience with Zaccheus took place, with Jesus even going to his house (Lk. 19:5).

At some point in time they made preparations to depart, and from whatever part of the city, when Jesus performed the Miracle as recorded by Matthew and Mark.

Consequently, all three were correct as they reported it.

The phrase, *"When they heard that Jesus passed by,"* contains a truth within itself.

How did they hear?

Of course the answer is obvious, with all the commotion taking place respecting the entrance of Jesus into the city. No doubt most everyone was discussing His Presence when the blind men overheard the conversations.

However, if they had not heard, and irrespective as to how, they would have not been healed. The world is in the same condition. Spiritually speaking, it is blind, and the only way it can receive its spiritual sight is through Christ. That's what Jesus meant when He said, *"The Spirit of the Lord is upon Me, because He hath anointed Me to . . . recover sight to the blind"* (Lk. 4:18).

Even though the account in Luke does speak

of physical sight, more than all, however, it speaks of *"spiritual sight."*

Paul said, *"How shall they hear without a Preacher?"* (Rom. 10:14). The primary business of the Church should be to take the Gospel to the world. Tragically, that is not so in many, if not most, cases.

The primary business of most of the Church runs the gamut from A to Z, with precious little priority given to World Evangelism, which is priority with the Lord.

Anyone who does not understand or believe that does not know or understand the Bible. The Great Commission, which is the taking of the Gospel to the world, is the last Message given by Christ to those who would constitute the Church (Mk. 16:15). Actually, the Holy Spirit was to be given, and was given, at least in part, for that very task (Acts 1:8).

The final words of anyone, just as Christ's were, are of supreme importance. This is evidenced by the action of the Early Church in placing total priority on taking the Gospel to the world of that day.

In fact, they were so successful that without the aid of modern transportation, the printing press, or modern communications, they were able by the end of the First Century to cover a good part of the civilized world of that day. They did it by the Power of the Holy Spirit, and because of a burden to carry out the last Command of Jesus Christ.

If our priorities are wrong, our aim is wrong, and the destination will be wrong as well! Tragically, the priority for the majority of the modern Church is wrong!

As it was imperative for those two blind men to *"hear,"* it is imperative for the whole world today to *"hear"* about the only One Who can save them, the Lord Jesus Christ.

The phrase, *"Cried out, saying, Have Mercy on us, O Lord, Thou Son of David,"* proclaims a request that could not be denied.

First of all, for them to refer to Jesus as *"Son of David"* was virtually to acknowledge Him to be the Messiah, Who, as the Prophets foretold, was to open the eyes of the blind (Isa. 29:18; 35:5).

How was it that these men who were blind had come to the conclusion that Jesus was the Messiah?

Quite possibly, and as it no doubt happened, they had heard many times of Jesus in these last three and a half years. The news had come to them of tremendous miracles taking place, even blinded eyes being opened.

Upon hearing this, Faith entered their hearts, and quite possibly they discussed it many times between themselves, coming to the conclusion that this Man must be the Messiah, the Promised One of Israel.

For whatever reason, they had no prior occasion to meet Christ. And now their opportunity will not be lost. There is an urgency in their heart evidenced in their *"cry."* There was no way they could know that this would be the last time He would come through Jericho, but quite possibly the Holy Spirit prompted them in their petition.

They would not be denied!

These blind beggars knew Who He was, but the Religious Leaders of Israel did not know!

(31) "AND THE MULTITUDE REBUKED THEM, BECAUSE THEY SHOULD HOLD THEIR PEACE: BUT THEY CRIED THE MORE, SAYING, HAVE MERCY ON US, O LORD, THOU SON OF DAVID."

The phrase, *"And the multitude rebuked them, because they should hold their peace,"* is normally the attitude of the *"multitude."*

When an individual reaches out for God, most of the time there will be very little encouragement. Many, as these, will seek to hinder, and in varied ways.

Many will say that the days of miracles are over; that God no longer answers prayer; or the person has done too bad for the Lord to hear him, etc., ...

The number of reasons as to why the Lord cannot be reached are endless. To listen to any one of them is to be denied. And, tragically, the Church and Preachers most of time are the biggest hindrance of all.

However, for all who will believe, and despite the discouragement and the demand for silence, Jesus, exactly as He passed by that day so long ago, is passing by again. If one has Faith and believes, he can reach out to Him and, to be certain, Jesus will stop. He ever heeds the cry of the distressed soul, for that is His very business.

The phrase, *"But they cried the more,"* represents Faith that will not be denied.

They would allow nothing to stop them, not even the taunts and discouragement of the crowd. To be sure, Faith will never allow hindrances to

stop its onward thrust. It will believe until the answer comes.

The phrase, *"Saying, Have Mercy on us, O Lord, Thou Son of David,"* represents the second time this is said. It should teach us a lesson.

If we ask and do not receive, ask again! Actually, we are admonished to keep asking until the answer comes (Lk. 11:5-13).

(32) "AND JESUS STOOD STILL, AND CALLED THEM, AND SAID, WHAT WILL YE THAT I SHALL DO UNTO YOU?"

The phrase, *"And Jesus stood still,"* represents one of the most poignant moments in history.

Jesus, as stated, was on His way to Calvary. The Salvation of mankind was at stake. Everything hung in the balance. However, Faith, even the Faith of two blind men, stopped Him momentarily, even though His task of the Redemption of mankind was the single greatest task ever devised by man or God. Such is the power of Faith. God will not overlook it because God cannot overlook it!

As Jesus stopped for these two men, He, as well, will stop for any who will dare to believe Him. God loves Faith!

The phrase, *"And called them, and said,"* would represent the greatest moment of their lives.

What must have been their thoughts when they heard His Voice?

Mark insinuates that at first they did not know it was Jesus Who had called them. But in a moment, the crowd, which at first had tried to still them, now proclaims the Good News of Jesus calling for them (Mk. 10:48-49).

The question, *"What will ye that I shall do unto you?",* was the greatest question they had ever heard in all of their lives.

As well, He is saying the same to all who would call unto Him. That means every sinner can be saved; every drunk can be delivered; every captive set free; every drug addict delivered by the Power of God; every sick person healed. He is still asking, as He asked so long ago, *"What will ye that I shall do unto you?"*

It is an open-ended request, and is limited only by our lack of Faith, at least if we ask in His Will, as these blind men.

As somebody wrote:

"Though millions have come, there is still room for one,
"There is room at the Cross for you."

(33) "THEY SAY UNTO HIM, LORD, THAT OUR EYES MAY BE OPENED."

The phrase, *"They say unto Him,"* will now occasion their request. At first they had asked for *"Mercy,"* and now they will ask for *"sight."*

As the correct *"order"* was then, so it is now!

The word, *"Lord,"* represents the cry of their heart, as it should represent the cry of all!

Truthfully, He is *"Lord!"* No other can honestly answer to that name; not Mohammed, not Buddha, not Confucius, nor anyone else. Only Jesus Christ can answer to *"Lord!"*

The phrase, *"That our eyes may be opened,"* proclaims exactly that which they needed.

As the crowd looks on, they make their request, and their request will not be denied.

(34) "SO JESUS HAD COMPASSION ON THEM, AND TOUCHED THEIR EYES: AND IMMEDIATELY THEIR EYES RECEIVED SIGHT, AND THEY FOLLOWED HIM."

The phrase, *"So Jesus had compassion on them,"* records Matthew only mentioning this attribute of the Lord.

To be sure, only Christ and those who truly follow Him have this attribute, *"compassion."* Their pitiful condition touched His Heart, as our pitiful condition touches His Heart. To be sure, this is the reason that God sent His Only Son (Jn. 3:16).

The phrase, *"And touched their eyes,"* as well, constituted the greatest touch they would ever know.

What must the Hand of Jesus felt like when it touched them?

To be sure, it was a *"touch"* as they had never experienced.

The phrase, *"And immediately their eyes received sight,"* proclaims their instant healing.

The song says:

"I got just what I wanted, I got just what I wanted,
"I got just what I wanted from the Lord.
"I got just what I wanted, I got just what I wanted,
"I got just what I wanted from the Lord."

As well, there was no gradual opening of their eyes, but an immediate sight. As well, when one comes to Jesus the Miracle of the New Birth transpires *"immediately."*

One can well imagine their joy that filled them from head to toe as they relished in this which Jesus had done for them.

The phrase, *"And they followed Him,"* proclaims them accompanying Him, possibly even to Jerusalem.

It is no wonder that they did so. Who would not want to follow One Who had done such great things for them?

They did not want to take their newly-opened eyes off Him. They, no doubt, feasted on His Person and relished in His Presence.

It is said that Bartimeus, who was one of these blind men, became known in the Early Church as a devoted follower of Christ, and hence his name is recorded for all time in the Sacred Narrative.

As someone wrote a long time ago:

"The windows of Heaven are open,
"The Blessings are falling tonight,
"There's joy, joy, joy in my heart,
"Since Jesus made everything right.
"I gave Him my old tattered garments,
"He gave me a robe of pure white,
"I'm feasting on manna from Heaven,
"That's why I'm happy tonight."

CHAPTER 21

(1) "AND WHEN THEY DREW NIGH UNTO JERUSALEM, AND WERE COME TO BETHPHAGE, UNTO THE MOUNT OF OLIVES, THEN SENT JESUS TWO DISCIPLES,"

The phrase, *"And when they drew nigh unto Jerusalem,"* concerns itself with the last week of the life of Jesus before the Crucifixion. Truly He would come unto His Own, and His Own would receive Him not (Jn. 1:11).

The phrase, *"And were come to Bethphage, unto the Mount of Olives,"* was a place very close to Bethany, and near the Mount of Olives. The name meant *"house of figs."*

Jesus and His Disciples were probably on their way to Bethany, the home of Lazarus, Mary, and Martha. When reaching *"Bethphage,"* He will now set in motion the *"Triumphant Entry."*

The phrase, *"Then sent Jesus two Disciples,"* proclaims them beginning the task — the Triumphant Entry — which would be so important to Jerusalem, but yet not recognized at all! Who the two Disciples were is not stated; however, tradition says that it was Peter and John.

(2) "SAYING UNTO THEM, GO INTO THE

VILLAGE OVER AGAINST YOU, AND STRAIGHTWAY YE SHALL FIND AN ASS TIED, AND A COLT WITH HER: LOOSE THEM, AND BRING THEM UNTO ME."

The phrase, *"Saying unto them,"* proclaims the identical manner in which He has always spoken to those who are His, and, in fact, does presently!

The sadness is that most are not near enough to Him to hear His Voice, and, therefore, have no idea as to what He wants and desires. To be frank, it takes a life of constant dedication, prayer, and attention to the Word, in order to hear His Voice.

The phrase, *"Go into the village over against you,"* no doubt refers to *"Bethphage."*

The phrase, *"And straightway ye shall find an ass tied, and a colt with her,"* refers to two animals, while Mark, Luke, and John only refer to one, and because Jesus probably only rode the *"colt."* However, both were brought to Christ in order to fulfill the Prophecy of Zechariah 9:9.

The phrase, *"Loose them, and bring them unto Me,"* is spoken with authority. The village was small, probably having only one main street, and, consequently, the *"colt"* being accompanied by its mother, and no doubt standing in a conspicuous place, was easily spotted.

(3) "AND IF ANY MAN SAY OUGHT UNTO YOU, YE SHALL SAY, THE LORD HATH NEED OF THEM; AND STRAIGHTWAY HE WILL SEND THEM."

The phrase, *"And if any man say ought unto you,"* refers to the owners or attendants.

If one is to notice, the terminology is strong, and because Christ assumes the role of Divine Messiah, King of His people. To be sure, this He always was, even though little explained at least in this manner. However, His manner and terminology will now reflect His Person for Who He really was!

The phrase, *"Ye shall say, The Lord hath need of them,"* actually means *"The Lord Messiah of Israel has need of them!"* Consequently, the owner of the animals would have absolutely no doubt as to Who was being referred to. A very valuable lesson should here be learned.

As these animals of so long ago, likewise, everything possessed by any and all Believers is, in effect, owned by the Lord. This refers to our time, money, ability, and even our very life (16:24-25).

Regrettably, many modern Christians

cannot be depended on to even pay their tithes, much less consecrating to the Lord all that they possess!

The phrase, *"And straightway He will send them,"* refers to perfect obedience.

Either the individual who owned the animals knew the Lord intimately, or else the pronouncement by the Disciples that the Lord Messiah wanted them was enough to bring about an instant acquiescence on the part of the owner. No doubt the Holy Spirit had previously proclaimed all of this to Christ by Divine Revelation.

In fact, Mark proclaims that certain ones did question their taking of the animals, but their doing as Jesus had spoken instantly brought about a release.

How many modern Believers follow Christ so closely that His every Word is instantly heard and obeyed?

The modern Christian mind upon thinking of this scenario would instantly exclaim the privilege of allowing Christ to use that which He needed for so important a task. However, the situation is no different now than then. The privilege is the same! Jesus said, *"Inasmuch as ye have done it unto one of the least of these My Brethren, ye have done it unto Me"* (Mat. 25:40).

This refers to both obedience and disobedience!

(4) "ALL THIS WAS DONE, THAT IT MIGHT BE FULFILLED WHICH WAS SPOKEN BY THE PROPHET, SAYING,"

This Passage proclaims the fact that Jesus guided His every footstep by the Word of God. The Bible, which consisted then of Genesis through Malachi, was His *"Lamp and Light"* (Ps. 119:105).

The word, *"fulfilled,"* does not necessarily mean that Christ engineered events so as to fulfill Prophecy, but that the events presented themselves, and guided by the Holy Spirit, He sought eagerly to do exactly that which the Prophets of old had foretold. Consequently, if the Religious Leaders of Israel had only bothered to investigate the Word of God, they would have instantly known exactly Who He was!

As well, the Disciples, even as John himself proclaimed, did not at this time know what was taking place, or that they were fulfilling Prophecy (Jn. 12:16). This would all fall into place some time later, but at the present they were only obeying, without really understanding the meaning of what was actually happening.

As Christ followed the Word minutely, likewise, every Believer is meant to do the same!

(5) "TELL YE THE DAUGHTER OF SION, BEHOLD, THY KING COMETH UNTO THEE, MEEK, AND SITTING UPON AN ASS, AND A COLT THE FOAL OF AN ASS."

The phrase, *"Tell ye the daughter of Sion,"* refers to Jerusalem and its inhabitants, including the Religious Leaders.

The word, *"Behold,"* refers to the suddenness of this happening, but even more so to its significance, which the Religious Leaders should have known, but did not!

The phrase, *"Thy King cometh unto thee,"* refers to the Messiah, One Who had been foretold by all the Prophets. He was to occupy the Throne of David, and reign forever (II Sam. 7:13).

This was Messiah's official presentation of Himself to Israel as the Great King, the Son of David. On this day, the 69th week of Daniel's prediction was completed (Dan. 9:27), as well as the Prophecies of Isaiah 62:11 and Zechariah 9:9 fulfilled.

The word, *"meek,"* is here used, while the word, *"lowly,"* is used in Zechariah 9:9. Both mean the same!

At least in part because of this *"meekness"* and *"lowliness,"* the Religious Leaders of Israel did not, and, in fact, would not recognize Christ as the Messiah. To them He was no more than a peasant, and a deluded one at that!

Their prideful self-righteousness had so placed them in opposition to the Word of God, and what it truly taught, that they no longer understood its meaning or Who it proclaimed! True *"meekness"* is ever a rebuke to evil pride. Actually, this is the only thing that Christ ever personally said of Himself, *"I am meek and lowly in heart"* (Mat. 11:29).

They had in mind a triumphant Messiah instead of a suffering Messiah. Consequently, the true mission of the Messiah as proclaimed by the Prophets, was totally lost upon them, and because of their self-will. Their interpretation of the Word of God was twisted and perverted, thereby *"making it of none effect"* (Mat. 15:6).

The phrase, *"And sitting upon an ass, and a colt the foal of an ass,"* probably refers to Christ riding the *"colt"* alone, with its mother following by its side.

NOTES

The two animals could well have represented both Israel and the Gentiles. In effect, the *"ass"* trotting along beside the *"colt,"* would denote Israel who would not accept Christ. The unbroken *"colt"* would denote the Gentile Church, which would, in effect, accept Christ.

Also, another great truth is here proclaimed. It is as follows:

In times of old, the riding of an *"ass"* denoted leadership and great importance (Jud. 5:10; 10:4). However, with the advent of Alexander the Great some 300 years earlier, the war-horse had replaced the lowly *"ass"* as a symbol of pomp, power, and majesty. In other words, where such a figure once rode an *"ass"* to signify his place and position, he now rides a war-horse.

Consequently, the riding of this *"colt the foal of an ass"* by Christ, proclaimed to all concerned that His Kingdom was not of this world, i.e., present world system, and, therefore, the accusations by the Jews of Him fomenting insurrection against Rome, had absolutely no basis in fact.

This lowly animal was meant to represent Christ as He truly was, *"meek and lowly,"* and, as well, to stifle any accusations of insurrection. Nevertheless, an evil eye can only see evil (Mat. 6:23).

(6) "AND THE DISCIPLES WENT, AND DID AS JESUS COMMANDED THEM,"

They did what the Lord told them to do, even though at the time, and as stated, they did not understand it.

(7) "AND BROUGHT THE ASS, AND THE COLT, AND PUT ON THEM THEIR CLOTHES, AND THEY SET HIM THEREON."

Both animals were brought, and both had garments laid on their backs to provide a saddle of sorts, for whichever one Christ intended to ride.

With the animals brought into the presence of Christ, He no doubt told them that one would be ridden, but without saying which. As His demeanor projected that of the Messiah, they probably did not feel free to ask which one, and, therefore, prepared both. Whatever type of outer garments they were wearing, some were quickly removed by the Disciples and placed on the backs of both animals.

The phrase, *"And they set Him thereon,"* refers to the one He selected, *"a colt the foal of an ass."* The other one, the mother, and as stated, probably walked alongside its *"foal"* and with its back prepared for a rider, but nevertheless absent, served as a symbol of Israel who rejected Christ.

(8) "AND A VERY GREAT MULTITUDE SPREAD THEIR GARMENTS IN THE WAY; OTHERS CUT DOWN BRANCHES FROM THE TREES, AND STRAWED THEM IN THE WAY."

The phrase, *"And a very great multitude spread their garments in the way,"* concerned the hundreds or even thousands who were coming into the city to celebrate the three great Feasts, *"The Passover, Unleavened Bread, and Firstfruits."* Little did they realize it, but Christ would fulfill all three.

1. His Death at Calvary would fulfill the Passover, as He would be the Lamb of God, Who would give His life.

2. The Feast of Unleavened Bread spoke of the perfect Body of Christ, which would serve as the Perfect Sacrifice, and because it had never been tainted by sin. As well, it would typify His perfect, sinless, spotless life.

3. The Feast of Firstfruits would typify His Resurrection, three days after the Crucifixion, which would serve as the *"Firstfruits"* of the coming Resurrection of Life, referred to as the Rapture of the Church (I Thess. 4:16-17).

Possibly having seen the Disciples place their garments on the backs of the animals, the multitude, likewise, began to do the same, spreading theirs on the road on which Christ was coming.

The phrase, *"Others cut down branches from the trees, and strawed them in the way,"* probably referred to palm fronds, which were stripped from nearby palm trees, and probably included the branches from olive trees, etc.

As Jesus, and riding the animal, begins to come into Jerusalem, and due to the meaning of this momentous event, no doubt, the Presence of God permeated the atmosphere. The crowd must have sensed it greatly, with some, if not many, having previously experienced His Healing Power as well! The results were that as proclaimed.

(9) "AND THE MULTITUDES THAT WENT BEFORE, AND THAT FOLLOWED, CRIED, SAYING, HOSANNA TO THE SON OF DAVID: BLESSED IS HE THAT COMETH IN THE NAME OF THE LORD; HOSANNA IN THE HIGHEST."

The phrase, *"And the multitudes that went before, and that followed, cried, saying,"* of course, spoke of the crowd before and behind the Master.

In a sense, it could refer to Israel which was before Him, and the Church which followed Him, combining both in that glad day when Israel will accept Him as Lord and Messiah. This will take place at the Second Coming.

Actually, the Scripture says, *"And the armies which were in Heaven followed Him upon white horses, clothed in fine linen, white and clean"* (Rev. 19:14).

As they followed Him on the occasion of the Triumphant Entry, the Church, of which these *"armies"* represent, and will include all the redeemed and resurrected Saints of all ages, will likewise follow Him at the Second Coming.

The phrase, *"Hosanna to the Son of David,"* actually means *"save now"* or *"help now"* Son of David. This was said once daily for seven days at the Feast of Tabernacles as they marched with palm and other branches around the Altar. On the eighth day they marched seven times, which was the Great Hosanna. The phrase is taken from Psalm 118:25-26.

As well, one can see by the phraseology of the people in their praises of Christ, that they were thinking of the *"Feast of Tabernacles,"* which actually symbolizes the coming Kingdom Age, with Christ the Messiah reigning supremely, and with Israel as the premier nation in the world. However, they were premature. Jesus must first be the *"Passover,"* which He was at the Crucifixion, but was rejected by Israel.

Nevertheless, this scene will one day be reenacted at the Second Coming of Christ, but this time with acceptance.

The phrase, *"Blessed is He that cometh in the Name of the Lord,"* actually means, *"The blessing of Jehovah rest on Him Who cometh!"* i.e., Messiah.

The phrase, *"Hosanna in the Highest,"* means that Salvation in the Form and Person of the Messiah will come from the *"Highest,"* i.e., Jehovah, and, in effect, will be the *"Highest!"*

Jesus accepts these accolades, and because He was the Messiah, although unrecognized by the Religious Leaders of Israel. By His actions, He even encourages that which is done.

Matthew does not mention Christ lamenting the fate of Jerusalem, as He passed the spot where Roman legions would, about 37 years later, lay siege to the doomed city.

It would not have been mentioned by Matthew as he, and guided by the Holy Spirit, presented Jesus as King, which a King, of course, would not do, while Luke does mention it, because he, and by the guidance of the Holy Spirit, presented Jesus as *"The Man!"* A man, even *"The Man, Christ Jesus,"* would lament the doomed city.

Some have claimed that the same crowd who shouted His praises here, would clamor some five days later for His life. However, that is incorrect.

Those who clamored for His life, *"crying, crucify Him,"* were the rabble who prowled the city at night, while these who shouted His praises were in their beds asleep!

(10) "AND WHEN HE WAS COME INTO JERUSALEM, ALL THE CITY WAS MOVED, SAYING, WHO IS THIS?"

The phrase, *"And when he was come into Jerusalem, all the city was moved,"* is exactly right, but in two directions.

The people who had come from all over Israel, and, in fact, from all over the Roman Empire, were exclaiming His praises, and because He had healed many of them. As well, many who had come from a far distance and were primarily unacquainted with His Miracles, would want to know as to Who He was?

However, the Pharisees vindictively exclaimed, *"Behold, the world is gone after Him!"*, proclaiming their opposition to Him. In effect, they hated Him!

The acclamation of the entirety of the city must have been great concerning His entrance, inasmuch as the words *"was moved"* really means to *"quake"* as in an earthquake. Therefore, there must have been several thousands of people before Christ and behind Him, who were exclaiming the great salutation, *"Hosanna in the Highest!"*

Regrettably, this adulation would have only increased the fervor of the Pharisees to kill Him. The Apostate Church must always attempt to kill the True Church!

The question, *"Saying, Who is this?"*, is the question of the ages!

Jesus Christ is God!

In Genesis He is the Creator.
In Exodus He is the Deliverer.
In Leviticus He is the Sacrifice.

In Numbers He is the Sanctuary.
In Deuteronomy He is the Word.
In Joshua He is the Victory.
In Judges He is the Judge.
In First and Second Samuel He is the Anointed One.
In First and Second Kings He is the King.
In First and Second Chronicles He is the Temple.
In Ezra He is the Restoration.
In Nehemiah He is the Wall.
In Esther He is the Unseen but Guiding Hand.
In Job He is our Sanctification.
In Psalms He is our Song.
In Proverbs He is Wisdom.
In Ecclesiastes He is the Preacher.
In Song of Solomon He is the Groom.
In Isaiah He is the Virgin-Born Son.
In Jeremiah He is the Balm of Gilead.
In Lamentations He is the Sorrowing Saviour.
In Ezekiel He is the Wheel in the middle of the Wheel.
In Daniel He is the Fourth Man in the fiery furnace.
In Hosea He is the Altar Call.
In Joel He is the Promise of the Holy Spirit.
In Amos He is Judgment.
In Obadiah He is Vengeance.
In Jonah He is the Presence of the Lord.
In Micah He is the Ruler in Israel.
In Nahum He is the Holiness of God.
In Habakkuk He is the Vision.
In Zephaniah He is the Day of the Lord.
In Haggai He is the Lord of Hosts.
In Zechariah He is Holiness unto the Lord.
In Malachi He is the Son of Righteousness Who arises with Healing in His Wings.
In Matthew He is the King.
In Mark He is the Servant.
In Luke He is the Man.
In John He is God.
In Acts He is the Baptizer in the Holy Spirit.
In Romans He is Justification by Faith.
In First Corinthians He is the Resurrection.
In Second Corinthians He is the Ministry of Reconciliation.
In Galatians He is Faith.
In Ephesians He is the One seated at the Father's Right Hand.
In Philippians He is the Exalted One.

In Colossians He is the Head of the Church.

In First Thessalonians He is the Rapture.

In Second Thessalonians He is Victor over the man of sin.

In First Timothy He is Sound Doctrine.

In Second Timothy He is Power, Love, and a Sound Mind.

In Titus He is the Pastor.

In Philemon He is the Saviour of Slaves.

In Hebrews He is a Better Covenant.

In James He is the Healer.

In First Peter He is Redemption.

In Second Peter He is All Things that pertain to Life and Godliness.

In First John He is Love.

In Second John He is Love.

In Third John He is Love.

In Jude He is the Common Salvation.

In Revelation He is King of kings and Lord of lords.

Jesus Christ is All in All; He is Our Everything!

(11) "AND THE MULTITUDE SAID, THIS IS JESUS THE PROPHET OF NAZARETH OF GALILEE."

In answer to the question as to Who He was, the *"multitude"* would choose the title most understandable to them, *"This is Jesus the Prophet of Nazareth of Galilee."*

If it is to be noticed, the enemies of Christ never referred to Him as *"Jesus,"* but rather used an appellative referring to Rabbi or Teacher.

"Jesus" being Joshua in the Hebrew, meant Saviour. Therefore, to refer to Him as such, would have, in essence, referred to Him as The Messiah.

As well, the multitude referring to Christ as *"The Prophet,"* did not necessarily mean they were refuting Him as the Messiah, but rather, and as stated, using a title with which they were much more familiar.

As well, the Name, *"Jesus,"* or Joshua, was quite common in Israel at that time, so He was clarified by the title *"Jesus of Nazareth."*

As Isaac Williams said, *"Friends and foes, Chief Priests in hate, Pilate in mockery, Angels in adoration, Disciples in Love, Christ Himself in lowliness"* (Acts 22:8), and now the multitudes in simplicity, all proclaim Him *"of Nazareth."*

(12) "AND JESUS WENT INTO THE TEMPLE OF GOD, AND CAST OUT ALL THEM THAT SOLD AND BOUGHT IN THE TEMPLE, AND OVERTHREW THE TABLES OF THE MONEYCHANGERS, AND THE SEATS OF THEM THAT SOLD DOVES."

The phrase, *"And Jesus went into the Temple of God,"* referred to the Temple built by Herod.

It was begun in 19 B.C., which was approximately 52 years before this particular time. Even though the main structure was finished within ten years (about 9 B.C.), work continued until 64 A.D.

The outer court of the Temple was surrounded by a portico inside the walls. As described by Josephus, the south porch had four rows of columns, and was called the Royal Porch. The porticos of the other side each had two rows.

Solomon's Porch stretched along the east side (Jn. 10:23; Acts 3:11; 5:12). In these colonnades the Scribes held their schools and debates (Mk. 11:27; Lk. 2:46; 19:47); and the merchants and moneychangers had their stalls (Lk. 19:45-46; Jn. 2:14-16), which is the subject of this Text.

This was the third Temple built on this site, with Solomon's being the first, and Zerubbabel's being the second, which was built after the dispersion.

Mark mentions that Jesus at this time did not cleanse the Temple, but *"looked round about on all things,"* and then returned to Bethany for the night.

He visited the Temple again on the following morning, and drove out those who profaned it.

Matthew omits the first visit and cuts straight to the Temple cleansing, perhaps intending to keep in mind the cleansing with the Triumphant Entry.

As well, this cleansing of the Temple was not the same as the earlier incident narrated in John 2:13. That cleansing commenced the beginning of the Ministry of Christ, while this cleansing commemorates its close.

The phrase, *"And cast out all them that sold and bought in the Temple,"* actually referred to the court of the Gentiles, which was separated from the Sanctuary by a stone partition, considered of lesser sanctity, and, therefore, a place where such activity could be carried forth. Irrespective, the Holy Spirit labeled that part of the Temple as important as any other part, i.e., *"in the Temple."*

In this area was sold about everything that one could imagine which was required for the Sacrifices. This meant lambs, meal, incense, salt, etc.

NOTES

In the manner of these types of activities, this entire area became the same as the bazaars in the city, with people shouting out what they had to offer, along with the prices and competition. As one would be about to purchase a lamb from one seller, another would shout out his *"better deal,"* with the entire scene taking on that which was the very opposite of what it was intended.

It seems that Christ, and as Mark stated, came and looked at this hullabaloo the day previous, but said or did nothing. However, during the night, righteous indignation filled his heart, which he placed into action the next day, of which this account proscribes.

The phrase, *"And overthrew the tables of the moneychangers,"* concerned the half shekel which every Jew had to pay on the 15th of March. In every city there were collectors to receive it. It was called tribute money in Matthew 17:24-27.

Many of the people in Israel at that time had Roman coins, of which most had idols stamped on them, and, consequently, could not be used in the Temple. Consequently, there were *"moneychangers"* who took advantage of this situation to practice fraud and get rich. As well, if one had been there, one would have heard the shouts of these *"moneychangers"* exclaiming their excellent rate of exchange, etc.

The phrase, *"And the seats of them that sold doves,"* concerned the most often used Sacrifices, because this was about all the poor could afford.

Consequently, and with a mixture of these commercial activities, coupled with the custom of loud, raucous haggling, the situation had become exactly as Christ called it, *"a den of thieves."*

(13) "AND SAID UNTO THEM, IT IS WRITTEN, MY HOUSE SHALL BE CALLED THE HOUSE OF PRAYER; BUT YE HAVE MADE IT A DEN OF THIEVES."

The phrase, *"And said unto them, It is written,"* places a Scriptural foundation for that which He is about to do.

One can see the startled looks on the faces of the people, when Jesus began to overturn the tables of the *"moneychangers,"* with coins being scattered in all directions, and with doves escaping out of the cages which were overturned and then flying in all directions.

As well, on His first cleansing of the Temple at the beginning of His Ministry, *"He made a scourge of small cords, and drove them all out."* However, it is not stated if He did this at this time or not!

The phrase, *"My House shall be called the House of prayer,"* is taken from Isaiah 56:7 and Jeremiah 7:11. Mark would add *"of all nations,"* meaning that the Temple was to be opened for both Jews and Gentiles. However, the Court of the Gentiles was now taken over by these *"moneychangers,"* which certainly precluded the worship of any Gentiles.

In other words, the statement, *"House of Prayer,"* meant that intercession, praise, and petition should be going up to God constantly from this place, and by both Jews and Gentiles. Instead, there was very little prayer, and possibly none at all by Gentiles, and for the reasons given.

The phrase, *"But ye have made it a den of thieves,"* means that these traffickers had turned these hallowed Courts into places of fraud and ill-gotten gain. As well, they were robbing the Gentiles of their place of prayer, which was a terrible offense to Righteousness.

The words, *"Ye have made it,"* mean that the Jews had turned the Temple into something it was not originally intended to be, i.e., *"a den of thieves."* In other words, the Temple became what they were, and by their actions, which spoke of greed, conveteousness, and blasphemy.

Then the phrase, *"My House,"* which referred to the Temple, was where God dwelt, or rather where He was supposed to dwell, which was between the Mercy Seat and the Cherubim in the Holy of Holies.

However, the Prophet Ezekiel saw the Lord leave Solomon's Temple, and in Truth, at least as far as that occupation was concerned, He has never returned (Ezek. 11:22-25). He will actually come back, even as Ezekiel also saw, to the coming Kingdom Temple, which will be built after the Second Coming (Ezek. 43:1-7).

However, the death of Christ on the Cross, which paid for the sins of man, and saved all who will believe, made it possible for the Holy Spirit Who once reigned in a Temple made with hands, now to rather reside in the hearts of men. This took place on the Day of Pentecost. Consequently, the *"House of the Lord"* is now the heart and life of the Believer. Paul said, *"Know ye not that ye are the Temple of God, and that the Spirit of God dwelleth in you?"*

He also said, *"If any man defile the Temple of God, him shall God destroy; for the Temple of God is holy, which Temple ye are"* (I Cor. 3:16-17).

In other words, exactly as the Lord destroyed the first Temple, and because of the unrepentant sin of the people, likewise, He will destroy the present House if it is defiled, and no repentance is forthcoming! Even though the statements of Christ were made regarding a building made with hands, still, the admonition is identical for the modern Believer. It is as follows:

1. His House, that where the Lord abides, is, as stated, the body, heart, and life of the Believer (I Cor. 3:16).

2. Everything in this Temple that defiles is to be *"cast out"* (II Cor. 6:14-18; 7:1).

3. As the Temple of old, the modern Spirit-filled Temple is to be a *"House of Prayer."* This speaks of unceasing prayer, or, instead, a constant prayerful attitude. Regrettably, such is scarce in most *"Houses."*

4. The *"Spiritually blind"* are to receive sight, and the *"physically lame"* are to be healed, as a result of Jesus being in the Temple, i.e., the heart of the Believer.

As an aside, many have misunderstood these Passages, thinking that the modern Church Building constitutes the same as the Temple of old, and, consequently, nothing should be sold in the Church, i.e., a bookstore, etc., or there should not be a kitchen in a Church, etc.

First of all, the modern Church Building has absolutely no relationship whatsoever to the Temple of old. As we have stated, the Temple where God now resides is the heart and life of the Believer.

In effect, the modern Church Building is in no way sacred or holy, but actually is only a place to keep out the weather. Just because Christians meet there to worship the Lord, does not make it holy. The Believer is the one who is to be holy, and not some building, etc. While particular places and things were holy under the Old Covenant, the Death and Resurrection of Christ fulfilled all of that, with such now transferred to the individual. Peter said, *"Because it is written, Be ye holy; for I am holy"* (I Pet. 1:16).

In fact, there were no Church Buildings during the time of the Early Church, and because such was not allowed by Roman authorities.

NOTES

Consequently, people met wherever they could to worship the Lord, whether in houses, caves, etc. Actually, the place had nothing to do with worship, only the fact of Believers gathering in His Name (Mat. 18:20).

In Truth, anything which is Scripturally done by any Believer any place, can be done likewise in a Church Building, without any violation of Scripture.

Many times people will go outside a Church Building in order to smoke a cigarette. They do this because they feel to do such inside the building would be desecrating the House of God. However, what they do not seem to realize is that the House of God is themselves, or else it is supposed to be, and, in reality, when they smoke a cigarette, and irrespective as to where they are, they are defiling that House.

While it would certainly be obnoxious seeing people smoke a cigarette inside a Church Building, still, in the eyes of God the damage done has nothing to do with the building, but rather with the individual, i.e., the True House of God.

So, it is not wrong to have a kitchen in a modern Church Building, to eat in a Church Building, or to have a bookstore offering Christian books and recordings, etc. for sale to those who would desire them. Such does not violate Scripture, and has absolutely nothing to do with the action of Christ concerning the Temple of old.

(14) "AND THE BLIND AND THE LAME CAME TO HIM IN THE TEMPLE; AND HE HEALED THEM."

Now the Temple is used for the purpose of which it was originally intended. Having condemned the wrong use of the Temple, He now showed them the right use of it.

What joy there must have been when blind eyes were instantly opened and lame legs were instantly made to walk. How much different this was, the joy and praise of the people, rather than the hawking of the traffickers.

(15) "AND WHEN THE CHIEF PRIESTS AND SCRIBES SAW THE WONDERFUL THINGS THAT HE DID, AND THE CHILDREN CRYING IN THE TEMPLE, AND SAYING, HOSANNA TO THE SON OF DAVID; THEY WERE SORE DISPLEASED,"

The phrase, *"And when the Chief Priests and Scribes saw the wonderful things that He did,"* should have made them know exactly as to Who He was!

They had witnessed the Triumphant Entry and the cleansing of the Temple, and now they see the healings. Nevertheless, these things did not move them because their hearts were evil.

These *"Chief Priests"* were probably members of the vaunted Sanhedrin, which in effect ruled Israel. They were supposed to be the spiritual leaders of Israel.

The *"Scribes"* were supposed to be protectors of the Sacred Text, the Bible. Regrettably, they were anything but! Both the Chief Priests and the Scribes were bitterly opposed to Christ.

Why?

They had a man-made religion, which, as well, characterizes almost all of the modern Church! They did not follow the Word of God, but rather twisted and turned it to their own devious ends.

The Holy Spirit specifically speaks of the *"wonderful things that He did,"* speaking of the miracles and the healings which brought untold joy to its recipients, but none at all to these wicked men of religion.

The phrase, *"And the children crying in the Temple, and saying, Hosanna to the son of David,"* spoke of scores of little children who were singing the praises of the Lord, and rightly so, while the Chief Priests and Scribes *"were sore displeased."* There you have it!

Most of the modern Church world is *"sore displeased"* as well, at any demonstration of the Holy Spirit, and especially people worshiping and praising God. It is sad, but most Churches in Christendom have never heard a *"Praise the Lord,"* but rather stilted formality which has no life of the Spirit.

These Religious Leaders were *"sore displeased"* for several reasons:

1. They did not know the Lord, and despite their profession, so any Praise to Him would have been foreign to their unspiritual ears and wicked hearts.

2. They could not stand the idea of Him being praised by anyone, even children, and because they were filled with envy.

3. They did not have the Power of God, and, consequently, they hated the One Who did!

4. As well, they were probably receiving a financial rake-off from the sales and the money exchange which Jesus had now shut down.

(16) "AND SAID UNTO HIM, HEAREST THOU WHAT THESE SAY? AND JESUS SAITH UNTO THEM, YEA; HAVE YE NEVER READ, OUT OF THE MOUTH OF BABES AND SUCKLINGS THOU HAST PERFECTED PRAISE?"

The question, *"And said unto Him, Hearest Thou what these say?"*, is said with an exclamation of feigned piety! They were speaking of the children, many who were in their pre-teens, and some even younger, who were praising the Lord, i.e., Jesus. In effect, by using the phrase, *"Hosanna to the Son of David,"* the children were exclaiming Jesus as the Messiah. The children were saying exactly what these Pharisees, and, in reality, the entirety of Israel should have been saying.

The phrase, *"And Jesus saith unto them, Yea,"* proclaims the entirety of this scenario of the children praising Christ, as being orchestrated by the Holy Spirit. Bible Prophecy, as the next phrase will bear out, is being fulfilled at this very moment, and the Pharisees and Scribes who claim to be such experts in the Word of God, did not even know it.

Deception is an awful thing. When the individual, as these Pharisees, begins to follow that which is Satanic, not only do they go in the wrong direction, but, as well, they lose all knowledge as to what the right direction is. In other words, they no longer, as these Pharisees, recognize the Lord when they are looking squarely at Him.

I have watched people in our local Church, even as every Godly Pastor has, as they would begin to lose their way. Irrespective as to how much the Spirit of God moves in a particular service and how mighty the Anointing of the Holy Spirit, and even though scores of others Believers are touched and moved greatly, these individuals are untouched, unmoved, and unimpressed. They have been deceived into accepting an *"Angel of light,"* and, consequently, they no longer recognize the True Light even when it is obvious (II Cor. 11:13-15).

Many, if not most of the times, such individuals, even as the Pharisees and Scribes, consider themselves to be spiritually deep, above others, and even above their Spiritual Leadership. It becomes a thing of pride exactly as the Pharisees of old, which makes them very susceptible to an *"Angel of light."*

The question, *"Have ye never read, Out of the mouth of babes and sucklings Thou hast perfected praise?"*, is taken from the 8th Psalm.

This Psalm was written by David approximately a thousand years before the First Advent of Christ.

As stated, the *"babes and sucklings"* refer to little fellows three and four years of age, and could include up to six and seven years old.

On this particular day, even hours before the Feast of Passover, the city and Temple were filled with worshipers. These children were there with their parents, and had quite possibly observed Jesus cleansing the Temple, and no doubt were witnesses of His performing miracles and healing the sick, immediately after the cleansing.

The Power of God must have been heavily present during these times, and especially during the miracles and healings. As the Spirit of God began to move, the innocent children probably sensed it more than all. As a result, they began to praise Christ, using the same terminology used by the adult worshipers a short time earlier at the Triumphant Entry, *"Hosanna to the Son of David!"*

When quite a number of these little ones began to praise the Lord using this phraseology, and inasmuch as there were many children present, others, no doubt, began to take up the chant of praise. What a sight and sound it must have been!

The words, *"Thou hast perfected praise,"* has several meanings, each more positive than the previous.

1. It means, *"Thou hast ordained strength,"* or, instead, great spiritual strength is found in Praise of the Lord.

2. The weak and simple, as evidenced by these very young children, give Glory to God by their praises, which serve as a rebuke to the strong and mature who for some see no need to praise the Lord.

This is evident in the modern Church, and, actually, has always been evident, in that the wealthy, noble, strong, and mature are oftentimes too prideful to praise the Lord. In other words, what would people think if they *"Let go, and let God . . . ?"*

3. Combining both languages of Hebrew and Greek, the explanation of the phrase is that *"The strength of the weak is praise, and worship of Christ is strength."*

Praise of God stills the enemy, even as the praises of these little children put to shame the objection of the Pharisees.

Every single Christian ought to be a perpetual praising Believer. Actually, the very word, *"Believer,"* lays the foundation for *"Praise to God!"*

It is impossible to praise and doubt at the same time. Praise always accompanies Faith, while lack of Praise always accompanies unbelief.

To be sure, even the most exuberant praise evidenced in some few Churches, even to the point that many, if not most, would consider fanaticism, in no way reaches the epitome of that which the Holy Spirit desires. In other words, it is impossible to praise God enough, or too much!

The Psalmist said, *"Enter into His gates with thanksgiving, and into His Courts with Praise: be thankful unto Him, and bless His Name."*

The reason? *"For the Lord is good; His Mercy is everlasting; and His Truth endureth to all generations"* (Ps. 100:4-5).

Even as I dictate these words, I can sense the Presence of the Lord. Our every word, even our every thought, ought to be a paean of Praise to the Lord.

It is sad when one realizes that in most Churches there has never been any type of Praise to the Lord even one time. There may be that which some call Praise, but, in reality, is only stilted formality, which does not come from the heart, and, consequently, is not considered as Praise by the Lord, and is not accepted as such.

It should be obvious that these children had no sense of shame or embarrassment, even though in a very public place. They were witnesses of a powerful moving and operation of the Holy Spirit, carried out by the Son of God, and they responded to it. This in a sense, is what is meant by *"perfecting praise,"* i.e., Praise unhindered and uninhibited!

(17) "AND HE LEFT THEM, AND WENT OUT OF THE CITY INTO BETHANY; AND HE LODGED THERE."

The phrase, *"And He left them,"* is bluntly given by the Holy Spirit, meaning that the Pharisees were silenced when Jesus directed that which was happening to the Word of God. Had they denied it, it would have been obvious to the people that they were denying that which they claimed to meticulously keep. Consequently, they said nothing; however, in a sense, their silence speaks volumes.

It spoke of hearts that had hardened to such an extent that even that which was obvious before their eyes was not seen nor recognized. The children would accept Christ, but they would not! Consequently, when it says, *"And He left them,"* it meant far more than mere physical absence. It meant He left them to go deeper into their spiritual darkness, in which some thirty-seven years later would ensure the destruction of their nation by the Romans.

An encounter with Christ never leaves one static. If Christ is accepted, the individual is immeasurably bettered, but if rejected immeasurably worsened!

The phrase, *"And went out of the city into Bethany,"* records Him leaving Jerusalem for the night, and, in fact, there is no record that Jesus ever spent the night in the city where God chose to put His Name forever (I Ki. 9:3; II Ki. 21:7).

The same can be said for many Churches, which exclaim the Name of the Lord, but which, in fact, He is not there, and because He is not welcome!

Lazarus, along with his two sisters, Mary and Martha, lived in Bethany, and quite possibly Jesus spent the night with them.

The phrase, *"And He lodged there,"* simply means this is where He spent the night, whether with His friends or even possibly in the open air. The sadness knows no bounds. There was no room for Jesus in the Inn when He was born, and, likewise, there is still no room for Him, even at the conclusion of His Ministry. However, Jerusalem's loss was Bethany's gain. Wherever He *"lodges"* there is blessing.

As you the reader look at these words, the question must be asked; *"Is there room in your heart for Jesus there to lodge?"*

(18) "NOW IN THE MORNING AS HE RETURNED INTO THE CITY, HE HUNGERED."

Mark has the illustration of the fig tree taking place immediately before the cleansing of the Temple (Mk. 11:12-14), while Matthew places it immediately after the cleansing of the Temple, while Luke did not mention it at all.

In studying the Gospels, and in fact the entirety of the Bible, it must be remembered that events as recorded are oftentimes done so in a moral sequence rather than a chronological sequence.

In other words, the Holy Spirit had the writer to place the event, whatever it may have been, in a particular sequence to make a moral point, and without specifically stating exactly when the event took place.

The moral sequence has the Pharisees and Scribes rejecting Christ, which is followed by the *"fig tree"* which had no fruit, thereby, representing Israel.

As stated, in Mark it is reversed, with the fig tree incident taking place immediately after the Triumphant Entry, which is probably the correct chronological sequence.

The phrase, *"Now in the morning as He returned into the city,"* proclaims Christ once again beginning another day facing the hostility of the Chief Priest and Pharisees, and this only hours before His Crucifixion. How saddened these hours must have been! The rejection was bad enough, but worse still, their rejection was ensuring their destruction, which would take place about thirty-seven years later. They desired to destroy Him, when in reality they were destroying themselves.

The words, *"He hungered,"* suggest that He did not spend the night with Lazarus, Mary, and Martha, but rather in the open. Had He stayed with His friends, no doubt they would have prepared breakfast for Him.

But then again, it is possible that He did stay with them, and arising very early, left before they even knew He was gone. This could very well have happened, explaining as to why He had had nothing to eat that morning.

(19) "AND WHEN HE SAW A FIG TREE IN THE WAY, HE CAME TO IT, AND FOUND NOTHING THEREON, BUT LEAVES ONLY, AND SAID UNTO IT, LET NO FRUIT GROW ON THEE HENCEFORWARD FOR EVER. AND PRESENTLY THE FIG TREE WITHERED AWAY."

The phrase, *"And when He saw a fig tree in the way, He came to it,"* proclaims expectation!

The *"fig tree"* in this episode will be used by the Lord as an object lesson representing the nation of Israel. As He came to the *"fig tree"* expecting fruit, likewise, He came to Israel in His First Advent expecting fruit, but found none!

The phrase, *"And found nothing thereon, but leaves only,"* means that outwardly the tree looked healthy, but upon inspection was found to have no fruit at all, i.e., *"leaves only."* Such was Israel!

As Israel of old, how many modern Believers so-called have all the outward accouterments, but no fruit? As said of Israel, it is said of many Believers, *"found nothing!"*

The phrase, *"And said unto it, Let no fruit grow on thee henceforward for ever,"* pertains to the season, even though early, but should have had fruit. As the *"fig tree"* did not function as it was supposed to, and, in fact, was created to, there was no point in its continued existence; therefore, Jesus pronounced a curse upon it which shortly culminated in its death. A powerful lesson is here portrayed, and, as such, it must be learned, and learned well!

As the *"fig tree"* did not serve its purpose, likewise, Israel did not serve its purpose, and, therefore, both were destroyed.

Some object to Christ taking such action against a mindless, senseless tree. However, they forget that Jesus was the Creator of the tree, as well as all other things, and inasmuch as it was not carrying out its intended purpose to bear fruit, there was no reason for its further existence. Consequently, He had the perfect right to do what He did, and, conversely, no one has the right to question His action.

Others have argued that the tree was someone else's property, and, as such, Jesus was out of bounds in His action.

Once again, such objections are wrong, inasmuch as the Text indicates that the *"fig tree"* was not a part of an orchard, or on anyone's property, but, instead, was growing wild, the property of no one.

The example here given by using the *"fig tree"* as an object lesson, proclaims that Israel not only had no fruit at the present, but, in fact, would have none forever, at least as long as they remained in this unbelieving state. It has now been nearly 2,000 years since this incident and Israel still has borne no fruit. To be sure, she will bear no fruit until Christ is accepted as Lord and Saviour, which will be done immediately after the Second Coming. Then they will bear much fruit, but only because they are a new Israel, with the old Israel being forever dead.

The phrase, *"And presently the fig tree withered away,"* actually pertained to the next day, with the *"fig tree"* dying overnight, even

beginning its *"withering"* immediately upon the Word of Christ.

As well, upon the advent and rejection of Christ, Israel immediately began to wither, and some thirty-seven years later was totally destroyed.

The lesson must not be lost on the modern Believer, in that the purpose of our Salvation is to bear fruit for Christ.

Jesus said, *"If a man abide not in Me, he is cast forth as a branch, and is withered; and men gather them, and cast them into the fire, and they are burned"* (Jn. 15:1-6).

Therefore, to how many modern Believers is the Lord speaking words of judgment exactly as He spoke to the *"fig tree"* of so long ago? It is a sobering thought and one that should be well contemplated. I am afraid that if the truth be known, the majority of that which calls itself *"Church"* falls into this same category! As a whole, but with some individual members excluded, it has been *"cursed"* by Christ, and for the reason of bearing no fruit. I think one could say, and without fear of contradiction, that entire Religious Denominations fall into this category. No, it doesn't mean that everyone in these particular Denominations, whatever they may be, are lost. It does mean that these individuals, whoever they may be, must find other pastures, that is, if they desire to bear fruit themselves (II Cor. 6:14-18). Otherwise they will *"wither away!"*

(20) "AND WHEN THE DISCIPLES SAW IT, THEY MARVELLED, SAYING, HOW SOON IS THE FIG TREE WITHERED AWAY!"

The phrase, *"And when the Disciples saw it, they marvelled,"* actually proclaims the true lesson of the fig tree being lost upon them. This would have happened the next day. They did not realize what Jesus meant by this object lesson, as to how it gave solemn warning of the certainty of judgment on the unfruitful Jewish nation.

In effect, they had the exact opposite in mind of what Christ was actually teaching. In their thinking, Jesus was going to use His power to restore Israel, with the nation becoming the premier nation on the face of the earth, as it had been in the time of Solomon. As well, they had imagined themselves holding high positions in this coming promotion. Therefore, they only saw the miracle, and not what the miracle was intended to teach.

I am afraid that many in the modern Church follow suit, failing to properly interpret these *"signs of the times,"* and because of self-will!

The exclamation, *"How soon is the fig tree withered away!",* was their response. They did not see what all of this represented, only the withering of the tree. In other words, they had very little spiritual insight, only seeing what could be observed physically.

They had heard Jesus' Word the day before, and now they marvel as to *"how soon"* His Word had taken effect. They were marvelling over the power and effectiveness of His Word, as they certainly should have, but more than all, they should have asked why He was doing what He did, instead of merely observing what He did!

(21) "JESUS ANSWERED AND SAID UNTO THEM, VERILY I SAY UNTO YOU, IF YE HAVE FAITH, AND DOUBT NOT, YE SHALL NOT ONLY DO THIS WHICH IS DONE TO THE FIG TREE, BUT ALSO IF YE SHALL SAY UNTO THIS MOUNTAIN, BE THOU REMOVED, AND BE THOU CAST INTO THE SEA; IT SHALL BE DONE."

The phrase, *"Jesus answered and said unto them,"* records the answer being given according to their level of Faith. In other words, they had no idea as to the object lesson He was presenting, consequently, He said nothing about it, dealing only at the level they could then comprehend.

Actually, it was Faith they now needed, and, therefore, the area in which Christ will expostulate. The more important prophetic lesson concerning Israel, and due to the passing of events, will later become much more clear to them. So, He deals with them according to their present need, and for the obvious reasons.

The phrase, *"Verily I say unto you, If ye have Faith, and doubt not,"* proclaims the necessary ingredient for victory in our lives, and victory in our work for God.

So as to not misunderstand, Jesus proclaims this foundation truth in a double form. It is as follows:

1. *"If you have Faith":* Faith is obtained by hearing, learning, and understanding the Word of God. Paul said, *"So then Faith cometh by hearing, and hearing by the Word of God"* (Rom. 10:17).

Personally, I have always been a student of the Word of God. However, in the last four years,

beginning in 1991, it seems the Holy Spirit has given me a voracious appetite for the Word of God. Time and time again in our daily prayer meetings, the Holy Spirit will bring a Passage of Scripture to my mind and enlarge upon it, taking me even deeper into the Word, and, above all, increasing my Faith. It has been, and is, the most enlightening, glorious, and wonderful experience that I have ever known. By God's Grace, I pray that such will continue until the Lord comes, or until He calls me home.

In all of this, He is teaching me to depend totally upon His Word, looking to no other source, believing Him for that which His Word promises, and, to be sure, He has never failed. We have literally seen this very Scripture, and in various ways, come to pass over and over again.

2. *"And doubt not":* One cannot have *"Faith"* and *"doubt"* at the same time! Doubting not here means that one does not debate in one's mind whether a thing can be done or not, but believes that all is possible.

To be sure, one does not come to this place of Faith instantly or easily, with all doubt dispelled and eradicated. As the Disciples, one has to grow in Grace and the knowledge of the Lord. However, it is a place that the Holy Spirit desires to bring us, and which is predicated on our knowledge of the Word of God. Regrettably, such knowledge is weak in the lives of most Christians, and, consequently, their Faith is weak as well!

The phrase, *"Ye shall not only do this which is done to the fig tree,"* in fact, would be fulfilled totally in the lives and ministries of the Apostles, as well as all others who closely follow Christ.

The true lesson of the *"fig tree"* was not its *"withering away,"* but what it represented. Actually, there is no record that the Disciples even at the height of their ministry, ever placed a *"curse"* on any *"fig trees"* or any other such objects. However, they greatly proclaimed the Gospel to Israel, which it continued to reject, and which resulted in her destruction, i.e., withering away exactly as Jesus stated!

In Truth, any God-called Preacher of the Gospel either brings life with his proclamation or death — life if accepted; death if rejected! Primarily, that is what Jesus was speaking of when He said, *"And whosoever shall not receive you, nor hear your words, when ye depart* out of that house or city, shake off the dust of your feet.

"Verily I say unto you, it shall be more tolerable for the land of Sodom and Gomorrah in the day of judgment, than for that city" (Mat. 10:14-15).

The phrase, "But also if ye shall say unto this mountain, Be thou removed, and be thou cast into the sea; it shall be done," proclaims an even greater miracle than the one just witnessed by the Disciples.

As well, there is no record that Jesus ever literally moved any mountains, nor did any of His Apostles, or anyone else for that matter, as far as I know! Consequently, as the real lesson behind the withering away of the fig tree must be sought, likewise, these statements must be looked at accordingly.

First of all, Jesus is proclaiming to His Disciples and, in effect, to all who will follow Him, the power of Faith derived from His Word. Of the religions of the world, all which have been instigated by Satan, none can remotely approach the power and veracity of True Bible Christianity. Bible Christianity is a miracle-working experience which has no counterpart. The trouble is there is not much True Bible Christianity around. Most have been so watered-down, compromised, and diluted until it bears no resemblance to the Book of Acts.

In the Book of Acts, the dead were raised, the sick were healed, and miracles were performed of varied types, which strengthened the proclamation of the Word of God. If they had it then, we should have it now!

In Truth, "mountains" of difficulties, circumstances, problems, and hindrances are removed and "cast into the sea" of victory by those who dare to believe the Word of God.

While it is true that many in Christendom do not believe, and, as a result, see no mountains or even tiny hills removed, etc. However, for the few who dare to believe the Word of God, great and glorious things always happen.

The closing statement in this Scripture, "It shall be done," means exactly what it says! Whatever is needed, and irrespective of its seeming impossibility, is possible with God if men will dare to believe Him. To be sure, the "mountain" may be moved a piece at a time, but persevering Faith guarantees that the task ultimately "shall be done."

NOTES

(22) "AND ALL THINGS, WHATSOEVER YE SHALL ASK IN PRAYER, BELIEVING, YE SHALL RECEIVE."

The phrase, "And all things," refers to "all things" of His Will, and not our will. Jesus said as much in the Garden of Gethsemanee, "Not My will, but Thine, be done" (Lk. 22:42).

Unfortunately, in the last few years many in the modern Church have attempted to extend the "all things" to any and everything they wanted, automatically assuming they knew what the Will of God was. Consequently, many foolish things which were not the will of God have been attempted, which have brought hurt and harm to the Kingdom of God, and, even more importantly, disillusionment to souls.

But yet, one must not allow a lack of wisdom as evidenced on the part of some to be the guiding rule of our spiritual quest. The Believer must attempt great things for God, and upon proper Faith great things will be brought about.

The phrase, "Whatsoever ye shall ask in prayer," proclaims the value of this all-important spiritual exercise.

Even last night in prayer (9-8-95), the Lord moved extensively so, even directing my request as He often does, toward that for which He desired that I ask. It was for a greater operation and moving of the Holy Spirit in my own life and Ministry. To be sure, He has poured through my heart over and over again in the last four years respecting this urgent need. Little by little, I have sensed an increase in the operation of the Spirit of God respecting many things, not the least being the Anointing of the Holy Spirit upon my Ministry.

Actually, as I dictate these words, Frances and I have just returned from South Africa, where we were privileged to conduct a series of meetings. In two or three of the services, the Anointing of the Holy Spirit was so strong that I have difficulty in describing that which the Lord did.

It was an Anointing stronger than I've ever experienced before, and accompanied by the convicting power of the Holy Spirit as well! Each time when I would give the Altar Call, and especially during these particular services, the Spirit of God would be moving so mightily upon the congregation that at times it seemed like over half the people would respond, even into the thousands.

Whether we were in an auditorium or in the open air, at these times the response of the people would be so moving that it was absolutely no doubt as to what was happening to them. The Holy Spirit would melt their hearts, with problems of every type and description being easily handled, as well as many being saved.

This has not come easily, even with some three or four years of importuning the Lord, but slowly and surely it is coming. I believe, as well, that it is just the beginning. That which I have asked and am presently asking, and at the instigating of the Holy Spirit, I believe is going to become so powerful that it will result in the greatest harvest of souls I personally have ever known, with, as well, bondages broken, sick bodies healed, along with every other thing the Spirit desires to do.

Actually, and as I have mentioned elsewhere in these Volumes, in October of 1991, the Lord specifically told me to call these prayer meetings twice a day, each and every day, with the exception of Saturday morning and service nights. This we have done, and it has resulted in a greater relationship with Christ than I have ever known before. Someone asked me some time ago as to exactly how long we plan to continue this frequency?

I looked at the Brother for a moment without answering because the question somewhat startled me. There had not been a thought in my mind about stopping the prayer meetings, and for the obvious reasons.

After getting over my being startled, I quickly answered, *"We do not plan to ever stop!"*

I will admit that we have had very little success in getting many people to pray with us. Most are too busy or else think they are.

Constantly, I watch people even in our own Church, who are facing tremendous problems, but yet with which I have little success in getting them to sincerely seek God.

Why?

I think if the truth was known, it would fall under the heading of the next word, *"believing."* In other words, they simply do not *"believe."*

Along with *"prayer,"* Jesus attached the word, *"believing,"* and for a purpose.

The act of prayer within itself carries no power or help. To be sure, tens of millions of Moslems pray five times a day, each and every day, with no results or answer whatsoever. It is

a fruitless exercise and that which is not of God, nor according to His Word. Consequently, it does no good.

I am persuaded that the prayers of many Christians, such as they are, probably have little more effect than the prayers offered by Moslems and other unbelievers. The cause is *"unbelief,"* which is the opposite of *"believing."*

Believing what?

Paul would later write, *"But without Faith it is impossible to please Him: for he that cometh to God must believe that He is, and that He is a rewarder of them that diligently seek Him"* (Heb. 11:6).

The *"Faith"* spoken of, is that which must be had in God's Word. If the Believer does not know the Word, the Believer cannot possibly have Faith, at least enough to do what Jesus is here speaking of.

Faith pleases God, and, consequently, He delights in honoring it.

To believe that *"He is,"* means to believe all that the Bible says about God. He is the Creator of all things, and minutely watches over His creation.

He is Omnipotent (all-powerful), Omniscient (all-knowing), and Omnipresent (everywhere).

Second, the Believer must understand that God desires to become a part of our lives, and in every capacity. In other words, He wants a relationship with us, with His Word outlining exactly as to how that relationship can be enjoined. It is through Christ.

As stated, He wants to be involved in every part of our lives, even the mundane, strongly desiring, and even demanding, that we allow His Will to be carried out in all that we do. He urges us to seek Him, even as these verses along with so many others proclaim, asking Him for all that we need, etc.

He has promised to be a *"Rewarder"* to them who diligently seek Him, and, of course, this speaks of prayer.

As well, the word, *"believing,"* carries in it the attributes of importunity and persistence. Many Believers will seek the Lord momentarily, but quickly grow discouraged and quit. They do so because they really do not *"believe."*

"Believing" demands that we continue to ask, that is if we are certain it is the Will of God, and not allow circumstances, hindrances, or what appears to be silence on the part of

the Heavenly Father to hinder us in any way. God is not Santa Claus, and neither is Jesus a glorified bell-hop. God is our Heavenly Father, and as such, He desires our good, and leads us accordingly.

"Believing" means to keep believing when circumstances scream the very opposite. It is here where most Christians break down. They simply don't believe, consequently, they cease to pray.

The phrase, *"Ye shall receive,"* is emphatic, meaning that the answer, though sometimes delayed, would most assuredly come. The directions are simple:

1. *"Ask in prayer"*;
2. *"Believe"*;
3. *"Ye shall receive"*;

In all of this, one easily detects Jesus proclaiming that His children should look directly to Him, and to Him alone as their Source.

This is the primary reason that the Children of Israel, after their deliverance from Egypt, were taken through the wilderness. There was absolutely no sustenance of any kind in this wasteland. In other words, they had to look to the Lord for everything.

This was the intention of the Holy Spirit, that they would be bereft of supply of any nature except from God. They were taught to look to Him for everything, as we are taught to look to Him for everything. In other words, we are not to depend on man, or even ourselves. We are to depend on God.

(23) "AND WHEN HE WAS COME INTO THE TEMPLE, THE CHIEF PRIESTS AND THE ELDERS OF THE PEOPLE CAME UNTO HIM AS HE WAS TEACHING, AND SAID, BY WHAT AUTHORITY DOEST THOU THESE THINGS? AND WHO GAVE THEE THIS AUTHORITY?"

The phrase, *"And when He was come into the Temple,"* is meant to proclaim the fact that the Temple being full of pilgrims who had come from all parts of the Roman Empire, Jesus was immediately given an audience, with the people, no doubt, hanging on to His every Word, as they should have been. This sight angered the Religious Leaders, and for many reason, all of them wrong.

First of all, they were envious of His miracles, considering that they could not perform any. As a result of those miracles, many of the people

gave Him instant audience. Also, when He spoke, His Words were with Power, actually anointed greatly by the Holy Spirit.

As stated, they had none of this, and in fact did not know God at all, even though they claimed great spirituality. Many things were involved here, not the least of them being the control of the people.

Religion must control people or else its claims are not valid. It will use any method to achieve its ends, irrespective of how evil they may be, as here evidenced by the Religious Leaders of Israel.

Religion controls people by fear, superstition, threat, blackmail, pseudo authority, pretention, wild claims, etc., although without substance or fact, and even with the threat of bodily harm. These Religious Leaders saw their control of the people threatened, therefore, they will resort to any means to counter this threat. They have no desire for God or His Ways, only their own ways. Religion always thinks of self-preservation, and will do anything to attain that end. God's Will is not in its thoughts, and, in reality, cannot be in its thoughts because it does not know God.

So, angry at what they are observing, they will empower their cleverest men to set a theological trap for Jesus.

The phrase, *"The Chief Priests and the Elders of the people came unto Him as He was teaching,"* means that they interrupted His *"teaching,"* which the people so desperately needed. Religion can only interrupt the Word of God, which by its design it attempts to do.

Even though what He was teaching would have been the greatest Word ever heard by these individuals who were privileged to hear Him, still, these *"Chief Priests and Elders"* had absolutely no regard for that. In Truth, it was because of the Anointing of the Holy Spirit greatly upon His *"teaching"* that aroused their anger. Otherwise, they would have given it little consideration. The Apostate Church has always attempted to stop the True Church. It, as stated, will use any means at its disposal.

At this late date in the Ministry of Christ almost every Synagogue in the land was closed to Him. Any Ruler of the Synagogue who allowed Him to speak, would have been subject to excommunication. Consequently, any and all followers, that is if they followed closely, were subject to the same discrimination.

It might also be quickly said that if one truly preaches the Word of God, and preaches it by the might and power of the Holy Spirit, that most of the Churches in the land will be closed to him as well! To be sure, the situation has little changed, if any at all, from then until now.

Almost anywhere in the world where we presently go to preach the Gospel, we have very little opposition from governments or the world in general, but much opposition from many of the Churches. They will do anything they can to keep their people from attending the meetings, and irrespective of the number of people being saved, etc.

If asked the reason why, their answers are revealing!

They will either give a reason that is totally untrue, or else an answer that makes little sense.

The real reason is the Anointing of the Holy Spirit. If they truly loved souls, desiring to see them saved, with bondages broken, and broken hearts healed, along with all the things that Christ can do in a person's life, there would be no objection, only willful cooperation.

As these Religious Leaders of Israel, they do not have the moving and operation of the Holy Spirit in their lives or ministries, therefore, they will oppose those who do.

To be sure, they are not of God, for if they were of the Lord, they would not oppose the Lord. The Lord does not oppose Himself!

If the Holy Spirit anointed Christ to preach the Word and heal the sick, He certainly could not anoint these *"Chief Priest and Elders,"* and irrespective of their religious position, to oppose Christ.

As well, even though these *"Chief Priests and Elders"* held high religious positions in Israel, still, they held no high positions with God. In fact, they held no position at all!

Tragically, most of the world, and even the Church, thinks that religious offices, which are devised by men, elected by men, and instituted by men, because of their religious nature, are, consequently, of God. Nothing could be further from the truth!

In Truth, any religious office in the world, and no matter how high or well thought of by men, if not Scriptural, is given no credence whatsoever by God. Actually, these *"Chief Priests"* were filling offices originally instigated by the Lord.

However, they had so deviated from the Word of God that they were no longer legitimate.

So, the criteria is not the acceptance by men or high religious office, but that which is appointed by the Lord which will be honored by His Presence. If His Presence is there, one can be certain that what is being done is according to the Word of God. His Presence can accompany nothing that is not anchored in the Word.

So, that should be the criteria, instead of some man-made religious office.

The question, *"And said, By what authority doest thou these things?",* pertains to the events recently occurred respecting the Triumphant Entry, the cleansing of the Temple, etc. In other words, they were saying that Jesus had no right to do these things, and because they, the *"Chief Priests and Elders"* had not given Him permission to do so. They were guardians of the Temple, consequently, He was usurping their authority.

As we have stated, men love control, and religious men most of all. These Religious Leaders had so controlled the Work of God in Israel, until Very God Himself was not welcome! Of course, that is the idea of Satan all along. In fact, Satan controls all the religions of the world, and even much, if not most of that which calls itself *"Christianity,"* inasmuch as it has also degenerated into mere religion.

Untold amounts of blood have been shed since the beginning of time over *"religious authority."* It began when Cain killed Abel, and has not ceased from that moment until this.

The question, *"And who gave thee this authority?",* now strikes at the very heart of the matter. They first asked *"What?"* and now they ask *"Who?"* Their trap is being cleverly sprung. They are attempting to make Him look like a lone ranger pitting Himself against the proper and legal authority of the Temple and even of Israel. The Triumphant Entry had been one thing, but the cleansing of the Temple was something else entirely! They could not brook nor tolerate such action, especially considering that it made them look very bad. Therefore, they were attempting to place Him in the position of opposing legal and constitutional authority.

Respecting the questions of these Religious Leaders of so long ago concerning *"spiritual authority,"* perhaps more should be said on the subject.

What is spiritual authority? And who has it?

FROM THE VERY BEGINNING

The subject of *"spiritual authority"* and as spoken by these Religious Leaders to Christ of so long ago, is perhaps one of, if not the most important subject in the Work of God. It is the area where Satan functions best, and where he has caused the most damage to the Work of God. Let's address ourselves to the first question.

WHAT IS SPIRITUAL AUTHORITY?

The very word, *"authority,"* means *"a decision,"* or to put it more perfectly, *"the power to make the decision."*

The Greek word for authority is *"exousia,"* which in its simplistic sense means *"freedom of choice."* As used in respect to God, one automatically assumes that He has ultimate authority. He is totally free to make decisions that cannot be frustrated by any natural or personal power in the universe.

An example of the authority held by Christ could be expressed respecting the Roman soldier who came to Jesus asking for His help concerning the healing of his servant. He said, *"I myself am a man under authority, with soldiers under me. I tell this one 'Go,' and he goes; and that one 'Come,' and he comes. I say to my servant, 'Do this,' and he does it"* (Mat. 8:9).

As a military officer, this man derived his authority from Rome, i.e., from the Empire itself, which had chosen to extend to him the freedom of action he enjoyed in controlling the behavior of his troops.

The officer recognized that the authority Jesus derived from God was so complete that He was able to exercise control even over diseases. Jesus spoke and acted with full Divine authority and authorization.

The Gospels are replete with the freedom of action that Jesus had in teaching and healing the people. Instead of constantly referring to tradition as the authority for His actions, Jesus relied on His Own unmistakable aura of power.

When Jesus scandalized His listeners by pronouncing the sins of a paralyzed man forgiven, He proved His authority to do so by healing him, *"So that you may know that the Son of Man has authority* (freedom of action) *to forgive sins..."* (Mat. 9:6-8; Mk. 2:10; Lk. 5:24).

Despite Jesus' miracles, at the end of His ministry on earth, as we see in this very Scripture, Matthew 21:23, He was still being challenged by the Religious Leaders who were unwilling to accept Him as God's Son and Messenger (Mk. 11:28-33; Lk. 20:2-8).

Nevertheless, the Gospels are replete with statements made by Christ that define His authority, and, as well, the Epistles extend the authority of the then and now-risen Lord. While Jesus was on earth, His miracles showed His authority over nature, sickness, sin, demons, and even death itself.

As well, Jesus has authority to judge all humankind (Jn. 5:27). The Father has *"granted Him authority over all people that He might give eternal life to all those the Father has given Him"* (Jn. 17:2).

Due to the Crucifixion of Christ, it may seem as if though human beings exerted a superior authority over Him in taking Him away from His Ministry, and crucifying Him on a Cross. But Jesus claimed, *"I lay down My life — only to take it up again. No one takes it away from Me, but I lay it down of My Own accord. I have authority to lay it down and authority to take it up again"* (Jn. 10:17-18).

After His Resurrection, Jesus told His followers, *"All authority in Heaven and on earth has been given to Me"* (Mat. 28:18). Jesus now has total freedom to act (Col. 2:10), and He does act on behalf of His Body, the Church (Eph. 1:21-23).

Ultimately, Jesus will exercise His freedom to act, and will destroy every competing power, making everything subject to the direct, active Will of God the Father (I Cor. 15:24-28).

WHO HAS SPIRITUAL AUTHORITY?

The Scriptures teach and assume that in a world warped by sin, governing authorities are necessary, especially as it relates to civil governments (Rom. 13:1-7). However, that is not the authority we are speaking of here, but rather the nature of authority within the Body of Christ.

In its philosophical and theological sense, as freedom of action to control or limit the freedom of action of others, do Christian Leaders really have authority within the Church?

The issue is an important one and deserves much study and debate, especially considering that Satan has used this very principle, albeit in a warped twisted way, to control untold numbers of people through pseudo Religious Leaders. The Catholic Church is a case in point, but with this spirit of control pandemic in Protestant circles as well!

Many Church people erroneously think that Church officials elected by popular ballot and holding religious offices, which, for the most part, are man-devised, by the virtue of these offices hold spiritual authority, and, consequently, must be obeyed. To defy them, irrespective as to how unscriptural their demands may be, many think that spiritual authority has been defied.

Is this true?

No it isn't! In fact, anything that is unscriptural must be opposed, with every unscriptural demand defied, and irrespective to its source.

In other words, the Bible teaches that no one has spiritual authority over another. For instance, Jesus delegated authority to His Disciples (Mk. 3:15; 6:7; Lk. 9:1; 10:19), but this was authority over demons and diseases. No Passage suggests freedom to exercise control over other human beings. In fact, the freedom of choice to whom these Disciples came is clearly protected (Mk. 6:11; Lk. 10:8-12).

One incident reported in the Synoptics is especially significant. Matthew 20, Mark 10, and Luke 22 all tell of a heated debate among the Disciples over which of them would be the greatest. Jesus took that opportunity to instruct them on leadership and its character within the Church. Each Passage reports that Jesus said, *"You know that the rulers of the Gentiles lord it over them, and their high officials exercise authority over them."* In each Passage, Jesus bluntly rules out this kind of leadership authority for His Disciples, or anyone else in the Church for that matter. He simply said, *"It is not to be so with you!"*

The alternative that Jesus spells out is *"servant leadership."* To be sure, a servant is a far cry from a ruler!

It is interesting to compare these three Passages and to note that one of them uses *"exousia"* to indicate the authority exercised by secular officials. The other two (Mat. 20:25; Mk. 10:42) used *"katexousiazo,"* and is found only here in the New Testament. This latter word means *"authority over,"* but it also implies a tendency toward whatever compulsion is required to gain compliance.

These Passages suggest strongly that whatever authority Christian leaders may have, their freedom of action does not include the right to control the actions and choices of their brothers and sisters in the Lord.

The Apostle Paul is deeply aware of the fact that as an Apostle he does have authority. He speaks of it in II Corinthians 10:13.

He told the Corinthians that the Lord gave him authority with a specific purpose: *"For building you up, not tearing you down"* (II Cor. 10:8; 13:10). In II Corinthians 13, Paul speaks of his concern not to be *"harsh in the use of his authority"* (II Cor. 13:10). The context shows that the Christians in Corinth refused to admit that Christ was speaking through this servant leader. Paul did not respond by threatening. He did not try to manipulate or to coerce. He simply reminded them, *"Christ is not weak in dealing with you, but is powerful among you"* (II Cor. 13:3).

Paul had no need to resort to manipulation or to coercion because Jesus was alive and acting as Head of His Church. Jesus remained powerful among His people and was free to exercise His authority in disciplining ways. Paul relied on Jesus to bring about a response to the words that He, Jesus, had given to Paul to speak to the Corinthians. Jesus was the Head of the Church, and would so act!

These Passages and studies of Paul's style of leadership suggest strongly that in the Church God limits the authority given to leaders. The leader's authority is not an authority to control, but an authority to help the Believer use his or her freedom to respond willingly to Jesus.

AND FINALLY

As is here noted, our primary insight into the nature of authority comes from the New Testament. There we see, as far as God is concerned, it is portrayed as unrestricted freedom of action. God has unlimited authority, which He exercises as He chooses to direct or to permit.

Jesus demonstrated His Deity by proving that His Own freedom of action was likewise unlimited. Although Jesus delegated authority to His Disciples, their freedom of action did not involve a right to manipulate or to coerce other persons. In fact, Jesus never acted in this way Himself. He, as our example, did not compel, but He invited His hearers to believe Him and to obey.

When Jesus taught His Disciples about how authority would be experienced in the Church, He specifically ruled out the kind of power-based authority that is exercised in the secular world for personal gain or glory, and, sadly, in much of the Church as well!

Jesus gives Christian leaders authority to build up Believers, not to enslave or smother them. Built up in the Faith, Christians will freely choose to be obedient to Jesus as living Lord.

As well, the Apostle Paul who certainly had spiritual authority as an Apostle, still, following the example of Christ, never exercised that authority in a demanding way. If his authority as an apostle was questioned, which it constantly was, he merely referred the matter to Christ, Who, as the active Head of the Church, would deal with the situation. Paul never threatened, coerced, demanded, or exercised any authority in a dictatorial manner.

If anyone would have had a right to have acted in this manner, Paul certainly would have. However, he did not do so, simply because it would have been unscriptural and an abrogation of the teaching of Christ.

Ephesians 4:11 names those to whom spiritual authority is given, *"And He gave some, Apostles; and some, Prophets; and some, Evangelists; and some, Pastors and Teachers."*

If one is to notice, the titles of Pope, Priest, Cardinal, Superintendent, or President, etc., are not given. Consequently, those particular offices, plus others not named, carry no spiritual authority, even though some of these offices may, in fact, be occupied by Godly men.

Religious men are fond of devising religious offices beyond that given by the Holy Spirit, and claiming spiritual authority. Outside of these offices or callings given in Ephesians 4:11, no other offices are Scriptural.

However, this does not mean that all Church offices other than these listed in Ephesians 4:11 are wrong and unscriptural, at least if understood in the proper context. There are many Church offices which are administrative, and, therefore, Scripturally legitimate, providing it is understood that they are administrative only, and not spiritual.

However, even with the legitimate Scriptural offices listed, still, and as we have hopefully brought out, even their authority is limited, *"For the perfecting of the Saints, for the work*

NOTES

of the Ministry, for the edifying of the Body of Christ" (Eph. 4:12).

There is absolutely nothing suggested in the New Testament concerning spiritual authority, which gives the right to anyone, and irrespective of their place or position, to tell anyone else if they can or cannot preach the Gospel, or what is to be preached. To do such is to abrogate the Headship of Christ! As well, to obey such unscriptural demands is an abrogation of the Headship of Christ.

(24) "AND JESUS ANSWERED AND SAID UNTO THEM, I ALSO WILL ASK YOU ONE THING, WHICH IF YE TELL ME, I IN LIKE WISE WILL TELL YOU BY WHAT AUTHORITY I DO THESE THINGS."

The phrase, *"And Jesus answered and said unto them,"* proclaims Christ turning their theological trap back on their own heads.

The phrase, *"I also will ask you one thing,"* proclaims the manner in which the Lord addressed Himself to their question.

In reality and Scripturally, the Miracles of Christ were in total fulfillment of the Prophecies concerning the Messiah, and, as well, His birth, place of birth, and genealogy proved beyond the shadow of a doubt as to exactly Who He was! He might, had he so desired, have mentioned these things, proving that His authority was directly from God, and, in effect, He was God. Nevertheless, the attitude of these Religious Leaders, and especially considering that they would even ask the question concerning authority, proved that their hearts were so hard and that they were in such a state of rebellion against God and His Word, that nothing that was said or done would satisfy them concerning Christ. Purely and simply they hated Him, and because their deeds were evil. In effect, there is no evil such as religious evil.

Such evil hides itself under a cloak of pretense and justifies its evil actions under the guise of religious authority. Consequently, Jesus will address their question in a way that would turn their theological trap, as stated, back on their own heads.

The phrase, *"Which if ye tell Me, I in like wise will tell you by what authority I do these things,"* now puts them on the spot!

No doubt, a great crowd of people had gathered and was overhearing this exchange.

It would seem by now that these Religious

Leaders would have understood that it was impossible for them to match wits with Him. And yet, and despite many previous confrontations in which they had always been stymied, they were so full of themselves that they seemed not at all to get the picture.

(25-26) "THE BAPTISM OF JOHN, WHENCE WAS IT? FROM HEAVEN, OR OF MEN? AND THEY REASONED WITH THEMSELVES, SAYING, IF WE SHALL SAY, FROM HEAVEN; HE WILL SAY UNTO US, WHY DID YE NOT THEN BELIEVE HIM?

"BUT IF WE SHALL SAY, OF MEN; WE FEAR THE PEOPLE; FOR ALL HOLD JOHN AS A PROPHET."

The question, *"The Baptism of John, whence was it? from Heaven, or of men?"*, took them down a road that was totally unexpected on their part.

As we have stated, as Jesus asked this question, the crowd was eagerly listening and watching as to what the answer would be! Consequently, and as is obvious, Jesus would use the crowd against these *"Chief Priests and Elders"* even as they had sought to use the crowd against Jesus.

The Baptism of John included the entirety of his Ministry and Message. The Message was singular in its operation and direction, in effect, the presentation of the Messiah. As well, it was unmistakable!

All of Israel had concluded John to be a Prophet sent from God, and even though these *"Chief Priests and Elders"* did not believe that, still, due to John's wide acceptance by the people, they were at least forced to pay lip service to his prophetic office.

The phrase, *"And they reasoned with themselves,"* proclaims them going into a huddle, and because they realize the potential of the question.

The question, *"If we shall say, From Heaven; He will say unto us, Why did ye not then believe Him?"*, puts them in an obvious dilemma!

John's testimony was unimpeachable. He had actually introduced Christ, saying, *"Behold the Lamb of God . . . !"* Consequently, if they believed in John, they, as well, had to believe in Jesus! As stated, they really did not believe John, and, consequently, did not believe His Message. In Truth, they did not believe anyone who truly came from the Lord, which places the deadly germ of unbelief in a category all its own.

This is the reason that unbelief respecting one part of the Word of God will ultimately fall out to disbelieving the entirety of the Word of God.

As an example, if Preachers, or anyone for that matter, disbelieve the plain Scriptural teaching of the physical evidence of the Baptism in the Holy Spirit, which is speaking with other tongues (Acts 2:4), shortly, other parts of the Bible will be disbelieved as well! It pertains to the Scriptural Law of a little leaven, unless removed, ultimately corrupting the whole (I Cor. 5:6; Gal. 5:9).

These Religious Leaders questioning Jesus, did not believe any part of the Bible, even though they loudly trumpeted the opposite!

The Chief Priests assumed to be judges, but their inability to answer the Lord's question proved them incapable to be such. It also exposed their hypocrisy and hatred, for they were bound to receive Jesus as the Messiah if they admitted that John was His predicated forerunner.

The phrase, *"But if we shall say, Of men; we fear the people,"* places them in the position of the people staring and waiting for their answer. The silence must have been pregnant!

The admiration of the people regarding John the Baptist had even increased after his death, with many of them even believing that Herod's present problems were a judgment upon him for this murder. Consequently, the Chief Priests are on the horns of a dilemma, with a negative answer placing the people in opposition to them, and a positive answer concerning John and his prophetic office, placing them in the position of being forced to accept Christ as well!

Their *"fear of the people"* persuaded their answer, but did not change their hearts. As subtle as these hypocrites were, the people little knew the depravity of their hearts. It is no less today!

How many modern Christians are supporting modern *"Chief Priests and Elders"* just because they hold some high religious office? Or else the people do not really know the evil hearts of those they are supporting?

And yet, it was very obvious that these Religious Leaders were bitterly opposed to Christ, which the people could easily have ascertained, had they any spirituality at all! Regrettably, it is no different at present! As someone said recently: *"The last generation lost the Anointing,* consequently, this present generation doesn't even know what it is or isn't!"

The phrase, "For all hold John as a Prophet," proclaims them knowing exactly how the people felt, which beliefs they did not share.

That is obvious! At the time of John's arrest by Herod, there is no evidence that any Religious Leaders of Israel lifted a hand to obtain his release. Were the truth known, they were probably happy that Herod had taken the steps he did, and were in total favor of John's execution.

(27) "AND THEY ANSWERED JESUS, AND SAID, WE CANNOT TELL. AND HE SAID UNTO THEM, NEITHER TELL I YOU BY WHAT AUTHORITY I DO THESE THINGS."

The phrase, "And they answered Jesus, and said, We cannot tell," was untrue! The truth was they would not tell, and because their answer would have incriminated them.

They were the Religious Leaders of Israel, and, consequently, were supposed to know what was right and wrong. They claimed to be scholars in the Scripture, and for them to answer accordingly, not only portrayed their evil hearts, but, as well, made it seem to the people who were intently watching that they had little knowledge of the Word of God.

It was the duty of these Leaders and Teachers of Israel to take a position concerning such things, and to pronounce a verdict on such claims, as of the veracity of the prophetic office of John the Baptist.

These hypocrites allowed the people to erroneously think that they, the Religious Leaders of Israel, concluded John to be a Prophet, when they believed no such thing. Jesus now will publicly expose them.

How many modern Christians are supporting Religious Leaders in particular Religious Denominations who do not really believe the Bible to be the inspired Word of God, or that Jesus is the Son of God and died on Calvary to save sinners, and was resurrected from the dead?

How many Missionaries are presently being supported, with people thinking a great Work for God is being carried out by these individuals, when, in reality, nothing for the Lord is being done?

Of course, some few Missionaries are doing a great Work for God, but that is hardly the point!

The idea is that millions support particular people and causes for all the wrong reasons.

They do so because it is "their Denomination" or it is the particular Doctrine they believe, etc. The evidence is replete, as with Israel of old, that precious few support something for the right reasons, i.e., it is Scriptural and they are led by the Spirit of God.

Most Believers so-called have a "me too" philosophy. If the conventional wisdom, and irrespective as to what it is, says a particular thing, they go along simply because it is the popular thing to do. Most have no idea as to what the Word of God says about a matter, neither are they led by the Spirit of God!

The phrase, "And He said unto them, Neither tell I you by what authority I do these things," in effect is saying, "If you will not be honest with Me and the people, it is pointless to continue this conversation."

In this exchange, Jesus showed that they knew and were unwilling to answer; and that they knew He knew that they refused to utter what they well knew respecting the veracity of John the Baptist.

Their question concerning authority was not truthfully asked, but only intended as a theological trap. So, to continue dialogue with someone who was so obviously dishonest was a pointless exercise in futility. Therefore, Jesus refuses to answer their dishonest question.

(28) "BUT WHAT THINK YE? A CERTAIN MAN HAD TWO SONS; AND HE CAME TO THE FIRST, AND SAID, SON, GO WORK TODAY IN MY VINEYARD."

The question, "But what think ye?", proclaims Jesus addressing the next two parables to these "Chief Priest and Elders," as well as the people! What He is about to say will be so startling that it will turn their self-righteousness upon its head.

The phrase, "A certain man had two sons," is meant to represent two classes of people, prominent then, and prominent now!

The "Man" represents the Lord, and the "Two sons" first, the lawless and ungodly who made no pretense at religion, while the second represented the Pharisees and their followers, who made every pretense of religion. This parable plus the following, will place everything in total clarity, totally exposing the self-righteous Pharisees as to exactly what they were. Sadly and regrettably, it exposes the modern Church as well!

The phrase, *"And He came to the first, and said,"* represents the ungodly and lawless, who, as stated, made no pretense at religion, and, consequently, no claim on God.

The phrase, *"Son, go work to day in My vineyard,"* respects the great invitation.

(29) "HE ANSWERED AND SAID, I WILL NOT: BUT AFTERWARD HE REPENTED, AND WENT."

The phrase, *"He answered and said, I will not,"* proclaims the answer of most individuals, at least at first, after they hear the Word of God, and are convicted by the Holy Spirit.

This parable will proclaim in detail the heart reaction of all, as well as the self-righteous Pharisees.

In my experience as an Evangelist, I have seen this repeated countless times. Through the years we have received into our office, multiple thousands of letters from individuals who heard us preach the Gospel over Television. Their first reaction, at least the far greater majority of the time, was exactly as here portrayed by Christ. They rebelled! Their answer was *"No!"* With many of these individuals, they would continue to say *"I will not,"* even for a lengthy period of time, i.e., years.

As an example, a short time ago my son Donnie was in a particular city in a revival meeting at one of the local Churches. A lady who attended the services gave him this testimony.

She said her Dad had started watching our Telecast in the early 1980's, even though he was an alcoholic. She went on to say how that he would not miss the program, demanding that full attention be given by all to the presentation of the Message. She went on to say how this went on for years, with him watching each program with a can of beer in his hand.

Actually, his alcoholism was acute, with her seldom, if ever, having seen him draw a sober breath. But yet he would watch the Telecast, even under great conviction.

In 1989, the Telecast went off the air in her area. She said that her Dad said very little, but she could tell from what little he did say that he was grieved that the program was no longer there. In effect, it was his one last hope, even though he probably would not have put it in those words. And then in 1992 the program came back on the air in his area.

Once again, she said, he took up his ritual in

watching the Telecast each and every week, even with a can of beer in his hand. And then one day it happened!

She said the program was especially anointed that day, with the Spirit of God seeming to fill the house as the Message was proclaimed. She looked over at her Dad, and to her amazement tears were rolling down his cheeks. She watched him set the can of beer down, and as I began to pray the sinner's prayer, she saw his lips begin to move as he began to pray with me. He had watched the program for years and had been under conviction for all of these years, but this was the first time he finally yielded.

There was no doubt as to his Salvation, the drinking instantly stopped, with him beginning to attend Church, etc. It was obvious that his life was changed, and that Christ had performed a miracle of Redemption in his heart. However, just a few months after his conversion, he died instantly with a heart attack.

It had taken all of these years, with him continuing to say, *"I will not,"* and then finally yielding. As stated, I have seen this happen countless times in one form or the other. Why it is that most upon hearing the Word of God and being convicted by the Holy Spirit, will automatically react in this manner, can probably only be understood in the realm of the rebellion of the human heart. More than likely, you, the reader, reacted the same way when Jesus spoke to you requesting your heart. Your answer probably was, *"I will not";* however, the next phrase proclaims your ultimate answer, *"But afterward he repented, and went."* As stated, almost all who come to Christ respond in this fashion.

(30) "AND HE CAME TO THE SECOND, AND SAID LIKEWISE. AND HE ANSWERED AND SAID, I GO, SIR: AND WENT NOT."

The phrase, *"And He came to the second, and said likewise,"* will produce a hypocritical answer. This *"second son"* represents the Pharisees and their ilk! As well, one must remember that as this parable was given for Israel of old, it is likewise given for any and all who follow thereafter, even presently!

The phrase, *"And he answered and said, I go, sir: and went not,"* concerns itself with a respectful answer, and because he is religious and knows how to employ all the correct terminology.

If one is to notice, the response of the first is curt and even caustic, with the second being smooth and acquiescent. Such were the Pharisees, and such is their modern counterparts.

As an example, since 1988, Jimmy Swaggart Ministries, in our efforts in World Evangelism, to which I might quickly add, the Lord has called us, has had to depend almost exclusively on those who have been brought to Christ as a result of this Ministry. These are individuals who, for the most part, at least at the first, rejected Christ, but later repented and went. They characterize perfectly this of which Christ speaks. As for the *"second son,"* i.e., the Church as a whole, they make all types of claims respecting World Evangelism, but in reality do little or nothing!

I might quickly add, and that despite the fact that we have seen hundreds of thousands of people brought to Christ, and continue to see such at the present, an appeal for help to the far greater majority of the modern Church, for the most part falls on deaf ears. The tragic conclusion, and exactly as Christ stated, is *"And went not."*

(31) "WHETHER OF THEM TWAIN DID THE WILL OF HIS FATHER? THEY SAY UNTO HIM, THE FIRST. JESUS SAITH UNTO THEM, VERILY I SAY UNTO YOU, THAT THE PUBLICANS AND THE HARLOTS GO INTO THE KINGDOM OF GOD BEFORE YOU."

The question, *"Whether of them twain did the will of his father?",* will receive its intended answer. These Pharisees had attempted to spring a trap on Jesus, while now He will spring a trap on them. To be sure, they will fall headlong into it.

The phrase, *"They say unto him, The first,"* proclaims the only answer that could be given, with them little realizing in their self-righteous piety that the parable was directed at them. They definitely were <u>not</u> the ones who *"afterward repented, and went."* They were the ones who smoothly proclaimed their allegiance to God and His Word, but, in reality, had no allegiance at all!

The phrase, *"Jesus saith unto them,"* has the emphasis on the word, *"them,"* and referring to the Pharisees, and is said with power and strength! Consequently, they had absolutely no doubt as to what He was talking about, or to

whom He was speaking. When He point blank told them that *"Publicans"* who were traitors and thieves in the eyes of the Pharisees, as well as *"harlots,"* who were sinful to say the least, would *"go into the Kingdom of God before you,"* and with the emphasis on *"you,"* which referred to the Pharisees, this amounted to the highest insult that could be uttered. If they hated Him before, they will hate Him with a passion now!

As is obvious in this Passage, the Lord has no rebuke for those who were disobedient, but afterwards repented. His stinging rebuke falls on the professors and self-righteous who ought to have been leaders, but, in effect, were the very opposite.

It must quickly be added that as the Church was then, the Church is now! That is sad, but true. It was not the *"Publicans and Harlots,"* as evil as their nefarious lifestyle was, who crucified Christ, but, instead, that which called itself *"the Church."* Let not the reader think that the situation has changed from then until now. It is actually as bad now as then, and, in Truth, will grow progressively worse. The Apostate Church will actually be the greatest promoter of the coming Antichrist. It will include the old-line Denominations, as well as the Pentecostals and Charismatics. I am Pentecostal, therefore, I take no delight in including my own, but the signs of the times demand that I be completely forthright. Most of the main-line Churches, such as the Baptist and Methodist, etc., having denied, at least for the most part, the Holy Spirit, basically deny the Power of God. Therefore, there is precious little of the moving of the Holy Spirit in these ranks.

As well, the Charismatics have for the most part totally embraced the prosperity and political message, which is *"another gospel"* pure and simple (II Cor. 11:4).

Sadly, and at least in America and Canada, there are precious few True Pentecostals left, with many of the few who remain, mired in legalism or else little believing the great Pentecostal Message. To be sure, in certain other parts of the world, the situation is different and in the positive. However, at least in America and Canada, and in the major Pentecostal Denominations, if the truth be known, less than fifty percent of the adherents to these particular Denominations even claim to be Baptized in the Holy Spirit with the evidence of speaking with other tongues.

Thankfully, there are exceptions to all of the above. There are definitely some few Preachers in the old-line Churches who truly know and love Jesus Christ and are being used by the Lord. The same can be said for the Pentecostals and Charismatics; however, as a whole my statements are true, and regrettably so!

How do I know these things?

I think what we have stated, as distasteful as it may be, would have to be admitted by anyone who knows the Word of God and is spiritually minded. As well, God does not oppose Himself. In other words, if His Spirit is moving and operating in the Salvation of souls, and the edifying of the Body of Christ, He at the same time will not oppose that which He is doing. In other words, the Chief Priests, Elders, and Christ, could not all be Scripturally correct, and, therefore, all of God, even though all professed. Of course it is obvious that Christ was of the Lord because He was the Lord. But, at the same time, those who opposed Him were of Satan, and despite their claims to the contrary!

(32) "FOR JOHN CAME UNTO YOU IN THE WAY OF RIGHTEOUSNESS, AND YE BELIEVED HIM NOT: BUT THE PUBLICANS AND THE HARLOTS BELIEVED HIM: AND YE, WHEN YE HAD SEEN IT, REPENTED NOT AFTERWARD, THAT YE MIGHT BELIEVE HIM."

The phrase, *"For John came unto you in the way of Righteousness, and ye believed him not,"* proclaims the veracity of the Prophet, as well as the Message he proclaimed, i.e., *"The Way of Righteousness."*

In effect, Christ is saying that the Pharisees were promoting a way of self-righteousness, which could not be accepted by God. John's presentation of *"Righteousness"* was from the Lord, and the only type that God would accept, but which the Pharisees would not accept.

The words, *"And ye believed him not,"* are emphatic, meaning that the Holy Spirit dealt with them, even with this Scriptural *"Way of Righteousness"* presented so succinctly. In other words, they could not deny what was being said, not only from the Scriptures, or the change brought about in the lives of those who yielded to the entreaty of the Holy Spirit. So, their unbelief was a studied, willful unbelief. They not only rejected the conviction, but they rejected the *"way."*

The phrase, *"But the publicans and the harlots believed him,"* which proclaims them admitting what they were, and, thereby, seeking God for help, Redemption, and His Way of Salvation. That is the reason they went into the *"Kingdom of God"* before these Religious Leaders. In effect, the Religious Leaders did not go in at all, but died eternally lost.

The phrase, *"And ye, when ye had seen it, repented not afterward, that ye might believe him,"* is a startling statement indeed!

The idea is that the Pharisees saw the result of the changed lives brought about by God's *"Way of Righteousness,"* and despite that infallible proof, still would not believe! Consequently, the Holy Spirit holds up this proof as irrefutable, and what will always accompany the True Gospel, i.e., changed lives.

In the last few years, I have marveled as I have watched this scene reacted over and over again, even in our own Ministry.

Despite the tremendous number of people who have come to Christ under this Ministry, whose lives have been gloriously and wondrously changed and are obvious for all to see, still, almost all the Religious Leaders reject this proof, even as the Pharisees rejected the same proof of long ago.

Why?

The same spirit of unbelief and self-righteousness that characterized the Religious Leaders of Jesus' day, characterizes their counterparts presently!

(33) "HEAR ANOTHER PARABLE: THERE WAS A CERTAIN HOUSEHOLDER, WHICH PLANTED A VINEYARD, AND HEDGED IT ROUND ABOUT, AND DIGGED A WINEPRESS IN IT, AND BUILT A TOWER, AND LET IT OUT TO HUSBANDMEN, AND WENT INTO A FAR COUNTRY:"

The phrase, *"Hear another parable,"* was, once again, directed toward the Pharisees. As the former, it would be a parable they did not desire to hear. However, by their efforts to snare Christ, they have placed themselves in a position to where they have no alternative or choice but to hear what He has to say. To be sure, He will pull no punches, making it unmistakably clear as to exactly what and who He is talking about. I wonder how many Preachers presently have the boldness to preach as Christ did?

The phrase, *"There was a certain householder,"*

is meant in this parable to represent God the Father. It begins in this manner so as to proclaim to all Who the Vineyard belongs to. In effect, Israel had attempted to wrest control from Him to themselves.

Regrettably, the modern Church follows suit in that it abrogates to a great degree the Headship of Christ. Christ is an active Head of the Church, and not a passive Head, as many seem to believe. So, immediately, Christ will let these *"Chief Priests and Elders"* know exactly as to Who owns the Vineyard.

The phrase, *"Which planted a Vineyard,"* represents two things:

1. The Lord had gone to much difficulty and trouble in planting this Vineyard, as is evidenced throughout the Old Testament, with the call of Abraham and David, etc. The Vineyard did not come into being on its own, but was the result of a planned, purposely designed program of Salvation.

2. The Vineyard illustrates the Kingdom of Heaven which was entrusted to the Jews, and was meant to yield fruit in order to be a great blessing not only to the Jews, but to the entirety of the world (Mat. 21:43; Mk. 12:1-9; Lk. 20:9-19; Rom. 3:1-2; 9:1-5).

The phrase, *"And hedged it round about,"* refers to the protection that the Lord gave it in His watchful care and provision, so that it would be free from the intrusion of wild beasts, i.e., demon spirits, who would attempt to destroy the fruit of the Vineyard.

The phrase, *"And digged a winepress in it,"* illustrates all the institutions and means of blessings for the entirety of the human race.

The phrase, *"And built a tower,"* represents the place and position of watchmen who were to serve as protectors of the Vineyard, i.e., the Prophets, etc.

The phrase, *"And let it out to husbandmen,"* illustrates Israel who had charge of the Vineyard to render unto the Householder the fruit in due season.

Consequently, Jesus tells this parable in a way that all would understand, reducing the great Plan of God to street terms.

The phrase, *"And went into a far country,"* refers to the Lord giving the rulership of Israel and His Great Plan on earth into the hands of Prophets and Kings. Regrettably, there were not many of the Prophets or the Kings who

NOTES

were Godly, which would bring about the related events.

(34) "AND WHEN THE TIME OF THE FRUIT DREW NEAR, HE SENT HIS SERVANTS TO THE HUSBANDMEN, THAT THEY MIGHT RECEIVE THE FRUITS OF IT."

The phrase, *"And when the time of the fruit drew near,"* illustrates the seasons in which the Lord expected results from the Jews in extending the Kingdom among other nations and doing those things required to bring the knowledge of God to others.

The phrase, *"He sent His servants to the husbandmen,"* refers to the Old Testament Prophets, Priests, and Teachers, that the Jews may know the way and do it.

The phrase, *"That they might receive the fruits of it,"* pertains to a set course of action, which, if followed, would definitely have rendered fruit.

As we have repeatedly stated, one of the primary tasks of Israel was to evangelize the world. Of course, to do this they would have to minutely follow the Lord, in effect, being a holy nation. But as it obvious, they miserably failed, and, consequently, brought forth no fruit of Evangelism. Actually, instead of showing the surrounding nations the way, they, instead, became like the other nations, which ultimately necessitated their destruction.

(35) "AND THE HUSBANDMEN TOOK HIS SERVANTS, AND BEAT ONE, AND KILLED ANOTHER, AND STONED ANOTHER,"

The *"servants"* representing the Godly Prophets, were subject to much abuse in Israel, consequently, enduring beatings and stonings, with some of them being killed.

For instance, with Judah standing on the very trembling edge of destruction, Jeremiah, the Prophet, was kept from death only by the preserving Hand of the Lord. If Judah had had her way, she would have killed this Prophet, the last one, in effect, sent to warn her of impending doom.

(36) "AGAIN, HE SENT OTHER SERVANTS MORE THAN THE FIRST: AND THEY DID UNTO THEM LIKEWISE."

The word, *"Again,"* further emphasizes the patience of the Lord, along with the increased number of Prophets sent to Judah the last 200 years before her defeat and destruction by the Babylonians. This is emphasized by the phrase,

"More than the first." (The most powerful Prophets such as Isaiah, Jeremiah, etc., were sent at that time.)

But tragically, the phrase, *"And they did unto them likewise,"* proclaims the nation growing increasingly harder. To sin against light does not leave one static, but, instead, worse! In other words, with each rejection of the Prophets sent by the Lord, their spiritual condition steadily deteriorated.

The writer of II Chronicles said, *"But they mocked the messengers of God, and despised His Words, and misused His Prophets, until the wrath of the Lord arose against His people, till there was no remedy"* (II Chron. 36:16).

(37) "BUT LAST OF ALL HE SENT UNTO THEM HIS SON, SAYING, THEY WILL REVERENCE MY SON."

The phrase, *"But last of all He sent unto them His Son,"* refers to John 3:16.

The Lord now brings the parable from the past to the present. The Religious Leaders listening to Christ, would have no doubt remonstrated greatly against Israel for her treatment of the Prophets, claiming that they would never have done such a thing. However, the Lord ushers them from this hypocrisy to the present, which will outline the wickedness of their evil hearts by proclaiming what they will do.

The phrase, *"Saying, They will reverence My Son,"* is said for many reasons, which surely seemed that such would be done.

Jesus absolutely fulfilled all the Prophecies concerning His birth and genealogy. As well, the miracles He performed were so outstanding that mere words could never begin to describe them. In other words, there was absolutely no reason that even the most spiritually illiterate among them could not know Who Jesus was, i.e., the Messiah. But the Truth is, they did not *"reverence God's Son,"* but actually treated Him with the worst type of contempt, and ultimately killed Him.

(38) "BUT WHEN THE HUSBANDMEN SAW THE SON, THEY SAID AMONG THEMSELVES, THIS IS THE HEIR; COME, LET US KILL HIM, AND LET US SEIZE ON HIS INHERITANCE."

The phrase, *"But when the husbandmen saw the Son,"* is a far stronger term than appears on the surface. It means that all the things we have mentioned, proof concerning His Virgin Birth, His genealogy, His fulfillment of Scripture, plus all the miracles, were seen, witnessed, and observed by them, but with a willful studied rejection. They *"saw"* the Son of God, and they could have known that Jesus was the Son, but unbelief prevailed!

They threw off the operation of the Holy Spirit, refusing to admit the proof that stared them in the face, and made a conscious, willful decision to their course of murder and rebellion.

The phrase, *"They said among themselves,"* proclaims a studied consultation, with plans made, not only to not accept God's Son, but, in reality, to kill Him.

The phrase, *"This is the heir,"* means that they not only knew exactly Who He claimed to be, but, as well, they knew He fit every Scriptural description. In other words, the proof was obvious, and beyond the shadow of a doubt, that He was *"The Son of God."*

The phrase, *"Come, let us kill Him,"* proclaims their murderous intent!

Why?

The phrase, *"And let us seize on His inheritance,"* gives us the answer, i.e., self-will.

Even though these individuals were the Religious Leaders of Israel, and as such claimed to be keepers of the Law of God, and, in fact, talked about God constantly, still, in reality, they were working for Satan. They were what Paul would later call, *"Satan's ministers"* (II Cor. 11:15).

As such, they were *"angels of light,"* and were able to deceive the people (II Cor. 11:14).

Consequently, Satan would project through *"his ministers,"* an alternate plan of Salvation, which, in reality, was no Salvation at all!

To do this, they had to have supremacy over the minds and consciences of the people, in effect, lording it over God's heritage.

They saw Jesus as the greatest threat to their hold over men, and if He was allowed to continue, they would lose their places as rulers, teachers, men of influence, as well as their authority over the people and their chief business. Incidentally, their chief business was ruling the people, occupying high places and position, and making lots of money!

They imagined that if they could destroy Christ, they could continue in their possession of the inheritance. They killed that they might possess, but killing was the road to their sure destruction.

NOTES

Religion is never content to allow God to have His Way, but, instead, seeks earnestly to control all people in their domain. Hence, Religious Denominations will go to almost any lengths to protect what they consider to be theirs. They will steal, slander, and even kill, that is, if the Law of the land allows. If they cannot kill physically, they will do all within their power to kill by slander.

(39) "AND THEY CAUGHT HIM, AND CAST HIM OUT OF THE VINEYARD, AND SLEW HIM."

The phrase, "And they caught Him," refers to that which will take place just hours from the time that Christ is uttering these words.

The phrase, "And cast Him out of the Vineyard," means that they not only killed Him, but, as well, excommunicated Him, in effect, claiming to Israel that He was an imposter, and that He died lost without God. Having branded Him as a heretic, a blasphemer, and a deceiver, they now felt justified in anything they did.

The phrase, "And slew Him," was done only after they had pronounced their curses upon Him, which in their minds legitimized their hideous action of murder.

As stated, they felt justified in what they were doing because they did it all in the Name of God.

This is the reason that the actions of religious men can be so murderous, evil, and wicked! They do what they do in the Name of God, thereby cloaking themselves in a garment of false piety, claiming to greatly regret what has to be done, but, nevertheless, pursuing its bloody end with relish and zeal!

However, it should be quickly noted that as these reprobates had no power to condemn Christ, likewise, no other man has that power as well! It does not matter what the Church so-called might say, or how many may voice their approval at such action, still, God is the Judge, and no other! Men cannot put one into the Kingdom of God, and men cannot take one out of the Kingdom of God.

(40) "WHEN THE LORD THEREFORE OF THE VINEYARD COMETH, WHAT WILL HE DO UNTO THOSE HUSBANDMEN?"

The phrase, "When the Lord therefore of the Vineyard cometh," proclaims a finality, which these hypocrites, at least at the moment, have not quite grasped.

NOTES

In other words, the Lord is pointedly telling them that such will not be allowed to continue, especially considering the great lengths gone to in order to secure the Vineyard.

The question, "What will He do unto those husbandmen?", is spoken directly to the "Chief Priests and Elders."

The words, "Those husbandmen," are emphatic, actually dripping with contempt!

The evidence is that at the moment they are not quite sure where He is going with this, and, consequently, will continue to bite until they hang themselves.

(41) "THEY SAY UNTO HIM, HE WILL MISERABLY DESTROY THOSE WICKED MEN, AND WILL LET OUT HIS VINEYARD UNTO OTHER HUSBANDMEN, WHICH SHALL RENDER HIM THE FRUITS IN THEIR SEASONS."

The phrase, "They say unto Him," presents them being drawn into the net, in which they will actually condemn themselves. Actually, their answer will be perfect. No one could have said it better.

The phrase, "He will miserably destroy those wicked men," proclaims exactly as to what is going to happen, with them little realizing, at least at this time, that they are speaking of themselves.

The phrase, "And will let out His Vineyard unto other husbandmen," is exactly what happened! The Lord turned from the Jews to the Gentiles (Acts 10).

The phrase, "Which shall render Him the fruits in their seasons," has proven to be exactly correct.

While it is true that the modern Church, at least for the most part, is Apostate, still, there is a Remnant which is not Apostate, and, consequently, is the True Body of Christ. It is made up of all Believers, whomever they may be, and in whatever Church organization they may be ensconced. It is this True Body of Christ that provides the "fruits in their seasons."

Actually, Israel was divided accordingly, at least in a spiritual sense. There was Apostate Israel, and there was the small True Remnant, who truly loved God, and attempted to follow Him. Regrettably, this Remnant became smaller and smaller, until there were not enough left to salvage the people and the nation.

Israel was "miserably destroyed" in 70 A.D.

by the Roman General Titus and his tenth legion. Over 1,000,000 Jews were killed, with well over 100,000 being crucified. As well, several hundreds of thousands of others were sold as slaves for trifling prices all over the world.

Also, they have wandered as outcasts among the nations of the world since that time, only becoming a nation once again in 1948, and this as a direct result of Bible Prophecy.

(42) "JESUS SAITH UNTO THEM, DID YE NEVER READ IN THE SCRIPTURES, THE STONE WHICH THE BUILDERS REJECTED, THE SAME HAS BECOME THE HEAD OF THE CORNER: THIS IS THE LORD'S DOING, AND IT IS MARVELLOUS IN OUR EYES?"

The phrase, *"Jesus saith unto them,"* presents Him about to spring the trap, but which is not meant in that way, but rather as a final warning. He will appeal to Scripture, which they professed to believe.

The question, *"Did ye never read in the Scriptures . . . ?"*, draws them directly to the Word of God on which everything is based. In other words, the Lord is telling them that it doesn't really matter what they think or say, but, instead, what the Scriptures say about it.

In fact, they claimed to be masters of the Scriptures, so, consequently, they should have known what it said about the coming Messiah, so there was no excuse for their ignorance.

The phrase, *"The Stone which the builders rejected,"* is taken from Psalm 118:22-23. The Stone spoken of was the cornerstone on which the superstructure rested, which was the most important stone in the building.

Tradition says that the builders of Solomon's Temple left out the cornerstone because they did not understand the head architect's plans. It is said that this stone was found later, and was found to be that on which the completeness of the structure depended — on which the two walls met and were bonded together. The Messiah of these Jews was compared to this stone. Christ warned them not to make the same mistake that the builders of the Temple had made.

The phrase, *"The same is become the Head of the corner,"* refers to everything hinging on Christ. He was the Law and He is Grace. Without Him the Law degenerated, which it did, into a meaningless burden grievous to be borne.

Without Jesus, Grace, in effect, is no Grace

at all! Consequently, Christianity is not a philosophy as religions are, but, instead, a relationship with a Man, the Man Christ Jesus.

I have had the privilege of ministering many times in the country of South Africa. A particular Jewish lady in that country told our Office Manager how much she enjoyed our Ministry.

She stated as to how the music was such a blessing to her, and especially the preaching. However, she objected to my strong promotion of the Lord Jesus Christ. She said to my Office Manager, Isaac Locke, *"Tell Brother Swaggart to go lightly on Jesus, and he will possibly win many more Jews."* In other words, she was saying that they did not believe in Jesus, and my strong emphasis on Him was an affront to them, etc.

When he humorously related this to me, my answer was: *"Jesus is my Song; Jesus is my Message; Jesus is my Power; Jesus is my Strength; Jesus is my All in All."* In other words, if Jesus were taken out, that which she enjoyed and was a blessing to her would be lost as well! He Alone is the *"Head of the corner."*

To accept Christianity without Christ, which is what actually happens in too many cases, is to accept nothing but a meaningless philosophy. Tragically, much of the modern Church has attempted to divorce Christ from Christianity. Little by little He has been relegated to an inferior position or no position at all. Consequently, as Israel of old, the individual who does such a thing is left with nothing at all.

The phrase, *"This is the Lord's doing,"* means that Jesus Christ as the *"Head of the corner,"* is the direct plan of Jehovah. As well, when He is rejected, Jehovah is rejected!

So, Israel was left with nothing, despite their claims. That is the reason that much of that which calls itself *"Christianity"* is, basically, nothing!

The phrase, *"And it is marvellous in our eyes,"* means that even though Israel did not think it marvellous at all, with almost all of the world following suit, still, Jesus, as the Head of the corner, is *"the Lord's doing,"* and, as such, it is *"marvellous"* beyond words!

The moment that men begin to look at Christ, they find their way.

(43) "THEREFORE SAY I UNTO YOU, THE KINGDOM OF GOD SHALL BE TAKEN FROM YOU, AND GIVEN TO A NATION BRINGING FORTH THE FRUITS THEREOF."

The phrase, *"Therefore say I unto you,"* presents Christ after proclaiming the sin, now proclaiming the punishment.

The phrase, *"The Kingdom of God shall be taken from you,"* once again presents *"you"* as emphatic. They know exactly of whom He is speaking.

This means their special place as God's chosen people has been abrogated, which resulted in them losing everything.

Consequently, and in grand style, these wicked Religious Leaders proved the statement of Christ, that in *"saving their lives they lost them"* (Mat. 16:25).

The phrase, *"And given to a nation bringing forth the fruits thereof,"* refers to the Gentiles, of which most of the Church consists, who took the place of the Jews in the Gospel Program (Acts 13:46-49; 15:13-18; Rom. 10:19-11:26).

The *"fruits"* spoken of consists of World Evangelism, i.e., the taking of the Gospel to the world.

The Church, although not nearly as proficient as it should be in this respect, still, has managed to touch a great part of the world with the Gospel of Jesus Christ. This proclaims to us — the fruits — the priority of God. It is the proclamation of the greatest story every told, and the taking of it to the whole world. Regrettably, a great part of the modern Church is expending its energy on other things, such as the prosperity message, i.e., getting rich, or the political message, i.e., getting certain men and women elected to high public office, which is construed in this erroneous gospel as *"Evangelism."*

The Lord's method of Evangelism, which is the only one that matters, is the preaching of the Gospel to a lost and dying world (Mk. 16:15). Any other method is an abrogation of God's method, and, consequently, becomes the work of Satan.

(44) "AND WHOSOEVER SHALL FALL ON THIS STONE SHALL BE BROKEN: BUT ON WHOMSOEVER IT SHALL FALL, IT WILL GRIND HIM TO POWDER."

The phrase, *"And whosoever shall fall on this Stone shall be broken,"* does not mean as some have claimed, that they will be saved, but rather the opposite.

In fact, the entirety of this Passage speaks of Judgment, and severe Judgment at that!

The idea is that those who found in Christ's low estate, *"a stone of stumbling and rock of*

offense," would destroy themselves, *"shall fall on,"* and because of their opposition.

The phrase, *"But on whomsoever it shall fall, it will grind him to powder,"* refers to those who put themselves in active opposition to Him and His Kingdom. They will be destroyed without hope of recovery, and will include every religion of the world.

The *"grinding to powder,"* portrays all such philosophies being totally destroyed without any chance of resurrection.

This coincides with the words of the Psalmist, *"Kiss the Son, lest He be angry, and ye perish from the way, when His Wrath is kindled but a little. Blessed are all they that put their trust in Him"* (Ps. 2:12).

(45) "AND WHEN THE CHIEF PRIESTS AND PHARISEES HAD HEARD HIS PARABLES, THEY PERCEIVED THAT HE SPAKE OF THEM."

The phrase, *"And when the Chief Priests and Pharisees had heard His parables,"* now mentions the Pharisees who actually made up the majority of the Sanhedrin, and guided the spiritual life of Israel.

The phrase, *"They perceived that He spake of them,"* means that their motive and conduct was now fully discovered, with there being absolutely no doubt as to whom He was speaking.

(46) "BUT WHEN THEY SOUGHT TO LAY HANDS ON HIM, THEY FEARED THE MULTITUDE, BECAUSE THEY TOOK HIM FOR A PROPHET."

The phrase, *"But when they sought to lay hands on Him,"* proclaims the wickedness of their evil hearts.

It is amazing as to how men can reject the Lord. This parable told them exactly who they were, and what they were thinking in their hearts, but yet, they did not allow this amazing perception as given by the Holy Spirit to bring them to repentance, but, instead, they hardened their hearts even further.

They grew exceedingly angry, and if the opportunity had presented itself, they would have arrested Him then and there.

Even after all had been said and done, and even with unmistakable evidence, they still would not believe that He was the Messiah, the Son of God.

Why not? Especially considering that the evidence was unmistakable!

Unbelief is an insidious thing, and is predicated on prejudice, bias, and self-will. The very nature of unbelief demands that evidence has been presented, and in overwhelming amounts, but yet rejected. Its very nature demands a willful, studied rejection. They closed their eyes, ears, and minds to all proof, purposely setting themselves on a course from which there was no return.

The phrase, *"They feared the multitude,"* was the only restraint, because their evil hearts would have killed Him then, had the opportunity presented itself.

The phrase, *"Because they took Him for a Prophet,"* spoke of the multitude, and not the Pharisees and Chief Priests, etc.

Going back to the 32nd verse, the drunks knew, but they, the Religious Leaders of Israel, did not know!

CHAPTER 22

(1) "AND JESUS ANSWERED AND SPAKE UNTO THEM AGAIN BY PARABLES, AND SAID,"

This will be the parable of the Marriage Feast.

Mark insinuates that after the parable of the householder, that the Pharisees and others of such ilk left. However, even though no doubt that happened, still, more than likely they quickly returned. Jesus now given this parable, directed at *"them,"* even as this first verse proclaims.

This is the third parable given to the Jews in the Temple, and will continue in the same vein.

This parable teaches the great doctrines of the Love of God, the Wrath of God, the Deity of Christ, the need of His justifying Righteousness, and the eternal doom of the self-righteous.

(2) "THE KINGDOM OF HEAVEN IS LIKE UNTO A CERTAIN KING, WHICH MADE A MARRIAGE FOR HIS SON."

The *"King"* is God the Father, and *"His Son"* is the Lord Jesus Christ.

The *"Marriage"* concerns the Church being married to Christ. In this case, the Church includes all in the great Plan of God, even from the very beginning, including the Jews and the modern Church, etc.

(3) "AND SENT FORTH HIS SERVANTS

TO CALL THEM THAT WERE BIDDEN TO THE WEDDING: AND THEY WOULD NOT COME."

The phrase, *"And sent forth His servants to call them that were bidden to the wedding,"* represents all the Prophets, as well as John the Baptist, and even the Disciples of Christ who were sent by Him to minister in Israel during the time of His earthly sojourn.

The word, *"them"* refers to Israel, and concerns the great invitation given to them first of all to become a part of the *"Kingdom of Heaven."*

The phrase, *"And they would not come,"* refers to Israel's rejection of the Prophets and even of their Messiah. The phrase proclaims a studied and deliberate rejection.

(4) "AGAIN, HE SENT FORTH OTHER SERVANTS, SAYING, TELL THEM WHICH ARE BIDDEN, BEHOLD, I HAVE PREPARED MY DINNER: MY OXEN AND MY FATLINGS ARE KILLED, AND ALL THINGS ARE READY: COME UNTO THE MARRIAGE."

The phrase, *"Again, He sent forth other servants,"* could well refer to the ministry of the Apostle Paul as well as the Disciples, after the Resurrection and Ascension of Christ.

The phrase, *"Tell them which are bidden,"* respects a studied invitation directed personally to the people of Israel. The first few Chapters of the Book of Acts will bear this out.

The phrase, *"Behold, I have prepared my dinner: my oxen and my fatlings are killed, and all things are ready,"* concerns itself with time that is running out. The word, *"Behold,"* emphasizes this fact, and even places a strong sense of urgency upon the invitation.

The phrase, *"Come unto the marriage,"* respects the very last invitation given to the Jews to accept that which God had provided, His Only Son, the Lord Jesus Christ.

This last invitation could well have been given by the Apostle Paul when he stood before the Jewish Sanhedrin as is recorded in Acts 23. Their answer to his message was, *"They would neither eat nor drink till they had killed Paul"* (Acts 23:12). They were not able to do so, but it was only for lack of opportunity.

(5) "BUT THEY MADE LIGHT OF IT, AND WENT THEIR WAYS, ONE TO HIS FARM, ANOTHER TO HIS MERCHANDISE:"

The phrase, *"But they made light of it,"* concerns Israel's response to the Gospel. They not only rejected it, but, as well, held it up to mockery, scorn, and ridicule.

The phrase, *"And went their ways,"* concerns exactly what it says, *"Their ways, instead of God's Ways."*

The phrase, *"One to his farm, another to his merchandise,"* respects what that way was, at least for this group.

Israel had no interest in the Gospel, they were more interested in money. Concerning the Ministry of Christ, the Scripture says, *"And the Pharisees also, who were covetous* (hungry for money and power), *heard all these things: and they derided Him"* (Lk. 16:14). This spirit continues to characterize Israel unto this day.

(6) "AND THE REMNANT TOOK HIS SERVANTS, AND ENTREATED THEM SPITEFULLY, AND SLEW THEM."

The phrase, *"And the Remnant took his servants,"* concerns the portion of Israel, who not only had no desire for the things of God, but, as well, actively opposed the Gospel and the bearers of that Light.

The phrase, *"And entreated them spitefully, and slew them,"* concerns the Apostles, who tradition says, all died martyrs deaths with the exception of John the Beloved. As well, unnumbered others, whose names are not mentioned in early Church history, but nevertheless paid the supreme price, the giving of their lives.

In fact, the times of the Early Church as recorded in the Book of Acts, was glorious to say the least. However, it was also a time of intense persecution with many giving their lives, exactly as here proclaimed.

(7) "BUT WHEN THE KING HEARD THEREOF, HE WAS WROTH: AND HE SENT FORTH HIS ARMIES, AND DESTROYED THOSE MURDERERS, AND BURNED UP THEIR CITY."

The phrase, *"But when the King heard thereof, he was wroth,"* concerns the response of the Heavenly Father toward those who had so brutally mistreated His servants, and rejected His invitation.

God's anger is always a righteous anger, and is not quickly manifested, as these Passages portray. Actually, tremendous patience is shown and over a long period of time, respecting rejection and even outright hostility. However, there will come a time, as here, that the

anger of God will manifest itself, and to be sure it is not something to be taken lightly.

In the coming Great Tribulation Period, the Scripture says, *"For the Great Day of His Wrath is come; and who shall be able to stand?"* (Rev. 6:17).

Even though this parable addresses itself primarily to the Jewish people, still, it will apply to the entirety of mankind in the very near future. Despite much of the modern Church denying the coming of Daniel's 70th week, the Great Tribulation, this period of time is very shortly to come upon this world.

For nearly 2,000 years, the Gospel has been proclaimed over a great part of this planet, and despite the glorious Truth that many have accepted, still, the far greater majority have conducted themselves in the same manner as Israel of old. They have met the Gospel with rebellion and hostility. Consequently, the Wrath of God is about to be poured out upon this world which has forgotten God days without number.

The phrase, *"And He sent forth His armies,"* actually respects the Roman Army that the Lord would use to carry out His Will.

The phrase, *"And destroyed those murderers, and burned up their city,"* speaks of the Roman General Titus and his Tenth Legion, which destroyed Jerusalem in 70 A.D. Over 1,000,000 Jews died in this carnage, with hundreds of thousands of others sold as slaves all over the world.

Jesus called Israel *"murderers,"* which they were! They murdered God's Son, as well as many of the Apostles and countless others!

"Their city was" Jerusalem. It was once His city, now theirs, and would consequently be destroyed.

(8) "THEN SAITH HE TO HIS SERVANTS, THE WEDDING IS READY, BUT THEY WHICH WERE BIDDEN WERE NOT WORTHY."

The phrase, *"Then saith He to His servants,"* proclaims a change of action. The Plan of God is not halted, only its direction.

The phrase, *"The wedding is ready,"* is spoken in a manner that lets us know the wedding will go on as planned, but with a change of guests.

The phrase, *"But they which were bidden were not worthy,"* concerns Israel which rejected the clarion call of the Gospel, which proved themselves to be unfit subjects, and hence, *"not worthy."*

Luke writes, *"Then Paul and Barnabas waxed bold, and said, It was necessary that the Word of God should first have been spoken to you: but seeing ye put it from you, and judge yourselves unworthy of everlasting life, lo, we turn to the Gentiles"* (Acts 13:46).

Even though, and as stated, this pertains to Israel of old, still, the principle continues to hold true with all of God's dealings.

If particular Religious Denominations will not accept the Move of God, the Lord simply moves on past them, and pours out His Spirit on those who will accept it. Consequently, most, if not all, of the old-line Religious Denominations are bereft of any semblance of a Move of God whatsoever! Jesus has simply *"removed their candlestick out of His place"* (Rev. 2:5).

Sadly and tragically, the modern Pentecostal Denominations which were once recipients of the mighty Move of God, and because it was rejected by those just mentioned, are now, at least for the most part, rejecting it themselves. I say this with no joy, and I pray there is still time for repentance, for that is the only thing that will save them. Jesus said, *"Except thou repent!"* (Rev. 2:5).

Regrettably, most of the modern Pentecostal and Charismatic efforts are attempting to substitute other things such as religious phenomenon in place of Bible Repentance. However, there is no substitute for Repentance!

(9) "GO YE THEREFORE INTO THE HIGHWAYS, AND AS MANY AS YE SHALL FIND, BID TO THE MARRIAGE."

The phrase, *"Go ye therefore into the highways,"* now concerns itself with the entirety of the world. In other words, Israel is no longer the focus, but the entirety of mankind.

Actually, God's Plan has always been for the entirety of mankind (Jn. 3:16), with Israel serving as a recipient of the Grace of God, and, thereby, giving it to the entirety of the world. However, Israel would not only not give it to the world, but would not even receive it herself.

Consequently, the Plan of God, at least as far as its over-all complexion is concerned, did not change, only its direction.

The phrase, *"And as many as ye shall find, bid to the marriage,"* saw its beginning with Peter preaching to the household of Cornelius,

as recorded in Acts 10. From then on, and especially with the Ministry of the Apostle Paul, a general evangelization was begun, with the major thrust pointed toward the Gentiles.

Of course, the thrust of the Gospel now includes all, both Jew and Gentile, and which in reality was supposed to have been all the time.

(10) "SO THOSE SERVANTS WENT OUT INTO THE HIGHWAYS, AND GATHERED TOGETHER ALL AS MANY AS THEY FOUND, BOTH BAD AND GOOD: AND THE WEDDING WAS FURNISHED WITH GUESTS."

The phrase, *"So those servants went out into the highways,"* concerns the beginning of World Evangelism as initiated by the Apostle Paul. It should be obvious to all, especially when reading the Book of Acts, that God's priority in His Great Plan is the taking of the Gospel to those who have not had the privilege to hear it. From the moment and time of the Early Church *"servants,"* i.e., Missionaries and Evangelists have been going out into the *"highways"* in order to proclaim the greatest story ever told. This is the thrust of the Holy Spirit, and whenever it ceases to be the major thrust in our lives and Churches, that is the greatest sign of all that we are losing our way with God.

The phrase, *"And gathered together all as many as they found,"* concerns the Gospel invitation given to everyone. None are excluded; none are placed in an inferior position; none are to be ignored.

The phrase, *"Both bad and good,"* proclaims a like invitation, but, as well, and more importantly, proclaims that the *"good"* needs Salvation, the same as the *"bad"*!

Actually, the manner in which the language proclaims this statement, *"bad and good,"* means that the designation is man's and not God's. In other words, even though men may designate some as *"good,"* still, in the eyes of God they need Salvation just as much as those who men may label as *"bad"*! Consequently, all are placed in the same category, as the word, *"both,"* means!

Men have little difficulty in understanding that the *"bad"* need Salvation, but have great difficulty in understanding that the *"good"* are in such need as well! Man does not understand that that which he labels as *"good"* is not labeled thusly by God. The Lord actually labels man's self-righteousness, i.e., *"good,"* as filthy rags (Isa. 64:6).

The phrase, *"And the wedding was furnished with guests,"* respects the redeemed who will be made up of both Jews and Gentiles.

In its stricter interpretation, the Jews, at least as a whole, did not desire to be a part of the wedding, so, consequently, it was open to the Gentiles, as stated, which the Lord intended from the very beginning, which *"furnished"* the house.

(11) "AND WHEN THE KING CAME IN TO SEE THE GUESTS, HE SAW THERE A MAN WHICH HAD NOT ON A WEDDING GARMENT:"

The phrase, *"And when the King came in to see the guests,"* respects the custom of those days. It was customary for hosts to come in and see their guests after they were assembled.

The phrase, *"He saw there a man which had not on a wedding garment,"* refers to a *"wedding garment"* supplied by the King.

Irrespective as to who the guests were, they were not allowed to wear their own *"wedding garments,"* as beautiful as they may have been, but must wear the *"wedding garment"* supplied by the King. The meaning is clear.

The ones who had on the *"wedding garments"* supplied by the King, are those who have accepted Christ's Salvation, and not depended on their own good works, etc.

The man who did not have on the King's *"wedding garment,"* but, instead, supplied his own, could not be accepted, as his own wedding garment typified self-righteousness, i.e., his own way of Salvation. Consequently, this man could not be accepted, and, in Truth, none can be accepted who refuse the *"wedding garment,"* i.e., Righteousness of the King, i.e., The Lord Jesus Christ.

In its strict interpretation, this *"man"* refers to Israel, who would not accept the *"wedding garment"* furnished by Christ, but demanded that they be able to use their own, and were summarily cast out.

However, it can, and in fact does, refer to any and all who refuse God's Way of Salvation, attempting to substitute their own. Regrettably, this *"Man which had not on a wedding garment"* furnished by the King, constitutes a huge number, even in modern Christendom.

(12) "AND HE SAITH UNTO HIM, FRIEND, HOW CAMEST THOU IN HITHER NOT HAVING A WEDDING GARMENT? AND HE WAS SPEECHLESS."

NOTES

The phrase, *"And he saith unto Him, Friend,"* is not spoken in kindness, but rather distrust. The word, *"Friend,"* actually has the opposite meaning than normally used. It is the same word used by Christ when confronting Judas at the betrayal (Mat. 26:50).

It means that he claimed to be God's Friend, but he really was not!

The question, *"How camest thou in hither not having a wedding garment?",* in effect says, *"How did you think you could come into this marriage feast wearing your own wedding garment, which is totally inappropriate, and refusing the one I have freely offered?"*

It speaks of a willful rejection of God's Righteousness, and, instead, parading self-righteousness as a sufficient covering.

The phrase, *"And he was speechless,"* proclaims this man deeming his own garment good enough for the feast; and it suited very well until the King came in, then was he exposed and cast out.

Self-righteousness may compare quite favorably between men. However, when compared to the Righteousness of Christ, i.e., His furnished wedding garment, it is woefully inadequate.

Regrettably, much of the Church is fond of comparing with others. Nevertheless, even though approved of men, it can never be approved of God. No Righteousness, i.e., wedding garment, furnished by man will be accepted by God, and irrespective of its claimed beauty. Only the Righteousness furnished by Christ is acceptable!

As this *"man"* was *"speechless,"* likewise, all of humanity who trusted in themselves will be *"speechless"* at the *"Great White Throne Judgment."* Man has no defense; there is no way he can justify himself.

(13) "THEN SAID THE KING TO THE SERVANTS, BIND HIM HAND AND FOOT, AND TAKE HIM AWAY, AND CAST HIM INTO OUTER DARKNESS, THERE SHALL BE WEEPING AND GNASHING OF TEETH."

The phrase, *"Then said the King to the servants,"* represents the Wrath demonstrated in the doom of the man not having *"the wedding garment"*; and it is the same doom as that of the men who murdered the servants and the son of the householder (21:41).

The phrase, *"Bind him hand and foot, and take him away,"* proclaims the Kingship and Godhead of the Son of Man.

In the parable of the prior Chapter (vss. 43-46), the Sonship of Christ is declared. This, as stated, affirms His Kingship and Godhead. As the Son, He has the bride, and as the King He comes in to see the guests, and as God He has power to cast into hell. He is at once the King and the King's Son (Ps. 72:1).

The phrase, *"And cast him into outer darkness, there shall be weeping and gnashing of teeth,"* refers to the end of those who attempt to effect their own salvation by their self-righteousness. As bluntly as it sounds, the end result is hellfire.

The *"servants"* mentioned in this verse, are not Prophets and Preachers, but, instead, the Angels of God, etc.

(14) "FOR MANY ARE CALLED, BUT FEW ARE CHOSEN."

The phrase, *"For many are called,"* does not refer to a select number, but really to the entirety of the human family. It is referred to as *"many"* because it is *"many"*! It means that every man, woman, boy, and girl in the world is *"called"* to the *"marriage feast,"* i.e., Salvation in Christ.

Love invites the *"many,"* that is, all, and provides a wedding garment free for everyone, welcoming sinners into Heaven's highest joys, and — most wonderful of all — regards those justly expelled as *"the many"* which they are, and the residue as *"the few"*; for love is not willing that even one should perish.

The phrase, *"But few are chosen,"* are those who are called, as the others, and who humbly accept Christ as their Righteousness, which the others would not do!

The many who are called, but not chosen, are the self-righteous. They are not *"chosen,"* because they do not *"choose"* God's Plan of Salvation, the Righteousness of Christ.

(15) "THEN WENT THE PHARISEES, AND TOOK COUNSEL HOW THEY MIGHT ENTANGLE HIM IN HIS TALK."

The phrase, *"Then went the Pharisees,"* speaks of the self-righteous hypocrites who Christ was speaking of in verses 11-14. Jesus is in the Temple when He is uttering these parables, along with the Pharisees. They now leave Him, knowing that He is speaking these parables of them (21:45).

The phrase, *"And took counsel how they might entangle Him in His talk,"* includes the Herodians, the Sadducees, and the Pharisees who tried to entrap Him in some statement that would give Him into the power of either the civil or religious authorities, but they failed.

It would seem by now that they would realize that it was impossible to *"entangle Him"* in His talk. In all of the exchanges with Him, they had not even come close to their intended goal, but, instead, had always found themselves greatly humiliated.

(16) "AND THEY SENT OUT UNTO HIM THEIR DISCIPLES WITH THE HERODIANS, SAYING, MASTER, WE KNOW THAT THOU ART TRUE, AND TEACHEST THE WAY OF GOD IN TRUTH, NEITHER CAREST THOU FOR ANY MAN: FOR THOU REGARDEST NOT THE PERSON OF MEN."

The phrase, *"And they sent out unto Him their disciples with the Herodians,"* concerns another well-laid trap, which will again be turned on their own heads.

Even though the Herodians and Pharisees hated each other, they made now an unholy alliance for the purpose of attacking Jesus.

There were actually three major parties in Israel:

1. Herodians: These were a political sect which supported the dynasty of Herod, and were more or less favorable to the dominion of Rome, as that was what preserved their authority in the country.

These individuals were not very religious, and advocated freedom to conform to pagan religion as well as to Judaism if it was more convenient and if it helped further their political fortunes and secular gain.

These would have been called the worldlings of this present time.

2. Sadducees: These individuals were a rationalistic sect who denied the supernatural, Angels, demons, and Resurrection. Most of the high religious offices in Israel were held by them.

They would have been called the modernists of our present time.

3. Pharisees: These were a sect of self-righteous and zealous Jews who held to the letter of their interpretations of the Law of Moses and to their own traditions, regardless of whether they nullified the Word of God or not. They were bitter enemies of Christ.

They would have been called the fundamentalists of our day.

The words, *"Saying, Master,"* begin the flattering approach to Christ. If one is to notice, none of these individuals ever referred to the Lord by His Name of *"Jesus."* The word, *"Master,"* simply meant *"Teacher."*

The phrase, *"We know that Thou art true,"* was exactly right, but yet not actually believed by these hypocrites. As stated, they were using flattery, completely misunderstanding the character of Jesus.

The phrase, *"And teachest the Way of God in Truth,"* was again totally correct, but yet a statement which they did not believe.

The phrase, *"Neither carest Thou for any man: for Thou regardest not the person of men,"* was again exactly right! However, it was something they did not believe.

They were only using this type of terminology in order to appeal to His ego, hoping He would answer their question in a way which would cause the Roman authorities to come down on His Head.

As stated, they did not know or understand the character of Christ. His character was one of *"meekness and lowliness,"* and not one of ego at all!

(17) "TELL US THEREFORE, WHAT THINKEST THOU? IS IT LAWFUL TO GIVE TRIBUTE UNTO CAESAR, OR NOT?"

The question, *"Tell us therefore, What thinkest Thou?",* is designed, as previous questions, to trap Him irrespective as to which way He answered.

The question, *"Is it lawful to give tribute unto Caesar, or not?",* was a question that now raged in Israel.

Had He said it was not lawful to pay tribute, they would at once have denounced Him to the Government.

Had He said it was lawful, He would have denied His claim as Messiah, the King of Israel.

Caesar, at this time, was Tiberius. The *"tribute"* here spoken of, was the poll-tax levied by the Romans to pay for the occupation troops, etc.

By asking concerning the lawfulness of the payment, they did not inquire whether it was expedient or advisable, but, instead, whether it was morally right!

As stated, this question was being debated by the religious parties of Israel, with some refusing to pay it, such as some of the Pharisees,

with others submitting without hesitation, such as the Herodians.

In their thinking, whichever way He answered, would cause Him great problems!

(18) "BUT JESUS PERCEIVED THEIR WICKEDNESS, AND SAID, WHY TEMPT YE ME, YE HYPOCRITES?"

The phrase, *"But Jesus perceived their wickedness,"* pertains to the hypocrisy which prompted their question.

They had no desire to have the true answer to this question, only to snare Christ and make Him look bad before the people, or even to be arrested by Rome.

The Holy Spirit, no doubt, informed Him exactly as to their design, and, as well, the answer to the dilemma.

Regarding their hypocrisy, such was obvious!

The question, *"And said, Why tempt ye Me, ye hypocrites?",* strikes at the very heart of the matter.

Little did these *"hypocrites"* realize it, but the character to which they had flatteringly given to Jesus, would prove all too true!

(19) "SHEW ME THE TRIBUTE MONEY. AND THEY BROUGHT UNTO HIM A PENNY."

The phrase, *"Shew Me the tribute money,"* referred to the coin in which the tribute was paid. His response was totally unexpected!

They were expecting a long dissertation, or maybe even embarrassed silence, but, instead, He requests a coin, which throws them completely off guard.

The phrase, *"And they brought unto Him a penny,"* was a coin worth approximately $2 in 1995 money. They no doubt handed Him the coin, which He took!

(20) "AND HE SAITH UNTO THEM, WHOSE IS THIS IMAGE AND SUPERSCRIPTION?"

The phrase, *"And He saith unto them,"* will once again supply an answer no doubt given to Him by the Holy Spirit, and which would answer their question, but, as well, provide a foundation of teaching regarding this subject for all time.

The question, *"Whose is this image and superscription?",* probably pertained to the image of Tiberius which was on the coin.

Actually, at this time the Jews had no coins of their own, and were forced to use Roman coins.

(21) "THEY SAY UNTO HIM, CAESAR'S. THEN SAITH HE UNTO THEM, RENDER

THEREFORE UNTO CAESAR THE THINGS WHICH ARE CAESAR'S; AND UNTO GOD THE THINGS WHICH ARE GOD'S."

The phrase, *"They say unto Him, Caesar's,"* respects Christ not taking any side whatsoever in the controversy which then raged concerning independence for Israel.

The phrase, *"Then saith He unto them, Render therefore unto Caesar the things which are Caesar's,"* answers several things:

1. Lawful government is here recognized, and support for government approved. As stated, Jesus was not taking sides in the matter respecting Israel's freedom from the subjection of Rome, which raged at that time, but was simply saying that government had to be supported, whether it was agreed with or not, and for obvious reasons.

Without government there is anarchy. Actually, civil government is ordained by God, with its foundation being given to Noah after the flood (Gen. 9:1-7).

This does not mean that God approves of bad government, which He, in fact, does not! It just simply means that government is ordained of God, and must be supported (Rom. 13:1-7).

This also means that local, state, and federal taxes, as grievous as they sometimes may be, must be paid by Christians. To be sure, the Christian has the right and the obligation to make government better by involvement.

2. There are certain things which belong to Caesar, i.e., government, and must be rendered to him. This speaks of the payment of taxes, as stated, and allegiance, as far as is possible.

Actually, the Early Church, just a little later, would face unjust and unscriptural laws made by Caesar, which they could not accept or obey. For instance, there came a time in the Empire, not long after the ascension of Christ, that Caesar demanded that he be called *"Lord."* Christians could not do this, instead saying, *"Jesus is Lord."* Consequently, multiple thousands died in the Roman arenas, torn by wild beasts, etc., simply because they would not obey this particular law.

And yet, if a law made by government, and no matter how distasteful or unfair, does not violate the Word of God and therefore one's conscience, it must be obeyed.

3. Human government, as stated, is in the Plan of God. He has determined that human

governments shall exist to help Him carry on moral government and enforce moral laws. They are appointed by God, but He is not responsible for their acts. If the government becomes unjust, the Lord will judge them, just as He will judge all.

Governments are instituted by God to guarantee freedom of the people, but, as well, to use force and to punish if necessary. This is to be carried out on individual criminals, but also universal and national criminals. This includes execution of war to put down criminal nations, as well as criminal individuals (Dan. 2:21; 4:17-25; 5:21; Rom. 13:1-5; I Pet. 2:13-17).

This means that America and other nations are Scriptural in putting down criminal nations such as Iraq under Saddam Hussein, etc.

It means that America and other nations were Scripturally right in their opposition to Germany and Japan in World War II. It was Scriptural to use whatever force was necessary to put down this terrible evil in the world. However, for such to be engaged, the cause must be just and the position Scripturally right.

As well, and as stated, Christians are not to leave popular government up to the ungodly. To neglect good government is to neglect the Salvation of souls.

Christians should vote and enter public life to promote good government so that the Gospel will not be hindered and stamped out. Both reason and experience, as well as the Bible make this obligatory upon all. Since government is necessary for the best good of all, it is the duty of every Christian to help bring about the best government to secure this end.

Human governments, therefore, are not founded upon the arbitrary Will of God, but upon the needs of humanity in securing their highest good.

If in a small family law and penalties are needed, how much more are they needed in communities, states, and nations.

If government needs reformation, then let the Christians bring about such reforms. If government requires nothing contrary to God, moral obligation and the conscience, and if they meet the needs of those governed, they should be perpetuated (Rom. 13:1-6).

Upon the grounds of the best public interests, it becomes the duty of human governments to use all necessary means to attain this end. It is absurd to believe that rulers have the right to govern, and not the right to use the necessary means to carry on good government. Such error or belief causes many Christians to object to the right of capital punishment, the right to deal with mobs, to suppress rebellion, and to make wars on criminal nations.

When a person or nation sells himself or itself to destroy the best good of others, it becomes necessary to take him or it from the society, or the community of nations he or it seek to destroy.

In such cases it becomes necessary to deal with these individuals, as well as bandit nations, to enforce law and order for the best good of all.

Rulers are God's Ministers to execute God's Wrath upon the ungodly and to preserve moral law and government for the good of all (Rom. 13:1-6; I Pet. 2:13-17).

The phrase, *"And unto God the things that are God's,"* refers to that which belongs to God, which actually pertain to ourselves — our life, powers, faculties, and means.

Actually, Jesus is teaching that there need be no conflict between God and Caesar. Of course, that does not hold true in all cases, as it would not hold true with Caesar just a little later, and as previously stated.

Consequently, if Caesar's Law abrogates God's Law, God's Law must be obeyed in preference to Caesar's Law. Of course, the consequences will have to be suffered, but better to give one's life, than to lose one's soul.

America's method of separation of Church and State is, I believe, Scriptural. However, this does not mean a separation of God and State, as some are attempting to do.

The Church has to do with particular organizations and Religious Denominations which should be separate from the State, and the State separate from it. However, at the same time, allegiance to God must reside in the spirit and fabric of government. Otherwise it becomes wholly a secular State, denying God, which abrogates His Blessings.

The State needs the help of God just as well as any and all other fabric of life.

Jesus here proclaims that allegiance to both can be maintained, even with great blessing to both, providing the Scripture is adhered to. If a citizen does his duty to God, he will find his obligations to the civil government also, at least

most of the time, coincident and harmonious. If the State respects the rights of God and of conscience, there will be no collision between itself and the Worship of God.

Actually, had the Jews rendered to God His dues, they would never have been reduced to their present state of subjection and debasement. They would never have had to pay tribute to a foreign nation.

Somebody has well said, that as long as the Gospel of Jesus Christ is the greatest commodity exported from the shores of America, that the jack-booted heel of foreign invaders will never pound American soil.

Actually, Jesus is saying that if a person *"renders unto God the things that are God's,"* he will, at the same time, *"render unto Caesar the things which are Caesar's,"* at least that which does not violate Scripture.

(22) "WHEN THEY HAD HEARD THESE WORDS, THEY MARVELLED, AND LEFT HIM, AND WENT THEIR WAY."

The phrase, *"When they had heard these words,"* even though brief, constituted some of the greatest teaching of all time.

In this short statement, a new sphere of government was introduced, which was completely novel to the Jews, the two spheres of Church and State to be distinct and not be joined. Under the Mosaic Law, the Church and the State, that is if we can use such terminology, were one and the same. He here proclaims that the two are distinct, and should be treated accordingly, consequently, proclaiming that which would begin in the very near future, at least that which pertained to the True Work of God.

(In countries where the State and Church are enjoined, there is very little freedom to render to God that which is due God. As well, even in countries which have a State Church, but, in fact, also allows freedom of worship, as in England, still, such is unscriptural.)

The phrase, *"They marvelled,"* means they were left speechless, actually overwhelmed by the wisdom of His answer. They had no answer in return. There was nothing in His Words they could condemn; nothing treasonable, nothing unpatriotic.

The phrase, *"And left Him, and went their way,"* does not pertain to conversion, but the opposite! While it is true they were silenced, still, their evil hearts were not changed.

To prove the case of their evil hearts, they had the brass to accuse Jesus of forbidding to pay tribute to Caesar at a later date (Lk. 23:2).

(23) "THE SAME DAY CAME TO HIM THE SADDUCEES, WHICH SAY THAT THERE IS NO RESURRECTION, AND ASKED HIM,"

The phrase, *"The same day came to Him the Sadducees,"* completes the Trinity of the three parties of Israel — Pharisees, Herodians, and Sadducees.

They too will present to Him a question, which they feel has no answer. It seems that they, as well, are very slow to learn!

The phrase, *"Which say that there is no Resurrection, and asked Him,"* proclaims the utter spiritual bankruptcy of these pretenders. They claimed to believe the Pentateuch, but like many modernists, they refused to accept the supernatural upon which the Scriptures are built.

They did not believe in a future life of the soul, or the resurrection of the body. Consequently, they would ply Christ with a question which they felt would reduce to an absurdity the doctrine of the Resurrection.

(24) "SAYING, MASTER, MOSES SAID, IF A MAN DIE, HAVING NO CHILDREN, HIS BROTHER SHALL MARRY HIS WIFE, AND RAISE UP SEED UNTO HIS BROTHER."

The phrase, *"Saying, Master, Moses said,"* proclaims these individuals studying the Bible, not for it to mold their lives, but, instead, for their thinking to mold and twist its teaching. They are not unlike many today who study the Bible attempting to make it conform to their doctrines, instead of allowing their doctrines to be conformed to its teaching.

The phrase, *"If a man die, having no children, his brother shall marry his wife, and raise up seed unto his brother,"* is taken from Deuteronomy 25:5-10.

The indication seems to be that the unmarried brother is to take his dead brother's place, marrying the widow, with the first son born to that union carrying the name of the dead brother. In this manner the family name would continue, with both families surviving, that of the dead brother and of the live brother who had married the widow.

This was only under the Old Covenant, and was not carried over into the New Covenant. It was done because of Israel's unique position in

NOTES

the Plan of God. In this Plan, the land was of extreme importance, because it was where God dwelt, as well as each allotment per family. The families were, above all, of supreme importance. The Messiah was to come through one of these families, which, in effect, was the family of David in the Tribe of Judah. Irrespective, each and every family in each and every Tribe was to play their part in taking the Gospel to the world. Regrettably, they failed, as is here portrayed!

(25) "NOW THERE WERE WITH US SEVEN BRETHREN: AND THE FIRST, WHEN HE HAD MARRIED A WIFE, DECEASED, AND, HAVING NO ISSUE, LEFT HIS WIFE UNTO HIS BROTHER:"

The phrase, *"Now there were with us seven brethren,"* is not the presentation of an actual case, but, instead, hypothetical.

The phrase, *"And the first, when he had married a wife, deceased,"* is a continuation of the story, as will become obvious.

The phrase, *"And, having no issue, left his wife unto his brother,"* continues the scenario.

(26) "LIKEWISE THE SECOND ALSO, AND THE THIRD, UNTO THE SEVENTH."

The scenario, as revolting and unlikely as it may be, is carried through until all seven brothers have been the husbands of one wife.

(27) "AND LAST OF ALL THE WOMAN DIED ALSO."

Now their little tale has concluded, and they plan to have a laugh at Jesus' expense concerning the Resurrection.

(28) "THEREFORE IN THE RESURRECTION WHOSE WIFE SHALL SHE BE OF THE SEVEN? FOR THEY ALL HAD HER."

The question, *"Therefore in the Resurrection whose wife shall she be of the seven?",* springs the trap, which they believe has no answer, because, so they teach, there is no Resurrection. They think their question repudiates any Resurrection, for if the doctrine was genuine, at least in their thinking, how could this matter be resolved?

The phrase, *"For they all had her,"* concluded the scenario.

To be sure, this was not a question that had been generated in the last few days, but one that had raged for many years. The Rabbis taught that if a woman has two husbands in this life, she will have the first only in the next life. However, this was only speculation, with no Scriptural foundation, and was not adhered to by many, with most not knowing the answer at all.

Inasmuch as this question had been debated for many years, even centuries, the Sadducees felt smug in their contest with Christ. In their minds, all the others may have failed, but they will succeed. The brightest theological minds had not been able to give a satisfactory answer to this perplexity, therefore, they were certain that Jesus could do no better. They would see that their certainty was not so certain after all!

(29) "JESUS ANSWERED AND SAID UNTO THEM, YE DO ERR, NOT KNOWING THE SCRIPTURES, NOR THE POWER OF GOD."

The phrase, *"Jesus answered and said unto them,"* portrays these things which seemed to be so unanswerable to others as simple for Him, and rightly so!

In fact and Truth, there was no question that any human being could have put to Him that He could not have answered. This was so, even though He was Very Man, and with all of man's limitations. But yet, He was filled with the Holy Spirit beyond measure (Jn. 3:34).

As such, He had perfect knowledge, and because He perfectly knew the Scriptures.

The phrase, *"Ye do err, not knowing the Scriptures,"* once again portrays Him going to the foundation of all knowledge, the Word of God.

Had they known the Scriptures, and especially about Him, they would have known that the Psalmist had written, and about Christ, *"Thou through Thy Commandments hast made Me wiser than Mine enemies: for they are ever with Me."*

As well, they would have known, *"I have more understanding than all My teachers: for Thy Testimonies are My meditation."*

And then, *"I understand more than the ancients, because I keep Thy precepts"* (Ps. 119:98-100).

So, they were speaking to the most brilliant, knowledgeable, and enlightened Individual Who ever lived. His knowledge was so far beyond theirs that it defied description.

I realize that many would not think that extraordinary simply because Jesus was God. While that is certainly true, Very God, nevertheless, His brilliance, wisdom, and understanding did not come from His position as Deity, for all of that was voluntarily laid aside (Phil. 2:6-7).

NOTES

Consequently, it was as a man, and a man only, in which He gained His super-intelligence. It came from two sources, which are available to all: A. The Holy Spirit; and, B. The Scriptures.

Of course, the knowledge, wisdom, and brilliance we speak of, pertains to that which addresses itself to *"Life and Godliness"* (II Pet. 1:3).

The question could be asked as to how far this knowledge extended? Did it cover modern-day understanding of physics, advanced mathematics, chemistry, etc.? Even though these matters are not addressed in the Gospels, still, I personally feel that the knowledge of Christ in all things, even including modern-day scientific advancement (true science), and technology, would have exceeded by far the most brilliant minds of our time.

While it is true that He did not address Himself to these things, and for two reasons:

First of all, it wasn't God's time for scientific and technological advancement to be introduced, and, as well, those questions really did not lead to the true problems of man, which were spiritual (Dan. 12:4).

Man's problem is sin, and his need is a Saviour. That Saviour is Christ. A man can be a brilliant scientist, and yet be a moral wreck. He can also be rich and fall into the same category. Consequently, Christ came to address Himself to man's true problem, which was sin, and to bring the solution, which was His Death at Calvary, and the Resurrection.

These Sadducees, even as the Pharisees, simply did not know the Scriptures, or they would not have asked such foolish questions.

Once again, allow us to declare that Christ always pointed men to the Scriptures.

The phrase, *"Nor the Power of God,"* addresses itself to the denial by the Sadducees of the supernatural. As stated, they had divorced the supernatural from the Scriptures, which, by and large, left them with nothing.

Tragically, this sin did not die with the Sadducees, as the majority of the Church world presently does the same thing. Paul said, *"They have a form of Godliness, but deny the power thereof"* (II Tim. 3:5).

Christianity without the *"Power of God"* is just another philosophy. With the *"Power of God,"* it is the most powerful life-changing principle the world has ever known.

(30) "FOR IN THE RESURRECTION THEY

NEITHER MARRY, NOR ARE GIVEN IN MARRIAGE, BUT ARE AS THE ANGELS OF GOD IN HEAVEN."

The phrase, *"For in the Resurrection,"* first of all proclaims that the Doctrine of the Resurrection is a valid Scriptural Doctrine, which is guaranteed by the Power of God.

Actually, there are two Resurrections which will take place in the future:

1. The Resurrection of Life: This pertains to every single Believer who has ever lived from the time of Adam extending through the Coming Great Tribulation.

While the bodies of the sainted dead go back to dust, the soul and the spirit immediately go to be with Christ at death (Phil. 1:23).

(Before Christ, all Believers upon death, went into Paradise which was in the heart of the earth, at least as far as their soul and spirit were concerned. At the Resurrection of Christ, which was a guarantee of the Resurrection of all Believers, these were liberated from this prison and taken to Heaven, Lk. 16:19-31; Eph. 4:8-9.)

The Rapture of the Church is actually the Resurrection (I Thess. 4:13-18). Then the Saints of God of all ages will receive a Glorified Body, which will be indestructible and eternal (I Cor. 15:50-56).

2. The Resurrection of Damnation: This Resurrection will take place approximately a thousand years after the First Resurrection. It will include all of the ungodly dead who have ever lived.

When the ungodly die, their soul and spirit automatically go to hell (Lk. 16), with their bodies going back to the dust of the earth exactly as the Godly, i.e., those who have accepted Christ.

At the Great White Throne Judgment, the Second Resurrection of Damnation will take place, with eternal bodies given to the souls and spirits of the ungodly, who will then live forever in eternal torment (Rev. 20:4-6, 11-15).

The Doctrine of the Resurrection, both for the Godly and ungodly, is one of the cardinal doctrines of the Bible.

The phrase, *"They neither marry, nor are given in marriage,"* completely debunks the idea as taught by some Rabbis of the wife having the first of two husbands in the next life, etc.

Jesus here teaches that there will not be marriage in the Resurrection, i.e., the next life. Consequently, earthly ties, as here known, will

NOTES

not exist then, but will be on an entirely different plain.

While it is true that all Believers at that time will have perfect knowledge, which will include knowledge of the husband, wife, children, parents, etc., which was prevalent in this life, but will then be on a higher plain in the Resurrection (I Cor. 13:12).

The purpose of marriage is several-fold.

1. To replenish the earth.

2. To keep the race going, which would otherwise be extinguished because of death.

3. The union of husband and wife is meant to serve as an example or symbol of Christ and the Church.

In the Resurrection, and inasmuch as Saints will not die, there will be no need to marry to keep their kind in existence. Hence, there is no marriage among Angels or resurrected men and women.

Then Christ will be the focal point of all, with everything and every relationship geared to Him.

The phrase, *"But are as the Angels of God in Heaven,"* is referred to only in the sense of Angels not having to marry to keep their kind in existence, because Angels do not die. The Resurrected Saints will be identical.

Consequently, Jesus also proclaims the existence of Angels, which the Sadducees denied.

As an aside, there is nothing said in this Passage about Angels being sexless. Actually, every indication is that all Angels are of the male variety.

It seems clear from Scripture that of some of the Angels who fell with Lucifer, some of them did leave their own first estate and marry the daughters of men, producing a race of giants (Gen. 6:1-4).

That they who did commit fornication are now in hell is clear in Jude 6-7 and II Peter 2:4. Actually, Angels are capable of many human activities.

(31) "BUT AS TOUCHING THE RESURRECTION OF THE DEAD, HAVE YE NOT READ THAT WHICH WAS SPOKEN UNTO YOU BY GOD, SAYING,"

The phrase, *"But as touching the Resurrection of the dead,"* will take the Sadducees to the very Books they felt which were inspired, the Pentateuch, and from these Five Books prove the Doctrine of the Resurrection.

The question, *"Have ye not read that which*

was spoken unto you by God, saying…?", shows the total inadequacy of these individuals concerning the Scriptures.

In fact, Christ is proving His statement, *"Ye do err,"* meaning that all are sure to err who do not know the Scriptures.

The Sadducees were like so many presently, who know the letter of the Bible, but know nothing of the Spirit of the Word of God. Actually, the key to the interpretation of the Scripture is Faith. It is not enough to be acquainted with the literal signification; this is always inadequate, and denotes not the chief matter intended.

To fully know the Scriptures, one must fully know Christ, which these Sadducees did not, nor the Pharisees, hence, their unbelief.

Christ will here proceed to demonstrate how the very Pentateuch, which was reverenced by this party, and which they deemed to be entirely silent on the subject of the life of the soul, but, in fact, will speak plainly on this matter to all who had Faith to understand and appreciate the Words of Divine Wisdom.

(32) "I AM THE GOD OF ABRAHAM, AND THE GOD OF ISAAC, AND THE GOD OF JACOB? GOD IS NOT THE GOD OF THE DEAD, BUT OF THE LIVING."

The phrase, *"I am,"* actually constitutes the Doctrine of the Resurrection. Jesus, in effect, is the Resurrection and the Life (Jn. 11:25).

The full phrase, *"I am the God of Abraham, and the God of Isaac, and the God of Jacob,"* is taken from Exodus 3:6 and 16.

As stated, the Sadducees held that the Books of Moses were the only Scriptures. Even though this was wrong, Christ would use them to prove His point.

The statement, *"God is not the God of the dead, but of the living,"* portrays the fallacy of the great Plan of God being built and predicated on *"the dead,"* i.e., having no existence. Such would be foolishness! Consequently, the Doctrine of the Resurrection, as stated, is the very foundation of the Faith.

In effect, the Lord is saying that these men, *"Abraham, Isaac, and Jacob,"* were then alive, and, in fact, are still alive, and will be ever alive.

Jesus here teaches the immortality of the soul and that God is the God of all departed souls. In Luke it is stated that *"all live unto Him"* (Lk. 20:38).

NOTES

Many other Scriptures teach immortality of the soul (Isa. 14:9; Mat. 17:3; Lk. 16:19-31; 23:43; II Cor. 4:18; 5:8; Eph. 4:8-10; Phil. 1:21-24; Heb. 12:22-23; I Pet. 3:4; 4:6; Rev. 6:9-11).

As we have stated, at death, it is actually only the body which dies, with the soul and spirit continuing to live, whether with Christ or in hell.

Regrettably, a great part of the world continues to believe as the Sadducees, that man really does not have a soul and spirit, or if he does, it dies along with the body at death, consequently, ceasing to exist. Of course, most who believe that, do not believe there is a God, and only looks at man as a higher form of animal life.

To believe there is a God, one as well must believe in His creation. As well, He has a plan for that creation. Man is created in God's Image, and, as such, he lives forever, whether eternally lost or eternally saved (Jn. 3:16).

Because of the Fall in the Garden of Eden, man lost his way, actually incurring upon himself eternal death, which means separation from God, and not cessation of existence. However, Jesus came to set men free from this terrible bondage of death, i.e., separation from God, and, in fact, restored man's dominion, and made it possible for him to have eternal life. This was done by Christ dying on Calvary, thereby, paying the price for man's Redemption, and then being raised from the dead.

Consequently, this is what Jesus meant when He said, *"God is not the God of the dead, but of the living."* He meant, and as stated, that the great investment He had made was not made in those who had ceased to exist, which would be a fruitless exercise, but, instead, that they may live forever with Christ.

(33) "AND WHEN THE MULTITUDE HEARD THIS, THEY WERE ASTONISHED AT HIS DOCTRINE."

The phrase, *"And when the multitude heard this,"* constitutes a Truth which opened up the Scriptures in a fashion they had never known before, and especially concerning one of the great foundation doctrines of the Bible, the Resurrection.

The phrase, *"They were astonished at His Doctrine,"* constitutes a double meaning.

1. They were *"astonished"* at the simplicity of what He said concerning the Resurrection, and by using examples from the Word of God which were so simple, and should have been

even to them so obvious! What point would Jehovah have in referring to individuals who had lived long before, such as Abraham, Isaac, and Jacob, if, in fact, they were dead and had actually ceased to exist? To be the God of something that did not exist, was of no consequence. Therefore, the continued statement of Jehovah, *"I am the God of Abraham . . . ,"* was actually saying, and which should have been so obvious, that these were not men who had ceased to exist, but were rather alive, even at that very moment!

As stated, when Jesus pointed it out, it became so obvious that as Luke noted, some of the Scribes who were undoubtedly of the Pharisees and, consequently, no friend of Christ, but overwhelmed by His Truth, cried out, *"Master, Thou hast well said!"* (Lk. 20:39).

2. Christ not only unfolded this cardinal Doctrine of the Resurrection, but, as well, dug deep into the hearts of these adversaries, exposing the cause of their error. Men who act as the Pharisees and Sadducees of old, interpreting the Scripture falsely, do so because their hearts are wicked and evil.

(34) "BUT WHEN THE PHARISEES HAD HEARD THAT HE HAD PUT THE SADDUCEES TO SILENCE, THEY WERE GATHERED TOGETHER."

The phrase, *"But when the Pharisees had heard that He had put the Sadducees to silence,"* should have served as a warning to them, but, instead, from their wicked hearts they went deeper into rebellion.

As we have repeatedly stated, Who Christ was should have been so obvious. However, the hearts of these wicked hypocrites could not be shown the True Ways of God, irrespective of what was done.

When men are wrong in their hearts, they cannot see God in anything. Irrespective of what He does, it is lost upon them, and because they are dishonest, wicked, and rebellious. In other words, the entirety of their being is opposed to God, which means they are opposed to His Ways, even though they are loudly trumpeting as to how spiritual they are!

The phrase, *"They were gathered together,"* means that both the Pharisees and Sadducees continued their amalgamation against Christ, even though they normally hated each other.

The awfulness of the actions of these men, even though the Religious Leaders of Israel,

NOTES

should be a warning to all as to how easy it is to fall into a state of rebellion, and ultimately lose one's soul.

(35) "THEN ONE OF THEM, WHICH WAS A LAWYER, ASKED HIM A QUESTION, TEMPTING HIM, AND SAYING,"

The phrase, *"Then one of them, which was a lawyer, asked Him a question,"* actually refers to a Scribe. These individuals, as formerly stated, were copyists, preservers, and interpreters of the Law.

The Scribe, as a person of education and means, was able to wear fine garments with a pen-case or *"ink horn"* hanging from his girdle (Ezek. 9:2). His equipment included reed-pens; a small knife for erasures and cutting papyrus, and, in some cases, styli for writing in the cuneiform script. They were supposed to be experts and scholars in the Law of Moses.

The phrase, *"Tempting Him, and saying,"* probably refers more to the Pharisees than this particular Scribe. Mark says that Jesus somewhat commended him, which would have placed him in a somewhat different category than all the others. Even though he was fronting for the Pharisees and Sadducees, still, there is some evidence that he, at least as far as his own person was concerned, was open, forthright, and honest.

(36) "MASTER, WHICH IS THE GREAT COMMANDMENT IN THE LAW?"

The title, *"Master,"* portrays Jesus once again alluded to as a Teacher.

The question, *"Which is the great Commandment in the Law?",* concerned itself with great theological discussions which raged at that particular time.

The Law of Moses had been so dissected and added to, that the Scribes and Pharisees claimed that there were now 614 Commandments. There were 249 affirmative Commandments, and 365 negative Commandments. Consequently, it is easy to see how the Religious Leadership of Israel had become bogged down in the letter of the Law, while altogether missing the Spirit of the Law.

They considered the breaking of some of these Commandments to be grievous, while others were of little consequence. In effect, this is what James was speaking of when he said, *"Whosoever shall keep the whole Law, and yet stumble in one point, he is become guilty of all"* (James 2:10).

(37) "JESUS SAID UNTO HIM, THOU SHALT LOVE THE LORD THY GOD WITH ALL THY HEART, AND WITH ALL THY SOUL, AND WITH ALL THY MIND."

The phrase, *"Jesus said unto him,"* proclaims a forthcoming answer, which will once again proclaim a tremendous Truth. However, *"Truth"* was not what the Pharisees and Sadducees were looking for!

The phrase, *"Thou shalt love the Lord thy God,"* places this as the foundation of all the Law, and, as well, applies to the present Day of Grace.

In this phrase, Jesus uses the title, *"Lord,"* which refers to Covenant, as it prefaces *"God"* as the Creator. Unless one really knows God, which the title *"Lord"* implies, one cannot really love Him. As *"Lord"* implies Covenant, it implies Relationship.

As such, to truly *"love"* Him, is to place Him first in all things.

The phrase, *"With all thy heart, and with all thy soul, and with all thy mind,"* proclaims the manner in which God is to be loved.

The *"heart"* pertains to all inward affections, while the *"soul"* pertains to all consciousness, with the *"mind"* pertaining to all thoughts.

As should be obvious, the manner in which God must be loved claims total allegiance. In other words, if God is not *"Lord"* of all, He is not *"Lord"* at all!

The quotation by Christ is taken from Deuteronomy 6:5, with Jesus once again, as always, going to Scripture for each and every answer.

(38) "THIS IS THE FIRST AND GREAT COMMANDMENT."

Consequently, Jesus answers the man's question as to the *"Great Commandment,"* but, as well, adds to it the word, *"first!"*

Why did He use the word, *"first?"*

It follows that the Love of God must be "first" before anything else can be claimed.

Solomon said, *"Let us hear the conclusion of the whole matter: Fear God, and keep His Commandments: For this is the whole duty of man"* (Ecc. 12:13).

(39) "AND THE SECOND IS LIKE UNTO IT, THOU SHALT LOVE THY NEIGHBOUR AS THYSELF."

The phrase, *"And the second is like unto it,"* takes this dissertation a step further than the Scribe had asked! Jesus gives this because it is very easy for people to say they love the Lord

with all their heart, soul, and mind; however, the second Commandment will serve as the proof.

The phrase, *"Thou shalt love thy neighbour as thyself,"* is actually the proof of whether the first and greatest Commandment is kept.

If Love of God does not show itself in the love of one's neighbor, then our claim is false.

Consequently, the Pharisees and Sadducees, as a result of Jesus' answer, would have been placed in an untenable position.

They claimed to love God, but they hated Christ, and were even then plotting His Death. Therefore, they had no Love of God! Consequently, the following question must be asked:

If a person truly loves the Lord, even as Jesus here commanded, will he slander his neighbor?

As well, if they see their neighbor in need, and as John the Beloved said, *"And shutteth up his bowels of compassion from him, how dwelleth the Love of God in him?"* (I Jn. 3:17).

The question must be asked, as one Scribe did ask (whether the same as this one is not known), *"And who is my neighbour?"*

Jesus answered that question by giving the parable of the Good Samaritan. Consequently, He took it much further than one might think, even referring to rank strangers (Lk. 10:25-37).

So, it is not too difficult to ascertain as to exactly how much love one has for God by looking at one's conduct toward their *"neighbour."*

Someone has well said that the greatest way one can show that one loves God is to love one's neighbor. When we love them, at least in a Christlike way, we are loving God. That should not be difficult to understand.

Man was originally made in God's Image, and is His highest creation. When man fell, he changed allegiance from Jehovah to Satan. However, Satan has been a hard taskmaster. Actually hating man, he steals, kills, and destroys (Jn. 10:10). Consequently, for someone to truly love man, is the same, at least in a sense, of someone truly loving God's children. Allow me to give an illustration.

A particular Preacher in California, who was a relative of one of my dear Preacher friends, had a Ministry of dealing with street children. In other words, he took in homeless young men and young ladies who had lost their way, and by the Grace of God was able to help some of them immeasurably so, even getting their lives straightened out.

One of these young men he greatly helped was of Chinese descent. My acquaintance knew very little about him, but did all he could to help him respecting victory over alcohol and drugs, which was brought about.

One fine day, he was visited by a man of Chinese descent, who introduced himself as this boy's Father.

To be very brief, this man was one of the wealthiest men in Hong Kong, but, in effect, had lost his son. And then miracle of miracles, he regained his son, and found out that the help had been provided by the Preacher of my acquaintance.

For quite some time the Chinese Brother sat there relating to my Preacher acquaintance, as to how grateful he was for what had been done, especially considering that he had come to the place that he didn't feel there was any hope. And then, miracle of miracles, his son was restored to him whole!

He asked my Preacher acquaintance and his wife to come with him, as he had something he desired to do. They did not understand the reason for his insistence, but went along.

He visited several beautiful homes which were for sale, and then at the end of the day turned to them and said, *"Choose the home you like, as I am purchasing it for you!"*

They sat there in open-mouthed astonishment for some time, and then finally selected the least expensive one. He turned to them and said, *"That's what I thought you would do, therefore, I have purchased the nicest one already."*

He told them that the home would remain in his name, but he would pay all insurance, upkeep, and taxes, and they could live in it as long as they desired as their very own.

That may be a crude illustration; however, as this man, even though having little knowledge of the Lord, was so appreciative of what had been done for his son, I think it is obvious as to how the Lord feels respecting those who would help His Children, wayward or not!

(40) "ON THESE TWO COMMANDMENTS HANG ALL THE LAW AND THE PROPHETS."

The phrase, *"On these two Commandments,"* proclaims this argument being settled in Israel once and for all, as to the Greatest Commandment, by adding the second one to it, thereby proving the validity of the *"First Commandment."*

The phrase, *"Hang all the Law and the Prophets,"* as well, includes the New Testament, which is the Great Covenant of Grace.

This answer given by Christ concerning the Great Commandment of the Law, projects Christianity as the most revolutionary concept in all ages. It so far eclipses every religion in the world, that, in effect, there is no contest.

Religions do one of two things:

1. They draw attention to the betterment of self, with little regard for others, as Buddhism, Shintoism, and Confucianism. The same can be said for Hinduism.

2. They teach hate for others, as Islam, etc.

Christianity has as its Founder the Lord Jesus Christ, Who fulfilled the Law. In effect, He was the Law, and, in effect, He was the only One Who could fully keep the Law, which He did! As such, He became our Substitute, with our Salvation demanding that we identify with the price He paid and the victory He won. Consequently, and as repeatedly stated, Christianity without Christ is just another philosophy, or another religion. With Christ, Christianity becomes a living organism, an all-powerful force which changes lives. It is all based on *"Love"* for God and man! Therefore, the foundation of True Christianity is *"Love."*

Consequently, this is the answer, and, in fact, the only answer for race relations, prejudice, bias, and hatred for others. Without the Love of God, it is impossible to love one's brother as oneself. Actually, this hit at the very heart of the Jewish problem, because they hated the Gentiles, thinking themselves to be superior and *"God's chosen."*

(41) WHILE THE PHARISEES WERE GATHERED TOGETHER, JESUS ASKED THEM,"

The phrase, *"While the Pharisees were gathered together,"* refers to Jesus speaking to the great crowd in the Temple, which contained many Pharisees. Actually, the question is directed toward the Pharisees, and not with malice or ensnarement as they had tendered toward Him, but, instead, as an appeal, even one of the last, for them to accept His claims which were so very obvious.

The phrase, *"Jesus asked them,"* will concern itself with the most important question they could be asked, because it concerned the Person of Christ, the Messiah.

As He had taken them into the depths of the Word of God as they had never known before, surely this must have left a mark upon them. They knew, and beyond the shadow of a doubt, that no one in Israel, even remotely so, had the knowledge of the Scriptures that He did. As well, this knowledge not only included the letter, but, as well, the Spirit. In other words, His answers to their questions were unimpeachable, and, as well, probed their hearts deeply. This that is now forthcoming will be the deepest probe of all!

(42) "SAYING, WHAT THINK YE OF CHRIST? WHOSE SON IS HE? THEY SAY UNTO HIM, THE SON OF DAVID."

The question, *"Saying, What think ye of Christ?"*, concerns the Messiah. The Prophets had foretold Him, with Daniel even proclaiming the approximate time of His Coming (Dan. 9:24-26).

As interpreters of the Law, their duty, first of all, was to alert the people as to His Coming in which they all expected Him at this particular time.

As well, they were to know Who He was, and by the Scriptures. Regrettably, they had so twisted the Word of God to suit their own ends, that they little knew its true purpose or meaning. It is the same at present!

The Bible plainly tells us of the Spirit of God being poured out upon humanity in the last days, but most Religious Leaders do not believe it or know it, exactly as the Pharisees of old (Joel 2:28-29; Acts 2:17-18; I Cor. 14:21).

The question, *"Whose Son is He?"*, would be easily answered by them, but as Christ will show, they did not fully understand at all the comport of their answer.

The phrase, *"They say unto Him, The Son of David,"* is the correct answer as outlined in II Samuel Chapter 7.

They knew this, as well as the Prophecy of Isaiah, concerning a Virgin who would conceive (Isa. 7:14); however, they did not fully understand the Incarnation, if at all! In fact, the type of Messiah they were looking for, the conquering Messiah, was a Messiah of their own invention, and not one outlined by the Scriptures.

As David defeated all the enemies of Israel, and, consequently, made the nation great, likewise, they expected the *"Son of David"* to do the same thing.

In Truth, this is what would happen, but in a

spiritual sense. Israel's greatest enemies were not Rome or others, but, instead, her sins. This, *"The Son of David,"* would overcome by defeating the greatest enemy of all, Satan! However, their self-righteousness would not allow them to admit that they needed deliverance from sin. Consequently, neither did they realize that their subjugation to Rome was the result of their sin.

(43) "HE SAITH UNTO THEM, HOW THEN DOTH DAVID IN SPIRIT CALL HIM LORD, SAYING,"

The phrase, *"He saith unto them,"* will now confound them with the question as to the Messiah being David's Son, and David's Lord, i.e., the great mystery of Christ's Humanity and Deity.

The question, *"How then doth David in Spirit call Him Lord, saying…?"*, refers to David making his statement of the next verse under the inspiration of the Holy Spirit. This spoke of the Divine Authority of the Old Testament.

(44) "THE LORD SAID UNTO MY LORD, SIT THOU ON MY RIGHT HAND, TILL I MAKE THINE ENEMIES THY FOOTSTOOL?"

This is quoted from Psalms 110:1, and is a Psalm, as stated, of David. It is referred to seven times in the New Testament (Mat. 22:44; Mk. 12:36; Lk. 20:42; Acts 2:34; I Cor. 15:25; Heb. 1:13; 10:13).

The Phrase, *"The Lord said unto My Lord,"* refers to God the Father speaking to God the Son. It is, as stated, a Prophecy given in Psalms concerning the coming Incarnation, which was fulfilled in Christ, as the balance of this Scripture shall show.

The phrase, *"Sit Thou on My Right Hand,"* refers to Christ being exalted to the highest position in Heaven, which immediately followed the Ascension (Phil. 2:9-11).

The phrase, *"Till I make Thine enemies Thy footstool,"* refers to all enemies being put down during the Millennium and at its conclusion (I Cor. 15:24-28; Eph. 1:10).

(45) "IF DAVID THEN CALLED HIM LORD, HOW IS HE HIS SON?"

This is the question that would help them understand the Incarnation, as well as His fulfillment of Bible Prophecy as the Messiah.

He, as these Passages and others bear out, was not so much trying to prove His claim of Messiahship, as much as He was pointing out the Scriptures which proved His position. They claimed to believe the Scriptures, therefore, He drew them to the Scriptures, which He would have done in any case.

The answer to this question is that He is David's Lord because He is God; He is David's son because He became man through Mary of the House of David (Lk. 1:34-35; 3:23-38).

As stated, this one question presents to them the Truth of His Incarnation, God becoming Man, as no other question or Passage in Scripture.

There is no way they can refute His claims! The evidence is irrefutable, as the evidence is obvious! He is the *"Son of David,"* and He is *"Lord!"* At the same time, it can be reversed and be equally true, He is *"Lord"* and He is the *"Son of David!"*

(46) "AND NO MAN WAS ABLE TO ANSWER HIM A WORD, NEITHER DURST ANY MAN FROM THAT DAY FORTH ASK HIM ANY MORE QUESTIONS."

The phrase, *"And no man was able to answer Him a word,"* means that they could not refute His arguments. As they did not desire to accept Him, and even though the evidence was irrefutable, they simply held their peace.

The phrase, *"Neither durst any man from that day forth ask Him any more questions,"* portrays these individuals finally realizing that His Spiritual and Scriptural intelligence far exceeded anything they had ever seen or known, and that they were continuing to look even worse in the eyes of the people with each confrontation.

So, they will cease all such activity, casting about for another method to silence Him. They would soon be rewarded with the perfidiousness of Judas.

How evil these religious individuals were! How ungodly and how wicked!

I realize the reader may tire of my repetition; however, religion is no different now than it was then. The cold-blooded calculations of these wicked hypocrites, even though mouthing the name of God constantly, in Truth, did not know Him at all! They were, as Jesus has said, *"Blind leading the blind, with all falling in the ditch."*

Regrettably and sadly, it has not changed even unto the present.

CHAPTER 23

(1) "THEN SPAKE JESUS TO THE MULTITUDE, AND TO HIS DISCIPLES,"

There is every evidence that Jesus is still in the Temple, and will now make a pronouncement of startling clarity!

The Jesus of this Chapter is not the Jesus of most books or of the fashionable pulpit, for this Jesus denounced woes upon the clergy of the Hebrew Church, and in terrific language condemned them to the damnation of hell (vs. 33).

The first 12 verses are addressed to the Disciples and the multitude; the remainder to the Scribes and Pharisees.

As well, the stinging accusations brought, will be to the faces of the Pharisees, and in front of the people.

(2) "SAYING, THE SCRIBES AND THE PHARISEES SIT IN MOSES' SEAT:"

The *"Scribes"* and *"Pharisees"* are singled out, because the Sadducees were not looked at as teachers of the Law, which they were not, and were never recognized as spiritual leaders.

To *"Sit in Moses' seat,"* means that they claimed to be the interpreters of the Law of Moses for the people. This Jesus did not deny!

Some think that there were only about 7,000 Pharisees in Israel at this particular time. Nevertheless, making up most of the Sanhedrin, the ruling body, and, consequently, serving as interpreters of the Law, they were, in effect, the leaders of Israel, and especially in a spiritual sense.

However, as the following will show, Christ blames the spiritual deterioration of Israel upon these individuals, and will now denounce them in no uncertain terms, and publicly!

(3) "ALL THEREFORE WHATSOEVER THEY BID YOU OBSERVE, THAT OBSERVE AND DO; BUT DO NOT YE AFTER THEIR WORKS: FOR THEY SAY, AND DO NOT."

The phrase, *"All therefore whatsoever they bid you observe, that observe and do,"* respected a correct interpretation of the Law of Moses, and not their glosses, additions, and evasions. They were to be respected only so far as their correct handling and interpretation of the Law was carried out.

The phrase, *"But do not ye after their works,"* is meant to distinguish between their preaching and their practice. The latter is to be avoided and shunned at all cost! In other words, they did not at all live what they preached.

The phrase, *"For they say, and do not,"* portrays their hypocrisy.

They loudly trumpeted their knowledge of

the Law, and their strict observance of it, but, in reality, they did not keep it at all, rather grossly violating it. They talked a good game, but that's about as far as it went!

Regrettably, this latter phrase, *"For they say, and do not,"* makes up a great majority of the modern Church, and, sadly, has probably characterized all of us at one time or the other.

However, there is a vast difference in a heart which cries out to God, although, at times, falling short, than a heart which has no desire for God, but actively seeks, as these Scribes and Pharisees, a way of corruption.

(4) "FOR THEY BIND HEAVY BURDENS AND GRIEVOUS TO BE BORNE, AND LAY THEM ON MEN'S SHOULDERS; BUT THEY THEMSELVES WILL NOT MOVE THEM WITH ONE OF THEIR FINGERS."

The phrase, *"For they bind heavy burdens and grievous to be borne, and lay them on men's shoulders,"* concerns the glosses and additions that had been made by these hypocrites to the Law.

For instance, a woman was not allowed to comb her hair on the Sabbath, because a speck of dirt might be in the hair, and this could be construed as plowing. (Plowing was forbidden on the Sabbath, Ex. 20:8-10.)

As well, one was not allowed to drag a chair across the floor on the Sabbath, because there may be dust on the floor, and, again, if the dust was moved, it could be construed as plowing.

Actually, there were a myriad of laws of this nature, which, in fact, had not been given by God, but were man-devised. As such, they were *"heavy burdens and grievous to be borne."*

What Christ is denouncing is not the Law itself, but the false inferences and deductions, leading to injunctions, as stated, which were insupportable and impracticable.

The phrase, *"But they themselves will not move them with one of their fingers,"* means that they made no effort to correctly interpret the Law, but, instead, insisted that all the additions and nuances be adhered to in totality, or else suffer the consequences!

In Truth, the Pharisees and Scribes enjoyed immensely, minutely watching people in order to catch them in an infraction of the Law, i.e., man-devised additions to the Law. They did this to Christ constantly, pointing out that which they considered to be infractions, such

NOTES

as healing on the Sabbath, which He studiously ignored. Men love to make rules, and religious men most of all! The modern Church, in some respects, is little different!

Attempting to legislate Holiness, as Israel of old, myriad rules are ensconced in the Constitution and Bylaws of many Church organizations — rules against the wearing of jewelry, make-up for ladies, etc. The doing or not doing of these things because of a rule, constitutes nothing in the eyes of God. These are man-devised additions, which, in effect, carry the same weight as the additions to the Law in olden times — none at all! Holiness cannot be legislated, actually, legislation will have the opposite effect.

When Family Worship Center was begun in 1982, discussion was engaged respecting the qualifications for joining the Church. Some were adamant that a long list of rules must be included, etc.

After listening to the pros and cons for some time, I finally asked the question to the brethren involved, *"Why not just have the qualifications that the Bible speaks of, accepting Christ as one's Saviour?"*

There was silence for a few moments, with some quickly saying that was not enough. I asked the question, *"If it was good enough for the Lord, why is it not good enough for man?"* (Rom. 10:9-13).

"The rules were needed," some said, to *"keep the Church pure!"* I sat there for a few moments, thinking of the utter hypocrisy of such a statement, plus the obvious ignorance of the Word of God.

First of all, the Church is not pure, at least as far as man is concerned, and will not be until the Trump sounds, and corruption then puts on incorruption, etc. (I Cor. 15:51-54).

As well, the purity of the Church is Faith in Christ (Gal. 2:20), and the Power of the Holy Spirit (Rom. 8:1).

Even though some did not agree with it at all, the qualifications for joining Family Worship Center is simply a confession of Faith in the Lord Jesus Christ.

Of course, we strongly preach a separated life, which can only be brought about by the Power of the Holy Spirit, and, at the same time, seek to have patience and understanding concerning those who are weak.

We have never excommunicated anyone from Family Worship Center, and will not do so unless there is open, unconfessed sin being habitually practiced, and in open defiance of the Word of God, as well as admonitions of the brethren (I Cor. 5:1-13).

Even then, and before the act of ex-communication would be carried out, every effort would be made to get the sinning brother (or sister) to see the error of his or her ways, and, consequently, to repent! If such were forthcoming, there would not, and, in effect, should not, be any excommunication. Paul said, *"Ye ought rather to forgive him, and comfort him, lest perhaps such a one should be swallowed up with overmuch sorrow"* (II Cor. 2:7).

Paul also said, *"Brethren, if a man be overtaken in a fault, ye which are spiritual, restore such an one in the spirit of meekness; considering thyself, lest thou also be tempted"* (Gal. 6:1).

Of course, this is predicated on one sincerely repenting before God and man.

(5) "BUT ALL THEIR WORKS THEY DO FOR TO BE SEEN OF MEN: THEY MAKE BROAD THEIR PHYLACTERIES, AND ENLARGE THE BORDERS OF THEIR GARMENTS,"

The phrase, *"But all their works they do for to be seen of men,"* is a scathing denunciation indeed!

This is the exact opposite of the teaching of Christ, and of True Bible Salvation (Mat. 6:1-4).

Things done supposedly for God in order to be *"seen of men,"* are not recognized by God at all. In other words, it is a fruitless exercise in vanity.

The phrase, *"They make broad their phylacteries,"* spoke of a small square box containing a parchment or skin, on which were written particular Scriptures taken from Exodus 13:1-10 and Deuteronomy 6:4-9; 11:13-21.

These were worn on the arm and forehead only during prayers, and only by men. However, they were worn continually by the Pharisees who also sought to enlarge the boxes so as to attract attention.

The terminology of the phrase suggests that Jesus did not condemn the wearing of these, but the manner in which they were worn, which was to make a great show to attract public attention.

The phrase, *"And enlarge the borders of their garments,"* had to do with fringes or tassels which were fastened to the corners of the outer garments, in accordance with Numbers 15:38-41, and were composed of white and blue threads. They were intended to remind the wearers of the Commandments of the Lord.

Christ did not condemn the wearing of these, as there is evidence that He wore them Himself, inasmuch as this seems to be what the woman touched with the *"issue of blood"* (Lk. 8:43-48).

What He condemned was the enlarging of these borders, in order that attention would be called to them, with people admiring the supposed consecration of the wearer.

(6) "AND LOVE THE UPPERMOST ROOMS AT FEASTS, AND THE CHIEF SEATS IN THE SYNAGOGUES,"

The phrase, *"And love the uppermost rooms at feasts,"* had to do with the most honored place at the table which was located at the right hand of the host.

The phrase, *"And the chief seats in the Synagogues,"* concerned the replica of the Ark of the Covenant which was in every Synagogue. The Ark contained the sacred scrolls of the Law and the Prophets.

Immediately before the Ark, and facing the people, were the seats of honor for the rulers of the Synagogue and the honorable. These were the places for which the Pharisees contended, thinking far more of these positions in the sight of the congregation, than of the Divine Worship which was supposed to be enjoined.

(7) "AND GREETINGS IN THE MARKETS, AND TO BE CALLED OF MEN, RABBI, RABBI."

The phrase, *"And greetings in the markets,"* respected flowery salutations in public places. In other words, the Scribes and Pharisees loved to be lauded in public.

The phrase, *"And to be called of men, Rabbi, Rabbi,"* actually meant *"teacher,"* and was the favorite title claimed by the Pharisees.

One was made a Rabbi by laying on of hands by the Sanhedrin who gave him a key as a sign of the authority conferred upon him to teach others, and a table-book as a sign of diligence in study.

The key was worn as a badge of honor and was buried with him. The Jews called John such

(Jn. 3:26) and Jesus (Jn. 1:38, 49; 3:2; 6:25) even though they were not ordained as Rabbis by the Sanhedrin.

The term *"Rabbi,"* and being used twice, or even more in many cases, was done for the sake of praise, and implied superiority in those thus called.

In effect, these greetings and salutations were enjoined on scholars and inferiors, under pain of ecclesiastical censure, or even loss of Salvation.

(8) "BUT BE NOT YE CALLED RABBI: FOR ONE IS YOUR MASTER, EVEN CHRIST; AND ALL YE ARE BRETHREN."

The phrase, *"But be not ye called Rabbi,"* was not so much a forbidding of this title, as it was the inordinate grasping at such personal distinctions. It concerned the greedy ambition which loved the empty title, and took any means to obtain it.

The phrase, *"For One is your Master, even Christ,"* refers to the One to Whom men must look. The title, *"Master,"* actually meant *"Leader,"* or *"Guide."*

Men, and especially religious men, have ever attempted to usurp authority over the Headship of Christ. It is plainly said here that such is not to be. Consequently, for anyone to take the title of *"Pope," "Cardinal,"* or *"Archbishop,"* is unscriptural, as should here be obvious. All of these titles incidentally imply spiritual authority, which is held only by Christ, and for the obvious reasons.

The title, *"Christ,"* means *"Anointed,"* and could be applied only to Jesus, at least in this context.

The phrase, *"And all ye are brethren,"* means that no one Believer is higher than another, and neither can have from Me any authority over other Believers (I Pet. 5:1-8).

At the same time, the Lord does not forbid respect for true Preachers of the Gospel, or even different grades, if one could refer such to that (I Cor. 12:28; Eph. 4:11-13)!

Even then, the Holy Spirit warned the Church through Paul not to place undue significance on particular Preachers. He said, *"Now this I say, that every one of you saith, I am of Paul; and I of Apollos; and I of Cephas"* (Peter), etc. This brings *"contentions among you"* he added (I Cor. 1:11-12).

Even though Preachers of the Gospel are to

be loved, respected, and held in high esteem, still, Paul would also ask, *"Is Christ divided? Was Paul crucified for you? Were you baptized in the name of Paul?"* (I Cor. 1:13).

In other words, never forget that Christ, Who gives these particular callings to the Church, is to be ever looked at as the *"Master"* or *"Leader,"* while, at the same time, the Preachers are loved and respected!

(9) "AND CALL NO MAN YOUR FATHER UPON THE EARTH: FOR ONE IS YOUR FATHER, WHICH IS IN HEAVEN."

The phrase, *"And call no man your father upon the earth,"* concerned the title given to eminent teachers and founders of schools, to whom the people were taught to look to rather than God.

The word, *"Father,"* in the Greek is *"Pater,"* and means *"generator, or nearest of ancestor,"* or even *"the founder of a race."*

THE SANHEDRIN

At the time of Christ, the lordly titles were common, with the Sanhedrin being referred to as *"fathers"* (Acts 7:2; 22:1), and with others being referred to by the same title or other similar titles.

Jesus condemned all of these titles; but Jewish leadership greatly cherished them, because they nourished their hypocrisy and religious pride.

The way that Christ uses the term *"father,"* He is not really referring to our earthly parents, but rather to these august titles.

The phrase, *"For One is your Father, which is in Heaven,"* means that all good Bible teachers must cause men to look to God, and not to themselves as the source of Power and Truth.

(10) "NEITHER BE YE CALLED MASTERS: FOR ONE IS YOUR MASTER, EVEN CHRIST."

The phrase, *"Neither be ye called masters,"* actually means that Preachers should not be referred to as spiritual leaders, for this is what the word, *"master,"* means!

The phrase, *"For one is your Master, even Christ,"* actually means that God and Christ are the only Ones Who have any right to these titles. God is the only Father of Christians, and Christ is the only Leader and Head of the Church (Eph. 2:20-23; Col. 1:18-24).

I think it is obvious that Jesus is censoring the sectarian spirit which was extremely present here, and even continued in the primitive Church, when Believers began to say, and as just stated, *"I am of Paul,"* etc.

Sadly, this division, and partly because of men taking undue honors upon themselves, has continued unto this day.

While much of the Church world is divided because of Doctrine, still, if one knew the Truth, one would probably find spiritual superiority as the greatest culprit of all!

(11) "BUT HE THAT IS GREATEST AMONG YOU SHALL BE YOUR SERVANT."

This statement, albeit so brief, is the definition of Christian greatness. It is the *"servant"* principle! Unfortunately, it is not a position to which many aspire.

(12) "AND WHOSOEVER SHALL EXALT HIMSELF SHALL BE ABASED; AND HE THAT SHALL HUMBLE HIMSELF SHALL BE EXALTED."

The phrase, *"And whosoever shall exalt himself shall be abased,"* in a direct way speaks of the Pharisees with their pride and vanity. Of course, it characterizes all, and for all time, who follow in their train.

The phrase, *"He that shall humble himself shall be exalted,"* is the universal Law of God's dealings with men.

Actually, this phrase illustrates the example of Christ Who humbled Himself in a manner that no human being could ever begin to imagine. He that was God, while never ceasing to be God, still, became man. There is no way the human mind can grasp such a thing! Not only did He become man, but, as well, suffered the horrible humiliation of the Cross. Consequently, He is our Example.

As someone has well said, *"My humility is my exaltation, and my exaltation is my humility."*

True humility and meekness does not defend itself, but leaves that to the Lord, while, at the same time, boldly standing for the defense of the Gospel (Jude 3).

True humility feels no slight, and because it is hidden in Christ.

True humility never exalts itself, but leaves such in the Hands of God.

True humility suffers in silence, that is, if suffering is called for.

True humility embarks on no self-improvement crusades, but, instead, hides self in Christ.

True humility trusts God implicitly in respect

to the past, present, and future, looking to Him exclusively for promotion.

(13) "BUT WOE UNTO YOU, SCRIBES AND PHARISEES, HYPOCRITES! FOR YE SHUT UP THE KINGDOM OF HEAVEN AGAINST MEN: FOR YE NEITHER GO IN YOURSELVES, NEITHER SUFFER YE THEM THAT ARE ENTERING TO GO IN."

The phrase, *"But woe unto you, Scribes and Pharisees, hypocrites,"* pronounces the first of eight *"woes"* on these Religious Leaders, and all who would follow in their train, and for all time.

It is even more remarkable when one considers that Christ said these things in the Temple, and in front of the great crowd which had gathered, and, as well, in the very face of the Pharisees and Scribes. The Temple was the logical place for these statements to be made, because it was in the Temple where the Holy Spirit was supposed to reside. It incorporated all that God was doing and had done under the Old Covenant. So these flaming statements will be made in its confines.

To be sure, the statements of Christ, even though directed at these individuals, and blatantly so, still, are meant to point out this false way to any and all.

This was the world of religion, and, as such, Satan used it in his grand scheme as he used nothing else. He does the same no less today! In these *"woes,"* Jesus will elucidate Satan's methods which the evil one, as stated, continues to follow to this present hour.

The phrase, *"For ye shut up the Kingdom of Heaven against men,"* is the first scheme of Satan through religion.

These individuals prevented men from accepting Christ, and, thereby, entering the Kingdom of Heaven, primarily by their false interpretation of Scripture.

They took away the key, i.e., the Bible, for they withheld it from the laity, and they nullified it with their own traditions.

The phrase, *"For ye neither go in yourselves, neither suffer ye them that are entering to go in,"* actually means that they refused to accept Christ, and stood in the door to bar access to any and all who would attempt to come in.

In Truth, there is ample evidence that the people were ready to acknowledge Christ and to follow Him as Messiah. A word from these authorized leaders would have tipped the scale in favor of Righteousness. However, the weight of religious authority was always placed on the opposite side, as it is most always placed on the opposite side presently! The only thing the Religious Leaders of Israel gave to Christ was animosity, slander, and prejudice.

Failure to properly interpret the Word of God, is listed as the foundation *"Woe,"* which keeps the far greater majority out of the Kingdom of Heaven. It continues to function in the same capacity at present, and, in fact, always has.

The greatest hindrance to people entering the Kingdom of Heaven is not the liquor business, drug business, or any other sinful vice, but, instead, religion. Preachers stand behind pulpits, but do not faithfully deliver the Word of God, and, consequently, cause their followers to be eternally lost.

Roman Catholicism is an excellent case in point. Its leaders will not go in, i.e., make the Bible the standard instead of the endless meanderings of the Church, and, consequently, they hinder all others in their wake from coming in as well!

In Truth, the world of Protestantism is little better! Of the hundreds of thousands of Protestant Churches in the land, precious few truly espouse the Word of God. The Religious Leaders will not believe it, and, consequently, do all within their power to keep their adherents from believing it.

As the Pharisees of old, it's not so much a disavowal of the Word of God, although that is prevalent, but more so a false interpretation which denies the Power of God (II Tim. 3:5).

In most of the modern old-line Churches, the Holy Spirit is all but totally disavowed, while in the modern Pentecostal ranks, at least for the most part, He is ignored. Other lights, albeit false, are held up, such as psychology, etc. The Word of God, at least in America and Canada, is less the standard today than ever before in the history of the Church, although, as the Pharisees of old, loudly trumpeting otherwise!

(14) "WOE UNTO YOU, SCRIBES AND PHARISEES, HYPOCRITES! FOR YE DEVOUR WIDOWS' HOUSES, AND FOR A PRETENCE MAKE LONG PRAYER: THEREFORE YE SHALL RECEIVE THE GREATER DAMNATION."

The phrase, *"Woe unto you, Scribes and*

Pharisees, hypocrites," pronounces the second Woe, which adds covetousness to hypocrisy.

As control is the first *"Woe,"* covetousness is the second *"Woe,"* i.e., greed and lust for money.

The phrase, *"For ye devour widows' houses, and for a pretence make long prayer,"* projects a false piety which deceives people, and the most helpless at that!

The *"widows"* stand not only for that group, but, as well, for all, who for whatever reason, are vulnerable to flattery and attention. To be sure, these individuals (the widows) should have been led by the Word of God, and if so, would not have fallen for this ruse. But, tragically, many Believers are not familiar enough with the Word of God to discern the true and the false.

Sadly and regrettably, the far greater majority of modern evangelism falls into this category. People give their money to support *"false apostles",* who, in effect, are doing the work of Satan, but yet under the cloak of Godliness.

Religious men want control and they want money, and will do anything to gain both!

The phrase, *"Therefore ye shall receive the greater damnation,"* pronounces a greater judgment upon these preachers of hypocrisy and covetousness, even above any other wickedness. This tells us that religious wickedness is the greatest wickedness of all.

The Salvation of souls and the edification of the True Body of Christ are of little concern to these religious hypocrites. As stated, control and money is their concern.

This is primarily what Jesus was speaking of when He said, *"Ye shall know them by their fruits"* (Mat. 7:16). But, sadly, much of the modern Church believes the false, bloated, swollen reports claiming *"good fruit,"* although completely lacking in Scriptural or physical evidence. Therefore, to support such, means that one enters into this *"greater damnation!"*

Is it possible for true Believers to be so deceived?

It is not possible if the Believer stays close enough to the Lord so that he can always hear His Voice, and if he is solidly anchored in the Word of God. However, most, and sadly so, do not fall into that category. Many follow afar off, and, tragically, are susceptible to the *"pretence"* of the modern Scribes and Pharisees.

"Pretence" is a powerful word, meaning that it looks right and sounds right, but, in reality,

is wrong! It is the *"false prophets, which come to you in sheep's clothing, but inwardly they are ravening wolves"* (Mat. 7:15).

(15) "WOE UNTO YOU, SCRIBES AND PHARISEES, HYPOCRITES! FOR YOU COMPASS SEA AND LAND TO MAKE ONE PROSELYTE, AND WHEN HE IS MADE, YE MAKE HIM TWOFOLD MORE THE CHILD OF HELL THAN YOURSELVES."

The phrase, *"Woe unto you, Scribes and Pharisees, hypocrites,"* pronounces the third *"Woe,"* and refers to sectarianism, i.e., drawing people to themselves instead of God.

How many in modern Christianity work diligently to draw people to their Denomination, their particular Church, their Ministry, while not at all drawing them to Christ?

The phrase, *"For ye compass sea and land to make one proselyte,"* refers to these individuals working much harder to draw people to themselves than most True Believers do to draw men to Christ.

The phrase, *"And when he is made, ye make him twofold more the child of hell than yourselves,"* is a startling statement indeed!

Why does Jesus place these individuals, adherents to this false piety, in this category?

The Woes of false doctrine and pretence now added to spiritual bankruptcy, locks them into a lost condition.

Previously, these converts were just lost and knew it. Now they are lost, while, at the same time, thinking they are saved, which adds a double jeopardy. As someone has said, there is nothing worse than a false way of Salvation, and, to be sure, this is what the Pharisees of old espoused, and this is what the modern Pharisees espouse as well!

It is probably even more subtle now than then. The Pharisees then opposed Christ, while now the modern Pharisees loudly mouth Him, just as the Pharisees of old mouthed God, but, in reality, did not know Him! The direction is the same, a false way!

Would it be too strong to say that many, if not most, Churches are presently filled with individuals who are *"twofold more the child of hell,"* than they previously had been?

Religion provides an excellent cloak for sin, and, to be sure, all sin does not reside in the category of alcohol, drugs, immorality, etc., but, much instead, in *"religious pretence."*

(16) "WOE UNTO YOU, YE BLIND GUIDES, WHICH SAY, WHOSOEVER SHALL SWEAR BY THE TEMPLE, IT IS NOTHING; BUT WHOSOEVER SHALL SWEAR BY THE GOLD OF THE TEMPLE, HE IS A DEBTOR!"

The phrase, *"Woe unto you, ye blind guides,"* pronounces the fourth *"Woe."* It concerns two things:

1. A devotion to externals!

2. An improper direction, even in that devotion!

To *"err"* and because one does not know the Scriptures, is to err indeed! If it's not according to the Word of God, which speaks of Godliness and life, it is error pure and simple!

For instance, Mormonism is error, because it substitutes another Bible and its false vision for the Word of God. The same can be said for Christian Science which seeks to take the teachings of Christ, making them a mental law in place of a spiritual change, which can only be brought about by the Holy Spirit. As such, it is error.

Jehovah's Witnesses fall into the same category, in fact, denying the Deity of Christ, and other plain teaching of the Word of God.

Seventh Day Adventism, although not falling into the category of those just mentioned; however, by inference, places Salvation in the realm of works, i.e., the seventh day, etc.

As well, Catholicism is a religion of the Church, instead of Salvation by the Word, through Christ.

All of these philosophies place undue attention on improper devotion, which constitutes wrong direction, and, consequently, make the individual a *"twofold more child of hell."*

If the leader is *"blind,"* there is no way that the recovery of the spiritually blind can be effected. Jesus said *"if the blind lead the blind, both shall fall into the ditch"* (Mat. 15:14). It is sad, and not pleasant to say, but one could probably say, and without any fear of contradiction or exaggeration, that most of the pulpits in America and Canada are occupied by *"blind guides."*

The phrase, *"Which say, Whosoever shall swear by the Temple, it is nothing,"* concerned the Temple, which is obvious, and especially that it was the most sacred place in Judaism. Consequently, to *"swear by the Temple,"* or its accoutrements, was to lend reinforcement to an oath. In other words, they would use the Temple or other things attached to the Temple, such as the gold, to reinforce a statement. They would say, *"I swear by the Temple,"* or *"The gift that is on the Altar,"* etc., that what I am telling you is true . . . .

This had become very prominent in Israel, with the things of God being pulled into the wickedness of the people. In other words, they made God a part of their lies and wickedness in taking an oath by using His Name, or that which belonged to Him, i.e, the Temple, etc. Jesus had already said, *"Swear not at all"* (Mat. 5:34-37).

The attitude of the people had so cheapened the things of God, that they meant little anymore.

The phrase, *"But whosoever shall swear by the gold of the Temple, he is a debtor,"* places the accouterments of the Temple in a greater position than the Temple itself.

In other words, if they <u>really</u> wanted to make an oath binding, they would *"swear by the gold of the Temple."*

(17) "YE FOOLS AND BLIND: FOR WHETHER IS GREATER, THE GOLD, OR THE TEMPLE THAT SANCTIFIETH THE GOLD?"

The phrase, *"Ye fools and blind,"* proclaims Christ adding to the epithets of hypocrites and blind, the word *"fools!"*

As we have previously stated, the Christ preached from behind most fashionable pulpits, is not the Christ of the Bible. Even though Jesus was the epitome of kindness, graciousness, love, and compassion, still, He was a defender of the Faith unparalleled. Not only did He point out the True Way of Righteousness, which, in reality, was Himself, but, as well, He pointed out the false way and even those who were instigators of the false way, as the Pharisees, etc. I suspect in these modern times, He would have been grossly accused of destroying the unity of the Body.

No! He did not destroy the unity of the Body, and because these individuals were not a part of the Body.

Is it the obligation of the modern Preacher of the Gospel to point out error and strongly so?

For anyone who knows anything at all about the Word of God, and seeks to follow it, they know, as Christ, it is the obligation and duty of all God-called Preachers to make clear the Way of Righteousness, and, as well, to clearly point

NOTES

out the error. Jesus is our example, and the true *"watchman"* will follow that example!

To be sure, there will be opposition, even if the True Way of Righteousness alone is expounded, but the wrath of hell unparalleled will be stirred up if the error, as well, is pointed out. Of that, one can be sure!

Someone has said that while Christ may have said these things, it is not proper for His Preachers to do so! However, those who would espouse such error, should study the Apostle Paul. He called such *"false apostles, deceitful workers, transforming themselves into the Apostles of Christ."*

He even said, *"Therefore it is no great thing if his ministers also be transformed as the ministers of Righteousness; whose end shall be according to their works"* (II Cor. 11:13-15).

In other words, he called them *"Satan's ministers,"* which they were!

To be sure, he, as Christ, suffered much for this stand, but it was that which the Holy Spirit demanded. Sheep must be led by a Godly Shepherd, and, as well, the Godly Shepherd will point out the wolves, even though they be dressed in sheep's clothing.

The question, *"For whether is greater, the gold, or the Temple that sanctifieth the gold?"*, is not meant to place a seal of approval on swearing by either, but, instead, the foolishness of such a position. It was not the *"gold"* which sanctified the *"Temple,"* but, instead, the *"Temple"* which sanctified the *"gold."*

(They were speaking of particular items of furniture which were overlaid with gold, or certain molding in the Temple which may have been overlaid with gold.)

These individuals, albeit very religious, had lost sight (blind), and understanding (fools), of what the Plan of God was all about. They professed to be great students of the Scripture, and were supposed to be interpreters of the Word, but as is here obvious, they did not know the Word of God.

Consequently, Jesus is attempting to show the people just how off base these Pharisees were!

Is it any different now?

Millions of people this Sunday morning will have a wafer placed on their tongue and will actually think it literally turns into the Body of Christ. Consequently, they make the wafer (the Lord's Supper) greater than Christ.

Many do the same respecting their Religious Denomination! People are encouraged to join their Church without ever having been born again, equating the joining of the Church actually with being born again, which it is not! Then the Church organization becomes greater than Christ. Consequently, all the *"blind fools"* of long ago did not end the species.

(18) "AND, WHOSOEVER SHALL SWEAR BY THE ALTAR, IT IS NOTHING; BUT WHOSOEVER SWEARETH BY THE GIFT THAT IS UPON IT, HE IS GUILTY."

The *"Altar"* here spoken of was the great Altar in front of the Temple on which the Sacrifices were offered. The Sacrifices were the *"gifts upon it."*

These individuals were concluding the lamb being offered on the Altar as more important than the *"Altar."* While it is true that the lamb represented Christ, still, the lamb was not Christ, hence, it was the Altar which sanctified the lamb, i.e., gift.

(At Calvary, Jesus sanctified the Cross, which is the opposite of this, but the lamb being only a representation, could not sanctify the Altar, but in turn was sanctified by the Altar, which represented Calvary.)

Concerning the error of the people, they were swearing by the Altar, which in their minds carried little force, while if they swore by the *"gift upon it,"* it was claimed to be a strong oath.

(19) "YE FOOLS AND BLIND: FOR WHETHER IS GREATER, THE GIFT, OR THE ALTAR THAT SANCTIFIETH THE GIFT?"

The phrase, *"Ye fools and blind,"* is used once again by Christ, and proclaims the people being wrong, not only by their direction, but that they should not swear at all.

The question, *"For whether is greater, the gift, or the Altar that sanctifieth the gift?",* is meant to point out the wrong direction of these Pharisees, as well as the wrongness of the entirety of the debacle.

(20) "WHOSO THEREFORE SHALL SWEAR BY THE ALTAR, SWEARETH BY IT, AND BY ALL THINGS THEREON."

Christ, while not placing any seal of approval whatsoever on swearing at all, nevertheless, uses the occasion to show these people exactly how far off base they were in their thinking. They had lost sight as to what the Temple was or the Altar, etc.

NOTES

A false way always perverts the true way as here, and actually turns it on its head.

Different types of animals were offered on the Altar as Sacrifices, such as bullocks, lambs, and goats. To be sure, and as stated, it was not these gifts which sanctified the Altar, but rather the Altar which sanctified the gifts. They were just symbols or representations, while the Altar represented Calvary and the Atoning Sacrifice that would ultimately be made by Christ in the Redemption of mankind.

In Truth, many modern Charismatics, and because of erroneous teaching, have, as these of old, placed Calvary, i.e., the Altar, in a secondary position. They erroneously claim that Calvary, while important as far as being saved is concerned, holds little significance thereafter. Consequently, all songs concerning the Cross or the Blood, are pretty much eliminated from their worship.

While it is certainly true that it is improper to leave Christ on the Cross, as do many Catholics, still, Paul said, *"I determined to know nothing among you save Christ and Him crucified,"* for purpose and reason. Not only were we saved by accepting what Christ did at Calvary, but, as well, the Cross is ever the example of the Christlike life, and, as well, every demon spirit which seeks to hinder the Believer, is defeated by what Christ did at Calvary and our appropriation of it.

That doesn't mean that the great Resurrection principle should not be applied to our lives, but means it cannot be applied unless we properly understand the Cross and the part it continues to play in the everyday life of every Child of God (I Cor. 2:2). Paul also mentioned, *"Enemies of the Cross of Christ"* (Phil. 3:18), of which some Charismatics come dangerously close.

Paul also said, *"But God forbid that I should glory, save in the Cross of our Lord Jesus Christ, by Whom the world is crucified unto Me, and I unto the world"* (Gal. 6:14).

As I have stated, the *"Cross of Jesus Christ"* is the secret not only of our Salvation, but, as well, our present victory.

(21) "AND WHOSO SHALL SWEAR BY THE TEMPLE, SWEARETH BY IT, AND BY HIM THAT DWELLETH THEREIN."

Several things are projected in these Passages, and some of them are as follows:

1. There are some things on earth which are

holy unto the Lord. Under the old economy of God, the Temple and everything in it was considered to be holy.

Under the New Covenant of Grace, no places are considered to be holy, but rather certain people — those who are saved and filled with the Spirit, who become Temples of the Holy Spirit (I Cor. 3:16).

Some time back, particular Preachers, going to Israel, were taking written prayer requests from their followers with them, where they would pray over them on the Mount of Olives, or some such place. While taking prayer requests and praying over them is certainly valid, still, the Lord will hear a prayer prayed in those places no more than He would any place else. Actually, if emphasis is placed on the praying over these requests at these particular places, insinuating that doing such carried with it some type of special favor from the Lord, such erroneous ideas would probably make the effort an exercise in futility.

While it was true that going to the Temple to pray was very Scriptural and right under the Old Covenant, much has now been changed.

Then, the Lord resided between the Mercy Seat and the Cherubim in the Holy of Holies in the Temple in Jerusalem, or was supposed to. Now that Jesus has been glorified, the Lord no longer dwells in a house made by hands, but, instead, and as stated, in the heart, soul, and spirit of the individual (I Cor. 3:16).

2. The Lord had already stated that it was not proper to swear by these sacred things (Mat. 5:33-37), and actually one should not swear or take an oath at all. A person's word should be such that a simple *"yes"* or *"no"* is sufficient.

However, if a vow is made, it should be kept (Num. 30:1-2).

3. We learn from these Passages that things dedicated to God should be treated accordingly. While at the present, such may not be considered holy as the Temple of old, still, if dedicated to God, it should not be treated lightly.

When I was eight years old, I asked the Lord to give me the talent to play the piano. I promised Him if He would do so, I would not use it in the service of the world in any fashion, but would use it exclusively for His service. By God's Grace, I have done that.

To say this gift that God gave me would be construed in the same capacity of holy as the

Temple of old, etc., I think would be Scripturally incorrect. However, inasmuch as it is given by God as a direct answer to prayer, and dedicated to Him, it must be treated accordingly.

(22) "AND HE THAT SHALL SWEAR BY HEAVEN, SWEARETH BY THE THRONE OF GOD, AND BY HIM THAT SITTETH THEREON."

Some of the Scribes insisted that swearing by Heaven or earth carried little weight, and, consequently, was not binding. However, Christ here says that to swear by *"Heaven,"* includes God and His Throne whether realized or not.

The idea as presented by Christ, is that a person should be so reverential of God that they would avoid all profaneness and carelessness in regard to things that are concerned with God. In effect, these individuals were taking God's Name in vain. The same can oftentimes be said presently.

To use the epithet, *"My God!"*, and in a slang fashion, as many people do without even thinking of it, especially when they see or hear something that is out of the ordinary, constitutes the profaning of God's Name.

As well, to use the name, *"Jesus,"* or *"Jesus Christ,"* in the capacity of slang, is constituted by God to be profanity.

The word, *"damn,"* whether people realize it or not, is a Scriptural word, and then to add the prefix *"God"* to it, constitutes profanity of the most sinful kind, and because one is wishing judgment or damnation on another individual who was originally created in the Image of God. Such damnation is God's prerogative alone, with no individual having the right to demand such.

As well, the word, *"hell,"* as is obvious, is a Scriptural term. Consequently, to use the word in the sense of *"go to hell,"* is, once again, a judgment of the highest order. It is the idea of desiring that someone go to hell and for all eternity, a prerogative, and as stated, which belongs only to God.

The use of the word, *"bitch,"* in modern thinking, has to do with a cur dog. However, its strict meaning and interpretation is that it refers to Mary the Mother of Christ.

The connotation carries with it the idea that Jesus was illegitimate, actually having been fathered by a man out of wedlock, hence the prefix of *"son of a"* to this word. It is an awful profanity, blaspheming the Name of God and

His Son the Lord Jesus Christ, in a fashion that is so reprehensible that it defies description. And yet, such epithets roll from the lips of much of the world constantly. It is the solemn breaking of the third Commandment, *"Thou shalt not take the Name of the Lord thy God in vain; for the Lord will not hold him guiltless that taketh His Name in vain"* (Ex. 20:7).

(23) "WOE UNTO YOU, SCRIBES AND PHARISEES, HYPOCRITES! FOR YE PAY TITHE OF MINT AND ANISE AND CUMMIN, AND HAVE OMITTED THE WEIGHTIER MATTERS OF THE LAW, JUDGMENT, MERCY, AND FAITH: THESE OUGHT YE TO HAVE DONE, AND NOT TO LEAVE THE OTHER UNDONE."

The phrase, *"Woe unto you, Scribes and Pharisees, hypocrites,"* constitutes the fifth *"Woe."* It pertains to the omission of things which really count, such as *"Judgment, Mercy, and Faith."*

The phrase, *"For ye pay tithe of mint and anise and cummin,"* had to do with small plants used for seasoning, etc. One can easily observe the Pharisees being scrupulously intent on making certain that they gave the tenth plant to the Priests in the Temple, while the far weightier things were ignored. This is a perfect picture of those who are mired in religion, with all the keeping of its rules and regulations, but, in fact, do not know Christ.

The phrase, *"And have omitted the weightier matters of the Law, Judgment, Mercy, and Faith,"* may have been taken from the words of the Prophet Micah. He said, *"What doth the Lord require of thee, but to do justly, and to love Mercy, and to walk humbly with thy God?"* (Micah 6:8).

The idea is that the keeping of these outward observances are worthless when the moral precepts are neglected.

1. Judgment: This speaks of being fair and honest, and treating one's neighbor right. It speaks of impartiality in our dealings with our fellowman.

2. Mercy: This simply speaks of love and kindness in one's conduct.

3. Faith: Such means a total trust in God, without which it is not possible to please Him, and which should underlie and influence all moral action.

The phrase, *"These ought ye to have done, and not to leave the other undone,"* places the

NOTES

seal of approval by Christ on the paying of tithe, even in the smallest matters, such as the tiny plants, but with the reminder that the *"weightier matters"* must not be neglected.

As *"tithing"* is here mentioned, it would be proper to proclaim its Scriptural standard.

TITHING BEFORE THE LAW OF MOSES

Some claim that tithing is a precept of the Law, and, as such, carries no Scriptural command in the New Testament. Such is error.

Tithing preceded the Law by approximately 430 years when Abraham paid Tithes to Melchizedek King of Salem (Gen. 14:18-20; 28:22; Heb. 7:1-11).

Some Hebrew Scholars even believe that the Lamb sacrificed by Abel, and called *"The firstlings of his flock,"* actually spoke of the Tithe, the first Lamb of ten (Gen. 4:4).

At any rate, the evidence is clear that Tithing was instituted by God long before the Law, even though it was continued under the Law.

TITHING UNDER THE LAW OF MOSES

1. It was commanded (Lev. 27:30; Mal. 3:10).
2. Five purposes:

A. A Tithe for the Levites and the Priests (Num. 18:21-26).

B. A Tithe of the income of every family was to be set aside each year, in order to pay their expenses in attending the various Feasts in Jerusalem (Deut. 14:22-26).

C. A Tithe was to be given every three years to be used as welfare for the *"stranger, and the fatherless, and the widow"* (Deut. 14:28-29).

The sum total of all the giving demanded by God under the Law, was 23 1/3 percent of one's income. As stated, 10 percent for the Priests, 10 percent for expenses used in attending the Feasts, and 3 1/3 percent each year to be used as welfare.

D. To supply God's house (Mal. 3:10).

E. To honor God (Prov. 3:9-10).

3. The Tithe was to be brought yearly, along with all other offerings for the Feasts (Deut. 12:6-7; 14:22-26).

4. The Tithe belonged to God, not the people who paid them (Lev. 27:30-34; Mal. 3:8).

5. The Tithe was to be brought to the Temple (II Chron. 31:12; Neh. 10:38; 12:44; 13:5, 12; Mal. 3:8).

6. If an individual borrowed his Tithe, in effect not paying it, when the Tithe was paid, 20 percent interest had to be added (Lev. 27:31).

TITHING IN THE NEW TESTAMENT

1. Christ taught it, as is here proclaimed (Mat. 23:23; Lk. 11:42. Compare Mat. 5:20 with Lk. 18:11-12. See Mat. 10:10; Lk. 10:7-8). Some claim that this was still under the Law; however, the teaching that Christ gave concerned the Kingdom of Heaven, which included the Covenant of Grace (Mat. 11:11-14; Lk. 16:16).

2. Paul taught it.

A. He condemned sacrilege (Rom. 2:22), and robbing Temples (Mal. 3:8-10) and using holy things (Lev. 27).

B. Teachers had to be paid, which was a part of the Tithing Program (Gal. 6:6).

C. God ordained the support of Ministers (I Cor. 9:7-14; I Tim. 6:17-18).

D. Christians are to give as God prospers them (I Cor. 16:2).

E. The Melchizedek Priesthood, as exampled by Christ, and which pertains to all Ministers of the Gospel, is eternal, and must be supported by children of Abraham, which includes modern Christians (Heb. 6:20; 7:1-11, 17, 21).

F. The children of Abraham, in Faith, which includes modern Christians, must walk in his steps, and he paid Tithe (Rom. 4:12; Heb. 7).

G. Tithing is proof of obedience and appreciation of God's Blessings (Rom. 4:12; Heb. 7:6-10; I Cor. 9:7-14; I Tim. 6:17-18, compare Mal. 3:8-10; Prov. 3:9-10; Gen. 14:20; Deut. 8:10-20).

THE BLESSINGS OF TITHING

1. Blessing for obedience, which includes the Scriptures just given.

2. So that God's Work will not want (Mal. 3:10).

3. So that God's Ministers will not want (Neh. 13:10; Mal. 3:8-10; I Cor. 9:7-14; I Tim. 5:17-18).

4. Tithing guarantees material and spiritual blessings from the Lord (II Chron. 31; Neh. 13; Prov. 3:9-10; Mal. 3:8-10).

EXAMPLES OF PAYING TITHE

1. Abraham (Gen. 14:20; Heb. 7:1-11).

2. Jacob (Gen. 28:22).

3. Levi and Abraham (Heb. 7:9).

NOTES

4. Hezekiah and Israel (II Chron. 31).

5. Nehemiah and Israel (Neh. 13).

6. Christians (I Cor. 9:7-14; 16:2; II Cor. 7:11; 8:1-15; Gal. 6:6; I Tim. 5:17-18; Heb. 7).

As stated, the program of Tithing as instituted by God, began long before the Law, and continues unto the present. There is no Scripture in the New Testament which mentions a substitute program for Tithing. Tithing is God's method of supporting His Work. As well, obedience in paying Tithe is the manner chosen by God to bless His Children materially and spiritually. As such, it ought to be practiced faithfully by every Christian, as well as the liberal giving of offerings other than the Tithe. Such, according to the Apostle Paul, proves the *"sincerity of one's love"* (II Cor. 8:8).

Actually, Paul calls giving a *"Grace,"* and places it in the same category as *"Faith, Utterance, and Knowledge"* (II Cor. 8:7).

The greatest dissertation respecting giving to God, is found in II Corinthians Chapters 8 and 9. It should be studied diligently by all Christians.

SOME QUESTIONS CONCERNING TITHING

1. What does the word, *"Tithing,"* mean? The word actually means a *"tenth"* of the total. In other words, one dollar out of ten, etc.

2. Of what does one owe Tithe on, the gross or the net? That should be left up to the individual, with the attitude being how much one can give instead of how little.

3. If one buys a house for $100,000, and sells it for $120,000, how much would the Tithe be on that transaction? The Tithe would be on the profit, which would be, at least in this case, $20,000, with the Tithe being $2,000, which is a tenth.

4. If a person buys a house for $100,000, and sells it for $100,000, would any Tithe be owed on such a transaction? No! No profit is made, so no Tithing is owed.

What if a person is given a house to live in, or a car to drive, etc., would Tithing be owed in such a case? Yes it would! If one is allowed such, the rental value should be ascertained, and Tithing paid on that. In other words, if someone is given a job with a house included, not only would Tithe be owed on the salary, but on the rental value of the house as well! If a person would normally pay $500 a month in rent, the house they are allowed to use is actually saving them that much money each month. Consequently, they would owe a tenth of that amount, which would be $50 a month, beside Tithe on the salary.

5. What happens if a Christian refuses to pay their Tithe? God is a merciful and gracious Benefactor. However, His Word implicitly says, *"Ye are cursed with a curse"* (Mal. 3:9). And there is nothing in the New Testament that says this curse is lifted, if one continues in disobedience.

6. What happens if an individual pays their Tithe to a Church or cause which is not truly preaching the Gospel? In the eyes of God, they have not given anything, and, worse still, many Christians actually aid and abet the Work of Satan by supporting false doctrine or that which is not truly called of God.

Jesus said, *"Beware of false prophets."* And does one honestly think that giving to such could be blessed by God? It is obvious that it would not be blessed by the Lord, and, furthermore, those individuals supporting such would actually be financing the Devil.

When *"false apostles"* came into the Church at Corinth and attempted to undermine the Apostle Paul, and, in effect, throw aside the great Covenant of Grace, sadly and regrettably, the people in the Church at Corinth were supporting these individuals. Paul called them *"Satan's ministers"* (II Cor. 11:12-15).

Consequently, not only was the money of the people in this Church thrown away, but, in effect, it was used to aid and abet the work of Satan in his efforts to steal, kill, and destroy. Consequently, every Believer must know <u>what</u> and <u>who</u> he supports. To be sure, each Believer is going to be held accountable not only for <u>what</u> is given, but <u>where</u> it is given!

(24) "YE BLIND GUIDES, WHICH STRAIN AT A GNAT, AND SWALLOW A CAMEL."

A gnat and a camel were both ceremonially unclean; the former was one of the smallest and the latter the largest living creature in Israel. The Pharisee, to avoid any possible defilement, poured all potables through fine gauze, but was guilty of extortion and incontinence. Thus he strained out a gnat (strained all wine through a gauze, to make certain it did not have a gnat in it, so the Law would not be broken respecting the eating of unclean things), and then swallowed a camel, i.e., had his heart filled with hate toward Christ, and others who did not totally agree with him.

NOTES

This was self-righteousness taken to an ultra extreme.

(25) "WOE UNTO YOU, SCRIBES AND PHARISEES, HYPOCRITES! FOR YE MAKE CLEAN THE OUTSIDE OF THE CUP AND OF THE PLATTER, BUT WITHIN THEY ARE FULL OF EXTORTION AND EXCESS."

The phrase, *"Woe unto you, Scribes and Pharisees, hypocrites,"* is the sixth *"Woe,"* and concerns itself with gross hypocrisy. In other words, the Pharisees took extreme caution to appear unto men to be ever so holy, and did so by addressing themselves totally to externals. Therefore, in this *"Woe,"* Jesus strongly denounces external formalism which in no way changes the heart. Such is religion!

Religion deals only with the externals, and because it is devised by man, therefore having no power to change the heart. Such is Islam, Mormonism, Catholicism, Buddhism, etc., and much of Christianity! Anything that is man-devised will always deal strongly with externals, because it can do nothing else.

The phrase, *"For ye make clean the outside of the cup and of the platter,"* concerned the cup they drank from and the platter they ate from, with its own set of rules for these externals.

Before they ate, they had to wash their hands a certain way, because it was thought that demon spirits could sit on the hands and be imbibed while eating, etc. As well, the dishes had to be washed a certain way, handled in a certain manner, with the drink and food placed in the receptacle in a certain manner as well!

Meticulous care was taken in order that all of these things would be done right, while, at the same time, the heart was full of wickedness, evil, and hate.

On reading these statements, many may have the idea that they are not so important, rather dealing with something that took place some 2,000 years ago. However, it is not the practice that Jesus is necessarily condemning, but, instead, the external formalism in which these individuals engaged themselves, thinking it denoted some type of righteousness. As He had just stated, they do all of these things, but *"omit the weightier matters of the Law, Judgment, Mercy, and Faith."*

Sadly and regrettably, the modern Church is filled with this type of external religion. Millions think that attending a certain Church, and especially engaging in its rituals, such as the Lord's Supper and Water Baptism, etc., surely makes them righteous and acceptable unto God.

The Truth is, it does not, not even by the greatest stretch of the imagination. Such rituals cannot change the heart, which can only be changed by the Power of God.

In reading the story a short time ago of one of the richest men in the world, he made a statement concerning *"joining the Church."*

He had relocated his merchandise headquarters to a particular small city, and which, I might quickly add, grew into one of the largest retail chains in the world.

After arriving in this little city, and getting his business going, he told his wife that they should join the Church. In his thinking, this was the proper thing to do, inasmuch as it would make him more acceptable in the community, etc.

There was not a word about being *"born again,"* or *"accepting Christ as one's Saviour."* It was merely a functional external, which, in this man's heart, no doubt, made him think and believe that such constituted Salvation.

It is obvious from his statements that he did not know the Lord, and, sadly, did not find the Lord in his Church joining. It was all a matter of externals, which, sadly, includes the far greater majority of those who call themselves *"Christians."*

The phrase, *"But within they are full of extortion and excess,"* proclaims that which is really important, and that which the Lord truly surveys, the heart. Ever how religious the externals, if the heart says something else, the external religious effort is of no consequence.

While, at the same time, if the heart is righteous, it will show itself externally as well!

"Extortion" actually refers to extreme covetousness, which has degenerated into fraud.

"Excess" speaks, as stated, of impurity, i.e., immorality.

Jesus is pointing out the fact that these individuals were laboring diligently in order that men think of them very highly, which was indicative of their self-righteousness, while they had little concern as to what God thought, and, in fact, knew!

(26) "THOU BLIND PHARISEE, CLEANSE FIRST THAT WHICH IS WITHIN THE CUP AND PLATTER, THAT THE OUTSIDE OF THEM MAY BE CLEAN ALSO."

NOTES

The phrase, *"Thou blind Pharisee, cleanse first that which is within the cup and platter,"* refers to spiritual blindness, which, in effect, was a willful blindness. In other words, they, of all people, should have known better, being the recipients of the Word of God from the mouths of the Prophets.

The idea is that food placed in a vessel with its interior dirty, and irrespective as to how clean the external is, will, as is obvious, contaminate the food.

The phrase, *"That the outside of them may be clean also,"* has to do with a moral purity which comes from within. Such inspires true spiritual cleanliness which will be obvious, and will have no resemblance whatsoever to the man-instituted efforts at cleansing the externals. In other words, clean the inside of the vessel, and the exterior will follow.

These statements are powerful to say the least, portraying that which is really within man. The Federal Government of America has spent, and is spending, hundreds of billions of dollars, attempting to assuage the drug problem, etc. They are no closer to success now than when they spent their first dollar. The reasons, at least to the spiritually minded are obvious!

Man can only deal with the externals, which addresses itself to the real need not at all! The only way that this problem, plus any other problem, can be cured, is for Jesus Christ to change the heart.

Just yesterday morning in service at Family Worship Center in Baton Rouge (9-17-95), Frances read a letter to the congregation which we had received a few days earlier. It concerned a 17-year-old girl who had been saved while watching the Telecast a short time earlier.

The girl wrote a lengthy letter (some 17 pages), telling how she was an alcoholic at 13 years old. She spoke of sexual abuse by her stepfather, which accelerated the decline of her life. In this atmosphere, she became pregnant by a young man she scarcely knew. Her mother made her leave home.

She went on to tell how she obtained employment at a service station, living in a tiny mobile home, paying some $60 a week in rent.

She had sought for and received a two or three day absence from her job in order to have an abortion.

She told how she came in from work, with

the abortion scheduled for the next morning, and laid down on the couch, after having turned on the small black and white Television set. She drank a glass of vodka, and then drifted off to sleep.

She told how she did not want to abort her baby, but she simply did not know what to do. When she awakened a couple of hours later, the Television set still on, our program had just come on the air. It was 4 p.m. on a Tuesday afternoon.

As she heard the music, and began to listen to the Message, the Spirit of God began to deal with her. In the course of the Message, I made the statement concerning abortion, that laying down in front of abortion clinics, or killing doctors who performed abortions, was not the answer to this terrible problem. I went on to say that the only answer was Jesus Christ Who Alone could produce a changed heart.

As she heard these words, conviction by the Holy Spirit seized her soul. As stated, she had not wanted to have an abortion, but she did not see any way out.

She went on to tell how she knew so little of Christianity, but now something was happening to her that she could not explain. She went on to say how she began to weep as the Spirit of God dealt with her, finally slipping to the floor on her knees, and praying with me as I closed the service with the Sinner's Prayer.

That which happened to her was so beautiful and so revolutionary that she had difficulty in trying to explain it. Once again she drifted off to sleep, and actually slept all night long. When she awakened the next morning, for the first time in a long time, there was no thirst or desire for alcohol.

She told how she only had $3 to her name, and decided to go to a nearby restaurant and get some breakfast, which she almost never did.

Sitting in the booth in the restaurant, a lady walked in with a Bible under her arm. The woman stood there a moment looking around, and then finally spotted the young lady whom she did not know, and walked over to her. This is what she said:

"Every morning I come into this restaurant and read my Bible, and sometimes the Lord gives me someone to witness to. The Lord has pointed you out to me, and I'm going to join you if you don't mind."

Without another word, she sat down in the other booth in front of the young lady. She then told the girl this remarkable story.

She said, *"Yesterday I saw Jimmy Swaggart over Television, and during the course of his Message he mentioned something about abortion. The Spirit of God spoke to me, and told me that this morning I would come in contact with a young lady who was pregnant and thinking of having an abortion. You are that young lady, aren't you?"*

The girl stammered out, *"Yes!"*

The lady then asked her if she had ever viewed our program. And, miracle of miracles, and just as we have related, she had seen it the day before, and had actually given her heart to Christ.

To make the story brief, the lady took this girl home with her, giving her a room, and purchased some clothes for her. She, as well, got her a better job, and, incidentally, a little later, a little baby boy was born to her.

In her letter, she went on to tell how beautiful he was, and how thrilled she was that Jesus had changed her life, and had given her this precious little boy. Without that, her life would have been totally destroyed, with her baby murdered.

However, Jesus Christ changed all of that, as He has changed the lives of untold millions. Nothing else could have brought this about but Christ. No power on earth could have changed this girl's situation except Jesus.

That's what Jesus was speaking of when He said, *"Cleanse first that which is within...."* That is the only answer to abortion, drugs, alcohol, immorality, hatred, or any other condition.

(27) "WOE UNTO YOU, SCRIBES AND PHARISEES, HYPOCRITES! FOR YE ARE LIKE UNTO WHITED SEPULCHRES, WHICH INDEED APPEAR BEAUTIFUL OUTWARD, BUT ARE WITHIN FULL OF DEAD MEN'S BONES, AND OF ALL UNCLEANNESS."

The phrase, *"Woe unto you, Scribes and Pharisees, hypocrites,"* proclaims the seventh *"Woe!"*

This *"Woe"* is similar to the last, but with a difference. It spells out in graphic terms the spiritual bankruptcy of these Pharisees, and all who follow in their train.

The phrase, *"For ye are like unto whited sepulchres, which indeed appear beautiful outward,"* pertains to the tombs and places where corpses were buried. Once a year, the Jews whitewashed these tombs in order to make them conspicuous, that men may not contract ceremonial defilement by touching or walking over them.

This was derived from Numbers 19:16.

Death was the result of sin, and, consequently, those who touched the dead, or even the tomb which contained them, were considered as defiled, and had to go through a ceremonial cleansing.

The horror of all the pain and heartache of this world, and even death, was brought about due to the Fall of man in the Garden of Eden. Consequently, everything is dying, with death being the most obvious result of sin in the world.

The phrase, *"But are within full of dead men's bones, and of all uncleanness,"* has reference to the fact that even though the tombs were whitewashed, etc., still, this did not at all negate the fact of what they contained, i.e., *"dead men's bones, and of all uncleanness."*

The idea was that the Pharisees, and all who like them attempted to polish up the exterior, were still full of death, and because they had not been changed by the Power of God. Regrettably, this emphasizes most modern professing Christians as well!

(28) "EVEN SO YE ALSO OUTWARDLY APPEAR RIGHTEOUS UNTO MEN, BUT WITHIN YE ARE FULL OF HYPOCRISY AND INIQUITY."

The phrase, *"Even so ye also outwardly appear righteous unto men,"* sadly and regrettably, and as stated, is the way of millions today in Churches where Christianity goes no deeper than what can be seen (I Sam. 16:7; II Cor. 10:7; II Tim. 3:5; I Pet. 3:3).

The phrase, *"But within ye are full of hypocrisy and iniquity,"* proclaims the spiritual bankruptcy of the human family. Without a life-changing experience, which can only be brought about by Christ, this terrible condition of death, and irrespective of the outward efforts, will remain unchanged. Islam, or Buddhism, Mormonism, Confucianism, etc., have no power to change the heart of man.

This is the reason that Preachers must preach Jesus. It is not the Church that saves, as the Catholics claim, nor is it the acquiescence to certain doctrines, but only Christ.

(29) "WOE UNTO YOU, SCRIBES AND PHARISEES, HYPOCRITES! BECAUSE YE BUILD THE TOMBS OF THE PROPHETS,

AND GARNISH THE SEPULCHRES OF THE RIGHTEOUS,"

The phrase, *"Woe unto you, Scribes and Pharisees, hypocrites,"* is the eighth and final *"Woe!"* It pertains to the hostility of self-righteousness as opposed to the imputed Righteousness of God. To be sure, it is hostility that has continued from the time Cain killed Abel, even unto the present!

The phrase, *"Because ye build the tombs of the Prophets, and garnish the sepulchres of the righteous,"* speaks of the honors paid to departed Saints, while, at the same time, planning to murder living Saints, even Christ!

The idea is that the Righteousness held by these Prophets of old was not at all desired by these hypocrites. Their action in building and restoring the *"tombs of the Prophets,"* was strictly a show in order to impress the people.

(Some think at this time, and along with Herod's massive building program, that many of the tombs of the Prophets were, as well, restored or completely rebuilt.)

(30) "AND SAY, IF WE HAD BEEN IN THE DAYS OF OUR FATHERS, WE WOULD NOT HAVE BEEN PARTAKERS WITH THEM IN THE BLOOD OF THE PROPHETS."

The two words, *"And say,"* in effect, says it all!

These hypocrites made long sermons and lamentations before the people, demeaning the acts of those who had killed the Prophets, whose tombs they were rebuilding, etc.

While they were touting the righteousness of the Prophets of old, and the utter wickedness of the *"fathers,"* who had murdered them, they were at the same time planning the same, i.e., the murder of Christ.

The emphasis of this Scripture is that it's not so much what one says, but, actually, what one does. The making all types of claims, in no way negated the wickedness of their evil hearts.

(31) "WHEREFORE YE BE WITNESSES UNTO YOURSELVES, THAT YE ARE THE CHILDREN OF THEM WHICH KILLED THE PROPHETS."

The phrase, *"Wherefore ye be witnesses unto yourselves,"* invites them to look at their own precarious spiritual condition. Actually, this is a command not only to the Pharisees of old, but, as well, to all men.

It is very easy to *"witness"* the spiritual destitution of others, but not so easy to witness the same in ourselves. And yet, this we are invited to do!

Self-righteousness will always extol its great virtues, and because of its externals, and, consequently, will not be honest. Actually, this is the terrible sin of self-righteousness. It so warps and twists the mind and heart that it no longer sees things through the Word of God, but, instead, through its own twisted version of the Bible, which always justifies self.

The idea is that a man witness unto himself, as to exactly what he is, which is very difficult for most to do.

Someone has said that Repentance is not really repenting over what we have done, but, instead, what we are!

The phrase, *"That ye are the children of them which killed the Prophets,"* proclaims them having the same wicked hearts as their fathers before them. They were travelling the same road of self-righteousness and hypocrisy which caused the conduct of their ancestors, but with one exception. They were, in fact, worse than their fathers!

(32) "FILL YE UP THEN THE MEASURE OF YOUR FATHERS."

As the Pharisees heard these words, little did they realize their import.

The implication is that there is a certain limit to iniquity; when this is reached, punishment falls. Jesus is here telling the Pharisees that they will, in fact, *"fill up that measure,"* and, consequently, suffer a just punishment. To be sure, such punishment will be awful indeed, completely destroying Jerusalem and the nation as a whole.

As spoken of Israel of so long ago, the same can be said of any nation, or even of any person.

As one looks at the rise and fall of nations, if the spiritual cover could be pulled aside, one would be able to see the Law of the measure of iniquity.

It was said of the Amorites of old, and their occupation of the Promised Land, *"But in the fourth generation they shall come hither again: for the iniquity of the Amorites is not yet full"* (Gen. 15:16).

The Lord was telling Abraham, that even though he and his descendants were guaranteed the Promised Land, still, it would be four generations before being brought about. The measure of the cup of iniquity was not yet full

NOTES

respecting the Amorites, who occupied at least a part of the land. At that time, four generations hence, which would be in the time of Moses, this measure would be filled, with the Amorites destroyed.

As stated, individuals fall into the same category. God's patience and longsuffering are extended; however, unless Repentance is engaged, judgment will ultimately come, with Repentance alone halting the Judgment.

This is the reason the Message of Repentance is so very important. It is the reason that both John the Baptist and Jesus came, *"Saying, Repent ye: for the Kingdom of Heaven is at hand"* (Mat. 3:2; 4:17).

Just as well, the Message could have been, *"Repent ye: for judgment is at hand!"*

If Israel had repented, the terrible judgment which fell upon them in 70 A.D., resulting in the loss of their nation, would not have fallen. But sadly, they did not repent.

As well, at the present time, Repentance is little preached from behind most pulpits in America and Canada. In fact, most of the Charismatic Churches do not even believe in Repentance, claiming it to be an Old Testament Doctrine, which has no relativity to the New Covenant. What they fail to understand is that the *"Kingdom of Heaven,"* as both John and Jesus preached, was the introduction to, and, in fact, the proclamation of, the New Covenant. And then, in many of the remainder of the Churches, and of whatever variety, self-righteousness is so predominant that Repentance, although not denied, still, is little engaged. Therefore, the only Message which can forestall the coming Judgment is abrogated.

(33) "YE SERPENTS, YE GENERATION OF VIPERS, HOW CAN YE ESCAPE THE DAMNATION OF HELL?"

The phrase, *"Ye serpents, ye generation of vipers,"* is the most powerful epithet uttered by Christ concerning these Religious Leaders.

In calling them this, He likened them to that old serpent, and their father, the Devil (Jn. 8:44; Rev. 12:9; 20:2).

The question, *"How can ye escape the damnation of hell?",* is meant to introduce the fact that they would not repent, and, consequently, the only alternative was hellfire. The idea of the entirety of this scenario is as follows:

Before sinning or disobeying God, the

individual ought to fear lest it be the filling up of the measure of iniquity, consequently, inducing Judgment.

God forbid that any Believer sin, but if such happens, Repentance must be enjoined immediately, because this is the only means to escape the *"damnation of hell."* But as someone else said, *"How rare is this Grace* (Repentance) *after a pharisaical life!"* Hypocrisy is always a bar to Repentance.

(34) "WHEREFORE, BEHOLD, I SEND UNTO YOU PROPHETS, AND WISE MEN, AND SCRIBES: AND SOME OF THEM YE SHALL KILL AND CRUCIFY; AND SOME OF THEM SHALL YE SCOURGE IN YOUR SYNAGOGUES, AND PERSECUTE THEM FROM CITY TO CITY:"

The phrase, *"Wherefore, behold, I send unto you Prophets, and wise men, and Scribes,"* affirms the Godhead of Christ.

The words, *"Behold, I send,"* actually say *"I am about to send."*

Such respects His Apostles, plus the Apostle Paul, and others!

The Book of Acts records the persecutions and deaths they suffered from the hands of men who here declared they would not have been guilty of the similar conduct of their fathers. But the hatred that motivated the murder of Abel and all the Prophets, reached its climax with the murder of the Messiah and His Apostles; hence the just judgment of verse 35.

The word, *"Scribes,"* was not in the Jewish sense of the Scribes who hated Christ, but, instead, instructors in the new Law of Life, the New Covenant.

The phrase, *"And some of them ye shall kill and crucify,"* could very well refer to Peter who tradition says, was crucified upside down. No doubt, others met the same fate!

The phrase, *"And some of them shall ye scourge in your synagogues, and persecute them from city to city,"* happened, as stated, exactly as the Book of Acts describes it.

If the Truth be arrived at, these Passages proclaim the constant war between self-righteousness, i.e., man's own devised way of Salvation, instigated by Satan, and God's imputed Righteousness. That war continues unto this moment, and will actually exacerbate in these, the last days. Much of the modern Church is mired in the same self-righteous mire as the Pharisees of old!

NOTES

How do we know that?

Whenever the Word of God is refused and rejected in favor of self-made rules, it is the greatest sign of all of self-righteousness. And this is exactly what is happening with the modern Church. In this self-righteousness, there is little or no moving and operation of the Holy Spirit, which should be obvious. Consequently, two things happen:

1. Things are projected as being a moving of the Holy Spirit, which, in reality, have little or no Scriptural support at all. As we have previously stated, the last generation lost the Anointing, consequently, this present generation doesn't even know what the Anointing is.

2. To the few who truly have the Anointing of the Holy Spirit in their lives and Ministries, every effort is made to neutralize these individuals, as few as they may be. To do this, any method which does not violate the Law of the Land will be used. As stated, it is a war which has raged from the very beginning, and is the dividing line of the Church, as it was the dividing line of Israel of so long ago. There are a few who have the imputed Righteousness of Christ, hence, Christ saying, *"And few there be that find it"*(Mat. 7:14). The far greater majority falls into the *"self-righteousness"* group, which always *"persecutes"*those with imputed Righteousness.

(35) "THAT UPON YOU MAY COME ALL THE RIGHTEOUS BLOOD SHED UPON THE EARTH, FROM THE BLOOD OF RIGHTEOUS ABEL UNTO THE BLOOD OF ZACHARIAS SON OF BARACHIAS, WHOM YE SLEW BETWEEN THE TEMPLE AND THE ALTAR."

The phrase, *"That upon you may come all the righteous blood shed upon the earth,"* speaks of their cup of iniquity being filled, with vengeance being taken in the destruction of Jerusalem and the slaughter of over one million Jews, which took place in 70 A.D.

To be sure, it definitely was not predestined by the Lord that this would happen, but that they instituted it themselves, because they rejected the greater Light of the Son of God. In doing so, they stubbornly refused all offers of God's Mercy confirmed by the greatest signs and wonders of all times. Consequently, Judgment was to fall in a greater measure than upon any other generation.

The phrase, *"From the blood of righteous*

Abel," proclaims Christ going back to the first murder of a man, and who died for Truth, i.e., for offering up the Sacrifice which was accepted by God (Gen. 4:8).

In effect, Jesus is saying, and as we have stated, that the cause of this great conflict is self-righteousness. Cain brought an offering as well, the labor of his own hands, which God would not, and, in Truth, could not accept. However, Abel brought a lamb of his flock, which constituted an innocent victim, and was not a product of his own labor and, as such, was accepted by the Lord. It was a type of Christ, as all sacrificed lambs or bullocks in the future, at least to God, would be types of Christ.

There was no excuse for Cain's actions, simply because the Lord had made it perfectly clear as to what He would accept or not accept, exactly as He always has done, even unto today (Gen. 4:7).

Incidentally, Abel was called *"Righteous"* because of his placing confidence in the right Sacrifice. The Righteousness given unto him was imputed Righteousness.

There are three types of righteousness in the world, one only of which the Lord will accept:

1. Works righteousness: This was typified by the Pharisee who talked about fasting twice a week and giving Tithes of all that he possessed. He thought by his good works that such guaranteed him Salvation. It did not!

Irrespective of his good works, and good they were, still, no individual can earn his Salvation by the act of good deeds, etc.

2. Relative righteousness: This is righteousness as well that is induced by man, which compares itself with others. The Pharisee also did this, saying, *"I thank Thee, that I am not as other men are, extortioners, unjust, adulterers, or even as this Publican"* (Lk. 18:11).

This is a favorite pastime among many Christians, comparing their righteousness with others, which the Lord will not accept.

3. Imputed Righteousness: This is the only type of Righteousness that God will accept, because it is His Righteousness and not man's. He freely gives it to those who admit they have none, and, in effect, cannot have any at least within themselves, thereby, placing their trust and confidence in Christ. Faith in Christ guarantees Righteousness (Rom. 4:9).

The phrase, *"Unto the blood of Zacharias son*

of Barachias, whom ye slew between the Temple and the Altar," seems without a doubt to be Zechariah the Prophet (Zech 1:1).

Some claim that it was the Zechariah of II Chronicles 24:20-21, and that is possible!

At any rate, and which ever Zechariah is being spoken of, he was the last Prophet to be murdered before John the Baptist.

Inasmuch as he was murdered *"between the Temple and the Altar,"* made the crime abnormally atrocious, and especially considering the sanctity of this spot.

(36) "VERILY I SAY UNTO YOU, ALL THESE THINGS SHALL COME UPON THIS GENERATION."

This *"generation"* being spoken, actually concerned the next generation after Christ, who would continue the murderous intent of their fathers, which would result in terrible persecutions of the Early Church.

About 37 years later, in 70 A.D., Jerusalem was totally destroyed.

(37) "O JERUSALEM, JERUSALEM, THOU THAT KILLEST THE PROPHETS, AND STONEST THEM WHICH ARE SENT UNTO THEE, HOW OFTEN WOULD I HAVE GATHERED THY CHILDREN TOGETHER, EVEN AS A HEN GATHERETH HER CHICKENS UNDER HER WINGS, AND YE WOULD NOT!

The phrase, *"O Jerusalem, Jerusalem,"* presents Jesus standing in the Temple when He gave this sorrowing account.

It is as if He suddenly turns from these blind and wicked hypocrites, and the sinless anger that burns on His Face and in His Eyes melts into anguish and pity, as it may be assumed, spreading out His Arms, He looks down and upon the city spread out before and beneath Him.

The phrase, *"Thou that killest the Prophets, and stonest them which are sent unto thee,"* presents the terrible animosity tendered toward these Messengers of God, and which resulted in the deaths of many.

In this statement, and in the account, it is obvious that the Lord notes each and every action of each individual carried out against those who are His Messengers. Nothing escapes His all-seeing eye, and, consequently, all will now be accounted for, as sooner or later all are accounted for!

The phrase, *"How often would I have gathered thy children together, even as a hen gathereth her chickens under her wings, and ye would not,"* proclaims every effort made by the Lord, and made *"often"* to bring Israel to her senses, but always ending in a stern rebellion, rejection, and refusal.

The words, *"And ye would not,"* speaks of a harsh rejection, even to the murdering of those sent with the appeal!

The metaphor of the *"wings"* is appropriate when, as it was put, the Roman Eagles were hovering near, and there was no hope of safety but under the Lord's wings. But, tragically, they would not resort to that safety.

It was always in their power to turn if they willed, but they willfully resisted Grace, and must suffer accordingly.

(38) "BEHOLD, YOUR HOUSE IS LEFT UNTO YOU DESOLATE."

If one is to notice, Jesus uses the words, *"Your house,"* which meant that the Temple, or Jerusalem, was no longer God's habitation. They did not want Him, and made it abundantly clear as to their feelings and thoughts, even by murdering Him. As such, their house was left *"desolate."*

It means the protecting wing is withdrawn, with the Divine Presence removed, and the house deserted. Consequently, Israel was doomed!

In this one sentence, the 38th verse, is found all the suffering and heartache that the Jews have had to undergo in the last 2,000 years. They have suffered as no people on the face of the earth have ever suffered, and for a reason!

Along with all the sorrow and heartache, the horror of World War II was certainly not the least. Over 6,000,000 Jews died in that hell, with Adolph Hitler attempting to destroy them all.

America and Canada does not stand innocent in that carnage, hardly lifting a hand, when Hitler began his horrid program of extermination. So as not to offend him, ship-loads of Jews were turned away from the harbor in New York City, as well as other ports, and eventually had to go back to Europe where most of them concluded their lives in Hitler's death camps.

Scores of times, the world has seen the newsreels of the thousands of dead bodies of Jews wasted and gaunt, being thrown into open pits.

As someone said, how many Jonas Salks and Albert Einsteins died in that horror? Men who may have brought great benefit to the world!

It is not that God would will this *"desolation"*

upon Israel, but that Israel would reject Him, and not being desired, He would depart. His departure, to be sure, would result in the only protection they had being lifted from them, with them now being at the mercy of Satan, who, to say the least, hated them. Hence, all the suffering and heartache which have ensued.

(39) "FOR I SAY UNTO YOU, YE SHALL NOT SEE ME HENCEFORTH, TILL YE SHALL SAY, BLESSED IS HE THAT COMETH IN THE NAME OF THE LORD."

The phrase, *"For I say unto you,"* is meant to announce a terrible horror, but with a gleam of hope!

The phrase, *"Ye shall not see Me henceforth,"* means that inasmuch as they did not want Him, they, in turn, would no more see Him.

While it was true that he appeared to chosen witnesses after His Resurrection, still, He was seen no more by the people as a whole after the Crucifixion (Acts 10:41).

The phrase, *"Till ye shall say, Blessed is He that cometh in the Name of the Lord,"* speaks of the beginning of the Kingdom Age, and immediately following the Second Coming. Consequently, a note of hope is enjoined.

These words, *"Blessed is He . . . ,"* were uttered by the people just a few days before. However, the Religious Leaders did not accept Him as the Messiah, and, therefore, the fulfillment of Bible Prophecies.

Instead of saying, *"Blessed is He,"* they, instead, by their action said, *"Cursed is He!"*

Nevertheless, Jesus here proclaims, and even as the Prophets had foretold, that Israel would ultimately repent of its rejection of her True Messiah, and will in bitter contrition look upon Him Whom they pierced, and on Him as the Son of God, the Messiah of Israel, and the Saviour of the world (Zech. 12:10; 13:6). Then, *"All Israel shall be saved"* (Rom. 11:26).

But before their coming Salvation, Christ here proclaims that both the Temple and Jerusalem would be destroyed, with Israel being officially cut off as a nation, which took place at the end of Daniel's 69th week. As such, Israel will not be dealt with again accordingly until Daniel's 70th week (Dan. 9:27).

This concerns the coming Great Tribulation, which will last for seven years, hence a *"week"* of years.

During this week of years, Israel will come

close to being destroyed, and, in fact, would be destroyed, but for the Second Coming of Christ (Rev. Ch. 19).

CHAPTER 24

(1) "AND JESUS WENT OUT, AND DEPARTED FROM THE TEMPLE: AND HIS DISCIPLES CAME TO HIM FOR TO SHEW HIM THE BUILDINGS OF THE TEMPLE."

The phrase, *"And Jesus went out, and departed from the Temple,"* is of far greater import than merely leaving the Temple in a physical sense. Men only saw a simple man leaving the Temple, but the Angels saw the God of Glory and the Glory of God forsaking it.

The Glory of God dwelt in Solomon's Temple, but the God of Glory Himself, in the Second Temple, as predicted by Haggai.

Jesus, the God of Israel, having forsaken His House, it became morally leprous — as all becomes that He forsakes — and in harmony with Leviticus 14:45, He predicted that not one stone of it should be left upon another.

The phrase, *"And His Disciples came to Him for to shew Him the buildings of the Temple,"* proclaims them digesting His Words concerning its destruction, but which they can hardly believe.

As they begin to climb the Mount of Olives which lay immediately east of the Temple and the Wall, upon coming to a place where the buildings of the Temple were plainly obvious, they drew Christ's attention to its beauty and magnificence.

It is said that the Temple was about 750 feet square, was made of white marble, and was one of the wonders of ancient times.

It was popularly said, *"He who never saw the Temple of Herod has never seen a building of grand design."*

(2) "AND JESUS SAID UNTO THEM, SEE YE NOT ALL THESE THINGS? VERILY I SAY UNTO YOU, THERE SHALL NOT BE LEFT HERE ONE STONE UPON ANOTHER, THAT SHALL NOT BE THROWN DOWN."

The phrase, *"And Jesus said unto them,"* begins the great Olivet discourse. As previously stated, Jesus began His Ministry with the Sermon on the Mount, and closes it with a Sermon

NOTES

on the Mount. The first was Grace, with the latter being Judgment, as a result of Grace refused!

The question, *"See ye not all these things?",* is asked in response to the remarks made by His Disciples concerning the beauty and glory of the Temple.

The phrase, *"Verily I say unto you,"* is meant to introduce a statement of powerful proportions.

The phrase, *"There shall not be left here one stone upon another, that shall not be thrown down,"* was fulfilled in total exactness. It took place in 70 A.D.

It is said that Titus, the Roman General who commanded the Tenth Legion, had given instructions that the Temple, and because of its great beauty, was to be spared.

However, he did not command the loyalty of his troops, as had his father, Vespasion. However, Vespasion had been called back to Rome, where he was now Caesar, with his son, Titus, having taken command of the Tenth Legion.

The Roman soldiers had heard that gold was mixed with mortar between the great stones of the Temple, and, consequently, it is said that they hooked yokes of oxen to these great stones, pulling them down one by one, until there was not *"one stone left upon another."*

It is said that a harrow was run over the ground where the Temple had sat, showing the utter destruction of the edifice.

Incidentally, there was no gold in the mortar between the great stones.

Josephus said that some stones were over 90 feet long and over 10 feet high, and some 13 feet wide. One hundred and sixty-two marble columns held up the porches which were 52 feet high. Every stone was removed.

The Apostate Julian, in the fourth century, endeavored to cast a slur upon the Prophecy of Christ by rebuilding the city and Temple. However, his design proved to be an ignominious failure.

(3) "AND AS HE SAT UPON THE MOUNT OF OLIVES, THE DISCIPLES CAME UNTO HIM PRIVATELY, SAYING, TELL US, WHEN SHALL THESE THINGS BE? AND WHAT SHALL BE THE SIGN OF THY COMING, AND OF THE END OF THE WORLD?"

The phrase, *"And as He sat upon the Mount of Olives,"* notes that the coming siege of Jerusalem by the Romans began on this very spot some 37 years later, where this Prophecy of its destruction was delivered by Christ.

Strategical reasons compelled the Romans to make their attack from this area.

As the buildings constructed of white marble sat so imposing in the setting of the sun, the scene must have been remarkable! It is said that the Temple walls were sculptured on their exterior as to resemble the waves of the sea. Consequently, the beauty was breathtaking.

The phrase, *"The Disciples came unto Him privately, saying,"* was carried out in this manner because of the explosive nature of His Words. No doubt, there were quite a number of people within hearing distance at this time, due to it being the Passover season, which glutted Jerusalem with pilgrims. As well, there could have been some who followed Christ and His Disciples, desiring to stay near Him as long as they could.

At any rate, the Disciples, not wanting anyone to overhear Jesus' predictions concerning the coming destruction of the Temple, pulls Him aside in order to explore His predictions even further. Consequently, this famous prophetic discourse concerning Israel in the last days, will be given only to His Disciples.

The question, *"Tell us, when shall these things be?"*, has to do with the utterance He had just given concerning the destruction of the Temple, and not one stone being left upon another.

This is totally contrary to their thoughts concerning Israel once again becoming the premier nation in the world. Strangely enough, He will not answer this question at this time, but will answer it in the Temple, as Luke records, which was probably the next day (Lk. 21:12-24).

The question, *"And what shall be the sign of Thy coming?"*, refers to the Second Coming, with the Disciples at this time having no understanding of the Rapture (I Thess. 4:16-18). Their minds are still on the ascension of Israel, which they felt Jesus would lead, and which they expected shortly!

At this time, they had no idea whatsoever of the coming destruction of Jerusalem, the Advent of the Church, and Israel's dispersion throughout the world, which has now lasted for nearly 2,000 years. However, this discourse, as here given, will give them the correct chronological course of events. No doubt, it was some time after the Day of Pentecost before they fully understood its meaning.

NOTES

The question, *"And of the end of the world?"*, really should have been translated, *"And of the end of the age."* The Greek word for *"world"* is *"aion,"* and means *"age, a period of time long or short."* This age will end at the Second Advent (Zech. 14:1-5; Mat. 24:29-31; 25:31-46; Rev. 19:11-21).

Actually, the world will never end, with the earth and man continuing forever (Gen. 8:22; 9:12; Ps. 104:5; Eccl. 1:4; Isa. 9:6-7; Dan. 7:13-14; Rev. 11:15, 21:3-22:5).

(4) "AND JESUS ANSWERED AND SAID UNTO THEM, TAKE HEED THAT NO MAN DECEIVE YOU."

The phrase, *"And Jesus answered and said unto them,"* gives the future of Israel, and how it will affect the entirety of the world. It is regrettable that this great discourse which fell from the lips of the Son of God, is given little credence in the world, and not much by the Church. It falls in perfectly with Daniel's Prophecies, as well as those given to John on the Isle of Patmos some 60 years later. The remarkable thing is that the fulfillment of these predictions is now very close at hand. As such, they completely refute the erroneous modern teaching of the *"Kingdom Now philosophy."*

This erroneous teaching, more or less, denies any future for Israel, claiming that these Prophecies by Christ were fulfilled in 70 A.D., when Titus destroyed Jerusalem, with Israel actually ceasing as a nation.

This error further claims that the world presently is improving in every way, with Christianity gradually overtaking the nations, and coming to terms with other religions. At some time in the near future, they claim, the Church will announce to Christ that He can now return to the earth. I refer to this throughout these Volumes as the *"political message,"* or, *"Kingdom Now."* Regrettably, it is believed by millions, even though total error!

The phrase, *"Take heed that no man deceive you,"* places deception as Satan's greatest weapon. Therefore, it is remarkable that Christ would begin this discourse with the warning of false ways tendered by the evil one. To be sure, it includes far more than that which I have just mentioned, but definitely does include the erroneous doctrine of *"Kingdom Now!"*

Jesus does not answer the question of the Disciples as to the exact time regarding these coming events, at least as far as year and month are concerned, but rather begins with the warning of deception. This, as would be obvious, was done purposely!

To be sure, in these last days *"deception"* is becoming more and more pronounced.

The Hebrew word for *"deceit"* is *"rama,"* which means *"treachery or guile"* (Ps. 34:13). Since the Devil is the arch-deceiver (Rev. 20:10), his children are described as *"full of deceit"* (Acts 13:10).

Conversely, in Christ's Mouth there is no deceit (I Pet. 2:22).

Inasmuch as spiritual declension is rampant at present, spiritual deception quickly follows in its train. It is the Anointing of the Holy Spirit which points the Believer toward Truth (I Jn. 2:27). However, if there is precious little or no Anointing, deception is made easy. Regrettably, and as previously stated, the last generation of Pentecostals lost the Anointing, and this present generation, consequently, little knows what it is.

As a result, the modern Church is accepting foolish phenomenon, which has little if any bearing in Scripture. Regrettably, and because of the signs of the times, this will only increase.

At present, there is almost no call for Repentance. Instead, prosperity schemes abound on every hand. Some time back while in a major American city, I had the occasion to tune in about five Preachers, with four of them telling people how to get rich. The fifth one, if I remember correctly, was espousing some psychological jargon respecting marriage, etc. There was no Gospel, at least among the ones I saw, only deception.

This deception is always cloaked in a heavy covering of religious terminology, and even papered with many Scriptures. Actually, the Scriptures are used to foment these unscriptural Doctrines, twisting them out of their proper context.

One must stay close to God, anchored in the Word, in order that he not be pulled away to fables (II Tim. 4:4).

(5) "FOR MANY SHALL COME IN MY NAME, SAYING, I AM CHRIST; AND SHALL DECEIVE MANY."

Three great signs will herald the Second Advent: the false Messiah (vs. 5); the abomination of desolation (vs. 15); and, lastly, the Second Coming itself (vs. 30).

The phrase, *"For many shall come in My Name,"* concerns itself primarily with the time immediately before the coming Great Tribulation, and especially its first half. As false Messiahs abounded prior to the destruction of Jerusalem in 70 A.D., likewise, immediately prior to the Second Advent the great false Messiah, i.e., the Antichrist, and the great false prophet will appear, deceiving the nations. This time is so close that the two individuals here mentioned could well be alive at this moment.

The phrase, *"Saying, I am Christ; and shall deceive many,"* actually refers to the Antichrist and all who will herald him as the Messiah. Israel will be quick to accept him.

The *"many"* here referred to, no doubt speaks of a number of false claimants, but, more so to those who will apply the title of *"Messiah"* to the Antichrist. Even though this applies primarily to Israel, still, its principle can, and, in fact, does presently apply to the modern Church.

The phrase could be translated, *"Saying, I am of Christ; and shall deceive many."*

In the modern Church, many abound in this mode. They are quick to claim they are of Christ, with some producing Religious phenomenon to prove it. As such, *"miracles,"* allegedly so, in these last days will abound!

Once again, and as Jesus proclaimed, the *"fruit"* must be inspected (Mat. 7:15-16), but is little done so by most Christians.

(6) "AND YE SHALL HEAR OF WARS AND RUMOURS OF WARS: SEE THAT YE BE NOT TROUBLED: FOR ALL THESE THINGS MUST COME TO PASS, BUT THE END IS NOT YET."

The phrase, *"And ye shall hear of wars and rumours of wars,"* concerns itself particularly with the first half of the Great Tribulation. However, the terrible problem of *"wars"* has abounded since the very beginning.

When Christ was born, peace reigned over the entirety of the world. It remained primarily so for the entirety of His life, which was only some 33 years. However, upon his Crucifixion, followed by the Resurrection and the Ascension, the Roman Empire was almost immediately thrown into military disturbance. Four Emperors — Nero, Galba, Otho, and Vitellius — died by violence within a short space of time. From that time scores of wars have raged all over the world, and continue unto this hour.

Former President Bush, upon the demise of the Soviet Union, declared that we had now come to a time of the *"New World Order."* It was to be a world without war or serious threat. However, almost immediately the Middle East erupted in flames, along with the continued fighting in Bosnia. Regrettably, and because man has rejected the Prince of Peace, the Lord Jesus Christ, these *"wars"* will only continue, and even at an accelerated pace.

The phrase, *"See that ye be not troubled,"* is directed totally to the Believer.

These Passages tell us, and in no uncertain terms, that society is not going to be changed by the Church, as some teach! In other words, the situation, and on a worldwide basis, is not going to get better and better, but, instead, worse and worse! (II Tim. 3:1-5).

In view of these troubled times, which, in effect, have always existed, but will exacerbate in these last days, the Believer is to not be troubled, knowing that his anchor is in Christ, and not the variations of this world's system.

Even though this prophetic discourse is directed exclusively toward Israel and its future, still, the Church is affected inasmuch as some of these events will affect the entirety of the world.

While it is true that the True Church of Jesus Christ will have been raptured away when most of these things are brought to pass, still, the events leading up to the Rapture and the preparation of Israel, as are now taking place, will greatly affect the Church, as should be obvious!

As Israel will be greatly deceived into accepting the Antichrist in the first half of the Great Tribulation, thinking he is the true Messiah, likewise, the spirit of this gross deception is already at work, affecting not only Israel, but the Church as well! Actually, there is every evidence that the Apostate Church will help usher in the Antichrist (II Thess. 2:3-12).

Nevertheless, the True Believer is not to be *"troubled,"* but, instead, *"When these things begin to come to pass, then look up, and lift up your heads; for your Redemption draweth nigh"* (Lk. 21:28).

(Even though this Passage in Luke speaks of Israel, still, it can apply to the Church relative to that of which we are speaking.)

The phrase, *"For all these things must come to pass,"* means that all these things spoken by Christ are sure to occur, not because it is

willed by God, but because of men's passions and perverseness.

In fact, one could probably say that all Prophecies concerning Judgment do not come to pass because God wills such, but, instead, due to the wickedness of the people. It is the same as a medical doctor excising a cancer from a patient. The doctor does such, not because he desires to do so, but because of the malignancy that threatens the life of the individual.

The phrase, *"But the end is not yet,"* means that the end of the age will not come until the Second Coming of the Lord. However, many things are to take place before that time, which are here enumerated by Christ.

As someone has well said, as the Rapture is the hope of the Church, likewise, the Second Coming is the hope of the world. The indication is that without the Rapture the Church would be destroyed, and without the Second Coming the world would suffer the same fate.

(7) "FOR NATION SHALL RISE AGAINST NATION, AND KINGDOM AGAINST KINGDOM: AND THERE SHALL BE FAMINES, AND PESTILENCES, AND EARTHQUAKES, IN DIVERS PLACES."

All of these things mentioned which pertain to wars, and include national disasters, have continued unabated to the present moment. The idea is this:

When Israel rejected Christ at His First Advent, this guaranteed the continuing of these disasters, which will exacerbate the closer the world gets to the Second Coming.

These things are brought about because of man's rebellion against God. Consequently, such events, and wherever they happen, proclaim the *"filling up of the measure of iniquity,"* as stated in Matthew 23:32.

"Divers places" mean that very few places in the world, if any, will be exempt from these Judgments — and Judgments they are!

Even at the present (1995), wars are taking place in several different parts of the world. As well, the world has just witnessed the horrible *"famine"* of Somalia, which resulted in approximately 500,000 people starving to death. Also, the AIDS epidemic rages throughout the world, increasing daily, i.e., *"pestilences."*

In the recent past, San Francisco, California, as well as Japan, have experienced terrible earthquakes, with Seismologists predicting that an earthquake could affect California so severely that it would actually break off a sizable part of the State, making it an island several miles into the Pacific.

As I write these words, the Caribbean, along with parts of the U. S. have witnessed one of the worst hurricane seasons ever!

For all of man's vaunted scientific and technological knowledge, he is unable to bring about peace, or to abate these disasters, which, as stated, will only increase!

(8) "ALL THESE ARE THE BEGINNING OF SORROWS."

The words, *"All these,"* refer to the happenings of the previous verse, and, as bad as they may be, still, that which is to come, which Jesus will call *"Great Tribulation,"* will be far worse! So, the world, as many in the modern Church presently teach, and as stated, is not going to get better and better, but, instead, worse and worse!

It is sinful, wicked pride which instigates claims by many in the Charismatic community, that their *"political message,"* i.e., the electing of *"good"* officials to public office, is going to Christianize the world, thereby ushering in the Millennium.

Instead, the Scripture declares that the *"Gospel"* must be preached to all the world, which contains not only the *"Good News"* of Salvation for all who will believe, but, as well, the Message of Judgment as here proclaimed! However, many if not most Preachers would rather proclaim the *"Prosperity Message"* which is of man, consequently error, rather than a Message of Judgment which no one desires to hear. Consequently, very little *"Gospel"* is presently preached, but, instead, *"another gospel"* (Gal. 1:6-9).

The phrase, *"Are the beginning of sorrows,"* refers, as stated, to the disasters of the previous verse, but more importantly, that they will exacerbate, and even greatly so, during the first part of the Great Tribulation Period, which is just ahead.

The word, *"sorrows,"* in the Greek is *"odin,"* and refers to birth pangs. It pertains to the troubles of Israel in the coming Great Tribulation.

However, these *"sorrows,"* and according to the Book of Revelation, will affect not only Israel, but, as well, the entirety of the world. Added to these, will be the Wrath of God, which during

this particular time will be poured out on the world, which will usher in a time of sorrow such as the world has never experienced (Rev. 6:17).

So, even though we applaud the efforts of men to bring about peace, as well as the efforts of scientists to ameliorate disasters, still, they will have no success at all! These things will only increase, instead of decreasing.

(9) "THEN SHALL THEY DELIVER YOU UP TO BE AFFLICTED, AND SHALL KILL YOU: AND YE SHALL BE HATED OF ALL NATIONS FOR MY NAME'S SAKE."

The word, *"Then,"* has to do with the previous two verses, and concerns the birth pangs of Israel during the coming Great Tribulation. However, even though its primary fulfillment will take place at that time, as well, it also refers to Israel from the time of her rejection of Christ some 2,000 years ago.

The full phrase, *"Then shall they deliver you up to be afflicted, and shall kill you,"* pertains primarily to the mid-point of the coming Great Tribulation, when the Antichrist, who Israel thought was the Messiah, will show his true colors, and will invade Israel, portraying his true intentions.

That's what Paul was speaking of when he said, *"For when they shall say, Peace and safety; then sudden destruction cometh upon them, as travail upon a woman with child; and they shall not escape"* (I Thess. 5:3).

The *"travail"* here mentioned, is basically the same as the *"sorrows"* of verse 8.

Nevertheless, and as stated, it also pertains to the treatment of Israel from the time of her rejection of Christ.

The phrase, *"And ye shall be hated of all nations for My Name's sake,"* has been borne out during the last 2,000 years, but, more perfectly, will take place even in a greater way during the coming Great Tribulation, when all the nations of the world will join the Antichrist in his efforts to destroy Israel, or at least offer her no help!

All of this will happen to Israel because of Jesus and His being rejected as the Messiah of Israel.

It is ironic! Israel hates the Name of Jesus, and yet because of this Name, they have suffered untold agony, which will only exacerbate in the near future!

The animosity of the world against Israel is fostered by Satan and because of who these people are. Their role in the Plan of God has been very obvious, and, as well, will continue, even as this discourse by Christ bears out.

Someone has said that Israel is God's prophetic time clock. While that is certainly true, still, their role is far greater than a mere *"sign,"* actually having to do with the entirety of mankind.

First of all, the world will not see an end to these disasters mentioned by Christ until Israel again realizes her place as the premier nation in the world (Gen. 12:3). And Israel cannot attain that place and position until she recognizes Christ as her Lord, Saviour, and Messiah.

When this happens, which it surely shall, the terrible disasters which constantly plague humanity will then be stopped. It is called the *"Kingdom Age!"*, and will be headed up by Christ, with the *"government of the world on His Shoulder"* (Isa. 9:6-7).

(10) "AND THEN SHALL MANY BE OFFENDED, AND SHALL BETRAY ONE ANOTHER, AND SHALL HATE ONE ANOTHER."

This Scripture proclaims that not only will the animosity of the world be directed toward the Jews, but, as well, there will be tremendous dissention even in their own ranks, which has been borne out, and graphically so, these last nearly 2,000 years. Nevertheless, in the coming Great Tribulation, these *"offenses and betrayals"* will exacerbate.

This will be understandable, especially considering the Salvation of the 144,000 who will accept Christ (Rev. 7:1-8; 12:4-5), and the *"two witnesses"* who will prophesy about Christ the last three and a half years of the Great Tribulation (Rev. 11:3-12).

In other words, at least some Jews in the coming Great Tribulation will accept Christ as their Saviour, which will, greater still, stir the hatred of the majority of Jews who hate Him.

(11) "AND MANY FALSE PROPHETS SHALL RISE, AND SHALL DECEIVE MANY."

The phrase, *"And many false prophets shall rise,"* refers to these who have always existed, but will increase manyfold at the outset of the coming Great Tribulation. These *"false prophets"* will, no doubt, exclaim that the Antichrist is the Messiah, and that Israel must accept Him, which they shall!

The phrase, *"And shall deceive many,"* refers to almost all in the nation being deceived at

that time, which will bring about the acceptance of the man of sin.

As the *"false prophets"* will increase the nearer the Second Coming, likewise, they will, and, in fact, are already increasing in the modern Church, with this at least one of the greatest indications of the coming Rapture of the Church.

Concerning the Church, it is very difficult for most Believers who really do not know their Bibles as they should to detect these *"false prophets."* Especially considering they are *"prophets,"* but not called by God, but, instead, are called by Satan, and, are *"angels of light"* (II Cor. 11:12-15).

Some of these *"false prophets"* will even perform miracles, which will be carried to even greater lengths by the greatest *"false prophet"* of them all, the man who will serve as the religious liaison for the Antichrist (Rev. 13:11-18).

Consequently, the Church must not make miracles its criteria, even though legitimate some may be, but, instead, the Word of God.

(12) "AND BECAUSE INIQUITY SHALL ABOUND, THE LOVE OF MANY SHALL WAX COLD."

The phrase, *"And because iniquity shall abound,"* refers to Israel's great sin in accepting the man of sin, i.e., the Antichrist, as the Messiah. At least for the first three and a half years, the nation of Israel, as well as the entirety of the world, will be plunged into an abyss of sin such as it has never known before.

Considering how iniquity abounds presently, and, in fact, has always done so, one is left aghast at this *"iniquity"* increasing, and greatly so!

Even now, the spirit of this exacerbated iniquity is already building. Consequently, the order is being inverted. Righteousness is called evil, while evil is called Righteousness. This will not abate, but will rather increase, finding its zenith during the coming Great Tribulation (II Thess. 2:6-12).

The phrase, *"The love of many shall wax cold,"* doesn't refer to a high percentage, as the word *"many"* seems to say, but, almost all of the world.

The Gospel of Jesus Christ, which in effect is the entirety of the Bible, greatly affects, in a positive way, the world.

When the True Church is raptured away, with the Gospel greatly restrained, *"false prophets"* are going to abound, and with no hindering of sin, which the True Church does, iniquity will be unrestrained. This is primarily what Paul was speaking of when he said, *"For the mystery of iniquity doth already work: only he who now letteth will let, until he be taken out of the way."*

And then he added, *"And then shall that wicked be revealed"* (II Thess. 2:7-8).

The one that *"letteth,"* or *"hindreth,"* is the True Church, with the *"taken out of the way"* referring to the Rapture.

At that time, there will be very little in the world left to hinder iniquity, which will cause the world to readily accept the Antichrist, as wicked as he may be!

(13) "BUT HE THAT SHALL ENDURE UNTO THE END, THE SAME SHALL BE SAVED."

The phrase, *"But he that shall endure unto the end,"* refers to the end of the Great Tribulation. Zechariah said that two-thirds of Israel will be killed during this time (Zech. 13:8). So, the Jews who actually survive the Great Tribulation, with the Antichrist attempting to annihilate them, could very well label their sojourn as an *"endurance."*

The phrase, *"The same shall be saved,"* actually speaks of survival, and not the Salvation of the soul.

However, in effect, it will amount to the Salvation of the soul, because the Scripture is replete with the information that the Jews who survive the Great Tribulation and come to the Second Coming, will, at least for the most part, accept Christ as their Saviour (Zech. 13:1, 9).

(14) "AND THIS GOSPEL OF THE KINGDOM SHALL BE PREACHED IN ALL THE WORLD FOR A WITNESS UNTO ALL NATIONS; AND THEN SHALL THE END COME."

The phrase, *"And this Gospel of the Kingdom,"* refers to the same type of Gospel preached by Christ, which includes preaching, teaching, and the healing of the sick, as it began, and as stated, with Christ in the Early Church (Mat. 4:23-24; 9:35; Lk. 4:18; I Cor. 4:20).

Regrettably, most of that which presently passes for *"Gospel"* is not Gospel at all, at least according to the Word of God. For the most part, it is a watered-down, compromised version, which in effect is really not Truth, and, consequently, is accompanied not at all by the Power of the Holy Spirit. Most Preachers deny the Holy Spirit respecting Acts 2:4, and, consequently, are bereft of all the Holy Spirit brings.

Most Preachers do not even believe that

NOTES

Jesus presently heals or that God even answers prayer. In effect, their presentation is mostly psychology papered over with a few Scriptures. As Paul said, *"They have a form of Godliness, but deny the power thereof."*

He then said, *"From such turn away"* (II Tim. 3:5).

That type of Gospel sees no one saved, healed, or delivered! So, that is not the Gospel that Jesus is speaking of.

To say it another way, if Preachers are not preaching the same Gospel preached by Christ and the Apostle Paul, and others as outlined in the Early Church, they, in effect, are not preaching the Gospel.

The phrase, *"Shall be preached in all the world for a witness unto all nations,"* does not actually mean every single person, but definitely does mean *"every nation."*

It probably can be said now that the Gospel has, in effect, gone to every nation in the world, with, of course, some nations having far greater opportunity than others.

In 1975, the Lord dealt with me strongly about going on Television with the Gospel. This we did, but with very humble beginnings.

In about 1979, the Lord began to deal with me about placing our Telecast in other countries of the world, actually translating into their language. This we did as well, ultimately translating into Spanish, German, Italian, French, Russian, Arabic, Portuguese, Japanese, and Chinese. If I remember correctly, we also translated into Turkish and Zulu. From the time of beginning this foreign programming unto the present (1995), we have received well over 4,000,000 letters, with many of these containing some of the greatest testimonies of conversion to the Lord Jesus Christ that one could ever read. Actually, in many countries of the world, it is difficult to find a city, town, or village, where one or more people haven't been saved as a result of the Telecast. How we thank the Lord for that, realizing that it is His Power upon His Word, and in the mighty Name of Jesus, which has brought about these astounding results. To this day, we continue to receive accounts of some of the most miraculous conversions that one could ever hear of. Actually, I believe that what is ahead is going to eclipse that which is past.

I am certainly not meaning that Television

is the only way to reach people with the Gospel, while any manner that gets the Gospel to anyone is very important indeed! However, given that the world's population is so large, it is very difficult, if not impossible, to reach vast numbers other than by Television or at least radio.

As well, just being on Television is definitely not enough! There must be a powerful Anointing of the Holy Spirit which accompanies the delivery of the Message, if results are to be forthcoming. Regrettably, such Anointing is as scarce as the proverbial hen's teeth!

Many Christians erroneously think that anyone on Television can accomplish the same task. However, nothing could be further from the Truth. The Preacher must be called of God to do so, in which the appropriate Message will be forthcoming, and accompanied by the Spirit. As well, if powerful conversions to Christ are to be brought about, the Preacher in question must of necessity have a very close walk with the Lord, engaging in constant prayer.

Such does not mean that one earns the moving and operation of the Holy Spirit, but rather that the vessel be a channel unobstructed through which the Holy Spirit can flow.

Respecting the presentation of the Gospel, we do not mean to say that Television can take the place of the local Church, even though used correctly, and with a strong Anointing of the Holy Spirit residing upon the Message, for it cannot! However, it definitely can be an Evangelistic arm of the Church, which it certainly should be!

I would ask the reader to pray for us, that God will greatly help us, and that we may follow Him closely in order that we may finish this course laid out for us respecting World Evangelism. I do not believe there is anything more important than the taking of the Gospel to those who have little had the privilege to hear it.

The phrase, *"And then shall the end come,"* concerns the prayer prayed by Christ, *"Thy Kingdom come, Thy will be done in earth, as it is in Heaven"* (Mat. 6:10).

The word, *"then,"* has to do with the Second Coming, and is tied, it seems, to the preaching of the Gospel to the world.

As well, the seed of another great outpouring of the Holy Spirit and a revival of the original New Testament program in all its fullness, is found in this Scripture!

NOTES

Time and time again, and especially in the last nearly four years, the Holy Spirit has dealt strongly with me concerning this very thing. I believe He has told me that a great outpouring is on the way!

(15) "WHEN YE THEREFORE SHALL SEE THE ABOMINATION OF DESOLATION, SPOKEN OF BY DANIEL THE PROPHET, STAND IN THE HOLY PLACE, (WHOSO READETH, LET HIM UNDERSTAND:)"

The phrase, *"When ye therefore shall see the abomination of desolation, spoken of by Daniel the Prophet,"* refers to Revelation 13:14. It speaks of the coming Great Tribulation, with the rebuilding of the Temple in Jerusalem on the exact spot where Solomon's Temple and succeeding Temples once stood! That spot is now occupied by the Moslem Dome of the Rock. As this is a source of great contention between Islam and Judaism, no one quite knows how this site can be procured for the building of a Jewish Temple. However, if the Scripture says it will be done, and it does, then it shall be done!

For the first three and a half years of the seven year period called the Great Tribulation, the Jews will reinstitute the offering of the Sacrifices exactly as they did thousands of years ago. At this time, they will have accepted the Antichrist as the Messiah, thinking he is the fulfillment of the Prophecies of old (Dan. 9:27).

Nevertheless, at the mid-point of the Great Tribulation, the Antichrist will invade Israel, with her suffering her first military defeat since her restoration as a nation in 1948. With a superior force, the Antichrist would completely destroy fleeing Israel then, but for pressing business otherwise (Dan. 11:44). Actually, great numbers of Jews will at that time seek refuge in the ancient ruins of Petra, which are now empty (Ps. 60:6-12; 108:8-13; Isa. 16:1-5; 26:20-21; 63:1-5; Ezek. 20:33-44; Dan. 11:36-45; Rev. 12:6).

The Antichrist will then make the newly-constructed Jewish Temple his headquarters, actually setting up a statue of himself in the Holy of Holies, demanding that it be worshiped (II Thess. 2:4). This is the *"abomination of desolation, spoken of by Daniel the Prophet"* (Dan. 8:9-14; 9:27; 11:45; 12:1, 7, 11).

The phrase, *"Stand in the Holy Place,"* refers to the Temple, and more particularly the Holy of Holies, where the Ark of the Covenant sat in Solomon's Temple.

The phrase, *"Whoso readeth, let him understand,"* refers to reading the Bible at that future point of time, and especially the Books of Daniel and Revelation. They will then understand, and recognize those events as being the fulfillment of these Prophecies.

Regrettably, much of the modern Church world does not *"understand,"* claiming that all of this was fulfilled in 70 A.D. when Titus destroyed Herod's Temple in Jerusalem.

However, at that time there was no *"abomination of desolation"* set up in the Temple, and neither was the Gospel preached to all the world for a witness. And as is quite obvious, the *"end"* did not at that time come, with Christ Personally beginning His reign in Jerusalem, which will happen when the end truly comes, i.e., the end of this Dispensation of the Day of Grace.

(To be sure, Grace will continue in the coming Kingdom Age as now, but will be joined by prevailing Righteousness.)

(16) "THEN LET THEM WHICH BE IN JUDAEA FLEE INTO THE MOUNTAINS:"

The word, *"Then,"* has to do with the time when the *"abomination of desolation"* is set up in the Temple in Jerusalem.

Actually, with the invasion of Israel by the Antichrist, with him breaking his seven-year pact, the Jews are to *"flee into the mountains."* Consequently, some 2,000 years before this event actually happens, Jesus gives the warning that, in effect, shall be followed. They will actually go into Edom and Moab (Petra), which is modern Jordan, and, consequently, escape the Antichrist. This will happen, and as stated, at about the mid-point of the coming Great Tribulation.

Even though the account in Matthew speaks of the coming Great Tribulation, in Luke, Jesus gave similar instructions concerning the siege of Jerusalem by the Romans which culminated in its destruction in 70 A.D.

Then He did not mention the *"abomination of desolation, spoken of by Daniel the Prophet,"* because He wasn't speaking of that particular time, but rather, the near destruction of the city. He used the phrase in Luke, *"And when ye shall see Jerusalem compassed with armies"* (Lk. 21:20).

He went on to say in Luke, *"Jerusalem shall be trodden down of the Gentiles, until the times of the Gentiles be fulfilled"* (Lk. 21:24).

Consequently, the two accounts in Matthew and Luke concern two different destructions.

Actually, the *"times of the Gentiles"* are still in effect, and will not end until the Second Coming.

(17) LET HIM WHICH IS ON THE HOUSETOP NOT COME DOWN TO TAKE ANY THING OUT OF HIS HOUSE:"

The idea is that upon the invasion by the Antichrist, the Jews should use such haste in fleeing that they would not even stop to *"take any thing out of the house."*

As would be obvious, modern mechanized warfare is carried out very swiftly, which will characterize the invasion of the Antichrist.

(18) "NEITHER LET HIM WHICH IS IN THE FIELD RETURN BACK TO TAKE HIS CLOTHES."

Again, the necessity of haste is enjoined!

(19) "AND WOE UNTO THEM THAT ARE WITH CHILD, AND TO THEM THAT GIVE SUCK IN THOSE DAYS!"

The idea is that the invasion will be so swift, with the necessity of fleeing so urgent, that it will be difficult for mothers with little babies, and even women who are pregnant.

(20) "BUT PRAY YE THAT YOUR FLIGHT BE NOT IN THE WINTER, NEITHER ON THE SABBATH DAY:"

"Winter" speaks of adverse weather, and especially the lack of shelter, at least at the beginning, in Petra. No doubt, at that particular time, multiple tens, if not hundreds, of thousands of Jews will have to exist at least for a time in the open air. Consequently, bad weather will definitely bring hardship.

The phrase, *"Neither on the Sabbath Day,"* concerns the strict religious observance of the Sabbath, as will then be demanded by certain Religious Leaders. According to the Law of Moses, Orthodox Jews held that it is unlawful to travel more than a mile on that particular day.

In effect, these statements as given by Christ are not meant to portray the actual conditions at that particular time, but to imply the rapidity by which the Antichrist will invade and take Jerusalem. The principle of the fleeing Jews will apply, even though modern equipment will definitely be used.

(21) "FOR THEN SHALL BE GREAT TRIBULATION, SUCH AS WAS NOT SINCE THE BEGINNING OF THE WORLD TO THIS TIME, NO, NOR EVER SHALL BE."

The phrase, *"For then shall be great tribulation,"* signals that by using the word, *"then,"* portrays when this will be, i.e., when the *"abomination of desolation, spoken of by Daniel the Prophet, stands in the Holy Place."* Consequently, we know for this to happen, the Temple has to be rebuilt, and then taken over by the Antichrist.

Even though this will be a seven-year period of time called *"Daniel's 70th week,"* still, the worst part, and by far, will be the last three and a half years, which Jesus called *"The Great Tribulation."* (As stated, the Antichrist will not break his covenant with Israel, actually invading her and taking over the Temple until the mid-point of this seven-year period.)

The *"abomination"* spoken of in verse 15 is derived by Christ from Daniel 9:27, *"And he* (Antichrist) *shall confirm the covenant with many* (Israel and other nations) *for one week* (a week of years — seven years)*: and in the midst of the week* (three and a half years) *he shall cause the sacrifice and the oblation to cease* (sacrifices as offered in the Temple), *and for the overspreading of abominations he shall make it desolate* (set up a statue of himself in the Temple, and demand worship), *even until the consummation* (till the end of the seven-year period), *and that determined shall be poured upon the desolate* (until all the judgments are poured out upon Israel)*."*

This *"week of years,"* and concerning Daniel's vision, is found in Daniel 9:24, and says, *"Seventy weeks* (seventy weeks of years, 490 years) *are determined upon thy people* (Daniel's people, Israel) *and upon the Holy City* (Jerusalem), *to finish the transgression* (the Crucifixion of Christ, followed by rebellion, and the ultimate acceptance of the Antichrist, which is yet to come), *and to make an end of sins* (for Israel's rebellion to end, which will conclude at the Second Coming), *and to make reconciliation for iniquity* (when Israel's sins are atoned for, which will take place at her repentance, immediately after the Second Coming of Christ), *and to bring in everlasting Righteousness* (upon Israel's acceptance of Christ, the Kingdom Age will commence, which will, in effect, last forever), *and to seal up the vision and Prophecy* (all the Prophecies given to the Prophets of old concerning Israel and Jerusalem, and their eternal restoration under the Messiah which will at that time be fulfilled), *and to anoint the Most Holy* (this concerns the building of the Millennial Temple as recorded in Ezekiel Chpts. 40-43; Zechariah 6:12-13)*."*

We know from Daniel's visions that the seventy weeks of years (490 years) do not concern or refer to the Church in any sense, but rather exclusively to Israel. Consequently, the prophetic part of the 24th Chapter of Matthew concerns only Israel, and is meant to partially answer the questions asked by the Disciples in verse 3.

This 490-year period of time, outlined by the Lord and given in a vision to Daniel, began with the Commandment to restore and to build Jerusalem (Dan. 9:25).

As Bible students know, this refers to the conclusion of Israel's Babylonian captivity. At the end of that period of time, Cyrus, King of Persia (Ezra 1:1-4; 3:8; Isa. 44:28; 45:1-4; 46:11), gave the commandment that Jerusalem was to be restored, which began the 490-year period.

However, the 490-year period did not run consecutively.

The first period of seven weeks (49 years), as given in Daniel 9:25, actually took some 141 years to complete. Only the time spent actually working was counted. It was somewhat like a clock which stops and starts several times during this 141-year period.

The second block of time called by Daniel, *"threescore and two weeks"* (434 years), started at the end of the forty-nine years and ended with the Crucifixion of the Lord Jesus Christ. Combining the forty-nine years with the 434 years, brings it out to a total 483 years.

(As we have stated, and due to the clock being stopped and started, etc., it took some 575 years to complete this 483-year period, which ended with the Crucifixion of Christ, leaving seven years yet to be fulfilled. When Christ was crucified, the clock stopped again, and has actually remained stopped for nearly 2,000 years now. The clock will start again, counting out the last seven-year period, when the Temple is built in Jerusalem, with Sacrifices beginning once more. This is the time of *"great tribulation"* spoken of by Christ, and what is meant by Daniel's 70th week. This seven-year period will probably commence shortly following the Rapture of the Church — I Thess. 4:16-17).

Much of the modern Church world denies this coming *"Great Tribulation,"* claiming it was fulfilled in 70 A.D. with the destruction of Jerusalem by the Roman General, Titus.

However, and as stated, the *"abomination of*

desolation, spoken of by Daniel," was not, at that time fulfilled. As well, Jesus, in Luke 21, makes it very clear that the destruction by Titus did not fulfill these Prophecies. He said, *"And they* (Israel) *shall fall by the edge of the sword* (the destruction by Titus in 70 A.D.), *and shall be led away captive into all nations* (which took place, with Israel scattered all over the world for these last 2,000 years): *and Jerusalem shall be trodden down of the Gentiles* (which she has for 2,000 years), *until the times of the Gentiles be fulfilled."* (For the last 2,000 years, Gentiles have pretty much controlled Jerusalem, with the city even now being hotly contested by both Israel and the Arabs. When the Temple is rebuilt in Jerusalem, every Scriptural evidence is that Israel will then control all of Jerusalem without question. However, and as stated, the Antichrist will break his covenant with Israel at the mid-point of the seven-year period, taking over Jerusalem for the last three and a half years of the coming Great Tribulation. His domain will come to an end at the Second Coming of Christ, which will fulfill the *"times of the Gentiles,"* and the conclusion of Daniel's 70th week, also ending the 490-year period of time spoken of by Daniel, with Israel once again, and forever, fully occupying her Land, her City, and her Temple. This will be done because Israel now accepts Christ, whereas she rejected Him some 2,000 years ago. Then, this *"Great Tribulation"* as spoken of by Christ and Daniel, along with many other Prophets, will come to an end with the Kingdom Age commencing.)

Especially considering that the Holy Spirit has given greater knowledge to God's people respecting the understanding of Prophecy in these last days (Dan. 12:4), there is no excuse for not understanding what the Bible plainly teaches. If its general thrust is misunderstood, such portrays an evil heart of unbelief, fostered and nurtured by spiritual pride. Such characterizes the *"Kingdom Now"* teaching, which is embraced by many, denying this coming Tribulation, claiming that the world will get better and better, with ultimately all false religions being taken over by Christianity, or else coming to a meeting of minds. If one misunderstands where one is going concerning Bible Prophecy, one may well misunderstand where one presently is, spiritually speaking. The *"Kingdom Now"* philosophy

NOTES

is a man-centered teaching, which denies the plain teaching of the Bible, placing man at the center instead of Christ.

Actually, it is true that all religions of the world are going to be terminated, with Christ-centered Christianity being all supreme, but this will not take place as a result of man's efforts, but rather by the Second Coming of Christ (Rev. 19). Daniel described the Second Coming of Christ, which will do away with all false religions, consequently, ushering in the True *"Kingdom Age,"* as a *"Stone"* (Christ) *"cut out without hands* (not of man's doings), *which smote the image upon his feet that were of iron and clay, and brake them to pieces* (will destroy the supremacy of Gentile nations, with Christ being supreme — Dan. 2:34)."

Daniel also said, *"And the stone that smote the image became a great mountain, and filled the whole earth,"* which speaks of the Kingdom Age brought about by the Second Coming of Christ (Dan. 2:35).

As these Passages, plus many others adequately prove, the world will ultimately be taken over by Christ, but it will be by a violent overthrow (the Second Coming, which will smite the nations), and not by the Christianizing of world cultures as taught by some.

The phrase, *"Such as was not since the beginning of the world to this time,"* refers to the time of the Garden of Eden to the coming Great Tribulation.

The world has seen many natural disasters, as well as tribulations sent by the Lord in this last some 6,000 years of recorded history. However, it has never seen a time such as that which is coming. John wrote, *"For the great day of His Wrath is come; and who shall be able to stand?"* (Rev. 6:17).

The Book of Revelation portrays this coming time when Judgment will be poured out upon the world by God in an unparalleled manner.

Why?

The coming Great Tribulation is called by Jeremiah, *"The time of Jacob's trouble"* (Jer. 30:7), and is therefore designed by the Lord to bring Israel back to God, and, consequently, an acceptance of Jesus Christ as Lord, Saviour, and Messiah.

However, Satan will oppose this greatly by raising up the Antichrist, who will be joined by many, if not most, of the nations of the world, attempting to abrogate these Prophecies concerning Israel, and even to completely destroy her. Consequently, the Lord will meet the Antichrist, and these rebellious nations setting themselves against God, with great and terrible judgment.

Even though Israel during this particular time will come close to annihilation, still, the Great Tribulation will serve its purpose, causing Israel to finally cry to God for deliverance from the Antichrist, which the Lord will answer with the Second Coming.

The phrase, *"No, nor ever shall be,"* means that such will never happen again, and because Jesus will reign supreme at that time over the world, with ultimately the Lord moving His Headquarters from Heaven to earth (Rev. Chpts. 21 and 22).

(22) "AND EXCEPT THOSE DAYS SHOULD BE SHORTENED, THERE SHOULD NO FLESH BE SAVED: BUT FOR THE ELECT'S SAKE THOSE DAYS SHALL BE SHORTENED."

The phrase, *"And except those days should be shortened,"* refers to the terrible persecution of Israel being shortened, and not the time period of the last three and a half years of the Great Tribulation, which will be the worst of all!

The phrase, *"There should no flesh be saved,"* actually refers to Israel coming close to annihilation.

At that time, the Antichrist will set out to completely annihilate Israel, exactly as Adolph Hitler attempted in World War II. He will come close, with some two-thirds of all Jews in Israel being killed, according to Zechariah 13:8. Actually, the Lord, and according to this verse, will cut short the persecution, or else the other third would die as well!

The phrase, *"But for the elect's sake those days shall be shortened,"* refers totally to Israel, and not the Church as some teach.

As stated, this is not the Church, and for the following reasons:

1. Jesus is answering a Jewish question asked by His Disciples (Mat. 24:3; 24:31-46; Acts 1:6).

2. The abomination of desolation concerns Israel only.

3. In the abomination of desolation, Jesus is speaking of the Jewish Temple.

4. Verse 16 proclaims Israel fleeing, and not the Church, etc.

5. The Second Coming of Christ is to deliver

NOTES

Israel, and not the Church, which will actually come back with Him (Zech. 14; Mat. 24:29-31; 25:31-46).

6. The Church will have already been raptured away before the events of this 24th Chapter of Matthew come about (II Thess. 2:7).

Why will the Antichrist hate Israel so much?

Actually, and as is obvious, this hatred has existed from the very beginning, and because of Israel's role in the Plan of God (Gen. 12:3). Consequently, it is a continuing hatred, but exaggerated greatly so by the Antichrist.

At this present time, Israel has few friends in the world. To be sure, America's friendship with Israel is predicated on the True Body of Christ in the United States. In other words, Spirit-filled Christians know and understand what Israel is, and her place in the fulfillment of Bible Prophecy. Consequently, the pressure is strong upon Washington to stand by Israel, and for the obvious Biblical reasons.

In 1987 (I believe it was), a Jewish American (who I will leave nameless), who served as the political liaison between Congress and Israel, asked to have a meeting with me. The meeting was extremely interesting, lasting for several hours.

This was during the Administration of President Reagan, with that Administration being very friendly toward Israel. Inasmuch as Reagan was very conservative, with most Jews having historically been liberal, this was confusing to this man.

He related to me how most Jews had strongly opposed the election of President Reagan, but now found him and his Administration to be the greatest friend that Israel had ever had. He had asked for a meeting with me to discuss these matters, seeking an answer to his question.

I related to him how that most True Christians who are, incidentally, mostly conservative, strongly supported Israel. Inasmuch as a great part of President Reagan's political strength was brought about by the Conservative Christian community, it was natural for him to be a strong friend of the State of Israel.

This brought on even more questions, because most Jews do not quite understand the term, *"Christian,"* actually blaming all of their troubles on this sector. (They even believe that Adolph Hitler was a Christian.)

I attempted to explain to him how that many

people who call themselves *"Christians,"* actually were not, and, in fact, were the very opposite!

I then explained how that True Christians love Israel, and because of Biblical reasons. Actually, all True Bible Christian roots are in Judaism. We serve the same God, but with a difference, in that Israel some 2,000 years ago rejected Jesus Christ, Who all True Christians conclude to be the Son of God, the Messiah of Israel, and the Saviour of mankind. Even though Israel has no regard for Christ, actually hating Him in many quarters, still, True Christians love Israel despite this, knowing that one day soon Israel, and according to the Bible, is going to accept Christ as Saviour and Messiah.

I asked him if he understood all these things I was saying, Israel's role in world events, and what the Bible said of her future.

He looked at me for some moments before answering, and finally said, *"No, I really don't understand these things; however, many times I find myself sitting in the Synagogue weeping, and not really knowing the reason why."*

When the Church is removed out of this world by the Rapture, the one great force which really loves Israel will be removed. Then the flood gates of hatred will open against these ancient people as never before! This is what Paul was speaking of when he said, *"Only He* (the Church) *who now letteth* (hinders iniquity) *will let* (hinder), *until He* (the Church) *be taken out of the way.*

"And then (after the Rapture) *shall that Wicked* (Antichrist) *be revealed* (make his debut), *whom the Lord will consume with the Spirit of His Mouth, and shall destroy with the brightness of His Coming* (the Second Coming — II Thess. 2:7-8)."

The Antichrist will know, and because he is inspired by Satan, that the Plan of God, as well as the restoration of all things, is tied up in the Prophecies made concerning Israel. Consequently, he feels that if Israel can be destroyed, then it will be impossible for these Prophecies to be fulfilled, thereby, abrogating the Plan of God. As stated, he has attempted this many times through the centuries, but will make his greatest effort in the coming Great Tribulation, hence, spoken of by Christ in these Passages.

The Antichrist will not succeed, and as said by Daniel, *"He* (the Antichrist) *shall also stand up against the Prince of princes* (Christ); *but he*

(the Antichrist) *shall be broken without hand* (killed at the Second Coming — Dan. 8:25)."

(23) "THEN IF ANY MAN SHALL SAY UNTO YOU, LO, HERE IS CHRIST, OR THERE; BELIEVE IT NOT."

The phrase, *"Then if any man shall say unto you,"* is speaking of the Great Tribulation days, as proven by the word, *"then."*

The phrase, *"Lo, here is Christ, or there; believe it not,"* means that irrespective of what is claimed respecting the appearance of the Messiah, and speaking of the Great Tribulation Days, it is not to be believed. The reason? Simply because it will not match up to the Word of God.

The title, *"Christ,"* means, *"the Anointing,"* or *"Anointed One,"* which actually did characterize Christ. Consequently, in using this title, impostors will claim to have the Anointing, which the next verse portrays.

(24) "FOR THERE SHALL ARISE FALSE CHRISTS, AND FALSE PROPHETS, AND SHALL SHEW GREAT SIGNS AND WONDERS; INSOMUCH THAT, IF IT WERE POSSIBLE, THEY SHALL DECEIVE THE VERY ELECT."

The phrase, *"For there shall arise false Christs, and false prophets,"* is actually saying that as prior to the destruction of Jerusalem in 70 A.D., false Messiahs appeared, so immediately prior to the Second Advent, the great false Messiah and the great false prophet will deceive the nations.

The phrase, *"And shall shew great signs and wonders,"* is the proof, they will say, that they are the Anointed one.

While it is certainly true that Christ performed *"great signs and wonders,"* as well as His Apostles, and many Believers down through the ages (Mk. 16:17), still, these things are not conclusive proof of the Anointing of the Holy Spirit. The miracles performed in the coming Great Tribulation by the false Messiah and the false prophet, will fulfill Revelation 13:13, *"And he doeth great wonders, so that he maketh fire come down from Heaven on the earth in the sight of men."*

And then it says, *"And deceiveth them that dwell on the earth by the means of those miracles which he had power to do in the sight of the Beast"* (Rev. 13:14).

The phrase, *"Insomuch that, if it were possible, they shall deceive the very elect,"* has reference to Israel. (The word, *"elect,"* does not refer to the Church as many have believed, as the prophetic part of this Chapter pertains solely to Israel.)

In effect, these *"signs and wonders"* will deceive much of the world, which will then turn on Israel, aiding and abetting the Antichrist.

No doubt, these miracles will be performed as well in the first three and a half years of the Great Tribulation, in effect, deceiving Israel, but every evidence is that the power of the Antichrist and the false prophet will increase in the last three and a half years, as the Beast comes down on Israel to destroy her.

With the Antichrist turning on Israel, and even attempting to annihilate her, it will then be obvious that he is not what Israel thought he was, i.e., the Messiah; however, his miracles will continue to deceive the rest of the world.

It is tragic, but the modern Church little knows or understands the Anointing of the Holy Spirit anymore, and because they little know the Word of God. As we have stated, one of the great functions of the Holy Spirit is to give the Anointing to Spirit-filled Believers in order that they may know what is Scripturally correct (I Jn. 2:27). However, if the Holy Spirit is not wanted or desired, or else He is given little opportunity to function, as in most Christian lives, this great office work will then be missing.

Since approximately 1990, much religious phenomenon has taken place in particular Churches or evangelistic meetings across the nation and other parts of the world. However, the biggest question to come out of these meetings is, *"Is it of God?"* And pertaining to some of the happenings in these meetings, this one thing is certain:

The Scripture, as is here obvious, plainly tells us that Satan's major device in these last days is *"deception."* Consequently, he will do his best to do things which closely resemble the True Moving and Operation of the Holy Spirit, but, in fact, will be false! Only those who truly know the Word of God and are led by the Spirit, will be able to detect this deception. In Truth, millions will be lost, thinking they are actually worshiping the Lord, when, in reality, they are worshiping Satan. As well, this increased deception is not something which will come in the near future, but, in fact, has already begun!

NOTES

(25) "BEHOLD, I HAVE TOLD YOU BEFORE."

This Scripture has reference to verse 23 and the words concerning false Christs, *"Believe it not,"* and pertains to verse 26, with the same admonition. It is meant to emphasize the seriousness of the matter, which a double command gives, and especially considering the pronouncement of verse 25.

(26) "WHEREFORE IF THEY SHALL SAY UNTO YOU, BEHOLD, HE IS IN THE DESERT; GO NOT FORTH: BEHOLD, HE IS IN THE SECRET CHAMBERS; BELIEVE IT NOT."

The phrase, *"Wherefore if they shall say unto you,"* is meant to pinpoint the error of Satan's claims concerning the coming Messiah.

To be sure, and concerning the last three and a half years of the coming Great Tribulation, with Israel staring annihilation in the face, and, in fact, crying for the Messiah to come because they realize He is their only hope, many false Christs, no doubt, at this time, will make their appearance claiming legitimacy.

The phrase, *"Behold, he is in the desert; go not forth,"* is meant to pronounce the fact that some such type of appearance is not Scriptural, and, therefore, will not be the Messiah. In other words, He is not going to come from *"the desert."*

The phrase, *"Behold, He is in the secret chambers, believe it not,"* refers to some alleged secret place in Israel where supposedly the Messiah has been waiting for some time, and will now make His appearance. Jesus said, *"Believe it not!"*

The next verse will tell the manner of His coming, which will so eclipse all pretenders that it defies description.

(27) "FOR AS THE LIGHTNING COMETH OUT OF THE EAST, AND SHINETH EVEN UNTO THE WEST; SO SHALL ALSO THE COMING OF THE SON OF MAN BE."

The phrase, *"For as the lightning cometh out of the east, and shineth even unto the west,"* is meant to proclaim the most cataclysmic event the world has ever known in all its history.

Considering that Christ will come back visibly (Zech. 14; II Thess. 1:7-10; Rev. 1:7; 19:11-21), and with brightness and fire (Ezek. 38:17-21; Mal. 4:1-6; II Thess. 1:7-10; 2:8), and with power and great glory (Mat. 16:27; 24:27-31; 25:31-46), this event will be something known and heralded all over the world.

As the Second Coming will take place in the midst of the Battle of Armageddon, no doubt, hundreds if not thousands of Television cameras will be present on the scene, in order to record the supposed victory of the Antichrist, with no doubt, virtually every Television set in the world tuned to this happening. However, the scene that fills the Television sets will not be the victory of the Antichrist as supposed, but rather the Coming of the Lord Jesus Christ, and with such Glory as the world has never known before, that is if the powerful atmospheric disturbances which will then occur do not disturb Television reception!

Coming back with Christ will be every Saint of God who has ever lived, along with myriads of Angels (Zech. 14:5; Mat. 24:29-31; 25:31-46; II Thess. 1:7-10; Jude 14; Rev. 17:14; 19:14). To describe the Glory that will fill the heavens respecting this greatest event of all time, would be impossible! No wonder the Holy Spirit through Christ described it *"as the lightning cometh out of the east, and shineth even unto the west."*

The phrase, *"So shall also the coming of the Son of Man be,"* proclaims this Coming to not be secret, but, in effect, worldwide. As stated, virtually every Television set in the world will record this event, an event we might quickly add which will cause the special effects people of Hollywood to pale by comparison. Even that is the understatement of all time.

Consequently, the ridiculous assertions of an appearance in the desert, or some secret place, is an absurdity in comparison to the real event.

(28) "FOR WHERESOEVER THE CARCASS IS, THERE WILL THE EAGLES BE GATHERED TOGETHER."

The phrase, *"For wheresoever the carcass is,"* has to do with the Battle of Armageddon, with the armies of the Antichrist, and the gathering of the nations. All of it, the world's assemblage, which have come together to annihilate Israel, for all its vaunted power, is looked at by the Lord of Glory as no more than a *"carcass."* For that's exactly what it will become at His Coming.

The phrase, *"There will the eagles be gathered together,"* should have been translated, *"There will the vultures be gathered together,"* because the Hebrew word, *"nesher,"* and translated, *"eagle,"* often signifies *"the vulture."*

This 28th verse has reference to Ezekiel 39:17, *"And thou son of man, thus saith the Lord*

God; Speak unto every feathered fowl, and to every beast of the field, Assemble yourselves, and come; gather yourselves on every side to My sacrifice that I do sacrifice for you, even a great sacrifice upon the mountains of Israel, that ye may eat flesh, and drink blood."

John also wrote, and concerning the Second Coming, *"Saying to all the fowls that fly in the midst of Heaven, Come and gather yourselves together unto the supper of the Great God"* (Rev. 19:17).

The idea according to the Prophet Ezekiel is that five out of every six men in the vast army of the Antichrist are going to be killed (Ezek. 39:2). This could easily number anywhere from one million to several million men.

No wonder it is called a *"carcass,"* and *"eagles,"* i.e., vultures, will come upon the dead. Actually, so many men will die that it will take *"seven months"* for Israel to bury them all, even using modern equipment such as bulldozers, etc. (Ezek. 39:12). One can well imagine the number of vultures gathered at such a feast.

(29) "IMMEDIATELY AFTER THE TRIBULATION OF THOSE DAYS SHALL THE SUN BE DARKENED, AND THE MOON SHALL NOT GIVE HER LIGHT, AND THE STARS SHALL FALL FROM HEAVEN, AND THE POWERS OF THE HEAVENS SHALL BE SHAKEN:"

The phrase, *"Immediately after the tribulation of those days,"* speaks of the days, or even hours, immediately preceding the Second Coming.

The phrase, *"Shall the sun be darkened, and the moon shall not give her light, and the stars shall fall from Heaven,"* proclaims this earth-shaking phenomenon taking place immediately before the Second Coming.

As well, this earth-shaking phenomenon concerning the *"sun,"* *"moon,"* and *"stars,"* will take place under the sixth seal, about two or two and a half years into the seven-year Tribulation. It will then be caused by a *"great earthquake,"* which is not mentioned by Christ concerning the Second Coming, but is spoken of in Revelation 16:18, and no doubt refers to that event.

Consequently, there will be a repeat of the events of the sixth seal at the Second Coming, which will greatly add to the Glory of this time.

The phrase, *"And the powers of the heavens shall be shaken,"* speaks of an upheaval in the very heavens themselves, affecting, and as stated, the *"sun, moon, and stars."* To describe such an event is impossible!

The word, *"stars,"* as here used, actually refers to meteorites, which will strike the earth, some, no doubt of great size!

Consequently, there is no need for Israel, or anyone else, to be deceived concerning some supposed appearance of Christ in *"the desert,"* etc., especially considering the earth-shaking phenomenon which will take place at the Second Coming.

(30) "AND THEN SHALL APPEAR THE SIGN OF THE SON OF MAN IN HEAVEN: AND THEN SHALL ALL THE TRIBES OF THE EARTH MOURN, AND THEY SHALL SEE THE SON OF MAN COMING IN THE CLOUDS OF HEAVEN WITH POWER AND GREAT GLORY."

The phrase, *"And then shall appear the sign of the Son of Man in Heaven,"* pertains to the Second Coming which will take place in the very midst of these earth and heaven-shaking events. In other words, these events will be the *"sign"* of the Coming of the Son of Man.

It is interesting that the title, *"Son of Man,"* is used, which denotes Christ in His human, glorified body. In other words, and exactly as the Angels said, the same Jesus Who left some 2,000 years ago is coming back (Acts 1:10-11).

The phrase, *"And then shall all the tribes of the earth mourn,"* concerns all the nations of the world which will see this phenomenon by Television, unless the shaking of the heavens destroys the Satellite reception, which it could well do! However, there is indication in this and the next phrase that Television transmission will possibly be continued.

This observance by Television, of course, will not include everybody in the world, but it definitely will include at least three-fourths of the population of the planet, that is, if Television transmission, as stated, is continued!

The nations of the world will *"mourn"* simply because they will then realize that the Jesus Who was born of the Virgin Mary, some 2,000 years ago and dying on Calvary, is actually the Son of God, exactly as the Bible states, and, in fact, was raised from the dead. They will now know that everything said about Him in the Bible is true down to the smallest detail, and that He, in effect, is God! They will *"mourn"*

because they have rejected Him, with all its disastrous consequences!

The phrase, *"And they shall see the Son of Man coming in the clouds of Heaven with Power and Great Glory,"* lends credence to the thought that much of the world will see Him, and by Television, as He makes His descent.

The *"Clouds of Heaven,"* no doubt refers to the Glory of His Coming, as He is accompanied by all the Resurrected Saints and the Angels.

At His Ascension, the *"cloud that received Him"* was not so much a literal cloud, but, instead, a *"cloud of Glory"* (Acts 1:9).

The *"power"* referred to will be without measure, and actually limitless, such as the world has never known before! Consequently, the Antichrist and his armies will be quickly defeated, and with any other opposition, whatever that may be, instantly put down. Actually, at this time, Satan and all his minions of darkness will be chained, and placed in the *"bottomless pit,"* where they will remain for the entirety of the Kingdom Age (Rev. 20:1-3).

(31) "AND HE SHALL SEND HIS ANGELS WITH A GREAT SOUND OF A TRUMPET, AND THEY SHALL GATHER TOGETHER HIS ELECT FROM THE FOUR WINDS, FROM ONE END OF HEAVEN TO THE OTHER."

The phrase, *"And He shall send His Angels,"* doesn't say whether they will be visible or not! However, inasmuch as many Angels will come with Him to earth (II Thess. 1:7-10), quite possibly they will be visible.

The word, *"Angels,"* in both the Old and New Testaments means *"Messenger."*

Jesus Christ is the Creator of all Angels, as well as all other things (Col. 1:15-16). It seems that all Angels were created in the distant past at one time, and fully mature. In other words, there is no Biblical record of a baby Angel, etc. However, there are ranks among Angels, with Michael being the only one who bears the title of *"Archangel"* (Jude 9). However, there are other chief Angels (Dan. 10:13).

Only four Angels are named in Scripture:

1. Lucifer (Isa. 14:12; Ezek. 28:11-17). This is Satan who seems to have once been the most powerful and beautiful Angel created by the Lord Jesus Christ, because the Scripture says of him, *"Thou sealest up the sum, full of wisdom, and perfect in beauty"* (Ezek. 28:12).

At some time in the distant past, Lucifer led

a revolution against God, drawing some one-third of the Angels into his rebellion (Rev. 12:4). This revolution is the cause of all the suffering, heartache, and death on planet earth, and has swallowed up billions of human beings into the abyss of darkness.

Even though Lucifer, i.e., Satan, was defeated by Jesus Christ at Calvary, still, he has been allowed to continue his deception, and will do so until the Second Coming, where he will then be locked away (Rev. 20:1-3). This is called the *"mystery of iniquity"* (II Thess. 2:7).

When Lucifer is locked away at the Second Coming, there is every evidence that all his fallen Angels and demon spirits as well, will be locked away with him. However, at the conclusion of the one-thousand-year Kingdom Age, he will be *"loosed out of his prison,"* and will be allowed one more brief effort on the earth, when he will be quickly subdued, and *"cast into the lake of fire and brimstone,"* where he will *"be tormented day and night for ever and ever"* (Rev. 20:7-10).

Thus will end his inglorious reign of terror and darkness, with Righteousness prevailing evermore thereafter! (Rev. Chpts. 21 and 22).

2. Michael: As stated, Michael is the only one called an *"Archangel,"* and seems to be the primary Angel under God who has to do with Israel, and is called in so many words, *"The Prince of Israel"* (Dan. 10:21).

3. Gabriel: Even though this Angel is not called an Archangel, still, he is said to *"stand in the Presence of God,"* which may possibly be even a higher rank. In this role, he announced the coming birth of John the Baptist, and, above all, of Christ (Dan. 8:16; 9:21; Lk. 1:19, 26).

4. Abaddon or Apollyon: This is a powerful fallen Angel who serves Satan (Rev. 9:11), and therefore, the Scripture, at least as far as names are concerned, presents two Righteous Angels and two unrighteous Angels.

Angels, as stated, are created beings with individuality and personal identity, who exist in a spiritual dimension that touches, but is not the same as our material universe. Even though our attention is not to be focused on these beings, still, the veil between us and the unseen world is pulled back slightly in the revelation of their activities.

What is seen is a spiritual universe within which an invisible war is continually being waged, which definitely translates into the

visible in the form of wasted lives, sorrow, heartache, and lost souls. Although hidden from us, Angels play a significant role both in our lives and in the whole course of history.

These supernatural beings are also referred to by other names. They are called *"sons of God,"* a phrase meaning direct creations of God (Gen. 6:2-4; Job 1:6; 2:1). They are also called *"mighty ones"* in Psalms 29:1 and *"heavenly beings"* in Psalms 89:6, as well as *"holy ones"* in Psalms 89:5, 7; and Daniel 4:13, 17, 23; 8:13.

Angels were witnesses to the creation of the material universe (Job 38:7). As well, they serve as members of God's eternal court (Job 1:6; Isa. 6:2-4), and they are exhorted to praise Him (Ps. 103:20-21; 148:2).

There seems to be different orders and different types of these powerful beings. The Cherubim, for example, have traits, seemingly, of both humans and animals (Gen. 3:24; Ps. 18:10; Isa. 6:2; Ezek. 1:5-14; 10:19-22).

The role of Angels in both Testaments is an indication of their importance to sacred history.

Angels were associated with God's deliverance of His people from slavery in Egypt. God promised Israel, *"I am sending an Angel ahead of you to guard you along the way and to bring you to the place I have prepared"* (Ex. 23:20).

On a similar mission of protection, an Angel aided Shadrach, Meshach, and Abednego in the fiery furnace (Dan. 3:28); however, this *"fourth man"* could well have been a pre-incarnate appearance of the Lord Jesus Christ. As well, an Angel helped Daniel in the lions' den (Dan. 6:22).

One of the most graphic illustrations of angelic protection is found in II Kings 6. Here, Elisha showed his servant *"the hills full of horses and chariots of fire all around them"* (II Ki. 6:17). It seems an angelic army was present to protect the Lord's Prophet.

As well, Angels were involved in God's dramatic judgments on sinful people as evidenced by the destruction of Sodom and Gomorrah (Gen. 19:1).

Also, Angels are clearly given assignments to guard and guide Believers (Gen. 24:7, 40).

Daniel 10 shows us, as well, that Angels were created by God with varying powers — or ranks — in angelic armies. This Chapter shows us that an invisible war is taking place between the Angel armies of God and those of Satan, and fought with forces whose numbers and power we cannot begin to imagine. It shows that nations as well as individuals are participants in this invisible war and that results of these conflicts influence political events in our world of space and time.

What we are shown is but a glimpse; however, what is seen is compelling evidence that there is a spiritual universe that exists alongside the universe we know through our senses. The Angels and other spiritual beings are real. God is the ultimate Ruler of the invisible as well as of the visible.

As is obvious in the Scriptures, Angels are closely associated with both the First and Second Comings of the Lord Jesus Christ. As well, they are *"all ministering spirits sent to serve those who will inherit Salvation"* (Heb. 1:14). Angels seem to have a special ministry in relation to children (Mat. 18:10). As well, Acts 12 proclaims an Angel as instrumental in releasing Peter from prison, and in preparing the way for the conversion of Cornelius (Acts 10).

In no way are Angels to be worshiped. When Believers at Colosse turned aside to follow a heresy that stressed special honor given Angels as Divine intermediaries, Paul sent a stern warning to them (Col. 2). Jesus Christ is to be the focal point of all the attention of every Believer. It was Jesus Who freed us from sin's deadly grip so that we might share through Him the fullness of all that God has for us. Angels, and as stated, play a role in the Plan of God, but they are all under the authority of the Lord Jesus Christ, *"Who is the Head over every power and authority"* (Col. 2:10). Jesus, not Angels, is the focus of our Faith. He is the One in Whom we find fulfillment (Col. 3:1-4).

It is clear from the Bible that Angels are now superior to human beings in many ways. As direct creations of God, these beings have unlimited lifetimes and unusual powers. Yet the writer to the Hebrews points out, in awed tones, that *"it is not to Angels that He* (God) *has subjected the world to come"* (Heb. 2:5).

Jesus chose to share our humanity so that He might free us from sin's grip. *"Surely it is not Angels He helps,"* the writer says in wonder, *"but Abraham's descendants"* (Heb. 2:16). Alive now in Jesus, we will be brought to Glory and lifted far above the Angels.

Angels, then, are not only God's Ministers, assigned to serve the heirs of Salvation; they

NOTES

are also eager witnesses to all that God is doing in this world (Lk. 15:10; I Cor. 11:10; I Tim. 3:16). Ultimately, human beings will be called on to judge the Angels (I Cor. 6:3). This pertains to those who fell with Lucifer.

However, throughout the entirety of the Bible, the thrust of both Testaments is clear. Human beings, not Angels, are the focus of God's concern. In return, God invites us to fix our thoughts and our Faith on Jesus, not on Angels. Consequently, we can trust Christ as Lord to supervise the unseen universe for His good purposes and for our benefit. Therefore, we can concentrate our efforts to better know and love the One Who truly is Lord of all, the Lord Jesus Christ.

(Many of the thoughts on Angels were derived from the writings of Dr. Lawrence O. Richards.)

The phrase, *"With a great sound of a trumpet,"* has to do with the announcement of an important event, the gathering of Israel at the Second Coming.

Trumpets always sounded at gatherings of Israel as outlined in the Old Testament (Ex. 19:13-19; Lev. 25:9; I Sam. 13:3; II Sam. 2:28).

The *"trumpet"* mentioned here is predicted in Isaiah 18:3; 27:13 and Zechariah 9:14. However, this trumpet is not the same as the seven trumpets of Revelation 8:2, 6, or the trumpets in connection with the Resurrection of the Righteous, which will have sounded at least seven years earlier (I Cor. 15:51-58; I Thess. 4:16).

The phrase, *"And they shall gather together His elect from the four winds, from one end of Heaven to the other,"* concerns Jews, for this is what the word, *"elect,"* means! The idea is this:

Immediately after the Second Coming, Israel, realizing that her Messiah is actually the Lord Jesus Christ, the One Who they rejected at His First Coming, will then accept Him as Lord and Saviour, as well as Messiah. Even though many Jews will then be in Israel, still, multiple millions will be scattered all over the world, as they are presently! Then, most, if not every Jew in the world, will strongly desire to be relocated in Israel and will be eager to come in order to worship the Lord, which will be their great restoration.

As eager as they are to come, the Lord will be more eager to gather them.

If one is to notice, the words are used *"His*

elect," meaning that He now owns them, as they own Him. Israel will then carry out her role as originally designed by God. Even as she has failed so much in the past, she will now succeed even more so, and because of Jesus Christ.

(32) "NOW LEARN A PARABLE OF THE FIG TREE; WHEN HIS BRANCH IS YET TENDER, AND PUTTETH FORTH LEAVES, YE KNOW THAT SUMMER IS NIGH:"

The phrase, *"Now learn a parable of the fig tree,"* is the first of five parables in Matthew 24 and 25.

The Bible presents three trees, the fig, the olive, and the vine, as representing the nation of Israel nationally, spiritually, and dispensationally as a witness for God in the earth.

The phrase, *"When his branch is yet tender, and putteth forth leaves,"* is meant to serve as the illustration of Israel nationally.

In 1948, Israel became a nation once again, after approximately 1900 years of being scattered all over the world. As well, their ancient homeland as originally given to them by God, and despite being contested bitterly by the Arabs, was once more occupied, at least in part, by Jews. For the first time in about 1900 years, it was once again known as the *"State of Israel."* Jacob's sons were coming home!

Since that time, and even though the *"branch is yet tender,"* still, it is now *"putting forth leaves."*

The phrase, *"Ye know that summer is nigh,"* refers to Israel as the greatest sign of all that we are now living in the last of the last days. The analogy is well taken.

As simple as ascertaining that summer is near due to the budding of the fig tree, likewise, the present development of Israel is the sign of all signs that several things are very near. Those things are: A. The Rapture of the Church; B. The rise of the Antichrist; C. The Coming Great Tribulation which will last for seven years; D. The Battle of Armageddon which will be fought at the conclusion of the Great Tribulation; and, E. The Second Coming of the Lord.

(33) "SO LIKEWISE YE, WHEN YE SHALL SEE ALL THESE THINGS, KNOW THAT IT IS NEAR, EVEN AT THE DOORS."

The phrase, *"So likewise ye,"* is meant to point to those alive at this particular time, whether Jews or Gentiles, i.e., the Church.

The phrase, *"When ye shall see all these things,"* is meant to point to the rise of Israel on to the last half of the *"Great Tribulation."* At this time, *"false Christs and false prophets"* will abundantly appear, *"showing great signs and wonders,"* etc. As well, tremendous disturbances in the heavens, and according to the Book of Revelation will be taking place. That is what is meant by *"these things."*

The phrase, *"Know that it is near, even at the doors,"* refers to the Second Coming, because this is what Jesus has just been referring to.

Consequently, there will be no excuse for Israel not knowing the approximate time of His Second Coming. They need not be deceived by false claims. Yet, Israel's animosity toward the New Testament may provide a hindrance; however, deep into the last half of the Great Tribulation, it will be glaringly obvious that the Antichrist is not the Messiah. Quite possibly many Jews will then turn to these very words in the New Testament.

Also, considering the plain teaching of Christ on this all-important subject, there is no excuse for the modern Church to continue to project its false interpretations concerning the end time. It should be glaringly obvious to all that these events did not transpire in 70 A.D., as many now claim! Israel was then destroyed with its people scattered all over the world, and as obvious, was not budding as the *"fig tree,"* symbolizing the rebirth of these people.

(34) "VERILY I SAY UNTO YOU, THIS GENERATION SHALL NOT PASS, TILL ALL THESE THINGS BE FULFILLED."

This Scripture has two meanings:

1. It speaks of the *"generation"* which will be alive at the time of the Great Tribulation, with all of these events happening in that particular time-frame. In other words, these things will not take place over a period of hundreds or thousands of years, but, instead, in a relatively short period of time, i.e., during the time-frame of one generation, but not necessarily that long!

2. The phrase, *"this generation,"* means that the Hebrew people shall continue as a people, even though greatly persecuted by Satan, but in unbelief, as they now are! This unbelief will last up to the Second Advent (Deut. 32:5, 20).

The phrase, *"Till all these things be fulfilled,"* demonstrates inspiration, and guarantees its fulfillment. In other words, these things will be fulfilled exactly as Jesus proclaimed!

(35) "HEAVEN AND EARTH SHALL PASS AWAY, BUT MY WORDS SHALL NOT PASS AWAY."

The phrase, *"Heaven and earth shall pass away,"* does not mean as some think, total annihilation, but rather a change from one condition or state to another.

The Greek word for *"pass away,"* is *"parerchomai,"* and means *"a change only,"* and not annihilation. Actually, the heavens and earth are eternal (Ps. 72:5-17; 89:3-37; 104:5; Eccl. 1:4), and cannot pass out of existence. However, they will be *"changed"* (Rom. 8:21-23; Heb. 1:10-12; 12:25-28), be renovated by fire (II Pet. 3:5-13), and be renewed (Rev. 21:1), but never pass out of existence.

The phrase, *"But My Words shall not pass away,"* means that even though the *"Heaven and earth"* may be changed, the *"Words of the Lord"* will not be changed. They are inviolable.

(36) "BUT OF THAT DAY AND HOUR KNOWETH NO MAN, NO, NOT THE ANGELS OF HEAVEN, BUT MY FATHER ONLY."

The phrase, *"But of that day and hour knoweth no man,"* does not refer to the approximate time, which will be at the conclusion of the Great Tribulation, but of the very *"day and hour."*

As well, when Jesus uttered these words, He gave no clue as to when they would begin to be fulfilled, i.e., the fig tree putting forth its leaves, etc. In fact, it has been almost 2,000 years from the time He gave these predictions, and they still have not been fulfilled, but are only in the beginning stages.

The phrase, *"No, not the Angels of Heaven, but My Father only,"* means there is a *"day and hour"* this will take place, but not known by men or Angels.

The phrase, *"My Father only,"* no doubt presently includes God the Son and God the Holy Spirit.

As well, many have misunderstood verse 33 and 36 as pertaining to the Rapture, which it does not! Actually, the Rapture is not mentioned whatsoever in the prophetic part of Matthew 24.

In Truth, there are no signs given in the Bible pointing to the Rapture. It, within itself, will, in fact, be one of the greatest signs of the soon to come Second Advent.

NOTES

There are no Prophecies to be fulfilled before the Rapture, for it can take place at any time without any sign or Prophecy coming to pass (Phil. 3:21; Tit. 2:13). All signs of the Coming of Christ point to the Second Advent and not the Rapture.

There will be at least seven years between the two events, and maybe even more (II Thess. 2:7).

The Rapture is not the Second Advent, nor one phase or stage of it, for Christ does not come to the earth at that time. He meets the Saints in the air and takes them back to Heaven (I Thess. 2:19; 3:13; Rev. 19:1-11).

The Saints will stay in Heaven with Christ for these years and then return to the earth with Him at the Second Advent (Zech. 14:5; Jude 14; Rev. 19:11-21).

(37) "BUT AS THE DAYS OF NOE WERE, SO SHALL ALSO THE COMING OF THE SON OF MAN BE."

The phrase, *"But as the days of Noe were,"* proclaims the fact that the men of Noah's day were insensible to the signs and Prophecies predicting the coming flood, and so will men be blind to the signs announcing the coming of the Son of Man.

The phrase, *"So shall also the coming of the Son of Man be,"* is meant to point not only to the world, but the Church as well!

The Message of the Rapture and the Second Coming is almost lost in the modern Church. Most who refer to themselves as Christians, have little or no knowledge at all of end time events. To be sure, and in a negative sense, that is a sign of the spiritual declension which will take place in these last days (II Tim. 4:3-4).

To use a particular Pentecostal Denomination as an example (the Assemblies of God), when I was a child, the soon and eminent return of the Lord Jesus Christ in the Rapture, and, as well, the Second Coming were proclaimed constantly. At that time, great segments of this particular Denomination were on fire for God, consequently, heralding this particular Message.

At the present, attention, and due to false teaching, is more and more being focused on *"this present world,"* instead of *"the world to come."* Consequently, the Message of the Rapture and the Second Coming is little preached in many, if not most, of these particular Churches, as well as many other Pentecostal and Charismatic Churches. Actually, and as previously stated, the *"Kingdom Now"* and *"Prosperity"* teaching have made great inroads into all of these religious bodies, consequently, undermining the all-important Doctrines of the Coming of the Lord. Such proclaims a terrible spiritual declension, which actually says that the Church is not too very interested in Jesus coming back. It shows a tremendously impaired spiritual relationship.

(38) "FOR AS IN THE DAYS THAT WERE BEFORE THE FLOOD THEY WERE EATING AND DRINKING, MARRYING AND GIVING IN MARRIAGE, UNTIL THE DAY THAT NOE ENTERED INTO THE ARK,"

The phrase, *"For as in the days that were before the flood,"* likens that cataclysmic event to the Second Coming of the Lord. Tragically, Noah had no favorable response at all concerning his Message of a coming flood. The people did not believe him, and, as a result of that unbelief, met his proclamation with derision. The next phrase proves that.

The phrase, *"They were eating and drinking, marrying and giving in marriage,"* refers to an absolute lack of concern respecting Noah's Message of a coming flood.

The word, *"eating,"* here implies eating gluttonously, meaning there was no thought of Repentance and no concern for the Message. In other words, it was business as usual.

The phrase, *"Until the day that Noe entered into the Ark,"* means they watched him build the Ark, and heard him preach Righteousness for many years, but still took no heed.

(39) "AND KNEW NOT UNTIL THE FLOOD CAME, AND TOOK THEM ALL AWAY; SO SHALL ALSO THE COMING OF THE SON OF MAN BE."

The phrase, *"And knew not until the flood came,"* means that even though they heard Noah's Message, still, it was to them as an idle tale, and they never for a moment believed that it had any validity. Consequently, when the *"flood came,"* as it most certainly did, it was something they never dreamed in a million years would happen. In other words, they had laughed about Noah's Message, as well as making fun of him, with his Message literally becoming a joke to them. They were to find out that it was no joke!

The phrase, *"And took them all away,"* means

they were destroyed, i.e., drowned, and, consequently, eternally lost.

The phrase, *"So shall also the coming of the Son of Man be,"* speaks of the similarity, and in the Words of Christ, of Noah's time and the Coming of the Lord.

As well, this notes the fact that as the flood was destructive, at least to evil, so shall the Coming of Jesus be.

The world of Noah's day was not getting better and better, but rather worse and worse. Likewise, this present world system is not getting better, i.e., Christianized, but rather more and more evil. To be sure, and sadly so, the Church is not going to change it. By the Power of Christ, and the moving of the Holy Spirit, individuals are saved out of this system of evil, which is really what the Church is called to do. However, the Church will not be successful in Christianizing the society, but, instead, if that tact is taken, as it now is, society will be successful in socializing Christianity. As we have repeatedly stated, it is not the business of the Church to save society, but, instead, to save men out of society, and by the preaching of the Gospel.

When the True Church is raptured away (I Thess. 4:16-17), as it will be in the near future, then the last restraint against evil and wickedness will be taken away, after which the deterioration of society will be rapid.

Great segments of the world will have so gone after the Antichrist, at that time, even declaring him to be God, that the idea of Christ's returning will be preposterous! In effect, and according to these Passages, during the Great Tribulation, there will be precious few who will be expecting the return of Christ. Nevertheless, it will happen!

(40) "THEN SHALL TWO BE IN THE FIELD; THE ONE SHALL BE TAKEN, AND THE OTHER LEFT."

This Scripture has absolutely nothing to do with the Rapture as some have been led to believe. It pertains solely to the Second Coming.

As Christ mentioned the people in the time of Noah being *"taken away"* by the flood, as well, He speaks here of some being taken in another kind of flood, i.e., the destruction at Armageddon.

As well, the Passages could also refer to the terrible destructive power of the *"seven seals,"* *"seven trumpets,"* and *"seven vials."* During the

Great Tribulation lasting for some seven years, counting these terrible judgments poured out by God, along with the horrible wars which will be fought, there is a possibility that half of the population of the world could be killed during this particular time. And if we are to take these Scriptures literally, that is exactly what it means!

(41) "TWO WOMEN SHALL BE GRINDING AT THE MILL; THE ONE SHALL BE TAKEN, AND THE OTHER LEFT."

This Scripture proclaims the fact that the terrible devastation coming at this time will affect not only the combatants in the field, but, as well, all domestic life. Of course, it would be obvious that the judgments would be indiscriminatory; however, war, as well, is now just as destructive to civilians as the soldiers in the field.

As should be obvious, this is not going to be a pleasant time, and, consequently, describes perfectly the Words of Christ, *"Great tribulation, such as was not since the beginning of the world to this time, no, nor ever shall be."*

(42) "WATCH THEREFORE: FOR YE KNOW NOT WHAT HOUR YOUR LORD DOTH COME."

The phrase, *"Watch therefore,"* means that the end will be sudden, i.e., the Coming of the Lord. This, as is obvious, is addressed to those who will be living at that particular time and most particular, the Jews.

The phrase, *"For ye know not what hour your Lord doth come,"* even though denying the reader the knowledge of the exact time, still, proclaims the certitude of His Coming!

The manner of withholding the exact time is done for a purpose. Israel, at this time, will be grievously affected by the Antichrist, and, consequently, will begin to cry unto the Lord, possibly as they have never sought Him before!

The Promise of the Coming, but yet the lack of knowledge respecting the exact time, only heightens the desperation and hence the pleading, which is the very posture desired by the Holy Spirit.

(43) "BUT KNOW THIS, THAT IF THE GOODMAN OF THE HOUSE HAD KNOWN IN WHAT WATCH THE THIEF WOULD COME, HE WOULD HAVE WATCHED, AND WOULD NOT HAVE SUFFERED HIS HOUSE TO BE BROKEN UP."

This is called the Parable of the Goodman

NOTES

of the House. It is meant to emphasize the readiness which should be engaged respecting the Second Coming.

The phrase, *"But know this,"* is said with strength, and is meant to signify the readiness which Christ is espousing respecting that particular time.

The phrase, *"That if the goodman of the house had known in what watch the thief would come,"* is meant to symbolize the fact that Christ will come in the same manner as a thief would come in the entering of a house. As is obvious, he will come at the time that is least expected.

As should be obvious, Christ is not placing any approval on such nefarious activity as theft, but, instead, is calling attention to the method.

The phrase, *"He would have watched, and would not have suffered his house to be broken up,"* means that the thief does not send a message that he is coming, but, instead, tries to come at a time least expected.

The moral of this Parable is that the world will not believe at all in the Coming of Christ, and, as well, the Antichrist will think he has successfully made his claim to deity, and, consequently, there is no fear from this sector.

The invasion of Israel by the Antichrist and his armies, will be a greatly thought-out plan. The Scripture says, *"And thou shalt think an evil thought"* (Ezek. 38:10).

As this massive army rolls down into Israel in order to bring about the final solution once and for all, there seems no stopping of the Antichrist from his goal of annihilating Israel, and, for that matter, taking over the entirety of the world. His arrogance will know no bounds, and victory is his, or so he thinks! As he comes against Jerusalem, with half of the city falling to him, to be sure, there is no thought of the Coming of the Lord. However, Zechariah writes, *"Then shall the Lord go forth, and fight against those nations, as when He fought in the day of battle"* (Zech. 14:3).

(44) "THEREFORE BE YE ALSO READY: FOR IN SUCH AN HOUR AS YE THINK NOT THE SON OF MAN COMETH."

The phrase, *"Therefore be ye also ready,"* speaks to Israel. They will be the ones under siege, consequently facing certain annihilation. Therefore, they are to believe that He is coming back, which He will, and because He has promised!

They are to be *"ready,"* not for annihilation by the Antichrist, but for the Coming of the Lord, which will be to their rescue, as well as to set up the Kingdom Age.

The phrase, *"For in such an hour as ye think not the Son of Man cometh,"* actually means that when they have about given up hope, Jesus will come!

In Truth, they will be very close to annihilation, and as we have stated, with all of Israel taken by the Beast, and with Jerusalem ready to fall at any hour, or possibly any minute.

Inasmuch as it is very late, even past the time when they can be rescued at least by any type of earthly army, Christ will come!

To be sure, it will be at the last minute, even at a time when most have given up hope. Nevertheless, He here says, *"The Son of Man cometh!"*, and come He shall!

(45) "WHO THEN IS A FAITHFUL AND WISE SERVANT, WHOM HIS LORD HATH MADE RULER OVER HIS HOUSEHOLD, TO GIVE THEM MEAT IN DUE SEASON?"

This is called the Parable of the Faithful Servant!

The question, *"Who then is a faithful and wise servant . . . ?"*, is meant to apply not only to Israel, but to the Church as well! Faithfulness as a quality is demanded of all, with Christ directing this Parable to all!

The Holy Spirit demands of all followers of Christ that we be *"faithful,"* i.e., faithful to Christ, and *"wise,"* i.e., put Christ first in all things, and, as well, know and understand His Word.

The question continued, *"Whom his Lord hath made ruler over His household, to give them meat in due season?"*, refers to all who follow Christ, seeking to carry out His Will.

The *"meat"* here spoken of, concerns the Word of God. It is the business of all God-called Preachers, whether they be Apostles, Prophets, Evangelists, Pastors, or Teachers, to give the *"household,"* i.e., Body of Christ, the *"strong meat"* of the Word (Heb. 5:12, 14).

(46) BLESSED IS THAT SERVANT, WHOM HIS LORD WHEN HE COMETH SHALL FIND SO DOING."

The phrase, *"Blessed is that servant,"* means those who are *"faithful and wise"* respecting the Word of God. This man is happy!

The phrase, *"Whom his Lord when He cometh shall find so doing,"* concerns either the

NOTES

Rapture or the Second Coming. The moral applies to all, whether Jews or Gentiles.

(47) "VERILY I SAY UNTO YOU, THAT HE SHALL MAKE HIM RULER OVER ALL HIS GOODS."

The phrase, *"Verily I say unto you,"* is spoken strongly, and is meant to denote the seriousness of this matter.

The phrase, *"That He shall make him ruler over all His goods,"* refers to the Resurrected Saints being made *"rulers"* in the coming Kingdom Age, and the faithful of Israel being placed in the same capacity as the premier nation in the world.

As to exactly how many Jews are going to be saved in the Great Tribulation is known only by the Lord. The Scripture is clear that 144,000 (12,000 from each Tribe) will come to Christ (Rev. 7:3-8). However, they will be raptured at about the mid-point of the Great Tribulation (Rev. 14:3-5).

As well, we are told of a *"great multitude, which no man could number, of all nations, and kindred, and people, and tongues,"* who will give their hearts to Christ, and will be killed by the Antichrist (Rev. 7:9-17). The implication is that at least some of the people will be Jews, because it says, *"All nations, and kindreds, and people, and tongues."*

Also, the *"two witnesses"* will prophesy in Jerusalem the last three and a half years of the Great Tribulation, whose Ministries will, no doubt, win some to Christ.

At any rate, there will certainly be some Jews who will be in this number, and will be made *"rulers"* in the Coming Kingdom Age.

(48) "BUT AND IF THAT EVIL SERVANT SHALL SAY IN HIS HEART, MY LORD DELAYETH HIS COMING;"

If the heart surrenders the hope of the Lord's Coming, it will not be long until the conduct be that of verse 49.

In this verse, and so many others, we find the tremendous emphasis placed by the Holy Spirit on the Coming of the Lord, and the heart's response to it. Consequently, those who hold to the erroneous *"Kingdom Now"* teaching, whether they understand it or not, are actually saying by their false beliefs, *"My Lord delayeth His Coming."* Of course, they would deny this; however, anything that places the Coming of the Lord, whether the Rapture or the Second

Advent in a position of denial or delay, has entered into unbelief.

The *"heart"* is here mentioned because unbelief begins here!

Irrespective of the reasons, whether false doctrine or spiritual declension, if the spiritual cover be pulled aside, one will find that self-will is the culprit. It is man's will versus God's Will.

If one is to notice, the *"evil servant"* still refers to God as *"My Lord,"* but yet he falsely interprets the Word of God respecting the all-important event of the Rapture or the Second Coming, hence, is called *"evil"* by the Holy Spirit.

(49) "AND SHALL BEGIN TO SMITE HIS FELLOWSERVANTS, AND TO EAT AND DRINK WITH THE DRUNKEN;"

This Passage tells us that the *"blessed hope"* of the Rapture and the Promise of the Second Coming is a tremendous inducement for spiritual consecration. John the Beloved said, *"And every man that hath this hope* (the Rapture) *in him purifieth himself, even as He* (Jesus) *is pure"* (I Jn. 3:3).

Not in modern times has this *"hope"* burned more feebly than now! As stated, the Rapture is little believed by the far greater majority of Christians, and, as well, false teaching has placed the Second Coming in a posture of the whim of man. As a result, and exactly as this Passage proclaims, two things are happening:

1. *"And shall begin to smite his fellowservants":* The maltreatment of fellow Christians has probably never been higher in Christendom, at least in modern times! Slander, gossip, and whispering, have never been more rampant than presently. The great Christian Graces, such as love, longsuffering, compassion, patience, forbearance, goodness, and grace, have never been in shorter supply.

2. *"And to eat and drink with the drunken":* Sadly and tragically, most modern Christians have little separation from the world. There was a time that most Believers felt that Hollywood was a negative influence on the Christian experience. Today it is very difficult to find many Christians who do not attend movies regularly, and despite the fact that they are more vulgar and obscene than ever! Social drinking is rampant, along with about anything else the world does. In other words, there is very little separation from the world in modern Christian circles!

NOTES

Jesus plainly says in these Passages, that an erroneous concept of the coming Rapture and the Second Coming, is greatly responsible for this.

(50) "THE LORD OF THAT SERVANT SHALL COME IN A DAY WHEN HE LOOKETH NOT FOR HIM, AND IN AN HOUR THAT HE IS NOT AWARE OF,"

The phrase, *"The Lord of that servant shall come,"* emphatically states that the time of the Lord's Coming, whether the Rapture or the Second Coming, has absolutely nothing to do with man's prognostications. The day and the hour is chosen exclusively by the Lord. As well, He is coming, and irrespective as to whether men are ready or not!

The phrase, *"In a day when he looketh not for Him,"* means that those who are not looking for the Rapture, and because they don't even believe in it, are going to be rudely awakened. The emphasis is that every Believer should *"look for Him"* at any time, and at all times!

The phrase, *"And in an hour that he is not aware of,"* means that the foolish prognostications of the *"Kingdom Now"* beliefs, are going to be rudely interrupted.

The Faith Message so-called, which has been heavily proclaimed throughout the Body of Christ in the last thirty years, has gradually changed the emphasis of Faith from the Lord to the Believer; from Heaven to earth; from spiritual things to material things; from looking to leave to looking to stay! The spiritual emphasis has become skewed, so much in fact that what is presently believed and practiced by most Christians has little resemblance to the Word of God.

Many, if not most Believers, at least in the Pentecostal and Charismatic realm, are little looking for the Rapture, but, instead, how they can believe God to give them a Cadillac in place of their Honda, or a $200,000 home in place of their $100,000 home! The emphasis, to use a cliche, is no longer on Jesus, but rather jewelry. Today, instead of Jesus using us, we use Him.

To be sure, it is a heady message and attracts many followers because it appeals to greed and pride, which, sadly, resides, at least somewhat, in most of us!

At the present, money and people are the criteria of the modern Church, with Righteousness and Holiness of little consequence, if any at all! And then too often, if these twin subjects of Bible Standards are approached at all, it is man's variety of righteousness and holiness, which, in effect, is self-righteousness, etc.

(51) "AND SHALL CUT HIM ASUNDER, AND APPOINT HIM HIS PORTION WITH THE HYPOCRITES: THERE SHALL BE WEEPING AND GNASHING OF TEETH."

The phrase, *"And shall cut him asunder,"* is chilling indeed!

This simply means that the individual, at least if engaging himself in the wickedness spoken of by the Lord, will lose his soul. Consequently, the fallacious Doctrine of Unconditional Eternal Security is refuted once again.

The phrase, *"And appoint him his portion with the hypocrites,"* tells us two things:

1. It is the Lord Who does the appointing. Too often, too many attempt to please men, without any thought of pleasing God.

However, and as here proclaimed, it is not man who does the appointing, whether good or bad, but God. If He is for us, who can be against us? Conversely, if He is against us, who can be for us? At least, that will do any good!

2. Even though he is not here called a hypocrite, still, his portion will be with them, meaning that the Lord places both in the same category.

The phrase, *"There shall be weeping and gnashing of teeth,"* tells us this is not just a loss of reward, but, instead, the loss of the soul. In other words, the individual, though professing to know the Lord all the time, even referring to Him as *"My Lord,"* still, will be judged by the Lord as having no Salvation, and, consequently, dying eternally lost!

CHAPTER 25

(1) "THEN SHALL THE KINGDOM OF HEAVEN BE LIKENED UNTO TEN VIRGINS, WHICH TOOK THEIR LAMPS, AND WENT FORTH TO MEET THE BRIDEGROOM."

This Chapter contains the Parable of the Ten Virgins, the Parable of the Talents, and the Judgment of the Living Nations at Christ's Second Advent.

The Parable of the Ten Virgins is very similar to the Parable of the Faithful (and unfaithful)

Servant, in that it stresses faithfulness, watchfulness, and consecration. Consequently, it concerns all who follow Christ, whether Gentiles or Jews. Actually, the Lord makes no distinction, with the exception of certain promises made to the Jews respecting future events, etc. Salvation has always been alike for all men (Jn. 3:16). In other words, the Lord does not have one Salvation for Gentiles and another for Jews. All must come the same way, which is by and through Jesus Christ, for, as Peter said, *"Neither is there Salvation in any other: for there is none other name under Heaven given among men, whereby we must be saved"* (Acts 4:12).

The phrase, *"Then shall the Kingdom of Heaven be likened unto ten virgins,"* is intended to illustrate watchfulness in view of His Coming. Consequently, once again the all-important Doctrine of the Rapture and the Second Coming are here expressed.

The number *"ten"* was looked at by the Jews as the number of perfection; such a number of persons was required to form a Synagogue, and to be present at any office, ceremony, or formal benediction.

Talmudic authorities affirm that the lamps used in bridal processions were usually ten in number.

The *"virgins"* here spoken of represent those who have accepted the Lord and, consequently, are cleansed from the pollution of the world.

If one is to notice, the bride is not here mentioned, and because the *"virgins"* are actually the bride, i.e., Church, one in unity, and members in particular, hence, ten.

The phrase, *"Which took their lamps,"* represents each as being responsible for their own preparation concerning the coming wedding.

The *"lamps"* represent the Light of Christ within us, and nurtured by the oil of the Holy Spirit.

The phrase, *"And went forth to meet the bridegroom,"* speaks of preparation of the Church to meet Christ at His Coming.

This preparation should be constant and ongoing, with an anticipation of His appearing at any time. The moral of these Parables, consequently, teaches constant consecration, and watchfulness for the Lord.

Some claim that these Parables are to be looked at only in the broad lesson they teach, such as the lesson of watchfulness as we have just stated, with the various parts of the story such as the *"virgins"* or *"oil,"* etc., as having no spiritual meaning. However, the method of the Holy Spirit in the entirety of the Bible lends no credence to this belief, but rather the opposite! The object is, and intended we believe, by the Holy Spirit, that the Parables be properly interpreted, even in their various parts, which will then convey a Truth far beyond the mere intent of the major thrust, as important as that may be!

As an example, when Jesus gave the Parable of the Tares and Wheat (Mat. 13:24-30), His Disciples came to Him at a private time, asking that He explain it to them.

He could have just said that the Parable illustrated the opposition of the powers of darkness to the presentation of the Gospel, and our response to it. However, He assigned a great significance to each part of the Parable, saying, *"He that soweth the good seed is the Son of Man."*

He then said, *"The field is the world; the good seed are the children of the Kingdom; but the tares are the children of the wicked one,"* etc.

In other words, each particular part of the Parable had a spiritual meaning, as is here obvious! Consequently, each one of His Parables certainly teach a particular Truth, but, as well, each part of the Parable presents a spiritual Truth, that is if properly interpreted, which lends emphasis to the over-all thrust.

(2) "AND FIVE OF THEM WERE WISE, AND FIVE WERE FOOLISH."

We know from verse 1, that all were *"virgins,"* consequently, belonging to Christ. We also know that all had *"lamps,"* which referred to the Light of Christ. Outwardly, all were the same, but there was a difference in their characters as proved by the results. The Holy Spirit gives them labels exactly as He does all Christians.

He labeled *"five of them as wise, and five as foolish!"*

Why?

The next verse tells us.

(3) "THEY THAT WERE FOOLISH TOOK THEIR LAMPS, AND TOOK NO OIL WITH THEM:"

The *"foolish"* as labeled by the Holy Spirit, are those who took no extra supply of oil, only what was already in their lamps.

The *"oil"* as should be obvious, is a symbol of the Holy Spirit. The moral should be well taken.

When the individual is saved and filled with

the Spirit, it is natural that the light of their life provided by the Spirit would, at that time, burn brightly. However, the manner in which the Holy Spirit functions within our lives, is designed that we should need and receive many fillings. In other words, the supply that is present now will not last forever, and actually only for a short while.

This is the reason that Paul said, *"Be filled with the Spirit,"* or as it should have been translated, *"Be being filled with the Spirit,"* which implies a constant refilling (Eph. 5:18).

This is the reason that Church attendance, one's prayer life, and study of the Word, are vastly important. For one to be as he ought to be in Christ, there must be many fillings of the Holy Spirit, which are actually replenishments. Tragically, the *"oil"* in many Christian lives has long since burned out, with no refilling, which has resulted in spiritual bareness. This is partly what Jesus was speaking of when He said, *"So then because thou art lukewarm, and neither cold nor hot, I will spew thee out of My Mouth"* (Rev. 3:16).

These *"foolish"* virgins, and as labeled by the Holy Spirit, *"took no oil with them,"* i.e., were not refilled! The result of this foolishness would be the eternal loss of their souls, which, once again, refutes the unscriptural doctrine of unconditional eternal security.

(4) "BUT THE WISE TOOK OIL IN THEIR VESSELS WITH THEIR LAMPS."

The Holy Spirit labels these *"virgins"* as *"wise."*

Why?

They not only had the *"oil,"* i.e., Holy Spirit, in their *"lamps,"* i.e., infilling of the Spirit, but, as well, they took extra oil in their *"vessels,"* i.e., refillings!

The emphasis is, and by the Holy Spirit, that it's not so much what we had yesterday, but what we have today!

To be sure, all professed, but all at the present time did not possess, even though all at one time did. Only those who continue to walk with the Lord, drawing ever nearer to Him, consequently, having many refillings of the Holy Spirit, are called wise. Jesus said, *"If ye continue in My Word, then are ye My Disciples indeed"* (Jn. 8:31).

The others retained the outward show and form of Faith, but neglected the true inward life of Faith; they had the appearance without

NOTES

the reality, and were called by the Holy Spirit *"foolish."* To be sure, just a little later, we will see exactly how foolish!

(5) "WHILE THE BRIDEGROOM TARRIED, THEY ALL SLUMBERED AND SLEPT."

The phrase, *"While the bridegroom tarried,"* refers to Jesus Who has not yet come, but, in effect, will come at any time; however, a time not known by the *"ten virgins,"* i.e., Body of Christ.

The phrase, *"They all slumbered and slept,"* concerns itself with the normal activities of life. It does not imply that by doing this, they did something wrong.

Actually, the phrase is intended to point to the readiness of the five wise virgins, and irrespective of their status or occupation in life. In other words, they did these other things, whatever they may have been, but their primary objectiveness was *"readiness"* for the Lord's return.

I wonder how many presently fall into the category of *"wise?"* If we are to take this Parable literally, it would mean only about half of those who claim to know the Lord actually do. And of course, even that number would have to be qualified.

The Holy Spirit used the word, *"virgins,"* which implies individuals who had truly once been saved and who truly once knew the Lord. This, within itself, would eliminate most of those who call themselves *"Christians,"* simply because many really have never known the Lord.

So, is He saying that only about fifty percent of those who truly once knew the Lord will actually be ready at His Coming?

It is a sobering thought!

(6) "AND AT MIDNIGHT THERE WAS A CRY MADE, BEHOLD, THE BRIDEGROOM COMETH; GO YE OUT TO MEET HIM."

The phrase, *"And at midnight there was a cry made,"* proclaims the time of the Coming of the Lord, i.e., *"midnight."* No, it does not literally refer to *"midnight,"* because, *"But of that day and hour knoweth no man, no, not the Angels of Heaven, but my Father only"* (Mat. 24:36). The idea is this:

Every Believer should live in their expectation of the Rapture as if it will happen any time, even at the most inopportune time. In other words, they must be ready at all times!

Many would like the Lord to come at the exact time they are praying, in Church, or in the midst of Holy Ghost Revival. In fact, for

some, that will happen! However, for many, it will be at *"midnight,"* i.e., *"when ye think not!"*

The phrase, *"Behold, the bridegroom cometh,"* refers to Christ and His Coming.

The phrase, *"Go ye out to meet Him,"* refers to the time that all should have been waiting for, but the five called *"foolish"* shows that they were not looking for Him, were not prepared for Him, and, consequently, were not ready for Him.

(7) "THEN ALL THOSE VIRGINS AROSE, AND TRIMMED THEIR LAMPS."

The *"trimming"* of the lamps consisted of removing (cutting off) the charred portion of the wick, and raising the wick itself by means of a pointed wire which was fastened by a chain to each lamp. This would be followed by the replenishment of oil from the vessel carried for that very purpose.

This was done twice a day in the Tabernacle and Temple of old.

If the wick was not trimmed, it would give off more smoke than light, and ultimately go out.

Even though *"all"* of the virgins arose and trimmed their lamps, still, there is evidence that the five foolish had not been trimming their wicks, and, consequently, had carried no extra oil.

Many Believers do not *"burn brightly"* for this very reason. They fail to lay aside every weight and sin that doth so easily beset them, i.e., do not trim the wick, and, consequently, the light is extinguished (Heb. 12:1).

(8) "AND THE FOOLISH SAID UNTO THE WISE, GIVE US OF YOUR OIL; FOR OUR LAMPS ARE GONE OUT."

The phrase, *"And the foolish said unto the wise, Give us of your oil,"* portrays an improper manner of obtaining *"oil,"* i.e., the Holy Spirit.

Regrettably, in most Churches, the spiritual load is carried by only a few, and irrespective of the size of the congregation.

The *"foolish"* tend to think that the spirituality of others will be a provision for them as well! However, these Passages tell us differently.

Each individual must have his own touch with the Lord, and irrespective of what others may do.

The phrase, *"For our lamps are gone out,"* should have been translated, *"are going out,"* for a wick will burn brightly for a short time, but not having oil, will ultimately go out.

Sadly and regrettably, the *"lamps"* of many

Christians are either going out or else have already gone out!

(9) "BUT THE WISE ANSWERED, SAYING, NOT SO; LEST THERE BE NOT ENOUGH FOR US AND YOU: BUT GO YE RATHER TO THEM THAT SELL, AND BUY FOR YOURSELVES."

The phrase, *"But the wise answered, saying, Not so,"* proclaims a Truth that spiritual energy cannot be derived from others. Once again, a close experience with the Lord by one individual, will in no way suffice for another individual, and irrespective as to how related they may be. In other words, consecration cannot be borrowed from someone else. The Lord judges each person individually, and each person, individually, will have to stand or fall on their own consecration, or the lack of it.

The phrase, *"Lest there be not enough for us and you,"* means that as they needed their supply of oil, likewise, whatever amount of Grace is given by the Lord to any particular individual, and irrespective of its abundance, is needed by that particular individual. For instance, Paul was no doubt given a large supply of Grace, but it was Grace that he needed, and, in fact, could not be passed on to others (II Cor. 12:7-12).

The entirety of the idea is that the Lord has designed His Salvation Plan in such a manner that each individual is responsible for his or her personal consecration, or the lack of it. As someone has said, God has no grandsons!

To be frank, there have been, and no doubt shall be, multiple millions, who, in a time of emergency, have said to a consecrated loved one, *"Give us of your oil,"* but such could not be done, and because they are not the supplier, but the Lord.

Each Salvation is enough only for the individual, and not for anyone else.

The phrase, *"But go ye rather to them that sell, and buy for yourselves,"* more perfectly explains the situation than many realize.

Basically, this is what Jesus was speaking of when He said, *"If any man will come after Me, let him deny himself, and take up his cross, and follow Me"* (Mat. 16:24).

Actually, this statement was made in the context of what is now being discussed, for Jesus then said, *"For the Son of Man shall come in the Glory of His Father with His Angels; and then He shall reward every man according to his works"* (Mat. 16:27).

The idea is not that one can purchase by merit or good works that which is desperately needed, but, instead, *"That he will lose his life, and by the losing of his life for Christ's sake, he shall find it,"* i.e., *"buy for yourselves"* (Mat. 16:25).

This is what the *"foolish"* have failed to do all along, and is typical of many Christians.

(10) "AND WHILE THEY WENT TO BUY, THE BRIDEGROOM CAME; AND THEY THAT WERE READY WENT IN WITH HIM TO THE MARRIAGE: AND THE DOOR WAS SHUT."

The phrase, *"And while they went to buy, the bridegroom came,"* portrays them doing what they should have done all along, but now too late! As after death, one cannot get right with God, for it is too late; likewise, at the Rapture of the Church, there will be no time to get ready then, as millions will no doubt try to do, for that preparation should have already been made. Actually, and as repeatedly stated, this is the moral of the Parable.

The phrase, *"And they that were ready went in with Him to the marriage,"* means exactly what it says, *"That were ready!"*

I think this Parable teaches us, and graphically so, that one having been truly saved at a point in time, does not ensure that he will make the Rapture. The teaching is here explicit, that many, although once having known the Lord, and even retaining the outward show and form of Faith, still, within, have no inward life of Faith, and, consequently, *"are not ready,"* i.e., are spiritually lost.

The idea is that having been ready twenty years ago, and even yesterday, is not sufficient. One must be ready now, i.e., when the bridegroom comes!

The phrase, *"And the door was shut,"* means that it had once been open, and for a protracted period of time. Consequently, there was ample time to get ready, but too late after it is *"shut."*

When Noah was commanded by the Lord to build the Ark, the door to that Ark was open all the time the Ark was in preparation. At that time, and sadly without success, the appeal was made for all to enter who so desired.

However, there came a time that the *"Lord shut the door,"* and when He did, no one else could come in (Gen. 7:16).

Millions who claim Christ, and even many, if not most Preachers, treat the present consecration of an individual in a cavalier fashion.

Too often Grace has been extended by man much further than God intended, claiming it covers sins which have never been confessed, repented of, and stopped, which it does not! As well, millions have died eternally lost, or else, are on their way to being eternally lost, because they believe an unscriptural doctrine called *"Unconditional Eternal Security,"* which in essence says, that once one is saved, there is no way one can lose his Salvation, and irrespective as to what type of life he may live. Such is error pure and simple, and, as stated, has caused millions to be lost.

As this Parable and others illustrate, there are many who truly were once saved, but presently have nothing in their hearts for Christ, but are rather depending on something that happened many years ago, which, because of their present conduct, has no bearing on their present condition. They, as these *"foolish virgins,"* will be caught exactly as here portrayed, unprepared and unready, and, therefore, lost!

(11) "AFTERWARD CAME ALSO THE OTHER VIRGINS, SAYING, LORD, LORD, OPEN TO US."

The phrase, *"Afterward came also the other virgins,"* portrays *"afterward"* as being too late!

After what?

After the Lord has dealt with the individual over and over again, and for years, and they have repeatedly spurned His clarion call. After the Rapture takes place, there will be no time to prepare for it, as will be obvious. The door will then be shut, and those who were prepared will have gone to be with the Lord, and, consequently, to the *"Marriage Supper of the Lamb."* As well, death claims many in the same lost condition!

Sadly, this scene will be repeated countless times when the Rapture actually does take place. Millions, having been left, will grieve because they thought they were ready, when they really were not!

Others will blame Preachers for telling them everything was all right, when, in reality, nothing was all right. They will then realize that the few Preachers who constantly reminded them that the vessels must be full of Holy Ghost oil, were right after all. But it will be too late to heed that Altar Call then, the door will be *"shut."*

The phrase, *"Saying, Lord, Lord, open to us,"* is an appeal that cannot now be answered.

The title, *"Lord,"* and especially its repetition,

which actually means *"Covenant Lord,"* speaks of their part of the Covenant as having been broken, which they now realize.

The Covenant was available all the time, but was little regarded by these *"foolish virgins,"* as it is little regarded by many presently.

In our own Church in Baton Rouge, Louisiana, where I am attempting to preach the Gospel without fear or favor, with many if not most, there seems to be little interest. Even though we have begun prayer meetings twice a day, which provides an excellent opportunity for any and all to draw closer to God, still, there is little desire!

I watch many with terrible problems in their lives, homes, or marriages, which only the Lord can handle, and still, there is precious little, if any, seeking of His Face. Too often, if someone does begin to seek Him, they will only do so for a very short period of time. If the answer is not forthcoming immediately, they soon tire and quit. This shows such a lack of Faith.

The time to call Him *"Lord"* is now! The time to draw nearer is now!

(12) "BUT HE ANSWERED AND SAID, VERILY I SAY UNTO YOU, I KNOW YOU NOT."

The phrase, *"But He answered and said,"* will now be Judgment, as it had been Mercy for so long, but yet unheeded.

The phrase, *"Verily I say unto you, I know you not,"* is chilling indeed! It means that despite their profession, and despite what they once had (virgins), they do not have it now, and, consequently, are excluded from the *"marriage"* of Salvation.

There could be no worse statement than, *"I know you not!"*

This means that these individuals, whoever they may be, will be eternally lost, just as lost as if they had never known the Lord. Consequently, their hell will be far worse than those who never knew!

To come so close and profess so long, and actually be deceived into believing that everything is fine, when, in reality, nothing is fine, at least in the spiritual sense, is the worst deception of all. And yet, as this Parable portrays, this number will not be few.

In reality, almost the entirety of the nation of Israel fell into this category, which Jesus was desperately trying to reach by the giving of this Parable.

Many in the modern Church, and as well for all time, fall into the same category.

(13) "WATCH THEREFORE, FOR YE KNOW NEITHER THE DAY NOR THE HOUR WHEREIN THE SON OF MAN COMETH."

The two words, *"Watch therefore,"* which are meant to portray the major thrust of this Parable, are as demanding now as then.

Watch for what?

Our lives are to be lived as if Jesus would come today. The imminent looking for Him, as we have already stated, provides an occupation of consecration which can be obtained in no other manner. It is sad, but most of the Church is not looking for Him now or tomorrow.

The phrase, *"For ye know neither the day nor the hour wherein the Son of man cometh,"* is meant to portray the fact that we are to live as though this is the *"day and the hour,"* of His return. Such occupation will cause one to be diligent, persevering, consecrated, and, therefore, ready!

Are you ready?

(14) "FOR THE KINGDOM OF HEAVEN IS AS A MAN TRAVELLING INTO A FAR COUNTRY, WHO CALLED HIS OWN SERVANTS, AND DELIVERED UNTO THEM HIS GOODS."

This is the Parable of the Talents, and expresses the necessity of man's accountability to God for that which the Lord has given unto him. In other words, proper stewardship.

Some have claimed that the Parable of the Pounds given in Luke 19 is one and the same with this Parable. However, the two, although similar, are different, and, in effect, are not the same! But Jesus often gave the same Truth in different ways, which I think these two Parables will illustrate.

The phrase, *"For the Kingdom of Heaven is as a man travelling into a far country,"* represents Christ at His First Advent, Who, in His earthly Ministry, gave instructions as here recorded regarding the accountability of His servants, of that which is given unto them, before He went back to Heaven.

The phrase, *"Who called His Own servants, and delivered unto them His goods,"* represents a studied knowledge of each servant, and, accordingly, the amount entrusted to each.

Inasmuch as these Parables were uttered just hours before the Crucifixion, one should well

NOTES

understand the tremendous significance of each. The lessons here taught are to be graphically learned and heeded. Every Believer, as this Parable proclaims, will give account for this Christian life. Consequently, even though the far greater number of Believers are not called to a Ministry office, still, all are called in some way, and must equip themselves accordingly!

Even though they may labor at some particular activity to make a living for themselves and their family, still, their primary occupation is the Work of the Lord, and that goes for each and every Believer, irrespective of his station in life. Regrettably, and in too many Christian circles, this Parable is little heeded at all, with far too many falling into the category of the last individual of verse 26 who showed no accountability at all!

Many, if not most, Believers function in the capacity of placing Christ and His Work in a minor capacity, if any capacity at all, even though it has eternal consequences, but rather give their total attention to secular matters, which are fleeting at best!

(15) "AND UNTO ONE HE GAVE FIVE TALENTS, TO ANOTHER TWO, AND TO ANOTHER ONE; TO EVERY MAN ACCORDING TO HIS SEVERAL ABILITY; AND STRAIGHTWAY TOOK HIS JOURNEY."

The phrase, *"And unto one He gave five talents, to another two, and to another one,"* represents the Lord giving this Parable in the symbol of money so as to make it very simple and easy to understand.

Each *"talent"* in 1995 money would be worth very near $500,000. Consequently, a high value is placed on these gifts.

It is from the use of this word *"talents"* that we derive its common meaning of natural gifts and endowments concerning our labor for the Lord.

Just yesterday, I listened as in a certain radio program a man mentioned a particular ability of some nature or type that every individual possesses. He was speaking in the secular sense, and was encouraging people to find their unique ability which they have and put it to *"golden"* use. Conversely, he was speaking as to how most never utilize their God-given talent, whatever it may be, for their benefit.

Whether he is correct (which he probably is), in that everyone has a natural ability in some measure, etc., this one thing is certain — every Believer, as here recorded, is given a particular Ministry by the Lord. Regrettably, most have no idea as to what it is, and are not even interested enough to seek the Lord respecting that knowledge.

It is obvious from these Passages, that the Lord gives more to some than to others. Consequently, He expects more from those to whom much is given; however, His judgment of their efforts is not dependent on the amount given, but on the faithfulness rendered.

The phrase, *"To every man according to his several ability,"* records the fact that every single Believer, with none excluded, is given a proper Ministry.

As well, the gifts are distributed, not to all alike, but in such proportions that men are able to bear and to profit by. Seemingly, everything about the individual's disposition, intellect, will, opportunity, position, etc., is taken into account, with distribution made accordingly.

The phrase, *"And straightway took His journey,"* represents the Lord setting the standards as here given at His First Advent, and then going back to Heaven, which He did, thereby leaving the trust and care of the Kingdom of Heaven in our hands.

What are these *"talents"* or Ministries as given by the Lord?

Paul said, *"Having then gifts differing according to the Grace that is given to us, whether Prophecy, let us prophesy according to the proportion of Faith;*

"Or Ministry, let us wait on our ministering: or he that teacheth, on teaching;

"Or he that exhorteth, on exhortation: he that giveth, let him do it with simplicity; he that ruleth, with diligence; he that sheweth mercy, with cheerfulness" (Rom. 12:6-8).

As is obvious in these Passages, the listing runs the gamut all the way from *"Prophecy"* (the gift of Prophecy), to *"Giving,"* and even the *"Shewing of mercy."*

Consequently, and even though by no means are all the gifts here given, still, one can easily ascertain the diversity.

Therefore, whatever the Lord has given unto us, should be used diligently. In other words, the Believer should seek the Lord earnestly regarding the use of his particular *"gift,"* seeking to utilize it to the utmost, and for the Glory of God.

As well, faithfulness in one area may well be rewarded by the addition of a gift in another area.

All of this is meant to portray the tremendous significance of our lives lived for God. In effect, the only light in this world is that which is carried by Believers. To be sure, Islam has no light, neither Buddhism, Shintoism, or Confucianism.

I think it should be obvious that Humanism or Spiritism carry no light as well! Jesus said, and speaking of His followers, *"Ye are the light of the world"* (Mat. 5:14). Consequently, if our light does not shine, there is no other light to take its place.

(16) "THEN HE THAT HAD RECEIVED THE FIVE TALENTS WENT AND TRADED WITH THE SAME, AND MADE THEM OTHER FIVE TALENTS."

There is indication in this Parable that the greater number of *"talents"* was given to the individuals with the greatest consecration and heart toward God. I think that ability and personal gifts definitely have some small part to do with it, but only a small part. The indication seems to be that mostly the talents were dispensed according to consecration and love for God. The reason I say this is because those who were given the *"five talents"* and *"two talents"* acquitted themselves admirably. It was the one who received the *"one talent,"* which I think was given to him because of lack of consecration, who did not acquit himself well at all!

(The word, *"ability,"* in verse 15 does pertain to personal ability, knowledge, and opportunity, but is given that way because of the nature of the Parable, with Jesus using it in the material sense so as to be easily understood. However, the Lord little operates His Work on that basis, rather dealing with individuals according to their consecration and faithfulness. In fact, the Scripture says, *"Not many wise men after the flesh, not many mighty, not many noble, are called."*

Then Paul said, *"But God hath chosen the foolish things of the world to confound the wise; and God hath chosen the weak things of the world to confound the things which are mighty"* — I Cor. 1:26-27.)

(17) "AND LIKEWISE HE THAT HAD RECEIVED TWO, HE ALSO GAINED OTHER TWO."

Both the one who received *"five talents"* and

the one who received *"two talents,"* show diligence in their labor for the Lord.

The idea is that whether our endowments are large or little, we are to use them all in the Lord's service. Jesus further said, *"To whomsoever much is given, of him shall be much required"* (Lk. 12:48); and it could well be said, *"To whomsoever less is committed, of him less shall be required."*

The Lord pays the same compliment to the one who gained *"two talents"* as He did to the one who gained *"five talents."* The amount gained was not necessarily the primary question, but rather the amount given and the consequent faithfulness.

(18) "BUT HE THAT HAD RECEIVED ONE WENT AND DIGGED IN THE EARTH, AND HID HIS LORD'S MONEY."

The phrase, *"But he that had received one went,"* portrays activity, but in the wrong direction.

The phrase, *"And digged in the earth, and hid his Lord's money,"* presents him preserving what he had been given, but adding nothing to it. Had he spent the same energy in adding to it as he did in attempting to preserve it, the results would have been far different.

Why did he do what he did?

Perhaps fear played some small part in his action, as it does in many.

There is some indication that this was the case with Timothy when Paul told him to *"Stir up the Gift of God, which is in thee by the putting on of my hands."*

He then went on to say, *"For God hath not given us the spirit of fear; but of power, and of love, and of a sound mind"* (II Tim. 1:6-7).

Incidentally, there is every evidence that Timothy heeded Paul's admonition.

Perhaps it was, as stated, a lack of consecration. To be frank, there seems to have been little, or else the Lord would have given him more talents to begin with.

This man's idea was one of preservation rather than multiplication. The 25th verse shows that he knew what the Lord expected of him, but *"feigned fear"* kept him from doing it. As such keeps many from doing what God has called them to do.

And then, again, we have many with *"one talent"* attempting to carry out a *"five talent"* Ministry. It is just as bad to try to do that which

the Lord has not called one to do, as to do nothing at all! Blessed is the man who knows what the Lord has called him to do and sets about with all his might to do it, irrespective of what it may be. If God has called one for a certain task, that task, although seemingly small to others, is never small to Him, but rather extremely important in the entire scheme of events. In other words, if the blacksmith does not properly shoe the horse, the General riding him and directing the battle could well lose that battle if the horse throws the shoe because it was improperly repaired. In God's eyes, which should be the only eyes that are important, everything has its place, and all who function in those capacities are extremely important in His sight.

We have scores of people who desire to preach, who God has never called to preach. Others desire to sing, who God has never given the talent to sing. The list is almost endless. Too many, and too often, do not properly use the talent God has given them.

Not only is it imperative that our talent be put to proper use, whatever that use may be, but, as well, that we know exactly what our talent is!

As an example, a dear friend of mine who is now with the Lord, spoke of the Lord's dealings with his mother many, many years ago.

In prayer and consecration, and sensing that the Spirit of God was dealing with her greatly, she asked the Lord as to what He wanted her to do.

The answer was almost instant, *"Raise the children!"*, the Lord said.

Somewhat taken aback by this answer, she thought in her mind, *"Lord, what do you think I'm going to do, kill them?"*

Of course, her answer was predicated on her lack of knowledge of what the Lord had in mind.

After further prayer and consecration, little by little she began to understand what the Lord had told her to do. This was her *"talent,"* or perhaps it was *"five talents."* At any rate, she raised those children for God, instilling in them the Word of God which generated Faith, and, consequently, her children, after becoming adults, had a tremendous impact on the Work of God all over the world.

One of her sons was A. N. Trotter, who was used of God in a tremendous way in Africa, and especially in America. Only the Lord knows the lives who have been touched and blessed as a result of his Ministry, including this Evangelist.

Also, one of her sons-in-law was H. B. Garlock, who, as far as I know, was the first man to open up West Africa to the great Pentecostal Message. The miracles that God performed through this man are straight out of the Book of Acts.

"Raising the children," was what God called her to do, and which many would have thought to have been very mundane, but which the Lord knew was extremely important. She was not unfaithful in this task, with the fruit having been borne resulting in miraculous proportions.

(19) "AFTER A LONG TIME THE LORD OF THOSE SERVANTS COMETH, AND RECKONETH WITH THEM."

The phrase, *"After a long time,"* pertains to a period of time which has now been nearly 2,000 years. When Christ ascended, the two Angels who then immediately appeared said, *"This same Jesus, which is taken up from you into Heaven, shall so come in like manner as ye have seen Him go into Heaven"* (Acts 1:11).

Even though the opportunity of working for Christ in the earthly life is ended at death, the reckoning is reserved for the Coming of the Lord, in this case the Rapture.

The phrase, *"The Lord of those servants cometh,"* refers to the Church.

The phrase, *"And reckoneth with them,"* has a double meaning:

1. For the group who professed to know the Lord, but yet had ceased to serve Him, and had, in effect, *"hid their talent,"* they will be treated according to verse 30. It will include all those who have ever lived, and were professors, but not possessors!

As an aside, when the Rapture takes place, all of these professors who are alive at that time, which will be many, will be left. Despite their profession, they really are not Believers, and will be treated accordingly by the Lord. And yet, many of these, no doubt, will come to Christ after this great event and will wholeheartedly live for Him, at least until they are martyred by the Antichrist. The Scripture says that many of these will come out of the Great Tribulation and will be mostly Gentiles, but certainly with some Jews (Rev. 7:9-17).

Actually, this will be the last group included in the Resurrection of Life.

2. Those who were given their *"five talents"*

NOTES

or *"two talents"* will appear at the Judgment Seat of Christ, where they will be rewarded. This will include every Saint of God who has ever lived from the time of Adam. It will even include these Tribulation martyrs we have just mentioned, for it seems that the Judgment Seat of Christ will take place immediately prior to the Second Coming (II Cor. 5:10).

(The Judgment Seat of Christ does not pertain to Believers' sins, for these were taken care of at Calvary, but has to do with rewards.)

Due to these Parables being given only for the purpose of proclaiming a particular Truth, various different subjects such as the Rapture, the manner of the Second Coming, the Great White Throne Judgment, or the Judgment Seat of Christ are little mentioned, if at all; however, these great events will certainly figure prominently in the overall fulfillment of these Parables.

(20) "AND SO HE THAT HAD RECEIVED FIVE TALENTS CAME AND BROUGHT OTHER FIVE TALENTS, SAYING, LORD, THOU DELIVEREDST UNTO ME FIVE TALENTS: BEHOLD, I HAVE GAINED BESIDE THEM FIVE TALENTS MORE."

The phrase, *"And so he that had received five talents came and brought other five talents,"* no doubt pertains to the Judgment Seat of Christ, where the acts and motives of all Believers will be judged.

The phrase, *"Saying, Lord, Thou deliveredst unto me five talents,"* is a simple presentation of that given by the Lord, but yet so important!

The very statement proclaims the high value placed upon this responsibility by the individual involved. It shows that this entrusted to him by the Lord was on his mind continually, and, as well, was discharged continually. In other words, service for the Lord, and irrespective as to who he was, was his primary occupation.

Let it ever be said that all the secular things in which men believe to be so very important on earth, will ultimately be found out to have little significance at all! Sadly, too many Believers give most all their time and diligence to things which will perish shortly, failing to lay up treasure in Heaven (Mat. 6:19-20). Wonder of wonders is the Christian businessman, while tending responsibly to his earthly occupation, yet has as his primary objective the business of the Lord.

The phrase, *"Behold, I have gained beside them five talents more,"* is not spoken boastfully, but simply as a matter of fact.

Of everything on earth, and the privilege of living this life, all will be reckoned at this time.

As every Believer stands at that time before the Lord, little mention will be made of the accomplishments on earth regarding secular matters, and irrespective as to how much money was involved. In other words, those things we think so grand here are so little thought of there, that no mention is even made of them. (If mention is made, it will only be in the manner as to how we allowed these things to help us carry out our work for the Lord.)

The only thing that will matter is the manner in which we acquitted ourselves for the Lord.

Sadly, many Believers who have no particular calling as a Preacher of the Gospel (Eph. 4:11), feel these matters do not apply to them. However, no distinction is made by the Lord, in effect, treating all alike. In other words, every single Believer is given a certain number of *"talents,"* and will be held responsible accordingly. Even though the Christian businessman or the Christian housewife may not pastor a Church or have any calling of that nature, still, they are definitely called, at least in some regard, which is very important in the Work of the Lord, and will be held responsible.

(21) "HIS LORD SAID UNTO HIM, WELL DONE, THOU GOOD AND FAITHFUL SERVANT: THOU HAST BEEN FAITHFUL OVER A FEW THINGS, I WILL MAKE THEE RULER OVER MANY THINGS: ENTER THOU INTO THE JOY OF THY LORD."

The phrase, *"His Lord said unto him,"* proclaims the single most important moment in the life and ministry of the Believer. This is the accounting time, the *"Judgment Seat of Christ."*

The words, *"Well done,"* is that which the Believer longs to hear.

As I dictate these words, I sense the Presence of the Lord in that the Holy Spirit denotes the tremendous significance of this moment.

With everything in me, those are the words I desire to hear. Nothing else matters and nothing else is of any significance.

As I have related elsewhere in these Volumes, some time ago we had the occasion to take quite a number of Bibles into Communist China. The man to whom we delivered them had spent about

20 years in a Communist prison, simply because of his testimony for Jesus Christ. Then I heard he was arrested again, being sent back to prison.

A short time later he was killed for his Testimony. He paid with his life the supreme sacrifice.

I related that again, simply to ask the question: *"If by the Grace of God we manage to ultimately hear from the lips of Christ, 'Well done,' how will that compare with his* (the man I spoke of above) *'Well done' and others like him?"*

The phrase, *"Thou good and faithful servant,"* proclaims this judgment as predicated on two things, *"goodness and faithfulness":*

1. *"Goodness":* If one truly follows Christ, one will be truly Christlike. This means to be kind, considerate, patient, longsuffering, gracious, and generous. It also means that one will not engage in gossip, slander, or anything that will hurt others. Since Christlikeness is the major thrust of the Holy Spirit within our lives, a person will work diligently toward this conclusion.

2. *"Faithfulness":* This means to be trusting and believing, but, as well, to be trustworthy, reliable, and faithful. It portrays an unshakable loyalty, which is displayed in a number of ways.

Paul, in taking up this subject, makes all of us aware that God has committed to him, as to every Believer, the responsibility of using our gifts to serve others. It is required that those who have been given a trust must prove faithful (I Cor. 4:2).

We know that we can trust God to remain faithful to His commitments. As well, it is wonderful that God entrusts so much to us, of which this entire Parable is all about!

The phrase, *"Thou hast been faithful over a few things,"* means that the Lord looks at these things as *"few,"* even though they are quite large to us, in fact, so large that it should take up the entirety of our lives.

The phrase is meant for us to understand that these responsibilities are given to us, not because the Lord has need of our efforts, but that we have need of this test and the doing of it. In other words, all of this is for our benefit, and not God's. The Lord needs nothing we have, and, consequently, nothing we do. It is somewhat like a test given to a student by a teacher. The test, as is obvious, is not needed by the teacher, but by the pupil.

So, if we have the idea that we are needed

in this great Work of God, then we do not fully understand Who God is, nor ourselves for that matter!

The phrase, *"I will make thee ruler over many things,"* proclaims a great reward all out of proportion to the small service rendered.

What does He mean by *"ruler?"*

Of course, the entirety of what the Lord means in respect to this word is known only by Him. This we do know, anything He does is always far larger than we can ever begin to imagine.

John wrote, *"Blessed and holy is he that hath part in the first Resurrection . . . They shall be Priests of God and of Christ, and shall reign with Him a thousand years"* (Rev. 20:6).

This pertains to the coming Kingdom Age, as is obvious, and what exactly is meant by *"reigning with Christ,"* is not totally known. However, it does speak of rulership and the government of the coming Kingdom Age.

It will as well extend over into the perfect age and perfect earth to come (Rev. Chpts. 21 and 22).

The phrase, *"Enter thou into the joy of thy Lord,'* is not really speaking of joy entering into the Believer, but is actually much greater because it is not measured by our capacity for receiving it, but, instead, absorbs us, envelops us, and becomes our atmosphere of life"* (Augustine).

It is somewhat the difference in drinking water, and going swimming in the ocean.

(22) "HE ALSO THAT HAD RECEIVED TWO TALENTS CAME AND SAID, LORD, THOU DELIVEREDST UNTO ME TWO TALENTS: BEHOLD, I HAVE GAINED TWO OTHER TALENTS BESIDE THEM."

This verse is identical, at least in principle, to verse 20.

It is repeated here by the Lord, in order that it be known that just as much diligence and attention are given to the one with *"two talents"* as the one with *"five talents."* He was faithful with what he had, and was rewarded exactly as the greater.

(23) "HIS LORD SAID UNTO HIM, WELL DONE, GOOD AND FAITHFUL SERVANT; THOU HAST BEEN FAITHFUL OVER A FEW THINGS, I WILL MAKE THEE RULER OVER MANY THINGS: ENTER THOU INTO THE JOY OF THY LORD."

The wording is identical in this verse to verse 21. Consequently, the reward is identical, *"Ruler over many things."*

NOTES

Again, the amount is not in question, but the *"goodness and faithfulness"* respecting the talents given.

(24) "THEN HE WHICH HAD RECEIVED THE ONE TALENT CAME AND SAID, LORD, I KNEW THEE THAT THOU ART AN HARD MAN, REAPING WHERE THOU HAST NOT SOWN, AND GATHERING WHERE THOU HAST NOT STRAWED:"

The phrase, *"Then he which had received the one talent came and said,"* will prove to be a totally unwarranted accusation regarding the character of the Lord. If one is to notice, the blame is placed elsewhere, instead of where it rightly belonged — the one with the one talent!

The phrase, *"Lord, I knew Thee that Thou art an hard Man,"* is a view of God, not as He actually is, but according to one's own perverted views. In other words, he read his own perverted character into his conception of Him.

In Truth, the Lord is not *"hard,"* but, in reality, the very opposite. His yoke is easy, and His burden is light (Mat. 11:28-30).

With every one of us, the Lord uses patience (much patience), kindness, longsuffering, and compassion.

After He gives us the *"talents,"* i.e., responsibilities, He then gives us power and wisdom to accomplish the task. Then, as we repeatedly fail, He patiently deals with us, giving us strength and guidance when we in no way deserve such, and gently shepherds us to the accomplished task.

So, for this man to say that the Lord is *"hard,"* is an outright lie! Tragically, men have been accusing God of this and much worse from the very beginning.

The phrase, *"Reaping where Thou hast not sown, and gathering where Thou hast not strawed,"* means that this man is bringing a twofold charge against the Lord:

1. He virtually accuses the Lord of fraud. To reap where one has not sown, means to profit at another's expense.

2. To *"gather where he has not planted,"* is the same as a mafia chieftain extorting money from businesses which he is not due.

Tragically, this man is not alone in his accusations, in that much of the world falls into this category. People blame God for every difficulty, refusing to acknowledge that man's problems are caused by man.

(25) "AND I WAS AFRAID, AND WENT AND HID THY TALENT IN THE EARTH: LO, THERE THOU HAST THAT IS THINE."

The phrase, *"And I was afraid,"* means that he did not have a legitimate fear, but, instead, claimed to be *"afraid"* because the Lord was so hard and harsh!

While *"fear"* is definitely a problem in many cases, still, this complaint is not genuine.

While individuals may truly be afraid of their lack of ability to perform, to claim that their fear is caused by the harshness of the Lord, only adds insult to injury.

The phrase, *"And went and hid Thy talent in the earth,"* means that the man totally ignored the previous instructions given. The very purpose of the *"talent"* was not preservation, nearly as much as it was multiplication. When he took the *"talent,"* he understood that, but now blames the Lord for his own indolence!

The phrase, *"Lo, there Thou hast that is Thine,"* proclaims not only indolence, but, as well, insolence. The talent was not given to him to bury, but to use for the Lord's profit. However, in reality, the profit was more so his than the Lord's, because the Lord actually had no personal need for it. So, when he cheated the Lord, he cheated himself!

(26) "HIS LORD ANSWERED AND SAID UNTO HIM, THOU WICKED AND SLOTHFUL SERVANT, THOU KNEWEST THAT I REAP WHERE I SOWED NOT, AND GATHER WHERE I HAVE NOT STRAWED:"

The phrase, *"His Lord answered and said unto him,"* respects One Who will call to account, and that to Whom an answer must be given. Every individual must understand this! What the Lord will answer is predicated on our responsibility, or the lack of it!

The phrase, *"Thou wicked and slothful servant,"* concerns appellatives which fit the evil heart of this individual.

The reason for his action was not that the Lord was *"hard,"* etc., but, instead, that this servant was *"wicked and slothful!"* That is the reason for the actions of all other servants of this character. They are *"wicked,"* i.e., evil, and *"slothful,"* i.e., lazy!

The phrase, *"Thou knewest that I reap where I sowed not, and gather where I have not strawed,"* doesn't mean that the Lord was actually this way, but that the man said He was!

So, the Lord is saying that if he really believed this, he would have taken other action, as the next verse suggests.

(27) "THOU OUGHTEST THEREFORE TO HAVE PUT MY MONEY TO THE EXCHANGERS, AND THEN AT MY COMING I SHOULD HAVE RECEIVED MINE OWN WITH USURY."

The phrase, *"Thou oughtest therefore to have put My money to the exchangers,"* proves that his accusations against the Lord concerning *"hardness"* had no substance in fact! He actually believed the very opposite.

His true thinking was that the Lord was so kind and gracious that He would take no offense at his action. And especially considering that he had no interest in what the Lord required of him, it became very easy for him to *"bury the talent."*

Using the language of the street, and concerning this Parable, the Lord tells him that the least he could have done was simply put the money in the bank and drawn interest.

The phrase, *"And then at My coming I should have received Mine Own with usury,"* means that if the money had been so employed, he would have at least received something for his investment.

The Lord does not say what He would have done had this tactic been employed; however, the idea is, and seems to be presented, that if a person doesn't give his all to the Lord, he most of the time gives nothing. In other words, a tepid consecration seems to be unlikely if not impossible! To use a crude expression, it's somewhat like saying a woman is a little bit pregnant. She either is, or isn't! As well, a person is either consecrated to the Lord, or not consecrated. There is no in between.

(28) "TAKE THEREFORE THE TALENT FROM HIM, AND GIVE IT UNTO HIM WHICH HATH TEN TALENTS."

The phrase, *"Take therefore the talent from him,"* refers to the significance of the matter, and, as well, the action of the Lord, which the one talent man did not foresee. The Lord is Gracious and Kind, as well as Patient and Long-suffering; however, He means what He says and says what He means! The talent was unused, therefore it must be taken away.

The phrase, *"And give it unto him which hath ten talents,"* is a startling revelation!

The implication is, and as the next verse

proclaims, the rewards that would have gone to these individuals had they proved faithful, will instead be given to the ones who, in fact, proved faithful, and in conjunction with the tremendous reward they already have. A life lived for Him is a life rewarded by Him.

(29) "FOR UNTO EVERY ONE THAT HATH SHALL BE GIVEN, AND HE SHALL HAVE ABUNDANCE: BUT FROM HIM THAT HATH NOT SHALL BE TAKEN AWAY EVEN THAT WHICH HE HATH."

The phrase, *"For unto every one that hath shall be given, and he shall have abundance,"* proclaims a Law of God which takes away from the unfaithful and gives to the faithful. The first concludes with nothing, and because they did nothing, while the latter concludes with everything, because they did everything they could with what the Lord gave them to do with.

The phrase, *"But from him that hath not shall be taken away even that which he hath,"* actually refers not only to the responsibility given him, but as the next verse portrays, even the loss of his soul.

Once again, we state that this pertains to those who truly once knew the Lord as their Saviour, but drifted from Him, and even though retaining all the outward signs of Faith, still, were bereft of any inward work. Even though they were religious and considered by the Church to be *"saved,"* nevertheless, they were not considered thusly by the Lord.

Sadly and regrettably, millions are basing their soul's Salvation on what man tells them, instead of what God's Word says. They will learn to their dismay that it's not what man says, but what God says!

(30) "AND CAST YE THE UNPROFITABLE SERVANT INTO OUTER DARKNESS: THERE SHALL BE WEEPING AND GNASHING OF TEETH."

The phrase, *"And cast ye the unprofitable servant into outer darkness,"* concerns, as is obvious, much more than the loss of reward, but the loss of the soul.

The phrase, *"There shall be weeping and gnashing of teeth,"* proclaims the destination as hell itself (Mat. 13:42).

Consequently, a tremendous lesson is taught in this Parable, that the slothful servant shall suffer punishment not because of evil committed, but of duty neglected. To merit

the fearful doom of this verse, it only needs inactivity (Heb. 2:3).

And yet, this tremendous Truth is proclaimed in another way by Christ concerning the failure to bear fruit. This is what He said:

"Every branch in Me that beareth not fruit He taketh away."

He then said, *"If a man abide not in Me* (continues to abide), *he is cast forth as a branch, and is withered; and men gather them, and cast them into the fire, and they are burned"* (Jn. 15:2, 6).

Consequently, this means there are millions of people in modern Churches (and always have been), who are committing no overt or covert sins, and as stated, with all the outward trappings of Faith, but bearing no fruit whatsoever. They've never borne any, and they are bearing none now. These Passages tell us that these people are lost.

No! It in no way means that Salvation is by works, but that proper Faith in the heart will always produce good works, i.e., bear fruit. If no works are forthcoming, i.e., the bearing of fruit, this means there is no Faith in the heart, but only an outward profession, hence the individual is lost!

(31) "WHEN THE SON OF MAN SHALL COME IN HIS GLORY, AND ALL THE HOLY ANGELS WITH HIM, THEN SHALL HE SIT UPON THE THRONE OF HIS GLORY."

The phrase, *"When the Son of Man shall come in His Glory,"* speaks of Jesus in His human, glorified body at the Second Coming.

His Coming the first time, even though of signal greatness to God and all the Holy Angels, still, was of small moment regarding man's concern. There was no room in the inn, and, as well, some time later Herod would seek to kill Him.

Even though Joseph, his foster father, would have been King of Israel had the dynasty continued, and because he was in the direct lineage of David, still, no royal splendor accompanied his present occupation as a carpenter. In other words, he was a peasant! Consequently, Jesus was raised in this atmosphere, doing exactly as Paul would later say, *"But made Himself of no reputation, and took upon Him the form of a servant"* (Phil. 2:7).

However, when He comes the second time, it will not be as a peasant, but as *"KING OF KINGS, AND LORD OF LORDS"* (Rev. 19:16).

The *"Glory"* accompanying His Presence will make the glory of every earthly king who has ever lived pale by comparison!

The phrase, *"And all the Holy Angels with Him,"* speaks of all the Angels assigned to His Second Coming, and not to all the Angels He originally created. Without a doubt, these Angels will be visible to all, and accordingly, will carry out the functions assigned to them. However, it must be quickly stated that they will add nothing to His Glory, and neither will the phenomenon taking place in the heavens respecting the *"sun, moon and stars"* (Mat. 24:29).

An idea of His Personal Glory can be obtained from Revelation 21:23, where it speaks of the New Jerusalem coming down from God out of Heaven, with John saying, *"And the city had no need of the sun, neither of the moon, to shine in it: for the Glory of God did lighten it, and the Lamb is the Light thereof."*

Even though Jesus will continue to occupy His human glorified body, as evidenced by the word, *"Lamb,"* still, His Glory will be so great that His very Presence will illuminate the city. Even though the sun and moon will continue to give their light, still, such will be of no consequence compared to His Light, i.e., Glory. Consequently, the Holy Spirit is here speaking of a *"Glory"* such as the world has never known before, even remotely so!

The phrase, *"Then shall He sit upon the Throne of His Glory,"* specifies the time by the word, *"Then,"* as referring to the beginning of the Kingdom Age.

His *"Throne"* will be of such magnificence that the earthly Jerusalem, no doubt, even as its heavenly counterpart which will come down to earth in the coming perfect age, will have no need of auxiliary light. Ezekiel tells us in his Book of the Glory of the Kingdom Temple, which will serve as the Headquarters for the *"Throne of His Glory"* (Ezek. Chpts. 40-48).

As someone has said, and referring to the terrible problems of this earth, down through the ages some few men have known the right, but they did not have the might. Now, Jesus will not only know the right, but He will have the might. From this *"Throne"* He will govern the entirety of the earth (Isa. 9:7).

(32) "AND BEFORE HIM SHALL BE GATHERED ALL NATIONS; AND HE SHALL SEPARATE THEM ONE FROM ANOTHER,

AS A SHEPHERD DIVIDETH HIS SHEEP FROM THE GOATS:"

This is called the *"Judgment of the nations,"* which will commence at the outset of the Kingdom Age.

It is falsely understood by some to be the final Judgment of Revelation 20:11. However, that Judgment comes at the conclusion of the Kingdom Age, while the *"Judgment of the nations,"* precedes the Millennium. The one, as stated, is a Judgment of the living nations; the other, the Judgment of the resurrected evil dead.

As well, it will not be the Judgment of the Church, for the Church is an election out of all nations, nor is it the Judgment of Israel, for they were not to be reckoned among the nations (Num. 23:9).

Also, the reward to Israel here is *"from the foundation of the world"* (vs. 34), while the Church was chosen from *"Before the foundation of the world."*

This Judgment, and as stated, will take place at Jerusalem, and at the Throne of Christ, attended by His Angels.

The Millennial Reign will be introduced by three general Judgments:

1. The Judgment of Israel: This will take place at the Second Coming, and is outlined in Matthew 24:27-44.

2. The Judgment of Christendom: This will take place in a sense at the Rapture, by many who claim to be Believers, but really are not, and will consequently be left (Mat. 24:45-51; 25:1-30).

3. The Judgment of the Living Nations: We will study this Judgment in these verses, Matthew 25:31-46.

The phrase, *"And before Him shall be gathered all nations,"* concerns all the nations of the world then existing, which will probably be very similar to the present nations.

This Judgment will not include all the people of all these nations, but, rather, official representatives such as Presidents, Premiers, Prime Ministers, etc. As stated, this will take place in Jerusalem, at the Throne of Christ, and at the beginning of the Kingdom Age.

The phrase, *"And He shall separate them one from another, as a shepherd divideth his sheep from the goats,"* proclaims such being done according to the treatment of Israel by these particular nations.

The leaders who helped Israel in any way and

at any time, will be blessed and allowed to continue, while the leaders of those which did the opposite and who basically sided with the Antichrist, will be severely judged.

(33) "AND HE SHALL SET THE SHEEP ON HIS RIGHT HAND, BUT THE GOATS ON THE LEFT."

The phrase, *"And He shall set the sheep on His Right Hand,"* refers primarily to the nations in the Great Tribulation, who would not throw in their lot with the Antichrist in his attempt to annihilate Israel. Even though there is little evidence, if any, that these nations, whichever they might be, actually helped Israel at this critical time, except in small ways, still, they did not overtly or covertly oppose her.

This proves that the entirety of the world will not be conquered by the Antichrist, as some teach. Of a certainty, he will be well on his way to doing such when he will be abruptly stopped by the Coming of the Lord.

The phrase, *"But the goats on the left,"* refers to those nations who actively sided with the Antichrist in his efforts to destroy Israel in the latter half of the Great Tribulation, and especially during the Battle of Armageddon.

There is no way that one can know exactly who these nations will be. However, the Bible does mention a few, *"Persia, Ethiopia, and Libya,"* and infers others, without specifically giving their names (Ezek. 38:5). No doubt, there will be many!

(34) "THEN SHALL THE KING SAY UNTO THEM ON HIS RIGHT HAND, COME, YE BLESSED OF MY FATHER, INHERIT THE KINGDOM PREPARED FOR YOU FROM THE FOUNDATION OF THE WORLD:"

The phrase, *"Then shall the King say unto them on His Right Hand,"* refers to the sheep nations.

Incidentally, the word, *"nations,"* in verse 32 is a neuter noun in Greek, and *"them,"* a masculine pronoun, indicating that each nation will be judged individually.

The phrase, *"Come, ye blessed of My Father,"* refers to a *"blessing"* bestowed upon these nations by God. This *"blessing"* has nothing to do with Salvation of the soul, but rather blessings as a nation, and being allowed to enter the Kingdom Age as such.

In the Kingdom Age, nations will exist then exactly as now, carrying on commerce, trade,

manufacturing, etc. However, all will look to Jesus Christ for leading, guidance, and prosperity. In this, they will be greatly *"blessed."*

However, within these Gentile nations, there will be at least some people who will not desire to live for the Lord, or even obey His rules, and will consequently be executed for their crimes, with, of course, the loss of their souls (Isa. 65:20). However, many of the people then on earth, if not most, will accept Christ as their Lord and Saviour, and, consequently, will live forever, although without a glorified body, and because they were not a part of the First Resurrection (I Thess. 4:16-17).

They will live forever by virtue of partaking of the *"fruit"* and *"leaves"* of the Tree of Life (Rev. 22:1-2).

Also, at the conclusion of the Kingdom Age, and immediately before the Perfect Age, Satan will be loosed out of the bottomless pit, where he will go forth to *"deceive the nations which are in the four quarters of the earth"* (Rev. 20:8-9).

This does not mean that these nations will be destroyed, but that all who live in them and who have not accepted Christ as their Saviour, will then throw in their lot with the evil one, then *"fire will come down from God out of Heaven and devour them."*

(It seems that these individuals, whoever they are, although unsaved, will obey the Laws during the Kingdom Age, and, consequently, will not be executed, but will now show their true colors by siding with Satan and be summarily destroyed and *"cast into the Lake of Fire along with Satan, the Beast, and the False Prophet,"* etc. — Rev. 20:10. Thus will conclude Satan's and man's sinful career on earth, with sin never again showing its ugly head. Consequently, these sheep nations, as described by Christ, will enter the perfect age without sin, and exist forever — Rev. 21:23-24.)

The phrase, *"Inherit the Kingdom prepared for you from the foundation of the world,"* concerns the Kingdom Age and their entrance into it, and, as stated, their continuance in the perfect age to come.

This one phrase proclaims the great Plan of God.

The Lord intended for Israel, which sprang from the loins of Abraham, to be a light unto the nations of the world, thereby bringing them to Christ. Sadly and regrettably, they miserably failed in this endeavor, and for some 2,000 years wandered as outcasts all over the world, losing, at least for this time, their place and position in the Plan of God.

However, at the Second Coming they will be restored, and because of their acceptance of the Lord Jesus Christ, Who they rejected at the first, and will then (during the Kingdom Age and forever) fulfill their mission on the earth as originally intended.

So, what will happen at the beginning of the Kingdom Age regarding the nations of the world and Israel is not something thrown together at the last minute, but, in effect, was the Plan of God all along.

The word, *"foundation,"* in the Greek, at least in this instance, is *"katabole,"* and means the disruption, overthrow, or ruin of the social system before Adam.

For instance, in Genesis 1:1, we have the word, *"themelioo,"* which means the founding of the earth (Heb. 1:10). In Genesis 1:2, we have the *"katabole,"* which means the overthrow of the social system on the earth by a flood, which does not refer to Noah's flood, but, instead, the flood that occurred in Genesis 1:2, which particular time the Bible does not give.

So, from the time that Lucifer fell from his lofty estate because of his rebellion against God, which resulted in the violent overthrow of Genesis 1:2, the Plan of God was devised for the earth and the entirety of the human family. This was long before Adam and Eve, as should be obvious!

In effect, Israel could have had this blessing at the First Advent of Christ, which, in turn, would have blessed all the nations of the world, exactly as here described. But, instead, they rebelled against Christ, actually murdering Him, and thus destroyed themselves and committed the world to continued violence, hate, and war, which has continued to be its offing until now. Therefore, from the Judgment of the Nations, as here described, we are given a brief preview of what the Plan of God was all along, and will now finally be carried out. Then the prayer of Christ will be answered, *"Thy Kingdom come, Thy will be done in earth, as it is Heaven"* (Mat. 6:10).

(35-36) "FOR I WAS AN HUNGERED, AND YE GAVE ME MEAT: I WAS THIRSTY, AND YE GAVE ME DRINK: I WAS A STRANGER, AND YE TOOK ME IN:

"NAKED, AND YE CLOTHED ME: I WAS SICK, AND YE VISITED ME: I WAS IN PRISON, AND YE CAME UNTO ME."

Even though Christ is here speaking of the kind treatment accorded Israel by these particular nations of the world, still, the phrases can definitely refer to the treatment of any and all Believers, which includes the Church.

To persecute the lowliest of Christ's brethren, is to persecute Christ Himself (Acts 9:5); and to minister to such is to minister to Him. Thus He makes Himself One with His people.

When one considers that Israel was far from God at the time these kind acts were carried out, one begins to understand how important kind treatment is to those who belong to the Lord, or even to those to whom God has made special promises as Israel. To lay a hand on God's is to lay a hand on God.

If one is to notice, even the slightest thing done for these in kindness is graphically noted by the Lord!

(37-39) "THEN SHALL THE RIGHTEOUS ANSWER HIM, SAYING, LORD, WHEN SAW WE THEE AN HUNGERED, AND FED THEE? OR THIRSTY, AND GAVE THEE DRINK?

"WHEN SAW WE THEE A STRANGER, AND TOOK THEE IN? OR NAKED, AND CLOTHED THEE?

"OR WHEN SAW WE THEE SICK, OR IN PRISON, AND CAME UNTO THEE?"

The word, *"righteous,"* in verse 37 does not pertain to the Righteousness of Christ given to Believers at Salvation, but, instead, the right or *"righteous"* dealings with Israel by these nations. While it is true that many, if not most, of these people will go on to accept Christ as their personal Saviour, and, consequently, receive His Righteousness as do all Believers, still, this Passage does not have that in mind.

The personal pronoun, *"Thee,"* and referring to Christ, and used so plentifully, means that these *"Righteous Nations"* are perplexed at the statements of Christ. In their minds they had not even seen Christ, much less having done all these good things to Him. However, the next verse will portray what He is speaking of.

As we have stated, and as is graphically explicit in this Judgment of the Nations, the Lord also minutely notes the injustices as well!

I have always found it very difficult to understand how one can be of God and still be greatly opposed, even persecuted, by others who also claim to be of God, that is, if they really are of God!

I certainly do realize how it is possible for people to have misunderstandings, as the Saints in Jerusalem did concerning the conversion of the Apostle Paul. They, at first, would not receive him, and because of the obvious reasons. Nevertheless, that was shortly cleared up with the help of Barnabas (Acts 9:26-28).

As well, one can have preferences respecting Preachers of the Gospel, although Paul took exception even to this, especially when it was carried too far (I Cor. 1:11-13).

But for one who calls himself a Believer to actively oppose the efforts of another God-called Believer in his Work for God, cannot be of God, but rather of Satan.

If this happens, as it did happen at Corinth when interlopers came in attempting to undermine Paul and his Message, and has happened countless times before and since, the situation can only be rectified by Repentance.

These individuals who Paul called *"false apostles and deceitful workers,"* attempted to demean Paul's character to the people of the Corinthian Church, and to change the Great Gospel of Grace to a mixture of Grace and Works. This was rectified only by the Repentance of those in that Church who were guilty of following these *"false apostles"* (II Cor. 7).

If the Church had not repented, those who involved themselves in this debacle would have ultimately lost their souls (Gal. 5:4).

Even in a deviation from correct Scriptural Doctrine, at least if it pertains to the Salvation of the soul, or, if for whatever reason the True Work of God is opposed, such individuals place themselves in the same position as Peter when he disagreed with Christ concerning the Crucifixion. Jesus said to him, *"Get thee behind Me, Satan: thou art an offense unto Me: for thou savourest not the things that be of God, but those that be of men"* (Mat. 16:22-23).

If Peter had not repented, and would have continued in that error, I think it is obvious to all who have even an elementary knowledge of the Word of God, that Peter would have lost his soul. Judas did lose his soul!

As well, any who fall into these same categories, and for whatever reason, placing themselves in opposition to God, if Repentance is

NOTES

not ultimately forthcoming, destruction ultimately is. To be sure, one would be shocked if one knew how many fell into this category of opposing God, while all the time claiming to be of God!

(40) "AND THE KING SHALL ANSWER AND SAY UNTO THEM, VERILY I SAY UNTO YOU, INASMUCH AS YE HAVE DONE IT UNTO ONE OF THE LEAST OF THESE MY BRETHREN, YE HAVE DONE IT UNTO ME."

The phrase, *"And the King shall answer and say unto them, Verily I say unto you,"* places Christ in the position of being Judge of all! As well, this Judge, *"shall not judge after the sight of His Eyes, neither reprove after the hearing of His Ears:*

"But, with Righteousness shall He judge . . ." (Isa. 11:3-4).

In this Judgment of the Nations, lawyers will not be able to side-step the real issue, nor will lies be believed. This Judge, the Lord Jesus Christ, will know everything, past, present, and future, even to the thoughts of the heart. Consequently, all His Judgments are Righteous, and, therefore, Perfect!

Jesus of Nazareth here declares Himself to be the King of Israel, and the Mighty God; for He will reward with everlasting life, and doom to everlasting death.

The phrase, *"Inasmuch as ye have done it unto one of the least of these My Brethren,"* refers to Israel. The Judgment of that day will be based upon the one test as to what was the conduct of people toward them.

The phrase, *"Ye have done it unto Me,"* is, and as we have stated, a solemn statement indeed!

Concerning Israel, every dollar in aid given by the Congress of the United States to Israel, as well as every other type of help, is at least one of the most important things America or any nation could ever do.

Not long before President Truman died, a reporter asked him in an interview what he considered to be his most important achievement respecting his tenure in office as President?

The former President of the United States answered and said, *"My involvement in helping Israel become a Sovereign State!"*

It took the reporter somewhat by surprise because this was an answer he did not expect. Quite possibly, the President, with this being just months before his death, was being dealt with by the Holy Spirit concerning spiritual things. Consequently, he answered accordingly!

While such did not save his soul, and I have no knowledge of his spiritual condition, still, what he did respecting Israel was, and exactly as he stated, so very important.

Any thing the Lord does, as should be obvious, is so very important! As such, anyone who aids and abets such a cause, will be signally honored and blessed by God.

(41) "THEN SHALL HE SAY ALSO UNTO THEM ON THE LEFT HAND, DEPART FROM ME, YE CURSED, INTO EVERLASTING FIRE, PREPARED FOR THE DEVIL AND HIS ANGELS:"

The phrase, "Then shall He say also unto them on the left hand," concerns those He has labeled as the "goat nations" (vs. 33).

The phrase, "Depart from Me, ye cursed, into everlasting fire," is the most chilling words that could ever be heard!

From this Passage, we also know, and alluded to, that no True Believer will oppose Israel, as is here obvious. As well, we know that kind treatment of Israel does not constitute Salvation, for to be saved one must accept Jesus Christ as one's Saviour (Jn. 3:16). Consequently, what did Jesus mean concerning the people of these various nations being lost?

It is somewhat like the not doing of certain bad things will not save one, while, at the same time, the doing of certain bad things, whatever they may be, will definitely cause one to be lost!

The Judgment of these nations will probably pertain only to the time-frame of the Great Tribulation. We know there are certain nations such as Egypt and Assyria, who persecuted Israel greatly in the past, but will be signally honored and blessed in the coming Kingdom Age (Isa. 19:24-25).

Therefore, it probably refers only to the leaders of these nations respecting their treatment of Israel in the Great Tribulation, and not the names of the nations themselves, which will continue on forever, enjoying the leadership of Godly men and women!

This somewhat seems to be the case, and, if so, means that these ungodly leaders, whoever they may be, will be consigned immediately to "everlasting fire." If such is the case, this means that these individuals will instantly die upon this pronounced Judgment.

NOTES

If that is the case, the possibility exists that they will not need to be resurrected and judged again in the Great White Throne Judgment described in Revelation 20:11-15.

The phrase, "Prepared for the Devil and his angels," means that hell was not originally prepared for man. Nevertheless, if man insists on following Satan, as most do, his abode, eternal hell, will be their abode. As well, it will be "everlasting!"

(42-43) "FOR I WAS AN HUNGERED, AND YE GAVE ME NO MEAT: I WAS THIRSTY, AND YE GAVE ME NO DRINK:

"I WAS A STRANGER, AND YE TOOK ME NOT IN: NAKED, AND YE CLOTHED ME NOT: SICK, AND IN PRISON, AND YE VISITED ME NOT."

As the leaders of the sheep nations were told what positive things they did do respecting Israel, and during the time of the Great Tribulation, likewise, the leaders of the goat nations are told exactly what they did not do respecting help they could have given to Israel.

What does this say about Christians who could have helped a very important Work of God, with it even being called to their attention, and with them amply able to do so, but would not?

I think the possibility definitely exists that such falls into the same category as these Passages concerning treatment of Israel.

The Lord is patient, kind, and longsuffering, but if individuals will not hear His Voice, thereby turning a deaf ear to His Call, ultimately, if this thing is not repented of, one could well find himself in the same straits as the man who buried his "one talent" (vs. 30).

(44) "THEN SHALL THEY ALSO ANSWER HIM, SAYING, LORD, WHEN SAW WE THEE AN HUNGERED, OR ATHIRST, OR A STRANGER, OR NAKED, OR SICK, OR IN PRISON, AND DID NOT MINISTER UNTO THEE?"

The phrase, "Then shall they also answer Him, saying, Lord, when saw we Thee . . . ?", is going to be the question of many. They were not feigning ignorance, for they actually did not know! However, ignorance is no excuse!

When Jesus told of Lazarus going to Paradise and the rich man going to hell, and him requesting of Abraham that he allow Lazarus to go back to earth in order to testify to his brothers who were unsaved, Abraham answered, *"They have Moses and the Prophets; let them hear them"* (Lk. 16:19-31).

The Bible has proliferated the entirety of the world, consequently, there is no excuse for not knowing what it says. So, their ignorance is no excuse, nor is the ignorance of anyone!

(45) "THEN SHALL HE ANSWER THEM, SAYING, VERILY I SAY UNTO YOU, INASMUCH AS YE DID IT NOT TO ONE OF THE LEAST OF THESE, YE DID IT NOT TO ME."

The only difference in this verse and verse 40, at least in a basic sense, is the word, *"not."* The Righteous Nations did good things for Israel, while the unrighteous nations did not do these things.

If one is to notice, there is no accusation here by Christ of hurt or intended harm, but, rather, that they simply did not do what they could have done to have been of service, i.e., *"I was a stranger, and ye took me not in."* When they refused Israel, they refused Christ! It was not so much the sin of comission, as it was the sin of omission!

As well, inclusion of the words, *"My Brethren,"* in verse 40, with it not being included in verse 45, gives us insight into the mind of unbelief.

The idea is that the leaders of nations who helped Israel did so because in some manner the tie to Christ was recognized, even though Israel would not admit to such. In other words, Israel doesn't quite understand that America's help for her is predicated on Believers in this country who love Jesus Christ.

The words, *"My Brethren,"* were not added in verse 45, because these unbelieving leaders, whoever they may be, placed little or no credence in Jesus Christ or His Word.

This portrays people who have absolutely no knowledge of the Word of God, and, consequently, make no decisions respecting its Truth.

(46) "AND THESE SHALL GO AWAY INTO EVERLASTING PUNISHMENT: BUT THE RIGHTEOUS INTO LIFE ETERNAL."

The same term that declares the eternal blessing of the one company is the same term which declares the eternal misery of the other.

The phrase, *"And these shall go away into everlasting punishment,"* means they go voluntarily, recognizing the justice of their doom.

The phrase, *"But the Righteous into life eternal,"* no doubt refers to the leaders of these

nations accepting Christ as their eternal Saviour, and, who consequently, will live forever!

CHAPTER 26

(1) "AND IT CAME TO PASS, WHEN JESUS HAD FINISHED ALL THESE SAYINGS, HE SAID UNTO HIS DISCIPLES,"

The phrase, *"And it came to pass,"* refers to the conclusion of Christ's public Ministry to Israel and begins His period of suffering.

However, its total meaning goes all the way back to the rebellion of Lucifer, of which there is no time-frame. The Scripture says, *"of the Lamb slain from the foundation of the world"* (Rev. 13:8). The word, *"foundation,"* here means the same as in 25:34.

So, it seems in the Mind of God that at the time of Lucifer's rebellion, God, knowing that He would restore the world and create man, and, as well, that man would fall, planned that God the Son, even at that early date, would die for lost humanity. How many thousands of years that entails, we are not told. However, ever how many the number, it has *"come to pass"* that this event of all events, the Redemption of mankind, will now take place.

The phrase, *"When Jesus had finished all these sayings,"* refers to Chapters 22-25. This concluded His public teaching, even though other discourses were given to the Disciples only (Jn. 13:31-17:26).

The phrase, *"He said unto His Disciples,"* will constitute words of such sadness, they defy description!

That God would become man, and die for humanity in order that they be redeemed, is beyond comprehension. However, for Him to die for those, who, in reality, hated Him, and, above that, to be murdered by His very Own, presents a love of which no human possessed, and, as well, could not even understand.

(2) "YE KNOW THAT AFTER TWO DAYS IS THE FEAST OF THE PASSOVER, AND THE SON OF MAN IS BETRAYED TO BE CRUCIFIED."

The phrase, *"Ye know that after two days is the Feast of the Passover,"* referred to the fourteenth of Nisan, which also began the Feast of Unleavened Bread which lasted eight days.

The *"Passover"* began in Egypt, and referred to *"the passing over"* of the destroying Angel, who killed all the firstborn of those who did not have the blood of the lamb sprinkled on the door posts of the houses (Ex. 12). The Egyptians had no blood sprinkled on their door posts, so, consequently, the firstborn of every one of their households died, even to the household of Pharaoh.

Many miracles were performed by the Lord in Egypt before the sprinkling of the blood. However, Israel was not delivered until the blood was applied.

Likewise, the sinner can only be redeemed by the precious shed Blood of the Lord Jesus Christ, as was done at Calvary.

To receive its vast benefits, the sinner only has to Believe, even though he little understands all that Christ has done for him (Jn. 3:16). Faith in Christ and what He did at Calvary effect the results of eternal life. Consequently, Jesus was the fulfillment of the Passover, and, in fact, was the Passover.

Likewise, the Feast of Unleavened Bread typified His sinless Body and spotless Life.

"Leaven" is a form of yeast, which, in a measure, rots or corrupts itself when placed in dough, consequently causing it to rise. It was then a type of sin. Consequently, the bread eaten during the Passover was to typify Christ Who had no sin, hence *"unleavened."*

There has been much argument as to the day Jesus uttered the words, *"after two days."* Some think He ate the Passover a day early, which well could have been. If, in fact, that was the case, He uttered these Words on Monday.

He would have eaten the Passover on Wednesday, being arrested that night in the Garden of Gethsemane. His trial was conducted early Wednesday morning before daylight. Consequently, He would have been crucified on Wednesday, which is contrary to the popular thinking that He was crucified on Friday.

For Jesus to remain in the tomb for three days and three nights, as He had stated, He would have been placed in the tomb late Wednesday afternoon, rising from the dead some time after sunset Saturday evening. The Jewish day began at sunset, whereas ours begins at midnight. Therefore, according to Jewish calendars, Sunday, the first day of the week, began at sunset Saturday. (As well, the Wednesday

NOTES

mentioned above, began at 6 p.m. on what we now call Tuesday evening.)

The phrase, *"And the Son of Man is betrayed to be crucified,"* portrays the manner in which He was delivered up to the Jews, with the word, *"betrayed,"* used in the present tense which denotes the certitude of the event. He sees the event as actually present, even though Judas at this time had not yet committed the foul deed.

The Greek word for *"crucified"* is *"stauroo,"* which means *"to impale on a cross."*

Crucifixion was, and without a doubt, the most cruel form of punishment that could be devised. It was borrowed by the Greeks and the Romans from the Phoenicians, who used it for the worst criminals and slaves until Constantine banned it in the fourth century.

(3) "THEN ASSEMBLED TOGETHER THE CHIEF PRIESTS, AND THE SCRIBES, AND THE ELDERS OF THE PEOPLE, UNTO THE PALACE OF THE HIGH PRIEST, WHO WAS CALLED CAIAPHAS."

The phrase, *"Then assembled together the Chief Priests, and the Scribes, and the Elders of the people,"* constituted the Religious Leaders of Israel.

The *"Chief Priests"* included the office of High Priest which had originally been held for life. However, the office was now political, and, consequently, was controlled by Rome. As such, it changed hands frequently, with these various individuals continuing to claim the title of *"Chief Priests."* They were all members of the Sanhedrin, the ruling body of Israel.

The *"Scribes"* and *"Elders"* would have constituted other members of the Sanhedrin.

The phrase, *"Unto the palace of the High Priest, who was called Caiaphas,"* means that it was not a formal meeting, or it would have been held in the hall Gazith, *"the hall of hewn stones."*

It was assembled at the house of the High Priest, which probably meant that some were present who were not members of the Sanhedrin.

"Caiaphas" was the son-in-law of Annas who had been appointed by Quirinius, but after nine years had been deposed. He was succeeded by Ishmael, Eleazar, his son, Simon, and lastly, Caiaphas.

Actually, there were some who continued to hold Annas as the High Priest, and he does appear to have possessed high authority (Jn. 18:13; Acts 4:6).

Two years after the crucifixion, both Caiaphas

and Pilate were deposed by Vitellius, then Governor of Syria, and afterwards Emperor. Caiaphas, unable to bear the disgrace and the stings of his conscience for the murder of Christ, committed suicide about 35 A.D.

(4) "AND CONSULTED THAT THEY MIGHT TAKE JESUS BY SUBTILTY, AND KILL HIM."

The two words, "And consulted," concerned these Religious Leaders of Israel. The topic of their conversation was the most diabolical crime ever conceived in the hearts of wicked men.

Even at the present time, and actually for all time, most "consulting" by Religious Leaders has been for the purpose of hindering the Work of God. It is a startling statement, but true!

This is the reason it is very difficult for the Lord to work in religious institutions. They become man-centered, consequently, taking over the Headship of Christ, with their goals and aspirations diametrically opposed to God.

The phrase, "That they might take Jesus by subtilty," meant that the act would not be carried out in an open above-board way, but by stealth. They would not do it out in the open, because they had no legal grounds to do so. Jesus had done nothing wrong, and, in Truth, had done everything right, and actually the greatest right there ever was. So, they would have to take Him in an unlawful manner because they were performing an unlawful deed!

The phrase, "And kill Him," actually means that they consulted to kill Him as men consulted to kill a wild beast.

Why?

Their hearts were evil, and there is no evil like religious evil! When men begin to commit dastardly crimes in the Name of God, there is no limit to what they will do because they feel justified in their actions. When men pull a cloak of religion over their evil actions, most never pull out of it. It is ironical, their plotting to kill Him, was, in reality, a plot to kill themselves. Their actions would result in the destruction of their nation, and in such a bloody way as to defy description!

(5) "BUT THEY SAID, NOT ON THE FEAST DAY, LEST THERE BE AN UPROAR AMONG THE PEOPLE."

The phrase, "But they said, Not on the Feast day," actually should have been translated, "Not during the Feast." This was the eight days of Passover celebration.

It is ironical, the very Feast day they were celebrating, the Passover, was a type of Jesus Christ, and had been observed for nearly 1600 years. While it commemorated the deliverance of the Children of Israel from Egyptian bondage, it in its broader scope was meant to represent the greater deliverance of all of humanity from sin, at least those who would believe!

Some may ask the question as to how Jesus would have died on Calvary to redeem man from the awful clutches of sin, if the Religious Leaders had not carried out this dastardly act?

As should be obvious, God being God, could have brought about this thing in any one of many ways, without His Own people doing it, and without tampering with the will of man. Jesus said, "For it must needs be that offenses come (due to the evil hearts of men); but woe to that man by whom the offence cometh!" (Mat. 18:7).

Sadly and regrettably, there were no lack of evil candidates for this evil task! But Israel, God's Own, stood at the head of that line as the most evil of all!

The phrase, "Lest there be an uproar among the people," concerned the many who loved Jesus, and had even been healed by His miracle-working Power. The city and the Temple being filled with these pilgrims, made it more difficult for them to carry out their nefarious activities. They knew if there was the slightest commotion, that Pilate would come down on the situation with a heavy hand. Consequently, whatever they did had to be by subterfuge.

(6) "NOW WHEN JESUS WAS IN BETHANY, IN THE HOUSE OF SIMON THE LEPER,"

John tells us that this incident took place six days before the Passover (Jn. 12:1-3). It seems that the Holy Spirit directed Matthew to place some of his accounts in spiritual rather than chronological order. Consequently, the order of this Anointing of Christ would be placed immediately prior to preparation for the Passover.

If all the Passages concerning the household at Bethany be put together, some conclude that Martha was the wife of Simon the leper, Lazarus and Mary being, consequently, brother-in-law and sister-in-law to Simon.

It seems that the house was evidently a large one, and Simon, therefore, would have been in comfortable financial circumstances. He was evidently one who had been healed by Christ of leprosy.

For someone to continue to be addressed according to past circumstances, such as Matthew the Publican, was common in those days. Therefore, Simon, although now healed and well, continues to be addressed as *"Simon the leper."*

As well, *"Simon"* was a common name, therefore, those carrying this name were often addressed as *"Simon the Canaanite, Simon the Tanner, Simon Bar-jona,"* etc.

(7) "THERE CAME UNTO HIM A WOMAN HAVING AN ALABASTER BOX OF VERY PRECIOUS OINTMENT, AND POURED IT ON HIS HEAD, AS HE SAT AT MEAT."

The phrase, *"There came unto Him a woman having an alabaster box of very precious ointment,"* points to Mary, the sister of Martha (Jn. 12:3). As well, there was only one anointing, with Matthew and John giving an account of the same incident.

It is said that the *"alabaster box"* was made of soft white marble. These were generally round-shaped with a long narrow neck, with the small opening being sealed.

The word, *"precious,"* adequately describes this *"ointment,"* and because in today's money (1995) it would have been worth approximately $12,000. Consequently, to own something of this nature, meant, no doubt, that this family was well off financially!

Mark called it *"pistic nard,"* and is rendered *"spikenard."* It was used for any salve or ointment which contained myrrh as one of its ingredients. It was not found in Israel, and had to be imported from a long distance, consequently adding to its cost.

The phrase, *"And poured it on His Head, as He sat at meat,"* has meaning of great import.

As well, John said that she poured it on His Feet, wiping them with her long flowing hair.

Even though the anointing of the head of very distinguished guests was not uncommon, still, Mary had other thoughts in mind.

She, no doubt, had been made aware of His statements concerning His coming death, with it possibly even having been made in her presence. I think it is obvious that she had a far greater grasp of what He was saying, even than His Disciples.

Living in the suburbs of Jerusalem, she no doubt knew of the terrible animosity and even hatred of the Religious Leaders for Christ. Considering His statements concerning His death,

she knew in her heart that such was eminent. However, the manner in which she anointed Him gives us insight into her Faith.

First of all, she anointed His Head, which spoke of His death. However, according to John, she then anointed His Feet, signifying His Resurrection. In other words, from the tomb in which they would place His dead Body, He would walk out of under His Own Power! (Jn. 12:3).

She remembered that just a few days before, and just prior to raising her brother Lazarus from the dead, Jesus had told her sister Martha, *"I am the Resurrection, and the Life"* (Jn. 11:25). Consequently, her anointing His Feet testified to her belief in the Resurrection. She seemed to be the only one who fully understood what He had said about His Death and Resurrection, with His Disciples little understanding it until after Pentecost.

(8) "BUT WHEN HIS DISCIPLES SAW IT, THEY HAD INDIGNATION, SAYING, TO WHAT PURPOSE IS THIS WASTE?"

The phrase, *"But when His Disciples saw it, they had indignation,"* points to Judas Iscariot who originated this complaint, which was quickly taken up by the other Disciples (Jn. 12:4).

The question, *"Saying, To what purpose is this waste?"*, proclaims an ignorance that was appalling! Several things are here said:

1. The disgruntled complaint of the traitor Judas will quickly spread to the other Disciples, portraying how error and fault-finding are so contagious.

When one member of a Church begins to find fault, and as here without justification, it soon spreads to others in the Church, creating an atmosphere of doubt and unbelief. Consequently, what every Believer says should be according to the words of Paul, *"Let no corrupt communication proceed out of your mouth, but that which is good to the use of edifying, that it may minister grace unto the hearers."* What Judas said did not *"edify"* or *"minister Grace."*

Then Paul said, *"And grieve not the Holy Spirit of God,"* which Judas did, with the other Disciples following suit (Eph. 4:29-30).

2. Anything done for God is never a *"waste,"* whereas much of that done for secular things definitely is.

These men were thinking in a very secular and carnal way, having been fueled by the traitor.

The world presently thinks that anything done for God is a waste. Consequently, the money spent to air the Gospel by Television is of absolutely no consequence to the world, and, sadder still, by most of the Church, and because they think in the ways of the world.

Countless times I have had newsmen refer to the money given by people for the Cause of Christ, and especially given by the elderly, to be but *"waste."* And yet, they think nothing, and even applaud, the billions spent by the poorest of the poor, as well as the elderly, to buy lottery tickets, etc.

3. Sadly, in the Church there is definitely much *"waste!"* How much money is needlessly spent on elaborate Church buildings, when much less ostentation would suffice? (To be sure, I stand condemned in this matter myself in the construction of Family Worship Center in 1982. In looking back, and through the years, hopefully having learned some things, a similar structure could have been built for much less.)

How much money is *"wasted"* by Churches supporting false doctrine?

If the Truth be known, it could probably be said that ninety percent of that given supposedly for the Cause of Christ is wasted. Money in the Church should go but for two purposes:

A. Simple structures which are adequate to meet the housing needs of the local Church, as well as its administrative costs.

B. Everything above that should go for the taking of the Gospel to the world. However, money given for World Evangelism must be spent on those who truly preach the Gospel, and, who consequently, *"bear fruit."*

As a case in point, I think it would be obvious that those who supported the Apostle Paul got their money's worth. This man won souls, and won souls, and won souls!

At the same time, when the Church at Corinth was supporting *"false apostles and deceitful workers,"* who were preaching *"another gospel,"* I think it should be obvious that not only was their money *"wasted,"* but, as well, it was actually supporting the work of Satan. As then, so now, much of that given which purports to be for the Work of God, is actually being given to modern *"false apostles and deceitful workers"* (II Cor. 11:12-15).

(9) "FOR THIS OINTMENT MIGHT HAVE BEEN SOLD FOR MUCH, AND GIVEN TO THE POOR."

This verse puts forth the argument of the

entirety of the world and much of the Church regarding service to God and to man. It must ever be understood that piety is not shown only in the giving of alms to the poor, but that the honor of God has a superior claim. As stated, the world does not understand or believe this, nor does many in the Church, and because they have the spirit of the world.

We must not neglect what we owe to Jesus Christ under pretense of what we owe His members. Many count it as waste what is expended in the worship of God, which proves they love neither God nor His worship.

As well, giving alms to the poor, which is important, in no way takes the place of worship of God.

In Truth, and sadly so, many Religious Denominations expend all their effort on giving to the *"poor,"* with no effort at all given to the worship of God. This is always a glaring sign of spiritual declension!

Proper worship of God will result in the poor not being neglected; however, if the True Worship of God is neglected, ultimately, the poor will be neglected as well!

It is the same as loving God first and your neighbor second, which means that the proper Love of God guarantees love for one's neighbor. Otherwise, all breaks down! (Mat. 22:37-40).

(10) "WHEN JESUS UNDERSTOOD IT, HE SAID UNTO THEM, WHY TROUBLE YE THE WOMAN? FOR SHE HATH WROUGHT A GOOD WORK UPON ME."

The phrase, *"When Jesus understood it,"* either referred to Him ultimately overhearing the negative statements, or it was revealed to Him by the Holy Spirit.

The question, *"He said unto them, Why trouble ye the woman?",* referred to Mary the sister of Martha and Lazarus.

Jesus, using the word, *"woman,"* is not meant as a negative, for in that culture it had no ulterior meaning, while, presently, it is a cold, impersonal reference.

As the Disciples then erroneously troubled *"Mary,"* likewise, many seek to trouble all who seek to worship God. Sometimes it is even by well-meaning people such as the Disciples.

The phrase, *"For she hath wrought a good work upon Me,"* refers to that which was so very important, His death on Calvary. Two things have happened here:

1. As we have stated, a disgruntled negative spirit, which was resident in Judas, quickly spread to all the Disciples, and because they entertained his thoughts. One negative person can spoil many good people. It is the old adage of one rotten apple being placed in a barrel of good apples. The good apples do not make the bad apple good, but rather the opposite! The bad apple, if not removed, will ultimately spoil the entirety of the good ones!

2. Many Believers, as the Disciples, do not think in a spiritual sense, but, instead, in a carnal sense. As such, they do not understand spiritual things, with almost all judgments being carnal, and, therefore, wrong. Such is the bane of the modern Church.

Paul said, *"But the natural man receiveth not the things of the Spirit of God: for they are foolishness unto him: neither can he know them, because they are spiritually discerned"* (I Cor. 2:14).

Thankfully, after the Day of Pentecost, the Disciples would quickly be pulled from the natural senses to the spiritual, which was done by the Holy Spirit.

The *"good work"* done to and for Christ, will never be recognized by the world, nor much of the Church. However, we must never forget that the labels we are interested in are those He provides, and not man!

(11) "FOR YE HAVE THE POOR ALWAYS WITH YOU; BUT ME YE HAVE NOT ALWAYS."

The phrase, *"For ye have the poor always with you,"* is, regrettably, a result of man's inhumanity to man.

As someone has said, *"If $1,000,000 was given in cash to every single person on the earth, at the end of about twelve months, about one percent would have it all, with most having little or none left."*

Democracy boasts of its equal opportunity for all, and, as well, of its care for those who do not know how to take advantage of opportunity, or else are deprived and dispossessed in some way. And, to be sure, it is the greatest system in the world. However, it is Bible Christianity which has produced it, and not vice versa.

Poverty is not of God! And, to be sure, during the coming Kingdom Age it will be totally eliminated.

No, that does not mean that poverty is a sin,

but it definitely is a terrible handicap, and, as well, a product of the Fall of man.

The phrase, *"But Me ye have not always,"* spoke of His bodily Presence. It spoke of His human Body being removed from the touch and sight of men, and is even now in Heaven.

The Catholic doctrine of Transubstantiation claims that the Catholic wafer actually turns in to the very flesh and Body of our Lord. That doctrine is here contradicted by Jesus Himself.

Regarding the Lord's Supper, the bread is but a symbol of His Broken Body and the Cup is but a symbol of His Shed Blood.

(12) "FOR IN THAT SHE HATH POURED THIS OINTMENT ON MY BODY, SHE DID IT FOR MY BURIAL."

As stated, Mary no doubt knew of Christ's statements respecting His Death and Resurrection. Consequently, she recognized that embalmment would be needless, therefore, she poured the ointment on His living Body, which, as well, testified of her belief in the Resurrection.

The phrase, *"She did it for My burial,"* as spoken by Christ, proclaims that which was normally done after death.

Actually, the women who had come with Him from Galilee, the Scripture says, *"Prepared spices and ointments,"* which they planned to use on His Body in the early hours of Sunday morning.

In the three days and nights that Christ was in the tomb, two Sabbaths fell which hindered the women from carrying out the embalming process before Sunday morning.

If our calculations are correct, Jesus was placed in the tomb late Wednesday afternoon. Thursday was a High Sabbath, which was the first day of the Feast, and not the ordinary weekly Sabbath, which was yet two full days away (Lk. 23:54).

The special Sabbath or the first day of the Feast of Unleavened Bread always came on the fifteenth of Nisan regardless of what day of the week it fell on. It was on Thursday at this time, which was from our Wednesday sunset to Thursday sunset.

On that day they were allowed to do no work, consequently, they could not prepare the *"spices and ointments"* until Friday, which they did. Then the next day being Saturday was the regular weekly Sabbath, which prevented them from applying to His Body what they had prepared.

Consequently, Sunday morning was the first opportunity they had, hence them coming early to the tomb. Nevertheless, they were late, Jesus had already risen from the dead, therefore, Mary's anointing of Him was the only anointing He received (Lk. 24:1-8).

(13) "VERILY I SAY UNTO YOU, WHERESOEVER THIS GOSPEL SHALL BE PREACHED IN THE WHOLE WORLD, THERE SHALL ALSO THIS, THAT THIS WOMAN HATH DONE, BE TOLD FOR A MEMORIAL OF HER."

The phrase, "Verily I say unto you," proclaims the announcement that proves Inspiration. Opponents of Inspiration deny the fact of prediction. They claim that all the Prophecies in the Bible were made after the events happened. But they cannot deny the fact of this Prophecy. It was made nearly 2,000 years ago, and no one can question its fulfillment today.

The phrase, "Wheresoever this Gospel shall be preached in the whole world," proclaims that it would be preached, and that Mary's story would ever be told!

The phrase, "There shall also this, that this woman hath done," proclaims Heaven's delight with her act of love and kindness.

The phrase, "Be told for a memorial of her," proclaims from the Mouth of Jesus how highly He thought of this which she had done. To be sure, it was far more than an act of kindness, but, rather, an understanding of Who He was and why He came! As stated, Mary's understanding of Him was far deeper at this time, even than His Own Disciples.

As well, it gives me great pleasure in the writing of these notes, as clumsy as they may be, to be able to share in the fulfillment of this Prophecy made by Christ nearly 2,000 years ago.

As I dictate these words, I strongly sense the Presence of God. I realize what Mary did on that day so long ago was so much more important even than she realized. And yet, with what little the Lord here allowed this door to be opened to the meaning of His Death and Resurrection, still, He only allowed us to know of its victory and so little of the darkness He entered and defeated. Hence, the fragrance of the costly "ointment" representing His spotless pure life, would fill the nostrils of all who were

in the room, whether they understood it at that time or not! It continues to do so today.

(14) "THEN ONE OF THE TWELVE, CALLED JUDAS ISCARIOT, WENT UNTO THE CHIEF PRIESTS,"

The phrase, "Then one of the Twelve, called Judas Iscariot," chronologically refers to the time-frame immediately following verses 3-5. The story of Mary is parenthetical, actually belonging to several days earlier. However, the Holy Spirit, at least in the Book of Matthew, had it placed immediately prior to the betrayal of Judas, which ties in, at least somewhat, to the indignation he showed respecting Mary's anointing of Jesus.

As well, the Holy Spirit, by using the phrase "One of the Twelve," portrays that he was one of the chosen companions of Christ, which emphasizes his crime, making it more heinous. To sin is bad enough, but to sin against Light is worse still! And Judas sinned against Light.

There is no way that one can excuse or dress-up this heinous crime committed by this man. Yes, had he repented, he would have been forgiven. But he did not repent, and went to his death and eternal doom by his own hand.

The phrase, "Went unto the Chief Priests," refers to those of verse 3. They were as wicked or more wicked than he was, and yet the Religious Leaders of Israel.

To betray Christ, it is ironical that Judas did not go to the thieves, harlots, or drunks, but rather to the Church! It is a point that should not be lost upon the reader.

The greatest hindrance to the Work of God is not that which we have just mentioned, even though woefully sordid, but, rather, pious self-righteousness, which has probably damned more people to hell than all the sins of passion put together!

Religion is an evil, wicked business, while relationship with Christ is the most glorious possession that a person could ever have, which Judas did not have!

(15) "AND SAID UNTO THEM, WHAT WILL YE GIVE ME, AND I WILL DELIVER HIM UNTO YOU? AND THEY COVENANTED WITH HIM FOR THIRTY PIECES OF SILVER."

The question, "And said unto them, What will ye give me, and I will deliver Him unto you?", portrays the evil of this man's heart! No wonder the Holy Spirit through Paul said, "For *the love of money is the root of all evil: which while some coveted after, they have erred from the Faith, and pierced themselves through with many sorrows"* (I Tim. 6:10). John said, regarding Judas and his complaint respecting the anointing of Jesus by Mary with the expensive ointment, *"Not that he cared for the poor; but because he was a thief, and had the bag, and bear what was put therein"* (Jn. 12:6).

Therefore it seems that Judas was the treasurer for Christ and the Apostles, and that he had been stealing for some time. Now he will commit the greatest crime of all, and for a paltry thirty pieces of silver.

The phrase, *"And they covenanted with him for thirty pieces of silver,"* is approximately $5000 in 1995 money. This was the legal price of a slave which had been gored by an ox, or killed in some other way (Ex. 21:32).

The Prophet Zechariah, about 500 years earlier, had prophesied, *"I said unto them, If ye think good, give Me My price; and if not, forbear. So they weighed for My price thirty pieces of silver"* (Zech. 11:12).

As well, this evil transaction had been foreshadowed when another Judas sold his brother, Joseph, for twenty pieces of silver (Gen. 37:27-28). Also, it was typified by Ahithophel giving counsel against David, his familiar friend (II Sam. 16).

The most foul deed in human history is now about to be carried out!

(16) "AND FROM THAT TIME HE SOUGHT OPPORTUNITY TO BETRAY HIM."

Why did Judas do such a thing?

Of course, only the Lord knows the answer in totality to this question. However, there are indications.

As the other Disciples, Judas envisioned a grand empire with Jesus at its Head, and His Disciples at His side, occupying positions of Power and Glory. Israel would once again regain her place and position as the premier people of the world, as it had been under David and Solomon. All the Prophets had spoken of this time, and surely this is what Jesus, especially considering His great Power, would do! However, as the months passed, lengthening into somewhat over three years, there was no indication from Christ that such would be done. Actually, if anything, Jesus was saying the very opposite! He was speaking of being killed, and

of late He had even mentioned that He would be crucified.

It was obvious that the Religious Leaders of Israel hated Christ, and were plotting constantly to bring His Ministry to an end. And then had come the Great Triumphant Entry!

Multiple thousands were cheering the Name of Jesus, but yet He made no gesture toward the usurpation of power. Beside that, He had ridden a lowly mule into the city, which was perplexing to Judas. This, within itself, was the very opposite of what a victorious conqueror would do!

And then Jesus had gone into the Temple, totally disturbing its activity by throwing out the moneychangers, which incensed the Religious Leaders even more!

In Judas' mind, it was now obvious that Jesus was not going to set up an earthly kingdom, thereby overthrowing Rome. As well, the hatred of the Sanhedrin against Christ was so strong that it seemed impossible for Christ's Ministry to go on much longer! Consequently, he would derive what he could out of a final transaction — thirty pieces of silver.

Now that the first question has been asked, please allow us to ask the second question:

How could he do it?

Jesus was the most kindest, gracious human being Who had ever lived, in effect, God manifest in the Flesh, Immanuel! Everything about Christ was perfect, His demeanor, character, nature, attitude, spirit, and, consequently, every act He committed. Judas had witnessed Him healing every manner and type of illness, sickness, and disease, even to the raising of the dead. He had seen it all, missing nothing! He had seen sad hearts made glad, and by the thousands. He had witnessed those in the terrible bondage of sin instantly set free by the Power of God. He had been privy to, and witness of, the greatest example of Love, Mercy, and Compassion, that the world had ever known in all its history. Everything that was good, noble, true, honest, and kind, was wrapped up in Jesus Christ.

Not one time in the three and a half years that Judas along with the other Disciples had travelled with Him, had Jesus treated him in any way except with the greatest love, regard, and respect. So how could he do this thing?

As well, he was perfectly aware of the wickedness and evil of the Religious Leaders of

Israel. He knew of their dishonesty, immorality, and evil intent. He knew they were liars and thieves! So how could he do this?

First of all, we learn that environment or association is not Salvation. Judas could not have had a better environment, actually the best that anyone has ever known. Neither would it have been possible to have had a better association. To be able to walk side by side with Christ was the greatest privilege ever afforded a human being.

We also learn that miracles, within themselves, as spectacular as they may be, are not the instrument which draws one to Salvation. Of course, the question must be asked, *"Was Judas a true follower of the Lord, and, therefore, saved when originally chosen by Christ?"*

There is every Biblical evidence that he was.

First of all, Jesus prayed all night, seeking the Will of His Heavenly Father respecting the ones to be chosen. There is nothing in the Word of God that would even remotely suggest that God would tell Christ to choose one who was even then a devil (Lk. 6:12-16). At a much later time Satan entered into Judas (Jn. 13:2).

Not too long after choosing the Twelve, Jesus *"gave them power against unclean spirits, to cast them out, and to heal all manner of sickness and all manner of disease"* (Mat. 10:1).

If Judas was a devil then, or rather used of Satan, Jesus would have been giving Satan power to cast out Satan, which of course is absurd! Jesus Himself said, *"And if Satan cast out Satan, he is divided against himself"* (Mat. 12:26).

He then said, *"But if I cast out devils by the Spirit of God, then the Kingdom of God is come unto you"* (Mat. 12:28).

So, the only way that devils could be cast out, and according to Christ, was by the Spirit of God. Consequently, Judas had the Spirit of God, and could not have had it unless he at that time was saved. Paul said, *"Now if any man have not the Spirit of Christ, he is none of His"* (Rom. 8:9). When Judas was chosen, and for some time thereafter, he had the *"Spirit of Christ."*

So, at some point in time he began to lose his way, and right in the middle of the greatest Move of God the world had ever known!

As to how he could do such a thing, I think one need look no further than *"self."* It was self-will which pulled him away from Christ, and by his own volition. This is what Jesus was

speaking of when He said, *"If any man will come after Me, let him deny himself, and take up his cross, and follow Me"* (Mat. 16:24).

This Judas did not do! Consequently, self-will became more and more prominent, because a little leaven ultimately corrupts the whole (I Cor. 5:6).

(17) "NOW THE FIRST DAY OF THE FEAST OF UNLEAVENED BREAD THE DISCIPLES CAME TO JESUS, SAYING UNTO HIM, WHERE WILT THOU THAT WE PREPARE FOR THEE TO EAT THE PASSOVER?"

The phrase, *"Now the first day of the Feast of Unleavened Bread the Disciples came to Jesus,"* actually meant that it was approaching, which would be on Thursday, and must be prepared for. It was on Tuesday that this question was asked.

The question, *"Where wilt Thou that we prepare for Thee to eat the Passover?"*, concerned the eating of the Passover and not the preparation of it, for Jesus would eat it a day early.

That Tuesday afternoon, Peter and John, who represented the company of Disciples, and, no doubt, instructed by Christ, went, as was customary, to the Temple with the Paschal Lamb. There, taking turns with others who thronged the Temple on the same errand, they killed the Lamb, the nearest Priest catching the blood in a gold or silver bowl, and passing it next in the row of Priests until it reached the one nearest the Altar, who instantly sprinkled it toward the Altar's base.

The Lamb was then flayed and the entrails removed, to be burnt with incense on the Altar. This was done, as we have stated, on Tuesday afternoon.

When evening came, the Lamb was roasted with great care. Unleavened bread, wine, bitter herbs, and sauce were also provided for the supper.

Josephus, the Jewish historian, said that approximately 250,000 lambs were offered up at this particular Passover. All as a type of Him, Who was in their very midst, and would in reality become the Passover, to Whom all the other Sacrifices had pointed, but yet not recognized by Israel.

Other than preparing the Lamb, as we have stated, the preparations for the place where the Passover would be eaten needed much preparation as well! A proper room had to be found and carefully cleansed from every particle of leaven. Tables and couches had to be arranged, with all the proper lighting, etc.

(18) "AND HE SAID, GO INTO THE CITY TO SUCH A MAN, AND SAY UNTO HIM, THE MASTER SAITH, MY TIME IS AT HAND; I WILL KEEP THE PASSOVER AT THY HOUSE WITH MY DISCIPLES."

The phrase, "And He said, Go into the city to such a man, and say unto him," refers to Jerusalem, for Jesus was presently at Bethany. Who the man was, is not known. Some think he was the father of John Mark, who wrote the Gospel of Mark.

The phrase, "The Master saith," is very similar to the instructions given respecting the animal used for the Triumphant Entry.

Every Believer should live so close to Him that His every Word would be our command. It is regrettable that many are not close enough to even hear His Voice, much less obey it!

The phrase, "My time is at hand," is a statement that carries with it the meaning of the ages. This was the time of His suffering and death. And yet to the Disciples, the expression was mysterious. The very reason for which He had come was now about to be fulfilled. It would be the greatest task every performed by God or man, the Redemption of mankind! To explain it, or even understand it, man can only go so far. He then loses his way in the mystery of the Love of God, which was more evident at Calvary than any place else!

Someone has well asked the question, "How horrible is sin?"

The answer to that question can only be found in the great price that Jesus paid to deliver man from sin. If we can fully understand the greatness of the price that was paid, then we can fully understand the horror of that for which it was paid.

The phrase, "I will keep the Passover at thy house with My Disciples," would bring honor to that house as it had never known before! To think of one having the privilege of Jesus and His Disciples eating the Last Supper at one's house, is beyond one's comprehension. And yet, that's what Jesus did, and, again, that's what Jesus does constantly with all who will invite Him in!

(19) "AND THE DISCIPLES DID AS JESUS HAD APPOINTED THEM; AND THEY MADE READY THE PASSOVER."

The phrase, "And the Disciples did as Jesus had appointed them," spoke of all the preparations for the most important Passover that had ever been kept. All the some 1600 previous years pointed toward this one moment, when Jesus would offer Himself on Calvary, which would be the True Passover. As the blood had been shed in Egypt as the result of a lamb being slain as an innocent victim, with its blood applied to the doorposts of the houses, with all in the houses being safe, and because the Lord said, "When I see the blood, I will pass over you" (Ex. 12:12-14). Likewise, when Jesus would die on Calvary, which would fulfill this which had taken place in Egypt so long before, all who would believe in Him, accepting what He did at Calvary as our Substitute, would be saved and safe exactly as those who had sought the protection of the blood those long years before (Jn. 3:16).

When Jesus died on Calvary, there would be no more need for other lambs to be offered, because His One Sacrifice would forever pay the price, that "Whosoever will, let him take the water of life freely" (Rev. 22:17).

The phrase, "And they made ready the Passover," speaks of the last Passover that would ever been offered, at least that God would recognize! Even though the Jews continued to keep the Passover, and still do in a limited manner, still, it is only because they do not recognize Jesus Christ as their Lord and Messiah, and what He did at Calvary. However, it is presently a fruitless exercise, and because Jesus fulfilled the type some 2,000 years ago.

(20) "NOW WHEN THE EVEN WAS COME, HE SAT DOWN WITH THE TWELVE."

The phrase, "Now when the even was come," was probably about 6 p.m. on Tuesday evening. It is obvious that Jesus ate the Passover early so that He could actually become "The Passover" at the regular time the Jews had always eaten it. Inasmuch that it was proper for the Jews to eat the Passover as much as a month late, providing circumstances demanded such, Jesus eating it early would not have been a violation of the Law in any way (II Chron. 30:2-5).

The phrase, "He sat down," has a beautiful spiritual significance as well!

When the Passover was originated in Egypt, it was ordered to be eaten standing (Ex. 12:11). However, after the Children of Israel had gained the Promised Land, the posture was changed to that of reclining in token of rest.

This posture representing the *"rest"* that one would find in Christ coincides with the words of the Apostle Paul, *"There remaineth therefore a rest to the people of God."*

He then said, *"For he that is entered into His rest, he also hath ceased from his own works, as God did from His"* (Heb. 4:9-10).

The phrase, *"With the Twelve,"* included Judas.

(21) "AND AS THEY DID EAT, HE SAID, VERILY I SAY UNTO YOU, THAT ONE OF YOU SHALL BETRAY ME."

The phrase, *"And as they did eat, He said,"* proclaims him eating that which had been prepared, including the Lamb.

Some claim that Jesus instituted a Supper after, and distinct from, the Paschal Supper. They claim that no lamb was prepared, with Jesus and the Disciples only partaking of the other ingredients. However, this belief was mainly derived from the corrupt Eastern Church, and has no Scriptural validity.

The eating of the Passover was on this fashion:

A cup was filled with wine for everyone. A blessing was pronounced, after which the wine was drunk. Then, unleavened bread, bitter herbs, and the lamb were brought in.

Thanksgiving was offered for the many blessings of life and the food handed around to each guest. A second cup of wine was drunk, after which an explanation of the Feast was given with Exodus 12:26-27.

The company then sang Psalms 113 and 114, followed by another blessing. Then the food was eaten. After this, a third cup of wine was drunk and Psalms 115 and 118 were sung. This is what is referred to in verse 30.

The phrase, *"Verily I say unto you, that one of you shall betray Me,"* presents Christ giving Judas a last chance of Repentance before the final act. Actually, Christ made seven efforts to win Judas from his fearful purpose; but in vain (Mat. 26:21, 23-25; Jn. 13:11, 18, 27).

(22) "AND THEY WERE EXCEEDING SORROWFUL, AND BEGAN EVERY ONE OF THEM TO SAY UNTO HIM, LORD, IS IT I?"

The phrase, *"And they were exceeding sorrowful,"* proclaims them realizing the import of the Words of Christ.

NOTES

The question, *"And began every one of them to say unto Him, Lord, is it I?",* presents the Eleven calling Him *"Lord,"* while Judas called Him *"Rabbi"* (vs. 25).

The question must be asked as to how Judas could get by so long without the other Disciples suspecting him? Of course, Jesus knew the heart of the traitor, but the others did not! Were there not tell-tale signs?

At this stage, the spirituality of the Disciples was such that they would not have picked up on these signs. In other words, they simply were not spiritual enough!

After the Day of Pentecost, and their being Baptized in the Holy Spirit, the entirety of their spiritual perception would be changed. The 5th Chapter of Acts bears this out, in that Peter instantly recognized the perfidy of Ananias (Acts 5:1-11). Such proclaims the veracity provided by the Holy Spirit. Without the Baptism in the Holy Spirit with the evidence of speaking with other tongues (Acts 2:4), not only is spiritual perception greatly hindered, but, as well, any and all capacities of the spiritual life is seriously weakened, even though one be truly born again! Consequently, most of the Church world stumbles along with no more spirituality than the Disciples before Pentecost. Sadly, this characterizes even most of the Religious Denominations who call themselves *"Pentecostal."* In Truth, with only about a third of the people in these particular Denominations even claiming to be Baptized in the Holy Spirit, one readily sees the terrible spiritual declension. Only a Holy Ghost Revival can change the situation!

(23) "AND HE ANSWERED AND SAID, HE THAT DIPPETH HIS HAND WITH ME IN THE DISH, THE SAME SHALL BETRAY ME."

The phrase, *"And He answered and said,"* proclaims another effort to pull Judas back from the abyss, but with no success!

If one is to notice, Jesus never one time, at least that is recorded, pulled Judas aside and talked with him privately about his perfidious action.

Why?

There is no record that Jesus ever counselled very much. Even when He took His Disciples aside privately, most of His conversations were to all of them, without singling out one or two. Actually, there is very little in the Bible that substantiates the modern counseling binge presently used by the Church. In the Early Church, there is very little evidence, if any, that Paul or Peter, or any of the other Apostles for that matter, devoted any time at all in one-to-one counseling.

There is every evidence given by the Holy Spirit, that the proclaimed Word of God given in public assemblies, wherever that may have been, was sufficient. In other words, if individuals would not heed the Word of God as it was proclaimed, and especially under the Anointing of the Holy Spirit, there is little evidence that they would have heeded a one-to-one encounter.

There certainly may have been a small amount of such counseling; however, it could not have been very much because the Holy Spirit would certainly have said more about it.

The methods of the modern Church, at least as a whole, little include the Bible anymore, but rather humanistic psychology, hence these unscriptural modern methods, which, in effect, offer no help at all!

On a recent radio talk program, I had the occasion to hear the exchange between one of the most noted psychologists in America and the host of the program. This man had written 32 books on psychology, so I would have to assume he had some credentials in that particular field. He made this humorous statement.

He asked the host and his radio audience as to what would happen if all psychologists were laid flat on their backs head to toe?

He then acclaimed in so many words that the mental health of America would greatly improve, and that it would be better off if they just stayed there.

He then went on to cite a fellow psychologist who had just written a book on the relationship of marriage. He went on to acclaim as to how she had been married five times, consequently, suffering four divorces! And yet, because she was a psychologist, people would buy her book telling them how to have a happy marriage.

Regrettably, this was ludicrous to this psychologist, as it should have been, but, seemingly, not so ludicrous to those who call themselves *"Christian Psychologists!"*

Another leading psychologist in America exclaimed that people are worse off after the counseling sessions than when they began. He

NOTES

went on to say, *"What we do, is little better than voodoo!"*

And yet, the Church falls for this fabrication of darkness.

Why?

As a whole, the Church has long since abandoned the Bible, which does hold all the answers for man's dilemma of life, and because it is the Word of God. As a substitute, psychology has taken its place, which I might hurriedly add is a sorry substitute!

To be sure, there certainly are times that one-on-one counseling is needed, but, in Truth, and as evidenced by the Word of God, very seldom!

If the Preacher will truly preach the Word of God, sooner or later every problem that may confront humanity is addressed. I might also quickly add that some have attempted to use the Bible without a proper relationship with Christ. Both go hand in hand!

Jesus said, *"Come unto Me, all ye that labour and are heavy laden, and I will give you rest.*

*"*Take My yoke upon you, and learn of Me; for I am meek and lowly in heart: and ye shall find rest unto your souls.

"For My yoke is easy, and My burden is light" (Mat. 11:28-30).

The phrase, *"He that dippeth his hand with Me in the dish, the same shall betray Me,"* was spoken to all the Disciples. Inasmuch as all had dipped into the dish, the information was not too revealing.

Actually, there was a dish of large dimensions sitting in the middle of the table, which contained the sauce in which the bread was dipped. Each guest, consequently, took his portion with his fingers.

(24) "THE SON OF MAN GOETH AS IT IS WRITTEN OF HIM: BUT WOE UNTO THAT MAN BY WHOM THE SON OF MAN IS BETRAYED! IT HAD BEEN GOOD FOR THAT MAN IF HE HAD NOT BEEN BORN."

The phrase, *"The Son of Man goeth as it is written of Him,"* refers to all that the Prophets had said concerning this time. Isaiah 53 proclaims this moment in such detail that no misunderstanding need occur. As well, and as we have stated, Zechariah prophesied that Jesus would be sold for *"thirty pieces of silver"* (Zech. 11:13).

As Abraham had told his son Isaac, when he asked, *"Where is the lamb for a burnt offering?",* he then said, *"My son, God will provide Himself a Lamb"* (Gen. 22:7-8).

That Lamb was Christ (Jn. 1:29).

Even at the very beginning, the Lord had told Satan, and concerning the great victory that Jesus would purchase at Calvary, *"And I will put enmity between thee and the woman, and between thy seed and her Seed; It shall bruise thy head, and thou shalt bruise His heel"* (Gen. 3:15). Now the time has come which was planned *"from the foundation of the world"* (Mat. 25:34).

The phrase, *"But woe unto that man by whom the Son of Man is betrayed!"*, gives us insight into the manner of God's dealings with the human family.

Does it mean that Judas was predestined to do this?

No! The Prophecies given many hundreds of years before concerning these things, and actually this very betrayal by Judas, are not the cause of men's wickedness, nor does it involve any necessity of it. Chrysostom said, *"Judas was not a traitor because God foresaw it, but He foresaw it because Judas would be so."*

Some would ask the question that if Judas had not done this, would not another have betrayed Him?

The idea is that if the Jews had not schemed the death of Christ, and Judas had not betrayed Him, how would all of this been carried out, which was necessary for the Redemption of man?

The question is moot, because God, in his foreknowledge, saw that these would do what they did, and of their own free will.

To ask such a question, is to show lack of understanding regarding God and His Omniscience and Omnipotence. His Wisdom is rich in contrivance, and, consequently, incomprehensible!

It was not God's Will for the Pharisees to murder Christ, nor for Judas to betray Him. It is His Will that all be saved, with Jesus making every effort to bring this to pass, at least without violating their free moral agency (II Pet. 3:9).

The Scriptures are replete with the Truth that God never tampers with one's will. He persuades, convicts, speaks, and moves in many and varied ways, that men may turn to Him, but never by violating their power of choice (Rev. 22:17).

The phrase, *"It had been good for that man if he had not been born,"* proclaims the eternal consequences of Judas' action, as well as all others who refuse Christ.

The gift of life is precious, and, as an aside, this is what makes the terrible crime of abortion so wicked. Regrettably, most waste the life God has given them, pursuing after that which is of no value. Solomon said, *"Let us hear the conclusion of the whole matter: Fear God, and keep His Commandments: for this is the whole duty of man"* (Ecc. 12:13).

The moment an individual is born, he becomes an eternal soul. In other words, even though the body will eventually die, the soul and spirit will live forever, finally being joined in the Resurrection with a body that cannot die, and irrespective of being saved or lost! Therefore, every human being that's ever been born will live forever with Christ or with Satan (Rev. 21:1-7; 20:10).

The choice is up to the individual, and not God. He made His choice a long time ago, *"Not willing that any should perish, but that all should come to Repentance"* (II Pet. 3:9).

(25) "THEN JUDAS, WHICH BETRAYED HIM, ANSWERED AND SAID, MASTER, IS IT I? HE SAID UNTO HIM, THOU HAST SAID."

The question, *"Then Judas, which betrayed Him, answered and said, Master, is it I?"*, portrays Judas asking last, after all the other Disciples had posed this question.

There is every indication that John the Beloved was on one side of Christ (Jn. 13:25), with Judas on the other side of the Master. Consequently, if that is correct, Judas was given a favored position at the Last Supper, hence fulfilling the Prophecy of David, *"Yea, Mine Own familiar friend, in whom I trusted, which did eat of My bread, hath lifted up his heel against Me"* (Ps. 41:9).

The phrase, *"He said unto Him, Thou hast said,"* proclaims the Lord's reply being so quiet that the others did not hear.

Now, and beyond the shadow of a doubt, Judas knows that Christ knows exactly what he is doing, and yet he continues on his evil course!

(26) "AND AS THEY WERE EATING, JESUS TOOK BREAD, AND BLESSED IT, AND BRAKE IT, AND GAVE IT TO THE DISCIPLES, AND SAID, TAKE, EAT; THIS IS MY BODY."

The phrase, *"And as they were eating,"* proclaims Jesus continuing the meal, even after this exchange, but no doubt with a heavy heart.

The Disciples had partaken of at least three Passovers with Christ in the preceding three years; however, at least at this time, they little knew that Jesus was the Passover, and that this would be the last one, with Him becoming the Sacrificial Lamb, fulfilling the Prophecies, and redeeming humanity, at least those who would believe (Jn. 3:16).

The phrase, *"Jesus took bread, and blessed it, and brake it, and gave it to the Disciples,"* proclaims the symbol of that which He would do, and become.

He was the *"Bread,"* and, consequently, *"blessed,"* inasmuch as He was God manifest in the Flesh.

Likewise, His Body was *"broken"* at Calvary, considering the wounds He experienced.

As well, He *"gave"* the results of this action at Calvary, not only to His Disciples, but, as well, to the entirety of the world.

As this was the example of Christ, likewise, it serves as the example for all Believers, and is as follows:

1. *"Jesus took bread"*: This is illustrative of Him taking the Believer upon Faith in Christ out of the terrible grip of sin, giving him Eternal Life.

2. *"And blessed it"*: Immediately after conversion to Christ, the Believer is blessed immeasurably. Not only does he have Eternal Life, and the privilege of being Baptized in the Holy Spirit, but, as well, experiences blessings in every realm.

3. *"And brake it"*: After conversion to Christ, and a time of great blessing, the Believer enters into a sanctifying process. While it is true that every Believer is sanctified at conversion, without which he cannot even be saved, still, this only begins the process, at least where Sanctification is concerned (I Cor. 6:9-11).

This is the Believer's *"standing"* in Christ, and cannot be changed, moved, or abrogated. However, the Believer's *"state,"* at least at this stage, is never up to his *"standing."* Therefore, the *"breaking"* or the sanctifying process, which brings our *"state"* up to our *"standing,"* is begun by the Holy Spirit. Paul alluded to this by saying, *"And the very God of Peace sanctify you wholly"* (I Thess. 5:23). Actually, this is a work of Grace which never ends, at least regarding this life, and will conclude only when we are *"presented faultless before the presence of His Glory with exceeding joy"* (Jude 24).

I'm sure the reader understands that the sanctifying process has nothing to do with

NOTES

one's Salvation, as that is sealed and secure the moment one accepts Christ, but, instead, that we *"be conformed to the image of His Son"* (Rom. 8:29).

The *"breaking"* is never pleasant, because it amounts to an abrogation of *"self,"* which must be hidden in Christ. Jesus died to save man from sin and self. However, even though sin is immediately washed away by the Blood of Christ, self is not so easily brought into line. Such was the purpose of Job's terrible ordeal, and such is the purpose in our own lives, although not nearly so severe as Job's.

4. *"And gave it"*: Until the Believer is properly *"broken,"* with all self hidden in Christ, he cannot be properly given unto the world. To give *"self"* to the world, affords no blessing whatsoever, but to give Christ affords all Blessings.

This is the reason that only a few Believers truly are a blessing, because it is only a few who are truly *"broken."*

This is what Jesus was actually speaking of when He said, *"If any man will come after Me, let him deny himself* (self), *and take up his cross, and follow Me"* (Mat. 16:24).

The *"Cross"* is to die on, and it speaks of the self-life, which, if properly crucified, brings on the exhibition of the Christ-life, which is the goal of the Holy Spirit in every life. It is regrettable that much of the Charismatic world totally negates the Cross, calling it *"past miseries."* Such portrays a lack of understanding of Bible Salvation and the teaching of Christ. Hence, there is not much *"breaking"* in those ranks, and, hence, not much of Christ given to the world, but only bloated, prideful, egotistical *"self."* The example of Christ as given here is meant for us to follow. If the Holy Spirit has His Way in our lives, we will *"Take up the cross and follow Jesus."*

The phrase, *"And said, Take, eat; this is My Body,"* spoke of the unleavened bread, which represented His perfect, sinless Body. The word, *"This,"* in the Greek is *"neuter,"* and therefore is not with *"bread,"* which is masculine. In other words, He is not saying that this bread is His literal Body, but, rather, that it symbolizes or represents His Body. Regrettably, on this simple action the monstrous Mass and its imitations in the Catholic Church have been founded!

Catholicism teaches the Doctrine of *"transubstantiation,"* which means that the bread or wafer placed on the tongue of the worshiper, actually turns into the literal, physical Body of Christ.

The Lutherans teach *"consubstantiation,"* which means that the bread turns into the Body of Christ in spirit.

Both are error, in that the *"bread"* was meant by Christ to serve only as a symbol or representation of His Body, which the language proves.

Consequently, both the Catholic and Lutheran error teaches that one is saved by partaking of such, or, in other words, that the taking of the Lord's Supper constitutes Salvation.

As stated, this is error pure and simple, inasmuch as it reduces Salvation to *"works,"* i.e., the works of man.

While it was true that man's Salvation is brought about by a *"Work,"* which Christ did at Calvary, but *"Faith"* alone in that *"Work"* is required for one to be saved. Hence, Paul would say, *"For by Grace are ye saved through Faith; and that not of yourselves: it is the Gift of God:*

"Not of works, lest any man should boast" (Eph. 2:8-9).

Therefore, as holy and sacred is the Lord's Supper, its holiness and sacredness reside in what Christ did at Calvary, of which the Supper is a symbol. To make more of it, abrogates the finished Work of Christ. To make less of it, denies what He did at Calvary and the Resurrection. It does not save, and in no way is meant to save, but merely to serve as a commemoration of what He did for lost humanity (I Cor. 11:24).

This is primarily what Jesus was speaking of when He said, *"Except ye eat the Flesh of the Son of Man, and drink His Blood, ye have no life in you"* (Jn. 6:53).

He wasn't speaking literally of His Flesh and Blood, for He also said, *"It is the Spirit that quickeneth; the flesh profiteth nothing: the Words that I speak unto You, they are Spirit, and they are Life"* (Jn. 6:63).

In other words, He was saying that if anyone could literally eat His Flesh and drink His Blood, it would not save their souls. It is the believing of His Word, which leads one to make Christ the Lord of one's life. Christ then forms a union with the Believer, in that by virtue of His Sacrificial Death, and Resurrection, Eternal Life is appropriated.

The idea is of a continuous action of making

Christ the Lord of one's life, i.e., the eating of His Flesh and the drinking of His Blood!

To be sure, the Lord's Supper has absolutely nothing to do with that, which is done alone by Faith, with the ordinance of that Supper serving as a memorial of His Death at Calvary, which made it all possible.

(27) "AND HE TOOK THE CUP, AND GAVE THANKS, AND GAVE IT TO THEM, SAYING, DRINK YE ALL OF IT;"

The phrase, *"And He took the cup, and gave thanks,"* is meant to serve as a symbol or representation of His shed Blood at Calvary. This was probably the third cup at the close of the Supper, and was called *"the Cup of Blessing"* (I Cor. 10:16). It followed the eating of the Lamb.

If one is to notice, in all of the accounts of the Lord's Supper, the word, *"wine,"* is not used, with the word, *"cup,"* being repeatedly used. Jesus called this drink the *"fruit of the vine"* (Mat. 26:29; Mk. 14:25; Lk. 22:18).

Actually, the Holy Spirit carried this directive right on through even into the Early Church. The Apostle Paul said, *"After the same manner also, He took the cup, when He had supped, saying, This cup is the New Testament in My Blood"* (I Cor. 11:25).

I think this was done because the Holy Spirit took particular pains not to use any words that could be construed as referring to any kind of intoxicating beverage.

The very meaning of fermented wine makes it unsatisfactory to represent the Blood of the Lord Jesus Christ. Fermented wine is grape juice in which decay (or rot) has taken place. In other words, the process of fermentation is the break-down of large molecules caused by the influence of bacteria or fungi. Wine, then, results from the degenerative action of germs on pure substances.

Fermented wine used in Communion would actually symbolize tainted, sinful blood, and not the pure and perfect Blood of Jesus Christ that had to be made evident to be a perfect cleansing for our sins.

Pure, fresh grape juice tends toward life, but fermented wine tends toward death. Alcohol used for drinking purposes is both a narcotic and a poison. It could hardly be used as a symbol for the Blood of the Lord Jesus Christ.

The Jews were required to use unleavened bread with the Passover Feast, and they were commanded that during that time, *"There shall no leavened bread be seen with thee, neither shall there be leaven seen with thee in all thy quarters"* (Ex. 13:7). As the unleavened bread symbolized the perfect Life and perfect Body of the Lord Jesus Christ, likewise, pure unfermented grape juice symbolized His shed Blood.

It would not make any sense for unleavened bread to be used symbolizing His Body, and then to use fermented wine to represent His Blood! Therefore, He used the word *"cup"* to symbolize pure, perfect shed Blood.

The phrase, *"And gave thanks,"* is meant to convey appreciation for the Blessings of the Lord. After the Death and Resurrection of Christ, it takes on a completely new meaning, giving thanks unto the Lord for all He did at Calvary in redeeming man from the terrible bondage of sin, and the impartation of new life.

The phrase, *"And gave it to them, saying, Drink ye all of it,"* completely negates the Roman Catholic assertion that the *"cup"* is for the Priests alone.

This is done because the Catholics claim that their Bishops and Priests are successors to the original Apostles in the Apostolic Line.

To do that, denies the shed Blood of Christ, at least by symbolism, to all who Jesus died for.

No! All the Apostles drank of the cup that day, and, as well, the account given by the Holy Spirit through the Apostle Paul plainly says that it is for *"All, because all are sinners in desperate need of a Redeemer, the Lord Jesus Christ"* (I Cor. 11:23-32).

(28) "FOR THIS IS MY BLOOD OF THE NEW TESTAMENT, WHICH IS SHED FOR MANY FOR THE REMISSION OF SINS."

The phrase, *"For this is My Blood,"* as with the broken bread and His Body, represented His Blood. It cannot be substituted by water, or, as we have stated, by intoxicants, or anything else.

Every Covenant or Testament of old was made with blood (Ex. 24:8; Heb. 9:20). As well, there can be no remission of sins without it (Lev. 17:11; Heb. 9:22).

The *"cutting of the Covenant,"* was an ancient ritual that was practiced between nations, or even between tribes or families. In such a case, an animal was killed, with its blood being shed, with its body actually parted into halves. One-half of the slain victim was placed on one side, with the other half on the other side, with

NOTES

the two participants pricking their fingers, and, consequently, drawing blood. They then pushed their fingers together, mixing the blood, and walked between the two halves of the slain animal.

The idea was, if the Covenant was broken by either party, the one that broke it could be torn apart exactly as the animal had been. The mixing of the blood sealed the Covenant.

There are four major Covenants outlined in the Bible respecting God and man. (There were other Covenants, but only these four were major, with the first three serving as major stepping-stones to the fourth and final Covenant, *"The New Covenant."*)

The four were the, *"Abrahamic, Mosaic, Davidic, and New."*

In each of these Covenants, God states what He will do.

In Genesis 15, we find that God passed between the halves of sacrificial animals as Abraham lay in a deep sleep. In this way God bound Himself to keep the Promises made to Abraham.

The Mosaic Covenant followed, but was somewhat different! This Covenant was bound only by the obedience of both parties, God and Israel. The Lord kept His part of the Covenant, while Israel did not at all obey, and ultimately suffered the consequences of the broken Covenant.

The David Covenant as the Abrahamic was unconditional (II Sam. 7). As the Abrahamic Covenant, it had to do with purposes which would be accomplished according to the very question asked of Jesus by His Disciples, *"And what shall be the sign of Thy coming, and of the end of the age?"* (Mat. 24:3). As stated, the Abrahamic and Davidic Covenants are unconditional, and will be fulfilled at the conclusion of this Dispensation.

The New Covenant was instituted by Christ (Mat. 4:17), and actually given in detail to the Apostle Paul. However, it was prophesied by Jeremiah about 600 years before Christ, but was not actually made at that time. The New Covenant was made and confirmed at the Cross.

At the Last Supper, as we are here studying, the night before the Crucifixion, Jesus explained the symbolism of the Communion Cup, by saying, *"This is the Blood of the 'New' Covenant, which is poured out for many for the forgiveness of sins"* (Mat. 26:28; Mk. 14:24; Lk. 22:20; I Cor. 11:25).

Just as the other Covenants were oath-confirmed, so the New Covenant would be made by a Covenant-initiating Sacrifice. But this time the Offerer and the Sacrifice were One, and the Blood that sealed God's Commitment was that of His Own Son.

The New Covenant has now been made and confirmed. The Promise of forgiveness is assured. As well, no one need ever fret or worry that Jesus will not keep His part of the Covenant, for His shed Blood has guaranteed the perpetuity of that Covenant. As stated, the Promise of Forgiveness is assured to all who will believe (I Jn. 1:9).

However, only at the First Resurrection of Life, will Believers realize the full meaning of what Jesus has done, even though today we are able to experience the Promised Forgiveness and Transformation made available in this glorious New Covenant.

The difference between the Old and New is striking! The Old Covenant knew a Law that was carved in cold stone. The New Covenant takes the Righteousness that was expressed in Law and supernaturally infuses that Righteousness into the very character of the Believer. Thus the Book of Hebrews quotes the Old Testament fore view as something that is now, through Christ, our own: *"I will put My Laws in their hearts, and I will write them on their minds… Their sins and lawless acts I will remember no more"* (Heb. 10:16-17).

Consequently, in this New Covenant, the Promise is given that every single sin properly confessed is not only forgiven, but forgotten.

The New Covenant is vastly different from the Old, in that the New has none of the Laws called *"Do this and live."* Instead, we meet again the great *"I will"* of God, Who promises that He Himself will transform us from within.

Paul carefully explains that all of God's Promises are appropriated by Faith. In other words, the Believer does not have to shed blood to ratify this Covenant, because the Blood shed by Christ sufficed for both, inasmuch as He was God manifested in the Flesh. In other words, He was both God and Man, which meant that the shedding of His Blood was the same as God and man shedding blood, ratifying the Covenant. In other words, He became our Substitute, and in our identifying with Him, and by Faith, we appropriate to ourselves the benefits

of this Covenant. It cannot fail, because it's all in Christ, and not in man.

Hallelujah!

Today, to us, who, like Abraham, are *"fully persuaded that* God (has) power to do what He Promises" (Rom. 4:21) comes the Promised Salvation, and with it comes forgiveness and inner transformation. Such are the benefits of Covenant relationship with the Lord.

In Romans 4 and Galatians 3, Paul argues that the essence of Covenant is Promise. What can we do to respond to the Promise of God? Only one thing.

We are to believe the Promise and consider God's Word trustworthy. We are to consider God's Word so trustworthy that we step out to act on what He says.

It was this Faith that saved Abraham long before either circumcision or Law was introduced. It is Faith alone — Faith in Jesus, the seal of God's New Covenant — that saves us today.

Faith enables Believers to appropriate God's Promises and experience their benefits personally. But whether or not we believe in God's Promises, His Covenant Promises stand. In other words, our unbelief does not nullify the Promises or the Covenant. While it is true that the Believer can fail to appropriate the Promises, and, consequently, will suffer loss, nevertheless, the moment he desires to believe God, appropriating these Promises by Faith, he will find that the Covenant still stands and has not been abrogated at all!

In simple terms, and even though a Believer should sin, still, the Covenant is not weakened by the number of times one pleads for forgiveness. Each and every time the repentant Believer will find, *"If we confess our sins, He is faithful and just to forgive us our sins, and to cleanse us from all unrighteousness"* (I Jn. 1:9).

Even though the Mosaic Covenant was broken by Israel, and because it was based on performance (the performance of Israel) and not on Promise, it was intended to define for Israel the lifestyle that would enable God to bless them until the New Covenant was made.

Even though Israel forfeited it, still, Jesus as the spiritual Israel, kept the Mosaic Law in all its fullness, thereby satisfying its demands. However, Israel would not accept His fulfilling of the Law, consequently, cutting themselves off from the New Covenant and, therefore, Salvation.

However, the Prophets proclaim that Israel ultimately will accept the New Covenant, which will be at the Second Coming, and the beginning of the Kingdom Age.

From the beginning, Faith has been the only correct response people can make when God speaks in Promise. Faith alone is able to bring human beings to personal relationship with God. It is through Faith that we today can experience the Blessings of God's New Covenant: the forgiveness of our sins and the Spirit's work of engraving Righteousness on our hearts.

So, when Jesus said, *"For this is My Blood,"* He was speaking of that which He would do at Calvary, which, in effect, would *"cut the Covenant,"* doing so for God and man.

Therefore, it is inviolable.

The phrase, *"Of the New Testament,"* is the New Covenant, which was carried out at Calvary, and ratified by the Resurrection of Christ from the dead (Mk. 14:24; Lk. 22:20; Jn. 6:53-56; 19:34; Acts 20:28; Rom. 3:24-25; 5:9; I Cor. 10:16; 11:25; Eph. 1:7; 2:13-16; Col. 1:14-20; Heb. 9:12-15; 10:19-29; 12:24; 13:12, 20; I Pet. 1:2, 18-23; I Jn. 1:7; 5:6; Rev. 1:5-6; 5:9; 7:14; 12:11).

This New Covenant takes the place of the old Mosaic Covenant which is now abolished (II Cor. 3:6-15; Gal. 3:13-25; 4:21-31; Eph. 2:14-15; Col. 2:14-17; Heb. 7:11-28; 8:8-13; 9:1-24; 10:1-23).

The phrase, *"Which is shed for many for the remission of sins,"* signifies the Lord using this term in the present tense, meaning that His death is certain — that the Sacrifice has already begun, that the *"Lamb is slain from the foundation of the world"* (Rev. 13:8).

The word, *"many,"* is equivalent to *"all,"* and irrespective as to how many it may be, or become! Redemption is universal, though all men, sadly and regrettably, do not accept.

The *"remission of sins,"* means that the blood of bulls and goats could not take away sin, with them at most, giving a ritual or ceremonial purification. In other words, the sins were not taken away at that time, only covered by the atoning blood of the innocent victim, typifying Christ. However, when Jesus made His Ministry debut, John said, *"Behold the Lamb of God, which taketh away the sin of the world"* (Jn. 1:29).

In other words, Jesus would not cover the sins, but, instead, take them away, i.e., remit them. The word, *"remittance,"* means to release from the guilt or penalty of sins. This could be

done because Christ satisfied the penalty by His death, and paid the price by the shedding of His Own Blood. So, no Believer need ever worry about sins which are properly confessed being dragged out again. They are gone! Even the Lord cannot remember them, for He said, *"And their sins and their iniquities will I remember no more"* (Heb. 8:12).

If Satan drags them out, which he always attempts to do, tell him to take them to the Lord, which he dare not do! With the Lord, there is no recollection of them, hence, *"Justification by Faith."*

Inasmuch as there are so many Catholics, and inasmuch as they depend upon the Mass for their Salvation, and inasmuch as verses 26-28 are claimed as a foundation for their Doctrine, perhaps the following would be helpful:

THE MASS, HOLY COMMUNION, THE LORD'S SUPPER, THE HOLY EUCHARIST, OR THE BLESSED SACRAMENT

All of the foregoing terms are used almost interchangeably to refer to the Lord's Supper. In fact, all Christians observe the Lord's Supper in one form or another, or certainly should!

While New Testament accounts of the inception of the Lord's Supper are wonderfully simple, very little within Catholic usage remains simple for long. Under Catholic Administration, it soon becomes complicated and barely recognizable as an extension of the same principles espoused within the Word of God.

To try to bring some coherence into the general subject under discussion, let us look at four areas in regard to the Roman Catholic Mass — or the Lord's Supper, if you prefer:

1. The Mass as observed in Roman Catholic ritual.

2. The Doctrine of Transubstantiation.

3. Salvation through participation in the Mass.

4. What the Bible teaches about the Lord's Supper.

THE MASS IN ROMAN CATHOLIC RITUAL

To begin with, it is (according to Catholic theology) a mortal (spiritually fatal) sin to miss Mass (without good and sufficient reason) on the Sabbath or on holy days of obligation. A mortal sin immediately consigns a person to hell, whatever his spiritual condition, until it is removed by participating in the Rite of Reconciliation — formerly referred to as confession, penance, absolution, and Communion.

The Roman Catholic Church teaches that the Holy Mass is an expiatory (sin-removing) Sacrifice, in which the Son of God actually is sacrificed anew on the Cross. He literally (according to this error) descends into the Priest's hands during the act of Transubstantiation, wherein the elements of the host (the wafer) literally are transformed into the Body, Blood, Soul, and Divinity of our Lord Jesus Christ. This was defined as such by the Counsel of Trent, although minor alterations were made in wording due to the Second Vatican Counsel.

Further, this repeated Sacrifice of Christ can be specifically applied to benefit deceased souls if this is the expressed wish of living persons who donate specified sums to help defray the cost of such Masses. The Catholic Church further teaches that the laity may receive full benefit of participation in the Mass by taking only the bread, while the Priest alone receives both the bread and the cup.

Bartholomew F. Brewer, former Catholic Priest, states:

"We are taught some incredible things about the host, the wafer that Catholics receive in Communion. Canon I, on the Most Holy Sacrament of the Eucharist, reads, 'If anyone denieth, that, in the Sacrament of the Most Holy Eucharist, are contained truly, really, and substantially, the Body and Blood together with the soul and Divinity of our Lord Jesus Christ, and consequentially the whole Christ; but saith that He is only therein as in a sign, or in figure, or virtue; let him be anathema.'"

(In other words, if the person fails to believe in the Doctrine of Transubstantiation, he is lost.)

"We were taught," Bartholomew Brewer further states, *"that when the Priest hovers over the wafer and says, 'This is my body,' it becomes the actual Flesh of Christ. Likewise, after the Priest says the words, 'This is my blood,' the wine is said to become the actual Blood of Jesus. It is true that Jesus said, 'This is My Body . . . This is My Blood,' but it is obvious that He was speaking figuratively, just as He did when He said, 'I am the True Vine, and My Father is the Husbandman'"* (Jn. 15:1).

"This dogma about the host — sometimes called the 'wafer — God,'" Dr. Brewer goes on to

state, *"has given rise to some strange doings. If, for example, the consecrated host is dropped and a mouse or other animal snatches the wafer away, the Priest is given a 40-day penance to perform. If the sacramental wine is spilt at Mass, the Priest is advised to lick it up and clean the place with a special cloth called a purificator. If the Priest vomits after consuming the bread or the wine, it is recommended that he consume the vomit, provided that he can do it without creating an embarrassing scene. The alternative is to burn what he vomited. And such things have happened many times; I, myself, recall times that the Mass was being said on tossing Navy ships and the Priests became seasick."*

IS THE LORD'S SUPPER A SACRAMENT OR AN ORDINANCE?

If the word, *"sacrament,"* is used to define a formal religious act used as *"a symbol or memorial to a spiritual reality,"* it could be called a *"sacrament"* without doing violence to Scripture. However, if the word, *"sacrament,"* is meant to indicate a *"sacrifice,"* wherein the Lord's death is repeated over and over again (as a formal religious act or as a sign instituted by Jesus Christ), then it should not be referred to as a *"sacrament."*

Perhaps the word, *"ordinance,"* would be more appropriate or acceptable for the New Testament Christian. This simply infers *"an act of arranging something ordained or decreed by Deity, a prescribed usage, a practice, or a ceremony."* However, it must be understood that to the Roman Catholic mind the Mass is a *"sacrament"* which implies a *"sacrifice."* This belief lies at the very heart of Catholicism.

Clark Butterfield, a former Roman Catholic Priest, who wrote about the Mass after his conversion to Christ in 1978, stated:

"If you . . . have been subjected to the Roman Catholic system, (you) will always be at somewhat of a loss to fully understand and empathize with the Catholic and his 'Jesus in the Blessed Sacrament' (Orientation). You may read about it, hear about it, and study it, but its subjective reality will ultimately elude you.

"Conversely," Clark Butterfield went on to say, *"you who have experienced the Catholic way will recognize immediately the reality of which I write. The reality is an enigma to all outside the Catholic tradition. It is an enigma to Evangelicals because they rightfully ask,*

'How can an idolatrous misconstruing of the Saviour's Words and Actions have aught of good in it? How can such folly be the very bedrock of the spiritual lives of countless millions of Roman Catholics?'

"But to the Catholic and to many former Catholics, it is the reality, the final refuge even beyond Mary and the Church itself."

Among the staggering millions of Roman Catholics throughout the world, there are, undoubtedly, untold numbers who are earnestly searching for a personal relationship with the One they perceive to be their Redeemer.

Regrettably, and for almost all of them, this will be in the figure of the transformed host on the Altar — where the prosaic bread and wine have supposedly been changed into the Living Body and Blood of the risen Jesus Christ. Sadly, that is no relationship at all!

It is said that with ex-Catholics the single most traumatic aspect of their separation from the Church lies in their new concept of Holy Communion. With an expanded and proper grounding in Holy Scripture, they can surrender their dependence on the mediation of Mary and the Saints. They can even survive without the cathartic effect of confession and penance. They eventually come to view the whole Church of Jesus Christ, along with the Catholic Church, in a new perspective based on Scriptural concepts. But there is a longer struggle and a greater psychological dependence on the *"Blessed Sacrament"* question than on any other single element of their changed situations.

Finally, Roman Catholic Doctrine says, *"Without equivocation"* that when Jesus Christ, on the night preceding His Crucifixion, said, *"This is My Body"* (Mat. 26:26), the bread He was holding literally became His physical Body. When He took the cup and said, *"This is My Blood"* (Mat. 26:28), He meant that the cup no longer contained the fruit of the vine, but suddenly contained His Blood (which does cause some conflict with Acts 15:20 in which the New Testament Church is forbidden to imbibe blood). And, when Christ added the words, *"This do in remembrance of Me"* (Lk. 22:19), He was actually ordaining the Apostles as Priests eternally to re-offer this sacrifice — or at least so says the Roman Catholic Church.

This esoteric sacrifice was to be a recreation of His suffering and death on Calvary,

NOTES

perpetually repeated within His Church until He should come again. Therefore, He is today the truly present Body, Blood, Soul, and Divinity (although, admittedly, disguised as wine and bread) on all Catholic Altars and in all Catholic Tabernacles, and will so remain until such time as He may choose to come again.

THE DOCTRINE OF TRANSUBSTANTIATION

The Catholic Doctrine of Transubstantiation is, without question, one of the most absurd doctrines ever imposed on a trusting public. As we have already discussed, this Doctrine states that the Priest is endowed with a power to transform bread and wine into the literal Body and Blood of Christ. The Roman Catholic Catechism of Christian Doctrine says:

"The Holy Mass is one and the same sacrifice as that of the Cross inasmuch as Christ, Who offered Himself, a bleeding victim on the Cross to His Heavenly Father, continues to offer Himself in the unbloodied manner on the Altar, through the Ministry of His Priests."

Roman Catholic errors are inevitably human innovations that were inserted into the Church during the early centuries. This teaching on the Eucharist (Lord's Supper) follows this pattern.

In the first century, as described in the New Testament, Holy Communion was a meal of fellowship eaten as a Memorial to the Death of Christ and a symbol of unity among Christians — both with each other and with Christ.

In the second century, it began to shift toward a ceremony, in which Christ was present in some undefined form. This was not yet the eventual Catholic Doctrine of Transubstantiation — which was a development of the Middle Ages — but it was a beginning in this unfortunate, unscriptural direction.

By the third century, the idea of Sacrifice began to intrude, wherein Christ's Body and Blood were mysteriously produced by an ordained Priest for the gratification and benefit of both the living and the dead.

Michael A. Smith, an English Ecclesiastical historian, tells it well in his essay on the worship patterns of early Christians:

"The central service of worship on Sunday in the Early Church was the 'breaking of bread' or 'Communion.' This was a fellowship meal, with preaching, Bible reading, and prayer, which

culminated in the formal acts taken over from the Last Supper. The aim was to remember Jesus' death, and to celebrate His Resurrection. Praise and thanksgiving were uppermost, and for this reason the name 'Eucharist' (Greek for thanksgiving) was often given to the occasion. Gradually, the Eucharist became more formal, and the meal aspect secondary.

"From the third century, Old Testament ideas of Priesthood were used by some to interpret the Eucharist as the 'Christian Sacrifice.' At first the Sacrifice was thought to consist of praises, but gradually it came to be held that an offering was made to God to gain forgiveness of sins. By the Middle Ages this had been developed to make the Eucharist a re-offering of Christ's Sacrifice on the Cross.

"There also arose magical ideas concerning the bread and wine. By the fourth century it was held that either when the words of the Last Supper were repeated...or when the Holy Spirit was invoked on the bread and wine...a change took place. It was felt right to venerate the bread and wine as representing Jesus visibly."

This Doctrine of Transubstantiation, which simply means that the bread and wine changed to His Body and Blood, was first formulated by Paschasius Radbertus, Abbot of Corbey, at the beginning of the ninth century. It was first named *"Transubstantiation"* by Hildebert of Tours in the early years of the twelfth century, and made an Article of Faith (official doctrine) by the Lateran Council in the beginning of the thirteenth century.

In all honesty, we must repudiate this dogma on two counts:

1. It is opposed to Scripture.

2. It is contradicted by the evidence of the senses. When a person handles the wine or the wafer, the textures remain the same. They taste the same. There is no transformation in odor. They are still bread and juice, with all the original qualities. They are physically unchanged and will ever remain unchanged, because they are unchanged. They are merely as blessed and holy as they might be, a memorial to our Saviour's Sacrifice as a sin-offering in our stead.

Therefore, we reject this erroneous doctrine because of its basically superstitious nature and the idolatrous connotations connected with it.

An elementary study of Paul's Epistle to the Hebrews should lead us at least to question the

NOTES

Roman Doctrine of the continuing Sacrifice of the Mass. Please note these verses:

"For such an High Priest became us, Who is holy, harmless, undefiled, separate from sinners, and made higher than the heavens;

"Who needeth not daily, as those High Priests, to offer up Sacrifice, first for His Own sins, and then for the people's: for this He did once, when He offered up Himself" (Heb. 7:26-27).

"But Christ being come an High Priest of good things to come, by a greater and more perfect Tabernacle, not made with hands, that is to say, not of this building;

"Neither by the blood of goats and calves, but by His Own Blood He entered in once into the Holy Place, having obtained eternal Redemption for us" (Heb. 9:11-12).

"For Christ is not entered into the Holy Places made with hands, which are the figures of the true; but into Heaven itself, now to appear in the Presence of God for us:

"Nor yet that He should offer Himself often, as the High Priest entereth into the Holy Place every year with blood of others;

"For then must He often have suffered since the foundation of the world: but now once in the end of the world hath He appeared to put away sin by the Sacrifice of Himself" (Heb. 9:24-26).

These verses confirm the *"Once-and-for-all"* character of Christ's Sacrifice. Obviously, this allows for no repetition. So the clear teaching of God's Word expressly contradicts any continuing sacrifice — after the manner of the Catholic Mass.

The teaching of the Bible is clear and concise. Any future sacrifices were repudiated when Jesus paid the price for all future sin and cried out, *"It is finished"* (Jn. 19:30).

Actually, this phrase uttered by Jesus (in the Greek, teleo) was a colloquial expression that meant *"paid in full,"* or *"the debt is cleared forever."*

So, how might a person explain this cleavage between New Testament teaching and Catholic dogma? Of course, we know that Scriptural error invariably stems from the evil one, Satan. In this case it was due, at least in part, to dabbling into the popular Eastern mystery religions, borrowing from Greek and Roman paganism and reverting to outmoded Old Testament, Mosaic customs — all of which demanded recurring sacrificial offerings.

It is just one more tragic example of what happens when man's misguided intellect strays from the Written Word of God.

The Catholic Doctrine of Transubstantiation forces a person to humiliate Christ, even beyond the supreme humiliation He suffered on the Cross at Calvary. The glorified, risen, and ascended Christ can never again be degraded by any force, human or spiritual. Yet the very concept of bread and wine, which He Himself created — being mysteriously transformed into His Living Body and Blood — forces Him into further humiliation, which is unacceptable and unthinkable.

SALVATION THROUGH THE MASS

To the Roman Catholic mind, the Blessed Sacrament, the Mass, is a critical element in his Salvation (being saved).

The Mass is the Catholic means of worshiping Jesus. Whatever the degree of involvement with Catholicism, the Catholic never trifles with the awesome concept of the Eucharist, or Blessed Sacrament, being Jesus. However misdirected he may be in his daily life, when it comes time to confront that Presence, he renounces all vices until he has received Jesus at Holy Communion.

As a logical extension of the Doctrine of Transubstantiation, it has also become dogma that consecrated bread and wine should be publicly and privately adored and venerated. As a result, the Roman Catholic Church has adopted a number of rituals (in the form of various feasts and devotions) to promote adoration and veneration of these physical elements that have been transformed, they say, into the Godhead.

The principle Feast is Holy Thursday or the Feast of Corpus Christi (Latin for *"The Body of Christ"*). The principle devotions are benediction of the Blessed Sacrament, Forty Hours Devotions, and Perpetual Adoration of the Sacrament (in certain designated Churches). Each Feast has its own particular rites and each devotion its individual ceremonies or customs.

At Mass, the Priest consecrates — in addition to the bread and wine he will consume during the Mass — the hosts to be received by the faithful at the Mass. (Because of the alcoholism problem among Priests, the Vatican now allows common grape juice to be substituted by alcoholic Priests.)

Each wafer is called a host. There are small

hosts for the congregation and a large host for the Priest. Moreover, the Priests may consecrate additional small hosts to be retained in a chalice held within the Tabernacle (container) between Masses. Furthermore, he may consecrate an additional large host, also to be reserved in the Tabernacle, but to be used later for public display and adoration. (As previously noted, nothing is ever simple within the rites of Roman Catholicism.)

So there is, almost always — in every Catholic Church — some consecrated bread reserved in the Tabernacle, which means that Jesus is physically present within the Church — although firmly locked within the interior of the Tabernacle (small container). This is the reason Catholics genuflect (touch their knee to the ground) as they enter and leave their Churches — even when no service is in progress.

It is also the reason Catholics maintain a somber silence in their Churches and why candles burn perpetually in the sanctuary. Jesus is present in the Tabernacle, although in the form of bread. (The Tabernacle, usually an ornate and expensive vault that maintains the security of the expensive chalices holding the hosts, represent the central focus of the Church arrangement and occupies a central position over the Altar.)

Although the hosts stored within the Tabernacle are not usually visible to the public, parishioners are encouraged to come to the Church at almost any hour to pray, to adore, and to be comforted by the consecrated hosts.

INDULGENCES

Numerous indulgences are granted to Catholics who observe this custom. (An indulgence is a reduction in the sentences imposed on Catholics, in purgatory, where past sins, which have been forgiven through confession and penance, are personally atoned for by torment imposed by God.)

In effect, the granting of indulgences suggests that the Church issues (and God affirms) these reductions in sentence.

Indulgences can be either saved up for personal use after death by the person earning the indulgence, or cashed in immediately by crediting them to the account of loved ones who already have died. As no one knows precisely how long sentences in purgatory run (perhaps for centuries), it is obviously prudent to save up as many indulgences as possible.

This Roman teaching (of purgatory and indulgences) blatantly ignores the fact that Jesus Christ accepted <u>all</u> the guilt for our sins. It further ignores God's statement:

"And their sins and iniquities will I remember no more" (Heb. 10:17).

It was scandals over the selling of indulgences that first enflamed Martin Luther against excesses within the Church, and indirectly brought about the Protestant Reformation.

One former Priest states that he made innumerable visits to countless cathedrals in Europe and in numerous Churches — where he would spend long hours kneeling in solitary prayer and adoration before Tabernacles — venerating the consecrated bits of bread. Basically, he went on to say, this was the only time he ever felt really close to Jesus Christ. And then he added the solemn truth that *"feeling close"* to Christ is a far cry from trusting Him for Salvation.

In addition to private and personal adoration of the Blessed Sacrament, ornate and ostentatious public ceremonies are calculated to promote fervid devotion to the Eucharist. On such occasions the larger host is brought out from behind the Altar and inserted in a glass-fronted receptacle within a monstrance.

The monstrance is a portable, ornate, and expensive device of precious metals (and sometimes jewels), which is shaped vaguely like a cross but with a prominent sunburst effect around the area where the host is displayed.

Because of the glass front, a person can actually see Jesus (or the bread) as it is transported about the premises by a Priest.

The monstrance routinely is paraded through Churches during benediction (usually after the last Mass on Sunday morning), during which a ceremony of sprinkling Holy Water and shaking vessels of incense accompanies the Lord's trip around the Church. The monstrance is also the vehicle for transporting the host for veneration during many festivals in Latin American countries.

And such is the average worshiper's relationship with the Jesus of the Eucharist. Clark Butterfield said it was a love-fear relationship: love because he was told it was Jesus, fear because he was terrified that he might dishonor

the sacrament through some carelessness, and continuing apprehension that he might at some time receive the sacrament unworthily in Communion.

To the convicted Catholic, Transubstantiation means that the bread and wine no longer remains; they have actually become the Body and Blood of Christ.

In addition, during the Mass, a True Sacrifice is constituted when the Priest pronounces the words of consecration. Calvary is renewed, restored, and replayed before the eyes of the assembled congregation. A person is physically there at the foot of the Cross as Jesus serves as propitiation for his sins.

In Roman Catholicism the Eucharist is central to all worship. It is an integral part of Salvation. What it amounts to is that this is the basic Catholic relationship with Jesus Christ, which, in Truth, is no relationship at all!

THE QUESTION MUST BE ASKED: IS THIS IDOLATRY?

The Catholic Catechism (the basic guidebook on Catholic Doctrine) defines *"idolatry"* as *"rendering to any creature the honor and adoration that are due to God Alone."* I think a person would have to agree that what we are describing constitutes idolatry — the worshiping of a piece of bread that a person has become convinced is the Lord Jesus Christ.

WHAT DOES THE BIBLE TEACH ABOUT THE LORD'S SUPPER?

Even though we have addressed ourselves to this subject in some detail, please allow me the latitude of addressing it again relative to Catholic Doctrine.

Luke, the Beloved Physician, said:

"And He took bread, and gave thanks, and brake it, and gave unto them, saying, This is My Body which is given for you: this do in remembrance of Me.

"Likewise also the cup after supper, saying, This cup is the New Testament in My Blood, which is shed for you" (Lk. 22:19-20).

Mark, the Evangelist, said:

"And they all drank of it" (Mk. 14:23).

The Apostle Paul said:

"For as often as you eat this bread, and drink this cup, ye do shew the Lord's death till He come.

"Wherefore whosoever shall eat this bread,

and drink this cup of the Lord, unworthily, shall be guilty of the Body and Blood of the Lord.

"But let a man examine himself, and so let him eat of that bread, and drink of that cup.

"For he that eateth and drinketh unworthily, eateth and drinketh damnation to himself, not discerning the Lord's Body" (I Cor. 11:26-29).

It is sad, but true, that tens (and even hundreds) of millions of Catholics drink the cup of the Lord unworthily — guilty of the Body and Blood of the Lord — simply because they do not rightfully discern the Lord's Body.

They think the host (little wafer) and the wine actually become His personal Flesh and Blood — which constitute a form of idolatry. They do not understand what the Lord said respecting the Sacrifice He would shortly offer at Calvary.

The words, *"This is My Body . . . This is My Blood"* (Mat. 26:26, 28), are accepted literally in Catholic dogma. On the same basis, we should accept without thinking that Jesus gave us literal living waters, which will produce Eternal Life (Jn. 4:14), or that Jesus is truly a Door (Jn. 10:7-9), that He is a Lamb (Jn. 1:29), or that He is a growing Vine (Jn. 15:5).

If the Catholic hierarchy is to be consistent, they should foster adoration of doors, vines, and lambs. Certainly, these figures of speech are descriptive and colorful, but they are transparently figurative, just as are the terms, *"My Body"* and *"My Blood,"* in relationship to the *"bread"* and the *"cup."* The New Testament Church and the Early Church understood and accepted this just as it was offered — as a figure of speech.

In Catholic theology, much is made of the 6th Chapter of the Gospel of John (which we have already mentioned), which recounts the discourse of Jesus in which He referred to Himself as *". . . The Living Bread which came down from Heaven"* (Jn. 6:51).

Catholic Doctrine states that Jesus was here depicting Himself as the Eucharist — to be literally consumed as a means to Eternal Life.

However, at the end of this discourse, Jesus demolished any such carnal interpretation by adding:

"Doth this offend you? . . . It is the Spirit that quickeneth; the flesh profiteth nothing: the words that I speak unto you, they are Spirit, and they are Life" (Jn. 6:61-63).

So how do we *"eat and drink"* of His Flesh and Blood?

By coming to Him to end our spiritual hunger, and by believing in Him to end our spiritual thirst. This does not come by eating some magically transformed bread and by drinking some magically changed wine.

But, insists the Roman Catholic, *"Why did Christ use the words 'hoc est corpum meum?' Why did He not say, 'This is a symbol of My Body?'"*

For all intents and purposes, this is an excellent question. But we must remember that when the Lord initiated this holy memorial to His Death, He was eating the Passover Feast with His Disciples. Passover was established centuries before as a memorial for Israel of the awesome event that had taken place while they were in bondage in Egypt. The firstborn of every family then residing in Egypt would be slain, except those who had established their Faith in God by trusting in the Blood placed on their doorposts as a sign that their house should be exempt.

Now, however, the Passover was to be abandoned as a memorial to the Saving Grace of God Almighty and a new memorial created — to the ultimate Salvation that had only been foretold by the original Passover. In effect, the Lord's Supper was to be the Christian replacement for the Hebrew Passover.

From that moment forward, the Christian community (God's New Israel) would be able to celebrate a greater liberation than that from Egyptian slavery. Finally, man was to be freed from the bondage of sin and condemnation through the Sacrifice of *". . . The Lamb of God, which taketh away the sin of the world"* (Jn. 1:29).

When the Israelites partook of the Passover meal, no one was confused. No one believed that the lamb they were eating was the true body of the Lord's Passover. They were fully aware that it was only a representation, a memorial of the event they were commemorating.

In view of this, it is perfectly clear why the Lord should employ, for the new commemoration, words that reflected the rites of the old. Nor did He doubt that the common sense of the Disciples would enable them to understand that this was a figurative and not a literal statement.

It is clear to anyone who has studied the New Testament that this is the manner in which the Apostles interpreted it. This is confirmed by the fact that their standard reference to this act was simply that of *"breaking bread."*

"And they continued steadfastly in the

Apostles' Doctrine and fellowship, and in breaking of bread, and in prayers . . . And many wonders and signs were done by the Apostles . . . And they, continuing daily with one accord in the Temple, and breaking bread from house to house, did eat their meat with gladness and singleness of heart.

"Praising God, and having favour with all the people. And the Lord added to the Church daily such as should be saved" (Acts 2:42-47; compare Acts 20:7).

"The Cup of Blessing which we bless, is it not the Communion of the Blood of Christ? The bread which we break, is it not the Communion of the Body of Christ?" (I Cor. 10:16).

No Roman Catholic would refer to the Holy Mass as *"breaking bread,"* without adding complicated explanations. Yet, in the New Testament the Apostle Paul twice referred to the Lord's admonition, *"This do in remembrance of Me"* (Lk. 22:19; compare I Cor. 11:24-25).

Paul then added (in the form of comment):

"For as often as ye eat this bread, and drink this cup, ye do shew the Lord's Death till He come" (I Cor. 11:26).

Please note several things. He did not say *"Ye shall eat His Body and drink His Blood."* He referred to the ritual as employing bread and a cup. If these were legitimately the Blood and Body of Christ, Paul would certainly have referred to them as such. Further, Paul did not say, *"Ye shall repeat the Sacrifice of Christ until He comes."* He said, *"Ye do shew the Lord's Death."* The Greek word here translated, *"shew"* is *"kataggello,"* which means *"to declare, preach, speak, or teach."* It does not mean to reenact or reproduce. Also, the words, *"Drink this cup"* are plural, which suggest that, at least in the Corinthian Church, all partook of the cup — not just one individual, the Priest, as in the Catholic Mass.

A COMMEMORATION — NOT A SACRIFICE

That the Communion should be a re-offering of the very Body of Christ to humiliation and Sacrifice, or as it is called within Catholic usage, a repetition of the Sacrifice, is an idea that is obviously variant with many Passages of Sacred Scripture. For example:

"If they shall fall away, to renew them again to Repentance; seeing they crucify to themselves the Son of God afresh, and put Him to an open shame" (Heb. 6:6).

NOTES

These Scriptures all assure us that the Death of Christ was a unique act, and, on that, would be sufficient for the remission of all sins for all time.

It seems obvious that if the expiatory death of Jesus was a perfect work, we have no need for additional Sacrifices. There should be no further need for even *"bloodless"* Sacrifices to finish any work of Redemption.

"The Blood of Jesus Christ His Son cleanseth us from all sin" (I Jn. 1:7).

If the celebration of the Mass were a True Sacrifice, it would be wicked and cruel for the Priests to repeat it so frequently. If, as argued, this is a mystic Sacrifice (rather than a real one) and the Son of God does not really suffer (as He did on Calvary), then why refer to it as a Sacrifice? No True Sacrifice exists without pain and suffering.

That the celebration of the Eucharist by the Roman Catholic Church is labeled a *"Sacrifice,"* rather than a *"Commemoration,"* is due partly to the pagan custom of calling everything offered to the gods a Sacrifice.

The New Testament clearly shows that the Lord's Supper was only a peripheral element in the overall majesty of the Gospel Message. It was obviously not considered an essential part of Salvation. There is no hint anywhere within God's Word that the edible elements involved with the Last Supper were ever adored (or meant to be adored) by Christians.

To be sure, the rite was commanded by the Lord. He did say, *"This do."* But to put everything into focus, He also said, *". . . in remembrance of Me"* (Lk. 22:19).

So we do exactly that!

We partake of the Holy Communion in remembrance of the Lord Jesus Christ. We recall and remember, and always will, that His Body was given as a Perfect Sin Offering, and that His Blood was shed for each and every one of us, and that He is coming again!

(29) "BUT I SAY UNTO YOU, I WILL NOT DRINK HENCEFORTH OF THIS FRUIT OF THE VINE, UNTIL THAT DAY WHEN I DRINK IT NEW WITH YOU IN MY FATHER'S KINGDOM."

The phrase, *"But I say unto you,"* is meant to add an element to the price which would be paid at Calvary and the Resurrection.

The phrase, *"I will not drink henceforth of*

this fruit of the vine," had reference to this Passover being the last one, at least recognized by the Heavenly Father, until the coming Kingdom Age.

The phrase, *"Until that day when I drink it new with you in My Father's Kingdom,"* refers to the Kingdom Age, which has not yet come, but most assuredly will! In effect, this is a solemn Promise that *"This day"* shall come. It is the *"day"* that the prayer of Christ will be answered, *"Thy Kingdom come. Thy Will be done in earth, as it is in Heaven"* (Mat. 6:10).

The word, *"new,"* and referring to the *"Lord's Supper,"* proclaims that whereas the Supper is now taken in commemoration of what Christ did at Calvary and the Resurrection, and that it is to continue until He comes, here proclaims to us that He will come, and that this scene will be reenacted.

At the time of the Last Supper, the Kingdom belonged to the Jews, but because they did not desire the Kingdom of God, it was taken from them and given to others (Gentiles). But in the coming Kingdom Age, and when the Lord eats the Supper again with His Disciples, it will definitely be the *"Father's Kingdom,"* i.e., thousand-year Millennial Reign.

(30) "AND WHEN THEY HAD SUNG AN HYMN, THEY WENT OUT INTO THE MOUNT OF OLIVES."

The phrase, *"And when they had sung an hymn,"* refers to Psalms 115 and 118.

In the 118th Psalm, the Messiah is named some thirty times as *"Jah, Elohim, and Jehovah."*

This being the last song sung at the Paschal Supper, as stated by Hebrew historians, it gives an added preciousness to the heart that knows the Lord to picture Him singing it immediately before setting out for Gethsemane.

As the True Israel, He could perfectly sing it, and as the High Priest of His people, thus express His Faith and Her Faith, and make real and bring near the joys of the morning which are predicted to follow the sorrows of that dark night and the afflictions of Jacob's long exile.

As well, there is every indication that this song will be sung by Israel on the happy morning of her renewed espousals. This will be at the Second Coming.

She will invite all to trust Jehovah and now to praise Him; she will testify that the Messiah is her One and efficient Saviour; she will

acknowledge the wisdom and love which permitted her sufferings at the hands of man; she will approve the moral lessons of that chastening; she will proclaim that the once rejected Saviour is now her God and Redeemer; that her Sabbath has at last dawned; that there is no Blessing apart from Him; that He is the One and only Gate into Righteousness; and that He is the Promised Deliverer Who comes with Blessing out of the House of Jehovah.

The great note of this particular Song is reserved to its close. It is that there is no restoration for Israel apart from the once-rejected Messiah. She will exclaim: *"Jehovah Messiah is God. He has shown us light. He is Blessed. He cometh in the Name of Jehovah"*; and Messiah will, for His part, say, *"Thou art My God, I will praise and exalt Thee,"* and then, altogether, He with them and they with Him, they will sing the words of this 118th Psalm.

Only the Faith of Him Who is the Author and Finisher of Faith could sing such a song of Promised Glory when descending into the horrors of Gethsemane and Calvary.

(Notes on the 118th Psalm were derived from Reverend George Williams.)

The phrase, *"They went out into the Mount of Olives,"* probably speaks of about 7 or 8 o'clock at night, or even later! This was Tuesday night, or rather Wednesday as the Jews tabulated it.

Jesus was crucified on Wednesday, actually dying at 3 p.m. that afternoon, and being put in the tomb about 5 or 5:30. As prophesied, He remained in the tomb three full days and three full nights, being raised from the dead some time after 6 p.m. on Saturday evening, or, as the Jews would have called it, Sunday, the First Day of the Week (Mat. 12:40).

It seems that Jesus spent every night of this final week, or at least most of them, in the open air. As there was no room for Him when He was born, likewise, there was no room for Him when He was to die, as there is no room for Him in most hearts today! However, for those who make room, inviting Him in, they truly know Life Eternal.

(31) "THEN SAITH JESUS UNTO THEM, ALL YE SHALL BE OFFENDED BECAUSE OF ME THIS NIGHT: FOR IT IS WRITTEN, I WILL SMITE THE SHEPHERD, AND THE SHEEP OF THE FLOCK SHALL BE SCATTERED ABROAD."

The phrase, *"Then saith Jesus unto them,"* will not be one of victory, at least regarding the Disciples, but, rather, defeat!

The phrase, *"All ye shall be offended because of Me this night,"* records Christ Alone standing, with all the other falling. They would forsake Him, but He would never forsake them.

At this time, most only think of Peter's denial; however, even though the remaining Ten did not deny Him, still, they did forsake Him. (Judas had already departed in order to betray Him.)

The phrase, *"For it is written, I will smite the Shepherd, and the sheep of the flock shall be scattered abroad,"* is derived from Zechariah 13:7. The exact words are, *"Awake, O sword, against My Shepherd, and against the Man that is My Fellow, saith the Lord of Hosts; smite the Shepherd, and the sheep shall be scattered."*

The *"Shepherd"* is Christ, and the *"sheep"* are the Disciples, who, *"forsook Him, and fled"* (vs. 56).

(32) "BUT AFTER I AM RISEN AGAIN, I WILL GO BEFORE YOU INTO GALILEE."

The phrase, *"But after I am risen again,"* portrays, without a doubt, the greatest event in human history, the Resurrection of Christ from the dead. Without the Resurrection, Calvary, as is obvious, would have been of no avail. In effect, the Resurrection ratified what Jesus did at Calvary.

The phrase, *"I will go before you into Galilee,"* records this appointed meeting. As obvious, it would be after the Resurrection.

Even though Jesus did appear to the Disciples in Jerusalem before this appointed meeting in Galilee, still, it would be at the meeting in Galilee that He would reunite the Apostolic Body, and renew the Apostolic Commission. John gave the greatest account of this (Jn. 21).

(33) "PETER ANSWERED AND SAID UNTO HIM, THOUGH ALL MEN SHALL BE OFFENDED BECAUSE OF THEE, YET WILL I NEVER BE OFFENDED."

The phrase, *"Peter answered and said unto Him,"* records good intentions, but is actually a boast which could not be kept.

The phrase, *"Though all men shall be offended because of Thee, yet will I never be offended,"* says several things, and all in error. It behooves us to take a lesson from the experience of the fisherman.

1. Once again, Peter fell into the trap of

disagreeing with Jesus and even rebuking Him (Mat. 16:22-23). As we blanch at Peter's statement, how often have we done the same thing!

Disobedience of the Word of God is in essence the same.

2. It seems that Peter's answer was the result of boastful pride, and was made after he had received the warning recorded by Luke (22:31-32), *"Simon, Simon, behold, Satan hath desired to have you, that he may sift you as wheat:*

"But I have prayed for thee, that thy Faith fail not."

3. Peter places himself above all the other Apostles, and, consequently, fell the hardest.

Possibly this occasioned the statement he later made, *"For God resisteth the proud, and giveth Grace to the humble"* (I Pet. 5:5).

4. He takes his boast even higher, claiming that irrespective of what came, he would *"never"* fail the Lord.

To be sure, if the Lord lifts His Hand even the slightest, thereby giving Satan greater latitude, there is no human being who can stand without falling. Only the prideful would doubt that statement!

It is very easy to reprimand Peter at this time, pointing to his cowardly conduct which would come in a matter of hours. However, if any one of us would have been placed in the same position as Peter at that particular time, would we have done any better?

The lessons we learn are seldom learned through victories, but most of the time through defeats. Admittedly, they are expensive lessons, but seemingly the nature of man is such, even Godly men, that such can be little learned any other way.

(34) "JESUS SAID UNTO HIM, VERILY I SAY UNTO THEE, THAT THIS NIGHT, BEFORE THE COCK CROW, THOU SHALT DENY ME THRICE."

The phrase, *"Jesus said unto him, Verily I say unto thee,"* is in reply to Peter's statement, and will portray exactly how weak Peter really was, at least within himself!

The phrase, *"That this night,"* refers to the hours just ahead. It would truly be *"night"* for Judas, for Israel, and for Peter and the other Disciples. However, for Peter and the remaining Ten that *"night"* would blessedly end, with that particular Sun never setting again!

The phrase, *"Before the cock crow, thou shalt*

deny Me thrice," refers to the early morning hours before daylight, with Peter denying three times that he knew the Lord, or had ever been His follower.

(35) "PETER SAID UNTO HIM, THOUGH I SHOULD DIE WITH THEE, YET WILL I NOT DENY THEE. LIKEWISE ALSO SAID ALL THE DISCIPLES."

The phrase, *"Peter said unto Him,"* records the opposite of what he should have done. He should have fallen on his face crying to the Lord for strength and help, especially considering what was about to happen. However, even though the Disciples understood what Jesus was saying concerning His near crucifixion, still, the full import of it was not even remotely understood by them. The depth of the trial that was about to break upon them was of far greater magnitude than they could ever begin to imagine!

The phrase, *"Though I should die with Thee, yet will I not deny Thee,"* reinforces his boastful claim, despite the words just uttered by Christ.

Why did he do this?

I think Peter really meant what he said. However, he, at least at this time, did not even remotely comprehend the degree of the powers of darkness which would soon come upon him. He would learn that it was not a matter of his will, but of something else entirely, his Faith!

He would find that his Faith was not nearly as strong as he thought it was, and would come close to breaking. However, it did not break, and because Christ prayed for Him (Lk. 22:32).

Someone has said, and rightly so, that every attack directed against the Child of God by Satan, is but for one purpose, to weaken and, if possible, destroy one's Faith in God.

The phrase, *"Likewise also said all the Disciples,"* proclaims them joining in with Peter with their boastful claims. As stated, they were now about to enter a trial where the Lord Alone could stand; and had Peter, therefore, made greater protestations, they would only have resulted in a deeper fall.

(36) "THEN COMETH JESUS WITH THEM UNTO A PLACE CALLED GETHSEMANE, AND SAITH UNTO THE DISCIPLES, SIT YE HERE, WHILE I GO AND PRAY YONDER."

The phrase, *"Then cometh Jesus with them unto a place called Gethsemane,"* spoke of the Garden just across the Kidron Valley from Jerusalem, about 200 yards from the city wall.

Gethsemane means *"the oil press,"* and would be a fit place for Jesus to spend His last hours before the Crucifixion.

Some think that the Garden may have belonged to Joseph of Arimathaea, or Nicodemus. At any rate, it was a favorite place of retirement when Christ was at Jerusalem (Lk. 22:39; Jn. 18:2).

The phrase, *"And saith unto the Disciples, Sit ye here, while I go and pray yonder,"* proclaims Christ resorting to that which offers the only comfort and solace in time of trouble — prayer. It is regrettable that the modern Church little recommends such anymore. Instead, the psychologists are recommended, with prayer given little, if any, credence! However, if men know God, they go to God. If they don't know Him, they go elsewhere!

(37) "AND HE TOOK WITH HIM PETER AND THE TWO SONS OF ZEBEDEE, AND BEGAN TO BE SORROWFUL AND VERY HEAVY."

The phrase, *"And He took with Him Peter and the two sons of Zebedee,"* referred to James and John.

It seems that the Eight were asked to wait at a particular place in the Garden, while Jesus and the Three went a little further.

Why did He single out these Three?

In fact, Jesus had taken these Three into a deeper confidence some two times previous:

1. When Jesus raised the daughter of Jairus from the dead, He took Peter, James, and John with Him (Lk. 8:51). There they were witnesses of His *"Power."*

2. As well, these three had witnessed His Transfiguration (Mat. 17:1-8). There they witnessed His *"Glory."*

3. Now He takes them with Him into the Garden. Here they will witness His *"Suffering."*

The only answer is that He evidently saw something in the hearts of these Three which leaned closer to Him than the others, and despite the present failure!

In the three episodes given, Suffering comes last, which is not understandable to the carnal mind. It would think maybe first, if at all! However, the Holy Spirit placed the *"Suffering"* last, and for reason!

If the Spirit of God truly works through an individual, ultimately it will lead to Suffering. The world is not in sympathy with that which is of the Lord, and neither is much of the modern

Church! Consequently, the Suffering will follow the Glory which follows the Power. This would prove the case in their own lives and Ministries, and will prove the case in all others as well!

The phrase, *"And began to be sorrowful and very heavy,"* proclaims Christ in the Garden of Gethsemane demonstrating His humanity as He demonstrated His Deity on the Mount of Transfiguration.

(38) "THEN SAITH HE UNTO THEM, MY SOUL IS EXCEEDING SORROWFUL, EVEN UNTO DEATH: TARRY YE HERE, AND WATCH WITH ME."

The phrase, *"Then saith He unto them,"* will present a side of Him they had never seen.

The phrase, *"My soul is exceeding sorrowful, even unto death,"* means that He, as a Man, could not have endured it but for added angelic strength (Lk. 22:43-44). In other words, Satan would try to kill Him before He reached Calvary, where He would pay the price for lost humanity.

What was it that brought such exceeding sorrow?

The nature of the agony which appalled the mind and tortured the Body of Jesus in Gethsemane, is, perhaps, impossible for man to know. That a sinless being should have any contact with sin (Jn. 8:46); and, further, should be loaded with sin (I Pet. 2:24); and, most dreadful of all, should be constituted sin (Jn. 3:14; II Cor. 5:21), even though He personally never sinned, must have been unspeakable agony.

As well, several of the Psalms support the belief that the horror of being forsaken by God was so great, especially considering they had never been separated (Ps. 22:1). However, bearing the sin of the world, the Father, for a short period of time, would forsake Him!

The phrase, *"Tarry ye here, and watch with Me,"* proclaims Christ longing for the companionship of these Three, even though it would prove to be of little solace.

However, I have to believe that His admonition to them respecting their *"tarrying and watching"* had more to do with them, than Him. They, as well, were about to enter into a place of spiritual darkness that they had never known before. Regrettably, they would fail! However, all failure has one of two tendencies. It either causes one to run away from the Lord, or to run to the Lord. Thankfully, the Disciples ran to Him!

(39) "AND HE WENT A LITTLE FARTHER, AND FELL ON HIS FACE, AND PRAYED, SAYING, O MY FATHER, IF IT BE POSSIBLE, LET THIS CUP PASS FROM ME: NEVERTHELESS NOT AS I WILL, BUT AS THOU WILT."

The phrase, *"And He went a little farther,"* records, as Luke said, *"He was withdrawn from them about a stone's cast"* (22:41).

However, the word, *"farther,"* has a much deeper meaning than just the physical sense. The distance He went in agony and prayer at this time, no human being could follow. Only One Who is Perfect, can, consequently, know such agony! And Christ is the only One Who was Perfect, and in every respect! Only he who has known such heights, can know such depths! And it all must be remembered that none of this was for Him, but, instead, for the world, those who did not love Him.

The phrase, *"And fell on His Face, and prayed, saying,"* means that He repeatedly did so. In other words, out of sheer weakness, He would fall to the ground, struggle to get up, and then fall again. This was repeated over and over!

His praying was not the following statement made one time, but made over and over.

The phrase, *"O My Father,"* was actually the Aramaic word, *"Abba."* To better understand it, it would probably have been better said, *"Abba Father!"*

As well, even though all Believers can use the same terminology, with it being true in every respect, still, Jesus could refer to the Heavenly Father as such, as no one else! God was His Father in a unique way, and respecting the Incarnation, that no mortal could claim.

And yet, because of what Jesus did for us, and our Faith in Him, we have become *"joint-heirs with Christ"* (Rom. 8:17).

The phrase, *"If it be possible,"* is said in Mark, *"All things are possible unto Thee"* (Mk. 14:36).

In other words, He is saying that He knows the Father in His Omnipotence and Omniscience, could carry out this Redemption of humanity in another way.

The phrase, *"Let this cup pass from Me,"* has to do with the prescribed manner that has been directed by the Father concerning the Redemption of mankind. This *"cup"* was one of *"bearing the sin of humanity," "separation from the Father,"* and *"death."* These three sufferings, man cannot comprehend.

Inasmuch as man is born in sin, he has no idea as to what it is to be untouched by sin.

As well, inasmuch as man was born with no relationship with God, and even if born again, has had relationship for only that period of time, whereas Christ actually had no beginning with the Father, but always was. This type of relationship man does not know, and, in Truth, cannot know.

Also, the death He died was a death loaded with sin, even suffering the terrible Judgment of God that we, instead, should have suffered.

An example is given at the dedication of Solomon's Temple, when the *"Fire came down from Heaven, and consumed the Burnt Offering and the Sacrifices"* (II Chron. 7:1).

That was a type of God's Judgment falling upon the innocent victim, instead of the sinner who offered the Sacrifice. Likewise, the Judgment of God fell on Christ, when, in reality, it should have fallen on us!

This *"cup"* was a cup that no human being has ever had to drink. And as well, Jesus did not drink it for Himself, but, instead, for lost humanity.

The phrase, *"Nevertheless not as I will, but as Thou wilt,"* proclaims the Divine Will, as the expression of Divine Righteousness and Love, which limits the exercise of the Divine Power, and therefore supplies a necessary check to the expectations which might otherwise arise from the belief in the Omnipotence.

In other words, even though it was possible for Redemption to be afforded in another manner, still, this way was the best way, and, consequently, the Will of the Father, and, consequently, the Will of the Son.

In this moment, the Believer is shown the rudiments of consecration, with Jesus setting the example. The Will of God is all that matters. Anything else is spurious! Consequently, the Father's Will was the Son's Will, as it must be our will as well!

The struggle that prevails in every heart can be found in this 39th verse. It is God's Will versus self-will in all of us. Therefore, the hardest thing to conquer in our lives is self-will. This is where Satan makes his final stand, just as he did here in the Garden of Gethsemane. The battleground for Christ was not the Cross, but the Garden. Consequently, for every Believer the battleground is not so much doing

NOTES

the Will of God, but, rather acquiescing to the Will of God.

(40) "AND HE COMETH UNTO THE DISCIPLES, AND FINDETH THEM ASLEEP, AND SAITH UNTO PETER, WHAT, COULD YE NOT WATCH WITH ME ONE HOUR?"

The phrase, *"And He cometh unto the Disciples, and findeth them asleep,"* presents to us the present spiritual condition of the Disciples. The reproof of Christ will show their acute danger, a danger we may quickly add, which they did not realize, and for which they were ill prepared!

Several things are said regarding this encounter:

1. The Church, as Christ, will, at times, face a crises. Satan makes an all-out attack, with the intent of destroying the Work of God.

2. At this time it is the duty of the Church to *"watch and pray,"* but, regrettably, such is little done.

3. As the Disciples were spiritually dull, especially at this time, likewise, the Church is too often in the same dilemma. Thankfully, the Day of Pentecost would change this for the Disciples; however, much, if not most, of the modern Church doesn't even believe in the Day of Pentecost, and most of those who claim to do so little rely upon the Presence and Strength of the Holy Spirit.

The question, *"And saith unto Peter, What, could ye not watch with Me one hour?"*, records the small amount the Lord asks of those who follow Him.

At this time, and as is obvious, Christ needed these Disciples, and, more importantly, for their own spiritual welfare they desperately needed to do what He was requesting.

Is He saying the same to the modern Church?

There comes times in the Work of God that the Church, under the Headship of Christ, is implored by the Holy Spirit to do exactly what Peter, James, and John were here requested to do, *"watch and pray,"* but to little avail! Regrettably, much of the modern Church is doing exactly as the Disciples did before the Crucifixion of Christ, where Luke said, *"And there was also a strife among them, which of them should be accounted the greatest"* (Lk. 22:24).

The majority of the modern Church, and of every stripe, feels that things have never been better. The Churches are full of people, and more money is coming in than ever before. Consequently, if it is judged by those two principles, then prosperity reigns! However, for all the crowds and money, as well as the religious hullabaloo of *"signs and wonders"* which are little from the Lord, spiritually speaking, the Church has never been in worse condition!

Of course, I speak mostly from the precepts of America and Canada, with my knowledge not so extensive regarding the rest of the world. However, I greatly suspect that a spiritual malaise covers the Church, at least for the most part, throughout the world. In America and Canada, very few people are being won to Christ. As well, these two countries, and especially America, that once sent Missionaries all over the world, can still claim high numbers in this regard, but with very little of the Spirit of God in their hearts. For the most part, it is a social effort, instead of proclamation of the Gospel.

(41) "WATCH AND PRAY, THAT YE ENTER NOT INTO TEMPTATION: THE SPIRIT INDEED IS WILLING, BUT THE FLESH IS WEAK."

The phrase, *"Watch and pray, that ye enter not into temptation,"* actually has a twofold thrust:

1. Spiritual *"watchfulness"* has to do with spiritual discernment, and, consequently, knows the areas of danger. Prayer provides spiritually-skilled direction, as well as power to overcome the temptation should such arise. Consequently, the first thrust concerns being led after the Spirit, which avoids temptation because of proper direction. Spiritual discernment (watchfulness) empowered by prayer, guarantees the consecration to be led accordingly.

2. At times, and for whatever reason, the temptation cannot be side-stepped, with the Lord allowing us to be led into certain spiritual circumstances, and for our own spiritual betterment. Of course, Satan means everything for the destruction of the Believer, while the Lord means everything for the edification of the Believer!

If, and despite the watchfulness and prayer, temptation comes our way, and even if it is our fault, still, the same ingredients are prescribed.

The phrase, *"The spirit indeed is willing, but the flesh is weak,"* presents the battleground of the spiritual man.

The *"spirit"* here spoken of is not the Holy

NOTES

Spirit, but, rather, the spirit of man. Here, it is a regenerated spirit, exercised by the Holy Spirit. However, the *"flesh,"* the area of self-will, is much, if not all, of the time antagonistic to the regenerated spirit. Almost, if not all the attacks by Satan are directed at the flesh, with its desires, passions, emotions, feelings, and hunger. It is the part of regenerated man which must be made subject to the spirit, instead of the spirit being subject to the flesh. As stated, this is a battleground that sees constant conflict. Paul said, *"For to be carnally minded is death; but to be spiritually minded is life and peace"* (Rom. 8:6).

Paul also said, *"For if ye live after the flesh, ye shall die: but if ye through the Spirit do mortify the deeds of the body, ye shall live"* (Rom. 8:13).

So, the Spirit of God working on our regenerated spirit, seeks to subdue the flesh. Actually, only the Spirit of God can do this!

Jealousy, envy, malice, uncontrollable temper, pride, etc., may begin in the spirit of man, but it must manifest itself in the *"flesh,"* i.e., self-will. Consequently, if the regenerated spirit has a proper relationship with Christ, precious few of these vices can have any sway, or will die aborning. And if the flesh is made subject to the spirit, as it certainly should be in Christ, and by the Power of the Holy Spirit, there will be no platform for the manifestation of evil impulses.

The meaning of the *"willing spirit"* is that it desires to carry out the Will of God once that Will is made known. However, the *"flesh"* being *"weak,"* cannot carry out what the regenerated spirit wants, unless heavily covered by watchfulness and prayer.

Regrettably, much of our efforts to overcome the flesh is by the flesh, consequently, we fail! Only the Spirit of God can carry out the Will of God in our lives, and overcome the flesh. Any other method, of which the Church abounds, is doomed to failure!

(42) "HE WENT AWAY AGAIN THE SECOND TIME, AND PRAYED, SAYING, O MY FATHER, IF THIS CUP MAY NOT PASS AWAY FROM ME, EXCEPT I DRINK IT, THY WILL BE DONE."

The phrase, *"He went away again the second time, and prayed,"* respects Christ praying in a different manner.

The first time He asked if the cup could pass from Him, while this time, knowing that it was not the Will of God for such to be, He, in essence, asks for strength to do that which must be done.

The phrase, *"Saying, O My Father,"* proclaims Him using the same expression of relationship, and because He is determined to do the Will of God. The Believer cannot readily say, *"My Heavenly Father,"* if every fiber in his being is not attempting to carry out the Will of God. If the Will of the Father is abrogated, likewise, the relationship with the Father is abrogated. Consequently, most Christians, I think one could say, have little relationship with Christ because His Will is not sought.

The phrase, *"If this cup may not pass away from Me, except I drink it,"* proclaims an acquiescence to God's Will, and irrespective as to what it may be.

From this Passage, some erroneous interpretations have resulted concerning the Will of God.

First of all, this of which the Father asked Christ to do, was unique with Christ. In other words, no Believer would ever be asked to do such a thing, as to drink that type of *"cup,"* even though every Believer is required to bear his cross.

Many have the idea that if God asks them to do something, it will always be something which they strongly detest.

Not so!

Anything God asks a Believer to do, and irrespective of what it may be, the Lord, as well, gives a desire to do that thing. In other words, nothing else will satisfy until that individual begins to carry out the Will of God. That's the reason so many Christians are unhappy, not because they are doing the Will of God, but because they are <u>not</u> doing it.

I remember asking the late Mark Buntain, who built such a great work in Calcutta, India, if he did not dread going back to that city?

At that time, he was in Baton Rouge, Louisiana, having preached for us at Family Worship Center. As well, he had been preaching in quite a few cities in the States. I will never forget his answer to my question!

He turned to me, and with a look of exclaim which filled his countenance, he said, *"Oh no, I can hardly wait to get back."* Looking at his face and feeling his spirit, I knew that what he was saying was the true feeling of his heart.

I have been to Calcutta, and I don't think I've ever seen anything quite like it in all the world. Even though the people of India are an extremely handsome people, with the children, at least in my opinion, being some of the most beautiful on earth, still, Satan has made his evil hand felt. Somebody once said, *"Until you have seen Calcutta, you have not seen hell!"*

Only God could make someone desire to minister in that place. And yet, when His Call is given, which constitutes His Will, as well, the desire and love for that particular direction is placed in the heart by the Lord.

The phrase, *"Thy Will be done,"* was the prayer of consecration of Christ, and must be the prayer of consecration for every Believer.

(43) "AND HE CAME AND FOUND THEM ASLEEP AGAIN: FOR THEIR EYES WERE HEAVY."

The phrase, *"And He came and found them asleep again,"* would have been better translated, *"And He came again and found them asleep."*

The phrase, *"For their eyes were heavy,"* places them in the same position as at the Transfiguration, where they experienced the same over-powering drowsiness, and, as well, the same inability to give expression to their thoughts.

I think the drowsiness had to do more with the tremendous spiritual agony of the moment than physical exhaustion. Not having the Holy Spirit at this time, at least in the fashion in which He would come on the Day of Pentecost, they were not equal to the task.

(44) "AND HE LEFT THEM, AND WENT AWAY AGAIN, AND PRAYED THE THIRD TIME, SAYING THE SAME WORDS."

The phrase, *"And He left them, and went away again,"* portrays a spiritual need that He felt was not yet quite met. We have to believe that the Holy Spirit guided Him in all that He did, and especially now. Consequently, the Spirit of God would have been urging Him to seek the Father once again, in that greater strength would be garnered for the task ahead.

The phrase, *"And prayed the third time, saying the same words,"* sets for us an example.

At times, a matter must be prayed over more than once, even several times. Even though each time the same words were said, still, a greater degree of spiritual direction was given with each petition.

First of all, He determined the Will of God,

while the second time He acquiesced to do that Will. The third time, He gained the strength to carry it out.

This is a form of supplication and intercession coupled with travail, which always secures an answer from the Lord. The Gethsemane experience, which the Believer can only enter into respecting the Will of God, is the area where great spiritual conflicts are fought and won. It is here where the great Work of God is realized, directed, and carried out. It is here where World Evangelism begins, with the results being the Salvation of many souls. It is here that the foundation is laid, direction given, and power developed.

Many claim that God never says, *"No,"* to a petition from His Child! However, the 39th verse tells us different.

While it is true that He never says *"No,"* if it is His Will, still, many times Believers pray outside of the Will of God. It is not wrong to do so if one is seeking direction, as Christ, but once that is ascertained, one must pray accordingly with the answer then always being *"Yes."* In other words, whenever we say *"Yes,"* He says *"Yes!"*

(45) "THEN COMETH HE TO HIS DISCIPLES, AND SAITH UNTO THEM, SLEEP ON NOW, AND TAKE YOUR REST: BEHOLD, THE HOUR IS AT HAND, AND THE SON OF MAN IS BETRAYED INTO THE HANDS OF SINNERS."

The phrase, *"Then cometh He to His Disciples, and saith unto them,"* will be carried out with the utmost tenderness. The battle with Satan is now won, with Jesus ready to go forward, even eager to carry out the great Plan of God ordained before the foundation of the world.

The phrase, *"Sleep on now, and take your rest,"* is not meant as a sarcastic statement, but, rather, as a parent would speak tenderly to a beloved child. In these words is a hurting heart concerning the trial they must endure. However, weeping may come for a night, but joy cometh in the morning.

The phrase, *"Behold, the hour is at hand,"* refers to that for which Christ had come! The many millennia, or even thousands of years, which had passed since the Plan of God originated for the Redemption of humanity, had all come down to the final *"hour."*

The phrase, *"And the son of Man is betrayed into the hands of sinners,"* refers to Judas having

carried out his treacherous act, and is even now entering the Garden with the Temple guard and others in order to arrest Christ.

(46) "RISE, LET US BE GOING: BEHOLD, HE IS AT HAND THAT DOTH BETRAY ME."

The phrase, *"Rise, let us be going,"* portrays Christ desiring to be ready, which He was, at the arrival of the multitude. They would not find Him and the Disciples sleeping, as they had supposed, but rather standing and awaiting their arrival.

The phrase, *"He is at hand that doth betray Me,"* speaks of Judas, and, at that time, coming deep into the Garden. The Holy Spirit has told Him everything they are about to do, and even the time of their arrival.

(47) "AND WHILE HE YET SPAKE, LO, JUDAS, ONE OF THE TWELVE, CAME, AND WITH HIM A GREAT MULTITUDE WITH SWORDS AND STAVES, FROM THE CHIEF PRIESTS AND ELDERS OF THE PEOPLE."

The phrase, *"And while He yet spake,"* refers to the very moment of the betrayal.

The phrase, *"Lo, Judas, one of the Twelve,"* is given in this fashion by the Holy Spirit in order to enhance his guilt. Never in human history has so perfidious an act been carried out against One Who was so good, kind, and gracious. To sin against man is bad enough, but to sin against God is to sin against Goodness and Light. And yet, all of us, in one way or the other, have some Judas in us, because in one way or the other we have all betrayed Him, at least in some fashion! It is hard to admit that, but I think it is necessary to do so.

As we stated elsewhere in this Chapter, the Disciples here entered a trial where the Lord Alone would stand. Sadly and regrettably, all of us have followed in that long train. However, because He stood and did not waiver, ultimately, they stood and would not waiver.

Likewise, every Believer!

The phrase, *"And with him a great multitude with swords and staves,"* represented, as stated, the Temple guards, as well as some Roman soldiers, etc.

The phrase, *"From the Chief Priest and Elders of the people,"* represents, in effect, His being arrested by the Church. This element, which is far larger than the True Remnant, has always been the greatest enemy of the Work of God. Ironically enough, it kills the Lord in the Name of the Lord!

(48) NOW HE THAT BETRAYED HIM GAVE THEM A SIGN, SAYING, WHOMSO-EVER I SHALL KISS, THAT SAME IS HE: HOLD HIM FAST."

The phrase, *"Now he that betrayed Him gave them a sign,"* speaks of the most despicable, treacherous moment in human history.

The phrase, *"Saying, Whomsoever I shall kiss,"* portrays the manner of betrayal.

Evidently, the guards were somewhat apprehensive that they not arrest the wrong one, thereby being embarrassed greatly in front of the *"Chief Priests and Elders of the people."*

The phrase, *"That same is He,"* portrays Judas as making certain by the kiss that they arrest the right man. Inasmuch as Judas knew Him, his foul deed was made even more wicked!

The phrase, *"Hold Him fast,"* is ironic!

Judas knew His Power. He had seen Jesus perform all types of miracles, even to the raising of the dead. So, how did he think that Jesus could be held unless He purposely chose to do so?

Who knows what was in the mind of Judas! Maybe he thought that Jesus would here use His great Power to overthrow this *"multitude,"* and finally take the leadership of Israel. At any rate, he understood Jesus not at all.

(49) "AND FORTHWITH HE CAME TO JESUS, AND SAID, HAIL, MASTER; AND KISSED HIM."

The phrase, *"And forthwith he came to Jesus,"* means that Judas, first of all and quickly, came directly to Jesus.

The phrase, *"And said, Hail, Master; and kissed Him,"* fulfilled the words of the Psalmist, *"The words of his mouth were smoother than butter, but war was in his heart: his words were softer than oil, yet were they drawn in swords"* (Ps. 55:21).

(50) "AND JESUS SAID UNTO HIM, FRIEND, WHEREFORE ART THOU COME? THEN CAME THEY, AND LAID HANDS ON JESUS AND TOOK HIM."

The phrase, *"And Jesus said unto him, Friend,"* is said in kindness and not sarcasm! It seems that even unto the last, Jesus was attempting to reach Judas, but to no avail!

The question, *"Wherefore art thou come?",* again, was not asked to secure knowledge, for Jesus knew why he was there, but was another attempt to make Judas stop and think what he was doing.

NOTES

Some may claim that it was too late to reach Judas, for the betrayal had already been carried out; however, if Judas had repented, even at this late hour, or any time immediately thereafter, he would have been instantly forgiven. But he would not repent!

The phrase, *"Then came they, and laid hands on Jesus and took Him,"* is the beginning of the action of the murderous hearts of the Religious Leaders of Israel. They hated Christ, and would have carried out this act much sooner had the opportunity presented itself.

Why?

Their religion was a philosophy of their own making, and not of the Bible. Despite their constant speaking of God, they really did not know Him. Had they known Him, they would have known His Son.

Likewise, men cannot be of the Lord, irrespective of how much they speak of Him, and oppose that which is of Him. The Spirit of God is identical everywhere, and irrespective of what Church a person may be in. So, the Spirit of God in one will recognize the Spirit of God in another! If it doesn't, it just might be possible that the Spirit of God is not there!

(51) "AND, BEHOLD, ONE OF THEM WHICH WERE WITH JESUS STRETCHED OUT HIS HAND, AND DREW HIS SWORD, AND STRUCK A SERVANT OF THE HIGH PRIEST'S, AND SMOTE OFF HIS EAR."

The phrase, *"And, behold, one of them which were with Jesus,"* is named by John as Simon Peter. As well, he gives the name of the servant as Malthus.

The phrase, *"Stretched out his hand, and drew his sword,"* was probably something new with Peter, the carrying of a sword. A few hours before, and according to Luke, Jesus had said, *"And he that hath no sword, let him sell his garment, and buy one"* (Lk. 22:36). However, it was only a symbolical expression respecting government and the power of the Magistrate, which was ordered by God. In effect, He was telling His Disciples that He was not going to take over Israel now, disturbing the government, but, in fact, that it would continue, and His Work and Ministry must be carried out by those He calls in these confines. In other words, the Church was to support good government, and work where possible within its framework. Peter misunderstood the Words of Christ, as His Disciples at that time misunderstood most of what He said, and went out and purchased a sword.

The phrase, *"And struck a servant of the High Priest's, and smote off his ear,"* actually proclaims Peter attempting to take off his head.

Peter did not lack physical courage, but he and the others did lack moral courage, for in a minute's time they *"All forsook Him, and fled."*

The carnal nature can never act aright. It is always too courageous or too cowardly, too wise or too foolish, too forward or too backward, too talkative or too silent.

Peter struck off the ear of Malthus the servant of the High Priest and then ran away, and later said: *"I know not the man"* (Jn. 18:10), referring to Jesus.

According to Luke, the Lord at once asked a moment's liberty from His captors and stretching out His Hand touched the ear and healed it (Lk. 22:51).

This particular *"servant"* was the body-servant of the High Priest, and a man of some importance.

What was his thought when Jesus healed his ear? Better yet, what did Caiaphas, the High Priest, think when his servant related this incident to him? Inasmuch as Caiaphas committed suicide not long after, and because of his burning conscience that could not be stilled because of what he had done to Christ, this incident probably weighed very heavily on his mind.

Incidentally, this was the last miracle performed by Christ before His Death. It was carried out on His enemies while they were engaged in hostility against Him.

(52) "THEN SAID JESUS UNTO HIM, PUT UP AGAIN THY SWORD INTO HIS PLACE: FOR ALL THEY THAT TAKE THE SWORD SHALL PERISH WITH THE SWORD."

The phrase, *"Then said Jesus unto him,"* refers to Peter and the action he had just taken.

The phrase, *"Put up again thy sword into his place,"* actually said, *"Turn away thy sword."*

In essence, He is saying that the sword is not to be used in this fashion, but only in its proper place. In other words, it does have a *"place,"* but not in the Work of God.

Many Believers do not understand the role of government in the world and how God has ordained such! Consequently, in the role that government plays, it has to have the necessary power to enforce its laws. Paul said this

is to be recognized by Believers and supported, at least if the laws do not violate the Word of God (Rom. 13:1-7).

In essence, Paul is saying, and carrying forth the Words that Christ uttered here, that it is absurd to believe that rulers have the right to govern, and not the right to use the necessary means to carry on good government. Such error or belief causes many Christians to object to the right of capital punishment, the right to deal with mobs, to suppress rebellions, and to make wars on criminal nations.

When a person or nation sells himself or themselves to destroy the best good of others, it becomes necessary to take the person or the nation from the society it seeks to destroy.

In such cases it becomes necessary to deal with individuals and nations to enforce law and order for the best good of all. It must be both the right and the duty of government and all its subjects to use every necessary and possible means to suppress unlawful and unbiblical rebellion and enforce respect for law and order.

Rulers are God's Ministers to execute God's Wrath upon the ungodly and preserve moral law and government for the good of all (Rom. 13:1-6; I Pet. 2:13-17).

The phrase, *"For all they that take the sword shall perish with the sword,"* has three meanings:

1. The sword is to have no place in the propagation of the Gospel. Consequently, many of the efforts in the Middle Ages, and other times, respecting the crusades in the Holy Land, etc., were unwarranted and unscriptural. The spread of Christianity is to be by the Power of God as a result of preaching the Word of God. It is to never be by the Sword!

2. Those who presumptuously resort to violence concerning criminal activity, etc., will, of necessity, meet with violence, i.e., *"Perish with the sword."*

3. Warring nations that expand by the sword, will ultimately die by the sword. Hence, Nazi Germany, etc., as well as philosophies such as Communism.

(53) "THINKEST THOU THAT I CANNOT NOW PRAY TO MY FATHER, AND HE SHALL PRESENTLY GIVE ME MORE THAN TWELVE LEGIONS OF ANGELS?"

The beginning of the question, *"Thinkest thou that I cannot pray to My Father . . . ,"* is spoken to Simon Peter, but as well to all! In times of crisis, and any other time for that matter, *"prayer"* is to be the weapon of the Child of God. Then the matter is placed in the Hands of God, with self-will having no place.

As well, and as this Scripture portrays, the real battle is in the spirit world, which unfolds itself, as here, in the natural world, and must really be addressed in the spiritual realm. A valuable lesson is here taught if we can only grasp it!

The Religious Leaders of Israel were being instigated by Satan and his minions of darkness. Opposing them were the forces of Heaven, plus Christ and His small group of followers. Even though that small group may have seemed to have been grossly outnumbered, the next phrase tells us that the opposite is true!

The conclusion of the question, *"And He shall presently give Me more than twelve legions of Angels?"*, refers to the actual power at the disposal of Christ.

A Roman legion was 6,000 men, consequently, Christ used the term *"legion"* with intention. According to John, Jesus was arrested by a military cohort of about 600 men, the tenth part of a legion (Jn. 18:3). Consequently, Jesus is saying that if He so chose, He could have *"twelve legions of Angels"* immediately by His side, which constituted 72,000.

So, the attempt to protect Christ by the use of a single sword was not only unnecessary, but senseless! Jesus was not lacking in power or protection. However, He would use that power and protection only in the Will of God. Consequently, the authority of the Believer is here brought into question.

As we have stated, the real struggle is spiritual, and irrespective as to how it may represent itself in the natural, whether physical, material, domestical, or financial! Consequently, the Believer is to address the problem first and foremost in the spiritual. This is done, as stated, by prayer, and taking authority over the spirits of darkness which seek to hinder (Mat. 18:18-19; Jn. 14:14; 15:7).

However, the authority given by the Holy Spirit to Believers is never over other people, but rather over spirits of darkness (Mk. 16:17).

(54) "BUT HOW THEN SHALL THE SCRIPTURES BE FULFILLED, THAT THUS IT MUST BE?"

The question, *"But how then shall the Scriptures be fulfilled . . . ,"* harks back to verse 39,

and the Words of Christ, *"Nevertheless not as I will, but as Thou wilt."*

Even though Jesus had supreme authority, as should be obvious, still, He acquiesced to the Will of God which was the Scriptures.

The authority we have spoken of as given to Believers, in Truth, is invalid in the lives of most, and because they desire to use it in the realm of self-will instead of God's Will. The Will of God, and in all things, must be primary at all times.

The conclusion of the question, *". . . That thus it must be?"*, emphasizes the word, *"must,"* and affirms the Divine Inspiration of the Scriptures. Had they been composed by men, there would have been no necessity compelling their fulfillment.

During the last day of His life and the first of His Resurrection, the Lord Jesus quoted about thirty Passages of Scripture; and several more are pointed to by the Holy Spirit when recording the occurrences of those days. Bible in hand, so to speak, He descended into, and rose out of, the tomb.

(55) "IN THAT SAME HOUR SAID JESUS TO THE MULTITUDES, ARE YE COME OUT AS AGAINST A THIEF WITH SWORDS AND STAVES FOR TO TAKE ME? I SAT DAILY WITH YOU TEACHING IN THE TEMPLE, AND YE LAID NO HOLD ON ME."

The phrase, *"In that same hour said Jesus to the multitudes,"* amounted to, and as we have stated, approximately 600 men. Luke said that in this *"multitude,"* were the *"Chief Priests, and Captains of the Temple, and the Elders,"* with the latter being the vaunted Sanhedrin, the ruling body of the nation (Lk. 22:52).

The question, *"Are ye come out as against a thief with swords and staves for to take Me?"*, is posed to direct their attention to Who He was! They were treating Him as a *"thief,"* apprehending Him as they would such an individual, and why!

They were thieves themselves, and in the worst sort of way, consequently, they treated Him accordingly. Many times people judge another as they are themselves.

To be sure, their *"thievery"* was much worse than that of a common criminal, in that they stole in the Name of God. The money the people of Israel gave to the Work of God was not at all used for that, but, rather, to support that wicked, ungodly religious regime. Actually, that is one of the reasons they hated Jesus so much, because they thought He just might use His Power to change the order of things, and this they did not desire! Or course, He had no intention of such a course of action, but, again, they judged Him as they would have done themselves, if in His place.

The phrase, *"I sat daily with you teaching in the Temple, and ye laid no hold on Me,"* refers to His activities in the Temple the past week, which were carried out openly, etc. His actions were not those of sedition, and neither did He have armed men around Him. So why did not they arrest Him then, instead of carrying it out in the darkness of night? Of course, the question posed by Christ, to which He already knew the answer, struck at the very heart of the problem.

They did not arrest Him in the Temple, even though they desired to do so, because they feared the people. Not being able to accuse Him of anything that would warrant such action, they were forced to resort to subterfuge and the cover of darkness. In other words, they had no proper charges to lay against Him, and, accordingly, the question posed by Christ, exposed their wicked hearts.

It is amazing the manner in which Christ approached this situation. Every single word He said revealed the wickedness of their hearts, but yet was designed in kindness. At any time they could have repented, but their hard-hearted self-will overrode His kindness, as well as the probing of their hearts. Consequently, they were without excuse!

(56) "BUT ALL THIS WAS DONE, THAT THE SCRIPTURES OF THE PROPHETS MIGHT BE FULFILLED. THEN ALL THE DISCIPLES FORSOOK HIM, AND FLED."

The phrase, *"But all this was done,"* could have been translated, *"All this has come to pass ...."* He was speaking of the manner in which He had been arrested. Had he been arrested in the Temple, and, consequently, died by stoning, it would not have fulfilled the Scriptures.

Many Believers misunderstand this, thinking that God consequently forced the action, and, thereby, the wills of the Religious Leaders. However, that is totally incorrect!

Through foreknowledge, God looked down through the ages and saw what these individuals would do, and gave it by inspiration to the Prophets, which they wrote down in Books, and were called the *"Scriptures."*

NOTES

Every single perfidious action taken by these Religious Leaders was all of their own doing. They did not have to do this, but did it because it is what they desired to do. The Holy Spirit, by Inspiration, only recorded their action beforehand. It was their will and not God's Will.

The phrase, *"That the Scriptures of the Prophets might be fulfilled,"* proclaims the Scriptures as a foundation for all His activities, as it must be the foundation for ours.

As one Preacher of old said, *"Again and again He declares that one thing which, nevertheless, Christian theology perpetually refuses to learn from the supreme Teacher and Doctor. He holds firmly to the Scripture, whether speaking to the exasperated Jews or the docile Disciples; He puts those to shame in their folly by proofs from Scripture, and strengthens these in their despondency by its consolatory promises. He appeals to Scripture in His vehement disputation with men, as He does in His solemn way of suffering to die for them; He confronts Satan with 'It is written,' and prays to the Father — that the Scripture may be fulfilled."*

The idea is this, if Christ, the Lord of Glory, adhered that strictly to the Scriptures, referring minutely to them, and based everything He did on them, how much more should the Believer do the same!

Tragically, one could probably say without fear of contradiction, that most Christians have never even read the Bible through once, much less making it a life study. Even those who make it a part of their daily lives, too often spend almost all of their time in certain parts of it, while ignoring the rest.

The Bible is the Word of God from Genesis through the Book of Revelation. Consequently, one should spend as much time in the Book of Leviticus as one does in the Gospel of John.

The Bible presents a story, the Redemption of man, which is carried through from its beginning to its conclusion. Consequently, Believers should read the Bible in that manner, from Genesis through the Book of Revelation. As well, they should do this habitually and with dedication. Even as our physical appetite is satisfied with three meals a day, likewise, every Believer should set aside a particular amount of time each and every day for the Word of God. Any Christian who reads newspapers more than he does the Bible, is greatly shortchanging himself.

Also, as one studies the Word, one should ask the Lord to give him understanding respecting the Word. This, He will do!

As should be obvious, two things are emphasized in these Passages, and especially as Jesus faced the terrible ordeal of the Crucifixion. Those two things are *"Prayer and the Word of God."* That should be our foundation as well!

The phrase, *"Then all the Disciples forsook Him, and fled,"* fulfilled that which was written (Zech. 13:7).

If one can imagine the scene that unfolded that night, it will not be a pleasant picture to behold.

More than likely, the soldiers bound Jesus, with Him, as is obvious, offering no resistance. The Disciples, overcome with fear, run away leaving Him alone. However, Mark records that *"A certain young man,"* did *"follow Him"* for a distance, before being stopped (Mk. 14:51). Who this young man was, is not known!

How this must have hurt the Heart of Christ, to be left alone in these circumstances, with not one soul standing up for Him! And yet, after the Day of Pentecost, these same men would be filled with boldness and power, and, in effect, would touch the world for Christ.

(57) "AND THEY THAT HAD LAID HOLD ON JESUS LED HIM AWAY TO CAIAPHAS THE HIGH PRIEST, WHERE THE SCRIBES AND THE ELDERS WERE ASSEMBLED."

The phrase, *"And they that had laid hold on Jesus led Him away to Caiaphas the High Priest,"* omits the account of Jesus being led before Annas the former High Priest, as recorded in John 18:13, 19-24. Annas held some sway with the Romans, and great sway over Caiaphas. Matthew, Mark, and Luke omit this meeting, cutting straight through to Caiaphas, because he was the High Priest at the time.

The phrase, *"Where the Scribes and the Elders were assembled,"* pertains to the palace or court of the High Priest.

A gated porch admitted to a central courtyard on one side which was the palace of Annas, and on the other side the palace of Caiaphas. Opposite the porch a raised columned pavement formed an audience chamber. Here Christ would stand as a prisoner before the High Priest, and thus Peter was enabled to see Him, and He to see Peter (Lk. 22:61). This midnight examination was preliminary to that of

the following morning when the whole council assembled for a public trial.

These *"Scribes"* and *"Elders"* consisted of an informal meeting of the leading Sanhedrists. It was here where the trial would be conducted.

(58) "BUT PETER FOLLOWED HIM AFAR OFF UNTO THE HIGH PRIEST'S PALACE, AND WENT IN, AND SAT WITH THE SERVANTS, TO SEE THE END."

The phrase, *"But Peter followed Him afar off,"* presents the Apostle turning back toward Christ from Whom he had fled at first. No doubt, he is ashamed of his actions, and now in a quandary, timidly follows the group taking Jesus to the palace.

The phrase, *"Unto the High Priest's palace, and went in,"* means that at first he could not get in, but as John recorded it, someone spoke to the keeper of the door and Peter was allowed in (Jn. 18:15-16).

Some have concluded that this was the Apostle John, while others feel it may have been Nicodemus or Joseph of Arimathaea. More than likely, it was one of these two, and not John, because the Scripture says that Joseph was *"A Disciple of Jesus, but secretly for fear of the Jews"* (Jn. 19:38).

The phrase, *"And sat with the servants, to see the end,"* seems ironic since Peter has not yet seen the end and, in Truth, never shall! His story will continue with verse 69.

(59) "NOW THE CHIEF PRIESTS, AND ELDERS, AND ALL THE COUNCIL, SOUGHT FALSE WITNESS AGAINST JESUS, TO PUT HIM TO DEATH;"

The phrase, *"Now the Chief Priests, and Elders, and all the Council,"* represented the Religious Leadership of Israel.

The *"Chief Priests"* were the heads of the twenty-four courses, which carried out the respective Temple services of Sacrifices, etc., throughout the year. In other words, all the Priests in Israel did not function all of the time, but a particular number at two-week intervals. There was a Chief Priest who headed up each course, and was in charge of the Priests who functioned at that particular time. (Chief Priests could also include former High Priests.)

The *"Elders"* were representatives of the people in the Sanhedrin, as the Chief Priests were of the Priesthood.

The *"Council"* was the Sanhedrin, made up

of all of these groups. It was the Supreme Court of the Nation which heard appeals from lower courts and tried cases of greater importance than the lower courts.

It consisted of seventy-one members headed by a President, Vice-president, and a Sage, or Referee, whose duty was to put into proper shape the subjects for discussion. The Vice-president led and controlled the discussions. The President represented the Nation before the Romans.

The phrase, *"Sought false witness against Jesus, to put Him to death,"* means that they did not care if the information against Christ was false, that is, if they could get two or three witnesses to swear falsely against Him. This, in their warped minds, would make it legal (Deut. 17:6).

It is amazing as to how they wanted to do everything according to the Scripture, but knowing all along it was a lie! They were so twisted and jaded, that they no longer had any idea as to what the Scripture taught. To them, the Scripture could be used, as it is by many, for their own nefarious purposes. They were determined to kill Jesus, and, consequently, they had no interest in Truth or what the Scriptures truly said. Their opportunity had come, and they would go forward with their mock trial, irrespective of how blasphemous, crooked, unscriptural, and ungodly it was!

(60) "BUT FOUND NONE: YEA, THOUGH MANY FALSE WITNESSES CAME, YET FOUND THEY NONE. AT THE LAST CAME TWO FALSE WITNESSES,"

The phrase, *"But found none,"* means they found none who would collaborate each other.

The phrase, *"Yea, though many false witnesses came, yet found they none,"* says the same thing again, but with greater explanation.

As stated, there were many witnesses who came forward with false stories, but they could not get any two to substantiate each other.

The phrase, *"At the last came two false witnesses,"* who seized upon a statement made by Christ, and twisted it out of context. They didn't dare bring up any of the questions they had asked Him in the Temple, because His answers then had silenced them, and they feared the same now.

As well, no favorable witnesses were allowed to testify on behalf of Christ. This shows how corrupt this high court so-called, actually was!

What kind of trial is it, when no one is allowed to speak on behalf of the accused, and when false testimony is accepted at face value, and without any proof?

It was no trial, but what is referred to in modern terminology as a *"kangaroo court!"*

(61) "AND SAID, THIS FELLOW SAID, I AM ABLE TO DESTROY THE TEMPLE OF GOD, AND TO BUILD IT IN THREE DAYS."

The phrase, *"And said, This fellow said,"* is spoken with dripping contempt. The word, *"fellow,"* was inserted by the translators, and was not in the original Text. The accuser must have pointed a finger at Christ, referring to Him contemptuously, as *"This!"*

The phrase, *"I am able to destroy the Temple of God, and to build it in three days,"* is a distorted account of what was actually said by the Lord. It concerned His first cleansing of the Temple.

Jesus had actually said, *"Destroy this Temple, and in three days I will raise it up"* (Jn. 2:19).

He was speaking of His Body, and being resurrected three days after His Death.

Even though they misunderstood His statement then, still, there is every evidence that He explained exactly what He was speaking of (Jn. 2:21).

Consequently, if they continued to misunderstand, it was because they desired to do so.

Actually, they really did not care! Whether the literal Temple or His physical Body, either way would give them excuse to accuse Him to the Romans.

As stated, they had no interest in the Truth, only in furthering their cause, which was to kill Him, and they little cared as to how it would be carried out. This is a picture of murderers hiding under the cloak of religion.

Regrettably, that brand of ilk did not die with these hypocrites!

(62) "AND THE HIGH PRIEST AROSE, AND SAID UNTO HIM, ANSWEREST THOU NOTHING? WHAT IS IT WHICH THESE WITNESS AGAINST THEE?"

The phrase, *"And the High Priest arose, and said unto Him,"* speaks of Caiaphas.

The question, *"Answerest Thou nothing?"*, presents Jesus answering His accusers not at all!

The question, *"What is it which these witness against Thee?"*, speaks of the accusation concerning the Temple. However, even this charge had broken down, owing to the disagreement of the two witnesses (Mk. 14:59). So, the High Priest will change his tactics, attempting to brow-beat Christ into saying something, which they could seize upon in order to incriminate Him.

(63) "BUT JESUS HELD HIS PEACE, AND THE HIGH PRIEST ANSWERED AND SAID UNTO HIM, I ADJURE THEE BY THE LIVING GOD, THAT THOU TELL US WHETHER THOU BE THE CHRIST, THE SON OF GOD."

The phrase, *"But Jesus held His peace,"* fulfilled the Scripture, *"He was oppressed, and He was afflicted, yet He opened not His Mouth"* (Isa. 53:7).

At any rate, the accusations were so absurd and ridiculous that to attempt to answer them in any manner would have dignified the lies. So, He said nothing, because nothing He said would have been accepted.

The scene is dramatic, as the High Priest questions Jesus concerning the accusations made against Him, with Jesus saying nothing. There is nothing but silence!

The phrase, *"And the High Priest answered and said unto Him,"* concerns the answer to the silence. Consequently, He must take another approach.

The phrase, *"I adjure Thee by the Living God,"* in effect, and in the way it was used, at least after a fashion, recognizes Christ as a Minister of God. Consequently, He must answer, because the Mosaic Law demanded that He do so, as all under such circumstances (Lev. 5:1).

The phrase, *"That Thou tell us whether Thou be the Christ, the Son of God,"* proved that they knew that the Messiah was to be the Son of God.

However, the interpretation of Caiaphas concerning the meaning of *"the Son of God,"* would probably not have claimed the Messiah as One in essence with the Father.

They believed, at this time, that when the Messiah came, although from God and having Divine attributes, He would still definitely, at least in their thinking, be inferior to God.

Without a doubt, he had heard that Jesus claimed Oneness with God, in that God was His Father, and if he could get Him to admit such in the presence of the Sanhedrin, he could then denounce Him as an imposter or a blasphemer. In doing this, the High Priest partially fulfilled Psalm 2:2.

(64) "JESUS SAITH UNTO HIM, THOU HAST SAID: NEVERTHELESS I SAY UNTO YOU, HEREAFTER SHALL YE SEE THE SON OF MAN SITTING ON THE RIGHT HAND OF POWER, AND COMING IN THE CLOUDS OF HEAVEN."

The phrase, *"Jesus saith unto him,"* constitutes a direct answer, with absolutely no doubt as to its meaning!

The phrase, *"Thou hast said,"* is a direct affirmation, with Mark saying it even clearer, *"I am"* (Mk. 14:62).

Unequivocally and without hesitation, Christ answers in the affirmative, which in effect means, and was understood by Caiaphas, *"I am the Messiah, the Son of the Blessed One, God of God, of one substance with the Father."*

The phrase, *"Nevertheless I say unto you,"* would have been better translated, *"But moreover."* In other words, *"And that's not all!"*

The phrase, *"Hereafter shall ye see the Son of Man sitting on the right hand of power,"* refers to the coming Crucifixion, Resurrection, and Ascension to God in Heaven, where He would be seated at the Right Hand of the Father.

The words, *"Shall ye see,"* refers to them seeing but not believing, or else having the opportunity to see, but refusing to do so.

They *"saw"* His Crucifixion, but would not believe what Isaiah had said of Him in Isaiah 53.

As well, they *"saw"* the Resurrection, but would not believe it, even though the proof was incontestable. They even gave a large sum of money to the soldiers who guarded the tomb not to tell the truth about the matter (Mat. 28:12).

Likewise, they *"saw"* Christ ascend to the Father from the Mount of Olivet, or at least a goodly number of people did see it, and they, as well, could have seen it had they so desired!

The title, *"Son of Man,"* denoted Christ in His Incarnation, in weakness and humility, but yet about to be Glorified.

In other words, what He was saying was, *"What you are looking at now is not really what I am, and one day you will see Me as I really am, but it will not be to your liking!"*

Concerning the *"right hand of power,"* He was really speaking of the coming *"Great White Throne Judgment,"* where and when these very men would be judged by Him (Rev. 20:11-15).

He was telling them that they were judging

Him now, and dishonestly; however, He would one day judge them, and with Power.

The phrase, *"And coming in the clouds of Heaven,"* concerns the Second Coming, and with all its attendant Glory. Then Israel would accept Him as the Messiah, realizing that the One they crucified is actually the One Who has come back.

(65) "THEN THE HIGH PRIEST RENT HIS CLOTHES, SAYING, HE HATH SPOKEN BLASPHEMY; WHAT FURTHER NEED HAVE WE OF WITNESSES? BEHOLD, NOW WE HAVE HEARD HIS BLASPHEMY."

The phrase, *"Then the High Priest rent his clothes,"* proclaimed him aghast at the answer given by Christ. He rips his garment in order to express his horror!

The phrase, *"Saying, He hath spoken blasphemy,"* means He had made Himself One with God. However, He was not blaspheming, and did not tell an untruth, but was exactly Who He said He was! As well, their reaction did not make Him any less so.

In effect, what man says is of little consequence. It is what God says that counts. And yet, most of the religious world base their conclusions on what man says, completely ignoring what God has said, i.e., His Word!

The question, *"What further need have we of witnesses?"*, means they can dispense with all the liars. Christ has played right into their hands, or so they think, by making the great admission of His Messiahship, and even more, claiming that the Messiah is God.

The phrase, *"Behold, now ye have heard His blasphemy,"* meaning that Caiaphas had witnesses in that the entire Sanhedrin had heard His statement.

It is obvious that Jesus did not whisper the words, but said them plainly and loudly in order that all may hear. Very shortly, those words came back to haunt Caiaphas, causing him to ultimately commit suicide. As well, those very words of the claims of Christ will face this Sanhedrin at the *"Great White Throne Judgment."* But then, and as stated, Jesus will be the Judge, instead of them!

(66) "WHAT THINK YE? THEY ANSWERED AND SAID, HE IS GUILTY OF DEATH."

The question, *"What think ye?"*, was spoken to all the members of the Sanhedrin who were present.

NOTES

The phrase, *"They answered and said, He is guilty of death,"* was the sentence demanded by the Law of Moses for the crime of blasphemy (Lev. 24:16). It was to be carried out by stoning, which, under the Romans, they really did not have the power to do.

Furthermore, He was exactly Who He said He was, and, therefore, no blasphemer, and had broken the Law of Moses not at all. By sentencing Him to death, they broke the Law of Moses, which they had sworn to uphold, and because He was innocent.

Furthermore, the entirety of this meeting was wrong, in that it was not a regular Council of the Sanhedrin, nor was it held in the appointed chamber, and, as well, was conducted at night when criminal processes were forbidden. Consequently, they would hold a meeting the next morning (27:1) attempting to legitimize what they had already done.

(67) "THEN DID THEY SPIT IN HIS FACE, AND BUFFETED HIM; AND OTHERS SMOTE HIM WITH THE PALMS OF THEIR HANDS,"

The word, *"Then,"* refers in the modern vernacular to *"fair game."* Now that sentence had been passed upon Him, He was *"fair game"* for anything they desired to do. No insult, indignity, or cruelty, were beyond their scope. So much for the Church of that day!

The phrase, *"Then did they spit in His Face,"* was considered to be the greatest insult to a person. How many did this is not known, with probably twenty to thirty, or even more, engaging in this vile act.

The phrase, *"And buffeted Him,"* means they hit Him with their fists. This was probably done by the Temple guards, but could well have included some members of the vaunted Sanhedrin. Without God, men are animals! Worse still, those who claim to know Him, but in reality do not, will stoop to any level. In other words, they are far worse than the worldling.

The phrase, *"And others smote Him with the palms of their hands,"* is felt by some that it should have been translated, *"Smote Him with rods."*

Inasmuch as the striking with the hands has already been mentioned, quite possibly the correct translation refers to the striking with rods.

The Temple guards had spears which had wooden handles, and are probably intended here. What He must have looked like at this time, would be beyond imagination. From the beating, His Face would have swollen immediately, and with the spittle running down His Face, mixing with His beard and even blood, the sight must have been grotesque.

The Prophet had said, *"As many were astonied at Thee; His visage was so marred more than any man, and His form more than the sons of men"* (Isa. 52:14).

(68) "SAYING, PROPHESY UNTO US, THOU CHRIST, WHO IS HE THAT SMOTE THEE?"

Mark and Luke said they blindfolded Him (14:65; 22:64).

The phrase, *"Saying, Prophesy unto us,"* had actually already been done, with the pronouncement by Jesus in verse 64. However, they would not accept that, therefore, they will sink to a level lower than animals.

The words, *"Thou Christ,"* are spoken contemptuously! Christ means *"The Anointed,"* and spoke of the Messiah. They are making fun of His claims, and, consequently, ridiculing the Anointing of the Holy Spirit upon Him. As a result, they were coming very close to blaspheming the Holy Spirit, if, in fact, they had not already done so!

The question, *"Who is he that smote Thee?",* was asked, no doubt, with hellish glee!

The awful depravity of man was never more shown than at this moment. The awful evil that registered in these religious hearts is indicative of the religious nature of Satan. How the evil one hated Christ, and, consequently, his children followed accordingly.

Now they smote Him, but about thirty-seven years later, they, in turn, would be smitten. As a direct result of this action against Christ, the vengeance of the Lord came upon them in a way that defies description. The siege of Jerusalem by the Roman Tenth Legion of Titus, completely decimated the city. Over 1,000,000 Jews were killed in that carnage, with multiple tens of thousands crucified on crosses exactly as they had crucified Christ.

To touch God, or that which belongs to God, is a frightful exercise indeed! Now these hypocrites were laughing, but soon they would not be laughing anymore.

(69) "NOW PETER SAT WITHOUT IN THE PALACE: AND A DAMSEL CAME UNTO HIM, SAYING, THOU ALSO WAST WITH JESUS OF GALILEE."

The phrase, *"Now Peter sat without in the palace,"* probably refers to him sitting by a fire in the courtyard as the night was cold (Jn. 18:18). There, in the company of servants, Peter attempted to warm himself. But how different was that *"fire of coals"* to the *"fire of coals"* of John 21:9!

At Satan's *"fire of coals,"* Peter sat with servants, and got no real warmth; and it was night in nature and in his soul; and three times he denied the Lord.

At Immanuel's *"fire of coals,"* there was warmth, and goodly company, and food, and sunshine in nature and in his soul, and three times he confessed the Lord (Jn. 21:9, 15-17).

These two coal fires are burning today.

The phrase, *"And a damsel came unto him, saying, Thou also wast with Jesus of Galilee,"* probably referred to *"the damsel that kept the door,"* which gave entrance into the courtyard. When it said that Peter *"sat without,"* it was speaking of the open court around which the palace was built.

How she knew Peter is anyone's guess, possibly having seen him with Christ in the Temple in the last few days. Others were no doubt with her when she points Peter out as a follower of Christ. She used the beautiful appellative, *"Jesus of Galilee,"* but it seems, with some sarcasm.

(70) "BUT HE DENIED BEFORE THEM ALL, SAYING, I KNOW NOT WHAT THOU SAYEST."

The phrase, *"But he denied before them all,"* spoke of a number of people standing with the damsel. This was his first denial of Christ.

The phrase, *"Saying, I know not what thou sayest,"* is an attempt to sidestep the issue.

While Jesus was being beaten inside, with spittle mixed with blood running down His Face, Peter outside was denying that he knew Him.

Lest we too sharply denounce Peter, I wonder if all of us, at one time or the other, have not in some way denied Him?

(71) AND WHEN HE WAS GONE OUT INTO THE PORCH, ANOTHER MAID SAW HIM, AND SAID UNTO THEM THAT WERE THERE, THIS FELLOW WAS ALSO WITH JESUS OF NAZARETH."

The phrase, *"And when he was gone out into the porch,"* referred to the passageway from the street to the court. He seemingly was attempting to remove himself from these who had just fingered him, but will find himself deeper into his dilemma.

The phrase, *"Another maid saw him, and said unto them that were there,"* concerns another group apart from the first one.

The phrase, *"This fellow was also with Jesus of Nazareth,"* is, as well, said with sarcasm. The word, *"fellow,"* was added by the translators, with the emphasis on the word, *"This."* So it is with contempt that she points to Peter.

She uses another appellative of Christ, *"Jesus of Nazareth!"*

(72) "AND AGAIN HE DENIED WITH AN OATH, I DO NOT KNOW THE MAN."

The phrase, *"And again he denied with an oath,"* does not tell us exactly what the oath was, but insinuates a much stronger denial.

The phrase, *"I do not know the Man,"* is emphatic, meaning that he claims not even to know His Name. Consequently, he calls his beloved Master, *"The Man!"*

(73) "AND AFTER A WHILE CAME UNTO HIM THEY THAT STOOD BY, AND SAID TO PETER, SURELY THOU ALSO ART ONE OF THEM; FOR THY SPEECH BEWRAYETH THEE."

The phrase, *"And after a while came unto him they that stood by, and said to Peter,"* represents, according to Luke, about an hour of time. Quite a few people were in the courtyard, and it seems they are all drawn to Peter.

The phrase, *"Surely thou also art one of them,"* proclaims the Apostle once again being fingered.

The phrase, *"For thy speech bewrayeth thee,"* shows him to be a Galilean, and from where most of the followers of Christ had come.

The accent of the northern part of Israel which incorporated the Galilee area, was quite different than the southern area which included Jerusalem. Actually, those in Jerusalem considered the Galileans to be somewhat uncouth and crude.

The word, *"bewrayeth,"* is an old English version of *"betrayeth."*

(74) "THEN BEGAN HE TO CURSE AND TO SWEAR, SAYING, I KNOW NOT THE MAN. AND IMMEDIATELY THE COCK CREW."

The phrase, *"Then began he to curse and to swear,"* presents the veracity of the denials increasing.

NOTES

First of all, he denied, then he denied with an oath, and lastly, he added curses to his oath.

The popular opinion is that Peter in his fear relapsed into the profane language that he may have used as a fisherman prior to his conversion. But all the evidence about him in the Sacred Records points to his having been a devout Hebrew, believing in, and awaiting, the Advent of the Messiah.

It seems, as well, that he was a follower of John the Baptist before following Christ (Jn. 1:35-42).

To have used vulgar oaths and curses would have been sad indeed, but to do as he did, that is, to take a solemn oath such as men do in a Court of Justice, and then to call upon God to curse him if the oath were false — was a sin of appalling magnitude and depth. It might even be termed *"spiritual suicide."*

The Greek word for *"curse"* is *"katanathematidzo,"* which means *"to call curses on himself if what he said was untrue."*

The phrase, *"Saying, I know not the Man,"* means that he swore by the Name of God that he did not know Christ.

The phrase, *"And immediately the cock crew,"* refers to the rooster crowing at daybreak. There is, therefore, no conflict between Mark 14:30 and Luke 22:34. Hence Mark says *"This night,"* and Luke, *"This day."*

During the night the rooster would crow twice, but at break of day, only once. Luke records with emphasis what happened at daybreak; and hence the accuracy of the record. *"The cock-crowing"* in the Bible means that which occurs at daybreak.

(75) "AND PETER REMEMBERED THE WORD OF JESUS, WHICH SAID UNTO HIM, BEFORE THE COCK CROW, THOU SHALT DENY ME THRICE. AND HE WENT OUT, AND WEPT BITTERLY."

The phrase, *"And Peter remembered the Word of Jesus, which said unto him,"* referred to the rooster crowing.

The phrase, *"Before the cock crow, thou shalt deny Me thrice,"* was now fulfilled, and exactly as Jesus had said it would be.

Peter had been told that Satan had been given permission to sift him as wheat (Lk. 22:31). God fans (Mat. 3:12) to get rid of the chaff; Satan sifts to get rid of the wheat.

But Peter had been given the Promise that in answer to the prayer of Jesus, his Faith would not fail, and that prayer contemplated the moment, when, in the dark night outside the court, and while Peter was weeping bitterly, Satan doubtless whispered to him: *"You have committed spiritual suicide, now you are mine!"* Had his faith then failed, he would possibly, like Judas, have destroyed himself.

However, when this happened, Jesus was being led out of the palace, and He turned, and from the chamber facing the court looked upon Peter (Lk. 22:61). The Scripture does not say that Jesus said anything to Peter, but the look that Jesus gave him, which was undoubtedly one of supreme kindness, would melt Peter's heart. Jesus, in the midst of all of His terrible sufferings and sorrows, had not forgotten the Apostle.

The phrase, *"And he went out and wept bitterly,"* proclaims his Repentance.

Tradition says that for the rest of his life, Peter could not hear a rooster crow without falling upon his knees and weeping.

CHAPTER 27

(1) "WHEN THE MORNING WAS COME, ALL THE CHIEF PRIESTS AND ELDERS OF THE PEOPLE TOOK COUNSEL AGAINST JESUS TO PUT HIM TO DEATH:"

The phrase, *"When the morning was come,"* referred to Wednesday morning. He would be crucified in a matter of hours.

It is ironical, this *"morning"* that would dawn so ignominious concerning the wickedness of Israel and the world, in another sense, would be the greatest day that had ever dawned. On this day, Jesus Christ, the Lord of Glory, would pay the price in full for man's Redemption, that all who will *"may come and drink of the Water of Life freely."*

The phrase, *"All the Chief Priests and Elders of the people,"* represented the Church of its day. Of all Satan's efforts to destroy men, his effort of religion is the greatest of all. Through this method, he has damned billions to an eternal hell, and does no less today!

This morning session was that of the entire Sanhedrin; it followed the unofficial meeting in the High Priest's house (26:57).

The phrase, *"Took counsel against Jesus to put Him to death,"* referred to the dealings of

the Sanhedrin in their efforts to formulate a political charge against Jesus, causing the Romans to carry out the death sentence.

They were determined that His death would be such that it would dispel any notion throughout Israel of Him being the Messiah. Consequently, they would demand crucifixion, hence the cry of verses 22 and 23. Their thinking was derived from Deuteronomy 21:23, *"For he that is hanged is accursed of God."*

If they had even one time in the last three and a half years taken *"counsel"* respecting the claims of Christ as Messiah, they would have known that the proof was irrefutable. However, no such counsel was taken, because they did not want the True Messiah sent from God, and, in reality, was God.

They did not realize that taking *"counsel"* to put Him to death, in effect, would put themselves to death!

(2) "AND WHEN THEY HAD BOUND HIM, THEY LED HIM AWAY, AND DELIVERED HIM TO PONTIUS PILATE THE GOVERNOR."

The phrase, *"And when they had bound Him, they led Him away,"* refers to His Hands being tied behind His back with a rope. What further indignities they heaped upon Him in this early morning session, Matthew does not relate, and Luke only alludes to. His appearance had to be extremely debilitating and disheveled to say the least! He had been up all night, and had been treated brutally in a physical sense by those who had passed sentence upon Him. Even though they had pummelled Him repeatedly with their fists and beaten Him severely with sticks, the horror of this treatment was only beginning.

The phrase, *"And delivered Him to Pontius Pilate the Governor,"* concerns the fifth (some say sixth) Roman Procurator of Judaea. He was appointed by Emperor Tiberius.

He had full powers of life and death in Judaea, and could reverse capital sentences passed by the Sanhedrin, which had to be submitted to him for ratification. He also appointed the High Priests and controlled the Temple and its funds: the very vestments of the High Priest were in his custody and were released only for festivals, when the Procurator took up residence in Jerusalem and brought additional troops to patrol the city.

Philo said of him, that he was *"By nature*

rigid and stubbornly harsh and of spiteful disposition and an exceeding wrathful man."

The verdict of the New Testament is that he was a weak man, ready to serve expediency rather than principle, whose authorization of the judicial murder of the Saviour was due less to a desire to please the Jewish authorities than to fear of imperial displeasure if Tiberius heard of further unrest in Judaea.

He held his office for some ten years, at the end of which time he was removed for cruelty and extortion, and banished to Vienne in Gaul, where he committed suicide.

Pilate usually resided at Caesarea, but came to Jerusalem at this great festival, as stated, to be ready to quell any fanatical outbreak that might occur. He was accompanied by his wife.

(3) "THEN JUDAS, WHICH HAD BETRAYED HIM, WHEN HE SAW THAT HE WAS CONDEMNED, REPENTED HIMSELF, AND BROUGHT AGAIN THE THIRTY PIECES OF SILVER TO THE CHIEF PRIESTS AND ELDERS,"

The phrase, *"Then Judas, which had betrayed Him,"* concerns itself now with the beginning of the horrible darkness which would invade Judas, which covers him even unto this moment, and will do so forever.

The phrase, *"When he saw that He was condemned,"* refers to what the Religious Leaders had done to Jesus in their brutal treatment of Him. It is not known if Judas actually saw Christ at this time, or only heard what happened; however, if he actually did see Him, which he probably did, even though sickened by what he saw, the sight of Jesus did not affect him as it had Simon Peter. Seeing Jesus brought Peter to repentance, while Judas would not allow himself to be brought to this place of mercy and forgiveness. He was morose and broody, and left to himself he became a helpless victim of Satan who kept him from turning to God, and who pressured him to destruction.

The words, *"Repented himself,"* in the Greek is *"metamelomai,"* and means, *"To have deep remorse at the consequence of sin, rather than a deep regret at the cause of it. It is never used of genuine repentance to God."*

Many erroneously feel that God at this time would not have considered true repentance from Judas. However, that is incorrect! The Lord has never turned anyone away who truly

came to Him in brokenness and contrition, and He would not have turned Judas away either. What Judas ultimately did was strictly of his own volition.

However, it should be brought out that once one gives oneself over to Satan, darkness fills the soul, making it extremely difficult to throw off. In all honesty, only a few are able to do so. Tampering with Satan is somewhat like taking a rattlesnake into one's bosom. The chances of not being bitten are slim indeed!

Solomon said, *"Can a man take fire in his bosom, and his clothes not be burned?"*

He then said, *"Can one go upon hot coals, and his feet not be burned?"* (Prov. 6:27-28).

Over the years, we have received thousands of letters from those who have been brought from the very brink of eternal darkness. The Word of God through the Telecast would reach out to them, many times at the last moment, bringing them to Christ. However, for every one who pulls back from the brink, only the Lord knows the countless others, as Judas, who are not brought back, but go into perdition!

The phrase, *"And brought again the thirty pieces of silver to the Chief Priests and Elders,"* concerns the blood money. After he had seen the results of his sin, such wages are not now so attractive. In Truth, it never is!

He traded the Love, Peace, Mercy, Grace, Compassion, and Salvation offered by Christ for the silver. He was to find that it was a sorry trade! It would not have mattered if he had been given the entirety of the world, he would still have come out the loser by far. Salvation afforded by Christ can take the place of anything else, but nothing else can take its place.

(4) "SAYING, I HAVE SINNED IN THAT I HAVE BETRAYED THE INNOCENT BLOOD. AND THEY SAID, WHAT IS THAT TO US? SEE THOU TO THAT."

The phrase, *"Saying, I have sinned,"* presents him confessing this sin to man, and evil man at that, but not to God. While it was true that sorrow filled his heart, still, it was not *"Godly sorrow which worketh repentance to Salvation,"* but rather, *"The sorrow of the world which worketh death"* (II Cor. 7:10).

The phrase, *"In that I have betrayed the innocent blood,"* presents a powerful statement within itself.

The word, *"The,"* emphasizes that the Blood

of Christ was the only truly innocent blood that had ever been. They accused Him of being illegitimate in His birth, but, in reality, His was the only truly legitimate birth that ever was.

Not only was He <u>not</u> guilty of what they were accusing Him of, sedition and insurrection, but, as well, He was not guilty of any sin whatsoever! He was the only Man who ever lived Who never sinned, and, therefore, these evil Religious Leaders killed the only Perfect Man that ever was.

Whether at this stage Judas truly believed that Christ was Divine, is open to question. However, having been by His side for three and a half years, He at least knew that Jesus was sinless. As well, he now knew they were going to kill Him.

Their question, *"What is that to us?"*, was coldly appropriate. They knew He was not guilty of these trumped-up charges. They also knew He had never done anything but good in all of His Life and Ministry. They simply did not care. They saw Him, as a threat, and, as well, they envied Him.

Consequently, they had no regard for Judas, him being only a tool for them to use. Now that they had used him, he was of no more value or concern to them.

As someone has well said, *"To sympathize with repentance is the duty and the privilege of the Christian; to deride and scoff at the returned sinner is devilish."*

(5) "AND HE CAST DOWN THE PIECES OF SILVER IN THE TEMPLE, AND DEPARTED, AND WENT AND HANGED HIMSELF."

The phrase, *"And he cast down the pieces of silver in the Temple,"* presents him flinging the shekels onto the marble floor. That which a person loses his soul for is lost as well!

The phrase, *"And departed, and went and hanged himself,"* concludes this perfidious transaction. Satan hated Judas, if possible, just as much as he hated Christ.

He probably hanged himself with his own girdle or sash, which was wound around his waist.

Peter mentioned this in Acts 1:18, *"Falling headlong, he burst asunder in the midst, and all his bowels gushed out."*

Tradition says that the limb broke from the tree to which the sash was tied, and he fell heavily to the rocks below, where a passing wagon, unable to stop, crushed and disembowelled him.

NOTES

Lightfoot, the Jewish Historian, said that Satan took the body of Judas the moment he fell, throwing it on the rocks below, with his very bowels gushing out.

At any rate, his death was awful!

He could have lived for God, spending the entirety of his life in the service of the Master Who chose him, with his name ultimately inscribed on the foundations of the New Jerusalem. But, instead, he chose self-will and thirty pieces of silver (Rev. 21:14).

On one of our trips to Israel, I had the occasion to be brought to the place where it was said that Judas hanged himself. Standing at the foot of the cliff, looking up to where he had stood when he tied the noose around his neck, I happened to look down at my feet.

An open sewer was running at the base of the cliff, with its foul odor filling the air. The symbolism was apt!

(6) "AND THE CHIEF PRIESTS TOOK THE SILVER PIECES, AND SAID, IT IS NOT LAWFUL FOR TO PUT THEM INTO THE TREASURY, BECAUSE IT IS THE PRICE OF BLOOD."

The phrase, *"And the Chief Priests took the silver pieces, and said,"* represents the blood money now in their hands where it rightfully belonged all the time! Judas was evil, but they were far more evil! So, the Holy Spirit returned it to its rightful owners.

The phrase, *"It is not lawful for to put them into the treasury,"* is ironic indeed!

They would bend over backwards to make certain they did not break the *"Law"* in this respect, and totally ignored the *"Law"* in condemning an innocent man to death. Such is religion!

It gags at a gnat, and swallows a camel!

This is the reason that religion is so ungodly! It minutely attends to the outward ceremony, while its heart is plotting the greatest of evil. That is the reason religion changes no one, except for the worse.

Concerning a noted athlete who had just become a Moslem, someone remarked that they hoped it would help him. However, there is no help from that source, because it only deals with the externals, which is not the real cause of man's problems. The real cause is an evil, wicked heart, which can only be changed by the Power of God. Hence, Jesus said, *"You must be born again"* (Jn. 3:3).

The phrase, *"Because it is the price of blood,"* spoke of the Blood of Jesus Christ. As well, they were the ones who shed it, but they felt no remorse whatsoever! Their action concerning the blood money not being put back into the treasury, was taken from Deuteronomy 23:18. However, their minutely adhering to the Law in this respect, in no way abrogated their terrible crime or their guilt. Paying tithe on stolen money does not legitimize the theft.

(7) "AND THEY TOOK COUNSEL, AND BOUGHT WITH THEM THE POTTER'S FIELD, TO BURY STRANGERS IN."

The phrase, *"And they took counsel,"* concerns what is to be done with this blood money. What makes it even more horrible is that this is the *"Church"* that is having this *"counsel."* The Church as we think of it, has always been divided into two entities. The larger part is the apostate Church, and was headed up by these Religious Leaders. Too often institutionalized religion falls into this category.

The True Church was those who were followers of Christ, ever how many that may have been. In Truth, that pretty well sums it up for all time, those who follow Christ and those who follow institutionalized religion.

What do we mean by institutionalized religion?

Pure and simple, it speaks of Church which is controlled by man, and in whatever capacity. As well, it does not necessarily refer to all religious institutions, but can as well, and often does, include those who come under no institutional heading.

In its simple form, any work that claims to be of God and is man-controlled, by its simple definition, is not God-controlled!

How can one tell the difference?

Quite a bit of what Christ taught had to do with this very thing. He warned repeatedly of *"false prophets," "corrupt trees,"* and *"evil fruit"* (Mat 7:15-20). As well, a great deal of everything else He taught addressed itself in some respect to this very subject, and because it is so very important.

To know the difference, one must stay close to the Lord and be thoroughly acquainted with His Word. Regrettably, most Christians do not fall into that category.

To take an example from Christ, which is the

greatest example of all, the pattern becomes a little more clear.

1. Despite the obvious moving of the Holy Spirit in the Ministry of Christ, and actually the greatest the world had ever known, Jesus was opposed by institutionalized religion from the very beginning. They opposed Him because they were not of God, and He was!

2. They lied about Him constantly, and their modern counterparts do the same. They did anything they could to hinder His support, or to hurt His influence with the people.

3. It came to the place in the last year of His public Ministry that institutionalized religion threatened or actually carried out excommunication against anyone who followed Christ. Consequently, and despite the greatest performing of miracles the world had ever known, the crowds thinned out considerably the last year of Jesus' public Ministry.

Therefore, as Satan's tactics were then, his tactics are now! The larger crowd will always be on the side of the apostate Church, exactly as they were during the time of Christ. And as well, most people demand to be on the popular side, and, to be sure, the popular side has never been that of Christ.

The phrase, *"And bought with them the potter's field, to bury strangers in,"* speaks of a spot that was on the south of Jerusalem, across the valley of Hinnom.

It is not known what was meant by the word, *"strangers,"* unless it spoke of Gentiles who died while in Jerusalem, etc.

(8) "WHEREFORE THAT FIELD WAS CALLED, THE FIELD OF BLOOD, UNTO THIS DAY."

The phrase, *"Wherefore that field was called, The field of blood,"* was not the name given to it by the Religious Leaders of Israel, but others! Consequently, the name would forever serve as a testimony to the treachery and wickedness of those who killed the Lord of Glory.

The phrase, *"Unto this day,"* referred to the time that Matthew wrote His Gospel, which tradition says was about 37 A.D. However, up to the mid 1800's, it was still being used for this purpose, the burying of the poor and unhonored dead of Jerusalem.

(9) "THEN WAS FULFILLED THAT WHICH WAS SPOKEN BY JEREMY THE PROPHET, SAYING, AND THEY TOOK THE

THIRTY PIECES OF SILVER, THE PRICE OF HIM THAT WAS VALUED, WHOM THEY OF THE CHILDREN OF ISRAEL DID VALUE;"

The phrase, *"Then was fulfilled that which was spoken by Jeremy the Prophet,"* has been debated for many centuries. This phrase is not found in Jeremiah, but in Zechariah 11:12-13. So, for those of us who definitely believe that the Bible is without error, how can this be explained? The following may provide some help:

1. Inasmuch as the original Texts of the Scriptures no longer exist, authenticity has to be derived from copies of the original, of which there are many.

The copyists who did their work by hand, on rare occasions could make a mistake.

For instance, in II Chronicles 36:9, it says, *"Jehoiachin was eight years old when he began to reign."*

In II Kings 24:8, it says, *"Jehoiachin was eighteen years old when he be began to reign."*

As stated, the error was made by a copyist, with such a mistake easy to make in transcribing numeral letters of the Hebrew Text. The correct number in both cases should have been *"eighteen."*

As stated, there is a possibility that a copyist by mistake put in the name *"Jeremiah,"* when he should have put in *"Zechariah."*

Of course, the skeptic could say that if God was able to make the original Text error-proof, He certainly could have done the same with the copies! Of course that it true; however, I suspect that oftentimes the Lord allows little things like this to happen by purpose and design. Such strengthens the Faith of the Believer, while, at the same time, doing the opposite to the unbeliever.

2. It is quite possible that this Prophecy was *"spoken"* through Jeremiah and not written down, but handed down by word of mouth, as here stated by the Holy Spirit, and was repeated and recorded by that same Spirit in Zechariah 11:12.

The phrase, *"Saying, And they took the thirty pieces of silver, the price of Him that was valued,"* was the price of an injured slave.

The phrase, *"Whom they of the children of Israel did value,"* is given by the Holy Spirit in order to emphasize the fact that this was the price or worth that Israel placed upon her Messiah. Such a thing is inconceivable, but yet this is what they did. It might be quickly asked as

to what kind of *"value"* does the world attribute to Christ? Or even the Church? Or even you the reader?

The world, as is obvious, places little value on Christ at all! Sadly and regrettably, most of the Church places little value on Him as well! He is supposed to be the Head of the Church, and certainly is of the True Church, but of the apostate Church, I think it is obvious that He is not. As an example, as long as the Catholic Church has an earthly Pope, they cannot have a heavenly Pope, i.e., Christ. The same goes for Protestant Popes as well!

(10) "AND GAVE THEM FOR THE POTTER'S FIELD, AS THE LORD APPOINTED ME."

The phrase, *"And gave them for the potter's field,"* is taken from Zechariah 11:13, *"And I took the thirty pieces of silver, and cast them to the potter in the House of the Lord."*

The phrase, *"As the Lord appointed me,"* is basically the same as Zechariah's, *"And the Lord said unto me,"* from the same verse.

Therefore, this action, as is obvious, was fore-ordained as to its destination. The money would go for the purchase of a potter's field.

Did not these Religious Leaders of Israel know about this Prophecy? Did it not at any time become obvious to them that they were fulfilling this hideous transaction?

Evidently not! Else they did not know the Bible well enough to know what it said, or in their eagerness to carry out this wickedness, they brushed aside that which was so obvious.

Men tend to justify themselves, and religious men most of all!

(11) "AND JESUS STOOD BEFORE THE GOVERNOR: AND THE GOVERNOR ASKED HIM, SAYING, ART THOU THE KING OF THE JEWS? AND JESUS SAID UNTO HIM, THOU SAYEST."

The phrase, *"And Jesus stood before the Governor,"* speaks of Pontius Pilate.

Matthew omits a number of things that took place while Jesus was before Pilate, but was related by John. Pilate seemed to be reluctant to involve himself in this situation. He felt it was a religious matter and did not involve Rome. Consequently, and according to Luke, the Jews accused Christ of making Himself a King, which would definitely involve Rome.

The phrase, *"And the Governor asked Him,*

saying," refers itself to this charge. Rome appointed all kings, and, consequently, if Jesus actually was calling Himself a King, this could cause much trouble. Therefore, He will do exactly what the Jews desired, involve Himself.

The question, *"Art Thou the King of the Jews?"*, is straight to the point, and will receive a like answer from Christ.

In effect, the last king to occupy a Throne in Judah was Zedekiah some 600 years before. In Truth, *"Jehoiachin,"* who preceded Zedekiah, was the last one to be recognized by God, who was actually in the lineage of David, for Zedekiah was his uncle (II Chron. 36:10). (The word, *"brother,"* in the 10th verse, actually means *"next of kin."* And in this case, Jehoiachin's uncle.)

So, in reality, Christ was to be the next One to sit on the Throne of David (II Sam. 7:12). However, Israel did not want Him as their King, stating rather, *"We have no king but Caesar"* (Jn. 19:15). Therefore, they have had Caesar for about 2,000 years, and, to say the least, it has brought them untold sorrow! Only when Jesus does actually reign as King, which He shall at the Second Coming, will Israel finally know what she has missed, and could have had all along.

The phrase, *"And Jesus said unto him, Thou sayest,"* in effect says, *"I am the King of the Jews."* As far as is recorded, this is the first time Jesus had made such a claim. Therefore, the Jews were lying when they charged that He had made such a claim prior to this time. Others may have said it about Him, but there is no record that He said it of Himself before now.

Jesus was a King, and, in reality, *"The King,"* but actually far more than that. He was *"The Messiah, The Son of the Blessed One, God of God, of one substance with the Father."*

He was *"KING OF KINGS, AND LORD OF LORDS!"* (Rev. 19:16).

(12) "AND WHEN HE WAS ACCUSED OF THE CHIEF PRIESTS AND ELDERS, HE ANSWERED NOTHING."

The phrase, *"And when He was accused of the Chief Priests and Elders,"* concerned false accusations. They were trying to convince Pilate that Jesus was claiming to be a King, usurping power over Rome. However, the manner in which Jesus had answered Pilate respecting this question, and as John recorded it, He had said, *"My Kingdom is not of this world"* (Jn. 18:36). Consequently, Pilate knew that His claims were spiritual, and, therefore, not of this world.

This examination was taking place within the Praetorium, with the Jews standing outside. They would be defiled if they went inside this Gentile judgment hall (Jn. 18:28). And yet they can murder the Lord of Glory! Such is religion.

All of these accusations took place as Pilate walked to the door of this judgment hall.

The phrase, *"He answered nothing,"* referred itself to these accusations.

He would not defend Himself before people who cared nothing for Truth, and, in fact, wanted no part of Truth. To have answered their accusations would have lent at least some small amount of dignity to them, therefore, Jesus said nothing.

(13) "THEN SAID PILATE UNTO HIM, HEAREST THOU NOT HOW MANY THINGS THEY WITNESS AGAINST THEE?"

The phrase, *"Then said Pilate unto Him,"* records this Governor not really realizing Who Jesus was, but yet suspicioning that something was different about Him, more so than anyone he had ever witnessed.

The question, *"Hearest Thou not how many things they witness against Thee?"*, concerned the accusation that Jesus stirred up the people, *"Beginning from Galilee to this place"* (Lk. 23:5).

It was at this stage that Pilate sent Jesus to Herod, because Galilee lay in Herod's jurisdiction (Lk. 23:6-7). However, Matthew did not mention the Herod episode.

(14) "AND HE ANSWERED HIM TO NEVER A WORD; INSOMUCH THAT THE GOVERNOR MARVELLED GREATLY."

The phrase, *"And He answered him to never a word,"* fulfilled the Prophecy of Isaiah, *"He was oppressed, and He was afflicted, yet He opened not His mouth: He is brought as a lamb to the slaughter, and as a sheep before her shearers is dumb, so He openeth not His mouth"* (Isa. 53:7).

The phrase, *"Insomuch that the Governor marvelled greatly,"* means that Pilate was struck dumb with astonishment that Jesus defended Himself not at all against these accusations, even though they could lead to His death. In effect, the Governor had never seen One such as Christ!

Despite Jesus having been severely beaten a few hours before, He no doubt had a regal bearing that could not be disguised even by His disheveled appearance. Even though He was truly Man, still, He was truly God. As such, His comportment, no doubt, was unlike any other human being who had ever lived. There was something about Him . . . .

We must not make more of His being than we should, but we dare not, at the same time, make less!

Considering that He had never been touched by sin, and which could be said of Him Alone, and inasmuch as He was filled with the Holy Spirit without measure, His Presence must have been something unlike any other human being who had ever lived, or would live! Pilate must have sensed this, and yet not realizing that he was standing within inches of his Creator.

(15) "NOW AT THAT FEAST THE GOVERNOR WAS WONT TO RELEASE UNTO THE PEOPLE A PRISONER, WHOM THEY WOULD."

The phrase, *"Now at that Feast,"* spoke of the Passover.

The phrase, *"The Governor was wont to release unto the people a prisoner, whom they would,"* meant that at this time each year a prisoner, chosen by the people would be released into their custody. No one knows how this practice began, whether instigated by Rome or Israel.

At any rate, Pilate seizes upon this opportunity, thinking this may be a solution to his dilemma. He did not want to condemn Christ, having already said to the Jews, *"I find no fault in this Man"* (Lk. 23:4). However, he did not realize the amount of hatred and animosity that filled the hearts of these Religious Leaders. In reality, Pilate was a Pagan, knowing little of the God of Israel, and actually a worshiper of many gods. However, he was a far less wicked man than these religious jackals who demanded the life of Christ.

(Some claim that the release of a prisoner at Passover time was begun by the Jews, and was a symbol of Israel's release from Egypt.)

(16) "AND THEY HAD THEN A NOTABLE PRISONER, CALLED BARABBAS."

Mark said that Barabbas was a murderer, and had led an insurrection against Roman authority (Mk. 15:7).

At any rate, the word, *"notable,"* should have been translated *"notorious,"* and because at that time his crimes against Roman authority

were known throughout Israel, and, evidently, some, if not many, sympathized with him.

The name, *"Barabbas,"* means *"son of the father."* In some manuscripts his name is given as *"Jesus Barabbas."* If that is correct, the people were faced with a choice of *"Jesus Barabbas,"* the murderer, or *"Jesus Christ,"* the Giver of Eternal Life.

(17) "THEREFORE WHEN THEY WERE GATHERED TOGETHER, PILATE SAID UNTO THEM, WHOM WILL YE THAT I RELEASE UNTO YOU? BARABBAS, OR JESUS WHICH IS CALLED CHRIST?"

The phrase, *"Therefore when they were gathered together, Pilate said unto them,"* will spark the doom that is about to fall heavily upon them. The Jews did not realize it, but every choice they now made would be given to them in totality, and would be a choice that would haunt them even unto this very day.

The question, *"Whom will ye that I release unto you? Barabbas, or Jesus which is called Christ?",* places the choice in their lap. As stated, Pilate could have said, *"Jesus Barabbas,"* or *"Jesus Christ?"*

"Christ" meant The Anointed, and spoke of the Messiah. Therefore, Pilate had at least some understanding of the Jews' claim of a coming Messiah, and of the possibility that Christ may be this One! Of course, he knew that they claimed that their coming Messiah would overthrow Rome, bringing Israel back to her days of glory and power. Naturally, this did not sit well with Rome! Pilate may very well have been goading the Jews by referring to Jesus as the possible Messiah, and especially considering His disheveled physical appearance, it would have been somewhat of a joke on them.

In other words, he may have been saying by his presentation of Christ, *"Is this the One Who is going to deliver you?" "Is this the One Who is going to overthrow mighty Rome?"*

Mark mentions that Pilate had used the title, *"King of the Jews,"* at this time. Quite possibly he used both *"Jesus Christ"* and *"King of the Jews!"*

His sarcasm would have been leveled more so at the Jews, for whom he had absolutely no respect, rather than Jesus. However, the joke was at the expense of Christ. As well, and what Pilate did not know, all of these names and titles that Pilate alluded to concerning Jesus, and in sarcasm we might add, Jesus actually was!

(18) "FOR HE KNEW THAT FOR ENVY THEY HAD DELIVERED HIM."

This verse states that irrespective of the accusations leveled against Christ by the Religious Leaders of Israel, Pilate saw through their flimsy facade, knowing that Jesus was innocent of all these charges.

Concerning the tremendous number of miracles that Christ had performed, even to the raising of the dead, some of this must have come to Pilate's ears. Consequently, he knew how these hypocrites hated Jesus, fearing that they would lose control of the people. They were jealous of Him, and, consequently, they wanted to kill Him.

What a horrible testimony offered to this Pagan! What must he have thought of the God of Israel, as he dealt with those who claimed to be His Children?

Consequently, in this, it becomes obvious that the Holy Spirit is dealing with this Governor, attempting to help him see through this hoax! The next verse will present an even greater effort by the Holy Spirit.

(19) "WHEN HE WAS SET DOWN ON THE JUDGMENT SEAT, HIS WIFE SENT UNTO HIM, SAYING, HAVE THOU NOTHING TO DO WITH THAT JUST MAN: FOR I HAVE SUFFERED MANY THINGS THIS DAY IN A DREAM BECAUSE OF HIM."

The phrase, *"When he was set down on the judgment seat,"* concerned a chair on a raised platform in front of the Praetorium. It was here that he gave judgment respecting all cases brought before him. When he sat down that day, little did he realize that this would be the greatest judgment he would ever make. As well, little did he realize that as he judged Christ, he judged himself!

He would never get over this judgment, a short time later committing suicide.

The phrase, *"His wife sent unto him, saying,"* proclaims the veracity of Matthew. Her name was Claudia Procula. It was only in the reign of Tiberias that wives of Governors were permitted to accompany their husbands. Tradition says that she ultimately became a Christian.

The phrase, *"Have thou nothing to do with that just man,"* is meant that Pilate should do nothing to harm Him. This was, as stated,

another effort by the Holy Spirit prompting Pilate to make the right decision.

The phrase, *"For I have suffered many things this day in a dream because of Him,"* presents the Holy Spirit working through Pilate's wife, dealing with her heart, of which there is some small evidence, as stated, of her ultimately becoming a Christian.

What her dream was, the record does not say. However, in all of the account of the sufferings of Christ this last week before His death, she, a Gentile, is the only one, it seems, who gave Him a kind word. This is remarkable, in that she was the wife of a heathen Governor, the deputy of the Emperor of the world.

(20) "BUT THE CHIEF PRIESTS AND ELDERS PERSUADED THE MULTITUDE THAT THEY SHOULD ASK BARABBAS, AND DESTROY JESUS."

The phrase, *"But the Chief Priests and Elders persuaded the multitude,"* proclaims the fact that the crowd of people who was there that early morning hour, seemed at first to be persuaded toward Jesus. Barabbas, being a notorious murderer, and the story of the many miracles and healings performed by Christ having reached the ears of at least some of these people, they seemed to be, at first, disposed toward Him. However, the Religious Leaders of Israel persuaded them otherwise.

Most people can be easily persuaded by Religious Leaders, even though it is the wrong direction! Most do not have an adequate knowledge of the Word of God themselves, and, as well, have a tendency to think that people such as these *"Chief Priests and Elders,"* must know the right way or else they would not be in this position. As it held true then, it holds true now! Consequently, millions have died lost following religious pied pipers. As well, whatever is popular is sought by many, and because it is not easy to go against popular opinion.

Others have remarked that these were the same people, who, a few hours earlier, were shouting the acclaims of Christ at the Triumphant Entry. However, that is incorrect, inasmuch as most, if not all, of those people were in bed, due to the early morning hour. This *"multitude"* was made up of a different type of people altogether.

The phrase, *"That they should ask Barabbas, and destroy Jesus,"* means that these Religious Leaders quickly sifted out through the crowd, using whatever persuasive powers they had to turn the crowd their way. They were thirsty for the blood of Christ, and would resort to any means to procure that end! What they did not realize was, that in destroying Jesus, they were destroying themselves.

(21) "THE GOVERNOR ANSWERED AND SAID UNTO THEM, WHETHER OF THE TWAIN WILL YE THAT I RELEASE UNTO YOU? THEY SAID, BARABBAS."

The phrase, *"The Governor answered and said unto them,"* proclaims the thought that the Governor thought surely they would request Jesus; however, he was to be disappointed!

The question, *"Whether of the twain will ye that I release unto you?",* presents no alternative but Jesus or Barabbas.

The death knell of doom is fastly descending upon all who participated in this, the most despicable crime of all eternity! Looking back, almost all would decry the action of these Religious Leaders. However, most Religious Leaders today, if the same occasion presented itself, would do accordingly! That is a strong statement, but true.

In the world of religion, if an individual is not following Christ, he is following Satan! As it was not possible to be neutral about Christ then, it is not possible to be neutral now.

The phrase, *"They said, Barabbas,"* presented the choice of the Religious Leaders of Israel. Jesus had God as His Father, while Barabbas had Satan. Israel preferred the later!

(22) "PILATE SAITH UNTO THEM, WHAT SHALL I DO THEN WITH JESUS WHICH IS CALLED CHRIST? THEY ALL SAY UNTO HIM, LET HIM BE CRUCIFIED."

The phrase, *"Pilate saith unto them,"* shows a disappointment in the Roman Governor. He had not planned on the situation going in this direction.

The question, *"What shall I do then with Jesus which is called Christ?",* is not only the greatest question ever asked by Pilate, but the greatest question that anyone may ask. The answer to it decides the eternal destiny of the human soul.

As well, and as alluded to, one cannot remain neutral! Silence is the same as the answer of Israel of that day.

The phrase, *"They all say unto him, Let Him be crucified,"* was the most horrifying answer that Israel could ever give.

They specified *"crucifixion,"* because such a death would cause all the people, they thought, to turn against Him. Most knew that the Law of Moses condemned anyone hanged upon a tree (crucified) as being cursed by God (Deut. 21:23). So, in their thinking, His reputation would be destroyed. Were He really the Messiah, such would not happen. Consequently, the very fact of its happening would prove Him to be an imposter and blasphemer, or so they thought!

As well, the method of execution by the Jews was stoning, so they had a further insulation inasmuch as Rome alone could crucify.

So their evil plan was being weaved out, as they worked behind the scenes, with most of their evil effort being carried out in the dead of night, or else the early morning hour, to fulfill their scheme. So now, the crowd roars, *"Let Him be crucified!"*

They had completely ignored the Sermon on the Mount given by Jesus some three years ago, and the words, *"And with what measure ye mete, it shall be measured to you again"* (Mat. 7:2). However, and irrespective of their ignorance of that statement, or their unbelief had they known it, it would be fulfilled upon them in frightful consequences.

When Titus destroyed Jerusalem some thirty-seven years later, of the 1,100,000 Jews who perished in that horror, tens of thousands of them were crucified by the Romans. It is said that so many perished in this manner, that there was simply no more places to put crosses, with every foot of ground being taken up for this gruesome task. Truly they were accursed!

So, once again, when they clamored for His Crucifixion, they were clamoring for their own!

(23) "AND THE GOVERNOR SAID, WHY, WHAT EVIL HATH HE DONE? BUT THEY CRIED OUT THE MORE, SAYING, LET HIM BE CRUCIFIED."

The phrase, *"And the Governor said,"* proclaims his indecisiveness. As well, the multitude senses it.

The question, *"Why, what evil hath He done?",* is a question they could not answer, and, therefore, did not answer, and because He had done no evil. He was perfect! He had never sinned.

There have been individuals down through history who have been executed for crimes they did not commit, but even though innocent of that particular crime, still, *"All have sinned, and come short of the Glory of God"*(Rom. 3:23), with the exception of Christ. He had not only not done any evil, but had rather done only good!

He never made an eye to be blind, but made many to see! He never made a leg to be lame, but many to walk! He never broke a heart, but healed many broken hearts! He never put one in prison, but opened the prison doors that any and all who would believe, may go free!

So, Pilate's question, as well, is a question that the entirety of the world will have to answer at one time or the other.

The phrase, *"But they cried out the more,"* proclaims them offering no answer, and because they had no answer. So they covered up the poverty of their accusation by its loudness!

The phrase, *"Saying, Let Him be crucified,"* proclaims their final choice!

As the morning sun begins to break over Olivet, it will dawn on a day of infamy such as the world had never seen before or since. Israel is fastly descending into a darkened night from which there is no escape! Her doom is being sealed, and in a way that she can never begin to imagine.

Please allow us to emphasize once again, that all who read this must either be for or against Him. To be for Him, is to love and follow Him. While being against Him means to clamor as those of old, *"Crucify Him!"*

(24) "WHEN PILATE SAW THAT HE COULD PREVAIL NOTHING, BUT THAT RATHER A TUMULT WAS MADE, HE TOOK WATER, AND WASHED HIS HANDS BEFORE THE MULTITUDE, SAYING, I AM INNOCENT OF THE BLOOD OF THIS JUST PERSON: SEE YE TO IT."

The phrase, *"When Pilate saw that he could prevail nothing,"* means that his persuasive powers, such as they were, had no effect upon the evil hearts of these murderers. The apostate Church would settle for no less than the Blood of Christ.

The action of Pilate shows the heart attitude of many. They don't want to oppose Christ, but, at the same time, and because of popular opinion which does oppose Christ, they will not, at the same time, take a public stand for Him. Sadly, as Pilate of old, this incorporates most of that which calls itself *"Church!"* Let all understand that such action now, as then, will *"prevail nothing."*

The phrase, *"But that rather a tumult was made,"* proclaims the ominous signs of a riot.

Most likely, he feared that if he did not give in to their demands, a riot might occur, and that he would be accused in Rome of refusing to punish a pretender to the Jewish Throne. Consequently, as the balance of the account portrays, he will attempt to satisfy the people, while absolving himself of blame. But such is not to be done!

The phrase, *"He took water, and washed his hands before the multitude,"* proclaims his effort to heed the admonition of his wife, and at the same time give the people what they wanted.

By carrying out this act, he attempted to cast the guilt upon the people, as if the administration of justice lay with them and not with him.

The phrase, *"Saying, I am innocent of the blood of this just person,"* did not make it so by him saying it. He was not innocent of the Blood of Christ, inasmuch as he had the necessary number of Roman soldiers at his beck and call, who would have quelled any type of riot at his command. Therefore, he was inexcusable!

The phrase, *"See ye to it,"* proclaims him about to give these evil men what they desired, the Crucifixion of Christ. He could wash his hands, but he could not purify his heart or remove the burning sting of his conscience from the stain of this foul murder.

Tens of millions have attempted to do the same, not opposing Christ, while not standing up for Him. Regrettably, their conclusion is not innocence as Pilate attempted to claim, but rather guilt — just as much as the people who screamed for His Crucifixion!

(25) "THEN ANSWERED ALL THE PEOPLE, AND SAID, HIS BLOOD BE ON US, AND ON OUR CHILDREN."

The phrase, *"Then answered all the people,"* proclaims a decision that would bring them such sorrow as the world has never known — a sorrow that continues unto this day. And yet, every single person on the face of the earth must *"answer"* regarding Christ.

What will your answer be?

The phrase, *"And said, His Blood be on us, and on our children,"* proclaims a statement so lightly said, but bearing such fearful consequences.

The malediction they invoked upon themselves and upon their children rests upon them still, and was, and is, a malediction of appalling horror and suffering.

No one was ever hated so much as Christ. He was hated by princes, both civil and ecclesiastical, e. g., by Pilate, Herod, and the two High Priests; He was hated by the mobs; He was hated by the soldiers; and He was hated by the malefactors. Criminals, when tortured, do not normally revile a fellow-sufferer. This depth of bitterness was reserved for Immanuel.

Some time ago, Frances and I, along with friends, were in Munich, Germany. A few miles from this great German city is *"Dachou,"* the first concentration camp built by Hitler.

Today it is peacefully still, but in the early 1940's it was a place of unspeakable horror. We walked into the crematorium, where the gas ovens were located, and where multiple thousands of Jews were disposed of. Standing before one of the ovens, I opened its door with my hands, realizing that countless bodies had been pushed into this particular oven, where they would be dissolved in a matter of minutes. The ovens ran twenty-four hours a day.

It is said that when the wind was blowing toward Munich, one could easily smell the burning of bodies from this hell called *"Dachou."* This was not the only camp of such horror, with many others being built in Germany and elsewhere! Over 6,000,000 Jews died in this carnage, and as a direct result of the acclaimed responsibility of that early morning hour so many years ago.

Modern Jewry attempts to abrogate this responsibility, claiming that they had nothing to do with that decision made so long ago. However, their modern hatred of Christ, at least as a whole, continues to echo the evil shout of their forefathers so many generations removed.

While it is true that this generation is not responsible for an act committed nearly 2,000 years ago, still, multiple hundreds of millions of every race suffer every day for things done, over which they did not do, and, in effect, have no control. Such is life!

However, the guilt of the Jews is of a different magnitude, and because the blood they took upon themselves was not the blood of an ordinary man, but, in fact, their very Messiah, the Lord Jesus Christ, the Lord of Glory, Jehovah.

As God, they rejected Him; and as Immanuel, God manifest in the flesh, they murdered Him!

I made these statements, or similar, in a Message preached some years ago in a crusade in Dallas, Texas. It was aired a short time later over Television. The anger of many Jews around the nation was aroused, with some of them even attempting to get the Telecast removed from their particular area. They claimed that I had said that God had brought this thing upon them, and because of this action committed nearly 2,000 years ago.

In dialogue with some of their leaders, my answer was according to the following:

No, it was not God Who brought this judgment upon Israel, but actually was the result of their own actions.

Upon this rejection of Christ, the Lord took His Hand of protection off Israel, and because that is what they demanded. Inasmuch as the Lord was their only protection, now they had no protection at all!

Consequently, and according to their own demands, Caesar became their protector, and, as is obvious, Caesar hates them and continues to do so (Jn. 19:15). Caesar has been a hard taskmaster, and will continue to be so until the Second Coming of Christ.

The Jews have a problem of admitting their culpability, but so does the entirety of humanity. It is not a problem indigenous only to these people. Men want to blame God, that is if they even believe in God, for their dilemma, whatever it may be, consequently, refusing to own up to their own responsibility. This began with Adam and Eve after the Fall in the Garden of Eden, when Adam blamed Eve for his failure, and Eve blamed the serpent (Gen. 3:12-13). Men are loathe to take the blame themselves, which is an absolute requirement for Repentance and Restoration.

Thankfully, Israel will repent of this rebellion at the Second Coming, but only after terrible tribulation.

Israel has tried to abrogate her position as a people chosen by God for a particular task. They may bridle and chaff at this fact, but fact it is! Consequently, having resisted it, has resulted in untold heartache and sorrow. As well, a restored Israel, which will take place at a coming glad time, will bring untold Blessing and Glory.

It is impossible for Israel to deny her calling or position in this world, despite her actions. These actions of rebellion must be remedied, even though it is going to take even greater tribulation in the near future (Mat. 24:21-22).

(26) "THEN RELEASED HE BARABBAS UNTO THEM: AND WHEN HE HAD SCOURGED JESUS, HE DELIVERED HIM TO BE CRUCIFIED."

The phrase, *"Then released he Barabbas unto them,"* proclaimed their choice. They desired a robber and a murderer, and they have been robbed and murdered ever since! It is a chilling knowledge to see how this has played out in their national existence from that time unto this.

Until 1948, consequently, for about 1900 years, Jews wandered all over the world in search for a home, and finding none. In country after country they have been persecuted and expelled for no reason than simply being Jews. Perhaps America has provided the safest haven of any nation in their long history. Even now in their own nation of Israel, which is according to the fulfillment of Bible Prophecy, it has been a constant struggle for survival.

And yet, God has promised to bless those who would bless Israel, and which at least has been the cause of some of America's great blessings (Gen. 12:3). Also, in that same verse, the Lord pronounced a curse upon all who would hinder or harm these ancient people, which is the cause of many nations being destroyed. Even though the blame may be laid at the doorstep of many things, still, if the Truth be known, the ill treatment of Jews has brought about the Judgment.

The phrase, *"And when he had scourged Jesus,"* proclaimed the usual preliminary to Crucifixion. It was one of the most cruel forms of punishment ever employed, and sometimes killed the victim before the act of crucifixion could be employed.

The whip used for this gruesome task was not ordinary, but a number of leather thongs loaded with lead or armed with sharp bones and spikes, so that every blow cut deeply into the flesh, causing intense pain.

The victim was stripped of his clothes, and bound to a post, with the whip applied to his bare back. As someone has said, *"To think that the Blessed Son of God was subject to such torture and indignity is indeed a lesson for us written in blood."*

Isaiah prophesied, *"I gave My back to the smiters, and My cheeks to them that plucked*

off the hair: I hid not My face from shame and spitting" (Isa. 50:6).

And then he said, *"And with His stripes we are healed"* (Isa. 53:5).

In reference to that, anyone, as I see it, who would deny that healing is in the Atonement, especially considering the tremendous price paid by Christ, may as well repudiate what He did at Calvary for our sins!

The phrase, *"He delivered Him to be crucified,"* concerns Pilate losing the battle for his own soul, and because he submitted to the demands of these hypocrites.

A few hours before, Jesus was *"fair game"* for the Jews, now He is *"fair game"* for the Romans. Anything they desire to do to Him is lawful, and, consequently, the venomous depravity of the human heart will express itself at Calvary, as no other time and place.

(27) "THEN THE SOLDIERS OF THE GOVERNOR TOOK JESUS INTO THE COMMON HALL, AND GATHERED UNTO HIM THE WHOLE BAND OF SOLDIERS."

This *"common hall"* was the *"praetorium"* which was the open courtyard or judgment hall. It was the residence of the Governor, and in this case Pontius Pilate, as well as the camp headquarters of the Roman Guard.

The *"soldiers"* as here represented, would have no mercy whatsoever on Christ. Inasmuch as whatever they did, and irrespective of what it was, was legal, the brutality of their hearts would quickly become obvious.

The *"whole band of soldiers"* spoken of here, probably represented about 200 men, which was the third part of a *"cohort."*

The Governor's guard summoned their comrades in the barracks to come join in their cruel sport.

(28) "AND THEY STRIPPED HIM, AND PUT ON HIM A SCARLET ROBE."

The phrase, *"And they stripped Him,"* referred to His robe, and not the inner garments. Considering the "scourging" He had just experienced, His back was no doubt cut to pieces, with the robe sticking to the blood, which when taken from Him, no doubt reopened the wounds.

The phrase, *"And put on Him a scarlet robe,"* represented either a worn-out officer's cloak, or else a cast-off garment from the wardrobe of Herod.

Irrespective, it suited their purpose of

mocking Him, having heard that He claimed to be a King. So in their minds He was just a poor deluded, deceived peasant, with visions of grandeur, Who now had these dreams brought to an abrupt conclusion!

They realized not at all that the One they were mocking was actually the Lord of Glory, the Creator of the heavens and the earth, and all therein. However, their guilt, as cruel and obvious as it was, was small in comparison to those who had delivered Him up.

(29) "AND WHEN THEY HAD PLATTED A CROWN OF THORNS, THEY PUT IT UPON HIS HEAD, AND A REED IN HIS RIGHT HAND: AND THEY BOWED THE KNEE BEFORE HIM, AND MOCKED HIM, SAYING, HAIL, KING OF THE JEWS!"

The phrase, "And when they had platted a crown of thorns, they put it upon His head," could have represented a particular type called "victor's thorns," and which grew up to six inches in length. Whatever type of thorn it was, pushed down upon His head, and if penetrating the scalp, would quickly cause swelling.

As well, as "thorns" were a part of the original curse, Christ, as the Second Adam, was now bearing that curse upon Himself, and, as a result, removing it!

The phrase, "And a reed in His right hand," was probably a simple cane placed in His hand, to look like a sceptre.

The phrase, "And they bowed the knee before Him," represented their mocking obeisance.

Little did they realize, "That at the Name of Jesus every knee should bow, of things in Heaven, and things in earth, and things under the earth;

"And that every tongue should confess that Jesus Christ is Lord, to the Glory of God the Father" (Phil. 2:10-11). Therefore, at the coming Great White Throne Judgment, these same soldiers will once again stand before Christ, and once again bow the knee to Him. But this time, it will not be in mocking tone, but, instead, the very opposite!

As well, in a coming day, "All the kindreds of the nations shall worship before Him" (Ps. 22:27).

The phrase, "And mocked Him, saying, Hail, King of the Jews," presents the farce being carried out to its mocking conclusion.

Some think that the soldiers cried to Him, "Ave Rex Judaeorum!" which was an imitation

of the "Ave Imperator!" which was addressed to the Emperor of Rome.

It was all a cruel joke, as they mockingly bowed the knee to this pathetic figure standing before them, Whose Blood was quickly staining the "scarlet robe." He really was the "King of the Jews," but yet of a magnitude such as no king had ever graced, but which one day will be obvious.

(30) "AND THEY SPIT UPON HIM, AND TOOK THE REED, AND SMOTE HIM ON THE HEAD."

The phrase, "And they spit upon Him," proclaims them doing the same as the Religious Leaders of Israel.

The phrase, "And took the reed, and smote Him on the head," undoubtedly caused the thorns to be driven deep into His scalp, which would have caused the head to swell to a disproportionate size.

It was also probably at this time that they pulled the beard from His face, fulfilling Isaiah 50:6. Consequently, "His visage was so marred more than any man, and His form more than the sons of men," fulfilling Isaiah 52:14.

As well, this would totally negate the alleged authenticity of the Catholic "Shroud of Turin," which supposedly was the burial Shroud placed over the face of Christ, thereby showing the imprint of His countenance. It should be obvious that such a disfigured face, as His certainly was, would have left no discernable imprint. Therefore it is a hoax!

The sight of His head swollen grotesquely, and with His beard pulled from His face, with blood and spittle mixed together, must have been horrifying to behold! As stated, at the Crucifixion of Christ, the utter depravity of both the religious and pagan hearts is quickly obvious!

(31) "AND AFTER THAT THEY HAD MOCKED HIM, THEY TOOK THE ROBE OFF FROM HIM, AND PUT HIS OWN RAIMENT ON HIM, AND LED HIM AWAY TO CRUCIFY HIM."

Immediately after the torture inflicted upon Him, Pilate, according to John, made another effort to release Him, thinking that surely the terrible torture and indignities would satisfy the blood lust of the Jews, but he was to be disappointed. Matthew does not mention this, cutting straight through to the Crucifixion.

The phrase, "And after that they had mocked

Him," speaks of these soldiers having vented their torture lust against Christ, and probably warned not to kill Him, now prepare Him for Crucifixion.

The phrase, *"They took the robe off from Him, and put His Own raiment on Him,"* proclaims them fulfilling Prophecy, even though not at all realized.

David had prophesied about a thousand years before, *"They part My garments among them, and cast lots upon My vesture"* (Ps. 22:18).

Had the soldiers not put His *"robe"* back on Him, David's Prophecy could not have been fulfilled, as it was at the Crucifixion site.

The phrase, *"And led Him away to crucify Him,"* represented one of, if not the most cruel and shameful deaths that could ever be devised by evil men.

Crucifixion is supposed to have been invented by Semiramis, Queen of Nimrod, who founded the Babylonian system of mysteries. It was a Roman practice inflicted only upon slaves and the worst criminals.

The victim was placed on the cross, each hand extended to the utmost stretch, and nailed to the wooden cross-bar. The feet were nailed together, and then the cross was lifted and dropped into the hole with a violent thud which disjointed the whole body. The weight of the body hung on nails through the hands and feet. The victim was left on the cross until he died of pain and untold sufferings.

This must have been approximately 9 a.m.

As well, the place of Crucifixion would have been outside the city walls, which would have, as well, fulfilled Prophecy.

The Scripture said, *"The bodies of those beasts, whose blood is brought into the sanctuary by the high priests for sin, are burned without the camp. Wherefore Jesus also, that He might sanctify the people with His Own Blood, suffered without the gate"* (Heb. 13:11-12).

The way He was led to the hill called Golgotha, was probably by a cordon of soldiers. A Centurion riding on horseback would have headed up the company. As well, a man walking directly in front of Jesus, would have constantly proclaimed His sentence. Jesus would have been bearing the Cross, with a small company of soldiers following Him.

(32) "AND AS THEY CAME OUT, THEY FOUND A MAN OF CYRENE, SIMON BY

NAME: HIM THEY COMPELLED TO BEAR HIS CROSS."

The phrase, *"And as they came out,"* referred to going out the city gate, which would lead to the place of Crucifixion.

The phrase, *"They found a man of Cyrene, Simon by name,"* spoke of the father of Alexander and Rufus, who Mark says were well-known Believers (Mk. 15:21; Rom. 16:13).

"Cyrene" was a province of Libya in North Africa. It was about eleven miles inward from the Mediterranean. There is some small evidence that Simon may have been a black man. If so, he would have represented his race in being the very first one to lend a helping hand to Christ.

Our black brothers and sisters have borne many a burden, many of them unjust, in the advancement of civilization. However, if, in Truth, Simon was a member of this particular race, the greatest and most noble burden ever borne by a human being in all the annals of human history, was this burden of the Cross borne for Christ by Simon of Cyrene. Tradition says that he became a devout follower of Christ.

The phrase, *"Him they compelled to bear His Cross,"* does not mean that they had difficulty in getting him to do it, but rather that they had the power to force him, or anyone else for that matter, to do whatever they desired.

This *"Cross"* was probably the ordinary Latin cross, which was shaped like a *"T."*

Even though Jesus could have been made to carry the entire Cross (and later Simon), most probably it was the *"patibulum,"* or the cross-bar which He carried. The manner of Crucifixion was carried out in one of two ways. It was as we have just mentioned in Commentary on verse 31, or as follows:

The condemned man was stripped naked, laid on the ground with the cross-beam under his shoulders, and his arms or his hands tied or nailed (Jn. 20:25) to it. (In Jesus' case, His hands were nailed.)

This cross-bar was then lifted and secured to the upright post, so that the victim's feet, which were then tied or nailed (in His place, nailed), were just clear of the ground, not high up as so often depicted.

The main weight of the body was usually borne by a projecting peg, astride which the victim sat. There the condemned man, and in the case of Christ, His wounds open and bleeding, he was left to die of hunger and exhaustion.

Death was sometimes hastened by the breaking of the legs, as in the case of the two thieves, but not done in our Lord's case, because He was already dead. However, a spear was thrust into His side to make sure of death, so that the body could be removed, as the Jews demanded, before the Sabbath (Jn. 19:31).

The method of Crucifixion seems to have varied in different parts of the Roman Empire. Secular writers of the time shrink from giving detailed accounts of this most cruel and degrading forms of punishment. However, new light has been thrown on the subject by archaeological work in Israel.

In the Summer of 1968, a team of archaeologists discovered four Jewish tombs near Jerusalem, with one containing the bones of a young crucified man, dating from probably between A.D. 7 and A.D. 66, judging from Herodian pottery found there. The name, "Jehohanan," is inscribed. Thorough research was made into the causes and nature of his death, and may throw considerable light on our Lord's form of death.

In this case, the young man's arms (not his hands) were nailed to the patibulum, the cross-beam, which might indicate that Luke 24:39; John 20:20, 25, 27, should be translated *"arms."* (Actually, most believe that the nails were driven into the wrists of Christ, instead of His palms which would have quickly been torn through.)

The weight of the body was probably borne by a plank nailed to the upright beam, as a support for the buttocks. The legs had been bent at the knees and twisted back so that the calves were parallel to the cross-bar, with the ankles under the buttocks. One iron nail had been driven through both his heels together, with his right foot above the left.

A fragment shows that the cross was of olive wood. His legs had both been broken, presumably by a forcible blow, like those of Jesus' two companions in John 19:32.

If Jesus died in this fashion, then His legs were not fully extended as in traditional Christian art. In that case, His contorted leg muscles would then have probably caused severe pain with spasmodic contractions and rigid cramps. This could have contributed to the shortened

time of His death in six hours or less, hastened doubtless by the earlier scourging.

Contemporary writers describe it as a most painful form of death. The Gospels, however, give no detailed description of our Lord's physical sufferings, but simply and reverently say, *"They crucified Him."*

According to Matthew 27:34, our Lord refused any form of alleviation for His sufferings, doubtless that He might preserve clarity of mind to the end, in doing His Father's Will. Hence the fact that He was able to comfort the dying thief, and pronounce the rest of the seven wonderful words from the Cross.

(For a detailed account of what His death may have been like, please see our Commentary on Isaiah 53.)

The New Testament writers' interest in the Cross is neither archaeological nor historical, but Christological. They are concerned with the eternal, spiritual significance of what happened once for all in the death of Jesus Christ, the Son of God, on the Cross. Theologically, the word, *"Cross,"* was used as a summary description of the Gospel of Salvation, that Jesus Christ *"Died for our sins."* So the *"Preaching of the Gospel"* is *"The Word of the Cross," "The preaching of Christ crucified"* (I Cor. 1:17). So the Apostle glories *"In the Cross of our Lord Jesus Christ,"* and speaks of suffering persecution *"For the Cross of Christ."* Clearly the word, *"Cross,"* here stands for the whole glad announcement of our Redemption through the Atoning Death of Jesus Christ.

"The Word of the Cross" is also *"The Word of Reconciliation"* (II Cor. 5:19). This theme emerges clearly in the Epistles to the Ephesians and Colossians. It is *"Through the Cross"* that God has reconciled Jews and Gentiles, abolishing the middle wall of partition, the Law of Commandments (Eph. 2:14-16). It is *"By the Blood of His Cross,"* that God has made peace, in reconciling *"All things unto Himself"* (Col. 1:20).

This reconciliation is at once personal and spiritual. It comes because Christ has set aside the bond which stood against us with its legal demands, *"Nailing it to His Cross"* (Col. 2:14). Consequently, all, both Jew and Gentile, may come alike, with Salvation offered to all who believe (Jn. 3:16).

The Cross in the New Testament is a symbol of shame and humiliation, as well as of God's

Wisdom and Glory revealed through it (I Cor. 1:24). Rome used it not only as an instrument of torture and execution, but also as a shameful execution of torture reserved for the worst and lowest. To the Jews it was a sign of being *"accursed"* (Deut. 21:23; Gal. 3:13).

This was the death Jesus died, and for which the crowd clamored. He *"Endured the Cross, despising the shame"* (Heb. 12:2). The lowest rung in the ladder of our Lord's humiliation was that He endured *"Even death on a Cross"* (Phil. 2:8). For this reason it was a *"stumbling-block"* to the Jews (I Cor. 1:23; Gal. 5:11), inasmuch as the Jews believed, which was true, that all who died on a cross were cursed by God (Deut. 21:22-23). (Jesus was cursed by God, but not for His sins, but for our sins, thereby, bearing the sin of the world, and paying the price for lost humanity.)

The shameful spectacle of a victim carrying a patibulum (cross-bar) was so familiar to His hearers that Jesus three times spoke of the road of discipleship as that of cross-bearing (Mat. 10:38; Mk. 8:34; Lk. 14:27).

Furthermore, the Cross is the symbol of our union with Christ, not simply in virtue of our following His example, but in virtue of what He has done for us and in us. In His substitutionary death for us on the Cross, we died *"In Him"* (II Cor. 5:14), and *"Our old man is crucified with Him,"* that by His indwelling Spirit we might walk in newness of life (Rom. 6:4; Gal. 2:20; 5:24; 6:14), abiding *"In Him."*

(Information on the Cross was derived from the Bible Dictionary.)

(33) "AND WHEN THEY WERE COME UNTO A PLACE CALLED GOLGOTHA, THAT IS TO SAY, A PLACE OF A SKULL,"

The phrase, *"And when they were come unto a place called Golgotha,"* means the place of a skull. Tradition says that Adam was buried here, and that his skull was found. Origin claimed this to be so, but other than that no evidence exists.

Inasmuch as this is where Jesus was crucified, it is said that it was congruous that the First Adam and the Second Adam should meet here in death, the latter winning the victory, where the former showed his defeat.

As well, it is said to have derived its name because of its skull-like appearance.

There are two places in Jerusalem claimed to be the correct site. The first one is the Church

of the Holy Sepulchre, and of Catholic origin, with the other being Gordon's Calvary, with the tomb nearby known as the Garden Tomb.

All that is known from the Scripture is that the correct site was outside Jerusalem, fairly conspicuous, probably not far from a city gate and a highway, and that a Garden containing a tomb lay nearby. As stated, this fits the description of Gordon's Calvary, and is accepted by most Protestants.

The phrase, *"That is to say, a place of a skull,"* represented its description.

On one of our trips to Israel, having flown most of the night, we arrived in Tel Aviv in the early afternoon. Some of our party boarded a bus, while Frances and I were taken by car to Jerusalem.

We arrived at about 5 p.m., when traffic was at its heaviest. Being extremely tired, I was not noticing too much about me, when the car stopped because of the traffic, sitting there for a few moments. I looked up, glancing out the right window, and to my amazement, stared at Calvary.

I had not realized where we were in Jerusalem, least of all that we were near the place where Jesus died for lost humanity. As many know, there is a city bus station located at the foot of Golgotha.

I cannot begin to relate as to exactly how I felt as I sat there for a few moments staring at this place that meant so much to me personally, and to the entirety of the world. For it was here that Jesus paid the price for the Salvation of man, the greatest act of love that the mind of man could ever begin to imagine.

As I looked at the place, for a few moments I felt several sensations that are difficult to describe. A part of me was upset over the din and racket caused by the bus station, with buses coming and going.

But then it was as if the Lord spoke to me, and which I believe He did! If, in Truth, it was the Lord and not merely my imagination, He spoke to my heart, saying, *"This bus station, along with all its activity, is not a reproach to Me, even though men may have intended for it to be. In one sense, it represents the activity of life, which I came to purchase. The place of My Death should not be a shrine, because in My Death I brought Life."*

(34) "THEY GAVE HIM VINEGAR TO

DRINK MINGLED WITH GALL: AND WHEN HE HAD TASTED THEREOF, HE WOULD NOT DRINK."

The phrase, *"They gave Him vinegar to drink mingled with gall,"* indicates the custom of giving a stupefying potion to an intoxicate which helped alleviate sufferings (Prov. 31:6). But Christ refused it so as to suffer the full penalty for sin, sober, and in His right mind.

It seems from the Scripture, that this drink was offered five times to the Lord: once certainly in mockery (Lk. 23:36), once in curiosity (vs. 48), and it may be hoped on the other three occasions, in pity.

The five occasions were: on the way to Calvary (Mk. 15:23; on arrival there (Mat. 27:33); and later on, after Crucifixion by the soldiers — probably at their own meal (Lk. 23:36); later still (Mat. 27:48); and for the last and fifth time in response to the Lord's cry (Jn. 19:29).

The phrase, *"And when He had tasted thereof, He would not drink,"* proclaims it being refused for several reasons.

As stated, He must suffer the full brunt of the penalty of sin, and, as well, His mind must be clear, inasmuch as He would shortly deal with the dying thief who was being crucified by His side (Lk. 23:43).

(35) "AND THEY CRUCIFIED HIM, AND PARTED HIS GARMENTS, CASTING LOTS: THAT IT MIGHT BE FULFILLED WHICH WAS SPOKEN BY THE PROPHET, THEY PARTED MY GARMENTS AMONG THEM, AND UPON MY VESTURE DID THEY CAST LOTS."

The phrase, *"And they crucified Him,"* is portrayed in simple words by the Holy Spirit. No effort is made to explain the suffering or its degree, nor to speak of the terrible humiliation of this form of death. The mere relating of the happenings, without giving any detail, possibly says more than if fully explained. The depths of the suffering can only be imagined, and because it far transcends that which normally happened. The death of Christ was totally unlike the death of any person who had ever died. In effect, Christ died by laying down His Own Life, after being smitten by His Own Father. There is no way that one can even begin to comprehend the agony of such a time. Perhaps Psalm 22, which portrays this hideous action, is meant to serve by the Holy Spirit, as its pure description.

NOTES

What more can be said! To fully describe it would sully its sacred moment. As well, to become lost in the *"manner"* of death, is not the intention of the Holy Spirit, but, rather, that we would ever remember the *"reason"* for His Death.

The phrase, *"And parted His garments, casting lots,"* spoke of the clothes of the condemned, which were divided among the soldiers. This was their extra *"pay"* for serving this ghastly duty.

Their *"casting lots"* was simply as one presently would *"draw straws."* The winner, at least in this case, would obtain the seamless robe worn by Christ. It was no doubt greatly stained with His Blood. Little did this soldier realize what he held in his hands!

The phrase, *"That it might be fulfilled which was spoken by the Prophet,"* pertained to David, and the 22nd Psalm.

The phrase, *"They parted My garments among them, and upon My vesture did they cast lots,"* is derived from Psalm 22:18.

Five Scriptures were quoted from Psalm 22 in the New Testament:

1. My God, My God, why hast Thou forsaken Me? (Mat. 27:46; Mk. 15:34).

2. He trusted on the Lord that He would deliver Him (Mat. 27:43; Mk. 15:29-30; Lk. 23:35).

3. They pierced My hands (Jn. 19:37).

4. They parted My garments (Mat. 27:35; Mk. 15:24; Lk. 23:34; Jn. 19:24).

5. I will declare Thy Name unto My brethren (Heb. 2:12).

I wonder how much David understood of the Prophecy given to him by the Holy Spirit, and concerning the Crucifixion of Christ?

How he must have poured over these words after they were written down, and how his heart must have broken. Quite possibly, and more than likely, the Holy Spirit gave him the full meaning of these Passages, with him understanding to a greater degree that which would befall the *"Son of David."*

(36) "AND SITTING DOWN THEY WATCHED HIM THERE;"

Their *"watching Him,"* was for reason.

At times, friends would come to remove the victim from the cross, if not carefully attended by the guards. Sometimes it took days for the victim to die, with the soldiers, at times, hastening the process by the breaking of the victim's legs. Actually, it would be done at this time, but not to Jesus, as He had already expired.

NOTES

Josephus, the Jewish Historian, relates how he took down three criminals from crosses, one of whom completely recovered, though the others died from their injuries.

Consequently, if the soldiers had not *"watched Him there,"* the Jews, no doubt, would have claimed that His friends spirited Him away, without Him seeing death. However, Rome could not be accused of a laxity of duty in this case!

Little did they realize Who they were watching! I cannot believe that they did not notice something different, much different about Him! I think the 54th verse bears this out, when the Centurion in charge said at the death of Christ, *"Truly this was the Son of God."*

(37) "AND SET UP OVER HIS HEAD HIS ACCUSATION WRITTEN, THIS IS JESUS THE KING OF THE JEWS."

The phrase, *"And set up over His head,"* pertained to a wooden tablet smeared with gypsum, which on it was written in black letters the charge on which the prisoner was condemned. This had either been hung about His neck, or held by a man for all to see, who walked in front of Him on the way to the Crucifixion.

When fastened to the top of the upright part of the Cross, it formed the part which protruded above His head.

The phrase, *"His accusation written,"* is said to have been written in three languages, Hebrew, Greek, and Latin; hence the three inscriptions and translations recorded in the Gospels.

These several superscriptions display accuracy and not, as some think, discrepancy; for the amount of space required for the writing in each language would be the same though the translation into other languages would be necessarily different.

The phrase, *"THIS IS JESUS THE KING OF THE JEWS,"* had been prepared by Pilate (Jn. 19:19, 22). It was meant to be offensive to the Jews, without thinking of Christ, but, in reality, proclaimed exactly Who and What He was.

Someone said that the three languages in which this inscription was written, gathered up the results of the religious, social, and intellectual preparation for Christ. And, as well, in each, witness was given to His office.

The Catholic Church in Rome claims to have a supposed fragment of this title, and is preserved in the Church of the Holy Cross. It

is declared by a papal bull to be authentic. However, in this case, infallibility has rather overstepped its limits. In other words, the claim is false!

(38) "THEN WERE THERE TWO THIEVES CRUCIFIED WITH HIM, ONE ON THE RIGHT HAND, AND ANOTHER ON THE LEFT."

The phrase, *"Then were there two thieves crucified with Him,"* was again a fulfillment of Bible Prophecy. The Holy Spirit through Isaiah gave the words, *"And He was numbered with the transgressors"* (Isa. 53:12). Only Luke mentions the Repentance of one of the thieves.

At this time, many were being crucified in Jerusalem, and because of insurrection carried out against Rome. As well, many criminals, as these thieves, were quickly dispatched and executed without the benefit of much of a trial, if any! Consequently, there may have been several crucified other than the two here mentioned.

The phrase, *"One on the right hand, and another on the left,"* is seen by Augustine as having a spiritual significance.

"The very Cross," he said, *"was the tribunal of Christ; for the Judge was placed in the middle; one thief, who believed, was saved; the other, who reviled, was condemned; which signified Christ as the Judge of all humanity."*

(39) "AND THEY THAT PASSED BY REVILED HIM, WAGGING THEIR HEADS."

The phrase, *"And they that passed by reviled Him,"* spoke of the Religious Leaders of Israel who came to mock a dying man. The heartless cruelty of these people knew no bounds! Even if one was a guilty criminal, such heartless response would be beyond contempt. But inasmuch as this was the Son of the Living God, and One Who had never done anything but good, such an act depicted the depraved hearts of those who had blasphemed the Holy Spirit, and, consequently, who were beyond Salvation.

The phrase, *"Wagging their heads,"* was, again, the fulfillment of Bible Prophecy. It is the words of David, *"All they that see Me laugh Me to scorn: they shoot out the lip, they shake the head"* (Ps. 22:7).

David also wrote, *"I became also a reproach unto them: when they looked upon Me they shaked their heads"* (Ps. 109:25).

(40) "AND SAYING, THOU THAT DESTROYEST THE TEMPLE, AND BUILDEST IT IN THREE DAYS, SAVE THYSELF. IF

THOU BE THE SON OF GOD, COME DOWN FROM THE CROSS."

The phrase, *"And saying, Thou that destroyest the Temple,"* is a statement that Jesus never made. He had said, *"Destroy this Temple, and in three days I will raise it up,"* which referred to His Own Body, with Him no doubt pointing to Himself at the same time. He was speaking of what the Jews would do to Him regarding the Crucifixion. It had nothing to do with the Temple structure on Mt. Zion. They perverted His Words as men are wont to do!

The phrase, *"And buildest it in three days,"* once again, were words He never said. He did say He would raise up His Body in the Resurrection, but was referring not at all to the Temple structure (Jn. 2:19-22).

The words, *"Save Thyself,"* represented a demand which He would not do. He did not come to *"save Himself,"* but rather to save others.

The phrase, *"If Thou be the Son of God,"* proclaims that there was absolutely no doubt as to What and Who He claimed to be. They questioned this claim to the point of total denial, while the Centurion on the Cross, a Pagan, confessed the opposite, *"Truly this was the Son of God"* (vs. 54).

Their outright blasphemy is amazing! They knew of His miracles, and probably had observed some of them being performed. Had they taken the time to check the genealogy in the Temple, they would have known that His family lineage was perfect.

As well, had they bothered to check the Scriptures, they would have seen that He fulfilled every Prophecy concerning the coming Messiah. Also, there was absolutely nothing in the realm of wrongdoing they could point to which He had done, other than some of their own silly rules which He had broken, and which they had made up themselves, which had no validity in the Word of God. So, their action was inexcusable!

The phrase, *"Come down from the Cross,"* is a striking taunt!

There is no way to know what went through His mind when the Religious Leaders of Israel were throwing this in His teeth. Was there a temptation to do what they said?

No! However, if the Prophets who had lived through the ages would have heard the mockings of these Religious Leaders, and had witnessed

that moment, they would have shouted, *"No! Don't come down from the Cross."*

Abel would have shouted, *"If You do, Faith in my Sacrifice was in vain!"*

Noah would have shouted, *"The preparing of the Ark was a futile gesture!"*

Abraham would have shouted, *"If You come down from that Cross, I will never see that city foursquare!"*

Isaac would have shouted, *"If You come down from the Cross, the statement, 'The God of Abraham, Isaac and Jacob,' is in vain!"*

Jacob would have shouted, *"Your changing of my life from Jacob, the schemer, to Israel, Prince with God, was all in vain!"*

The list is endless concerning the sainted multitudes, who, through the ages, placed their Faith and Trust in that One Who was to come. If He did not pay the price, the price could not be paid, because man was helpless to pay it!

So, if they had witnessed that moment, all would have shouted with voices that sounded like thunder, and would have echoed through the ages, *"Don't come down from that Cross!"*

As well, unborn millions, if such a thing could be, would have shouted across the recesses of time, and concerning the Salvation of their souls, *"Don't come down from that Cross!"*

At this juncture, as the reader, I must add my feeble voice to those sainted millions as well, but yet with the realization that this is an acclamation that I nor others will ever have to make. Even though He had the power to do what they taunted a million times over, instead He suffered the insults of those who should have been praising Him, and died for the sins of the world, theirs included!

Therefore, the entirety of the world can sing, if they so desire:

"Amazing Grace how sweet the sound,
"That saved a wretch like me.
"I once was lost, but now I'm found,
"I was blind, but now I see."

(41) "LIKEWISE ALSO THE CHIEF PRIESTS MOCKING HIM, WITH THE SCRIBES AND ELDERS, SAID,"

The two words, *"Likewise also,"* present the Church of that day. It was not a pretty picture.

The phrase, *"The Chief Priests mocking Him,"* represented in their office, whether they knew it or not, the very types of His Person. Actually, every single Priest in the Aaronic

Priesthood from the time of Moses, had been a type of Christ. As well, these *"Chief Priests"* officiated over the twenty-four courses, which divided each year into twenty-four parts of fifteen days each, which pertained to the Sacrifices, which were also types of Christ. (The Jews had only 360 days in their calendar year.)

Even though these individuals were constantly involved in things pertaining to God, the simple fact is they did not know God. Had they known God, they would have known His Son.

The phrase, *"With the Scribes and Elders, said,"* fills out the compliment which included the entirety of the Sanhedrin. Therefore, every group of Religious Leaders mocked Him as He died on the Cross. As I have said many times, please allow me to say it again:

There is no evil such as religious evil. It transcends all other efforts of Satan to steal, kill and destroy. Religion has been the cause of almost all the bloodshed in the world. It is Satan's greatest trump card! Inasmuch as he is a religious being himself, he is a master of subverting the True Plan of God, as given in the Word of God, thereby causing billions to be eternally lost.

Even as I dictate these words, religion dominates almost all the world, with all of its participants lost and undone without God. This includes the followers of Islam, Buddhism, Hinduism, Shintoism, Confucianism, Mormonism, along with almost all of Catholicism. As well, it includes most of that which calls itself *"Christian!"*

There is no way to God except through Jesus Christ. He Himself said, *"I am the Door: by Me if any man enter in, he shall be saved, and shall go in and out, and find pasture."*

He then said, and concerning the religions of the world. *"The thief cometh not, but for to steal, and to kill, and to destroy: I am come that they might have life, and that they might have it more abundantly"* (Jn. 10:9-10).

These very *"Priests, Scribes, and Elders,"* who were supposed to represent God, in fact represented Him not at all, and, therefore, ultimately died lost without God.

(42) "HE SAVED OTHERS; HIMSELF HE CANNOT SAVE. IF HE BE THE KING OF ISRAEL, LET HIM NOW COME DOWN FROM THE CROSS, AND WE WILL BELIEVE HIM."

The phrase, *"He saved others,"* was totally true, even though they meant it as a mockery.

They were aware that He had raised Lazarus and others from the dead. They were aware that He had changed the lives of countless numbers in His earthly Ministry. They were aware of all His miracles, but still would not believe.

The word, *"others,"* means that they would not allow themselves to be included in that group.

The phrase, *"Himself He cannot save,"* was in a sense true, but yet not in the way they meant it.

If they had said, "Himself He would not save," their statement would have been one-hundred percent true. In Truth, He could have saved Himself, but had He done so, He could not have saved others, which was the very reason for which He came.

If one is to notice, their taunts are blasphemous to say the least, and actually represent individuals who have blasphemed the Holy Spirit.

There is little evidence that the Romans engaged in such blasphemy. It remained for the Church of that day to stoop to such a level of cruelty.

The phrase, *"If He be the King of Israel,"* is said with a sneering taunt, because in their minds if He really was a King, what was He doing on the Cross?

Even though they were so sure of their position, still, their position had no assurance. They were so jaded and deceived, that they did not realize their actions of taunting a dying man, even the Son of God, were so ungodly. Their thinking was so skewed, which religion will do to a person, that right was wrong, and wrong was right! Millions, if not billions, fall into the same category at present!

The phrase, *"Let Him now come down from the Cross, and we will believe Him,"* is an addition to the first taunt.

At first, they just taunted Him to *"Come down from the Cross,"* while now, they claim that if He does so, *"They will believe Him."* However, blasphemers are also liars!

In reply to this taunt, which, in effect, had nothing to do with its claim, He would do even greater than they suggested. He would rise from the dead on the third day, which was far and away greater than what they suggested. And yet they still would not believe.

Men find it easy to explain away that which is <u>of</u> God, and, as well, to believe that which is <u>not</u> of God.

(43) "HE TRUSTED IN GOD; LET HIM DELIVER HIM NOW, IF HE WILL HAVE HIM: FOR HE SAID, I AM THE SON OF GOD."

The phrase, *"He trusted in God,"* is another direct fulfillment of Bible Prophecy.

David had prophesied about a thousand years before that these reprobates would say these very words. The Holy Spirit through Him, and about them said, *"He trusted on the Lord that He would deliver Him: let Him deliver Him, seeing He delighted in Him"* (Ps. 22:8).

Even though these Religious Leaders claimed to be the keepers of the Word of God, in Truth, they did not know the Word of God. They had some small head knowledge of its content, but no Spirit knowledge whatsoever! They had no idea as they threw these words in His teeth, that they were directly fulfilling that which the Holy Spirit had predicted of them so long before. As well, even at the present, Religious Leaders mock the Baptism in the Holy Spirit with the evidence of speaking with other tongues, not realizing they are fulfilling Bible Prophecy. Paul said, *"In the Law it is Written, with men of other tongues and other lips will I speak unto this people; and yet for all that will they not hear Me, saith the Lord"* (I Cor. 14:21).

The phrase, *"Let Him deliver Him now, if He will have Him,"* shows a complete misunderstanding of Who Christ was, and Who God the Father was, for that matter! Had they read and believed Isaiah 53, they would have known Who Jesus was, and what He was doing.

As well, they would have known that not only would God not deliver Him, but, in effect, would smite Him (Isa. 53:4).

However, God would not smite Him because of His sins, for He had none! He would smite Him for our sins, with Him, consequently, taking our place.

If God had delivered Him from the Cross, Jesus could not have delivered us from our sins.

To be sure, Jehovah would *"have Him,"* and grandly so, for He had said, *"This is My Beloved Son, in Whom I am well pleased"* (Mat. 3:17).

As well, the Holy Spirit would say through Paul, *"Wherefore God also hath highly exalted Him, and given Him a Name which is above every name"* (Phil. 2:9).

Yes, they would not have Him, but God, His Father, certainly would.

As well, multiple tens of millions would *"have*

Him," and I, and with all the strength I have, will shout it now and forever, *"I will have Him."*

The fact that so many would *"have Him,"* is no wonder at all! The wonder is that He would have us!

The phrase, *"For He said, I am the Son of God,"* represents exactly what He said!

They are implying that if He was what He pretended to be, He would not now be dying on the Cross.

Yes, He did say, *"I am the Son of God"* (Mk. 14:62), but His Father, and as we have stated, said it as well! So do I, and so have, and so do, billions of others.

(44) "THE THIEVES ALSO, WHICH WERE CRUCIFIED WITH HIM, CAST THE SAME IN HIS TEETH."

The phrase, *"The thieves also, which were crucified with Him,"* pertains, at least at this time, to all of them, ever how many there were.

More than likely, the meaning is that all of them joined in with their mockery, but one of them, even as Luke records, upon observing the demeanor and meekness of Christ, repented and was instantly granted Eternal Life (Lk. 23:39-43).

The phrase, *"Cast the same in His teeth,"* means that they picked up the mocking, taunting insults of the Religious Leaders.

(45) "NOW FROM THE SIXTH HOUR THERE WAS DARKNESS OVER ALL THE LAND UNTO THE NINTH HOUR."

The phrase, *"Now from the sixth hour,"* represented 12 o'clock noon. Jesus was crucified at about 9 a.m., which was the time of the morning Sacrifice, and died at 3 p.m., which was the time of the evening Sacrifice. Consequently, He stayed on the Cross about six hours.

The phrase, *"There was darkness over all the land unto the ninth hour,"* did not speak of an ordinary eclipse, for then the moon was full, it being the Passover time. Nor did it have any connection with the subsequent earthquake (vs. 51).

In Truth, the *"darkness"* was brought on by God, in that He could not look upon His Son as He bore the sin of the world.

As well, God would hide this shameful scene from the mocking eyes of the Religious Leaders of Israel, as well as all others!

Whether this darkness extended beyond Judaea is not known for certain, however, there is some small evidence that it did.

Some of the ancient Fathers claimed it to have been universal.

Tertullian claims that a notice of this darkness was found in the archives of Rome.

"It is related," Dionysius, the Areopagite, said, "either the God of nature is suffering, or the machinery of the world is being dissolved."

At this time, Jesus suffered the darkness which shrouded Him, that you and I, and all who would believe for that matter, would not have to suffer eternal darkness.

Not only was the "darkness" a shroud brought on by God in order that He would not have to look at His sin-laden Son, but, as well, represented all the sin, corruption, sickness, bondage, and iniquity of Satan's kingdom. Consequently, what Jesus did not only defeated Satan, but, more importantly, satisfied the claims of heavenly justice. Sin had to be paid for, and Jesus was the only One Who could do it.

Even though the "darkness" filled the land, which, in its supernatural element was a striking sign which should have been obvious to all, still, the 49th verse proclaims these Religious Leaders continuing to mock. To explain the depths of the unbelief of these reprobates is impossible!

(46) "AND ABOUT THE NINTH HOUR JESUS CRIED WITH A LOUD VOICE, SAYING, ELI, ELI, LAMA SABACHTHA-NI? THAT IS TO SAY, MY GOD, MY GOD, WHY HAST THOU FORSAKEN ME?"

The phrase, "And about the ninth hour," records the hour of His death, and, as stated, the time of the evening Sacrifice.

The phrase, "Jesus cried with a loud voice," proclaims the vitality of His Life, and despite His mangled form, meaning that in His perfect, pure, and stainless Life and Body, man could not have killed Him. For Him to die, He had to lay down His Life freely (Jn. 10:17-18).

The question, "Saying, Eli, Eli, Lama Sabachtha-ni?", represents the language as Aramaic, which is what was commonly used by the Lord.

The question, "That is to say, My God, My God, why hast Thou forsaken Me?", speaks of the darkness, and that God, His Father, had turned His back on Him, and because He was bearing the sin of the world.

The Prophet Habakkuk had said about 650 years before, "Thou art of purer eyes than to

NOTES

behold evil, and canst not look on iniquity" (Hab. 1:13). (The Hebrew language refers that God does materially and spiritually see sin and iniquity, and because such is obvious; however, the meaning is that He cannot countenance such.) Inasmuch as Jesus was now being "made to be sin for us," even though He "knew no sin," God could no longer look upon Him, at least at this particular time (II Cor. 5:21).

The sufferings of Christ on the Cross are immeasurable to human intelligence; but the abyss of horror into which He ascended under the Wrath of God was far more terrible and inscrutable. The floods lifted up their voices; and none can fathom His suffering at the bottom of that abyss into which He descended in order to save men from going there.

Where sin had brought man, love brought Him; that His apprehension of being cut off from, and forsaken by, God, that is, His consciousness of hell and its horror, was infinitely beyond that of ordinary men. No one but He could fully feel or fathom such a doom.

It is a wonderful fact that the One Righteous Man Who ever lived should, at the close of His Life of perfect obedience and moral perfection, have declared that He was forsaken of God. But here Faith triumphed, for though forsaken on the Cross and shut up in the pit, He still trusted.

Made to be sin, and that in the Presence of God, with no veil to hide its defilement, and no mercy to cover or forgive it, He suffered, and believed, and triumphed as no other could have done.

The "Fathers" in their distress cried, and were delivered, but He cried in vain to God, Who forsook Him though He trusted Him. In that He took the penalty of sin, which, in effect, we should have taken, guaranteed, by His being forsaken, that we would not be forsaken!

The use of the Name or Title, "God," at this time, and especially that it was said twice, denoted this rupture. This designation points to God as the Creator and Maker of all things, but denotes no relationship whatsoever as does "Lord," or "Father."

This question as to why God had forsaken Him, was not asked in a sense of not knowing, but rather in a sense of acknowledging the act. For three hours the land was shrouded in darkness, which constituted Jesus fulfilling all the Levitical Offerings. He would bear the sin of the world, as the lambs through the centuries as innocent victims had suffered the Judgment of God in place of the sinner. Consequently, for this three hours, God forsook Him!

As well, what this meant, and as we have stated, man will never fully know.

(47) "SOME OF THEM THAT STOOD THERE, WHEN THEY HEARD THAT, SAID, THIS MAN CALLETH FOR ELIAS."

The phrase, *"Some of them that stood there,"* represents the Jews. The Romans would not have answered accordingly, because they would have had no knowledge of Elijah.

The phrase, *"When they heard that,"* refers to what Jesus said on the Cross.

The phrase, *"Said, This Man calleth for Elias,"* referred to the Prophet Elijah.

As Jesus *"Cried with a loud voice,"* the words, *"Eli, Eli,"* there is no reason they should have misunderstood what He said, inasmuch as it was the language they spoke.

Quite possibly they spoke of Elijah as they did because he had been translated by a chariot of fire, and maybe they were thinking that Christ was thinking that such would happen to Him, and maybe even Elijah would be the instrument in this rescue.

If, in fact, this was their thought, it only shows how little they knew and understood the Word of God.

As well, the word, *"Man,"* was inserted by the translators, and was not in the original, therefore, they alluded to Jesus as *"This,"* and with great contempt!

(48) "AND STRAIGHTWAY ONE OF THEM RAN, AND TOOK A SPONGE, AND FILLED IT WITH VINEGAR, AND PUT IT ON A REED, AND GAVE HIM TO DRINK."

The phrase, *"And straightway one of them ran, and took a sponge,"* possibly shows a small act of mercy shown by at least *"one"* of them.

The phrase, *"And filled it with vinegar,"* was a stupefying intoxicant that would deaden the senses.

The phrase, *"And put it on a reed, and gave Him to drink,"* was in response to His *"I thirst,"* as recorded by John. He *"received the vinegar"* according to John, which probably meant that some of it touched His lips, and then He died (Jn. 19:28-30). John called the *"reed"* a stalk of *"hyssop."* This is interesting inasmuch as hyssop was used to apply the blood to the doorposts

of the houses in Egypt when Israel was delivered (Ex. 12:22-23).

(Hyssop was a small bushy plant, which stalks produced a healthy growth of leaves which had a pungent taste.)

So, when the reed of hyssop touched His lips, due to the wounds on His face, especially considering the pulling out of His beard, blood must have been oozing from the wounds, and, thereby, stained the hyssop, which fulfilled the symbol of the hyssop dipped in the blood of the basin and applied to the doorposts. Now it is applied by Faith to our hearts.

(49) "THE REST SAID, LET BE, LET US SEE WHETHER ELIAS WILL COME TO SAVE HIM."

The phrase, *"The rest said,"* refers to all the others other than the *"one"* who had offered the vinegar.

The phrase, *"Let be, let us see whether Elias will come to save Him,"* represents the rest addressing the one who had offered the drink, meaning, in effect, *"Leave Him alone, and let's see if Elijah will come to save Him."* The words were said in mockery!

As well, Mark said that the one who offered the vinegar made this statement, with Matthew saying that all joined in.

Consequently, we do not know if that which the *"one"* did was an act of mercy or derision. Hopefully it was mercy, but probably it was derision.

(50) "JESUS, WHEN HE HAD CRIED AGAIN WITH A LOUD VOICE, YIELDED UP THE GHOST."

The Name, *"Jesus,"* is here used, in that it means *"Saviour,"* and, consequently, the greatest Name of all! Even though He was *"Jehovah-Jirah,"* and, *"Jehovah-Shalom,"* as well as all the other Names given to Him in the Old Testament, still, it was as the *"Saviour,"* hence *"Jesus,"* that He died. In that Name all the other Names were fulfilled.

The phrase, *"When He had cried again with a loud voice,"* represents the second time He cried loudly. It was probably the words, *"Into Thy Hands I commend My Spirit"* (Lk. 23:46), followed by *"It is finished,"* which were His last words (Jn. 19:30).

As well, the loud cry at the last moment proved that He laid down His Life voluntarily, and that no man took it from Him (Jn. 10:17-18).

Consequently, He did not die from His wounds, or from physical exhaustion, but from determined purpose.

The phrase, *"Yielded up the ghost,"* means that He *"dismissed His Spirit."*

We know that His heart broke, because the spear which pierced His side after His death, producing blood and water, proves this fact (Jn. 19:33-34). However, it is not known if the breaking of His heart was what actually caused His death. If it did, which was most likely the case, He willed it, and brought it about by the last agonizing cry, *"It is finished!"*

As we have stated, His agonizing but triumphant shout *"Finished,"* showed that His death was not due to exhaustion, but to self-surrender. It was not suicide, for He did not *"take"* His Life as a man does who cannot restore it, but He laid it down of Himself because He had power to take it again, and in so doing perfected a Sacrifice for the expiation of man's guilt.

There were actually seven sayings on the Cross as recorded in the four Gospels:

1. My God, My God, why has Thou forsaken Me (Mat. 27:46; Mk. 15:34; Ps. 22:1).

2. Father, forgive them; for they know not what they do (Lk. 23:34).

3. Verily, I say unto thee, to day shalt thou be with Me in Paradise (Lk. 23:43).

4. Father, into Thy Hands I commend My Spirit (Lk. 23:46).

5. Woman, behold thy Son . . . Behold thy mother (Jn. 19:26-27).

6. I thirst (Jn. 19:28).

7. It is finished (Jn. 19:30).

As *"Seven"* is God's number of perfection, likewise, His *"Seven sayings on the Cross,"* proclaimed His perfect reaction.

1. He reacted to God forsaking Him by admitting that it had to be.

2. He reacted to sinners by asking forgiveness for them.

3. He reacted to the petition of the thief by giving him Salvation.

4. He reacted to death by commending His Spirit to the Father.

5. He reacted to His mother by providing for her.

6. He reacted to His humanity by exclaiming *"I thirst."*

7. He reacted to the great Plan of God and God's Will for His life, by saying, *"It is finished."*

It is remarkable that the first recorded Words of Jesus are, *"Wist ye not that I must be about My Father's business?"* (Lk. 2:49). His last words before His death, and concerning His *"Father's business,"* were *"It is finished!"* (Jn. 19:30).

(51) "AND, BEHOLD, THE VEIL OF THE TEMPLE WAS RENT IN TWAIN FROM THE TOP TO THE BOTTOM; AND THE EARTH DID QUAKE, AND THE ROCKS RENT;"

The words, *"And, behold,"* proclaim an event of startling consequence, hence prefaced by this exclamation!

The phrase, *"The Veil of the Temple,"* spoke of the curtain which hid the Holy of Holies from the Holy Place.

In the Holy Place were the ten *"Tables of Shewbread"* and the ten *"Candlesticks of Gold,"* or rather, were supposed to have been.

There seemed to have been only one Altar of Worship.

The *"Veil"* was supposed to be made of *"blue, and purple, and crimson, and fine linen, and wrought Cherubims thereon"* (II Chron. 3:14; 4:6-8).

Only once a year was the Holy of Holies to be entered, and that by the High Priest, who was to offer up Blood on the Mercy Seat of the Ark of the Covenant. This was on the Great Day of Atonement (Heb. 9:2-9).

(There were two Veils; one at the entrance of the Holy Place, and this *"Veil,"* as stated, between the Holy Place and Holy of Holies.)

It is said that the Holy of Holies in Herod's Temple was empty. When the Roman soldiers broke into it in A.D. 70, they found nothing. So, this which was commanded by God respecting the High Priest entering once a year, no longer was carried out, and because the Ark of the Covenant was no longer there. What happened to it, no one knows!

Prior to the army of Nebuchadnezzar breaking into Solomon's Temple, which took place approximately 600 years before Christ, it is said that Jeremiah took the Ark out of the Holy of Holies and hid it. Where is not known.

It is almost positive that the Babylonians did not take it, and for the reason mentioned, so, as far as is known, there was no Ark of the Covenant in the Temple built by Zerubbabel, which was constructed immediately after the dispersion, or, as stated, in Herod's Temple.

The phrase, *"Was rent in twain from the top*

to the bottom," represented an impossible feat, at least within itself. The Veil was 60 feet high from the ceiling to the floor, and according to Josephus, the Jewish Historian, 4 inches thick. It was so strong, it is said that four yoke of oxen could not pull it apart. Consequently, the *"renting"* of this huge partition had to have been by a supernatural act of God. It happened the moment that Jesus died.

The rending of the Veil signified that the middle wall of partition between Jews and Gentiles was broken down (Eph. 2:14-18) and that each Believer now could have personal access to God, without going through a Priest as an intermediary (Eph. 2:14-18; Heb. 9:8; 10:19-23).

The Incarnation of Christ, as wonderful and glorious as that was, did not rend the Veil; nor did the Lord's sinless life of perfect moral beauty; nor His anguish in Gethsemane; nor His agony on the Cross. These never could have rent that Veil; for the curse resting upon the sinner being the sentence of death, Jesus must actually die in order to redeem the sinner from that curse by suffering it Himself on behalf of, and for the benefit of, the sinner.

Hence the Veil did not rend, so permitting the sinner to approach to God, and God to come forth in Grace to the sinner, until Christ had actually died.

The transgressor of Leviticus 4:27 was not loosed from the sentence of death until the Sin Offering was slain and all its blood — the demonstration of its actual death — poured out at the base of the Altar; nor was the manslayer of Joshua 20 liberated from the sword of the avenger of blood until the death of the High Priest who was a type of Christ.

Therefore, the *"Rending"* of the *"Veil,"* and by the supernatural Power of God, took place upon the death of Christ, and made it possible for *"whosoever will, to take the Water of Life freely"* (Rev. 22:17).

How this great occurrence of the *"Rending of the Veil"* was discovered, no one knows. However, any Priest who would have been in the Holy Place, which they were constantly, would have instantly seen it, with some possibly even there when it happened.

The phrase, *"And the earth did quake, and the rocks rent,"* represented an earthquake which took place at the Death of Christ. However, it seems that this eruption had nothing

NOTES

to do with the rending of the Veil, and that the rending took place immediately before this phenomenon.

With these ominous signs, it seems that Israel would have taken note, but unbelief had already sealed their doom.

It is said, even though I have no proof, that this earthquake was different in that the rending of the rocks was horizontal instead of vertical, which is the normal manner.

(52) "AND THE GRAVES WERE OPENED; AND MANY BODIES OF THE SAINTS WHICH SLEPT AROSE,"

The phrase, *"And the graves were opened,"* proclaims Matthew alone giving this account.

The phrase, *"And many bodies of the Saints which slept arose,"* actually refers to all who had been in Paradise.

Before the Resurrection of Christ, every Saint who died went to Paradise, instead of Heaven. Paradise was actually in the heart of the earth, and was separated from the burning side of hell only by a great gulf (Lk. 16:19-31). Even though the Saints were comforted in this place, still, it was actually a part of hell, even though not the burning side, but yet, with all in this compartment being held captive by Satan.

Now when Christians die, they no longer go into the lower parts of the earth, as then, and held captive by the Devil against their will, but go to Heaven to await the Resurrection of the body (II Cor. 5:8; Phil. 1:21-24; Heb. 12:22; Rev. 6:9-11).

The wicked continue to go to hell to await their resurrection of damnation (Lk. 16:19-31; Rev. 20:11-15).

Every evidence is that Jesus visited this place after His death and before His Resurrection. This is what He meant when He said, *"For as Jonas was three days and three nights in the whale's belly; so shall the Son of Man be three days and three nights in the heart of the earth"* (Mat. 12:40).

When He was resurrected, at the same time, He resurrected all of those Saints in Paradise and took them immediately to Heaven. This is what Paul was speaking of when he said, *"Wherefore He saith, When He ascended up on High, He led captivity captive* (these Saints in Paradise who had been held captive by Satan), *and gave gifts unto men."*

He then said, *"Now that He ascended, what*

is it but that He also descended first into the lower parts of the earth?" (Eph. 4:8-9).

The word, *"many,"* does not mean only a percentage of the whole, but actually all, which constituted *"many."*

The *"Saints"* were all those who trusted Christ as their Saviour from the time of Abel to the Resurrection of Christ. This would have included the penitent thief, who, for all practical purposes, would not have stayed in Paradise but a few hours, when he, with the others, would have been taken to Heaven.

Of course, as the reader understands, the Name, *"Christ,"* or, *"Jesus,"* would have been unknown to this great multitude before the Ministry of Christ; however, Salvation would have been by Faith in Whom the Sacrifices represented, namely Christ, although at the time only understanding such dimly. Salvation has always been through Christ and no other way. Before Calvary, people were saved by looking forward to that event, and after Calvary, people are saved by looking backward to that which Jesus did.

(53) "AND CAME OUT OF THE GRAVES AFTER HIS RESURRECTION, AND WENT INTO THE HOLY CITY, AND APPEARED UNTO MANY."

The phrase, *"And came out of the graves after His Resurrection,"* pinpoints the time! The Resurrection of Christ was *"The Firstfruits of them that slept"* (I Cor. 15:20).

The phrase, *"And went into the Holy City, and appeared unto many,"* represents an occurrence that was astounding to say the least! It doesn't mean that all stopped over in Jerusalem, but only some. Who these were, the Scripture does not say, or to whom they appeared. It just says *"many."*

These who appeared, could well have been some of the Patriarchs of old, such as Abraham, Isaac, or Jacob, or even David, or Ruth, etc. As to their identification, the Scripture is silent, therefore, we can only speculate.

As well, how they were recognized by the living Saints, we are not told. Perhaps they introduced themselves. At any rate, and in whatever manner it happened, and to whomever they appeared, this had to be one of the most astounding events of all time!

Can you imagine what the little group of Saints in Jerusalem must have thought when word came to them that Jesus was not dead,

but alive! And then, on top of that, certain individuals would walk up to them, introducing themselves as one of the Bible Greats of old. No doubt the astonishment of such an appearance would have been great, and even with some skepticism. However, in whatever manner it happened, it became quickly obvious that these individuals were actually who they said they were. And then as quickly as they came, they were gone!

As well, the words, *"Holy City,"* describe the earthly Jerusalem, and would have been referred to in this manner because of its long history.

At that time, Christ was rejected. However, in a coming Glad Day, He will be accepted, and gladly; then that which was said by Faith will be reality.

(54) "NOW WHEN THE CENTURION, AND THEY THAT WERE WITH HIM, WATCHING JESUS, SAW THE EARTHQUAKE, AND THOSE THINGS THAT WERE DONE, THEY FEARED GREATLY, SAYING, TRULY THIS WAS THE SON OF GOD."

The phrase, *"Now when the Centurion, and they that were with him,"* spoke of the cordon of Roman soldiers officiating at the Crucifixion of Christ.

A *"Centurion"* was normally in charge of 100 men, but it is doubtful that this many served at the Crucifixion. Pilate probably assigned this Centurion to this duty, and for his own particular reasons. At any rate, even though it was an awful day, still, it was to be the greatest day for him, he would ever know.

The phrase, *"Watching Jesus, saw the earthquake, and those things that were done, they feared greatly,"* pertained to the strange phenomenon that took place before and after the death of Christ.

The fear that gripped their hearts when the darkness came at noon, was only exacerbated at the earthquake some three hours later.

These men had seen many things, and were no doubt hardened by their lot in life. However, they had never seen, witnessed, or experienced anything of this nature.

The phrase, *"Saying, Truly this was the Son of God,"* with the word, *"the,"* meaning in a sense no other man ever was or ever will be — the Only Begotten Son (Jn. 1:14, 18; 3:16, 18; Col. 1:15-18). He was begotten, while we are adopted (Rom. 8:14-16; Gal. 4:5; Eph. 1:5).

Jesus predicted that if lifted up from the earth, He would draw all men unto Him — all men without distinction, not all men without exception — so the Centurion who had charge of His Crucifixion testified: *"Truly this was the Son of God."* He was the first Gentile to render this testimony of Faith.

Tradition affirms that the Centurion's name was Longinus, that he became a devoted follower of Christ, preached the Faith, and died a martyr's death.

When the Centurion used the word, *"the,"* he was distinguishing Jesus from the many called by the Romans (a) son of god. Even Caesar claimed to be God! So, his exclamation in effect said, *"Many have claimed to be, but this is 'The One'."*

The testimony of the Centurion is conclusive of the fact that Jesus really died, for his evidence was official, impartial, and independent.

(55) "AND MANY WOMEN WERE THERE BEHOLDING AFAR OFF, WHICH FOLLOWED JESUS FROM GALILEE, MINISTERING UNTO HIM:"

The phrase, *"And many women were there beholding afar off,"* concerns those who came from Galilee, and were with Him unto the end, seeing things even the Apostles did not see. They showed more courage and affectionate concern for their Lord than the men who had promised to die with Him.

The phrase, *"Which followed Jesus from Galilee, ministering unto Him,"* concerns them coming with Him from Galilee to this last Passover, and, as well, doing what they could to help, and in any way. What a privilege it was to do such, and how so few took advantage of it.

As then, so now! Many have the opportunity, but most little take advantage of that privilege. Thank God for those who do.

(56) "AMONG WHICH WAS MARY MAGDALENE, AND MARY THE MOTHER OF JAMES AND JOSES, AND THE MOTHER OF ZEBEDEE'S CHILDREN."

The phrase, *"Among which was Mary Magdalene,"* concerns her name mentioned first by Matthew, while Mary, the Mother of Christ, was mentioned first by John (Jn. 19:25).

Mary Magdalene was a native of the small village of Magdala which was located on the shore of the Sea of Galilee.

Concerning her background, we know little,

only that from her Jesus had cast out seven devils (Mk. 16:9; Lk. 8:2).

The horror of this bondage would know no bounds. Her life must have been a living hell on earth. What had happened to bring about this terrible condition is not related to us. Therefore, the Holy Spirit desired that it not be known, and all further speculation is valueless. However, this we do know!

When Jesus set her free, every indication is that she was so grateful that she desired that her eyes never depart from Him. And no wonder!

"Once like a bird in prison I dwelt,
"No freedom from my sorrow I felt.
"But Jesus came, and listened to me,
"Praise the Lord, He set me free."

The phrase, *"And Mary the mother of James and Joses,"* probably referred to the wife of Cleophas (Jn. 19:25). She is thought by some to have been the sister of Mary the Mother of Jesus. If that is correct, the two Disciples here mentioned would have been the first cousins of Christ.

The phrase, *"And the mother of Zebedee's children,"* was Salome (Mk. 15:40), the mother of James and John.

(The first James mentioned was *"James the Less,"* Mk. 15:40.)

(57) "WHEN THE EVEN WAS COME, THERE CAME A RICH MAN OF ARIMATHAEA, NAMED JOSEPH, WHO ALSO HIMSELF WAS JESUS' DISCIPLE."

The phrase, *"When the even was come,"* referred to a period of time beginning at 3 p.m. until sunset, when the Sabbath would begin.

The phrase, *"There came a rich man of Arimathaea, named Joseph,"* speaks of this man who was a member of the vaunted Sanhedrin. However, he and Nicodemus did not at all consent to the counsel and deed of the rest of the rulers. They were probably not even present when this monstrosity of a trial was held the night before.

The Scripture proclaims him being *"rich,"* because he was, and that he owned a beautiful tomb which had never been used, and in which Jesus would be buried, fulfilling Isaiah 53:9, *"And He made His grave with the wicked* (meaning that He was buried along with the criminals who were crucified with Him), *and with the rich in His death."* This was the tomb of Joseph.

The actual meaning is that the Jews appointed Him a grave with criminals, but at the last moment Joseph, a rich man, begged the Body of Jesus so he could put it in his own tomb, as predicted.

The place called *"Arimathaea,"* was located in Mount Ephraim, and was the birthplace of the Prophet Samuel.

The phrase, *"Who also himself was Jesus' Disciple,"* means that he was a follower of Christ, and thereby had accepted Him as Lord, Saviour, and Messiah.

(58) "HE WENT TO PILATE, AND BEGGED THE BODY OF JESUS. THEN PILATE COMMANDED THE BODY TO BE DELIVERED."

The phrase, *"He went to Pilate,"* proves he had access to the Governor, and probably because he was a *"rich man,"* and a member of the Sanhedrin.

It seems that his devotion to Christ had previously been *"in secret for fear of the Jews"* (Jn. 19:38).

But now he lays aside his timidity, and becomes bold toward the Crucified One.

The phrase, *"And begged the Body of Jesus,"* concerned the approaching Sabbath.

It was the Roman custom to leave criminals hanging on the Cross for days, until their bodies were devoured by birds and wild animals. However, as the Passover Sabbath was approaching at sunset (Thursday), the bodies must be taken down.

The phrase, *"Then Pilate commanded the body to be delivered,"* proclaimed the Roman Governor as the only one who could give such an order.

To be sure, the Jewish Priests could not have cared less if He had been left on the Cross, but Joseph and others desired that he be taken down immediately in order that His Body could be properly attended.

Pilate gave his permission, but only after ascertaining that Jesus was really dead. He sent for the officer in charge of the execution, which well could have been the Centurion of verse 54, who confirmed the fact of the death of Christ.

(59) "AND WHEN JOSEPH HAD TAKEN THE BODY, HE WRAPPED IT IN A CLEAN LINEN CLOTH,"

The phrase, *"And when Joseph had taken the Body,"* represented one of the most holy and sacred things ever done.

Joseph, and no doubt others, with even maybe the Roman soldiers helping, had to pull the Cross out of the ground which contained the Body of Jesus, or at least have taken the cross-bar with Jesus' Body off the main beam. They would have laid it gently on the ground, and then as tenderly as they could, removed the spikes from His Hands as well as His Feet.

As well, they would have gently wiped the blood from His pierced Hands and Feet, as well as His wounded Side. They probably were able to do very little with His Back which had been cut to pieces with the Roman whip. As well, what they could have done with His Face from which His Beard had been plucked, would have been very little.

The phrase, *"He wrapped it in a clean linen cloth,"* would have been a fine Indian cloth or muslin, much used for such purposes in Egypt. This would have been done gently, carefully, and tenderly.

How the Angels at this time must have hovered near, for this was the *"Body"* that God had prepared for the Perfect Sacrifice, which would redeem fallen humanity (Heb. 10:5).

To touch a dead body, according to Mosaic Law, meant that one would be ceremonially defiled for seven days. Consequently, Joseph or Nicodemus could not partake of the Passover Feast, with all its solemn and joyful observances. However, they no doubt realized that this *"Body"* they touched, in no way defiled them, but did the very opposite. As well, He was the *"Passover,"* therefore they were, in a sense, partaking of it in a way that no one ever had.

(60) "AND LAID IT IN HIS OWN NEW TOMB, WHICH HE HAD HEWN OUT IN THE ROCK: AND HE ROLLED A GREAT STONE TO THE DOOR OF THE SEPULCHRE, AND DEPARTED."

The phrase, *"And laid it in his own new Tomb,"* has tremendous meaning.

John said it was nearby, therefore, making Gordon's Calvary the most likely place for the Crucifixion, as well as Gordon's Tomb.

The Tomb, as well as the place thought to be Golgotha, was first pointed out in 1849 by a British Army Officer by the name of Gordon. The site accords with the Biblical data.

The Tomb was *"new"* in that it had never been used, which also ensured that no other body could rise thence except His, Who Alone was buried therein.

The phrase, *"Which he had hewn out in the rock,"* means that it had been cut out of solid rock.

I have had the privilege of walking into this Tomb several times, as have hundreds of thousands of others. Thank God it is empty, with no remains to mark the spot.

It was probably at this time that Nicodemus performed a temporary embalming with, as John put it, *"A mixture of myrrh and aloes"* (Jn. 19:39). However, as the Passover High Sabbath was fastly approaching, this could not be finished. Therefore, their efforts, as stated, were only temporary, with plans to finish shortly.

The phrase, *"And he rolled a great stone to the door of the sepulchre, and departed,"* is the same *"great stone"* that the Angel rolled away (28:2).

The following seems to be the order of events of Wednesday (our Tuesday sunset to Wednesday sunset) and following:

1. Sat down to eat (Mat. 26:20; Mk. 14:17-18; Lk. 22:14; Jn. 12:1-2).

2. Jesus washed the Disciples' feet (Jn. 13:2-20).

3. Passover eaten, Lord's Supper instituted, betrayal announced, and the New Covenant made (Mat. 26:21-29; Mk. 14:18-25; Lk. 22:15-23; Jn. 13:21-30).

4. First Prophecy of Peter's denials (Jn. 13:21-38).

5. Strife among Disciples (Lk. 22:24-30).

6. Second Prophecy of Peter's denials (Lk. 22:31-34).

7. Final instructions about their commission (Lk. 22:35-38; Jn. 14:1-31).

8. Departure from Upper Room (Mat. 26:30; Mk. 14:26; Lk. 22:39; Jn. 14:31).

9. Last discourse and prayer on the way to the Garden (Jn. 15:1-17:26).

10. Third Prophecy of Peter's denials (Mat. 26:31-35; Mk. 14:27-31).

11. Arrival and agony at Gethsemane (Mat. 26:36-46; Mk. 14:32-42; Lk. 22:40-46; Jn. 18:1).

12. Betrayal and arrest early Tuesday evening (actually their Wednesday — Mat. 26:47-56; Mk. 14:43-52; Lk. 22:47-53; Jn. 18:2-11).

13. Trials throughout Tuesday night (their Wednesday night) and early morning on Wednesday (Mat. 26:57-27:26; Mk. 14:53-15; Lk. 22:54-23:25; Jn. 18:12-19:15).

NOTES

14. The Crucifixion (Mat. 27:27-56; Mk. 15:16-41; Lk. 23:36-49; Jn. 19:16-36).

15. Burial Wednesday about sunset (Mat. 27:57-66; Mk. 15:42-47; Lk. 23:50-56; Jn. 19:38-42).

16. The Resurrection early Sunday morning or sometime after sunset on Saturday night, which would have been their Sunday (Mat. 28:1; Mk. 16:1-2; Lk. 24:1; Jn. 20:1-2).

(61) "AND THERE WAS MARY MAGDALENE, AND THE OTHER MARY, SITTING OVER AGAINST THE SEPULCHRE."

The phrase, *"Sitting over against the Sepulchre,"* referred to *"Mary Magdalene,"* and *"Mary,"* the mother of James and Joses. They could not bring themselves to leave the Tomb where Christ was buried. They were the last to leave Him dead, and they were the first to see Him risen.

It should be added that the temporary preparations of embalmment provided by Joseph and Nicodemus, as well as that of Mary Magdalene and others, showed that they had no Faith in the Resurrection of Jesus from the dead. Seeing His mutilated Body, they no doubt felt that such was impossible.

Even though they had no doubt heard Him mention His Resurrection, still, His Death was so final and so horrible, that they probably dismissed these statements as something spiritual and which they did not understand. At any rate, their actions prove that they did not take Him literally. How surprised they were to be!

(62) "NOW THE NEXT DAY, THAT FOLLOWED THE DAY OF THE PREPARATION, THE CHIEF PRIESTS AND PHARISEES CAME TOGETHER UNTO PILATE,"

The phrase, *"Now the next day, that followed the day of preparation,"* referred to the High Sabbath and the Chief Day of the Passover Festival. This would have been Wednesday sunset to Thursday sunset.

The phrase, *"The Chief Priests and Pharisees came together unto Pilate,"* referred to the next day after the Crucifixion, and a large deputation of these chief men who presented themselves before the Procurator.

(63) "SAYING, SIR, WE REMEMBER THAT THAT DECEIVER SAID, WHILE HE WAS YET ALIVE, AFTER THREE DAYS I WILL RISE AGAIN."

The phrase, *"Saying, Sir, we remember that*

that deceiver said, while He was yet alive," concerned the prediction made by Christ that He would rise from the dead after three days and three nights.

As well, their testimony here confirms that Jesus died, and did not merely swoon as some modern unbelievers claim.

The phrase, *"After three days I will rise again,"* proclaims that the Jews understood Him to have said three days and three nights as given in Matthew 12:40, proving the Crucifixion could not possibly have been on Friday and the Resurrection one day and one night after His death.

(64) "COMMAND THEREFORE THAT THE SEPULCHRE BE MADE SURE UNTIL THE THIRD DAY, LEST HIS DISCIPLES COME BY NIGHT, AND STEAL HIM AWAY, AND SAY UNTO THE PEOPLE, HE IS RISEN FROM THE DEAD: SO THE LAST ERROR SHALL BE WORSE THAN THE FIRST."

The phrase, *"Command therefore that the Sepulchre be made sure until the third day,"* once again ensures the three days and three nights in the Tomb.

Inasmuch as Jesus had been crucified by the Romans and was considered, therefore, a State criminal, they felt that the Romans must assume responsibility of guarding His Tomb.

They were only interested in this being done until the three days and nights were concluded, which would prove His prediction wrong, or so they thought!

The phrase, *"Lest His Disciples come by night, and steal Him away,"* is something that could have scarcely happened!

The Disciples had all fled, fearing, it seemed, that if they associated themselves with Jesus in any way, even during His Crucifixion, that possibly they might meet the same fate. Consequently, they were utterly demoralized and depressed. To be sure, they would not, and in fact, could not, have tried such a thing, even if Jesus had not been Who He said He was.

However, these scheming Priests and Pharisees were trying to ward off any possibility of anything happening which could perpetuate His Name.

The phrase, *"And say unto the people, He is risen from the dead,"* is actually the lie that these Priests and Pharisees continued to proclaim, even after the Resurrection of Christ.

NOTES

Their scheme of getting the Roman soldiers to guard the Tomb was carried out; however, as we shall see, it did not work. But still, it did not keep them from continuing this lie of His stolen Body, and claimed Resurrection, even though there was no proof of such a thing, with actually every proof of the opposite!

The phrase, *"So the last error shall be worse than the first,"* actually meant that the people's belief in Him had been an *"error,"* and if they in any way thought He had risen from the dead, this would be even a greater *"error"* and *"worse then the first."*

The manner in which they proposed this to Pilate furthered their accusation of Christ as being injurious to the interests of Caesar. Therefore, as they had hooked Pilate the first time by accusing Jesus of kingly claims, which would have usurped authority over Rome, they now hook Him again by the danger of a proposed Resurrection.

(65) "PILATE SAID UNTO THEM, YE HAVE A WATCH: GO YOUR WAY, MAKE IT AS SURE AS YE CAN."

The phrase, *"Pilate said unto them,"* proves that at least in some way he bought their story concerning the proposed danger to Rome.

The phrase, *"Ye have a watch,"* referred to a guard of four soldiers which was changed every three hours, meaning that it was continuous.

The phrase, *"Go your way, make it as sure as ye can,"* means that they not only had the soldiers at their command, but were free to do whatever else they saw fit to guarantee the security of the Tomb.

(66) "SO THEY WENT, AND MADE THE SEPULCHRE SURE, SEALING THE STONE, AND SETTING A WATCH."

The phrase, *"So they went, and made the Sepulchre sure,"* means they did everything that possibly could be done to secure the Tomb.

The phrase, *"Sealing the stone,"* proclaims that they passed a cord around the stone that closed the mouth of the Sepulchre to the two sides of the entrance. This was sealed with wax or prepared clay in the center and at the ends, so that the stone could not be removed without breaking the seals or the cord.

The phrase, *"And setting a watch,"* proclaims that the four soldiers took up their position at the mouth of the Tomb and in front of the stone. Consequently, with all these preparations, His enemies made the proof of His Resurrection incontrovertible.

Inasmuch as the Tomb was sealed, this meant there was no unfair dealing, and it was not humanly possible for His Disciples, or any other human, to break this seal in the face of the guards, and steal His Body.

However, all the efforts made by man, and no matter how secure, could not stop that which God was about to do. The next Chapter will tell us of the greatest miracle the world has ever known, the Resurrection of Christ from the dead!

CHAPTER 28

(1) "IN THE END OF THE SABBATH, AS IT BEGAN TO DAWN TOWARD THE FIRST DAY OF THE WEEK, CAME MARY MAGDALENE AND THE OTHER MARY TO SEE THE SEPULCHRE."

Now begins the greatest day the world has ever known! And yet one certainly could call the day that Jesus died, some three days and nights earlier, as the greatest day; however, if it had not been for the Resurrection, as would be obvious, Calvary would have been in vain. In effect, the Resurrection ratified Calvary. Consequently, we serve not a dead Lord, but a risen Saviour!

In piecing together the narrative of the Four Evangelists respecting the events of the Resurrection, some claim discrepancies. However, such discrepancies do not really exist, for details not being needed in any respective Gospel, such are not given.

Not only can the statements be properly pieced together, but it is remembered that the Lord, in Resurrection, was no longer confined to an ordinary human body of flesh and blood, but had a Resurrection body of flesh and bone, and what the powers of that body were (Lk. 24:39) is not known, only it is stated that He was the "same Jesus" (Acts 1:11). Consequently, He was able to pass through locked doors (Jn. 20:19), and to assume "another form" (Mk. 16:12).

That all the details given by the four Evangelists are somewhat dissimilar are to be ascribed to the facts that the writers did not depend on one another, nor draw their accounts from one source; that each gives only an incomplete

history, introducing those details with which he was familiar, or which it suited for the plan of the Holy Spirit to recount in that particular instance.

However, and as alluded to, there are no discrepancies or contradictions, with each difference easily reconciled when all the facts are known.

The phrase, "In the end of the Sabbath," refers to the end of the day, and, in effect, the end of the week.

As previously stated, the Jewish Sabbath began on Friday at sunset, and ended on Saturday at sunset.

The phrase, "As it began to dawn toward the first day of the week," refers to very early in the morning (Mk. 16:2; Lk. 24:1) and when yet dark (Jn. 20:1).

This "first day of the week," which is Sunday, and because it was the day of the Resurrection of Christ, took the place of the old Jewish Sabbath of Saturday. (Christ rose from the dead some time after sunset on Saturday evening, which was actually the beginning of the Jewish Sunday at that time.) We find throughout the New Testament that this day, Sunday, was the principle day that was kept, henceforth proclaiming among other things that the old Mosaic Law had been fulfilled by Christ, and, consequently, "blotted out," i.e., abolished (Col. 2:14).

As a result, Luke wrote, "And upon the first day of the week, when the Disciples came together to break bread, Paul preached unto them . . ." (Acts 20:7).

Paul also writes, "Upon the first day of the week let every one of you lay by him in store, as God hath prospered him" (I Cor. 16:2).

John the Beloved, in writing the Book of Revelation, said, "I was in the Spirit on the Lord's Day, and heard behind me a great voice, as of a trumpet" (Rev. 1:10).

The term, "The Lord's Day," was used by early Christians of the first day of the week, commemorating the Lord's Resurrection. Romans set aside certain days for Emperor worship, and called them "The Augustean Day," etc., so Christians set aside Sunday as a special day each week to worship God and Christ, calling it "The Lord's Day."

Some claim that modern Christians are to continue to keep the Old Jewish Sabbath, claiming that it was Constantine who changed the day of worship from Saturday to Sunday in

321 A.D. They also claim that the Catholic Church recognized this law of Constantine in 364 A.D. However, the following facts from history will prove that as error:

JEWISH CHRISTIANS

Early Jewish Christians continued to keep the Mosaic Law, including the Sabbath, which brought untold trouble to the Early Church. But Paul, on the other hand, taught from the very beginning that the Jewish Sabbath wasn't binding on Christians because Christ totally had fulfilled all of the Law (Col. 2:16).

In 321 A.D., Constantine made Sunday the rest day for the Roman Empire. But Sunday had been observed by Christians for nearly 300 years before it became a law by Constantine. So the claim that Constantine instituted "Sunday" as a day of worship is completely false. As stated, Christians had been observing Sunday for some 300 years by the time of Constantine.

IGNATIUS, BISHOP OF ANTIOCH

Ignatius lived at the time of the Apostles, 30-107 A.D. He was a Disciple of John the Beloved and one who certainly knew what Christians were practicing in the Early Church.

He wrote, *"And after the observance of the Sabbath of the Jews, let every friend of Christ keep the Lord's day as a festival, the Resurrection Day, the Queen and Chief of all days of the week . . . on which our life sprang up again, and victory over death was obtained in Christ . . . it is absurd to speak of Jesus Christ with the tongue and to cherish in the mind a Judaism which has come to an end. . . . If any man preach the Jewish Law unto you, listen not to him."*

JUSTIN MARTYR

This man was a Gentile, born near Jacob's Well about 110 A.D.

He wrote, *"And on the day called Sunday, all who lived in cities or in the country gathered together in one place, and the memoirs of the Apostles or the writings of the Prophets are read. This is the day (Sunday) on which we hold our common assembly, because it is the first day on which God, having wrought a change in the darkness and matter, made the world; and Jesus Christ our Saviour, on the same day, rose from the dead"* (Vol. I, page 186).

IRENAEUS

In 178 A.D., Irenaeus made the following statement. He said, *"The mystery of the Lord's Resurrection may not be celebrated on any other day than the Lord's Day, and on this alone should we observe the breaking of the Pascal Feast* (Lord's Supper) . . . *Pentecost fell on the first day of the week, and was therefore associated with the Lord's Day."*

EUSEBIUS

Eusebius is given up to be the Father of Church History. He lived from 265-340 A.D. He said, *"From the beginning, Christians assembled on the first day of the week, called by them 'The Lord's Day,' for the purpose of religious worship, to read the Scriptures, to preach and to celebrate the Lord's Supper . . . the first day of the week on which the Saviour obtained the victory over death. Therefore, it has the preeminence, first in rank, and is more honorable than the Jewish Sabbath."*

THE SABBATH, A TYPE OF CHRIST

The Jewish Sabbath, which was Saturday, was not a day of worship, but rather a day of rest. It was that for the sole purpose of being a Type of Christ, Who would bring rest to the soul, Who did so by the giving of Himself on the Cross of Calvary. The Law could not give rest simply because animal blood was insufficient to take away sin. But Jesus took away sin, leaving the Believer free of condemnation.

For all time since the Cross, when a Believer follows Christ, he is actually keeping the Sabbath, of which the old Jewish Sabbath was a type. The Sabbath is a type of the *"rest"* which is produced by Christ and His Sacrificial Offering of Himself. To make any more of the Sabbath than that is to make more of that particular day than God intended. Every part and particle of the Jewish Law pointed in some way to Christ — either in His Atoning, Mediatorial, or High Priestly Work.

The phrase, *"Came Mary Magdalene and the other Mary to see the sepulchre,"* proclaims these as the first two to see the empty tomb. Someone has said that love could not abandon its object, living or dead.

There is inference that there may have been

other women with these two (Lk. 24:1-10), or that a second group of women came shortly after *"Mary Magdalene and the other Mary, the mother of James and Joses"* (Mat. 27:56).

However, among all of these women who came, whoever they may have been, Mary Magdalene stands prominently forward, first in love and first in care. According to John the Beloved, she was the first to herald the Gospel Message of the Resurrection of Jesus Christ (Mk. 16:9-10; Jn. 20:1-18).

However, it should be noted that their early arrival at the Tomb was not because they believed that Christ would actually rise from the dead, but actually to embalm His Body, for which necessary preparations had been made.

Mark tells us they were perplexed about the difficulty of removing the stone, seemingly not knowing anything of the sealing of the stone or the posting of guards.

Matthew does not mention the proposed embalmment, because, whether he realized it or not, the Holy Spirit directed his Gospel to be written in the realm of Jesus as King. Consequently, no mention would be made of this as the Resurrection rendered it impracticable.

(2) "AND, BEHOLD, THERE WAS A GREAT EARTHQUAKE, FOR THE ANGEL OF THE LORD DESCENDED FROM HEAVEN, AND CAME AND ROLLED BACK THE STONE FROM THE DOOR, AND SAT UPON IT."

The phrase, *"And, behold, there was a great earthquake,"* presents the second earthquake, with the first taking place when Christ died (Mat. 27:51).

There is no record that these particular earthquakes caused any damage or deaths in Jerusalem, nor was the earthquake the occasion for the removal of the stone from the door of the Tomb, for the Angel did this.

It seems that the earthquakes which occasioned the Death and Resurrection of the Lord, proclaim these great acts of Christ in the deliverance of humanity, as being the Lord Creator of the earth. Consequently, it would record this the greatest of all occurrences, by these actions.

The phrase, *"For the Angel of the Lord descended from Heaven,"* was probably observed by the Roman soldiers, who alone witnessed it and gave the account.

The phrase, *"And came and rolled back the*

stone from the door," was <u>not</u> done in order that Christ may walk out of the tomb, because His Glorified Body was not restricted by such obstacles. Actually, Christ had already risen from the dead and had left the Tomb when the stone was rolled away.

This was done in order to give the women and others entrance to the empty Tomb, and, as well, to strike terror into the hearts of the soldiers. As stated, it was not done to let Jesus out, but, rather, to let the women and Disciples in.

The phrase, *"And sat upon it,"* is not without spiritual significance. This was done as a show of triumph, and to show that it was not to be replaced. In other words, death was vanquished!

Angels were present at the Birth of Christ, at His temptation, as well as His agony in the Garden of Gethsemane. Now they guard His empty Tomb, with the soldiers having fled in terror.

(3) "HIS COUNTENANCE WAS LIKE LIGHTNING, AND HIS RAIMENT WHITE AS SNOW:"

There is no evidence that any of the women or Disciples saw this glorious coming of the Angel. However, the next verse tells us that the Roman guards did see it, and were terrified!

The phrase, *"His countenance was like lightning,"* is a description difficult for humans to comprehend. No doubt this Angel had been in the Presence of God, and, consequently, reflected that startling glory. To describe it as *"like lightning,"* also reflected power such as is beyond comprehension.

The phrase, *"And His raiment white as snow,"* as well, proclaimed His absolute purity!

Matthew described the Transfiguration of Jesus in a very similar manner, *"And His Face did shine as the sun, and His raiment was white as the light"* (Mat. 17:2).

However, there is no record that Matthew personally saw the Angel, but that the women who did see him, described his appearance to the Apostle. (They did not see his descending and rolling back the stone from the door as the soldiers, but only after this was done.)

(4) "AND FOR FEAR OF HIM THE KEEPERS DID SHAKE, AND BECAME AS DEAD MEN."

The phrase, *"And for fear of him the keepers*

did shake," means, as stated, they saw him descend from Heaven, and with his appearance so glorious and startling, they began to tremble and *"shake."* They no doubt stood there petrified by fear, as he quickly moved the stone from the entrance of the Tomb. There was absolutely nothing they could do about it, with that, of course, being an understatement!

The phrase, *"And became as dead men,"* means these four soldiers fainted from fear. Inasmuch as this happened at night, the situation was even more frightful.

Exactly how long they remained in this state of immobility is unknown; however, the moment they were able to arise to their feet, they fled in terror.

As they related this story to the officials, there is no record that they were even reprimanded for deserting their post, therefore, whatever they did and however they looked was so convincing that no action was taken against them.

(5) "AND THE ANGEL ANSWERED AND SAID UNTO THE WOMEN, FEAR NOT YE: FOR I KNOW THAT YE SEEK JESUS, WHICH WAS CRUCIFIED."

The phrase, *"And the Angel answered and said unto the women,"* was at their arrival, which was just before dawn, and after the soldiers had run away.

(Some claim that the women actually saw the soldiers, witnessing their hasty departure, which may well have been the case, but of which there is no record.)

Luke and John mentioned that there were two Angels, with Matthew only mentioning one, which well could have been a different appearance than the two. There were doubtless innumerable Angels in this vicinity, which could have, and no doubt, did occasion different appearances.

The phrase, *"Fear not ye,"* speaks of the natural reaction of the women. Actually, the entirety of the scene occasioned fear.

They had come expecting to embalm the Body of Christ, and, instead, find the stone rolled away, with the Tomb empty, and the Angel in glorious appearance sitting on the stone, who probably illuminated the entire area dispelling the darkness. Consequently, their *"fear"* was understandable! Therefore, he calms them by his admonition.

The phrase, *"For I know that ye seek Jesus,*

which was crucified," proclaims the Angel knowing all their intentions for embalming the Body. However, he does not in any way seek to reprimand them, but rather to comfort.

Even though crucifixion was a horrible form of death, and administered supposedly only to the vilest of criminals, still, the Angel now uses this word, *"crucified,"* in a most glorious manner. It is now *"The Power of God and the Wisdom of God"* (I Cor. 1:23-24).

As someone has brought out, the Crucifixion was not simply a temporary incident in the life of Christ, but an eternal principle in His Kingdom.

The Crucifixion of Christ satisfied the claims of heavenly justice, and, as well, destroyed the powers of darkness and Satan's stranglehold on humanity. Consequently, the vileness of this manner of death, was turned by Christ into a thing of glory and victory.

(6) "HE IS NOT HERE: FOR HE IS RISEN, AS HE SAID. COME, SEE THE PLACE WHERE THE LORD LAY."

The phrase, *"He is not here,"* and speaking of the Tomb, is the beginning of the most glorious statement that could ever fall upon the ears of mere mortals.

The body of Vladimir Lenin, one of the founders of Communism, is in his tomb in Moscow, for I have seen it. The same can be said for every other mortal who has lived and died; however, the Tomb of Christ is empty!

Consequently, Christians do not relate to a dead founder, but, rather, to a risen and, thereby, living Christ.

The phrase, *"For He is risen,"* completes the phrase, *"He is not here."* A dead and risen Saviour is the life and substance of the Gospel (I Cor. 15:1-4).

The word, *"risen,"* means that His dead Body was not merely moved to another place, but, rather, had actually been raised from the dead.

The phrase, *"As he said,"* means that the Angel brought to the attention of the women the fact that Christ had stated several times that He would be crucified and rise from the dead. He is reminding them that they should have believed Him, but, sadly, they did not, as their actions prove!

The phrase, *"Come, see the place where the Lord lay,"* proclaims their unbelief and the necessity for the Angel to show them that no corpse was in the Tomb.

Unbelief regarding the Word of God is a terrible thing. It causes the actions of even the most devoted to be totally contrary to the Truth. Consequently, they were looking for a dead body, but, instead, would find a risen Lord. They were looking for a Tomb containing a corpse, but, instead, would find it empty.

They were conducting themselves as if everything had ended, when, in reality, it had only begun!

Verses 6 and 7 proclaim the Gospel in four words, *"Come," "See," "Go," "Tell."*

Whatever the Lord does, is always open, observable, and plain for all to see, which is totally unlike the mystery religions with their secret societies, etc.

(7) "AND GO QUICKLY, AND TELL HIS DISCIPLES THAT HE IS RISEN FROM THE DEAD; AND, BEHOLD, HE GOETH BEFORE YOU INTO GALILEE; THERE SHALL YE SEE HIM: LO, I HAVE TOLD YOU."

This verse is freighted with meaning, and quickly establishes the beginning of the proclamation of the Gospel Message as heralded by the Holy Spirit.

The phrase, *"And go quickly,"* was spoken first to women. There is a reason for that, as we shall soon see.

They have come and seen, and now they should go and tell.

The following proclaims what is said:

1. *"Go"*: So followed the Great Commission, *"Go ye into all the world, and preach the Gospel to every creature"* (Mk. 16:15).

Spiritual declension is quickly obvious as portrayed by the lack of *"Go"* on the part of the Church. When the Church becomes introverted as it has in the past few years, as is obvious by its *"prosperity message,"* there is very little concern for the advancement of the Gospel to the parts of the world which are lacking this all-important Word. Today, and sadly, the criteria of much of the Church is to confess a Honda into a Cadillac, etc. As stated elsewhere in these Volumes, Frances and I were in a major American city a short time ago, and, consequently, had the opportunity to view several Preachers over what is proposed to be *"Christian Television."* If I remember correctly, I viewed a part of some five messages. Four of them were telling people how to get rich, with the fifth seeming to be some type of psychological mishmash.

To properly proclaim my feelings would be difficult. A grief filled my heart to such an extent that I could not sleep that night. No souls would be saved or lives changed by this perversion of the Gospel. I think I must have felt somewhat like Paul felt when, *"His spirit was stirred in him, when he saw the city* (Athens) *wholly given to idolatry"* (Acts 17:16).

I do not personally believe that the idolatry spoken of by Paul in Athens, was any different than the idolatry I witnessed respecting that which proposed to be the Gospel Message. Actually, if anything, the modern version is more ungodly because of being more subtle. Everything in Athens was a lie, while part of what these Preachers proclaim is Truth, which makes their lie even more plausible and, consequently, acceptable! A half truth is always more subtle, and, therefore, destructive, than a whole lie!

Any way that one may look at it or label it, the modern *"prosperity message"* is a selfish, self-willed greed posing as the Gospel, which, in reality, is *"another gospel,"* projected by *"another spirit"* and proclaiming *"another Jesus"* (II Cor. 11:4).

2. *"Quickly"*: The emphasis respecting this grand and glorious Message, as is obvious, is on speed and haste! Why not? It is truly the Greatest Story ever told.

Some time back, Frances and I, if I remember correctly, on our way to Australia for meetings, stopped over in the Fiji Islands. At the time we were on Television there. Someone told me this story concerning that beautiful place.

Years before, a Missionary had come to the Fiji Islands, bringing with him the grand and glorious story of Jesus Christ and His Power to save. It is said that the Chief of the largest Tribe in the Islands accepted Christ, along with many of his people. He then asked this question:

"When did Jesus come to die on Calvary in order to save lost humanity, last year?"

The Missionary said, *"No!"*

The Chief then said, *"Five years ago?"*

Again, the answer was *"No!"*

"Ten years ago?", the Chief remonstrated!

Once again the Missionary answered, *"No!"*

"Well when did He come?", the Chief asked!

"About 1900 years ago," the Missionary answered!

"And you are just now coming to tell us about it?", the Chief said!

And then he added, *"What about all the generations who lived before me?"*

There was no answer that could be given from the Missionary.

Of course, the Chief was right. Thank God for the Missionary who did answer the call, but as the Chief asked, *"What about all the generations who came before him and never had the opportunity to hear, and, consequently, died lost?"*

Too often, the Church takes the attitude that the responsibility is not ours. However, it is!

Heaven has already done everything it can do to save humanity, by God sending His Only Son to die for this fallen race. He simply asks that we tell the story. However, and sadly, most are little interested in telling that story.

As I dictate these words, it is possible at this present time to reach from fifty percent to two-thirds of the world with Television. The doors are open, many hearts are hungry, but most Believers have little interest! Most of the money from Christian pockets is rather going to propagate false doctrine, or to build entertainment centers, or other such foolishness! Very little money truly goes to proclaim the True Gospel of Jesus Christ.

As I have related elsewhere in these Volumes, as far as I know, we were the first to begin airing the Gospel by Television in the area formerly known as the Soviet Union. This is a vast area covering approximately one-sixth of the world's land surface, as well as approximately 250,000,000 people. Television went to virtually all of these, with most of them having little or no knowledge at all of Jesus Christ. Needless to say, the response was absolutely phenomenal to say the least. Even our enemies admitted that tremendous strides were being made, with literally multiple thousands coming to the Lord Jesus Christ as a result of the Gospel we preach over the Telecast. Among the many testimonies we received, one pastor from the States told me that in a Seminar he conducted in Moscow, with Pastors coming from all over the former Soviet Union, that over half of these Pastors had been saved as a result of the Telecast.

How we thank the Lord for the privilege of doing this, and how we thank Him for the tremendous results given.

One would think in a circumstance such as

NOTES

this, with a door now open to people who had had very little opportunity to hear the Gospel in the past, that an appeal for funds to pay for this effort which was reaching so many people, would meet with great success. However, the response has been almost nothing. Somehow the Lord has made a way for this expense to be met each month, but time and time again we would come down to the very day that the funds must be paid, but yet with only a part in hand. Time and again, we would have to plead for extra time to try to raise the funds.

And yet there is generally plenty of money for false doctrine, or for schemes which have no Scriptural validity, but very little for the presentation of the True Gospel of Jesus Christ delivered by the Power of the Holy Spirit!

As we have stated, the proper or improper response by the Church to this all-important task of World Evangelism, portrays its spiritual temperature.

The phrase, *"And tell His Disciples,"* is an irony to say the least! The Disciples should have been the ones telling others, but because of their unbelief, this great and glorious Message would be delivered to them by two women. They had deserted Christ in His hour of need, had not stood by His Cross, nor aided in His burial. So they would not be the first ones to see the risen Lord. This honor would go to these handmaidens.

Such should be a lesson that Faith is always rewarded, and no matter how feeble it may be. These women, and as we have stated, did not believe He would rise from the dead anymore than the Disciples. However, their love overrode their fear, and they would attempt to be close to Jesus, although dead, or so they thought!

The phrase, *"That He is risen from the dead,"* is without a doubt the greatest Message that man has ever heard. As someone has said, the Resurrection of Christ ratified all that was done at Calvary. Of course, it would be obvious that if Jesus had not risen from the dead, Calvary would have been in vain. Consequently, this would be the crowning Message of the Early Church, *"He's alive again!"*

The phrase, *"And, behold, He goeth before you into Galilee,"* proclaims the area where most of His Ministry was carried out, and which would be rewarded accordingly. It was ordained by the Holy Spirit that this would be. Years later

Peter would say, *"That Word, I say, ye know, which was published throughout all Judaea, and began from Galilee"* (Acts 10:37).

Two appearances of Christ after the Resurrection are mentioned respecting Galilee. One is mentioned in the last Chapter of John, and another in verse 17 of this last Chapter of Matthew.

Why Galilee?

This area was looked at with contempt by the Religious Leaders in Jerusalem. Consequently, the Lord would choose this humble and despised Galilee as the starting-point of his Church. He Who was despised and rejected of men, would, as well, choose a place that was despised and rejected of men (Isa. 53:3; Jn. 7:41).

As a Preacher of old said, *"As in all things God sets at naught the pride of mankind, and chooses persons, instruments, and places mean in the eyes of the world, teaching us that in humbler and more retired abodes, secret from the world, we are to seek for the strength of God, Who hideth Himself."*

The phrase, *"There shall ye see Him,"* would certainly be true, and respecting the things we have said; however, the women and the Disciples would, as well, see Him this very day.

The phrase, *"Lo, I have told you,"* guarantees the certitude of this action.

Of course, some would ask the question as to why Jesus did not rise from the dead in a manner which would have electrified Jerusalem? Such could have been easily done, but yet was not done.

Why?

Everything done by the Lord is to nurture Faith, which, at the same time, will give an occasion for unbelief, if, in fact, that is what men desire. The Truth is, the plainest evidence will not persuade against willful blindness. Jesus had already stated, *"If they hear not Moses and the Prophets, neither will they be persuaded, though one rose from the dead"* (Lk. 16:31).

God does not satisfy idle curiosity, nor does He reward unbelief!

The manner of His Resurrection was the manner of His Ministry. He performed no miracles to answer the argument of unbelief, but performed many miracles for the truly needful.

(8) "AND THEY DEPARTED QUICKLY FROM THE SEPULCHRE WITH FEAR AND GREAT JOY; AND DID RUN TO BRING HIS DISCIPLES WORD."

The phrase, *"And they departed quickly from the sepulchre,"* means according to verse 6, that they had actually gone into the burial chamber, and had seen with their own eyes that Jesus was not there (Lk. 24:3).

The phrase, *"With fear and great joy,"* is certainly understandable under the circumstances. They had spoken with an Angel, and no doubt greatly feeling the Presence of God, had heard a Message which was the greatest that would ever fall upon human ears, and had verified the fact that Jesus was no longer in the Tomb. It is no wonder that they did *"fear!"*

However, this was a healthy *"fear,"* which every Believer ought to have.

And yet, there was *"great joy"* and understandably so!

An hour earlier their world had fallen to pieces, with actually little reason or purpose for continuing to live. And now, miracle of miracles, the sun is not setting, but rather rising. Everything is not lost, but rather the opposite. As well, that reaction should fill the heart of every Believer.

The phrase, *"And did run to bring His Disciples word,"* would be the greatest word the Disciples would ever hear. They *"did run"* because they had a Message to tell, and what a Message it was!

One can see these two Marys as they hurriedly leave the Tomb in obedience to the words of the Angel. Maybe in their reverence they attempted to show a restraint immediately upon leaving, but in moments threw all restraint aside. They must tell any and all, *"He is risen!"*

As they ran, the tears of joy must have flowed down their cheeks, with their hearts racing with anticipation.

The events of the day may be thus outlined:

Before daybreak the Angel rolled back the stone from the door of the sepulchre. The terrified soldiers left the Garden by one exit as the women (Lk. 23:55; 24:10 — four of them are named) entered by another.

Mary Magdalene directly she saw the empty Tomb, hastened to where John and Peter lodged, presumedly nearby, told them that the Lord's Body had been stolen, and returned with them to the Garden as the other women were leaving it by a different path for the Upper Room, which it may be assumed was at another and distant part of the city (Jn. 20:1-2).

The Apostles finding the Tomb empty believed with Mary that the Body had been taken away, and went home much perplexed (Lk. 24:12). Directly they left, the Lord showed Himself to Mary Magdalene, then to the women as they were approaching the Upper Room, then to Peter, then to the Emmaus Disciples, and lastly to all in the evening meeting.

The appearance to Mary Magdalene as given in John 20:11-17 must only have occupied a few moments thus permitting the appearance to the women as they were on their way to the Apostles (Mat. 28:8) at the very time that the soldier deputation was on its way to the High Priests (Mat. 28:11).

(9) "AND AS THEY WENT TO TELL HIS DISCIPLES, BEHOLD, JESUS MET THEM, SAYING, ALL HAIL. AND THEY CAME AND HELD HIM BY THE FEET, AND WORSHIPPED HIM."

The phrase, *"And as they went to tell His Disciples, behold, Jesus met them,"* proclaims the only appearance of the Resurrected Christ in Jerusalem, which Matthew would relate. However, this was not the first appearance of Jesus, that being to Mary Magdalene (Mk. 16:9).

So we are given to understand that Matthew did not relate everything in chronological order, as did none of the accounts. Matthew's account would coincide with the theme of his Gospel, of Jesus as King, even though he probably would have had no idea of such an emphasis. However, the Holy Spirit Who superintended these accounts, most certainly did have that idea!

The phrase, *"Saying, All hail,"* actually meant, *"All joy!"* However, these were not the first recorded words spoken by Christ after the Resurrection, with that honor going to the account of the appearance first to Mary Magdalene. The first words of Christ after the Resurrection were, *"Woman, why weepest thou?"*, (Jn. 20:13). However, that question would coincide with the acclamation, *"All joy!"*

To be sure, this *"joy"* was far more than an outward exhilaration on the receiving of good news. It was far deeper than that! It was a *"joy"* that bubbled up from the heart, which could only be given by God. It is as if Jesus is saying, *"I am alive, and the future is secure!"*

This is no time for the weeping of sorrow, but, rather, for the exclamation of joy! As well, one must hurriedly add, that this *"joy"* has not

subsided from that day until this. If Jesus truly reigns within the heart, *"joy"* will reign as well!

The phrase, *"And they came and held Him by the feet, and worshipped Him,"* proclaims to us several things.

1. They would find that they were touching a human body of flesh and bone, and that it was not an apparition or ghostly figure. The attitude of the women relates to us that even though they now believed He was risen from the dead, still, they were not at all certain as to what was meant by that. His appearance to them, with them touching Him, and thereby satisfying their question, would remove all doubts as to what the Resurrection meant.

There is some evidence that in the appearance of Jesus to Mary Magdalene a short time earlier, that she had actually touched Him, even trying to cling to Him, when He said to her, *"Touch Me not; for I am not yet ascended to My Father"* (Jn. 20:17).

No doubt she had told the others of this meeting, and His response to her, which could have made the other women think that His Body was not real. Consequently, upon His appearance to them, not at all to satisfy curiosity, but out of sheer joy, they would *"hold Him by the feet."* Then realizing that they were not holding a ghost, but rather a real human body, they remained at His feet in profound worship.

Why did Jesus say to Mary Magdalene, *"Touch Me not,"* or, *"Do not cling to Me,"* when He made no such requirement of this appearance?

According to the account given in John 20:17, when Jesus first appeared to Mary Magdalene, He was actually about to ascend to the Father in Heaven, which He did do so, coming back almost immediately.

Quite possibly this was when He applied the Blood to the Mercy Seat. However, it is not certain if this quick ascent to Heaven took place immediately after the appearance to Mary Magdalene or this appearance as recorded by Matthew. Very little information is given, consequently, there is much that is simply not known.

(10) "THEN SAID JESUS UNTO THEM, BE NOT AFRAID: GO TELL MY BRETHREN THAT THEY GO INTO GALILEE, AND THERE SHALL THEY SEE ME."

The phrase, *"Then said Jesus unto them, Be not afraid,"* proclaims an understandable statement.

These women had seen Jesus die on Calvary. They had seen His Body terribly wounded and mutilated. Not only did He die, but He died a horrible death.

They were no doubt there when Joseph of Arimathaea and Nicodemus took Jesus from the Cross after His death. They must have witnessed the removal of the spikes from His Hands and Feet. They must have stood close, or even helped, when Joseph and Nicodemus attempted to clean the Blood from the Body before *"wrapping it in a clean linen cloth."* The shock of what they saw was horrifying to say the least! And now they see Him standing before them, and, as well, they must have seen the nail prints in His Hands and Feet. Consequently, they, or anyone else for that matter, would *"be afraid."*

However, when He said, *"Be not afraid,"* it is assured that a calmness came over them, as His Presence filled every fiber of their being. They did not understand everything, but they now knew that everything was going to be all right.

The phrase, *"Go tell My Brethren,"* is beautiful indeed!

They had deserted Him, with Peter even denying Him, and yet He calls them *"Brethren!"* He had called them *"Friends"* before His death (Jn. 15:14-15). Now He gives them a greater title. *"He is not ashamed to call them Brethren"* (Heb. 2:11).

There was no reprimand, scolding, condemnation, or reproof. However, at the same time, He knew they loved Him. He knew they wanted to do that which was right. Consequently, His Love was not wasted on unrepentant ones.

The phrase, *"That they go into Galilee, and there shall they see Me,"* means more than just an appearance. Actually, he would appear to them in Jerusalem, even proclaiming great Truths (Jn. 20:19-23). However, that which would be given to them in Galilee, would amount to a re-commissioning, and even though mentioned by Matthew, is given in detail by John in the last Chapter of his Book.

(11) "NOW WHEN THEY WERE GOING, BEHOLD, SOME OF THE WATCH CAME INTO THE CITY, AND SHEWED UNTO THE CHIEF PRIESTS ALL THE THINGS THAT WERE DONE."

The phrase, *"Now when they were going,"* refers to the women after seeing Jesus, going to the Disciples to bring them the great and glorious news.

The phrase, *"Behold, some of the watch came into the city,"* speaks of the four soldiers who had actually seen the coming of the Angel and him rolling the stone away from the mouth of the Tomb. (Four soldiers guarded the Tomb, changing the watch every three hours, which was to be done for some seventy-two hours, or a little longer.)

After these four soldiers revived from their experience, they quickly leave the empty Tomb, going to the Chief Priests to tell them what had occurred.

The phrase, *"And shewed unto the Chief Priests all the things that were done,"* proclaims them relating the account of these incidents to these Religious Leaders. They related as to how the Angel had *"descended from Heaven, and rolled back the stone from the door, and sat upon it."* They, as well, told what his countenance was like, and how the light which emanated from him filled the area. As well, they saw there was no corpse in the Tomb!

Upon hearing this, these Priests knew that these Roman soldiers were not making up this story. For them to desert their post was a capital offense. In other words, they could be executed for such an act.

However, even though these Chief Priests knew this account to be true, their hearts were further hardened instead of terrified. Such is the spirit of unbelief.

(12) "AND WHEN THEY WERE ASSEMBLED WITH THE ELDERS, AND HAD TAKEN COUNSEL, THEY GAVE LARGE MONEY UNTO THE SOLDIERS,"

The phrase, *"And when they were assembled with the Elders,"* referred to a hurried meeting of the Sanhedrin.

The phrase, *"And had taken counsel,"* once again was in the negative. They now knew, and beyond the shadow of a doubt, that Jesus was the Son of God. They knew the testimony of these soldiers was true. And yet, all of their *"counsel"* was not pertaining to their desperately needed repentance, but how they could make the people believe their concocted lie.

As we have stated, the plainest evidence will not persuade against willful blindness.

Also, a group of men meeting together in a religious hierarchy will almost always cause them to do things far more evil than normal. This is for two reasons:

1. Religions hierarchies are not Scriptural. This pertains not only to the Sanhedrin of old, but, as well, to modern Denominational Boards. In Truth, there is no evidence in the Word of God that the Lord speaks to boards, committees, groups, etc. The Truth is, He speaks to individuals.

About the only gathering of a group of Preachers recorded in the New Testament, that is sanctioned by the Holy Spirit, is recorded in Acts 15. However, this was done to discuss points of Doctrine which were critical to the Work of God. And yet it is the only such meeting recorded.

Oftentimes, Religious Leaders elected by popular ballot begin to think their man-made office holds some spiritual significance. Consequently, they begin to conduct themselves in a manner that is dictatorial, and, thereby, unscriptural.

Thankfully, some few Godly men fill such positions; however, the number is few.

2. Men meeting as this Sanhedrin, will almost always be far more harsh than if they were making a decision alone. It is almost as if a mob spirit takes control of such meetings, with things done that are contrary to common sense, and, above all, the Word of God.

It is as if a wicked decision made by a large group is sanctioned because it is made by a group!

The phrase, *"They gave large money unto the soldiers,"* means that they did not doubt the facts to which the guards bore witness. As well, they did not attempt to discredit their story by any type of accusation. They accepted it as Truth, which it was, and then set about to shut the mouths of these men by giving them large sums of money.

Did they not stop to consider that if One could rise from the dead, as Christ, that whatever feeble steps they were taking would be of no avail?

(13) "SAYING, SAY YE, HIS DISCIPLES CAME BY NIGHT, AND STOLE HIM AWAY WHILE WE SLEPT."

This was the story concocted by the Sanhedrin, and a poor one at that. When one considers that this was the best they could come up with, one begins to consider how desperate they were. Let's look at their story:

1. If the soldiers were asleep, how could they know that the Disciples stole the body?

2. All knew that the penalty for a Roman soldier going to sleep on his watch, or deserting his post, was punishable by death. How could this be explained?

3. How could these Disciples secure the Body from the Tomb without awaking the soldiers?

4. Why would the Disciples now risk their lives to do this thing, when they would not even stand up for Christ at His Crucifixion?

5. If, in fact, they had done such a thing, what had they done with the Body?

6. Why did not these soldiers put up a fight after they were awakened, especially considering that they were heavily armed, while the Disciples were not armed at all?

No, their story was absurd, but, sadly, many Jews believe it even unto this very day.

(14) "AND IF THIS COME TO THE GOVERNOR'S EARS, WE WILL PERSUADE HIM, AND SECURE YOU."

The phrase, *"And if this come to the Governor's ears,"* refers to Pilate.

The phrase, *"We will persuade him, and secure you,"* meant that the Sanhedrin would take full responsibility for this action, and do whatever was necessary to appease the Governor, even to paying another large sum of money if necessary!

Considering that the offense of the soldiers of deserting their post was punishable by death, the matter was serious indeed, and, no doubt, took some doing on the part of the Sanhedrin to convince these men. However, the following verse proves they were very convincing.

Pilate, however, later learned the great fact of Christ's Resurrection. As far as is known, however, he took no steps toward punishing the guards who had forsaken their post. He was probably convinced that their story was real and Jesus had really risen from the dead.

It is said in one of the chronicles of that time, that he sent an account of this matter to Tiberius, who, in consequence, we are told, endeavored to make the Roman Senate pass a decree enrolling Jesus in the list of Roman gods. This fact is attested by Tertullian.

Nevertheless, even though he was obviously convinced as to Who Jesus really was, still, he never sought forgiveness, and died of suicide a short time later.

(15) "SO THEY TOOK THE MONEY, AND DID AS THEY WERE TAUGHT: AND THIS

SAYING IS COMMONLY REPORTED AMONG THE JEWS UNTIL THIS DAY."

The phrase, *"So they took the money, and did as they were taught,"* means that the matter was rehearsed with them over and over again by the Sanhedrin until all had the same story. The *"money"* would ensure the story, but would not make it true. How men love to believe a lie!

The phrase, *"And this saying is commonly reported among the Jews until this day,"* was true in Matthew's time, and is true presently.

It is said that the Jews at that time sent emissaries in all directions to spread this false report. Consequently, the Holy Spirit through Matthew throws light on this lie, and exposes the perfidiousness of the reprobate Sanhedrin.

(16) "THEN THE ELEVEN DISCIPLES WENT AWAY INTO GALILEE, INTO A MOUNTAIN WHERE JESUS HAD APPOINTED THEM."

The phrase, *"Then the Eleven Disciples went away into Galilee,"* does not tell us exactly when this happened. However, the sequence seems to indicate that it took place at least a week after the Resurrection of Christ (Jn. 20:26; 21:1). The number *"Eleven"* is specifically mentioned, in that the Holy Spirit desires that the betrayal not be forgotten. The number was brought back up to Twelve just before Pentecost (Acts 1:15-26).

The phrase, *"Into a Mountain where Jesus had appointed them,"* gives no evidence as to exactly where this Mountain was.

Some have thought it may have been Mt. Tabor, which was near Nazareth, and where more than likely the Transfiguration took place. Others have suggested the Mt. of Beatitudes. However, the Scripture does not say, and all conjecture is pointless. This much we do know:

The word, *"appointed,"* specifies that this was a designated meeting, which would have ensured a definite place.

(17) "AND WHEN THEY SAW HIM, THEY WORSHIPPED HIM: BUT SOME DOUBTED."

The phrase, *"And when they saw Him,"* refers to this meeting on the Mountain in Galilee.

The inference by the words, *"saw Him,"* is that He may have emanated glory to such an extent that some were awed while others were affected differently. As well, it seems for certain that the *"Eleven"* were not the only ones there, with the crowd somewhat enlarged.

The phrase, *"They worshipped Him,"* proclaims

the far greater number realizing exactly Who they were seeing, the Lord of Glory. Consequently, *"worship"* was not only the normal thing to do, but, as well, that desired of the Holy Spirit. Jesus is God, therefore, He demands worship!

The phrase, *"But some doubted,"* would not have included any of the *"Eleven Disciples."* Who these doubters were, we do not know; and, as well, it is not known why they *"doubted."*

The Greek word for doubt in this instance is *"distazo,"* and means *"to hesitate."* It does not refer to the type of doubt that registers unbelief.

As we have stated, quite possibly they now saw Jesus in a form or manner to which they were unaccustomed, and, consequently, they hesitated in their recognition and worship. However, every evidence is that this was soon corrected.

(18) "AND JESUS CAME AND SPAKE UNTO THEM, SAYING, ALL POWER IS GIVEN UNTO ME IN HEAVEN AND IN EARTH."

The phrase, *"And Jesus came and spake unto them,"* continues to speak of this meeting on the Mountain in Galilee, and actually refers to the Great Commission.

In Truth, there were three Commissions given by Jesus shortly before His ascension. They are as follows:

1. The first seemed to have been given in Jerusalem, and pertained to the Eleven receiving the proclamation of the Holy Spirit, as well as the privilege of announcing the proclamation of sins forgiven or retained, according to the acceptance or rejection of the Gospel as ministered (Jn. 20:22-23).

2. The second Commission as well seemed to take place in Jerusalem, and concerned the *"preaching the Gospel to every creature."* It also pertained to *"signs following them that believe"* (Mk. 16:14-18).

3. The third Commission is the one noted by Matthew on the Mountain in Galilee, which may have very well included more than the Eleven. It, as well, proclaimed the absolute necessity of taking the Gospel to the world (Mat. 28:19-20).

Also, it should be noted that these Commissions (and they should not be confounded), even though given to only the Eleven in two cases, still applies to any and all who follow Jesus Christ, and for all time!

Inasmuch as it was given three times, with each time presenting a different occasion, the contents should be understood as extremely important, but, as well, the absolute necessity of carrying it out. This is the duty of the Church, the taking of the Gospel to the world, and, as such, must not in any way be hindered, weakened, or abrogated.

Jesus paid the great price of Redemption, and it's up to the Church to tell the world about it. Considering that He has given us the Holy Spirit to help in this great endeavor, there is no excuse for failure.

The phrase, *"All power is given unto Me in Heaven and in earth,"* is the assertion that Jesus Christ, the Son of Man, has received from the Father supreme authority in Heaven and earth, and over the entirety of the whole Kingdom of God in its fullest extent.

A. L. Williams said, *"This is not given to Him as Son of God; for, as God, nothing can be added to Him or taken from Him; it is rather a power which He has merited by His Incarnation, Death, and Passion (Phil. 2:8-10), which was foretold in the Old Testament, by Psalmist (Ps. 2:8; 8:5-8) and Prophet (Dan. 7:13-14), and with which He was endued on the day that He rose victorious from the grave."*

Williams went on to say, *"So the verb 'was given' is in the past tense, because it refers to the Plan of God arranged in God's eternal purpose, and to the actual investiture at the Resurrection. The power is exercised in His mediatorial Kingdom, and will continue to be exercised till He hath put all enemies under His Feet, and destroyed death itself (I Cor. 15:24-27); but His absolute Kingdom is everlasting; as God and Man He reigns forever and ever."*

He then closed by saying, *"This mediatorial authority extends not only over men, so that He governs and protects the Church, disposes human events, controls hearts and opinions; but the forces of Heaven also are at His Command, the Holy Spirit is bestowed by Him, the Angels are in His employ as ministering to the members of His Body."*

Consequently, when He said, *"All power,"* He meant, *"All power!"*

However, this does not mean that Satan does not retain power, for he does! It does mean that while his power is limited, the power of Jesus Christ is absolutely unlimited, therefore, *"Omnipotent!"*

Some of this *"power"* is given to the Saints, upon their being baptized in the Holy Spirit

with the evidence of speaking with other tongues (Acts 1:8; 2:4).

This *"power"* is to be used in many capacities; however, its major thrust is always to be centered on World Evangelism, i.e., the proclamation of the Gospel of Jesus Christ all over the world.

Regrettably, great segments of the modern Church, and especially in the Charismatic community, have attempted to use this power for things other than its intended purpose. Even though the material prosperity of the Saints is important in the eyes of God, still, such is not priority, nor anything close to priority. And yet, segments of the Church have made it priority!

When the Church of Jesus Christ stands at the Judgment Seat of Christ, it will not really matter as to what model of car we drove, or the price of our suit of clothes, but only our efforts at telling others about Jesus, and our motives for doing so! (Lk. 12:15).

Even though the Bible does not specifically say, there seems to have been about twelve appearances of Christ after the Resurrection. They are as follows:

1. Mary Magdalene (Mk. 16:9; Jn. 20:15-16).
2. Women at the Tomb (Mat. 28:9).
3. Two Disciples on the road to Emmaus (Lk. 24:13-31).
4. Peter (Lk. 24:34; I Cor. 15:5).
5. The Ten (Jn. 20:19).
6. The Eleven (Jn. 20:26).
7. The Seven (Jn. 21:1-22). This was after the second Sunday.
8. The Eleven on a certain Mountain in Galilee (Mat. 28:16).
9. The Twelve, including Matthias (Acts 1:26; I Cor. 15:5).
10. Above 500 Brethren (I Cor. 15:6).
11. James, the Lord's brother (I Cor. 15:7; Gal. 1:19).
12. All the Apostles (Mk. 16:19-20; Lk. 24:50-53; Acts 1:3-12, 26; I Cor. 15:7).

(19) "GO YE THEREFORE, AND TEACH ALL NATIONS, BAPTIZING THEM IN THE NAME OF THE FATHER, AND OF THE SON, AND OF THE HOLY GHOST:"

The phrase, *"Go ye therefore,"* even though addressed to the group on the Mountain, nevertheless, applies to any and all who follow the Lord Jesus Christ, and, as stated, in all ages.

It is interesting that the very first word in this *"Great Commission,"* is *"Go!"*

As well, the pronoun, *"ye,"* or *"you,"* refers to all, and with no exceptions. In other words, it is the duty of every single Believer, and irrespective as to whom they may be, or what station in life they occupy, to do their part in helping to take the Gospel to the world.

The following is an idea of what Jesus is saying:

1. For those who are specifically and personally called to go to certain places in the world in order to take the Message, they must, without fail, obey that call. It is an apostolic call, and must not be denied or hindered.

2. While most Believers are not personally called respecting a preaching or teaching Ministry, still, every single Believer can give at least some of their income to help finance this most important of all tasks. That means everyone!

If God blesses some with a greater than normal income, as He occasionally does, whatever is reasonably needed for one's sustenance should be used, but the rest should be given to the Cause of Christ. It is regrettable that most large estates are ultimately wasted on lawyers, or given to children or others, who most of the time are corrupted by it. While parents should definitely care for their children, still, it should be done in a reasonable way, with at least a percentage going to help take the Gospel to the world.

Even those who are blessed with a mediocre or even small income, a portion must be set aside for this all-important purpose. What that portion is to be, should be left up to the Lord. However, every single individual, and irrespective as to how small the gift each month would be, should specifically lay aside a certain amount for this cause.

3. As well as giving, and being dedicated to the task, every Believer should earnestly seek the Lord as to where this money should go. Tragically and regrettably, one could probably say that ninety-nine cents out of every dollar given to that which proposes to be the Work of God, is, in Truth, not the Work of God at all! Consequently, and as would be obvious, most is wasted, if not actually aiding and abetting the work of Satan.

Many Believers give to their particular Church regarding World Evangelism, without really knowing where their money goes. In other words, whatever Religious Denomination they are associated with, is that which they support, and

irrespective of what is preached, proclaimed, or done! Giving to God, which is extremely important, should never be done in this manner.

While the Believer certainly should support his local Church, and in some cases all of his missions' dollars going there as well, still, in most cases that is improper.

This matter is so important, that every Believer should earnestly seek the Lord, and thoroughly investigate where his money goes, in order that it be used as it should. If one sincerely seeks the Lord about these matters, and especially considering how important they are, the Lord will, and without fail, give needed direction.

Jesus encouraged all to investigate the *"Fruit."* The Fruit will be, and as we have stated, saved souls, changed lives, broken bondages, Believers edified and filled with the Holy Spirit, and sick bodies healed (Mat. 7:15-20).

As well, bloated reports should not be taken at face value, but the *"Fruit"* must be personally inspected where at all possible.

Actually, that is not too difficult to do, especially if we are concerned enough to investigate.

4. The last, but by no means the least is *"prayer."* Actually, it is the most important thing that one could ever do respecting World Evangelism.

Every Believer can give something, and every Believer can pray. Those who truly pray, seeking God earnestly regarding this all-important task, will find the Ministry of Intercession given unto them. To be sure, this is the bedrock and foundation of all Revivals and Moves of God.

Even though the Intercessor may have never been to a certain country in his or her life, the Holy Spirit will oftentimes give that person a burden for a particular place, which cannot be satisfied without crying to God for a move in these areas. I am convinced that every single Move of God that's ever taken place in the world, has been preceded by Saints on their faces before God interceding for these areas, as the Holy Spirit laid such on their hearts.

Regrettably, that of which I speak is almost unknown in today's modern Church. Consequently, there is very little of a True Move of God around the world.

Just last night in our prayer meeting (10-16-95), the Spirit of God moved upon me personally in a manner that I have seldom experienced.

For a few minutes I sensed the terrible lostness of the lost, and their bondage, as never before. Even though the Holy Spirit has affected me in this manner many times, I do not believe He has ever done so to a degree of this magnitude. For a few minutes it seemed as though I would not be able to physically endure the pressure which was applied by the Holy Spirit. Consequently, there was a cry to God for those in this terrible condition, who actually number into the hundreds of millions and suffer such pain and heartache.

In the last few months, we have begun to receive some of the greatest testimonies regarding precious souls coming to Christ, and being brought out of the most horrifying bondages of darkness. I speak of our Telecast that airs in many parts of the world. I firmly believe that these conversions have a lot to do with the Intercession I have just mentioned.

Paul said, *"Who now rejoice in my sufferings for you, and fill up that which is behind of the afflictions of Christ in my flesh, for His Body's sake, which is the Church"* (Col. 1:24).

Paul was not here speaking of the sufferings of Christ for our sins, but that which all Believers are called to suffer for the Church and Truth (Rom. 8:18; II Tim. 3:12).

The words, *"fill up,"* have to do with that of which I speak, interceding and sometimes suffering, on behalf of those who cannot intercede for themselves.

The word, *"therefore,"* in *"Go ye therefore,"* refers to the authority of the Lord Jesus Christ given with full power of attorney to Believers to carry on the work that He has begun. Consequently, there is no excuse for us not getting it done!

The phrase, *"And teach all nations,"* refers to all the people on the face of the earth. Consequently, the Jews were not to be the only ones to receive the Gospel, but Gentiles as well, and not just some Gentiles, but all Gentiles.

This means that there is no such thing as some have claimed as a *"Western Gospel."* While it is true that more people in the West have received the Gospel than in the East, still, the Gospel is for all mankind, and, consequently, is a Northern, Southern, Eastern, and Western Gospel. It is for all men of *"all nations."* Jesus died for all (Jn. 3:16), consequently, all must have the privilege to hear whether they accept or not!

NOTES

The phrase, *"Baptizing them in the Name of the Father, and of the Son, and of the Holy Ghost,"* is the only formula for Water Baptism given in the Word of God.

First of all, the word, *"Baptizing,"* means to be immersed completely under the water. The Greek word is *"Bapto,"* and means to *"dip under,"* or *"immerse,"* and to *"cover wholly with water."* It does not mean to sprinkle.

As well, this statement by Christ does not teach that one enters into Salvation by Water Baptism, but that one is baptized in water as a result of having already come to Jesus Christ in Salvation.

One is always required to repent before Water Baptism (Rom. 10:9-10; I Jn. 1:9). Then, and then only, is one a fit candidate for Water Baptism, which is an outward symbol of the Death, Burial, and Resurrection of Jesus Christ (I Pet. 3:21). It testifies to the world that one has already repented and been forgiven by Faith in Christ (Rom. 1:16; 3:24-25; 5:1; Eph. 2:8-9).

As well, Water Baptism is <u>not</u> a Sacrament, but rather an Ordinance. As the word, *"Sacrament,"* is presently used, it basically refers to Water Baptism and the Lord's Supper, and means that by engaging in these rites, one has incurred Salvation, and that one cannot be saved unless engaging in these rites. Also, it means that Salvation is maintained by continuing to engage in the rite of the Lord's Supper.

All of this is spurious, and has no foundation in Scripture. Water Baptism along with the Lord's Supper, are extremely important, as should be obvious; however, to link either one to Salvation is unscriptural. Salvation comes by simple Faith in Christ, for the Scripture says, *"For by Grace are ye saved through Faith; and that not of yourselves: it is the Gift of God.*

"Not of works, lest any man should boast" (Eph. 2:8-9).

As a result of believing that Water Baptism is a Sacrament, i.e., plays a part in one's Salvation, Infant Baptism is practiced in some Churches.

Is Infant Baptism a Scriptural Doctrine? No!

HISTORY OF INFANT BAPTISM

Infant Baptism appeared in Church history about the year A.D. 370. It came about as a result of the Doctrine of Baptismal Regeneration

— the teaching, as we have been discussing, that Baptism is essential to Salvation; or if you want to turn it around, that Water Baptism saves the soul, or at least is a part of one's Salvation. So, consequently, as the teaching of Baptismal Regeneration began to be propagated, it was natural for those holding to this Doctrine to believe that everyone should be baptized as soon as possible. Thus, baptism of infants still in the innocent state (and yet unaccountable for their actions) came into vogue among many of the Churches. Consequently, these two grievous errors (Baptismal Regeneration and Infant Baptism) have probably caused more people to go to hell than any other Doctrine.

MORE HISTORY

The professed conversion of Emperor Constantine in A.D. 313 was looked upon by many persons as a great triumph for Christianity. However, it more than likely was the greatest tragedy in Church history because it resulted in the union of Church and State in the establishment of a hierarchy that ultimately developed into the Roman Catholic system.

There is great question that Constantine was ever truly converted. At the time of his supposed vision of the Sign of the Cross, he promised to become a Christian. But he was not baptized in water until near death, having postponed the act in the belief that Baptism washed away all past sins, and he wanted all his sins to be in the past tense before he was baptized. In other words, it seemed he wanted the freedom to sin as much as he desired; and then when he was too old or too sick to care, he would have them all washed away by the act of Baptism.

In A.D. 1416 Infant Baptism was made compulsory throughout the Roman Empire. This filled the Churches with unconverted members as would be obvious. So whatever power the Church had in the past relative to actual conversions was now null and void. The world, consequently, was plunged into the gloom of the Dark Ages, which endured for more than twelve centuries, until the Reformation.

During this time, God had a Remnant who remained faithful to Him; they never consented to the union of Church and State, or to Baptismal Regeneration, or to Infant Baptism. These people were called by various names, but probably could better be summed up by their generic

name, *"Anabaptists,"* meaning rebaptizers. These people ignored Infant Baptism and rebaptized those who had been saved through personal Faith. They also had a generic name for themselves, *"Antipedobaptists,"* meaning *"against Infant Baptism."*

THE STRANGE THING

The strange thing about these two diabolical doctrines of Baptismal Regeneration and Infant Baptism (and diabolical they are), is that the great Reformers (Martin Luther, for one) brought with them out of Rome these two dreaded errors: the union of Church and State and Infant Baptism. Strangely enough, in those days not only did the Roman Catholic Church persecute those who would not conform to its ways, but after the Lutheran Church became the established Church of Germany, it persecuted the nonconformists as well — of course, not as stringently so and not in such numbers as those before them.

John Calvin, as well as Cromwell in England and John Knox in Scotland, all stuck to the union of Church and State and Infant Baptism, and used their power when they had power, to seek to force others to conform to their own views.

Unaware to a lot of people, this thing came to the Americas well in the early days of this Republic. Before the Massachusetts Bay Colony was twenty years old, it was decreed by statue that *"If any person or persons within this jurisdiction shall either openly condemn or oppose the baptizing of infants, or go about secretly to seduce others from the approbation or use therefore, or shall purposely depart from the congregation at the administration of the ordinance — after due time and means of conviction — every such person or persons shall be subject to banishment."*

Religious persecution existed even in the early days of the United States of America. Roger Williams and others were banished (when banishment meant to go and live with the Indians) because they would not submit to the Doctrine of Baptismal Regeneration, or the baptizing of infants.

However, it was the Constitution of the Rhode Island Colony (founded by Roger Williams, John Clark, and others) that established religious liberty by law for the first time in 1300 years (over the world). Thus Rhode Island, founded by a small group of Believers, was the first spot on earth where religious liberty became the Law of the Land. The settlement was made in 1638, and the colony was legally established in 1663. Virginia followed, to be the second, in 1786.

As you can see, the Doctrine of Infant Baptism has a long and bloody history, and it has been one of Satan's chief weapons to condemn untold millions of people to eternal perdition.

FURTHER EXPLANATION

What does the above have to do with us today? A great deal!

You see, the union of Church and State continues today in many countries of the world. In the State Churches, Pastors and Leaders christen babies, which means they make them *"Christians"* by baptizing them; thus the person having been christened as a baby believes he is on his way to Heaven simply because he was christened (or baptized) in infancy. Having been taught all his life that this saved him, he naturally considers himself saved by the act of Infant Baptism. The Roman Catholic Church teaches Baptismal Regeneration and practices Infant Baptism. Its Statement of Doctrine says, *"The Sacrament of Baptism is administered by the pouring of water and the pronouncement of the proper words, and cleanses from original sin."*

The Reformed Church says, *"Children are baptized as heirs of the Kingdom of God and of His Covenant."*

The Lutheran Church teaches that Baptism, whether of infants or adults, is a means of Regeneration.

Because of the following declaration, I believe the Episcopal Church teaches that Salvation comes through Infant Baptism. In his Confirmation, the Catechist answers a question about his Baptism in infancy, by saying, *"In my Baptism . . . I was made a member of Christ, a Child of God, and an inheritor of the Kingdom of God."* (This is printed in the prayer book and can be read there by anyone interested enough to look for it.)

In fact most people who practice Infant Baptism believe the ceremony has something to do with the Salvation of the child. However, these are traditions of men. Consequently, we can follow the Commandments of God or follow after

NOTES

the traditions of men; it is up to us. We cannot follow both!

CLEAR BIBLE TEACHING

The Word of God is clear regarding the matter of Salvation. Jesus said, *"He that believeth on the Son hath everlasting life: and he that believeth not the Son shall not see life; but the Wrath of God abideth on him"* (Jn. 3:36).

"He that believeth on Him is not condemned: but he that believeth not is condemned already, because he hath not believed in the Name of the Only Begotten Son of God" (Jn. 3:18).

Basically, there are two groups of people in the world today: those who do believe on the Son and those who do not. Those who believe are not condemned; they have everlasting life (whatever Church they may belong to). Those who believe not on the Son are condemned already, and they shall not see life, but the Wrath of God abides on them.

This is the clear, unmistakable teaching and language of the Bible.

If you will notice, the Word of God never says simply believe and be saved, but rather believe *"on the Lord Jesus Christ"* and be saved. The Word of God always identifies the object of Faith, which is the Lord Jesus Christ Himself. *"For God so loved the world, that He gave His Only Begotten Son, that whosoever believeth in Him should not perish, but have everlasting life"* (Jn. 3:16). It is not enough just to believe; a person must believe *"in Him."*

When the Philippian jailer asked, *"Sirs, what must I do to be saved?",* Paul answered, *"Believe on the Lord Jesus Christ, and thou shalt be saved"* (Acts 16:30-31). It was not enough simply to believe; such belief, such trust, such dependence had to be *"in Him."*

If a person is trusting in Baptism for Salvation, he cannot be trusting *"in Him."* Christ is not one way of Salvation; He is the Only Way of Salvation (Jn. 14:6; 10:1, 7, 9). There is no promise in the Word of God to those who believe partially in Christ. In other words, a person cannot trust the Lord Jesus Christ ninety percent and Baptism ten percent, or Jesus fifty percent and Baptism fifty percent, or Jesus ninety-five percent and some Church five percent, etc. As a matter of fact, there is no such thing as partially trusting Christ. The man who is partially trusting is not trusting at all! Yet the sad fact is that the majority of people in Churches in America and the world today are not trusting Christ at all — they are trusting Him plus Water Baptism for Salvation, which is no trust at all!

It is even sadder to realize that more people are going to hell through Religious Organizations than any other way. This is a shocking, startling statement, but it is true. Jesus said, *"Many will say to Me in that day, Lord, Lord, have we not prophesied in Thy Name? and in Thy Name have cast out devils? and in Thy Name done many wonderful works?*

"And then will I profess unto them, I never knew you: depart from Me, ye that work iniquity" (Mat. 7:22-23).

You see, any works offered to Christ for Salvation are called by Jesus Himself, *"Works of iniquity."*

There's an old song that expresses what we are saying:

"My hope is built on nothing less,
"Than Jesus' Blood and Righteousness;
"I dare not trust the sweetest frame,
"But wholly lean on Jesus' Name.
"On Christ, the solid Rock, I stand;
"All other ground is sinking sand,
"All other ground is sinking sand."

(Portions of source material for the information on *"Infant Baptism"* were derived from a Message by the late Dr. William Pettingill.)

The phrase, *"In the Name of the Father, and of the Son, and of the Holy Ghost,"* as stated, is the only formula given in the Bible for Water Baptism. Consequently, several things should be said:

1. It is true that we read, in the Early Church, of persons being baptized *"In the Name of the Lord Jesus,"* and *"In the Name of the Lord"* (Acts 8:16; 10:48); but this expression by no means assumes that the Names of the other Divine Persons were not used; it denotes that those who had accepted Christ as their Saviour, were brought into the great Salvation experience purchased by Christ at Calvary's Cross.

The phrases in the Book of Acts were never intended to be used as a formula. If they had, they would have been identical, which they are not.

2. The phrase as used here by Christ, does not mean merely invoking the Name, under the sanction of the Great Name, but something more than this. It signifies into the power and influence of the Holy Trinity, into Faith in the

three Persons of God, and the duties and privileges consequent on that Faith, into the family of God and obedience unto its Head, the Lord Jesus Christ.

3. The *"in"* or *"into"* actually means *"by the authority of."* Here it means by the authority of all three Persons and not by the authority of Jesus only. He is the One authorizing us to recognize the others as well as Himself.

This will help us to understand Acts 2:38; 8:16; 10:48; and 19:5. It is by the authority of Jesus Christ that we baptize at all, and it is by His authority that we baptize in the Name of, or by the authority of all three Persons.

4. Inasmuch as the Believer is baptized into something, this formula given by Christ shows the end and aim of the consecration of Baptism. The *"Name"* of God is that by which He is known to us — that which connotes His Being and His Attributes, that by which there exists a conscious connection between God and ourselves.

So being baptized into the Name of God (for that is what it is), implies being placed in subjection to and communion with God Himself, admitted into Covenant with Him.

5. It is to be observed that the term is *"Name"* not *"Names,"* thus denoting the <u>unity</u> of the Godhead in the Trinity of Persons.

The three Divine Persons were revealed at the Baptism of Jesus (Mat. 3:16-17); consequently, they are invoked at every Christian Baptism in Water.

As well, the *"Father"* is *"God the Father,"* and the *"Son"* is *"God the Son,"* and the *"Holy Spirit"* is *"God the Holy Spirit."*

(20) "TEACHING THEM TO OBSERVE ALL THINGS WHATSOEVER I HAVE COMMANDED YOU: AND, LO, I AM WITH YOU ALWAY, EVEN UNTO THE END OF THE WORLD. AMEN."

The phrase, *"Teaching them to observe all things whatsoever I have commanded you,"* presents a different word than *"teach"* in verse 19. The Greek word in that verse is *"matheteuo,"* and means *"to make Disciples."* Therefore, it should have been translated, *"And preached to all nations."*

The word, *"teaching,"* in verse 20 in the Greek is *"didasko,"* and means *"to give instruction,"* and is therefore translated properly. So, in verses 19 and 20, the method of the Holy Spirit is given in that first of all the Gospel is *"preached"* to the lost in order to call their attention to Truth, while after they are converted, they are *"taught,"* which means to explain Truth.

That which is to be taught, is that which Christ has given, which actually includes the entirety of the New Testament, from Matthew 1:1 to Revelation 22:21.

No individual has the right to qualify or limit, or to add to, or take from any of that which is taught in the New Testament.

The Old Testament should be taught and practiced as well, as Jesus is the Author of it also, as it was given by the Holy Spirit (Jn. 1:1).

While it is true that many of the Old Testament Principles (the Law) and Types have been fulfilled in Christ, still, if we properly understand what they truly represented, then Christ, as well as all He did, becomes much more understandable.

Someone has said that the Old Testament is the New Testament concealed, while the New Testament is the Old Testament revealed!

One might could say that the Old Testament is the House, while the New Testament is the Furnishings in the House. Neither one is complete without the other.

One of the reasons why many Charismatics improperly interpret some of the New Testament is because they do not properly understand the Old. If the understanding of the foundation, which is the Old Testament, is improper, that which is built upon it is improper also!

Also, Jesus used the word, *"commanded,"* in reference to His Word, which means, and as we have stated, that they are not to be countermanded. In other words, they are not suggestions, but commands.

As well, the word, *"whatsoever,"* means that everything is to be included, with no part of the Gospel being eliminated or ignored.

Consequently, whenever modern Believers claim that Jesus no longer Baptizes in the Holy Spirit with the evidence of speaking with other tongues, they are abrogating that which John the Baptist said that Jesus would do (Mat. 3:11).

It should be quickly added, if anything is excluded, all that remains will be weakened as well! Hence, weak Christians and weak Churches!

The phrase, *"And lo, I am with you alway, even unto the end of the world,"* actually means *"age,"* for the world will never end.

In this phrase, every word is emphatic. Even

though Matthew did not mention the Ascension, still, it was at hand, with the Visible Presence of Jesus to be taken from His followers. Yet, Jesus comforts them with the assurance that His Spiritual Presence will be of far greater magnitude even than His Physical Presence. Then He could only be in one place at one time, where with His Spiritual Presence, He is everywhere.

In effect, He is saying, *"It is I Myself, I, God and Man, Who am* (not *"will be"*) *hence forever present among you, and with you as Companion, Friend, Guide, Saviour, God."*

Also, He is saying that He will be with His followers, not only with His Glorious Presence, and in every capacity, but, as well, He will help and strengthen in every single Righteous activity. He is promising that His Presence will not be withdrawn for a single moment, and irrespective of what the situation may be!

Consequently, this Promise, which has been gloriously and wonderfully carried out, is something unknown in Old Testament history. As someone has said, it is a nearness unspeakable, in the Church at large and in the Christian's heart as well!

When He uses the phrase, *"Unto the end of the world,"* i.e., *"age,"* He is referring to the time He will return. This speaks of the Second Coming, which will usher in a new age, or *"Kingdom Age."*

To be sure, His Presence and activity will be no less then, but the assurance of this Promise is, that during the meantime when He is bodily in Heaven, He will be no less present with us on earth. Through the Person and Agency of the Holy Spirit, His Spiritual Presence is guaranteed on a constant basis.

The word, *"Amen,"* closes out Matthew's Gospel, and is a fitting word at the conclusion of the Great Commission and this Great and Glorious Promise given by Christ of His Promised Presence.

In effect, it says several things:

1. *"Amen":* What I have told you, you can count on it!

2. *"Amen":* It is the guarantee of My Promise!

3. *"Amen":* I have left nothing hanging, all is complete!

As we have alluded to, there is no Ascension in this Gospel, for all in it relates to the King and to the Kingdom which He proposed to set up upon the earth; and so He promised to be with them until the predicted hour came of the establishment of that Kingdom.

As well, there is no account of the Ascension in the account of John the Beloved, for as Matthew's account related to Jesus as King, John's relates to Jesus as God. As such, the last Chapter of His Book is a prophetic picture of the Millennial Kingdom. The dawn of that morning, which is to follow the toil of this present night, will reveal the Messiah.

Conversely, both Mark and Luke speak of His Ascension, because Mark spoke of Jesus as *"The Servant,"* while Luke spoke of Him as *"The Man!"* As such, both spoke of His Incarnation, and of necessity, would include the Ascension. As a result of what Jesus did:

*"There's a peace in my heart that the
    world never gave,*
"A peace it cannot take away;
*"Tho' the trials of life may surround like
    a cloud,*
"I've a peace that has come there to stay!"

"Constantly abiding, Jesus is mine;
"Constantly abiding, rapture divine;
*"He never leaves me lonely, He whispers
    oh so kind:*
"I will never leave thee, Jesus is mine."

NOTES

INDEX

The index is listed according to subjects. The treatment may include a complete dissertation or no more than a paragraph. But hopefully it will provide some help.

As well, even though extended treatment of a subject may not be carried in this commentary, one of the other commentaries may well include the desired material.

For all information concerning the *Jimmy Swaggart Bible Commentary,* please request a Gift Catalog.

You may inquire by using Books of the Bible.

- Genesis (639 pages) (11-201)
- Exodus (639 pages) (11-202)
- Leviticus (435 pages) (11-203)
- Numbers
  Deuteronomy (493 pages) (11-204)
- Joshua
  Judges
  Ruth (329 pages) (11-205)
- I Samuel
  II Samuel (528 pages) (11-206)
- I Kings
  II Kings (560 pages) (11-207)
- I Chronicles
  II Chronicles (528 pages) (11-226)
- Ezra
  Nehemiah
  Esther *(will be ready Summer 2011)* (11-208)
- Job (320 pages) (11-225)
- Psalms (688 pages) (11-216)
- Isaiah (688 pages) (11-220)
- Jeremiah
  Lamentations (456 pages) (11-070)
- Ezekiel (508 pages) (11-223)
- Daniel (403 pages) (11-224)
- Matthew (625 pages) (11-073)
- Mark (606 pages) (11-074)

- Luke (626 pages) (11-075)
- John (532 pages) (11-076)
- Acts (697 pages) (11-077)
- Romans (536 pages) (11-078)
- I Corinthians (632 pages) (11-079)
- II Corinthians (589 pages) (11-080)
- Galatians (478 pages) (11-081)
- Ephesians (550 pages) (11-082)
- Philippians (476 pages) (11-083)
- Colossians (374 pages) (11-084)
- I Thessalonians
  II Thessalonians (498 pages) (11-085)
- I Timothy
  II Timothy
  Titus
  Philemon (687 pages) (11-086)
- Hebrews (831 pages) (11-087)
- James
  I Peter
  II Peter (730 pages) (11-088)
- I John
  II John
  III John
  Jude (377 pages) (11-089)
- Revelation (602 pages) (11-090)

For telephone orders you may call 1-800-288-8350 with bankcard information. All Baton Rouge residents please use (225) 768-7000. For mail orders send to:

Jimmy Swaggart Ministries
P.O. Box 262550
Baton Rouge, LA 70826-2550

Visit our website: www.jsm.org

NOTES

NOTES

NOTES

NOTES

NOTES